Western Civilizations

Their History & Their Culture

Joshua Cole

Carol Symes

Western Civilizations

Their History & Their Culture

BRIEF FOURTH EDITION

W. W. Norton & Company ▪ NEW YORK ▪ LONDON

W. W. Norton & Company has been independent since its founding in 1923, when William Warder Norton and Mary D. Herter Norton first published lectures delivered at the People's Institute, the adult education division of New York City's Cooper Union. The firm soon expanded its program beyond the Institute, publishing books by celebrated academics from America and abroad. By midcentury, the two major pillars of Norton's publishing program—trade books and college texts—were firmly established. In the 1950s, the Norton family transferred control of the company to its employees, and today—with a staff of four hundred and a comparable number of trade, college, and professional titles published each year—W. W. Norton & Company stands as the largest and oldest publishing house owned wholly by its employees.

Editor: Jon Durbin

Project Editor: Christine D'Antonio

Associate Editor: Justin Cahill

Editorial Assistant: Travis Carr

Manuscript Editor: Michael Fleming

Managing Editor, College: Marian Johnson

Managing Editor, College Digital Media: Kim Yi

Production Manager: Andy Ensor

Media Editor: Laura Wilk

Assistant Media Editor: Chris Hillyer

Marketing Manager, History: Sarah England

Design Director: Rubina Yeh

Book Designer: Judith Abbate / Abbate Design

Photo Editor: Evan Luberger

Photo Research: Rona Tucillo

Permissions Manager: Megan Jackson

Permissions Clearer: Bethany Salminen

Composition: Cenveo Publisher Services

Cartographers: Mapping Specialists

Manufacturing: LSC Communications—Willard

Permission to use copyrighted material is included in the credits sections of this book, which begin on page A56.

The Library of Congress has cataloged an earlier edition as follows:

Library of Congress Cataloging-in-Publication Data

Cole, Joshua, 1961–
Western civilizations : their history & their culture / Joshua Cole and Carol Symes.—Eighteenth edition.
    pages cm
Includes bibliographical references and index.
ISBN 978-0-393-92213-4 (hardcover)
 1. Civilization, Western—Textbooks.   2. Europe—Civilization—Textbooks.   I. Symes, Carol.   II. Title.
CB245.C56   2013
909'.09821—dc23   2013029952
This edition: ISBN 978-0-393-26532-3

W. W. Norton & Company, Inc., 500 Fifth Avenue, New York, N. Y. 10110
www.wwnorton.com

W. W. Norton & Company Ltd., 15 Carlisle Street, London W1D 3BS

4 5 6 7 8 9 0

To our families:

Kate Tremel, Lucas and Ruby Cole
Tom, Erin, and Connor Wilson

with love and gratitude for their support.
And to all our students, who have also been
our teachers.

JOSHUA COLE (Ph.D., University of California, Berkeley) is professor of history at the University of Michigan, Ann Arbor and the former director, Center for European Studies at the University of Michigan. His publications include work on gender and the history of the population sciences, colonial violence, and the politics of memory in nineteenth- and twentieth-century France, Germany, and Algeria. His first book was *The Power of Large Numbers: Population, Politics, and Gender in Nineteenth-Century France* (Ithaca, NY: Cornell University Press, 2000).

CAROL SYMES (Ph.D., Harvard University) is associate professor of history and former director of undergraduate studies in the history department at the University of Illinois, Urbana-Champaign, where she has won the top teaching award in the College of Liberal Arts and Sciences. Her main areas of study include medieval Europe, the history of information media and communication technologies, and the history of theater. Her first book was *A Common Stage: Theater and Public Life in Medieval Arras* (Ithaca, NY: Cornell University Press, 2007). She is the founding editor of *The Medieval Globe,* the first academic journal to promote a global approach to medieval studies.

Brief Contents

Contents

Chapter 9 ▪ THE CONSOLIDATION OF EUROPE, 1100–1250   223

Chapter 10 ▪ THE MEDIEVAL WORLD, 1250–1350   255

Chapter 11 ▪ REBIRTH AND UNREST, 1350–1453   285

Chapter 16 ■ THE NEW SCIENCE OF THE SEVENTEENTH CENTURY   425

Chapter 17 ■ EUROPE DURING THE ENLIGHTENMENT   449

Chapter 27 ▪ THE COLD WAR WORLD: GLOBAL POLITICS, ECONOMIC RECOVERY, AND CULTURAL CHANGE   727

Chapter 28 ▪ RED FLAGS AND VELVET REVOLUTIONS: THE END OF THE COLD WAR, 1960s–1990s   753

Chapter 29 ▪ A WORLD WITHOUT WALLS: GLOBALIZATION AND THE WEST   779

Maps

Documents

Preface

This new Brief Fourth Edition of *Western Civilizations* sharpens and expands the set of tools we have developed to empower students—our own and yours—to engage effectively with the themes, sources, and challenges of history. It presents a clear, vigorous, and coherent narrative, supplemented by a compelling selection of primary sources and visually striking images. At the same time, as the authors of this book's previous edition we have worked to develop a unified program of pedagogical elements that guide students toward a more thorough understanding of the past, and of the ways that historians reconstruct that past. This framework helps students to analyze and interpret historical evidence on their own, encouraging them to become active participants in the learning process. We have also worked hard to overcome one of the major shortcomings of most brief editions—the lack of a coherent narrative Here we used our innovative pedagogical tools as guides, particularly the Story Lines, Chronologies, and Core Objectives, to ensure that the chapter themes and core content remain fully present. Moreover, we cut the narrative by 25 percent, rather than the more traditional 40 percent, which again helps to retain a more coherent reading experience.

Moreover, the wide chronological scope of this book offers an unusual opportunity to trace central human developments (population movements, intellectual currents, economic trends, the formation political institutions, the power of religious belief, the role of the arts and of technologies) in a region of the world whose cultural diversity has been constantly invigorated and renewed by its interactions with peoples living in other places. Students today have a wide selection of introductory history courses to choose from, thanks to the welcome availability of introductory surveys in Latin American, African, and Asian history, alongside both traditional and innovative offerings in the history of the United States and Europe. Global history has also come into its own in recent years. But our increasing awareness that no region's history can be isolated from global processes and connec-

tions has merely heightened the need for a richly contextualized and broad-based history such as that represented in *Western Civilizations*. As in previous editions, we have attempted to balance the coverage of political, social, economic, and cultural phenomena with extensive treatment of material culture, daily life, gender, sexuality, art, science, and popular culture. And following the path laid out in the book's previous editions, we have insisted that the history of European peoples must be understood through their interactions with peoples in other parts of the world. Accordingly, our treatment of this history, attentive to the latest developments in historical scholarship, is both deep and dynamic.

Given the importance of placing human history in a global context, those of us who study the histories of ancient, medieval, and modern Europe are actively changing the ways we teach this history. The title of this book reflects the fact that, for good reasons, few historians today would uphold a monolithic vision of a single and enduring "Western civilization" whose inevitable march to domination can be traced chapter by chapter through time. This older paradigm, strongly associated with the curriculum of early-twentieth-century American colleges and universities, no longer conforms to what we know about the human past. Neither "the West" nor "Europe" can be seen as a distinct, unified entity in space or time; the meanings attributed to these geographical expressions have changed in significant ways. Moreover, historians now agree that a linear notion of any civilization persisting unchanged over the centuries was made coherent only by leaving out the intense conflicts, extraordinary ruptures, and dynamic changes that took place at the heart of the societies we call "Western." Smoothing out the rough edges of the past does students no favors; even an introductory text such as this one should present the past as it appears to the historians who study it—that is, as a complex panorama of human effort, filled with possibility and achievement but also fraught with discord, uncertainty, accident, and tragedy.

Highlights of the New Brief Fourth Edition

The new Brief Fourth Edition makes history an immersive experience through its innovative pedagogy and digital resources. InQuizitive—Norton's groundbreaking, formative, and adaptive new learning program—enables both students and instructors to assess learning progress at the individual and classroom level. The Norton Coursepack provides an array of support materials FREE TO INSTRUCTORS who adopt the text for integration into their local learning-management system. The Norton Coursepack includes valuable assessment and skill-building activities like New Primary Source Exercises, Guided Reading Exercises, Review Quizzes, and Interactive Map Resources. In addition, we've created new Office Hours and Present and Past videos that help students understand the core objectives and make history relevant for them (see page xxx for information about student and instructor resources).

We know that current and future users of our text will welcome the efforts we made in this new edition to update and reorganize the Late Medieval and Early Modern periods in order to place them in a larger Atlantic World context. The major highlight of this reorganization is a brand-new chapter, entitled "Europe in the Atlantic World, 1550–1650." It places the newly integrated space of the Atlantic at the center of the story, exploring the ways that nation building, religious warfare, economic developments, population movements, and cultural trends shaped—and were shaped by—historical actors on this dynamic frontier. Another significant result of the reorganization of these two periods is to provide a clearer chronological framework for the narrative, so that the students can better see how major topics and events emerge from their historical context. This, of course, was part of a larger effort begun across the entire text in the previous edition. These revisions demonstrate our dual commitment to keep the book current and up to date, while striving to integrate strong pedagogical features that help students build their study and history skills (see chapter-by-chapter revisions further below).

NEW AND REVISED PEDAGOGICAL FEATURES

In our ongoing effort to shape students' engagement with history, this book is designed to reinforce your course objectives by helping students to master core content while challenging them to think critically about the past. In order to achieve these aims, our previous edition augmented the traditional strengths of *Western Civilizations* by introducing several exciting new features. These have since been refined and revised in accordance with feedback from both teachers and student readers of the book. The most important and revolutionary feature is the pedagogical structure that supports each chapter. As we know from long experience, many students in introductory survey courses find the sheer quantity of information overwhelming, and so we have provided guidance to help them navigate through the material and to read with greater engagement.

At the outset of each chapter, the ***Before You Read This Chapter*** feature offers three preliminary windows into the material to be covered: *Story Lines*, *Chronology*, and *Core Objectives*. The *Story Lines* allow the student to become familiar with the primary narrative threads that tie the chapter's elements together, and the *Chronology* grounds these *Story Lines* in the period under study. The *Core Objectives* provide a checklist to ensure that the student is aware of the primary teaching points in the chapter. The student is then reminded of these teaching points upon completing the chapter in the ***After You Read*** This Chapter section, which prompts the student to revisit the chapter in three ways. The first, *Reviewing the Core Objectives*, asks the reader to reconsider core objectives by answering a pointed question about each one. The second, *People, Ideas, and Events in Context*, summarizes some of the particulars that students should retain from their reading, through questions that allow them to relate individual terms to the major objectives and story lines. Finally, *Thinking about Connections*, new to this edition, allows for more open-ended reflection on the significance of the chapter's material, drawing students' attention to issues that connect it to previous chapters and giving students insight into what comes next. As a package, the pedagogical features at the beginning and end of each chapter work together to enhance the student's learning experience by breaking down the process of reading and analysis into manageable tasks.

A second package of pedagogical features is designed to capture students' interest and compel them to think about what is at stake in the construction and use of historical narratives. Each chapter opens with a vignette that showcases a particular person or event representative of the era as a whole. Within each chapter, an expanded program of illustrations and maps has been enhanced by the addition of ***Guiding Questions*** that urge the reader to explore the historical contexts and significance of these visual features in a more analytical way. The historical value of images, artifacts, and material culture as types of primary sources is further emphasized in another feature we introduced in our previous edition, ***Interpreting Visual Evidence***. These carefully crafted features provide discussion leaders with a provocative departure point for conversations about the key issues raised by visual sources, which students often find more approachable than texts. Once this conversation has begun, students can further develop their skills by **Analyzing Primary Sources** through close readings of primary texts accompanied by cogent interpretive questions. The dynamism and diversity of Western civilizations are also illuminated through a look at **Competing Viewpoints** in each chapter, in which specific debates are presented through paired primary source texts. The bibliographical **For Further Reading**, now located at the end of the book, has also been edited and brought up to date.

In addition to these tools that have proven very successful, we are delighted to introduce an entirely new feature with this Brief Fourth Edition. The new **Past and Present** features in the main text prompt students to connect events that unfolded in the past with the breaking news of our own time, by taking one episode from each chapter and comparing it with a phenomenon that resonates more immediately with our students. To bring this new feature to life for students, we have also created a new series of *Past and Present* Author Interview Videos in which we describe and analyze these connections across time and place. There are a number of illuminating discussions, including "Spectator Sports," which compares the Roman gladiatorial games with NFL Football; "The Reputation of Richard III," which shows how the modern forensics we see on numerous TV shows were recently used to identify the remains of Richard III; "The Persistence of Monarchies in a Democratic Age," which explains the origins and evolution of our ongoing fascination with royals from Louis XIV to Princess Diana; and "The Internet and the Enlightenment Public Sphere," which compares the kinds of public networks that helped spread Enlightenment ideas to the way today's Internet can be used to spread political ideas in movements such as the Arab Spring and Occupy Wall Street. Through this new feature not only do we want to encourage students to recognize the continuing relevance of seemingly distant historical moments, we want to encourage history-minded habits that will be useful for a lifetime. If students learn to see the connections between their world and that of the past, they will be more apt to comprehend unfolding developments and debates in a more informed and complex historical context.

A TOUR OF NEW CHAPTERS AND REVISION

Our previous edition of *Western Civilizations* featured significant changes to each of the book's first five chapters, and this process of revision has continued in the present edition. In Chapter 1, the challenge of locating and interpreting historical evidence drawn from nontextual sources (archaeological, environmental, anthropological, mythic) is a special focus. Chapter 2 further underscores the degree to which recent archeological discoveries and new historical techniques have revolutionized our understanding of ancient history. Chapter 3 offers expanded coverage of the diverse polities that emerged in ancient Greece, and of Athens' closely related political, documentary, artistic, and intellectual achievements. Chapter 4's exploration of the Hellenistic world includes an unusually wide-ranging discussion of the scientific revolution powered by this first cosmopolitan civilization. Chapter 5 emphasizes the ways that the unique values and institutions of the Roman Republic are transformed through imperial expansion under the Principate.

With Chapter 6, more-extensive revision has resulted in some significant reshaping and reorganization in order to reflect recent scholarship. The story of Rome's transformative encounter with early Christianity has been rewritten to enhance clarity and to emphasize the fundamental ways that Christianity itself changed through both its changing status within the Roman Empire and also its contact with peoples from northwestern Europe. Chapter 7, which examines Rome's three distinctive successor civilizations, now offers more-extensive coverage of the reign of Justinian and emergence of Islam. Balanced attention to the interlocking histories of Byzantium, the Muslim caliphates, and western Europe has been carried forward in subsequent chapters. Chapters 8 contains an entirely new section, "A Tour of Europe around the Year 1000," with coverage of the Viking diaspora, the formation of Scandinavian kingdoms and the empire of Cnute, early medieval Rus' and eastern Europe, and the relationships among Mediterranean microcosms. Chapter 8 also features greatly expanded coverage of economy, trade, and the events leading up to the First Crusade. Chapter 9, which now covers the period 1100–1250, features a new segment on the Crusader States and crusading movements within Europe.

Chapter 10's treatment of the medieval world between 1250 and 1350 is almost wholly new, reflecting cutting-edge scholarship on this era. It includes a fresh look at the consolidation of the Mongol Khanates, new images and maps, some new sources, and a new **Interpreting Visual Evidence** segment on seals and their users. Chapters 11 and 12 have been thoroughly reorganized and rewritten to ensure that the narrative of medieval Europeans' colonial ventures (from the western Mediterranean to the eastern Atlantic and Africa, and beyond) is integrated with the story of the Black Death's effects on the medieval world and the impetus for the intellectual and artistic innovations of the Renaissance. In previous editions of the book, these concurrent phenomena were treated as separate, as though they took place in three separate periods (the later Middle Ages, the Renaissance, and the "Age of Exploration"). This divided treatment made the connections among them almost impossible to explain or appreciate. In this Brief Fourth Edition, therefore, the voyages of Columbus are firmly rooted in their historical contexts while the religious social and cultural upheavals of the Reformation (Chapter 13) are more clearly placed against a backdrop of political and economic competition in Europe and the Americas.

This program of revisions sets the stage for the most significant new chapter in the book: Chapter 14, "Europe in the Atlantic World, 1550–1650." This chapter, the hinge between the book's first and second halves, resulted from a close collaboration between us. It is designed to function either as the satisfying culmination of a course that surveys the history of western civilizations up to the middle of the seventeenth century (like that taught by Carol Symes) or to provide a foundation for a course on the history of the modern West (like that taught by Joshua Cole). The chapter illuminates the changing nature of Europe as it became fully integrated into a larger Atlantic World that dramatically and how that integration impacted all of its internal political, social, cultural, and economic development. In addition to greatly enhanced treatment of the transatlantic slave trade and the Columbian Exchange, Chapter 14 also features new sections on the different models of colonial settlement in the Caribbean and the Americas, as well as expanded coverage of the Thirty Years' War.

The new emphasis on the emergence of the Atlantic World carries over to Chapter 15, which covers the emergence of powerful absolutist regimes on the continent and the evolution of wealthy European trading empires in the Americas, Africa, and Asia. This material has now been reorganized to clarify developments over time, as the early successes of the Spanish Empire are gradually eclipsed by the successes of the Dutch, the French, and the British Empires. A new document on the *streltsy* rebellion, meanwhile, allows students to better understand the contested nature of power under the Russian tsars during the absolutist period. We have retained the emphasis on intellectual and cultural history in Chapter 16, on the Scientific Revolution, and in Chapter 17, on the Enlightenment. In Chapter 16 we have enhanced our treatment of the relationship between Christian faith and the new sciences of observation with a new primary source document by Pierre Gassendi. In Chapter 17, meanwhile, we have sought to set the Enlightenment more clearly in its social and political context, connecting it more explicitly to the theme of European expansion into the Americas and the Pacific. This helps, for example, in connecting a document like the American Declaration of Independence with the ideas of European Enlightenment thinkers.

Chapters 18 and 19 cover the political and economic revolutions of the late eighteenth and early nineteenth centuries. Chapter 18 covers the French Revolution and the Napoleonic empire in depth, while also drawing attention to the way that these central episodes were rooted in a larger pattern of revolutionary political change that engulfed the Atlantic world. Chapter 19 emphasizes both the economic growth and the technological innovations that were a part of the Industrial Revolution, while also exploring the social and cultural consequences of industrialization for men and women in Europe's new industrial societies. The *Interpreting Visual Evidence* feature in Chapter 19 allows students to explore the ways that industrialization created new perceptions of the global economy in Europe, changing the way people thought of their place in the world.

Chapters 20 and 21 explore the successive struggles between conservative reactionaries and radicals in Europe as the dynamic forces of nationalism unleashed by the French Revolution redrew the map of Europe and threatened the dynastic regimes that had ruled for centuries. Here, however, we have sought to clarify the periodization of the post-Napoleonic decades by focusing Chapter 20 more clearly on the conservative reaction in Europe after 1815, and the ideologies of conservatism, liberalism, republicanism, socialism, and nationalism. By setting the 1848 revolutions entirely in Chapter 21 (rather than splitting them between two chapters, as in previous editions), we've helped instructors to demonstrate more easily the connection between these political movements and the history of national unification in Germany and Italy in subsequent decades. While making these changes in the organization of the chapters, we have retained our treatment of the important cultural movements of the first half of the nineteenth century, especially romanticism.

Chapter 22 takes on the history of nineteenth-century colonialism, exploring both its political and economic origins and its consequences for the peoples of Africa and Asia. The chapter gives new emphasis to the significance of colonial conquest for European culture, as colonial power became increasingly associated with national greatness, both in conservative monarchies and in more-democratic regimes. Chapter 23 then brings the narrative back to the heart of Europe, covering the long-term consequences of industrialization and the consolidation of a conservative form of nationalism in many European nations even as the electorate was being expanded. This chapter emphasizes the varied nature of the new forms of political dissent, from the feminists who claimed the right to vote to the newly organized socialist movements that proved so enduring in many European countries.

Chapters 24 and 25 bring new vividness to the history of the First World War and the intense conflicts of the interwar period, while Chapter 26 uses the history of the Second World War as a hinge for understanding European and global developments in the second half of the twentieth century. The *Interpreting Visual Evidence* feature in Chapter 24 focuses on the role of propaganda among the belligerent nations in 1914–18, and the chapter's section on the diplomatic crisis that preceded the First World War has been streamlined to allow students to more easily comprehend the essential issues at the heart of the conflict. In Chapter 25 the *Interpreting Visual Evidence* feature continues to explore a theme touched on in earlier chapters—political representations of "the people"—this time in the context of fascist spectacles in Germany and Italy in the 1930s. These visual sources help students to understand the vulnerability of Europe's democratic regimes during these years as they faced the dual assault from fascists on the right and Bolsheviks on the left.

Chapters 27–29 bring the volume to a close in a thorough exploration of the Cold War, decolonization, the collapse of the Soviet Union and the Eastern Bloc in 1989–1991, and the roots of the multifaceted global conflicts that beset the world in the first decade of the twenty-first century. Chapter 27 juxtaposes the Cold War with decolonization, showing how this combination sharply diminished the ability of European nations to control events in the international arena, even as they succeeded in rebuilding their economies at home. Chapter 28 explores the vibrancy of European culture in the crucial period of the 1960s to the early 1990s, bringing new attention to the significance of 1989 as a turning point in European history. Finally, extensive revisions to Chapter 29 add to the issues covered in our treatment of Europe's place in the contemporary globalized world. The chapter now includes a new section on efforts to deal with climate change, as well as expanded discussion of both the impact of global terrorism and recent developments in the Arab-Israeli conflict. The discussion on the financial crisis of 2008 and the presidency of Barack Obama has been brought up to date and two new sections have been added to allow students to think about the Arab Spring of 2011 and the European debt crisis of recent years in connection with the broader history of European democracy, nation building, and colonialism in the modern period.

Media Resources for Instructors and Students

History becomes an immersive experience for students using Norton's digital resources with the Brief Fourth Edition of *Western Civilizations*. The comprehensive ancillary package features a groundbreaking new formative adaptive system as well as innovative interactive resources, including maps and primary sources, to help students master the core objectives in each chapter and continue to strengthen the skills they need to do the work of historians. Norton is unique in partnering exclusively with subject-matter experts who teach the course to author these resources. As a result, instructors have all of the course materials they need to successfully manage their Western Civilization course, whether they are teaching face-to-face, online, or in a hybrid setting.

INSTRUCTOR RESOURCES

LMS Coursepacks: Strong Assessment and Lecture Tools

- **New! Author Office Hour Videos:** These segments feature the authors speaking for 90 seconds on the Core Objectives of each chapter. There are nearly 100 of these new video segments.
- **New! Past and Present Author Interview Videos:** These videos connect topics across time and place and show why history is relevant to understanding our world today. Examples include "Spectator Sports," "Medieval Plots and Modern Movies," "Global Pandemics," and "The Atlantic Revolutions and Human Rights."
- **New! Guided Reading Exercises:** These exercises are designed by Scott Corbett (Ventura College) to help students learn how to read a textbook and, more importantly, comprehend what they are reading. The reading exercises instill a three-step Note-Summarize-Assess pedagogy. Exercises are based on actual passages from the textbook, and sample feedback is provided to model responses.
- **New! StoryMaps:** These presentations break complex maps into a sequence of four or five annotated screens that focus on the *story* behind the *geography*. The ten StoryMaps include such topics as the Silk Road, the spread of the Black Death, and nineteenth-century imperialism.

- **Interactive iMaps:** These interactive tools challenge students to better understand the nature of change over time by allowing them to explore the different layers of the maps from the book. Follow-up map worksheets help build geography skills by allowing students to test their knowledge by labeling.
- **Review Quizzes:** Multiple-choice, true/false, and chronological-sequence questions allow students to test their knowledge of the chapter content and identify where they need to focus their attention to better understand difficult concepts.
- **Primary Sources:** Over 400 primary source documents and images

Instructor's Manual

The Instructor's Manual for *Western Civilizations*, Brief Fourth Edition, is designed to help instructors prepare lectures and exams. The Instructor's Manual contains detailed chapter outlines, general discussion questions, document discussion questions, lecture objectives, interdisciplinary discussion topics, and recommended reading and film lists. This edition has been revised to include sample answers to all of the student-facing comprehension questions in the text.

Test Bank

The Test Bank contains over 2,000 multiple-choice, true/false, and essay questions. This edition of the Test Bank has been completely revised for content and accuracy. All test questions are now aligned with Bloom's Taxonomy for greater ease of assessment.

Lecture PowerPoint Slides

These ready-made presentations provide comprehensive outlines of each chapter, as well as discussion prompts to encourage student comprehension and engagement.

STUDENT RESOURCES

New! Norton InQuizitive for History This groundbreaking formative, adaptive learning tool improves student understanding of the core objectives in each chapter. Students receive personalized quiz questions on the topics with which they need the most help. Questions range from vocabulary and concepts to interactive maps and primary sources that challenge students to begin developing the skills necessary to do the work of a historian. Engaging game-like elements motivate students as they learn. As a result, students come to class better prepared to participate in discussions and activities.

New! Student Site

wwnorton.com/college/history/western-civilizationsBrief4

Free and open to all students, Norton Student Site includes additional resources and tools to ensure they come to class prepared and ready to actively participate in discussions and activities.

- **Office Hour Videos:** These segments feature the authors speaking for 90 seconds on the Core Objectives of each chapter. There are nearly 100 of these new video segments.
- **Western Civilizations Tours powered by Google Earth:** This new feature traces historical developments across time, touching down on locations that launch images and primary source documents
- **iMaps:** Interactive maps challenge students to explore change over time by navigating the different layers of the maps from the book. Practice worksheets help students build their geography skills by labeling the locations.
- **Online Reader:** The online reader offers a diverse collection of primary source readings for use in assignments and activities.

A Few Words of Thanks

Our first edition as members of the *Western Civilizations* authorial team was challenging and rewarding. Our second edition has been equally rewarding in that we have been able to implement a number of useful and engaging changes in the content and structure of the book, which we hope will make it even more student- and classroom-friendly. We are very grateful for the expert assistance and support of the Norton team, especially that of our editor, Jon Durbin. Christine D'Antonio, our fabulous project editor, has driven the book beautifully through the manuscript process. Travis Carr has provided good critiques of the illustrations in addition to all the other parts of the project he has handled so skillfully. Laura Wilk, our amazing new emedia editor, has assembled a great team to successfully deliver InQuizitive and all the carefully crafted new elements in the Norton Coursepack. Andy Ensor has masterfully marched us through the production process. Michael Fleming and Bob Byrne were terrific in skillfully guiding the manuscript through the copyediting and proofreading stages. Finally, we want to thank Sarah England for spearheading the marketing campaign for the new Brief Fourth Edition. We are also indebted to the numerous expert readers who commented on various chapters and who thereby strengthened the book as a whole. We are thankful to our families for their patience and advice, and to our students, whose questions and comments over the years have been essential to the framing of this book. And we extend a special thanks to, and we hope to hear from, all the teachers and students we may never meet—their engagement with this book will frame new understandings of our shared past and its bearing on our future.

REVIEWERS

Brief Third Edition Consultants

Paul Freedman, Yale University
Sheryl Kroen, University of Florida
Michael Kulikowski, Pennsylvania State University
Harry Liebersohn, University of Illinois, Urbana-Champaign
Helmut Smith, Vanderbilt University

Brief Third Edition Reviewers

Donna Allen, Glendale Community College
Marjon Ames, Appalachian State University
Eirlys Barker, Thomas Nelson Community College
Matthew Barlow, John Abbot College
Ken Bartlett, University of Toronto
Volker Benkert, Arizona State University
Dean Bennett, Schenectady City Community College
Patrick Brennan, Gulf Coast Community College
Neil Brooks, Community College of Baltimore County, Essex
James Brophy, University of Delaware
Kevin Caldwell, Blue Ridge Community College
Keith Chu, Bergen Community College
Alex D'erizans, Borough of Manhattan Community College, CUNY
Hilary Earl, Nipissing University
Karin Enloe, Arizona State University
Kirk Ford, Mississippi College
Michael Gattis, Gulf Coast Community College
David M. Gallo, College of Mount Saint Vincent
Jamie Gruring, Arizona State University
Tim Hack, Salem Community College
Bernard Hagerty, University of Pittsburg
Paul T. Hietter, Mesa Community College
Paul Hughes, Sussex County Community College

Lacey Hunter, Caldwell College
Kyle Irvin, Jefferson State Community College
Lloyd Johnson, Campbell University
Llana Krug, York College of Pennsylvania
Guy Lalande, St. Francis Xavier University
Chris Laney, Berkshire Community College
Charles Levine, Mesa Community College
Heidi MacDonald, Lethbridge University
Steven Marks, Clemson University
James Martin, Campbell University
Michael Mckeown, Daytona State University
Dan Puckett, Troy State University
Dan Robinson, Troy State University
Craig Saucier, Southeastern Louisiana University
Aletia Seaborn, Southern Union State College
Nicholas Steneck, Florida Southern College
Victoria Thompson, Arizona State University
Donna Trembinski, St. Francis Xavier University
Pamela West, Jefferson State Community College
Scott White, Scottsdale Community College
Aaron Wilson, Creighton University
Julianna Wilson, Pima Community College

Brief Fourth Edition Reviewers

Matthew Barlow, John Abbott College
Ken Bartlett, University of Toronto
Bob Brennan, Cape Fear Community College
Jim Brophy, University of Delaware
Keith Chu, Bergen Community College
Geoffrey Clark, SUNY Potsdam
Bill Donovan, Loyola University Maryland
Jeff Ewen, Sussex County Community College
Peter Goddard, University of Guelph
Paul Hughes, Sussex County Community College
Michael Kulikowski, Penn State University
Chris Laney, Berkshire Community College
James Martin, Campbell University
Derrick McKisick, Fairfield University
Dan Puckett, Troy University
Major Ben Richards, US Military Academy
Bo Riley, Columbus State Community College
Kimlisa Salazar, Pima Community College
Sara Scalenghe, Loyola University Maryland
Suzanne Smith, Cape Fear Community College
Bobbi Sutherland, Dordt College
David Tengwall, Anne Arundel Community College
Pam West, Jefferson State Community College
Julianna Wilson. Pima Community College
Margarita Youngo, Pima Community College

Western Civilizations

Their History & Their Culture

Before
You
Read
This
Chapter

Early Civilizations

CORE OBJECTIVES

- **UNDERSTAND** the challenges involved in studying the distant past.

- **DEFINE** the key characteristics of civilization.

- **IDENTIFY** the factors that shaped the earliest cities.

- **EXPLAIN** how Hammurabi's empire was governed.

- **DESCRIBE** the main differences between Mesopotamian and Egyptian civilizations.

There was a time, the story goes, when all the peoples of the earth shared a common language and could accomplish great things. They developed new technologies, made bricks, and aspired to build a fortified city with a tower reaching to the sky. But their god was troubled by this, so he destroyed their civilization by making it hard for them to understand one another's speech.

We know this as the legend of Babel. It's a story that probably circulated among peoples of the ancient world for thousands of years before it became part of the Hebrew book we call by its Greek name, Genesis, "the beginning." This story lets us glimpse some of the conditions in which the first civilizations arose, and it also reminds us of the ruptures that make studying them hard. We no longer speak the same languages as those ancient peoples, just as we no longer have direct access to their experiences or their beliefs.

Such foundational stories are usually called *myths*, but they are really an early form of history. For the people who told them, these stories helped to make sense of the present by explaining the past. The fate of Babel conveyed a crucial

3

message: human beings are powerful when they share a common goal, and what enables human interaction is civilization. To the peoples of the ancient world, the characteristic benefits of civilization—stability and safety, government, art, literature, science—were always products of city life. The very word "civilization" derives from the Latin word *civis*, "city." Cities, however, became possible only as a result of innovations that began around the end of the last Ice Age, about 13,000 years ago, and that came to fruition in Mesopotamia 8,000 years later. The history of civilization is therefore a short one. Within the study of humanity, which reaches back to the genus *Homo* in Africa, some 1.7 million years ago, it is merely a blip on the radar screen. Even within the history of *Homo sapiens sapiens*, the species to which we belong and which evolved about 50,000 years ago, civilization is a very recent development.

The study of early civilizations is both fascinating and challenging. Historians still do not understand why cities developed in the region between the Tigris and the Euphrates rivers, in what is now Iraq. Once developed, however, the basic patterns of urban life quickly spread to other parts of the ancient world, both by imitation and by conquest. A network of trading connections linked these early cities, but intense competition for resources made alliances among them fragile. Then, around the middle of the second millennium B.C.E. (that is, "Before the Common Era," equivalent to the Christian dating system B.C., "Before Christ"), emerging powers began to shape some fiercely independent cities into empires. How this happened—and how we know that it happened—is the subject of Chapter 1.

BEFORE CIVILIZATION

More than 9,000 years ago, a town began to develop at Çatalhöyük (*CHUH-tal-hih-yik*) in what is now south-central Turkey. Over the next 2,000 years, it grew to cover an area of thirty-three acres, within which some 8,000 inhabitants lived in more than 2,000 separate houses. If this seems small, consider that Çatalhöyük's population density was actually twice that of today's most populous city, Mumbai (in India). It was so tightly packed that there were hardly any streets. Instead, each house was built immediately next to its neighbor, and generally on top of a previous house.

The people of Çatalhöyük developed a highly organized and advanced society. They wove wool cloth; they made kiln-fired pottery; they painted elaborate hunting scenes on the plaster-covered walls of their houses; they made weapons and tools from razor-sharp obsidian imported from the nearby Cappadocian mountains. They honored their ancestors with religious rites and buried their dead beneath the floors of their houses. Settled agriculturalists, they grew grains, peas, and lentils and tended herds of domesticated sheep and goats. But they also hunted and gathered fruits and nuts, like their nomadic ancestors, and their society was egalitarian, another feature common to nomadic societies: both men and women did the same kinds of work. But despite their relatively diverse and abundant food supply, their life spans were very short. Men died, on average, at the age of thirty-four. Women, who bore the additional risks of childbirth, died at around age thirty.

The basic features of life in Çatalhöyük are common to all subsequent human civilizations. But how, when, and why did such settlements emerge? And how do we have access to information about this distant past? The era before the appearance of written records, which begin to proliferate around 3100 B.C.E., is of far greater duration than the subsequent eras we are able to document—and no less important. But it requires special ingenuity to identify, collect, and interpret the evidence of the distant past. In fact, historians have just begun to explore the ways that climatology, neuroscience, evolutionary biology, and genetics can further illuminate this period, augmenting the older findings of paleontology, archaeology, and historical anthropology.

Societies of the Stone Age

Primates with human characteristics originated in Africa 4 to 5 million years ago, and tool-making hominids—species belonging to the genus *Homo*, our distant ancestors—evolved approximately 2 million years ago. Because these early hominids made most of their tools out of stone, they are designated as belonging to the Stone Age. This vast expanse of time is divided into the Paleolithic ("Old Stone") and the Neolithic ("New Stone") Eras, with the break between them falling around 11,000 B.C.E.

As early as 164,000 years ago, hominids in Africa were kindling and controlling fire and using it to make tools. The Neanderthals, a hominid species that flourished about 200,000 years ago, made jewelry, painted on the walls of caves, and buried their dead in distinctive graves with meaningful objects such as horns (blown to make music)

CAVE PAINTINGS FROM LASCAUX. These paintings, which date to between 10,000 and 15,000 B.C.E., show several of the different species of animals that were hunted by people of the Ice Age. The largest animal depicted here, a species of long-horned cattle known as the *auroch*, is now extinct.

and, in one case, flowers. Could these hominids speak? Did they have a language? At present, there is no way that we can answer such questions.

However, archaeology has shown that in the last phase of the Paleolithic Era, around 40,000 B.C.E., the pace of human development began to accelerate dramatically. Human populations in Africa expanded, suggesting that people were better nourished, perhaps as a result of new technologies. In Europe, *Homo sapiens* began to produce finely crafted and more-effective tools such as fishhooks, arrowheads, and sewing needles made from wood, antler, and bone. The most astonishing evidence of this change was produced by these new tools: cave paintings like those at Lascaux and Chauvet (in France). These amazing scenes were purposefully painted in recesses where acoustic resonance is greatest, and were probably intended to be experienced as part of multimedia musical ceremonies. This is almost certain evidence for the development of language.

Despite these changes, the patterns of human life altered very little. Virtually all human societies consisted of bands of a few dozen people who moved incessantly in search of food. As a result, these groups left no continuous archaeological record. Their lifestyle also had social, economic, and political limitations which help to explain the differences—both positive and negative—between these subsistence societies and those that can be called "civilizations." Early humans had no domestic animals to transport goods, so they could have no significant material possessions aside from basic tools. And because they could not accumulate goods over time, the distinctions of rank and status created by disparities in wealth could not develop.

Hierarchical structures were therefore uncommon. When conflicts arose or resources became scarce, the solution was probably to divide and separate. And although scholars once assumed that men did the hunting and women the gathering, it is more likely that all members of a band (except for the very young and very old) engaged in the basic activity of acquiring food.

THE BUILDING BLOCKS OF CIVILIZATION

What changes allowed some hunter-gatherer societies to settle and build civilizations? The historical divide between the Paleolithic and Neolithic Ages, around 11,000 B.C.E., reflects very evident developments brought about by changes in the climate, which led to the development of managed food production, which in turn fostered settlements that could trade with one another, both locally and over long distances. For the first time, it became possible for individuals and communities to accumulate and store wealth on a large scale. The results were far-reaching. Communities became more stable, and human interactions more complex. Specialization developed, along with distinctions of status and rank. Both the rapidity and the radical implications of these changes have given this era its name: the Neolithic Revolution.

The Neolithic Revolution

The artists who executed the cave paintings at Lascaux and Chauvet were able to survive in harsh climatic conditions. Between 40,000 and 11,000 B.C.E., daytime temperatures in the Mediterranean basin averaged about 60° F (16° C) in the summer and about 30° F (–1° C) in the winter. These are very low compared to today's temperatures in the city of Marseilles, not far from Lascaux, which average about 86° F (30° C) in summer and 52° F (11° C) in winter. This means that cold-loving reindeer, elk, wild boar, bison, and mountain goats abounded in regions now famous for their beaches and vineyards. But as the glaciers receded northward with the warming climate, these species retreated with them, all the way to Scandinavia. Some humans moved north with the game, but others stayed behind to create a very different world.

Within a few thousand years after the end of the Ice Age, peoples living in the eastern Mediterranean and

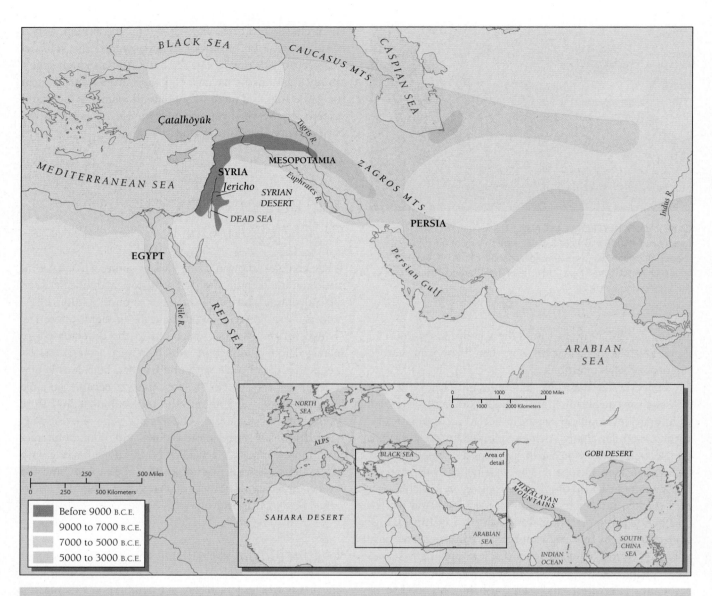

THE GROWTH OF AGRICULTURE. Examine the chronology of agriculture's development in this region. ▪ *What areas began cultivating crops first, and why?* ▪ *How might rivers have played a crucial role in the spread of farming technologies?*

some other regions of the world accomplished the most momentous transformation in human history: a switch from food-gathering for subsistence to food production. The warmer, wetter climate allowed wild grains to flourish, geometrically increasing the food supply. People began to domesticate animals and cultivate plants. Stable settlements grew into cities. This process took several thousand years, but it still deserves to be called "revolutionary." In a relatively short time, people altered patterns of existence that were millions of years old.

This revolution produced new challenges and inequalities. For example, well-nourished women in sedentary communities can bear more children than women in hunter-gatherer groups, and so the women of this era became increasingly sequestered from their male counterparts, who in turn gave up an equal role in child care. The rapid increase in population was also countered by the rapid spread of infectious diseases, while dependence on carbohydrates resulted in earlier deaths than were typical among hunter-gatherers.

Eventually, increased fertility and birthrates outweighed these limiting factors, and by about 8000 B.C.E. human populations were beginning to exceed the wild food supply. They therefore had to increase the food-growing capacity of the land and devise ways of preserving and storing grain between harvests. Some peoples had learned how to preserve wild grain in storage pits as early as 11,500 B.C.E., and they discovered that they could use this seed to produce even more grain the following year. The importance of the latter discovery cannot be overstated: deliberate cultivation could support larger populations and could also compensate for disasters (such as flooding) that might inhibit natural reseeding. Even more important, intensified seeding and storage provided humans with the stable and predictable surpluses needed to support domestic animals. This brought a host of additional benefits, guaranteeing a more reliable supply of meat, milk, leather, wool, bone, and horn, and also providing animal power to pull carts and plows and to power mills.

The Emergence of Towns and Villages

The accelerating changes of the Neolithic Revolution are exemplified by towns like Çatalhöyük and by the simultaneous rise of trade and warfare—sure signs of increased specialization and competition. Hundreds, and probably thousands, of settlements grew up in western Asia (the "Near East") between 7500 and 3500 B.C.E. Some of these can be classified as cities: centers of administration and commerce with a large and diverse population, often protected by walls. Among the earliest of these was Jericho, in the territory lying between modern Israel and Jordan. Jericho emerged as a seasonal grain-producing settlement, and by 6800 B.C.E. its inhabitants were undertaking a spectacular building program. Many new dwellings were built on stone foundations, and a massive dressed stone wall was constructed around the western edge of the settlement. It included a circular tower whose excavated remains still reach to a height of thirty feet, a powerful expression of its builders' wealth, technical prowess, and political ambitions.

Jericho covered at least eight acres and supported 3,000 people, so it was even more densely settled than Çatalhöyük. It was sustained by intensive cultivation, made possible by irrigation, of recently domesticated strains of wheat and barley. Jericho's inhabitants also produced some of the earliest-known pottery, which allowed them to store grain, wine, and oils more effectively. Pottery's most important benefits, however, were in cooking. For the first time, it was possible to produce nourishing stews, porridges, and ales. (The capacity to produce beer is a sure sign of civilization.) Pottery production was not only vital to ancient civilizations, it is vital to those who study them. As the techniques for making pottery spread throughout the Near East and Asia, identifiable regional styles also developed. By studying the different varieties, archaeologists can construct a reasonably accurate chronology and can also trace the movements of goods and people.

Jericho and Çatalhöyük illustrate the impact that stored agricultural surpluses have on human relations. For the first time, significant differences began to arise in the amount of wealth individuals could stockpile for themselves and their heirs. Dependence on agriculture also made it more difficult for individuals to split off from the community when disputes and inequities arose. The result was the construction of a much more stratified society, with more opportunities for a few powerful people to become dominant. The new reliance on agriculture also meant a new dependence on the land, the seasons, and the weather, which in turn led to new speculations about the supernatural. Different life forces were believed to require special services and gifts, and the regular practice of ritual and sacrifice ultimately produced a priestly caste of individuals or families who seemed able to communicate with these forces. Such spiritual leadership was allied to more worldly forms of power, including the capacity to lead war bands, to exact tribute from other settlements, to construct defenses, and to resolve disputes.

Trade was another important element in the development of early settlements. Local trading networks were already established around 9000 B.C.E., and by 5000 B.C.E., long-distance routes linked settlements throughout the region. Long-distance trade accelerated the exchange of ideas and information within the Fertile Crescent, and it further increased social stratification. Because status was enhanced by access to exotic goods from afar, local elites sought to monopolize trade by organizing and controlling the production of commodities within their own communities and by regulating their export. Certain people could now devote at least a portion of their labor to pursuits other than agriculture: making pottery or cloth, manufacturing weapons or tools, building houses and fortifications, or facilitating trade. Thus the elites who fostered and exploited the labor of others eventually became specialized themselves, with the leisure and resources to engage in intellectual, artistic, and political pursuits. The building blocks of civilization had been laid.

THE WHITE TEMPLE AT URUK, c. 3400 B.C.E. This temple may have been dedicated to the sky god, An, or designed to provide all the region's gods with a mountaintop home in a part of the world known for its level plains.

water into irrigation canals. Despite the hostility of the environment, Ubaid communities were soon producing surpluses sufficient to support specialists in construction, weaving, pottery, metalwork, and trade: the typical attributes of Neolithic village life.

Yet there is also early evidence of something quite new: central structures that served religious, economic, and administrative functions, something not found in Çatalhöyük. Starting out as shrines, these structures soon became impressive temples built of dried mud brick, like the bricks described in the story of Babel—and unlike the plentiful stone used at Jericho (the scarcity of stone meant that builders in this region had to be more resourceful). Each large settlement had such a temple, from which a priestly class acted as managers of the community's stored wealth and of the complex irrigation systems that would make the civilization of Sumer possible.

URBAN DEVELOPMENT IN MESOPOTAMIA

The Greeks called it Mesopotamia, the "Land between Rivers." It was a land that received only about eight inches (20 cm) of rainfall per year. Its soils are sandy, and summer temperatures exceed 110° F (44° C). The two rivers supplying water—the Tigris and Euphrates—are noted for their violence and unpredictability. Both are prone to flooding, and the Tigris was liable to change its course from year to year. It was in this challenging environment that the urban society of Sumer flourished.

Early Ubaid Settlements

The earliest cities of Mesopotamia were founded by the Ubaid peoples, so called because of their settlement at al-Ubaid (now in Iraq), which dates to around 5900 B.C.E. In this era, the headwaters of the Persian Gulf extended at least 100 miles farther inland than they do today, so some Ubaid settlements bordered on fertile marshlands, which enabled them to develop irrigation systems. Although these began as relatively simple channels and collection pools, Ubaid farmers quickly learned to build more sophisticated canals and to line some pools with stone. They also constructed dikes and levees to control the seasonal flooding of the rivers and to direct the excess

Urbanism in Uruk, 4300–2900 B.C.E.

After about 4300 B.C.E., Ubaid settlements developed into larger, more prosperous, and more highly organized communities. The most famous of these sites, Uruk, became the first Sumerian city-state. Its sophistication and scale is exemplified by the White Temple, built between 3500 and 3300 B.C.E. Its massive sloping platform looms nearly forty feet above the surrounding flatlands, and its four corners are oriented toward the cardinal points of the compass. Atop the platform stands the temple proper, dressed in brick and originally painted a brilliant white.

Such temples were eventually constructed in every Sumerian city, reflecting the central role that worship played in civic life. Uruk in particular seems to have owed its rapid growth to its importance as a religious center. By 3100 B.C.E. it encompassed several hundred acres, enclosing a population of 40,000 people within its massive brick walls. The larger villages of Sumer were also growing rapidly, attracting immigrants just as the great cities did. Grain and cloth production grew tenfold. Trade routes expanded dramatically. And to manage this increasingly complex economy, the Sumerians invented the technology on which most historians now rely: writing.

CUNEIFORM WRITING. The image on the left shows a Sumerian clay tablet from about 3000 B.C.E. Here, standardized pictures are beginning to represent abstractions: notice the symbol *ninda* (food) near the top. On the right, carvings on limestone from about 2600 B.C.E. reveal the evolution of cuneiform. ■ *Why would such standardized pictograms have been easier to reproduce quickly?*

The Development of Writing

In 4000 B.C.E., the peoples of Sumer were already using clay tokens to keep inventories. Within a few centuries, they developed a practice of placing tokens inside hollow clay balls and inscribing, on the outside of each ball, the shapes of all the tokens it contained. By 3300 B.C.E., scribes had replaced these balls with flat clay tablets on which they inscribed symbols representing the tokens. These tablets made keeping the tokens themselves unnecessary, and they could also be archived for future reference or sent to other settlements as receipts or requests for goods.

Writing thus evolved as a practical recording technology to support economic pursuits. Because it existed to represent real things, its system of symbols—called *pictograms*—was also realistic: each pictogram resembled the thing it represented. Over time, however, a pictogram might be used not only to symbolize a physical object but to evoke an idea associated with that object. For example, the symbol for a bowl of food, *ninda*, might be used to express something more abstract, such as "nourishment." Pictograms also came to be associated with particular spoken sounds, or *phonemes*. Thus when a Sumerian scribe needed to employ the sound *ninda*, even as part of another word, he would use the symbol for a bowl of food to represent that phoneme. Later, special marks were added so that a reader could tell whether the writer meant it to represent the object itself, a larger concept, or a sound used in a context that might have nothing to do with food.

By 3100 B.C.E., Sumerian scribes also developed a specialized tool suited to the task of writing, a stylus made of reed. Because this stylus leaves an impression shaped like a wedge (in Latin, *cuneus*), this script is called *cuneiform* (*kyoo-NAY-i-form*). Cuneiform symbols could now be impressed more quickly into clay. And because the new stylus was not suited to drawing pictograms that accurately represented things, the symbols became even more abstract. Meanwhile, symbols were invented for every possible phonetic combination in the Sumerian language, reducing the number of necessary pictograms from about 1,200 to 600. Whereas the earliest pictograms could have been written and read by anyone, writing and reading now became specialized, powerful skills accessible only to a small and influential minority who were taught in special scribal schools.

THE CULTURE OF SUMER

The great centers of Sumerian civilization shared a common culture and a common language. They also shared a set of beliefs. However, this common religion did not produce peace. The residents of each city considered themselves to be the servants of a particular god, whom they sought to glorify by exalting their own city above others. The result was intense competition that frequently escalated into warfare. There was also an economic dimension to this conflict, since water rights and access to arable land and trade routes were often at stake.

Much of the economic production of a city passed through the great temple warehouses, where priests

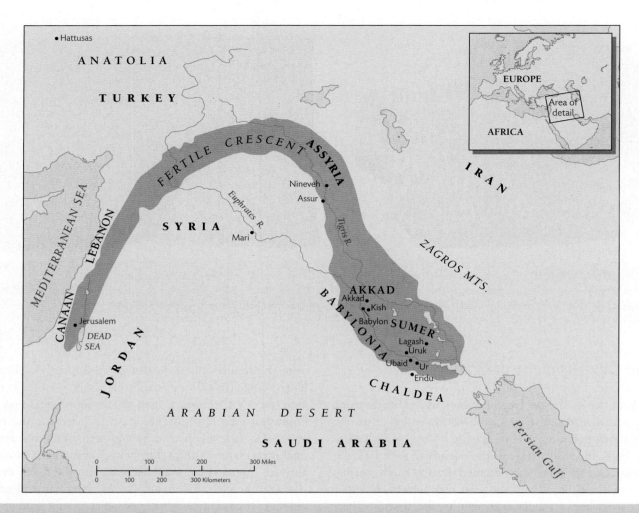

THE FERTILE CRESCENT. Notice the proximity of cities to rivers; consider the vital role played by the Tigris and Euphrates in shaping Mesopotamian civilizations. ■ *How many city-states can you identify on the map?* ■ *Why would these city-states have been clustered so closely together?* ■ *What challenges and opportunities would this present?*

redistributed the city's produce. During the third millennium, these great temples began to control the production of textiles, employing thousands of servile women and children. Temple elites also played a key role in long-distance trade, as both buyers and sellers of goods. So for any city-state to surrender its independence would not only offend the conquered city's god, it would jeopardize its entire economy and the power of its ruling class.

Each Sumerian city had its own aristocracy, the group from which priests were drawn. As much as half the population consisted of free persons who held parcels of land sufficient to sustain themselves, but the rest were dependents of the temple who worked as artisans or as agricultural laborers, and many of these dependents were slaves. Most of these slaves were prisoners of war from other Sumerian city-states whose bondage was limited to three years, after which time a slave had to be released.

But non-Sumerians could be held indefinitely, although a few might manage to buy their freedom. In either case, slaves were the property of their owners. They could be beaten, branded, bought, and sold like any other form of merchandise. Perhaps the only positive thing to say about slavery in antiquity is that it was egalitarian: anyone could become a slave. It was not until the beginning of the modern era that slavery became linked to race (see Chapter 14).

The Early Dynastic Period, 2900–2500 B.C.E.

Around 2900 B.C.E., conflicts among the growing Sumerian city-states became more acute. Competition for resources intensified and warfare became more frequent and destructive. A new type of military leadership began to emerge and eventually evolved into a form of kingship. Historians refer to this phase as the Early Dynastic Period because it was dominated by family dynasties, each headed by a war leader whose prestige earned him the title *lugal*: "big man." Unlike the priestly rulers of the Uruk Period, lugals did not see themselves as humble servants of the city's god. Rather, they believed that success in battle had earned them the right to exploit the city's wealth for their own glory.

The most striking expression of this development is the *Epic of Gilgamesh*, a series of stories recited over many generations and eventually written down on cuneiform tablets: the first literary monument in world history. It recounts the exploits of a lugal named Gilgamesh, who probably lived in Uruk sometime around 2700 B.C.E. Gilgamesh earns his legendary reputation through military conquest and personal heroism, particularly in campaigns against uncivilized—that is, nonurban—tribes. But he becomes so powerful that he ignores his own society's code of conduct; he disrespects the priesthood and commits acts of sacrilege. So the people of Uruk pray to the gods for retribution, and the gods fashion a wild man named Enkidu to challenge Gilgamesh.

The confrontation between Gilgamesh and Enkidu reveals the core values of Sumerian society. Gilgamesh is a creature of the city; Enkidu is a creature of the past, a hunter-gatherer. But then Enkidu has a sexual encounter with a beguiling woman and is unable to return to the wilderness: his urban initiation has civilized him and allowed him to befriend the lord of Uruk. Together they have many adventures. But Enkidu is eventually killed by the goddess Inanna, who punishes the friends for mocking her powers. Gilgamesh, distraught with grief, attempts to find a magical plant that will revive his friend. He finds it at the bottom of a deep pool, only to have it stolen from him by a water snake. In the end, he is forced to confront the futility of all human effort. He becomes "The One Who Looked into the Depths," the name by which his story was known to Sumerians. The larger message seems to be that not even civilization can shield humans from the forces of nature and the inevitability of death.

Sumerian Religion

In the Uruk Period, the Sumerians identified their gods with the capricious forces of the natural world. In the Early Dynastic Period, however, they came to imagine their gods as resembling the lugals who now ruled the city-states. Like these kings, the gods desired to live in the finest palaces and temples, to wear the costliest clothing and jewels, and to consume the tastiest foods. According to this new theology, which clearly reflects changes in Sumerian society, humans exist merely to provide for their gods. This was, indeed, why the gods had created people in the first place. There was thus a reciprocal relationship between humanity and divinity. The gods depended on their human servants to honor and sustain them; and in return, the gods occasionally bestowed gifts and favors.

As the gods' representatives on Earth, lugals bore special responsibilities and also enjoyed special privileges. Kings were thus set apart from all other men, including priests. But kings were also obliged to honor the gods through offerings, sacrifices, festivals, and massive building projects. Kings who neglected these duties, or who exalted themselves at the expense of the gods, were likely to bring disaster on themselves and their people. And even kings could not evade death.

Science, Technology, and Trade

The Sumerians' worldview was colored by their adversarial relationship with their surroudings. Precisely because neither their gods nor their environment were trustworthy, Sumerians cultivated a high degree of self-reliance and ingenuity. These qualities made them the most technologically innovative people of the ancient world.

For example, despite the fact that their land had no mineral deposits, the Sumerians became skilled metallurgists. By 6000 B.C.E., a number of cultures throughout

SUMERIAN WAR CHARIOTS. The earliest known representation of the wheel, dating from about 2600 B.C.E., shows how wheels were fashioned from slabs of wood. (For a later Mesopotamian wheel with spokes, see the illustration on page 51.)

The Flood: Two Accounts

One of the oldest stories in the world tells of a great flood that devastated the lands and peoples of the earth, an event that can be traced to the warming of the earth's climate at the end of the last Ice Age. Many ancient cultures told versions of this story, and two of these are excerpted below. The first, included in the Epic of Gilgamesh, *was written down during the first half of the third millennium B.C.E., making it at least 1,500 years older than the similar account in the Hebrew Bible. But both are probably the products of much older storytelling traditions. The hero of the Sumerian story is Utnapishtim. The Hebrew story's hero is Noah.*

The Epic of Gilgamesh

Utnapishtim spoke to Gilgamesh, saying: "I will reveal to you, Gilgamesh . . . a secret of the gods. . . . The hearts of the Great Gods moved them to inflict the Flood. Their Father Anu uttered the oath (of secrecy). . . . [But the god] Ea . . . repeated their talk [to me, saying]: 'O man of Shuruppak, son of Ubartutu: Tear down the house and build a boat! . . . Spurn possessions and keep alive living beings! Make all living beings go up into the boat. The boat which you are to build, its dimensions must measure equal to each other: its length must correspond to its width. Roof it over like the Apsu.' I understood and spoke to my lord, Ea: 'My lord, thus is the command which you have uttered. I will heed and will do it.' . . . On the fifth day I laid out her exterior. It was a field in area, its walls were each 10 times 12 cubits in height. . . . I provided it with six decks, thus dividing it into seven (levels). . . . Whatever I had I loaded on it. . . . All the living beings that I had I loaded on it. I had all my kith and kin go up into the boat, all the beasts and animals of the field and the draftsmen I had go up.

"I watched the appearance of the weather—the weather was frightful to behold! I went into the boat and sealed the entry. . . . All day long the South Wind blew . . . , submerging the mountain in water, overwhelming the people like an attack. . . . Six days and seven nights came the wind and flood, the storm flattening the land. When the seventh day arrived . . . the sea calmed, fell still, the whirlwind and flood stopped up. . . . When a seventh day arrived, I sent forth a dove and released it. The dove went off, but came back to me, no perch was visible so it circled back to me. I sent forth a swallow and released it. The swallow went off, but came back to me, no perch was visible so it circled back to me. I sent forth a raven and released it. The raven went off, and saw the waters slither back. It eats, it scratches, it bobs, but does not circle back to me. Then I sent out everything in all directions and sacrificed (a sheep). I offered incense in front of the mountain-ziggurat. . . .

"The gods smelled the savor . . . and collected like flies over a sacrifice. . . . Just then Enlil arrived. He saw the boat and became furious. . . . 'Where did a living being escape? No man was to survive the annihilation!' Ea spoke to Valiant Enlil, saying . . . 'How, how could you bring about a Flood without consideration? Charge the violation to the

western Asia and Europe had learned how to produce weapons and tools using copper. By the Uruk Period (4300–2900 B.C.E.), trade routes were bringing this raw element into Sumer, where it was processed into weapons and tools. Shortly before 3000 B.C.E., people further discovered that copper could be alloyed with arsenic (or later, tin) to produce bronze. Bronze is almost as malleable as copper, and it pours more easily into molds; but when cooled, it maintains its rigidity and shape even better than copper. For almost two thousand years, until about 1200 B.C.E. and the development of techniques for smelting iron, bronze was the strongest metal known to man—the most useful and, in war, the most deadly. Following the Greeks (see Chapter 3), we call this period the Bronze Age.

Alongside writing and the making of bronze, the invention of the wheel was the fundamental technological

violator, charge the offense to the offender, but be compassionate lest (mankind) be cut off, be patient lest they be killed.' Enlil went up inside the boat and, grasping my hand, made me go up. He had my wife go up and kneel by my side. He touched our forehead and, standing between us, he blessed us. . . ."

Source: Maureen Gallery Kovacs, trans., *The Epic of Gilgamesh*, Tablet XI (Stanford, CA: 1985, 1989), pp. 97–103.

The Book of Genesis

The Lord saw that the wickedness of humankind was great in the earth and . . . said, "I will blot out from the earth the human beings I have created . . . for I am sorry I have made them." But Noah found favor in the sight of the Lord. . . . God saw that the earth was corrupt and . . . said to Noah, "I have determined to make an end to all flesh. . . . Make yourself an ark of cypress wood, make rooms in the ark, and cover it inside and out with pitch. . . . Make a roof for the ark, and put the door of the ark in its side. . . . For my part I am going to bring a flood on the earth, to destroy from under heaven all flesh. . . . But I will establish a covenant with you, and you shall come into the ark, you, your sons, your wife, and your sons' wives with you. And of every living thing you shall bring two of every kind into the ark, to keep them alive with you. . . . Also take with you every kind of food that is eaten." . . . All the fountains of the great deep burst forth, and the windows of the heavens were opened. . . . The waters gradually receded from the earth. . . . At the end of forty days, Noah opened a window of the ark . . . and sent out the raven, and it went to and fro until the waters were dried up from the earth. Then he sent out the dove from him, to see if the waters had subsided from the face of the ground, but the dove found no place to set its foot, and it returned. . . . He waited another seven days, and again sent out the dove [which] came back to him . . . and there in its beak was a freshly plucked olive leaf, so Noah knew the waters had subsided from the earth. Then he . . . sent out the dove, and it did not return to him anymore. . . . Noah built an altar to the Lord . . . and offered burnt offerings. And when the Lord smelled the pleasing odor, the Lord said in his heart, "I will never again curse the ground because of humankind . . . nor will I ever again destroy every living creature as I have done." . . . God blessed Noah and his sons.

Source: Genesis 6:5–9:1, *The New Oxford Annotated Bible* (Oxford: 1994).

Questions for Analysis

1. What are the similarities and differences between these two accounts?

2. What do these differences or similarities reveal about the two societies that told these stories? Does one seem to derive from the other? Why or why not?

3. How is the geography and climate of Mesopotamia reflected in the Sumerian version of the story?

achievement of the era. The Sumerians were using potter's wheels by the middle of the fourth millennium B.C.E. and could produce high-quality clay vessels in greater quantity than ever before. By around 3200 B.C.E., the Sumerians were also using two- and four-wheeled chariots and carts drawn by donkeys. (Horses were unknown in this region until sometime between 2000 and 1700 B.C.E.). Chariots were another new and deadly military technology, giving warriors a tremendous advantage over armies on foot: the earliest depiction of their use, dating from 2600 B.C.E., shows one trampling an enemy. At the same time, wheeled carts dramatically increased the productivity of the Sumerian workforce.

Other inventions derived from the study of mathematics. In order to construct their elaborate irrigation systems, the Sumerians had to develop sophisticated

Engineering Nature

Humans have been manipulating our planet's environment since the Neolithic Revolution. The image on the left shows the irrigation canals that enabled ancient Egyptians to channel the Nile's life-giving waters into the desert. The image on the right shows a storm-surge barrier in the Netherlands, which protects reclaimed land from rising sea levels (ironically) caused by the cumulative results of man-made climate change.

Watch related author videos on the Student Site
wwnorton.com/college/history/western-civilizationsBrief4

measuring and surveying techniques as well as the art of map making. Agricultural needs may also lie behind the lunar calendar they invented, which consisted of twelve months, six lasting 30 days and six lasting 29 days. Since this produced a year of only 354 days, the Sumerians eventually began to add a month to their calendars every few years in order to predict the recurrence of the seasons with sufficient accuracy. The Sumerian practice of dividing time into multiples of sixty has lasted to the present day, not only in our notion of the 30-day month but also in our division of the hour into sixty minutes, each comprised of sixty seconds. Mathematics also contributed to Sumerian architecture, allowing them to build domes and arches thousands of years before the Romans would adopt and spread these architectural forms throughout their empire (Chapter 5).

Sumerian technology depended not only on ingenuity but also the spread of information and raw materials through trade. Sumerian pioneers traced routes up and down the rivers and into the hinterlands of Mesopotamia, following the tributaries of the Tigris and Euphrates. They blazed trails across the deserts toward the west, where they interacted with and influenced the Egyptians. By sea, they traded with the peoples of the Persian Gulf and, directly or indirectly, with the civilizations of the Indus Valley (modern Pakistan and India). And, along with merchandise, they carried ideas: stories, art, the use of writing, and the whole cultural complex that arose from their way of life. The elements of civilization, which had fused in their urban crucible, would thus come together in many other places.

THE FIRST EMPIRES

Evidence shows that competition among Sumerian city-states reached a new level around 2500 B.C.E., as ambitious lugals vied to magnify themselves and their kingdoms. Still, it seems that no Sumerian lugal ever attempted to create an empire by imposing centralized rule on the cities he conquered. As a result, Sumer remained a collection of interdependent but mutually hostile states whose rulers were unable to forge any lasting structures of authority. This pattern would ultimately make the people of Sumer vulnerable to a new style of imperial rulership imposed on them from the north in the person of Sargon the Akkadian.

Sargon and the Akkadian Empire, 2350–2160 B.C.E.

The Akkadians were the predominant people of central Mesopotamia. Their Sumerian neighbors to the south had greatly influenced them, and they had adopted cuneiform script along with many other elements of Sumerian culture. Yet the Akkadians preserved their own Semitic language, part of the linguistic family that includes Hebrew and Arabic. Sumerians tended to regard them as uncivilized, but in the case of the lugal whom the Akkadians called "great king," this probably meant not being bound by the conventions of Sumerian warfare. For Sargon initiated a systematic program of conquest designed to subject all the neighboring regions to his authority. By 2350 B.C.E., he had conquered the cities of Sumer and then moved to establish direct control over all of Mesopotamia.

From his capital at Akkad, Sargon installed Akkadian-speaking governors to rule the cities of Sumer, ordering them to pull down existing fortifications, collect taxes, and obey his will. Sargon thus transformed the independent city-states of Sumer and Akkad into a much larger political unit: the first known empire, a word derived from the Latin *imperium*, "command." This enabled him to manage and exploit the network of trade routes crisscrossing the power broader area known as the Near East. So although his political influence was felt only in Mesopotamia, his economic influence stretched from Ethiopia to India. Sargon's capital became the most splendid city in the world, and he exercised unprecedented power for a remarkable fifty-six years.

Sargon's imperialism also had a marked effect on Sumerian religion. To unite the two halves of his empire, Sargon merged Akkadian and Sumerian divinities. He also tried to lessen the rivalry of Sumerian cities by appointing a single Akkadian high priest or priestess, often a member of his own family, to preside over several local temples.

Sargon's successor, his grandson Naram-Sin, extended Akkadian conquests and consolidated trade, helping to stimulate the growth of cities throughout the Near East and binding them more closely together. By 2200 B.C.E., most people in central and southern Mesopotamia would have been able to converse in the language of either the Sumerians or the Akkadians. Indeed, the two civilizations became virtually indistinguishable except for these different languages.

The Dynasty of Ur and the Amorites, 2100–1800 B.C.E.

After Naram-Sin's death, Akkadian rule faltered. Around 2100 B.C.E., however, a new dynasty came to power in Ur under its first king, Ur-Nammu, and his son Shulgi. Ur-Nammu was responsible for the construction of the great ziggurat at Ur, a massive temple complex that originally rose seventy feet above the surrounding plain. Shulgi continued his father's work, subduing the lands up to the Zagros Mountains northeast of Ur and demanding massive tribute payments from them; one collection site accounted for 350,000 sheep per year, and Shulgi built state-run textile-production facilities to process the wool. He promulgated a code of law, calling for fair weights and measures, the protection of widows and orphans, and limitations on the death penalty for crimes. He also pursued military conquests, the centralization of government, commercial expansion and consolidation, and the patronage of art and literature. Shulgi thus established a pattern of rule that influenced the region for centuries to come.

The Empire of Hammurabi

In 1792 B.C.E., a young Amorite chieftain named Hammurabi (*hah-muh-RAH-bee*) became the ruler of Babylon, an insignificant city in central Mesopotamia. The Amorites, like the Akkadians, were a Semitic people. Until this period they had largely been nomads and warriors, but now they came to control the ancient cities of Mesopotamia.

THE ZIGGURAT OF UR. Built around 2100 B.C.E., this great temple is the best-preserved structure of its kind. It is located at Nasiriyah, in what is now Iraq. Archaeological research (see diagram) reveals that its central shrine, the most sacred part of the temple, was reached by climbing four sets of stairs and passing through a massive portal.

Hammurabi may have been the first ruler in history to understand that power need not be based on force. He recognized that military intelligence, diplomacy, and strategic planning might accomplish what his small army could not. For Hammurabi used writing itself as a weapon. He did not try to confront his mightier neighbors directly. Rather, through letters and embassies, double-dealing and cunning, he induced his stronger counterparts to fight each other. While other Amorite kings exhausted their resources in costly wars, Hammurabi fanned their mutual hatred and skillfully portrayed himself as a friend and ally to all sides. Meanwhile, he quietly strengthened his kingdom, built up his army, and, when the time was right, fell on his depleted neighbors. By such policies, he transformed his small state into what historians call the Old Babylonian Empire.

Under Hammurabi's rule, Mesopotamia achieved an unprecedented degree of political integration. Ultimately, his empire stretched from the Persian Gulf into Assyria. To help unify these territories, Hammurabi introduced another innovation, promoting the worship of the little-known patron god of Babylon, Marduk, and making him the ruler-god of his entire empire. Although he also paid homage to the ancient gods of Sumer and Akkad, Hammurabi made it clear that all his subjects now owed allegiance to Marduk.

The idea that political power derives from divine approval was nothing new, but Hammurabi's genius was to use Marduk's supremacy over all other gods to legitimate his own claim to rule in Marduk's name, because he was king of Marduk's home city. Hammurabi thus became the first known ruler to launch wars of aggression justified in the name of his primary god. This set a precedent for colonial expansion that would become a characteristic feature of Near Eastern politics, as we will see in Chapter 2, and that lies behind nearly all imperial ventures down to the present day.

Yet Hammurabi did not rely solely on religion to bind his empire together. Building on the precedents of past rulers, he also issued a collection of laws, copies of which were inscribed on stone and set up in public places throughout his realm. The example that survives (see page 19) is an eight-foot-tall *stele* (*STEH-leh*) made of gleaming black basalt, originally erected in a central marketplace. The upper portion shows Hammurabi consulting with the god of justice. The phallic form on which the laws were inscribed would have been immediately recognizable as a potent symbol of Hammurabi's authority, obvious even to those who could not read the laws themselves. (It still makes a strong impression on visitors to the Louvre museum in Paris.)

It is impossible to overemphasize the importance of Hammurabi's decision to become a lawgiver. By collecting and codifying legal precedents, like those of Shulgi, Hammurabi declared himself to be (as he stated in the code's preamble) "the shepherd of the people, the capable king"— not a lugal ruling through fear and caprice. This set a new standard of kingship, and expressed a new vision of empire as a union of peoples subject to the same laws.

Centralizing rulers could project their power quickly and effectively up and down its course. Within a remarkably short time, just a century or two after the first cities' appearance in Upper Egypt, they had banded together in a confederacy. The pressure exerted by this confederacy in turn forced the towns of Lower Egypt to adopt their own form of political organization. By 3100 B.C.E., the rivalry between these competing regions had given rise to the two nascent kingdoms of Upper and Lower Egypt.

The Power of the Pharaoh, c. 3100–c. 2686 B.C.E.

With the rise of powerful rulers in these two kingdoms, Egyptian history enters a new phase, one that can be chronicled with unusual precision. The system for numbering the ruling dynasties that emerged in this era—known as the Archaic Period—was actually devised nearly three thousand years later by an historian named Manetho (*mahn-EH-thoh*), who wrote in the third century B.C.E. By and large, Manetho's work has withstood the scrutiny of modern historians and archaeologists, although recent research has added a "Zero Dynasty" of early kings who were instrumental in bringing about the initial unification of Egypt.

Manetho did not record these rulers because he didn't know about them; we know them almost exclusively from archaeological evidence. Among them was an Upper Egyptian warlord known to us as King Scorpion, because the image of a scorpion accompanies engravings that assert his authority. Another warlord, King Narmer, appears to have ruled both Upper and Lower Egypt. His exploits, too, come down to us in powerful pictures (see **Interpreting Visual Evidence** on page 22). Both of these kings probably came from Abydos in Upper Egypt, where they were buried. Their administrative capital, however, was at Memphis, the capital city of Lower Egypt and an important center for trade with the Sinai Peninsula and the Near East.

Following the political unification of Upper and Lower Egypt, the basic features of Egypt's distinctive centralized kingship took shape along lines that would persist for the next 3,000 years. The title used to describe this kingship was *pharaoh*, a word that actually means "great household" and thus refers not to an individual king but to the whole apparatus that sustains his rule. This fact, in turn, helps to explain the extraordinary stability and longevity of Egyptian civilization, which could survive even a dynastic takeover by Macedonian Greeks in the century before Manetho wrote his chronicle (Chapter 4). Indeed, it is comparable to some modern forms of government—none of which has yet lasted so long. As we have seen, kingship in Mesopotamia tended to be a form of personal rule, dependent on the charisma of a particular individual. But in Egypt, the office of the pharaoh was durable enough to survive the deaths of individual successors, facilitating the peaceful transition of power to new rulers and withstanding the incompetence of many.

This was accomplished, as we shall see, by the efficiency of palace bureaucracy, but it was also a function of the pharaoh's close identification with the divine forces credited with renewing Egypt every year. Like the seasons, the pharaoh died only to be born again, renewed and empowered. Egyptian rulers thus laid claim to a sacred nature quite different—and much more benign—than that governing Sumeria. And they were more powerful than any Sumerian lugal, who was never more than a mortal who enjoyed (an all-too-temporary) divine favor.

How the earliest kings of Egypt came to be distinguished as pharaohs and to establish their claims to divinity is still not well understood. We do know, however, that legitimating their rule over all Egypt was difficult. Local civic and religious loyalties remained strong, and for centuries Lower Egyptians would continue to see themselves as distinct from their neighbors to the south. Indeed, it seems probable that the centralization of government in the person of the pharaoh and his association with divinity were related approaches to solving the problem of political unity. And together, these measures had astonishing success. By the end of the Second Dynasty, which coincides with the end of the Archaic Period (2686 B.C.E.), the pharaoh was not just the ruler of Egypt, he *was* Egypt: a personification of the land, the people, and their gods.

The Old Kingdom, c. 2686–2160 B.C.E.

Because so few written sources from the Old Kingdom survive, historians have to rely on funerary texts from the tombs of the elite. These sources are hardly representative, and they have tended to convey the impression that Egyptians were obsessed with death; they also tell us little about the lives of ordinary people. Further complicating the historian's task is the early Egyptians' own belief in the unchanging, cyclical nature of the universe. This makes it difficult for us to reconstruct their history in detail.

However, the surviving inscriptions, papyri, and art of the Third Dynasty (c. 2686–2613 B.C.E.) do tell us a great deal about the workings of the "great household" that undergirded individual rulers' power. This power was vast because the pharaoh was considered to be the intermediary between the land, its people, and their gods, so all the resources of Egypt belonged to him. Long-distance trade

The Narmer Palette

he Narmer Palette (c. 3100 B.C.E.) is a double-sided carving made of green silt-stone. Palettes were used to grind pigments for the making of cosmetics, but the large size (63 cm, over 2 feet) of this one is unusual. It was discovered in 1897 by archaeologists excavating a temple dedicated to the god Horus at Nekhen, the capital of Upper Egypt. Found nearby were other artifacts, including the so-called Narmer Macehead, thought to depict the marriage of Narmer, king of Upper Egypt, to a princess of Lower Egypt.

On the left, dominating the central panel, Narmer wears the White Crown of Upper Egypt (image A). He wields a mace and seizes the hair of a captive kneeling at his feet. Above the captive's head is a cluster of lotus leaves (a symbol of Lower Egypt) and a falcon representing the god Horus, who may be drawing the captive's life force (*ka*) from his body. The figure behind Narmer is carrying the king's sandals; he is depicted as smaller because he is an inferior. The two men in the lower panel are either running or sprawling on the ground, and the symbols above them indicate the name of a defeated town. On the right, the other side of the palette shows Narmer as the chief figure in a procession (image B). He now wears the Red Crown of Lower Egypt and holds a

A. Narmer wearing the White Crown of Egypt.

B. Narmer wearing the Red Crown of Egypt.

mace and a flail, symbols of conquest. Behind him is the same servant carrying his sandals, and in front of him are a man with long hair and four standard-bearers. There are also ten headless corpses. Below, the entwined necks of two mythical creatures (serpopards, leopards with serpents' heads) are tethered to leashes held by two men. In the lowest section, a bull tramples the body of a man whose city the bull is destroying.

Questions for Analysis

1. This artifact has been called "the first historical document in the world," but scholars still debate its meanings.

For example, does it represent something that actually happened, or is it political propaganda? In your view, is this proof that Narmer has united two kingdoms? Why or why not?

2. Do the two sides of the palette tell a coherent story and, if so, on which side does that story begin?

3. What might be significant about the site where the palette was found? Should the palette be interpreted as belonging with the mace found nearby? If so, how might that influence your interpretation of the palette's significance?

was entirely controlled by the pharaoh, as were systems for imposing taxation and conscripting labor. To administer these, the pharaohs installed provincial governors, known to the Greeks as *nomarchs*, many of whom were members of the pharaoh's own family.

Old Kingdom pharaohs kept tight control over the nomarchs and their armies of lesser officials in order to prevent them from establishing local roots in the territories they administered. Writing was therefore critical to internal communication and the management and exploitation of Egypt's vast wealth. This gave rise to a whole class of scribal administrators who enjoyed the power, influence, and status that went along with literacy, a skill few people could command—especially in Egypt, since only experts could master the intricacies of hieroglyphic reading or writing. Even a child just beginning his scribal education was considered worthy of great respect because the training was so difficult. But it carried great rewards. Indeed, the scribal author of a document from the Middle Kingdom called "The Satire of the Trades" exhorted the beginning student to persevere by reminding him how much better off he would be than everyone else.

The Power of Writing

Among the many facets of Egyptian culture that have fascinated generations of scholars is the Egyptian system of pictographic writing. Called *hieroglyphs* (HI-eroh-glifs) or "sacred carvings" by the Greeks, these strange and elaborate symbols remained completely impenetrable (and thus all the more mysterious) until the nineteenth century, when a French

THE ROSETTA STONE. This famous *stele*, carved in 196 B.C.E., preserves three translations of a single decree in three different forms of writing: hieroglyphs (top), demotic Egyptian (middle), and classical Greek (bottom). ■ *Why would scholars be able to use the classical Greek text to decipher the hieroglyphic and demotic scripts?*

scholar named Jean-François Champollion deciphered them with the help of history's most famous decoding device, the Rosetta Stone. This *stele* preserves three versions of the same decree issued in 196 B.C.E., written in ancient Greek, demotic (a later Egyptian script), and hieroglyphics—still in use after more than 3,000 years. Because he could read the text in Greek, Champollion was eventually able to translate the demotic and hieroglyphic texts as well. From this beginning, generations of scholars have added to and refined the knowledge of ancient Egyptian language.

The development of hieroglyphic writing in Egypt dates to around 3200 B.C.E., when pictograms begin to appear in Mesopotamia. But the uses of writing for government and administration developed far more quickly in Egypt than in Sumer. And unlike Sumerian cuneiform, Egyptian hieroglyphics never evolved into a system of phonograms. Instead, the Egyptians developed a faster, cursive script for representing hieroglyphics, called *hieratic* script, which they employed for the everyday business of government and commerce. They also developed a shorthand version that scribes could use for rapid note-taking. Little of this hieratic script remains, however, due to the perishable nature of the medium on which it was usually written: papyrus.

Produced by hammering, drying, and processing river reeds, papyrus was much lighter, easier to write on, and more transportable than the clay tablets used by the Sumerians. When sewn together into scrolls, papyrus also made it possible to record and store large quantities of information in very small packages. Production of this versatile writing material remained one of Egypt's most important industries and exports throughout antiquity and into the Middle Ages. Yet even in the arid environment of Egypt, which has preserved so many ancient artifacts, papyrus is fragile and subject to decay. Compared to the huge volume of papryrus documents that would have been produced, therefore, the quantity that survives is small, and this significantly limits our understanding of Old Kingdom Egypt.

The origins of the ancient Egyptian language in which these texts were written has long been a matter of debate, and it can be plausibly linked to both the Semitic languages of the Near East and a number of African language groups. Whatever its origins, the Egyptian language has enjoyed a long history. Eventually, it became the tongue known as Coptic, which is still used today in the liturgy of the Coptic Christian church in Ethiopia.

Imhotep and the Pyramids

One of the greatest administrative officials in the history of Egypt exemplifies both the skills and the possibilities for advancement that the consummate scribe could command. Imhotep (*im-HO-tep*) rose through the ranks of the pharaoh's administration to become a sort of prime minister to Djoser (*ZOH-ser*), a pharaoh of the Third Dynasty around 2650 B.C.E. Imhotep's learning included medicine, astronomy, theology, and mathematics—but above all he was an architect. Earlier pharaohs had already devoted enormous resources to their burial arrangements at Abydos. It was Imhotep, however, who designed the Step Pyramid, the first building in history constructed entirely of dressed stone. It was not only to be the final resting place of Djoser but an expression of his transcendent power as the pharaoh.

Built west of the administrative capital at Memphis, the Step Pyramid towers 200 feet over the desert. Surrounding this structure was a huge temple and mortuary complex, perhaps modeled after Djoser's palace. These buildings served two purposes. First and foremost, they would provide Djoser's *ka*, his spirit or life force, with a habitation and sustenance in the afterlife. Second, the design of the buildings, with their labyrinthine passageways, would (it was hoped) thwart tomb robbers, a chronic problem as pharaonic burials became more and more tempting to thieves.

Imhotep set a precedent to which all other Old Kingdom pharaohs would aspire. The pyramids on the plain of Giza, built during the Fourth Dynasty (2613–2494 B.C.E.), are a case in point. The Great Pyramid itself, built for the pharaoh Khufu (*KOO-foo*, called Cheops by the Greeks), was originally 481 feet high and 756 feet along each side of its base, constructed from more than 2.3 million limestone blocks and enclosing a volume of about 91 million cubic feet. In ancient times, the entire pyramid was encased in gleaming white limestone and topped by a gilded capstone,

as were the two massive but slightly smaller pyramids built for Khufu's successors. During the Middle Ages, the Muslim rulers of nearby Cairo had their builders strip off the pyramid's casing stones and used them to construct and fortify their new city. (The gold capstones had probably disappeared already.) But in antiquity these pyramids would have glistened brilliantly by day and glowed by night, making them visible for miles in all directions. The Greek historian Herodotus (*heh-RAH-duh-tuhs*), who toured Egypt more than 2,000 years after the pyramids were built, estimated that it must have taken 100,000 laborers 20 years to build the Great Pyramid. This is probably an exaggeration, but it is a measure of the impression these monuments made.

Once thought to have been the work of slaves, the pyramids were in fact raised by tens of thousands of peasant workers, who labored most intensively on the pyramids while their fields were under water during the Nile's annual flood. Still, the investment of human and material resources required to build the great pyramids put grave strains on Egyptian society. Control over the lives of individual Egyptians increased and the number of administrative officials employed by the state grew ever larger. So too did the contrast between the lifestyle of the pharaoh's splendid court at Memphis and that of Egyptian society as a whole.

The End of the Old Kingdom

For reasons that are not entirely clear, the Fifth and Sixth Dynasties of the Old Kingdom (2494–2181 B.C.E.) witnessed the slow erosion of pharaonic power. Although pyramid construction continued, the monuments of this period are less impressive in design, craftsmanship, and size, perhaps mirroring the diminishing prestige of the pharaohs who ordered them built. Instead, the priesthood of Ra at Nekhen, which was the center of worship for the god Horus and the place where Narmer's unification of Egypt was memorialized, began to assert its own authority over that of the pharaoh. Ultimately, it declared that the pharaoh was not an incarnation of Horus or Ra, but merely the god's earthly son. This was a blow to the heart of Egyptian political theology. More practically threatening was the growing power of the pharaoh's nomarchs, whose increased authority in the provinces allowed them to become a hereditary local nobility: precisely what the vigorous kings of earlier dynasties had refused to permit.

Scholars are uncertain as to how some priests and local officials were able to take power away from the pharaonic center. It may be that the costly building efforts of the Fourth Dynasty had overstrained the economy, while the

STEP PYRAMID OF KING DJOSER. This monument to the pharoah's power and divinity was designed by the palace official Imhotep around 2650 B.C.E. It served as a prototype for the pyramids constructed at Giza in the following century.

PYRAMIDS AT GIZA. The Great Pyramid of Khufu (Cheops) is in the center, and was completed c. 2560 B.C.E. The pyramids are not only monuments to pharaonic power, they also exemplify the enormous wealth and human resources of Egyptian society.

continued channeling of resources to the royal capital at Memphis increased shortages and resentments in the provinces. Other evidence points to changing climatic conditions that may have disrupted the regular inundations of the Nile, leading to famine in the countryside. Meanwhile, small states were beginning to form to the south in Nubia. With better organization and equipment, the Nubians may have restricted Egyptian access to precious metal deposits, further crippling the Egyptian economy.

As a result, the pharaoh's power diminished. Local governors and religious authorities began to emerge as the only effective guarantors of stability and order. By 2160 B.C.E., which marks the beginning of what historians call the First Intermediate Period, Egypt had effectively ceased to exist as a united entity. The central authority of the pharaoh in Memphis collapsed, and a more ancient distribution of power reemerged: a northern center of influence based at Herakleopolis (*her-ah-clay-OH-polis*) was opposed by a southern regime headquartered at Thebes, with families from each region claiming to be the legitimate pharaohs of all Egypt.

Compared to the centralized authority of the Old Kingdom, this looks like chaos. But redistribution of power always leads to some important developments in any society. In Egypt, wealth became much more widely and evenly diffused than it had been, as did access to education, the opportunities for the creation of art, and the possibilities for personal advancement. Resources that the pharaoh's court at Memphis had once monopolized now resided in the provinces, enabling local elites to emerge as both protectors of society and as patrons of local artisans. Many arts and luxuries—including elaborate rites for the dead—were developed originally at the pharaoh's court, and had been limited to it. Now, however, they became available to Egyptian society as a whole.

EGYPTIAN CULTURE AND SOCIETY

As already noted, the environment of Egypt and the special benefits it conferred on its inhabitants were construed as peculiar divine gifts, renewed each year through the mediation of the pharoah, who was god on earth. Although the Egyptians told a variety of stories that dealt with the creation of their world, these were not greatly concerned with how humanity came to exist. Rather, what mattered was the means by which all life was created and re-created in an endless cycle of renewal.

Egyptian Religion and Worldview

At the heart of Egyptian religion lay the myth of Osiris and Isis, two of the gods most fundamental to Egyptian belief. Osiris was, in a sense, the first pharaoh: the first god to hold kingship on earth. But his brother, Seth, wanted the throne for himself. So Seth betrayed and killed Osiris, sealing his body in a coffin. Then his loyal sister Isis retrieved the corpse and managed to revive it long enough to conceive her brother's child, the god Horus. Enraged by this, Seth seized Osiris' body and hacked it to pieces, spreading the remains all over Egypt. Still undeterred, Isis sought the help of Anubis, the god of the afterlife. Together, they found, reassembled, and preserved the scattered portions of Osiris' body, thus inventing the practice of mummification. Afterward, Horus, with the help of his mother, managed to defeat Seth. Osiris was avenged and revived as god of the underworld, and the cycle of his death, dismemberment, and resurrection was reflected in the yearly renewal of Egypt itself.

Life and Death in Ancient Egypt

In addition to embodying Egypt's continual regeneration, Osiris exemplified the Egyptian attitude toward death, which was very different from the Sumerians' bleak view. For the Egyptians, death was a rite of passage, a journey to be endured on the way to an afterlife that was more or less like one's earthly existence, only better. To be sure, the journey was full of dangers. After death, the individual body's *ka*, or life force, would have to roam the Duat, the underworld, searching for the House of Judgment. There, Osiris and forty-two other judges would decide the ka's fate. Demons and evil spirits might try to frustrate the ka's quest to reach the House of Judgment, and the journey might take some time. But if successful and judged worthy, the deceased would enjoy immortality as an aspect of Osiris.

Egyptian funerary rites aimed to emulate the example set by Isis and Anubis, who had carefully preserved the parts of Osiris' body and enabled his afterlife. This is why the Egyptians developed their sophisticated techniques of embalming, whereby all of the body's vital organs were removed and then treated with chemicals—except for the heart, which played a key role in the ka's final judgment. A portrait mask was then placed on the mummy before burial, so that the deceased would be recognizable despite being wrapped in hundreds of yards of linen. To sustain the ka on his or her journey, food, clothing, utensils, weapons, and other items of vital importance would be placed in the grave along with the body.

"Coffin texts," or books of the dead, also accompanied the body and were designed to speed the ka's journey. They contained special instructions that would help the ka travel through the underworld and prepare it for the final test. They also described the "negative confession" the ka would make before the court of Osiris, a formal denial of offenses commited in life. The god Anubis would then weigh the deceased's heart against the principle of *ma'at*: truth, order, justice. Because ma'at was often envisioned as a goddess wearing a plumed headdress, a feather from this headdress would be placed in the scales opposite the heart; only if the heart was light (empty of wrongdoing) and in perfect balance with the feather would the ka achieve immortality.

As previously noted, this manner of confronting death has often led to the erroneous assumption that the ancient Egyptians were pessimistic, but in actuality their practices and beliefs were inherently life affirming, bolstered by confidence in the renewal of creation. Binding together this endless cycle was ma'at, the serene order of the universe, and embodying ma'at on earth was the pharaoh. But when that order broke down, so too did their confidence in the pharaoh's power.

Egyptian Science

Given the powerful impression conveyed by their monumental architecture, it may seem surprising that the ancient Egyptians lagged far behind the Sumerians and Akkadians in science and mathematics, as well as in the application of new technologies. Only in the calculation of time did the Egyptians make notable advances, since their close observation of the sun for religious and agricultural reasons led them to develop a solar calendar that was far more accurate than the Mesopotamian lunar calendar. Whereas the Sumerians have bequeathed to us their means of dividing and measuring the day, the Egyptian calendar is the direct ancestor of the Julian Calendar adopted for Rome by Julius Caesar in 45 B.C.E. (see Chapter 5) and later corrected by Pope Gregory XIII in 1582 C.E.; this is the calendar we use today.

The Social Pyramid

The social pyramid of Old Kingdom Egypt was extremely steep. At its apex stood the pharaoh and his extended family, whose prestige and power set them entirely apart from all other Egyptians. Below them was a class of nobles, whose primary role was to serve as priests and officials of the pharaoh's government; scribes were usually recruited and trained from among the sons of these families. All of these Egyptian elites lived in considerable luxury. They owned extensive estates, exotic possessions, and fine furniture. They kept dogs, cats, and monkeys as pets, and hunted and fished for sport.

Beneath this tiny minority was everyone else. Most Egyptians lived in crowded conditions in simple mud-brick dwellings. During a period of prosperity, master craftsmen—jewelers, goldsmiths, and the like—could improve their own conditions and those of their familes by fulfilling the needs of the wealthy, but they did not constitute anything like a middle class. Other skilled professionals—potters, weavers, masons, bricklayers, brewers, merchants, and schoolteachers—also enjoyed some measure of respect as well as a higher standard of living. The vast majority of Egyptians, however, were laborers who provided the brute force necessary for agriculture and construction. Beneath them were slaves, typically captives from foreign wars rather than native Egyptians.

Yet despite the enormous demands the pharaohs placed on Egypt's wealth, their rule does not appear to have been perceived as particularly oppressive. Commoners' belief in the pharaoh's divinity made them willing subjects, as did the material benefits of living in a stable, well-governed society. Even slaves had certain legal rights, including the ability to own, sell, and bequeath personal property.

Unfortunately for historians, the written laws and other documentary practices produced by the lugals of Mesopotamia do not have any Old Kingdom parallels. This makes it difficult to reconstruct social values or the daily lives of commoners through reference to such sources.

The Status of Women

Despite the absence of written laws, there is evidence that Egyptian women enjoyed unusual freedoms by the standards of the ancient world. Female commoners were recognized as

The Instruction of Ptah-Hotep

Egyptian literature often took the form of "instructions" to or from important personages, offering advice to those in public life. This document declares itself to be the advice of a high-ranking official of the Old Kingdom to his son and successor, perhaps composed around 2450 B.C.E. However, the earliest surviving text dates from the Middle Kingdom period.

Be not arrogant because of your knowledge, and be not puffed up because you are a learned man. Take counsel with the ignorant as with the learned, for the limits of art cannot be reached, and no artist is perfect in his skills. Good speech is more hidden than the precious greenstone, and yet it is found among slave girls at the millstones.

. . . If you are a leader commanding the conduct of many, seek out every good aim, so that your policy may be without error. A great thing is *ma'at*, enduring and surviving; it has not been upset since the time of Osiris. He who departs from its laws is punished. It is the right path for him who knows nothing. Wrongdoing has never brought its venture safe to port. Evil may win riches, but it is the strength of *ma'at* that endures long, and a man can say, "I learned it from my father." . . . If you wish to prolong friendship in a house which you enter as master, brother, or friend, or anyplace that you enter, beware of approaching the women. No place in which that is done prospers. There is no wisdom in it.

A thousand men are turned aside from their own good because of a little moment, like a dream, by tasting which death is reached. . . . He who lusts after women, no plan of his will succeed. . . . If you are a worthy man sitting in the council of his lord, confine your attention to excellence. Silence is more valuable than chatter. Speak only when you know you can resolve difficulties. He who gives good counsel is an artist, for speech is more difficult than any craft.

Source: Nels M. Bailkey, ed., *Readings in Ancient History: Thought and Experience from Gilgamesh to St. Augustine*, 5th ed. (Boston, MA: 1995), pp. 39–42.

Questions for Analysis

1. According to Ptah-Hotep, what are the most important attributes of a man engaged in public life? What are the most dangerous pitfalls and temptations he will encounter?

2. Why does Ptah-Hotep emphasize the importance of acting in accordance with *ma'at*? How does this idea of *ma'at* compare to that described elsewhere in the chapter?

3. Based on what you have learned about the changes in Egyptian politics and society, what might indicate that Ptah-Hotep lived during the time of the prosperous Fifth Dynasty of the Old Kingdom? How might these instructions have resonated differently with later readers of the Middle Kingdom?

---

persons in their own right and were allowed to initiate complaints (including suits for divorce), to defend themselves and act as witnesses, to possess property of their own, and to dispose of it, all without the sanction of a male guardian or representative, as was typically required in other ancient societies—and in most modern ones until the twentieth century. Women were not allowed to undergo formal scribal training, but surviving personal notes exchanged between high-born ladies suggest at least some could read and even write.

Normally women were barred from holding high office, apart from that of priestess and also, importantly, queen. Indeed, queens are often represented as the partners of their royal husbands and were certainly instrumental in ruling alongside them. And occasionally, a woman from the royal family might assume pharaonic authority for a time, as did Queen Khasekhemwy (*kah-sehk-KEM-wee*, d. 2686 B.C.E.) on behalf of her son Djoser before he came of age. Some may even have ruled in their own right; this was certainly the case under the New Kingdom (see Chapter 2).

Gender divisions were less clearly defined among the peasantry. The limitations of our sources, however, means that we can only glimpse the lives of peasants through the eyes of their social superiors. Whatever their status, it seems that women did not enjoy sexual equality. While most Egyptians practiced monogamy, wealthy men could and did keep a number of lesser wives, concubines, and female slaves; and any Egyptian man, married or not, enjoyed freedoms that were denied to women, who would be subject to severe punishments under the law if they were viewed as guilty of any misconduct.

The Widening Horizons of the Middle Kingdom (2055–c. 1650 B.C.E.)

After the disruption of Old Kingdom authority around 2160 B.C.E., warfare between competing pharaonic dynasties would continue for over a century. Then, in 2055 B.C.E., the Theban king Mentuhotep II conquered the northerners and declared himself the ruler of a united Egypt. His reign marks the beginning of Egypt's Middle Kingdom and the reestablishment of a unified government, but this time centered in Thebes rather than Memphis. The architect of this new government was Mentuhotep's chief supporter, Amenemhet (*ah-meh-NEHM-het*), who seized power after the king's death and established himself and his descendants as Egypt's Twelfth Dynasty.

This succession of remarkable pharaohs remained in power for nearly 200 years, and under them the Egyptians began to exploit more thoroughly the potential for trade to the south. They secured their border with Nubia

and began to send mounted expeditions to the land they called Punt, probably the coast of Somalia. By the middle of the nineteenth century B.C.E., Nubia was firmly under Egypt's control. Meanwhile, diplomatic relations with the smaller states and principalities of Palestine and Syria led to decisive Egyptian political and economic influence in this region. These lands were not incorporated into Egypt; instead, Amenemhet constructed the Walls of the Prince in Sinai to guard against incursions from the Near East.

The huge fortifications built along Egypt's new frontier demonstrate the great resourcefulness of the Twelfth Dynasty, and their very different ways of allocating resources and expressing ambition. As such, they also display a marked shift in the Egyptian outlook on the world. The placid serenity epitomized by ma'at, and the shared devotion to the pharaoh that had built the pyramids, had been challenged. Egyptians could no longer be dismissive of outsiders or the world beyond their borders. Unlike their Old Kingdom ancestors, the Egyptians of the Middle Kingdom were not turned inward. Their attitude to the pharaoh also seems to have changed. Although they continued to enjoy special position as divine representatives, the pharaohs of the Middle Kingdom represented themselves as what they were expected to be—good shepherds, tenders of their flock. Only by diligently protecting Egypt from a hostile outside world could a pharaoh provide the peace, prosperity, and security desired by his

After You Read This Chapter

 Go to **INQUIZITIVE** to see what you've learned—and learn what you've missed—with personalized feedback along the way.

REVIEWING THE OBJECTIVES

- The study of the distant past is challenging because written sources are rare. What other sources of information do historians use?
- All civilizations require the same basic things and share certain characteristics. What are they?
- The cities of Mesopotamia remained largely independent from one another, yet shared a common culture. Why was this the case?
- Hammurabi's empire created a new precedent for governance in Mesopotamia. How did he achieve this?
- The civilizations of ancient Mesopotamia and Egypt differed in profound ways. What were the major causes of their differences?

subjects; his alignment with ma'at was now conditional, and it had to be *earned*.

The literature of the Middle Kingdom expresses the general change in attitude. Among the most popular literary forms were manuals ostensibly written by or for kings, detailing the duties and perils of high office and offering advice for dealing with difficult situations. These include *The Instruction of Ptah-Hotep* (see **Analyzing Primary Sources** on page 27), an example of Egyptian "wisdom literature" attributed to a court official of the Old Kingdom, which achieved a wider readership in this new era. Ptah-Hotep's teaching is upbeat and practical; by contrast, the examples of this genre produced under the Middle Kingdom are bleakly pragmatic. Reading between the lines, we discern that Egyptians' sense of their own superiority—a product of their isolation and their comparatively benign environment—had been shattered. They saw themselves being drawn into a much wider world, and in the course of the next millennium, they would become more fully a part of it.

CONCLUSION

While the story of Babel records the legendary loss of communication, this chapter shows that people of the distant past can still speak to us. The marks they have left on the landscape, the remains of their daily lives, their written records, and their very bodies make it possible for historians to piece together the evidence and to make sense of it. And every year new sources come to light, meaning that we have to be ready to revise, constantly, our understanding of what happened in the past.

Although this chapter has emphasized the differences between the early civilizations of Mesopotamia and Egypt, it is worth noting some significant similarities. Both developed the fundamental technologies of writing at about the same time, and this facilitated political alliances, long-distance trade, and the transmission of vital information to posterity. During the third millennium, both underwent a process of political consolidation, an elaboration of religious ritual, and a melding of spiritual and political leadership. Both engaged in massive building and irrigation projects, and both commanded material and human resources on an enormous scale. At the same time, each of these civilizations cultivated an inward focus. Although they had some contact with each other, and some transfers of information and technology probably took place, there were few significant political or cultural interactions. For all intents and purposes, they inhabited separate worlds. This relative isolation was about to change, however. The next millennium would see the emergence of large-scale, land-based empires that would transform life in Mesopotamia, Egypt, and the lands that lay between them. These are the developments we examine in Chapter 2.

PEOPLE, IDEAS, AND EVENTS IN CONTEXT

- What fundamental changes associated with the **NEOLITHIC REVOLUTION** made early civilizations possible?
- What new technologies allowed the **SUMERIANS** to master the environment of **MESOPOTAMIA**, and how did these technologies contribute to the development of a new, urbanized society?
- By contrast, why did the Nile River foster a very different civilization and enable the centralized authority of the **PHARAOH**?
- How do the differences between **CUNEIFORM** and **HIEROGLYPHS** reflect the different circumstances in which they were invented and the different uses to which they were put?
- In what ways are the *EPIC OF GILGAMESH* and the *CODE OF HAMMURABI* rich sources of information about the civilizations of Sumer and **BABYLON**?
- How do the **ZIGGURATS** of Mesopotamia and the **PYRAMIDS** of Egypt exemplify different forms of power, different ideas about the gods, and different beliefs about the afterlife?
- Why was the worldview of ancient Egyptians, which was strongly reflected in the concept of **MA'AT** during the **OLD KINGDOM**, altered in significant ways by the time of the **MIDDLE KINGDOM**?

THINKING ABOUT CONNECTIONS

- How do the surviving sources of any period limit the kinds of questions that we can ask and answer about the distant past? In your view, are there sources for this early era that have been undervalued? For example, if writing had not been developed in Mesopotamia and Egypt, what would we still be able to know about the civilizations of these two regions?
- What features of ancient civilizations do modern civilizations share? What might be the implications of these shared ideas, social structures, and technologies?
- In particular, what lessons could we draw from humans' tendency to manipulate their environment? How should knowledge of the distant past influence current debates over sustainability and climate change?

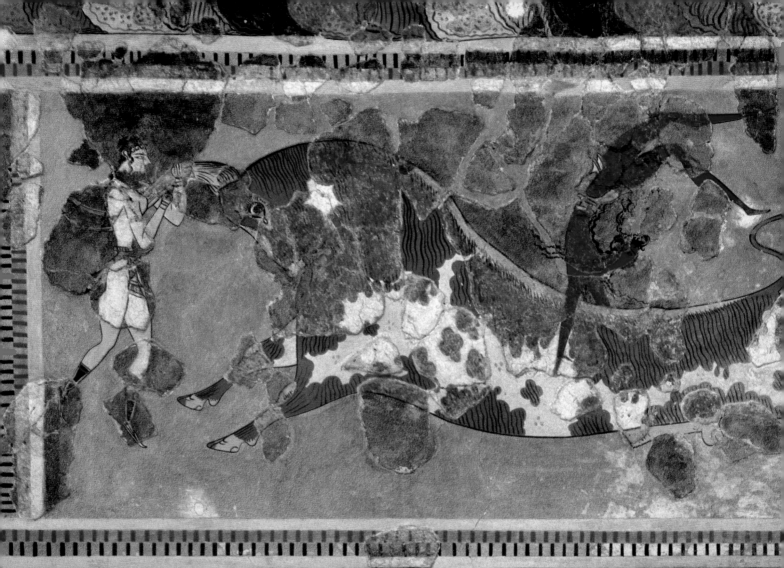

STORY LINES

- During the second millennium B.C.E., new peoples settled in the Near East, spreading a related set of languages known as Indo-European, the ancestor of several major modern language groups.

- In Egypt, the rise of the Eighteenth Dynasty fostered imperial expansion beyond the Nile Valley for the first time.

- During the late Bronze Age, an interconnected network of alliances bound peoples together in new ways. But this civilization was eventually destroyed by the raids of mysterious Sea Peoples.

- In the wake of these invasions, both oppressive new empires and smaller-scale states emerged.

- The worship of Yahweh among the Hebrews and of Ahura-Mazda among the Persians fostered a new view of the world, one in which a single creator god ruled over all peoples.

CHRONOLOGY

1900–1500 B.C.E.	Minoan civilization flourishes
1800–1400 B.C.E.	Creation of the Hittite Empire
1792 B.C.E.	Rise of Babylon under Hammurabi
1650–1550 B.C.E.	Hyksos invasion of Egypt and Second Intermediate Period
1600–1200 B.C.E.	Mycenaean civilization flourishes
1550–1075 B.C.E.	New Kingdom of Egypt established
c. 1200 B.C.E.	Invasions of the Sea Peoples begin
1100–1000 B.C.E.	Philistine dominance in Palestine
1000–973 B.C.E.	Hebrew kingdom consolidated
924 B.C.E.	Israel and Judah divided
883–859 B.C.E.	Neo-Assyrian Empire founded
722 B.C.E.	Kingdom of Israel destroyed
612–605 B.C.E.	Fall of the Neo-Assyrian Empire
586 B.C.E.	Fall of the kingdom of Judah
539–486 B.C.E.	Persian Empire consolidated

Before You Read This Chapter

Peoples, Gods, and Empires, 1700–500 B.C.E.

CORE OBJECTIVES

- **DESCRIBE** the impact of new migrations and settlements on the ancient Near East.

- **DEFINE** the differences between Egypt's New Kingdom and the previous Old and Middle Kingdoms.

- **EXPLAIN** the workings and importance of transnational networks in the late Bronze Age.

- **IDENTIFY** the new empires and kingdoms that emerged in the Iron Age.

- **UNDERSTAND** the historical importance of monotheism.

A ccording to Hesiod, a Greek poet who flourished during the eighth century B.C.E., all of human history falls into five ages. The dawn of time was a golden age, when men lived like gods. Everything was good then, food was plentiful, and work was easy. The next age was silver, when men took gods for granted, killed one another, and lived in dishonor. So the gods destroyed them, sending a mighty flood that spared only the family of Deucalion, who built an ark. Then came the age of bronze, when everything was made of bronze—houses and armor and weapons and tools—and giants fought incessantly from huge strongholds, causing destruction so great that no man's name survives. The time following was short but bright, a heroic age, the time of men who ventured with Theseus and fought beside Achilles and sailed with Odysseus, men whose names will live forever. But Hesiod's own age was iron: a dull age, a time of tedium and strife and bickering and petty feuds.

Hesiod's periodization captures an understanding of history that had evolved with humanity itself and that reflects actual developments. The stories he knew told of a time before cities.

They recalled times of environmental catastrophe. They chronicled the wars of the age we still call Bronze, when the enormous abandoned palaces visible in Hesiod's day were built. And they remembered the race of heroes whose glory was measured by their abiding fame, and who bequeathed a further round of stories. Thanks to new archaeological finds, new linguistic discoveries, and new efforts at decoding the historical record, we can both confirm and correct Hesiod's perspective on the past.

In the second millennium B.C.E., the ancient Near East was transformed by the arrival of new peoples and by the emergence of extensive land-based empires built up through systematic military conquest. These migrations and conquests caused upheaval, but they also led to cultural contact and economic integration that extended from Scandinavia to China. By the thirteenth century B.C.E., nations from the southern Balkans in Europe to the western fringes of Iran in the Ancient Near East had been drawn into a wide-ranging web of relationships.

Yet this extraordinary system proved more fragile than its participants could have imagined. Around 1200 B.C.E., a wave of mysterious invasions led to the destruction of nearly every Bronze Age civilization. As a result, around the turn of the first millennium B.C.E. we enter a new world organized along profoundly different lines. In this new age, iron would slowly replace bronze as the primary component of tools and weapons. New and more brutal empires would come to power, while new ideas about the divine and its relationship to humanity would emerge. Two of the Western world's most enduring religious traditions— Judaism and Zoroastrianism (*zoh-roh-AHS-tree-anism*)— were born, fundamentally altering conceptions of ethics, politics, and the natural world. This Iron Age would prove a fateful historical crossroads, as elements both old and new combined to reconfigure the ancient world.

INDO-EUROPEAN LANGUAGES AND PEOPLES

In 1786, a British judge serving in India made a discovery that transformed the understanding of history. Turning his spare time to the study of Sanskrit, the ancient language of South Asia, Sir William Jones discovered that it shares the same grammar and vocabulary as ancient Greek and Latin—to an extent inexplicable by sheer coincidence. He then examined the early Germanic and Celtic languages of Europe and the Old Persian language of the Near East, and found that they also exhibit marked similarities. He concluded that all of these languages must have evolved from

a common source. Within another generation, the ancient language whose existence Jones had hypothesized, and the later languages derived from it, would be labeled Indo-European, reflecting their wide distribution from India to Ireland. The Biblical story of mankind's shared language, the story of Babel, turns out to be partly true.

Since then, scholars have greatly enlarged our understanding of Indo-European languages and their speakers. Yet much remains controversial. It is certain that Indo-European linguistic forms begin to appear in the Near East and eastern Mediterranean shortly after 2000 B.C.E. Around this same time, a group of Indo-European speakers also moved into the Aegean basin, where the resulting language became an early form of Greek. Other Indo-European speakers went east; some may have reached western China.

These were not the only new peoples moving into the Near East. As we noted in Chapter 1, Semitic-speaking peoples were also making their mark, beginning with the Akkadians and the Amorites, from whose ranks Hammurabi came. The Assyrians, the Phoenicians, and the Canaanites would also become prominent. These newcomers did not wipe out existing cultures; rather, they built on established patterns of urban life and organization. But their collective impact was enormous.

New Settlers in Anatolia

By 1900 B.C.E., the nomadic Assyrians had become caravan merchants whose extensive trade networks stretched across Anatolia and Mesopotamia. They relied on the protection of local rulers and, in turn, they made these rulers rich. They also served as advisers and officials, and married into important urban families. In the process, they carried Mesopotamian civilization and its trappings into far-flung regions.

In their wake, new population groups were attracted to Anatolia, northern Syria, and Mesopotamia. The most formidable of these were the Hittites, an Indo-European-speaking people who arrived around 2000 B.C.E. In contrast to the Assyrians, the Hittites were conquerors and colonists who imposed themselves and their language on the peoples they vanquished. By 1700 B.C.E., they had integrated many city-states into a larger kingdom.

The Hittites' warrior aristocracy fielded the most fearsome army of the Bronze Age. They were quick to adopt the latest technologies, including the chariot and (eventually) the use of iron for weaponry. But the Hittites also adopted the more peaceful practices of those they conquered, using cuneiform to record their own language and laws. And they sought to control trade routes, particularly the overland trade in copper and arsenic, the raw materials for making bronze. By 1595 B.C.E., they had captured Babylon.

A century later, the Kassites, another new people, moved into that devastated city. For the next 500 years, they presided over a largely prosperous Babylonian realm. The Hittites, however, continued to destabilize the region, until they were themselves checked by the arrival of a people known as the Mitannians, whose initial advantage was their use of horses, hitherto unknown outside the steppes of Asia. Their light, horse-drawn chariots became terrifying death-machines, transporting archers rapidly around the battlefield. The Mitannians also pioneered cavalry tactics. Eventually, however, their opponents adopted these same technologies, and the Hittites once again achieved the advantage and turned their attention to Egypt.

THE NEW KINGDOM OF EGYPT

As we have seen, Egypt's Middle Kingdom had been formed by the many internal changes of the First Intermediate Period, chiefly the redistribution of wealth and power. Now it was further transformed by external forces, through the dynamic movement of new peoples. Some of these came to Egypt as immigrants; others were hired as mercenaries. And for a while, a strategy of accommodation preserved Egypt from large-scale armed attack and fostered commercial exchange with neighboring regions. But around 1700 B.C.E., Egypt was invaded for the first time since the unification of the Upper and Lower Kingdoms. These invaders' origins and identity remain mysterious; the Egyptians called them simply Hyksos (HIHK-sohs), "rulers of foreign lands." The Hyksos began to project their authority over most of Lower Egypt.

With this conquest, the central authority of the pharaoh once again dissolved and Egypt entered what scholars call the Second Intermediate Period (c. 1650–1550 B.C.E.). Significantly, however, the Hyksos took over the machinery of pharaonic government in Lower Egypt and took steps to legitimize their rule. In Upper Egypt, by contrast, Hyksos power was weak. Here, a native pharaonic regime maintained a tenuous independence at the traditional capital of Thebes.

Although the Hyksos established Lower Egypt as the most significant power in the Near East, their conquest also weakened the dominion of Upper Egypt over the Nubians, who eventually founded an independent kingdom called Kush. This Nubian kingdom posed a much greater threat to the native dynasty at Thebes than to the Hyksos in Lower Egypt—but it also provided additional incentive to southern pharaohs determined to oust the Hyksos. By the end of the sixteenth century B.C.E., the pharaoh Ahmose had driven them out, establishing the Eighteenth Dynasty and the New Kingdom of Egypt.

The Pharaohs of the Eighteenth Dynasty

Under the Eighteenth Dynasty, Egyptian civilization reached the height of its magnificence and power. Although many Egyptian traditions were renewed and strengthened, the dynamism of the New Kingdom—particularly its new focus on imperial expansion—changed the very fabric of Egyptian life, which had never before looked beyond the narrow world of the Nile Valley.

Among the striking developments that took place during this period was the rise of a new aristocracy whose wealth was acquired through warfare and the winning of lands (with slaves to work them), which they received from the pharaoh as rewards for service. The Eighteenth Dynasty itself was forged in battle. Ahmose, the man who expelled the Hyksos, had been reared by the warrior queen Ahhotep. His eventual successor, Thutmose I (r. 1504–1492 B.C.E.), was the son of an unknown warrior who married Ahmose's daughter.

Under Thutmose's leadership, the Egyptians subdued the Nubians to the south, seizing control of their gold mines. They also penetrated beyond their northeastern frontier, driving deep into Palestine and Syria. By the time of his death, Thutmose could claim to rule the land from beyond the Nile's Fourth Cataract to the banks of the Euphrates. Never had Egypt so clearly declared its imperial ambitions. Nor was this success fleeting. The Egyptians would sustain a strong military presence in the Near East for the next 400 years.

The Legacy of Hatshepsut

The early death of Thutmose's son and successor could have resulted in a crisis for the Eighteenth Dynasty. Instead, it led to one of the most remarkable reigns in Egypt's history, for Thutmose II (r. 1492–1479 B.C.E.) passed the power of pharaoh to his sister, wife, and co-ruler Hatshepsut (haht-SHEHP-suht, r. 1479–1458 B.C.E.). Such brother-sister unions were common in the Egyptian royal family, although they do not appear to have been the routine way to produce royal children: pharaohs customarily kept a harem of subsidiary wives and concubines for this purpose. However, Thutmose II and Hatshepsut did conceive at least one child together, Neferure; in fact, she may have been their designated heir. For 21 years, Hatshepsut ruled as pharaoh in her own right, while her daughter took on the usual duties of queen.

Like her great-grandmother Ahhotep, Hatshepsut was a warrior. Moroever, she was routinely protrayed on

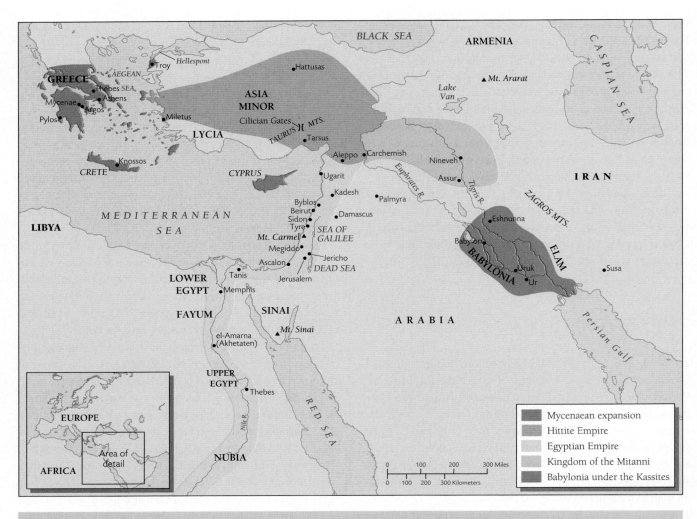

Map labels:

BLACK SEA · ARMENIA · CASPIAN SEA
Troy · Hellespont · Hattusas · ▲Mt. Ararat · Lake Van
GREECE · AEGEAN SEA · ASIA MINOR
Thebes · Athens · Mycenae · Argos · Miletus · Pylos
Cilician Gates · TAURUS MTS. · Tarsus · Aleppo · Carchemish · Nineveh · Assur · IRAN
LYCIA · Ugarit · Kadesh · Palmyra · ZAGROS MTS.
Knossos · CRETE · CYPRUS · Euphrates R. · Tigris R.
MEDITERRANEAN SEA · Byblos · Beirut · Sidon · Damascus · Eshnunna · Babylon · Uruk · ELAM · Susa
LIBYA · Tyre · Mt. Carmel ▲ · SEA OF GALILEE · BABYLONIA · Ur
Megiddo · Jericho · DEAD SEA
Ascalon · Jerusalem · ARABIA
LOWER EGYPT · Tanis · Memphis · SINAI
FAYUM · el-Amarna (Akhetaten) · ▲Mt. Sinai · Persian Gulf
UPPER EGYPT · Thebes · RED SEA · Nile R.
NUBIA

Area of detail · EUROPE · AFRICA

Legend:
Mycenaean expansion
Hittite Empire
Egyptian Empire
Kingdom of the Mitanni
Babylonia under the Kassites

0   100   200   300 Miles
0   100   200   300 Kilometers

EGYPT AND ITS NEIGHBORS, c. 1400 B.C.E. ▪ *What factors appear to shape patterns of conquest and settlement in the Mediterranean?* ▪ *What political developments dominate this map?* ▪ *What developments would have enabled trade to flourish during this period?*

monuments and in statuary with the masculine figure and ceremonial beard characteristic of pharaohs. She did not pretend to be a man: inscriptions almost always indicate her sex, and she herself claimed to be the most beautiful woman in the world. But it was important to Egyptians that she use the conventional iconography of power to locate herself firmly within a long history of male dynastic rule.

Hatshepsut's statecraft proved crucial to the continuing success of Egypt. With her stepson/nephew, Thutmose III, she launched several successful military campaigns and extended trade. The arts also flourished, setting standards that would be emulated for a thousand years. Indeed, Hatshepsut was one of the most ambitious builders in Egyptian history, which is saying something. Her own mortuary temple was probably the first tomb constructed in the Valley of the Kings, the New Kingdom's answer to the pyramids.

Yet after Hatshepsut's death in 1458 B.C.E. her legacy was called into question. At some point late in her nephew's reign, attempts were made to remove her name from inscriptions and to destroy her images (see **Interpreting Visual Evidence** on page 36). Scholars used to assume that Thutmose himself was responsible for this, because he resented his stepmother/ aunt's power over him. But more recent research has suggested that the culprit was his son, Amenhotep II (r. 1427– 1400 B.C.E.), who was thereby blocking the claims of royal rivals, possibly Hatshepsut's daughter, Neferure.

Religious Change and Political Challenges

The great conquests of the Eighteenth Dynasty brought mind-boggling riches to Egypt. Much of this wealth went to the glorification of the pharaoh in the form of grand temples, tombs, and other monuments, including the thousands of steles that provide us with so much information about this era. Another significant portion of the plunder went to the military aristocracy that made such conquests possible. But the lion's share went to the gods as offerings of thanks. As the temples became wealthy and powerful, so too did their priests. But no temple complex was so well endowed as that of Amon at Thebes.

Thebes was not only the capital of New Kingdom Egypt, it was also the place most sacred to Amon (or Amun), the god of creation, who played an important role in the dynasty's self-image. Amon had come into prominence when the political center of gravity shifted to Thebes during the Middle Kingdom, and his cult had steadily increased in status and popularity. By 1550 B.C.E. he had become identified as another manifestation of the sun god Ra, and was believed to be the divine force behind the Eighteenth Dynasty's triumph over the Hyksos. This accounts for the favor shown to his priests at Thebes, who became a formidable political force. Eventually, they surpassed even the military aristocracy in importance and influence.

AKHENATEN, HIS WIFE NEFERTITI, AND THEIR CHILDREN. The Aten is depicted here as a sun disk, raining down power on the royal family. ■ *What messages might this image have conveyed to contemporary Egyptians?* ■ *How does this depiction of the pharaoh differ from earlier precedents?*

The Reign of Akhenaten (1352–1336 B.C.E.)

All of these factors are important when we consider the reign of Amenhotep IV, who inherited the vast, well-governed kingdom assembled by his predecessors. This young pharaoh showed an early inclination toward the worship of the sun, but not as an aspect of Amon. Instead, Amenhotep (whose dynastic name means "Amon Is Pleased") exalted Ra as a discrete divinity and laid aside the traditional iconography of this god as a falcon (or a falcon-headed man), replacing it with the symbol *Aten*, the hieroglyph representing the sun's rays. He then went farther, changing his own name to Akhenaten (*AH-keh-NAH-ton*), "He Who Is Profitable to the Aten," and building a new capital to honor the god. Located halfway between Memphis and Thebes, it was called Akhetaten ("The Horizon of the Aten").

Although the priesthood of Amon exalted Amon-Ra, it also recognized all the other gods of Egypt. Akhenaten's theology, by contrast, was closer to monotheism. And unlike traditional Egyptian deities, the Aten could not be imagined as taking on human or animal form. Akhenaten also celebrated his new religion by representing himself in a very unconventional way. In a complete departure from the divine virility of his ancestors—which even

his ancestor Hatshepsut had emulated—Akhenaten had himself pictured as a family man enjoying the company of his wife, Nefertiti, and their children. This emphasis on his own humanity might have been an extension of his theology, which honored the life force within every being. But it was also dangerous to the ideology of royal power. The pharaoh was not supposed to be a man with quirky personality. He was supposed to be a god on earth.

Akhenaten's spiritual revolution therefore had enormous political implications. Not surprisingly, the priesthood of Amon also put up strenuous resistance. To make matters worse, Akhenaten did not balance his theological enthusiasm with attention to Egypt's interests abroad. This cost him the support of his nobility and may even have led to his deposition. He was ultimately succeeded by one of his younger sons, Tutankhaten ("Living Image of the Aten"), a child of nine whose name was quickly changed to reflect the restoration of the god Amon and his priesthood. He became Tutankhamun (r. 1333–1324 B.C.E.), the boy king whose sumptuous tomb was discovered in 1922. After his early death, he was succeeded by a general called Horemheb, who reigned as the last pharaoh of the Eighteenth Dynasty. When he died, he passed his office to another general. This was Ramses, the founder of the Nineteenth Dynasty, who would restore Egypt to glory in the Near East.

Remembering Hatshepsut

he pharaohs of Egypt's New Kingdom carefully controlled their public images. The visual language they used was highly symbolic, an iconography (vocabulary of images) intended to make each successive pharaoh look as much like his royal predecessors as possible: godlike, steadfast, virile, authoritative—even when the pharaoh was a woman, Hatshepsut (r. 1479–1458 B.C.E., images A and B). So many statues and portraits of her survive that nearly every major museum in the world has at least one (the Metropolitan Museum of Art in New York has a whole room set aside for them). But many of these images show signs of having been defaced during the reign of her successor, Thutmose III, who was also her nephew and stepson. Until very recently, scholars assumed that Hatshepsut must have usurped his powers, and that this was his revenge. Yet the evidence clearly shows that Hatshepsut was Egypt's legitimate ruler. Why, then, would Thutmose III or his heirs have tried to efface her memory?

The two unblemished *steles* shown here depict Hatshepsut and Thutmose III. In the *stele* on the left (image C), Hatshepsut is placed in the center of the frame, wearing a royal helmet; she is offering wine to the god Amun. Behind her stands Thutmose III, wearing the crown of Upper Egypt. In the *stele* on the right (image D), Thutmose III wears the warrior's crown, while Hatshepsut wears the double crown of Upper and Lower Egypt and wields a mace.

Questions for Analysis

1. Bearing in mind that few Egyptians could read the hieroglyphs accompanying these images, how might they

A. Defaced head of Hatshepsut.

B. Undefaced statue of Hatshepsut.

TRANSNATIONAL NETWORKS OF THE LATE BRONZE AGE

Bronze Age history must be understood within the context of what we might call international relations. Yet it is more accurate to call the political and economic networks of this period *transnational*, because this web of alliances and relationships transcended any idea of national identity.

This Late Bronze Age was an age of superpowers. The great pharaohs of the Eighteenth Dynasty had transformed Egypt into a conquering state, and the Hittites had created an empire out of the disparate city-states and kingdoms of Anatolia. The Assyrians controlled Near Eastern trade, and the Kassite kingdom of Babylonia remained a significant force in economic and military relationships. In addition to these imperial entities, numerous smaller states flourished and extended their influence. Holding it all together was a

have "read" the relationship between these two royal relatives? Does this evidence support the hypothesis that Thutmose was slighted by Hatshepsut?

2. What can these images tell us about gender roles? What else would we need to know before making a judgment about masculine and feminine characteristics in ancient Egypt?

3. Given that Hatshepsut was Egypt's legitimate pharaoh, what might have motivated either Thutmose III or his son Amenhotep II to deface her image many years after her death?

C. *Stele* of Hatshepsut and Thutmose.

D. *Stele* of Thutmose and Hatshepsut, from the Red Chapel at Karnak.

network of trade that created an interdependent Afro-Eurasian world.

Transnational Diplomacy

Although warfare remained the fundamental mode of interaction, a balance of power among the larger empires gradually helped to stabilize the region. By the fourteenth century B.C.E., a wide-ranging correspondence was binding leaders together and promoting a set of mutual goals and understandings. Surviving letters show that the most powerful rulers address one another as "brother," while lesser princes and chieftains show their deference to the pharaoh, the Hittite king, and other sovereigns by using the term "father." Rulers of this period also exchanged lavish gifts and entered into marriage alliances with each other. Professional envoys journeyed back and forth, conveying gifts and handling politically sensitive missions. Some of these emissaries were also merchants, sent to explore the possibility of trading opportunities as well as to cement alliances.

Transnational Trade

Indeed, it was trade that allowed smaller communities to become integral parts of this transnational network. Seaside cities such as Ugarit and Byblos became centers for the exchange of dazzling commodities. A single vessel's cargo might contain scores of distinct items originating anywhere from the interior of Africa to the Baltic Sea, as demonstrated by the contents of a merchant ship discovered at Uluburun off the Turkish coast in 1982. The region was also supplied with goods brought in overland, via contacts reaching into India and the Far East.

Trade was not only the basis for a new economy, but the conduit for art, ideas, and technology. In the past, such influences spread slowly and unevenly; now, the societies of the late Bronze Age could keep abreast of all the latest developments. This trend was particularly marked in large coastal towns. At Ugarit, on the coast of modern-day Syria, the swirl of commerce and the multiplicity of languages spoken by traders even propelled the development of a simpler form of writing than the cuneiform still in use throughout most of the Near East. The Ugaritic alphabet consisted of about thirty symbols representing the sounds of consonants. (Vowels had to be inferred.) This system was far more easily mastered and more flexible than cuneiform, and it would become the model for the development of all modern alphabets.

The search for markets, resources, and trade routes also promoted greater understanding among cultures. After a great battle between Egyptians and Hittites near Kadesh (c. 1275 B.C.E.), the pharaoh Ramses II realized that more was to be gained through peaceful relations with his northern neighbors than through warfare. The treaty he established with the Hittites fostered stability and allowed further economic exchanges to flourish.

But greater integration also meant greater mutual dependence. If one economy suffered, the effects of that decline were sure to be felt elsewhere. And the farther this transnational system spread, the more vulnerable it became. Many of the new markets depended on emerging societies in far less stable regions, where civilization was also new.

AEGEAN CIVILIZATIONS: MINOAN CRETE, MYCENAEAN GREECE

Greek poets like Hesiod described a heroic age when great men mingled with gods and powerful kingdoms contended for wealth and glory. For a long time, modern scholars dismissed these stories as fables. Tales of Theseus and the Minotaur, the Trojan War, and the wanderings of Odysseus were regarded as reflecting no historical reality. Greek history was assumed to begin in 776 B.C.E., when the first recorded Olympic Games occurred. The Greece of the Bronze Age was considered a primitive backwater that played no significant role in the Mediterranean world or in the later, glorious history of classical Greece.

But in the late nineteenth century, an amateur archaeologist named Heinrich Schliemann became convinced that these myths were really historical accounts. Using the epic poems of Homer as his guide, he found the site of Ilium (Troy) near the coast of northwest Anatolia. He also identified a number of once-powerful citadels on the Greek mainland, including the home of the legendary king Agamemnon at Mycenae (*MY-seh-nee*). Soon afterward, the British archaeologist Sir Arthur Evans took credit for discovering the remains of a great palace at Knossos on the island of Crete that predated any of the major citadels on the Greek mainland. He dubbed this magnificent culture—which no modern person had known to exist—"Minoan," after King Minos, the powerful ruler whom the ancient Greeks described as dominating the Aegean, and the man for whom the engineer Daedalus had designed the Labyrinth. Although some of their conclusions have proven to be false, the discoveries of Schliemann and Evans forced scholars to revise, entirely, the history of Western civilizations. It is now clear that Bronze Age Greece—or, as it is often termed, Mycenaean Greece—was an important and integrated part of the Mediterranean world during the second millennium B.C.E.

The Minoan Thalassocracy

In the fifth century B.C.E., the Athenian historian Thucydides wrote that King Minos of Crete had ruled a *thalassocracy*, an empire of the sea. We now know that he was correct, that a very wealthy civilization began to flourish on the island of Crete around 2500 B.C.E. Thereafter, for about a millennium, the Minoans controlled shipping around the central Mediterranean and the Aegean, and may have exacted tribute from many smaller islands. At its height between 1900 and 1500 B.C.E., Minoan civilization was the contemporary of Egypt's Middle Kingdom and the Hittite kingdom. And unlike them, it was virtually unassailable by outside forces, protected by the surrounding sea.

Analyzing Primary Sources

The Diplomacy of the Mycenaeans and the Hittites

Around 1260 B.C.E., the powerful Hittite king Hattusilis III sent the following letter to a "King of Ahhiyawa," identifiable as a leader of the Mycenaean Greeks, who often called themselves Akhaiwoi, Achaeans. This fascinating document exemplifies the tangle of close ties that bound powerful men together within the transnational system of the Late Bronze Age, as well as the problems and misunderstandings that could arise from the misbehavior of men under their command. The events referenced here all occurred in western Anatolia (Turkey), a region controlled partly by the Hittites and partly by the Greeks, the same region in which Troy (Ilium) was located. (See the map on page 34.)

... have to complain of the insolent and treacherous conduct of one Tawagalawas [*tah-wah-GAH-la-wahs*]. We came into contact in the land of Lycia, and he offered to become a vassal of the Hittite Empire. I agreed, and sent an officer of most exalted rank to conduct him to my presence. He had the audacity to complain that the officer's rank was not exalted enough; he insulted my ambassador in public, and demanded that he be declared vassal-king there and then, without the formality of an interview. Very well: I order him, if he desires to become a vassal of mine, to make sure that no troops of his are found in Iyalanda when I arrive there. And what do I find when I arrive in Iyalanda?— the troops of Tawagalawas, fighting on the side of my enemies. I defeat them, take many prisoners ... scrupulously leaving the fortress of Atriya intact out of respect for my treaty with you. Now a Hittite subject, Piyamaradus [*pie-yah-ma-RA-dus*] by name, steals my 7,000 prisoners, and makes off to your city of Miletus. I command him to return to me: he disobeys. I write to you: you send a surly message unaccompanied by gift or greeting, to say that you have ordered your representative in Miletus, a certain Atpas, to deliver up Piyamaradus. Nothing happens, so I go fetch him. I enter your city of Miletus, for I have something to say to Piyamaradus, and it would be well that your subjects there should hear me say it. But my visit is not a success. I ask for Tawagalawas: he is not at home. I should like to see Piyamaradus: he has gone to sea. You refer me to your representative Atpas: I find that both he and his brother are married to daughters of Piyamaradus; they are not likely to give me satisfaction or to give you an unbiased account of these transactions. ... Are you aware, and is it with your blessing, that Piyamaradus is going round saying that he intends to leave his wife and family, and incidentally my 7,000 prisoners, under your protection while he makes continual inroads on my dominion? ... Do not let him use Achaea [in Greece] as a base for operations against me. You and I are friends. There has been no quarrel between us since we came to terms in the matter of Ilios [the territory of Troy]: the trouble there was my fault, and I promise it will not happen again. As for my military occupation of Miletus, please regard it as a friendly visit. ... [As for the problems between us], I suggest that the fault may not lie with ourselves but with our messengers; let us bring them to trial, cut off their heads, mutilate their bodies, and live henceforth in perfect friendship.

Source: Adapted from Denys Page, *History and the Homeric Iliad* (Berkeley, CA: 1959), pp. 11–12.

Questions for Analysis

1. Reconstruct the relationship between Hattusilis III and the Achaean king, based on the references to people and places in this letter. What picture emerges of their interactions, and of the connections between the Hittite Empire and Mycenaean Greece?

2. Why is Hattusilis so concerned about the disrespect shown to him by the Achaeans? Reading between the lines, what do you think he wanted to accomplish by sending this letter?

3. Based on this letter, what can you deduce about the standards of behavior expected of civilized participants in the transnational system of the Late Bronze Age? Within this code of conduct, what sanctions or penalties could be imposed on individuals or their nations?

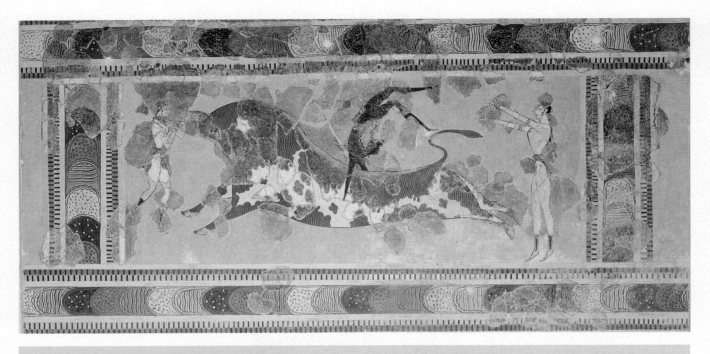

MINOAN FRESCO, C. 1500 B.C.E. A stylized representation of bull-leaping, painted into the plaster of a wall at Knossos. ■ *Is this likely to represent real practices?* ■ *Why or why not?*

Thanks to its strategic position, Crete was not only a safe haven but also a nexus of vibrant economic exchange. Like its counterparts in the Near East, it acted as a magnet for the collection of resources which were then redistributed by its rulers and their emissaries. Knossos was also a production center for textiles, pottery, and metalwork. Minoan merchants traded these with Egypt, southwest Anatolia, and Cyprus for a range of exotic goods. Artistic influences also traveled along these routes; among much else, Minoan-style paintings from this period appear regularly in the Nile Delta and the Levant.

Traces of the bright colors and graceful lines of these paintings are still evident on the ruined walls of the palace at Knossos (*Kuh-NOSS-oss*). Furnished with indoor plumbing, among other luxuries, it covered several acres and comprised hundreds of rooms joined by an intricate network of winding hallways that inspired the famous story of the Labyrinth. The Minoans probably worshiped a god in the form of a bull or bull-man, and they appear to have devised an elaborate ritual sport known as bull-leaping, similar to bull-fighting but involving an element of athletic dance. There is also some evidence that they practiced human sacrifice (possibly facilitated by the dangers of bull-dancing) as a religious rite.

Despite all these fascinating remains, Minoan culture remains mysterious because its language has yet to be decoded. Its script is called Linear A, to distinguish it from

Linear B, used in Mycenaean Greece—a script that *has* been deciphered. Although Linear A and Linear B represent different languages, the formal relationship between them reflects the fact that Minoan commercial activity engaged the mainland of Greece. The presence of a wide variety of Minoan objects on the Greek mainland corroborates this.

Yet the dynamics of the relationship between Minoans and Mycenaeans remains debatable. Before 1600 B.C.E., the Minoans were clearly much more sophisticated and may have dominated their Greek neighbors. One story told of Theseus describes how the hero was sent to Crete as a hostage, intending to free Athens from the heavy tribute imposed by King Minos. Given what we have already learned about the close relationship between myth and history, it is probable that this story preserves ancient memory, just as the story of Daedalus is an attempt to explain the technological marvels of the palace at Knossos.

Mycenaean Greece

When Linear B was deciphered in the early 1950s, the texts written in this script spurred scholars to reconsider the history of ancient Greece. Since then, new research shows that the Indo-Europeans whose language became Greek entered the region in several waves after the turn of the second

LINEAR B TABLET FROM KNOSSOS. Unlike cuneiform, whose characters are formed using the wedge-shaped tip of a reed, the scripts of Linear A and B used a sharp stylus that incised fine lines in clay or soft stone.

The basic political and commercial unit of the Mycenaean world—a powerful king and war leader, a warrior aristocracy, a palace bureaucracy, a complex economy, large territorial kingdoms—differs markedly from the Greek city-state of the classical age (Chapter 3). However, we can trace some features of this later civilization back to the Mycenaeans, including the Greek language. Linear B tablets speak of a social group with considerable economic and political rights, the *damos*; this may be the precursor of the *demos*, the urban population that sought political empowerment in many Greek cities. The tablets also preserve the names of several gods familiar from the later period, such as Zeus, Poseidon, and Dionysos. And later Greeks believed themselves to be descended from these legendary forebears, whom they credited with superhuman achievements. Although they knew little about their Mycenaean ancestors in fact, the impact of what they imagined about them was considerable.

The Sea Peoples and the End of the Bronze Age

The civilization of Mycenaean Greece seems to have collapsed around the end of the thirteenth century B.C.E. What triggered this cannot be determined with any certainty, but the consequences of the collapse are clear. Because Mycenaean Greece was an integrated part of a transnational network, the effects of its demise were felt throughout the Mediterranean and the Near East. Thereafter, a wave of devastation swept from north to south, caused by a group of people so thoroughly destructive that they obliterated everything in their path. We might know nothing about them were it not for a narrow victory by the pharaoh Ramses III around 1176 B.C.E.

In the *stele* set up to commemorate his triumph, Ramses III referred to these invaders as "Sea Peoples" and named several groups as part of a coalition. Some were familiar to the Egyptians, and it seems that many were from the Aegean. Most notable were the Philistines who, after their defeat, withdrew to populate the coast of the region named after them: Palestine.

Because the Sea Peoples' arc of annihilation started in the north, it may have been one of the factors contributing to the collapse of Mycenaean Greece. Disruption of northern commercial networks would have devastated the Mycenaean kingdoms, which could not support their enormous populations without trade. Suddenly faced with an apocalyptic combination of overpopulation, famine, and violence, bands of desperate refugees would have fled the Aegean basin. Meanwhile, the damage to commerce devastated the

millennium, dominating and displacing the indigenous inhabitants. By 1500 B.C.E., huge citadels dotted the Greek landscape, ruled by warriors whose epitaphs boast of their martial prowess and who were buried with their weapons. The power of these rulers was based on their leadership and their ability to reward followers with plunder. The most successful of them gained control of strategic sites from which they could exploit major trade routes, engaging in both trade and piracy.

Over time, and perhaps under the influence of Minoan culture, the Mycenaean citadels developed into much more complex societies. They served as both centers of government and warehouses for storage. By the thirteenth century B.C.E., some rulers had carved out territorial kingdoms with as many as 100,000 inhabitants; later, Hesiod would imagine their citadels to have been built by giants. These palace centers were adapted from Near Eastern models and their massive size was not ideally suited to the Greek landscape. In war also, Mycenaean imitation of Near Eastern examples had its limits. For example, Mycenaean kings cherished the chariots used by their contemporaries on the plains of Anatolia, yet such chariots were highly impractical on rocky terrain.

Despite these and other differences from their Mediterranean neighbors, the Mycenaean Greeks played an important role in Bronze Age networks. By about 1400 B.C.E., they had subjugated Crete, taking over Knossos and using it as a Mycenaean center. In western Anatolia, not far from Troy, at least one Mycenaean king exercised enough influence for a Hittite ruler to address him as "my brother." This evidence suggests that the Mycenaeans earned prestige as warriors and mercenaries, as the Greeks' heroic poems attest.

MYCENAEAN GREECE. ▪ *What are the main geographical features of Greece?* ▪ *How might this dry, mountainous country surrounded by the sea determine the nature of Greek civilization and economic interests?* ▪ *How might geography have allowed Mycenaean culture to spread so widely?*

of the networks that had undergirded the transnational system, had to fight for their very existence. In Babylon, the peaceful and prosperous rule of the Kassites withered. In the vacuum left behind, new political configurations took shape and a new metallurgical technology began to supplant the use of bronze. Out of the ashes arose the culture of the Iron Age.

THE STATES OF THE EARLY IRON AGE

With the destruction of transnational networks, the geopolitical map of the Near East changed significantly. In Anatolia, a patchwork of small kingdoms grew up within the territories once controlled by the Hittites. Similar developments took place in the Levant: the eastern Mediterranean coastline that today comprises Israel, Lebanon, and parts of Syria. For centuries, this region had been controlled either by the Egyptians or the Hittites. With the collapse of these empires, new states began to emerge here, too. They were small, but they had a huge impact on the history of Western civilizations.

The Phoenicians

The most influential civilization of this period was that of a people whom the Greeks called Phoenicians. They are also known as Canaanites, and were speakers of a Semitic language closely related to Hebrew. During the Late Bronze Age, most Phoenician cities had been controlled by Egypt. But the erosion of Egyptian imperial power after 1200 B.C.E. gave these cities the opportunity to forge a new independence and to capitalize on their commercial advantages. One Phoenician city was a clearing house for papyrus, the highly prized Egyptian writing material. This explains why the Greek name for this city, Byblos, became the basis for the Greek word *biblion*, meaning "book." (The Bible is so called from the plural *biblia*, "the books.") Another valuable commodity came to be the name by which the Phoenicians themselves were known: a rare purple dye derived from the shells of snails culled from seabeds off the Levantine

economy of the Hittites, whose ancient kingdom rapidly disintegrated. Along the Mediterranean coast we find other clues. The king of Ugarit wrote a letter to a "brother" king on the island of Cyprus, begging for immediate aid because he had sent all his own warriors to help the Hittites. Poignantly, however, we have his letter only because the clay tablet on which it was written baked hard in the fire that destroyed his palace. The letter was never sent.

In the end, the Sea Peoples destroyed the civilizations that had flourished in the Near East and Mediterranean for over 2,000 years. The devastation was not total; not all cities disappeared, and trade did not cease entirely. But the Hittite Empire was gone, leaving behind it many weak, short-lived principalities. The great cosmopolitan cities of the eastern Mediterranean lay in ruins, and new groups—sometimes contingents of Sea Peoples like the Philistines—populated the coast. The citadels of Mycenaean Greece were depopulated by as much as 90 percent over the next century, and Greece entered into a period of cultural and economic isolation that would last for 250 years.

The victorious Egyptians survived, but with their major trading partners diminished or dead their civilization suffered. The Assyrians, the original architects

The Fragility of Global Networks

In the late Bronze Age, the destruction of transnational commercial networks had a domino effect on the interlocking civilizations of the West, plunging many into a "dark age" of isolation and impoverishment. The global economic crisis of our own day was caused by a similar phenomenon: the 2008 collapse of mutually dependent financial systems that proved more fragile than anyone had anticipated.

Watch ralated author videos on the Student Site
wwnorton.com/college/history/western-civilizationsBrief4

coast. So as far as the Greeks were concerned, those who supplied this dye were *phoinikeoi*, "purple people." The Phoenicians also became expert metalworkers, ivory carvers, and shipbuilders.

Phoenician Colonies and Cultural Influence

The Phoenicians were also aggressive colonists. By the end of the tenth century B.C.E., they had planted settlements from one end of the Mediterranean to the other and had begun to venture out into the Atlantic Ocean.

The widespread colonial and mercantile efforts of the Phoenicians meant that they influenced cultures across the Mediterranean. Among their early overseas trading partners were the Greeks, and the Phoenicians may have played an important role in reintroducing urban life

to Greece after the collapse of the Mycenaean citadels. While each city of the Phoenician mainland had its own hereditary royal government, in the Phoenicians' overseas colonies a new type of political system emerged in which power was shared among a handful of elite families. This aristocratic form of government would become a model for many other Western societies, including those of Greece and Rome.

Without question, however, the most important contribution of the Phoenicians was their alphabet. As we noted earlier, a thirty-character system had evolved at Ugarit by the end of the Bronze Age. Around 1100 B.C.E., the Phoenicians refined this writing system to twenty-two characters. This simpler alphabet further facilitated trade and accounting, and the Phoenicians may have wanted to encourage similar practices among their partners to safeguard their own interests. The Greeks certainly remained aware of their debt to the Phoenicians: their legends ascribe the invention of the

Phoenician	Hebrew	Classical Greek	Modern Alphabetic
𐤀	א	A	A
𐤁	ב	B	B
𐤂	ג	Γ	G
𐤃	ד	Δ	D
𐤄	ה	E	E
𐤅	ו	Y	V
𐤆	ז	Z	Z
𐤇	ח	H	H
𐤈	ט	Θ	TH
𐤉	י	I	Y
𐤊	כ	K	K
𐤋	ל	Λ	L
𐤌	מ	M	M
𐤍	נ	N	N
𐤎	ס	Ξ	S
𐤏	ע	O	O
𐤐	פ	Π	P
𐤑	צ		TZ
𐤒	ק	Ϙ	Q
𐤓	ר	P	R
𐤔	ש	Σ	S
𐤕	ת	T	T

THE EVOLUTION OF THE ALPHABET. This table shows how the shapes of letters changed as the Phoenician alphabet was adapted by the Hebrews, the Greeks, and eventually the Romans (from whom our modern alphabet derives).

alphabet to Cadmus, a Phoenician who settled in Greece. Their debt is also clear in the close relationship between the names of letters in Greek (alpha, beta, gamma, delta . . .) and Phoenician letter names (aleph, bayt, gimel, dalet . . .), and from the obvious similarities in letter shapes.

The Philistines

Southward along the Levantine coast from Phoenicia lay the land of the Philistines, descendants of the Sea Peoples defeated by Ramses III. Their bad reputation is the result of their dominance over their neighbors, the herdsmen known as the Hebrews, who used writing as an effective weapon against them: the Philistines are the great villains of the

Hebrew scriptures, and the word *philistine* has accordingly come to mean a boorish, uncultured person. Because the Philistines do not appear to have made use of the same powerful technology to record their own outlook on the world, and almost everything we know about them comes from the work of archaeologists, or has to be sifted through the bad press of their detractors. We know little about their language, but their material culture, behavior, and organization exhibit close affinities with Mycenaean Greece.

Philistine power was based on five great strongholds, the so-called Pentapolis (Greek for "five cities"): Gaza, Ashkelon, and Ashdod on the coast, and the inland cities of Ekron and Gath. Again, these citadels are strikingly similar to the fortified palaces of Mycenaean civilization, and they appear to have served many of the same functions. From these strongholds, the Philistines dominated the surrounding countryside by organizing agricultural production and controlling trade routes. An independent lord ruled over each citadel, and no doubt tensions and rivalries existed among them. But much like the heroes of Greek epic, the Philistines could set aside differences when facing a common enemy.

Because we see the Philistines primarily through the eyes of their Hebrew enemies, we must be careful about drawing conclusions about them from the stories of Goliath's brutality or Delilah's sexual treachery. Yet the Hebrews had good reason to fear the Philistines, whose pressure on the Hebrew hill country was constant and who threatened the Hebrews' holy sanctuary at Shiloh, where the sacred Ark of the Covenant was said to contain the original tablets of the law given to Moses on Mount Sinai. In Hebrew tradition, the tribes of Israel had once carried the Ark before them into battle against the Philistines, only to lose it in the fray and to witness thereafter the destruction of Shiloh. The Philistines then established garrisons throughout the land of the Hebrews, exacted tribute, and denied them access to weapons.

The Hebrews and Their Scriptures

The central feature of Hebrew culture, their conception of and relationship to their god, will be discussed at greater length toward the end of this chapter. In this section, we focus our attention on the development of Hebrew society— while acknowledging that religion is always related to politics, as well as to economic conditions and the concerns of everyday life. Indeed the Hebrews, like all ancient peoples, could not have distinguished among these phenomena.

In reconstructing the early history of the Hebrews, we are indebted to an unusual textual source: a series of scriptures (literally "writings") that comprise mythology, laws

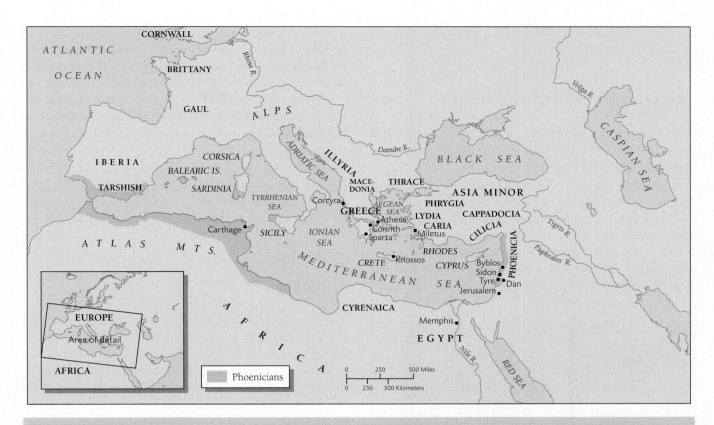

PHOENICIAN COLONIZATION. Compare this map to the more detailed one of the Hebrew kingdoms on page 46. ▪ *What part of the Mediterranean served as the homeland for the Phoenician city-states, and where did Phoenicians establish colonies?* ▪ *Why would overseas colonization be of such crucial importance to Phoenician city-states?* ▪ *What does their westward colonization imply about the Phoenicians' aims and about the different opportunities available in the West, as compared with the East?*

and ritual practices, genealogical records, books of prophecy, proverbs, poetry, and royal chronicles. These are collectively known as the Hebrew Bible or (among Christians) as the Old Testament. The books of the Bible were assembled over many centuries, mostly by unknown authors, copyists, and editors. Like other sources, they have to be treated as artifacts produced by particular historical circumstances, which also governed the way that certain texts were preserved and put together.

The first five books of the Hebrew Bible are traditionally attributed to Moses, but most of the materials in these books were borrowed from other Near Eastern cultures, including the stories of creation and the flood, which parallel those of Sumer (as we saw in Chapter 1). The story of Moses's childhood draws on a legend told about the Akkadian king Sargon the Great. And the story of the exodus from Egypt is fraught with problems. Although the later Book of Joshua claims that the Hebrews who returned from Egypt conquered and expelled the native Canaanites, archaeological and linguistic evidence suggests that the Hebrews were essentially Canaanites themselves. They may have merged with scattered refugees from Egypt in the aftermath of the

Sea Peoples' invasions, but for the most part they had been continuously resident in Canaan for centuries. In other words, the first five books of the Bible constitute a retrospective history whose purpose was to justify Hebrew traditions and claims to territory.

Among the other writings included in the Hebrew Bible are a group of texts which record events of the more recent past, those of the period we are considering now. These "historical books" are more straightforwardly verifiable, even if many details are difficult to confirm. According to the Book of Judges, the Hebrews were wandering herdsmen who had just begun to establish permanent settlements around the time of the Philistines' arrival in the Levant. They had organized themselves into twelve tribes—extended clan units whose families owed one another mutual aid and protection in times of war, but who frequently fought over cattle and grazing rights. Each tribe was ruled by a patriarch known as a judge, who exercised the typical functions of authority in a clan-based society: war leadership, high priesthood, and dispute settlement. By the middle of the twelfth century B.C.E., these tribes occupied two major territories, with those settled in the south calling themselves the tribes of Judah, and those in the north the tribes of Israel.

The Struggle for Hebrew Identity

The Hebrew tribes of this period had little experience of organized activity. This made them highly vulnerable, especially when the Philistines conquered the Levantine coast around 1050 B.C.E. To counter the Philistine threat effectively, they needed a leader. Accordingly, around 1025 B.C.E., an influential tribal judge called Samuel selected a king to lead the Hebrew resistance against the Philistines. His name was Saul. However, Saul proved to be an ineffective war-leader. So Samuel withdrew his support from Saul and threw it behind a young warrior in Saul's entourage, Saul's

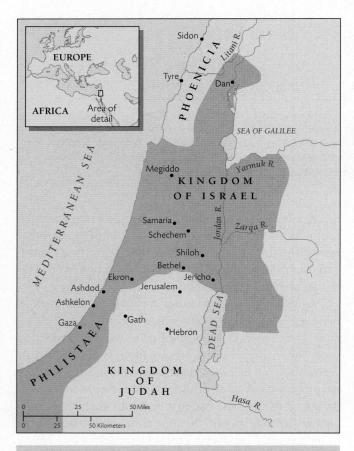

THE HEBREW KINGDOMS, c. 900 B.C.E. Notice the scale of the map and consider the comparatively small size of the Hebrews' world. ▪ *What advantages did the Philistines and Phoenicians possess, geographically and otherwise?* ▪ *Why did they present such a challenge to the Hebrews?* ▪ *What political and religious consequences might have resulted from the division of the kingdom after the death of King Solomon, given the location of Jerusalem?*

son-in-law David. Waging his own independent military campaigns, David achieved one triumph after another over the Philistines—that is, according to those chroniclers of the Bible who wrote their accounts under David's patronage.

These same books reveal that David was a man on the make; and when Saul finally drove him from his court, he became an outlaw on the fringes of Hebrew society and then a mercenary in Philistine service. It was as a Philistine mercenary that David fought against Saul in the climactic battle in which Saul was killed. Soon thereafter, David himself became king, first over the tribes of Judah, his home territory, and later over Saul's territory of Israel as well.

The Consolidation of a Hebrew Kingdom

After David's victory around 1000 B.C.E., he took advantage of the opportunity afforded by Egypt's decline to expand his control southward, eventually confining the Philistines to an inconsequential strip of coastal land. By the time of his death in 973 B.C.E., David's kingdom stretched from the middle Euphrates in the north to the Gulf of Aqaba in the south, and from the Mediterranean coast eastward into the Syrian deserts.

As David's power and prestige grew, he was able to impose on his subjects a highly unpopular system of taxation and forced labor. His goal was to build a glorious capital at Jerusalem, a Canaanite settlement that he designated as the central city of his realm. It was a shrewd choice. As a newly conquered city, Jerusalem had no previous affiliation with any of Israel's twelve tribes and so stood outside the ancient rivalries that divided them. Geographically too, Jerusalem was a strategic choice, lying between the southern tribes of Judah (David's people) and the northern tribes of Israel. David also took steps to exalt the city by making Jerusalem the resting place of the sacred Ark and reorganizing the priesthood of the Hebrew god, Yahweh. By these measures, he sought to forge a new collective identity centered on his own family and its connections to Yahweh. To this end, he also encouraged the writing of histories and prophecies that would affirm this identity and his central role in forging it.

The Reign of King Solomon (r. 973–937 B.C.E.)

Continuing his father's policies, but on a much grander scale, David's son Solomon built a great temple complex at Jerusalem to house the Ark. Such visible support of Yahweh's cult was approved by the historians whose works are included in the Bible, and who portray Solomon's reign as a golden age. However, Solomon was a ruthless and often brutal ruler whose promotion of Yahweh coincided with a program of despotism. To finance his expensive tastes and programs, Solomon instituted oppressive taxation and imposed customs duties on the lucrative caravan trade that passed through his country. With the help of the Phoenician king of Tyre, Solomon constructed a commercial fleet whose ships plied the waters of the Red Sea and beyond, trading—among other commodities—the gold and copper mined by Solomon's slaves.

Solomon also maintained a large standing army of conscripts from his own people. To undertake his ambitious building projects, Solomon required many of his subjects to perform forced labor four months out of every year. This level of oppression was too much for many Israelites, and the north seethed with rebellion against the royal capital. Within a decade or so of Solomon's death, in fact, the fragile monarchy split in two. The dynasty descended from David continued to rule the southern kingdom of Judah with its capital at Jerusalem, but the ten northern tribes banded together as the kingdom of Israel, with their capital at Shechem. In the meantime, the changing political situation of the Near East made the Hebrew kingdoms increasingly vulnerable.

cycle of violent oppression and rebellion continued until the reign of a military commander who took the name Sargon II (r. 722–705 B.C.E.). He claimed to be the direct successor of Sargon of Akkad, the first great king in Mesopotamian history, nearly 1,500 years earlier (Chapter 1).

Like the Hebrews, Sargon and his heirs skillfully deployed history as a political tool. And eventually, they extended the frontiers of the Neo-Assyrian Empire from western Iran to the shores of the Mediterranean. Briefly, they even subjugated parts of Egypt. Sargon himself put an end to the kingdom of Israel in 722 B.C.E., enslaving and deporting most of the population, and he terrified the southern kingdom of Judah into remaining a quiet vassal. By the seventh century B.C.E., Assyria was the unrivaled power of the ancient Near East.

Neo-Assyrian Government and Administration

The Neo-Assyrian Empire was built on the ability of its army to oppress both enemies and subjects alike. At its head was a hereditary monarch regarded as the earthly representative of the Assyrians' patron god, Assur. Supporting the

THE REVIVAL OF THE ASSYRIAN EMPIRE

The Assyrians had long played an important role in spreading trade and promoting urban settlements. But like the other great powers of the Near East, their civilization had been devastated by the Sea Peoples. For several centuries afterward they struggled for survival. Then, in the ninth century B.C.E., a brilliant but brutal ruler laid the foundations of what historians call the Neo-Assyrian Empire. Under the leadership of Assurnasirpal II (*ah-sur-NAH-sur-PAHL*, r. 883–859 B.C.E.), these "new" Assyrians began to conduct aggressive military campaigns against their neighbors. Those whom they defeated either had to pay tribute or face the full onslaught of the Assyrian war machine, which under Assurnasirpal acquired a deserved reputation for savagery.

Despite their military successes, Assurnasirpal and his successors inspired stiff resistance. The northern kingdom of Israel formed an alliance with other small states to halt Assyrian expansion. This coalition ultimately forced the Assyrians to settle for smaller victories against the Armenians to the northwest and the Medes to the northeast. Thereafter, a

ASSYRIAN ATROCITIES. Judean captives whose city has fallen to the Assyrian king Sennacherib (r. 704–681 B.C.E.) are shown being impaled on stakes. This triumphal carving comes from the walls of Sennacherib's palace at Nineveh. ▪ *What would be the purpose of advertising these captives' fates?*

empire's centralized authority was an extensive bureaucracy of governors, high priests, and military commanders—professions by no means mutually exclusive. These administrators exercised local authority on behalf of the king. They maintained lines of transport and communication and they oversaw construction of an extensive network of roads across the Near East. The Neo-Assyrian state also deployed a system of spies and messengers to report on the activities of subjects and provincial governors.

Not surprising for a people so mindful of historical precedent, the Neo-Assyrians modeled their laws on the code of Hammurabi, though many of their penalties were more severe. Neo-Assyrian law was also rigidly patriarchal, which entailed substantial revision of Hammurabi's code: now only husbands had the power of divorce, and they were legally permitted to inflict a variety of penalties on their wives, ranging from corporal punishment to mutilation and death.

The Neo-Assyrian Military-Religious Ethos

The Neo-Assyrians' new religious, political, and military ideology took shape during the long centuries when they fought for survival. Its two fundamental tenets were the waging of holy war and the exaction of tribute through terror.

The Neo-Assyrians were convinced that their god demanded the constant expansion of his worship through military conquest. Ritual humiliation of a defeated city's gods was therefore a regular feature of Neo-Assyrian conquests. Statues of conquered gods would be carried off to the Neo-Assyrian capital, where they would remain as "hostages." Meanwhile, an image of Assur himself—usually represented as a sun disk with the head and shoulders of an archer—would be installed in the defeated city, and the conquered people would be required to worship him. Although subject peoples did not have to abandon their previous gods altogether, they were made to feel their gods' inferiority. The Neo-Assyrians were therefore strict *henotheists*, meaning that they acknowledged the existence of other gods but believed that one god should be the supreme deity of all peoples.

Rather than defeating their foes once and imposing formal obligations, the Neo-Assyrians raided even their vanquished foes each year. This strategy kept the Neo-Assyrian military machine primed for battle, but it did little to inspire loyalty among subject peoples. Assyrian battle tactics were notorious even by the standards of ancient warfare, in which the mutilation of prisoners, systematic rape, and mass deportations were all commonplace. Moreover, the Neo-Assyrian army was not a seasonal army of part-time conscripts or peasants, but a massive standing force of more than 100,000 soldiers. And because the Neo-Assyrians mastered iron-smelting techniques on a large scale, they could equip their fighting men with high-quality steel weapons that overwhelmed opponents still reliant on bronze.

The organization of this army also contributed to its success. At its core were heavily armed and armored shock troops, the main force for crushing enemy infantry in the field and for routing the inhabitants of an enemy city once inside. To harass enemy infantry, the Neo-Assyrians deployed light skirmishers with slings and javelins, combined archery and chariotry, and also developed the first true cavalry force in the West. They even trained a highly skilled corps of combat engineers to undermine city walls and to build catapults, siege engines, battering rams, and battle towers.

The Legacy of Neo-Assyrian Power

The successors of Sargon II continued Neo-Assyrian military policies while devoting great energy to promoting an Assyrian cultural legacy. Sargon's immediate successor, Sennacherib (*sen-AH-sher-ib*, r. 704–681 B.C.E.), rebuilt the ancient Assyrian city of Nineveh, fortifying it with a double wall for a circuit of nine miles. He constructed an enormous palace there, and he ordered the construction of a massive irrigation system, including an aqueduct that carried fresh water to the city from thirty miles away. His son rebuilt the conquered city of Babylon along similar lines. His grandson Assurbanipal (*ah-sur-BAHN-uh-pahl*, r. 669–627 B.C.E.) was perhaps the greatest of all the Assyrian kings. For a time, he ruled the entire delta region of northern Egypt. He also enacted a series of internal reforms, seeking ways to govern his empire more peacefully.

By Neo-Assyrian standards, Assurbanipal was an enlightened ruler, and one to whom all students of history owe a tremendous debt. Like his grandfather Sargon II, he had a strong sense of the rich traditions of Mesopotamian history and laid claim to them. But he did this much more systematically: he ordered the construction of a magnificent library at Nineveh, where all the cultural monuments of Mesopotamian literature were to be copied and preserved. This library also served as an archive for the correspondence and official acts of the king. Fortunately, this trove of documentation has survived. Our knowledge of history, not to mention all modern editions of the *Epic of Gilgamesh*, derive from the library at Nineveh.

When Assurbanipal died in 627 B.C.E., the Neo-Assyrian Empire appeared to be at its zenith. Its kings had adorned their capitals with magnificent artwork, and the Hanging Gardens of Babylon were already famous: these were artificial slopes whose cascading flowers and trees were fed by irrigation systems that pumped water uphill, an amazing marriage of engineering and horticulture. The collapse of this empire is therefore all the more dramatic for its suddenness. Within fifteen years of Assurbanipal's reign, Nineveh lay in ruins. An alliance had formed between the Indo-European Medes of Iran and the Chaldeans, a Semitic people who controlled the southern half of Babylonia. By 605 B.C.E., the Chaldeans occupied Babylon itself and had become the predominant imperial power in Mesopotamia and the Levant. In 586 B.C.E., they captured Jerusalem, destroyed the Temple, and deported the population of Judea to Babylon. Meanwhile, the Medes retired to the Iranian Plateau to extend their dominion there.

THE RISE OF THE PERSIANS

The Persian Empire emerged as the successor state to the empire of the Neo-Assyrians, after the region was ruled for a few decades by the Chaldeans and Medes. On these foundations, the Persians would construct the largest empire known to humanity up until that time.

The Persian Empire of Cyrus the Great

The Persians came to power rather suddenly, under an extraordinary prince named Cyrus who succeeded to the rule of a single Persian tribe in 559 B.C.E. Shortly thereafter, Cyrus made himself ruler of all the Persians and then, around 549 B.C.E., threw off the lordship of the Medes and began to claim dominion over lands stretching from the Persian Gulf to the Halys River in Asia Minor.

This brought the Persians into close contact with the kingdom of Lydia. The Lydians had attained great prosperity as producers of gold and silver and as intermediaries for overland commerce between Mesopotamia and the Aegean. Most important, they were the first people in the ancient Near East to use precious-metal coinage as a medium of exchange for goods and services. When Cyrus came to power, their king was Croesus (*CREE-suhs*), a man whose reputation as the possessor of untold riches survives in the expression "rich as Croesus." Distrusting his new neighbor, Croesus decided to launch a preemptive strike against the Persians to preserve his own kingdom from conquest. According to the Greek historian Herodotus, he took the precaution of asking the oracle of Apollo at Delphi whether this strategy was

a good one, and was told that he would destroy a great nation if he pursued it. The oracle's pronouncement was both ambiguous and true: the nation that Croesus destroyed was his own. Cyrus defeated his forces in 546 B.C.E.

Cyrus then invaded Mesopotamia in 539 B.C.E., striking so quickly that he took Babylon without a fight. Once in Babylon, the entire Chaldean Empire was his, and his imperial policies proved very different from those of his predecessors in that region. Cyrus freed the Hebrews who had been held captive in Babylon since 586 B.C.E. and sent them back to Jerusalem, helping them to rebuild their temple and allowing them to set up a semi-independent vassal state. Cyrus also allowed other conquered peoples considerable self-determination, especially with respect to cultural and religious practices, a marked reversal of Assyrian and Chaldean policies. Two hundred years later, a young Macedonian king, Alexander, would emulate many of his exploits and build an empire sustained by many of the same strategies (see Chapter 4).

The Consolidation of Persia

When Cyrus died in battle in 530 B.C.E., Persian expansion continued, and his son conquered Egypt in 525 B.C.E. But although Cambyses (*kam-BY-sees*) was a warrior king like his father, he left the Persian Empire a poorly organized collection of rapid conquests. After a short period of civil war, the aristocratic inner circle that had served both Cyrus and his son settled on a collateral member of the royal family as the new king. This was Darius, whose long reign of 35 years (r. 522–486 B.C.E.) consolidated his predecessors' military gains by improving the administration of the Persian state. Darius divided the empire into provinces, each of which was administered by an official called a *satrap*. Satraps enjoyed extensive powers and considerable political latitude, yet they owed absolute loyalty to the central government, as did vassal states such as the technically autonomous Hebrew kingdom.

Adhering to the tolerant policy of Cyrus, Darius allowed the various peoples of the empire to retain most of their local institutions but enforced a standardized currency and a system of weights and measures. Beyond this, he had little interest in imposing onerous taxes, martial law, or hegemonic religious practices. After centuries of Neo-Assyrian and Chaldean tyranny, the light hand of Persian rule was welcomed throughout the empire's far-reaching lands.

Darius was also a great builder. He erected a new royal residence and ceremonial capital which the Greeks called Persepolis ("Persia City"). He ordered a canal dug from the Nile to the Red Sea to facilitate trade with

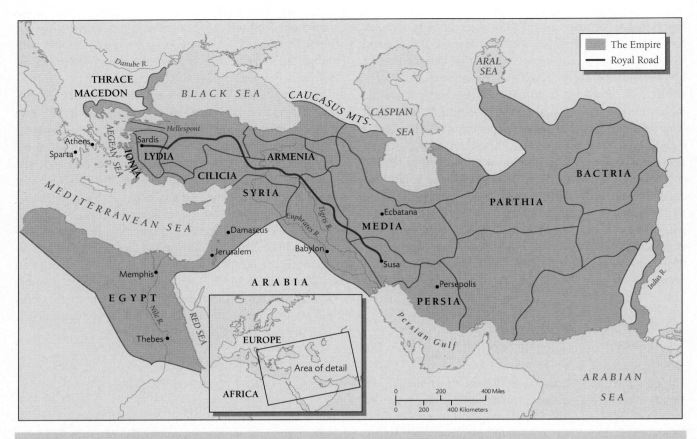

THE PERSIAN EMPIRE UNDER DARIUS I, 521–486 B.C.E. Consider the location of the Persian heartland and the four administrative centers of Persepolis, Susa, Ecbatana, and Sardis. ■ *What older kingdoms and empires did the Persian Empire contain?* ■ *Why is the Royal Road especially noted on this map?* ■ *How did Darius I successfully rule such a large and complex empire?*

the Egyptian interior, and directed the installation of irrigation systems on the Persian plateau and the fringes of the Syrian desert to increase agricultural production. Darius also expanded the existing Assyrian road system to enhance trade and communications throughout his huge realm. The most famous artery was the Royal Road, stretching 1,600 miles from Susa, near the Persian Gulf, to Sardis (the old Lydian capital) near the Aegean. Government couriers along this road constituted the first postal system, carrying messages and goods in relay stages from one post to another. Each post was a day's horseback ride from the next, where a fresh horse and rider would be ready to carry the dispatches brought by the postman before him. An extensive imperial spy network also used this postal system, famed throughout Persia as "the eyes and ears of the king."

Clearly, Darius was a gifted administrator. But as a military strategist he made an enormous mistake when he attempted to extend Persian rule into Greece. Cyrus's conquest of Lydia had made the Persian king the overlord of some long-established Greek-speaking cities on the eastern coast of the Aegean Sea, a region called Ionia. But these cities resisted even the easy terms of Persian rule, desiring instead to model themselves on the self-governing city-states across the Aegean. Consequently, between 499 and 494 B.C.E., the Greeks of Asia waged a war for independence and briefly gained the support of troops from Athens. Darius quelled this uprising and then decided to send a force to punish Athens and serve notice of Persian dominion over all Greek states. But at the battle of Marathon in 490 B.C.E., the Athenians dealt Darius the only major setback of his reign. And when his son and successor, Xerxes (*ZEHRK-zees*), attempted to avenge this humiliation in 480 B.C.E., a resistance led by both Athens and Sparta forced him to retreat and abandon his plans a year later. (We will discuss these events at greater length in Chapter 3.)

The Persians were thus compelled to recognize that they had reached the limits of their expansion. Thereafter, they concentrated on their Asian possessions and used money and diplomacy to keep the Greeks in check. This was not difficult, because the Greeks' hasty union in the face of Persian hegemony was short-lived, and they were too embroiled in wars with one another to pose any real threat to Persia.

The richness of their culture and the general tolerance they exhibited served the Persians well in maintaining their enormous empire. Unlike the Assyrians or Chaldeans, the Persians could count on the loyalty and even the affection of their subjects. In fact, their imperial model—the accommodation of local institutions and practices, consistent administration through a trained bureaucracy, and rapid communications between center and periphery—would be the one adopted by the great and lasting empires of the near and distant future.

The Spiritual Legacy of Zoroastrianism

Persia's political and cultural achievements were paralleled by a spiritual one, Zoroastrianism. This important religion was one of the three major universal faiths known to the world before Christianity and Islam, along with Buddhism and Judaism (to be discussed later in this chapter). Its founder was Zarathustra, known to the Greeks as Zoroaster, a Persian who probably lived shortly before 600 B.C.E. Zarathustra sought to reform the traditional customs of the Persian tribes by eradicating polytheism, animal sacrifice, and magic. That is, he wanted to redefine religion as an ethical practice common to all, rather than as a set of rituals and superstitions that caused divisions among people.

Zoroastrianism teaches that there is one supreme god in the universe, whom Zarathustra called Ahura-Mazda,

A CYLINDRICAL SEAL OF DARIUS THE GREAT (r. 522–486 B.C.E.). Seals were used in place of signatures to authenticate documents and correspondence. The cylindrical matrix (right) was rolled in soft wax to create an impression. This finely wrought example shows the king in a chariot, hunting lions with a bow. A winged representation of the god Ahura-Mazda rises above the scene.

"Wise Lord." Ahura-Mazda is the essence of light, truth, and righteousness; there is nothing wrathful or wicked about him, and his goodness extends to everyone, not just to one people or tribe. How, then, can there be evil and suffering in the world? Because, Zarathustra posited, there is a counter deity, Ahriman, who rules the forces of darkness. Yet he also posited that Ahura-Mazda must be vastly stronger than Ahriman.

Later teachers and priests of Zoroastrianism, the magi, placed greater emphasis on the dualism of these divine forces. They insisted that Ahura-Mazda and Ahriman are evenly matched, engaged in a desperate and eternal struggle for supremacy. Accordingly, light will not triumph over darkness until the Last Day, when the forces of Ahura-Mazda vanquish those of Ahriman forever. This vision of the universe would prove enormously influential, later informing the developing theologies of Christianity and Islam—not to mention the plots of much modern science fiction, fantasy literature, and film.

The devotion of the Persian imperial dynasty to Zarathustra's teachings made Zoroastrianism important to the conduct of Persian government, and also helps to explain the moderation of Persian rule. Unlike the Assyrians, the Chaldeans, or even the Egyptians, Persian kings saw themselves as presiding over an assemblage of different nations whose customs and beliefs they were prepared to tolerate. Whereas Mesopotamian potentates characteristically called themselves "true king," Persian rulers took the title "king of kings" or "great king," implying that they recognized the legitimacy of other kings who ruled under their canopy.

Unlike other ancient religions, then, Zoroastrianism did not exalt the power of a godlike ruler or support any particular regime. It was a personal religion, making private, spiritual demands as opposed to public, ritual ones. Its Wise Lord supported neither tribes nor states, but only individuals who serve the cause of truth and justice. According to its tenets, individuals possess free will and can choose to sin or not to sin; they are not compelled by an array of conflicting gods to act in particular ways. Zoroastrianism thus urges its adherents to choose good over evil, to be truthful, to love and help one another to the best of their powers, to aid the poor, and to practice generous hospitality. Those who do so will be rewarded in an afterlife, when the dead are resurrected on Judgment Day and consigned either to a realm of joy or to the flames of despair. In the scriptures of the Zoroastrian faith, known as the Avesta (compiled, like the Bible, over the course of many centuries), the rewards for righteousness are great, but not immediate. They are spiritual, not material.

Two Perspectives on Imperial Rule

> *These two inscriptions exemplify two very different attitudes toward imperial power and two very different methods of achieving it. The first glorifies the victories of the Neo-Assyrian king Esarhaddon in Syria, and is one of the most important records of his reign (r. 681–669 B.C.E.). The second commemorates the taking of Babylon by the Persian king Cyrus the Great (r. 559–530 B.C.E.), whose empire came to encompass and surpass that of the Neo-Assyrians.*

The *Stele* of King Esarhaddon at Senjirli, c. 680 B.C.E.

To Assur, father of the gods, lover of my priesthood, Anu mighty and preeminent, who called me by name, Ba'al, the exalted lord, establisher of my dynasty, Ea, the wise, all-knowing . . . Ishtar, lady of battle and combat, who goes at my side . . . all of them who determine my destiny, who grant to the king, their favorite, power and might . . . [I am] the king, the offering of whose sacrifices the great gods love . . . [he] who has brought all the lands in submission at his feet, who has imposed tribute and tax upon them; conqueror of his foes, destroyer of his enemies, the king, who

as to his walk is a storm, and as to his deeds, a raging wolf; . . . The onset of his battle is powerful, he is a consuming flame, a fire that does not sink: son of Sennacherib, king of the universe, king of Assyria, grandson of Sargon, king of the universe, king of Assyria, viceroy of Babylon, king of Sumer and Akkad. . . . I am powerful, I am all-powerful, I am a hero, I am gigantic, I am colossal, I am honored, I am magnified, I am without an equal among all kings, the chosen one of Assur . . . the great lord [who], in order to show to the peoples the immensity of my mighty deeds, made powerful my kingship over the four

regions of the world and made my name great.

. . . Of Tirhakah, king of Egypt and Kush, the accursed . . . without cessation I slew multitudes of his men, and him I smote five times with the point of my javelin, with wounds, no recovery. Memphis, his royal city, in half a day . . . I besieged, I captured, I destroyed, I devastated, I burned with fire. . . . The root of Kush I tore up out of Egypt and not one therein escaped to submit to me.

Source: Daniel David Luckenbill, ed., *Ancient Records of Assyria and Babylonia,* Vol. 2 (Chicago: 1926–27), pp. 224–27.

Inscription Honoring Cyrus, c. 539 B.C.E.

He [the god Marduk] scanned and looked (through) all the countries, searching for a righteous ruler who would lead him. (Then) he pronounced the name of Cyrus, king of Anshan [Persia], declared him to be the leader of the world. . . . And he (Cyrus) did always endeavor to treat according to justice the black-headed [people] whom he (Marduk) made him conquer. Marduk, the great lord, a protector of his people/worshipers, beheld with pleasure his good deeds and his upright mind, (and therefore) ordered him to march

against his city Babylon. He made him set out on the road to Babylon, going at his side like a real friend. His widespread troops—their number, like the water of a river, could not be established—strolled along, their weapons packed away. Without any battle, he made them enter his town Babylon, sparing Babylon any calamity. He delivered into his hands Nabonidus, the king who did not worship him. All the inhabitants of Babylon as well as of the entire country of Sumer and Akkad, princes and governors (included), bowed to him and kissed his feet, jubilant

that he (had received) the kingship, and with shining faces. Happily they greeted him as a master through whose help they had come (again) to life from death (and) had all been spared damage and disaster, and they worshiped his name.

I am Cyrus, king of the world, great king, legitimate king, king of Babylon, king of Sumer and Akkad, king of the four rims (of the earth), son of Cambyses, great king, king of Anshan, grandson of Cyrus, great king, king of Anshan, descendent of Teipes, great king, king of Anshan, of a family (which) always (exercised) kingship;

whose rule Bel and Nebo love, whom they want as king to please their hearts.

When I entered Babylon as a friend and (when) I established the seat of the government in the palace of the ruler under jubilation and rejoicing. . . . My numerous troops walked around Babylon in peace, I did not allow anybody to terrorize (any place) of the (country of Sumer) and Akkad. I strove for peace in Babylon and in all his (other) sacred cities. . . . I abolished the . . . [yoke] which was against their (social) standing, I brought relief to their dilapidated housing, putting (thus) an end to their (main) complaints. . . . All the kings of the entire world from the Upper to the Lower Sea, those who are seated in throne rooms, (those who) live in other (types of buildings as well as) all the kings of the West living in tents, brought their heavy tributes and kissed my feet in Babylon.

Source: Excerpted from James B. Pritchard, ed., *Ancient Near Eastern Texts Relating to the Old Testament*, 3rd ed. (Princeton, NJ: 1969), pp. 315–16.

Questions for Analysis

1. Both of these inscriptions constitute propaganda, but of different kinds. How do they differ? What audience(s) are they addressing? What function(s) does each inscription serve?

2. Each of these rulers claims to have a close relationship with the divine. How do those relationships differ, and what do those differences reveal about their attitudes to kingship and its sources of power?

3. Both of these kings boast of their royal lineage and their connections to past rulers. How different or similar are these perspectives? What do they reveal about these kings' awareness of history?

THE DEVELOPMENT OF HEBREW MONOTHEISM

Of all the important trends that we have traced in our study of the Iron Age Near East, perhaps none is of greater significance to the civilizations of the West than monotheism: the belief in a single god, the creator and ruler of all things. This development is traditionally associated with the Hebrews, but even the Hebrews were not always monotheists. Those who argued for the exclusive worship of Yahweh were a minority within Hebrew society, albeit a vocal and assertive one. How the Hebrews came to regard Yahweh as the only divine being in the universe, and to root their identity in such an exclusive religious outlook, is therefore a phenomenon that can only be understood within its historical context.

From Monolatry to Monotheism

For those who later advocated the exclusive worship of Yahweh, the early history of the Hebrews was full of embarrassments. Even the Hebrew scriptures reveal their propensity for the worship of many gods. Yahweh himself, in commanding that his people "have no other gods before me," acknowledged the attraction of those gods. The older, polytheistic Hebrew religion honored nature spirits such as Azazel and the Canaanite deity El, whose name is an important element in many Hebrew place-names (for example, Bethel) and became a synonym for "God." The temple built by Solomon at Jerusalem even included altars to Ba'al and his wife Asherah, a fertility goddess. Later Hebrew kings continued such practices, overriding the protests of religious purists devoted to Yahweh.

THE GODDESS ASHERAH. The Canaanite fertility goddess, Asherah, was the wife of the god Ba'al (or of his father, El), but she also figures in some inscriptions as the wife of the Hebrew god Yahweh. One Hebrew king even placed an image of her in the temple of Yahweh at Jerusalem. ■ *Why would this be viewed as controversial?*

By the beginning of the first millennium, however, the Hebrews living under the rule of David began to practice monolatry, meaning that they worshiped one god exclusively without denying the existence of others. Although the legendary prophet Moses is often credited as the first promoter of Yahweh's cult, sometime around the middle of the second millennium B.C.E., the ascendancy of Yahweh actually took place much later under the influence of the Levites, a tribe who claimed unique priestly authority and sought to enhance their own power and prestige by discrediting other gods.

The success of their campaign rested on the Levites' access to writing. The written word was especially potent in the ancient world because the skills necessary for its mastery were rare. In an age of constant threats to Hebrew religious and political sovereignty, the literacy of the Levites helped to preserve and promote Yahweh's worship. So did the political supremacy of the House of David, which bolstered its own legitimacy by allying itself with the Levites. The result was a centralized cult situated in the new royal capital of Jerusalem, which linked the political and the religious identity of the Hebrews to the worship of Yahweh as the supreme god.

Nevertheless, the worship of other gods actually increased in the eighth and seventh centuries B.C.E., perhaps in reaction to the austere morality demanded and imposed by the Yahwists. Thus, religious figures like Jeremiah (c. 637–587 B.C.E.) railed against "foreign" cults and warned of the disastrous consequences that would arise if Yahweh's people did not remain faithful to him. Moreover, Yahweh remained a somewhat conventional god, even in the eyes of his promoters. He was conceived as possessing a physical body and was often capricious and irascible. Further, he was not omnipotent; his power was largely confined to the territory occupied by the Hebrews.

Still, some of the Hebrews' most important contributions to subsequent Western religions crystallized by the middle of the eighth century B.C.E. One was their theology of Yahweh's transcendence: the teaching that God is not part of nature but exists outside of it. God can therefore be understood in purely intellectual or abstract terms, as entirely separate from the operations of the natural world.

Complementing this principle was the belief that Yahweh had appointed humans to be the rulers of nature by divine mandate. When Yahweh orders Adam and Eve to "replenish the earth and subdue it, and have dominion over . . . every living thing," his injunction stands in striking contrast to other accounts of creation in which humans are made to serve the gods. Finally, Hebrew religious thought was moving in this period toward the articulation of universal ethics—a universal theory of justice and righteousness. According to the Babylonian flood story, for example, a particularly petulant god destroys humanity because their noise deprives him of sleep. In Genesis, Yahweh sends a flood in punishment for human wickedness but saves Noah and his family, because "Noah was a just man."

The Hebrews honored Yahweh during this period by subscribing to certain moral precepts and taboos. The Ten Commandments as they now appear in Exodus 20:3–17 may not have existed, but they certainly reflect earlier ethical injunctions against murder, adultery, lying, and greed. In addition, the Hebrews observed an array of ritual practices unusual in the ancient world, such as infant circumcision, adherence to strict dietary laws, and refraining from labor on the seventh day of the week.

Yet the moral standards imposed by Yahweh on the Hebrew community were not binding when the Hebrews dealt with outsiders. Lending at interest, for example, was not acceptable among Hebrews, but was quite acceptable between a Hebrew and a non-Hebrew. Such distinctions applied also to more serious issues, such as the killing of civilians in battle. When the Hebrews conquered territories in Canaan, they took "all the spoil of the cities, and every man they smote with the sword . . . until they had

RECONSTRUCTION OF THE ISHTAR GATE. This is a reconstruction of one of the fifty-foot-high entrance gates built into the walls of Babylon by King Nebuchadnezzar around 575 B.C.E. About half of this reconstruction, in the Pergamon Museum of Berlin, is original.

The foremost Hebrew prophets of this era were Amos and Hosea, who preached in the kingdom of Israel before it fell to the Neo-Assyrians in 722 B.C.E.; Isaiah and Jeremiah, who prophesied in Judah before its fall in 586 B.C.E.; and Ezekiel and the "second Isaiah" (the Book of Isaiah had at least two different authors), who continued to preach "by the waters of Babylon" during the exile there. Despite some differences in emphasis, these prophets' messages consistently emphasize three core doctrines:

1. Yahweh is the ruler of the universe. He even makes use of peoples other than the Hebrews to accomplish his purposes. The gods of other nations are false gods. There has never been and never will be more than this one god.
2. Yahweh is exclusively a god of righteousness. He wills only the good, and evil in the world comes from humanity, not from him.
3. Because Yahweh is righteous, he demands ethical behavior from his people. Over and above ritual and sacrifice, he requires that his followers "seek justice, relieve the oppressed, protect the fatherless, and plead for the widow."

destroyed them." Far from having any doubts about such a brutal policy, the Hebrews believed that Yahweh had inspired the Canaanites to resist so that the Hebrews could slaughter them: "For it was the Lord's doing to harden their hearts that they should come against Israel in battle, in order that they should be utterly destroyed, and should receive no mercy but be exterminated" (Joshua 11:20).

With the political fragmentation of the Hebrew kingdoms after Solomon's death, important regional distinctions arose within Yahweh's cult. As we noted previously, the rulers of the northern kingdom discouraged their citizens from participating in ritual activities at Jerusalem, thereby earning the disapproval of the Jerusalem-based Yahwists who shaped the biblical tradition. The erosion of a cohesive Hebrew identity was further accelerated by the Neo-Assyrians, who under Sargon II absorbed the northern kingdom as a province and enslaved nearly 28,000 Hebrews. The southern kingdom of Judah survived, but political collaboration with the Neo-Assyrians meant acceptance of the god Assur.

This was the whetstone on which the Yahwist prophets sharpened their demands for an exclusive monotheism that went beyond monolatry. Hebrew prophets were practical political leaders as well as religious figures, and most of them understood that military resistance to the Assyrians was futile. So if the Hebrews were to survive as a people, they had to emphasize the one thing that separated them from everyone else in the known world: the worship of Yahweh and the denial of all other gods. The prophets' insistence that Yahweh alone should be exalted was thus an aggressive reaction to the equally aggressive promotion of Assur by the Assyrians.

Judaism Takes Shape

Through their insistence on monotheism as the cornerstone of Hebrew identity, the Yahwists made it possible for the Hebrews to survive under Neo-Assyrian domination. And as the Assyrian threat receded in the late seventh century B.C.E., so the Yahwists triumphed religiously and politically. The king of Judah during the waning years of the Neo-Assyrian Empire, Josiah (r. 621–609 B.C.E.), was a committed monotheist whose court employed prominent prophets, including Jeremiah. With Assyrian power crumbling, Josiah found himself in a position to pursue significant reforms. He presided over the redrafting and revision of the "Law of Moses" to bring it into line with current policies, and it was during his reign that the Book of Deuteronomy was "discovered" and hailed as Moses' "Second Law." Deuteronomy is the most stridently monotheistic book of the Hebrew Bible, and it lent weight to this new political program.

But within a generation of King Josiah's death, the Chaldeans under Nebuchadnezzar (as discussed earlier in the chapter) conquered Jerusalem, destroyed the Temple, and carried thousands of Hebrews off to Babylon in 587/586 B.C.E. This Babylonian Captivity brought many challenges, paramount among them the maintenance of the Hebrews' identity. The leading voices in defining that identity continued to be the patriotic Yahwists, the same people who would later spearhead the return to Palestine after Cyrus of Persia captured Babylon and liberated the Hebrews two generations later.

Among the Yahwists, the prophet Ezekiel stressed that salvation could be found only through religious purity, which meant ignoring all foreign gods and acknowledging only Yahweh. Kingdoms and states and empires came to nothing in the long run, Ezekiel said. What mattered for those living in exile was the creature God had made in his image—man—and the relationship between God and his creation.

The period of captivity was therefore decisive in forging a universal religion that transcended politics. Just as Yahweh existed outside creation, so the people who worshiped him could exist outside of a Hebrew kingdom. In Babylon, the worship of Yahweh therefore became something different: it became Judaism, a religion that was not tied to any particular political system or territory, for after 586 B.C.E. there was neither a Hebrew ruling class nor a Hebrew state. Outside of Judah, Judaism flourished. This was an unparalleled achievement in the ancient world: the survival of a religion that had no political power to back it and no holy place to ground it.

After 538 B.C.E., when Cyrus permitted the Hebrews of Babylon to return to their lands and to rebuild the Temple, Jerusalem became once again the central holy place of Hebrew religious life. But the new developments that had fashioned Judaism during captivity would prove lasting, despite the religious conflicts that soon erupted. These conflicts led to ever more specific assertions about the nature of Judaism, and to religious teachings that focused on ethical conduct as an obligation owed by all human beings toward their creator, independent of place or political identity. The observance of ritual requirements and religious taboos would continue, but not as the essence of religious life; rather, they would be symbolic of the special relationship binding Yahweh to the Hebrews. Eventually, the transcendental monotheism that emerged from these historical processes would become common to the worldview of all Western civilizations.

CONCLUSION

The centuries between 1700 and 500 B.C.E. were an epoch of empires. While the two great powers of the second millennium were New Kingdom Egypt and the Hittite Empire

REVIEWING THE OBJECTIVES

- The settlement of Indo-European peoples in the Near East had marked effects on the older civilizations there. What were some major consequences?
- Egypt's New Kingdom differed profoundly from the Old and Middle Kingdoms that preceded it. Why was this the case?
- The civilizations of the late Bronze Age were bound together by transnational networks. What were the strengths and fragilities of these relationships?
- What kingdoms and empires emerged in the Near East after the devastation caused by the Sea Peoples?
- Monotheism was a significant historical development of the first millennium B.C.E. Why is it so important?

in Anatolia, a host of lesser empires also coalesced during this period, including Minoan Crete, Mycenaean Greece, and the trading empire of the Assyrians. All were sustained by a sophisticated network of trade and diplomacy. But between 1200 and 1000 B.C.E. the devastation wrought by the Sea Peoples brought this integrated civilization to an end. These invasions cleared the way for many new, small states, including those of the Phoenicians, the Philistines, the Lydians, and the Hebrews. Many crucial cultural and economic developments were fostered by these small states, including alphabetic writing, coinage, mercantile colonization, and monotheism. Yet the dominant states of the Iron Age continued to be the great land empires centered in western Asia: first the Neo-Assyrians, then briefly the Chaldeans, and finally the Persians.

The empires of the early Iron Age were quite different from those that had formed an integrated Near East a thousand years before. These new empires were much more highly unified. They had capital cities, centrally managed systems of communication, sophisticated administrative structures, and ideologies that justified their aggressive imperialism as a religious obligation imposed on them by a single, all-powerful god. They commanded armies of unprecedented size, and they demanded from their subjects a degree of obedience impossible for any previous Bronze Age emperor to imagine or enforce. Their rulers declared themselves the chosen instruments of their gods' divine will.

At the same time, we can trace the emergence of more personalized religions. Zoroastrian dualism and Hebrew monotheism added an important new emphasis on ethical conduct, and both pioneered the development of authoritative written scriptures that advanced religious teachings. Zoroastrianism, despite its radical re-imagining of the cosmos, proved fully compatible with imperialism and became the driving spiritual force behind the Persian Empire. Judaism, by contrast, was forged in the struggle to resist the imperialism of the Neo-Assyrians and Chaldeans. Both systems of belief would exercise enormous influence on future civilizations. In particular, they would provide the models on which Christianity and Islam would ultimately erect their own traditions, just as the models of imperial governance forged in this period would become the template for future empires. In Chapter 3, we will look at the ways in which the city-states of ancient Greece both built on and departed from these models.

PEOPLE, IDEAS, AND EVENTS IN CONTEXT

- How did the Hittite Empire integrate the cultures of **INDO-EUROPEAN PEOPLES** with the older civilizations of this region?
- What do the reigns of **HATSHEPSUT** and **AKHENATEN** tell us about the continuities and limitations of pharaonic power?
- What factors produced the transnational networks of the Late **BRONZE AGE**?
- How did the civilizations of **MINOAN CRETE** and **MYCENAEAN GREECE** differ from one another, and from the neighboring civilizations of the Near East?
- In what ways do the **PHOENICIANS**, the **PHILISTINES**, and the **HEBREWS** exemplify three different approaches to state-building at the beginning of the first millennium B.C.E.?
- What was new about the **NEO-ASSYRIAN EMPIRE**? How do its methods of conquest and its military-religious ethos compare to the **PERSIAN EMPIRE** that followed it?
- How and why did monotheism develop in the Hebrew kingdoms? In what ways might **JUDAISM** have been influenced by **ZOROASTRIANISM**?

THINKING ABOUT CONNECTIONS

- In the religions of Akhenaten, Zoroaster, and the Hebrews we see a rejection of polytheism. What cultural factors may have contributed to this? What would you consider to be the long-term effects of monotheism as a motivating force in history?
- What patterns of success or failure appear to be emerging when we consider the empires that flourished in the Iron Age, particularly those of the Assyrians and the Persians? Are similar patterns visible in other periods of history, including our own?

STORY LINES

- The emergence of democracy was dependent on the historical circumstances of the ancient Greek world, including slavery and the exclusion of women from public life. It therefore differs markedly from the political system(s) described as democratic today.

- The Greeks were united only through a shared language and culture. The lack of a common political structure made it difficult for them to work toward a common goal except when faced with annihilation.

- The Athenians' leadership in the Persian Wars enabled them to dominate the Mediterranean, and also to influence our understanding of their historical legacy.

- The cultural achievements of the fifth century B.C.E. glorified the individual male and his role in the community, and also valorized Athenian imperial ambitions.

CHRONOLOGY

800–400 B.C.E.	Rise of the polis
c. 750 B.C.E.	Homeric epics transcribed
725–650 B.C.E.	Hoplite tactics become standard
c. 600 B.C.E	Militarization of Sparta
600–500 B.C.E.	Emergence of the Milesian School (pre-Socratic philosophy)
594 B.C.E.	Solon's reforms in Athens
546 B.C.E.	Cyrus of Persia conquers Lydia and controls the Greek cities of Ionia
510 B.C.E.	Overthrow of the Peisistratid tyrants in Athens
499–494 B.C.E.	Ionian Revolt
490 B.C.E.	Battle of Marathon
480 B.C.E.	Battles of Thermopylae and Salamis
479 B.C.E.	Battle of Plataea
478 B.C.E.	Formation of the Delian League
431 B.C.E.	Peloponnesian War begins
404 B.C.E.	Defeat of Athens by Sparta
399 B.C.E.	Death of Socrates

Before You Read This Chapter

The Civilization of Greece, 1000–400 B.C.E.

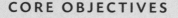

CORE OBJECTIVES

- **DESCRIBE** the factors that led to the emergence of the Greek polis.

- **DEFINE** hoplite warfare and its effects on the development of democracy.

- **EXPLAIN** the key differences among the poleis of Athens, Sparta, and Miletus.

- **IDENTIFY** the ways in which Athenian culture, philosophy, and art reflect political and social ideals.

- **UNDERSTAND** the impact of the Persian and Peloponnesian Wars and their different outcomes.

In the fifth century B.C.E., a Greek-speaking subject of the Persian Empire began to write a book. He had been to Egypt and along the African coast, to the Greek colonies of Italy, the cities of Persia, the wilds of Thrace and Macedonia, and all over the Aegean. He had collected stories about peoples and places even farther afield: Ethiopia, India, the Black Sea. We have already met this intrepid traveler, Herodotus (c. 484–c. 425 B.C.E.), who marveled at the pyramids of Giza (Chapter 1) and who told how the king of Lydia lost his power to the Persians (Chapter 2). His reason for compiling this information was timely: he wanted to write a history of recent events. As he put it, "Herodotus of Halicarnassus here sets forth the results of his research, with the aim of preserving the remembrance of what men have done, and of preventing the great and wonderful deeds of both Greeks and barbarians from losing their glory; and in particular to examine the causes that made them fight one another."

Herodotus's fascination with the Persians, Phoenicians, and Egyptians underscores the extent to which all Greek-speakers regarded themselves as different from other peoples. In fact, they had responded very differently to the Bronze Age collapse.

THE ACROPOLIS OF ATHENS AND THE PARTHENON. Many Greek cities were built upon mountain strongholds, but the most famous of these is the Acropolis of Athens. First settled in the Neolithic Period, during the Bronze Age it became a fortified palace—allegedly that of the hero Theseus—and then a precinct sacred to the goddess Athena, for whom the city was named. The Parthenon, its most important surviving structure, was built on the site of an older temple after the Athenian victory over the Persians at Marathon in 490 B.C.E., and then rebuilt after the Persians sacked Athens ten years later. Most of the damage it sustained thereafter occurred during modern wars. ▪ *Why was this site the focal point of so much activity?* ▪ *What do these successive events tell us about the relationship between place and identity?*

off from trade and communication. The use of writing declined to such an extent that knowledge of Linear B disappeared. Archaeological evidence suggests a world in stasis, isolated from the centers of civilization that were reemerging in the Near East.

The material realities of life in this era profoundly shaped the civilization that emerged from it. This civilization would emphasize political equality and modest display, principles that formed the basis of early democracies. At the same time, the hardships of daily life, which contrasted sharply with stories of a heroic and opulent past, made the Greeks suspicious of their gods. They came to rely far more on the power of individual human beings than on divine intervention in human affairs. They also developed an awareness that excessive pride in one's own accomplishments could be dangerous. While the gods favored those who showed initiative and daring, they would punish the *hubris* of those who failed to acknowledge their own limitations.

While they struggled to cooperate politically, they were able to unite around a common language and culture, and their shared values were distinct from those of the people they called *barbarians*: peoples whose speech, to Greek ears, sounded like gibberish ("bar-bar-bar"). They cherished individual liberty, participatory government, artistic innovation, scientific investigation, and the creative powers of the human mind. Although the practical implementation of these ideals would prove problematic—and continues to be so—our own civilization would be unimaginable without the political experiments and cultural achievements of ancient Greece.

FROM CHAOS TO POLIS

By the end of the twelfth century B.C.E., Mycenaean civilization had vanished. Except at Athens, the great citadels that had crowned the heights of mainland kingdoms were destroyed. Settlements shrank in size and moved inland, away from vulnerable coastlines, thus cutting themselves

Homer and the Heroic Tradition

Around the year 1000 B.C.E., the chaotic conditions that had contributed to the isolation of Greece were alleviated by a period of relative peace. The standard of living improved, artisans developed their crafts, and increased contact among individual settlements fostered trade. Greek pottery, in particular, became a sophisticated and sought-after commodity, which Greek merchants could exchange for luxury goods from abroad.

As trade became an increasingly important feature of the new economy, the personal fortunes of those who engaged in trade increased accordingly, leading to a new kind of social stratification based on wealth. The men who controlled that wealth were aware that their status was not founded on warfare or noble birth, as had been the case in the past. Instead, they began to justify their preeminence as a reflection of their own superior qualities as "best men" (*aristoi*). Wealth was one sign of this superiority, but it was not sufficient in itself as a claim to aristocracy, which literally means "the rule of the best." Those who aspired to this status were therefore expected to emulate, as far as possible, the heroes of old, whose stories lived on in the prodigious memories and agile voices of the singers of tales.

These singers, the guardians of a rich oral history that had never been written down, were part poets in their own right and part *rhapsodes*, "weavers of songs." The most famous is Homer, the poet credited with having woven together the mesh of stories that we know as the *Iliad* and the *Odyssey*, which crystallized around 800 B.C.E. The epics ascribed to Homer are vast encyclopedias of lore set at the end of the Bronze Age, the time his contemporary Hesiod called "the Age of Heroes" (Chapter 2): the age of Achilles and his Trojan rival, Hector; the age of Odysseus.

But these stories were not fixed in that time. Over centuries of retelling, the social and political relationships portrayed in the poems changed to reflect the assumptions and agendas of later ages. Treating these epics as historical sources, therefore, requires the historian to peel back layers of meaning. For example, Homer depicts a world in which competition and status are of paramount importance to the warrior elite, just as they were of vital concern to the aristocrats of his own day. Through the exchange of expensive gifts and hospitality, men aspiring to positions of power sought to create strong ties of guest friendship (*xenia*, *zeh-NEE-ah*) with one another, and thus to construct networks of influence that would support their economic, social, and political ambitions. This suggests that aristocrats in the Greek world conceived of themselves as having more in common with each other than they did with the local societies they dominated, something that is also reflected in the essential similarity of Trojans and Greeks in the *Iliad*.

However, the shared sense of a common culture among aristocratic households did not lessen the competition among them. Indeed, it led to competition over the epic past, as fledgling aristocratic clans vied to claim descent from one or another legendary hero. A hero cult might begin when an important family claimed an impressive Mycenaean tomb as that of their own famous ancestor, someone named in the *Iliad* and said to have come from that place. They would then develop a pious tradition of devotion that would extend to their followers and dependents; eventually, an entire community might come to identify itself with the famous local hero. The heroic ideal thus became a deeply ingrained feature of Greek society.

The Rise of the Polis

In the ninth century B.C.E., contacts between Greeks and Phoenicians intensified. Most crucially, the Greeks adopted the Phoenician alphabet, which replaced the long-disused Linear B. The Phoenicians also pointed the way to the revival of another lost art among the Greeks: seafaring. After the devastation of the late Bronze Age, Greek vessels hugged the shoreline and traveled only short distances. By the tenth century, however, Greeks were copying Phoenician designs for merchant vessels, which allowed them to set out on trading ventures of their own. As commercial activity increased, significant numbers of Greeks began to move to the shores of the mainland, to outlying islands, and to the eastern coast of the Aegean.

These economic and cultural developments were accompanied by dramatic growth in the Greek population, which placed heavy demands on the resources of a mountainous country with limited agricultural land. Soon, some degree of economic, political, and social cooperation among the inhabitants of rival communities became necessary. But the values that had developed during centuries of isolation did not make such cooperation easy. Each local community treasured its autonomy and independence, celebrated its own rituals, and honored its own heroes. On what basis could such communities unite?

The Greek solution to this challenge was the *polis*, the root from which we derive the words *politics* and *political*. The Greeks considered the polis to be a social collectivity, first and foremost—not a place. For this reason, our sources speak of groups of people ("the Athenians," "the Spartans") rather than individual cities. *Poleis* (the plural of *polis*) came to be so essential to Greek identity that Aristotle (see Chapter 4) would later define man as "a political animal," someone who participates in the life of the polis and who cannot survive outside it.

In practice, poleis combined both formal institutions and informal structures that could differ widely. Most poleis were organized around a social center known as the *agora*, where markets and important meetings were held. Surrounding the whole urban settlement, the *asty*, was the *khora*, "land." The khora of a large polis might support several other towns or smaller poleis, as well as numerous villages. The Greeks described this early process of community building as the "bringing together of dwellings" (*synoikismos*, synoecism).

Polis formation could also come about through the conquest of one settlement by another and/or through the gradual alliance of neighboring communities. Some poleis took shape around fortified hilltops, such as the Athenian acropolis (literally, the "high city"). Other communities may have borrowed a Near Eastern (and particularly Phoenician) practice of orienting the urban center around a temple precinct. In many Greek cities, however, temple building may have been a consequence of polis formation rather than a cause, as elites competed with one another to exalt their poleis and glorify themselves.

THE CULTURE OF ARCHAIC GREECE, 800–500 B.C.E.

Scholars date the Archaic Period of Greek history to the emergence of the polis and the return of writing, which the Greeks would put to a wide variety of uses. The Athenians, in particular, used writing to establish their cultural dominance over other Greek poleis, controlling the inscription of the Homeric canon, promoting the work of contemporary poets, and fostering the writing of prose histories, which allowed them to pass on to posterity a narrative of history in which they played the central role. It is therefore important to bear in mind that much of what we know about this early period derives from the work of later authors who wrote from this Athenian perspective: these include the Ionian-born Herodotus, who spent much of his later life in Athens; the historians Thucydides (c. 460–c. 395 B.C.E.) and Xenophon (430–354); and the philosophers Plato (c. 428–348) and his pupil Aristotle (384–322).

Colonization and Panhellenism

In the eighth and seventh centuries B.C.E., small-scale Greek trading ventures and settlements had developed into a full-fledged colonial enterprise that followed the example of the Phoenicians. Many larger poleis competed with one another to establish colonies, with Athens and Corinth being particularly successful in such ventures.

Although each of these colonies was an independent foundation, it sustained familial and affective ties to its mother polis; so it was often called upon to support the polis and could become entangled in the political and military affairs of the mainland. At the same time, these individual Greek colonies celebrated their shared language and heritage, which was exported to far-flung reaches of the known world, creating a Panhellenic ("all-Greek") culture that eventually stretched from the Black Sea to the Mediterranean coastlines of modern France and Spain.

Greek colonization permanently altered the cultural geography of the Mediterranean world. The western shores of Anatolia would remain a stronghold of Greek culture for the next 2,000 years. So many Greeks settled in southern Italy that later Romans called the region Magna Graecia, "Greater Greece"; Greek-speaking enclaves would survive there into the twentieth century of our era. By the fourth century B.C.E., more Greeks lived in Magna Graecia than in Greece itself.

Motives for colonization varied. Some poleis, such as Corinth, were blessed by their strategic location on the land bridge between Attica and the Peloponnesus (*pel-oh-poh-NEE-suss*; the large peninsula of mainland Greece), but cursed by the poverty of their land. Trade therefore became the lifeblood of this polis and of the ruling aristocracy who bankrolled the ambitious planting of colonies. Other poleis, confronted by the pressures of growing populations and political unrest, sponsored new colonies as outlets for undesirable elements or unwanted multitudes. These colonial projects parallel, in many ways, those of modern nation-states.

Colonial expansion also intensified Greek contacts with other cultures. Phoenician pottery brought new artistic motifs, while Egypt profoundly influenced early Greek sculptural representations of the human form (see **Interpreting Visual Evidence** on page 64). However, intensified contact with other cultures simultaneously sharpened Greeks' awareness of their own identity as Hellenes (the Greeks' name for themselves). Such self-conscious Hellenism did not lead to greater political cooperation, but it did encourage the establishment of Panhellenic festivals, such as the Olympic Games, and of holy sites.

The most important of these was the temple of Apollo at Delphi, home to the oracle of the sun god. Suppliants who sought to have their questions answered would offer gifts to the shrine and then wait while the god spoke through his priestess, whose mysterious answers would be translated into enigmatic Greek verse by an attending priest. The resulting advice was essentially a riddle that called for further interpretation on the part of the recipient—who often misconstrued it: as we noted in Chapter 2, Croesus of Lydia thought that he was following the advice of the oracle when he attacked the Persians, but the great nation he destroyed turned out to be his own.

At the Olympic Games, Greeks honored the king of the gods, Zeus, near the giant temple dedicated to him at Olympia. The Greeks took great pride in these athletic competitions, and only Hellenes were permitted to participate in them. Like colonization, these games did little to alleviate rivalry among the poleis; in fact, they often increased it. But they further strengthened the Greeks' awareness of their common culture, an awareness that could be harnessed when they faced a common threat.

Hoplite Warfare

In the centuries immediately following the calamities of the late Bronze Age, the defense of surviving Greek communities rested with the few elite warriors who had the resources to invest in armor, chariots, and weaponry. This monopoly on military prowess gave the aristocracy

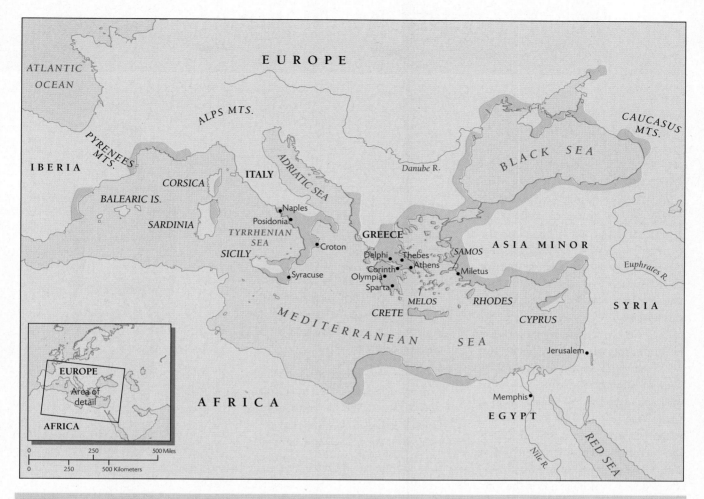

EUROPE

ATLANTIC OCEAN

ALPS MTS.

PYRENEES MTS.

CAUCASUS MTS.

BLACK SEA

IBERIA

Danube R.

CORSICA   ITALY

ADRIATIC SEA

BALEARIC IS.

SARDINIA

TYRRHENIAN SEA

Naples

Posidonia

GREECE

ASIA MINOR

Euphrates R.

SICILY

Croton

Delphi   Thebes

Corinth   Athens   SAMOS

Olympia

Sparta

Miletus

SYRIA

Syracuse

MELOS   RHODES

CRETE

CYPRUS

MEDITERRANEAN   SEA

Jerusalem

EUROPE

Area of detail

AFRICA

AFRICA

Memphis

EGYPT

Nile R.

RED SEA

0   250   500 Miles

0   250   500 Kilometers

GREEK COLONIZATION, C. 550 B.C.E. Compare this map with that on page 45. ▪ *How do you account for the differences in Greek and Phoenician patterns of colonization?* ▪ *Were Greek colonies likely to compete with Phoenician colonies?* ▪ *Where were such conflicts most likely to erupt?*

tremendous political and social leverage. As a result, aristocrats dominated political offices and priesthoods in the poleis, as well as economic life.

But during the Archaic Period, a revolution in military tactics brought aristocratic military dominance to an end. Increasingly, the effective defense of a polis required that it be able to call on a standing militia. Accordingly, able-bodied citizens began to equip themselves for battle and to train alongside one another. These citizen-soldiers became known as *hoplites*, from the large round shield (*hoplon*) carried by each. In battle, hoplites stood shoulder to shoulder in a close formation called a *phalanx*, several columns across and several rows deep, with each hoplite carrying his shield on the left arm to protect the unshielded right side of the man next to him. In his right hand, each hoplite carried a spear or sword, so that an approaching phalanx presented a nearly impenetrable wall of armor and weaponry to its opponents. If a man in the front rank fell, the one behind him stepped up to take his place; as a result, the weight of the entire phalanx was literally behind the front line, with each soldier leaning with his shield into the man in front of him.

This tight formation required only one shared skill: the ability to stay together. As long as the phalanx remained intact, it was nearly unbeatable. But like the polis itself, it could fall apart if its men did not share a common goal. The hoplite revolution was therefore bound up with a parallel revolution in politics. As a polis came increasingly to draw upon the resources of more and more citizens, it was forced to offer them a larger part in the exercise of political power. By the seventh century B.C.E., these citizen-soldiers formed a hoplite class that could demand a say in decision making and thereby challenge the hegemony of old elites.

The Ideal of Male Beauty

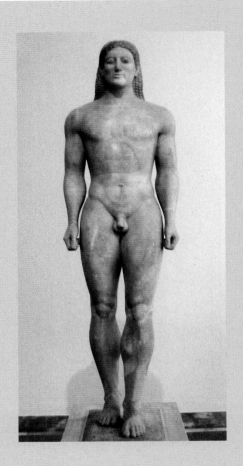

he Greek word *kouros* ("young man" or "youth") is now applied to a whole series of life-sized statues from the Archaic Period. The one shown here comes from Anavyssos in Attica, and was made between 540 and 515 B.C.E. (it is now in the National Archaeological Museum of Athens). Although scholars used to believe that such statues were meant to represent the god Apollo, further research has shown that most were made to commemorate the dead, especially young warriors who had fallen in battle. This one appears to be walking forward, smiling, but his eyes are closed. The accompanying inscription reads: "Stop and show your pity here for Kroisos, now dead, who once fighting in the foremost ranks of battle was destroyed by raging Ares."

Questions for Analysis

1. What aspects of the body does the kouros emphasize? If this is intended to be a model of Greek manhood, what values would it convey to contemporary youths?

2. Is this a representation of the young man as he was when living, or in death? How do your conclusions about the ideal of male beauty change if this is a glorification of death?

3. Compare this image to the values expressed in the verses by Tyrtaeus of Sparta on "The Beautiful and the Good" (page 67). How do these two perspectives complement one another?

Aristocracy, Tyranny, and Democracy

For the better part of the seventh and sixth centuries B.C.E., aristocrats continued to dominate the Greek poleis. Struggles for influence among competing families were commonplace, and these differences affected polis government at every level, not least because aristocrats were the only members of society who could afford to hold unpaid and time-consuming political offices.

The aristocrats of this period pursued not only wealth, power, and fame; they also cultivated a distinctive lifestyle. Participating in politics and holding office was part of this lifestyle. So too was the *symposium*, a "drinking party" at which elite men would enjoy wine, poetry and poetic competition, performances by trained dancers and acrobats, and the company of *hetaeras* (courtesans) who provided witty conversation, music, and physical intimacy.

Respectable women were excluded from such meetings, as they were from nearly all other aspects of public and political life (as will be discussed later). So too were non-aristocratic men. The symposium was thus an arena for the display of aristocratic masculinity.

The glorification of male sexuality was another important aspect of this homosocial aristocratic culture. Typically, a man in his late twenties to late thirties, who had just begun to make his career in political life, would take as his lover and protégé an aristocratic youth in his early to mid-teens. The two would form an intimate bond in which sexual intercourse played an important role. This benefited both partners and their familes, and allowed the younger partner to learn the workings of politics while making valuable social connections. Many later philosophers, including Plato, argued that true love could exist only between such lovers, because only within such

HOPLITE INFANTRY ADVANCING INTO COMBAT. This Corinthian vase, dating from around 650 B.C.E., displays the earliest-known depiction of hoplites fighting in a phalanx formation.

a relationship could a man find a partner worthy of his affections.

A whole complex of values, ideas, practices, and assumptions thus shaped aristocratic identity. As a result, it was impossible for those outside this elite world to participate fully in the public life of the polis. By the middle of the Archaic Period, moreover, the circle of the aristocratic elite tightened even further, as smaller and smaller groups came to dominate higher offices. Many aristocrats found themselves on the outside of their own culture, looking in.

For these men, one remedy lay close at hand: an alliance with the rising class of hoplites. And occasionally, a single aristocrat with the backing of the hoplites would succeed in setting up an alternative form of government, a *tyranny*. The word *tyrannos* had been borrowed from the Lydians, and it signified someone who ruled outside the traditional framework of the polis.

A tyrant in Archaic Greece was not necessarily an abusive ruler. Indeed, tyranny often led the way to wider political enfranchisement because anyone who sought the support of the hoplite class would have to appease that class by extending further rights of political participation, while all the time striving to keep the reins of power in his own hands. But this was an inherently unstable state of affairs, because the continuance of tyranny became an obstacle to even greater power for the hoplite class. For this reason, tyrannies rarely lasted for more than two generations and could serve as a stepping-stone from aristocracy to a more broadly participatory form of government: democracy.

It is important to stress that our notion of democracy is quite different from that of the Greeks. In fact, Aristotle denegrated this form of government as "mob rule," because it gave too much power to the *demos*, a word meaning "neighborhood" or "affinity group." He saw it as a system too easily controlled by a particular faction. Our ideal of democracy is closer to what Aristotle would have called a *polity*—governance by the polis as a whole.

The Power of Poetry

The aristocracy of the Archaic Period were deeply invested in the heroic ideal enshrined in the Homeric epics. But they also strove to express their unique culture in newer poetic forms. The most characteristic of these is the lyric, a series of rhythmic verses sung to the music of the lyre. Because these songs would have been composed orally, even improvised, relatively few survive. But those that do are valuable historical sources. Because they were the focus of entertainment at gatherings, they are often politically charged, sexually explicit, or daringly subversive. For example, the poet Archilochus of Paros (c. 680–640 B.C.E.) flouts the conventions of epic poetry by mocking his own failures on the battlefield: "Some barbarian waves my shield, since I had to abandon it / . . . but I escaped, so it scarcely matters / . . . I can get another just as good." So much for the heroic ideal of returning either with one's shield, or on it! In another lyric, Archilochus

Songs of Sappho

Although Sappho of Lesbos (c. 620–550 B.C.E.) was a prolific poet and skilled musician, we know very little about her life, and only a few examples of her extraordinary verse survive. Of the nine books collected in the third century B.C.E., we now have just one complete lyric and a series of fragments, some consisting of only two or three words, often preserved because they were quoted admiringly by other authors. Astonishingly, though, a papyrus scroll containing a previously unknown part of a poem was identified in 2004. Another has since been found.

Fragment 16

Some say thronging cavalry, some say
  foot soldiers,
others call a fleet the most beautiful of
sights the dark earth offers, but I say it's
  whatever you love best.

And it's easy to make this understood by
everyone, for she who surpassed all
  human
kind in beauty, Helen, abandoning her
  husband—that best of
men—went sailing off to the shores of
  Troy and
never spent a thought on her child or
  loving
parents: when the goddess seduced her
  wits and left her to wander,
she forgot them all, she could not
  remember
anything but longing, and lightly straying
aside, lost her way. But that reminds me
  now: Anactória,

she's not here, and I'd rather see her lovely
step, her sparkling glance and her face
  than gaze on
all the troops in Lydia in their chariots
  and glittering armor.

Source: Translated by Jim Powell, *The Poetry of Sappho* (New York: 2007), pp. 6–7.

The New Fragment (2004)

Live for the gifts the fragrant-breasted
  Muses
send, for the clear, the singing lyre, my
  children.
Old age freezes my body, once so lithe,
rinses the darkness from my hair, now
  white.
My heart's heavy, my knees no longer
  keep me
up through the dance they used to
  prance like fawns in.
Oh, I grumble about it, but for what?
Nothing can stop a person's growing old.

They say that Tithonus was swept away
in Dawn's passionate, rose-flushed arms
  to live
forever, but he lost his looks, his youth,
failing husband of an immortal bride.

Source: Translated by Lachlan Mackinnon, *Times Literary Supplement*, July 15, 2005.

Questions for Analysis

1. How does Sappho use stories from the older tradition she has inherited to address her own concerns? How does the perspective of the female poet transform masculine ideas about heroism, beauty, warfare, and aging?

2. What are the challenges of working with such fragmentary sources as these? If these were the only pieces of evidence to survive from Archaic Greece, what conclusions could you draw about the society and its values?

castigates his faithless (female) lover and his even more faithless (male) lover with whom she has run off.

Given the male domination of Greek culture, it is paradoxical that the most famous lyric poet of this age was not a man. Rather, it was Sappho (SAF-foh, c. 620–550 B.C.E.), who lived in the polis of Mytilene on the island of Lesbos. Revered by her contemporaries, Sappho composed songs for a wide array of occasions and a range of moods: songs of courtship and marriage, longing and desire, loss, old age, and death. Often, they are passionately dedicated to women: both the women whom Sappho loved and the historical women who occupy the margins of masculine epic. Frequently, they take some image or incident from that inherited tradition and give it a distinctive spin. In one song, Sappho compares herself to Agamemnon, who was only able to return from Troy after he prayed to Hera, a goddess worshiped at Lesbos; Sappho now prays that her beloved will arrive safely with the goddess's help. In another, she imagines a scene not included in the *Iliad*, the joyous wedding of the Trojan Hector and his bride, Andromache. The intimacy of lyric thus reveals something that few sources from antiquity are able to convey: the feelings and desires of individuals who were often at odds with the dominant culture of their time.

"The Beautiful and the Good"

The poet known as Tyrtaeus of Sparta flourished during the middle of the sixth century B.C.E. He may originally have come from Athens, but whatever his origins he expressed ideas of honor, beauty, and virtue that were universal among the hoplite warriors of the new poleis. The key terms he uses in the following verses cannot be adequately translated into English, since these short Greek adjectives are freighted with ancient meanings: kalos *(beautiful, honorable), and* agathos *(good, brave, manly). They stand in opposition to the term* aischros *(shameful, ugly, mean).*

alos it is for an *agathos* warrior to die, fallen among the foremost fighters, in battle for his native land; but to leave his polis and rich fields and beg—that is most painful of all, as he wanders with his dear mother and aged father, his small children and his wedded wife. Detested he will be in the eyes of all those to whom he comes, constrained by need and hateful poverty. He shames his birth and belies his glorious appearance; dishonor and misery are his companions.

If no account is taken of a warrior who is a wanderer, if there is no respect for him or his family in the future, then let us fight with all our hearts for this land and die for our children, no longer hesitating to risk our lives. Young men, stand firm beside each other and fight.

Do not begin shameful flight or fear. Rather, create a mighty, valorous spirit in your breasts, and show no love for your lives when you are fighting. Do not flee, abandoning the older men, whose knees are no longer nimble.

For *aischros* it is for an older warrior to fall among the foremost fighters and lie out ahead of the young men—a man whose hair is already white and his beard grey—as he breathes out his valorous spirit in the dust, holding his bloody guts in his own hands, his body laid bare. *Aischros* is this to the eyes, and a cause of resentment to look upon.

But to the young men all is seemly, while the glorious flower of lovely youth is theirs. To men the young man is admirable to look upon, and to women lovable while he lives and *kalos* when he lies among the foremost fighters. So let a man take a firm stance and stand fast, with both feet planted upon the ground, biting his lip with his teeth.

Source: Excerpted and modified from *The Greek Polis*, eds. W. H. Adkins and Peter White (Chicago: 1986), pp. 23–24.

Questions for Analysis

1. How does Tyrtaeus characterize defeat? How does this poem exemplify the values and tactics of hoplite warfare?

2. Why is so much emphasis placed on physical beauty and youth? What other qualities are associated with the word *kalos*? Why is old age potentially *aischros*?

3. How does this ideal of male beauty compare with that made visible in the kouros of Anavyssos (page 64)?

PORTRAITS OF THREE POLEIS

The poleis of the Archaic Period developed in very different ways. To illustrate this diversity, we will examine three particularly well-documented examples: Athens, Sparta, and the Ionian city of Miletus. None of these, however, can be considered typical. There were approximately one thousand poleis in Greece, and about most of them we know almost nothing. But at least we can survey some of the features that, with variations, made each polis unique—and yet comparable, in some ways, to its neighbors.

Athens

The Athenians liked to boast that their city had been a great metropolis since the Bronze Age. But although Attica had long been a populous and prosperous region, Athens itself was of no great significance during the Mycenaean Era. When Athenians first came together to form a polis, theirs was a distinctly agricultural economy. Whatever profits aristocrats acquired through trade, they reinvested in land. Indeed, Athenian elites came to regard commerce as a disreputable means of earning a living, a mentality that persisted even when the city's excellent harbors made Athens famous as a mercantile polis.

THE ATHENIAN PNYX, WITH A VIEW OF THE ACROPOLIS. The Athenian assembly, the *ekklesia*, met on the sloping hill of the Pnyx. A speaker standing on the *bema* ("stepping stone," to the right) would have to make himself heard by all the citizens gathered in front of this platform, and all proceedings would have been plainly visible to noncitizens and foreigners in the *agora* (central marketplace) at the foot of the hill (off to the left). Overlooking it all was the temple of the city's patron goddess, Athena, on the crest of the Acropolis. ■ *How is the relative openness and accessibility of Athenian democracy symbolized by this chosen site?*

In the Archaic Period, aristocratic dominance over this polis rested on the monopolization of elected offices and control of the city's council, the Areopagus (*ah-ree-OH-pah-gus*). By the early seventh century B.C.E., an even smaller group of aristocratic officials wielded executive authority in Athens: the *archons*, or "first men." Ultimately, nine archons presided over the entire governance of the polis. Although each served for only one year, all became lifetime members of the Areopagus. And because the Areopagus appointed the archons, it could therefore control its own future membership.

As power was consolidated by this small group, deep economic and social divisions developed. A significant proportion of the population fell into slavery through debt, while struggles among aristocratic families destabilized the government and fomented cycles of revenge killings. Finally, this situation inspired Athens' first attempt to promulgate a set of written laws. In 621 B.C.E., an aristocrat named Drakon sought to control civic violence through harsh punishments: hence our use of the term "draconian" to describe any severe penalty or regime. This attempt failed, but ultimately led both aristocrats and hoplites to an agreement. In 594 B.C.E., they elected one man, the poet Solon, as the sole archon for one year, and they gave him sweeping powers. Solon was an aristocrat, but he had made his fortune as a merchant and did not hold that vocation in

contempt; this meant that he was not allied with any single interest.

Solon's political and economic reforms laid the foundations for the later development of Athenian institutions. He forbade the practice of debt slavery and set up a fund to buy back Athenian slaves who had been sold abroad. He encouraged the cultivation of olives and grapes, thus spurring cash-crop farming and urban industries such as oil and wine production, as well as the manufacture of pottery storage jars and decorative drinking cups. He also broadened rights of political participation and set up courts in which citizens served as jurors and to which any Athenian might appeal. He based eligibility for political office on property qualifications, not birth, thus making it possible for someone not born into the aristocracy to gain access to power. Moreover, he convened an Athenian assembly, the *ekklesia* (*eh-KLAY-see-a*), and gave it the right to elect archons. Now all free-born Athenian men over the age of eighteen could participate in government. Even those who were not eligible for citizenship were able to see the workings of government for themselves, since the assembled citizens met on the slopes of the Pnyx (*pNIX*), a hill visible from the central marketplace and overlooked by the sacred precincts of the Acropolis.

Yet Solon's reforms were not widely accepted. The aristocracy thought them too radical; the people of the demos, not radical enough. In the resulting generation of turmoil, an aristocrat named Peisistratos (*pi-SIS-trah-tohs*) succeeded in establishing himself as tyrant in 546 B.C.E. Somewhat ironically, Peisistratos then proceeded to institute Solon's reforms. But the apparent mildness of his rule was undergirded by the quiet, persistent intimidation of his fellow Athenians by foreign mercenaries and the ruthlessness with which he crushed any dissent. Still, by enforcing Solon's laws, he strengthened the political role of the demos and remained a popular ruler until his death. His sons, however, were less able to control the various factions that threatened their rule: one was assassinated and the other ousted with the help of the Spartans in 510 B.C.E.

But the following period of Spartan-sponsored oligarchy ("rule of the few") was brief. Two generations of increasing access to power had left the Athenian demos with a taste for self-government. For the first time in recorded history, a group of commoners can be credited with the overthrow of a regime. The hoplites rallied behind Cleisthenes

(CLIE-sthen-ees), an aristocrat who had championed the cause of the demos after the fall of the Peisistratids. Once voted in as archon in 508/7 B.C.E., Cleisthenes took steps to limit aristocratic power. By reorganizing the Athenian population into ten voting districts, he suppressed traditional aristocratic loyalties. He also introduced the practice of ostracism, whereby Athenians could decide each year whether they wanted to banish someone for a decade and, if so, whom. With this power, Cleisthenes hoped that the demos could prevent the return of a tyrant and quell factional strife.

By 500 B.C.E., these struggles had given Athens a far more populist government than any other Greek polis, and had strengthened its political institutions. In the meantime, Athens had become the principal exporter of olive oil, wine, and pottery in the Greek world. It was poised to assume the role it would claim for itself during the fifth century B.C.E. as the exemplar of Greek culture.

Sparta

Located in the southern inland part of the Peloponnesus, Sparta took shape when four villages (and ultimately a fifth) combined to form a single polis. Perhaps as a relic of this unification process, Sparta retained a dual monarchy throughout its history, with two royal families and two lines of succession: a situation that often led to political infighting among their respective supporters.

According to local tradition, Spartan hegemony in the surrounding region of Laconia began with the conquest of Messenia, one of the mainland's few agriculturally viable territories. Around 720 B.C.E., the Spartans subjugated and enslaved the indigenous people there, the *helots*, who were forced to work under Spartan lordship. Around 650 B.C.E., however, the helots revolted, briefly threatening Sparta with annihilation. Eventually, Sparta triumphed; but the shock of this rebellion brought about a permanent transformation.

Determined to prevent another uprising, Sparta became the most militarized polis in Greece. By 600 B.C.E. everything was oriented to the maintenance of its hoplite army, a force so superior that Spartans confidently left their city unfortified. At a time when Athenian citizens spent more time legislating than fighting, Spartan society was becoming increasingly devoted to an older aristocratic ideal of perpetual warfare.

The Spartan system made every male citizen a professional soldier of the phalanx. At birth, every Spartiate child was examined by officials who determined whether it was healthy enough to raise; if not, the infant was abandoned in the mountains. This was a custom observed elsewhere in the ancient world, but only in Sparta was it institutionalized. If deemed worthy of upbringing, the child was placed at age seven in the polis-run educational system. Boys and girls trained together until age twelve, participating in exercise, gymnastics, and other physical drills and competitions. Boys then went to live in barracks, where their military training would commence in earnest. Girls continued their training until they became the mates of eligible Spartiate males.

Barracks life was designed to accustom youths to physical hardship. At age eighteen, the young man who survived this training would try for membership in a brotherhood whose sworn comrades lived and fought together. Failure to gain acceptance would mean that the young man would lose his rights as a citizen. If accepted, he remained with his brotherhood until he was thirty years of age. He was also expected to mate with a Spartiate woman, but occasions for this were few—a fact that partially accounts for the low birthrate among Spartan citizens. After age thirty, a Spartiate male could opt to live with his family, but he was still required to remain on active military duty until he was sixty.

All Spartiate males over the age of thirty were members of the citizens' assembly, the *apella*, which voted on matters proposed to it by the two kings and twenty-eight elders. This *gerousia* (gher-oo-SEE-ah, "council of elders") was the main policymaking body of the polis and also its primary court. Its members were elected for life, but had to be over the age of sixty before they could stand for office. Meanwhile, five *ephors* (overseers), elected annually, supervised the educational system and acted as guardians of Spartan tradition. In the latter role, ephors could even depose an errant king from command of the army while on campaign. The ephors also supervised the Spartan secret service, the *krypteia*. Agents spied on citizens, but their main job was to infiltrate the helot population and identify potential troublemakers.

Spartan policy hinged on the precarious relationship between the Spartiates and the helots, who outnumbered the Spartiates ten to one. Helots accompanied the Spartiates on campaign as shield bearers and baggage handlers. At home, however, the helots were a constant security concern. Every year the Spartans ritually declared war on them as a reminder that they would not tolerate dissent. Ironically, the threat of unrest meant that the polis was notoriously reluctant to send its army abroad.

Helot slavery therefore made the Spartan system possible, but Sparta's reliance on a hostile population of slaves was also a serious limitation. This system also limited Spartans' contact with the outside world in other respects. Spartiates were forbidden to engage in commerce, because wealth might distract them from the

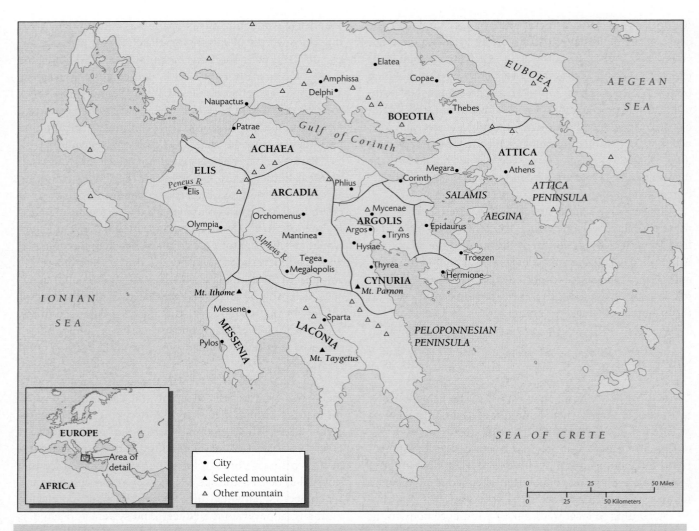

THE PELOPONNESUS. Located on the Peloponnesian peninsula, the highly militarized society of Sparta dominated the region known as Laconia. ▪ *Where is Sparta located?* ▪ *How might Sparta's inland situation have influenced its outlook on foreign affairs?* ▪ *Did geography make conflict between Athens and Sparta inevitable?*

pursuit of glory. Nor did Spartiates farm their own lands, as Athenians did. Economic activity fell either to the helots or to the free residents of other Peloponnesian cities, who were known as *perioikoi (pair-ee-OY-koy)*, "those dwelling round about." Unlike the residents of Attica, the perioikoi exercised no political rights.

The Spartans also self-consciously rejected innovation, styling themselves as the protectors of the "traditional customs" of Greece. In this role, Sparta tried to prevent the establishment of tyrannies in neighboring states and tried to overthrow them when they arose: hence their willing intervention in the affairs of Athens under the Peisistratids. Indeed, Sparta's stern defense of tradition made it an object of admiration throughout the Greek

world, even though few Greeks had any desire to live as the Spartans did.

The fatal flaw in the Spartan system was demographic. There were many ways to fall from the status of Spartiate, but the only way to become one was by birth—and the Spartan birthrate simply could not keep pace with the demand for trained warriors. As a result, the number of full Spartiates declined from perhaps as many as 10,000 in the seventh century to only about 1,000 by the middle of the fourth century B.C.E. Another flaw is historical: because the Spartans placed little value on written records, almost everything we know about them (including the summary offered here) must be gleaned from archaeological investigations or the propaganda of their rivals, notably the Athenians.

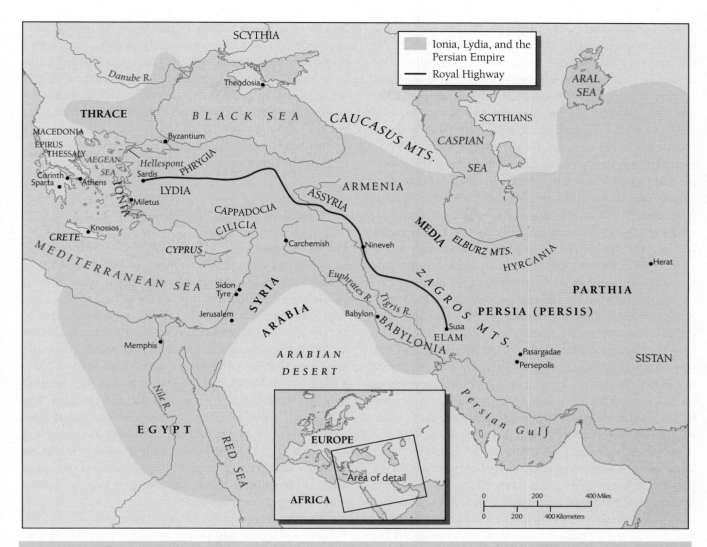

IONIA, LYDIA, AND THE PERSIAN EMPIRE. During the seventh and sixth centuries B.C.E., the Greek cities of the Ionian coast were the cultural and commercial leaders of Greece. But during the fifth century B.C.E., after the Persians conquered Lydia, they lost this position to Athens. ▪ *Where are Ionia, Lydia, and Miletus on this map?* ▪ *How does Ionia's geographical position help to explain the change in its fortunes?* ▪ *How might this change have influenced Ionian attitudes toward the Persian Empire?*

Miletus and the Ionian Revolution in Thought

Across the Aegean from the Greek mainland lay the Greek cities of Ionia on the central part of the Anatolian coast. Here, Miletus was the foremost commercial and cultural power. Long a part of the Greek world (see **Analyzing Primary Sources** in Chapter 2, page 39), it had also been shaped by Mesopotamian and Egyptian influences, and Milesian intellectuals were well aware of Near Eastern literature and learning. Some even echoed the vaunting rhetoric of Persian imperial decrees ("thus speaks Darius the Great King . . .") to make their own, quite different observations ("thus speaks Hecataeus of Miletus: the sayings of the Greeks are many and foolish").

The relationship between the Ionians of the coast and the interior kingdom of Lydia was close but difficult. It was through the Ionians that the Lydian invention of coinage was introduced to the Greek world, where it revolutionized trade, made wealth portable for the first time, and introduced a host of new philosophical and ethical problems. The Ionians, in turn, played a crucial role in Hellenizing western Asia while at the same time insisting on their independence. The major cities of Ionia ultimately banded together to form the Ionian League, a political and religious confederation of poleis pledged to support each other. This was the first such organization in the Greek world.

The Milesians founded many colonies, especially in and around the Black Sea. They were also active in Egypt.

These colonial efforts, combined with its advantageous position for trade, brought Miletus extraordinary wealth. At the same time, it became a center for what the Greeks called *philosophia*, "the love of wisdom." Beginning in the sixth century B.C.E., a series of intellectuals now known as the pre-Socratics (because they came before Socrates) raised new and vital questions about the relationship between the natural world (the *kosmos*), the gods, and men. Often, their explanations moved the direct influence of the gods to the margins or removed it altogether, something that other Greeks regarded as blasphemous. For example, Milesian philosophers sought physical explanations for the movements of the heavens, and did not presume that heavenly bodies were divine. By making human observations the starting point for their knowledge, they began to formulate scientific explanations for the working of the universe.

Stimulated by the cultural diversity of their city, Milesian philosophers also began to rethink humans' place in the cosmos. When Hecataeus (*heck-ah-TAY-us*) remarked that "the sayings of the Greeks are many and foolish," he was deriding his contemporaries' unquestioning acceptance of a narrow worldview. He set out to expand their horizons by traveling extensively and studying the customs and beliefs of other cultures. The philosopher Xenophanes (*zee-NOFF-uh-nees*) further posited that all human knowledge is relative and conditioned by experience: he observed that the Thracians (a people living north of Greece) believed that the gods had blue eyes and red hair as the Thracians themselves did, whereas Ethiopians portrayed the gods as dark skinned and curly haired, as they themselves were. He concluded that human beings make gods in their own image, not the other way around. If oxen could pray, Xenophanes declared, they would pray to gods who looked like oxen.

Such theories would become a distinctive strand in later Greek philosophy, yet they would continue to be regarded as disturbing and dangerous—dangerous enough to warrant the execution of Socrates in Athens a hundred years later (as will be discussed later). By that time, the Persian conquest of Lydia had made Miletus and its sister cities subject to that great empire. Ultimately, those poleis' resistance to Persian rule would trigger a momentous struggle for dominance and survival.

THE CHALLENGE OF THE PERSIAN WARS

The two major wars fought between the Greeks and the Persians were construed as defining events by those who witnessed and looked back on them. From the first, the contest was unequal. Persia was the largest and most efficient state the world had ever seen, capable of mustering over a million armed men. The Greeks, by contrast, remained a collection of disparate communities, fiercely competitive and suspicious of one another. An exceptionally large polis, such as Athens or Sparta, might put 10,000 hoplites in the field; but the vast majority of Greek states could only provide a few hundred each. So the threat of Persian conquest loomed large on the Greek horizon.

The Ionian Revolt (499–494 B.C.E.)

For the first time in the history of Western civilizations, we can follow the unfolding of events through the narrative of a contemporary historian. Herodotus self-consciously set out to write an account of his own times in careful, unambiguous prose, rather than in the form of heroic poetry or the boastful language of victorious inscriptions. And luckily for us, Herodotus was uniquely qualified to probe the long-term and more immediate causes of the Persian Wars. Raised in the Ionian polis of Halicarnassus, he regarded both the Greeks and the Persians as great peoples. Yet, as a Greek himself—albeit one born within the Persian dominion—he was not impartial. Indeed, his surviving account reflects the intellectual currents of Athens, where he spent the better part of his career, as well as many Athenian prejudices. This is something we must be bear in mind when reading his work.

Herodotus was careful to show that the war between the Persians and Greeks had ancient roots, but his narrative also shows that the catalyst was a political conflict in Miletus. In 501 B.C.E., the city was governed by Aristagoras (*ah-ris-TAG-or-us*), a tyrant who owed his power to the backing of the Persian emperor, Darius. But apparently Aristagoras came to believe that his days as the emperor's favorite were numbered. So he turned abruptly from puppet to patriot, rousing the Milesians and the rest of Ionia to revolt against Persian rule. As a safeguard, he also sought military support from sympathetic poleis on the Greek mainland. The Spartans refused to send their army abroad, but Athens and Eretria, on the island of Euboea, agreed to send twenty-five ships and crews. This small force managed to capture the old Lydian capital of Sardis (by then a Persian administrative center) and burn it to the ground. Then the Athenians and Eretrians went home, leaving the Ionian colonies to their own devices. In 494 B.C.E., these rebellious poleis were finally overwhelmed by the vastly superior might of Persia.

Darius realized, however, that as long as his Greek subjects could cast a hopeful eye to their neighbors across the Aegean, they would forge alliances. He therefore decided

A MODERN REPLICA OF AN ATHENIAN TRIREME. These versatile warships were much more powerful than the old 50-oared pentakonters that had been in use for centuries. As the name suggests, a trireme featured three banks of oars on each side, 170 oars in total. These were manned by citizen rowers seated on benches at three different levels in the vessel's hold. In battle, rowers could help power a ship forward, turn it, and keep it on course in a chase, even when sailing into the wind. In favorable winds, sails could be used to add speed. ■ *How does this new military technology build on some of the same strategies as hoplite warfare?*

the Athenians had defeated the world's major imperial power, and they had done it without Spartan help. It was a vindication of hoplite tactics and a tremendous boost to Athenian confidence.

Yet the Athenian politician Themistocles (*theh-MIS-toh-klees*) warned that the Persians would retaliate with an even larger force. So when the Athenians discovered a rich vein of silver ore in the Attic countryside a few years later, they used the windfall to finance a fleet of 200 triremes, state-of-the-art warships.

Xerxes' Invasion

Darius the Great was succeeded by his son Xerxes (*ZERK-sees*), who almost immediately began preparing a massive invasion of Greece to avenge his father's shame. Supported by a fleet of 600 ships, this grand army set out in 480 B.C.E., crossing the narrow strait separating Europe from Asia. But unlike his father, who had dispatched talented generals to lead the earlier attack on Athens, Xerxes led this campaign himself.

Many Greek poleis capitulated immediately. But Athens, Sparta, Corinth, and some thirty others hastily formed a Hellenic League: an unprecedented alliance. In August

to launch a preemptive strike against Athens and Eretria, to teach these upstart poleis a lesson. In the summer of 490 B.C.E., a punitive expedition of 20,000 soldiers crossed the Aegean. Their forces sacked and burned Eretria to the ground, sending its population into captivity in Persia. They then crossed the narrow strait to Attica, landing on the plain of Marathon, approximately 26 miles from Athens.

Marathon and Its Aftermath

In this emergency, the Athenians sought help from the only polis that could conceivably help them avoid annihilation: Sparta. But the Spartans responded that they were unable to assist—they were celebrating a religious festival. Only the small, nearby polis of Plataea offered the Athenians aid. Heavily outnumbered and without effective cavalry to counter that of the Persians, the Athenian hoplites took a position between two hills blocking the main road to the polis. After a standoff of several days, the Athenian general Miltiades (*mil-TIE-uh-dees*) received word that the Persians were watering their horses, and that the Persian infantry was vulnerable. Miltiades led a charge that smashed the Persian force and resulted in crippling losses. Almost unbelievably,

GREEK FORCES DEFEAT PERSIANS. This detail from a bowl commemorating the defeat of Xerxes' army depicts an Athenian hoplite poised to strike a death-blow to his Persian opponent. The artist has carefully delineated the differences between the enemies' dress and weaponry. To the Greeks, the Persian preference for trousers over short tunics seemed particularly barbaric and effeminate.

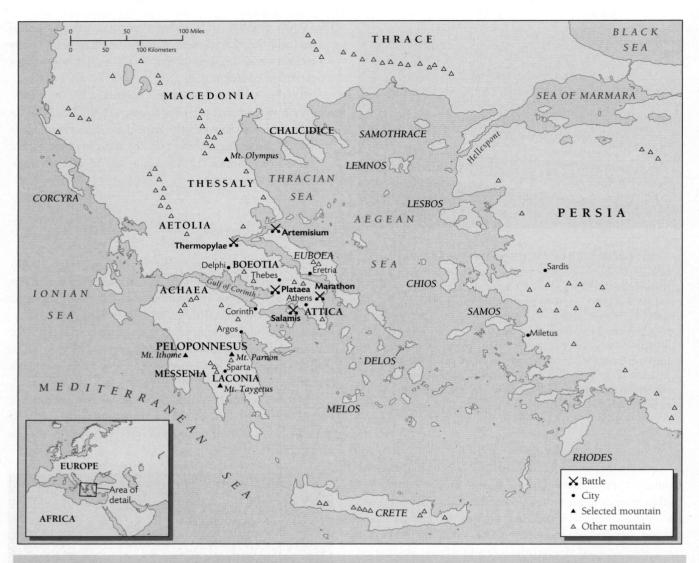

of 480, a major Persian offensive was held at bay when the outnumbered Greek allies, under the military leadership of Sparta, confronted Xerxes at the mountain pass of Thermopylae (*ther-MO-pih-lie*). For three days, they valiantly held off the Persian multitude. Meanwhile, a Greek fleet led by Athens engaged a Persian flotilla. The Spartans' defense of Thermopylae ultimately failed, but their sacrifice of some 300 warriors allowed the new Athenian warships to inflict heavy losses on the Persians.

However, these engagements left Athens without any men to defend their city. Themistocles therefore persuaded the entire population to abandon Athens for the island of Salamis. From there, the Athenians watched the Persians torch their city. Time, however, was on their side. Xerxes'

massive army depended on his damaged fleet for supplies, and the Persians' military tactics—which included a heavy reliance on cavalry and chariots—were not adapted for the rocky terrain of Greece.

In late September, the numerically superior Persian fleet sailed into the straits of Salamis. So confident was Xerxes that he had a throne placed above the bay, where he would have a good view of his victory. Instead, he watched as the Athenian triremes demolished the Persian fleet. This was the turning point of the war. When the allied Greek army met the Persians on favorable terrain the next spring—an open plain near Plataea—the Greeks prevailed. Against all odds, the small, fractious poleis had defeated the mightiest army of the known world.

THE GOLDEN AGE OF CLASSICAL GREECE

In the half century after the Persian Wars, Athens enjoyed a meteoric rise in power and prestige, becoming the premier naval power of the eastern Mediterranean. Athens also emerged as leader of the Delian League, a group of poleis whose representatives met on the sacred island of Delos and pledged to continue the war against Persia. The fifth century B.C.E. also witnessed the greatest achievements in Athenian culture and politics.

Periclean Athens

The reforms of the decades before the Persian Wars continued to encourage further experiments in democracy, including the selection of major officeholders by lot. Only one key position was now filled by traditional voting: the office of *strategos*, or general. This office became the career goal of Athens' most ambitious men.

Meanwhile, new voices were demanding a greater role in government. Most prominent were the *thetes* (THAY-tees), the class of free men that provided the triremes' rowers, the backbone of the all-important Athenian fleet. Like the hoplites of the Archaic Period, who had achieved citizenship because they were indispensible to the defense of the poleis, thetes wanted higher status and equal representation. The man who emerged to champion their cause was Pericles (PEHR-eh-klees), an aristocrat from one of Athens' most prestigious families.

Pericles advocated a foreign policy that was oriented away from cooperation with Sparta. In 462–461 B.C.E. he was elected strategos and immediately used his position to push through reforms that gave every Athenian citizen the right to propose and amend legislation, not just to vote yes or no in the citizens' assembly. And by paying an average day's wage for attendance, he made it easier for poorer citizens to participate in the assembly and in courts of justice. Through such measures, the thetes and other free men of modest means became a dominant force in politics—and loyal to the man who had made that dominance possible.

Athenian Literature and Drama

Pericles glorified Athens with an ambitious scheme of public building and lavish festivals honoring the gods. The most important of these was the Dionysia, a great spring feast devoted to the god Dionysus, which became a forum for the presentation of drama. From the beginning, Greek theater was closely connected to the political and religious life of the state that sponsored it. Indeed, the very format of classical tragedy replicates the tensions of democracy, showcasing the conflict among opposing perspectives. This format was perfected under the great tragedian Aeschylus (EYE-skihl-us, 525–456 B.C.E.) and his younger contemporary, Sophocles (496–406 B.C.E.). Their dramas made use of two and eventually three professional actors (each of whom could play numerous roles) and a chorus of Athenian citizens, which represented collective opinion and could comment on the action.

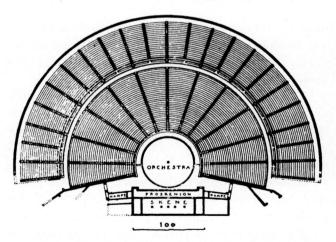

THE THEATER AT EPIDAUROS. Greek dramas were invariably presented in the open air, usually at dawn. Since these were civic spectacles, theaters had to be large enough to accommodate all citizens. Most, like this one at Epidauros (right), took advantage of the natural slope of a hill. The plan for the theater is shown above (left). The acting area would have been backed by a high wall, the *skene*, which housed stage machinery and enhanced the acoustics. A trained actor standing in the circular *orchestra* would have been audible even to those seated in the top tier. ▪ *How would the size and setting of such a theater enhance the political character of the plays performed within it?*

Past and Present

Political Satire

In the fifth century B.C.E., the playwright Aristophanes took an older form of comedy, the satyr play, and turned it into a vehicle for what we still call satire. Instead of gently mocking the gods, he lampooned the politics, popular culture, and current events of his own day—and so made his fellow citizens take a fresh look at themselves. If he were alive today, he might be working for *The Daily Show*.

Watch related author videos on the Student Site
wwnorton.com/college/history/western-civilizationsBrief4

Tragedies were almost always set in the distant or mythical past, yet were intended to address the cutting-edge issues of their day. However, the very earliest of all surviving tragedies, Aeschylus's *The Persians*, represents events of the playwright's own lifetime. (We know for certain that he fought at Marathon, because he had this fact proudly recorded on his tomb.) Performed for the first time in 472, it tells the story of the great Athenian victory at Salamis, but through the eyes of the defeated Xerxes, who thus becomes its tragic hero.

But even when its subject matter was derived from the epics of Homer, the fundamental themes of tragedy—the conflicting demands of personal desire and public duty, the unforeseen consequences of human actions, the brutalizing effects of power—addressed problems of immediate concern. For example, *Oedipus at Colonus*, one of Sophocles' later tragedies, used a story of the mythical king of Thebes to comment bitterly on Athens' disastrous war with Sparta (to be discussed later in the chapter). Similarly, the *Trojan Women* of Euripides (485–406 B.C.E.), presented in 415, marks the tragic

turning point in the Athenians' march toward defeat in that war. By looking back at the capture, rape, and enslavement of Troy's women, Athenians were forced to look ahead to the consequences of their own imperial policies.

Comedy was even more obviously a genre of political commentary, and could deal openly with the absurdities and atrocities of current events. Indeed comedy—then as now—could be effectively deployed to deal with issues that were too hot to handle in any other form: sexual scandals, political corruption, moral hypocrisy, intellectual pretension, popular fads. Aristophanes (*EHR-ih-STOFF-ah-nees*, c. 446–386 B.C.E.), the greatest of the Athenian comic playwrights, lampooned everything from the philosophy of Socrates to the tragedies of his contemporary Euripides, and was an especially outspoken critic of Athenian warmongers and their imperialist aims. He was repeatedly dragged into court to defend himself against the demagogues he attacked, but the power and popularity of comic theater was such that politicians never dared to shut it down for long.

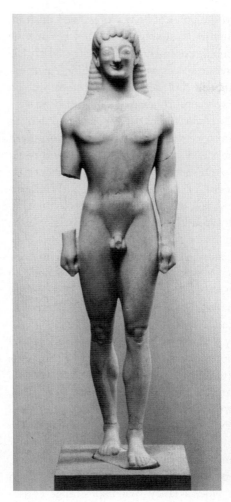

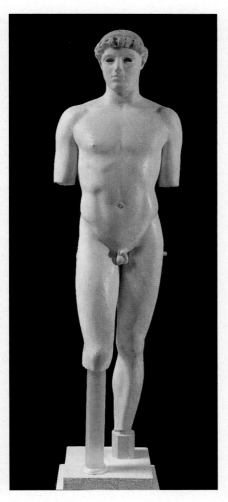

APOLLO OF TENEA, APOLLO OF PIOMBINO, AND THE CRITIAN BOY. These three statues, dating from about 560, 500, and 480 B.C.E., respectively, display the development of Greek statuary art. The first rather stiff and symmetrical statue (left) is imitative of Egyptian sculpture. Roughly half a century later, the second representation (middle) of Apollo begins to display motion, not unlike the *kouros* on page 64. The last figure (right), showing a boy standing in a relaxed posture with his weight resting on one leg, displays even greater naturalism.

Periclean Athens was also fertile ground for the development of new literary forms. Even though the Greeks were becoming more dependent on writing for legal and commercial transactions, intellectuals had long been used to expressing themselves through poetry, which was always intended to be sung and enjoyed in performance, not to be read. Now, though, the rise of functional literacy in Athens encouraged the emergence of prose as a distinct literary form. Herodotus found a ready market for his histories in Athens. His younger contemporary Thucydides (*thu-SID-ih-dees*) followed suit, using his time in exile to write a masterful—and scathingly critical—history of the war between his polis and Sparta.

Between them, these two historians developed a new approach to the study of the past, emphasizing the need to collect and interpret multiple sources and focusing on human agency as the driving force of history (rather than divine intervention). Both conceived the historian's role as distinct from that of a mere storyteller. The word *historia* would continue to mean both "story" and "history" in Greek, but for Herodotus and Thucydides the historian's task was to investigate and critically reflect on the events of his own time, as well as to illuminate those of the past. These methods and goals would increasingly come to inform other prose genres, including the philosophical writings of Plato and Aristotle (see Chapter 4).

Art and Architecture

The artists of fifth-century B.C.E. Athens revealed the same range of talents in the visual arts as poets did in their dramas. Perhaps the most striking development was the new attention paid to the crafting of naturalistic figures, both clothed and nude. Nothing like it had ever been seen before, although it is a trend already discernible in the figure of the *kouros* examined earlier in the chapter (page 64). What hastened the acceptance of naturalism is a matter of intense debate, but scholars have long wanted to link this innovation to the triumphant victories over the Persians. Greeks tended to regard the Persian male's modesty of dress, preference for trousers, fondness for jewelry, and luxurious long hair as proofs of effeminacy (see the vase painting on page 73), whereas Greek men took pride in exercising, sculpting their physiques, and participating in athletic contests in the nude. A Greek might have said that only barbarians covered their shameful bodies in constricting clothes; free men celebrate their individuality in the care of the body and its representation in art.

The Athenians also made exceptional contributions to architecture in this period. All Greek temples sought to create an impression of harmony, but the Parthenon of Athens, built between 447 and 438 B.C.E., is generally considered the finest example (see page 60). Construction of this expensive and structurally ambitious building was urged on the Athenians by Pericles as a tribute to their patron goddess, Athena Parthenos ("Athena the Virgin"), and as a symbol of their own power, confidence, and genius.

The Daily Life of Athens: Men, Women, and Slaves

Toward the end of his famous funeral oration, which Thucydides quotes in his history, Pericles addresses only a few brief remarks to the women of Athens who mourn their fallen fathers, husbands, and sons in the first year of the disastrous war with Sparta. He urges them to do three things: rear more children for the support of Athens and its wars, show no more weakness than is "natural to their sex," and attract no attention to themselves. His remarks reveal widely held attitudes toward women in classical Greece, although they may not reflect complex historical realities.

The growth of democracy did not lead to greater equality between the sexes; in fact, it had the opposite result. In Mycenaean Greece, women had been viewed as possessing extraordinary funds of courage and wisdom. They were prized for their shrewd advice on political and military matters, and they played an active role in the world. Sometimes they ruled kingdoms in their own right. But as aristocratic ideals gave way to more democratic ones, Greek women increasingly spent their lives in the confinement of the home.

The importance of the hoplite infantry and its spirit of shared purpose encouraged men to train together and to develop close relationships. At the same time, that spirit of equality discouraged the political agency of women. Instead, the production of children to supply the infantry became the female imperative. Public spaces were largely restricted to male activities, while domestic spaces were reserved for female endeavors such as child care and weaving. Respectable women lived in seclusion, rarely venturing forth from their homes.

In Athens, girls could be married at age fourteen, to husbands more than twice their age. A girl's father arranged her marriage and provided a dowry that her husband could use for her support. And shortly after a wife entered her new home, a regular schedule of childbirth would begin. The average young wife would bear between four and six children before she died, usually around the age of thirty-five. Her place might then be taken by another, younger woman.

Because respectable women seldom went beyond their neighborhoods, since it was thought immodest for them to be seen by men outside their immediate families, slaves did most shopping or marketing for the household. Even at home, women were expected to withdraw into private rooms if visitors arrived. But they were not supposed to sit around idly, and their main occupation was spinning and weaving. This was true of all women, from royalty to slaves. And since women's work was basically menial, men looked down on them for it, even though their own livelihoods and comfort depended on it.

There is even evidence suggesting that husbands were not encouraged to form emotional attachments to their wives, although some obviously did. In a revealing passage, Herodotus reports of a certain Lydian king that he "fell in love with his own wife, a fancy that had strange consequences." By contrast, an Athenian orator remarked that "we have prostitutes for pleasure, concubines for daily physical attendance, and wives to bear us legitimate children and be our faithful housekeepers." However, these perspectives are offset by a range of archaeological and material evidence (such as funerary monuments) that testify to women's valued social roles, the affection of their husbands and children, and even their wider economic and legal powers.

In addition to depending on the labor and fertility of women, Athenians were as reliant on slaves as Spartans were on helots. Without slavery, none of the Athenian accomplishments in politics, philosophy, or art would have been possible. The Athenian ideal of dividing and rotating governmental duties among all free men depended on slaves who worked in fields, businesses, and homes. In fact, the Athenian democratic system began to function fully only with the expansion of Athenian commerce around 500 B.C.E., which enabled Athenians to buy slaves in larger numbers. Freedom and slavery were thus inescapably, and paradoxically, linked in this democracy—much as they would be many centuries later in the United States before the Civil War.

Although widespread, Athenian slavery was modest in scale. Slaves did not ordinarily work in teams or in factories; the only exceptions were the state-owned silver mines, where large numbers of slaves toiled in miserable conditions. Most slaves were owned in small numbers by a wide range of Athenian families, including the relatively poor. As domestic servants and farm laborers, slaves might even be considered trusted members of the household, although their masters were legally empowered to beat them or abuse them; concubines were often drawn from among this class of slaves. Yet slaves could never be entirely dehumanized, as they were in modern slaveholding societies; the misfortune of becoming a slave through debt was a reality of Athens'

recent past, and the real possibility of being enslaved in war would become a widespread consequence of Athens' over-reaching ambitions.

"THE GREATEST WAR IN HISTORY" AND ITS CONSEQUENCES

Ultimately, Athens' foreign policy and imperial ambitions undermined its civic and cultural achievements. Since the 470s, Athens had begun crushing those allies who

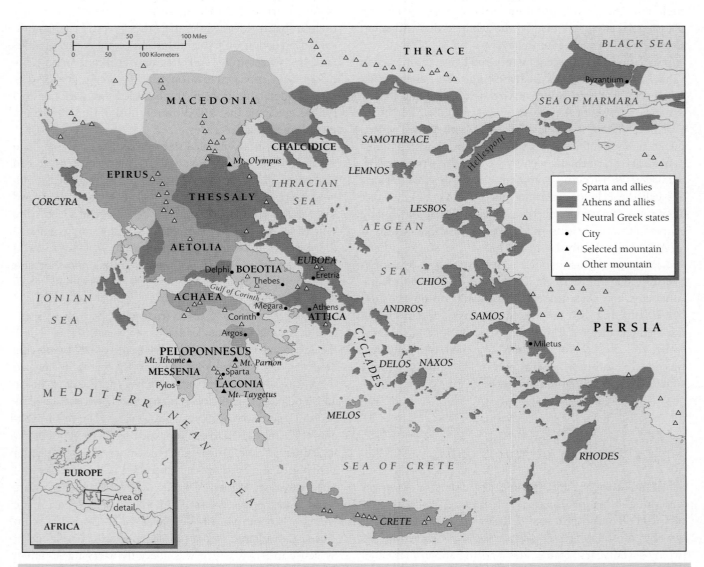

THE PELOPONNESIAN WAR. This map shows the patchwork of colonies and alliances that bound together the supporters of Sparta and Athens at the outbreak of the Peloponnesian War in 431 B.C.E. ▪ *Which side had the geographical advantage?* ▪ *Which neutral powers might have been able to tip the balance by entering the war on one side or the other?* ▪ *What strategic and military choices did geography impose on the two combatants and their allies?*

attempted to break from its control. By the early 440s, its only rival for supremacy in the Greek world was Sparta. Rather than attempting to maintain a balance of power, however, Pericles adopted a more aggressive policy. In order to ensure that military resources would be directed toward any Spartan opposition, he concluded a formal peace with Persia. Yet the sole purpose of the Delian League had been the defense of Greece against Persian aggression, so Athens now had no justification for compelling its members to maintain their allegiance. Many remained loyal nonetheless, enjoying the economic benefits of warm relations with Athens. Others, however, did not, and Athens found itself increasingly having to force its allies back into line, often installing Athenian garrisons and planting Athenian colonists—who retained their Athenian citizenship—to ensure future loyalty.

In the context of recent history and longstanding Greek values, such behavior was disturbing. The Persian wars had been fought to preserve Greek independence. Now Athens itself was becoming an oppressive, imperial power. Foremost among its critics were the Corinthians, whose own economic standing was threatened by Athenian dominance. The Corinthians were close allies of the Spartans, who were in turn the dominant power in what historians call the Peloponnesian League. (The Greeks called it simply the "Spartans and their allies.") When war finally erupted between Athens and Sparta, Thucydides—himself an Athenian—ascribed it to the growing power of Athens and the anxiety this inspired in other poleis. No modern historian has improved on Thucydides' thesis. Yet for the Athenians and their leaders, there could be no question of relinquishing their empire, or the dream of dominating the Mediterranean world. For Sparta and its allies, meanwhile, the prospect of relinquishing their independence was equally unthinkable. Two very different ideas of Greek superiority were about to fight to the death.

The Peloponnesian War Begins

When the Athenians and Spartans found themselves at war with one another in 431 B.C.E., both sides believed a conclusion would come quickly—a delusion common to many of history's pivotal contests. Instead, the war dragged on for twenty-seven years. Thucydides, writing about it in exile, recalled that he knew from the time of its outbreak that it was going to be "the greatest war in history," amounting to the first world war. He also meant that it was the worst, so devastating to both sides that it destroyed the Greeks' proud heritage of freedom. By the time Athens was forced

to concede defeat, all the poleis were weakened to such an extent that they would never again be able to withstand outside threats.

From the beginning, Athens knew that it could not defeat Sparta on land; and neither Sparta nor its allies had a fleet capable of challenging the Athenians at sea. Pericles therefore developed a bold strategy: he would pull the entire population of Attica within the walls of Athens and not attempt to defend the countryside against Sparta. For sustenance, Athens would rely on supplies shipped in by its fleet, which would also be deployed to ravage the coasts of the Peloponnesus.

The Spartans duly plundered the farms and pastures of Attica, frustrated that the Athenians would not engage them in battle. Meanwhile, the Athenians inflicted significant destruction on Spartan territory in a series of raids and by successfully encouraging rebellion among the helots. Time appeared to be on Athens' side. But in 429 B.C.E. the crowded conditions of the besieged city gave rise to a typhus epidemic that killed over a third of the population, including the aged Pericles.

Pericles' death revealed that he had been the only man capable of managing the dangerous political forces he had unleashed. His successors were mostly demagogues, ambitious men who played to the worst instincts of the crowd (the demos). The most successful of these was Cleon, who refused a Spartan offer of peace in 425 B.C.E. and continued the war until his own death in battle four years later. It was under Cleon that Thucydides was given the impossible task of liberating a city under Spartan control; his failure in 423 led to his exile.

After the death of Cleon, a truce with Sparta was negotiated by an able Athenian leader named Nicias (NICK-ee-ahs). But Athenians continued to pursue a "dirty war" by preying on poleis that it feared might support the Spartans. This led to atrocities like the destruction of the entire city of Melos, an island colonized by the Spartans that had maintained its neutrality since the beginning of the war. When the inhabitants of Melos refused to compromise this position by accepting Athenian rule, Athens had the entire male population slaughtered and every woman and child sold into slavery.

Thereafter, Athens' policy of preemptive warfare proved destructive to itself. In 415 B.C.E., a charismatic young aristocrat named Alcibiades (al-ki-BY-uh-dees) convinced the Athenians to attack the powerful Greek city of Syracuse in Sicily, which was allegedly harrying Athenian allies in the western Mediterranean. The expedition ended disastrously, with the death or enslavement of thousands of Athenian warriors.

News of the Syracusan disaster shattered the Athenians. Many political leaders were driven from the polis as scapegoats, and in 411 B.C.E. a hastily convened assembly of citizens voted the democracy out of existence, replacing it with an oligarchy of 400 men, many of whom had been present at this vote. The remains of the Athenian fleet, then stationed in Samos on the Ionian coast, responded by declaring a democratic government in exile under the leadership of none other than Alcibiades. The oligarchy proved to be brief, and democracy was restored to Athens by 409. But a pattern of self-destruction had been established, making it difficult for anyone in Athens or outside it to believe in the possibility of restored greatness.

SOCRATES. According to Plato, Socrates looked like a goatman but spoke like a god.

THE FAILURE OF ATHENIAN DEMOCRACY

The Spartans too despaired of bringing the war to an end. Even in its weakened condition, the Athenian fleet was invincible. Finally, Sparta turned to the Persians, who were glad to avenge themselves on Athens and agreed to supply the gold and expertise necessary to train an effective Spartan navy. Meanwhile, Athenians were turning against each other and making the Spartans' task easier. In 406 B.C.E., a rare Athenian naval victory ended in a sudden storm that prevented Athenian commanders from rescuing the sailors whose ships had been wrecked. A firestorm of protest was fanned by demagogues who insisted on making an example of those generals brave enough to return to Athens. One of these was Pericles' son Pericles, who died a victim of his father's policies. Through such measures, the Athenians executed or exiled the last of their able commanders.

The poorly led Athenian fleet was destroyed in 404 B.C.E. Without ships, the Athenians could neither feed themselves nor defend their city. The Spartans sailed the Aegean unopposed, installing pro-Spartan oligarchies. Finally, they besieged Athens, which surrendered. Corinth and Thebes, remembering the ruthless treatment of Melos, called for Athens' destruction. The Spartans refused, but imposed harsh terms: the dismantling of Athens' defensive walls, the scrapping of its fleet, and the acceptance of an oligarchy under Spartan supervision. These so-called Thirty Tyrants confiscated private property and murdered their political opponents. Their excesses drove committed democrats to plan a desperate coup, a bloodbath averted only through the intervention of the Spartan king.

By the end of 401 B.C.E., Athens had restored a semblance of democratic governance, but it was never more than a shadow of its former self. Meanwhile, Sparta succeeded Athens as the arbiter of the Greek world. But this was a thankless job, made worse by the losses the Spartans had suffered during the war and by the fact that they were even more aggressive in their control than the Athenians had been. In fact, the Spartans found themselves in a position they had avoided throughout their history, because their far-flung interests now sapped their manpower and undermined their control over the helots. They also faced a reinvigorated Persian Empire, which increased its naval presence in the Aegean.

These were the circumstances in which the Athenian philosopher Socrates (469–399 B.C.E.) attempted to reform his city's ethical and political traditions. To understand something of his accomplishments, and to assess the reasons for his tragic death, we must trace briefly the history of philosophical speculation in the half century before his birth.

The Pythagoreans and the Sophists

After the Persian conquest of Ionia, many Milesian philosophers fled to southern Italy. Philosophical speculation thus continued in the Greek "far west." A major figure here was Pythagoras (*pith-AG-or-us*), who founded a philosophical community. Pythagoras and his followers regarded the speculative life as the highest good, and believed that one must be purified of fleshly desires in order to achieve this. Just as the essence of life lay in the mind, they believed that the essence of the universe was to be found not in the natural world but in the study of abstractions. The Pythagoreans established the key properties of odd and even numbers and also proved an old Babylonian hypothesis in geometry, known today as the Pythagorean theorem. Even though they shunned the material world, they still exhibited the characteristic Greek quest for regularity and predictability in that world.

Two Views of Socrates

Socrates as a Sophist

Most people regard Socrates as the sage thinker who challenged the prevailing prejudices of his day. During his own time, however, he was not so universally admired. In Aristophanes' comedy The Clouds, *the protagonist, Strepsiades (strep-SIGH-uh-dees), goes to Socrates and his "Thought Shop" to ask that Socrates make him and his son, Pheidippides (phi-DIP-pid-ees), orators capable of winning lawsuits and growing rich. Aristophanes implies throughout that Socrates is a charlatan who teaches word games and tricks for hire.*

STREPSIADES: See that he [Pheidippides] learns your two Arguments, whatever you call them—oh yes, Right and Wrong—the one that takes a bad case and defeats Right with it. If he can't manage both, then at least Wrong—that will do—but that he must have.

SOCRATES: Well, I'll go and send the Arguments here in person, and they'll teach him themselves.

STREPSIADES: Don't forget, he's got to be able to argue against any kind of justified claim at all.

RIGHT: This way. Let the audience see you. . . .

WRONG: Sure, go wherever you like. The more of an audience we have, the more soundly I'll trounce you.

RIGHT: What sort of trick will you use?

WRONG: Oh, just a few new ideas.

RIGHT: Yes, they're in fashion now, aren't they, [*to the audience*] thanks to you idiots. . . . [*to Pheiddipides*] You don't want to be the sort of chap who's always in the agora telling stories about other people's sex lives, or in the courts arguing about some petty, filthy little dispute. . . .

WRONG: People here at the Thought Shop call me Wrong, because I was the one who invented ways of proving anything wrong, laws, prosecutors, anything. Isn't that worth millions—to have a really bad case and yet win? . . . Suppose you fall in love with a married woman—have a bit of fun—and get caught in the act. As you are now, without a tongue in your head, you're done for. But if you come and learn from me, then you can do whatever you like and get away with it . . . and supposing you do get caught with someone's wife, you can say to him . . . "What have I done wrong? Look at Zeus; wasn't he always a slave of his sexual passions? And do you expect a mere mortal like me to do any better than a god?" . . .

STREPSIADES [*to Socrates*]: I wonder if you'd accept a token of my appreciation? But my son, has he learned that Argument we were listening to a moment ago?

SOCRATES: Yes, he has.

STREPSIADES: Holy Fraud, how wonderful!

SOCRATES: Yes, you'll now be able to win any case at all.

Source: Aristophanes, *The Clouds*, trans. Alan H. Sommerstein (New York: 1973), pp. 148–50, 154, 159–60 (slightly revised).

Socrates and the Laws of Athens

According to his pupil Plato, Socrates spent the last days of his life in conversation with his friends and followers, some of whom urged him to escape from captivity and live in exile. In the dialogue Crito, *a young aristocrat of that name argues that the very laws that have condemned Socrates are unjust, and that by choosing to obey them Socrates is giving them a legitimacy they do not deserve. Halfway through the debate, Socrates turns the tables on him.*

SOCRATES: I should like you to consider whether we are still satisfied on this point: that the really important thing is not to live, but to live well.

CRITO: Why, yes.

SOCRATES: And that to live well means the same thing as to live honorably, or rightly?

CRITO: Yes.

SOCRATES: Then in light of this agreement we must consider whether or not it is right for me to try to get away without an official pardon. If it turns out to be right, we must make the attempt; if not, we must let it drop. . . .

CRITO: I agree with what you say, Socrates. . . .

SOCRATES: Well, here is my next point, or rather question. Ought one to fulfill all one's agreements, provided they are right, or break them?

CRITO: One ought to fulfill them.

SOCRATES: Then consider the logical consequence. If we leave this place without first persuading the polis to let us go . . . are we or are we not abiding by our just agreements?

CRITO: I can't answer your question, Socrates. I am not clear in my mind.

SOCRATES: Look at it this way. Suppose that while we were preparing to run away (or however one should describe it), the Laws of Athens were to come and confront us with this question: "Now, Socrates, what are you proposing to do? Can you deny that by this act which you are contemplating you intend, so far as you have the power, to destroy us, the Laws, and the whole polis as well? Do you imagine that a city can continue to exist and not be turned upside down, if the legal judgments which are pronounced in it have no force but are nullified and destroyed by private persons?"—How shall we answer this question, Crito, and others of the same kind? . . . Shall we say, "Yes, I do intend to destroy the Laws, because the polis has wronged me by passing a faulty judgment at my trial"? Is this to be our answer, or what?

CRITO: What you have just said, by all means, Socrates.

SOCRATES: Then supposing the Laws say, "Was there provision for this in the agreement between you and us, Socrates? Or did you pledge to abide by whatever judgments the polis pronounced? . . . [I]f you cannot persuade your country you must do whatever it orders, and patiently submit to any punishment it imposes, whether it be flogging or imprisonment. And if it leads you out to war, you must comply, and it is right that you should do so; you must not give way or retreat or abandon your position. Both in war and in the law courts you must do whatever your city and your country commands."

Source: Plato, *Crito*, excerpted (with modifications) from *The Last Days of Socrates*, trans. Hugh Tredennick (New York: 1969), pp. 87–91.

Questions for Analysis

1. Socrates actually refused to teach the art of "making the weaker argument defeat the stronger." But in *The Clouds*, Aristophanes shows him teaching how "to win any case at all." Why were the powers of persuasion considered potentially dangerous in democratic Athens? Why might Aristophanes choose to represent Socrates in this way?

2. How do the arguments of Plato's Socrates compare to those of Aristophanes' character?

3. How does Socrates' sense of honor and his duty toward the polis compare to that of Tyrtaeus of Sparta (page 67)?

Meanwhile, philosophy as it developed in mainland Greece was more attuned to questions of ethics and politics. The increasing power of individual citizens begged the question of how a man should conduct himself, in public and private life, so as to embrace "the beautiful and the good"—or at least to advance himself by the use of his wits. To answer this latter need were a new group of teachers known as Sophists, a term meaning "wise men." Unlike the Milesian philosophers or the Pythagoreans, however, the Sophists made a living from selling their knowledge. Their teachings are best exemplified by Protagoras (*pro-TAG-or-us*), an older contemporary of Socrates. His famous dictum, "man is the measure of all things," means that goodness, truth, and justice are relative concepts, adaptable to the needs and interests of human beings. They are not moral absolutes, established by the gods. Indeed, Protagoras declared that no one could know whether the gods existed or, if they did, what they wanted. He thus concluded that there could be no absolute standards of right and wrong. Empirical facts, established by the perception of the senses, were the only source of knowledge. And because each man experienced the world in a different way, there could be only particular truths valid for the individual knower.

Such teachings struck many Athenians as dangerous. Sophists like Protagoras made everyday life a subject for philosophical discussion, but their relativism could too easily degenerate into a conviction that the wise man (or the wise polis) is the one best able to manipulate others. Both individually and collectively, this conviction could rationalize monstrous acts of brutality—like those committed by Athens in the case of Melos. Indeed, the lessons of the Peloponnesian War went a long way toward demonstrating the disastrous consequences of this self-serving logic: if justice is merely relative, then neither personal morality nor society can survive. This conviction led to the growth of a new philosophical movement grounded on the theory that absolute standards do exist, and that human beings can determine what these are, through the exercise of reason. The initiator of this trend was Socrates.

The Life and Thought of Socrates

Socrates was not a professional teacher, like the Sophists. He may have trained as a stonemason, and he certainly had some sort of livelihood that enabled him to maintain his status as a citizen and hoplite. Having fought in three campaigns as part of the Athenian infantry during the war with Sparta, he was both an ardent patriot and a sincere critic of Athenian policy. His method of instruction was conversation: through dialogue with passers-by, he submitted every presumed truth to examination in order to establish a firm foundation for further inquiry. Everything we know about Socrates' teachings comes from the writings of younger men who considered themselves his pupils, and who participated in these conversations. The most important of these followers was Plato.

According to Plato, Socrates sought to show that all supposed certainties are merely unexamined prejudices inherited from others. Socrates always said that he himself knew nothing, because this was a more secure place from which to begin the learning process. He sought to base his speculations on sound definitions of key concepts—justice, virtue, beauty, love—which he and his pupils could arrive at only by investigating their own assumptions. And

he focused his attention on practical ethics rather than the study of the physical world (like the Milesians did) or abstractions (like the Pythagoreans). He urged his listeners to reflect on the principles of proper conduct, both for their own sakes and for that of society as a whole. One should consider the meaning and consequences of one's actions at all times, he taught, and be prepared to take responsibility for them. According to one of his most memorable sayings, "the unexamined life is not worth living."

It is bitterly ironic that such a man, the product of Athenian democracy, should have been put to death by democratic processes. Shortly after the end of the Peloponnesian War in 399 B.C.E., when Athens was reeling from the shock of defeat and from violent internal upheavals, a democratic faction decided that Socrates was a threat to the state. A democratic court agreed, condemning him to death for denying the gods, disloyalty to the polis, and "corrupting the youth." Although his friends made arrangements for him to flee the city and thus evade punishment, Socrates insisted on abiding by the laws, proving himself true to his own principles and setting an example for future citizens. He died calmly by the prescribed method, self-administered poison.

According to Socrates, the goal of philosophy is to help human beings understand and apply standards of absolute good, rather than to master a series of mental tricks that facilitate personal gain at the expense of others. The circumstances of his death, however, show that it is difficult to translate this philosophy into principles that can be widely accepted. This would be the task of Plato, who would lay the groundwork for all subsequent Western philosophy (see Chapter 4).

After You Read This Chapter

 Go to **INQUIZITIVE** to see what you've learned—and learn what you've missed—with personalized feedback along the way.

REVIEWING THE OBJECTIVES

- The Greek polis was a unique form of government. What factors led to its emergence?
- Hoplite warfare had a direct effect on the shaping of early democracy. Why?
- Poleis could develop in very different ways. What are some of the reasons for this?
- In what ways did Athenian culture, philosophy, and art reflect democratic ideals?
- The Persian and Peloponnesian Wars affected Greek civilization in profound ways. Describe some of the consequences of Athens' victory in the former and its defeat in the latter.

CONCLUSION

There are many striking similarities between the civilization of ancient Greece and our own–and many stark differences. Perhaps the most salient example of both is the concept of democracy, which in ancient Greece was ruled by a class of propertied male citizens supported by slavery. In theory and in practice, this class amounted to only a small percentage of the population in Athens, whereas in Sparta the vast majority were subject to the rule of an even smaller class of Spartiates. At the same time, the growth of Athenian democracy meant, increasingly, the exploitation of other poleis and the spread of imperialism, a ruinous policy of preemptive warfare, and increased intolerance and paranoia. (Socrates was not the only man put to death for expressing his opinions.) Finally, the status of women in this "golden age" was lower than it had been in earlier periods of history, and women had fewer personal rights than in any of the ancient societies we have studied so far.

And yet the profound significance of Greek experiments with new forms of governance, and new ideas about the world, is undeniable. This can be seen with particular clarity if we compare the Greek poleis with the empires and kingdoms of Mesopotamia and ancient Egypt. The typical political regime of the ancient Near Eastern world was, as we have seen, that of a monarch supported by a powerful priesthood. In this context, cultural achievements were mainly instruments to enhance the prestige of rulers, and economic life was controlled by palaces and temples.

By contrast, the core values of the Greeks were the primacy of the human male and the principles of competition, individual achievement, responsibility, and human freedom. (The very word for freedom—*eleutheria*—cannot be translated into any ancient Near Eastern language, not even Hebrew.) In his history, Herodotus records a conversation between a Greek (in this case a Spartan) and a Persian, who expresses surprise that the Greeks should raise spears against the supposedly benign rule of his emperor. The Spartan retorts, "You understand how to be a slave, but you know nothing of freedom. Had you tasted it, you would advise us to fight not only with spears but with axes." The story of how the Greeks came to turn those spears on one another within a few generations of their united victory is worthy of one of their own tragedies.

Another way of appreciating the enduring importance of Greek civilization is to recall the essential vocabulary we have inherited from it: not only the word *democracy* but *politics*, *philosophy*, *theater*, *history*. The very notion of humanity comes to us from the Greeks. For them, the fullest development of one's potential should be the aim of existence: every free man is the sculptor of his own monument. This work of growing from childishness to personhood is what the Greeks called *paideia* (*pie-DAY-ah*); the Romans called it *humanitas*. How this and other ideas came to be disseminated beyond Greece, to be adopted by the peoples and places of a much wider world, is the subject of Chapter 4.

PEOPLE, IDEAS, AND EVENTS IN CONTEXT

- How did the epics of **HOMER** transmit the values of the Bronze Age to the **ARISTOCRACY** of the new Greek **POLEIS**?
- How did the spread of **PANHELLENIC** Greek culture transform the Mediterranean, even as the adoption of **HOPLITE** military tactics transformed Greek politics?
- Compare and contrast the historical circumstances that led to the development of **ATHENS**, **SPARTA**, and **MILETUS**. What were the main differences among them?
- What were the different motives for the invasions of **DARIUS** and **XERXES**? By what methods did the Greek poleis manage to emerge victorious from the **PERSIAN WARS**?
- What were the triumphs and limitations of **DEMOCRACY** in **PERICLEAN ATHENS**?
- How did the **PELOPONNESIAN WAR** transform Athens and affect the balance of power in the Mediterranean?

THINKING ABOUT CONNECTIONS

- The trial and execution of Socrates can be seen as a referendum on the relationship between the individual and the state. What does this incident reveal about the limitations of personal power and individual rights? To what degree was this incident a product of Athenian losses during the Peloponnesian War? To what extent does it reflect long-term trends in the Greek world?
- We like to think that we can trace our democratic ideals and institutions back to Athens, but does this mean that the failings of Athenian democracy also mirror those of our own? What parallels can you draw between ancient Athens and today's United States? What are some key differences?

Before You Read This Chapter

The Greek World Expands, 400–150 B.C.E.

CORE OBJECTIVES

- **EXPLAIN** the reasons for Macedonia's rise to power and its triumph over the Greek poleis.

- **DESCRIBE** Alexander's methods of conquest, colonization, and governance.

- **IDENTIFY** the three main Hellenistic kingdoms and their essential differences.

- **DEFINE** the main characteristics of the Hellenistic world and explain their significance.

- **UNDERSTAND** how new philosophies and artistic movements reflect historical changes.

When the young Alexander of Macedonia set out for Persia in 334 B.C.E., he brought along two favorite books. The first was a copy of the *Iliad*, which his teacher Aristotle had given him. The second was the *Anabasis*, "The Inland Expedition," by an Athenian called Xenophon (ZEN-oh-fon, 430–354 B.C.E.). Both choices are significant. The *Iliad* recounts the story of a much earlier Greek assault on Asia, and its protagonist is the hero Achilles—a figure with whom Alexander identified: consummate warrior, favorite of the gods, a man who inspired passionate loyalty. It is also full of information useful to someone planning a long campaign in foreign lands against a formidable enemy, with a fractious army drawn from all parts of Greece and little prospect of bringing them home safely or soon. The *Anabasis* was an even more practical choice. Its author had been one of 10,000 Greek mercenaries hired by a Persian prince to overthrow his older brother, the Great King. The attempted coup failed, but Xenophon's book made the prince, Cyrus, another role model for Alexander. It also told, in detail, how Persians fought, how they lived, how they were governed, and what the terrain of their vast empire was like. Moreover, it showed what a dedicated army of hoplites could accomplish on Persian soil. This book would be Alexander's bible for the next ten years.

By the time of Alexander the Great's early death, a united Greek and Macedonian army had extended Greek culture and Greek governance from Egypt to the frontiers of India. This personal empire, the empire of Alexander, could not last. But the cultural empire built upon it did. This Hellenistic ("Greek-like") civilization joined disparate lands and peoples, forming the basis of the Roman Empire and mirroring the cosmopolitan world of our own time. How this happened is the subject of Chapter 4.

THE DOWNFALL OF THE GREEK POLIS

The Peloponnesian War had left Sparta the dominant power in the Greek world. But by 395, a significant number of poleis were aligned against Sparta in the so-called Corinthian War (395–387 B.C.E.). To quell this rebellion, the Spartans turned once again to Persia, as they had done in the final stages of the Peloponnesian War. This pattern of violence, temporarily halted by the intervention of Persia, would be repeated time and again over the next fifty years.

The Struggle for Dominance

After the Corinthian War, the Spartans punished the most dangerous of their rivals, Thebes, by occupying the city for four years. But when the Thebans regained their autonomy they elected as their leader a fierce patriot who was also a military genius, Epaminondas (*eh-pa-min-OHN-das*, c. 410–362 B.C.E.). In imitation of the Spartan system, he formed an elite hoplite unit known as the Theban Sacred Band, made up of 150 male couples: sworn lovers who pledged to fight to the death for their polis and for each other's honor.

When the Theban and Spartan armies met at Leuctra in 371 B.C.E., the Sacred Band helped carry the Thebans to victory. Epaminondas then marched through the Spartan territory of Messenia and freed the helots. Spartan power—and the unique social system that had supported it—was thereby brought to an end. But as Theban power grew, so did the animosity of the other Greek poleis. In 362, when Epaminondas fell in battle, Athens attempted—and failed—to fill the vacuum by establishing

a naval confederacy. Greece thus remained a constellation of petty warring states.

Social and Economic Crises

Meanwhile, the poleis were also riven by internal turmoil. Incessant warfare and political struggles profoundly affected their economic and social infrastructures. Many people were driven from their homes or reduced to slavery. Country towns had been ravaged, as had farmlands throughout Greece. Prices rose while standards of living declined. Taxes increased.

Unemployment was also widespread, and many men turned to mercenary service. As we have already noted, Cyrus, brother of the Persian emperor Artaxerxes II, even hired a Greek mercenary force of 10,000 men in an attempt to seize the throne in 401 B.C.E. But when Cyrus was killed in battle, the army—marooned in a hostile country—had to fight its way out under elected leaders. One of these was Xenophon, a former pupil of Socrates, and it was his account of this expedition that would become Alexander's guidebook.

RE-IMAGINING THE POLIS: THE ARTISTIC AND INTELLECTUAL RESPONSE

The year of Socrates' execution, 399 B.C.E., marks the end of an era—that of the polis. This basic engine of Greek life had continued to drive innovation and cultural production even during the Peloponnesian War. But now, the failure of democracy had a profound impact on the arts, philosophy, and especially political thought.

The Arts of the Fourth Century

As we observed in Chapter 3, the painters and sculptors of the fifth century B.C.E. were already working to achieve a heightened appearance of realism in their works. This experimentation continued in the fourth century, especially in the relatively new art of portraiture. Artists also grew bolder in their use of tricky techniques, like the casting of full-size statues in bronze. This was a medium in which the era's most famous sculptor, Praxiteles, excelled. Praxiteles (*prak-SIT-el-eez*) was bold, too, in his choice of subjects, and is widely regarded as the first artist to create full-size female nudes (see *Interpreting Visual Evidence* on page 91).

In contrast to the visual arts, the forms and functions of drama changed considerably. Tragedy and comedy were no

Analyzing Primary Sources

Xenophon Describes an Ideal Leader

In his history of "The Inland Expedition" undertaken by the Ten Thousand, Xenophon (430–354 B.C.E.) mourns the death of Cyrus the Younger, whom he believes would have made a better Great King of Persia than the brother he challenged, Artaxerxes II. The following description of the prince's character and leadership became very famous in its time, often circulating as a separate booklet. It is likely to have influenced the young Alexander.

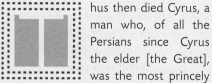

hus then died Cyrus, a man who, of all the Persians since Cyrus the elder [the Great], was the most princely and the most worthy of rule, as is agreed by all who appear to have had personal knowledge of him. In the first place, while he was yet a boy, and when he was receiving his education with his brother and other youths, he was thought to surpass them all in everything. For all the sons of the Persian nobles are educated at the gates of the king, where they may learn many a lesson of virtuous conduct, but can see or hear nothing disgraceful. Here the boys see some honored by the king, and others disgraced, and hear of them, so that in their very childhood they learn to govern and to obey.

Here Cyrus, first of all, showed himself most remarkable for modesty among those of his own age, and for paying more ready obedience to his elders than even those who were inferior to him in station; and next, he was noted for his fondness for horses, and for managing them in a superior manner. They found him, too, very desirous of learning, and most assiduous in practicing, the warlike exercises of archery and hurling the javelin. When it suited his age, he grew extremely fond of the chase and of braving dangers in encounters with wild beasts. On one occasion he did not shrink from a she-bear that attacked him, but, in grappling with her, was dragged from off his horse, and received some wounds, the scars of which were visible on his body, but at last killed her. The person who first came to his assistance he made a happy man in the eyes of many.

When he was sent down by his father, as satrap of Lydia and Great Phrygia and Cappadocia, and was also appointed commander of all the troops whose duty it is to muster in the plain of Castolus, he soon showed that if he made a league or compact with anyone, or gave a promise, he deemed it of the utmost importance not to break his word. Accordingly the states that were committed to his charge, as well as individuals, had the greatest confidence in him; and if anyone had been his enemy, he felt secure that if Cyrus entered into a treaty with him, he should suffer no infraction of the stipulations. When, therefore, he waged war against Tissaphernes, all the cities, of their own accord, chose to adhere to Cyrus in preference to Tissaphernes, except the Milesians; but they feared him, because he would not abandon the cause of the exiles; for he both showed by his deeds and declared in words that he would never desert them, since he had once become a friend to them, not even though they should grow still fewer in number, and be in a worse condition than they were.

Whenever anyone did him a kindness or an injury, he showed himself anxious to go beyond him in those respects; and some used to mention a wish of his that he desired to live long enough to outdo both those who had done him good, and those who had done him ill, in the requital that he should make. Accordingly to him alone of the men of our days were so great a number of people desirous of committing the disposal of their property, their cities, and their own persons.

Source: Excerpted from Xenophon, *Anabasis*, ed. M. I. Finley in *The Portable Greek Historians* (New York: 1959), pp. 383–84.

Questions for Analysis

1. According to Xenophon, what are the attributes of a great leader? How would Alexander have applied these to his own situation?

2. What seems to be Xenophon's attitude toward the Persians? How might his portrayal of them have been influenced by his travels among them? How might it have been colored by his attitude toward his own countrymen?

3. In what ways does Cyrus the Younger appear to have followed the example of his ancestor, Cyrus the Great (Chapter 2, page 52)?

longer mounted as part of publicly funded festivals, but were instead financed by private individuals who could exercise greater control over the content of performances. As a result, fourth-century playwrights did not have the freedom to use drama as a vehicle for political and social critique, as earlier dramatists had done. Instead, the "New Comedy" of this era relied more and more on mistaken identities, tangled familial relationships, and breaches of etiquette. Similar trends toward escapism are also apparent in a new literary genre: the prose novel. These pleasant fictions targeted an increasingly literate audience, including (as with many modern romance novels) an audience of women.

Philosophy after Socrates: The Schools of Plato and Aristotle

The intellectual and political legacy of Socrates was carried forward by Plato (429–349 B.C.E.), who as a young man witnessed the trial and death of his mentor. Plato strove to vindicate Socrates by constructing a philosophical system based on his precepts. He did this by founding an informal school called the Academy and by writing a series of dramatic dialogues that feature Socrates as the central character.

The longest and most famous of these dialogues is now known by its Latin title, the *Republic*. In it, Plato argues that social harmony and order are more important than individual liberty or equality. He imagines an ideal polis governed by a superior group of "guardians" chosen in their youth for natural attributes of intelligence and character. Those found to be the wisest would ultimately become "philosopher-kings." This imaginary system is clearly a response to the failures of Athenian democracy. But whether Plato himself believed in it is open to question. For such a system presumes that properly educated rulers will never be corrupted by power, a proposition that has yet to be sustained in practice.

The practical application of philosophy would be the preoccupation of Plato's own student, Aristotle (384–322 B.C.E.).

PLATO AND ARISTOTLE. Although many artistic representations of Plato and Aristotle were made in antiquity, the image that best captures the essential difference between their philosophies is this one, the focal point of a fresco by the Renaissance painter Raphael Sanzio (1483–1520 C.E., to be discussed further in Chapter 12). Plato is the older central figure to the viewer's left, who points with his right hand to the heavens; Aristotle is the younger man beside him, gesturing with an open palm to the earth. ▪ *How does this double portrait reflect these philosophers' teachings and perspectives?*

Reconstructing an Ideal of Female Beauty

The lost statue known as the Aphrodite of Knidos was considered the most beautiful in the ancient world, but we can only study it by looking at later copies. It was the work of the fourth century's most renowned sculptor, Praxiteles, who was reputed to have modeled it after the Athenian courtesan known as Phryne, a renowned beauty who inspired several contemporary artists and many apocryphal stories. The most reliable of these concerns the riches she accrued: apparently she became so wealthy that she offered to finance the rebuilding of Thebes in

336—on the condition that the slogan "destroyed by Alexander, restored by Phryne the Courtesan" be prominently displayed on the new walls. (Her offer was rejected.)

Praxiteles' original statue is thought to have been the first monumental female nude fashioned in antiquity. According to one authority, he had initially received a commission from the island of Kos, for which he made both clothed and naked versions of Aphrodite. Apparently, the scandalized citizens approved only the draped version and refused to pay for the nude. It was purchased instead by the city of Knidos on Cyprus, where it was displayed in an

open-air temple so that it could be seen from all sides. It quickly became a tourist attraction and was widely copied and emulated. Two of the more faithful replicas, made by artists working in Rome, are pictured here.

Questions for Analysis

1. As we have seen, the male nude was a favorite subject of Greek artists from the Archaic Period onward. Based on your knowledge of contemporary Greek culture and society, why was it only in the fourth century B.C.E. that a life-size female nude could be publicly displayed? Are there any precedents for statues like this?

2. Compare and contrast the ideal of female beauty suggested by the Knidian Aphrodite with the male ideals shown in Chapter 3. What can you conclude about the relationship between these ideals and the different expectations of male and female behavior in Greek society? Why, for example, would ancient sources insist that the model for the original statue was a courtesan?

3. Among the Romans, a statue like the Knidian Aphrodite was called a *Venus pudica*, a "modest Venus" (image A). Yet the citizens of Kos were allegedly shocked by its indecency, while old photographs of the copy in the Vatican Museum (image B) show that it was displayed until 1932 with additional draperies made of tin. How do you account for these very different standards of decency? To what degree do they suggest that concepts of "beauty" or "modesty" are historically constructed?

A. Roman copy of the Aphrodite of Knidos.

B. Second century C.E. copy of the Aphrodite of Knidos.

The son of a physician, Aristotle learned from his father the importance of observing natural phenomena. His own philosophical system was geared toward understanding the workings of the world through empirical knowledge—that is, information gained through sensory experience. In contrast to Plato, who taught that everything we see and touch is an untrustworthy reflection of some intangible ideal, Aristotle advocated the rigorous investigation of real phenomena. His method of instruction was also different. Unlike Socrates and Plato, whose dialogues were witty and often playful, Aristotle delivered lectures on which his students took detailed notes, and which eventually became the basis of treatises on politics, ethics, logic, metaphysics, and poetics.

Aristotle taught that the highest good consists in the harmonious functioning of the individual human mind and body. Good conduct is therefore rational conduct, and consists in acting moderately. And whereas Plato conceived of politics as a means to an end which could never be achieved in this life, Aristotle thought of politics as an end in itself: the collective exercise of moderation.

Yet Aristotle also took it for granted that some people—like barbarians—are not fully human, and so are intended by nature to be slaves. He also believed that women are not endowed with a full measure of humanity. So when Aristotle asserted that "man is by nature a political animal" (or, to be more faithful to the Greek, "a creature of the polis"), he meant only Greek males of privileged status. Nor did he believe that the best form of political organization is a democracy. Like Plato, he saw that as a "debased" form of government.

Men of Thought, Men of Action

For all their brilliance, Plato and Aristotle offered few prescriptions for reforming their own societies. But there were other intellectuals who were considering more radical alternatives. One was Xenophon, the veteran of the Ten Thousand and another product of the Socratic tradition. An exact contemporary of Plato, he spent much of his adult life in Sparta, and it is thanks to his admiring account that we know anything about the Spartiate system described in Chapter 3. He intended his description to be a rebuke to democratic Athens and a model for a different kind of ideal society.

The Athenian orator Isocrates (436–338 B.C.E.) was another direct contemporary of Plato. But rather than imagining an ideal polis, he proposed instead that the Greeks stage a massive invasion of Persia. This assault, he prophesied, should be led by a man of vision and ability who could unite the Greek world behind his cause. Isocrates spent most of his life casting about to find such a leader. Finally, he began to think that the man for the job

was someone most Greeks considered no Greek at all: the king of Macedonia, Philip II.

THE RISE OF MACEDONIA

Until the fourth century, Macedonia (or Macedon) had been a weak kingdom, regarded by most Greeks as a throwback to the "dark ages" before the emergence of enlightened poleis. As recently as the 360s, it had nearly succumbed to the even smaller kingdoms and predatory tribes that surrounded it. No one knows whether the ancient Macedonians were Greek-speaking during this period, but the royal family and nobility would at least have spoken Greek as a second language. Still, they were definitely outsiders. So when a young and energetic king consolidated the southern Balkans under his rule, many Greeks saw it as an alarming development.

The Reign of Philip II (359–336 b.c.e.)

Philip II of Macedonia was not supposed to be its ruler. Born in 382, he was the third and youngest son of King

PHILIP II OF MACEDONIA. This tiny ivory head was discovered in a royal tomb at Vergina and is almost certainly a bust of the king himself. Contemporary sources report that Philip the Great had his right eye blinded by a catapult bolt, a deformity visible here—and testimony to the unflinching realism of Greek portraiture in the fourth century B.C.E.

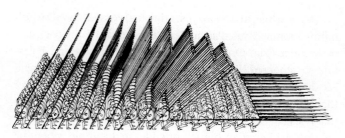

MACEDONIAN PHALANX. Philip of Macedonia's hoplite infantry—the model for Alexander's—was armed with two-handed pikes of graduated lengths, from 13 to 21 feet, and was massed in squares sixteen rows deep and wide. Members of the phalanx were trained to wheel quickly in step formation and to double the width of their front rank as needed, by filing off in rows of eight. The reach of their spears, called *sarissas*, extended the phalanx's fighting range.

Amyntas III, and was considered so dispensable that he was sent to Thebes as hostage when he was fourteen. This turns out to have been the making of him: he became the protégé of the brilliant Epaminondas and may even have trained in the Theban Sacred Band. By the time he returned to the Macedonian capital of Pella, he had received a more thorough education than any Macedonian before him. He was also ambitious. So when both of his older brothers died in battle, Philip was not content with the role of regent for an infant nephew. By 356, he was reigning as king, the same year that his queen, Olympias, bore him an heir. The boy was given the dynastic name Alexandros, "leader of men."

The first problem of Philip's reign was the fragility of Macedonia's northern borders. Through a combination of warfare and diplomacy, he subdued the tribes of the southern Balkans and incorporated their territory into his kingdom. His success had much to do with his reorganization of Macedonian warriors into a hoplite infantry along Theban lines, as well as access to mineral resources that he used to pay and equip a standing professional army. Philip also organized an elite cavalry squad—the Companions—who fought with and beside the king, perhaps in emulation of the Sacred Band. These young men were drawn exclusively from the nobility, and Philip thereby gained valuable young hostages to ensure the good conduct of fractious men. Their sons were now being brought up alongside Alexander and sharing his lessons with Aristotle, who had arrived at the Macedonian court in 343 B.C.E.

Isocrates saw in Philip a potential savior of Greece, but many Athenians believed that his ultimate aim was to conquer them. In actuality, he was probably trying to forge an alliance with Athens, whose fleet could facilitate an invasion of Persia by sea; in return, Philip promised to support Athens' old claim to lordship over Greece. But the Athenians refused to cooperate. This miscalculation ultimately led to war, which sent the Athenians scrambling to ally with Thebes. At the battle of Chaeronea in 338 B.C.E., an army led jointly by Philip and Alexander (aged 18) won a narrow victory, decimating the Athenian forces and destroying the Theban Sacred Band. In the aftermath, Philip called delegates from around mainland Greece to Corinth, where he established a new league whose main purpose was to provide forces for the planned invasion of Persia and maintain peace among the rival poleis.

But Philip never realized his dream of Persian conquest. Two years later, in 336 B.C.E., he was assassinated during a festival. The kingship now fell to Alexander. Among the Greeks, he would be known as Alexander, the Sacker of Cities. To the Romans, he was Alexander the Great.

THE CONQUESTS OF ALEXANDER, 336–323 B.C.E.

By the time of Alexander's early death at the age of 32, a monumental legend had already built up around him. This makes it all the more ironic that no contemporary account of his life and achievements survives. The great library assembled in his capital of Alexandria in Egypt—the repository of all Greek learning and literature—was destroyed or dispersed centuries later, and with it a great portion of assembled knowledge. So when we try to reconstruct the history of Alexander, we are depending on the writings of men who lived and worked under the Roman Empire, notably Plutarch (46–120 C.E.) and Arrian (c. 86–160 C.E.), both of whom were separated from their subject by a distance of four hundred years. Luckily, they were basing their histories on sources derived from two first-hand accounts, one written by Alexander's general (and alleged half-brother) Ptolemy (*TOHL-eh-me*, c. 367–c. 284 B.C.E.), who founded a new dynasty of Egyptian pharaohs, and another by Æschines Socraticus (c. 387–322 B.C.E.), an Athenian statesman.

It is a salutary reminder of how fragile the historical record of antiquity is, that the sources for the life of the era's most famous man are so hard to come by.

The Conquest of Persia

When Alexander succeeded his father in 336 B.C.E., he had to put down the revolts that erupted immediately after Philip's death—notably at Thebes, which he punished by destroying its famous walls. Two years later, he was crossing the Hellespont (literally the land bridge from Greece to Asia) to challenge the Great King of Persia.

Darius III was a minor member of the royal family who had been placed on the throne after a palace coup, at the relatively old age of 45—in the same year that

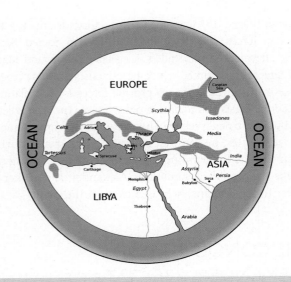

ALEXANDER'S WORLD. This view of the world, modeled on maps made in antiquity, represents what intellectuals of Alexander's own time knew about geography. ▪ *Comparing it to the map of Alexander's campaigns on page 99, how do you think this worldview affected the planning of his route?* ▪ *Based on available knowledge, why would he have traveled down the Indus river (near the marking India) and traveled overland to Susa?* ▪ *What similarities and differences do you find generally, comparing this ancient map with the other maps that appear in this book?*

Alexander himself became king at 20. Darius and his advisors failed to take the Macedonian threat seriously, despite the Persians' past history of defeat at the hands of Greek armies. Perhaps they assumed that the enormous forces they could rally in defense of their empire would easily overwhelm a comparatively small army of 42,000; perhaps they misunderstood Alexander's aims.

In any event, Alexander soon achieved a series of extraordinary victories, beginning in northwest Anatolia, near the site of the epic field of Troy, and continuing down the Ionian coastline. A year later, in 333 B.C.E., Darius was persuaded to engage Alexander personally. But the chosen site, on the banks of a river near Issus, favored Alexander's fast-moving infantry, not the heavy cavalry and chariots of the Persians. No warrior, Darius disgraced himself by fleeing the battlefield, abandoning not only his army but his entire household, which included his wife and his mother. (They were captured by Alexander and treated with great respect.) Darius spent the remainder of his life running from Alexander's advancing forces, until his decisive defeat at Gaugamela (near Mosul in modern Iraq) in 331, when he was killed by a local chieftain who hoped to win Alexander's favor. Instead, Alexander—acting as the new Great King—had the chieftain executed for treason. The next spring, Alexander destroyed the royal capital of Persepolis, lest it serve as a rallying point for Persian resistance.

Meanwhile, in the two years that had passed since Darius's humiliation at Issus, Alexander had completed his conquest of western Asia. One by one, the cities of Syria and Palestine surrendered. Following the example of Cyrus the Great, Alexander had developed a policy of offering amnesty to cities that submitted peacefully—but dealing mercilessly with those that resisted. The fortified city of Gaza, the last Persian stronghold on the Egyptian border, provides an example: when the fortress was finally taken, Alexander's troops slew all the adult males and enslaved the women and children. According to a later Roman historian, Alexander also dragged the body of the commander around the city's walls behind his chariot, imitating Achilles' legendary treatment of Hector.

Alexander in Egypt

After this, Alexander marched into Egypt unopposed. In fact, he was welcomed as a liberator: Egypt had been governed as a Persian satrapy since 525 B.C.E. Now Alexander himself was hailed as pharaoh and given the double crown of Upper and Lower Egypt, becoming the latest in a succession of rulers reaching back three thousand years. The "barbarian" chieftain of a backwater kingdom had become pharaoh of the oldest civilization on earth and heir to its immense riches and extraordinary history.

While the Persians had long been the Greeks' traditional enemies, the Egyptians had always been too far away to pose a threat; indeed, they were an object of awe. This may help to explain Alexander's response to the oracle of Ammon, the name the Greeks gave to the Egyptian sun god Amun-Ra, whom they identified with Zeus. At the oracle's desert oasis of Siwa, Alexander was reportedly told that he was "son of Ammon" and a god himself. Ever mindful of historical precedent, Alexander seems to have decided at this point that Egypt should be the capital of his new empire: it was in Egypt that he would build his shining new city of Alexandria. In the end, he just had time to lay out a plan for the streets before he left for the East. When he finally returned, he was in his sarcophagus.

Alexander's Final Campaigns

Over the ensuing five years, Alexander campaigned in the far reaches of the Persian Empire, in the mountainous regions that had been only loosely yoked with the more settled lands of Mesopotamia. This is the region encompassed today by Afghanistan, and a terrain famous for defeating every attempt at conquest. Here, Alexander and his army experienced the hardest fighting of their long campaign. Indeed, they never succeeded in getting more than a tenuous hold on the

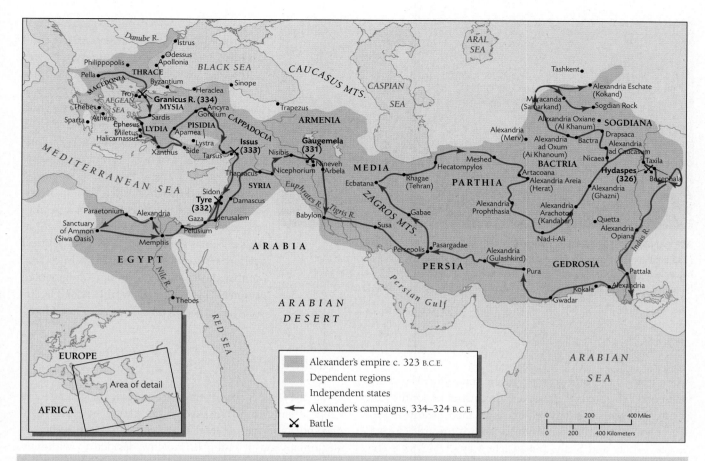

THE CAMPAIGNS OF ALEXANDER. The conquests of Alexander the Great brought Greek culture to the vast expanse of the former Persian Empire, as far east as the Indus River. Trace Alexander's route with your finger. ▪ *Where did he start and end?* ▪ *What was the farthest point east that he traveled on his conquests?* ▪ *Why might Alexander have chosen to found so many cities named after him, and what can you conclude about the purposes of these cities, based on their locations?*

territory, despite Alexander's marriage to Roxane, daughter of a local chieftain. Thereafter, Alexander moved down through what is now Pakistan to the Indus Valley, meeting stiff resistance from its warlords but eventually defeating their leader, Porus, at the Battle of Hydaspes in 326 B.C.E.

This was to be the last major battle of his career, and the one in which his famous warhorse, Bucephalus ("Thundercloud"), was killed. And it was here that Alexander's exhausted army refused to go on, thousands of miles and eight years from home. He was forced to turn back, and rather than attempting to recross the mountains, he pressed southward to the shores of the Arabian Sea—what was then the end of the world. The ensuing march through the Gedrosian Desert, combined with a decade of continuous fighting, weakened him and his army considerably.

When Alexander reached the Persian royal palace of Susa he took steps that indicate how he would have tried to combine his Greco-Macedonian Empire with that of Persia, had he lived. He announced that he would

begin training Persian youths to fight alongside Greeks and Macedonians in hoplite formation. He arranged a mass marriage between hundreds of his officers and a corresponding number of Persian noblewomen. Most controversially, he showed respect for his Persian subjects by adopting Persian dress—considered by Greeks to be effeminate and barbaric—and by encouraging those around him to perform the ritual of *proskynesis* (*pros-kin-EE-sis*). This was a gesture of bodily submission performed by those of lesser social standing when they met their superiors, and by all Persians—even those of royal rank—to honor the Great King. The person paying homage would bow deeply, in some cases prostrating himself entirely. To the Greeks, this practice suggested that the Persians worshiped their king as a god. To Alexander and his close advisers, it was more likely intended to level cultural differences. In any case, it was not a success, and it fueled a mutiny among the Macedonians, which Alexander himself had to quell.

ALEXANDER DEFEATS KING DARIUS OF PERSIA AT THE BATTLE OF ISSUS (333 B.C.E.). This Roman mural, discovered at Pompeii, shows Darius fleeing from the battlefield in his chariot (right), pursued by Alexander, the mounted figure on the far left. Note the reflection of Alexander and his horse in Darius's large round shield.

Alexander's Death

Apart from these attempts to create cohesion, Alexander took no realistic steps to create an administration for his vast empire. He seems to have fixed his sights more clearly on further conquests, perhaps in Arabia, perhaps toward "Greater Greece"—Italy and Sicily. But in late May of 323 B.C.E., he began to show signs of what may have been malarial fever. Some ancient sources even suggest that he was poisoned; his closest companion, Hephaistion, had died the year before at Ecbatana, leaving Alexander without his most vigilant bodyguard. In any case, Alexander ignored the advice of his doctors. His condition worsened, and he died on June 10 or 11, 323 B.C.E., in the palace built by the Chaldean king Nebuchadnezzar in Babylon, the ancient capital of Hammurabi. He was not yet thirty-three years old.

THE HELLENISTIC KINGDOMS

According to one account—by a later Roman historian—Alexander's officers gathered around his bed as he lay dying and asked to whom he wished to leave his empire. He had replied, "To the strongest." According to other sources, he was actually incapable of speech. According to still other sources, he silently gave his signet ring to a Macedonian called Perdiccas, the leader of his cavalry.

It was certainly Perdiccas who attempted to arrange a settlement among all the possible claimants for power, albeit unsuccessfully. It was eventually decided that the infant Alexander IV, his son by Roxane, should rule jointly with Alexander's half-brother, Philip, the son of Philip II by one of his lesser wives. But this solution was never put into effect, because both the child and his uncle were soon murdered, as was Perdiccas. Meanwhile, the Persian satrapies that had been alloted to various leaders of Alexander's armies became the bases from which these men attempted to seize control.

The turmoil lasted for two generations. By about 275 B.C.E., however, three separate axes of military and political power had emerged, each headed by a Greco-Macedonian ruling class but with a distinctive character. Indeed, a striking feature of this period is the renewal of ancient political patterns within the common culture that continued to unite Alexander's fragmented empire. This is why the world created by his conquests is called Hellenistic, "Greek-like."

Ptolemaic Egypt

By far the most stable of these three Hellenistic states was Egypt, thanks in large part to the canny governance of Alexander's former general Ptolemy, who was possibly an illegitimate son of Philip II. Ptolemy decided to withdraw from the contest over the larger empire and asked only to be given Egypt as his satrapy. Clearly, he recognized Egypt's virtual invulnerability to attack. He also seems to have appreciated, as had Alexander, its historical cachet. And he may already have been planning to make Egypt an independent monarchy and a shrine to Alexander's memory. It was thanks to Ptolemy, in fact, that Alexander's embalmed body was brought to Egypt in 323 B.C.E. It was supposed to have gone to the royal burial ground in Macedonia, but Ptolemy hijacked the funeral cortege and brought it to Memphis. Later, his son Ptolemy II moved the sarcophagus to a tomb in Alexandria, where it became a pilgrimage site and an object of veneration.

The Ptolemies ruled for 300 years, until Egypt became a Roman province in 30 B.C.E. (see Chapter 5). This dynasty, the thirty-second since the fourth millennium B.C.E., would be the last. The male heirs of the line all took the name Ptolemy (hence the term "Ptolemaic Egypt"). Many of their sisters were called Cleopatra, the name of Alexander's own sister and a dynastic name among Macedonian royal women. Beginning in the reign of Ptolemy II Philadelphus ("sibling-lover"), the Ptolemies even began to follow ancient Egyptian custom by marrying their sisters. And in many other ways, they showed reverence for the culture of their kingdom while bringing it within the ambit of the wider Hellenistic world.

Alexander Puts Down a Mutiny

The following account comes from the history of Alexander's campaigns by the Greek-speaking Roman historian Arrian (c. 86–160 C.E.), who lived in the Roman province of Bythinia in northern Anatolia. This is the closest thing we have to a primary source, since histories written by Alexander's own contemporaries have not survived. The following passage describes Alexander's response to a mutiny among his troops after his return from India in 324 B.C.E.

y countrymen, you are sick for home—so be it! I shall make no attempt to check your longing to return. Go wherever you will; I shall not hinder you. But if go you must, there is one thing I would have you understand—what I have done for you, and in what coin you have repaid me. . . .

"Marching out from a country too poor to maintain you decently, [I] laid open for you at a blow, and in spite of Persia's naval supremacy, the gates of the Hellespont. My cavalry crushed the satraps of Darius, and I added all Ionia and Aeolia, the two Phrygias and Lydia to your empire. . . . I took them and gave them to you for your profit and enjoyment. The wealth of Egypt and Cyrene, which I shed no blood to win, now flows in your hands; Palestine and the plains of Syria and Mesopotamia are now your property; Babylon and Bactria and Susa are yours; you are the masters of the gold of Lydia, the treasures of Persia, the wealth of India—yes, and the seas beyond India, too. You are my captains, my generals, my governors of provinces.

"From all this that I have labored to win for you, what is left for me myself except the purple and the crown? I keep nothing for my own. . . . Perhaps you will say that, in my position as your commander, I had none of the labors and distress which you had to endure to win me what I have won. . . . Come now—if you are wounded, strip and show your wounds, and I will show mine. There is no part of my body but my back which does not have a scar; not a weapon a man may grasp or fling, the mark of which I do not carry on me . . . and all for your sakes: for your glory and your gain. Over every land and sea, across river, mountain, and plain, I led you to the world's end, a victorious army. I marry as you marry, and many of you will have children related by blood to my own. . . . But you all wish to leave me. Go then! And when you reach home, tell them that Alexander your king, who vanquished the Persians and Medes and Bactrians . . . tell them, I say, that you deserted him and left him to the mercy of barbarian men, whom you yourselves conquered. . . ."

On the Macedonians, the immediate effect of Alexander's speech was profound. . . . But when they were told [three days later that] . . . command was being given to Persian officers, foreign troops drafted into Macedonian units, a Persian corps of Guards called by a Macedonian name, Persian infantry units given the coveted title of Companions, . . . every man of them hurried to the palace . . . and [they] swore they would not stir from the spot until Alexander took pity on them.

Source: Arrian, *The Campaigns of Alexander*, trans. Aubrey de Selincourt (New York: 1958), pp. 360–65 (slightly modified).

Questions for Analysis

1. What qualities of leadership does Alexander display in this speech? How do these qualities compare to those of Cyrus the Younger, in Xenophon's description of him (page 89)?

2. Given the circumstances that precipitated this mutiny, why does Alexander use the term *barbarians* to describe the Persians and other conquered peoples? What does he hope to convey by using this word, and then by reorganizing his forces to replace Macedonians with Persians?

3. Histories written well into the nineteenth century of our era feature speeches that were allegedly spoken by historical characters on momentous occasions. How closely do you think Arrian's reconstruction of this speech reflects historical reality? How might you go about arguing that it is, in fact, an accurate reflection of what Alexander actually said?

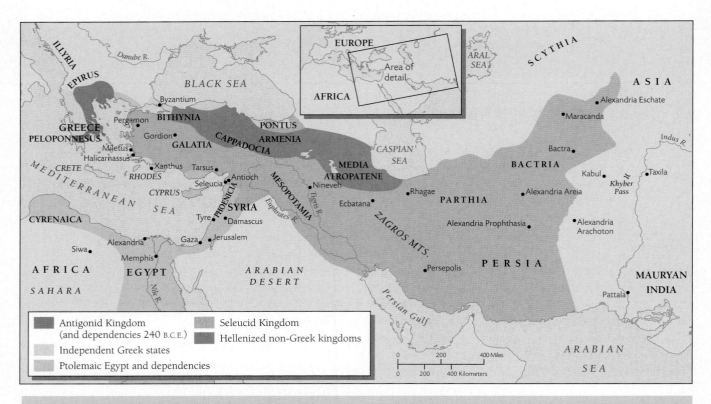

THE HELLENISTIC WORLD. Each of the three successor kingdoms to Alexander's empire was based in one of the three major civilizations we have studied so far: Egyptian, Mesopotamian, and Greek. ▪ *Based on the map above, what were the names of the three main successor states and where were they located?* ▪ *What might the division of Alexander's empire along such lines suggest about the lasting cultural differences among these regions?* ▪ *What might it suggest about the likelihood of forging a united empire, had he lived?*

They achieved this, in part, by ruling from the new city of Alexandria on the Mediterranean coast. In Alexandria, they acted as Macedonian kings toward their Greek and Macedonian citizens; outside of Alexandria, they played the role of pharaohs, surrounding themselves with the trappings and symbols of Egypt's heritage. But until the last Ptolemaic ruler, Cleopatra VII (69–30 B.C.E.), none of them bothered to learn the Egyptian language—although, as the Rosetta Stone attests (Chapter 1), they had able administrators who could communicate effectively with their multilingual and multicultural subjects.

For the Ptolemies, as for the ancient pharaohs, all of Egypt was land to be exploited for the benefit of the royal house. Supporting this tradition was the Macedonian idea that conquered land was plunder, to be used for personal enrichment and glorification. Accordingly, the Ptolemies exploited the wealth of the Egyptian countryside to the fullest. Most of this wealth ended up in Alexandria, which became the brilliant hub of the Hellenistic world. But there was little interest in improving the lives of the Egyptian peasantry, whose bread-winning labors made their rulers rich. So although the third century was a prosperous and relatively peaceful one in Egypt, future pharoahs would face regular and dangerous revolts.

Nevertheless, Ptolemaic Egypt was the most succesful of the Hellenistic kingdoms. It was also the most influential, because of its key role in preserving and transmitting the accumulated heritage of the civilizations that had preceded it: Egyptian, Mesopotamian, and Greek. The Ptolemies used much of their wealth to patronize science and the arts, and they established a great Museum ("home of the Muses") and library which attracted the greatest minds of the Hellenistic world. Many breakthroughs in astronomy, mechanical engineering, and physics occurred in Alexandria. In particular, the study of medicine advanced greatly: freed from the taboos of their homeland, Greek researchers were permitted to perform autopsies, making it possible for anatomy to become a scientific discipline in its own right. It was also in Alexandria that the texts of Greek poetry, drama, history, and philosophy were copied and preserved in the forms in which we know them, and here that the Hebrew scriptures were translated into Greek for a wider audience. Any history of Western civilizations would be impossible without these initiatives.

TWO PORTRAITS OF PTOLEMY I OF EGYPT. The Ptolemaic rulers of Egypt represented themselves as pharaohs to their Egyptian subjects (as in this bust) and as Greeks to their Macedonian and Greek subjects (as on this gold coin). ▪ *Why would it have been important to project these two very different images?*

Seleucid Asia

The vast possessions that Alexander had accumulated in Asia—both within the Persian Empire and outside of it—eventually fell to another Macedonian, Seleucus (*seh-LOO-kus*). Seleucus had navigated the turmoil after Alexander's death successfully and exploited the connections he made through his Persian wife. At his death in 281 B.C.E., his half-Persian son Antiochus (*an-TIE-oh-kuhs*) inherited an expansive realm whose capital was the city named after him, Antioch.

Throughout its history, the dynasty founded by Seleucus (known as the Seleucids) struggled with the problem of holding the disparate parts of this realm together. Seleucus himself solved part of this problem by ceding much of the Indus Valley to the great warrior-king Chandragupta in exchange for a squad of war elephants. By the middle of the third century B.C.E., the Seleucids had also lost control of Bactria (in modern Afghanistan), where a series of Indo-Greek states were emerging with a uniquely complex culture of their own. The Seleucid heartland now became northern Syria, parts of Anatolia, Mesopotamia, and the western half of Persia: still a great, wealthy kingdom, but far less than what Alexander had left.

Like the Ptolemies, the Seleucids presented two faces to their subjects, one looking to ancient Mesopotamian tradition, another looking to Greece. In his proclamations, Antiochus used terms reminiscent of Sargon, Hammurabi, and Cyrus: "I am Antiochus, Great King, legitimate king . . . king of Babylon, king of all countries." But on his coins, he wore his hair short in the fashion of the Greeks and styled himself *basileus*, the Greek word for "king." Although the Seleucids' bureaucracy was less organized than that of the Ptolemies, even haphazard tax collection could reap huge rewards in an empire of 30 million inhabitants. They had more than enough cash to defend their borders through the third century, a period of regular warfare with Egypt. It was not until the second century, when Antiochus III lost a costly war with a new imperial power, the Romans, that he had to plunder temples and private wealth to pay off the indemnity imposed on him.

Antigonid Macedonia and Greece

The Macedonian homeland did not possess the vast wealth of the new kingdoms carved from Alexander's conquests. It also remained highly unstable from the time of Alexander's death until 276 B.C.E., when a general named Antigonus finally established his own dynasty (known as the Antigonids). Thereafter, Macedonia drew its strength from its considerable natural resources and from its influence over Aegean trade, as well as its status as overlord of Greece. Moreover, the Macedonians continued to field the most effective army in the Hellenistic world.

Antigonus himself was influenced by a philosophical outlook called Stoicism (discussed later in this chapter) and viewed kingship as a form of noble servitude, to be endured rather than enjoyed. This perspective, combined with his modest resources, convinced him not to compete with the Seleucids and Ptolemies for dominance. Instead, Antigonid policy was to keep these other two powers at war with one another and away from the Macedonian sphere of influence. Antigonus and his successors thus pursued a strategy more reminiscent of Philip II than of his son. They secured the northern frontiers, maintained a strong standing army, and kept the fractious Greeks at heel.

The Greeks, however, were restive under the Antigonids, and two emergent powers served as rallying points for those who resented "barbarian" rule. These two forces, the Aetolian League and the Achaean League, were a departure in Greek political organization. Unlike the defensive alliances of the classical period, each represented a real political federation, with some centralization of governance. Citizens of the leagues' member poleis participated in councils of state that dealt with foreign policy and military affairs. New members were admitted on an equal footing with existing members, and all citizens of the various poleis enjoyed joint citizenship throughout the league. The same laws, weights and measures, coinage, and judicial procedures also applied throughout each federation. So effective was this mode of cooperation that James Madison, John Jay, and Alexander Hamilton employed it as one of their models for federalism in the United States.

FROM POLIS TO COSMOPOLIS

So what became of the polis, that building-block of classical Greece? As we have seen, the changes of the fourth century B.C.E. were already disrupting patterns of social and political life. Alexander's conquests hastened this process of transformation, and they also opened up a wider world—a world that came to admire all things Greek. By 300 B.C.E., a common Hellenistic culture was transcending political and geographical boundaries. It was fueled by the hundreds of thousands of adventurers who joined the Greek *diaspora* ("dispersion"), and whose emigration reduced the population of the Greek mainland by as much as 50 percent in the century after 325 B.C.E.

This exciting, urbane world was made up of interconnected cities whose scale surpassed anything imaginable in Periclean Athens. In the fifth century B.C.E., direct participation in government had meant that every male citizen had some share in his society, its institutions, its gods, its army, and its cultural life. In the huge and cosmopolitan Hellenistic city, by contrast, all these ways of defining oneself were no longer relevant. The individual male's intimate connection with the state was broken, as was his nexus of social relationships. An average Greek in one of the Hellenistic kingdoms might have only his immediate family to rely on, if that. Very often, he was alone. What resulted was a traumatic disjunction between the traditional values and assumptions of Greek life and these new realities—and a host of entirely new opportunities.

Commerce and Urbanization

The Hellenistic world was prosperous. Alexander's conquests had opened up a vast trading area stretching from Egypt to the Persian Gulf, dominated by Greek-speaking rulers and well-established merchant communities. These conquests also stimulated the economy by putting into circulation hoards of Persian gold and silver coins, jewelry, and other commodities acquired through plunder. Industries benefited too, because autocratic rulers found manufacturing to be a further means of increasing their revenues.

Every facility was provided by the Ptolemies and the Seleucids for the encouragement of commerce. Harbors were improved, warships were sent out to police the seas, roads and canals were built. The Ptolemies even employed geographers to discover new routes to distant lands. As a result of such methods, Egypt developed a flourishing commerce in the widest variety of products obtainable. Into the port of Alexandria came spices from Arabia, gold from Ethiopia and India, tin from Britain, elephants and ivory from Nubia, silver from Spain, fine carpets from Anatolia, and even silk from China.

The rapid growth of cities had both political and economic ramifications. Greek rulers imported Greek officials and especially Greek soldiers to maintain their control over non-Greek populations, making many new settlements necessary. Alexander himself had founded some 70 cities as outposts of domination and administration; in the next two centuries, his successors founded about 200 more. Urbanization also increased due to the expansion of commerce and industry, but the most significant factors were the Greek diaspora and the migration of workers from rural areas.

Population growth in some centers was explosive. At Antioch, the population quadrupled during a single century. Seleucia on the Tigris grew from nothing to a metropolis of several hundred thousand in less than two centuries. Alexandria in Egypt had half a million inhabitants; in ancient times, only imperial Rome would surpass it in size, and it would not be until the eighteenth century of our era that European cities like London and Paris were as large. Alexandria was not only populous, it was magnificent and spacious—which Rome never was. Its wide streets were paved and laid out in an orderly grid. It had splendid public buildings and parks, the great Museum, and the famous library containing half a million books. It was the storehouse and showcase of Greek culture.

Not everyone enjoyed prosperity. Agriculture remained the major occupation, and small farmers in particular suffered severely from exploitative taxation. Although industrial production increased, it continued to be based on manual labor by individual artisans, most of whom lived in poverty. Among the teeming populations of Hellenistic cities, unemployment was a constant concern. Even those who prospered in the new economy were subject to drastic fluctuations in their fortunes, owing to the precarious nature of mercantile endeavors. Merchants were also vulnerable to the boom-and-bust syndrome: an investor, thinking he could make a fortune during an upward price spiral, might go into debt to take advantage of the trend, only to find that supply exceeded demand, leaving him nothing with which to pay his creditors. The economic landscape of the Hellenistic world was therefore one of contrasting extremes. In many ways, this was also the case with respect to its culture.

HELLENISTIC WORLDVIEWS

Life in the Hellenistic boomtowns produced new worldviews and new philosophies that differed significantly from those of Plato and Aristotle. Another major departure was the separation of philosophy from scientific inquiry, which now became its own field of study. Despite these differences, however, scientists, philosophers, and religious

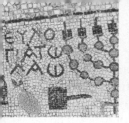

Past and Present

Assimilation and Difference

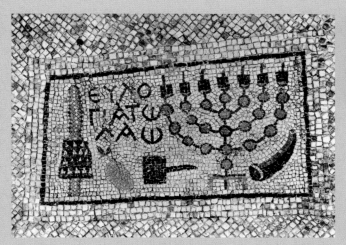

The Greek diaspora ("dispersion") that bound the Hellenistic kingdoms together would eventually lead to the emergence of distinctive new hybrid cultures. The mosaic on the left comes from an ancient synagogue and shows Jewish ritual objects (including a menorah and shofar) accompanied by a Greek inscription. The image on the right shows one manifestation of the modern Turkish diaspora: a clothing store in a district of Berlin called "Little Istanbul," where many Turkish "guest workers" settled in the 1960s.

Watch related author videos on the Student Site
wwnorton.com/college/history/western-civilizationsBrief4

teachers were all motivated by the same thing: the need to make human existence meaningful in a new age that lacked traditional civic structures and social values.

Two Paths to Tranquility: Stoicism and Epicureanism

The two strains of philosophy that dominated the Hellenistic world both originated in Athens around 300 B.C.E.: Stoicism and Epicureanism. Their teachings had several features in common. Both were concerned with the well-being of the individual, not with the welfare of society as a whole. Both were firmly rooted in the material world; even the soul was considered to be part of the mortal body. Both responded to the new cosmopolitan age by promoting universal values: they taught that people are the same the world over, and recognized no distinctions between Greeks and the peoples hitherto known as "barbarians."

But in other ways the two systems were radically different. The Stoics who followed Zeno of Citium (c. 335–c. 263 B.C.E.)—they took their name from the *stoa* ("colonnade") in which he regularly taught—believed that the cosmos is an ordered whole in which all contradictions are resolved for ultimate good. Evil is only relative; the particular misfortunes that befall human beings are merely incidents that will lead to the final perfection of the universe. Everything that happens is therefore predetermined. People are free only in the sense that they can accept fate or rebel against it. By freely submitting to the workings of the universe, and by acknowledging that whatever happens must be for the best, one can attain true happiness: tranquility of mind.

The Stoics' theory of ethics and social responsibility grew out of this personal philosophy. Believing that the highest good is serenity of mind, they emphasized self-discipline and the fulfillment of one's duties. They taught tolerance and forgiveness, and they also urged participation in public affairs as a special responsibility for those with able minds. They condemned slavery and violence, although they took no real actions against these evils because they saw them as inevitable— and because extreme social change might be worse.

With some later modifications, Stoic philosophy became the driving force behind the values of the Roman Republic and of early Christianity, and can be considered one of the most important products of the Hellenistic world. Even those who do not embrace its tenets or its perspective may not recognize that they have been influenced by it.

The teachings of Epicurus (341–270 B.C.E.) were based on the atomic theory of an earlier Greek philosopher called Democritus, who lived in the latter part of the fifth century B.C.E. According to his central thesis, the universe is made up entirely of atoms, and every individual object or organism is therefore the product of a combination of atoms. Studying Democritus's writings, Epicurus reached a conclusion exactly opposite to that of the Stoics: he interpreted the atomic theory to mean that there is no ultimate purpose in the workings of the universe. So the highest good cannot come of submitting oneself stoically to the endurance of hardship, because suffering is not part of a larger plan: it is merely the chance by-product of random atomic actions. The highest good, then, must be pleasure: the moderate satisfaction of bodily appetites, the intellectual pleasure of contemplating excellence and remembering past enjoyments, and serenity in the face of death. Indeed, an individual who understands that the soul itself is material, that the universe operates at random, and that no gods intervene in human affairs will have no fear of death or any other supernatural phenomenon.

The Epicureans thus came by a very different route to the same general conclusion as the Stoics: nothing is better than tranquility of mind. In contrast to the Stoics, however, they did not insist on virtue as an end in itself, or on the fulfillment of one's duties. For an Epicurean, the only duty a person has is to the self, and the only reason to act virtuously is to increase one's own happiness. Similarly, Epicureans denied that there is any such thing as justice; laws and political institutions are "just" only insofar as they contribute to the welfare of the individual. Yes, certain rules have been found necessary for the maintenance of order, but these rules should be obeyed solely because that is to one's advantage. The state is, at best, a mere convenience, and the wise man should take no active part in politics. Instead, he should withdraw to study philosophy and enjoy the fellowship of a few congenial friends. Modern libertarian and anarchic movements share many characteristics with Epicureanism.

Extreme Doubt: Skepticism

The most pessimistic philosophy generated by the Hellenistic era was propounded by the Skeptics, whose name means "those on the lookout" or "the spies." Skepticism reached the zenith of its popularity in the second century under the influence of Carneades (*car-ne-AH-dees*, c. 214–129 B.C.E.), a man born in the Greek city of Cyrene, in North Africa, who spent his youth in Athens. His chief teaching (adopted from Aristotle) was that all knowledge is based on sense perception and is therefore limited and relative. From this, the Skeptics concluded that no one can prove anything. Moreover, because our senses can deceive us, we cannot even be certain about the truth we think we have gained by observation of the world. All we can say is that things *appear* to be such and such; we do not *know* that they really *are* that way. It follows, furthermore, that we can have no definite knowledge of the supernatural, of the meaning of life, or of right and wrong.

The only sensible course for the Skeptic is therefore to suspend judgment. If we abandon the fruitless quest for truth and cease to worry about good conduct and the existence of evil, we can at least attain a certain peace of mind, the highest satisfaction that an uncertain life affords. Needless to say, the Skeptics were even less concerned than the Epicureans with political and social problems, from which they felt wholly alienated. Their ideal was one of escape from an incomprehensible world. In some key respects they anticipated modern existentialism and nihilism.

Varieties of Religion

Like Epicureanism and Skepticism, Hellenistic religion tended to offer vehicles of escape from political commitments. When we think back to how close was the link between Greek selfhood and politics down to the middle of the fourth century B.C.E.—"man is a creature of the polis"—we can begin to appreciate what a radical change had occurred in just a few generations. In all the societies we have studied so far, religion was wholly interconnected with politics. Divine worship centered on the gods who protected a community and furthered its interests. Hence, the most serious of the charges brought against Socrates was that he had "denied the gods of the polis" and thus committed treason. Religious crimes were political crimes, and piety was the same as patriotism.

Although this sense of a vital connection between a place and its gods persisted to a certain extent during the Hellenistic period, civic-oriented worship was compromised by rootless multiculturalism. In place of a shared religion, some elite members of society gravitated toward one of the philosophies discussed above. Ordinary people, though, were more likely to embrace religious cults that offered emotional gratification or the diversion of colorful rituals, as well as some assurance of an afterlife.

Cults that stressed extreme methods of atonement, mystical union with the divine, or contact with supernatural forces accordingly attracted many followers. Among these so-called mystery religions was the cult of Dionysus, which celebrated the cyclical death and resurrection of that Greek god. The Egyptian cult of Isis (Chapter 1) also revolved around rituals of death and rebirth. So too did Zoroastrianism (Chapter 2), which became increasingly dualistic: its magi now taught that the material world was entirely evil and urged believers to adopt ascetic practices that would purify their souls and prepare them for ethereal joy in the afterlife.

Like the peoples who worshiped them, the gods of the Hellenistic world were often immigrants from other lands. Temples to Greek gods and goddesses were dedicated throughout the Near East and Egypt; conversely, temples to Near Eastern divinities were constructed in the cities of the Greek homeland. In Alexandria, scholars of religion collected Egyptian and Near Eastern mythologies, which were recorded and reformulated for Greek-speaking audiences.

Even among the Jews, who resisted assimilation and the adoption of foreign customs, Hellenistic culture put down deep roots. This was especially true among elite Jews living outside Palestine, who outnumbered the Palestinian Jewish population by a considerable margin. To meet the needs of these Greek-speaking Jews, and to satisfy the curiosity of Gentiles interested in Jewish beliefs, scholars working in Alexandria produced a Greek version of the Hebrew scriptures. It is known as the Septuagint (*sep-TOO-ah-gint*), from the Greek word meaning "the seventy"; legend has it that seventy scribes, each working independently, produced individual translations from Hebrew to Greek that were identical in every respect. This meant that the Septuagint could be regarded as no less a product of divine inspiration than the original books that made up the Hebrew Bible, and could be treated as an authoritative text in its own right. For Jews concerned about their social and cultural standing vis-à-vis their Greek neighbors, the Septuagint was proof of their Hellenistic values—although, ironically, some of the very portions of scripture that were now written in Greek disapproved strongly of those values.

THE SCIENTIFIC REVOLUTION OF ANTIQUITY

The Hellenistic period was the most brilliant age in the history of science before the seventeenth century of our era (see Chapter 16). There are three major reasons for this. First, there was the stimulus to intellectual inquiry caused by the fusion of Mesopotamian and Egyptian science with the philosophical methods of the Greeks. Second, as in the more famous scientific revolution, the use of a common language (in the seventeenth century it was Latin) and the ease of communication facilitated by affordable travel made the circulation of knowledge and sharing of ideas easier (in the seventeenth century, communication was greatly enabled by the printing press). Finally, as in the seventeenth century, the competition among patrons of science was intense: every ruler wanted to be thought enlightened and to be associated with new discoveries. Even purely theoretical advances were so much admired that a Hellenistic prince who had bank-rolled such a breakthrough would share the glory of it. It was especially profitable to subsidize research that led to the development of new technologies, because they might have military applications.

The arts were also transformed by the economic and political conditions of the Hellenistic world. Artists working in various media strove to demonstrate their mastery of difficult techniques and so to attract the notice of potential patrons. New markets for art also changed *what* was being made, how, and for whom. In all of the civilizations we have studied so far, artists worked directly for royal or civic patrons. In the Hellenistic world, art became commodified. Sometimes a work would be made expressly for a particular patron, but many works of art were fashioned for the open market. They were also designed to suit the tastes and lifestyles of those merchant classes who had disposable income and wanted to increase their social standing through conspicuous consumption. This was as true of literature as of sculpture or the decorative arts: we know the names of over a thousand Hellenistic authors. Indeed, the number of texts and *objets d'art* that exist from this period is huge when compared to earlier eras.

Measuring and Mapping: Astronomy, Geography, and Mathematics

Hellenistic scientists took a major interest in measurements and mapmaking, whether of the heavens (astronomy), the earth (geography), or the forms occuring in nature (geometry). The most renowned—and most wronged—of the Hellenistic astronomers was Aristarchus of Samos (310–230 B.C.E.), whose major discovery anticipated that of Copernicus by 1,700 years: he deduced that the earth and other planets revolve around the sun. Unfortunately, however, this view was not accepted by many of his contemporaries or successors because it conflicted with the teachings of Aristotle, which in turn reflected the Greek conviction that humanity, and therefore the earth, must be at the center of the universe. The sad fate of his discovery was sealed in the second century C.E., when the Alexandrian scholar Claudius Ptolemaeus (known as

Debating the Education and Role of Women

The drastic political, social, and economic changes of the fourth century led philosophers to reimagine the traditional structures of the polis, and to debate the proper role of women within these structures. Meanwhile, the cosmopolitan culture of the expanding Hellenistic world made it increasingly difficult to limit women's access to public spaces. The following excerpts represent two philosophical responses to these problems. The first comes from Plato's treatise on "Polis-matters" (Politeía), known to us as The Republic, *the longest of his philosophical dialogues and the most influential work of political thought in history. Its conceptual narrator and protagonist is Socrates, who engages in a series of debates with his pupils. The second excerpt is taken from a philosophical treatise attributed to a female follower of Pythagoras (see Chapter 3), but it was really written around 200 B.C.E. in Hellenistic Italy, and by a man.*

Plato, *The Republic*, c. 380 B.C.E.

SOCRATES: For men born and educated like our citizens, the only way, in my opinion, of arriving at a right conclusion about the possession and use of women and children is to follow the path on which we originally started, when we said that the men were to be the guardians and watchdogs of the herd.

GLAUCON: True.

SOCRATES: Let us further suppose the birth and education of our women to be subject to similar or nearly similar regulations; then we shall see whether the result accords with our design.

GLAUCON: What do you mean?

SOCRATES: . . . The education which was assigned to the men was music and gymnastic[s].

GLAUCON: Yes.

SOCRATES: Then women must be taught music and gymnastic[s] and also the art of war, which they must practice like the men?

GLAUCON: That is the inference, I suppose.

SOCRATES: I should rather expect . . . that several of our proposals, if they are carried out, being unusual, may appear ridiculous.

GLAUCON: No doubt of it.

SOCRATES: Yes, and the most ridiculous thing of all will be the sight of women naked in the *palaestra*, exercising with the men, especially when they are no longer young; they certainly will not be a vision of beauty, any more than the enthusiastic old men who in spite of wrinkles and ugliness continue to frequent the gymnasia. . . . [Yet] not long ago, as we shall remind them, the Hellenes were of the opinion, which is still generally received among the barbarians, that the sight of a naked man was ridiculous and improper; and when first the Cretans and then the Lacedaemonians [Spartans] introduced the custom, the wits of that day might equally have ridiculed the innovation.

GLAUCON: No doubt . . .

SOCRATES: First, then, whether the question is to be put in jest or in earnest, let us come to an understanding about the nature of woman: Is she capable of sharing either wholly or partially in the actions of men, or not at all? And is the art of war one of those arts in which she can or cannot share? That will be the best way of commencing the enquiry, and will probably lead to the fairest conclusion. . . .

GLAUCON: I suppose so. . . .

SOCRATES: And if . . . the male and female sex appear to differ in their fitness for any art or pursuit, we should say that such pursuit or art ought to be assigned to one or the other of them; but if the difference consists only in women bearing and men begetting children, this does not amount to a proof that a woman differs from a man in respect of the sort of education she should receive; and we shall therefore continue to maintain that our guardians and their wives ought to have the same pursuits.

GLAUCON: Very true.

SOCRATES: Next, we shall ask . . . how, in reference to any of the pursuits or arts of civic life, the nature of a woman differs from that of a man? . . .

GLAUCON: By all means.

SOCRATES: . . . When you spoke of a nature gifted or not gifted in any respect, did you mean to say that one man will acquire a thing easily, another with difficulty; a little learning will lead the one to discover a great deal; whereas the other, after much study and application, no sooner learns than he forgets? Or again, did you mean, that the one has a body which is a good servant to his mind, while the body of the other is a hindrance to him? Would not these be the sort of differences which distinguish the man gifted by nature from the one who is ungifted?

GLAUCON: No one will deny that.

SOCRATES: And can you mention any pursuit of mankind in which the male sex has not all these gifts and qualities in a higher degree than the female? Need I waste time in speaking of the art of weaving, and the management of pancakes and preserves, in which womankind does really appear to be great, and in which for her to be beaten by a man is of all things the most absurd?

GLAUCON: You are quite right . . . in maintaining the general inferiority of the female sex: although many women are in many things superior to many men, yet on the whole what you say is true.

Source: Excerpted from Plato, *The Republic*, Book V, trans. Benjamin Jowett (New York: 1982), pp. 170–76.

Treatise Attributed to Phintys, Third/Second Century B.C.E.

Now some people think that it is not appropriate for a woman to be a philosopher, just as a woman should not be a cavalry officer or a politician. . . . I agree that men should be generals and city officials and politicians, and women should keep house and stay inside and receive and take care of their husbands. But I believe that courage, justice, and intelligence are qualities that men and women have in common. . . . Courage and intelligence are more appropriately male qualities because of the strength of men's bodies and the power of their minds. Chastity is more appropriately female.

Accordingly, a woman must learn about chastity and realize what she must do quantitatively and qualitatively to be able to obtain this womanly virtue. I believe that there are five qualifications: (1) the sancity of her marriage bed, (2) the cleanliness of her body, (3) the manner in which she chooses to leave her house, (4) her refusal to participate in secret cults . . . , (5) her readiness and moderation in sacrificing to the gods.

Of these, the most important quality for chastity is to be pure in respect of the marriage bed, and for her not to have affairs with men from other households. If she breaks the law in this way she wrongs the gods of her family and provides her family and home not with its own offspring but with bastards. . . . She should

also consider the following: that there is no means of atoning for this sin; no way she can approach the shrines or the altars of the gods as a pure woman. . . . The greatest glory a freeborn woman can have—her foremost honor—is the witness her own children will give to her chastity toward her husband, the stamp of the likeness they bear to the father whose seed produced them. . . .

As far as adornment of her body is concerned . . . her clothes should not be transparent or ornate. She should not put on silken material, but moderate, white-colored clothes. In this way, she will avoid being overdressed or luxurious or made-up, and not give other women cause to be uncomfortably envious. . . . She should not apply imported or artificial coloring to her face—with her own natural coloring, by washing only with water, she can ornament herself with modesty. . . .

Women of importance leave the house to sacrifice to the leading divinity of the community on behalf of their husbands and their households. They do not leave home at night nor in the evening, but at midday, to attend a religious festival or to make some purchase, accompanied by a single female servant or decorously escorted by two servants at most. . . . They keep away from secret cults . . . particularly because these forms of worship encourage drunkenness and ecstasy. The mistress of the house and head of the household should be chaste and untouched in all respects.

Source: From Mary R. Lefkowitz and Maureen B. Fant, eds., *Women's Life in Greece & Rome: A Source Book in Translation*, 2nd ed. (Baltimore, MD: 1992), pp. 163–64.

Questions for Analysis

1. Follow the steps of the argument made by Socrates. How does he go about proving that women and men are different, and should have different roles in society? Are there flaws in this argument? What are they?

2. How does the author of the treatise seem to define "chastity," and why does "she" (actually he) say that it corresponds to more masculine qualities of courage and intelligence? Why would this author have wanted to attribute these reflections to female members of the community founded by the philosopher Pythagoras (c.570–c. 495), three centuries earlier? How might this treatise be responding to the changes brought about by the expansion of the Greek world in the fourth and third centuries B.C.E?

3. What are main points on which these two perspectives agree? How might ideas like those expressed here have influenced contemporary ideas of female beauty and modesty (see *Interpreting Visual Evidence*, page 91)?

Ptolemy) unequivocally argued that Aristotle was correct, and that all heavenly bodies revolve around the earth. This mistaken view would not be overturned until the much later scientific revolution occurred.

Closely allied with astronomy were geography and mathematics. The most influential Hellenistic mathematician was Euclid, whose *Elements of Geometry* (c. 300 B.C.E.) remained the basic textbook of that subject until the twentieth century of our era. In the field of geography—and in a host of other pursuits, too—the most original thinker was Eratosthenes of Alexandria (*air-ah-TOS-then-ees*, c. 276–c. 196 B.C.E.). Not only did he accurately calculate the circumference of the earth (within a tiny margin of error, less than 200 miles), he was the first to suggest the possibility of reaching eastern Asia by sailing west. In addition, he founded the science of chronology by attempting to establish the dates of major events reaching back to the siege of Troy. Students of history are forever in his debt.

Medicine and Mechanics: The Sciences of Physiology and Physics

Before the third century B.C.E., physics had been a branch of philosophy. Now it became a separate, experimental science thanks to the genius of one man, Archimedes of Syracuse (c. 287–212 B.C.E.). It was he who discovered the law of floating bodies, or specific gravity, now known as 'Archimedes'

principle." According to legend, the idea came to him when he was in his bath, and the stunning insight so excited him that he lept from the water and dashed out naked into the street, shouting "*Eureka!*" ("I have found it!"). Archimedes also established the principles of the lever, the pulley, and the screw, and he invented both a compound pulley and a propeller. All of these discoveries had numerous practical uses in the construction of buildings, ships, and military machinery.

Extraordinary advances were also made in the field of medicine. Especially significant was the work of Herophilus of Chalcedon (c. 335–c. 280 B.C.E.), the greatest anatomist of antiquity and probably the first to practice human dissection. Herophilus's achievements included a detailed description of the brain, which allowed him to prove that it was the engine of human intellect (Aristotle thought that the seat of intelligence was the heart), as well as the discovery that the arteries contain blood alone (not a mixture of blood and air, as Aristotle had taught), and that their function is to carry blood from the heart to all parts of the body. His colleague Erasistratus (*air-ah-sis-STRAH-tus*) made allied discoveries, establishing that the heart was a pump and not an organ of emotion. Erasistratus also rejected the widely held theory of the physician Hippocrates (c. 460–c. 370), who had posited that the body consists of four "humors" which need to be kept in balance through bloodletting and other invasive practices. Unfortunately, this discovery went the way of the heliocentric universe posited by Aristarchus: another encyclopedist

THE CITADEL OF PERGAMON. An artist's reconstruction of Pergamon in the second century B.C.E., based on the work of nineteenth-century German archaeologists. High atop the hill is the massive altar of Zeus (now in the Pergamon Museum in Berlin) and below it slope the tiers of the theater. Other features include fortifications, terraces, and artificial landscaping for public gardens. ▪ *How does this complex of buildings compare to that of another citadel, the Acropolis of Athens (see Chapter 3, page 60)?*

DYING GAUL. The original (now lost) statue on which this Roman copy was based was sculpted in Pergamon around 220 B.C.E. The sculptor clearly wished to exhibit skill in depicting an unusual subject: the Gauls were a Celtic people about whom very little was known in this era. ▪ *How does this sympathetic representation of a "barbarian" express the new values of Hellenistic philosophy?*

of the second century c.e., Galen, preferred the erroneous theory of Hippocrates. The practice of bloodletting thus persisted into the nineteenth century of our era.

Urban Architecture and Sculpture

Hellenistic architecture drew on Greek models, but it was also influenced by tastes more characteristic of Egypt and Persia. The best surviving example comes from Pergamon, a city on the coast of Anatolia that became the capital of a new kingdom wrested from the control of the Seleucids in the second century B.C.E. It boasted an enormous altar dedicated to Zeus that crowned the heights of the city, below which an open-air theater was built into the steep slope of the hill. In Ephesus, not far away, the streets were not only paved, they were paved with marble.

But the most influential of all Hellenistic arts was sculpture, which placed even more emphasis on realism than the fourth-century sculptures discussed earlier in this chapter. And because awkward human postures offered the greatest technical challenges, sculptors often preferred to show people stretching themselves or balancing on one leg or performing other unusual feats. It is clear that the goal was to create something unique in both conception and craftsmanship—something a collector could show off as the only one of its type. It is not surprising, therefore, that complexity came to be admired for its own sake, and extreme naturalism sometimes teetered on the brink of absurdity. Yet to our eyes, such works appear familiar because of the influence they exerted on later sculptors like Michelangelo (see Chapter 12) and Auguste Rodin. Three of the most famous examples are pictured here, each exhibiting different aesthetic qualities and artistic techniques: the *Dying Gaul*, made in Pergamon around 220 B.C.E.; the *Winged Victory of Samothrace*, dating from around 200 B.C.E.; and the *Laocoön* group, from the first century B.C.E.

THE WINGED VICTORY OF SAMOTHRACE (left). This marble sculpture of the goddess Nike (Victory) may originally have been displayed on the prow of a monumental ship. It formed part of a temple complex on the island of Samothrace in the northern Aegean, and dates to around the year 200 B.C.E. It is now in the Louvre Museum, Paris. **LAOCOÖN AND HIS SONS (right).** In sharp contrast to the serene and confident *Winged Victory* is this famous sculpture group from the first century B.C.E. According to legend, Laocoön warned the Trojans not to accept the wooden horse sent by the Greeks and was accordingly punished by the sea-god Poseidon, who sent two serpents to kill him and his sons. The intense physicality of this work was an important influence on Michelangelo, a millennium and a half later.

Literary Fantasy and Historical Reality

In the sixth century B.C.E. it was the lyric, in the fifth century it was tragedy, and in the fourth century it was the novel; but in the Hellenistic era, the new literary genre was pastoral verse. These poems tapped into a strong vein of nostalgia for rural pastimes and simple pleasures, a make-believe world of shepherds and wood nymphs. The most important pastoral poet of the age was Theocritus, who flourished around 270 B.C.E. in the big-city environment of Alexandria. In the midst of urban bustle and within sight of overcrowded slums, he celebrated the charms of country life and lazy summer afternoons. He thereby founded an enduring tradition that would be taken up by poets from the Roman Virgil to the Englishman (and classical scholar) A. E. Houseman, which has provided a wealth of themes for the visual arts. Even composers like Beethoven and Debussy owe a debt to Theocritus.

By contrast, Hellenistic prose literature was dominated by historians who modeled their work on earlier pioneers, especially Thucydides. By far the most important was Polybius (c. 203–120 B.C.E.), a well-born Greek whose father was a prominent politician in the Achaean League. Polybius himself was trained as a cavalry officer at a time when the Achaean League was trying to position itself favorably in ongoing wars between the rising republic of Rome and the various kingdoms of northern Greece. In 168 B.C.E., the Romans became suspicious of the Achaeans' declared neutrality and demanded that a thousand noble hostages be sent to Rome as a guarantee of the League's good behavior. Polybius was one of those hostages, and he spent the next seventeen years living in Rome, where he became a fervent admirer of its unique form of government (see Chapter 5).

The result was a series of histories that glorified the achievements of Rome and its political system. Polybius also attempted to account for the patterns that he discerned in the history of Greece since the Peloponnesian War. He argued that historical developments follow regular cycles, and that nations pass inevitably through stages of growth and decay. Hence, it should be possible to predict exactly where a given state is heading if one knows what has happened to it in the past. Yet Polybius also argued that the special character of Rome's constitution would allow it to break the cycle, because it combined all of the different forms of government that Aristotle had outlined in his *Politics*. This view of history galvanized the framers of the United States Constitution, directly influencing their conception of our own political institutions.

CONCLUSION

Judged from the perspective of classical Greece, Hellenistic civilization seems strange. The autocratic governments of

After You Read This Chapter

 Go to **INQUIZITIVE** to see what you've learned—and learn what you've missed—with personalized feedback along the way.

REVIEWING THE OBJECTIVES

- Macedonia's successful conquest of the Greek poleis can be attributed to several factors. What are they?
- Alexander the Great's imperial policies were influenced by his own upbringing, the different cultures he encountered, and some key historical precedents. Give at least one example of each type of influence.
- Explain how the three Hellenistic kingdoms reflect the differences among the three main civilizations we have studied so far.
- Why is the Hellenistic world described as "cosmopolitan"? How did this urban culture differ from that of the Greek poleis?
- The philosophies of Plato and Aristotle both derive from the teachings of Socrates, but they diverge in some important ways. What are those main differences?

the age that followed Alexander's conquests would probably appear repugnant to a staunch proponent of Athenian democracy, and the Hellenistic love of extravagance can contrast strikingly with the tastes of the fifth century B.C.E. Yet Hellenistic civilization had its own achievements that the classical age could not match. Most Hellenistic cities offered a greater range of public facilities than any Greek cities of the previous period, and the numerous advances in science and technology are astonishing when compared to anything that came before, or even after.

But the most important contribution of the Hellenistic era to subsequent historical developments was its role as intermediary between the nascent empire of Rome and the older civilizations of Mesopotamia, Egypt, and Greece. The economic and political infrastuctures that were put in place after Alexander's conquests would form the framework of Roman imperial government. The Romans would also take advantage of the common language and cultural expectations that bound the far reaches of the Greek-speaking world together. Their own Latin language would never supplant Greek as the preeminent language of scholarship and administration in the eastern portions of their empire.

The Hellenistic era must also be recognized as the bridge that connects us to the earlier ages of antiquity: most of what is contained in the first four chapters of this book is known to us because older texts and artifacts were copied and collected by the scholars of Alexandria and other Hellenistic cities. And it was Hellenistic art and architecture, Hellenistic city planning and civic culture, that the Romans strove to emulate—not those of Periclean Athens. The same can be said of drama and poetry.

For us, two further aspects of Hellenistic culture deserve special mention: its cosmopolitanism and its modernity. The word *cosmopolitan* means "universal city," and it was the Hellenistic period that came closest to turning this ideal of globalization into reality. Around 250 B.C.E. a Greek tourist could have traveled from Sicily to the borders of India—the two ends of the earth—and never have found himself among people who did not speak his language or share his basic outlook. Nor would this tourist have identified himself in ethnic or nationalist terms, or felt any exclusive loyalty to a city-state or kingdom. He would have considered himself a citizen of the world. He would also have considered himself a modern man, not bound by the old prejudices and superstitions of the past. It is for these reasons that Hellenistic civilization seems so closely related to our own. It was a world of stark contrasts and infinite possibilities, where economic instability, extremism, and authoritarian regimes existed side by side with unprecedented prosperity, rational inquiry, and extraodinary freedoms. In Chapter 5, we will see how this world adapted itself to the dominion of a single Italian city.

PEOPLE, IDEAS, EVENTS IN CONTEXT

- How did the philosophies of **PLATO** and **ARISTOTLE** respond to the crisis of the polis?
- In what ways were the military strategies of **PHILIP II OF MACEDONIA** variations on older forms of hoplite warfare? How did the rise of mercenary armies and of **THEBES** further change military strategies in the fourth century?
- To what degree did the conquests of **ALEXANDER THE GREAT** unite Mesopotamia, Egypt, and Greece?
- Why and how did the three **HELLENISTIC KINGDOMS** emerge? How were the **AETOLIAN** and **ACHAEAN LEAGUES** new models for governance and cooperation in Greece?
- In what ways were **STOICISM**, **EPICUREANISM**, and other new philosophies a response to **COSMOPOLITANISM** and the breakdown of traditional societies and values?
- What were the driving forces behind the **SCIENTIFIC REVOLUTION OF ANTIQUITY**? What were its main achievements?
- What are some essential characteristics of **HELLENISTIC ART**? In what ways did it differ from that of the fifth century B.C.E. (Chapter 3)?

THINKING ABOUT CONNECTIONS

- "The history of the world is but the biography of great men"—so the Scottish historian Thomas Carlyle (1795–1881) summarized the impact of figures like Alexander the Great. How would you construct an argument in support of this proposition, using what you've learned in this chapter? How would you refute it?
- In what ways do Alexander's actions demonstrate his own knowledge of history, as well as a capacity to apply that knowledge to his own circumstances? Can you identify leaders of our own day who have mobilized their understanding of history in similar ways?
- In your view, which civilization more resembles our own: classical Athens or the Hellenistic world? Why? What characteristics make an era seem "modern"?

STORY LINES

- Romans were proud of their unique history, especially the legend that they had overthrown their kings. They clung to this story even when individual men came to wield kingly powers.

- Roman identity, religion, and politics were intimately bound up in the worship of ancestors, especially male ancestors. As a result, fathers (living and dead) wielded extraordinary power in early Rome.

- Roman women enjoyed more freedoms than the women of ancient Greece, but they were still subject to the authority of their male relatives.

- Paradoxically, the Romans celebrated their farming heritage even as they built a highly urbanized society. At the same time, they regarded Greek culture as both superior and dangerous.

- The Roman army had unprecedented strength and importance in this civilization, but the army's relationship to Roman politics and society changed drastically as Rome's empire grew.

CHRONOLOGY

753 B.C.E.	Legendary founding of Rome
c. 509 B.C.E.	Roman Republic established
c. 450 B.C.E.	Law of the Twelve Tables
287 B.C.E.	"Struggle of the Orders" ends
264–146 B.C.E.	Punic Wars
134–104 B.C.E.	Slave revolts in Sicily
133–122 B.C.E.	Reforms of the Gracchi
107–86 B.C.E.	Consulship of Marius
82–79 B.C.E.	Dictatorship of Sulla
73–71 B.C.E.	Rebellion of Spartacus
52–48 B.C.E.	Struggle of Pompey and Caesar
48–44 B.C.E.	Dictatorship of Caesar
44–30 B.C.E.	Rivalry of Octavian and Antony
27 B.C.E.–14 C.E.	Principate of the Emperor Augustus
27 B.C.E.–180 C.E.	Flowering of the *Pax Romana*
79 C.E.	Eruption of Mount Vesuvius destroys (and preserves) Pompeii
117 C.E.	Roman Empire reaches its greatest extent under Trajan

Before You Read This Chapter

The Civilization of Ancient Rome

CORE OBJECTIVES

- **IDENTIFY** the factors that influenced the formation of the Roman Republic.

- **UNDERSTAND** the basic elements of Roman identity.

- **DEFINE** the classes of people who struggled for power in Rome and **EXPLAIN** their different objectives.

- **DESCRIBE** the impact of territorial expansion on Roman society.

- **TRACE** the events leading up to the establishment of the Principate.

"Could anyone be so indifferent or slow-witted as not to care how, and under what system of government, the Romans managed to bring nearly the whole inhabited world under their rule? Can anything be more important than understanding this?" So the Greek soldier Polybius (c. 203–120 B.C.E.) addresses Greek readers in a history celebrating the achievements of the Roman Republic. Polybius had witnessed some of these firsthand: on the battlefield, in Rome itself as a hostage and guest, and on a visit to newly conquered Carthage. What better testament could there be to the success of a small Italian city than the admiration of a cultivated Greek aristocrat who, having been subjected to Roman authority, wholeheartedly embraced it? None, unless we cite the equally enthusiastic endorsement of the same Jews who had rebelled against Greek influence in 164 B.C.E. They, too, could not say enough in praise of the Romans, and they willingly placed themselves under Roman protection:

> Those whom they wish to help and to make kings, they make kings, and those whom they wish they depose; and they have been greatly exalted. Yet for all that, not one of

111

them has put on a crown or worn purple as a mark of pride, but they have built for themselves a senate chamber and every day three hundred and twenty senators constantly deliberate concerning the people, to govern them well. (1 Maccabees 8:12–15)

The only people who could say more in praise of Rome were the Romans themselves. To them, the enormous success of their empire meant that they were divinely chosen to colonize the world. This was the message conveyed by the poet Virgil (70–19 B.C.E.), commissioned by the Emperor Augustus to tell the story of Rome's rise to glory in a manner imitating the epics of Homer. In one key passage, the father of Aeneas, Virgil's epic hero, "foretells" the future and addresses posterity: "Remember, Roman, you whose power rules / all peoples, that these are your arts: plant peace, / make law, spare subjects, and put down the proud" (*Aeneid*, Book VI, lines 851–3).

While the Greeks struggled against the Persians and against each other, a new civilization emerged beyond the northern fringes of the Greek world, on the banks of the river Tiber in central Italy. By 300 B.C.E. Rome was the dominant power on the Italian peninsula. Two centuries later, it had conquered Greece itself. For the next three centuries after that—an unprecedented period of sustained expansion—its power steadily increased. In the first century of our era, it ruled the Hellenistic world as well as a vast region that Greek culture had never touched: western Europe. Eventually, Rome's empire united the entire Mediterranean and most of Asia Minor, while at the same time embracing provinces that are now parts of France, Spain, Portugal, Britain, Belgium, Germany, Switzerland, and the Balkans. Rome thus built a historical arch that enabled Europe to share in a rich heritage reaching back to ancient Mesopotamia and Egypt. Without Rome, European culture as we know it would not exist, and neither would the political and legal institutions that formed the United States. To echo Polybius: "Can anything be more important than understanding this?"

THE TIME OF THE KINGS

Romans looked back uneasily on their early history, for this was the time when they were ruled by kings. It may have been necessary in those days: Romans had never been peaceful settlers, and their land did not yield an easy living. Although Italy had much more fertile land than Greece, its extensive coastline boasts only a few good harbors, and most of these are on the western side, away from the commercial hubs of Greece and the Near East. Nor does the length of this coastline offer secure natural defenses. So the Romans

were a warlike people from the first, continually forced to defend their own conquests against other invaders.

Early Influences

When the Romans arrived in Italy, the dominant inhabitants of the peninsula were the Etruscans, a people who remain mysterious despite the rich archaeological record they left behind. This is because their language (not a branch of Indo-European) has never been fully deciphered, even though the Etruscans used an alphabet borrowed from the Greeks. By the sixth century B.C.E., the Etruscans had established a confederation of independent city-states in north-central Italy. They were skilled metalworkers, artists, and architects, from whom the Romans later took their knowledge of the arch and the vault, among much else, including the bloody sport of gladiatorial combat.

The two most important foundation myths told by the Romans were also derived from Etruscan tradition: the story of Aeneas's escape from Troy, which became the basis of Virgil's *Aeneid*, and also the story of the infant twins Romulus and Remus, abandoned at birth and then raised by a maternal wolf, afterward founding a fledgling city. Both legends would be mined by Rome's historians for their metaphorical significance, and further details would be added to increase their relevance for a changing audience. For example, the story of Aeneas's seduction and abandonment of Dido, queen of Carthage, reflected Rome's defeat of that powerful North African civilization.

In marked contrast to Greek society, Etruscan women enjoyed a very high status and played important roles in public life. Etruscan wives even ate meals with their husbands, another departure from both Greek and Roman custom. After death, devoted couples were buried together in the same mortuary vaults, and their tombstones and sarcophagi often emphasize mutual affection. Some of these practices certainly affected the Romans, whose women were less sequestered than their Greek counterparts. Yet Rome's women did not enjoy the same freedoms as Etruscan women until very late in Roman history, and by then such freedoms were condemned as signs of decadence (as will be discussed later in the chapter).

The Romans also borrowed ideas from the Greek settlers who had begun to colonize southern Italy and Sicily during the eighth century B.C.E. From them, Romans derived their alphabet, many of their religious beliefs, and much of their art. But the Romans downplayed Greek influence in their founding mythology, preferring to emphasize their alleged descent from the Trojans and also from an Italic people called the Sabines, from whom (according to legend) Romulus and his

CINCINATTUS THE STATESMAN-FARMER. This bronze statue of Cincinnatus is prominent in Cincinnati, Ohio, which was named after the Roman hero (and in honor of George Washington) in 1790. In his right hand he holds the *fasces*, symbolizing his powers as dictator. In his left, he grasps the handle of a plow. ▪ *Why would this figure have fired the imagination of Americans after their War of Independence?*

commercial port and was not threatened by attack from the sea. Rome also sat astride the first good ford across the Tiber, making it a major crossroads. Further, there were strategic advantages to the seven hills among which Rome was nestled. Eventually, its central markeplace—the *forum* or "open space"—would become the beating heart of the world's most populous and powerful city, with approximately a million people crowded into an area of five square miles.

At an early date, the Romans negotiated a series of agreements with their neighbors which were collectively known as the Latin Right: a trading pact called the *commercium*, provisions for intermarriage called the *connubium*, and the *migratio*, which allowed a Latin resident of one settlement to emigrate to another and, after a year's residence, to have the full rights of a citizen there. These privileges contrast strongly with the mutual suspicion that divided the cities of ancient Sumer or Greece. Indeed, the Romans' later willingness to extend the Latin Right far beyond their homeland of Latium was a key factor in the success of their empire.

According to their own legends, the Romans' early government mirrored the structure of Roman households, with a patriarchal king whose power was checked only by a council of elders, the Senate (from the Latin *senex*, "old man"). Seven kings, including Romulus, are said to have ruled in succession. The last, Tarquinus Superbus (Tarquin the Arrogant), is reputed to have been an Etruscan who paved the way for Rome's imperial expansion by dominating the agriculturally wealthy district of Campania to the south. But his power came at the price of Roman freedom and dignity, as was made clear when Tarquin's son allegedly raped a virtuous Roman wife, Lucretia, around 510 B.C.E. When she commited suicide to avoid dishonor, the Romans—led by Lucretia's kinsman, Lucius Junius Brutus—rose up in rebellion, overthrowing not only the Etruscan dynasty but rejecting the very idea of monarchy as a legitimate form of government. Henceforth, any claim to royal authority in Rome was considered anathema, and the very word "king" (*rex*) was a term of insult. The Brutus who would be instrumental in the assassination of Julius Caesar nearly five centuries later was a descendant of that same Brutus who had driven out the Tarquin kings—something he and his contemporaries never forgot.

men had forcibly abducted their wives. This was a practice Romans would continue, as the legions who planted new colonies intermarried with indigenous populations from the Persian Gulf to the lowlands of Scotland.

The Founding of Rome

The real founders of Rome were a tribe called the Latins, descendents of Indo-European-speaking peoples who crossed the Alps into Italy and settled on the banks of the Tiber by the tenth century B.C.E. This location was advantageous. Trading ships (but not large war fleets) could navigate the river as far as the city, yet no farther; Rome could thus serve as a

THE TRIUMPH OF THE EARLY REPUBLIC

The story of Lucretia was both a patriotic myth and a potent statement of Roman attitudes toward female chastity and family honor. And it coincided with a radical change in Roman governance. This change was so radical, in fact, that it did not match any of Aristotle's political categories (Chapter 4), but instead combined elements of them all. The Romans themselves didn't know what to call their political system: they spoke of it merely as *res publica*, "the public thing."

The Territorial Expansion of Rome

The early Roman Republic was marked by almost constant warfare aimed at stitching together a patchwork of valuable territories that could support Rome's growing population. Gradually, Romans came to control the valuable port of Ostia at the mouth of the Tiber, about twenty miles from their city. They also pushed northward into Etruscan territory, and southward to Naples, another good port. By 300 B.C.E., Rome had absorbed or allied itself with all of central Italy and began to look even farther south, to the wealthy Greek colonies of Sicily.

The Romans' rapid success is remarkable when compared to the patterns familiar to us from our study of classical Greece. What was the secret of it? For one thing, the Romans did not impose heavy burdens of taxation and tribute on the settlements they conquered. More often, they demanded only that they contribute soldiers to the Roman army. Rome also extended the Latin Right to many of these conquered territories, giving them a further stake in Rome's political and military expansion.

Rome thus gained for itself nearly inexhaustible reserves of fighting men. By the middle of the third century B.C.E, its army may have numbered as many as 300,000—a huge force even by modern standards. As we have seen, the Greeks had eventually turned to paid soldiering out of economic necessity, but they fought in smaller numbers; Xenophon's army was 10,000 and Alexander's 100,000. The Great King of Persia could claim to muster a million men, but these were private or tribal armies commanded by his satraps, not a standing army loyal to him.

The Romans also devoted themselves to the discipline of warfare in ways the Greeks (except for the Spartans) and the Persians did not. Although they originally used the phalanx formation, they quickly replaced it with smaller, more flexible divisions that could adjust to the hilly conditions of central Italy. While the major unit of the Roman army was always the legion (5,000 men), the combat unit was the *maniple* ("handful"), a group of 120 infantrymen who trained together and who often performed specialized tasks or used special weaponry. The Greek Polybius could not say enough in praise of this system, which made the army adaptable to climate, terrain, and new military techniques.

The republic's early history reinforced not only the military character of the Roman nation but its commitment to agriculture as the only proper peacetime employment for a Roman. The acquisition of new lands made it possible for citizens to maintain themselves as farmers. As a result, Romans developed an interest in commerce fairly late when compared with the Greeks or Phoenicians. And they would continue—even at the height of their empire—to valorize rural life over that of the city.

The paragon of Roman heroism in this era was Lucius Quinctius Cincinnatus (519–c. 430 B.C.E.), a stouthearted citizen-farmer who reluctantly accepted political office when Rome was threatened by attack. According to legend, he was found plowing his fields when a delegation of senators arrived to bring him to Rome, where he found that he had been named *dictator* ("decider"). This was a position of power to which the Romans elected one man during times of crisis that required decisive leadership. As legend has it, Cincinnatus dutifully performed this role, led Rome in wars with hostile neighbors—and then went back to his plow. If Lucretia was the Roman ideal of female fortitude, Cincinnatus was the paradigm of manly virtue. George Washington was frequently compared to him, to his own satisfaction.

The Constitution of the Early Republic

During this period of expansion, Rome's political system evolved accordingly. Initially, the overthrow of the monarchy had resulted in only moderate changes; instead of a king, the republic was headed by two elected officers called *consuls*. Although the consuls of the infant republic were supposedly chosen by all citizens, they were inevitably members of aristocratic families, known in Rome as *patricians* because they traced descent from a famous ancestor or *pater* ("father"). During his term of office, which lasted for one year, each consul exercised essentially the same power as a king: dealing justice, making law, and commanding the army. The only limit on power was the right of each consul to veto the actions of the other, which often led to stalemate or violent conflict. In times of grave emergency, such as that resulting in Cincinnatus's election, a dictator might be appointed for a term not longer than six months.

By the early fifth century, within a generation after the establishment of the republic, patrician dominance of the government began to be challenged by the *plebs* ("people"). This was the first stage in a centuries-long contest known as the Struggle of the Orders. The plebeian classes made up nearly 98 percent of the Roman population. Some had grown wealthy through trade, but most were smallholding farmers, artisans, or the urban poor. Their causes for grievance were numerous. Although they were forced to serve in the army, they were nevertheless excluded from holding office. They were also the victims of discriminatory decisions in judicial trials, which were judged by patricians. They did not even know what their legal rights were, because Rome had as yet no established laws: there were only unwritten customs whose meaning was interpreted by the patricians to their own advantage. The plebians were also, like the poorer citizens of Greek poleis, threatened with debt slavery.

These wrongs prompted a rebellion in the early fifth century B.C.E., when plebeians refused to join in the defense of Rome and instead seceded from the city, camping out on the Aventine hill (see the map of Rome on page 134). This general strike of military labor forced the patricians to allow the people to elect of their own officers, who were known as *tribunes* (tribal leaders). The job of each tribune was to protect his constituents from patrician injustice. Moreover, the plebeians guaranteed the safety of these officers by vowing to kill any person who hindered the exercise of their powers.

The plebs' victory led to the codification of the Law of the Twelve Tables, issued around 450 B.C.E. and inscribed on wooden tablets (hence "tables"). Although it was really a perpetuation of ancient custom, the fact that the law was now *defined* made it a significant improvement. Plebeians were made eligible to hold elected offices and they gradually gained access to the Senate. A further victory came in 287 B.C.E., when they succeeded in passing a law that made decisions enacted in their own assembly binding on the Roman government—whether the Senate approved them or not. It was at this time that the phrase *Senatus Populusque Romanum* came into regular use, abbreviated *SPQR* and designating any decree or decision made by "the Roman Senate and People." Visitors to Rome will still find *SPQR* emblazoned on everything from public buildings to the manhole covers of Rome's sewers.

These reforms had several important consequences. Successful plebeians could now work their way into the upper reaches of Roman society, which loosened the hold of patrician families. At the same time, laws prevented senators from engaging directly in commerce. This restriction had the effect of creating a new social order, that of the equestrians ("horsemen" or knights): men whose wealth made it possible for them to own and equip warhorses, and thus to provide Rome's cavalry. But the equestrians and the senators were never wholly distinct. Often, some members of a wealthy family would underwrite the political careers of their brothers and cousins. Those families who managed to win election by such means, generation after generation, became increasingly influential. Meanwhile, patricians who chose politics over wealth became impoverished and resentful. By the first century B.C.E., many were tempted to pursue their political agendas by styling themselves champions of the people (as will be discussed later in the chapter).

Later Roman patriots would regard this as a golden age of shared government, but Rome was never a democracy. A republic differs from a monarchy only because power is exercised by officers whose offices are not (at least in theory) hereditary. It is essentially a system for reserving power to an oligarchy or privileged group. The constitution that emerged in these key centuries therefore broadened and stabilized oligarchy by the balance it struck between competing institutions: the assembly, the Senate, and executive officeholders. Thanks to this distribution of powers, no single individual or clique could become overwhelmingly strong; but neither could direct expressions of the popular will affect Roman policy.

For the Greek historian Polybius, this was an ideal system, combining elements of the monarchy (executive officeholders, the consuls), the aristocracy (the Senate), and the polity (the people's assembly and the tribunes). For the framers of the United States Constitution, it was a model for the three branches of a new government designed to *prevent* the vast majority of Americans from participating directly in politics, while allowing some citizens (white men with sufficient property) a say in choosing their representatives. Polybius prophesied that such a system would break the political cycle that had destroyed the Greek poleis—that it could last forever. He was wrong.

THE ESSENCE OF ROMAN IDENTITY

Romans accepted new things reluctantly but then preserved them fiercely. The prevailing force was the *mos maiorum*, "the custom of the ancestors" or even—to use a word derived from the Latin *mos*—"morality." This unwritten code was essential to Roman identity. It accounts for the remarkable coherence of Roman culture, religion, and law, all of which rested on ancestor worship. The Latin word *pietas* ("piety") meant reverence for family traditions and for one's fathers—living and dead. What made the legendary Aeneas "pious Aeneas" was his devotion to his father, Anchises, whom he carried to safety while Troy burned. Metaphorically, this meant that Aeneas was the carrier of

FROM REPUBLIC TO EMPIRE

For more than two centuries after the founding of the republic, warfare and agriculture remained the chief occupations of most Romans. The fact that Rome had no standard system of coinage until 289 B.C.E suggests strongly that commerce was an insignificant component of its economy. Apparently, Romans didn't need portable wealth; when they weren't fighting, they wanted to be home on the farm, not gadding about the world. If they had money, they put it into real estate: land or slaves.

All of this changed rapidly when Romans began to look beyond Italy. In 265 B.C.E., they controlled most of the peninsula. A year later, they were already embroiled in a war overseas. For a home-loving people with ample resources, this seems paradoxical. Indeed, historians still argue about the motives for Roman expansion. Did Rome constantly extend its rule as a matter of policy, to feed a collective appetite for warfare and plunder? Or was it an accidental empire, built up in a series of reactions to changing pressures and threats—real and imagined? No definitive answer is possible, but it is in this crucial period that the Roman Republic began to transform Western civilizations, and to transform itself into the Roman Empire.

The Punic Wars, 264–146 B.C.E.

In 265 B.C.E. Roman territory extended to the tip of Italy's "boot," but there it ended. Just off its coast, the large islands of Corsica and Sardinia and the western half of Sicily were part of another state, much older and far wealthier. This was the great maritime empire of Carthage, which stretched along the northern coast of Africa from modern-day Tunisia through the Straits of Gibraltar and into modern Spain. Carthage itself had been founded around 800 B.C.E. as a Phoenician colony (see Chapter 2). It had the largest and most effective navy of its day, and it commanded the vast resources of commercial networks that reached as far north as Britain and deep into Egypt and the Near East. In every respect but one it was far superior to Rome. Yet that one factor was decisive: Carthage had no standing army. It relied on mercenaries bankrolled by the enormous profits of its merchants.

The epic struggle between Rome and Carthage lasted well over a century. It crystallized in three periods of concentrated warfare known as the Punic Wars (because the Romans called their enemies Poeni, "Phoenicians"). The first of these wars began in 264 B.C.E. Twenty-three years of bitter fighting were protracted because the Carthaginians only needed to suffer one defeat in a land battle before resolving to engage the Romans solely at sea. There, they had the advantage—until the Romans built their own navy. Eventually, in 241 B.C.E., Carthage was forced to cede all of her Sicilian lands to Rome and to pay reparations.

Thereafter, the Romans were determined not to let Carthage revive its maritime power. So when Carthage attempted to expand its presence in Spain, Rome intepreted this as a threat and declared a new war that lasted for sixteen years: the Second Punic War. This time, Rome was thrown entirely off its guard by the brilliant exploits of the Carthaginian commander Hannibal (247–183 B.C.E), who very nearly defeated the Romans at their own game. Daringly, Hannibal raised an army in Spain and equipped it with dozens of war elephants and siege engines. He then led this entire force across the Pyrenees into Gaul (now southern France), and then over the Alps into Italy. There, he harried Roman forces in their home territories for nearly sixteen years, from 218 to 202 B.C.E.

Hannibal was challenged more by the difficulty of supplying his army than by the Romans themselves. He also seems to have counted on winning the support of the Italian provinces that Rome had conquered, but Rome's generous treatment of its Latin allies kept them loyal. As a result, Rome could call on vast resources while Hannibal had only his exhausted army and no reserves forthcoming. Nevertheless, he won several amazing victories in Italy before retreating—technically undefeated—in 203. He also won the admiration of the Romans themselves, whose own histories frankly acknowledge his genius.

This phase of warfare ended only when a Roman general, Publius Cornelius Scipio (*SKIP-ee-oh*), took a leaf out of Hannibal's book. After campaigning successfully in Spain, he crossed into Africa and met Hannibal at Zama, near Carthage, in 201 B.C.E. His victory ended the Second Punic War and won him a new name, "Africanus," in honor of his conquest.

Carthage was now compelled to abandon all of its possessions except the city itself and its immediate hinterlands, and to pay an indemnity three times greater than the already crippling reparations demanded after the First Punic War. Yet Roman suspicion remained obsessive, and by the middle of the second century, some warmongers were urging a preemptive strike. Among the most vocal was an elderly patrician called Marcus Porcius Cato, who ended every speech he gave—no matter what the topic— with the words: "And furthermore, I strongly advise that Carthage be destroyed." This won him the nickname Cato the Censor, from the Latin verb "to advise."

In 149 B.C.E. the Senate seized on a minor pretext to demand that the Carthaginians abandon their city and settle at least ten miles from the sea. Of course, this absurd mandate amounted to a death sentence for a city dependent on maritime commerce, and it was refused—as the Romans knew it would be. The result was the Third Punic War and the siege of Carthage, which ended in 146 B.C.E. Those who survived the ensuing massacre were sold into slavery, and their once-magnificent city was razed to the ground. The legend that the Romans sowed the land with salt (to make it infertile) is apocryphal, but it vividly describes the successful eradication of an entire civilization. It would stand as a warning to Rome's other potential enemies.

Roman Control of the Hellenistic World

Rome's victories over Carthage led to the creation of new colonial provinces in Sicily, North Africa, and Hispania (Spain). This not only brought Rome great new wealth, it was also the beginning of the westward expansion that became Rome's defining influence on the history of Western civilizations.

At the same time, Rome's expansion brought it into conflict with eastern Mediterranean powers. During the Second Punic War, for example, Philip V of Macedonia had entered into an alliance with Carthage. Rome sent an army to stop him, and later foiled the plans of the Achaean League

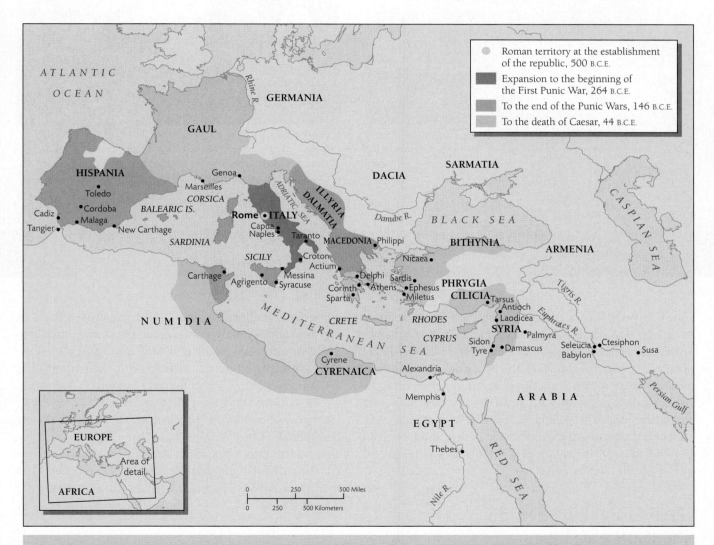

THE EXPANSION OF ROME, 264–44 B.C.E. The rapid increase of Rome's territories opened up new opportunities and challenges.
■ *Looking at the phases of expansion on this map, in what directions did Roman dominion move?* ■ *Why was this the case?* ■ *What particular problems might have been created by the eventual extension of Roman rule into Gaul, well beyond the "Roman lake" of the Mediterranean?*

Past and Present

Spectator Sports

Like the Romans' love for gladiatorial combat, Americans' love of football is inextricably tied to a sense of shared identity and fascination with violence and warfare. Although American football is not a bloodsport in a technical sense, part of its allure stems from the very great physical risks taken by its players, whose careers are often cut short by injury. Both pastimes form the core of far-reaching entertainment economies that would be dismantled by any attempts at reform: concessions, advertising, merchandising, and an array of other money-making activities.

Watch related author videos on the Student Site
wwnorton.com/college/history/western-civilizationsBrief4

(see Chapter 4). This was when Polybius was sent to Rome as a hostage, and became a guest-friend in the family of Scipio Africanus, later witnessing the destruction of Carthage. Rome also thwarted similar efforts by the Seleucid monarch Antiochus III. In neither of these cases did Rome set out to conquer the eastern Mediterranean. By 146 B.C.E., however, both Greece and Macedonia had become Roman provinces, Seleucid Asia had lost most of its territories, and Ptolemaic Egypt had largely become a pawn of Roman interests.

THE CONSEQUENCES OF IMPERIALISM

Rome's seemingly inadvertent conquest of Greece and western Asia transformed the republic. New wealth poured in, increasing the inequalities within Roman society and challenging traditional values. Small farmers left the land and swelled the impoverished urban population, unable to compete with huge plantations worked by gangs of slaves. Slaves also played an increasing role in Roman cities as artisans, merchants, and household servants.

Roman rule over the Hellenistic world had a particularly pervasive impact—so much so that many Romans considered themselves to have been "conquered" by Greece. Hitherto self-assured and self-satisfied, they now felt their own language and customs to be uncouth and barbaric compared to those of their cultivated colonial subjects.

Economic Change and Social Upheaval

Like all peoples of the ancient world, Romans took slavery for granted. But they were not prepared for the huge

meant "worthy of honor"—they now became attached to the person of the sole ruler. Rome had long been an empire, but it was only now that it had a single emperor. To avoid confusion, historians therefore refer to this phase of Rome's history as the Principate, from the title Augustus himself preferred: *princeps*, or "first man."

Because Augustus was determined not to be regarded as a tyrant or (worse) a king, he left most of Rome's republican institutions in place—but emptied them of their power. In theory, the emperor served at the will of "the Roman Senate and People." In practice, though, he controlled the army, which meant that he also controlled the workings of government. Fortunately, Augustus was an able ruler. He introduced a range of public services, including a police force and fire brigade; he reorganized the army; and he allowed cities and provinces more substantial rights of self-government than they had enjoyed before. He instituted a new system of coinage throughout the empire, and he abolished the old, corrupt system of taxation, whereby tax collectors were compensated by being allowed to keep a portion of what they collected. Instead, Augustus appointed his own representatives, paid them regular salaries, and kept them under strict supervision. He also conducted a census of the empire's population, and it was during one of these "enrollments" that the birth of Jesus occurred, according to the gospel of Luke (see Chapter 6). Augustus also established new colonies in the provinces, encouraging the emigration of Rome's urban and rural poor, thereby removing a major source of social tension and promoting the integration of the Roman heartland with its far-flung hinterland.

Although his rule had definitively ended the republic, Augustus represented himself as a stern defender of the *mos maiorum* and traditional Roman virtues. He rebuilt many of the city's ancient temples and prohibited the worship of foreign gods. In an attempt to increase the birthrate of Rome's citizens, he penalized men who failed to marry, required widows to remarry within two years of their husbands' deaths, and rewarded women who gave birth to more than two children. He also introduced laws punishing adultery and making divorces more difficult to obtain. To hammer the message home, Augustan propaganda portrayed the imperial family as a model of domestic virtue and propriety, despite the emperor's own notorious extramarital affairs and the well-known fact that the sexual promiscuity of his daughter Julia finally forced Augustus to have her exiled.

More land was gained for Rome in the lifetime of Augustus than in that of any other ruler. His generals advanced into central Europe, conquering the modern-day territories of Switzerland, Austria, and Bulgaria. Only in Germania did Roman troops meet defeat, when three legions were slaughtered in 9 C.E., a setback that convinced Augustus to hold the Roman borders at the Rhine and Danube rivers. Subsequently, though, the emperor Claudius would begin the conquest of Britain in 43 C.E., while the Emperor Trajan (r. 98–117 C.E.) would push beyond the Danube to add Dacia (now Romania) to the empire. Trajan also conquered territories in the heartland of Mesopotamia, but in so doing aroused the enmity of the Parthians, who now ruled in Persia. His successor, Hadrian (r. 117–138 C.E.), accordingly halted Rome's expansion and embarked on a defensive policy epitomized by the construction of Hadrian's Wall in northern Britain. The empire had now reached its greatest extent; in the third century, as we shall see (Chapter 6), the tide would turn and these limits would recede.

HADRIAN'S WALL. Stretching 73.5 miles across northern England, this fortification (begun in 122 C.E.) marked the frontier of Britain as established by the emperor Hadrian. (A later wall, built farther north by Antoninus Pius in 142, was quickly abandoned.) Long stretches of the wall still exist, as do many of the forts built along it. The tree in this photograph stands on the site of a "mile castle," one of the smaller watchtowers built at intervals of a Roman mile and garrisoned by sentries.

Competing Viewpoints

Two Views of Augustus's Rule

Augustus Speaks for Himself

The emperor Augustus was a master propagandist with an unrivaled capacity for presenting his own actions in the best possible light. This list of his own deeds was written by Augustus himself and was displayed on two bronze pillars set up in the Roman forum.

Below is a copy of the accomplishments of the deified Augustus by which he brought the whole world under the empire of the Roman people, and of the moneys expended by him on the state and the Roman people. . . .

1. At the age of nineteen, on my own initiative and at my own expense, I raised an army by means of which I liberated the republic, which was oppressed by the tyranny of a faction.

2. Those who assassinated my father I drove into exile, avenging their crime by due process of law.

3. I waged many wars throughout the whole world by land and by sea, both civil and foreign. . . .

5. The dictatorship offered to me . . . by the people and by the Senate . . . I refused to accept. . . . The consulship, too, which was offered to me . . . as an annual office for life, I refused to accept.

6. Though the Roman Senate and people together agreed that I should be elected sole guardian of the laws and morals with supreme authority, I refused to accept any office offered me which was contrary to the traditions of our ancestors.

7. I have been ranking senator for forty years. . . . I have been *pontifex maximus*, augur, member of the college of fifteen for performing sacrifices, member of the college of seven for conducting religious banquets, member of the Arval Brotherhood, one of the *Titii sodales*, and a *fetial* [all priestly offices].

9. The Senate decreed that vows for my health should be offered up every fifth year by the consuls and priests. . . . The whole citizen body, with one accord, . . . prayed continuously for my health at all the shrines.

17. Four times I came to the assistance of the treasury with my own money . . . providing bonuses for soldiers who had completed twenty or more years of service.

20. I repaired the Capitol and the theater of Pompey with enormous expenditures on both works, without having my name inscribed on them. I repaired . . . the aqueducts which were falling into ruin in many places . . . I repaired eighty-two temples. . . . I reconstructed the Flaminian Way. . . .

34. Having attained supreme power by universal consent, I transferred the state from my own power to the control of the Roman Senate and people. . . . After that time I excelled all in authority, but I possessed no more power than the others who were my colleagues in each magistracy.

35. At the time I wrote this document I was in my seventy-sixth year.

Source: "Res Gestae Divi Augusti," in *Roman Civilization, Sourcebook II: The Empire,* ed. Naphtali Lewis and Meyer Reinhold (New York: 1966), pp. 9–19.

When Octavian died in 14 C.E. he was not only Caesar, Imperator, and Augustus; he was *pontifex maximus* (high priest) and "father of the fatherland" (*pater patriae*). He was even deified by the Senate. These titles would be passed on to his successors, as would the system of government he had devised. And even those who mourned the passing of the republic and loathed these displays of imperial *hubris* had to admit that the system worked. Rome enjoyed nearly two centuries of peace, prosperity, and stability because of it. For the true test of any political institution

The Historian Tacitus Evaluates Augustus's Reign

Writing in the first decades of the second century C.E., the senatorial historian Tacitus (c. 56–117) began his chronicle of imperial rule, the Annals, *with the death of Augustus a century earlier.*

Intelligent people praised or criticized Augustus in varying terms. One opinion was as follows. Filial duty and a national emergency, in which there was no place for law-abiding conduct, had driven him to civil war—and this can be neither initiated nor maintained by decent methods. He had made many concessions to Antony and to Lepidus for the sake of vengeance on his father's murderers. When Lepidus grew old and lazy, and Antony's self-indulgence got the better of him, the only possible cure for the distracted country had been government by one man. However, Augustus had put the State in order not by making himself king or dictator but by creating the Principate. The empire's frontiers were on the ocean, or on distant rivers. Armies, provinces, fleets, the whole system was interrelated. Roman citizens were protected by the law. Provincials were decently treated. Rome itself had been lavishly beautified. Force had been sparingly used—merely to preserve peace for the majority.

The opposite view went like this. Filial duty and national crisis had been merely pretexts. In actual fact, the motive of Octavian, the future Augustus, was lust for power. Inspired by that, he had mobilized ex-army settlers by gifts of money, raised an army—while he was only a half-grown boy without any official status—won over a consul's brigade by bribery, pretended to support Sextus Pompeius [the son of Pompey], and by senatorial decree usurped the status and rank of a praetor. Soon both consuls . . . had met their deaths—by enemy action; or perhaps in the one case by the deliberate poisoning of his wound, and in the other at the hand of his own troops, instigated by Octavian. In any case, it was he who took over both their armies. Then he had forced the reluctant Senate to make him consul. But the forces given him to deal with Antony he used against the State. His judicial murders and land distributions were distasteful even to those who carried them out. True, Cassius and Brutus died because he had inherited a feud against them; nevertheless, personal enmities ought to be sacrificed to the public interest. Next he had cheated Sextus Pompeius by a spurious peace treaty, Lepidus by spurious friendship. Then Antony, enticed by treaties and his marriage with Octavian's sister, had paid the penalty of that delusive relationship with his life. After that, there had certainly been peace, but it was a bloodstained peace. . . . And gossip did not spare his personal affairs—how he had abducted [Livia] the wife of Tiberius Claudius Nero, and asked the priests the farcical question whether it was in order for her to marry while pregnant. Then there was the debauchery of his friend Publius Vedius Pollio. But Livia was a real catastrophe, to the nation, as a mother and to the house of the Caesars as a stepmother.

Source: Tacitus, *Annals* i.9–10. Based on *Tacitus: The Annals of Imperial Rome*, trans. Michael Grant (New York: 1989), pp. 37–39.

Questions for Analysis

1. How does Augustus organize his list, and why? What does he leave out and what does he choose to emphasize?

2. Tacitus presents two contrasting views of Augustus's motives. Which does he himself seem to believe? How does his account complement or undermine that of Augustus himself?

3. Could you write a new account of Augustus's life making use of both sources? How would you strike a balance between them? What would your own conclusion be?

is its capacity to survive incompetent officeholders. Aside from one brief period of civil war in 68 C.E., the transition of power between emperors was generally peaceful and the growing imperial bureaucracy could manage affairs competently even when individual emperors proved vicious and ineffectual, as did Caligula (r. 37–41 C.E.). Nevertheless, the fact that Rome had become an autocratic state became harder and harder to conceal.

The height of the Augustan system is generally considered to be the era between 96 and 180 C.E., often known as the reign of the "Five Good Emperors": Nerva (r. 96–98 C.E.), Trajan (r. 98–117 C.E.), Hadrian (r. 117–138 C.E.), Antoninus Pius (r. 138–161 C.E.), and Marcus Aurelius (r. 161–180 C.E.). All were capable politicians, and since none but the last had a son that survived him, each adopted a worthy successor—a policy that avoided the messy family dysfunctions that absorbed Augustus and his immediate heirs. They also benefited from the fact that Rome had few external enemies left. The Mediterranean was under the control of a single power for the first time in history. On land, Roman officials ruled from Britain to Persia. Now was the *Pax Romana*, the time of Roman Peace.

MAKING THE WORLD ROMAN

Occasionally, the Roman Peace was broken. In Britannia, Roman legions had to put down a rebellion led by the Celtic warrior queen Boudica (*boh-DI-kah*; d. 60/61 C.E.), a war that ended in a massacre of the defiant tribes. Another rebellion was violently quashed in Judea, the most restive of all Roman provinces, leading to the destruction of the Temple at Jerusalem in 70 C.E. In 135 C.E., a second rebellion completed the destruction of the city. Although Jerusalem was later refounded by Hadrian as Aelia Capitolina, a colony for veterans of Rome's army, Jews were forbidden to settle there.

Such rebellions were not the norm, however. Although the Roman Empire had been gradually achieved by conquest, it was not maintained by force. Instead, Rome controlled its territories by offering incentives to assimilation. Local elites were encouraged to adopt Roman modes of behavior and dress in order to gain entrance to political office. Local gods became Roman gods and were adopted into the Roman pantheon. Cities were constructed on a set model of urban planning, and the amenities of urban life were introduced: baths, temples, amphitheaters, aqueducts, and paved roads (see *Interpreting Visual Evidence* on page 134). Rights of citizenship were extended, and able provincials could rise far in the imperial government. Some, like the emperors Trajan and Hadrian—both raised in Hispania—came to control it. Meanwhile, tens of thousands of army veterans were settled in the provinces, marrying local women and putting down local roots. It was common for soldiers born in Syria to end their days peacefully in northern Gaul. In Camulodunum (now Colchester, England), the gravestone of a legionnaire called Longinus

SPOILS FROM JERUSALEM. A bas-relief inside the triumphal Arch of Titus in the Roman forum shows plundered treasures from the Temple at Jerusalem, including the Menorah, being carried in triumph through Rome.

Analyzing Primary Sources

Rome's Party Girls

The Satires *of the poet Juvenal circulated around the year 100 C.E. and attacked everything from the general erosion of public morality to the effete tastes of the elite. Some of his most pointed criticism was directed at contemporary women.*

 hat conscience has Venus, when she is drunk? Our inebriated beauties can't tell head from tail at those midnight oyster suppers when the best wine's laced with perfume, and tossed down neat from a foaming conch-shell, while the dizzy ceiling spins round, and the tables dance, and each light shows double. Why, you may ask yourself, does the notorious Maura sniff at the air in that knowing, derisive way as she and her dear friend Tullia pass by the ancient altar of Chastity? And what is Tullia whispering to her? Here, at night, they stagger out of their litters and relieve themselves, pissing in long hard bursts all over the goddess's statue. Then, while the Moon looks down on their motions, they take turns to ride each other, and finally go home. So you, next morning, on your way to some great house, will splash through your wife's piddle. Notorious, too, are the ritual mysteries of the Good Goddess, when flute-music stirs the loins, and frenzied women, devotees of Priapus, sweep along in procession, howling, tossing their hair, wine-flown, horn-crazy, burning with the desire to get themselves laid. . . . So the ladies, with a display of talent to match their birth, win all the prizes. No make-believe here, no pretense, each act is performed in earnest, and guaranteed to warm the age-chilled balls of a Nestor or a Priam.

Source: Juvenal, *Sixth Satire* 301–26; based on *Juvenal: The Sixteen Satires*, trans. Peter Green (New York: 1974), pp. 138–39 (modified).

Questions for Analysis

1. Compare Juvenal's account of female behavior to the legend of Lucretia, on the one hand, and Plutarch's description of Cleopatra, on the other. What can you conclude about attitudes to women and to sexual morality? Why and on what grounds would men living under the Principate hold women responsible for society's ills?

2. In your view, what are the benefits and the drawbacks of the *Satires* as a historical source?

---

sketches a typical career: born in Serdica (modern Sofia, in Bulgaria) to a local man named Szdapezematygus, he rose through the ranks to become sergeant of the First Thracian Cavalry under the emperor Claudius and one of the first Roman colonists of Britannia.

Even the outer fringes of the empire need to be understood as part of Rome's orbit. Although historians speak of the empire's "borders" for the sake of convenience, these were in fact permeable zones of intensive interaction. Roman influence reached far beyond these zones, into the heartland of Germania and lands farther to the east. By the middle of the third century C.E., when some frontier garrisons were withdrawn to take part in civil wars within the empire, many of these peoples moved southward, too, sometimes as plunderers but more often as aspiring Romans (see Chapter 6).

The Entertainments of Empire

The cultural and intellectual developments of the late republic came to fruition during the Principate, and are richly reflected in its literature. For the first time, Latin began to replace Greek as a language of learning and poetry—much of it, not surprisingly, propagandistic: its purpose was to advertise and justify Rome's achievements. The poetry of Publius Virgilius Maro (Virgil, 70–19 B.C.E.) is typical, and we have already noted his strategic use of "prophecy" in the story of Aeneas. Other major poets of the Augustan age were Quintus Horatius Flaccus (Horace, 65–8 B.C.E.) and Publius Ovidius Naso (Ovid, 43 B.C.E.–17 C.E.): the former a master of the lovely short lyric and the latter our major source for Greek mythology, which he retold in a long poem called the *Metamorphoses* ("Transformations").

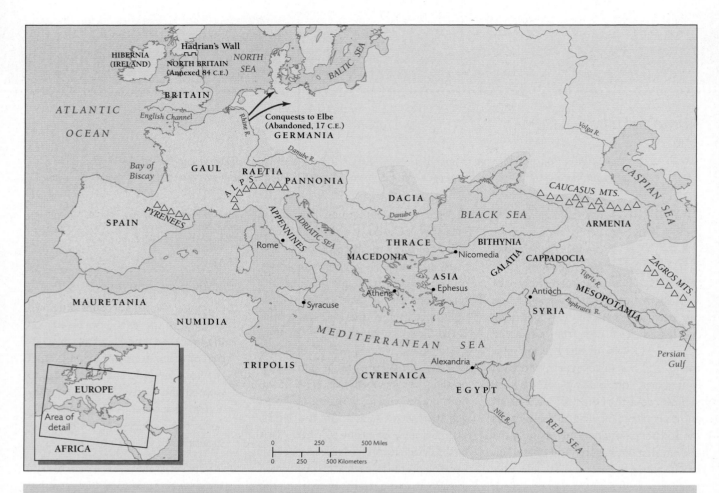

THE ROMAN EMPIRE AT ITS GREATEST EXTENT, 97–117 C.E. ▪ *How much farther north and west does the empire now reach compared to its earlier extent (see map on page 119)?* ▪ *How did geography influence the process of expansion?* ▪ *How did it dictate its limits?* ▪ *For example, what role do major river systems seem to play?*

After Augustus's death, Roman authors had more license and became important cultural critics. The tales of Petronius and Apuleius describe the more bizarre and sometimes sordid aspects of Roman life, and the satirist Juvenal (60?–140 C.E.) wrote with savage wit about the moral degeneracy he saw in his contemporaries. A similar attitude toward Roman society characterizes the writings of Tacitus (55?–117? C.E.), an aristocratic historian who describes the events and people of his age largely for the purpose of passing judgment on them. His *Annals* offer a subtle but devastating portrait of the political system constructed by Augustus and ruled by his heirs; his *Germania* contrasts the manly virtues of northern barbarians with the effeminate vices of the decadent Romans.

To many people today, the most fascinating (and repellant) aspect of Roman culture during the Principate was its spectacular cruelty. Gladiatorial contests were not new, but they were now presented in ampitheaters built to hold tens of thousands. Everyone, even emperors, attended these events, and they became increasingly bloody and brutal as people demanded more and more innovative violence. Individual gladiators fought to the death with swords or the exotic weapons of their homelands. Teams of gladiators fought pitched battles, often simulating historic Roman victories. Occasionally, a wealthy entrepreneur would fill an arena with water and stage a naval battle. Hundreds of men would die in these organized slaughters. On other occasions, hundreds of half-starved animals imported from Africa, India, or the forests of Germania would tear one another—or their human victims—apart. When a fighter went down with a disabling wound, the crowd would be asked to decide whether to spare his life or to kill him. If the arena floor became too slippery with blood, a fresh layer of sand would be spread over the gore so that the performance could continue.

Roman Art, Architecture, and Engineering

Like Latin literature, Roman art assumed its distinctive character during the Principate. Before this time, most artworks displayed in Roman homes were Hellenistic imports. As demand for such works increased, hundreds of copies were made by Roman artisans. In many cases, these copies proved more durable than their originals; in Chapter 4, for example, we were able to examine the lost Aphrodite of Knidos, courtesy of Roman sculptors.

Encouraged by the patronage of Augustus and his successors, artists began to experiment with more distinctively Roman styles and subjects. The relief sculpture of this period is particularly notable for its delicacy and naturalism, and sculptors also became adept at portraiture. Painting, however, was the Romans' most original and most intimate art. Romans loved intense colors, and those who could afford it surrounded themselves with brilliant wall paintings and mosaics made of tiny fragments of glass and stone, which were often set into the floors of houses or which formed the centerpieces of gardens. Lavish mosaics have been found in the remains of Roman

ROMAN AQUEDUCT IN SOUTHERN GAUL (FRANCE). Aqueducts conveyed water from mountains and lakes to the larger cities of the Roman Empire. The massive arches shown here were originally part of a 31-mile-long complex that supplied water to the city of Nemausus (Nîmes). It is now known as the Pont du Gard (Bridge of the Gardon), reflecting the use to which it was put after the aqueduct ceased to function, some eight centuries after its construction in the first century C.E. Many Roman aqueducts remained operational into the modern era: the one at Segovia, Spain was still in use at the end of the twentieth century. ▪ *What does the magnitude and longevity of such projects tell us about Roman power and technology?*

villas in all the territories of the empire, and similar design features indicate that many were mosaic "kits" that could be ordered from a manufacturer, who would ship out all the necessary components, along with a team of workmen to assemble them.

Augustus liked to boast that he had found Rome a city of clay and left it a city of marble. But in reality, marble was too precious to be used in common construction. Instead, marble panels or ornaments were added to the facings of buildings that were otherwise made of concrete. For the Roman had discovered how to make a mixture of quicklime, volcanic ash, and pumice, and it was this—along with superior engineering skills—that allowed them to build massive structures like the Colosseum, which could accommodate 50,000 spectators at gladiatorial combats.

Roman engineers also excelled in the building of roads and bridges, many of which were constructed by Rome's armies as they moved into new territories. Like the Persian Royal Road of the sixth century B.C.E. or the German Autobahn of the 1930s and the interstate highways of the United States begun in the 1950s, roads have always been, first and foremost, a device for moving armies and then, secondarily, for moving goods and people. Many of these Roman roads still survive, or form the basis for modern European highways. In Britain, for example, the only major thoroughfares before the building of high-speed motorways were based on Roman roads, to which the motorways now run parallel.

THE COLOSSEUM. Constructed between 75 and 80 C.E., this was the first amphitheater in Rome purposely built to showcase gladiatorial combats. Prior to this, gladiators would often fight in improvised arenas in the Forum or in other public places. ▪ *How does this fact change your perception of Roman history?*

Interpreting Visual Evidence

Roman Urban Planning

Prior to Roman imperial expansion, most cities in the ancient world were not planned cities—with the exception of the new settlements established by Alexander the Great, notably Alexandria in Egypt. Rome itself was not carefully planned, but grew up over many centuries, expanding outward and up the slopes of its seven hills from the nucleus of the Forum. By the time of Augustus, it was a haphazard jumble of buildings and narrow streets. Outside of Rome, however, the efficiency of Roman government was in large part due to the uniformity of imperial urban planning. As their colonial reach expanded, Romans sought to ensure that travelers moving within their vast domain would encounter the same amenities in every major city. They also wanted to convey, through the organization of the urban landscape, the ubiquity of Roman authority and majesty.

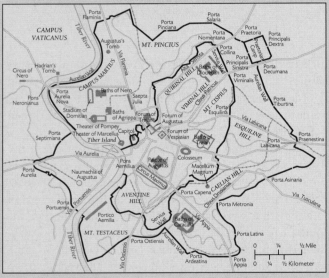

A. Imperial Rome

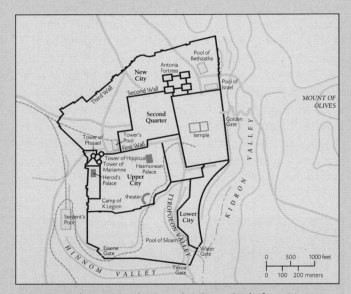

B. Roman settlement in Aelia Capitolina (Jerusalem) after 135 C.E.

The inhabitants of Roman cities also enjoyed the benefits of a public water supply. By the early decades of the second century C.E., eleven aqueducts brought water into Rome from the nearby hills for drinking and bathing and for flushing a well-designed sewage system. These amenities were common in cities throughout the empire, and the homes of the wealthy even had indoor plumbing and central heating. Water was also funneled into the homes of the rich for private gardens, fountains, and pools. The emperor Nero (54–68 C.E.) built a famous Golden House with special pipes that sprinkled his guests with perfume, baths supplied with medicinal waters, and a pond "like a sea." "At last," said Nero on moving day, "I can live like a human being."

The Reach of Roman Law

Roman architecture and engineering are impressive, but the most durable and useful of this civilization's

Questions for Analysis

1. Looking closely at the map of Rome (map A), how have topographical features—like the river Tiber and the seven hills—determined the shape and layout of the city? What are the major buildings and public areas? What were the functions of these spaces, and what do they reveal about Roman society and values?

2. Compare the plan of Rome to those of Roman Jerusalem (map B) and London (map C). What features do all three have in common, and why? What features are unique to each place, and what might this reveal about the different regions of the empire and the needs of the different cities' inhabitants?

3. Given that all Roman cities share certain features, what message(s) were Roman authorities trying to convey to inhabitants and travelers through urban planning? Why, for example, would they have insisted on rebuilding Jerusalem as a Roman city—Aelia Capitolina—after the rebellion of 135 C.E.?

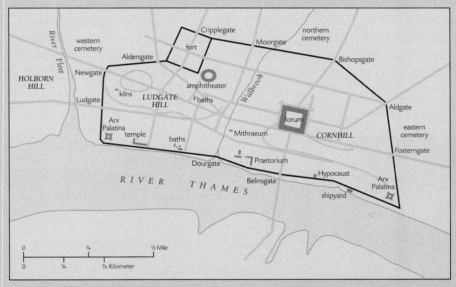

C. London under the Romans, c. 200 C.E.

legacies was its legal system. Over the course of several centuries, the primitive code of the Twelve Tables was largely replaced by a series of new laws that reflect the changing needs of Rome's diverse and ever-growing population.

The most sweeping legal changes occurred during the Principate. This was partly because the reach of Roman law had to match the reach of the empire. But the major reason for the rapid development of Roman legal thinking during these years was the fact that Augustus and his successors appointed a small number of eminent jurists to deliver opinions on the issues raised by cases under trial in the courts. The five most prominent of these experts flourished in the second century C.E.: Gaius (only this most common of his names is known), Domitius Ulpianus (Ulpian), Modestinus, Aemelianus Papinianus (Papinian), and Paulus. Taken together, their legal opinions constitute the first philosophy of law and the foundation for all subsequent jurisprudence, a word derived from the Latin phrase meaning "legal wisdom."

As it was developed by the jurists, Roman law comprised three great branches: civil law, the law of nations, and natural law. Civil law was the law of Rome and its citizens, both written and unwritten. It included the statutes of the Senate, the decrees of the emperor, the edicts of magistrates, and ancient customs that had the force of law (like the *mos maiorum*). The law of nations was not specific to Rome but extended to all people of the world regardless of their origins and ethnicity: it is the precursor of international law. This law authorized slavery; protected the private ownership of property; and defined the mechanisms of purchase and sale, partnership, and contract. It supplemented civil law and applied especially to those inhabitants of the empire who were not citizens, as well as to foreigners.

The most interesting (and in many ways the most important) branch of Roman law was natural law, a product not of judicial practice but of legal philosophy. Roman Stoics, following in the footsteps of Cicero, posited that nature itself is rationally ordered, and that careful study will reveal the laws by which the natural world operates, including natural justice. They affirmed that all men are by nature equal, and that they are entitled to certain basic rights that governments have no authority to transgress. Accordingly,

no person or institution has the authority to infringe on this law, repeal it, or ignore it. This law supersedes any state or ruler; a ruler who transgresses it is a tyrant.

Although the practical law applied in local Roman courts often bore little resemblance to the law of nature, the development of a concept of abstract justice as a fundamental principle was one of the noblest achievements of Roman civilization. It has given us the doctrine of human rights, even if it has not resulted in ending abuses of those rights.

CONCLUSION

The resemblances between Rome's history and that of Great Britain and the United States have often been noted. Like the British Empire, the Roman Empire was founded on conquest and overseas colonization intended to benefit both the homeland and its colonial subjects, who were seen as the beneficiaries of a "civilizing mission." Like America's, the Roman economy evolved from agrarianism to a complex system of domestic and foreign markets, problems of unemployment, gross disparities of wealth, and vulnerability to financial crisis. And like both the British and the American empires, the

After You Read This Chapter

 Go to **INQUIZITIVE** to see what you've learned—and learn what you've missed—with personalized feedback along the way.

REVIEWING THE OBJECTIVES

- The founding of the Roman Republic was both a cherished myth and a series of events. What factors contributed to this unique system of government?
- The shared identity and values of the Roman people differed in many ways from those of other ancient civilizations. What were some of these major differences?
- Rome's population was divided among classes of people who often struggled with one another for power. Identify these classes and their points of contention.
- The expansion of Rome's empire had a profound impact on Roman society. Why?
- The establishment of the Principate ushered in a new era in the history of Rome. What events led to this?

Roman Empire justified itself by celebrating the peace its conquests allegedly brought to the world.

Ultimately, however, such parallels break down when we remember that Rome's civilization differed profoundly from any society of the modern world. It was not an industrialized society. Its government never pretended to be representative of all its citizens. Roman class divisions are not directly comparable to ours. The Roman economy rested on slavery to a degree unmatched in any modern state. As a result, technological advances were not encouraged, social stratification was extreme, and gender relations were profoundly unequal. Religious practice and political life were inseparable.

Nevertheless, the civilization of ancient Rome continues to structure our everyday lives in ways so profound that they often go unnoticed. Our days are mapped onto the Roman calendar. The constitution of the United States is largely modeled on that of the Republic, and Roman architecture survives in the design of our public buildings. Roman law forms the basis of most European legal codes, and American judges still cite Gaius and Ulpian. Virtually all modern sculpture is inspired by Roman sculpture, and Roman authors continue to set the standards for prose composition in many Western countries. Indeed, most European languages are either derived from Latin—Romance languages are so called because they are "Roman-like"—or have borrowed Latin grammatical structures or vocabulary. As we shall see in the following chapters, the organization of the modern Roman Catholic Church can be traced back to the structure of the Roman state: even today, the pope bears the title of Rome's high priest, *pontifex maximus*.

But perhaps the most important of all Rome's contributions was its role as mediator between Europe and the civilizations of the ancient Near East and Mediterranean. Had Rome's empire not come to encompass much of Europe, there would be no such thing as the concept of Western civilization and no shared ideas and heritage to link us to those distant places and times. Although we shall pursue the history of Rome's fragmentation and witness the emergence of three different civilizations in the territories once united by its empire, we shall see that they all shared a common cultural inheritance. In this sense, the Roman Empire did not collapse. But it was transformed, and the factors driving that transformation will be the subject of Chapter 6.

PEOPLE, IDEAS, AND EVENTS IN CONTEXT

- In what ways were the early Romans influenced by their **ETRUSCAN** neighbors and by their location in central **ITALY**?
- What were the components of the **REPUBLIC'S CONSTITUTION**? What was the relationship between **ROMAN CITIZENSHIP** and the **ROMAN ARMY** in this era?
- How do the stories of **AENEAS**, **LUCRETIA**, and **CINCINNATUS** reflect core Roman values? How did those values, summarized in the phrase *MOS MAIORUM*, set the Romans apart from the other civilizations we have studied?
- Why did the Romans come into conflict with **CARTHAGE**? How did the **PUNIC WARS** and Rome's other conquests change the balance of power in the Mediterranean?
- How did **IMPERIALISM** and contact with **HELLENISTIC CULTURE** affect the core values of Roman society, its economy, and its political system? What role did **SLAVERY** play in this civilization?
- What were the major crises of the late republic, and what were the means by which ambitious men achieved power? How did **JULIUS CAESAR** emerge triumphant, and why was he assassinated?
- In what ways did the **PRINCIPATE** differ from the **REPUBLIC**? What were the new powers of the **EMPEROR**, and how did **AUGUSTUS** exemplify these?
- How did the Romans consolidate their **EMPIRE** during the *PAX ROMANA*? By what means did they spread Roman culture?

THINKING ABOUT CONNECTIONS

- Polybius believed that the Roman Republic would last forever, because it fused together aspects of monarchy, aristocracy, and polity. What were the chief factors that led to its demise in the first century B.C.E.? Could these have been avoided—and if so, how?
- In what ways does the Roman Empire share the characteristics of earlier empires, especially that of Alexander? In what ways does it differ from them?
- The Roman Empire could be said to resemble our own civilization in different ways. What features does today's United States share with the Republic? With the Principate? What lessons can we draw from this?

CONSTANTINVS MINOR IMPERATOR
HERACLII ET TIBERII IMPERATOR

AR
COP
VS

PRIVILEGIA

STORY LINES

- In a little over three centuries, Christianity grew from obscure beginnings in a small Roman province to become the official religion of the empire.

- Meanwhile, the Roman Empire was becoming too large and diverse to be governed by a single centralized authority. Significant political, military, and economic changes occurred during the third century in response to these challenges.

- In the fourth century, the founding of a new capital at Constantinople shifted the focus of imperial administration to the East. At the same time, mass migrations of frontier peoples created new settlements within the western half of Rome's empire.

- Christianity's eventual association with political power changed the religion in profound ways. At the same time, Christian intellectuals adapted Rome's traditional culture to meet Christian needs.

CHRONOLOGY

c. 4 B.C.E.–c. 30 C.E.	Lifetime of Jesus
46–67 C.E.	Paul's missionary career
66–70	Jewish rebellion
132–135	Expulsion of Jews from Jerusalem
203	Death of Perpetua at Carthage
235–284	Rule of the "barracks emperors"
284–305	Diocletian divides the empire
312	Constantine's victory at the Battle of the Milvian Bridge
313	Edict of Milan
325	Council of Nicaea convened
c. 370–430	Careers of Jerome, Ambrose, and Augustine
c. 376	Frontier migrations begin
391	Pagan religion outlawed
410	Visigoths sack Rome
476	Odovacer deposes Romulus Augustulus
493–526	Rule of Theodoric the Ostrogoth
c. 500–583	Careers of Boethius, Benedict, and Cassiodorus

The Transformation of Rome

CORE OBJECTIVES

- **IDENTIFY** the historical factors that shaped early Christianity.

- **DESCRIBE** the pressures on Roman imperial administration during the third century.

- **TRACE** the ways that Christianity changed after it became a legal religion.

- **EXPLAIN** how barbarian migrations affected the empire.

- **UNDERSTAND** the difference between traditional Roman and Christian worldviews.

I n the year 203 C.E., a young woman was arrested and brought before the Roman governor at Carthage. She was twenty-two years old, from a respectable family. She had an infant child who was still nursing and a father who doted on her. She must have had a husband, too, but he is conspicuously absent from Perpetua's own firsthand account. Instead, Perpetua emphasizes her father's grief and the efforts he made to free her. But, clearly, he had failed as a father: a Roman *paterfamilias* should kill his daughter with his own hands if she disgraced the family. For Perpetua's crime was terrible, punishable by a death so debasing that it was reserved for slaves and barbarian prisoners—to be stripped naked before a holiday crowd and mauled by wild beasts in the arena of her own city. That was the death Perpetua died. Perpetua was a Christian.

Early Christianity posed a challenge to the Roman Empire at almost every level. To be a Christian was to be, by definition, an enemy of Rome, because Christians refused to venerate the emperor as the embodiment of Rome's gods. Moreover, Jesus Christ had himself been a criminal duly tried and put to

139

death by the Roman state. Also disturbing was the way that Christians flouted the conventions of Roman society. Perpetua was young, yet she defied her father. She was well born, yet she chose a common jail. She was a woman, yet she died in the dust like a gladiator. If this was what it meant to be a Christian, then being a Christian was incompatible with being a Roman.

How, then, did a Roman emperor become a Christian just a century or so after Perpetua's death? What changes did both Rome and Christianity have to undergo in order for this to happen? The Rome in which Perpetua was raised stretched from central Asia to the British Isles, from the Rhine to her own province of North Africa. But the governance of this enormous state and its diverse population was straining the bureaucracy built on the foundations of the old Republic. By the fourth century, Rome itself even ceased to be the capital and hub of the empire. At the same time, Rome's settled provinces were coming under increased pressure from groups of people who had long lived along its borders but who now moved toward its center. These peoples would also challenge what it meant to be Roman, and they too would contribute to the transformation of the Roman world.

THE CHALLENGE OF CHRISTIANITY

Like the Hebrew monotheism that undergirds Judaism (see Chapter 2), Christianity was (and is) the product of historical processes. It began with the teachings of Jesus, who lived and worked among his fellow Jews around the year 30 C.E. It took root, however, in the Hellenistic world we studied in Chapter 4: the cosmopolitan, Greek-speaking cities around the eastern Mediterranean, which had been absorbed into the Roman Empire.

The Career of Jesus

Yeshua bar Yosef (Joshua, son of Joseph), known in Greek as Jesus, is one of the few figures of the ancient world about whose life we know a great deal. The earliest writings that mention him are the letters of Paul, a Hellenized Jew who was active during the 50s and 60s C.E. There were also many different narratives of Jesus's life written between c. 70 and 100 C.E. Four such accounts were eventually included in the New Testament, a collection of Christian scriptures codified around the third century C.E. In their original Greek, they were called *evangelia* ("good messages"); we know them as *Gospels*, an Old English word that means the same thing.

Jesus was born around the year 4 B.C.E., a generation or so after Augustus came to power in Rome. (He was not born precisely in the first year of the Common Era as we now reckon it.) When he was about thirty years old, he was endorsed by a Jewish preacher, John the Baptist, whom some considered to be a prophet. Thereafter, Jesus traveled around rural areas of Galilee and Judea, teaching and displaying unusual healing powers. He accumulated a number of disciples, some of whom had political ambitions.

Around the year 30 C.E., Jesus staged an entry into Jerusalem during Passover, a major religious holiday.

JUDEA AND GALILEE IN THE TIME OF JESUS. ■ *What are the major Judean cities in first century C.E.?* ■ *What do they indicate about the effects of Roman occupation on the lives of Jews?* ■ *Given what you have learned about their history, why would some Jews resist Roman rule?*

This was interpreted as a bid for political power by both the Roman colonial government and the high-ranking Jews of the Temple. Gospel accounts say that Jesus also drew attention to himself by attacking merchants and bankers within the Temple. The city's religious leaders therefore arrested him and turned him over to the Roman governor, Pontius Pilatus (Pilate).

Pilate's main concern was to preserve peace during a volatile religious festival. His authority depended on maintaining good relations with local Jewish elites and with Herod, a recent convert to Judaism who ruled the province of Galilee as a client king of the Roman Empire. And because Jesus was a resident of Galilee, not a citizen of Roman Judea, Pilate sent Jesus to Herod for sentencing. But Herod sent him back, indicating that dealing with Jesus fell under Roman jursidiction. So Pilate chose to make an example of Jesus by condemning him to death by crucifixion, the standard penalty for those judged guilty of sedition.

That might have been the end of the story. But soon after Jesus's execution, his followers began to assert that he had risen from the dead. Moreover, they said that Jesus had promised to return again at the end of time. Meanwhile, he had promised spiritual support to his followers, who now reinterpreted the meaning of his entire career. In life, Jesus had been a teacher and healer; in death, he had been revealed as divine. The evidence of this reinterpretation has come down to us in the letters of Paul and in the Gospel narratives.

Jesus and Judaism

In the decade after 1947, many extraordinary parchment and papyrus scrolls were discovered in caves near Qumran, on the shores of the Dead Sea. Written in Hebrew, Greek, and Aramaic, at various times between 100 B.C.E. and 70 C.E., they have revolutionized our understanding of religious practice in the lifetime of Jesus, a period of intense competition among groups of Jewish believers.

Roman rule in this region was controversial. Jewish elites reaped the rewards of participation in the Roman economy and administration, but there was talk of rebellion among rural communities and the urban poor. Many hoped for a messiah, an inspired leader who would establish a new Jewish kingdom. The most extreme were the Zealots, who eventually led two disastrous revolts. The first, between 66 and 70 C.E., ended in the Romans' destruction of the Temple that had been rebuilt after Cyrus the Great released the Jews from Babylon (see Chapter 2). The second, in 132–35 C.E., destroyed Jerusalem itself and prompted the Romans to expel the entire population.

Whereas the first exile of the Jews had ended after fifty years, this new diaspora would not be reversed until the modern state of Israel was established in 1948. For over 500 years, Jerusalem even ceased to exist; on its ruins, the Romans built the colony of Aelia Capitolina (see Chapter 5). It was only in 638, when the Islamic Caliphate restored Jerusalem as a holy site, that Jews were allowed to settle there again (see Chapter 7).

This context is essential to understanding the circumstances of Jesus's death and the different messages conveyed by his words and actions. Significant divisions had arisen among the various Jewish communities with whom Jesus interacted. The hereditary Temple priesthood was controlled by a group known as the Sadducees, who collaborated closely with Rome; the high priest was even appointed by the Roman Senate. Their chief rivals were the Pharisees, who were teachers of religious doctrine. Although the Sadducees claimed the right to control the interpretation of the Torah, the Pharisees argued that Yahweh had given Moses an oral Torah as well as a written one, and that this had been handed down from teachers to students and was now the special inheritance of the Pharisees.

The oral Torah of the Pharisees enabled the flexible application of religious law to daily life. It also supported belief in a life after death, a day of judgment, and the damnation or reward of individual souls. The Pharisees even actively sought out converts and looked forward to the imminent arrival of the Messiah. In all these respects they differed significantly from the Sadducees, who interpreted the Torah more strictly, considered Judaism closed to anyone who had not been born a Jew, and who had a vested interest in maintaining the political status quo.

Even more radical than the Pharisees was a faction known as the Essenes, a separatist group that hoped for spiritual deliverance through repentance and self-denial. Although some scholars see Essene influence behind the career of Jesus, his Jewish contemporaries probably saw him as some sort of Pharisee: a similar emphasis on the ethical requirements of the law, rather than its literal interpretation, is reflected in many of his teachings. Jesus's apparent belief in the imminent coming of "the kingdom of God" also fits within a Pharisaic framework, as does his willingness to reach out to people beyond the Jewish community. But he seems to have carried these principles considerably further than did the Pharisees.

For most Jews at this time, Judaism consisted of going up to the Temple on holy days; paying the annual Temple tax; reciting the morning and evening prayers; and observing fundamental laws, such as circumcision (for men), ritual purity (especially for women), and prohibitions on the consumption of certain foods. Jesus deemphasized such observances, and it may have seemed that he wished to abolish them. But what made him most controversial was his followers' claim that he was the promised Messiah.

Such claims grew more assertive after Jesus's death, yet they never persuaded more than a small minority of Jews. But when Jesus's followers began to preach to non-Jewish audiences, they found many willing listeners. So they began to represent Jesus in terms that made sense to Greek-speaking communities. Jesus, his followers now proclaimed, was not merely a savior for the Jews. He was the "anointed one" (in Greek, *Christos*), the divine representative of God who had suffered and died for the sins of all humanity. He had now ascended into heaven, and he would return to judge all the world's inhabitants at the end of time.

Christianity in the Hellenistic World

The key figure to develop this new understanding of Jesus's divinity was his younger contemporary, Paul of Tarsus (c. 10–c. 67 C.E.). Named Saul when he was born in the Roman province of Cilicia (now south-central Turkey), he was the son of a Pharisee. The Acts of the Apostles, a major source for Saul's early life, says that he was dedicated to stamping out the cult of the crucified Jesus. But at some point in his mid-twenties—a few years after Jesus's death—he underwent a dramatic conversion, changed his name to Paul, and devoted his life to spreading the new faith to Greek-speaking, mainly non-Jewish communities.

Unlike Peter and his other early followers, Paul had never met Jesus. Instead, he claimed to have received a direct revelation of his teachings. This led to a number of major disputes. For example, the disciple Peter and his companions believed that followers of Jesus had to be Jews. Paul declared that Jewish religious law was now irrelevant; Jesus had made a new covenant possible between God and humanity, and the old covenant between God and the Jews no longer applied. This position was also vehemently opposed by the Jewish Christians of Jerusalem, a group led by Jesus's brother, James. But after a series of difficult debates that took place around 49 C.E., Paul's position triumphed. Although some early Christians would continue to obey Jewish law, most of the converts who swelled the movement were not Jews. Paul began to call this new community of believers an *ekklesia*, the Greek word for a legislative assembly (see Chapter 3). The Latinized form of this word is translated as "church."

These early converts were attracted to Christianity for a variety of reasons. Some were Hellenized Jews like Paul himself, who had already begun to adapt their lifestyles and beliefs through contact with other cultures. Christianity also appealed to groups of non-Jews who admired the Jews for their loyalty to ancestral tradition and their high ethical standards. Christianity was even attractive to those who saw Jesus as living by Stoic principles (Chapter 4) or as the embodiment of Ahura-Mazda, the good god of Zoroastrianism (Chapter 2). Others were already devotees of mystery religions, like the very old cult of the Egyptian goddess Isis (Chapter 1) or the newer worship of the warrior-god Mithras, popular among Rome's professional soldiers. Both of these religions revolved around stories of sacrifice, death, and regeneration that prepared their adherents to embrace the worship of Jesus. At the same time, there were significant differences between Christianity and these other religions. Most mystery cults stressed the rebirth of the individual through spiritual transformation, but Christianity emphasized the importance of community.

Women were especially prominent in these churches, not only as patrons and benefactors (a role Roman women often played in religious cults) but also as officeholders. This high status was unusual: in other ancient religions, women could be priests only in cults open solely to women; they never took precedence over men and many cults denied them access entirely. The fact that Christianity drew its adherents from a broad range of social classes also distinguished it from other cults. In time, these unusual features were distorted by Christianity's detractors, who alleged that Christians were political insurgents like the Jesus they worshiped.

As both Christianity and Judaism redefined themselves, they grew further apart. Judaism was adapting to the Romans' destruction of the Temple and the mass exile of Jews from Jerusalem. By and large, the scholars who reshaped Jewish doctrine during these difficult years ignored Christianity. Christians, however, could not ignore Judaism. Their religion rested on the belief that Jesus was the savior promised by God to Israel in the Hebrew Bible.

For Christians, the heroes of Jewish scripture prefigured Jesus, while the major events of Hebrew history could be read, allegorically, as Christian paradigms. Christ was the new Adam, reversing man's original sin; wood from the fateful Tree in Eden became the wood of the Cross on which Jesus died. Christ, like Abel, had been slain at the hands of a brother. Christ was the new Noah, saving creation from its sins. Christ was prefigured in Isaac, Joseph, and Moses. According to Christians, all the words of the Hebrew prophets pointed to Jesus, as did the Psalms and the Proverbs.

In short, Christian theologians argued that the Christian church is the true Israel and that when the Jews rejected Jesus, God rejected the Jews. The Hebrew Bible was henceforth the Old Testament, vital to understanding Christianity but superseded by the New Testament. At the end of time, the Jews would see their

Analyzing Primary Sources

The Prosecution of a Roman Citizen

The Acts of the Apostles *was written by the same author as Luke's Gospel and was intended as a continuation of that book. It recounts the adventures and ministry of Jesus's original disciples and also follows the career of Paul, a Hellenized Jew who became a missionary to Gentiles throughout the Roman world. It offers fascinating glimpses into the workings of the Roman legal system because Paul, depicted here as a Roman citizen, would have had special rights under Roman law (as Jesus had not). In this passage, Paul has been accused of treason against the emperor by a group of Pharisees and has been sent to Felix, the governor of Judea. These events took place between 57 and 59 C.E.*

So the soldiers, according to their instructions, took Paul and brought him by night to [the city of] Antipatris. The next day, they let the horsemen go on with him, while they returned to the barracks. When they came to Caesarea and delivered the letter to the governor, they presented Paul also before him. On reading the letter, he asked what province he belonged to, and when he learned that he was from Cilicia he said, "I will give you a hearing when your accusers arrive." Then he ordered that he be kept under guard in Herod's headquarters.

Five days later, the high priest Ananias came down with some elders and an attorney, a certain Tertullus, and they reported their case against Paul to the governor. When Paul had been summoned, Tertullus began to accuse him, saying: "Your Excellency, because of you we have long enjoyed peace, and reforms have been made for this people because of your foresight. We welcome this in every way and everywhere with utmost gratitude. But, to detain you no further, I beg you to hear us briefly with your customary graciousness. We have, in fact, found this man a pestilent fellow, an agitator among all the Jews throughout the world, and a ringleader of the sect of the Nazarenes. He even tried to profane the temple, and so we seized him.

By examining him yourself you will be able to learn from him concerning everything of which we accuse him." The Jews also joined in the charge by asserting that all this was true.

When the governor motioned to him to speak, Paul replied: "I cheerfully make my defense, knowing that for many years you have been a judge over this nation. As you can find out, it is not more than twelve days since I went up to worship in Jerusalem. They did not find me disputing with anyone in the temple or stirring up a crowd either in synagogues or throughout the city. Neither can they prove to you the charge that they now bring against me. But this I admit to you, that according to the Way, which they call a sect, I worship the God of our ancestors, believing everything laid down according to the law or written in the prophets. I have hope in God—a hope that they themselves also accept—that there will be a resurrection of both the righteous and the unrighteous. Therefore I do my best always to have a clear conscience toward God and all people. . . ."

But Felix, who was rather well informed about the Way, adjourned the hearing with the comment, "When Lysias the tribune comes down, I will decide your case." Then he ordered the centurion to keep him in custody, but to let him have some liberty and not to prevent any of his friends from taking care of his needs.

When some days later Felix came with his wife Drusilla, who was Jewish, he sent for Paul and heard him speak concerning faith in Christ Jesus. And as he discussed justice and self-control and future judgment, Felix was alarmed and said, "Go away for the present; when I have an opportunity I will summon you." At the same time he hoped that money would be given him by Paul. So he sent for him often and conversed with him. But when two years had elapsed, Felix was succeeded by Porcius Festus; and desiring to do the Jews a favor, Felix left Paul in prison.

Source: Acts of the Apostles 23:31–24:27, in *The New Oxford Annotated Bible*, New Revised Standard Version, ed. Bruce M. Metzger and Roland E. Murphy (New York: 1994).

Questions for Analysis

1. Based on this account, what legal procedures are in place for dealing with any Roman citizen accused of a crime?

2. What seems to be the relationship between the Jewish elite of Judea and the Roman governor? What is the role of their spokesman, Tertullus?

3. What is the nature of the accusation against Paul, and how does he defend himself?

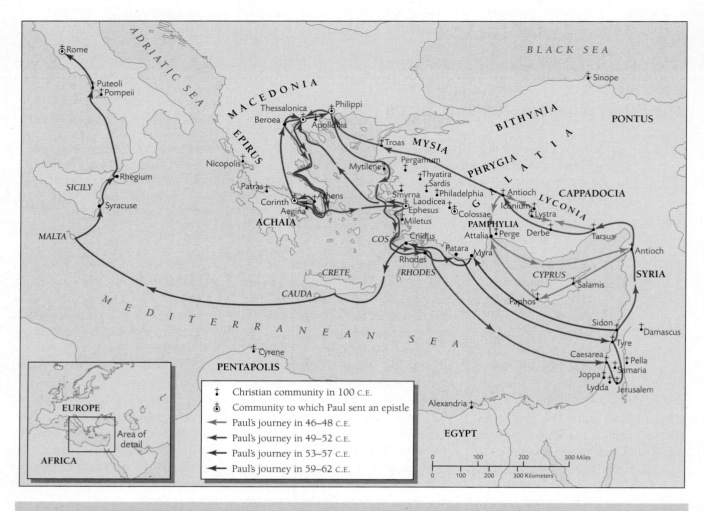

PAUL'S MISSIONARY JOURNEYS. Quite apart from its religious importance, Paul's career offers fascinating glimpses into the life of a Hellenized Roman citizen from one of the empire's eastern provinces. ▪ *What were the main phases of Paul's travels in the eastern Mediterranean?* ▪ *How were his itineraries shaped by geography and by various modes of transport?* ▪ *What conclusions about his mission can you draw from the extent of his travels and his major destinations?*

error and convert. From a Christian perspective, the Jews' own impiety had caused their exile from the Holy Land and would continue to bring suffering down on their descendants.

Christianity and the Roman State

Unlike Christianity, though, Judaism remained a legally recognized religion and many Jews were further protected by their Roman citizenship. Indeed, the Acts of the Apostles represents Paul as a Roman citizen who could not be put to death without trial (as the noncitizen Jesus had been) when brought up on charges of treason. Instead, Acts follows Paul's progress through the Roman judicial system, until he is finally brought to

trial at Rome and executed (by beheading) under Nero. Even after their rebellion, the Jews of the diaspora were allowed to maintain the special status they had always had under Roman rule.

Christianity, by contrast, was an upstart religion and raised suspicions on many levels. It encouraged women and slaves to hold office; it revolved around the worship of a criminal condemned by the Roman state; its secret meetings could be breeding grounds for rebellion. Nevertheless, the official attitude toward Christians was largely one of indifference. There were not enough of them to matter, and few of them had any political power. During the first and second centuries, therefore, Christians were tolerated by Roman officials, except when local magistrates chose to make an example of someone who flouted authority.

A FRESCO FROM THE CATACOMBS OF ROME. This image shows a catechumen (Greek for "instructed one") being baptized by the Holy Spirit in the form of an eagle. It is one of many paintings to be found in the ancient catacombs around Rome: subterranean burial and meeting places where Christians also hid during times of persecution. ■ *Why would such images have been important?*

THE CHALLENGE OF IMPERIAL EXPANSION

The emergence of Christianity coincided with the Roman Empire's most dramatic period of growth and a variety of challenges. For a long time, Rome's administrators clung to methods of governance put in place under Augustus, methods based on a single centralized authority. In reality, however, Rome's empire was no longer centered on Rome, or on Italy. It embraced ethnicities, cultures, economies, and political systems of vastly different kinds. More and more people could claim to be Roman citizens, and more and more people wanted a share of Rome's power. This placed enormous stress on the imperial administration. The fact that the empire had few defensible borders was another problem. Hadrian had attempted to establish one after 122, by building a wall between Roman settlements in southern Britannia and the badlands of northern tribes (see Chapter 5); but this act was more symbolic than effective.

For much of the second century, such stresses had been masked by the peaceful transfer of power among the so-called Five Good Emperors: Nerva, Trajan, Hadrian, Antoninus Pius, and Marcus Aurelius. This was partly accidental. None of these first four rulers had a surviving male heir, and so a custom developed whereby each adopted a young man of a good family and trained his successor in the craft of government. This sensible practice changed with the death of Marcus Aurelius in 180 C.E.

Although he was the closest Roman equivalent to Plato's ideal of the philosopher-king, Marcus was not wise enough to recognize that his own son, Commodus, lacked the capacity to rule. After his father's death, Commodus alienated the army by withdrawing from costly wars along the Danube. This move was also unpopular with the Senate, as were Commodus's violent tendencies and his scorn for the traditional norms of aristocratic conduct, including an alleged appearance as a gladiator in the Colosseum. In 192, a conspiracy was hatched inside his own palace, where he was strangled to death by his wrestling coach.

The Empire of the Severan Dynasty

Because Commodus had no obvious successor, the armies stationed in various provinces of the empire raised their own candidates. Civil war ensued, as it had during the crises of the late republic and again in 68 C.E., when three men had struggled for imperial power. In this case, there were five major contenders. The eventual victor was a North African general called Septimius Severus (r. 193–211 C.E.).

Under Severus (*SEH-ver-uhs*) and his successors, the administration of Rome's empire changed to a greater extent than it had since the time of Augustus. In many respects, changes were long overdue. Even the "Five Good Emperors" had been somewhat insulated from the realities of colonial rule. But Severus had been born and raised in Leptis Magna (in present-day Libya) and identified strongly with his father's Punic ancestors. Unlike Trajan and Hadrian, who had also grown up in the provinces, Severus did not regard Rome as the center of the universe.

Severus represents the degree to which the Roman Empire had succeeded in making the world Roman—succeeded so well that Rome itself was becoming practically irrelevant. One could be as much a Roman in Britannia or Africa as in central Italy. Severus's second wife, Julia Domna, exemplifies this trend in a different way. Descended from the Aramaic aristocracy who ruled the Roman client kingdom of Emesa (Syria), her father was the high priest of its sun-god, Ba'al. She was highly educated and proved an

The Development of an Imperial Policy toward Christians

It was not until the third century that the Roman imperial government began to initiate full-scale investigations into the activities of Christians. Earlier, the official position had been akin to a policy of "don't ask, don't tell." Local administrators handled only occasional cases, and they were often unsure as to whether the behavior of Christians was illegal or criminal. The following letter was sent to the emperor Trajan by Gaius Plinius Caecilius Secundus (Pliny the Younger), the governor of Bithynia-Pontus (Asia Minor), around 112 C.E. Pliny was anxious to follow proper procedures in dealing with the new sect and wanted advice about this. His letter indicates what Romans did and didn't know about early Christian beliefs and practices.

From Pliny to Trajan

It is my regular custom, my lord, to refer to you all questions which cause me doubt, for who can better guide my hesitant steps or instruct my ignorance? I have never attended hearings concerning Christians, so I am unaware what is usually punished or investigated, and to what extent. . . . In the meantime, this is the procedure I have followed in the cases of those brought before me as Christians. I asked them whether they were Christians.

If they admitted it, I asked them a second and a third time, threatening them with execution. Those who remained obdurate I ordered to be executed, for I was in no doubt . . . that their obstinacy and inflexible stubbornness should at any rate be punished. Others similarly lunatic were Roman citizens, so I registered them to be sent back to Rome.

Later in the course of the hearings, as usually happens, the charge rippled outwards, and more examples appeared.

An anonymous document was published containing the names of many. Those who denied that they were or had been Christians and called upon the gods after me, and with incense and wine made obeisance to your statue . . . and who moreover cursed Christ . . . I ordered to be acquitted.

Others, who were named by an informer, stated that they were Christians and then denied it. They said that they had been, but had abandoned their

effective governor during her husband's almost perpetual absence from Rome.

Severus largely ignored the politics of the Senate. He preferred to rule through the army, which he reorganized and expanded. Two of his reforms had long-term consequences. The first was a drastic raise in army pay, probably as much as 100 percent, which had the effect of securing the soldiers' absolute loyalty and reducing their need to augment their wages through plunder. The other was a relaxation of the long-standing rule forbidding soldiers to marry while in service. This dispensation encouraged men to put down roots in local communities, but it also made them reluctant to move when their legion was called up. On the one hand, this domesticated the army (hitherto a highly mobile fighting machine) and may have made it less effective. On the other, it gave the army a stake in the

peaceful governance of Rome's colonies and further contributed to the decentralization of power.

Severus spent most of his imperial career with his army. He died at Eboracum (York, England) in 211, after negotiations with tribes north of Hadrian's Wall. On his deathbed, he is reported to have said to his two sons, "Get along together, keep the soldiers rich, and don't bother about anyone else." His elder son, Caracalla, didn't heed the first of these injunctions for long: by the end of the year, he had assassinated his brother, Geta, and attempted to erase him from the historical record by declaring a *damnatio memoriae* ("a condemnation of memory") that banned the mention of Geta's name and defaced his image on public monuments. The second of his father's orders he obeyed in a certain sense, by extending the rights of Roman citizenship to everyone, including the entire army. His father's final piece of advice helped to shorten

allegiance some years previously. . . . They maintained, however, that all that their guilt or error involved was that they were accustomed to assemble at dawn on a fixed day, to sing a hymn antiphonally to Christ as God, and to bind themselves by an oath . . . to avoid acts of theft, brigandage, and adultery. . . . When these rites were completed, it was their custom to depart, and then reassemble again to take food, which was, however, common and harmless. They had ceased, they said, to do this following my edict, by which in accordance with your instructions I had outlawed the existence of secret brotherhoods. So I thought it all the more necessary to ascertain the truth from two maidservants [i.e., slaves], who were called deaconesses, even by employing torture. I found nothing other than a debased and boundless superstition. . . .

From Trajan to Pliny

You have followed the appropriate procedures, my Secundus. . . . No general rule can be laid down which would establish a definite routine. Christians are not to be sought out. If brought before you and found guilty, they must be punished, but in such a way that a person who denies that he is a Christian, and demonstrates this by his action . . . may obtain pardon for his repentance, even if his previous record is suspect. Documents published anonymously must play no role in any accusation, for they give the worst example, and are foreign to our age.

Source: Excerpted from *Pliny the Younger: The Complete Letters*, trans. P. G. Walsh (Oxford: 2006), pp. 278–79 (X.96–97).

Questions for Analysis

1. How does Pliny's treatment of Christians differ according to their social class? How does it differ from Felix's treatment of Paul (p. 143)?

2. Why would Trajan insist that anonymous accusations, like those discussed by Pliny, should not be used as evidence? Why is this "foreign to our age"?

3. What do you conclude from this exchange about the relationship between religion and politics under the Roman Empire?

Caracalla's reign significantly, since he alienated everyone who disagreed with him. He was assassinated in 217.

Caracalla's true successor was his mother's sister, Julia Maesa, who ruled through her adolescent grandson. This youth was known as Heliogabalus (or Elagabalus, r. 218–22) because of his devotion to the sun-god. But when Heliogabalus caused controversy by attempting to replace Jupiter, Rome's patron god, with a Latinized version of this eastern deity, Sol Invictus ("Invincible Sun"), his own grandmother engineered his assassination. Another of her grandsons, Alexander Severus (r. 222–35 C.E.), took his place. Alexander, in turn, was ruled by his mother Julia Mamea, the third in a succession of strong women behind the Severan dynasty, who even traveled with her son on military campaigns. This eventually proved fatal. The new prominence of the army made Rome's legions engines of political advancement, and many aspiring generals could harness this. In 235, in consequence, Alexander and his mother were murdered at Moguntiacum (Mainz) in Upper Germania, when the army of the region turned against them. Nearly fifty years of civil unrest ensued.

The Test of Rome's Strength

From 235 to 284 C.E. there were no fewer than twenty-six "barracks emperors": military commanders, each backed by a few loyal legions, who struggled with one another and an array of problems. This period is sometimes called the "Third-Century Crisis" and interpreted as a time when the Roman Empire was nearly destroyed. It is more accurately interpreted as a time when the consequences of Roman imperialism made themselves acutely felt. Those aspects of the empire that were strong survived. Those that had always been fragile were further strained.

For example, inflation caused by the devaluation of currency under Severus nearly drained Roman coinage of its value. Meanwhile, rival emperors levied exorbitant taxes on civilians in their provinces, while warfare destroyed crops and interrupted trade, causing food shortages. Because Rome itself was almost entirely dependent on Egyptian grain and other goods shipped in from the East, its inhabitants suffered accordingly. Poverty and famine even led to a new form of slavery in Italy, as free artisans, local businessmen, and small farmers were forced to labor on the estates of large landholders in exchange for protection and food.

In 251, a terrible plague, probably smallpox, swept through the empire's territories and recurred in some areas for almost two decades. A similar plague had ravaged Rome a century earlier, but its effects had been mitigated by sound governance. Now, with an estimated 5,000 people dying every day in the crowded city, people sought local scapegoats. Christians were among those targeted. Beginning in the short reign of Decius (r. 249–51), all Roman citizens were required to swear a public oath affirming their loyalty to Rome, which meant worshiping Rome's gods. Large numbers of Christians were implicated when this edict was put into effect and the enlightened policies of earlier emperors were abandoned.

The Reorganized Empire of Diocletian

As it happens, the most zealous persecutor of Christians was also responsible for reining in these destructive forces. Diocletian (*die-oh-KLEE-shan*, r. 284–305) was a cavalry officer from the Roman province of Dalmatia (modern Croatia).

THE EMPEROR SEPTIMIUS SEVERUS. This statue, carved during the emperor's lifetime, emphasizes his career as a military commander, showing him in the standard-issue uniform of a Roman legionnaire. How does this image of Severus compare to that of Augustus (see Chapter 5, page 125)? ■ *What do these differences suggest about the emperor's new role in the third century?*

THE TETRARCHY: DIOCLETIAN AND HIS COLLEAGUES. This grouping, carved from a valuable purple stone called porphyry, shows the two augusti, Diocletian and Maximian, embracing their younger caesars, Galerius and Constantius. ■ *Why do you think that these rulers are portrayed with identical facial features and military regalia?* ■ *What message does this convey?*

He could have been another "barracks emperor." Instead, he embraced the reality of Rome as a complex state that could not be governed from one place by one centralized bureaucracy. He appointed a fellow officer, Maximian, as co-emperor, putting him in charge of the western half of the empire and retaining the wealthier eastern half for himself. In 293, he delegated new authority to two junior emperors or "caesars," Galerius and Constantius. The result was a tetrarchy, a "rule of four," with each man governing a quarter of the empire, further subdivided into administrative units called *dioceses*.

This system not only responded to the challenges of imperial administration, but was also designed to secure a peaceful transfer of power, since the two young "caesars" were being groomed to take the place of the two senior "augusti." Diocletian apparently recognized that disputes over succession had been a fatal flaw of the Augustan system. Also unlike Augustus, who had cloaked the reality of his personal power in the trappings of the republic, Diocletian presented himself as an undisguised autocrat. His title was not *princeps* ("first man"), but *dominus* ("lord"). In fact, his style of imperial rule borrowed more from the Persian model than it did from the Roman. Gone were the days of simplicity and the scorn of kingly pomp: Diocletian wore a diadem and a purple gown of silk interwoven with gold. Under the Principate, the emperor's palace had been run like the household of any well-to-do Roman, only on a large scale. Diocletian, however, introduced Persian-style ceremonies in his lavish palace. Too much familiarity with their soldiers had bred contempt for the "barracks emperors." Diocletian was able to avoid this mistake.

Although Diocletian retained close personal control over the army, he took steps to separate military from civilian chains of command. To control the devastatingly high rates of inflation that were undermining the economy, Diocletian stabilized the currency and reformed the tax system. He even moved the administrative center of the empire from Italy to Nicomedia in the Roman province of Bithynia (modern Turkey). Rome remained the symbolic capital of the empire, not least because the Senate continued to meet there. But Diocletian had little need for the Senate's advice. The real power lay elsewhere.

THE CONVERSION OF CHRISTIANITY

By the beginning of the fourth century, the number of Christians living within the jurisdiction of Rome was statistically insignificant: probably no more than 5 percent of the total population in the West and possibly 10 percent of the Greek-speaking East. Still, one of Diocletian's methods for promoting unity was to take a proactive stance against any group perceived as subversive. Those who could not show proof of their loyalty to Rome's gods were stripped of their rights as citizens. Christians who had been serving in the army or in government offices were dismissed. So were Manicheans, followers of the Persian prophet Mani (c. 216–276), whose teachings paralleled Zoroastrianism by positing an eternal struggle between the forces of good and evil. Indeed, Christianity and Manichaeism must have seemed very similar, and both were implicated in a full-scale purge of religious dissidents in 303. This was the Great Persecution, a time when many became martyrs—a Greek word meaning "witnesses"—to their faith.

Christianity and Neoplatonism

Ironically, the very crises that prompted Diocletian's Great Persecution were contributing to a growing interest in Christianity. Its message of social justice and equality was attractive to those suffering from hardship. It also appealed to followers of a new and influential philosophy called Neoplatonism ("New Platonism"), which drew upon the more mystical aspects of Plato's thought. Its founder was Plotinus (204–270 c.e.), a Hellenistic philosopher from Egypt who had many followers among the Roman upper classes.

Plotinus taught that everything has its source in a single supreme being. The material world is part of this creation, but it is merely the residue of divinity. Human beings are composed of matter (bodies) and emanations of the divine (souls). This means that the individual soul, originally a part of God, is separated from its divine source. The highest goal of life is therefore to attain spiritual reunion with the divine through acts of self-denial that will liberate the soul from its earthly bondage. Asceticism (from the Greek word meaning "exercise" or "training") was therefore a major focus, because the body could be tamed by fasting and other forms of self-denial and thus made a more fitting vessel for the soul.

Neoplatonism became so popular in Rome that it almost supplanted Stoicism. (Although the two philosophies shared some fundamental characteristics, Stoicism did not hold out the hope of union with the divine.) Neoplatonism also struck a blow at traditional Roman worship of ancestors and the devotion to the empire's gods. It was thus a natural ally of Christianity, and many important Christian theologians would be influenced by it, while many educated Romans found their way to Christianity because of it. This was not, however, the path by which Christianity's first imperial convert reached the new faith.

Constantine's Vision

In 305, Diocletian built a palace near his hometown of Split, on the Adriatic coast, and retired there—the first time a Roman ruler had voluntarily removed himself from power since Sulla had resigned his dictatorship, nearly four centuries earlier (see Chapter 5). Diocletian obliged Maximian to retire at the same time, and the two caesars Galerius and Constantius moved up the ladder of succession, becoming augusti of the East and West, respectively. But the transfer of power was not as orderly as Diocletian had intended. One of the candidates to fill the vacant post of caesar was Constantius's son, Constantine, who was being trained at Galerius's court. But he was passed over, and Galerius pursued his own imperial agenda. So Constantine left the court at Nicomedia and joined his father in Gaul. From there, father and son went to Britannia and campaigned on the northern borders until 306, when Constantius died and named Constantine as his successor. This left Constantine in control of a large army: the legions of Gaul and the Rhineland, as well as Britannia.

Meanwhile, war had broken out among several other claimants to imperial power. Constantine remained aloof from this struggle, waged mostly in Italy, and concentrated on securing his quarter of the empire. Beginning around 310, he also began to promote himself as a favored devotee of the sun-god Sol Invictus, whose cult had been revived by the emperor Aurelian (r. 270–75). This was a smart move. Increasingly, the "Invincible Sun" was associated not only with the Roman gods of light and war, Apollo and Mars, but also with Mithras, whose cult was popular with soldiers. It was increasingly popular in Rome as well, where the feast long dedicated to the sky-god Saturn, the Saturnalia, was now being celebrated as the rebirth of the sun after the winter solstice, on December 25.

From the worship of Sol Invictus to the worship of Christ was, for Constantine, a small step (see **Interpreting Visual Evidence** on page 151). In 312, Constantine decided to march on Italy, which was now in the hands of a general called Maxentius, who had declared himself emperor and was trying to build up a coalition whose supporters included the Christian community of Rome. It may have been this that inspired Constantine to emblazon Christian symbols on his banners and shields the night before a battle north of Rome, at the Milvian Bridge over the Tiber. According to later legend, Constantine had seen a vision of two intertwined Greek letters inscribed on the sky, the first two letters in the name of Christ, and was told that "In this sign, you will conquer." He did.

In gratitude for his victory, Constantine showered benefits on the Christian clergy of Rome and patronized the construction of churches throughout the empire. He also forced Licinius, the augustus of the East, to join him in promoting religious tolerance when they met at Milan in 313. This Edict of Milan guaranteed freedom of worship to all Rome's citizens, Christian and non-Christian. But it was apparent that Christianity was the favored faith and thus the pathway for anyone with political ambitions. Almost overnight, then, Christians ceased to be members of an illegal and despised cult and became affiliates of a prestigious and profitable religion. The entire basis of Christianity's appeal had changed.

From Illegal Sect to Imperial Institution

Early Christianity had grown organically; it had not been designed as a religious system. It had no absolute teachings, and not all Christian communities had access to the same scriptures. Some churches had a few of Paul's letters; others had none. Some had bishops, priests, and deacons; others had only a handful of believers. Some counted women as their leaders; others disapproved of women in authority. Some had come under the influence of Neoplatonism or Manichaeism; others considered these to be perversions.

In every respect, then, the Christianity that emerged after Constantine's conversion had to reinvent itself. Doctrines formulated to suit the needs of small, scattered communities had to be reconciled. Members of this new institutional Church needed to agree on a shared set of beliefs. They needed a chain of command. All of these fundamentals had to be hammered out in a painful process that never quite managed to forge a common understanding, because the different varieties of Christianity had been too separate for too long: products of the same diversity that made the Roman Empire hard to govern.

The Hierarchy of the Church

When it came to organization, Rome's administration provided practical models. Because the empire's basic unit of governance was the city, the city became the basic unit of ecclesiastical administration. Each major city now had a bishop (from the Greek for "overseer") who also oversaw the rural areas of his diocese (a term borrowed from Diocletian). Bishops of the oldest and most prestigious Christian communities were called *patriarchs*, and their cities also jockeyed for preeminence. The main contenders were Rome, Alexandria, and Constantinople, a new city founded by Constantine (as will be discussed later).

Which of these Roman cities should be the capital of the Roman Church? Rome had long been venerated as the place where both Peter and Paul were martyred.

The Power of the Invincible Sun

Roman emperors often linked their power with those of Rome's traditional gods, and they were also worshiped as gods in their own right. Look carefully at the following images and consider the visual language of power that came to be associated with Sol Invictus, "the Invincible Sun," and eventually with Jesus Christ.

Questions for Analysis

1. How did Constantine invoke the iconography of Sol Invictus (image A)? What messages does this image convey?

2. How might Constantine's use of this imagery—after his initial conversion to Christianity—have been interpreted by Christians? How might it have been interpreted by followers of Rome's other religions? Do you think it was designed to be ambiguous?

3. Scholars dispute both the dating and the significance of this mosaic found beneath St. Peter's Basilica in Rome (image B). Is it likely that this is a representation of Jesus as Sol Invictus? If not, how would you explain the later association of this pagan deity with the Christian God?

A. This gold medallion was issued by Constantine in 313, a year after his victory at the Battle of the Milvian Bridge. The legend calls him "Invincible Constantine."

B. This mosaic comes from a necropolis (cemetery) found beneath St. Peter's Basilica in Rome. Its precise dating is in dispute, but it was made sometime between the mid-third and mid-fourth century.

And according to one of the Gospels (Matthew 16:18–19), Jesus had designated Peter as his representative on earth. Peter's successors, the subsequent bishops of Rome, thus claimed to exercise the same powers. Rome's bishop also enjoyed some political advantages over other patriarchs. Unlike the bishop of the new imperial capital at Constantinople, he could act with more freedom because he didn't have to deal directly with the emperor. But as far as eastern bishops were concerned, the patriarch of Constantinople should be the one to exercise control over the entire Church. This division—the product of cultural differences and contemporary politics—would continue to affect the development of Christian institutions. In time, it would lead to a very real division within Christianity that has never been resolved.

Orthodoxy, Heresy, and Imperial Authority

Christianity's new prominence raised the stakes of disputes over its basic teachings. While followers of Jesus had disagreed about such matters since the time of his death, these were of little political consequence. Under Constantine, however, doctrinal disputes had the potential to undermine the emperor. It was imperative, therefore, that these disputes be resolved.

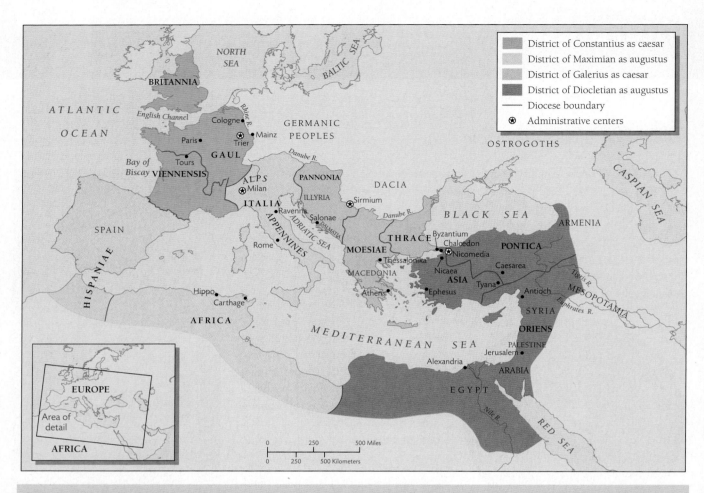

DIOCLETIAN'S DIVISION OF THE EMPIRE, C. 304 C.E. ▪ *What areas did each of the four divisions of the empire cover?* ▪ *What seems to be the strategy behind the location of the four major capitals, both within their respective quarters and in relation to one another?* ▪ *What is the status of Rome itself, according to this map?*

The most divisive issue concerned the nature of God. Jesus had taught his followers that he was the Son of God, and that after his death he would leave behind a comforting spirit that would also be an emanation of God. Accordingly, many Christians believed that God encompassed a Trinity of equal persons: Father, Son, and Holy Spirit. But other Christians, influenced by Neoplatonism, rejected the idea that Jesus could be equal with God. Instead, they maintained that Jesus was part of God's creation and shared in his divine essence, but was not equal to God. This belief was called Arianism, after the Christian teacher Arius who espoused it. (It should not be confused with Aryanism, a modern racial concept.) After protracted struggles, Arianism was condemned as a heresy, a word that comes from the Greek verb meaning "to choose for oneself." This became the Church's term for false beliefs punished with damnation. Yet many Christians continued to adhere to the Arian view.

This new emphasis on orthodoxy (Greek for "correct teaching") was another major consequence of Christianity's

conversion. So was the growing complexity of Christian theology, because Christian intellectuals had to demonstrate that Christianity was superior to Hellenistic philosophy. Just as there were many different schools of Greek and Roman thought, so there arose many different interpretations of Christian doctrine. Before Christianity became a legal religion, these differences could only be addressed informally, by small groups of bishops that had no power to enforce their decisions. In the fourth century, doctrinal disputes had real political consequences.

As a result, the Roman state became increasingly enmeshed in the governance of the Church. Constantine began this process in 325 C.E., when he summoned Christian representatives to the first ecumenical ("worldwide") meeting of the Christian community, the Council of Nicea, where Arianism was condemned and discrepancies over the canon of the Christian Bible were resolved. Constantine's successors carried this intervention much further. Gradually, they claimed to preside over Church councils as Christ's

CONSTANTINE'S CHRISTIAN SYMBOL. This fourth-century fresco shows the chi-rho symbol that Constantine claimed to have seen in the sky before his victory at the Milvian Bridge. (Chi and rho are the first two letters in the Greek word *Christos*.) Flanking this monogram are the first and last letters of the Greek alphabet, alpha and omega, which also refer to Jesus, "the beginning" and "the end."

representatives. Some even violently suppressed Christian groups who refused to accept imperial mandates. Essentially, these interventions were an extension of Augustan policies, which had made the emperor *pontifex maximus*, Rome's high priest. It began to look as though secular and spiritual authority would be combined in the person of the emperor. But this would change in later centuries, as we shall see.

New Attitudes toward Women and the Body

Women were conspicuously absent from the new hierarchy of the Christian Church. Even though they had long been deacons and may even have performed priestly duties, women were now firmly and completely excluded from any position of power.

This was perhaps the largest change brought about by Christianity's conversion. Jesus had included many women among his close followers, yet one of the gospels now rejected from the biblical canon was ascribed to Mary Magdalene. Paul had relied on women to organize and preside over churches and to finance his missionary journeys; he had declared in one letter (Galatians 3:28) that there should be no distinctions of gender, rank, or ethnicity among Christians. Women like Perpetua were prominent among the early martyrs and were often regarded as prophets. These strong female roles had always set Christianity apart from the traditional values of Roman society and had also been one of its main attractions.

What accounts for this drastic change? Three factors can be clearly identified. When Christianity was absorbed into the staunch patriarchy of Rome, it could no longer promote the authority of women. As the Church came to mirror the imperial administration, it replicated the structures of governance that had been the province of men since the founding of the republic. The Church now had the capacity to exclude or censor writings that represented women as the companions of Jesus and cofounders of the religion based on his teachings. These efforts were so successful that it was not until the very end of the nineteenth century that a gospel attributed to Mary Magdalene (among other writings) was known to exist.

The second factor leading to the marginalization of women was the growing identification of Christianity with Roman cults that emphasized masculinity, particularly the worship of Sol Invictus and the soldier-god Mithras. This was a deliberate strategy: it is easier to convert people to a new religion if that religion embraces elements of other religions. In common with many of the other religions we have studied, Christianity emphasized the heroic suffering and death of a male god and his eventual victory over death. Christ was increasingly identified with Sol Invictus, and his birthday came to be celebrated on the old Roman Saturnalia of December 25, which marked the passing of the winter solstice and the return of lengthening days.

The third factor contributing to women's exclusion from power was a growing emphasis on asceticism ("self-denial"), which changed attitudes toward the body. As we noted earlier, Neoplatonism taught that the goal of life was to liberate the soul from the tyranny of bodily desires, a teaching it shared with Stoicism. None of this was emphasized in the teachings of Christ. Quite the contrary: the body was celebrated as God's creation, and Christ himself had encouraged feasting, touching, bathing, and marriage. His followers insisted that he had been bodily resurrected, and that the bodies of all the faithful would be resurrected, too. Although early Christians had to be willing to sacrifice their lives, if need be, they were not required to renounce pleasures.

After Christianity became legal, however, there were few opportunities to "bear witness" to the faith through martyrdom. Instead, some Christians began to practice asceticism as an alternative path to sanctity. This meant renunciation of the flesh, especially sex and eating, activities both associated with women, who were in charge of any household's food supply and who were (obviously) sexual partners. A new spiritual movement, monasticism, also took hold, providing an alternative lifestyle for men who wanted to reject the world entirely; the word *monasticism* comes from the Greek word *monos*, "alone." Early monks lived as hermits and practiced extraordinary feats of self-abasement. Some tried to eke out a life in the desert; others penned themselves into small

SAINT SIMEON THE STYLITE. This gold plaque dating from the sixth century depicts the exertions of the ascetic saint who defied the devil (shown as a huge snake) by abusing his own body. Admirers wishing to speak to the saint could climb the ladder shown on the left. • *What do you make of the relationship between the precious medium of this image (gold) and the message it conveys?*

more lustful than men, the denigration of sexuality had a disproportionately negative effect on attitudes toward women.

Christians and Pagans

The urban focus of Christianity is reflected in the Latin word referring to a non-Christian: *paganus*, someone who lives in the countryside. It implies that only an uncivilized rustic would cling to the old Roman religion and thus spoil his chances of advancement. As Christians came to occupy positions of power within the empire, men with political ambitions were increasingly forced to convert—or at least conform—to Christian norms.

Constantine had retained both pagan and Christian officials in his court, but his successors were less inclined to tolerate competing faiths. An interesting exception was Julian "the Apostate" (r. 360–63), Constantine's nephew, who abandoned Christianity and attempted to revive traditional Roman piety. But when Julian was killed in a battle with the Persians, his pro-pagan edicts were allowed to lapse. By 391, the emperor Theodosius (r. 379–95 c.e.) had prohibited pagan worship of any sort within the empire. In just three generations, Christianity had gone from being a persecuted faith to a persecuting religion. Theodosius even removed the sacred altar of the goddess Victory from the Senate chamber in Rome, prompting pagan loyalists to prophesy the end of the empire. Fifteen years later, Rome fell to a barbarian army.

SHIFTING CENTERS AND MOVING FRONTIERS

In 324, Constantine broke ground for the capital city he named after himself. It was built on the site of a settlement called Byzantium, chosen for its strategic location at the mouth of the Black Sea and at the crossroads between Europe and Asia: the Hellespont (literally "the bridge to Greece"). This site gave Constantinople commanding advantages as a center for communications and trade. It also made the city readily defensible, surrounded on three sides by water and protected on land by walls. It would remain the political and economic center of the Roman Empire until 1453, when the city was conquered by the Ottoman Turks (see Chapter 11).

East or West?

The founding of Constantinople epitomizes the shift in Rome's center of gravity from Italy and western Europe to the eastern

cages; still others hung heavy weights around their necks. A monk named Cyriacus would stand for hours on one leg, like a crane. Another, Simeon "the Stylite," lived on top of a high pillar for thirty-seven years, punishing his lice-infested flesh while crowds gathered below to marvel.

This extreme denial of the body was a departure from most previous Christian practices and from those of many ancient religions, which often celebrated sexuality as a delight as well as a necessity. Even Roman religion had a place for priestesses and female prophets. Moreover, marriage was so important that Romans had regarded citizens' bodies as being at the service of the state: men as soldiers and fathers, women as mothers and wives. Now, however, some elite Christians were asserting that their bodies belonged to God, and that to serve God fully meant not bearing children.

Virginity for both men and women was accordingly preached as the highest spiritual standard, with celibacy for those who had once been married valued almost as highly. Marriage remained acceptable for average people, the laity, but was often represented as a second-best option. Moreover, because Aristotle had posited that women were inherently

Mediterranean. It also signaled Constantine's intention to abandon the political precedents set by Diocletian. Instead, imperial succession became hereditary. Even more ominously, he divided the empire among his three sons. Civil war ensued, each son aligned with a different faction within the Church. In the meantime, the empire became more and more fragmented. The last ruler who could claim to govern a united Rome was the same Theodosius who outlawed its venerable religion. Then he, too, divided the empire between his sons.

As we have seen, there had always been linguistic and cultural differences between the Greek- and Latin-speaking regions under Roman rule. Now, however, these differences became heightened. The eastern empire was becoming more populous, more prosperous, and more central to imperial policy; the western provinces were becoming poorer and more peripheral. Many western cities now relied on transfers of funds from their eastern counterparts, and they suffered when these funds dried up, when trade or communication failed, or when Roman legions were transferred elsewhere. Rome itself, which had been demoted to provincial status under Diocletian, now lost even that nominal position: the Italian city of Ravenna on the Adriatic coast became the new capital of the region and a more convenient stopping place for those traveling from Constantinople to the administrative centers of Milan and Trier. Only two of Constantine's successors ever visited Rome itself, and none of them lived there.

Internal and External Pressures

The new center of the empire and the widening gap between the eastern and western provinces were not the only fault lines emerging in this period. Beneath the surface of imperial autocracy, the empire was slowly dissolving into its constituent parts. It was also coming under renewed pressure from its borders. Since the third century, the growing power of a new Persian dynasty, the Sassanids, had prompted a shift of Roman military weight to the eastern frontier, reducing the number of troops stationed elsewhere. During the fourth century, relations between assimilated Romans and their barbarian neighbors along the porous frontier of Germania were generally peaceful. But starting in the early fifth century, a new wave of settlers moved in.

From the Periphery to the Center

The tribes that lived along the empire's northern frontiers were barbarians in the pure sense of that term: they did not speak either of the empire's civilized languages and they did not live in cities. But they were sophisticated agriculturalists and metalworkers who had enjoyed trading relationships with the Roman world for centuries. Many had been settled within Roman provinces for generations. Legionnaires from the hinterlands of Germania were core components in Roman armies. In some frontier areas, entire tribes had become Roman *foederati*: allied troops in the service of the empire. Many of these tribes even adopted the form of Christianity preached by disciples of Arius. Although this made them heretics from the perspective of the institutional Church, it also tied them more closely to Roman civilization.

What altered this relatively peaceful coexistence? Our study of previous civilizations has prepared us to answer this question: the arrival of new peoples and the subsequent struggle for land and resources. During the mid-fourth century, a group of nomadic herdsmen known as the Huns began to migrate westward from central Asia, into the region north of the Black Sea. Around 370, their arrival forced a number of other groups, notably the Goths, to migrate south and west. The Goths had been clients of the Roman state for several centuries, but now they were refugees. The Romans permitted them to cross the Danube River and settle within the empire. In return for food and other supplies, they were to guard the region against other migrant groups. Local officials, however, failed to uphold their end of the bargain. Instead, they forced the starving Goths to sell themselves and their children into slavery in return for food. In 378, the Goths revolted and the Roman army sent to suppress them was defeated at the battle of Adrianople.

Peace was restored by accommodating the Goths' demands for goods and farmland and by enrolling them in the Roman army under their own military leaders. This provided an opening for Alaric, a young leader of the Goths. Taking advantage of the fact that the empire was divided, he targeted the wealthier eastern provinces and led his army into Greece, looting and capturing many ancient cities, including Athens. In a desperate attempt to halt these incursions, Alaric was offered a Roman military command and encouraged to move into Italy, meaning that the price of peace in the eastern empire was Rome itself.

Meanwhile, the Huns had arrived in the region corresponding to modern-day Hungary, forcing several other peoples westward toward the Rhine. On New Year's Eve in the year 406, a people known as the Vandals crossed the frozen Rhine and invaded Gaul. To repulse them, the imperial military commander in the West, Flavius Stilicho (whose own father had been a Vandal) made an alliance with Alaric and his Goths. But when Stilicho fell from imperial favor just a few months later, there was no one else who could restrain Alaric.

Analyzing Primary Sources

A Senator Defends the Traditional Religion of Rome

In 382, the Emperor Theodosius ordered the removal of the ancient altar dedicated to the goddess of Victory (Nike) from the Senate chamber in Rome as part of his efforts to make Christianity the dominant religion in the empire. This controversial move sparked heated debate and elicited strong protests from Rome's senatorial elites. The following statement of their case was made by Quintus Aurelius Symmachus (c. 345–402), who was at that time prefect of the city of Rome. It is principally addressed to the young Western emperor, Valentinian.

To what is it more suitable that we defend the institutions of our ancestors, and the rights and destiny of our country . . . than to the glory of these times, which is all the greater when you understand that you may not do anything contrary to the custom of your ancestors? We demand then the restoration of that condition of religious affairs which was so long advantageous to the state. . . . Who is so friendly with the barbarians as not to require an Altar of Victory? . . . But even if the avoidance of such an omen were not sufficient, it would at least have been seemly to abstain from injuring the ornaments of the Senate House. Allow us, we beseech you, as old men to leave to posterity what we received as boys. The love of custom is great. . . . Where shall we swear to obey your laws and commands? By what religious sanction shall the false mind be terrified, so as not to lie in bearing witness? All things are indeed filled with God, and no place is safe for the perjured, but to be urged in the very presence of religious forms has great power in producing a fear of sinning. That altar preserves the concord of all, that altar appeals to the good faith of each, and nothing gives more authority to our decrees than that the whole of our order issues every decree as it were under the sanction of an oath. . . .

Let us now suppose that Rome is present and addresses you in these words: "Excellent princes, fathers of your country, respect my years to which pious rites have brought me. Let me use the ancestral ceremonies, for I do not repent of them. Let me live after my own fashion, for I am free. This worship subdued the world to my laws, these sacred rites repelled Hannibal from the walls, and the Senones [Gauls] from the capital. Have I been reserved for this, that in my old age I should be blamed? I will consider what it is thought should be set in order, but tardy and discreditable is the reformation of old age." We ask, then, for peace for the gods of our fathers and of our country. It is just that all worship should be considered as one. We look on the same stars, the sky is common, the same world surrounds us. What difference does it make by what pains each seeks the truth? We cannot attain to so great a secret by one road; but this discussion is rather for persons at ease, we offer now prayers, not conflict.

Source: Excerpted from *A Select Library of the Nicene and Post-Nicene Fathers,* 2nd Series, Vol. X (New York: 1896), pp. 411–14.

Questions for Analysis

1. How does Symmachus's defense exemplify the traditional values of the Roman Republic?

2. How does Symmachus justify the coexistence of Christianity and Rome's state religion? How would a Christian refute his position?

3. Less than a decade after the altar's removal, Theodosius outlawed all religions but Christianity. Based on your reading of this letter, how would that edict have affected Romans like Symmachus?

Like Stilicho, Alaric seems to have wanted to win a permanent place for himself in the imperial hierarchy. But unlike Stilicho—and many other generals—he did not understand how to use military power as a means toward that end. His assault on Rome made him Rome's destroyer, not its conqueror. In 410, after a protracted period of siege, Alaric's army captured and sacked the city. Many of the Goths then moved on, eventually settling in southern Gaul and Hispania, where they established what came to be known as the Visigothic kingdom. Others, later labeled as the Ostrogoths, remained in Italy. The Vandals ultimately crossed the Strait of Gibraltar to settle in North Africa. Other tribes, including the Franks and the Burgundians, then followed the Vandals across the Rhine into Gaul and

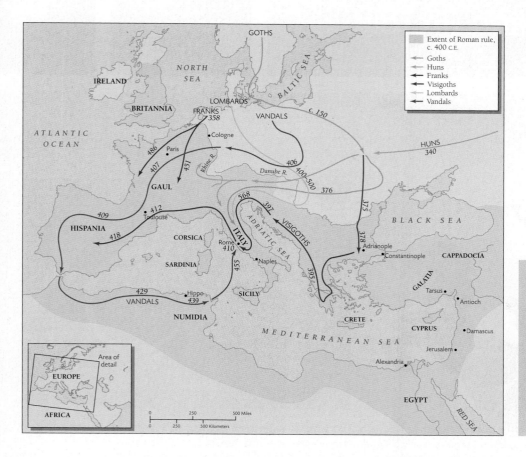

THE MIGRATIONS OF ROME'S
FRONTIER PEOPLES. ▪ *What
do the routes followed by these
different peoples suggest
about their destinations and
motives?* ▪ *Why did so many
converge on Rome, even though
the city was no longer the capital
even of the Western Roman
Empire?* ▪ *Why did the Romans
refer to them as "barbarians"?*

established kingdoms of their own. A generation later the Huns—whose migrations had set all of these gears in motion—themselves invaded Roman territory under the leadership of their warlord, Attila.

In Britannia, meanwhile, remaining legions were hastily withdrawn in 410, sent to embattled territories in Rome's older provinces. In the ensuing centuries, a mixed population of Romans and Celts eventually intermingled with invaders from northwestern Germania and Scandinavia: Angles, Saxons, and Jutes. These tribes' movements were so far-reaching that they dominated all but the westernmost and northern portions of the island within a few generations. Many Celts retreated to the regions where Celtic languages are still spoken in Britain today, including Wales and Scotland. The rest of Britain would become Angleland: England.

The last western Roman emperor was an ineffectual usurper known derisively as Romulus Augustulus ("Little Romulus Augustus"). In 476 he was deposed by Flavius Odovacer, a chieftain who headed a mixed band of barbarians, Huns, and disgruntled Romans. From the perspective of the East, this event was decisive: now Constantinople was not only "New Rome," it was the only viable capital. And the best way for its imperial agenda to be carried forward in the western provinces was through a strong barbarian ruler. Luckily, the emperor Zeno (r. 474–91) knew just the man: Theodoric, the son of a Gothic king, who had been sent to Constantinople as a hostage and raised in the civilized surroundings of the imperial court. After a decade of fierce fighting, Theodoric and his imperially equipped Gothic army managed to drive the Huns from Italy and establish a kingdom based in Ravenna, which he ruled (with imperial support) until his death in 526.

The Impact of the Fifth-Century Migrations

The migrations of the fifth century penetrated to Rome's core western provinces: Italy, Gaul, Hispania, North Africa. Yet the groups that moved through these territories were small, never more than war bands. Why couldn't long-established imperial cities defend themselves?

As the strongest legions were withdrawn from frontier western provinces, they were dispatched to protect richer eastern ones. Those that remained were integrated into local civilian populations, staffed by married men who grew their own food and lived with their families, making it difficult to move troops in an emergency. And even

Past and Present

Resisting Imperialism

Attempts at conquest are always met with resistance. In the Roman province of Britannia, a Celtic warrior queen named Boadicea led an armed uprising against the imperial army that is still celebrated as a proud example of British independence—as this modern statue in London indicates. A more peaceful uprising against American imperialism took place in Manila on the eve of President Barack Obama's first inauguration in 2008.

Watch related author videos on the Student Site
wwnorton.com/college/history/western-civilizationsBrief4

if the citizens of Rome's western provinces had been able to maintain a crack fighting force on the frontier, there would have been little reason for them to think that it was necessary. Their "barbarian" neighbors hadn't seemed threatening for generations. Many were so Romanized that differences between the groups are difficult to detect in surviving archaeological evidence.

In the eastern Roman Empire, by contrast, a thriving economy made it easier to equip and maintain a strong fighting force. Cities remained centers of commerce and industry, which meant that citizens possessed greater taxable wealth and could sustain the burdens of the imperial bureaucracy more easily. Moreover, potential invaders could be bought off or bribed to direct their attention elsewhere—as Alaric had been. For all these reasons, the eastern empire prospered during the fifth century, while the western empire floundered. After the fifth-century migrations, these differences were exacerbated. Ten years

after the Goths sacked Rome, the area was capable of producing only 15 percent of the revenues it had generated before. Similar reductions in revenues resulted from attacks on Gaul and Hispania. After 420 or so, as the newcomers began to set up their own kingdoms, these areas ceased to pay any taxes at all to imperial authorities. When the Vandals captured North Africa in 439, the richest of all Rome's western provinces was lost.

The consequences of these structural changes were far-reaching. In the year 400, the economy of the western Roman Empire was characterized by the mass production of low-cost, high-quality consumer goods that circulated in massive quantities. Although regional and local systems of exchange continued after 500, long-distance trade in bulk goods could be sustained only in the Mediterranean. As markets disappeared in northwestern provinces, skilled artisans either had to find other ways to make a living or had to emigrate. Standards of living gradually declined, and

THEODORIC THE OSTROGOTH. This coin shows the king in Roman dress but with the long hair characteristic of a barbarian nobleman. The inscription reads REX THEODERICVS PIVS PRINCIS—"King Theodoric, pious prince." ■ *How does this image compare to that of Constantine (see page 151)?*

so did the overall population. It is likely that the population of western Europe did not return to its fourth-century levels for a thousand years, until just before the Black Death (see Chapter 10).

Other aspects of Roman life in these regions changed, too, but almost imperceptibly. Roman bureaucracies often survived, although the proceeds from taxes now went into the purses of the new barbarian rulers or Christian bishops. Roman agricultural patterns continued in most areas, local Roman elites continued to dominate civic life, and Roman cities continued to dominate their surrounding regions. Nor did the invasions bring an end to Roman culture or to the influence of Roman values. As King Theodoric the Goth was fond of remarking: "An able Goth wishes to be like a Roman; but only a poor Roman would want to be like a Goth."

THE SHAPING OF A NEW WORLDVIEW

As the empire sustained attack from external forces and began to fragment along old fault lines, it seemed that a new age was beginning. Christ had promised to come again at the end of time, when all human souls would be judged. How, then, should Christians live in this new world and prepare for that imminent event? The men who forged answers to this question were contemporaries who knew

and influenced one another, though they did not always agree. They are now regarded as "fathers" of the Church: Jerome (c. 340–420), who came from the northeastern edge of Italy; Ambrose (c. 340–397), who grew up in Trier and was eventually named bishop of Milan; and Augustine (354–430), born and raised in North Africa.

Jerome: Translating the Christian Message

Jerome's signal contribution to the culture of the Roman West was his translation of the Bible from Hebrew and Greek into Latin. Known as the Vulgate or "common" version, it was not the first attempt to produce a Latin Bible—but it quickly became the standard, and remained so until the sixteenth century (see Chapter 13). Jerome was also an influential commentator on the Bible's interpretation, arguing that pagan learning could and should be adapted to Christian aims. The perennial problem, of course, was that one was always tempted to appreciate classical literature for its own sake, and not for the light it shed on Christian truths. Jerome himself never entirely succeeded in subordinating his love for classical authors, especially Cicero, to his love for God. Perhaps in an effort to compensate for this, Jerome became a rigorous ascetic and a fervent promoter of monasticism. He also held a narrow view of women's roles that exercised a strong influence on some later Christian teachers.

Ambrose and the Authority of the Church

Jerome was primarily a scholar. Ambrose, by contrast, was an aristocratic man of the world who helped to define the relationship between the sacred authority of the Church and the secular authority of worldly rulers. As patriarch of the imperial administrative capital at Milan, he fearlessly rebuked the pious emperor Theodosius. On matters of faith, he declared, "The emperor is within the Church, not above the Church."

Ambrose was also an admirer of Cicero—but because of Cicero's Stoicism, not his prose. Ambrose wrote an ethics handbook, *On the Duties of Ministers*, which drew heavily on Cicero's treatise *On Duties*, written nearly four centuries earlier for the senatorial elite of the Roman republic. Unlike Cicero, however, Ambrose argued that the goal of human conduct should be reverence for God, not social or political advancement. Even more fundamentally, Ambrose argued that God assists all Christians by sharing with them the power of divine grace, but extends more grace to some Christians than to others. This doctrine would be refined and amplified by his disciple, Augustine.

The Salvation of Saint Augustine

Apart from Jesus, Augustine is often considered the greatest of all Christianity's founders. He may be the most important Christian thinker of all time. His theology is essential to the doctrine of the medieval Church and thus to modern Roman Catholicism, and it also had a profound effect on Martin Luther and on the development of Protestant Christianities (see Chapter 13). Even today, many Christian philosophers describe themselves as neo-Augustinians.

Augustine's understanding of Christianity was the result of a long process of self-discovery, which he described in a remarkable book, the *Confessions*, a series of autobiographical reflections addressed to God. Augustine was not, as Jerome and Ambrose were, a confident Christian from the cradle. His father was not a Christian, and although his mother was, he scorned her influence and refused baptism. Full of ambition, he left North Africa for Italy as a young man, winning early fame as a teacher and charismatic orator. All the while, he gravitated from one philosophical system to another without finding intellectual or spiritual satisfaction. He regarded Christianity as a religion for fools, and only the appeal of Ambrose's teachings drove him to enquire further. After a spiritual epiphany described in his *Confessions*, Augustine decided to embrace Christianity. Yet his struggle to grasp and explain its paradoxes occupied him for the rest of his life. His skills as a preacher and commentator led to his rapid advancement in the Church hierarchy, and he returned to North Africa as the bishop of Hippo Regis in 395.

Although he led an extremely active life—when he died in 430, he was defending Hippo against the Vandals—Augustine still found time to write more than a hundred treatises analyzing the problems of Christian belief. All of these grapple with a basic question: if humanity is the creation of an omnipotent God whose nature is entirely good, why are human beings so profoundly sinful? Augustine adduced himself as a supreme example. In the *Confessions*, he remembers that he and a few other boys once stole some pears from a neighbor's garden, simply for the sake of doing something bad. He also recounted his many sexual adventures as a young man and recalled that he had prayed, "O God, give me chastity—but not yet!" In short, he argued that the human inclination toward evil is innate. But how, if we are the creatures of a good God?

Augustine traced the origin of evil back to the Garden of Eden, where God had given Adam and Eve, the first human couple, the freedom to follow his will or their own. He concluded that all the evils of the world are the result of this Original Sin: the human propensity to place our own desires ahead of God's. This fact alone would justify God's condemnation. But because God is merciful, he chose instead to save some human beings through the sacrifice of his son, Jesus.

Why only some? Because human beings are inherently sinful, Augustine reasoned, they cannot achieve salvation on their own; they need to be led to accept Jesus by an act of God's grace—hence the power of Augustine's own transformative experience, which led him to embrace Christianity *against his own will* but in accordance with God's. God alone makes this choice, and by granting grace to some and not to others he allows a portion of the human race to achieve salvation. If this seems unfair, Augustine would answer that strict fairness would condemn everyone to hell and that the basis for God's choice is a mystery far beyond the realm of human comprehension.

Defending the City of God

After the sack of Rome in 410, Augustine knew that some staunchly traditional Romans blamed Christianity for it. According to them, the attack on their city resulted from the removal of the altar of Victory from the Senate chamber. In response, Augustine wrote one of his most famous works, *The City of God*, a new interpretation of human history. He argued that mankind has always been divided into two opposing societies: those who live for the world and those who seek eternal life. The former belong to the City of Man, and their rewards are the riches, fame, and power they may win on earth, all tainted by sin. Only those who live in the City of God will be saved on Judgment Day.

CLASSICAL LEARNING AND THE CHRISTIAN LIFE

Jerome, Ambrose, and Augustine were members of the first generation to grow up in a world where Christianity was legal, even normal. For three centuries there had been no such thing as a Roman Christian: this was a contradiction in terms. Now, however, many Romans *were* Christians. How could these identities be reconciled? None of these influential teachers wanted to discard the heritage of the past. Since the time of Socrates, philosophy had been characterized by its capacity to absorb and blend many competing ideas. Christian intellectuals wanted to be regarded as philosophers, but they also wanted to replace the doctrines of pagan philosophy with the doctrine of Christ. To do this, they needed to make pagan learning applicable to a Christian way of life.

Preserving and Recycling the Classics

Reinterpreting classical culture for a Christian audience involved careful selection. Those pagan authors whose works were most immediately useful to Christians, like Cicero and Virgil, enjoyed continued celebrity. Those texts that had long educated students in the liberal arts were also preserved, alongside major classics of Latin poetry as well as histories that recorded the errors of Rome's pagan past. But texts that could not be readily adapted to Christian purposes were subjected to rigorous editing. One of the men who undertook this task was Anicius Manlius Severinus Boethius (*boh-EE-thee-uhs*, c. 480–524), an aristocrat attached to the court of Theodoric. His goal was to preserve the best aspects of ancient learning by compiling a series of handbooks and anthologies that packaged pagan texts in ways he deemed appropriate for Christian readers.

This is most evident in *The Consolation of Philosophy*, which Boethius wrote in prison after Theodoric condemned him to death for treason. (The justice of the charge is unclear.) In this treatise, he concludes that happiness is not found in earthly rewards such as riches or fame but in the "highest good," which is God. He comes to this realization through a series of imaginary conversations with "Lady Philosophy," the embodiment of wisdom. For the next millennium, Boethius's *Consolation* was one of the most read and imitated books in the West: the ultimate example of classical philosophy's absorption into the Christian worldview.

Monastic Education

The vital work of preserving selected classics was increasingly done by monks, whose way of life had undergone some significant changes. Leaders of the monastic movement recognized that few men were capable of ascetic feats, and some disapproved of them. Rather, they advocated a more moderate approach and emphasized the benefits of communal life.

In the Roman West, the most influential proponent of the monastic movement was a contemporary of Boethius, Benedict of Nursia (c. 480–c. 547), the son of a Roman aristocrat. Benedict founded a monastery at Monte Cassino, southeast of Rome, where he urged his followers to adopt "a simple rule for beginners." Benedict's *Rule* is notable for its brevity and practicality. It established a carefully defined cycle of daily prayers, lessons, and worship. Physical labor was encouraged—idleness, Benedict declared, was "an enemy of the soul"—but there was also time for private study and contemplation. In all such matters, Benedict left much to the discretion of the leader of the monastery. This man was the abbot, from the Syriac word *abba*, "father."

Cassiodorus and the Classical Canon

Benedict believed that monks must study the Bible in order to participate fully in a life of worship. And because many monks entered religious life as children, the monastery would need to provide schooling. Through this somewhat roundabout path, classical learning entered the monastic curriculum.

The man largely responsible for this was Flavius Magnus Aurelius Cassiodorus Senator (c. 490–c. 583), a younger contemporary of Benedict. Like Boethius, Cassiodorus (*cass-ee-oh-DOHR-uhs*) was attached to Theodoric's court

CASSIODORUS. This frontispiece from a Bible, produced in a monastery in Britain around the year 700, depicts Cassiodorus as a copyist and keeper of books. Monasteries were instrumental in changing the form of the book from the ancient scroll to the modern codex. Because their parchment pages were heavy, codices were customarily stored in cupboards, lying flat, as we see them here.

and was for many years the secretary in charge of the king's correspondence. He also wrote a *History of the Goths*, which depicted Theodoric's people as part of Rome's history. After Theodoric's death, Cassiodorus founded an important monastery where he composed his most influential work, the *Institutes*.

Cassiodorus believed that study of classical literature was an essential preliminary to a proper understanding of the Bible. The *Institutes* is essentially a syllabus, a list of readings arranged to begin with simpler, straightforward works before moving on to more difficult studies and finally to the demanding study of theology. Cassiodorus thereby defined a classical canon that formed the basis of Christian education in the Roman West.

In order to ensure that his monks had access to the necessary readings, Cassiodorus also encouraged the copying of books. Under his influence, monasteries thus became engines for the collection, preservation, and transmission of knowledge. It is worth noting that nearly all the Greek and Latin texts on which we rely for our study of western civilizations survive because they were copied in monasteries.

Monasteries also developed and disseminated an important new information technology: the codex. For millennia, the book had been a scroll, a clumsy format that made searching for a particular passage difficult and confined the reader to one passage at a time. The codex facilitates indexing (from the Latin word for "finger") because a reader can flip back and forth among various pages and keep a finger in one place while looking at another. Codices also store information more safely and efficiently, because they compress many hundreds of pages within protective bindings. They are less wasteful, too, because texts can be copied on both sides of a page. They even make finding a given book easier, since titles can be written on the codex's spine. It's arguable, in fact, that the invention of the codex was more revolutionary than the invention of printing a thousand years later. Unless you are scrolling through a digital version, your copy of *Western Civilizations* is a codex.

After You Read This Chapter

 Go to **INQUIZITIVE** to see what you've learned—and learn what you've missed—with personalized feedback along the way.

REVIEWING THE OBJECTIVES

- A number of historical factors shaped the way that Jesus's teachings were received. Describe the most important of these.
- The expansion of Rome and the strain on its central government posed significant challenges in the third century. How did Roman emperors respond?
- Christianity's acceptance as a legal religion changed it in profound ways. Why was this?
- In the fourth and fifth centuries, a new wave of migrations penetrated to the very heart of the empire. What made this possible?
- The differences between traditional Roman and Christian cultures were gradually reconciled through the efforts of Christian intellectuals. Why was this considered necessary?

CONCLUSION

Since the English historian Edward Gibbon published the first volume of *The Decline and Fall of the Roman Empire* in 1776, a year when Britain's own empire suffered a setback, more has been written about "the fall of Rome" than on the passing of any other civilization. Gibbon himself blamed Christianity, depicting it as a debilitating disease that sapped the empire's strength. Others have accused the barbarians whose movements put pressure on Rome's frontiers. But even in the time of Julius Caesar, Roman moralists had declared that Rome was in decline. Any self-respecting Roman republican would say that Rome fell when Augustus came to power.

More recent scholarship has argued that transformation is a more accurate model for understanding this period. No civilization is static and unchanging; civilizations, like human beings, are living organisms. Indeed, any evidence of Rome's decline can also be read as evidence of its adaptability. The imperial policies of Septimius Severus and Diocletian responded to the realities of Rome's size and diversity. The settlement of frontier peoples in Rome's western provinces gave rise to hybrid polities that found new uses for Roman buildings, political offices, and laws. Through Christianity, the Latin language as well as the administrative structures and culture of ancient Rome were preserved and extended. The flexibility of the Roman political system made this possible, because it was inclusive to a degree that no modern empire has ever matched.

Still, this transformation changed what it meant to be Roman, to the extent that historians now call this period "late antiquity" to distinguish it from the classical world that preceded it. By the seventh century, indeed, so much had changed that the contours of three distinctive civilizations can be discerned, each one exhibiting different aspects of Roman influence and crystallizing around different regions of the former empire. We will explore each of these civilizations in Chapter 7.

PEOPLE, IDEAS, AND EVENTS IN CONTEXT

- What were the main differences between **JESUS** and the Jewish leaders of his day?
- How did **PAUL OF TARSUS** reach out to the peoples of the Hellenistic world? How did his teachings influence the development of early Christianity?
- In what ways did **DIOCLETIAN**'s division of the empire and his institution of the **TETRARCHY** respond to longstanding problems?
- How and why was Christianity changed under **CONSTANTINE**? What effects did this have on attitudes toward women and their role in the church?
- How did the relocation of the imperial capital to **CONSTANTINOPLE** contribute to the growing divide within the Roman Empire? How did the mass migrations of frontier peoples then transform the Latin West?
- What were the key contributions of **JEROME**, **AMBROSE**, and **AUGUSTINE** to the development of a specifically Christian outlook by the end of the fourth century?
- How did **BOETHIUS**, **BENEDICT**, and **CASSIODORUS** reshape classical culture in the fifth century?

THINKING ABOUT CONNECTIONS

- In your opinion, which phenomenon had a more profound impact on Rome: the overextension of imperial power or the mass migration of peoples from Rome's frontier? Why?
- Few historians would now agree with the judgment of Edward Gibbon, who posited that Christianity destroyed the Roman Empire. But to what extent did Christianity alter the traditional values and infrastructure of the Roman state? Were these alterations inevitable?

Before You Read This Chapter

Rome's Three Heirs, 500–950

A round the year 600, the peoples of Britain were approached by missionaries from Rome. These Latin-speaking evangelists had to find a way to translate the central ideas of their faith into languages and concepts that made sense in a new context. So they looked for ways to meld Roman practices with indigenous ones, building churches on sacred sites and turning the worship of pagan gods into Christian rituals. An account of these negotiations comes down to us in a remarkable book written several generations later. In *The History of the English Church and People*, a monk named Bede (c. 672–735) described how Celtic and Anglo-Saxon tribes were uneasily united under the Roman Church. But he also shows how Roman Christian ideals were changed in the process.

This is just one example of the way that Rome's legacy was transmitted and transformed during the era known as the Middle Ages. This term is a problematic one because it is a later invention: in the seventeenth century, intellectuals began to argue that an intermediate, "medieval period" (*medium ævum*) separated their own "modern age" from the empire of ancient Rome, which many European states were trying to emulate. But it is arguable that the period between 500 and 1500 was the beginning of that "modern age." It was during this millennium that the foundations of modern states were laid and when the relationships among Judaism, Christianity, and Islam were first negotiated. In fact, three new civilizations became heirs of the Western civilizations formerly encompassed by Rome: the New Rome of Byzantium, the new religious empire of Islam, and the western European territories loyal to the Roman Church. Each of these interlocking civilizations preserved and modified different aspects of their shared Roman inheritance. Our world is still being shaped by the interactions among them.

JUSTINIAN'S IMPERIAL AMBITIONS

As we observed in Chapter 6, the eastern and western territories of Rome's empire were becoming divided along linguistic, cultural, and economic lines. By the end of the fourth century, this division also started to become political, as the imperial capital at Constantinople exercised less and less influence over the emerging barbarian kingdoms of western Europe. And when a new emperor attempted to reverse that trend and reunify the disparate parts of the empire, his efforts actually made that division permanent.

Justinian's Attempted Reconquest

Justinian (r. 527–65) was the most ambitious emperor since Constantine, and his drive for reunification was at least partly driven by his own background. Although the territories that he ruled were largely Greek-speaking, Justinian himself came from the Latin-speaking province of Dardania (now Serbia) and was an outsider to the elite Hellenistic culture of his capital. He became even more of an outsider when he married a former entertainer, Theodora, who alienated the cultivated aristocrats of the court.

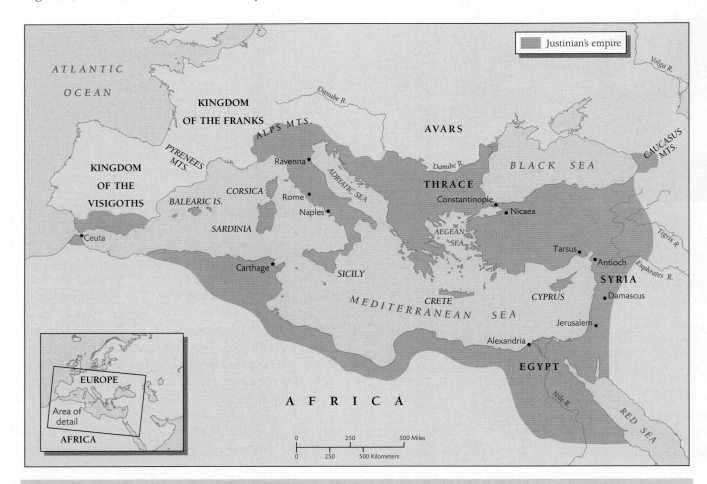

THE MEDITERRANEAN WORLD UNDER JUSTINIAN, 527–565. Compare this map with the one on page 152. Here, the green shading represents those regions controlled by Justinian. ▪ *What was the geographical extent of Justinian's empire?* ▪ *Which areas of the former Roman Empire did Justinian not attempt to reconquer?* ▪ *What may have been the strategy behind these campaigns?*

In 533, Justinian sent his general Belisarius to conquer the Vandal kingdom of northwest Africa, and his initial victory led to campaigns in Ostrogothic Italy and Visigothic Spain. But these early victories were illusory, because they drastically strained imperial resources and destroyed the very infrastructures of old Roman heartlands: roads, aqueducts. Justinian's need to levy soldiers led to oppressive taxes on vitally important regions like Egypt and Syria, which undermined support for his imperial project. These campaigns also distracted attention from dangers closer to Constantinople: the developing strength of the Persian Sassanids, which began to encroach on the eastern frontier.

The pressures of war were further exacerbated by the outbreak of a terrible plague pandemic in 541–42, now considered the first global catastrophe of this kind. Indeed, researchers in 2013 confirmed that it was caused by the same bacterium that spawned the terrible Black Death of the fourteenth century (see Chapter 10). It may have been just as deadly, affecting regions from central Asia to Scandinavia and reaching down into Africa and the Indian Ocean. It is estimated to have killed a large portion of the world's population at that time, some 25 million people; and it would recur in some places every generation or so for the next 200 years. Justinian himself was stricken with the disease, and though he recovered from it, this pandemic is still known as the Justinianic Plague.

Justinian's Impact on the West

Justinian's wars proved more devastating to Italy than the previous incursions of barbarian peoples had been. Around Rome, vital water supply lines were cut as the elaborate system of conduits and reservoirs were damaged and never repaired. Parts of the Italian countryside returned to marshland, and some areas would not be drained again until the twentieth century. In 568, a new people, the Lombards, took advantage of the situation and occupied the northern third of the peninsula. Thereafter, Italy would be divided between Lombard territories in the north and imperial territories in the southeast, with the city of Rome and its region precariously sandwiched between them. This tripartite division remained the essential political configuration of Italy until the nineteenth century. In fact, it still divides Italian politics to this day.

Imperial control over North Africa lasted only a few generations longer. Weakened by religious conflict and heavy taxation, this area fell to invading Muslims in the seventh century, along with Egypt and the rest of Roman Africa (as will be discussed later). When it did, Christianity in these regions largely disappeared, too, although a vibrant Christian community continued to flourish in Ethiopia. Meanwhile, tensions between the Visigoths and their Roman subjects in Spain continued, making it another territory easily absorbed by Islam.

The Codification of Roman Law

Justinian's most positive and lasting accomplishment to the legacy of imperial power was his codification of Roman law. This was project long overdue: since the time of the third-century jurists (see Chapter 5), the number of statutes, edicts, and legal decisions had multiplied, and the resulting body of law was both massive and self-contradictory. Moreover, conditions had changed so radically within the empire that many legal principles could no longer be applied. When Justinian came to power in 527, one of his first initiatives was to bring existing precedents into harmony with actual historical conditions and thereby to restore the prestige and power of the law.

This work was undertaken by a team of Latin-speaking lawyers under the supervision of a jurist called Tribonian. Its first publication was the Code, a systematic compilation of older imperial statutes. This was later supplemented by another book, the Novels (*Novellae*, "new laws"), containing the legislation of Justinian and his immediate successors. The commission also completed a summary of the writings of Rome's great legal authorities, the Digest. Its final product was the *Institutes,* a textbook of legal principles. Together, these four volumes constitute the *Corpus Juris Civilis*, the "body of civil law."

The *Corpus* was an extraordinary achievement, and it became the foundation on which all subsequent imperial law would rest. It eventually influenced the legal systems of many nations. The nineteenth-century Napoleonic Code—still the basis of law in France, Spain, much of Latin America, and the state of Louisiana—is essentially based on the *Corpus* of Justinian. The canon law of the medieval Roman Church would too be influenced by it (see Chapter 9).

The *Corpus* also had a profound impact on political philosophy. Starting from the maxim that "what pleases the prince has the force of law," it granted unlimited powers to the emperor and would therefore become a foundation for absolutism (see Chapter 15). Yet the *Corpus* also provided support for constitutional forms of government, because it maintained that a sovereign's powers are delegated by the people. Equally important is the fundamental principle that the state is a corporate body, not the extension of an individual's private property. The modern conception of the state as a public entity derives from the Roman law codified in the *Corpus*.

THE ROMAN EMPIRE OF BYZANTIUM

With the failure of imperial reunification, the history of the eastern Roman Empire enters a new phase. Indeed, it has usually been regarded as a new entity, the Byzantine Empire, a name derived from the ancient port where Constantinople was situated. But according to the citizens of this empire, it never ceased to be Rome, and they were never anything but Romans—even though their official language was Greek. It was they who carried forward Roman traditions, values, and institutions.

Initially, however, this new Rome was struggling for survival. By 610, its influence extended only as far west as the Adriatic and a few parts of southern Italy. On its south-eastern border, the Persians had conquered almost all of Syria and Palestine. They had even plundered Jerusalem. With an enormous effort, the emperor Heraclius (r. 610–41) rallied his remaining military powers and routed the Persians, recapturing Jerusalem in 627. But these gains were short-lived. A wave of Arab armies, inspired by the new religion of Islam, soon occupied the recently reconquered territories and claimed Jerusalem as a holy site for Muslims, too. They also absorbed the entire Persian Empire and rapidly made their way westward to North Africa.

The Arabs then took to the sea and, in 677, attempted a naval conquest of Constantinople. Repulsed, they made another attempt in 717 by means of a concerted land and sea operation. This new threat was countered by the emperor Leo III (r. 717–41). Deploying keen strategy and a secret incendiary mixture known as "Greek fire," imperial forces were able to defeat the Arabs. Over the next few decades, Byzantium reconquered most of Asia Minor, which became the core of the empire.

in times of upheaval. No polity in western Europe had anything resembling such effective mechanisms of government until a much later period.

Strong, self-perpetuating political institutions thus constituted a major source of stability in the eastern Roman Empire, which survived for more than a thousand years after the founding of Constantinople (see Chapter 12). The imperial bureaucracy regulated prices and wages, maintained systems of licensing, and controlled exports and trade. Its highly educated officials also supervised many aspects of social and cultural life, overseeing schools, the organization of the Orthodox Church, and the observance of religious rites and holidays. Even the popular sport of chariot racing—New Rome's exciting answer to gladiatorial combat—fell under strict supervision, as did the regulation of the various teams' fiercely competitive fans. Efficient bureaucracies also regulated the army and navy, the courts, and the diplomatic service, endowing these agencies with organizational strengths incomparable in their time.

Another source of stability was Byzantium's well-managed economy, which was far superior to that of western Europe. Commerce and cities continued to flourish as they had done in late antiquity. Constantinople became a central emporium for exotic eastern luxury goods and western raw materials. The empire also nurtured and protected its own industries, most notably the manufacture and weaving of silk, and it was renowned for its stable gold and silver coinage. Nor was Constantinople the only great urban center. The Hellenistic capital Antioch and the bustling cities of Thessalonica and Trebizond were very large and prosperous. Any one of them would have dwarfed any western European city; Constantinople may have had a population of close to a million. In the West at this time, Paris was a tiny village and Rome had a few thousand people living among the ruins.

Sources of Stability

In some ways, the internal politics of the Byzantine Empire were as tumultuous as its changing neighborhood. All power was concentrated in the imperial court, around emperors who claimed to rule autonomously, and this meant that opposition usually took the form of intrigue, treason, and violence. (The very word *byzantine* has come to denote cloak-and-dagger machinations or elaborate systems of hierarchy and bureaucracy.) In reality, though, many able rulers wielded their powers very effectively, through a centralized government that continued to function even

Orthodoxy, Iconoclasm, and Identity

Strong governance and a healthy economy: viewed from our perspective, these seem to be the most important aspects of a thriving society. Yet the inhabitants of New Rome also placed a high value on religious cohesion. In old Rome, the *mos maiorum* had undergirded Roman pride and superiority; in New Rome, Orthodox Christianity occupied the same fundamental place. The stakes of Byzantine doctrinal disputes were therefore high, and they were further heightened because emperors took an active role in them.

The most contentious issue was the meaning and use of religious images, and in the eighth century this broke out in a violent clash known as the Iconoclast ("image-breaking") Controversy. Christians had been accustomed to expressing their devotion to Christ and the saints through the making and veneration of images. At the same time, however, there was always an awareness that any representation of a holy person came close to being a form of idolatry—something that Jewish tradition strongly condemned, as did the new religion of Islam. Although Christians insisted that images were only *aids* to worship, not *objects* of worship, the line between the two was very fine.

In Byzantium, the veneration of icons was an especially potent part of daily devotion; any attempt to suppress them was bound to be contentious. But that is precisely what the Iconoclasts advocated. They argued

DEVOTIONAL IMAGE—OR DANGEROUS IDOL? This icon of *Christos Pantokrator* ("Christ the Almighty") was painted in the sixth century and is one of the oldest such images in existence. It is preserved at the Orthodox monastery of St. Catherine on Mount Sinai (Egypt). ■ *According to the proponents of iconoclasm, why would such an image be considered blasphemous?*

that honoring images was blasphemous. For their part, traditionalist Iconodules ("image servants") retorted that images were never objects of worship; rather, icons were windows through which a glimpse of Heaven might be granted to humans.

The Iconoclast movement was initiated by the same Emperor Leo III who had saved Constantinople from invasion by Muslims, and it is even possible that Muslim doctrine played a role in his thinking; by cracking down on icons, he may have been attempting to answer a major Muslim criticism of Christianity. There may also have been political and financial considerations behind the campaign, as the emperor tried to strengthen his control over the Orthodox Church and combat the growing power of monasteries, which were major producers of icons. So when the monasteries rallied to protect icons, Leo and his successors retaliated by confiscating much of their wealth.

The Iconoclast Controversy was resolved toward the end of the eighth century in favor of the Iconodules. But it had some long-lasting effects. One was the destruction of many artworks produced or preserved in Byzantium. This means that examples of Christian artistry from the first eight centuries after Jesus's death are very rare and can be found mainly in Italy, Palestine, or Egypt, which were beyond the reach of the Iconoclast emperors. A second consequence was the widening of a religious and political breach between the Greek East and the Latin West. Prior to Emperor Leo's initiatives, the patriarch of Rome—known familiarly as "papa" in Latin slang—had often been a close ally of Byzantium's rulers. But iconoclasm called into question not only the veneration of images but the cult of the saints, and by extension the claims of papal primacy that were based on the Roman patriarch's claim to be Saint Peter's successor (see Chapter 6).

The ultimate defeat of iconoclasm crystallized some aspects of belief and practice that came to be characteristic of Byzantine identity. One was a renewed emphasis on the Orthodox faith as the key to political unity and military success. This subsequently enforced the hegemony of Constantinople's own Christian traditions, marginalizing those of Syria and Armenia. Fear of heresy also tended to inhibit freedom of expression, and not just in religious matters.

Tradition and Innovation

If Orthodoxy was central to the identity of Byzantium, so was its direct link with the Hellenistic past and the heritage of ancient Greece. Byzantine schools based their instruction on classical Greek literature to a degree that might seem

Competing Viewpoints

Debating the Power of Icons

> The Iconoclast Controversy of the eighth century divided Byzantine society and was a factor in the growing division between the Latin Church of Rome and the Greek Orthodox Church. The excerpts below are representative of the two main arguments voiced at the time. The first is from a treatise by John of Damascus (c. 675–749), a Christian in the service of the Muslim Umayyad caliphs. The second is an official report issuing from the synod convened by the emperor Constantine V (r. 741–75) in 754. Constantine was carrying forward the iconoclastic policies of his father, Leo III.

John of Damascus, On Holy Images

Now adversaries say: God's commands to Moses the law-giver were, "Thou shalt adore the Lord thy God, and thou shalt worship him alone, and thou shalt not make to thyself a graven thing that is in heaven above, or in the earth beneath." . . .

These injunctions were given to the Jews on account of their proneness to idolatry. Now we, on the contrary, are no longer in leading strings. . . . We have passed the stage of infancy, and reached the perfection of manhood . . . and know what may be imaged and what may not. . . . An image is a likeness of the original with a certain difference, for it is not an exact reproduction of the original. Thus, the Son is the living, substantial, unchangeable Image of the invisible

God, bearing in Himself the whole Father, being in all things equal to Him, differing only in being begotten by the Father. . . . That which is divine is immutable; there is no change in Him, nor shadow of change. . . . God has noted and settled all that He would do, the unchanging future events before they came to pass. In the same way, a man who wished to build a house, would first make and think out a plan. Again, visible things are images of invisible and intangible things, on which they throw a faint light. Holy Scripture clothes in figure God and the angels. . . . If, therefore, Holy Scripture, providing for our need, ever putting before us what is intangible, clothes it in flesh, does it not make an image of what is thus invested

with our nature, and brought to the level of our desires, yet invisible? . . . For the invisible things of God since the creation of the world are made visible through images. We see images in creation which remind us faintly of God, as when, for instance, we speak of the holy and adorable Trinity, imaged by the sun, or light, or burning rays, or by a running fountain, or a full river, or by the mind, speech, or the spirit within us, or by a rose tree, or a sprouting flower, or a sweet fragrance. . . .

Source: Excerpted from *St. John Damascene on Holy Images*, trans. Mary H. Allies (London: 1898), pp. 6–12.

surprising given the more tentative attitude toward classical learning in western Europe (see Chapter 6). Educated people around the Byzantine court who quoted only a single line of Homer could expect their listeners to recognize the entire passage from which it came. In the English-speaking world, only the King James Bible has ever achieved the same degree of cultural saturation. For the intellectuals of Byzantium, indeed, Homeric epics were a kind of sacred text.

Byzantine scholars also intensively studied the philosophy of Plato and the historical prose of Thucydides.

By contrast, Aristotle's works were less well known, while many other philosophical traditions of antiquity were deemed dangerous to Orthodox belief. Somewhat paradoxically, Justinian—who had presided over the codification of ancient Roman (and thus pagan) law—registered his distrust of philosophy by shutting down the Athenian academies that had existed since Plato's day. Eventually, the emperor Alexius Comnenus (d. 1118) would ban the teaching of Aristotelian logic. The traditions of Greek scientific inquiry and the advances of Hellenistic science were also neglected.

Canons of the Synod of 754

t is the unanimous doctrine of all the holy Fathers and of the six Ecumenical Synods, that no one may imagine any kind of separation or mingling in opposition to the unsearchable, unspeakable, and incomprehensible union of the two natures in the one *hypostasis* or person. What avails, then, the folly of the painter, who from sinful love of gain depicts that which should not be depicted—that is, with his polluted hands he tries to fashion that which should only be believed in the heart and confessed with the mouth? He makes an image and calls it Christ. The name *Christ* signifies *God and man.* Consequently it is an image of God and man, and consequently he has in his foolish mind, in his representation of the created flesh, depicted the God-head which cannot be represented, and thus mingled what should not be mingled. Thus he is guilty of a double blasphemy—the one in making an image of the Godhead, and the other by mingling the Godhead and manhood . . . like the Monophysites, or he represents the body of Christ as not made divine and separate and as a person apart, like the Nestorians.

The only admissible figure of the humanity of Christ, however, is bread and wine in the holy Supper. This and no other form, this and no other type, has he chosen to represent his incarnation. Bread he ordered to be brought, but not a representation of the human form, so that idolatry might not arise. And as the body of Christ is made divine, so also this figure of the body of Christ, the bread, is made divine by the descent of the Holy Spirit; it becomes the divine body of Christ by the mediation of the priest who, separating the oblation from that which is common, sanctifies it. . . .

Source: Excerpted from *The Seven Ecumenical Councils of the Undivided Church*, trans. H. R. Percival, in *Nicene and Post-Nicene Fathers*, 2d Series, ed. P. Schaff and H. Wace (repr. Grand Rapids, MI: 1955), pp. 543–44.

Questions for Analysis

1. To what other phenomena does John of Damascus compare the making of images? How do these comparisons help him to make his argument in favor of them?

2. To what phenomena do the theologians of the synod compare the making of images? Why do they declare the bread and wine of the Eucharist to be the only legitimate representations of Christ?

3. What is the significance of the fact that John of Damascus did not fall under the jurisdiction of the emperor of Byzantium but that of the Muslim Umayyad caliph? What conclusions can you draw about the relative freedoms in these two realms?

Tradition was more highly prized than innovation. The benefit of this, for posterity, was the rescue of Greek and Hellenistic writings for later ages. The vast majority of ancient Greek texts known today survive only because they were copied by Byzantine scribes.

In further contrast to western Europe, as we shall see, the Byzantine educational system extended to many commoners and was open to women as well as to men. Although most girls from aristocratic or prosperous families were educated at home by private tutors, they nevertheless mingled freely with their male counterparts at court or on social occasions, and many female intellectuals were compared to Plato or Pythagoras. There were even female physicians in the Byzantine Empire, another extraordinary departure both from ancient tradition and from the practices of western Europe until the latter part of the nineteenth century.

Byzantine achievements in the realms of architecture and art are also remarkable. The finest example of both may be the church of Hagia Sophia ("Holy Wisdom") in Constantinople, constructed at enormous cost under the patronage of Justinian. It quickly came to define an architectural style unique to Byzantium. Its purpose was to symbolize the mysteries of the Christian religion and the holy knowledge imparted by Christ to the soul of the believer. For this reason, the architects paid little attention to the external appearance of the building. The interior, however, was decorated with richly colored mosaics, gold leaf, colored marble columns, and bits of tinted glass set on edge to refract rays of sunlight, like sparkling gems. Light appeared to be generated from within. The magnificent dome over its central square represented an unprecedented engineering feat and was upheld by four great arches springing from pillars at the four corners of the square. Its effect is heightened by the many windows placed around the dome's rim, which convey the impression that it floats in mid-air.

Many aspects of Byzantine arts and learning exerted strong influence on the craftsmen and scholars of western Europe through continued economic and cultural contact. The basilica of San Marco in Venice (c. 1063) reflects this influence distinctly, as do medieval mosaics in such cities as Ravenna and Palermo. Greek-speaking monasteries in southeastern Italy maintained especially close ties with their counterparts in the eastern empire, and many were allowed to practice the rituals of the Orthodox Church. Greek books—including the comedies of Aristophanes (Chapter 4)—were copied and preserved there. But much of the heritage of Western civilizations that was cultivated in Byzantium was largely inaccessible elsewhere in Europe, as the knowledge of Greek became increasingly rare.

MUHAMMAD AND THE TEACHINGS OF ISLAM

The civilization that formed around the religion of Islam mirrors the Roman Empire in its global reach and longevity; in this, it is truly one of Rome's heirs. Islam (Arabic for "submission") also resembles the early republic of Rome in that it was based on adherence to certain social and cultural norms. But whereas the Roman Empire was the vehicle for the spread of Christianity, the Islamic faith was itself the engine of imperial expansion. It has created empires, rather than depending on them.

The Revelations of Muhammad

Islam had its beginnings in Arabia, a desert land that neither the Romans nor the Persians had ever tried to conquer.

Arabian society was tribal; it did not revolve around urban settlements, and many Arabs were herdsmen living off the milk of their camels and the produce of desert oases. But like the Hittites in the second millennium B.C.E. (Chapter 1), their very mobility and ingenuity made them excellent explorers and long-distance traders. In the second half of the sixth century, when constant wars between Byzantium and Persia made travel dangerous, the Arabs quickly established themselves as guides and guardians of land routes between Africa and Asia.

As part of this process, towns began to emerge. The most prominent of these was Mecca, an ancient sacred site that lay at the crossroads of major caravan routes. Mecca was home to the Kaaba (*KAH-ah-bah*), a shrine housing the Black Stone. (It may be an ancient meteorite.) This was a powerful object of devotion, and the tribe that controlled this shrine, the Quraish (*kur-AYSH*), thus came to dominate the region, forming an aristocracy of traders and religious leaders.

Muhammad, the founder of Islam, was a member of this tribe. He was born in Mecca around 570 C.E. Orphaned early in life, he entered the service of a rich widow whom he later married. Until middle age he lived as a prosperous merchant. Then, around 610, he experienced a spiritual epiphany: the gods of his people were not many, they were one. This supreme God (in Arabic, *Allah*) was the sole ruler of the universe, like the Hebrews' Yahweh. But whereas the Hebrews' embrace of monotheism had been a long and gradual process, Muhammad's conversion was sudden and led to further revelations and his calling as a prophet.

At first, he was not successful in gaining converts. In Mecca, tribal leaders feared that his teachings would

HAGIA SOPHIA. This great monument to the artistry, engineering skill, and spirituality of Byzantium was built during the reign of Justinian. The four minarets at its corners were added in 1453, after Constantinople was absorbed into the empire of the Ottoman Turks. Hagia Sophia is now a mosque and a museum.

diminish the importance of the Kaaba. But the town of Yathrib, to the north, had no such concerns. Its representatives invited Muhammad to live among them, to serve as judge and arbiter in local rivalries. Muhammad and a few loyal friends accepted this invitation in the year 622. Because this migration—in Arabic, the Hijrah (HIJ-ruh)—marks the beginning of Muhammad's wider influence, Muslims regard this year as the first of their religion, just as Christians date all events to the birth of Jesus (see Chapter 6).

Muhammad changed the name of Yathrib to Medina ("City of the Prophet") and organized his followers into a community held together by shared economic ambitions as well as by a shared set of beliefs. Yet he did not abandon his desire to exercise political and prophetic authority among his own people. So he and his followers began raiding Quraish caravans traveling beyond Mecca. The Quraish could not continue to operate an extensive commercial enterprise in the face of these threats, and by 630 Muhammad had triumphed. He was invited back to Mecca and his kinsmen submitted themselves to his authority. Muhammad responded by promoting the Kaaba as Islam's holiest place, a status it maintains today. And because Mecca had long been a pilgrimage site for tribes throughout Arabia, many people were exposed to his teachings when they assembled there. At the time of Muhammad's death in 632, Islam had become an established faith.

Muhammad and the Qur'an

As its name indicates, Islam calls for submission to Allah, the same God worshiped by Jews and Christians. The Muslim saying "there is no god but Allah" is more accurately translated as "there is no divinity but God." For Muslims, the history and prophecies of the Hebrews are important components of their religion, as are the teachings of Jesus, who is venerated as a great prophet. But they consider Muhammad to be the last and greatest prophet, and the closest to God.

Muhammad's teachings are preserved in the sacred scripture of Islam, the Qur'an (kuhr-AHN), an Arabic word meaning "recitations." This is because Muhammad recited his revelations to listeners, who eventually gathered them together and transcribed them. This process continued after Muhammad's death and is renewed each time a Muslim memorizes and recites verses from the Qur'an. Unlike the Christian Gospels, which offer different perspectives on Jesus's ministry recorded a generation or two after his death, the Qur'an is considered a direct link with Muhammad. It is also unlike most books of the Bible because it is highly poetic, drawing on ancient genres of Arabic song.

Like Christianity, Islam teaches that a day of judgment is coming—soon. On this day, the righteous will be granted eternal life in a paradise of delights, but wrongdoers will be damned to a realm of eternal fire. Every person is therefore offered a fundamental choice: to begin a new life of divine service or to follow their own path. If they choose to follow God, they will be blessed; if they do not, God will turn away from them. The only sure means of achieving salvation is observance of the Five Pillars of the faith: submission to God's will as described in the teachings of Muhammad, frequent prayer, ritual fasting, the giving of alms, and an annual pilgrimage to Mecca (the Hajj).

Unlike Christianity, Islam is a religion without sacraments or priests. Although Muslims value the opportunity to come together for prayer, there is no prescribed liturgy. Islam more closely resembles Judaism as it developed after the Diaspora, when Jews no longer had access to the Temple priesthood but instead gathered around a master teacher (rabbi). Similarly, Muslims rely on a community leader (imam) or scholar qualified to comment on matters of faith. Like Judaism, Islam also emphasizes the inextricable connection between religious observance and daily life, between spirituality and politics. There is no opposition of sacred and secular authority, as in Christianity. But in marked contrast to Judaism, Islam is a religion that aspires to unite the world in a shared faith. This means that Muslims, like Christians, consider it their duty to engage in the work of conversion.

THE WIDENING ISLAMIC WORLD

The death of any charismatic leader is a moment of crisis. Muhammad and Alexander the Great represent very different types of leadership, but both were at the center of ambitious enterprises created by that leadership. Neither designated a successor, and both left behind close followers determined to inherit their power. Although the very survival of Islam seemed unlikely after Muhammad's death, within a generation it had come to encompass the oldest Western civilizations.

The Arabic Conquest of the West

Muhammad's closest allies were his father-in-law, Abu-Bakr (ah-boo-BAHK-uhr), and an early convert named Umar. After Muhammad's death, these two men agreed that Abu-Bakr

A Sura from the Qur'an

The Qur'an *preserves the teachings of Muhammad in a series of* suras, *or chapters. Composed in verse forms that draw on much older traditions of Arabic poetry, they are meant to be sung or chanted. Indeed, the word* Qur'an *means "recitations," referring both to Muhammad's method of revealing divine truths and to the Muslim practice of memorizing and repeating portions of this sacred scripture.*

Sura 81: The Overturning

In the Name of God the Compassionate
　the Caring

When the sun is overturned
When the stars fall away
When the mountains are moved
When the ten-month pregnant camels
　are abandoned
When the beasts of the wild are herded
　together　　　　　　　　　　　　　　　　5
When the seas are boiled over
When the souls are coupled
When the girl-child buried alive is asked
　what she did to deserve murder
When the pages are folded out
When the sky is flayed open
When Jahím [the Day of Reckoning]　10
　is set ablaze
When the garden is brought near

Then a soul will know what it has pre-
　pared
I swear by the stars that slide,　　　15
　stars streaming, stars that sweep
　along the sky
By the night as it slips away
By the morning when the fragrant air
　breathes
This is the word of a messenger enno-
　bled, empowered, ordained before
　the lord of the throne, holding sway
　there, keeping trust
Your friend [Muhammad] has not gone
　mad
He saw him on the horizon clear
He does not hoard for himself the
　unseen　　　　　　　　　　　　　　20
This is not the word of a satan struck
　with stones
Where are you going?

This is a reminder to all beings
For those who wish to walk straight
Your only will is the will of God lord of all
　beings　　　　　　　　　　　　　　25

Source: From *Approaching the Qur'an: The Early Revelations*, trans. Michael Sells (Ashland, OR: 1999), pp. 48–50.

Questions for Analysis

1. What impressions of Arab culture emerge from this sura? What does the litany of unlikely or mystical events reveal about the values of Muhammad's contemporaries?

2. How does Muhammad speak of himself and his role in society?

---

should be the prophet's *caliph*, a word meaning "deputy" or "representative," and began a campaign to subdue those Muslims unwilling to accept the caliph's authority. Abu-Bakr's forces began to move beyond the borders of Arabia, where they met only minimal resistance from Byzantine and Persian armies.

When Abu-Bakr died two years later, Umar succeeded as caliph and his followers continued northward. In 636, they routed a Byzantine army in Syria and quickly swept over the entire region, occupying the cities of Antioch, Damascus, and Jerusalem. In 637, they destroyed the main army of the Persians and took the Persian capital. By 651, the Arabian conquest of the ancient Persian Empire was virtually complete.

Muslim forces also turned westward toward North Africa, capturing Byzantine Egypt and extending their control throughout the rest of North Africa. Unable to take Constantinople from the sea, they crossed from North Africa into Visigothic Spain in 710, and quickly absorbed most of that territory. Within less than a century, followers of Islam had conquered the Near East and much of the Roman Mediterranean; in the process, the desert-dwelling Arabs had transformed themselves into the world's most daring seafarers.

How can we explain this achievement? On a basic level, the motivations are familiar: the search for richer territory and new wealth. There is little evidence that Arab Muslims attempted to convert subject peoples to the faith of Islam at this time. Instead, they aimed to establish themselves as a superior ruling class. Yet religion certainly played a crucial role in forging a shared identity among tribes used to fighting one another. This identity and sense of superiority must have been further strengthened by the absence of any serious opposition. Many peoples living within the Persian and Byzantine empires were restive and exhausted by the demands of far-reaching imperial bureaucracies. Moreover, Muslim leaders were more tolerant of different Christian sects and of their Jewish subjects. For all these reasons, Islam quickly spread over the territory between Egypt and Iran, and has been rooted there ever since.

The Shi'ite–Sunni Schism

But as these conquests widened the reach of Islam, disputes divided the Muslims of Mecca. When the caliph Umar died in 644, he was replaced by a member of the Umayyad (*oo-MY-yad*) family, a wealthy clan that had resisted Muhammad's authority. Opponents of this new caliph, Uthman, rallied instead around Muhammad's son-in-law, Ali, whose family ties to Muhammad made him seem a more appropriate choice. When Uthman was murdered in 656, Ali's supporters declared him the new caliph. But Uthman's powerful family refused to accept this. Ali was murdered and another member of the Umayyad family replaced him. From 661 to 750, this Umayyad dynasty ruled the Islamic world, establishing the caliphate's new capital at Damascus in Syria.

Ali's followers, however, did not accept defeat. They formed a separate group known as the Shi'ites (from *shi'a*, the Arabic word for "faction"). The Shi'ites insisted that only descendants of Ali and Muhammad's daughter Fatimah could legitimately rule the Muslim community. Moreover, the Shi'ites did not accept the customs (*sunna*) that had developed under the first two caliphs. Those Muslims who supported the Umayyad family and followed these customs were therefore known as Sunnis. This division between Shi'ites and Sunnis has lasted until the present day. The Shi'ites predominate

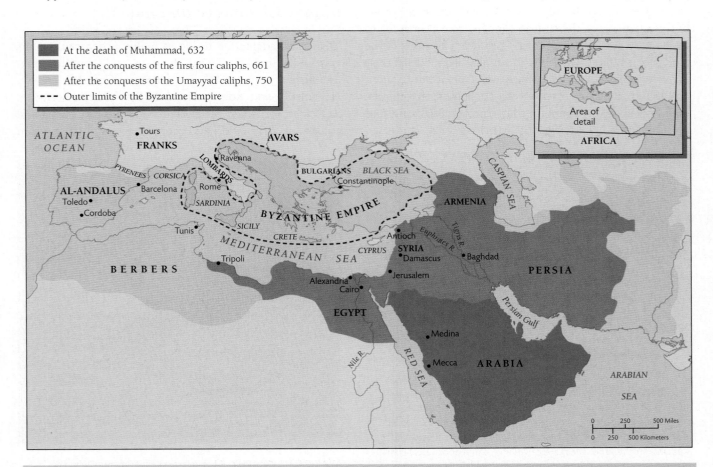

THE EXPANSION OF ISLAM TO 750. This map shows the steady advance of Islam, through Arab conquests, from the time of Muhammad to the middle of the eighth century. ▪ *What was the geographical extent of Islam in 750?* ▪ *What role did the Byzantine Empire play in the expansion of Islam?* ▪ *What conclusions can you draw regarding the period of especially rapid expansion in the generation after Muhammad's death?*

in Iran and are the largest single Muslim group in Iraq, yet they constitute only one-tenth of the world's Muslims and are often persecuted minorities in Sunni states.

The Umayyad and Abbasid Dynasties

The Umayyad capital at Damascus was a major Hellenistic and Roman city. And in many ways, the Umayyad Caliphate functioned as a Roman successor state; it even continued to employ Greek-speaking bureaucrats trained in the techniques of governance. But the failure of Umayyad attacks on Constantinople checked their power, which was also being challenged by a rival Sunni dynasty. The Abbasid clan claimed descent from one of Muhammad's uncles, and in 750 they led a successful rebellion that forced the Umayyads to retreat westward to their territories in Al-Andalus: the name for Muslim Spain.

In contrast to the Umayyads, the Abbasid Caliphate stressed Persian influences over Roman ones. Symbolic of this change was the shift in capitals from Damascus to Baghdad, where a new city was built near the ruins of the old Persian capital. The Abbasid caliphs also modeled their behavior on that of Persian princes and their administration on the autocratic rule of the former Persian Empire, imposing heavy taxation to support a large professional army and presiding over an extravagantly luxurious court. This is the caliphate that produced the *Arabian Nights*, a collection of stories written in Baghdad under the Abbasids. A dominating presence in these tales is Harun al-Rashid (r. 786–809), whose reign marked the height of Abbasid power.

Meanwhile, the Umayyad dynasty continued to rule Al-Andalus and to claim legitimate descent from Muhammad. Relations between the Muslims of Spain and Persia were therefore very cold; but because their realms were far apart, the hostility between them rarely erupted into war. Instead, the two courts competed for preeminence through literary and cultural patronage, much as the Hellenistic kingdoms had done. Philosophers, artists, and especially poets flocked to both. The *Arabian Nights* was one product of this rivalry in Baghdad. Meanwhile, the caliphs at the Spanish capital of Córdoba amassed a library of more than 400,000 volumes—at a time when a European monastery with 100 books qualified as a major center of Christian learning.

Islamic Commerce and Industry

The Arabs' adaptation to life in highly urbanized regions was swift, and it allowed them to build on the long-established commercial infrastructures of the Persian, Hellenistic, and Roman empires. By the tenth century, Arab merchants had penetrated into southern Russia and equatorial Africa and had become masters of the caravan

THE GREAT UMAYYAD MOSQUE AT DAMASCUS. This mosque was built by Caliph al-Walid between 705 and 715. Byzantine influence is apparent in its arched colonnades, its mosaics, and its series of domes, all of which were replicated in much subsequent Islamic architecture. The mosaic over the central doorway, shown here, indicates that the visitor is entering paradise. The mosque was constructed on the foundations of a Roman temple and also incorporates a later Christian shrine dedicated to Saint John the Baptist. ▪ *Why would the caliph have chosen this site for his mosque?*

ARABIC CALLIGRAPHY. Muslim artists experimented with the art of calligraphy to make complex designs, sometimes abstract but often representing natural forms. This ink drawing on paper actually incorporates Arabic words. It dates from the seventh century, and also represents the Muslim mastery of papermaking.

routes that led eastward to India and China. Muslim ships established new trade routes across the Indian Ocean, the Persian Gulf, and the Caspian Sea, and dominated the southern Mediterranean as well.

The growth of Muslim commerce in this period was driven and sustained by a number of important new industries. Mosul, in Iraq, was a center for the manufacture of cotton cloth; Baghdad specialized in glassware, jewelry, pottery, and silks; Damascus was famous for its fine steel and for its woven-figured silk known as "damask"; Morocco was noted for leather-working; Toledo produced excellent swords. Drugs, perfumes, carpets, tapestries, brocades, woolens, satins, and a host of other products turned out by skilled artisans were carried throughout the Mediterranean world and into central Asia along the network of roads to China that came to be known as the Silk Road. With them went the faith of Islam, which took root among peoples of India, Pakistan, and Afghanistan.

One commodity in particular deserves special mention: paper. Arabs and Persians had learned papermaking from the Chinese and became masters of the art. By the end of the eighth century, Baghdad alone had more than a hundred shops where blank paper or books written on paper were sold. Paper was cheaper to produce, easier to store, and far easier to use than papyrus or parchment. As a result, paper replaced papyrus in the Muslim world by the early eleventh century—even in Egypt, the heartland of papyrus production for almost 4,000 years.

The ready availability of paper brought about a revolution. Many of the characteristic features of Islamic civilization— bureaucratic record keeping, high levels of literacy and book production, even the standard form of cursive Arabic script—would have been impossible without the widespread availability of paper. Europeans would continue to rely on the more durable, but much more expensive, parchment made from animal hides for the copying of most books and documents. It was not until the advent of print that paper began to replace parchment as the reading and writing material of western Europe (see Chapter 12).

Mobility, Opportunity, and Status

The preeminence of trade and ease of travel in the cosmopolitan Muslim world not only increased geographical mobility, it fostered social mobility too. The Qur'an stressed the equality of all Muslim males, and all careers were open to men of talent, regardless of birth or wealth.

For those men wishing instead to embrace a religious life, Islam offered two main alternatives. One was that of the ulama, an influential class of learned men qualified to offer advice on aspects of religious law and practice. The other was that of the Sufis, mystics devoted to the cultivation of spiritual ecstasy. Some were Dervishes known for their trancelike whirling dances; others were faqirs whose powers of concentration are associated with snake charming; still others were quiet, meditative men. Sufis were usually organized into brotherhoods and eventually made many successful efforts to convert the peoples of Africa and India. The coexistence of the ulama and the Sufis is testimony to the cultural pluralism of Islam.

There were no comparable careers for Muslim women, parallel to the (admittedly narrow) options of their Christian counterparts. There are significant exceptions, of course. For example, Muhammad's favored wife, Aisha (ah-EE-sha, d. 678), was revered as a scholar and played an important role in the creation and circulation of hadith: stories and sayings that shed light on the Prophet's life and teachings. But in general, women could not take advantage of widening opportunities. They were considered valuable as indicators of a man's wealth and status.

The Qur'an allowed any Muslim man to marry as many as four wives, which meant that the number of women suitable for marriage was far smaller than the number of men who desired to marry. This made for intense competition, and men who had wives and daughters needed to ensure that their prized assets were safeguarded. So women were usually kept away from men who were not members of the family or trusted friends. Along with female servants and the concubines also owned by a wealthy man, they were housed in a segregated part of the residence called the haram ("forbidden place"), guarded by eunuchs (men, usually sold as slaves, who had been castrated prior to adolescence). Within these enclaves, women vied with one another for precedence and worked to advance the fortunes of their children. This was often the only form of power they could exercise.

Islam's Neighbors

For the inhabitants of Byzantium, the triumph of the Abbasid Caliphate alleviated the pressures of Umayyad expansion. Farther west, the Franks of Gaul also benefited from the Abbasids. Because an Umayyad dynasty controlled Al-Andalus, the great Frankish ruler Charlemagne (SHAHR-leh-mayn, r. 768–814) could counter neighboring Muslims' power by maintaining strong diplomatic and commercial relations with the more distant caliphate in Baghdad. The most famous symbol of

The Meanings of Medievalism

The people who lived during the thousand-year period that we call the Middle Ages didn't think of themselves as "medieval." And indeed, this modern term tends to be used to describe modern phenomena—whether things that we seek to condemn (terrorism, persecution) or that we wish to glorify. The romantic image of Joan of Arc, on the left, was used to rally Americans to the cause of France and its allies during World War I. The image on the right shows warfare as imagined by the game called *Arthur II*.

this connection was an elephant called Abul Abbas, a gift from Harun al-Rashid to Charlemagne. More important, however, was the flow of silver that found its way from the Abbasid Empire north through Russia and the Baltic into the Rhineland, where it was exchanged for Frankish exports of furs, wax, honey, leather, and especially slaves—Europeans, often Slavic peoples, who were captured and sold for profit by other Europeans. Through these channels, jewels, silks, spices, and other luxury goods from India and the Far East flowed north and west into Frankish territory. These trading links with the Abbasid world helped fund the extraordinary achievements of Charlemagne's own empire, which had a lasting effect on the culture and politics of Europe.

THE CONVERSION OF NORTHWESTERN EUROPE

At the end of the sixth century, the chronicler Gregory of Tours (c. 538–594) considered himself a Roman, living in a Roman world. He was proud of his family's senatorial status and took it for granted that he and his male relatives should be bishops who ruled, by right of birth and status, over their cities and the surrounding countryside. Although Gregory was aware that his own ruler was a Frankish warlord, he regarded barbarian kings as Roman successors. In the case of the Franks, the king even ruled with the approval of the Roman emperor in Constantinople. It was also a source of satisfaction to Gregory that these barbarian kings had converted to Roman Christianity. This, too, reinforced their *romanitas* and lent legitimacy to their rule.

Two hundred years later, the greatest of all Frankish kings, Charlemagne (742–814), was crowned as a new kind of Roman emperor in the West. By this time, there was no longer a sense of direct continuity with the earlier Roman world or a sense of obligation to the Roman emperor in Byzantium. When intellectuals at Charlemagne's court set out to rejuvenate cultural life, they sought a *renovatio Romanorum imperii*, "a renewal of the empire of the Romans." This awareness of a break with the Roman past developed during the seventh century, and was the consequence of profound economic and political changes.

Economic and Political Instability

Even though the Roman economy became increasingly regionalized after the third century C.E. (see Chapter 6), the Mediterranean remained a crucial nexus of trade and communication. Gold coinage continued to circulate; luxuries like silks and spices moved westward while staples like slaves, wine, grain, and leatherwork moved eastward. But this integrated Mediterranean world became increasingly disjointed after Justinian's failed efforts to reconquer the empire's western territories. Temporary disruptions to traditional trade routes were also caused by Arab raiders—temporary, because Muslim merchants and rulers would soon do much to reconstruct and extend patterns of commerce.

The most significant causes of economic instability in northwestern Europe were internal. The cities of Italy, Gaul, and Hispania could no longer maintain their walls, their public buildings, and their urban infrastructures. Although Christian bishops and their aristocratic kin still governed from these cities, barbarian kings and their followers were moving to the countryside, living off the produce of their own estates. At the same time, some agricultural land was passing out of cultivation. The slaves or servile peasants who had farmed Rome's large plantations for hundreds of years had no efficient state to enforce their obedience. They were able to become more independent—yet they were also less effective, working just a few acres by themselves. Productivity declined, and so did tax revenues.

The systems of coinage that circulated in western Europe were also breaking down, which meant that wealth ceased to be readily portable: a hindrance to long-distance exchange. The supply of gold available in western

Europe was now being channeled eastward to Muslim realms. But in any case, gold coins were too valuable to be useful in a local market economy. When we find evidence of such coins in western Europe at this time, they are more likely to have been plundered or given as gifts than to have been used for commerce. Those rulers who were still in a position to mint money and guarantee its value shifted from gold to silver coinage. Europe would remain a silver-based economy for the next thousand years, until the supply of gold from European conquests in Africa and America once again made a gold standard viable (see Chapter 12).

As a result of these processes, western Europe came to rely on a two-tier economy of a kind that had not been necessary for centuries. Gold, silver, and luxury goods circulated among the very wealthy, but most people relied on barter and various substitute currencies. Lords collected rents in food or labor, but then found it difficult to convert these payments into the weapons, jewelry, and silks that brought prestige in aristocratic society. This was problematic not only for social reasons but for political ones: the power of lords depended on their ability to bestow rich gifts on their followers (see *Interpreting Visual Evidence* on page 182). When they could not acquire these items through trade, they had to win them through plunder and extortion. Either way, the process led to violence.

The successful chieftains of this era therefore tended to be those whose areas of influence adjoined wealthy but poorly defended territories that could be easily attacked or subjugated. Such "soft frontiers" provided warlords and kings with land and booty which they could then distribute to their followers. Successes of this sort would bring more followers to a lord's service, allowing him to further extend his influence; and as long as more conquests were made, the process of amassing power and wealth would continue. But power acquired through plunder was inherently unreliable and it did not secure long-term loyalties.

Another factor contributing to the instability of power was the difficulty of ensuring its peaceful transfer. The barbarian rulers who had established themselves after the mass migrations of the fifth and sixth centuries did not come from the traditional royal families of their peoples, and thus they faced opposition from many of their own warriors. Moreover, the groups who took possession of territories were usually made up of many different tribes, including a sizable number of Romans. Whatever unity they possessed was largely the creation of the charismatic chieftain who led them, and this charisma was not easily passed on to heirs.

The Prosperous Kingdom of the Franks

Of all barbarian kingdoms planted in western Europe in this era, only the Franks were able to establish a dynasty from which leaders would be drawn for 250 years. This family reached back to Clovis (r. c. 481–511), a warlord who established an alliance with the powerful bishops of Gaul by converting to Roman Christianity. Clovis's lineage came to be known as the Merovingians, after his legendary grandfather Merovech, said to have been fathered by a sea monster (meaning that no one really knew where he came from). Clovis's own name proved even more long-lasting than his dynasty. As the Germanic language of the Franks merged with the Latin of Gaul, the name "Clovis" lost its hard *C* and *V* and became "Louis," the name borne by French kings up to the time of the French Revolution over a millennium later (see Chapter 18).

The Merovingians' success was due, in part, to the successful transfer of power between generations. Among Europe's barbarian peoples, the right of inheritance was not limited to the eldest male. All sons—and frequently all male kin and even daughters—could consider themselves rightful heirs. So even when rule was not threatened by outsiders, the transfer of power was almost always bloody. In Gaul, however, the often brutal conflicts between rival Merovingian claimants did not materially disrupt their governance. Many elements of late Roman local administration therefore survived throughout this period.

Latin literacy, fostered by a network of monasteries linked to the Frankish court, remained an important element in this administration. These monasteries grew remarkably during the seventh century and made Merovingian Gaul wealthier and more stable than other regions of northwestern Europe. Approximately 550 monasteries were thriving by the year 700, more than 300 of which had been established in the preceding century alone. Frankish bishops also prospered, amassing vast estates from which their successors would continue to profit—again, until the time of the French Revolution.

Such massive redistributions and concentrations of wealth reflected a fundamental shift in the economic gravity of the Frankish kingdom. In the year 600, the wealth of Gaul was concentrated in the south, as it had been throughout the late Roman period. By the year 750, however, the economic center of the kingdom lay north of the Loire, in the territories that extended from the Rhine westward to the North Sea. It was here that most of the new monastic foundations of the seventh century were established.

Behind this shift in prosperity lay a long and successful effort to bring under cultivation the rich, heavy soils of north-ern Europe. This effort was largely engineered by the new monasteries, which harnessed the peasant workforce and pioneered technologies adapted to the climate and terrain. The most important invention was a heavy, wheeled plow capable of cutting grassland sod and clay: soils very different from those of the Mediterranean. This innovation in turn necessitated the development of more efficient devices for harnessing animals (particularly oxen) to these plows. Gradually warming weather also improved the fertility of northern lands. As food became more plentiful, the population began to expand. Although much of Frankish Gaul remained a land of scattered settlements separated by dense forests, it was far more populous by 750 than it had been in the time of Clovis. All of these developments would continue during the reign of Charlemagne, and beyond (see Chapter 8).

The Power of Monasticism

Although monasteries had existed since the fourth century, most were located in highly Romanized areas. Then, in the fifth century, a powerful monastic movement began in Ireland, and eventually spread to the Celtic regions of Britain and from there to the Continent. The Irish missionary Columbanus (540–615), for example, was the founder of Merovingian monasteries in what is now France. Important monasteries were also established on the island of Iona, off the western coast of Scotland, and at Lindisfarne, off Britain's northeastern coast. In all of these cases, close ties were forged between monks and local tribal leaders or kings, much to the political and economic gain of all parties.

Most of these new monastic foundations were deliberately located in rural areas and at strategic crossroads, where they played a crucial role in trade. Indeed, the material advantages of monastic innovation were a powerful incentive to Christian conversion in the communities directly affected by improved living conditions. Prosperity was also a powerful advertisement for authority: a lord or chieftain who had the support of a monastery and its wealth was obviously worthy of loyalty. Because monasteries played such a key role in economic and political development, lords often granted them special privileges, helping to free them from the control of local bishops and giving them jurisdiction over their own lands. Thus monasteries became powerful not only because of their wealth and alliances, but because they were lordships in their own right.

Frequently, these monasteries housed women as well as men. Often they were established for women only.

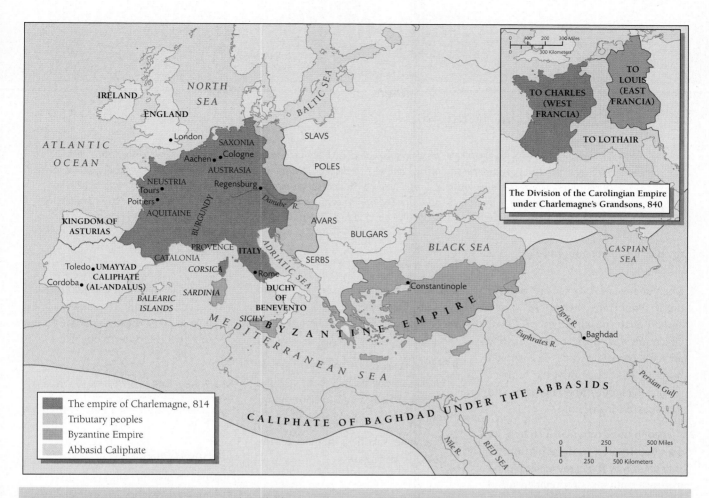

THE EMPIRE OF CHARLEMAGNE IN 814. When Charlemagne died in 814, he had created an empire that embraced a large portion of the lands formerly united under the western Roman Empire. ■ *What were the geographical limits of his power?* ■ *How were these limits dictated by the historical forces we have been studying?* ■ *Along what lines was Charlemagne's empire divided after his death?*

religious conformity. It became a settled assumption that the subjugation of a vanquished people should be accompanied by their religious conversion, and this became the settled policy of Europeans even in the New World (see Chapter 14).

To rule his enormous empire, Charlemagne enlisted the help of the Frankish warrior class he had enriched. These counts (*comites*, "followers") were given the task of supervising local governance within their territories, overseeing justice, and raising armies. Charlemagne also established a network of officials who convened local courts, established tolls, administered royal lands, and collected taxes. To facilitate transactions and trade, he created a new coinage system based on a division of the silver pound into units of twenty shillings, each worth twelve pennies—a system that would last in parts of continental Europe and in Britain into the 1970s (when it was replaced by a decimal-based currency). Much of the silver for this new

coinage originated in the Abbasid Caliphate, and was payment for furs, woolen cloth, and especially slaves captured in Charlemagne's wars, who were now being transported to Baghdad. The silver, in turn, circulated as far north as Scandinavia and the Baltic Sea.

Like Carolingian administration generally, this new monetary system depended on the regular use of written records, which means that sources supporting historical research on Charlemagne's empire are relatively abundant. But Charlemagne did not rely on the written word alone. Periodically, his court sent special messengers, known as *missi*, to relay his instructions and report back on the conduct of local administrators throughout the realm. This was the most thorough system of governance known in Europe since the height of the Roman Empire, reaching many parts of the Continent that the Romans had never occupied. It set a standard for royal administration that would be emulated and envied for centuries.

Analyzing Primary Sources

The Capitularies of Charlemagne

Charlemagne's careful governance of his domains would set a high standard for other rulers far into the future. One of the means by which this governance was carried out was through capitularies (from a Latin word denoting a document divided into chapters), which contained instructions issued by the central administration of the court to local counts and other authorities. The following are directives addressed in 785 to the administrators of Saxony, a region recently conquered by Charlemagne, whose inhabitants were forcibly converted to Christianity.

Capitulary Concerning the Parts of Saxony

1. Decisions were taken first on the more important items. All were agreed that the churches of Christ which are now being built in Saxony and are consecrated to God should have no less honor than the temples of idols had, but rather a greater and more surpassing honor.

2. If anyone takes refuge in a church, let no one presume to drive him out of that church by force; rather let him be in peace until he is brought to plead his case, . . . and after this let him be brought to the presence of our lord the king. . . .

3. If anyone makes forcible entry to a church, and steals anything from it by violence or stealth, or if he sets fire to the church, let him die.

4. If anyone in contempt of the Christian faith should spurn the holy Lenten fast and eat meat, let him die; but let the priest enquire into the matter, lest it should happen that someone is compelled by necessity to eat meat.

* * *

6. If anyone is deceived by the devil, and believes after the manner of pagans that some man or some woman is a witch and eats people, . . . let him pay the penalty of death.

7. If anyone follows pagan rites and causes the body of a dead man to be consumed by fire, . . . let him pay with his life.

8. If there is anyone of the Saxon people lurking among them unbaptized, and if he scorns to come to baptism, . . . let him die.

9. If anyone sacrifices a man to the devil, . . . let him die.

* * *

12. If anyone rapes the daughter of his lord, he shall die.

13. If anyone kills his lord or his lady, he shall be punished in the same way.

* * *

18. On Sundays there are to be no assemblies or public gatherings, except in cases of great need or when an enemy is pressing; rather let all attend church to hear the word of God. . . .

* * *

33. With regard to perjury, the law of the Saxons is to apply.

34. We forbid the Saxons to come together as a body in public gatherings, except on those occasions when our *missus* [messenger] assembles them on our instructions; rather, let each and every count hold court and administer justice in his own area. And the clergy are to see to it that this order is obeyed.

Source: From *The Reign of Charlemagne: Documents on Carolingian Government*, ed. and trans. H. R. Loyn and John Percival (New York: 1975), pp. 31–34.

Questions for Analysis

1. What types of behavior does this capitulary attempt to regulate? What seem to be the major challenges faced by Charlemagne's administrators in this new territory?

2. In only one case does this capitulary mention the law of the Saxon people themselves, in the clause relating to perjury (number 33). Why would Charlemagne's administrators consider it advisable to punish this particular crime in accordance with Saxon custom?

3. How would you characterize Charlemagne's method of dealing with a conquered people? In your estimation, is this policy likely to be effective?

Christianity and Kingship

Charlemagne took his responsibilities as a Christian king very seriously. As his empire expanded, he came to see himself as the leader of a unified Christian society, Christendom, which he was obliged to defend. Like his contemporaries in Byzantium and the Muslim world—as well as his Roman predecessors—he recognized no distinction between religion and politics. He conceived kingship as a sacred office created by God to protect the Church and promote the salvation of his people. Religious strength was therefore as central to proper kingship as justice and warfare.

These ideas were not new, but they took on a new importance because of the extraordinary power Charlemagne wielded. Like other rulers of this period, Charlemagne was able to appoint and depose bishops and abbots, just as he did his counts and other officials. He further extended his authority by glorifying the rituals of churches, reforming the rules of worship in monasteries, ruthlessly prohibiting pagan practices, and forcibly imposing basic Christian observances on all his subjects, especially the restive Saxons. As the dominant political power in northern and central Italy, Charlemagne was also the protector of the papacy, and he dealt with the bishop of Rome much as he did with other bishops in his empire. He supervised and approved papal elections, and he also protected the pope from his many enemies.

The Carolingian Renaissance

Bolstering these political, economic, and religious institutions was a phenomenon known as the Carolingian Renaissance: a cultural and intellectual flowering that took place around the Carolingian court and radiated from it. Like their biblical exemplars David and Solomon, Charlemagne and his son Louis the Pious considered it a crucial part of their role to be patrons of learning and the arts. In doing so, they created a courtly ideal that would profoundly influence European culture until the First World War (see Chapter 24).

Behind the Carolingians' support for learning was the conviction that education was essential to salvation. Charlemagne therefore recruited talented men from all over Europe to further the cause of scholarship. Foremost among these was the Anglo-Saxon monk Alcuin, whose command of classical Latin established him as the intellectual leader of Charlemagne's court. Under Alcuin's direction, Carolingian scholars produced much original Latin poetry and an impressive array of writings on many subjects. But their primary efforts were devoted to collating, correcting,

CHARLEMAGNE'S IMAGE OF AUTHORITY. A silver penny struck between 804 and 814 in Mainz (as indicated by the letter *M* at the bottom) represents Charlemagne in a highly stylized fashion, as a Roman emperor with a military cloak and laurel wreath. The inscription reads *Karolus Imp Avg* (Charles, Emperor, Augustus). Charlemagne's portrait is closely modeled on both Hellenistic and Roman coins.

and recopying ancient Latin texts, including, most importantly, the text of the Latin Bible, which had accumulated many generations of copyists' mistakes in the 400 years since Jerome's translation (see Chapter 6).

To detect and correct these errors, Alcuin and his associates gathered as many different versions of the biblical text as they could find and compared them, word by word. After determining the correct version among all the variants, they made a new, corrected copy and destroyed the other versions. They also developed a new style of handwriting, with simplified letter forms and spaces inserted between words, so as to reduce the likelihood that subsequent copyists would misread the corrected texts. Reading was further facilitated by the addition of punctuation. This new style of handwriting, known as Carolingian miniscule, is the foundation for the typefaces of most modern books—including this one.

The Revival of the Western Roman Empire

On Christmas Day in the year 800, Charlemagne was crowned emperor by Pope Leo III. Centuries later, popes would cite this event as precedent for the political superiority they claimed over all rulers. In the year 800, however, Pope Leo was entirely under Charlemagne's thumb. Yet Charlemagne's biographer, Einhard, would later claim that the coronation was planned without the emperor's knowledge.

This may have been true, or it may have been advantageous to insist that it was. For one thing, the crowning of a new emperor of the Romans was certain to anger the Roman imperial government in Constantinople, with which Charlemagne had strained relations. Nor did the imperial title add much to Charlemagne's position; he was already an emperor in his own right. Why, then, did he accept the title and, in 813, transfer it to his son Louis?

Historians are still debating this question. But the symbolic significance of the action is clear. Although the Romans of Byzantium no longer influenced western Europe directly, they continued to regard it (somewhat vaguely) as an outlying province of their empire. Charlemagne's assumption of the title was therefore a clear slight to the reigning empress Irene (r. 797–802), whose occupation of the imperial throne was controversial because she was a woman. It also deepened Byzantine suspicion of Charlemagnes' cordial relationship with Harun al-Rashid, the Abbasid caliph in Baghdad.

But for Charlemagne's followers—and for all the medieval rulers who came after him—the imperial title was a declaration of independence and superiority. With only occasional interruptions, western Europeans would continue to crown Roman emperors until the nineteenth century, while many territorial claims and European concepts of national sovereignty continued to rest on Carolingian precedent. Whatever his own motives may have been, Charlemagne's revival of the western Roman Empire was crucial to the developing self-consciousness of western Europe.

DISPUTED LEGACIES AND NEW ALLIANCES

When Charlemagne died in 814, his empire descended to his only surviving legitimate son, Louis the Pious. When Louis died in 840, however, the empire's unity had dissolved and it was divided among his three sons. Western Francia (the core of modern France) went to Charles the Bald; eastern Francia (which became key principalities of Germany) went to Louis the German; and a third kingdom (stretching from the Rhineland to Rome) went to Lothair, along with the imperial title. But when Lothair's line died out in 856, this fragile compromise dissolved into open warfare, as the East and West Franks fought over Lothair's former territories and the imperial power that went with them. The core of this disputed domain, known to the Germans as Lotharingia and to the French as Alsace-Lorraine, would continue to be a site of bitter contention until the end of the Second World War (see Chapter 26).

The Collapse of the Carolingian Empire

Louis faced an impossible situation of a kind we have studied many times before: the task of holding together an artificial constellation of territories united by someone else. Charlemagne's empire had been built on successful conquest, but it had pushed beyond the practical limits of his administration. To the southwest, he now faced the Umayyad rulers of Al-Andalus; to the north, the pagan inhabitants of Scandinavia; and in the east, the Slavic lands that lay beyond. At the same time, the pressures that had driven these conquests—the need for land and plunder to secure the allegiance of followers—had become ever more pronounced as a result of their very success. The number of counts had tripled, and each of them wanted more wealth and power.

Frustrated by their new emperor's inability to reward them, the Frankish aristocracy turned against him and on each other. Smoldering hostilities, which Charlemagne had stifled by directing their energies elsewhere, flared up again. As centralized authority broke down, the vast majority of the empire's free inhabitants found themselves increasingly dominated by local lords who treated them as if they were unfree serfs. At the same time, internal troubles in the Abbasid Caliphate caused a breakdown in the commercial system through which Scandinavian traders brought Abbasid silver into Carolingian domains. Deprived of their livelihood, these traders turned to raiding, which is what the Norse word *viking* means. Under these combined pressures, the Carolingian Empire fell apart, and a new political map of Europe began to emerge.

The Impact of the Viking Invasions

Scandinavian traders were already familiar figures in the North Sea and Baltic ports of Europe when Charlemagne came to power. They had begun to establish strategic settlements from which they navigated down the rivers to Byzantium (through the Black Sea) and to the Abbasid Caliphate (through the Caspian Sea). But when the power of the Abbasids declined, Viking raiders turned to plunder, ransom, and slaving. At first, these were small-scale operations. But soon, some Viking attacks involved organized armies numbering in the thousands. The small tribal kingdoms of the Anglo-Saxons and Celts made the British Isles easy targets, as were the divided kingdoms of the Franks.

By the tenth century, the Vikings controlled independent principalities in eastern England, Ireland, the islands of Scotland, and the region of France that is still called "Norseman-land"—Normandy. A Viking people known as

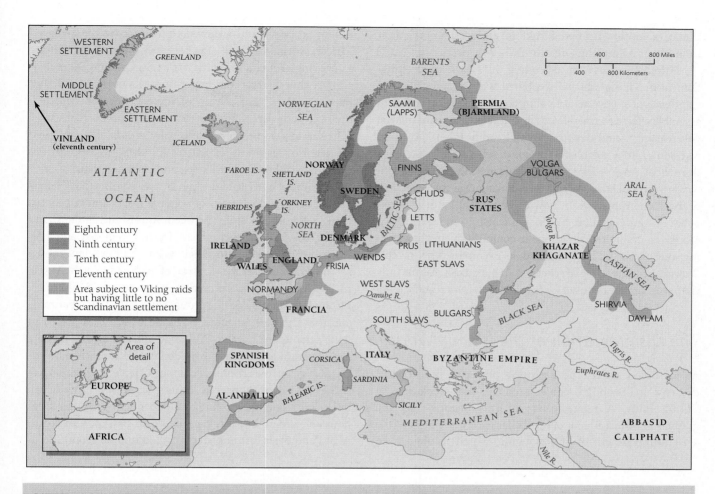

PATTERNS OF VIKING ACTIVITY AND SETTLEMENT, C. 700–1100. The Vikings were instrumental in maintaining commercial contacts among northern Europe, Byzantium, and Islam until the eighth century, when changing historical forces turned them into raiders and colonists. ▪ *What area was the original homeland of the Vikings?* ▪ *What geographic region did the Vikings first conquer, and why?* ▪ *The areas marked in green show territories that were later targeted by pillagers. Why would the Vikings have avoided settlement in these areas?*

the Rus' established the beginnings of a kingdom that would become Russia. At the end of the tenth century, Vikings ventured farther west and colonized Iceland, Greenland, and a distant territory they called Vinland (Newfoundland, Canada). In 1016, a Viking army placed a Danish king on the English throne.

The threat of Viking attacks began to lessen with Scandinavia's conversion to Christianity, which proceeded rapidly from the late tenth century onward. But it was more effectively mitigated by the fact that Viking populations quickly assimilated into the cultural and political world of northwestern Europe. By 1066, when the "Norsemen" of Normandy conquered England, the English—many of whom were descended from Vikings themselves—perceived them to be French. Driving this rapid assimilation may have been the raids of the Magyars, a non-Indo-European people who crossed the Carpathian Mountains around 895 and carried out a number of devastating campaigns in central

and eastern Europe before settling in what is now Hungary (which Hungarians call *Magyarország*).

The overall effect of the Vikings on Europe continues to be a matter of scholarly controversy. The mayhem they caused is undeniable, and many settlements and monasteries were destroyed—along with countless precious books and historical artifacts. Yet the Vikings were not a source of disorder only. In Ireland and eastern England, Vikings founded a series of new towns. As long-distance traders, Vikings transported large quantities of silver into western Europe, fueling the European economy. In those few regions where people did succeed in fending off Viking attacks, the unifying force of victory was strong. The best example of this phenomenon is England, which had never been part of Charlemagne's empire and which had remained divided into small kingdoms at war with one other—despite Bede's wishful history of "an English church and people." Yet in a direct response to the Viking threat, a loosely unified kingdom emerged for the first time under Alfred the Great (r. 871–99).

Alfred's success in defending his own small kingdom from Viking attacks, combined with his emulation of Charlemagne's governance, allowed him and his heirs to assemble effective armed forces, institute mechanisms of local government, found new towns, and codify English laws. In addition, Alfred established a court school and fostered a distinctive Anglo-Saxon literary culture. While the Anglo-Saxon vernacular had been a written language since the time of the Roman missions, it now came to rival Latin as a language of administration, history, scholarship, and spirituality. Moreover, oral traditions of poetic composition and storytelling were preserved and extended, as exemplified by the epic *Beowulf*. Until the eleventh century, Anglo-Saxon was the only European vernacular used for regular written communication.

The Disintegration of the Islamic World

As we noted above, the declining power of the Abbasid dynasty in Baghdad contributed to the escalation of Viking raids. A major cause of this decline was the gradual impoverishment of the Abbasids' economic base, the agricultural wealth of Mesopotamia, which resulted from ecological crises and a devastating revolt by the enslaved African workforce there. Tax revenues were also declining as provincial rulers in North Africa, Egypt, and Syria defiantly retained larger and larger portions of those revenues for themselves. As sources of income became depleted, the Abbasids were unable to support either their large civil service or the mercenary army on which they relied for defense. Massively expensive building projects further exacerbated the fiscal, military, and political crisis.

Behind the Abbasid decline lay two significant developments: the growing power of regional rulers and the sharpening religious divisions between Sunnis and Shi'ites, and among the Shi'ites themselves. In 909, regional and religious hostilities came together when a Shi'ite clan known as the Fatimids seized control of Abbasid North Africa. In 969, the Fatimids succeeded in conquering Egypt also. Meanwhile, another Shi'ite group, rivals of both the Fatimids and the Abbasids, attacked Baghdad in 927 and Mecca in 930, seizing the Kaaba. Although an Abbasid Caliphate would continue to exist in Baghdad until 1258, when invading Mongol armies conquered it (see Chapter 10), its empire had effectively disappeared. In its place a new order began to emerge, centered around an independent Egyptian kingdom and a new Muslim state based in Persia, with North Africa and Syria forming an embattled middle ground.

After You Read This Chapter

 Go to **INQUIZITIVE** to see what you've learned—and learn what you've missed— with personalized feedback along the way.

REVIEWING THE OBJECTIVES

- Justinian's attempted reunification of the Roman Empire proved destructive. What were its effects in the East? In the West?
- What were some important features of Byzantine culture, and how did it build on that of Rome?
- The rapid expansion of Islam can be explained with reference to several historical factors. What were they?
- What accounts for the close relationship between monasticism and secular power in early medieval Europe?
- What was the Carolingian Empire, and why is it important?

In Al-Andalus, disputes over succession within the Umayyad dynasty were matched by new external pressures. Beginning in the mid-ninth century, the small Christian kingdoms of northern and eastern Iberia began to encroach on Muslim territory. By the opening years of the eleventh century, the Umayyad Caliphate had been replaced by a host of smaller Muslim kingdoms, some of which paid tribute to the Christian rulers of the north.

These fractures deepened divisions that had always existed. While Islamic rulers were extremely tolerant of religious and cultural differences when dealing with their Jewish and Christian subjects, dissent within Islam itself was another matter. Under the strong rule of the caliphates, some different groups had learned to coexist; but with the disappearance of these centralized states it would be difficult to reconcile the ideal of universality with the realities of regional and ethnic differences.

CONCLUSION

The three civilizations that emerged as Rome's heirs each exhibit aspects of Roman civilization. Which was Rome's true successor? It depends on the criteria used to make this evaluation. If imperial Rome's most fundamental characteristics were the maintenance of legal and political institutions, the answer is Byzantium. If one is looking for a civilization that combines the rich legacies of the ancient Near East, Egypt, and the Hellenistic world, the answer is Islam, which also emulated Rome in promoting commerce and cultural exchange. If one associates Rome chiefly with the city itself and the Latin language of the first Romans, the answer is northwestern Europe.

There were also many connections among these heirs of Rome. Muslim traders were common in the ports of southern Italy and Gaul. Anglo-Saxon merchants were regular visitors to the Mediterranean. Jewish merchants in the Rhineland were carrying on an active trade with the communities of Muslim Egypt, while Viking traders had opened routes from the Baltic to the Black Sea and were busily founding cities from Novgorod to Dublin.

But developments of the ninth and tenth centuries would disrupt these networks and create new centers of power, as western Europe became a society mobilized for war to a degree unmatched in either Byzantium or the Islamic world. In the centuries to come, this militarization was to prove a decisive factor in the shifting relationship among Rome's heirs.

PEOPLE, IDEAS, AND EVENTS IN CONTEXT

- In what ways do **JUSTINIAN'S CODE OF ROMAN LAW** and the building of **HAGIA SOPHIA** reflect his desire to revive the glories of ancient Rome?
- What were **BYZANTIUM**'s sources of stability, and of dissent? What effect did the **ICONOCLAST CONTROVERSY** have on Byzantine society?
- What factors contributed to **MUHAMMAD**'s rise to power? What are the **FIVE PILLARS OF ISLAM**, and what is the role of the **QUR'AN**?
- To what extent were the **UMAYYAD** and **ABBASID CALIPHATES** heirs of Rome? What made Islamic culture of this period distinctive?
- How did the **MEROVINGIAN** kings of the Franks acquire and hold power? How did **BENEDICTINE MONASTICISM** contribute to the economy of western Europe, and how was it linked to politics?
- How did **CHARLEMAGNE** build an empire, and how did the **CAROLINGIAN RENAISSANCE** revive and extend **CLASSICAL LEARNING**?
- How did the **VIKINGS** contribute to the developments of the ninth and tenth centuries?

THINKING ABOUT CONNECTIONS

- Arguably, each of these three civilizations could claim the mantle of the Roman Empire. In your view, which one has the strongest claim to carrying forward the legacies of the classical past?
- How do the historical circumstances in which Islam emerged compare to those that shaped early Christianity? What are some key similarities and differences?

Before
You
Read
This
Chapter

The Expansion of Europe, 950–1100

CORE OBJECTIVES

- **EXPLAIN** the reasons for the fragmentation of political power in Europe during this period and **UNDERSTAND** the implications of this trend.

- **IDENTIFY** the most important outcomes of the medieval agricultural revolution and their effects.

- **DESCRIBE** the reforming movement with the Church and assess its consequences.

- **UNDERSTAND** the motives behind the First Crusade.

- **TRACE** the political, economic, social, religious, and cultural effects of the Crusades.

In the version of history popularized by medieval minstrels, Charlemagne and his knights are able to defeat a Muslim army in the mountainous borderlands between France and Spain. Their remaining obstacle is the castle of a Muslim king whose courage commands the Christians' respect. So when ambassadors from the king promise his conversion in exchange for the safety of his people, Charlemagne readily agrees. One of his men must now negotiate the terms of surrender. Roland, Charlemagne's bravest knight, suggests that his stepfather Ganelon be the chosen messenger. But Ganelon secretly resolves to betray his hated stepson and his liege lord: he convinces the Muslim king that Charlemagne's offer is a trick, and incites him to attack the Christian warriors as they travel homeward through the Pyrenees. Ganelon knows that Roland will volunteer to command the rear guard.

And so it happens. Roland's men are ambushed and his companion, Olivier, urges him to blow his horn and call for help. But Roland refuses: he will never endanger his lord by any such dishonorable deed. Instead, he will fight to the death and, with his last ounce of strength, break his sword. For it would never do to have this sacred gift of Charlemagne—made holier still by the relic in its pommel—fall into the hands of heathens. As Roland reminds Olivier, "We must not be the theme of mocking songs."

Like Homer's *Iliad*, *The Song of Roland* is the product of an oral storytelling tradition that took shape over hundreds of years. Written down around the year 1100, it reflects the many ways in which the world had changed since the time of the real Charlemagne. Its very language exemplifies one such change: the language we call French, no longer the Frankish tongue of Charlemagne. In Charlemagne's time, moreover, there was no such thing as knighthood, there were no major castles, there was no holy war against Muslims. All of these features were added to the story over time, to mirror a new reality and the ethos of the First Crusade (1095–99).

In this chapter, we will begin to trace the processes that transformed western Europe into the premier power among the three successor civilizations of the Roman Empire. In the centuries after the year 1000, European Christendom came to embrace the formerly outlying provinces of Scandinavia, Hungary, Poland, and Bohemia. Christian colonists would also push eastward into Prussia, Lithuania, Livonia, and the Balkans. Crusading knights would establish (and eventually lose) a Latin kingdom centered on Jerusalem. This expansion would be accompanied by a revolution in agricultural production, significant urbanization, and population growth. It would foster the rise of territorial monarchies, create a new social order, and spur remarkable intellectual and cultural achievements.

A TOUR OF EUROPE AROUND THE YEAR 1000

We have seen that many of Europe's territories were gradually brought into the orbit of Western civilizations through trade and imperial conquest. Meanwhile, the Jewish diaspora, the spread of Islam, and waves of immigration from the steppes of Asia increased the already rich ethnic and cultural diversity of Europe, as did the movements of the Vikings. While Charlemagne had tried to promote an idea of Europe as Christendom, Europe was not (and could never be) wholly Christian; and it was certainly not unified. So what was it?

This chapter is entitled "The Expansion of Europe" for two main reasons: because the very idea of Europe gained increasing coherence during this period and because

Europeans' forceful annexation of neighboring territories is a crucial development. Some influential historians argue that Europe was actually invented in this era, through an ongoing process of internal and external colonization. New kingdoms and communities were being created by conquest and settlement within Europe, but also well beyond it. Europeans were becoming the agents of imperialism, not its targets. This is a striking change. The West's center of gravity had always been the Mediterranean and its adjacent lands; it was from there that influences flowed farther west and north. Now that trajectory was being reversed.

Viking Initiatives

After the Viking invasions, new polities began to emerge. Some were formed when the Vikings became colonists: Iceland, Greenland, and (briefly) Newfoundland. Indeed, Iceland can claim to be Europe's oldest state and the world's first parliamentary democracy. In the year 930, its settlers formed a legislative assembly called the Althing, a Norse word with the same meaning as the Latin *res publica*. Icelanders would also produce a fascinating and influential body of poetic forms and literary entertainments, notably the *sagas*: sprawling family histories that unfold over generations, ranging from the hilarious to the ruthless. Modern action films and movie epics are heavily indebted to the sagas.

In regions where Vikings settled among more established groups—throughout the British Isles and the Low Countries—they both absorbed and affected these cultures. In Normandy, for example, the descendants of Vikings maintained alliances and kinship ties with the rest of the Norse world while at the same time intermarrying with the Franks and adopting their language.

The Rise of Rus' and the Kingdoms of Eastern Europe

One group of Vikings established an important kingdom in a region that still bears their name: Russia. The Rus' were active raiders and traders in the Baltic region, where they came to dominate the Finns and Slavic peoples who lived along the seaboard. They extended their reach through the navigation of Eurasian waterways while also moving farther inland, to Novgorod. By the year 1000, they had conquered the fortress of Kiev.

LINGSBERG RUNESTONE. This is one of two commemorative runestones erected at Lingsberg, Sweden, at the beginning of the eleventh century. The runic inscription records that a woman named Holmfríðr had it placed here in memory of her husband, Halfdan, whose father had been a Viking raider in England. Runic alphabets were in use among Germanic-speaking peoples of the North prior to the adoption of the Latin alphabet. Some runic letters survive in Anglo-Saxon and Old Norse, including the *edh*—the letter ð in the name of Holmfríðr—which is pronounced *th* as in *the*.

Kiev was a key outpost on the frontier controlled by the Khazars, a Turkic people with a trading empire along the Silk Road to China. From Kiev, on the shores of the river Dneiper, the Rus' also had easy access to the Black Sea and thence to Constantinople and Baghdad. They were thus in a position to trade directly and indirectly with much of Eurasia. Through a series of strategic intermarriages, moreover, they forged further connections with many powerful European families. This placed Kievan Rus' at the heart of the medieval world.

Yet the dominion of the Rus' was countered by the crystallization of Slavic kingdoms farther to the south: Serbia and Croatia on the Adriatic, which grew up within provinces of the old Roman Empire, and Poland. The ruling families of Croatia embraced the Latin Christianity of

Rome in this period; so did those of Poland. The Serbians, however, were drawn into the orbit of Byzantium and Greek Orthodoxy. Between them, and on the borders of Rus', was Hungary, comprising the former Roman province of Pannonia and stretching eastward toward the Carpathian mountains. It had been conquered by the Huns in the late fourth century and had since attracted new immigrants: the Magyars, a nomadic people from the region of the Urals whose language, like that of the Finns, was non-Indo-European.

The Magyars were expert herdsmen and horsemen. They also served as mercenaries fighting for various warring states. Around 895, they united under a leader called Arpád and settled in the fertile land of the Danube river basin, where they became farmers and ranchers. Arpád's descendants would embrace Latin Christianity, and would integrate the kingdom of Hungary with its neighbors through dynastic marriage and diplomacy.

New Scandinavian Kingdoms and the Empire of Cnut the Great

Meanwhile, powerful Norse lords were establishing control over parts of the Vikings' homeland. Around the year 1000, three strong kingdoms had emerged: Norway, Sweden, and Denmark. Each built on their kings' reputation for fearlessness in battle and generosity afterward, their capacity to dominate seas and riverways, and their canny practices of adaptation and intermarriage.

What made these new states distinctive was their rulers' very deliberate manipulation of this heritage, blended with the strategic decision to convert their followers to Christianity and to the political conventions of the Continent. They simultaneously glorified their own culture and achievements while tying them to newer models of government. For these reasons, scholars have often spoken of this as the "Viking Age." On the one hand, older Western civilizations can be said to have colonized Scandinavia; on the other hand, it was really Scandinavians who were doing the colonizing.

The empire forged by Cnut (*kuh-NOOT*) the Great is a good example of this. At the time of his death in 1035, Cnut ruled over Norway, much of Sweden, and England as well as his native Denmark; he had a controlling interest in large parts of Ireland and portions of the Low Countries; and he also had diplomatic and family ties to the independent principalities of Flanders and Normandy, the new kingdom of Poland (his mother was a Polish princess), and to the imperial family of Germany (through his daughter, who became empress). Although his was a short-term personal empire, it had long-term effects on the political organization of Europe.

Mediterranean Microcosms

The dynamism of these new states stands in contrast to the very different dynamics that governed relations in the medieval Mediterranean. No map could convey the political, religious, cultural, and economic affinities of this maritime world. It is more useful to imagine coastal regions and islands as interlocking components of the same civilization, and to further imagine that a community on the shores of North Africa—say, Muslim Tunis—would have more in common, and more contact, with Christian Barcelona than with another African community farther inland. The medieval Mediterranean was thus made up of diverse microcosms whose contours and interrelationships were more determined by prevailing winds, trading patterns, and climate than by the control of a particular ruler. In many places, it made little difference who the rulers were, especially since the forms of rule changed so often.

Take Sicily, for example: the first overseas colony of Rome (Chapter 5), it had been part of the Phoenician maritime empire of Carthage and, before that, a major Greek settlement (Chapters 2 and 3). All of those elements would still have been part of Sicily's historical DNA when it was invaded by the Vandals in the fifth century and afterward by the Goths. It was then reconquered by Justinian and became part of Byzantium—so important a part that one Byzantine emperor tried to move the capital from Constantinople to Palermo. Then, in the course of the tenth century, it became an emirate of the Fatimid Caliphate based in Egypt. In the eleventh, it was progressively infiltrated by Norman mercenaries who established a Norman (but only nominally Christian) kingdom there in 1072. So who were the Sicilians? More important, who did they think they were—and how stable was that identity over this long period of continual change? These are not easy questions to answer.

In any such case, it is better to think in terms of influences, connections, and orbits of exchange than about stable borders or identities; this holds true of many areas of Europe in this period but is especially true when speaking of regions joined by water. Gaining "control" of any Mediterranean community meant harnessing its commercial power, something not best done through violent conquest or military occupation. An exemplary light-handed interference was what enabled the Venetians to build a successful and long-lived trading empire in the Adriatic and then in the eastern Mediterranean and Aegean Seas.

The Heirs of Charlemagne

What had become of the former Carolingian empire? The Saxon kings of eastern Francia (now part of Germany) modeled themselves on Charlemagne, who had conquered Saxony, by extending their domains farther eastward, into Slavic lands. They also nurtured their image as guardians of Christendom: in 955, King Otto I defeated the then-pagan Magyars while carrying a sacred lance that had belonged to Charlemagne. In 962, he went to Rome to be crowned emperor by Pope John XII, who hoped Otto would help him defeat his own enemies. But Otto turned the tables on the pope, deposing him and selecting a new pope to replace him.

Otto thereby laid the foundation for his successors' claims to imperial autonomy. He also advertised his inheritance of Carolingian and Roman power through his patronage of arts and learning. The first known female playwright, Hrotsvitha of Gandersheim (c. 935–c. 1002), was raised in his court, and grew up hearing the works of classical authors read aloud. When she entered a royal convent, she wrote plays blending Roman comedy with the stories of early Christian martyrs, for the entertainment and instruction of her fellow nuns. Otto also presided over the establishment of cathedral schools and helped the bishops of his domain turn their own courts into cultural centers.

However, Otto could not control either the papacy or the independent towns of northern Italy unless he maintained a permanent presence there. And if he remained in Italy too long, his authority in Saxony broke down. The result was a gradually increasing rift between local elites and the king in his guise as emperor. This conundrum would deepen in the eleventh century, when the imperial crown passed to a new dynasty, the Salians, based in neighboring Franconia. When this Salian emperor attempted to assert control over Saxony, he touched off a war that was to have momentous repercussions (as will be discussed later).

Aspects of Charlemagne's legacy also survived in the highly effective administration of Anglo-Saxon England and in parts of the Mediterranean world. In Catalonia, counts descended from Carolingian appointees continued to administer justice in public courts of law and to draw revenues from tolls and trade. The city of Barcelona grew rapidly as both a long-distance and a regional market under the protection of these counts. In Aquitaine (southwestern France), the counts of Poitiers and Toulouse also continued to rest their authority on Carolingian foundations.

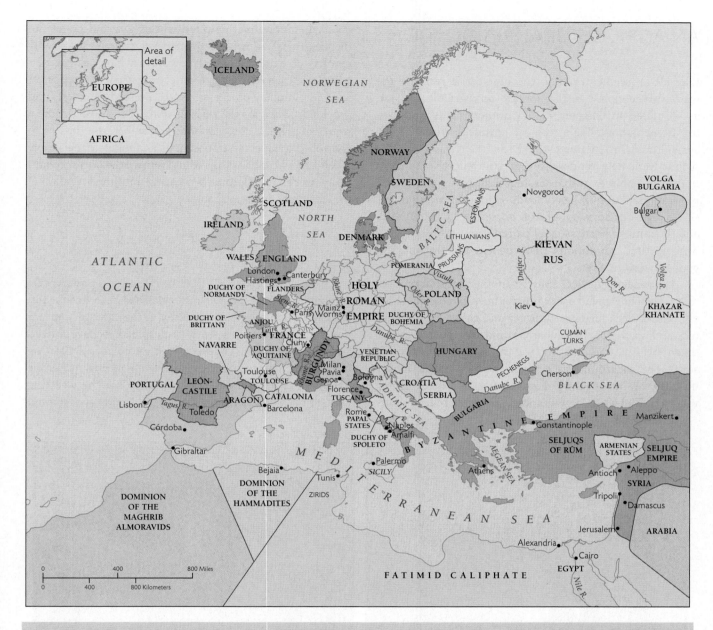

EUROPE, C. 1000. This map shows the patchwork of political power in western Europe after the millennium, although it cannot accurately illustrate the degree of fragmentation within these major territories, especially those of the Holy Roman Empire. ▪ *What factors account for the close relationship between Italy and the German principalities?* ▪ *How are they related to the northwestern regions of the Continent and the British Isles?* ▪ *Which geopolitical entities would you expect to emerge as dominant in the following centuries?*

In Charlemagne's own west Frankish kingdom, however, Carolingian rule collapsed under the combined weight of Viking raids, economic disintegration, and the growing power of local lords. A few Carolingian institutions—such as public courts and a centrally minted coinage—survived in new, autonomous principalities such as Anjou and Flanders. The Norse-Frankish rulers of Normandy also used these techniques effectively. But in the Franks' heartland, even this modicum of authority disappeared. The local count, Hugh Capet, had managed to defend his territory against the Vikings and, in 987, this modest feat earned him the title King of the Franks. Marooned on this Ile de France (literally, "island of France"), a tiny territory around Paris, the Capetian kings clung to the fiction that they were the heirs of Charlemagne's greatness. It would be another 200 years before one of them made this fiction a political reality (see Chapter 9).

AN AGRICULTURAL REVOLUTION

Like all economies prior to the nineteenth century, the medieval economy rested largely on agriculture. But, as we noted in Chapter 7, that economy was undergoing a revolution. Technological advances that boosted agricultural productivity—such as the heavy-wheeled plow—were now rendered even more effective through improved methods of harnessing, making it possible for plow animals to pull heavy loads without choking themselves. The development of iron horseshoes (around 900) and the tandem harnessing of paired teams (around 1050) were further innovations that enabled the transport of goods to new markets.

Labor-saving devices spurred another boost in productivity. The widespread use of iron for hoes, pitchforks, shovels, and scythes made work faster and easier for humans, too, and so did the wheelbarrow and the harrow (a tool drawn over plowed fields to level the earth and mix in the seed). The watermill was perhaps the most revolutionary invention. Although the Romans had known that running water was a potential power source, they had relied mainly on slave- and animal-powered wheels to grind grain. But the lack of slave labor led medieval engineers—usually monks—to experiment with new ways of harnessing water. Mills were then adapted to a variety of purposes: they drove saws for lumber, processed cloth, pressed olive oil, and provided power for the forging iron. They thus became a source of political and economic power, because those who controlled them could impose tolls and regulate the supply of food and weapons. Mills would remain the only mechanical power sources for manufacturing until the invention of the steam engine (see Chapter 19).

New Conditions for Growth

Although many of these technologies had been invented in the early Middle Ages, it was only in the eleventh century that they became sufficiently widespread to have a decisive impact. Climate change played a role in this. Starting in the late eighth century, average temperatures in Europe gradually rose by about 1° or 2°C (3.6°F). The warming climate benefited northern Europe by drying the soil and

EMPEROR OTTO THE GREAT. In this opening from a deluxe set of Gospels he commissioned for himself, Otto is shown seated on a throne and vested with the regalia of imperial and royal authority, surrounded by clerical and secular counselors, and receiving tribute from a procession of deferential women representing the four regions of his domain: Slavinia, Germania, Gallia, and Roma. • *What claims to power is Otto making through this imagery?*

lengthening the growing season, while hotter summers and diminishing rainfall hurt Mediterranean agriculture in equal measure. For several centuries, it was possible to raise crops as far north as Greenland.

These new technologies also took hold because the settlement of Viking and Magyar peoples decreased the threat of invasion and the disruption of planting cycles. Left in relative peace, monasteries could develop and implement the tools described above, which were then copied by entrepreneurial peasants and local lords who saw the benefits of managing their own lands more efficiently, rather than raiding others'.

Harnessing People

All of this productivity led to population increases, fundamental changes in patterns of settlement, and the organization of the peasant workforce. In the centuries after the fragmentation of Roman imperial power, most people lived on individual plots of land that they worked by themselves and with their families. Starting in the ninth century, however, many of these individual holdings merged into large, common fields that could be farmed collectively by the inhabitants of entire villages. The resulting complex is sometimes called a *manor* (from the Latin verb *manere*, meaning "to dwell").

In many cases, the impetus for consolidation came from the peasants themselves. Large fields could be farmed more efficiently and investment costs could be shared: a single plow and a dozen oxen might suffice for an entire village, obviating the need for every farmer to maintain his own plow and team. Common fields were potentially more productive, allowing villagers to experiment with new crops and to support larger numbers of animals on common pastures. In time, prosperous peasants might be able to establish a parish church, a communal oven, a blacksmith, a mill, and a tavern. They could socialize and assist their neighbors.

In other cases, a manor could be created or co-opted by a local lord or a monastery. Manors were attractive because their greater productivity meant that lords could take a larger share of the peasants' surplus; it was also easier to control and exploit peasants who lived together in villages and who were bound by ties of kinship and dependence. Over time, some lords were able to reduce formerly free peasants to the status of serfs. Like slaves, serfs inherited their servile status; unlike slaves, they were attached to the lands they worked. Practically speaking, there may have been little difference between a serf and a free peasant—indeed, some serfs may

have been better off. But, as we have seen, social mobility is often tied to geographical mobility; the inability of serfs to move freely would prevent them from achieving the liberties of those who could (as will be discussed later).

The Conquest of the Land

For centuries, farmers had known that sowing the same crop in the same field year after year would eventually exhaust the soil. The traditional solution was to divide one's land, planting half and leaving the other half to lie fallow. In the dry, thin soils of the Mediterranean, this remained the most common cropping pattern throughout the Middle Ages. In the more fertile soils of northern Europe, however, the organization of labor opened up more land for cultivation, and made that cultivation more efficient. Farmers discovered that a three-field crop-rotation system could produce a sustainable increase in overall production. One-third of the land would lie fallow or be used as pasture, so that manure would fertilize the soil; one-third would be planted with winter wheat or rye, sown in the fall and harvested in the early summer; and one-third would be planted in the spring with another crop to be harvested in the fall. These fields were then rotated over a three-year cycle.

This system increased the amount of land under cultivation, while the two separate growing seasons provided some insurance against loss due to natural disasters or inclement weather. The system also produced higher yields per acre, particularly if legumes or fodder crops like oats were a regular part of the crop-rotation pattern to replace the nitrogen that grains leach out of the soil. Both humans and animals could eat oats, and legumes provided a source of protein to balance the intake of carbohydrates from bread and beer, the two main dietary staples in northern and central Europe. Additional fodder supported more and healthier animals, increasing the efficiency of plow beasts and providing an additional source of protein through meat and milk. The new crop-rotation system also helped spread labor more evenly over the course of the year.

THE GROWTH OF TOWNS AND TRADE

As we observed in Chapter 7, the urban infrastructure of the western Roman Empire was weakened in the course of the fifth and sixth centuries. A few Roman cities

1. Cathedral
2. Alt St. Thomas
3. Alt St. Peter
4. Jung St. Peter
5. St. Nikolaus
6. St. Johann
7. St. Wilhelm
8. St. Stephen

0 50 100   200   300m

☐ Roman fortification, the 'city'

▨ Frankish settlement, called 'New City', walled at end of ninth century

☐ Extension of Frankish settlement before 1200 to include Alt St. Peter's parish

▥ Jung St. Peter's parish, walled 1202–1220

▨ St. Nikolaus parish, walled thirteenth and fourteenth centuries

▨ St. Johann Parish, walled 1374–1390

▪▬▪ St. Wilhelm parish, walled 1387–1441

THE METAMORPHOSIS OF A MEDIEVAL CITY. The city of Strasbourg, on the long-disputed border between modern Germany and France, exemplifies the multilayered dynamics of urban change throughout the Middle Ages. It began as a Roman settlement, which became the nucleus for an episcopal see—hence the cathedral (1) located in the ancient precinct. It was fortified with new walls at the end of the ninth century, as the Carolingian Empire was collapsing and the Vikings were on the move. It then responded to the renewed prosperity of the eleventh and twelfth centuries, far outgrowing its original bounds, and continued to expand for several centuries thereafter. ▪ *Note the scale of the map. What can you conclude from this about the density of settlement in a medieval city?*

continued to thrive, but many—including Rome itself—crumbled. Their depleted populations could no longer maintain public buildings, services, and defensive walls. In most areas of northwestern Europe, monasteries replaced cities as the nuclei of civilization. Then, under Charlemagne and his successors, towns were planted as centers for markets and administration. In Anglo-Saxon England, too, King Alfred and his heirs established new towns in strategic locations while at the same time fostering older Roman cities.

Fostering Commerce

Although many of towns were devastated by the Viking raids of the tenth century, the agricultural revolution

helped to revitalize them. The rapid urbanization of the eleventh and twelfth centuries was also fostered by monasteries and secular lords who provided safe havens for travelers and trade. This was especially true in the principalities of the Rhineland, the Low Countries, and the independent counties of Flanders and Champagne. In southwestern Europe, existing towns prospered from their status as ports or their location along the overland routes connecting the Mediterranean with the Atlantic.

In Italy, which had been decimated by five centuries of warfare and invasion, renewed prosperity initially depended on the Byzantine emperors' suppression of piracy in the eastern Mediterranean. Around the turn of the millenium, therefore, the most successful cities were situated in Byzantine-controlled areas: Venice in the north and Amalfi, Naples, and Palermo in the south. These were the trading posts that brought silks, spices, and other luxuries into western Europe. In the eleventh century, however, the Norman conquests of southern Italy frequently disrupted this trade, while Turkish invasions of Asia Minor turned Byzantium's attention to the empire's eastern frontier. This opened new opportunities to the northern ports of Genoa and Pisa, whose merchant navies took over the task of policing the eastern Mediterranean.

From Italy and other Mediterranean ports, exotic goods flowed northward to the towns of Flanders and to the organized system of fairs—international markets convened at certain times of the year—that enriched the county of Champagne. Flemish towns, in turn, kept up a brisk trade with England, processing English wool into cloth.

"Town Air Makes You Free"

To our eyes, most medieval towns would have seemed half rural. Streets were unpaved, houses had gardens for raising vegetables, and animals were everywhere. Sanitary conditions were poor, and the air reeked of excrement, both animal and human. (Even in 1900, this was also true of New York, where 150,000 horses produced 45,000 tons of manure each month.) Under these conditions, disease could spread rapidly. Fire was another omnipresent danger, because wooden and thatched buildings were clustered close together.

But these inconveniences were far outweighed by the advantages of urban life. As a German adage puts it, "Town air makes you free" (*Stadtluft macht Frei*). This is because the citizens of most medieval towns were not subject to the arbitrary power of a lord—or if they were, the lord realized that rewarding initiative with further freedoms fostered still more initiative and produced more wealth. Many towns accordingly received charters of liberty from local rulers and were given the right to govern themselves. Others seized that right: in 1127, for example, the people of Flemish Arras declared that they were no longer the serfs of the local monastery and they banded together to form a commune, setting up their own form of representative government. The monastery was forced to free them and was then free to tax them. By the end of the century, Arras was the wealthiest and most densely populated town in northern Europe.

Urban areas further expanded through the constant immigration of free peasants and escaped serfs in search of a better life. For once a town had established its independence, newcomers could claim the status of citizens after a year and a day. For this reason, some powerful lords and rulers resisted the efforts of towns to claim independence. Almost inevitably, though, they paid a high price for this. In Rome, the pope's claim to secular authority over the city led to frequent uprisings. In the French city of Laon, the bishop who asserted his lordship over a newly formed commune was murdered in 1112. In 1127, the count of Flanders was assassinated in Bruges by a family of powerful officials who denied that they were his serfs.

Portable Wealth: Money and Credit

The growth of these medieval towns depended on initiative, social mobility, and surplus goods. It also depended on money: reliable currencies and the availability of credit. It is no accident that the wealthiest cities were located in regions whose rulers minted and regulated a strong coinage: Byzantium, Al-Andalus and the Christian kingdoms of Spain, the old Roman region of Provence (southern France), Anglo-Saxon England, and Flanders. Yet precisely because there were so many currencies in circulation, the medieval economy also depended on moneychangers and on bankers who could extend credit to merchants.

Many sophisticated financial mechanisms for extending credit had long been in place throughout the Islamic world and Byzantium. In western Europe, though, much of this crucial activity was carried forward by Jewish bankers situated within a close-knit network that connected cities like Constantinople, Baghdad, and Córdoba to the burgeoning cities of the north. In many regions, Jews had a virtual monopoly on these activities, because Christians were technically forbidden to lend money at interest or to make a profit from investments: a practice called *usury* (from the Latin word for "interest"). In reality, however, the Roman Church turned a blind eye to such practices. Indeed, many prominent churchmen, including bishops, made fortunes lending money—especially in banking towns like Arras and Florence.

Still, the moral stigma attaching to this necessary practice meant that Jews were often the ones targeted in times of crisis, just as they were the people to whom rulers would turn most readily when they needed funds. This helps to explain why many rulers protected the Jewish communities in their realms and often extended special privileges to them in exchange for money. The unfortunate result of this Christian hypocrisy was the circulation of conspiracy theories harmful to Jews, who were perceived as exercising control over finance. Jewish communities' reliance on the protection of powerful men also made

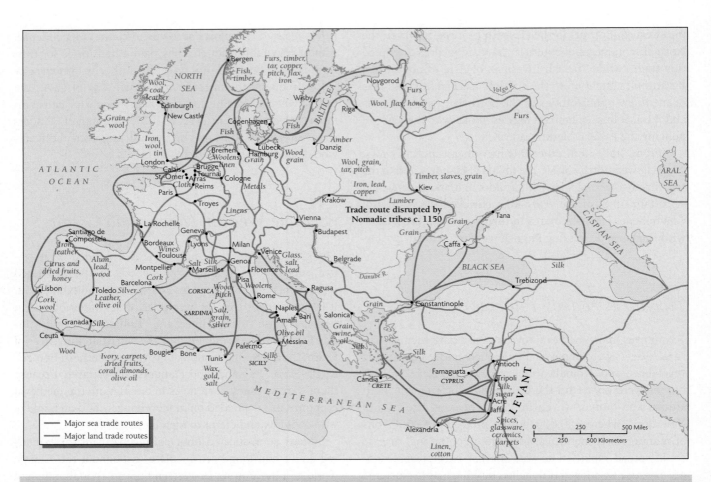

MEDIEVAL TRADE ROUTES. ■ *What does this map reveal about the relationship between waterways and overland routes during the eleventh and twelfth centuries?* ■ *Which regions appear to be most extensively interconnected, and why?* ■ *How does the trade in certain specialized goods create unique commercial patterns?*

them vulnerable when those men withdrew their support or were incapable of controlling the violence unleashed by their own policies.

VIOLENCE, LORDSHIP, AND MONARCHY

The new wealth of medieval Europe fostered social mobility, yet it also created a more stratified society. During the tenth and eleventh centuries, territorial lords and princes came to rival and often to surpass older aristocratic families in power and wealth. Some were descended from lesser officeholders in the Carolingian royal administration, men who had established independent powers after the empire collapsed and

who used their public offices for private gain. Others were successful interlopers who seized control of undefended manors and sustained war-bands of treasure-hungry young men.

Tools of Power: Castles and Knights

The predatory lords who emerged in this period protected their territories, their families, and their followers by building strongholds: castles, from the Latin word *castellum*, "little fortress." The stone castle, a structure seldom known in Europe before the Viking invasions, was both defensive and offensive. It rendered its keeper more secure from attack—though it was vulnerable to siege—and it enabled him to dominate the surrounding countryside, literally: the territory of a lord (*dominus*) was his dominion.

Indeed, castles often formed the nucleus of a new town by providing protection for the peasants and merchants who clustered close to its walls. In case of attack, these outliers could move inside.

Although most early castles were modest structures built of wood, situated on earthwork mounds surrounded by a ditch or moat, stone walls and keeps (fortified towers) soon replaced wooded palisades as the level of competitive violence increased. In Italy, rival families even built castles and towers in the middle of towns. Eventually, some castellans ("castle-holders") acquired enough power and booty to challenge more-established lords. These new lords didn't descend from Roman senators or Carolingian counts; instead, they boasted of lineages reaching back to successful warlords like Rollo the Viking, whom the Normans claimed to be their first duke (from the Latin word *dux*, "leader").

Both the older aristocracy and these self-made lords needed the help of warriors to enforce their claims to power. Accordingly, each lord maintained a private army of men heavily equipped with the new weaponry and armor made possible by the widespread availability of iron and new techniques for smelting it. These men fought on horseback and were therefore called "horsemen": in French, *chevaliers*, and in English, *knights*.

Knighthood was a career that embraced men of widely varying status. Some eleventh-century knights were the younger sons of noblemen who sought wealth by attaching themselves to the household of a great warlord. Others were youths recruited from the peasantry, mounted and armed. All that bound them together was their function, which was the violent prosecution of their lord's interests. Gradually, though, they came to regard themselves as belonging to a special military caste with its own rules of conduct. The beginnings of this process are discernible in *The Song of Roland*, a process that transformed the meaning of chivalry from "horsemanship" to something more refined (as will be discussed later).

Kings, Lords, and Vassals

Despite the emergence of self-governing cities and predatory lordships, the idea of kingship remained a powerful one. The weak Capetian rulers of Paris pretended that the lands once ruled by Frankish kings still owed allegiance to them, while the Ottonians claimed to be kings in northern Italy as well as in their own Saxon domain. In practice, however, neither was able to control the territories

YORK CASTLE (ENGLAND). This fortification exemplifies some of the major phases of medieval castle-building. The large mound is the remains of an earthwork erected on the orders of William the Conqueror in 1068, when it would have been crowned by a wooden palisade: this most basic type of construction is called a motte-and-bailey castle. York's castle remained a wooden tower until it was destroyed by fire and rebuilt in stone after 1245. It is now known as Clifford's Tower, after a rebel leader called Sir Roger Clifford, who was held prisoner there prior to his execution in 1322.

they claimed to rule. Real power lay in the hands of dukes, counts, castellans, and knights, all of whom channeled the increasing wealth of the countryside into their own hands. From their castles, these lords maintained the rights to mint money, dispense justice, raise troops, wage war, collect taxes, and impose tolls.

The Problem of "Feudalism"

The diffused distribution of power in this era is conventionally known as *feudalism*, but this term is misleading. For one thing, it is a modern construct that would have meant nothing to the people whose history we are discussing. Moreover, it has been used to mean many different things. Those influenced by the work of Karl Marx (1818–1883; see Chapter 20) used the term to describe an economic system based entirely on agriculture; as we have seen, this does not reflect the historical reality of medieval Europe or explain the importance of cities and trade. For others, "feudalism" means an aristocratic social order in which propertied men are bound together by kinship and shared interests; again, this does not match the varieties of power wielded in this period. Still others have seen "feudalism" as a system of landholding in which lesser men hold land from greater men in return for military service; and yet it was not always the greater men who held the most land.

Although people living at this time would never have heard the term *feudalism*, they would have understood the

Interpreting Visual Evidence

The Graphic History of the Bayeux Tapestry

One of the most famous historical documents of all time is not a document at all: it is an embroidered strip of linen 231 feet long (originally much longer) and 20 inches wide. It is also not an actual tapestry, as its name misleadingly implies, but an elaborate exercise in needlepoint. It tells the story of the Norman Conquest of England and the events leading up to it. The circumstances of its making remain mysterious, but it was certainly commissioned by someone close to William the Conqueror (1027–1087), the Norman duke who claimed the throne of England in 1066. Indeed, its purpose was to demonstrate the truth of William's claim and to justify his invasion of England when Harold Godwinson (c. 1022–1066), was crowned king of England in his place (image B). One likely patron is Queen Edith of England, the widow of the late King Edward (r. 1042–66) and sister of Harold, who became a friend and adviser to William. Edith was noted for her skill in embroidery as well as for her political acumen, and she would have been able to oversee the making of this visual history by the women of her household. Two of its evocative scenes, with translations of accompanying Latin texts, are reproduced here.

A. Here Harold Sails the Sea. In this scene from the first portion of the Tapestry, Harold has been sent on an embassy by King Edward. He feasts with friends in a hall on the English coast before crossing the Channel.

B. Here Is Seated Harold, King of the English. Although Harold may have promised to relinquish his claim to the English throne in William's favor, the central scene of the tapestry is his coronation. Stigant, the archbishop of Canterbury, stands on his right. Outside the cathedral, the people of London look on curiously. Some appear to be surprised or alarmed.

Questions for Analysis

1. Like a graphic novel or a comic strip, the Bayeux Tapestry tells its story through images; words (in very simple Latin) play a minor role. What do the Tapestry's artists choose to express exclusively through visualization? When do they choose to state something verbally? What might be the motivation behind these choices? What is left out of the story, or left ambiguous? What might be the reason(s) for this?

2. In addition to being a source for political and military historians, the Bayeux Tapestry provides us with fascinating glimpses into the daily life and material culture of the Middle Ages. What, for example, can you conclude about the necessary preparations for a voyage by sea? About the history of clothing, or weaponry, or animals?

3. If Queen Edith is responsible for making the Tapestry, it would constitute one of the few surviving historical accounts by a woman prior to the twentieth century. Would the fact of the creator's gender change your perception of this artifact or of these particular scenes? Why or why not?

word at its root: *feudum*, usually translated as "fief" (FEEF). A fief is a gift or grant that creates a kind of contractual relationship between the giver and receiver. This gift could be land, but it could also be the revenues from a toll or a mill, or an annual sum of money. In return, the recipient owed the giver loyalty or services of some kind.

In many cases, the recipient of a fief was subordinate to the giver and was said to be the giver's *vassal*, from a Celtic word meaning "boy." This relationship was dramatized in an act of *homage*, a ceremony that made the vassal "the man" (in French, *homme*) of his lord. Typically, the vassal would kneel and place his hands together in a position of prayer, and the lord would cover the clasped hands with his own. He would then raise up his new man and exchange a kiss with him. The symbolic importance of these gestures is clear: the lord could protect and elevate his man—but could also discipline him or bring him down.

In regions where no centralized authority existed, such relationships were essential to creating and maintaining order. However, these relationships were not understood in the same ways all over Europe. Many castellans and knights held their lands freely, owing no service whatsoever to the count or duke within whose territories their lands lay. Nor were these relationships neatly hierarchical. "Feudalism" created no "feudal pyramids," in which knights held fiefs from counts, and counts held fiefs from kings, all in an orderly fashion. Sometimes, kings would insist that the world *should* be structured this way, but they were seldom able to enforce this.

A New Type of Monarchy: England

The first place where we can observe a king's attempt to dominate other powerful lordships is England. In 1066, Duke William of Normandy claimed that he was the rightful successor of the Anglo-Saxon king, Edward, who had just died. But the English ignored this claim and elected a new king, Harold. So William crossed the English Channel to take the kingdom by force, defeating Harold's army at the Battle of Hastings (see **Interpreting Visual Evidence** on page 204). Now, however, William had to subjugate all of the Anglo-Saxon chieftains who held power in England, many of whom also aspired to be king.

William accomplished this by asserting that he was king by imperial conquest as well as by succession, and that all the land of England thereby belonged to him. Then William rewarded his Norman followers with fiefs: extensive grants of land taken from their Anglo-Saxon holders, which the Norman lords were allowed to exploit and

subdue. In return, William received their loyalty and a share of their revenues.

The Norman conquerors of England were already accustomed to holding land in return for service to their duke, back in Normandy. But in England, their subordination to the king was further enforced by the effective machinery of the previous Anglo-Saxon state. As king of England, therefore, William was able to exercise a variety of public powers that he could not have enjoyed in Normandy. In England, only the king could coin money and only the king's money was allowed to circulate. As kings of England, William and his successors also inherited the sole right to collect a national land tax, the right to supervise justice in royal courts, and the right to raise an army. They also retained the Anglo-Saxon officers of local government, known as sheriffs, to help them administer and enforce these royal rights.

William was thereby able to insist that all the people of England owed ultimate loyalty to the king, even if they did not hold a scrap of land from him. William's kingship thus represented a powerful fusion of Carolingian-style traditions of public power with the new forms of lordship that had grown up in the tenth and eleventh centuries, bolstered by indigenous Anglo-Saxon forms of governance. It was a new type of monarchy.

The Struggle for Imperial Power

We can contrast the wide-ranging powers of the new Norman kings of England with those of Germany. Any German king who claimed the title of emperor owed his imperial authority to a close alliance with the Church; he had no authority over any German principality but his own. For this reason, the emperor relied heavily on ecclesiastical leaders: his chief administrators were archbishops and bishops whom the emperor appointed and installed in their sacred offices, just as Charlemagne had done. Even the pope was frequently an imperial appointee. The fact that leading churchmen were often members of the emperor's own family also helped to counter the power of regional rulers.

But in the latter half of the eleventh century, this close cooperation between imperial and ecclesiastical authority was fractured. In 1056, the six-year-old Henry IV (1050–1106) succeeded his father as king of Saxony and emperor of the Romans. As we will observe, political competition among the advisers of underage rulers often escalates into larger conflicts. In this case, the German rulers of various other regions—led by some members of the Saxon nobility—tried to gain control of the royal government.

Gregory installed at the castle of Canossa under the protection of one of Europe's most powerful rulers, Matilda of Tuscany.

Encouraged by Matilda, who interceded on his behalf, Henry performed an elaborate ritual of penance, standing for three successive days outside the gates of the castle, barefoot, stripped of his imperial trappings, clad in the sackcloth of a suppliant. This performance forestalled his deposition, but it did not resolve his dispute with the nobility. And it also symbolically reversed the relationship between secular power and religious power. Since the time of Constantine, popes had been dependent on the rulers who protected them. Now an emperor had been bested by the pope. For the other kings and lords of Europe, Henry's humiliation was a chilling example of what could happen when a king became a vassal of the Church.

RELIGIOUS REFORM AND PAPAL POWER

The increased power of the papacy in the eleventh century was a result of the processes we have been surveying in this chapter. In the wake of the Viking invasions and the redistribution of power within the former Carolingian Empire, no ruler could maintain Charlemagne's hold on the Church. Many local churches had been abandoned or destroyed, while those that survived were often regarded as the personal property of some local family. Bishoprics, too, were co-opted by families who regarded Church lands and offices as their private property. Monasteries also underwent a process of privatization. Meanwhile, the holders of papal office were its worst abusers. Most were incompetent or corrupt, the sons or tools of powerful Roman families. Many fathered sons who themselves succeeded to high ecclesiastical office, including that of pope. The bishop of Rome had long occupied a privileged position, as the successor of St. Peter and the guardian of his tomb. Now, however, the papacy's credibility had been severely compromised.

MATILDA OF TUSCANY MEDIATES BETWEEN EMPEROR AND POPE. Matilda was one of the most powerful rulers in eleventh-century Europe, controlling many strategic territories in northern Italy. Fluent in German as well as Latin and Italian, she was a key mediator in the struggle between the emperor and the pope and a supporter of the reforming movement within the Church. The Latin inscription accompanying this manuscript miniature reads: "The King entreats the Abbot [i.e., the pope] and even humbles himself before Matilda." ■ *How does this image represent the relationships among these figures?* ■ *Which appears to be the most powerful, and why?*

When Henry began to rule in his own right, in 1073, these hostilities escalated into a civil war.

At the same time, the newly elected pope, Gregory VII (r. 1073–85), began to insist that no layman—not even a king—should have any influence within the Church. (This movement toward increased papal power will be discussed further in the next section.) For King Henry, this meant that he could no longer select his own key administrators—and course, he resisted. So Pope Gregory allied himself with the rebellious Saxon nobility, and together they moved to depose Henry. In order to save his crown, Henry was therefore forced to acknowledge the pope's superiority. Crossing the Alps into Italy in 1077, in the depths of winter, he found

The Monastic Reform Movement

The first successful attempts to restore the spiritual authority of the Roman Church can be traced to the founding of a new kind of monastery in Burgundy (now southeastern France). In 910, a Benedictine abbey called Cluny freed itself from any obligation to local families by placing itself under the direct protection of the papacy. And although it had a wealthy benefactor, that benefactor relinquished control over Cluny's property; instead, Duke William of Aquitaine and his family gained the spiritual support of the monks, whose prayers might save warlike men from eternal damnation.

This arrangement set a new precedent for the relationship between monasteries and powerful families, as Cluny began to sponsor other monasteries on the same model. This was another innovation: prior to this, all Benedictine monasteries had been independent of one another, united only by their observance of Benedict's *Rule* (Chapter 6). Now, Cluny established a network of Cluniac "daughter" monasteries across Europe, all of which remained subordinate to the mother house. By 1049, there were sixty-seven such priories, each one performing the same elaborate liturgy for which Cluny became famous, and each one entirely free from the control of local lords.

Cluniac influence was strongest in the former Frankish territories and in Italy, where the virtual absence of effective kingship allowed monastic power to thrive unchecked. In Germany and England, by contrast, fostering monastic reform emerged as an essential responsibility of any Christian ruler whose role model was the pious Charlemagne. Yet because these rulers were the guarantors of the monasteries' freedom, it was they who appointed the abbots, just as they also appointed the bishops of their kingdoms. As a result of this and of the Norman conquest, kings of England would have more direct control over Church lands than other European rulers. In Germany, as we have already noted, a prince's right to appoint spiritual leaders would be the central cause of Henry IV's strife with the papacy.

Despite the differences in sponsorship, these parallel reform movements made monasticism the dominant spiritual and intelletual force in western Europe. Monasteries also had an important influence on the piety of ordinary people, because many monastic communities maintained parishes that ministered directly to the laity. The spiritual practices that had been unique to monks and nuns in earlier centuries therefore came to influence daily life outside the cloister.

Relics and Pilgrims

One potent example of this new popular spirituality was the growing devotion to relics. Monasteries were the repositories of cherished objects associated with saints, such as fragments of bone or pieces of cloth cut from the garments of some holy person. These souvenirs were believed to possess special protective and curative powers. A relic was always buried beneath the altar of a church during the ceremony of its consecration, and relics were also collected and displayed in elaborate vessels (reliquaries) made of precious metals and studded with jewels. Indeed, relics were so valuable that monasteries and cathedral churches competed with one another for their acquisition and even plotted the "holy theft" of a particularly prized treasure. For instance, the relics of Nicholas, a fourth-century bishop of Myra (in Turkey), were stolen from the saint's tomb during the eleventh century. These were brought to Bari in southeastern Italy, where Benedictine monks built a magnificent church to house them. It became a major—and lucrative—attraction for pilgrims.

The possession and display of relics thus became a way to attract attention and generate revenue, since those who sought cures or favors at the shrine of a saint would often make a donation to the church in the saint's honor. If a saint was especially famous for a particular type of miracle, pilgrims might travel thousands of miles to visit a shrine. Saint Nicholas was famous for increasing the wealth of his suppliants, and for bestowing gifts—hence his later nickname, Santa Claus. The relics of Sainte Foy ("Saint Faith") of Conques (southern France) were renowned for their power to rectify injustices, restore order, and heal the maladies that afflicted the poor. Those of the apostle James at Compostela (in northwestern Spain) became the chief destination on a major pilgrimage route, rivaling even the holy sites of Rome and Jerusalem.

The Reform of the Secular Clergy

Eventually, the movement toward spiritual renewal in the monasteries of Europe began to influence the sees of bishops as well. This was a major change: bishops and the priests who served in their dioceses were secular clergy, living in the world (*saeculum* in Latin); it had long been expected that they would share some worldly preoccupations. But as the values and priorities of monasticism began to spread outward, abbots were more frequently appointed to episcopal office. Meanwhile, other bishops were forced to adopt stricter standards of personal conduct.

As their influence grew, the monasteries under the sway of Cluny began to push for even larger reforms, amounting to a fundamental dismantling of customs that reached back to the organization of the Church under Constantine, seven centuries earlier. They centered their attacks on the practice

A Miraculous Reliquary

Although pilgrimages had been a part of Christian religious practice for centuries, they became much more central elements of popular piety from the tenth century on. Pilgrims brought money and spiritual prestige to the monasteries and cathedrals that housed miracle-working relics, and competition among monastic houses sometimes led one house to steal the relics of another. But some critics worried that these newly popular shrines were encouraging idolatry. Bernard of Angers (c. 960–1028) was one such critic. His account of a visit to the shrines of several saints, including that of Sainte Foy ("Saint Faith") at Conques, reveals the negative impression that ornate reliquaries made on him—and the power of wonder-working relics to correct that impression.

t is an ancient custom in all of Auvergne, Rodez, Toulouse, and the neighboring regions that the local saint has a statue of gold, silver, or some other metal . . . [that] serves as a reliquary for the head of the saint or for a part of his body. The learned might see in this a superstition and a vestige of the cult of demons, and I myself . . . had the same impression the first time I saw the statue of Saint Gerard . . . resplendent with gold and stones, with an expression so human that the simple people . . . pretend that it winks at pilgrims whose prayers it answers. I admit to my shame that turning to my friend Bernerius and laughing, I whispered to him in Latin, "What do you think of the idol? Wouldn't Jupiter or Mars be happy with it?" . . .

Three days later we arrived at [the shrine of] St. Faith. . . . We approached [the reliquary] but the crowd was such that we could not prostrate ourselves like so many others already lying on the floor. Unhappy, I remained standing, fixing my view on the image and murmuring this prayer, "St. Faith, you whose relics rest in this sham, come to my assistance on the day of judgment." And this time I looked at my companion . . . because I found it outrageous that all of these rational beings should be praying to a mute and inanimate object. . . .

Later I greatly regretted to have acted so stupidly toward the saint of God. This was because among other miracles [that] Don Adalgerius, at that time dean and later . . . abbot [of Conques], told me [was] a remarkable account of a cleric named Oldaric. One day when the venerable image had to be taken to another place, . . . he restrained the crowd from bringing offerings and

The Reliquary of Sainte Foy, Early Tenth Century.

he insulted and belittled the image of the saint. . . . The next night, a lady of imposing severity appeared to him: "You," she said, "how dare you insult my image?" Having said this, she flogged her enemy with a staff. . . . He survived only long enough to tell the vision in the morning.

Thus there is no place left for arguing whether the effigy of St. Faith ought to be venerated since it is clear that he who reproached the holy martyr nevertheless retracted his reproach. Nor is it a spurious idol where nefarious rites of sacrifice or of divination are conducted, but rather a pious memorial of a holy virgin, before which great numbers of faithful people decently and eloquently implore her efficacious intercession for their sins.

Source: Bernard of Angers, "The Book of the Miracles of St. Faith," in *Readings in Medieval History*, 3rd ed., ed. and trans. Patrick J. Geary (Peterborough, ON., Canada: 2003), pp. 333–34 (slightly modified).

Questions for Analysis

1. Why does Bernard initially object to the display of relics in ornate reliquaries? Why would he consider this practice blasphemous? How does he become reconciled to it?

2. Can you think of present-day practices that resemble the medieval fascination with collecting, displaying, and venerating relics? What do such practices reveal about any society?

of simony (*SIGH-mony*), a term describing the use of ecclesiastical office for personal gain, including the purchase or sale of a bishopric. In other words, the reform movement targeted the very structure of the Roman Church as a network of lordships held by powerful men in trust for their families.

Even more radical was the reformers' demand that secular priests share the lifestyles of monks, taking vows of personal poverty and celibacy. Although some early councils of the Church had attempted to regulate the marriage of bishops and priests, these efforts had largely been abandoned. For a thousand years, it had been conceded that to demand priestly celibacy was unreasonable, and would also deprive a priest's parishioners of an additional resource and ministry—that of his wife. In the eleventh century, therefore, the vast majority of priests all across Europe were married. Married bishops were rarer, but not unknown. In Brittany, the bishop of Dol and his wife publicly celebrated the marriages of their daughters, endowing them with lands belonging to the bishopric; in Milan, the archbishops flatly rejected reformers' calls for celibacy on the grounds that their patron saint, Ambrose (see Chapter 6), had been married, too.

The Reform of the Papacy

In Rome, the most powerful bishopric of all remained resolutely unreformed until 1046, when the German king Henry III, who also bore the title of emperor, deposed three rival Roman nobles who claimed to be pope and appointed instead his own cousin, a monk who adopted the name Leo IX (r. 1049–54). Leo and his supporters began to promulgate decrees against simony and clerical marriage. They then took steps to enforce these decrees by traveling throughout the Continent, disciplining and removing from office priests deemed guilty of simony or obstinately determined not to "put away" their wives—whom the reformers insisted on calling "concubines."

Implicit in Leo's reforming efforts was a new vision of the Church as a type of monarchy, with the pope at the apex of a spiritual pyramid. Not surprisingly, therefore, Leo and his successors met with considerable opposition from powerful leaders within the Church itself, and they could only enforce their claims in regions where they had the support of secular rulers. Chief among these was the pious emperor Henry III, whose protection insulated papal reformers from the Roman nobility, who would otherwise have deposed or assassinated them.

But when Henry III died in 1056, the regents of his child heir Henry IV (whose reign we discussed above) were neither able nor willing to stand behind the reforming movement. In 1058, the Roman aristocracy seized this opportunity to regain control of the papal throne. By this time, however, the reform movement had gathered momentum; a year later, a new pope had been installed and was determined to counter any interference from either the German or Italian nobility. To this end, Nicholas II (r. 1059–61) created a new legislative body, the College of Cardinals (the Latin for "gathering of leaders"). The College became the nexus for creating papal policy and it also ensured the continuity of the papal office by overseeing elections, a role it still plays today.

Needless to say, this novel arrangement infuriated the advisers of the young Henry IV, since it removed the emperor's prerogative to oversee the process of papal elections himself. And it set the stage for the confrontations that were to follow.

The Investiture Conflict

In 1073, a few years after Henry IV began his adult rule, the new College of Cardinals elected a zealous reformer called Hildebrand, a Cluniac monk of Tuscan origins who took the name Gregory VII. Two years later, relations between papacy and empire were riven by a conflict that would permanently alter the political and religious landscape of western Europe. Superficially, the issue that divided Gregory and Henry was that of investiture: the right to appoint bishops and to invest them with the trappings of office. Since the time of the Carolingians, this had been the prerogative of the emperor—as it was in Byzantium. But to Pope Gregory, this practice smacked of simony, since a lay lord would obviously choose bishops who would be politically useful to him, regardless of their spiritual qualifications.

The real issue, however, was not the political power of bishops; it was the control of that power. For the papal reform movement under Gregory was predicated on liberating the Church from powerful influences in order that the papacy itself might become more powerful. This was the principle that lay behind the discouraging of clerical marriage, too: Church offices and Church property had to be protected by the Church for the Church. Allowing priests to marry might encourage the handing down of offices to sons, just as allowing rulers to appoint bishops encouraged these bishops to act as the rulers' agents. These practices tainted the austere authority that Gregory was trying to cultivate, and it also threatened to alienate property and power that he wanted to harness for the papacy.

Gregory therefore took the reform movement to a new level, insisting that adherence to these principles was not just a matter of policy but a matter of religious dogma, a term defined as "a truth necessary for salvation." When Henry IV refused to accept this and proceeded to invest the new archbishop of Milan, Gregory reminded him that he himself had the power to save or damn all souls as the successor of Saint Peter and the representative of Christ on earth. To drive the point home, Gregory excommunicated a number of Henry's advisers, including several of the bishops who had participated in the investiture at Milan. Henry countered by renouncing his obedience to Gregory, calling on him to resign. Gregory responded by excommunicating Henry, along with his supporters.

In itself, the excommunication of a king was not terribly unusual. Gregory, however, went much further by equating excommunication with deposition: since Henry was no longer a faithful son of the Church, he was no longer a king or the emperor, and his subjects had a sacred duty to rebel. It was this that occasioned Henry's humiliating stand before the castle at Canossa in January of 1077. But the story does not end there, because Henry used his restored powers to crush his Saxon opponents and to drive Gregory from Rome. In 1085, the aged pope died in exile in southern Italy.

By then, however, Gregory had established the principles on which papal governance would be based until the Reformation (see Chapter 13). In 1122, the conflict over investiture was provisionally resolved through compromise at the Concordat of Worms (*VOHRMS*) in Germany. Its terms declared that the emperor was forbidden to invest prelates with the *religious* symbols of their office but was allowed to invest them with the symbols of their rights as *temporal* rulers, in his capacity as their overlord. In practice, then, the rulers of Europe retained a great deal of influence over ecclesiastical appointments. But they also had to acknowledge that bishops were now part of a clerical hierarchy headed by the pope, and that they owed loyalty to the Church in Rome and not to the ruler of the region in which they lived.

CRUSADING CAUSES AND OUTCOMES

Gregory VII's equation of excommunication with deposition had given the pope a powerful new weapon, but his immediate successors would struggle to establish the credibility of his claims. In the end, it took the appeal of a Byzantine emperor and the preaching of a crusade to unite western Christendom under the papal banner.

The Expansion and Limitations of Byzantium

As Europe expanded, the eastern Roman Empire was undergoing its own series of transformations. The decline of the Abbasid Caliphate in Baghdad had relieved some of the pressures on its borders, but Muslims from North Africa had captured the Byzantine islands of Sicily and Crete, which later fell to the Normans. Meanwhile, the migration of pagan Slavs was undermining Byzantine control of the Balkans; and a formidable power was also emerging in the north, as the Viking Rus' established themselves along the river systems that fed into the Black and Caspian Seas. In 860, a fleet of them sailed into the Black Sea and sacked Constantinople.

The Byzantine response was to make these new enemies into allies. Missionaries began the process by converting some of the Balkan Slavs to Orthodox Christianity, devising for them a written language known as Old Church Slavonic and creating the Cyrillic alphabet (based on Greek) still used in Bulgaria, Serbia, and Russia. The empire also established a military and commercial alliance with the kingdom centered on Kiev. In 911, hundreds of Rus' served with the Byzantine navy in an attack on Muslim Crete. In 957, a Kievan princess named Olga was lavishly entertained on a state visit to Constantinople. And in 989, Vladimir of Kiev helped Basil II win a civil war against an imperial rival; in exchange, Basil married him to his sister Anna and Vladimir accepted baptism into the Orthodox Church.

The eastern Roman Empire simultaneously strengthened and weakened its position by reconquering territories that had been lost to the Abbasids since the seventh century. Although most peoples of this region had remained Christian through three centuries of Islamic rule, the Armenians and the Syrians had their own distinctive and ancient Christian traditions that were at odds, doctrinally and linguistically, with the Greek-speaking church at Constantinople. Reincorporating these "heretics" into the empire strained the limits of Orthodoxy and also created centers of power that lay outside the imperial capital. Rivalries divided the eastern nobility and the imperial court, eventually erupting into warfare.

By the eleventh century, these projects of reconquest and expansion were overextending the Byzantine military and treasury. In an effort to raise cash, some emperors began to debase the gold coinage that had kept the empire competitive with the Islamic Caliphate in Baghdad, thus undermining Byzantine commerce at the very moment when Venice, Genoa, and Pisa were consolidating their control in the eastern Mediterranean and taking over the lucrative trade between Muslim North Africa and western Europe.

A failing economy, ongoing dynastic civil war, a weakened army, and uneasy relations with the new kingdoms of the Balkans proved nearly fatal to Byzantine sovereignty. And then the empire was confronted with yet another threat. The Seljuq Turks, a powerful dynasty of Sunni Muslims who were building their own empire based in Persia, began to move westward. In 1071, they captured Armenia and moved swiftly into the Byzantine heartland of Anatolia (Turkey), where they destroyed a Byzantine army. In the same year, the Seljuqs captured Jerusalem, which had been part of the Shi'ite caliphate based in Egypt, ruled by the Fatimids. By 1081, when the eastern nobility of Byzantium finally emerged triumphant in their ongoing bid for the imperial throne, the new emperor Alexius Comnenus (r. 1081–1118) found himself at the head of a crippled state.

THE BYZANTINE EMPIRE, C. 1025. ▪ *As suggested by the map, what political challenges faced the Byzantine Empire in the eleventh century?* ▪ *How was the long-standing influence of Muslims in this region likely to affect the character of Byzantine culture?* ▪ *How did the domain of Kievan Rus' potentially create additional economic and military pressure on Byzantium, directly as well as indirectly?*

The Call for a Crusade

In the first decade of his rule, Alexius managed to shore up the failing economy and secure his hold over Bulgarian territory in the Balkans. He then began to plan a campaign against the Seljuqs. But with what forces? In 1085, the Byzantine army in Greece had been challenged by a far superior cavalry of Norman knights—for by this time, the Normans had established independent principalities in southern Italy and Sicily and were moving farther east. As it happened, this encounter convinced Alexius that such heavily armed horsemen would be successful if pitted against the lightly armored Seljuqs.

In the hopes of recruiting a mercenary force, Alexius approached Pope Urban II (r. 1088–99). Urban was trying to realize some of the powerful claims that Gregory VII had made on behalf of papal authority, and this seemed like a golden opportunity: by coming to the aid of the eastern Roman Empire, he could show the restive princes of western Europe that the papacy was a force to be reckoned with. At the same time, he could show that Latin military

Preaching the First Crusade: Two Accounts

We owe the following account of Urban II's call for a crusade to Fulcher of Chartres, a priest who was present at the Council of Clermont in 1095 and who later served as a chaplain to the first Norman king of Jerusalem, Baldwin. It forms part of Fulcher's contemporary chronicle of the First Crusade. The second account of the motives behind the crusade comes from a biography of the Byzantine emperor Alexius I Comnenus, written by his daughter Anna (1083–1153), who also lived through these events.

Pope Urban II's Call at Clermont, November 1195

Most beloved brethren: Urged by necessity, I, Urban, by the permission of God chief bishop and prelate over the whole world, have come into these parts as an ambassador with a divine admonition to you, the servants of God. . . .

Although, O sons of God, you have promised more firmly than ever to keep the peace among yourselves and to preserve the rights of the Church, there remains still an important work for you to do. Freshly quickened by the divine correction, you must apply the strength of your righteousness to another matter which concerns you as well as God. For your brethren who live in the east are in urgent need of your help, and you must hasten to give them the aid which has often been promised them. For, as most of you have heard, the Turks and Arabs have attacked them and have conquered the territory of Romania [the Byzantine Empire] as far west as the shore of the Mediterranean and the Hellespont. . . . They have occupied more and more of the lands of those Christians, and have overcome them in seven battles. They have killed and captured many, and have destroyed the churches and devastated the empire.

If you permit them to continue thus for a while with impunity, the faithful of God will be much more widely attacked by them. On this account I, or rather the Lord, beseech you as Christ's heralds to publish this everywhere and to persuade all people of whatever rank, footsoldiers and knights, poor and rich, to carry aid promptly to those Christians and to destroy that vile race [and remove it] from the lands of our friends. I say this to those who are present, but it is meant also for those who are absent. Moreover, Christ commands it.

All who die by the way, whether by land or by sea, or in battle against the pagans, shall have immediate remission of sins. This I grant them through the power of God with which I am invested. O what a disgrace, if such a despised and base race, which worships demons, should conquer a people which has the faith of omnipotent God and is made glorious with the name of Christ! With what reproaches will the Lord overwhelm us if you do not aid those who, with us, profess the Christian religion!

Let those who have been accustomed to wage unjust private warfare against the faithful now go against the infidels and end with victory this war which should have been begun long ago. Let those who for a long time have been robbers now become knights. Let those who have been fighting against their brothers and relatives now fight in a proper way against the barbarians. Let those who have been serving as mercenaries for small pay now obtain the eternal reward. Let those who have been wearing themselves out in both body

and spiritual might was greater than that of the weakened Greeks of Byzantium, thereby realizing the centuries-old dream of a united Christian Church based in Rome, with the pope at its head. In addition, Urban could support another reform that had gained momentum in recent years: a peace movement that was attempting to quell the violence unleashed by competitive bands of knights and their rapacious lords. What better way to defuse the situation than to ship those violent energies overseas, deploying them against a common enemy?

So Alexius received a favorable reply, but he got far more than he had asked for—or wanted. He had needed a modest contingent of a few thousand troops, to help him reconquer Anatolia. What he got was a vast

and soul now work for a double honor. Behold! On this side will be the sorrowful and poor, on that, the rich; on this side, the enemies of the Lord, on that, his friends. Let those who go not put off the journey, but rent their lands and collect money for their expenses; and as soon as winter is over and spring comes, let them eagerly set out on the way with God as their guide.

Source: S. J. Allen and Emilie Amt, eds., *The Crusades: A Reader* (Peterborough, ON, Canada: 2003), pp. 39–40.

Anna Comnena Describes the Beginnings of the First Crusade

[Alexius] had no time to relax before he heard a rumour that countless Frankish armies were approaching. He dreaded their arrival, knowing as he did their uncontrollable passion, their erratic character and their irresolution, not to mention . . . their greed for money. . . . So far from despairing, however, he made every effort to prepare for war if need arose. What actually happened was more far-reaching and terrible than rumour suggested, for the whole of the West and all the barbarians who lived between the Adriatic and the Straits of Gibraltar migrated in a body to Asia, marching across Europe country by country with all their households. The reason for this mass-movement is to be found more or less in the following events. A certain Kelt, called Peter [the Hermit] . . . left to worship at the Holy Sepulchre and after suffering much ill-treatment at the hands of the Turks and Saracens who were plundering the whole of Asia, he returned home with difficulty. Unable to admit defeat, . . . he worked out a clever scheme. He decided to preach in all the Latin countries. A divine voice, he said, commanded him to proclaim to all the counts in France that all should depart from their homes, set out to worship at the Holy Shrine, and . . . strive to liberate Jerusalem. . . . Surprisingly, he was successful. . . . Full of enthusiasm and ardour they thronged every highway, and with these warriors came a host of civilians, outnumbering the sand of the sea shore or the stars of heaven, carrying palms and bearing crosses on their shoulders. There were women and children, too, who had left their own countries. . . .

The upheaval that ensued as men *and* women took to the road was unprecedented within living memory. The simpler folk were in very truth led on by a desire to worship at Our Lord's tomb and visit the holy places, but the more villainous characters . . . had an ulterior purpose, for they hoped on their journey to seize the capital [Jerusalem] itself, looking upon its capture as a natural consequence of the expedition. . . .

Source: Excerpted from Anna Comnena, *The Alexiad*, trans. E. R. A. Sewter (New York: 1969), pp. 308–11.

Questions for Analysis

1. Given Urban II's explanation of the problems confronting the Byzantine Empire, how do you account for the fact that the Crusades were directed toward the Holy Land and not to the relief of Byzantium?

2. How does Anna Comnena represent the motives of Peter the Hermit and the crusaders? What distinctions does she make among the participants?

3. Are there points of comparison between these two accounts? On what do they agree? How would you explain the differences between them?

army of 100,000 men, charged to retake the holy city of Jerusalem for Christendom. For Urban appears to have interpreted Alexius's request very loosely. Speaking before an assembled crowd at an ecclesiastical council at Clermont (central France) in 1095, he announced that he fully supported the peace movement. He said, furthermore, that any knights who wished to fight for a just and Christian cause could liberate the Holy Land from its Muslim captors. At home, said Urban, most knights were riffraff and marauders, destined for damnation; abroad, fighting or dying in the service of Christ would win absolution for sins. By taking up the cross (*crux*, hence "crusade"), a warrior might attain salvation, as well as booty and glory.

ROLAND AS A CRUSADING KNIGHT. The association between knighthood and crusading helped to raise the social status of knights and contributed to the refinement of a chivalric ethos. Here, a crusading knight, dressed head to foot in expensive chain mail, is shown kneeling in homage to his lord, God.

Consequently, the ultimate response to Urban's call exceeded all expectations. Indeed, his message was amplified by other preachers, including a zealous priest called Peter the Hermit, who claimed (falsely) that he had been prevented by the Seljuqs from visiting the Holy Land. Within a year, thousands of seasoned warriors and a large number of untrained, untried men were on the march toward Constantinople, where they intended to gather before departing for Jerusalem. As with any large enterprise, the participants' motives must have varied. Some may have hoped to win lands for themselves. Others were drawn by the prospect of adventure. Many were the dependents of greater men, who had no choice but to accompany their lords; some hoped to free themselves from dependence by fighting. Most had no idea how long the journey would be or knew anything about the places for which they were destined.

But except for a few of the warlords—mostly Normans from Sicily and southern Italy—the prospect of winning new territory was both unlikely and even undesirable. In fact, one of the greatest challenges facing the Christian kingdom established in Jerusalem after 1099 was that crusaders so rarely wanted to stay. After fulfilling their vows, the vast majority went home. So why did they go crusading in the first place? The risks of dying on the journey were high; the costs of embarking were enormous. Crusading knights needed a minimum of two years' revenues in hand to finance the journey. To raise such sums, most were forced to mortgage lands and borrow heavily from family, friends, monasteries, and merchants. They then had to find some way to pay back these loans if and when they returned home. By any rational assessment, the Crusade was a fool's errand.

The seeming irrationality of this endeavor underscores the importance of reckoning with the crusaders' piety, and their desire to emulate legendary heroes like Roland. Crusading was the ultimate pilgrimage, the holy places of Jerusalem the ultimate Christian shrines. If anyone could receive special blessings by traveling to Compostela, Conques, or Bari, how much more blessed would be those who fought their way through to the Holy Land? Urban II made this point explicit at Clermont, and some agitators went even further, promising that the souls of those who died on crusade would go straight to heaven.

Crusade preaching also emphasized the vengeance that Christ's soldiers should exact on his pagan enemies. To some crusaders, accordingly, it seemed absurd to wait until they arrived in the Holy Land to undertake this aspect of their mission. Muslims might hold Jesus's property at Jerusalem, but Christian theology held Jews responsible for the death of Jesus himself. Assaults against Jewish communities therefore began in the spring of 1096 and quickly spread eastward with the crusaders. Hundreds of Jews were killed in the German towns of Mainz, Worms, Speyer, and Cologne. Many individual churchmen attempted to prevent these attacks, among them the bishops in whose dioceses Jews lived. But the Church's own negative propaganda thwarted these efforts, and pogroms against Europe's Jews would remain a regular and predictable feature of Christian crusading.

The Christian Conquest of Jerusalem

Surprised by the scale of the response to his appeal, Emperor Alexius did his best to move the crusaders

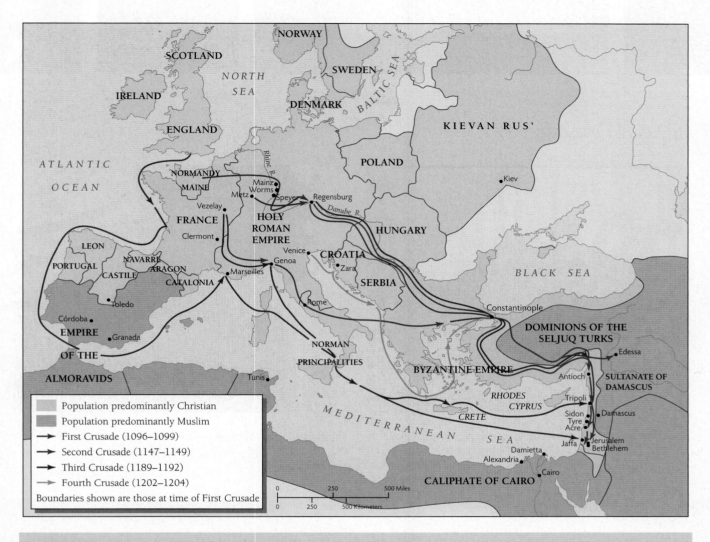

THE ROUTES OF THE CRUSADERS, 1096–1204. Compare the routes followed by participants in the first three Crusades. ▪ *What were the three main routes followed by crusaders?* ▪ *What geographical and political factors appear to be determining these trajectories?*

quickly through Constantinople and into battle with the Seljuqs. But he had little interest in an expedition to Jerusalem, and insisted that the expedition's leaders promise to restore any territory they captured to him. To the crusaders, this seemed like treachery. Furthermore, they did not understand the Byzantine emperor's willingness to make alliances with some Muslim rulers (the Shi'ite Fatimids of Egypt and the Abassids of Baghdad) against other Muslim rulers (the Sunni Seljuqs). Some warlords ignorantly concluded that the Byzantines were supporting the Muslims against them. These suspicions fed a growing conviction that the eastern Roman Empire was itself an obstacle to the recovery of Jerusalem.

Viewed from the perspective of Alexius, the Crusade was a disaster. But from that of the crusaders themselves,

it was a triumph. In 1098, crusaders captured the old Hellenistic city of Antioch and with it most of the Syrian coast. At the end of 1099, they took Jerusalem, indiscriminately slaughtering Muslim, Jewish, and Christian inhabitants. Their quick success stemmed mainly from the fact that their Muslim opponents were at that moment divided among themselves: the Fatimids had in fact recaptured Jerusalem just months before the crusaders arrived, and the defeated Seljuqs were at war with one another. Western military tactics, in particular the dominance of heavily armored knights, also played an important role in the crusaders' success. Equally critical was the naval support offered by Genoa and Pisa, whose merchant adventurers hoped to control the Indian spice trade that passed through the Red Sea and on to Alexandria in Egypt. The Crusade

Past and Present

Ideas of Crusade

The launching of the First Crusade was the beginning of a trend that decisively shaped the relations between western Europeans and their neighbors, and that continues today. The very use of the word "crusade" is apt to cause trouble—as when President George W. Bush spoke of "this crusade, this war on terrorism" to which he pledged the United States after September 11, 2001.

Watch related author videos on the Student Site
wwnorton.com/college/history/western-civilizationsBrief4

thereby contributed to the further decline of Byzantine commerce and decisively altered the balance of power between Byzantium and western Europe.

The Consequences of Crusade

For Byzantium, the consequences of the crusading movement were clearly negative. On the Muslim world, however, the impact was more modest. The crusader kingdoms established by victorious Norman and Frankish warlords were never more than a sparsely settled cluster of colonies along the coastline of Syria and Palestine. Because the crusaders did not control the Red Sea, the main routes of Islamic commerce with India and the Far East were unaffected by the change in Jerusalem's religious allegiance.

In any case, those crusaders who remained to settle in the region did not *want* to interfere with the caravan routes that wound through their new territories. Trade brokered by Arab, Persian, and Jewish merchants therefore continued. But the greatest economic gains went to the Italian maritime republics of Venice and Genoa, and to the western markets now open to Muslim merchants for their goods. Both sides also gained in military terms: western Europeans learned new techniques of fortification, and Muslims learned new methods of siege warfare and the uses of heavy cavalry.

The larger impact of the Crusades on western Europe is more difficult to assess. On the one hand, the establishment of the short-lived crusader states represents the limits of Europe's expansion during this otherwise extraordinary period of growth. On the other, trade with the Islamic world, and beyond it with India and the Far East, brought enormous prosperity to some. And yet these trading links had existed before the Crusades, and continued after they ended.

In the long run, the most lasting consequence of the First Crusade was the deadly escalation of both Christian and Muslim doctrines of holy war. Almost immediately, crusading rhetoric began to dictate the terms of western Europeans' attitudes toward the wider world and even toward one another, as we shall see in the following chapters. By 1108, it fostered a new ideology that would justify warfare against the Slavs, and it would continue to inform the "reconquest" of the Iberian Peninsula by the Christian rulers of Spain, leading to the massacre or forced conversion of Muslims and Jews. It would later fuel English wars against the Welsh and the Scots, and foment the massacre and dispossession of "heretics" in southern France by northern French colonists. It justified the conquest of the Baltic region and, later, the subsequent conquest of the Americas and the colonization of Asia, Africa, and Australia. And it has continued to exacerbate global animosities to this day.

THE CULTURE OF THE MUSLIM WEST

Not all the consequences of crusading were negative. The positive outcomes were hugely important, especially for western Europe. Increased intellectual and cultural contact with the Islamic world had an enormous impact on learning, literature, music, and art. Even Christian theology was transformed by contact with Islam. Europeans had been almost entirely ignorant of Muslim beliefs prior to the Crusade, assuming that Muslims were pagans who worshiped a god called Mahomet or Mahoun. But by 1143, a scholar called Robert of Ketton (c. 1100–c. 1160), originally from a small town in England, had completed a Latin translation of the Qur'an, working in Spain with the encouragement of the abbot of Cluny. In the 1130s, he and a friend, Hermann of Carinthia (in Slovenia), had traveled to Byzantium and the crusader kingdoms, where they became students of Arabic. And because Muslim scholars had inherited, preserved, and developed not only Hellenistic medicine and science but the teachings of Aristotle, this learning would form the basis of a new Christian philosophy.

Muslim Philosophy and Christian Theology

As we noted in Chapter 7, the scholars of Byzantium had taken a conservative approach to Greek philosophy, in every sense of the word. The dialogues of Plato and some works of Aristotle were copied and studied, but the latter's ideas were so hard to reconcile with Orthodox theology that Emperor Alexius eventually banned the teaching of Aristotelian logic. Ironically, then, it was through Arabic translations that western European intellectuals became acquainted with these ideas—thanks to the labor of Arabists like Robert and Hermann.

Even before the rise of Islam, a number of Greek philosophical texts had been translated into Syriac, a Semitic language closely related to Arabic. Arabic translations soon followed, many sponsored by the Abbasid court at Baghdad, which established a special school for this purpose: the House of Wisdom. By the end of the tenth century, Arabic translations of Greek authors were widely available and intensively studied throughout the Muslim world. Even in the remote Persian city of Bukhara, the great Muslim philosopher and physician Avicenna (Ibn Sīnā, 980–1037) was able to read all of Aristotle's works before he reached the age of eighteen.

Like their counterparts in Byzantium, Muslim philosophers strove to reconcile Greek and Hellenistic philosophical traditions and to match them with the tenets of their theology. Reconciling Aristotelianism and Neoplatonism was the easier task, because these schools of thought shared a number of common assumptions, including the eternity of the world and the capacity of the human mind to understand the principles that govern the world's workings. Both traditions also stressed the freedom of individual humans to choose between good and evil.

But combining Greek philosophy with Islamic theology was more difficult. Like Judaism and Christianity, Islam holds that a single omnipotent God created the world; this runs counter to the classical Greek view of the world as eternal. Moreover, both Christian and Islamic theology emphasize the immortality of the individual human soul, another doctrine in conflict with Aristotelian and Neoplatonic thought. With respect to the concept of free will, Muslims and Christians also had more in common with one another than with Greek tradition. Muslim philosophers had already adopted an array of different intellectual tactics to deal with these challenges, and thereby laid the groundwork for the Christian theologians who relied on them (see Chapter 9).

An Arab Aristocrat Encounters the Crusaders

Usama ibn Munqidh (1095–1188) was an Arab Muslim from Syria, whose family maintained a prominent place in the local administration even after the conquests of the Seljuqs and the Christian crusaders. He traveled widely and worked in various Islamic cities as a diplomat and scholar. He ended his life in the service of Salāḥ ad-Dīn (Saladin), the great Muslim leader who reconquered Jerusalem the year before Usama's death. The following excerpt is from Usama's memoir, which he called The Book of Contemplation. *The Templars mentioned in the account are the Christian military order of the Knights of the Temple, who dedicated themselves to protecting pilgrims in Jerusalem and guarding the holy sites. Their headquarters was in the main mosque of the city, which stood on the Temple Mount.*

nyone who is recently arrived from the Frankish lands is rougher in character than those who have become acclimated and have frequented the company of Muslims. Here is an instance of their rough character (may God abominate them!):

Whenever I went to visit the holy sites in Jerusalem, I would go in and make my way up to the al-Aqsa Mosque, beside which stood a small mosque that the Franks had converted into a church. When I went into the al-Aqsa Mosque—where the Templars, who are my friends, were—they would clear out that little mosque so that I could pray in it. One day, I went into the little mosque, recited the opening formula 'God is great!' and stood up in prayer. At this, one of the Franks rushed at me and grabbed me and turned my face towards the east, saying, 'Pray like *this!*'

A group of Templars hurried towards him, took hold of the Frank and took him away from me. I then returned to my prayers. The Frank, that very same one, took advantage of their inattention and returned, rushing upon me and turning my face to the east, saying, 'Pray like *this!*'

So the Templars came in again, grabbed him and threw him out. They apologized to me, saying, 'This man is a stranger, just arrived from the Frankish lands sometime in the past few days. He has never before seen anyone who did not pray towards the east.'

'I think I've prayed quite enough,' I said and left. I used to marvel at that devil, the change of his expression, the way he trembled and what he must have made of seeing someone praying towards Mecca.

Source: Usama ibn Munqidh, *The Book of Contemplation: Islam and the Crusades*, trans. Paul M. Cobb (New York: 2008), p. 147.

Questions for Analysis

1. What does Usama's account reveal about the variety of relationships among Christians and Muslims in the crusader kingdom of Jerusalem?

2. Who is the true outsider in this scenario? What does Usama's treatment by the Templars suggest about the policy of Christian leaders toward the city's Muslim residents?

Muslim Science, Medicine, and Mathematics

Many Muslim philosophers were also distinguished physicians and scientists. Both astrology and medicine were applied sciences that relied on careful, accurate observation of natural phenomena. Muslim observations of the heavens were so accurate, indeed, that some astronomers had corroborated the findings of Hellenistic scientists, positing that the earth must rotate on its axis and revolve around the sun (Chapter 4). But because these theories conflicted with the (mistaken) assumptions of Aristotle—that the earth remained stationary with the sun and planets revolving around it—they were not generally accepted in the Muslim world or in Europe.

Muslim accomplishments in medicine were equally remarkable. Avicenna discovered the contagious nature

MUSLIM ARCHITECTURE AND GARDEN DESIGN. Both images display how Muslim architects and designers borrowed features from many cultures but combined them in distinctively graceful ways.

of tuberculosis and noted that many diseases could spread through contaminated water and soil. His *Canon of Medicine* would remain an authoritative medical textbook in the Islamic world and Europe until the seventeenth century. Muslim physicians also studied cauterization and the use of styptic agents, diagnosed cancer, prescribed antidotes in cases of poisoning, and made notable progress in treating eye diseases. They recognized the infectious character of plague, pointing out that it could be transmitted by clothing. Muslim physicians were even pioneers in medical administration. At least thirty-four great hospitals were located in the principal cities of Persia, Syria, and Egypt, each with separate wards for particular illnesses, a dispensary for giving out medicine, and a library. Chief physicians and surgeons lectured to students, examined them, and issued licenses to practice medicine. Even the owners of leeches (used for bloodletting, a standard medical practice of the day) had to submit their medicinal worms for inspection at regular intervals.

Islamic scientists made important advances in optics and chemistry, but their most significant contribution was to the study of mathematics. Using Arabic numerals— actually adopted from the Hindus—mathematicians developed a decimal arithmetic based on place values and hinged on the concept of the zero. Their work enabled fundamental advances in entirely new areas, both of which bear Arabic names: algebra and algorithms. These advances revolutionized both the theoretical and practical applications of mathematics in Europe. They were first promoted beyond the Islamic world by the son of a Pisan merchant who grew up in Algeria, Leonardo Fibonacci

(c. 1170–c. 1250), and they made an indispensible contribution to the burgeoning European economy. The sophisticated accounting systems that supported commerce would have been impossible if merchants and bankers had continued to use the clumsy numerical system of the Romans. Thanks to Arabic mathematics, western Europeans could now add, subtract, divide, and multiply quickly and accurately, with or without the help of another Muslim invention, the abacus.

Muslim Literature and Art

Poetry was integral to Muslim culture. It had been a highly developed Arabic art form long before the emergence of Islam, and it became even more important because it was the form in which Muhammad framed the Qur'an (see Chapter 7). Like medicine and astronomy, poetry was also a route to power. Particularly around the Abbasid court, poets composing in both Arabic and in Persian enjoyed great renown. The best known of these is Umar Khayyam (d. 1123), whose *Rubaiyat* was turned into a popular English verse cycle by the Victorian poet Edward Fitzgerald (1809–1883). Fitzgerald's sensual translation ("a jug of wine, a loaf of bread—and thou") reflects themes that were common to much Muslim poetry, but it masks the fact that much of this poetry was addressed by men to other men. Jews also participated in this elite literary world, especially in Al-Andalus, where their Hebrew and Arabic lyrics celebrated wine, sexual intimacy, and the art of poetic composition.

The distinctive architectural and decorative arts of Islam also flourished at this time, and created the spaces in which poets and scientists interacted with their patrons. Many characteristic elements of Muslim architecture (the dome, the column, and the arch) had been adapted from Byzantine models, but were then combined with the intricate tracery and ambitious scale of Persian buildings to form a new architectural vocabulary. Building styles were further inflected by the many different cultures that embraced Islam, from Spain to Egypt to India and beyond. Muslim artistry was also expressed in the magnificent gardens and fountains that adorned palaces, and in the portable magnificence of gorgeous carpets, tooled leather, brocaded silks and tapestries, inlaid metalwork, enameled glassware, and painted pottery—all decorated with Arabic script, interlacing geometric designs, plants, fruits, flowers, and fantastic animal figures (another Persian influence). These complex designs anticipate the abstract forms that were considered new in the twentieth century and can often seem strikingly modern.

The Muslim Influence on Western Europe

Prior to the contacts facilitated by crusading, the cultural, economic, and intellectual achievements of Muslim civilization completely overshadowed those of western Europe. Thereafter, Europeans would continue to rely heavily on what they had learned from the Islamic world, and this is reflected in the large number of Arabic and Persian words that passed into European languages. Essential words for commerce and trade include *traffic, tariff, alcohol, muslin, orange, lemon, alfalfa, saffron, sugar, syrup,* and *musk,* to name just a few. The word *admiral* also comes from Arabic (from the title *emir*), as do words that tell the story of Europe's reliance on Muslim science and technology: *alchemy, algebra, algorithm, alkali, almanac, amalgam, cipher, soda, magazine,* and *zero*—not to mention the names of stars, such as Aldebaran and Betelgeuse.

After You Read This Chapter

 Go to **INQUIZITIVE** to see what you've learned—and learn what you've missed—with personalized feedback along the way.

REVIEWING THE OBJECTIVES

- The fragmentation of power in the ninth and tenth centuries created a world very different from that of Charlemagne. Describe some of the key changes. What were their causes?
- The agricultural revolution of the Middle Ages had far-reaching economic, social, and political consequences. What were they?
- The reforming movement with the Church changed the relationship between the papacy and the secular rulers of Christendom. Explain why. What were the larger implications of this shift?
- The motives behind the First Crusade were political as well as religious. Why was this the case?
- The crusading movement had profound effects on western Europe and Byzantium, as well as on the relationship between the Latin Christian and Muslim worlds. In what ways were these three civilizations transformed?

The Muslim world also had an enormous influence on the imagination of Christian Europe. Western Christians tended to look down on the Byzantine Greeks, but they respected and feared the civilization that brought Arabs, Persians, Turks, Egyptians, Africans, Indians, and Asians together in a common cultural and religious system, creating a diverse society and a splendid legacy of original discoveries and accomplishments. The expanding Europe of the Middle Ages reaped the benefits of its interactions with this rich culture.

CONCLUSION

Before the year 1000, western Europe was the least powerful, least prosperous, and least sophisticated of the three civilizations that had emerged from the Roman world. A hundred years later, it was a force to be reckoned with. This metamorphosis rested on economic foundations: increasingly efficient agriculture, a growing population, and expanding trade. These changes produced a dynamic, mobile society. No less important, however, were the political and military changes that began to alter the map of Europe in these centuries. By 1100, the mounted, heavily armored knight had emerged as the most formidable military weapon of the day, and new conceptions of power—both spiritual and temporal—were being articulated and contested.

Where, then, do the emerging kingdoms of medieval Europe fit into this picture? How would the struggle for the control of western Europe's expanding resources be carried forward in the wake of the Crusades? And what cultural, spiritual, social, and intellectual innovations would result? These are the questions we address in Chapter 9.

PEOPLE, IDEAS, AND EVENTS IN CONTEXT

- How was Europe affected by **VIKING** raids and settlements? Which territorial rulers imitated **CAROLINGIAN** models in the wake of these initiatives?
- What new technologies drove the **AGRICULTURAL REVOLUTION** of the Middle Ages? Why did the organization of labor on **MANORS** sometimes lead to **SERFDOM**?
- What conditions led to the growth of medieval **TOWNS** and why did the formation of urban **COMMUNES** foster new types of liberty? How were money and credit essential to medieval commerce?
- Why is **FEUDALISM** a problematic concept? How did the ceremony of **HOMAGE** symbolize the relationship between a **VASSAL** and his lord?
- What were the causes of the **INVESTITURE CONFLICT**?
- Why did **ALEXIUS COMNENUS** ask **POPE URBAN II** for assistance? Why did the pope use this as a pretext for urging the **FIRST CRUSADE?**
- How and why did **MUSLIM LEARNING AND CULTURE** exercise a profound influence on western Europeans?

THINKING ABOUT CONNECTIONS

- In what ways does the Investiture Conflict reflect the unique historical circumstances of the late eleventh century, and in what ways can it be viewed as an extension of longer-term phenomena?
- Based on what you have learned about the relationship between political power and religious power in previous chapters, would you say that the clash between the papacy and the Holy Roman Empire was inevitable?
- Given the many negative aspects of the crusading movement—and its eventual failure—how might you explain the continuing appeal of crusading rhetoric down to the present day?

STORY LINES

- The power of Europe's new monarchies and of the papacy depended on new methods of oversight, administration, and documentation.

- Continued crusading movements in the twelfth and thirteenth centuries intensified contacts between Latin Christendom and the Muslim world while posing a threat to many minority groups within Europe, and to the Byzantine Empire.

- The Church's presence in the daily lives of the laity produced vibrant forms of spirituality yet placed strict limitations on women, religious dissidents, and non-Christians.

- Schools and universities were crucial to the development of secular and ecclesiastical institutions, and they also provided ambitious men with unprecedented intellectual, social, and political opportunities.

- Meanwhile, Europe's princely courts, wealthy towns, universities, and cathedrals fostered new forms of entertainment, art, and architecture.

CHRONOLOGY

1079–1142	Lifetime of Peter Abelard
c. 1090–c. 1164	Lifetime of Heloise
1098–1179	Lifetime of Hildegard of Bingen
1099	First Crusade ends
1122–1204	Lifetime of Eleanor of Aquitaine
c. 1140	Gratian's *Concordance of Discordant Canons*
1152–1190	Reign of Frederick II Barbarossa
1180–1223	Reign of Philip II Augustus
1187	Muslim reconquest of Jerusalem
1192–1194	Alfonso II of Aragon compiles the *Liber feudorum maior*
1194–1250	Lifetime of Emperor Frederick II
1198–1216	Reign of Pope Innocent III
1204	Capture and sack of Constantinople
1209	Franciscan order established
	Beginning of the Albigensian Crusade
1215	Magna Carta and the canons of the Fourth Lateran Council are both formulated
1216	Dominican order established

Before
You
Read
This
Chapter

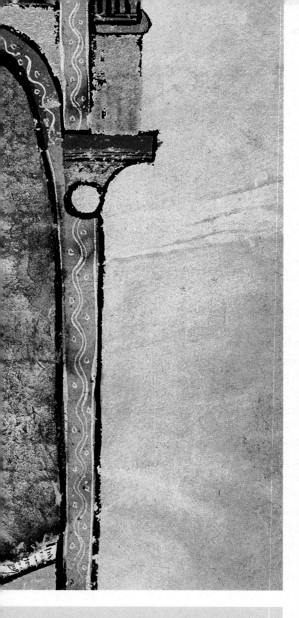

The Consolidation of Europe, 1100–1250

At the turn of the twelfth century, the eldest son of a nobleman did something unusual: he traded lordship for scholarship. His name was Peter Abelard, and after besting all the teachers in Paris he was appointed master of the cathedral school: the highest academic post of the time. There he met Heloise, the niece of a priest called Fulbert.

Heloise had received an excellent education in a nearby convent, but the path of higher learning—Abelard's school—was closed to her. Instead, she became his private pupil and, in time, his intellectual partner, lover, and wife. This last step was particularly problematic, because marriage was no longer an option for clerics like Abelard, and would ruin his chances of a brilliant career. So it remained a secret, as did Heloise's pregnancy and the birth of their son. But then her uncle found out and took revenge on Abelard, sending some local thugs to castrate him. What we know of these events comes from letters exchanged by the couple years later, when Heloise was the leader of a new religious community and Abelard was laying the intellectual foundations of the first university.

ABELARD AND HELOISE. This image from a thirteenth-century manuscript shows Abelard in a scholar's gown and cap and Heloise wearing a nun's habit; their gestures indicate that they are engaged in debate. The story of their fervent attraction and doomed marriage was already famous during their lifetimes, and by the time this manuscript was copied, theirs had become the ultimate example of star-crossed love.

The twelfth and thirteenth centuries witnessed the emergence of large-scale territorial monarchies as dominant political forces, with cathedral schools and the new universities turning out the skilled clerical professionals needed to run these growing bureaucracies, and that of the Church. But at the same time that new opportunities for advancement were available to men, those open to women were being closed down. Meanwhile, deepened connections between Europe and the wider medieval world were creating an integrated and far-reaching economy of goods and ideas. Novel literary forms took shape as the spoken vernaculars of Europe came to challenge Latin, becoming languages of commerce, devotion, and entertainment. By the middle of the thirteenth century, the political institutions and cultural identities that still define Europe had been formed.

THE MAKING OF MEDIEVAL MONARCHIES

As we learned in Chapter 8, power was highly decentralized and diffused for much of the tenth and eleventh centuries. Independent towns and lords often refused to acknowledge

royal authority and kings could no longer rely on close-knit kin groups or the broad powers wielded by Charlemagne. How, then, did some rulers build the foundations of states that continue to exist today? For crucially, the *idea* of a national state—a state that consolidates a shared identity and destiny—was an idea forged in the twelfth and thirteenth centuries. Thereafter, it become so vital for modern European states to trace their origins to the medieval past that those nations without a medieval pedigree would be obliged to invent one.

England: From Lordship to Government

After 1066, the conquest of England (Chapter 8) allowed its first Norman ruler, William, to experiment with a new type of kingship. In theory, he commanded the allegiance of every person dwelling in his kingdom. In practice, however, William needed to impose his will on his new subjects, either through force or through the highly effective administrative structures of his Anglo-Saxon predecessors, which he adapted to his own needs. This process was carried forward by his son Henry I (r. 1100–35), whose approach to kingship was unusual in its focus on governance rather than warfare. Henry strengthened local administration and instituted a system of traveling judges to administer royal justice. He also introduced a method of fiscal accounting carried out by an office known as the Exchequer, so called because clerks moved counters around on a checkered cloth to calculate receipts and expenditures.

But Henry's hands-on approach to royal lordship was both new and unpopular. Then, as now, those opposed to "big government" could react violently against it, and after Henry's death those reactions provoked a civil war that lasted throughout the reign of his cousin and successor, Stephen (r. 1135–54). Yet this period of relative chaos merely underscored the need for strong, centralized rule, a need that was finally met by Henry's grandson and namesake.

Henry II and the Extension of Royal Power

At the age of twenty-one, the new King Henry II (b. 1133, r. 1154–89) was already the duke of Normandy and the lord of two other independent French counties, Anjou and Maine. He also controlled the Aquitaine, thanks to his recent marriage to its powerful and brilliant ruler, Eleanor (1122–1204), who had annulled her first marriage to the French king Louis VII in order to create this alliance.

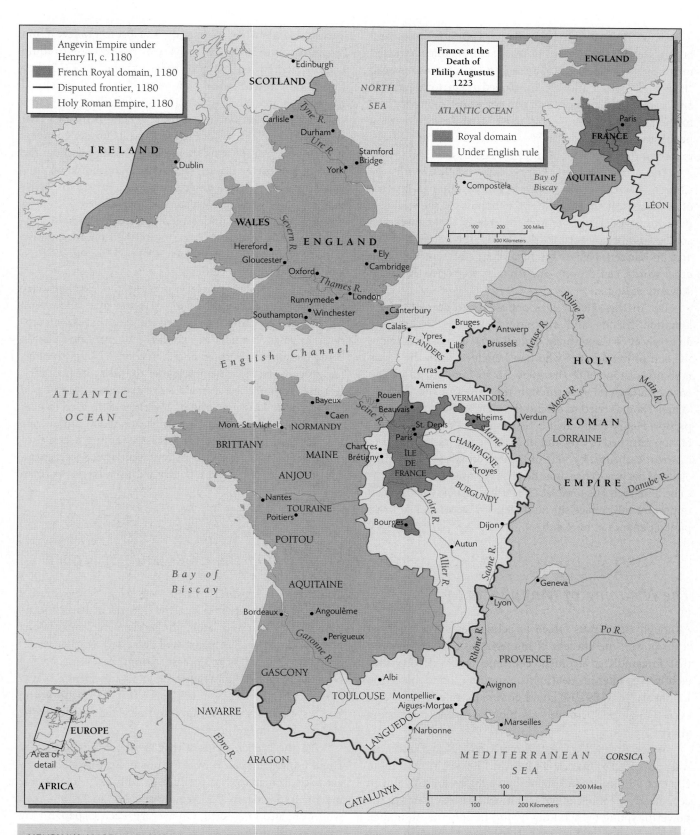

Map legend (main map):
- Angevin Empire under Henry II, c. 1180
- French Royal domain, 1180
- Disputed frontier, 1180
- Holy Roman Empire, 1180

Inset map (top right): France at the Death of Philip Augustus 1223
- Royal domain
- Under English rule

Inset map (bottom left): EUROPE — Area of detail — AFRICA

Labels on main map include: SCOTLAND, Edinburgh, NORTH SEA, Carlisle, Tyne R., Durham, Ure R., Stamford Bridge, York, IRELAND, Dublin, WALES, ENGLAND, Hereford, Gloucester, Severn R., Ely, Cambridge, Oxford, Thames R., London, Runnymede, Winchester, Southampton, Canterbury, Calais, English Channel, ATLANTIC OCEAN, Bruges, Ypres, Lille, Antwerp, Brussels, FLANDERS, Arras, Amiens, Meuse R., Rhine R., HOLY ROMAN EMPIRE, Bayeux, Rouen, Beauvais, VERMANDOIS, Rheims, Verdun, Mosel R., Main R., LORRAINE, Caen, Mont-St. Michel, NORMANDY, Seine R., St. Denis, Paris, Marne R., CHAMPAGNE, BRITTANY, MAINE, Chartres, Brétigny, ÎLE DE FRANCE, Troyes, ANJOU, BURGUNDY, Danube R., Nantes, TOURAINE, Poitiers, Bourges, Loire R., Dijon, Autun, POITOU, Allier R., Saône R., Geneva, Bay of Biscay, AQUITAINE, Lyon, Bordeaux, Angoulême, Périgueux, Garonne R., Rhône R., Po R., PROVENCE, GASCONY, Albi, Avignon, TOULOUSE, Montpellier, Aigues-Mortes, Marseilles, NAVARRE, Ebro R., LANGUEDOC, Narbonne, MEDITERRANEAN SEA, CORSICA, ARAGON, CATALUNYA

Inset map labels: ENGLAND, ATLANTIC OCEAN, FRANCE, Paris, AQUITAINE, Bay of Biscay, Compostela, LÉON

HENRY II'S ANGEVIN EMPIRE AND THE KINGDOM OF FRANCE, 1180–1223. ▪ What areas did Henry II's empire control in 1180? ▪ What advantages would the king of France have when challenging English control over continental territories—even though his own power was confined to the "island" (Île) of France around Paris?

Henry II restored his grandfather's administration and began, steadily, to extend its reach. He organized trusted men from every locale into juries (the Latin *jus* means both "law" and "oath") and commissioned them to adjudicate civil cases and to report every major crime that occurred in their districts. Henry also made it easier for common people to seek justice in the royal courts. These innovations represent the origin of our modern legal system.

They also brought Henry into conflict with the Church, because royal justice began to impinge on that of ecclesiastical courts: bishops' tribunals for the trial and punishment of clerics. Henry had declared that churchmen convicted of serious crimes should lose their clerical status and be handed over to his royal court for sentencing; in other words, clerics were English subjects before they were servants of Rome.

But in this, Henry was opposed by one of his own longtime friends and supporters: Thomas Becket, the archbishop of Canterbury. Thomas was a self-made man, the son of immigrants who had benefited from the social mobility of town life (he grew up in London) to obtain an education and rise through the ranks of the Church. When Thomas tried to defend the clergy's allegiance to the papacy, Henry responded by exiling him. When the archbishop returned to England in 1170, he was assassinated in his own cathedral by four of Henry's knights. Henry proclaimed his innocence, but the papacy pronounced Thomas to be a martyr. His tomb at Canterbury quickly became an important pilgrimage site, and Henry was compelled to do public penance at his tomb.

The Meaning of Magna Carta

Although Henry was forced to acknowledge the limits of royal power, the success of his legislative efforts ensured that England's government continued to work very efficiently even after his death: his crusading son Richard "the Lionheart" (r. 1189–99) could nominally rule for ten years even though he spent only six months in England during all that time.

When Richard was killed while besieging a castle, he was succeeded by his brother John (r. 1199–1216), a far more efficient administrator. But military losses forced John to cede nearly all of his father's Continental possessions to the powerful young French king, Philip II; only the Aquitaine, the inheritance of his mother Eleanor, remained of his father's original empire. This was politically disastrous for John. Not only did it deplete his resources, it angered the most powerful Norman lords of England, who lost their ancestral lands when Normandy was lost to France. John's response was to attempt a recovery by raising taxes to equip an army, thereby enraging the barons further. In 1215, they forced John to set his seal on a "great charter" that defined their own rights while limiting those of the king.

Magna Carta established some general principles that still undergird the laws of England and its former colonies. It stipulated that the king should levy no taxes without the consent of those he taxed, that no free man should be punished until he had been judged guilty by a jury of his peers, that no one should be arrested or imprisoned without a warrant, and that no unqualified person should hold public office. The great charter also established a representative body of barons called Parliament (derived from the French word for "speaking together").

In sum, Magna Carta expressed the extraordinary idea that a king should be subject to the rule of law. And further, Magna Carta normalized the idea that strong representative government is a good thing. Since no taxation could be imposed without common consent, English kings had to convene Parliament in order to justify its necessity. In time, Parliament became a legislative body that helped to govern the kingdom, and its meetings were used to hear judicial cases, review local administration, and promulgate new laws. Gradually, England was becoming a constitutional monarchy grounded in representative government, rather than a conquered territory within a larger Norman empire.

Philip II and the Emergence of France

Compared to England's rulers, the king of the Franks exercised little control in his tiny domain of Paris and its immediate hinterland. Most of Charlemagne's institutions of governance in that region had collapsed, further weakened by Viking raids and pressure from the Viking state of Normandy. When the empire of England's Henry II was at its height, the kingdom of Louis VII (r. 1137–80)—who had lost both his wife Eleanor and her lands to that same Henry—was insignificant.

But the French dynasty that had been established by Hugh Capet (Chapter 8) was fortunate. Against all biological odds, it managed to produce an unbroken line of able male heirs for nearly 350 years (from 987 to 1328)—men who were also long-lived. On average, each Capetian king ruled for thirty years, which contributed greatly to political stability. And this kingdom, though small, was a rich center of agriculture and trade. Its prestige was also enhanced by royal patronage of the arts and of the new university of

Paris founded by Abelard, which made Paris the intellectual capital of Europe (as will be discussed later).

Beyond all this, the Capetians proved to be shrewd politicians. Louis VII's son Philip II (r. 1180–1223) styled himself "Augustus" and was the first to use the title "King of France": king of a sovereign state (rather than "King of the Franks," leader of a tribe). Philip came to the throne at the age of eighteen, having witnessed the struggles of his father against the superior strength of Henry II. He understood that he could not win a direct military confrontation. Instead, Philip declared that John owed him homage and allegiance in return for Normandy and its adjacent territories, and then took advantage of his position as John's overlord to undermine John's control over these lands. When John objected, Philip declared all his lands to be forfeit to the French crown and backed this declaration with armies that won decisive victories.

In the new territories of his domain, Philip wisely maintained the bureaucratic structures put in place by generations of Anglo-Norman rule. But he also appointed royal overseers, known as *bailiffs*, who had full judicial, administrative, and military authority there. Philip drew these men from among the needy knights and lesser nobility of his own domain and rotated them frequently from region to region. This ensured their loyalty to Philip and also prevented them from developing personal ties to the regions they governed.

France and England Compared

Philip's administrative pattern, which recognized regional diversity while promoting centralized royal control, would continue to characterize French government until the time of the French Revolution (see Chapter 18). But the French Parlement never played the crucial role in French government that Parliament did in England. A fundamental reason for this was the French nobility's successful claim to exemption from taxation, something that would long remain a political and financial problem for the crown.

Other significant points of comparison between England and France still mark their intertwined histories. England, a far smaller country, was much more tightly unified at a much earlier date; English nobles could and did rebel against their kings, but they could rarely count on sustained regional support. In France, however, regional separatism and resentment of Parisian control remained (as it also remains) a significant force. English kings could rely on local men to do much of the work of local government without pay. This made English administration

inexpensive, and it also meant that royal policies had to be popular in order to be implemented. French kings, by contrast, ruled through salaried officers who had little connection to local communities. As a result, their government lacked effective mechanisms for mobilizing public support. Eventually, these features would be the undoing of the French monarchy.

Frederick Barbarossa and the Holy Roman Empire

We have seen that struggles with the papacy ultimately led to the weakening of imperial authority in Germany and northern Italy. But in the middle of the twelfth century, a newly elected emperor made an ambitious attempt to free his office from papal control. This was Frederick, later known as Barbarossa ("Red Beard," r. 1152–90). Frederick coined the term "Holy Roman Empire" to describe his realm, asserting that its holiness derived directly from God and did not depend on the blessing of the pope.

Frederick forged a close alliance with other German princes by supporting their efforts to control their own territories. In exchange, he exacted their support of his efforts to reassert imperial control over the wealthy cities of northern Italy. This strategy worked, but it sparked a series of destructive wars. Sanctioned by the pope, the cities of northern Italy formed an alliance, the Lombard League, which finally forced Frederick to guarantee their political independence in return for large cash payments.

Meanwhile, Frederick attempted to bypass the papacy by supporting a series of rival popes (or "antipopes"). This move was successfully countered by the reigning pope, Alexander III (r. 1159–81), who drove a shrewd bargain: if Frederick would concede the sovereignty of the pope's rule within Rome and its adjacent territories—lands that came to be known as the Papal States—then Alexander would concede the emperor's sovereignty within his domains, and even his overlordship of the Church in those domains. Frederick agreed and so gained the pope's support for his rule in northern Italy.

When Frederick left for the Holy Land in 1189—joining Richard the Lionheart and Philip Augustus on a (failed) crusade to reconquer Jerusalem (to be discussed later)—he left his realm in a powerful position. Although he died on that venture, his son, Henry VI, succeeded to the throne without opposition and enjoyed a huge income from the northern Italian towns; he ultimately became the king of Sicily, too. This strengthened the empire's position even further, for now the Papal States were surrounded by

KINGDOM OF ENGLAND

NORTH SEA

BALTIC SEA

London

FRIESLAND

Elbe R.

DUCHY OF POMERANIA

DUCHY OF SAXONY

MARCH OF BRANDENBURG

KINGDOM OF POLAND

DUCHY OF LOTHARINGIA

THURINGIA

MARCH OF LUSATIA

Oder R.

Seine R.

Paris

KINGDOM OF FRANCE

DUCHY OF FRANCONIA

KINGDOM OF BOHEMIA

MARCH OF MORAVIA

Loire R.

Rhine R.

Danube R.

DUCHY OF SWABIA

DUCHY OF AUSTRIA

Vienna

ATLANTIC OCEAN

COUNTY OF BURGUNDY

AQUITAINE

DUCHY OF BAVARIA

KINGDOM OF HUNGARY

Rhône R.

KINGDOM OF ARLES

LOMBARDY

Po R.

Venice

Genoa

ADRIATIC SEA

Marseilles

Bologna

Florence

PAPAL STATES

CORSICA

Rome

Holy Roman Empire, c. 1200

SARDINIA

KINGDOM OF THE TWO SICILIES

EUROPE

Area of detail

AFRICA

MEDITERRANEAN SEA

Palermo

SICILY

0   100   200   300 Miles
0   100   200   300 Kilometers

THE HOLY ROMAN EMPIRE AND ITS NEIGHBORS, c. 1200. ▪ *How would the borders of the Holy Roman Empire have been defined during the Middle Ages?* ▪ *Why were the German states not able to unify during this period?* ▪ *Why would the prospect of a single heir to the Holy Roman Empire and to the kingdom of the Two Sicilies have been a threat to the papacy?*

the lands of a single powerful ruler. However, Henry VI died in 1197 at the age of thirty-two, leaving only a three-year-old son, the future Frederick II, as his heir apparent.

The Reign of Frederick II and the Fragmentation of Imperial Power

Frederick II is one of the most fascinating of all medieval rulers. Having grown up in Sicily, at the heart of the multicultural Mediterranean, he spoke Arabic and Italian as well as Latin, German, and French. He was both a patron of learning and a scholar, author of a treatise on falconry that is still considered a model of scientific investigation. He maintained a menagerie of exotic animals, a troop of Muslim archers, and a harem of women, all of whom traveled with him on his journeys.

Frederick was devoted to pursuing his grandfather's policies, supporting the territorial princes in Germany while enforcing imperial rights in Italy. Much had changed, however, as a result of the two decades' civil war that followed his own father's death. In Germany, the princes had become so autonomous that all Frederick could do was confirm their privileges in exchange for their loyalty. In Italy, the cities of the Lombard League had ceased to pay their taxes and were striving for independence. Meanwhile, the powerful administrative structure of Sicily had fallen into chaos.

Frederick tackled all these problems and restored control over the disparate territories of his empire. In 1237, though, he asserted his right to rule the northern Italian cities directly, bypassing their own independent governments. The result was a lengthy war, which continued until Frederick's death in 1250. The papacy took every advantage of this situation, even excommunicating Frederick and, after his death, denying the rights of his heirs. When Frederick's last legitimate son died in 1254, the prospect of effective imperial rule died with him. For the next 500 years, until the founding of the modern German and Italian states, political power in the lands of the Holy Roman Empire would be divided among several hundred territorial princes.

The "Reconquest" of Spain

By the end of the Middle Ages, a unified kingdom of Spain would emerge as the most powerful monarchy in Europe and the wider Atlantic world (a process we will continue to trace in subsequent chapters). The key to this development lay in the successful alliances forged among the peninsula's

Christian rulers as well as their eventual defeat of neighboring Muslim kingdoms. This process is somewhat misleadingly termed the *Reconquista*, the "reconquest" of Christian lands. In reality, the Roman province of Hispania was only barely Christian when the Visigoths settled there in the fifth century (Chapter 6), and the Visigoths had barely converted before the Muslims arrived in 711 (Chapter 7). But conceptualizing this struggle as a holy war to "reconquer" Christian territory allowed Christian propagandists to cast it as another Crusade and thereby win support for these efforts.

There were four major Christian kingdoms in Iberia by the mid-twelfth century. In the far north was Navarre, which straddled the Pyrenees. In central Iberia were León and Castile, states that were governed as a united kingdom after 1037. Beyond these kingdoms' frontiers lay a broad swathe of Muslim territory. In the northeast was the Christian Crown of Aragon, formed in 1137 when the count of Barcelona, who ruled Catalonia, married the queen of Aragon. Farthest to the west was the new kingdom of Portugal, which had been the first new territory gained by Christian conquests and which won independence from León-Castile in 1139.

Like their counterparts elsewhere in Europe, the kings of Spain struggled to control the power of great lords. Centuries of warfare between Muslims and Christians and among competing Christian clans had left the landscape dotted with enormous castles that could be used as power bases. A ruler seeking to establish sovereignty thus had to use a combination of force and political cunning to bring rivals to heel. We have already seen these tactics at work in England: violent conquest followed by the establishment of effective administrative structures that made royal power a fact of daily life.

This pattern is exemplified by King Alfonso II of Aragon (r. 1162–96), who was also the count of Barcelona and the first to rule the united Crown of Aragon. Alfonso used documentation as the ultimate tool of power, presiding over the compilation of a richly illuminated "big book of fiefs" (*Liber feudorum maior*) between 1192 and 1194 (see **Interpreting Visual Evidence** on page 231). This book recounted property transactions and family lineages dating back centuries, citing documents in the royal archives. Alfonso thereby grounded his authority on his command of written records.

Papal Dominion and the Development of Canon Law

Like secular rulers, the popes of this era were attempting to establish greater authority by building up bureaucratic structures that increased the visibility of papal power. The pope in Rome began to send out specially commissioned

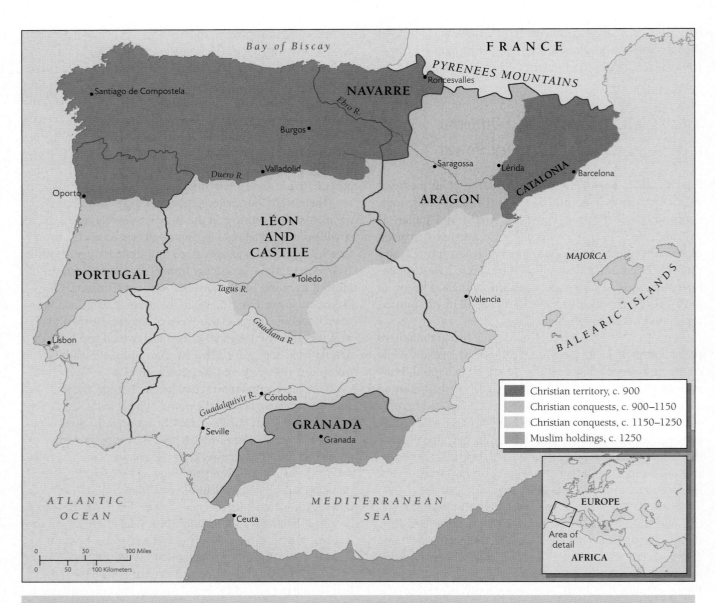

THE "RECONQUEST" OF SPAIN, 900–1250. ▪ *Where were the frontiers of the Christian kingdoms in 900? 1150? 1250?* ▪ *What geographical factors might have helped to sustain these small kingdoms?* ▪ *Why might Castile have become the largest of the Christian kingdoms over time?* ▪ *How could Aragon and Catalonia have maintained important positions as wealthy and significant powers?*

papal legates ("legal representatives") to convey and enforce papal commands, many of which arose from the legal cases that poured into Rome as the pope sought to establish a reputation for justice.

This extension of the papacy's jurisdiction required the development of a systematic body of law. A crucial step in this process was the codification of papal decrees and the decisions of Church councils reaching back to the second century—a thousand years. These formed a body of legal precedents known as *canons*, from the Greek word meaning "rules" or "supports." The problem, though, was that these precedents often contradicted one another, and so any usable compilation had to determine which was most authoritative. The resulting *Concordance of Discordant Canons*, first redacted around 1139 and later known as the *Decretum*, is attributed to a jurist known as Gratian, who may have been from Bologna.

Significantly, Gratian's codification was influenced by the *Corpus Juris Civilis* codified under Justinian (Chapter 7). This was another outcome of the Crusades and of increased contact with Byzantium, and it revitalized the study of Roman law in western Europe. The *Decretum* was also made possible by the new intellectual trends that were simultaneously giving rise to the universities of Europe (as will be discussed later).

Picturing Legal Transactions

Between the years 1192 and 1194, King Alfonso II of Aragon (r. 1162–96) and his court scribes compiled a remarkable book. The codex known today as "the big book of fiefs" (*Liber feudorum maior*) may have been made to assist Alfonso and his descendants in legitimizing their authority over the many areas they controlled. But it was also a way of expressing that authority: its very existence represented a new claim to royal power. In its original form, it consisted of 888 parchment folios (1,776 pages) on which 903 separate documents were copied.

This "big book" represents a new trend in Europe. In most places, claims to property were made on the basis of custom and memory, not on documentation. When property changed hands, the chief witnesses were people, and when questions arose it was these people (or their heirs) whose testimony proved ownership. In Catalonia, the habit of documenting things had a long history, and it was not unusual for individual families to keep archives of documents. At the same time, however, documentation was never sufficient on its own: verbal exchanges of agreement and the public performance of transactions constituted legally binding ceremonies meaningful to the entire community, and the validity of these actions was not dependent on the making of a written record.

With all this in mind, it is striking that seventy-nine of the documents copied into the book are accompanied by images that convey important messages about documentation and its limitations.

On the book's opening frontispiece (image A), King Alfonso consults with his chief archivist, Ramón de Caldes. Ramón discusses one of the charters taken from a large pile at his elbow, while a scribe makes copies behind him—perhaps to aid in the compilation of the "big book." The king is backed by men who look on approvingly.

One of the charters copied into the "big book" is accompanied by the second image (B). It records that the viscount of Nîmes betrothed his daughter, Ermengarde of Carcassone, to the count of Roussillon. Ermengarde, her flowing hair uncovered as a sign of her maidenhood, stands between her bearded father and her seated mother, Cecilia of Provence.

Questions for Analysis

1. Why would a book designed to document property transactions contain images, too? What functions could they have served?

2. Why would the artist of the "big book" have depicted the king consulting his archivist in the very first image? How does he depict the relationship between them? Why does he include a group of men as witnesses to their discussion?

3. Women figure prominently in many of the book's images, including the one below. On what basis could you argue that their active presence is crucial to the transactions being described?

A. King Alfonso and Ramón de Caldes.

B. Betrothal of Ermengarde to the Count of Roussillon.

The *Decretum* claimed ecclesiastical jurisdiction for many vital matters, including marriage and inheritance. Although such cases were often heard in local ecclesiastical courts overseen by bishops, popes increasingly insisted that they alone could issue dispensations that established precedents—such as the annulment of Eleanor's marriage to Louis VII—and that the papal court should function as a final court of appeals in all cases touching the Church. Thinking back to the dispute between Henry II of England and Archbishop Thomas Becket, we can better understand what was at stake: both secular and ecclesiastical rulers now defined their power in terms of law, and they naturally sought to defend their rights against encroachment. And just as kings had to become more skillful administrators, so the popes of this era were almost invariably trained as canon lawyers, which was a real departure from the monastic origins of the reforming movement discussed in Chapter 8. One of this new breed of popes was Alexander III, who dealt so skillfully with Frederick Barbarossa. Another was Innocent III (r. 1198–1216), who combined an expertise in canon law with a zeal for continuing the work of the Crusades.

CONTINUING THE CRUSADES

In 1095, when Pope Urban II urged the quarrelsome knights of northwestern Europe to take up the cross against the enemies of Christ, he was responding to the Byzantine emperor's request for reinforcements in his war with the Seljuq Turks. But the crusaders' reach quickly extended beyond the frontiers of Byzantium to the great cities of Antioch and Jerusalem. And as we saw in Chapter 8, many crusaders acted on a still broader interpretation of their mission by attacking the Jewish communities of the Rhineland.

So from the first, both the reasons for crusading and the outlets for aggression were apt to change. In the centuries following the First Crusade, violence was directed against many different kinds of people who could be construed as "enemies of Christ." While historians, for convenience, often speak of the Crusades as divided into seven or more distinct phases (the Second Crusade, the Third Crusade, etc.), the people of the time—both aggressors and victims—experienced crusading as a continuous, snowballing movement.

Crusader States and Crusading Orders

On the coasts of Palestine and Syria, the fragile principalities known as the Crusader States laid a thin veneer of

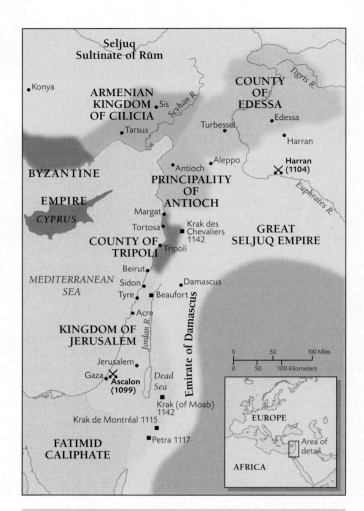

THE CRUSADER STATES. This map shows the fragile colonies known as the Crusader States at their greatest extent, around 1100. ■ *What geographical, political, and military factors would make these states vulnerable?*

western European influence on top of the much older western civilizations whose development we have been studying since Chapter 1. The relatively few veterans of the First Crusade who stayed and flourished were those who were able to adapt themselves. Most probably retained some aspects of their former identities, but they quickly became intertwined with local peoples, intermarrying and adopting their fashions, food, and outlook. Soon they had more in common with their immediate neighbors (Syrian and Armenian Christians, Shi'ite and Sunni Muslims) than with their distant families "back home." Second- and third-generation settlers might never visit western Christendom in the course of their lives.

The four main Crusader States were thus very different from the bureaucratic monarchies that were being consolidated in Europe at this time. They were more like the loosely configured, combative lordships of the tenth and eleventh centuries, and they were mostly short-lived. The largest, the inland county of Edessa, stretched as far east as the Tigris River and had to be heavily fortified against internal uprisings and external threats. Its Latin Christian population was a tiny minority, and by 1150 it had been mostly subsumed into the empire of the Seljuq Turks, with some portions reverting to Byzantium.

Edessa's position was precarious because its Frankish rulers had friendlier relations with their Armenian subjects (with whom they intermarried) than with the crusader principality of Antioch to the west, which comprised parts of what is now Syria and Turkey. Antioch also had a minority Latin Christian population and was largely dependent on Constantinople, and later Armenia, for protection from the Seljuqs. It ceased to exist in 1268, when its lands became part of a vast new empire, that of the Mongols (see Chapter 10).

The third major state, the county of Tripoli, was founded in 1109 to link these two northern states with the kingdom of Jerusalem. But its strategic commercial position exposed it to constant raids, and so its rulers entrusted its defense to a new military order dedicated to perpetual crusading: the Knights Hospitaller. Originally charged with care of pilgrims in the Hospital of St. John at Jerusalem, founded in 1023, members of this religious community became militarized after 1099 and came to control the islands of Rhodes and Malta as well as many strategic fortifications in Syria, like the massive *Krak des Chevaliers* ("Castle of the Knights," so called in a mixture of Arabic and French). In fact, the Hospitallers long outlived the Crusader States they served, maintaining a sovereign presence in the eastern Mediterranean into the early nineteenth century; the order is now headquartered in Rome.

The Kingdom of Jerusalem and the Conquest of Saladin

The kingdom of Jerusalem, the fourth and most symbolically important of the Crusader States, was really a network of cities and fortresses that constantly changed hands. Its cosmopolitan population testifies to the number of peoples who claimed it for their own: Muslims (both Sunni and Shi'a), Orthodox Christians (Greek and Syrian), alongside smaller communities (Jews, Samaritans)—all of whom dwarfed the Latin Christian population. As a result, those who claimed kingship in Jerusalem were heavily dependent on support from other Crusader States as well as from Europe; yet the cachet of Jerusalem was

KRAK DES CHEVALIERS. The necessity of securing hard-won territory in the Holy Land led to the construction of enormous castles like this one in present-day Syria, built by the Knights Hospitaller in the early twelfth century. When crusading movements were launched in Europe itself, similar castles would be built to subjugate peoples deemed rebellious or heretical.

such that ambitious allies often attempted to seize power there. Once again, defense of the kingdom came to rest on another new crusading order, the Knights Templar. Founded during the reign of King Baldwin II (r. 1118–31), the Templars were based in a wing of the captured Al-Aqsa Mosque, which was now the royal palace and thought to be part of King Solomon's original Temple complex: hence the order's name.

Although the kingdom of Jerusalem persisted in theory for almost two hundred years, it ceased to have any purchase on Jerusalem itself after 1187. In this year, a remarkable Kurdish chieftain called Salāḥ ad-Dīn (c. 1138–1193), who had become the Sunni sultan of both Egypt and Syria, succeeded in recapturing the Holy City. He became the target of a renewed crusading effort (the Third Crusade, 1189–92), which spurred three kings to take the cross: Richard the Lionheart, Philip Augustus, and Frederick Barbarossa. (Frederick was killed, Philip left early, and Richard was captured on the way back.)

Meanwhile, the victorious Saladin (as he was known in Europe) became celebrated among crusaders, who considered him a paragon of chivalry. Richard even considered arranging a marriage between his own sister, the widowed Queen Joan of Sicily, and Saladin's brother, to establish joint rule in Jerusalem. But this never happened, and the city of Acre (Akko, in northern Israel) became the new capital of the Christian kingdom. Its fall in 1291 marked the end of any viable western European presence in the region until the short-lived conquests of Napoleon at the end of the eighteenth century (see Chapter 18).

The Canons of the Fourth Lateran Council

In 1215, Innocent III presided over an ecumenical assembly of Church leaders in the papal palace and church of Saint John Lateran in Rome. The resulting canons both reaffirmed older legislation and introduced a number of new laws that responded to widespread social, economic, and cultural changes. Published in the same year as Magna Carta, they too became a standard set of principles and continued to be applied within the Church until they were modified by the Council of Trent in the sixteenth century.

Canon 1

. . . There is one Universal Church of the faithful, outside of which there is absolutely no salvation. In which there is the same priest and sacrifice, Jesus Christ, whose body and blood are truly contained in the sacrament of the altar under the forms of bread and wine; the bread being changed *(transsubstantiatio)* by divine power into the body, and the wine into the blood, so that to realize the mystery of unity we may receive of Him what He has received of us. And this sacrament no one can effect except the priest who has been duly ordained in accordance with the keys of the Church, which Jesus Christ Himself gave to the Apostles and their successors. . . .

• • •

Canon 3

We excommunicate and anathematize every heresy that rises against the holy, orthodox, and Catholic faith . . .

condemning all heretics under whatever names they may be known, for while they have different faces they are nevertheless bound to each other by their tails, since in all of them vanity is a common element. Those condemned, being handed over to the secular rulers of their bailiffs, let them be abandoned, to be punished with due justice, clerics being first degraded from their orders.

• • •

Canon 9

Since in many places within the same city and diocese there are people of different languages having one faith but various rites and customs, we strictly command that the bishops of these cities and dioceses provide suitable men who will, according to the different rites and languages, celebrate the divine offices for them, administer the sacraments of the Church and instruct them by word and example.

Canon 10

. . . It often happens that bishops, on account of their manifold duties or bodily infirmities, or because of hostile invasions or other reasons, to say nothing of lack of learning, which must be absolutely condemned in them and is not to be tolerated in the future, are themselves unable to minister the word of God to the people, especially in large and widespread dioceses. Wherefore we decree that bishops provide suitable men, powerful in work and word, to exercise with fruitful result the office of preaching; who in place of the bishops, since these cannot do it, diligently visiting the people committed to them, may instruct them by word and example. . . .

Canon 11

Since there are some who, on account of the lack of necessary means, are unable to acquire an education or to meet opportunities for perfecting themselves, the Third Lateran Council in a salutary

The Extension of Crusading Ideas within Europe

Once unleashed, the crusading ethos could not be contained by efforts to liberate the Holy Land. Within a decade after the First Crusade, it was being applied to a host of other initiatives that could open new lands for

European settlement and bring more peoples into the orbit of the Roman Church. In 1108, a crusade was called against the Slavs. In the 1160s, the rulers of Denmark and German Saxony began to colonize the Baltic coast and lands between the Elbe and Oder Rivers, again using the rhetoric of crusade.

These were represented as missionary efforts, but they were not carried forward peacefully and their goals were decree provided that in every cathedral church a suitable benefice be assigned to a master who shall instruct *gratis* the clerics of that church and other poor students, . . . we, confirming the aforesaid decree, add that, not only in every cathedral church but also in other churches where means are sufficient, a competent master be appointed . . . who shall instruct *gratis* and to the best of his ability the clerics of those and other churches in the art of grammar and in other branches of knowledge.

• • •

Canons 14–16

That the morals and general conduct of clerics may be better, let all strive to live chastely and virtuously, particularly those in sacred orders, guarding against every vice of desire. . . .

. . . All clerics shall carefully abstain from drunkenness. . . .

We forbid hunting and fowling to all clerics; wherefore, let them not presume to keep dogs and birds for these purposes. . . .

Clerics shall not hold secular offices or engage in secular and, above all, dishonest pursuits. They shall not attend the performances of mimics and buffoons, or theatrical representations. They shall not visit taverns except in case of necessity, namely, when on a journey. They are forbidden to play games of chance or be present at them. They must have a becoming crown and tonsure and apply themselves diligently to the study of the divine offices and other useful subjects. Their garments must be worn clasped at the top and neither too short nor too long. They are not to use red or green garments or curiously sewed-together gloves, or beak-shaped shoes . . .

• • •

Canon 68

In some provinces a difference in dress distinguishes the Jews or Saracens from the Christians, but in certain others such a confusion has grown up that they cannot be distinguished by any difference. Thus it happens at times that through error Christians have relations with the women of Jews or Saracens, and Jews and Saracens with Christian women. Therefore, that they may not, under pretext of error of this sort, excuse themselves in the future for the excesses of such prohibited intercourse, we decree that such Jews and Saracens of both sexes in every Christian province and at all times shall be marked off in the eyes of the public from other peoples through the character of their dress. . . .

Moreover, during the last three days before Easter and especially on Good Friday, they shall not go forth in public at all, for the reason that some of them on these very days, as we hear, do not blush to go forth better dressed and are not afraid to mock the Christians who maintain the memory of the most holy Passion by wearing signs of mourning. . . .

Source: Excerpted from H. J. Schroeder, *Disciplinary Decrees of the General Councils: Text, Translation, and Commentary* (St. Louis, MO: 1937), pp. 236–96.

Questions for Analysis

1. Based on this selection of canons, how would you characterize the main concerns of the Fourth Lateran Council? What is it attempting to regulate, and why? What changing historical circumstances do the canons reflect?

2. In what ways do the canons distinguish between clergy and laity? How does legislation work to maintain those distinctions?

3. Why do the canons place so much emphasis on clothing and appearance? Why would it be important for both clerics and "infidels" (Jews and Muslims) to dress in distinctive ways?

the conquest and occupation of pagan lands. At the same time, the English were launching crusades against the "infidel" Irish and Welsh (who were actually Christian), justifying this on the grounds that Celts were barbarians who would benefit from a superior civilizing influence. It had been a short step from the calling of a crusade against foreigners to those aimed at fellow European Christians.

Venice and the Crusade against Constantinople

The First Crusade had begun as an attempt to aid Constantinople; the Fourth Crusade (1202–4) ended in its destruction. The object of this expedition, called by Pope

Innocent III in 1198, was Egypt, where Saladin's successors continued to hinder European colonial efforts. This meant launching an attack by sea, because the remaining crusader outposts were too weak to support the movement of land armies.

The natural embarkation point was Venice. A major player in maritime trade since the ninth century, Venice had benefited enormously from the Crusades, supplying ships and supplies while reaping the benefits of closer ties with Byzantium. But relations with Constantinople worsened throughout the twelfth century, as the Crusades damaged Byzantine trade and threatened its security. In 1182, enraged citizens of Constantinople had attacked enclaves of Italian merchants and seamen; those who were not killed were banished, the Venetians among them.

The Venetians therefore had a reason for desiring revenge, and they were now confronted with an army of impoverished crusaders who could not pay for passage to Cairo. So instead, the crusaders paid the Venetians with the services they could render. Rather than sailing for Egypt, the expedition was diverted to Zara on the Dalmatian coast of the Adriatic, a former Venetian port that had rebelled and sought protection from the king of Hungary. Despite the fact that Hungary was loyal to Rome, the city was attacked and taken.

From there, the crusaders moved on to Constantinople. After a terrible siege, the city was savagely overrun in 1204, its people killed or left homeless, its churches and public buildings damaged, and its books and artworks consigned to flames or seized as loot. (See, for example, the porphyry statue shown in Chapter 6 on page 148, which is still in Venice). Then the Venetians colonized the city, controlling its shipping as well as that of Byzantine Crete and many Greek ports. Only in 1261 was imperial rule reestablished in the capital; but by that time, the eastern Roman Empire had shrunk to a fraction of its former size.

Innocent III's Crusade for a Unified Christendom

Pope Innocent III expressed alarm at the turn taken by his crusade, but he accepted the spoils of war and approved Venetian occupation of Byzantine territory. He was an ambitious man. Newly elected to the papacy at the age of thirty-seven, probably the youngest holder of the office in history, his goal was to unify all Christendom—and the wider world—under papal hegemony. But unlike Gregory VII (Chapter 8), Innocent never questioned the rights of secular rulers. Instead, he saw his role as regulatory and disciplinary: when rulers sinned, they should be reprimanded or excommunicated, thereby calling their legitimacy into question. Indeed, Innocent insisted that every Christian was obliged to obey the pope as Jesus Christ's representative on earth.

Innocent pressed these claims in many different ways. He made the papacy financially and politically independent by expanding and consolidating papal territories in central Italy. He proclaimed his power as king-maker and king-breaker by brokering the selection of the Holy Roman Emperor and compelling John of England to grant England to the papacy, as a fief. Innocent also asserted lordship over Aragon, Sicily, and Hungary. He even levied the first income tax on the clergy, in order to support the crusade against Constantinople and its Orthodox Christians.

His crowning achievement was the ratification of his agenda at a representative assembly of the Roman Church, the Fourth Lateran Council of 1215 (held in the Roman palace and church of St. John Lateran). This council defined the central dogmas of Christianity and made one of them the acknowledgment of papal supremacy. Since a dogma is defined as "a truth necessary for salvation," this meant that all Christians had to acknowledge the pope's ultimate power; those unwilling to do so (including the Christians of Byzantium) were, by definition, heretics—and as heretics, they could be punished.

In a further effort to achieve unity within Christendom, the Fourth Lateran Council (known as Lateran IV) took an unprecedented interest in the religious education of average men and women. It responded to the urbanization of Europe by establishing free primary schools (for boys) in all major cities, requiring bishops to recruit effective preachers, and outlawing all kinds of clerical misbehavior. It also sought to increase the distance between Christians and their Muslim and Jewish neighbors by discouraging social relationships, economic exchanges, and intermarriage. Most disturbingly, Innocent's council mandated that "infidels" be visibly distinguished from Christians by the wearing of distinctive clothing: the origins of the infamous "Jewish badge" (see Chapter 26).

The Crusade against Heresy

Innocent's reign marks the height of papal power, but it also sowed seeds of dissent. When Innocent's immediate successors came into conflict with Frederick II over control of Italian territories, the emperor opposed them; and instead of excommunicating him and encouraging rebellion, they called a crusade against him.

Innocent himself had paved the way for this move by launching a series of crusades against heretics, now defined as any group or individual who did not fall into line with the papacy's policies. The most notorious of these campaigns was the Albigensian Crusade, launched in 1209 and ostensibly directed against a heretical sect called the Cathars. In reality, it justified the colonization of what is now southern France by land-hungry knights from northern France, and its terrible violence created lasting tensions that would lead the inhabitants of this devastated region to ally with the English during the Hundred Years' War (see Chapter 10) and to embrace Protestant religion during the Reformation (see Chapter 13). In order to understand how this happened, we must turn to some larger religious developments in Europe as a whole.

UNITY AND DISSENT IN THE WESTERN CHURCH

The Investiture Conflict (Chapter 8) had engaged both clergy and laity in debates over the papacy's claim to supremacy, and in many places there was resistance to its encroachment on centuries-old regional customs and social networks. Bishops had been drawn from local elites since the time of Constantine, and it was normal for these offices to be controlled by certain families. Meanwhile, priests had been married men since the establishment of the first Christian churches, and the wives of priests were not only their husbands' partners, they were also ministers to their communities. When the papacy preached against "fornicating priests" and "concubines," it was condemning relationships that had been essential and accepted for generations.

On the one hand, then, the reforms that culminated in the reign of Innocent III gave the common people an important role to play, by urging them to reject certain practices and weed out offenders. Combined with the fervor that had been whipped up by the Crusades, the result was more widespread interest and increased participation in religious life—as well as increased violence in the name of religion. On the other hand, the reforming movement severely limited the laity's ways of expressing their spirituality, and it placed more controls on daily life.

THE MYSTERY OF THE MASS. In this manuscript illumination, the visionary Hildegard of Bingen (to be discussed later) illustrates the doctrine of transubstantiation. In the lower register, the bread and wine of the Mass have been placed on the altar and are being transformed into the body and blood of the crucified Christ, depicted in the upper register. Paired scenes from Christ's life (his birth and death, his ministry and resurrection) emphasize the fact that earthly substances—bread and wine—participate in a divine cycle of regeneration. Note that Hildegard does not imagine the mediating figure as a priest, but as the (female) Church, represented as a crowned queen and associated with the Virgin Mary. ■ *What might be the significance of this choice?*

The New Monasticism

One manifestation of the new popular piety was the growth and diversification of monastic movements. Many of these rejected the worldliness of Cluny and its daughter monasteries, which had (ironically) started the reforming movement by becoming independent lordships and acquiring extensive lands and enormous wealth. Those seeking holiness had to look elsewhere. The result was the founding of new monastic orders.

The most influential of these was founded at the monastery of Cîteaux in 1098. Cistercian monks followed Benedict's *Rule* in the most austere way possible, founding monasteries in wildernesses and remote areas. They also shunned all unnecessary decoration and elaborate rituals. Instead, they practiced private prayer and committed themselves to hard manual labor. Under the charismatic leadership of Bernard of Clairvaux (1090–1153), a spellbinding preacher and one of the most influential personalities of his age, the Cistercian order grew exponentially, from 5 houses in 1115 to 343 by 1153. This astonishing increase meant that many more people were becoming professional religious, and that still more were donating funds and lands to share indirectly in a life of devotion.

The Magic of the Mass

Another manifestation of popular piety was a new focus on the sacrament of the Mass: the liturgical reenactment of Christ's last meal with his disciples. This celebration, also known as the Eucharist, had always been an important Christian practice (Chapter 6); but in the twelfth century it became the central act of worship in the western Church. Bernard of Clairvaux was instrumental in making it so, by developing and popularizing the doctrine of transubstantiation. According to this teaching, every Mass is a miraculous event because the priest's blessing transforms the bread and wine on the altar into the body and blood of Christ: hence the term *transubstantiation*, since earthly substances thereby become the substance of Christ's divine body.

Popular reverence for the Eucharist became so great that the Church initiated the practice of elevating the consecrated bread, known as the Host, so that the whole congregation could see it. Not incidentally, this new doctrine further enhanced the prestige of the priesthood by seeming to endow it with wonder-working powers. In later centuries, the Latin words spoken at the consecration of the

Host, *Hoc est corpus meum* ("This is my body"), were understood as a magical formula: *hocus pocus.*

The Cult of the Virgin

Popular devotion to the Eucharist was matched by another new and hugely influential religious practice: the veneration of Jesus's mother, Mary. Bernard of Clairvaux played an important role in this, too, traveling around Europe to promote a theology that made Mary the very embodiment of the Church. Eventually, Catholic teaching would hold that Mary had not only given birth to Jesus while still a virgin but that she remained a virgin even after Jesus's birth— and, more radically, that she herself had been conceived without sin. This made Mary the exact opposite of Eve, the woman whose disobedience had (according to Judeo-Christian tradition) brought sin into the world for the first time; for through God's grace, Mary had given birth to

VIRGIN AND CHILD. This exquisite ivory sculpture (just over seven inches high) was carved in Paris in the mid to late thirteenth century as an aid to private devotion and prayer. The mother of Jesus, Mary, was also regarded as the mother of all humanity, the *alma mater* ("nourishing mother") who could be relied on to protect and heal those who asked for her help.

Christ, a second Adam, whose sacrifice of himself atoned for that Original Sin.

This theology raised Mary from the position of God's humble servant to that of heaven's queen, with the power to intercede on behalf of even the worst sinners. Her soaring reputation as a miracle worker and advocate is amply testified by the thousands of devotional images created during this period, the many stories and hymns celebrating her miracles, and the fact that practically all the magnificent new cathedrals of the age were dedicated to "Our Lady." This explains the many churches of Notre Dame in France, the Frauenkirchen of Germany, and so on.

The burgeoning cult of the Blessed Virgin had two contradictory effects. First, it elevated a female figure to a prominent place in the official Church for the first time, and thereby celebrated virtues associated with femininity: motherhood, healing, nourishment, mercy, kindness. But at the same time, it made Mary an unobtainable model of female perfection: she alone could be both virgin and parent, mother and bride. No real woman could emulate her, and thus real women were increasingly compared to Eve and perceived as weak and deceitful. Moreover, the veneration of a lone idealized woman coincided exactly with the suppression of most real women's access to positions of power within the Church. As the cult of the Blessed Virgin grew, so the opportunities for aspiring holy women shrank.

Heloise, Hildegard, and the Challenge to Women

This did not go unremarked at the time. The career of Heloise (c. 1090–1164), sketched at the beginning of this chapter, exemplifies both the avenues of advancement for women and the successful blocking of those avenues by new constraints on women's activities. Heloise's exact contemporary, Hildegard of Bingen (1098–1179), also struggled to make a place for herself and her female followers, and she was more outspoken than Heloise in her criticism of these trends. Like Heloise, she was an abbess and a highly original thinker. She was also a mystic who claimed to receive regular revelations from God.

Hildegard expressed these visions in writings on subjects as diverse as cosmology and medicine, which were transcribed and illustrated under her close supervision. She also composed hymns and ambitious musical dramas for her nuns—music now widely available. Her advice was frequently sought by religious and secular leaders, including Bernard of Clairvaux and Frederick Barbarossa, and she even received a special papal dispensation that allowed her to preach publicly.

Despite all this, Hildegard had to fight constantly for her rights and those of her nuns during her lifetime, and after her death efforts to have her recognized as a saint were thwarted by the papacy. A new canonization process was instituted by the papal curia (court) as a way of controlling the popular veneration of charismatic figures whom the Church considered threatening. Hildegard was one of them. It would take 800 years for her to be officially canonized, in 2012.

Heresy or Piety?

For a thousand years, as we have seen, Christianity had been transmitted to many different civilizations and had changed to absorb new influences. In this era, however, the medieval Church began to lose its capacity to respond

HILDEGARD OF BINGEN'S DIVINE INSPIRATION. This portrait of Hildegard and her male secretary, Volmar, appears in her book *Scivias* ("Know the Ways"). It shows Hildegard as the recipient of a divine vision (represented by tongues of heavenly fire) which she transcribes onto a wax tablet using a stylus—a common method for creating the first draft of a written work. Volmar is placed outside the frame in which her vision occurs, but he is prepared to copy it onto parchment. ■ *What does this image tell us about medieval ideas of authorship and authority?* ■ *What does it suggest about the relationship and status of the two figures?*

inclusively to change. This trend would eventually lead to a challenge so intense that it could not be contained: the Protestant Reformation (see Chapter 13). In the twelfth and thirteenth centuries, resistance was manifested in waves of popular opposition to centralized authority, which prompted the calling of crusades aimed at harnessing popular piety to that same authority.

The best way to understand this is through Innocent III's very different treatment of rather similar popular movements. On the one hand, the pope resolved to crush all disobedience; on the other, he wanted to support idealistic groups that could be made to acknowledge papal authority. So, as we already noted, Innocent condoned a crusade against the "heretics" of southern France, the Cathars (from the Greek word for "purity"); the fact that many Cathar leaders were women made the movement heretical by definition. Another related movement, Waldensianism, was also condemned. Its teachings can be traced back to a merchant called Waldes who wished to imitate the life of Christ and whose followers were active in the vernacular translation and study of the Gospels, and dedicated to lives of poverty. But when they began to preach without authorization they were branded as heretics. Many of their leaders, too, were women.

At the same time, however, Innocent embraced two other popular movements and turned them into new religious orders: the Dominicans and the Franciscans. Like the Waldensians, the friars ("brothers") of these orders imitated the life of Jesus by wandering the countryside and establishing missions in Europe's growing towns, preaching and offering assistance to the poor. They also begged for a living, hence their categorization as *mendicants*, from the Latin verb "to beg" (*mendicare*). In the end, what set these orders apart from "heretics" was their willingness to subject themselves to papal authority.

New Religious Orders

The Dominican order, formally known as the Order of Preachers, was founded by Dominic of Osma (1170–1221), a Castilian theologian. Approved in 1216, it was particularly dedicated to the prosecution of heretics and the conversion of Jews and Muslims. At first, the Dominicans hoped to achieve these ends by preaching and public debate, and so many of its members pursued academic careers in the new universities (as will be discussed later). The most influential intellectual of the Middle Ages, Thomas Aquinas (1225–1274), was a Dominican. But the Dominicans soon became associated with the use of other persuasive techniques through the administration of the Inquisition.

(It is now called the Congregation for the Doctrine of the Faith and is still staffed by members of the order.)

The Franciscans, formally known as the Order of the Friars Minor ("Little Brothers"), were committed to the welfare of the poor and the cultivation of personal spirituality. Whereas Dominic and his followers had been priests, the founder of the Franciscans was the ne'er-do-well son of an Italian merchant, Francis of Assisi (1182–1226), who eventually rebelled against the materialistic values of his father. Stripping himself (literally) of his possessions, he began to preach salvation in town squares. And he did this without official approval, thereby risking the same fate as a heretic. But when he showed himself willing to profess obedience in 1209, Innocent granted Francis and his followers permission to preach. Many Franciscans continued to engage in revivalistic outdoor preaching and to offer a model for apostolic living.

This was not, however, an approved religious lifestyle for women. Francis's most important female follower, Clare of Assisi (1194–1253), wanted to emulate Francis's example, but the Order of Poor Ladies (also known as the Poor Clares) was not allowed to work directly among the people and instead lived in cloistered convents. In northwestern Europe, however, there were communities of laywomen who did minister directly to the poor: the Beguines. But their relationship with Church was always strained. The Beguines embraced many of the practices associated with heresy, including the translation and study of the Bible. The fact that they were women made them even more suspect.

Christians against Jews

Violence and exploitation shaped the experiences of Europe's Jewish communities after the First Crusade. The Church never explicitly endorsed this, yet it did little to combat it. As a result, many Christians came to believe that their Jewish neighbors were capable of crucifying and eating Christian children, profaning the Eucharist, and poisoning wells. Stories of Jewish wealth added an economic element to these fears, as did the fact that Jewish social networks were the engine of the medieval economy. Conspiracy theorists inferred the existence of organized Jewish plots to undermine Christendom, and cited these as justifications for violence.

This situation worsened throughout the twelfth and thirteenth centuries, as both secular and ecclesiastical authorities devised more systematic mechanisms for policing undesirable segments of society: not only heretics but the indigent poor, prostitutes, "sodomites," and lepers. The Fourth Lateran Council had mandated that Jews be exposed through the wearing of the Jewish badge, and this made them easier targets in times of unrest. Meanwhile, the protections which Europe's rulers had once extended to their Jewish subjects were gradually withdrawn. In Spain, the Reconquista absorbed many of the Muslim kingdoms in which Jews had enjoyed a measure of tolerance, and they were not easily accommodated within the emerging monarchies of Christian Spain. Starting in the 1280s, rulers elsewhere in Europe began to expel their Jewish subjects from their kingdoms altogether, in most cases because they could no longer pretend to repay the enormous sums they had extorted from Jewish moneylenders: this was the case in the kingdoms of Sicily (1288), England (1290), and France (1306). The Jews were finally expelled from Spain in 1492 (see Chapter 12). By 1500, only northern Italy, parts of Germany, and central and eastern Europe were home to sizable Jewish communities.

AN INTELLECTUAL REVOLUTION

The Fourth Lateran Council mandated the education of the laity and more rigorous training for all clergy. These measures responded to a number of factors that were transforming the cultural landscape of Europe. The growth of towns had led to the growth of schools in those towns, for the most part founded by local bishops or monasteries. Meanwhile, the crusades became conduits for the transmission of Muslim learning and, through Muslim mediation, the precepts of ancient Greek philosophy. The infusion of these new ideas created an extraordinary new forum for intellectual endeavor: the university. In much the same way that ease of travel and communication had fostered a scientific revolution in the cities of the Hellenistic world (see Chapter 4), so the conditions that gave rise to the university mark the beginning of a revolution in the intellectual history of Europe.

Access to Education

In 1179, Pope Alexander III decreed that all cathedrals should set aside income for at least one schoolteacher, whose task would be to accept all comers, rich or poor, without fee. He predicted, correctly, that this measure would increase the number of well-trained clerics to staff the growing bureaucracy of the Church. The recently martyred Thomas Becket had been an early beneficiary of such schooling.

At first, cathedral schools existed almost exclusively for the training of parish priests, but their curriculum was soon broadened to provide more men with sophisticated skills. The most fundamental elements of learning were known as

the *trivium*, "the three ways": grammar, logic, and rhetoric. This meant a thorough grounding in Latin and training in the formulation of sound arguments. Those who mastered the trivium could move on to the *quadrivium* or "four ways": arithmetic, geometry, astronomy, and music. Together, these seven liberal arts—so called because they promised liberation from menial labor—were the prerequisites for advanced study in philosophy, theology, law, and medicine.

Until about 1200, most students would have belonged to the minor orders of the clergy. This means that they took vows of obedience and were immune from prosecution by secular authorities, but they were not required to remain celibate—unlike priests and bishops, who were in major orders. Even those who hoped to become lawyers or bureaucrats found it advantageous to "take orders" in case powerful ecclesiastical offices became open: Heloise tried to discourage Abelard from marrying for this very reason. Abelard, a nobleman's son, is by no means typical of the men who rose to prominence in this era through education. His contemporary and rival, Suger, is more representative: an orphan of obscure origins, he became abbot of the royal monastery of Saint-Denis and chancellor of two French kings.

Later, in the thirteenth century, boys who entered schools were usually not members of the clergy and never intended to be. Some regarded Latin literacy as a badge of status and a practical necessity. Others were future notaries, estate managers, and merchants who wanted to succeed in these careers. Many alternative schools were established to cater to these vocational students and, in many cases, Latin ceased to be the language of instruction and was replaced by the vernacular language of the region.

Formal schooling remained restricted to males. Yet many girls and women reared in convents or princely courts became highly learned. Heloise had clearly received excellent preparatory training in the convent before she began her studies with Abelard. Most laywomen were taught at home, sometimes by private tutors but more often by other women. In fact, laywomen were more likely to be literate than laymen, and it is for this reason that women were often the patrons of poets and the primary readers and owners of books.

Abelard and the Rise of Scholasticism

This educational revolution led to the development of new critical methods for framing and resolving complex intellectual and practical problems. These methods are collectively known as *scholasticism*, because they had their origins in the medieval schools. Scholastic methods are highly systematic and respectful of authority, but they also rely on rigorous

Competing Viewpoints

Two Conversion Experiences

> *Both Peter Waldo (or Waldes), later branded as a heretic, and Francis of Assisi, later canonized as a saint, were moved to take up a life of preaching and poverty after undergoing a process of conversion. These experiences exhibit some striking similarities, despite the different fates of these two men. The first account is that of an anonymous chronicler in Peter's home town of Lyons; the second is by Francis's contemporary and hagiographer, Thomas of Celano (c. 1200–c. 1260/70).*

The Conversion of Peter Waldo

At about this time, in 1173, there was a citizen of Lyons named Peter Waldo, who had made a great deal of money by the evil means of usury. One Sunday he lingered by a crowd that had gathered round a traveling storyteller, and was much struck by his words. He took him home with him, and listened carefully to his story of how St. Alexis had died a holy death in his father's house. Next morning Waldo hastened to the schools of theology to seek advice about his soul. When he had been told of the many ways of coming to God he asked the master whether any of them was more sure and reliable than the rest. The master quoted to him the words of the Lord, "If thou wilt be perfect, go sell what thou hast and give it to the poor, and thou shalt have treasure in heaven. And come follow me."

Waldo returned to his wife and gave her the choice between having all his movable wealth or his property in land. . . . She was very upset at having to do this and chose the property. From his movable wealth he returned what he had acquired wrongly, conferred a large portion on his two daughters, whom he placed in the order of Fontevrault without his wife's knowledge, and gave a still larger amount to the poor.

At this time a terrible famine was raging through Gaul and Germany. . . . Waldo generously distributed bread, soup, and meat to anyone who came to him. On the [Feast of the] Assumption of the Virgin [August 15] he scattered money among the poor in the streets saying, "You cannot serve two masters, God and Mammon." The people around thought he had gone out of his senses. Then he stood up on a piece of high ground and said, "Friends and fellow-citizens, I am not mad as you think. . . . I know that many of you disapprove of my having acted so publicly. I have done so both for my own sake and for yours: for my sake, because anybody who sees me with money in future will be able to say that I am mad; for your sake, so that you may learn to place your hopes in God and not in wealth." . . .

1177: Waldo, the citizen of Lyons whom we have already mentioned, who had vowed to God that he would possess neither gold nor silver, and take no thought for the morrow, began to make converts to his opinions. Following his example they gave all they had to the poor, and willingly devoted themselves to poverty. Gradually, both in public and in private they began to inveigh against both their own sins and those of others. . . .

1178: Pope Alexander III held a council at the Lateran palace. . . . The council condemned heresy and all those who fostered and defended heretics. The pope embraced Waldo, and applauded the vows of voluntary poverty which he had taken, but forbade him and his companion to assume the office of preaching except at the request of the priests. They obeyed this instruction for a time, but later they disobeyed, and affronted many, bringing ruin on themselves.

Source: Excerpted from *Chronicon universale anonymi Laudunensis*, ed. and trans. Robert I. Moore in *The Birth of Popular Heresy* (London: 1975), pp. 111–13 (slightly modified).

The Conversion of Francis of Assisi

There was a man by the name of Francis, who from his earliest years was brought up by his parents proud of spirit, in accordance with the vanity of the world. . . . These are the wretched circumstances among which the man whom we venerate today as a saint, for he is truly a saint, lived in his youth; and almost up to the

twenty-fifth year of his age, . . . he outdid all his contemporaries in vanities and he came to be a promoter of evil and was more abundantly zealous for all kinds of foolishness. . . . And while, not knowing how to restrain himself, he was . . . worn down by a long illness, [he] began to think of things other than he was used to thinking upon. When he had recovered somewhat and had begun to walk about the house with the support of a cane to speed the recovery of his health, he went outside one day and began to look about at the surrounding landscape with great interest. But the beauty of the fields, the pleasantness of the vineyards, and whatever else was beautiful to look upon, could stir in him no delight. He wondered therefore at the sudden change that had come over him. . . . From that day on, therefore, he began to despise himself. . . .

Now since there was a certain man in the city of Assisi whom he loved more than any other because he was of the same age as the other, and since the great familiarity of their mutual affection led him to share his secrets with him; he often took him to remote places, places well-suited for counsel, telling him that he had found a certain precious and great treasure. This one rejoiced and, concerned about what he heard, he willingly accompanied Francis whenever he was asked. There was a certain grotto near the city where they frequently went and talked about this treasure. The man of God, who was already holy by reason of his holy purpose, would enter the grotto, while his companion would wait for him outside; and filled with a new and singular spirit, he would pray to his Father in secret. . . .

One day, however, when he had begged for the mercy of God most earnestly, it was shown to him by God what he was to do. . . . He rose up, therefore, fortified himself with the sign of the cross, got his horse ready and mounted it, and taking with him some fine cloth to sell, he hastened to the city called Foligno. There, as usual, he sold everything he had with him . . . and, free of all luggage, he started back, wondering with a religious mind what he should do with the money. . . . When, therefore, he neared the city of Assisi, he discovered a certain church . . . built of old in honor of St. Damian but which was now threatening to collapse because it was so old. . . . And when he found there a certain poor priest, he kissed his sacred hands with great faith, and offered him the money he had with him, . . . begging the priest to suffer him to remain with him for the sake of the Lord. . . .

When those who knew him . . . compared what he was now with what he had been . . . they began to revile him miserably. Shouting out that he was mad and demented, they threw the mud of the streets and stones at him. . . . Now . . . the report of these things finally came to his father . . . [who] shut him up mercilessly in a dark place for several days. . . . It happened, however, when Francis' father had left home for a while on business and the man of God remained bound in the basement of the house, his mother, who was alone with him and did not approve of what her husband had done, spoke kindly to her son. . . . and loosening his chains, she let him go free. . . .

He [the father] then brought his son before the bishop of the city, so that, renouncing all his possessions into his hands, he might give up everything he had. . . . Indeed, he [Francis] did not wait for any words nor did he speak any, but immediately putting off his clothes and casting them aside, he gave them back to his father. Moreover, not even retaining his trousers, he stripped himself completely naked before all. The bishop, however, sensing his disposition and admiring greatly his fervor and constancy, arose and drew him within his arms and covered him with the mantle he was wearing. . . .

Source: Excerpted from Thomas of Celano, "The First Life of Saint Francis" in *Saint Francis of Assisi: Writings and Biographies*, ed. Marion A. Habiq (Chicago: 1973), pp. 229–41.

Questions for Analysis

1. How do the conversions of Peter and Francis reflect the social and economic changes of the twelfth century? What new sources of tension and temptation are evident?

2. How do these two accounts describe these new converts' relationship(s) with their families, communities, and Church authorities? What are the similarities and differences, and why would these be important factors in determining the sanctity of either?

3. The story of Peter's conversion is written by an anonymous chronicler of Lyons, that of Francis by his follower and official biographer. How do these different perspectives shape these two accounts? Which is the more reliable, and why?

questioning and argumentation. They therefore place great emphasis on evidence derived from reason. Indeed, scholasticism can be defined as the creation of knowledge through logical debate, often called *dialectic*.

The earliest practitioner of the scholastic method is often considered to be Anselm of Canterbury (1033–1109), a Benedictine monk from northern Italy who became archbishop of Canterbury. The central premise of Anselm's teaching was that the human mind can combine knowledge gained through education and experience with divine revelation. Building on the writings of Augustine and Boethius (Chapter 6), Anselm developed various rational proofs for the underlying truths of Christian doctrine. The most famous of these is his proof for the existence of God, known as the ontological proof ("proof from the fact of existence") because it reasons that human beings could not have ideas of goodness or truth or justice unless some higher being had instilled these ideas in us. He further reasoned that God must be "that than which nothing greater can be conceived" and, as such, must exist.

The philosopher who popularized the scholastic method was Abelard, and it was largely thanks to him that Paris became the intellectual capital of Europe. As a cathedral town and seat of the French monarchy, it had a number of schools when Abelard arrived there, but it was his appointment to the schoolmaster's chair at Notre-Dame that made Paris a magnet for ambitious young men attracted to his unorthodox teaching style. We can glimpse it through an audacious treatise called the *Sic et Non* ("Yes and No"), in which Abelard gathered a collection of contradictory statements from the Church Fathers, organized around 150 key theological problems. Like his contemporary Gratian, the codifier of canon law, his ultimate ambition was to show that these divergent authorities could be reconciled—in this case, through the skillful use of dialectic. Yet Abelard did not propose any solutions in this work, which caused grave concern. More inflammatory still were his meditations on the doctrine of the Trinity, which circulated in a book of lectures that was denounced and burned as heretical in 1121. Twenty years later, Bernard of Clairvaux had Abelard condemned for heresy a second time.

Bernard's own mystic spirituality stood in direct opposition to Abelard's tireless quest for reasoned understanding. Abelard, for his part, found no solace in the monastic life beloved by Bernard: teaching was the activity that nurtured his faith. Luckily, teaching also expanded his fame and allowed him to train many pupils who eventually vindicated his teachings. After Abelard's death, his student Peter Lombard would ask the same fundamental questions that his master had done, but he took care to resolve the tensions which the *Sic et Non* had left open-ended. His great work, known as the *Sentences*, became the standard theological textbook of the medieval university, on which all aspirants to the doctorate were required to comment.

The Birth of the University

The emergence of the university—a unique forum for advanced study and the questioning of received wisdom—was the natural extension of Abelard's teachings. His reputation and that of his students attracted many other intellectuals to Paris, and together they began to offer more varied and advanced instruction than anything obtainable in the average cathedral school. By 1200, this loose association of teachers had formed themselves into a *universitas*, "a union of diversity," and the resulting faculty began to collaborate in higher academic study, with a special emphasis on theology. At about the same time, the students of law based in Bologna came together in a *universitas* whose speciality was law.

Paris and Bologna provided the two basic models on which all medieval universities were based. In southern Europe, universities at Montpellier, Salamanca, and Naples were patterned after Bologna, where the students themselves were the university: they hired the teachers, paid their salaries, and fined or discharged them for poor instruction. The universities of northern Europe were like that of Paris: guilds of teachers who governed themselves and established fees for tuition and rules of conduct. They eventually embraced four faculties—liberal arts, theology, law, and medicine—each headed by a dean. By the end of the thirteenth century, the northern universities also expanded to include separate, semi-autonomous colleges, which provided housing for poorer students and were often endowed by a private benefactor. Over time, these colleges became centers of instruction, too. The universities of Oxford and Cambridge still retain this pattern of organization.

Medieval Student Life

Most of the degrees granted in our own universities derive from those awarded in the Middle Ages, even though the courses of study are very different. No university curriculum included history or vernacular languages or anything like the social sciences prior to the nineteenth century. The medieval student was assumed to know Latin grammar thoroughly before admission; he had learned it in the primary (or "grammar") schools discussed above. He was then required to spend about four years studying the basic liberal arts, which meant doing advanced work in Latin rhetoric and the rules of logic. If he passed his examinations, he received the apprentice degree: bachelor

THE SPREAD OF UNIVERSITIES. This map shows the geographical distribution of Europe's major universities and indicates the dates of their foundation. ▪ *Where were the first universities founded, and why?* ▪ *Notice the number and location of the universities founded in the fourteenth and fifteenth centuries.* ▪ *What pattern do you see in these later foundations?* ▪ *What might explain this?*

of arts. If he wanted a professional career, he had to devote additional years to the pursuit of an advanced degree, the master of arts or the doctorate in law, medicine, or theology. This was accomplished by reading and commenting on standard texts such as Peter Lombard's *Sentences* (theology), Gratian's *Decretum* (law), or Aristotle's *Physics*

(medicine). The requirements for the degree of doctor of philosophy included even more specialized training, and those for the doctorate in theology were particularly arduous: it could take twelve or thirteen years to earn this degree, over and above the eight years required to earn the MA.

Student life in medieval universities was rowdy. Since many students began their studies between the ages of twelve and fifteen, they were working through all the challenges of adolescence and early adulthood as they worked toward their degrees; this helps to explain the many prohibitions against drunkenness, gambling, and sexual pursuits included among the canons of Lateran IV. Moreover, because university students constituted an independent and privileged community apart from the towns in which they lived (technically immune to prosecution by secular authorities), there were often riots or pitched battles between "town" and "gown."

That said, study had to be intensive. Because handcopied books were expensive, the primary mode of instruction was the lecture (Latin for "public reading") in which a master would perform an authoritative work and comment on it, while the students took notes. As students advanced in their disciplines, they were expected to develop their own skills of analysis and interpretation in formal, public disputations. Advanced disputations could become extremely complex; sometimes they might last for days. Often they sparked debates of great magnitude. The Ninety-Five Theses posted by Martin Luther in 1517 were actually a set of debating points organized along these lines (see Chapter 13).

Classical Thought, Arabic Philosophy, Jewish Learning, and Christian Theology: The Synthesis of Thomas Aquinas

The intellectual revolution of the Middle Ages was hugely indebted to the learning and legacy of Muslim scholars. As we saw in Chapter 8, Muslim philosophers had been honing an array of different techniques to deal with the challenge of reconciling classical thought with Islamic belief, and these techniques contributed fundamentally to the development of Christian theology in the wake of the Crusades.

The most influential of these Muslim philosophers was Ibn Rushd, known to his Christian disciples as Averroès (ah-VER-oh-ayz, 1126–1198). Born in the Andalusian capital of Córdoba, Averroès single-handedly advanced the study of logic by publishing a series of careful commentaries that sought to purge Aristotle's works of all later and confusing influences. Soon translated from Arabic into Latin, these commentaries were received in western Europe alongside new translations of Aristotle's texts and fundamentally influenced the way all subsequent scholars

understood Greek philosophy. The prestige of Averroès was so great that Christian intellectuals called him simply "the Commentator," just as they called Aristotle "the Philosopher"—as if there were no others.

Ultimately, Averroès's learning was suppressed by the new Muslim dynasty that came to power in his lifetime, the Almohads, who demanded that all philosophy be subordinated to orthodox belief. After burning several of Averroès's works, they exiled him to Morocco. The greatest Jewish scholar of this period, Moses Maimonides (my-MAHN-eh-dees, c. 1137–1204), was also driven into exile by the Almohads; he traveled first to North Africa and then to Egypt, where he became famous as a teacher, jurist, and physician. Like Averroès, he exercised great influence on Christian theologians through his systematic exposition of Jewish law, the *Mishneh Torah*.

Because many aspects of the rabbinic tradition, Greek philosophy, and Arabic learning were not readily compatible with Christian doctrine, they all had to be filtered through the dialectical methods pioneered by Abelard and his pupils. The greatest proponent of this endeavor was Thomas Aquinas (1225–1274), a Dominican who became the leading theologian at the University of Paris. Thomas was committed to the defense of the Roman Church, but he also believed that the study of the physical world was a way of gaining knowledge of the divine. Thomas worked quietly and steadily on his two great summaries of theology, the *Summa contra Gentiles* (a compendium of arguments for refuting non-Christian religions) and the comprehensive *Summa Theologiae*. The theology of the modern Roman Catholic Church still rests on Thomistic methods, doctrines, and principles.

COURTS, CITIES, AND CATHEDRALS

In the eleventh century, it would have been possible to describe European society as divided among those who worked, those who prayed, and those who fought. By 1200, such a description no longer bore much relationship to reality. New elites had emerged, and the wealthiest members of society were merchants and bankers; aristocrats either had to best them by engaging in trade or join them through strategic intermarriage. The aristocracy still fought, but so did upwardly mobile knights, rural archers, citizen militias, and peasant infantries. Meanwhile, the pupils of the new schools made up a growing professional class that further defied categorization. We have already observed that careers in the Church or royal bureaucracies were open to self-made, educated men. But princely courts and cities also provided opportunities for advancement.

From Chevalerie to Chivalry

The transformation of chivalry and the emergence of medieval court culture were connected to the growing wealth of Europe, the competition among territorial rulers, and contemporary developments in military technology. In 1100, a knight could get by with a woolen tunic and leather corselet, a horse, and a sword. A hundred years later, a knight needed full-body armor made of iron, a visored helmet, a broadsword, a spear, a shield, several warhorses capable of carrying all this gear, and a groom or squire to care for everything. By 1250, a knight also had to keep up appearances at tournaments, which meant maintaining a string of horses, sumptuous silk clothing for himself and caparisons for his steeds, and a retinue of liveried servants. As the costs of a warrior's equipment rose, the number of men who could personally afford it declined dramatically, which made knightly display something increasingly prized by the nobility and upstart merchants alike. Knights who did not inherit property or gain sufficient wealth to support themselves had to seek wealthy brides or the protection of a lord who could afford to equip them.

There were still other factors contributing to the prestige of knighthood. As part of the larger effort to control violent competition for land, both secular and ecclesiastical rulers had begun to promote a new set of values that would redefine chivalry: bravery, loyalty, generosity, and civility. This new chivalry appealed to knights because it distinguished them from all the other "new men" who were emerging as powerful in this period, especially merchants and clerics. It also appealed to the nobility whose status in this socially mobile world no longer depended on descent from high-born ancestors. Families who *did* have such ancestors did not necessarily have the wealth to maintain a noble lifestyle.

What, then, was "nobility"? Was high status a matter of birth or was it the result of individual achievement? The amalgamation of knighthood and nobility offered something to those on both sides of the question. To the older aristocracy, it was a visible sign of good breeding. To professional warriors like many crusaders, and to the merchants and bureaucrats who later adopted its language and customs, chivalry offered a way of legitimizing social positions attained through bravery or skill. As a result, mounted combat—whether on the battlefield, in tournaments, or in the hunt—would remain the defining pastime

MAKING A KNIGHTLY APPEARANCE. The costs of maintaining a chivalric lifestyle rose steeply in the twelfth and thirteenth centuries, not only because a knight needed the most up-to-date equipment but also because he was expected to cut a gallant figure at tournaments and to dazzle female spectators. This image is one of many sumptuous full-page illuminations in the Manesse Codex, made in Zurich in the early fourteenth century and preserving the compositions of earlier courtly poets.

of European gentlemen until the end of the First World War (see Chapter 24).

The Culture of the Court

Closely linked to this new ideology of chivalry was a new emphasis on *courtoisie*, "courtliness," the refined behavior appropriate to a court. This stemmed in part from practical necessity. Those great lords who could support a knightly retinue would have households full of energetic, lusty young men whose appetites had to be controlled. Hence, the emerging code of chivalry encouraged its adherents to view noble women as objects of veneration who could only be wooed and won by politesse, poetry, and valiant deeds;

Past and Present

Medieval Plots and Modern Movies

From westerns to science fiction to action movies to romantic comedies, most of the films that draw big audiences today are based loosely or closely on literary genres that were popularized during the Middle Ages: tales of chivalry and heroism, forbidden love, supernatural events, and magical adventures.

Watch related author videos on the Student Site
wwnorton.com/college/history/western-civilizationsBrief4

they had to be courted. Non-noblewomen, though, were fair game and could be taken by force if they did not yield willingly to the desires of a knight.

Whole new genres of poetry, song, and storytelling emerged in the twelfth century to celebrate the allied cultures of chivalry and courtliness. These stand in marked contrast to the older entertainments of Europe's warrior class, the heroic epics that are often the earliest literary artifacts of various vernacular languages: the Anglo-Saxon *Beowulf*, *The Song of Roland*, the Norse sagas, the German *Song of the Nibelungs*, and the Spanish *Poem of the Cid*. These epics portray a virile, violent society. Gore flows freely; skulls are cleaved; manly valor, honor, and loyalty are the major themes. If women are mentioned, it is often as prizes to be won in battle.

The courtly entertainments introduced in the twelfth century are very different in style, subject matter, and authorship. Many of them were addressed to, and commissioned by,

women. In some cases, they were even composed by women or in close collaboration with a female patron. An example of the former is the collections of *lais* (versified stories) of Marie de France, who was active during the reigns of Henry II and Eleanor of Aquitaine, and who may have been an abbess as well as a member of the Anglo-Norman aristocracy. An example of the latter are the Arthurian tales composed by Marie's contemporary, Chrétien de Troyes (*KRAY-tyan duh TWAH*, fl. 1165–90), who spent time working under the patronage of Eleanor's daughter (by her first husband, Louis VII), Marie of Champagne.

Romances were engaging tales of love and adventure, often focusing on the exploits of King Arthur and his knights or some other heroic figure of the past, like Alexander the Great. But they were also attuned to the interests and concerns of women: threats to women's independence, enforced or unhappy marriages, disputed inheritances, fashion, fantasies of power. The heroine of one anonymous romance is a woman who dresses as a knight and travels the world performing valiant deeds. Other heroines accompany their husbands on crusades or quests, or defend their castles against attack, or have supernatural powers. Following in Chrétien's footsteps, the German poets Wolfram von Eschenbach and Gottfried von Strassburg vied to produce romances that retained the scope and complexity of heroic epics while featuring women in strong, central roles: Wolfram's *Parzival*, the story of the search for the Holy Grail, and Gottfried's *Tristan*, which retold the Celtic story of the adulterous love between Tristan and Isolde. Both inspired the operatic reconceptions of Richard Wagner (1813–1883).

The poetic tradition initiated by the southern French troubadours and northern French trouvères (terms deriving from the verbs *trobar/trouver*: "to discover, to invent") also contributed to the culture of chivalry and inspired the work of German *minnesänger* ("love singers"). Much troubadour poetry displays sensitivity to feminine beauty and the natural world. Take, for example, a lyric of Bernart de Ventadorn (c. 1135–1195), one of Eleanor's protégés:

> When leaves and grass are lush with renewed growth
> The beauty of my Lady blossoms forth . . .
> I am her slave, her vassal, she my lord;
> I pay her homage, hope to have a word
> Of kindness, or of love, exchanged for mine
> But she is cruel: she will not make a sign.

Other troubadour songs celebrated old-fashioned warlike virtues, as in the verses of Bernart's contemporary, Bertran de Born (c. 1140–1214), a friend of Eleanor's son Richard the Lionheart:

> It pleases me to hear the mirth and song
> Of birds, filling the wood the whole day long.
> But more it pleases me to see the fields
> All planted thick with tents, to see the shields
> And swords of my companions ranged for war,
> To hear the screams, to see the blood and gore.

To what extent do courtly entertainments reflect reality? Certainly, as the first song reveals, there were women throughout this period who wielded tremendous power, particularly in Scandinavia and parts of southern Europe, where women could inherit property, rule in their own right, and be treated as lords in fact and in name (as in Bernart's song). Queen Urraca ruled the combined kingdom of León-Castile from 1109 until 1126. Ermengarde of Narbonne (c. 1127–1197) ruled her strategically placed county from early adolescence to the time of her death. Eleanor remained sole ruler of Aquitaine throughout her long life, and she played a crucial role in the government of England at various times. The strong-willed Blanche of Castile (1188–1252), Eleanor's granddaughter, ruled France during the minority of her son Louis IX and again when he went on crusade.

Queens are not, of course, typical, but their activities in this period reflect some of the opportunities open to well-born women—and the freedoms that set most western European women of this time apart from their counterparts in the Byzantine and Muslim worlds. A striking symbol of this is the figure of the queen in the game of chess. In the Muslim courts where the game originated, the equivalent of the queen was a male figure, the king's chief minister, who could move only diagonally and only one square at a time. In twelfth-century Europe, this piece became the queen. She was the only figure versatile enough to move all over the board.

Urban Opportunities and Inequalities

In 1174, a cleric called William FitzStephen wrote a biography of his former employer, Thomas Becket, who had recently been canonized. In it, William went out of his way to extoll the urban culture of London that had produced this saintly man and other men of superior quality, as well as all the splendid sights and pastimes to be had there. Towns were crucibles of activity, and as such became cultural powerhouses as well as economic ones.

As we noted in Chapter 8, many of the towns that had emerged in the eleventh century were governed by associations of citizens who undertook a wide variety of civic responsibilities. But urban governance was also apt to fall into the hands of oligarchs, a trend that became increasingly marked during the thirteenth century when the enormous wealth generated by some forms of commerce led to stark social inequalities. In Italy, some cities sought to control the resulting violence by turning to an outsider who would rule as a dictator. Other cities adopted the model of Venice and became formal oligarchies, casting off all pretense to egalitarianism. Some cities remained republics in principle, like Florence, but became increasingly oligarchical in practice.

But even in places where town governance was controlled by a powerful few, there were many meaningful opportunities for collective activity. Urban manufacturing was regulated by professional associations known as guilds or (in some regions) confraternities. Guilds promoted the interests of their members by trying to preserve monopolies and limit

Analyzing Primary Sources

Illicit Love and the Code of Chivalry

Little is known about Marie de France, author of a series of popular verse tales that are among the earliest chivalric romances, but she may have been a nun or abbess living in the Anglo-Norman realm of Henry II and Eleanor of Aquitaine. The following excerpt is from her Lais (Ballads), adapted from stories told in the Franco-Celtic county of Brittany (Abelard's home).

 he Bretons, who lived in Brittany, were fine and noble people. In days gone by these valiant, courtly and noble men composed lays for posterity and thus preserved them from oblivion. . . . One of them, which I have heard recited, should not be forgotten. It concerns Equitan, a most courtly man, lord of Nantes, justiciary, and king.

Equitan enjoyed a fine reputation and was greatly loved in his land. He adored pleasure and amorous dalliance: for this reason he upheld the principles of chivalry. Those who lack a full comprehension and understanding of love show no thought for their lives. Such is the nature of love that no one under its sway can retain command over reason. Equitan had a seneschal, a good knight, brave and loyal, who took care of his entire territory, governing it and administering its justice. Never, except in time of war, would the king have forsaken his hunting, his pleasures, or his river sports, whatever the need might have been.

As his wedded wife the seneschal had a woman who was to bring great misfortune to the land. She was a lady of fine breeding and extremely beautiful with a noble body and good bearing. Nature had spared no pains when fashioning her: her eyes sparkled, her face and mouth were beautiful, and her nose was well set. She had no equal in the kingdom, and the king, having often heard her praised, frequently sent her greetings and gifts. . . . He went hunting in her region on his own and on returning from his sport took lodging for the night in the place where the seneschal dwelt, in the very castle where the lady was to be found. He had ample occasion to speak with her, to express his feelings and display his fine qualities. He found her most courtly and wise, beautiful in body and countenance. . . .

That night he neither slept nor rested, but spent his time reproaching and reprimanding himself. "Alas," he said, "what destiny brought me to this region? Because of this lady I have seen, my heart has been overwhelmed by a pain so great that my whole body trembles. I think I have no option but to love her. Yet, if I did love her, I should be acting wrongly, as she is the seneschal's wife. I ought to keep faith with him and love him, just as I want him to do with me. . . ."

Source: From "Equitan," in *The Lais of Marie de France*, trans. Glyn S. Burgess and Keith Busby (Harmondsworth, UK: 1985), pp. 56–57.

Questions for Analysis

1. Despite the king's initial misgivings, he and the seneschal's wife eventually have an affair and plot to murder her husband, only to be caught in their own trap. Given this outcome, how would you interpret Marie's remarks about courtliness and "the code of chivalry"? What are the tenets of this code, according to the king?

2. What social tensions does this story reflect, and how might it shed light on historical realities? What moral might contemporary readers draw from it?

---

outside competition. To these ends, terms of employment and membership were strictly regulated. If an apprentice or a journeyman worker (from the French *journée*, meaning "day" and, by extension, "day's work") wished to become a master, he had to produce a "masterpiece" to be judged by the masters of the guild. If the market was considered too weak to support additional master craftsmen, even a masterpiece would not secure a man the coveted right to set up his own shop and earn enough to marry. Most guilds were closed to Jews and Muslims and they also restricted the opportunities available to women.

Guilds and confraternities were therefore instruments of economic control, but they were also important social, political, and cultural institutions. Most combined the functions of religious association, drinking club, and benevolent society, looking after members and their families in hard times, supporting the dependents of members who died, and helping to finance funerals. Guilds also empowered their members in much the same way that unions do today, providing them with political representation and raising their social status. In the wealthy city of Arras, there was even a guild of professional entertainers, the confraternity of jongleurs, which became the most powerful organization in the town.

The Varieties of Urban Entertainment

Like courts, towns fostered new kinds of vernacular entertainment. Even the genres of Latin poetry, song, and drama produced in this period can be considered "vernacular" because they made use of vernacular elements (like rhyme, not a feature of classical Latin poetry), dealt with current events, and were popular with a wide audience. In one of Heloise's letters to Abelard, she recalls that he was so renowned for his love songs that "every street and tavern resounded with my name." It's possible that some of Abelard's songs were sung in French but more probable that they used the edgy, colloquial Latin popular among the student singer-songwriters known as "goliards," which means something like "daredevils." Their lyrics glorified the carefree life of youth, the pleasures of drinking and dice, the joys of love, and the agonies of poverty.

Perhaps the genre most representative of urban culture is the fabliau—a short story in verse with a salacious or satirical ending. Medieval fables lampooned the different types of people who were striving to reinvent themselves in the permissive world of the town: the oafish peasant, the effete aristocrat, the corrupt priest, the sex-starved housewife, the wily student, the greedy merchant, the con man. Gender-bending and reversals of fortune are common themes. In one fabliau, a young noblewoman is forced by her impoverished father to marry a buffoonish shopkeeper who thereby gains a knighthood. To shame him, she dresses herself as a knight and beats her husband in a jousting match. In another, a priest tricks a poor peasant out of his cow by promising that God will reward him by doubling his "investment" in the Church. When the cow breaks out

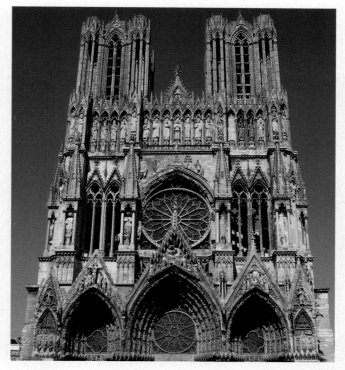

ROMANESQUE AND GOTHIC. Some distinguishing features of the Romanesque and Gothic styles are exhibited in these two churches, both dedicated to the Virgin Mary and built within a century of one another. On the left is the west front of the Church of Notre-Dame-la-Grande in Poitiers, the ancestral domain of Eleanor of Aquitaine. Constructed between 1135 and 1145, it featured rounded arches, strong stone walls, massive supporting pillars, and small windows. On the right is the cathedral of Notre-Dame at Reims in Champagne, built between 1220 and 1299. The emphasis on stolid, horizontal registers is here replaced by soaring, vertical lines. The gabled portals, pointed arches, and bristling pinnacles all accentuate the height of this structure, while the multitude of stained-glass windows—chiefly the enormous rose window—flood the vast interior with colored light.

of the priest's pasture and runs for home, she brings the priest's cow along, too, and the peasant is delighted by the fulfillment of the promised miracle.

The Medieval Cathedral

The cathedrals constructed in Europe's major cities during this period exemplify the ways in which the cultural communities of the court, the schools, and the town came together. For although any cathedral-building campaign would have been spearheaded by a bishop looking to glorify his episcopal see, it could not be completed without the support of the nobility, the resources of the wealthy, the learning of trained theologians, and the talents of urban craftsmen. And cathedrals were not merely edifices: they were theaters for the performance of liturgy, music, drama, and preaching.

Cathedrals were not, in themselves, new: the seat of a bishop had long been known as his *cathedra*, his throne, and the church that housed it was the principal church of the diocese. But the size, splendor, and importance of cathedrals increased exponentially in the twelfth and thirteenth centuries alongside the growing power of the Church, the population of cities, and the wealth and knowledge necessary for their construction. Indeed, the cathedrals of this period are readily distinguishable from their predecessors by their architectural style, which came to be called "Gothic," while the style of earlier buildings is known as "Romanesque."

As the term suggests, Romanesque buildings use the basic elements of public architecture developed under the Roman Empire: massive stone walls, the rounded arch, and sturdy supporting columns. These features convey stability, and they also enabled churches to be fortified and defended in troubled times. By contrast, the structural elements of Gothic architecture are the pointed arch, groined and ribbed vaulting, and the flying buttress, an external support that strengthened the much thinner stone walls and enormous stained-glass windows whose light illuminated elaborate decorative programs that made the cathedral a microcosm of the medieval world and an encyclopedia of medieval knowledge.

These new Gothic cathedrals were not buildings that could be defended in wartime and, it was thought, they would never have to be: they were manifestations of urban pride, expressions of practical and intellectual genius, symbols of a triumphant and confident Church. Their builders would have been dismayed to learn that the modern term *Gothic* was actually intended to be derogatory, the name for art forms that Renaissance artists—who favored Roman models—considered barbaric (see Chapter 12). They would have been still more shocked to learn that cathedrals were among the first monuments targeted for destruction during the Reformation, the revolutions of the

After You Read This Chapter

 Go to **INQUIZITIVE** to see what you've learned—and learn what you've missed—with personalized feedback along the way.

REVIEWING THE OBJECTIVES

- The emerging monarchies of Europe shared certain features but differed from one another in significant ways. What were the major similarities and differences of kingship in England, France, and Spain? Why are they important?
- How did the meaning and purposes of crusading change in the twelfth and thirteenth centuries?
- The growth of papal power made religion an important part of daily life for all Christians in unprecedented ways, but it also limited lay spirituality and the rights of non-Christians. How?
- Scholasticism was the method of teaching and learning fostered by medieval schools and it was also a method of debating and resolving problems. How did scholasticism assist in the reconciliation of classical and Christian thought?
- Why did the meaning of chivalry change in the twelfth century? What new literary genres and art forms of the High Middle Ages were fostered by courts, universities, and towns?

eighteenth and nineteenth centuries, and the wars of the twentieth. One of the prime examples of Gothic architecture, the cathedral dedicated to the Virgin Mary at Reims (shown on page 251), was almost entirely destroyed during World War I; what visitors see today is a reconstruction.

CONCLUSION

A century ago, the American medievalist Charles Homer Haskins described the intellectual, religious, and cultural changes of this era as "the Renaissance of the twelfth century" and the beginning of northwestern Europe's enduring cultural prestige. A generation later, his student Joseph Strayer located "the medieval origins of the modern state" in this same period and, with them, the modern ideas of national sovereignty and national identity. In recent decades, the British medievalists R. I. Moore and Robert Bartlett have also argued that this era marks the beginning of the modern world, though not in positive ways. Moore sees the growth of strong institutions like the Church and the state as leading to "the formation of a persecuting society" in which governmental bureaucracies are used to identify, control, and punish groups of people deemed threatening to those in power through a never-ending "war on heresy." Bartlett views this era as the key phase in a brutal process of "conquest and colonization" visible in the eastern expansion of the Holy Roman Empire, the Norman conquest of England, the growth of papal power, the Crusades, and other movements.

Common to all of these different paradigms is a recognition that the expansion of European power began around the year 1000, continued into the twelfth century, and was consolidated in the thirteenth. By 1250, Europe had taken on the geographic, political, linguistic, and cultural characteristics that continue to define it today. Many European states still look to these centuries for their origins and for the monuments of their cultural heritage. The doctrines crystallized in medieval canon law and scholastic theology are still the core doctrines of the Roman Catholic Church, and devotion to the Virgin Mary is still central to the piety of millions. The religious orders that emerged to educate and curb a burgeoning medieval population continue their ministries. The daughter houses of medieval monastic orders continue to proliferate in lands unknown to medieval Europeans: Japan, Australia, New Zealand, the Americas. Students still pursue the degrees granted in medieval universities, and those who earn them wear the caps and gowns of medieval scholars. Meanwhile, poets aspire to the eloquence of troubadours, singers record the music of Hildegard, and Hollywood films are based on chivalric romances. It is difficult to tell where the Middle Ages end and the modern world begins.

PEOPLE, IDEAS, AND EVENTS IN CONTEXT

- What was at stake in the clash between **HENRY II** of England and **THOMAS BECKET**?
- What was **MAGNA CARTA** and why was it made? How did **PHILIP AUGUSTUS** consolidate royal authority in France, and why were the German emperors unable to do so?
- Why were the **CRUSADER STATES** short-lived and fragile? How did the **RECONQUISTA** continue the Crusades?
- What were the main goals of **INNOCENT III**? How did the **FRANCISCANS** and **DOMINICANS** advance his agenda?
- How do the **CULT OF THE VIRGIN** and the careers of **HILDEGARD OF BINGEN** and **HELOISE** exemplify the ideals and realities of women's roles in the Church?
- Why were **PETER ABELARD'S** teachings condemned by the Church? In what sense can he be considered the founder of the **UNIVERSITY OF PARIS**?
- What is **SCHOLASTICISM**? How did **THOMAS AQUINAS** respond to the influence of Classical and Muslim philosophies?
- How did noblewomen like **ELEANOR OF AQUITAINE** contribute to the emergence of a new vernacular culture? What types of entertainment are characteristic of medieval cities?

THINKING ABOUT CONNECTIONS

- The growth of towns, monarchies, and the Church increased the degree of control that those in power could exercise; but this growth also increased access to education and new forms of social mobility. Is this a paradox, or are these two phenomena related?
- The U.S. Constitution is based on the legal principles and institutions that emerged in medieval England, but it also drew on Roman models. Which do you consider to be more influential, and why?
- Some historians have argued that the extent and methods of persecution discernible in the Middle Ages are unprecedented in the history of Western civilizations. How would you support or refute this thesis? For example, does the persecution of Jews in medieval Europe differ from their treatment under the neo-Assyrians and Chaldeans, or under the Roman Empire? Why or why not?

Before You Read This Chapter

The Medieval World, 1250–1350

When Christopher Columbus set out to find a new trade route to the East, he carried with him two influential travel narratives written centuries before his voyage. One was *The Book of Marvels*, composed around 1350 and attributed to John de Mandeville, an English author (writing in French) who claimed to have reached the far horizons of the globe. The other was Marco Polo's account of his journey through the vast Eurasian realm of the Mongol Empire to the court of the Great Khan in China. The Venetian merchant had dictated it to an author of popular romances around 1298, when both men were in prison—in Columbus's own city of Genoa, coincidentally. Both of these books were the product of an extraordinary era of unprecedented interactions among the peoples of Europe, Asia, and the Mediterranean world. And both became extraordinarily influential, inspiring generations of mercantile adventurers, ambitious pilgrims, and armchair travelers (see Chapter 12).

These narratives are representative of an era that seemed wide open to every sort of influence. This was a time when ease of communication and commercial exchange made Western civilizations part of an interlocking network that potentially spanned the globe. Although this network would prove fragile in the face of a large-scale demographic crisis, the Black Death, it created a lasting impression of infinite possibilities. Indeed, it was only *because* of the medieval network's connective channels that the Black Death was able to wreak such devastation in the years around 1350.

Europeans' integration with this widening world not only put them into contact with unfamiliar cultures and commodities, it opened up new ways of looking at the world they already knew. New artistic and intellectual responses are discernible in this era, as are a host of new inventions and technologies. At the same time, involvement in a wider world placed new pressures on long-term developments within Europe: notably the growing tensions among large territorial monarchies, and between these secular powers and the authority of the papacy. By the early fourteenth century, the papal court would literally be held hostage by the king of France. A few decades later, the king of England would openly declare his own claim to the French throne. The ensuing struggles for sovereignty would have a profound impact on the balance of power in Europe, and further complicate Europeans' relationships with one another and with their far-flung neighbors.

THE MONGOL EMPIRE AND THE REORIENTATION OF THE WEST

In our survey of Western civilizations, we have frequently noted the existence of strong links between the Mediterranean world and East Asia. Trade along the network of trails known as the Silk Road can be traced far back into antiquity, and we have seen that such overland networks were extended by Europe's waterways and by the sea. But it was not until the late thirteenth century that Europeans were able to establish direct connections with India, China, and the so-called Spice Islands of the Indonesian archipelago. For Europeans, these connections would prove profoundly important, as much for their impact on the European imagination as for their economic significance. For the peoples of Asia, however, the more frequent appearance of Europeans was less consequential than the events that made these journeys possible: the rise of a new empire that encompassed the entire continent.

The Expansion of the Mongol Empire

The Mongols were one of many nomadic peoples inhabiting the vast steppes of Central Asia. Although closely connected with Turkic peoples, the Mongols spoke their own distinctive language and had their own homeland, located to the north of the Gobi Desert in what is now known as Mongolia. Essentially, their daily lives and wealth depended on the sheep that provided shelter (sheepskin tents), woolen clothing, milk, and meat. But the Mongols were also highly accomplished horsemen and raiders. Indeed, it was to curtail their raiding ventures that the Chines had fortified their Great Wall, many centuries before. Primarily, though, China relied on the Mongols' tribal feuds, which kept their energies turned against each other.

In the late twelfth century, however, a Mongol leader named Temujin (c. 1162–1227) began to unite the various tribes under his rule. He did so by incorporating the warriors of each defeated tribe into his own army. In 1206, his supremacy over all these tribes was reflected in his new title: Genghis Khan, from the Mongol words meaning "universal ruler." This new name also revealed wider ambitions: in 1209, Genghis Khan began to direct his enormous army against the Mongols' neighbors.

Taking advantage of the fact that China was then divided into three warring states, Ghengis Khan launched an attack on the Chin Empire of the north, managing to penetrate deep into its interior by 1211. These initial attacks were probably looting expeditions rather than deliberate attempts at conquest, but the Mongols' aims were soon sharpened under Genghis Khan's successors. Shortly after his death in 1227, a full-scale invasion of both northern and western China was under way. In 1234, these regions also fell to the Mongols. By 1279, one of Genghis Khan's numerous grandsons, Kublai Khan, would complete the conquest by adding southern China to this empire.

For the first time in centuries, China was reunited—but under Mongol rule. And it was now connected to western and central Asia in ways unprecedented in its long history, since Genghis Khan had brought crucial commercial cities and Silk Road trading posts (Tashkent, Samarkand, and Bukhara) into his empire. One of his sons, Ögedei (*EHRG-uh-day*), building on these achievements, laid plans for an even more far-reaching expansion of Mongol influence. Between 1237 and 1240, the Mongols under his command conquered the capital of the Rus' at Kiev and then launched a two-pronged assault directed at the rich lands of the eastern European frontier. The smaller of the two Mongol armies swept through Poland toward Germany; the larger army went southwest toward Hungary. In April of 1241, the smaller Mongol force met a hastily assembled army of Germans and Poles at the battle of Liegnitz, where the two sides fought to a bloody standstill. Two days later, the larger Mongol army annihilated the Hungarian army at the river Sajo. It could have moved even deeper into

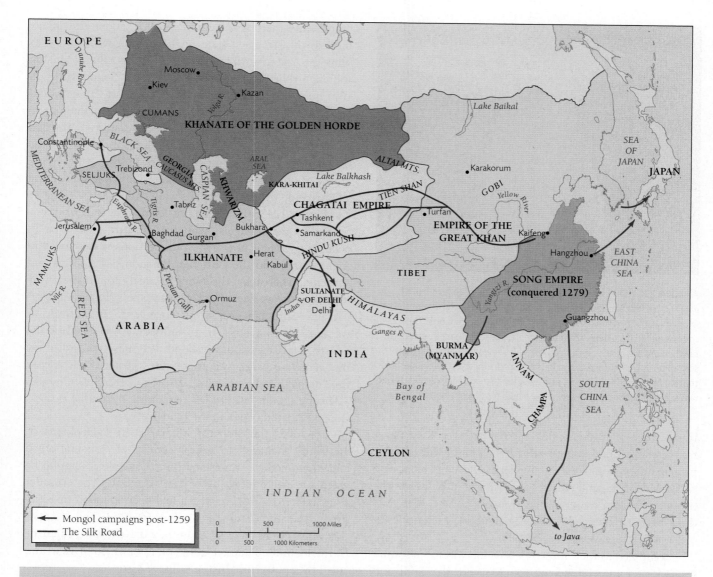

THE STATES OF THE MONGOL EMPIRE. Like Alexander's, Genghis Khan's empire was swiftly assembled and encompassed vast portions of Europe and Asia. ▪ *How many different Mongol khanates were there after 1260, when Kublai Khan came to power, and were these domains mapped onto older divisions within Western civilizations?* ▪ *How might the Mongol occupation of the Muslim world have aided the expansion of European trade?* ▪ *At the same time, why would it have complicated the efforts of crusader armies in the Holy Land?*

Europe after this important victory, but it withdrew when Ögedei Khan died in December of that same year.

Muscovy and the Mongol Khanate

As we have seen in previous chapters, the Rus' of Kiev had fostered crucial diplomatic and trading relations with both western Europe and Byzantium, as well as with the Islamic Caliphate at Baghdad. That dynamic changed with the arrival of the Mongols, who shifted the locus of power

from Kiev to their own camp on the lower Volga River. This became known as the Khanate of the Golden Horde. Its magnificent name evokes the impression made by tents that shone with wealth, some literally hung with cloth of gold. It derives from the Mongol word meaning "encampment" and the related Turkish word *ordu* ("army").

Initially, the Mongols ruled their westernmost territories directly, installing their own administrative officials and requiring local princes to show their obedience by traveling in person to the Mongol court in China. But after Kublai Khan's death in 1294, the Mongols began to tolerate the existence of several semi-independent principalities

A MONGOL ROBE IN CLOTH OF GOLD. The majestic term *Khanate of the Golden Horde* captures both the power and the splendor of the Mongol warriors who conquered Rus' and many other lands. The robe depicted here dates from the late thirteenth or early fourteenth century and was made from cloth of gold: silk woven with gold (and sometimes silver) thread, a precious but surprisingly durable material that was also used for banners and even tents. A robe similar to this one was sold at auction in 2011 for nearly a quarter of a million dollars.

Empire and then by the empires of Alexander and Rome. Indeed, the strongest state in this region was known as Rûm, the Arabic word for "Rome." This was a Sunni Muslim sultanate that had been founded by the Seljuq Turks in 1077, just prior to the launching of the First Crusade, and consisted of Anatolian provinces formerly belonging to the eastern Roman Empire. It had successfully withstood waves of crusading aggression while capitalizing on the misfortunes of Byzantium, taking over several key ports on the Mediterranean and the Black Sea while cultivating a flourishing overland trade as well.

But in 1243, the Seljuqs of Rûm were forced to surrender to the Mongols, who had already succeeded in occupying what is now Iraq, Iran, portions of Pakistan and Afghanistan, and the Christian kingdoms of Georgia and Armenia. Thereafter, the Mongols easily found their way into regions weakened by centuries of Muslim infighting and Christian crusading movements. Byzantium, as we noted in Chapter 9, had been fatally weakened by the Fourth Crusade: Constantinople was now controlled by the Venetians, and Byzantine states centered on Nicaea (in Anatolia) and Epirus (in northern Greece) were fragile. The capitulation of Rûm left remaining Byzantine possessions in Anatolia open to the Mongols.

In 1261, the emperor Michael VIII Palaeologus (r. 1259–82) managed to regain control of Constantinople and its immediate hinterland, but the depleted empire he ruled was surrounded by hostile neighbors. The crusader principality of Antioch, which had been founded in 1098, finally succumbed to the Mongols in 1268. The Mongols themselves were only halted in their drive toward Palestine by the Mamluk Sultanate of Egypt, established in 1250 and ruled by a powerful Muslim military caste.

All of these disparate territories came to be called the Ilkhanate, the "subordinate khanate," meaning that its Mongol rulers paid deference to the Great Khan. The first Ilkhan was Hulagu, brother of China's Kublai Khan. His descendants would rule this realm for another eighty years, eventually converting to Islam but remaining hostile toward the Mamluk Muslims, who remained their chief rivals.

from which they demanded regular tribute. Kiev never recovered its dominant position, but one of these newer principalities would eventually form the core of a state called Muscovy, centered on the duchy of Moscow. As the tribute-collecting center for the Mongol Khanate, Moscow's dukes were encouraged to absorb neighboring territories in order to increase Moscow's security.

Compared to Kiev, Moscow's location was less advantageous for forging commercial contacts with the Baltic and Black Sea regions. Its direct ties with western Europe were also less developed, but this had little to do with geography. The Moscovites were staunchly loyal to the Orthodox Church of Byzantium and had watched relations between the Latin West and the Greek East deteriorate drastically during the Crusades. They became openly hostile to western Europeans after Constantinople was captured and sacked by crusaders in 1204 (see Chapter 9), an event that led Moscovites to see themselves as the last remaining protectors of the Orthodox Church. Eventually, as we shall see in Chapter 12, they would claim to be the heirs of Roman imperial power.

The Making of the Mongol Ilkhanate

As Ögedei Khan moved into the lands of Rus' and eastern Europe, Mongol armies were also sent to subdue the vast territory that had been encompassed by the former Persian

The Pax Mongolica and Its Price

Although the Mongols' expansion of power into Europe had been checked in 1241, their combined conquests made them masters of territories that stretched from the Black Sea to the Pacific Ocean: one-fifth of the earth's surface, the largest land empire in history. Within this domain, no single Mongol ruler's power was absolute. Kublai Khan

THE MONGOL RULER OF MUSLIM PERSIA, HIS CHRISTIAN QUEEN, AND HIS JEWISH HISTORIAN. The *Compendium of Chronicles* by the Jewish-born Muslim polymath Rashid al-Din (1247–1318) exemplifies the pluralistic culture encouraged by Mongol rule: written in Persian (and often translated into Arabic), it celebrates the achievements of Hulagu Khan (1217–1265), a grandson of Genghis and brother of Kublai, who consolidated Persia and its neighboring regions into the Ilkhanate. But it also embeds those achievements within the long history of Islam. This image depicts Hulagu with his wife, Dokuz Khatun, who was a Turkic princess and a Christian.

■ *Why would Rashid al-Din have wanted to place the new Mongol dynasty in this historical context?*

(r. 1260–94), who took the additional title *khagan*, or "Great Khan," never claimed to rule all Mongol khanates directly. In his own domain of China and Mongolia, his power was highly centralized and built on the intricate (and ancient) imperial bureaucracy of China; but elsewhere, Mongol governance was directed at securing a steady payment of tribute from subject peoples, which meant that local rulers could retain much of their power.

This distribution of authority made Mongol rule flexible and adaptable to local conditions. Indeed, the Mongol khans differed from most contemporary rulers in being highly tolerant of all religious beliefs. This was an advantage in governing peoples who observed an array of Buddhist, Christian, and Muslim practices, not to mention Hindus, Jews, and the many itinerant groups and individuals whose languages and beliefs reflected a melding of many cultures.

This acceptance of cultural and religious difference, alongside the Mongols' encouragement of trade and love of rich things, created ideal conditions for some merchants and artists. Hence, the term *Pax Mongolica* ("Mongol Peace") is often used to describe the century from 1250 to 1350. No such term should be taken at face value, however: this peace was bought at a great price. Indeed, the artists whose

varied talents created the gorgeous textiles, utensils, and illuminated books prized by the Mongols were not all willing participants. Many were captives or slaves subject to ruthless relocation. The Mongols would often transfer entire families and communities of craftsmen from one part of the empire to another. The result was an intensive period of cultural exchange that might combine Chinese, Persian, Venetian, and Slavic influences (among many others) in a single work of art.

The Mongol Peace was also achieved at the expense of many flourishing Muslim cities that had preserved the heritage of even older civilizations and that were devastated or crippled during the bloody process of Mongol expansion. The city of Herat, situated in one of Afghanistan's few fertile valleys and described by the Persian poet Rumi as "the pearl in the oyster," was entirely destroyed in 1221 and did not fully recover for centuries. Baghdad, the splendid capital of the Abbasid Caliphate and a haven for artists and intellectuals since the eighth century (Chapter 8), was savagely besieged and sacked in 1258. The capture of the city resulted in the destruction of the House of Wisdom, the library and research center where Muslim scientists, philosophers, and translators preserved classical knowledge and advanced cutting-edge scholarship in such fields as mathematics, engineering, and medicine. Baghdad's fall is held to mark the end of Islam's golden age, since the establishment of the Mongol Ilkhanate in Persia eradicated a continuous zone of Muslim influence that had blended cultures stretching from southern Spain and North Africa to India.

Bridging East and West

To facilitate the movement of people and goods within their empire, the Mongols began to control the caravan routes that led from the Mediterranean and the Black Sea through Central Asia and into China, policing bandits and making conditions safer for travelers. They also encouraged and streamlined trade by funneling many exchanges through the Persian city of Tabriz, on which both land and sea routes from China converged. These measures accelerated and intensified economic and cultural connections.

Prior to Mongol control, such networks had been inaccessible to most European merchants. The Silk Road was a tangle of trails and trading posts, and there were few outsiders who understood its workings. Now travelers at both ends of the route found their way smoothed. Among the first were Franciscan missionaries whose journeys were sponsored by European rulers. In 1253, William of Rubruck was sent by King Louis IX of France as his ambassador to the Mongol court, with instructions to make a full report of his findings. Merchants quickly followed. The most famous of these are three Venetians: the brothers Niccolò and Matteo Polo, and Niccolò's son, Marco (1254–1324).

Marco Polo's account of his travels (which began when he was seventeen) includes a description of his twenty-year sojourn in the service of Kublai Khan and the story of his journey home through the Spice Islands, India, and Persia. As we noted above, this book had an enormous effect on the European imagination; Christopher Columbus's copy still survives. Even more impressive in scope than Marco's

travels are those of the Muslim adventurer Ibn Battuta (1304–1368), who left his native Morocco in 1326 to go on the sacred pilgrimage to Mecca—but then kept going. By the time he returned home in 1354, he had been to China and sub-Saharan Africa as well as to the ends of both the Muslim and Mongolian worlds: a journey of over 75,000 miles.

The Disintegration of Mongol Rule

The window of opportunity that made such impressive journeys possible was relatively narrow. By the middle of the fourteenth century, hostilities among and within various components of the Mongol Empire were making travel along the Silk Road perilous. The Mongols of the Ilkhanate came into conflict with merchants from Genoa who controlled trade at the western ends of the Silk

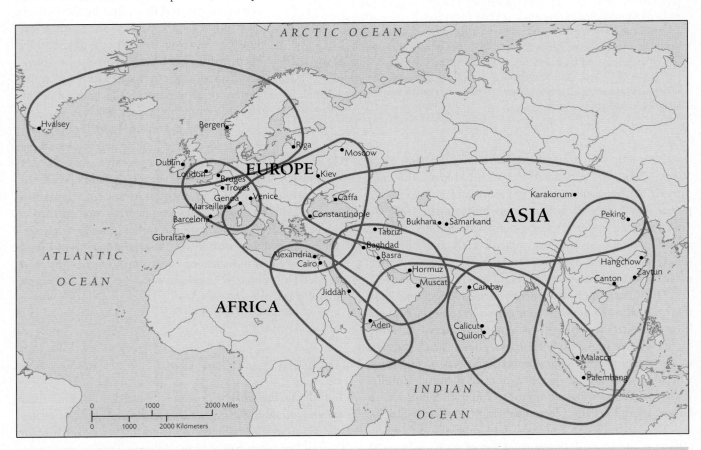

THE MEDIEVAL WORLD SYSTEM, c. 1300. At the turn of the fourteenth century, Western civilizations were more closely connected to one another and to the rest of the world than ever before. This map shows the major interlocking contact zones of the medieval world, showing how trade and travel within each zone could be extended to other zones and foster connections among all of them. ▪ *How has Europe's relationship with its neighbors changed as a result of its integration into this wider world?* ▪ *How might we need to see seemingly marginal territories (like Rus' or Hungary, Scotland or Norway) as central to one or more interlocking components of this system?*

THE EXTENSION OF EUROPEAN COMMERCE AND SETTLEMENT

Western civilizations' increased access to East Asia during the *Pax Mongolica* ran parallel to a number of ventures that were extending Europeans' presence in the Mediterranean and beyond it. These endeavors were both mercantile and colonial. Indeed, the language of crusading, with which we have become familiar, now came to be applied to these economic and political initiatives, whose often violent methods could be justified on the grounds that they were supporting Christian causes. To take one prominent example, the strategic goal of the Crusades that targeted North Africa in this era was to cut the economic lifelines that supported Muslim settlements in the Holy Land. Yet the only people who stood to gain from this were the merchants who dreamed of controlling the commercial routes that ran through Egypt: not only those that connected North Africa to the Silk Road, but the conduits of the sub-Saharan gold trade.

VENETIAN AMBASSADORS TO THE GREAT KHAN. Around 1270, the Venetian merchants Niccolò and Matteo Polo returned to Europe after their first prolonged journey through the empire of the Great Khan, bearing with them an official letter to the Roman pope. This image, from a manuscript of Marco Polo's *Description of the World*, shows his father and uncle at the moment of their arrival in the Great Khan's court, to which they have seemingly brought a Christian cross and a Bible. ▪ *Based on what you've learned about the Mongols and the medieval world, is it plausible that the Polo brothers would have carried these items with them?*

Road, especially in the transport depot of Tabriz. Mounting pressures finally forced the Genoese to abandon Tabriz, thereby breaking one of the major links in the commercial chain forged by the Mongol Peace. Then, in 1346, the Mongols of the Golden Horde besieged the Genoese colony at Caffa on the Black Sea. This event simultaneously disrupted trade while serving as a conduit for the Black Death, which passed from the Mongol army to the Genoese defenders, who returned with it to Italy (as will be discussed later).

Over the next few decades, the peoples of Eurasia and Africa would struggle to overcome the devastating effects of the massive depopulation caused by plague. In the meantime, in 1368, the last Mongol rulers of China were overthrown. Most Westerners were now denied access, while the remaining Mongol warriors were restricted to cavalry service in the imperial armies of the new Ming dynasty. The conditions that had enabled an integrated trans-Eurasian cultural and commercial network were no longer sustainable. Yet the view of the world that had been fostered by Mongol rule continued to exercise a lasting influence. European memories of the Far East would be preserved and embroidered, and the dream of reestablishing close connections between Europe and China would survive to influence a new round of commercial and imperial expansion in the centuries to come (Chapter 12).

The Quest for African Gold

The European trade in African gold was not new. It had been going on for centuries, facilitated by Muslim middlemen whose caravans brought a steady supply from the Niger River to the North African ports of Algiers and Tunis. In the early thirteenth century, rival bands of merchants from Catalonia and Genoa had established trading colonies in Tunis to expedite this process, exchanging woolen cloth from northern Europe for both North African grain and sub-Saharan gold.

But the medieval demand for gold accelerated during the late thirteenth and fourteenth centuries and could not be satisfied by these established trading relationships. The luxuries coveted by Europeans were now too costly to be bought solely with these goods. Although precious textiles (usually silk) were a form of wealth valued by the Mongols, the burgeoning economy of the medieval world demanded a reliable and abundant supply of more portable currency.

Silver production, which had enabled the circulation of coinage in Europe, fell markedly during the 1340s as Europeans reached the limits of their technological capacity to extract silver ore from deep mines. This would lead to a serious cash-flow problem, since more European silver was moving east than could now be replenished from existing sources. Gold therefore represented an obvious alternative currency for large transactions, and in the thirteenth century some European rulers began minting gold coins. But Europe itself had few natural gold reserves. To maintain and expand these currencies, new sources of gold were needed. The most obvious source was Africa, especially Mali and Ghana—which was called "the Land of Gold" by Muslim geographers.

Models of Mediterranean Colonization: Catalonia, Genoa, and Venice

The heightened European interest in the African gold trade, which engaged the seafaring merchants of Genoa and Catalonia in particular, coincided with these merchants' creation of entrepreneurial empires in the western Mediterranean. During the thirteenth century, Catalan adventurers conquered and colonized a series of western Mediterranean islands, including Majorca, Ibiza, Minorca, Sardinia, and Sicily. Except in Sicily, which already had a large and diverse population that included many Christians (see Chapter 8), the pattern of Catalan conquest was largely the same on all these islands: expulsion or extermination of the existing population, usually Muslim; the extension of economic concessions to attract new settlers; and a heavy reliance on slave labor to produce foodstuffs and raw materials for export.

These Catalan colonial efforts were mainly carried out by private individuals or companies operating under royal charters; they were not actively sponsored by the state. They therefore contrast strongly with the established colonial practices of the Venetian maritime empire, whose strategic ventures were focused mainly on the eastern Mediterranean, where the Venetians dominated the trade in spices and silks. Venetian colonies were administered directly by the city's rulers or their appointed colonial governors. These colonies included long-settled civilizations like Greece, Cyprus, and the cities of the Dalmatian coast, meaning that Venetian administration laid just another layer on top of many other economic, cultural, and political structures.

The Genoese, to take yet another case, also had extensive interests in the western Mediterranean, where they traded bulk goods such as cloth, hides, grain, and timber. They, too, established trading colonies, but these tended to consist of family networks that were closely integrated with the peoples among whom they lived, whether in North Africa, Spain, or the shores of the Black Sea.

From the Mediterranean to the Atlantic

For centuries, European maritime commerce had been divided between this Mediterranean world and a very different northeastern Atlantic world, which encompassed northern France, the Low Countries, the British Isles, and Scandinavia. Starting around 1270, however, Italian merchants began to sail through the Straits of Gibraltar and up to the wool-producing regions of England and the Low Countries. This was a step toward the extension of Mediterranean patterns of commerce and colonization into the Atlantic Ocean. Another step was the discovery (or possibly the rediscovery) of the Atlantic island chains known as the Canaries and the Azores, which Genoese sailors reached in the fourteenth century.

Efforts to colonize the Canary Islands, and to convert and enslave their inhabitants, began almost immediately. Eventually, the Canaries would become the focus of a new wave of colonial settlement sponsored by the Portuguese, and the base for Portuguese voyages down the west coast of Africa. They would be the point from which Christopher Columbus would sail westward across the Atlantic Ocean in the hope of reaching Asia (see Chapter 12).

There was also a significant European colonial presence in the northern Atlantic, as there had been for centuries. Viking settlers had begun to colonize Greenland in the late tenth century, and around 1000 they had established a settlement in a place they called Vinland: the coast of Newfoundland in present-day Canada. According to the sagas that tell the story of these explorations, written down in the late twelfth and thirteenth centuries, a band of adventurers led by Leif Eiriksson had intended to set up a permanent colony there. Numerous expeditions resulted in the construction of houses, a fortification, and even attempts to domesticate livestock transported from Scandinavia. Yet North America did not become home to a permanent European population at this time; the sagas report that relations with indigenous peoples were fraught, and there may have been other factors hindering settlement, such as malnutrition, disease, and the challenges of transatlantic travel.

However, Norse settlers did build a viable community on Greenland, which eventually formed part of the kingdom of Norway. This was facilitated by the warming of the earth's climate between 800 and 1300—the same

THE CHURCH AT HVALSEY, GREENLAND. Located on the southern tip of Greenland, Hvalsey was originally a farmstead established in the late tenth century by the uncle of Eirik the Red, father of the explorer Leif. The church at Hvalsey, pictured here, was built in the twelfth century and would have been roofed with turf. It was the site of the last documented event in the history of Norse settlement on the island, a wedding that took place in 1408. By that time, the population had largely died out due to starvation and disease.

phenomenon that partly enabled the agricultural revolution discussed in Chapter 8. For several centuries, these favorable climatic conditions made it possible to sustain some farming activities on the southern coastline of that huge island, supplemented by fishing, hunting, and foraging. But with the gradual cooling of the climate in the fourteenth century, which caused famines even in the rich farmlands of Europe, this fragile ecosystem was gradually eroded and the Greenlanders died out.

WAYS OF KNOWING AND DESCRIBING THE WORLD

The success of European commercial and colonial expansion in this era both drove and depended on significant innovations in measuring and mapping. It also coincided with intellectual, literary, and artistic initiatives that aimed to capture and describe the workings of this wider world.

Economic Tools: Balance Sheets, Banks, Charts, and Clocks

The economic boom that resulted from the integration of European and Asian commerce called for the refinement of existing business models and accounting techniques. New forms of partnership and the development of insurance contracts helped to minimize the risks associated with long-distance trading. Double-entry bookkeeping, widely used in Italy by the mid-fourteenth century, gave merchants a much clearer picture of their profits and losses by ensuring that both credits and debits were clearly laid out in parallel columns, a practice that facilitated the balancing of accounts. The Medici family of Florence established branches of their bank in each of the major cities of Europe and were careful that the failure of one would not bankrupt the entire firm. Banks also experimented with advanced credit techniques borrowed from Muslim and Jewish financiers, allowing their clients to transfer funds without any real money changing hands. Such transfers were carried out by written receipts: the direct ancestors of the check, the money order, and the currency transfer.

Other late medieval technologies kept pace in different ways with the demands for increased efficiency and accuracy. Eyeglasses, first invented in the 1280s, were perfected in the fourteenth century, extending the careers of those who made a living by reading, writing, and accounting. The use of the magnetic compass helped ships sail farther away from land, making longer-distance Atlantic voyages possible for the first time. And as more and more mariners began to sail waters less familiar to them, pilots began to make and use special charts that mapped the locations of ports. Called *portolani*, these charts also took note of prevailing winds, potential routes, good harbors, and known perils.

PORTOLAN CHART. Accurate mapping was essential to the success of maritime colonial ventures in the thirteenth and fourteenth centuries. The chart shown here is the oldest surviving example of a map used by mariners to navigate between Mediterranean ports. (The word *portolan* is used to describe such charts.) It dates from the end of the thirteenth century, and its shape clearly indicates that it was made from an animal hide. Although parchment was extremely durable, it would have slowly worn away owing to prolonged exposure to salt water and other elements—hence the rarity of this early example.

The Pursuit of Holiness

The fundamental theme of preachers in this era, that salvation was open to any Christian who strove for it, helps to explain the central place of the Mass and other sacraments in daily life. It also led many to seek out new paths that could lead to God. As we noted in Chapter 9, some believers who sought to achieve a mystical union with God were ultimately condemned for heresy because they would not subordinate themselves to the authority of the Church. But even less radical figures might find themselves treading on dangerous ground. For example, the German preacher Meister ("Master") Eckhart (c. 1260–1327), a Dominican friar, taught that there is a "spark" deep within every human soul and that God lives in this spark. Through prayer and self-renunciation, any person could therefore retreat into the inner recesses of her being and access divinity. This conveyed the message that a layperson might attain salvation through her own efforts, without the intervention of a priest. As a result, many of Eckhart's teachings were condemned. But views like these would find support in the teachings of popular preachers after the Black Death (see Chapter 11).

STRUGGLES FOR SOVEREIGNTY

When the French king Philip IV transplanted the papal court from Rome to Avignon, he was not just responding to previous popes' abuse of power: he was bolstering his own. By the middle of the thirteenth century, the growth of strong territorial monarchies had given some secular rulers a higher degree of power than any European ruler had wielded since the time of Charlemagne (see Chapter 7). Meanwhile, monarchs' willingness to support the Church's crusading efforts not only yielded distinct economic and political advantages, it also allowed them to assert their commitment to the moral and spiritual improvement of their realms. A king's authority in his own realm rested on the acquiescence of the aristocracy and on popular perceptions of his reputation for justice, piety, and regard for his subjects' prosperity. On the wider stage of the medieval world, it also rested on his successful assertion of his kingdom's sovereignty.

The Problem of Sovereignty

Sovereignty can be defined as inviolable authority over a defined territory. In Chapter 9, we noted that Philip

Augustus was the first monarch to call himself "king of France" and not "king of the French." In other words, he was defining his kingship in geographical terms, claiming that there was an entity called France and that he was king within that area.

But what was "France"? Was it the tiny "island" (Île-de-France) around Paris, which had been his father's domain? If so, then France was very small—and very vulnerable, which would make it hard to maintain any claim to sovereignty. Or did it comprise, rather, any region whose lord was willing to do homage to the French king, like Champagne or Normandy? In that case, the king would need to enforce these rights of lordship constantly and, if necessary, exert his rule directly. But what if some of France's neighboring lords ruled in their own right, as did the independent counts of Flanders, thus threatening the security of France's borders? In that case, the king would either need to forge an alliance with these borderlands or negate their independence. He would need to assert his sovereignty by absorbing these regions into an ever-growing kingdom.

The problem of sovereignty, then, is a zero-sum game: one state's sovereignty is won and maintained by diminishing that of other states. France and every other modern European state was being cobbled together in the medieval period through a process of annexation and colonization—just as the United States was assembled at the expense of the empires that had colonized North America and through the killing or displacement of autonomous native peoples.

The process of achieving sovereignty is thus an aggressive and often violent one. In Spain, the "Reconquest" of Muslim lands, which had accelerated in the twelfth century, continued apace in the thirteenth and fourteenth, much to the detriment of these regions' Muslim and Jewish inhabitants. German princes continued to push northward into the Baltic region and into Slavic lands, where native peoples' resistance to colonizing efforts was met with brutal force. Meanwhile, the Scandinavian kingdoms that had been forming in the eleventh and twelfth centuries were warring among themselves and their neighbors for the control of contested regions and resources. Italy and the Mediterranean also became a constant battleground, as we have observed. Among all emerging states, the two most strident in their assertion of sovereignty were France and England.

The Prestige of France: The Saintly Kingship of Louis IX

After the death of Philip Augustus in 1223, the heirs to the French throne continued to pursue an expansionist policy,

Rebirth and Unrest, 1350–1453

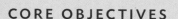

CORE OBJECTIVES

- **TRACE** the economic and social effects of the Black Death, and **EXPLAIN** their importance.

- **EXPLAIN** the relationship between the concepts of the Middle Ages and the Renaissance.

- **DESCRIBE** the intellectual, cultural, and technological innovations of this era.

- **DEFINE** the concept of national monarchy and **SUMMARIZE** its implications.

- **UNDERSTAND** the significance of the conciliar movement and its defeat by the papacy.

n June 1381, thousands of English workers rose in rebellion against royal authorities. Most were peasants or craftsmen who were dismissed as ignorant by contemporary chroniclers, and yet their revolt was carefully coordinated. Plans were spread in coded messages circulated by word of mouth and by the followers of a renegade Oxford professor, John Wycliffe, who had called for the redistribution of Church property and taught that common people should be able to read the Bible in their own language. The rebellion's immediate catalyst had been a series of exorbitant taxes, but its fundamental cause was a pandemic that had occurred thirty years earlier. The Black Death had reduced the entire population of Europe by 30 to 50 percent and had drastically altered the world of those who survived it. In this new world, workers were valuable and could stand up to those who paid them poorly or treated them like slaves. Although the leaders of this rebellion were eventually captured and executed, it made the strength of the common people known.

The fourteenth century is often seen as a time of crisis. Famine and plague decimated the population and war was a brutally recurrent fact of life. But this was also a time of extraordinary opportunity. The exhausted land of Europe recovered from centuries of overfarming, while workers gained the economic edge; some even gained social and political power. Meanwhile, popular and intellectual movements sought to reform the Church. A host of intellectual, artistic, and scientific innovations contributed to all of these phenomena.

This time of rebirth and unrest has been called by two different names: the later Middle Ages and the Renaissance. But these are not two separate historical periods; rather they reflect two different ways of looking back at an era considered to be the precursor of modernity. To understand it, we need to study it holistically.

LIFE AFTER THE BLACK DEATH

By 1353, when plague began to loosen its death grip on Europe, the Continent had lost nearly half of its population within a half century, owing to a combination of famine and disease (Chapter 10). In the century to come, recurring outbreaks of the plague and frequent warfare in some regions would result in further losses. In Germany, some 400,000 villages disappeared. Around Paris, more than half of the farmland formerly under cultivation became pasture. Elsewhere, abandoned fields returned to woodland, increasing the forested areas of Europe by about a third.

Life after the Black Death would therefore be radically different for those who survived it, because this massive depopulation affected every aspect of existence. First and foremost, it meant a relative abundance of food. The price of grain fell, which made it more affordable. At the same time, the scarcity of workers made peasant labor more valuable, and wages rose accordingly. Ordinary people could now afford more bread and could also spend their surplus cash on dairy products, meat, fish, fruits, and wine. As a result, the people of Europe were better nourished than they had ever been—better than many are today. A recent study of fifteenth-century rubbish dumps has concluded that the people of Glasgow (Scotland) ate a healthier diet in 1405 than they did in 2005.

The Rural Impact

In the countryside, a healthier ecological balance was reestablished in the wake of the plague. Forests that

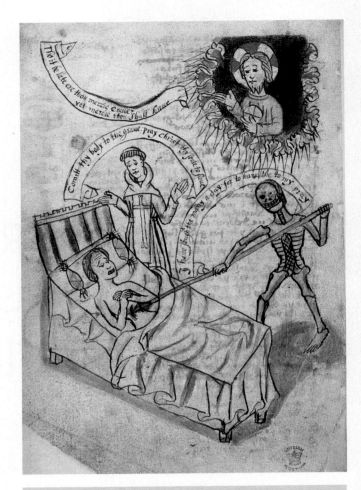

THE PLAGUE CLAIMS A VICTIM. A priest gives last rites to a bedridden plague victim as a smiling devil pierces the dying man with a spear and as Christ looks mercifully down from heaven. ■ *What are the possible meanings of this image?* ■ *What does it reveal about contemporary attitudes toward death by plague?*

had almost disappeared began to recover and expand. Meanwhile, the declining demand for grain allowed many farmers to expand their livestock herds, which also improved the fertility of the soil through manuring. Some farmers were even able to enlarge their holdings, because so much land had been abandoned.

Many of these innovations were made by small farmers, because many great lords—individuals as well as monasteries—were slower to adjust. But some large landholders responded to the shortage of workers by forcing their tenants to perform unpaid labor. In parts of eastern Europe, many free peasants became serfs for the first time: in Poland and Germany, and also in Castile, lords succeeded in imposing new forms of servitude.

In France and the Low Countries, by contrast, peasants experienced new freedoms. In England, where bondage had been common in some regions, serfdom eventually disappeared altogether. Although the Peasants' Revolt of 1381 was ultimately unsuccessful, increased economic opportunity allowed English workers to move to town or to the lands of a lord who offered more favorable terms, despite repeated attempts by Parliament to prevent this, as in the Statute of Labourers enacted in 1351. Geographical mobility and social mobility are, as we have often noted, intertwined.

The Urban Impact

Mortality rates were high in some of the crowded cities and towns of Europe, but not all cities were equally affected and many recovered quickly. In London and Paris, for example, immigration from the countryside reversed the short-term declines caused by the plague. Other urban areas suffered more from internal violence or warfare than from disease. In Florence, for example, the population rebounded quickly after the Black Death but was eventually depleted by civil unrest: by 1427, it had dropped from around 300,000 to about 100,000. In Toulouse (southwestern France), the population remained fairly stable until 1430, when it was reduced by a staggering 75 percent as a result of the ravages of the Hundred Years' War.

So while the overall population of Europe declined drastically because of the plague, a far larger percentage of all people were living in towns by 1500: approximately 20 percent as opposed to 10 or 15 percent prior to the Black Death. Fueling this urban growth was the increasing specialization of the late-medieval economy. With farmers under less pressure to produce grain in bulk, land could be devoted to livestock, dairy farming, and the production of a more diverse array of fruits and vegetables; and these could now be exchanged more efficiently on the open market.

Towns with links to extant trading networks benefited accordingly. In northern Germany, a group of entrepreneurial cities formed a coalition to build an entirely new mercantile corporation, the Hanseatic League, which came to control commerce from Britain and Scandinavia to the Baltic. In northern Italy, the increased demand for luxury goods—which even some peasants and urban laborers could now afford—brought renewed wealth to the spice- and silk-trading city of Venice and also to the fine-cloth manufacturers of Milan

and the jewelers of Florence. Milan's armaments industry also prospered, supplying its warring neighbors and the armies of Europe.

Popular Revolts and Rebellions

Although the consequences of the Black Death were ultimately beneficial for many, survivors did not adjust easily to this new world. Established elites resisted the demands of newly powerful workers; and when these demands were not met, violence erupted. Between 1350 and 1425, hundreds of popular rebellions challenged the status quo in many regions. In 1358, peasants in northeastern France rose up, destroying property, burning buildings and crops, and even murdering targeted individuals. This incident is known as the Jacquerie Rebellion, because all French peasants were caricatured by the aristocracy as "Jacques" ("Jack").

In England, as we have already noted, a very different uprising occurred in June of 1381, far more organized and involving a much wider segment of society. Thousands of people marched on London, targeting the bureaucracies of the government and the Church, capturing and killing the archbishop of Canterbury, and meeting personally with the fourteen-year-old king, Richard II, to demand an end to serfdom and to call for the redistribution of property. In Florence, cloth-industry workers—known as the Ciompi (chee-OHM-pee)—protested high unemployment and mistreatment by the manufacturers who also ran the Florentine government. They seized control of the city and maintained power for a remarkable six weeks before their reforms were revoked.

The local circumstances behind each of these revolts were unique, but all of them exhibit certain common features. Those who took part were empowered by new economic conditions and wanted to enact even larger reforms. Some revolts were touched off by resistance to new and higher taxes. Others took place at moments when governments were weakened by factionalism and military defeat. The English revolt was also fueled by the widespread perception of corruption within the Church.

Behind this social and political unrest, therefore, lies the growing prosperity and self-confidence of village communities and urban laborers who were taking advantage of the changed circumstances that arose from the plague. This tradition of popular rebellion would remain an important feature of Western civilizations. It would eventually fuel the American War of Independence and the French Revolution (see Chapter 18), and it continues to this day.

Aristocratic Life in the Wake of the Plague

Although the elites of Europe did not adapt easily to "the world turned upside down" by the plague, many great families became far wealthier and more dominant than their ancestors had ever been. However, their situations did become more complex and uncertain.

Across Europe, noble families continued to derive much of their revenue from vast land holdings. Many also tried to increase their sources of income through investment in trading ventures. In Catalonia, Italy, Germany, and England, this became common practice. In France and Castile, however, direct involvement in commerce was regarded as socially demeaning. Commerce could still be a route to ennoblement in these kingdoms; but once aristocratic rank was achieved, one was expected to abandon these employments and adopt an appropriate way of life: acquiring a rural castle or urban palace surrounded by a lavish household, embracing the values and conventions of chivalry (engaging in the hunt, commissioning a family coat of arms), and serving the ruler at court and in war.

What it meant to be "noble" became, as a result, even more difficult to define than it had been during previous centuries. In countries where noble rank entailed clearly defined legal privileges—such as the right to be tried only in special courts—proven descent from noble ancestors might be sufficient. Legal nobility of this sort was, however, a somewhat less exclusive distinction than one might expect. In fifteenth-century Castile and Navarre,

A HUNTING PARTY. This fifteenth-century illustration shows an elaborately dressed group of noblemen and noblewomen setting out with falcons, accompanied by their servants and their dogs. Hunting, an activity restricted to the aristocracy, was an occasion for conspicuous consumption and display.

10 to 15 percent of the total population had claims to be recognized as noble on these terms. In Poland, Hungary, and Scotland, the legally privileged nobility was closer to 5 percent.

Fundamentally, however, nobility was expressed by lifestyle and conspicuous consumption. This means that, in practice, the distinctions between noble and wealthy non-noble families were very hard to discern. Even on the battlefield, where the mark of nobility was to fight on horseback, the supremacy of mounted knights was being threatened by the growing importance of professional soldiers, archers, crossbowmen, and artillery experts. There were even hints of a radical critique of the aristocracy's claims to superiority. As the English rebels put it in 1381, "When Adam dug and Eve spun / Who then was a gentleman?"

Precisely because nobility was contested, those who claimed it took elaborate measures to assert their right to this status. This accounts, in part, for the extraordinary number, variety, and richness of the artifacts and artworks that survive from this period. Aristocrats—or those who wanted to be viewed as such—vied with one another in hosting lavish banquets, which required numerous costly utensils, special dining chambers, and the most exotic foods attainable. They dressed in rich and extravagant clothing: close-fitting doublets and hose with long pointed shoes for men, multilayered silk dresses with ornately festooned headdresses for women. They maintained enormous households: in France, around 1400, the Duke of Berry had 1,000 servants and 400 matched pairs of hunting dogs. They took part in elaborately ritualized tournaments, in which the participants pretended to be the heroes of chivalric romances. Noble status had to be constantly reasserted and displayed.

Rulers contributed to this process. Kings and princes across Europe competed in founding chivalric orders such as the Knights of the Garter in England and the Order of the Star in France. These orders honored men who had demonstrated the idealized virtues of knighthood. By exalting the nobility as a class, chivalric orders helped cement the links that bound the nobility to their kings and princes. These bonds were further strengthened by the gifts, pensions, offices, and marriage prospects that kings and princes could bestow.

Given the decline in the agricultural revenues of many noble estates, such rewards of princely service were critically important to maintaining noble fortunes. Indeed, the alliance that was forged in the fifteenth century between kings and their noble supporters would become one of the most characteristic features of Europe's ruling class. In France, this "Old Regime" (*ancien régime*) alliance lasted

A NOBLE BANQUET. Uncle of the mad king Charles VI of France, the Duke of Berry left politics to his brothers, the Duke of Burgundy and the Duke of Anjou. In return, he received enormous subsidies from the royal government, which he spent on sumptuous buildings, festivals, and artworks, including the famous Book of Hours (prayer book, c. 1410), which includes this image. Here, the duke (seated at right, in blue) gives a New Year's Day banquet for his household, who exchange gifts while his hunting dogs dine on scraps from the table. In the background, knights confront one another in a tournament.

until the French Revolution of 1789. In Germany, Austria, central Europe, and Russia, it would last until the outbreak of World War I.

Capturing Reality in Writing

The writings of literary artists who survived the Black Death, or who grew up in the decades immediately following it, are characterized by intense observations of the world and their appeal to a far larger and more diverse audience than that of their predecessors. We have noted that vernacular languages were becoming powerful vehicles for poetry and narrative in the twelfth century (see Chapter 9). Now they were being used to critique changing social mores and regimes. Behind this phenomenon lie three interrelated developments: the growing identification between vernacular language and the community of a realm, the still-increasing accessibility of education, and the rise of

a substantial reading public. We can see these influences at work in three of the major authors who flourished during this period: Giovanni Boccaccio, Geoffrey Chaucer, and Christine de Pisan.

Boccaccio (*boh-KAHT-chee-oh*, 1313–1375) is best known for *The Decameron*, a collection of prose tales about sex, adventure, and trickery. He presents these stories as being told over a period of ten days (hence the title, which means "work of ten days") by a sophisticated group of young women and men who have fled to a country villa outside Florence in order to escape the Black Death. Boccaccio borrowed the outlines of these tales from many earlier sources, especially the fabliaux discussed in Chapter 9, but he couched them in colloquial Italian. Whereas Dante had used the same Florentine dialect to evoke the awesome landscape of sacred history in his *Divine Comedy* (Chapter 10), Boccaccio used it to capture the foibles of human beings in plainspoken prose.

The English poet Geoffrey Chaucer (c. 1340–1400) was highly influenced by Boccaccio. Chaucer was among the first generation of English authors whose compositions can be understood by modern readers of that language with relatively little effort. By the late fourteenth century, the Anglo-Saxon (Old English) tongue of England's preconquest inhabitants had mixed with the French dialect spoken by their Norman conquerors, to create the language which is the ancestor of our own: Middle English.

Chaucer's masterpiece is *The Canterbury Tales*. Like *The Decameron*, this is a collection of stories held together by a framing narrative. In this case, the stories are told by travelers on a pilgrimage from London to the shrine of Thomas Becket at Canterbury. But there are also significant differences between *The Decameron* and *The Canterbury Tales*. Chaucer's stories are in verse, for the most part, and they are recounted by people of all different classes—from a high-minded knight to a poor university student to a lusty widow. Each character tells a story that is particularly illustrative of his or her own outlook on the world, forming a kaleidoscopic human comedy.

The generation or so after the Black Death also saw the emergence of authors who made their livings through the patronage of the aristocracy and the publication of their works. One of the first of these literary professionals was Christine de Pisan (c. 1365–c. 1434). Although born in northern Italy, Christine spent her adult life in France, where her husband was a member of the king's household. When he died, the widowed Christine wrote to support herself and her children. She mastered a wide variety of literary genres, including treatises on chivalry and warfare, which she dedicated to King Charles VI of

CHRISTINE DE PISAN. One of the most prolific authors of the Middle Ages, Pisan used her influence to uphold the dignity of women and to celebrate their history and achievements. Here she is seen describing the prowess of an Amazon warrior who could defeat men effortlessly in armed combat.

France. She also wrote for a more popular audience. For example, her imaginative *Book of the City of Ladies* is an extended defense of the capacities and history of women, designed to help female readers refute their male detractors. Christine also took part in a vigorous pamphlet campaign that condemned the misogynistic claims made by influential male authors like Boccaccio. This debate became so famous that it was given a name: the *querelle des femmes*, "the debate over women." Remarkably, Christine also wrote a song in praise of Joan of Arc. Sadly, she probably lived long enough to learn that this other extraordinary woman had been put to death for behaving in a way that was considered dangerously unwomanly (as will be discussed later).

Visualizing Reality

Just as the desire to capture real experiences and emotions was a dominant trait of the literature produced after the Black Death, so it was in the visual arts. This is evident both in the older arts of manuscript illumination and in the new kinds of sculpture we discussed in Chapter 10. A further innovation in the early fifteenth century was the technique of painting in oils, a medium pioneered in Flanders, where artists found a ready market for their works among the nobility and wealthy merchants.

Oil paints were a revolutionary artistic development: because they do not dry as quickly as water-based pigments, a painter can work more slowly and carefully, taking time with difficult aspects of the work and making corrections as needed. Masterful practitioners of this technique include Rogier van der Weyden (c. 1400–1464), who excelled at communicating spiritual messages through the details of everyday life (see **Interpreting Visual Evidence** on page 293). Just as contemporary saints saw divinity in all things, so too an artist could portray the Virgin and Child against a background of ordinary life: people going about their business or a man urinating against a wall. This conveyed the profound message that sacred events are constantly present, here and now: Christ is our companion, such artworks suggest, not some distant figure irrelevant to us.

The same immediacy is also evident in medieval drama. Plays were often devotional exercises that involved the efforts of an entire community, but they also celebrated that community. In the English city of York, for example, an annual series of pageants reenacted the entire history of human salvation from the Creation to the Last Judgment in a single summer day, beginning at dawn and ending late at night. Each pageant was produced by a particular craft guild and showcased that guild's special talents: "The Last Supper" was performed by the bakers, whose bread was used to reenact the first Eucharist, while "The Crucifixion" was performed by the nail makers and painters, whose wares were thereby put on prominent display. In Italy, confraternities competed with one another to honor the saints with songs and processions. In Catalonia and many regions of Spain, elaborate dramas celebrated the life and miracles of the Virgin; one of these is still performed every year in the Basque town of Elche, and is the oldest European play in continuous production. In northern France, the Low Countries, and German-speaking lands, civic spectacles were performed over a period of several days, celebrating both local history and sacred history at once. But not all plays were pious. Some honored visiting kings and princes. Others celebrated the flouting of social conventions, featuring cross-dressing and the reversal of hierarchies. They were further expressions of the topsy-turvy world created by the Black Death.

THE BEGINNINGS OF THE RENAISSANCE IN ITALY

Rummaging through the old books in a cathedral library, an Italian bureaucrat attached to the papal court at Avignon was surprised to find a manuscript of Cicero's letters—letters

Why a Woman Can Write about Warfare

Christine de Pisan (c. 1365–c. 1434) was one of the West's first professional writers, best known today for her Book of the City of Ladies *and* The Treasure of the City of Ladies, *works that aimed to provide women with an honorable and rich history and to combat generations of institutionalized misogyny. But in her own time, Christine was probably best known for the work excerpted here,* The Book of the Deeds of Arms and of Chivalry, *a manual of military strategy and conduct written at the height of the Hundred Years' War, in 1410.*

 s boldness is essential for great undertakings, and without it nothing should be risked, I think it is proper in this present work to set forth my unworthiness to treat such exalted matter. I should not have dared even to think about it, but although boldness is blameworthy when it is foolhardy, I should state that I have not been inspired by arrogance or foolish presumption, but rather by true affection and a genuine desire for the welfare of noble men engaging in the profession of arms. I am encouraged, in the light of my other writings, to undertake to speak in this book of the most honorable office of arms and chivalry. . . . So to this end I have gathered together facts and subject matter from various books to produce this present volume. But inasmuch as it is fitting for this matter to be discussed factually, diligently, and sensibly . . . and also in consideration of the fact that military and lay experts in the aforesaid art of chivalry are not usually clerks or writers who are expert in language,

I intend to treat the matter in the plainest possible language. . . .

As this is unusual for women, who generally are occupied in weaving, spinning, and household duties, I humbly invoke . . . the wise lady Minerva [Athena], born in the land of Greece, whom the ancients esteemed highly for her great wisdom. Likewise the poet Boccaccio praises her in his *Book of Famous Women*, as do other writers praise her art and manner of making trappings of iron and steel, so let it not be held against me if I, as a woman, take it upon myself to treat of military matters. . . .

O Minerva! goddess of arms and of chivalry, who, by understanding beyond that of other women, did find and initiate among the other noble arts and sciences the custom of forging iron and steel armaments and harness both proper and suitable for covering and protecting men's bodies against arrows slung in battle—helmets, shields, and protective covering having come first from you—you instituted and gave directions for drawing up a battle order, how to begin an assault and to engage in

proper combat. . . . In the aforementioned country of Greece, you provided the usage of this office, and insofar as it may please you to be favorably disposed, and I in no way appear to be against the nation from which you came, the country beyond the Alps that is now called Apulia and Calabria in Italy, where you were born, let me say that like you I am an Italian woman.

Source: From *The Book of the Deeds of Arms and of Chivalry*, ed. Charity Cannon Willard and trans. Sumner Willard (University Park, PA: 1999), pp. 11–13.

Questions for Analysis

1. Christine very cleverly deflects potential criticism for her "boldness" in writing about warfare. What tactics does she use?

2. The Greco-Roman goddess Athena (Minerva) was the goddess of wisdom, weaving, and warfare. Why does Christine invoke her aid? What parallels does she draw between her own attributes and those of Minerva?

---

that no living person had known to exist. They had probably been copied in the time of Charlemagne, and then forgotten for hundreds of years. How many other works of this great Roman orator had been lost to posterity? Clearly, thought Francesco Petrarca (1304–1374), he was living in an age of

ignorance. A great gulf seemed to open up between his own time and that of the ancients: a middle age that separated him from those well-loved models.

For centuries, Christian intellectuals had regarded "the dark ages" as the time between Adam's expulsion from

PETRARCH'S COPY OF VIRGIL. Petrarch's devotion to the classics of Roman literature prompted him to commission this new frontispiece for his treasured volume of Virgil's poetry. It was painted by the Sienese artist Simone Martini, who (like Petrarch) was attached to the papal court at Avignon. It is an allegorical depiction of Virgil (top right) and his poetic creations: the hero Aeneas (top left, wearing armor) and the farmer and shepherd whose humble labors are celebrated in Virgil's lesser-known works. The figure next to Aeneas is the fourth-century scholar Servius, who wrote a famous commentary on Virgil. He is shown drawing aside a curtain to reveal the poet in a creative trance. The two scrolls proclaim (in Latin) that Italy was the country that nourished famous poets and that Virgil helped it to rival the glories of classical Greece. ▪ *How does this image encapsulate and express Petrarch's devotion to the classical past?*

Petrarch was famous in his own day as an Italian poet, Latin stylist, and a tireless advocate for the resuscitation of the classics. The values that he and his followers began to espouse would give rise to a new intellectual and artistic movement in Italy, a movement strongly critical of the present and admiring of a past that had disappeared with the western Roman Empire and the end of Italy's greatness. We know this movement as "the Renaissance," from the French word for "rebirth" that was applied to it in the eighteenth century and popularized in the nineteenth, when the term "medieval" was also invented. It has since become shorthand for the epoch *following* the Middle Ages—but it was really part of the same era.

Renaissance Classicism

Talking about "the Renaissance," then, is a way of talking about some significant changes in education and artistic outlook that transformed the culture of northern Italy from the late fourteenth to the early sixteenth centuries and that eventually influenced the rest of Europe in important ways. The term has often been taken literally, as though the cultural accomplishments of antiquity had ceased to be appreciated and needed to be "reborn." Yet we have been tracing the enduring influence of classical civilization for many chapters, and we have constantly noted the reverence accorded to the heritage of antiquity, not to mention the persistence of Roman law and Roman institutions.

That said, one can certainly find traits that make the concept of "renaissance" newly meaningful in this era. For example, there was a significant quantitative difference between the ancient texts available to scholars in the first thousand years after Rome's fragmentation and those that became accessible in the fourteenth and fifteenth centuries. The discovery of "new" works by Livy, Tacitus, and Lucretius expanded the canon considerably, supplementing the well-studied works of Virgil, Ovid, and Cicero.

More important was the expanded access to ancient Greek literature in western Europe. In the twelfth and thirteenth centuries, as we have seen in Chapters 8 and 9, Greek scientific and philosophical works became available to western Europeans thanks to increased contact with Islam, via Latin translations of Arabic translations of the original Greek. Yet no Greek poems or plays were yet available in Latin translations, and neither were the major dialogues of Plato. Moreover, only a handful of western Europeans could read the language of classical Greece. But as the Mongols and, after them, the Ottoman Turks put increasing pressure on the shrinking borders of Byzantium

Eden and the birth of Christ. But now, Petrarch (the name by which English-speakers know him) redefined that concept. According to him, this age was not the pagan past but the time that separated him from direct communion with the classics. Yet this did not stop him from trying to bridge the gap. "I would have written to you long ago," he said in a Latin letter to the Greek poet Homer (dead for over 2,000 years), "had it not been for the fact that we lack a common language."

Interpreting Visual Evidence

Realizing Devotion

These two paintings by the Flemish artist Rogier van der Weyden (*FAN-der-VIE-den*, c. 1400–1464) capture some of the most compelling characteristics of late medieval art, particularly the trend toward realistic representations of holy figures and sacred stories. On the left (image A), the artist depicts himself as the evangelist Luke, regarded in Christian tradition as a painter of portraits; he sketches the Virgin nursing the infant Jesus in a town house overlooking a Flemish city. On the right (image B), van der Weyden imagines the entombment of the dead Christ by his followers, including the Virgin (left), Mary Magdalene (kneeling), and the disciple John (right). Here, he makes use of a motif that became increasingly prominent in the later Middle Ages: Christ as the Man of Sorrows, displaying his wounds and inviting the viewer to share in his suffering. In both paintings, van der Weyden emphasizes the humanity of his subjects rather than their iconic status (see Chapter 7), and he places them in the urban and rural landscapes of his own world.

Questions for Analysis

1. How are these paintings different from the sacred images of the earlier Middle Ages (see, for example, page 169)? What messages does the artist convey by setting these events in his own immediate present?

2. In what ways do these paintings reflect broad changes in popular piety and medieval devotional practices? Why, for example, would the artist display the dead and wounded body of Christ—rather than depicting him as resurrected and triumphant, or as an all-seeing creator and judge?

3. In general, how would you use these images as evidence of the worldview of the fifteenth century? What do they tell us about people's attitudes, emotions, and values?

A. Saint Luke drawing the portrait of the Virgin.

B. The Deposition.

(to be discussed later), more and more Greek-speaking intellectuals fled to Italy, bringing their books and their knowledge with them.

Thanks to these developments, some Italian intellectuals had access to more classical texts and they also used these texts in new ways. For centuries, Christian scholars had worked to bring ancient writings and values into line with their own beliefs (Chapter 6). By contrast, the new reading methods pioneered by Petrarch and others fostered an awareness of the conceptual gap that separated the contemporary world from that of antiquity. This awakened a determination to recapture ancient worldviews and value systems. In the second half of the fifteenth century, classical models would also contribute to the strikingly distinctive artistic style that is most strongly associated with the Renaissance (something we will address in Chapter 12).

Another distinguishing feature of this new perspective on the classical past was the way that it became overtly materialistic and commercialized. The competition among and within Italian city-states fostered a culture that used the symbols and artifacts of ancient Rome as pawns in an endless power game. Meanwhile, the relative weakness of the Church contributed to the growth of claims to power based on classical models—even by Italian bishops and Church-sponsored universities. When the papacy was eventually restored to Rome, it too had to compete in this Renaissance arena by patronizing the artists and intellectuals who espoused these aesthetic and political ideals.

Renaissance Humanism

The most basic feature of this new intellectual and political agenda is summarized in the term *humanism*. This was a program of study that aimed to replace the scholastic emphasis on logic and theology—central to the curriculum of universities like Paris and Oxford—with the study of ancient literature, rhetoric, history, and ethics. The goal of a humanist education was the understanding of human experience through the lenses of the classical past, in the service of man's individual potential in the present. By contrast, a scholastic education filtered human experience through the teachings of scripture and the Church fathers, with the salvation of humankind as the ultimate goal.

Some intellectuals also believed that the university curriculum concentrated too much on abstract speculation rather than the achievement of virtue and ethical conduct. Petrarch felt that the true Christian thinker must cultivate literary eloquence and so inspire others to do good through the pursuit of beauty and truth. According

to him, the best models of eloquence were to be found in the classics of Latin literature, which were also filled with ethical wisdom. Petrarch dedicated himself, therefore, to rediscovering such texts and to writing his own poems and moral treatises in a Latin style modeled on that of classical authors.

Humanists therefore preferred ancient writings to those of more recent authors, including their own contemporaries. And although some early humanists wrote in Italian dialects as well as Latin, most regarded vernacular literature as a lesser diversion for the uneducated; serious scholarship and poetry could be written only in Latin (or Greek). Proper Latin, moreover, had to be the classical Latin of Cicero and Virgil, not the evolving language of their own day, which they derided as a barbarous departure from "correct" standards of Latin style.

But ironically, their determination to revive this older language eventually helped to kill the lively Latin that had continued to flourish in Europe. By insisting on outmoded standards of grammar, syntax, and vocabulary, they turned Latin into a fossilized discourse that ceased to have any relevance to real life. They thus contributed, unwittingly, to the ultimate triumph of the various European vernaculars they despised.

Because humanism was an educational program designed to produce able public men, it largely excluded women because women were largely excluded from Italian political life. Here again is a paradox: as more and more Italian city-states fell into the hands of autocratic rulers, the humanist educational curriculum lost its immediate connection to the republican ideals of ancient Rome. Nevertheless, humanists never lost their conviction that the study of the "humanities" (as the humanist curriculum came to be known) was the best way to produce leaders.

Why Italy?

These new attitudes toward education and the antique models were fostered in northern Italy for historically specific reasons. After the Black Death, this region was the most densely populated part of Europe; other urban areas, notably northeastern France and Flanders, had been decimated by the Great Famine as well as the plague. Northern Italy also differed from the rest of urbanized Europe because aristocratic families customarily lived in cities and consequently became more fully involved in public affairs than their counterparts north of the Alps. Moreover, many town-dwelling aristocrats were engaged in banking or mercantile enterprises, while many rich mercantile families imitated the manners of the aristocracy. The Florentine ruling family, the Medici, originally made their fortune in banking and commerce.

These factors help to explain the emergence of the humanist ideals described above. Newly wealthy families were not content to have their sons learn only the skills necessary to becoming successful businessmen; they sought teachers who would impart the knowledge and finesse that would enable them to cut a figure in society, mix with their noble neighbors, and speak with authority on public affairs. Consequently, Italy produced and attracted a large number of independent intellectuals who were not affiliated with monasteries, cathedral schools, or universities—many of whom served as schoolmasters for wealthy young men while acting as cultural consultants and secretaries for their families. These intellectuals advertised their learning by producing political and ethical treatises and works of literature that would attract the attention of patrons or reflect well on the patrons they already had. As a result, Italian schools and private tutors turned out the best-educated laymen in all of Europe, men who also constituted a new generation of wealthy, knowledgeable patrons ready to invest in the cultivation of new ideas and new forms of artistic expression.

A second reason why late-medieval Italy was the birthplace of the Renaissance movement has to do with its vexed political situation. Unlike France and England, or the kingdoms of Spain, Scandinavia, and central Europe, Italy had no unifying political institutions. Italians therefore looked to the classical past for their time of glory, dreaming of a day when Rome would be, again, the center of the world. They boasted that ancient Roman monuments were omnipresent in their landscape and that classical Latin literature referred to cities and sites they recognized as their own.

Italians were also intent on reappropriating their classical heritage because they were seeking to establish an independent cultural identity that could counter the intellectual and political supremacy of France. The removal of the papacy to Avignon (Chapter 10) had heightened antagonism between the city-states of Italy and the burgeoning kingdom beyond the Alps. This also explains the Italians' rejection of the scholasticism taught in northern Europe's universities and their embrace of models that could create an artistic alternative to the dominant French school of Gothic architecture.

Finally, this Italian Renaissance could not have occurred without the underpinning of Italian wealth gained through the commercial ventures described in Chapter 10. This wealth meant that talented men seeking employment and patronage were more likely to stay at home, fueling the artistic and intellectual competition that arose from the intensification of urban pride and the concentration of individual and family wealth in urban areas. Cities themselves became primary patrons of art and learning in this era.

The Renaissance of Civic Ideals

For the intellectuals of Florence, in particular, the goal of classical education was civic enrichment. Humanists such as Leonardo Bruni (c. 1370–1444) and Leon Battista Alberti (1404–1472) valued eloquence and classical literature, but they also taught that man's nature should be cultivated for service to the state—ideally a city-state after the Florentine model. Ambition and the quest for glory are noble impulses, but they ought to be encouraged and channeled toward these ends. They also argued that the history of human progress is inseparable from the human dominion of the earth and its resources.

Many of the humanists' civic ideals are expressed in Alberti's treatise *On the Family* (1443), in which the nuclear family is presented as the fundamental unit of the city-state and, as such, is to be governed in such a way as to further the state's political and economic goals. He therefore consigned women—who, in reality, governed the household—to childbearing, child rearing, and subservience to men even within this domestic realm. He asserted, furthermore, that women should play no role whatsoever in the public sphere. Although such dismissals of women's abilities were fiercely resisted by actual women, the humanism of the Renaissance was characterized by a pervasive denigration of women.

The Emergence of Textual Criticism

The humanists' project was aided by a number of Byzantine scholars who emigrated to Italy in the first half of the fifteenth century and who gave instruction in the ancient form of their own native language. Wealthy, well-connected Florentines also increasingly aspired to acquire Greek literary masterpieces for themselves, which often involved journeys back to Constantinople. In 1423, one adventurous bibliophile managed to bring back 238 manuscript books, among them rare works of Sophocles, Euripides, and Thucydides. These were quickly paraphrased in Latin and made accessible to western Europeans for the first time.

This influx of new classical texts spurred a new interest in textual criticism. A pioneer in this activity was

Lorenzo Valla (1407–1457). Born in Rome and active primarily as a secretary to the king of Naples and Sicily, Valla turned his skills to the painstaking analysis of Greek and Latin writings in order to show how the historical study of language could discredit old assumptions and even unmask some texts as forgeries. For example, some propagandists argued that the papacy's claim to secular power in Europe derived from rights granted to the bishop of Rome by the emperor Constantine in the fourth century, enshrined in a document known as "The Donation of Constantine." By analyzing the language of this spurious text, Valla proved that it could not have been written in the time of Constantine because it contained more recent Latin usages and vocabulary.

This demonstration not only discredited more traditional scholarly methods, it made the concept of anachronism (the detection of historical errors) central to all subsequent textual criticism and historical thought. Indeed, Valla even applied his expert knowledge of Greek to elucidating the meaning of Saint Paul's letters, which he believed had been obscured by Jerome's Latin translation (see Chapter 6). This work was to prove an important link between Italian Renaissance scholarship and the subsequent Christian humanism of the north, which in turn fed into the Reformation (see Chapter 13).

THE END OF THE EASTERN ROMAN EMPIRE

The Greek-speaking refugees who arrived in Italy after the Black Death were self-made exiles. They were responding to the succession of calamities that had reduced the once-proud eastern Roman Empire to a scattering of embattled provinces. As we've noted, when Constantinople fell to western crusaders in 1204, the surrounding territories of Byzantium were severed from the capital that had held them together (see Chapter 9). When the Latin presence in Constantinople was finally expelled in 1261, imperial power had been so weakened that it extended only into the immediate hinterlands of the city and parts of Greece. The rest of the empire had become a collection of small principalities in precarious alliance with the Mongols and dependant on the Pax Mongolica for survival (see Chapter 10). Then, with the coming of the Black Death, the imperial capital suffered the loss of half of its inhabitants and shrank still further. Meanwhile, the disintegration of the Mongol Empire laid the larger region of Anatolia open to a new set of invaders.

The Rise of the Ottoman Turks

Like the Mongols, the Turks were originally a nomadic people. When the Mongols arrived in northwestern Anatolia, the Turks were already established there and were being converted to Islam by the resident Muslim powers of the region: the Seljuq Sultanate of Rûm and the Abbasid Caliphate of Baghdad. But when the Mongols toppled these older powers, they eliminated the two traditional authorities that had kept Turkish border chieftains in check. Now they were free to raid, unhindered, along the soft frontiers of Byzantium. At the same time, the Turks remained far enough from the centers of Mongol authority to avoid being destroyed themselves. One of their chieftains, Osman Gazi (1258–1326), established his own independent kingdom. Eventually, his name was given to the Turkish dynasty that would control the most ancient lands of Western civilizations for six centuries: the Ottomans.

By the mid-fourteenth century, Osman's successors had captured a number of important cities. These successes brought the Ottomans to the attention of the Byzantine emperor, who hired a contingent of them as mercenaries in 1345. They were extraordinarily successful—so much so that the eastern Roman Empire could not control their movements. They then struck out on their own and began to extend their control westward. By 1370, their holdings stretched all the way to the Danube. In 1389, they defeated a powerful coalition of Serbian forces at the battle of Kosovo, which enabled them to begin subduing Bulgaria, the Balkans, and eventually Greece. In 1396, the Ottoman army even attacked Constantinople itself, although it withdrew to repel an ineffectual crusading force that had been hastily sent by the papacy.

In 1402, another attack on Constantinople was deflected—this time, by a more potent foe who had ambitions to match those of the Ottomans. Timur the Lame (Tamerlane, as he was called by European admirers) was born to a family of small landholders in the Mongol Khanate of Chagatai. While still a young man, he rose to prominence as a military leader and gained a reputation for tactical genius. He was no politician, though, and never officially assumed the title of khan in any of the territories he dominated. Instead, he moved ceaselessly from conquest to conquest, becoming the master of lands from the Caspian Sea to the Volga River, as well as most of Persia. For a time, it looked briefly as if the Mongol Empire might be reunited under his reign. But Timur died in 1405, on his way to invade China, and his various conquests fell into the hands of local rulers. Mongol influence continued in the Mughal Empire of India, but in Anatolia the Ottoman Turks were once again on the rise.

The Fall of Constantinople

During the 1420s and 1430s, Ottoman pressure on Constantinople escalated. Monasteries and schools that had been established since the fourth century found themselves in the path of an advancing army, and a steady stream of fleeing scholars strove to salvage a millennium's worth of Byzantine books—many of them preserving the heritage of ancient Greece and the Hellenistic world. Then, in 1451, the Ottoman sultan Mehmet II turned his full attention to the conquest of the imperial city. In 1453, after a brilliantly executed siege, his army succeeded in breaching its walls. The Byzantine emperor was killed in the assault, the city itself was plundered, and its remaining population was sold into slavery. The Ottomans then settled down to rule their new capital in a style reminiscent of their Byzantine predecessors.

The Ottoman conquest of Constantinople was an enormous shock to European Christians. Yet its actual political and economic impact on western and central Europe was minor. Ottoman control may have reduced some Europeans' access to the Black Sea, but Europeans got most of their spices and silks through Venice anyway. Moreover, as we saw in Chapter 10, Europeans already had colonial ambitions and significant trading interests in Africa and the Atlantic that connected them to far-reaching networks.

But the effects of the Ottoman conquest on the Turks themselves were transformative. Vast new wealth poured into Anatolia, which the Ottomans increased by carefully tending to the industrial and commercial interests of their new capital city, which they also called Istanbul—the Turkish pronunciation of the Greek phrase *eis tan polin* "in (to) the city." Trade routes were redirected to feed the capital, and the Ottomans became a naval power in the eastern Mediterranean as well as in the Black Sea. As a result, Constantinople's population grew rapidly, from fewer than 100,000 in 1453 to more than 500,000 by 1600, making it the largest city in the world outside of China.

Slavery and Social Advancement in the Ottoman Empire

Despite the Ottomans' new attention to commerce, their empire continued to rest on the spoils of conquest.

To manage its continual expansion, the size of the Ottoman army and administration grew exponentially, drawing more and more manpower from conquered territories. And because both army and bureaucracy were largely composed of slaves, the demand for more soldiers and administrators could best be met through further conquests, requiring a still larger army and even more extensive bureaucracy—and so the cycle continued. It mirrors, in many respects, the dilemma of the Roman Empire in the centuries of its rapid expansion beyond Italy (see Chapter 5), which also created an insatiable demand for slaves.

Not only were slaves the backbone of Ottoman government, they were critical to the lives of the Turkish upper class. Indeed, one of the important measures of status in Ottoman society was the number of slaves in one's household. After the capture of Constantinople, new wealth would permit some elites to maintain households in the thousands. By the sixteenth century, the sultan alone possessed more than 20,000 slave attendants, not including his bodyguard and elite infantry units, both of which also comprised of slaves.

Where did all of these slaves come from? Many were captured in war. Many others were taken on raiding forays into Poland and Ukraine and sold to Crimean slave merchants, who shipped their captives to the slave markets of Constantinople. But slaves were also recruited (some willingly, some by coercion) from rural areas of the Ottoman Empire itself. Because the vast majority of slaves were household servants and administrators rather than laborers, some men willingly accepted enslavement, believing that they would be better off as slaves in Constantinople than as impoverished peasants in the countryside. In the Balkans especially, many people were enslaved as children, handed over by their families to pay the "child tax" that the Ottomans imposed on rural areas too poor to pay a monetary tribute. Although an excruciating experience for families, this practice did open up opportunities for social advancement. Special academies were created at Constantinople to train the most able of the enslaved male children, some of whom rose to become powerful figures in the Ottoman Empire.

For this reason, slavery carried relatively little social stigma (the sultan himself was most often the son of an enslaved woman). And because Muslims were not permitted to enslave other Muslims, the vast majority of Ottoman slaves were Christian—although many eventually converted to Islam. And because so many of the elite positions within Ottoman government were held by these slaves, the paradoxical result was that Muslims, including the Turks themselves, were effectively excluded from the main avenues of social and political influence in the Ottoman Empire. Avenues to power were therefore remarkably open to men of ability and talent, most of them non-Muslim slaves.

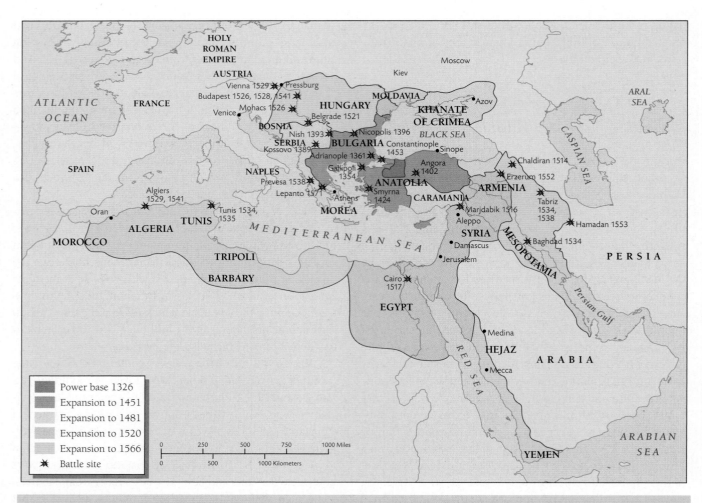

THE GROWTH OF THE OTTOMAN EMPIRE. Consider the patterns of Ottoman expansion revealed in this map. ▪ *Where is Constantinople, and how might the capture of Constantinople in 1453 have facilitated further conquests?* ▪ *Compare the extent of the Ottoman Empire in 1566 with that of the Byzantine Empire under Justinian (see the map on page 166). How would you account for their similarities?*

Nor was this power limited to the government and the army. Commerce and business also remained largely in the hands of non-Muslims, most frequently Greeks, Syrians, and Jews. Jews in particular found in the Ottoman Empire a welcome refuge from the persecutions that had characterized Jewish life in western Europe. After their expulsion from Spain in 1492 (see Chapter 12), more than 100,000 Spanish (Sephardic) Jews ultimately immigrated to the territories of the Ottoman Empire.

Because the Ottoman sultans were Sunni Muslims, they often dealt harshly with other Muslim sects. But they were tolerant of Christians and Jews. They organized the major religious groups of their empire into legally recognized units and permitted them considerable rights of self-government. They even promoted the authority of the Greek Orthodox patriarch of Constantinople. As a result, the Ottomans enjoyed staunch support from

their Orthodox Christian subjects for their wars with the Christians of western Europe.

Russia: "The Third Rome"

The Orthodox Church also received staunch support from the peoples of Rus' whose own Church had been founded by Byzantine missionaries (see Chapter 8) and whose written language was based on the Greek alphabet. Indeed, the emerging duchy of Muscovy (see Chapter 10) saw itself as the natural protector and ally of the eastern Roman Empire. After Constantinople fell to the Turks—predictably, without any help from Latin Christendom—the Russian Church emerged as the strongest proponent of Orthodoxy.

SULTAN MEHMET II, "THE CONQUEROR" (r. 1451–81). This portrait, executed by the Ottoman artist Siblizade Ahmed, exhibits features characteristic of both Central Asia and Europe. The sultan's pose—his aesthetic appreciation of the rose, his elegant handkerchief—are indicative of the former, as is the fact that he wears the white turban of a scholar and the thumb ring of an archer. But the subdued coloring and three-quarter profile may reflect the influence of Italian portraits. ▪ *What did the artist achieve through this blending of styles and symbols?* ▪ *What messages does this portrait convey?*

Muscovy's distrust of western Europe was increased by developments on its western borders. In the thirteenth century, the small kingdom of Poland had struggled to defend itself from absorption by German princes. When the Holy Roman Empire's strength waned after the death of Frederick the Great (see Chapter 9), Poland's situation grew more secure. In 1386, its female King, Jadwiga, strengthened its power when she married Jagiello, the grand duke of neighboring Lithuania. Lithuania had begun to carve out an extensive territory in the Baltic (modern-day Belarus and Ukraine) and this momentum increased after its union with Poland. In 1410, a combined Polish and Lithuanian force defeated the Teutonic Knights at the Battle of Tannenberg, crushing the military order that controlled a crucial region lying between the allied kingdoms. Thereafter, Poland-Lithuania began to push eastward toward Muscovy.

Although many of Lithuania's aristocratic families were Orthodox Christians, the established church in Poland was loyal to Rome, and Duke Jagiello was a pagan convert to Latin Christianity. For the rulers of Muscovy threatened by Poland-Lithuania, it therefore seemed expedient to take up the imperial mantle that had been abandoned when Constantinople fell, and to declare the Muscovite state the successor to Rome. To drive the point home, Muscovite dukes began to take the title of tsar, "caesar." "Two Romes have fallen," said a Muscovite chronicler, "the third is still standing, and a fourth there shall not be."

WARFARE AND NATION-BUILDING IN EUROPE

War has always been an engine for the development of new technologies. This is something we have noted since Chapter 1, but the pace and scale of warfare escalated to an unprecedented degree in the era after the Black Death. Although explosives had been invented in China, and were originally deployed in displays of fireworks, they were first put to devastating and destructive use in Europe. In fact, the earliest cannons were as dangerous to those who fired them as to those they targeted. But by the middle of the fifteenth century, they were reliable enough to revolutionize warfare. In 1453, heavy artillery played a leading role in the outcomes of two crucial conflicts: the Ottoman Turks breached the ancient defenses of Constantinople with cannon fire and the French captured the English-held city of Bordeaux, bringing an end to the Hundred Years' War.

Thereafter, cannons made it more difficult for rebellious aristocrats to hole up in their stone castles and consequently facilitated their subjugation by powerful monarchies. Cannons placed aboard ships made navies more effective. A handheld firearm, the pistol, was also invented in the fourteenth century, and around 1500 the musket ended forever the military dominance of heavily armored cavalry.

Indeed, there is a symbiotic relationship between warfare and politics as well as between warfare and technology. Because Europeans were almost constantly at war from the fourteenth century to the middle of the twentieth, governments claimed new powers to tax their subjects and to control their subjects' lives. Armies became larger, military technology deadlier. Wars became more destructive, society more militarized. As a result of these developments, the most successful European states were aggressively expansionist.

The Hundred Years' War Resumes

The hostilities that make up the Hundred Years' War can be divided into three main phases (see the maps on page 303). The first phase dates from the initial declaration of war in 1337 (Chapter 10), after which the English won a series of startling military victories. The war then resumed in 1356, with another English victory at Poitiers. Four years later, in 1360, Edward III decided to leverage his strong position: he renounced his larger claim to the French throne, and in return he was guaranteed full sovereignty over a greatly enlarged duchy of Gascony and the promise of a huge ransom for the king of France, whom he held captive.

But the terms of this treaty were never honored, nor did it resolve the underlying issues that had led to the war itself: namely, the problem of sovereignty in contested territory and the question of the English king's place in the French royal succession. The French king continued to treat the English king as his vassal, while Edward's heirs renewed their claim to the throne of France.

Although there were no pitched battles for two decades after this, a destabilizing proxy war developed during the 1360s and 1370s. Both the English troops (posted in Gascony) and the French troops (eager to avenge their losses) were organized into "Free Companies" of mercenaries and hired themselves out in the service of hostile factions in Castile and competing city-states in northern Italy. By 1376, when the conflict between England and France was reignited, the Hundred Years' War had become a Europe-wide phenomenon.

England's Disputed Throne and the Brief Victory of Henry V

In this second phase of the war, the tide quickly shifted in favor of France. The new king, Charles V (r. 1364–80), imposed a series of taxes to fund an army and disbanded the Free Companies, hiring the leader of one band as his commander. He thereby created a professional military that could match the English in discipline and tactics. By 1380, English territories in France had been reduced to a core area around the southwestern city of Bordeaux and the port of Calais in the extreme northeast.

Meanwhile, the aging Edward III has been succeeded by his nine-year-old grandson, Richard II (r. 1377–99), who was too young to prosecute a claim to the French crown. This was problematic, because the war had been extremely popular in England. And when Richard came

A FIFTEENTH-CENTURY SIEGE WITH CANNONS. Cannons were an essential element in siege warfare during the Hundred Years' War.

of age and showed no signs of martial ambition, many of his own aristocratic relatives turned against him. Richard retaliated against the ringleader of this faction, his cousin Henry of Lancaster, by sending him into exile and confiscating his property. Henry's supporters used this as pretext for rebellion. In 1399, Richard was deposed by Henry and eventually murdered.

As a usurper whose legitimacy was always in doubt, Henry IV (r. 1399–1413) struggled to maintain his authority. The best way to unite the country would have been to renew the war against France, but Henry was frequently ill and in no position to lead an army into combat. So when his son Henry V succeeded him in 1413, the new king immediately began to prepare for an invasion. His timing was excellent: the French royal government was foundering due to the insanity of the reigning king, Charles VI (r. 1380–1422). A brilliant diplomat as well as a capable soldier, Henry V sealed an alliance with the powerful Duke of Burgundy, who was allegedly loyal to France but stood to gain from its defeat. Henry also made a treaty with the German emperor, who agreed not to come to France's aid.

When he crossed the English Channel in the autumn of 1415, Henry V's troops thus faced a much-depleted French army that could not rely on reinforcements. Although it was still vastly larger and boasted hundreds of mounted knights, it was undisciplined. It was also severely hampered by bad weather and deep mud when the two armies clashed at Agincourt on October 25 of that year—conditions that favored the lighter English infantry. Henry's men managed to win a crushing victory.

Then, over the next five years, Henry conquered most of northern France. In 1420, the ailing Charles VI was forced to recognize him as heir to the throne of France, thereby disinheriting his own son. (This prince bore the ceremonial title of *dauphin*, "the dolphin," from the heraldic device of the borderland province he inherited.) Henry sealed the deal by marrying the French princess, Catherine, and fathering an heir to the joint kingdom of England and France.

Joan of Arc's Betrayal and Legacy

Unlike his great-grandfather Edward III, who has used his claim to the French throne as a bargaining chip to secure sovereignty over Gascony, Henry V honestly believed himself to be the rightful king of France. And his astonishing success in capturing the kingdom seemed to put the stamp of divine approval on that claim. But Henry's successes in France also transformed the nature of the war, turning it from a profitable war of conquest and plunder into an extended and expensive military occupation. It might have been sustainable had Henry been as long-lived as many of his predecessors. But he died early in 1422, just short of his thirty-sixth birthday. King Charles VI died only a few months later.

The new king of England and France, Henry VI (r. 1422–61), was only an infant, and yet the English armies under the command of his regents continued to press southward into territories held by the dauphin. Although it seemed unlikely that English forces would ever succeed in dislodging him, confidence in the French prince's right to the throne had been shattered by his own mother's declaration that he was illegitimate. It might have happened that England would once again rule an empire comprising much of France, as it had for a century and a half after the Norman conquest.

But this scenario fails to reckon with Joan of Arc. In 1429, a peasant girl from Lorraine (a territory only nominally part of France) made her way to the dauphin's court and announced that an angel had told her that he, Charles, was the rightful king, and that she, Joan, should drive the English out of France. The fact that she even got a hearing underscores the hopelessness of the dauphin's position, as does the extraordinary fact that he gave her a contingent of troops. With this force, Joan liberated the strategic city of Orléans, then under siege by the English, after which a series of victories culminated in Charles's coronation in the cathedral of Reims, the traditional site for crowning French kings.

Despite her miraculous success, Joan was an embarrassment whose very charisma made her dangerous. She was a peasant leading aristocrats, a woman leading men, and a commoner who claimed to have been commissioned by God. When, a few months later, the Burgundians captured her in battle and handed her over to the English, the king she had helped to crown did nothing to save her. Accused of witchcraft, condemned by the theologians of Paris, and tried for heresy by an English ecclesiastical court, Joan was burned to death in the market square at Rouen in 1431. She was nineteen years old.

The French forces whom Joan had inspired, however, continued on the offensive. In 1435, the duke of Burgundy withdrew from his alliance with England. When the young English king, Henry VI, proved first incompetent and then insane, a series of French military victories brought hostilities to an end with the capture of Bordeaux in 1453. English kings would threaten to renew the war for another century, and Anglo-French hostility would last until the defeat of Napoleon in 1815. But after 1453, English control over French territory would be limited to the port of Calais (which eventually fell, in 1558).

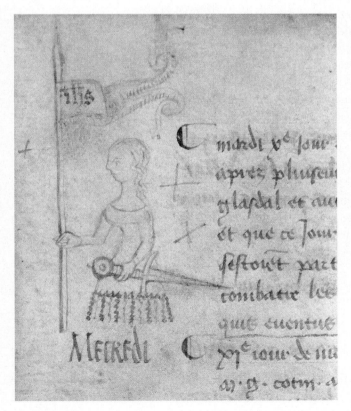

JOAN OF ARC. A contemporary sketch of Joan was drawn in the margin of this register documenting official proceedings at the Parlement of Paris in 1429.

The Long Shadow of the Hundred Years' War

The Hundred Years' War challenged the very existence of France. The disintegration of that kingdom glaringly revealed the fragility of the bonds that tied the king to

The Condemnation of Joan of Arc by the University of Paris, 1431

After Joan's capture by the Burgundians, she was handed over to the English and tried for heresy at an ecclesiastical court set up in Rouen. It was on this occasion that the theology faculty of Paris pronounced the following verdict on her actions.

You, Joan, have said that, since the age of thirteen, you have experienced revelations and the appearance of angels, of St. Catherine and St. Margaret, and that you have very often seen them with your bodily eyes, and that they have spoken to you. As for the first point, the clerks of the University of Paris have considered the manner of the said revelations and appearances. . . . Having considered all . . . they have declared that all the things mentioned above are lies, falsenesses, misleading and pernicious things and that such revelations are superstitions, proceeding from wicked and diabolical spirits.

Item: You have said that your king had a sign by which he knew that you were sent by God, for St. Michael, accompanied by several angels, some of which having wings, the others crowns, with St. Catherine and St. Margaret, came to you at the chateau of Chinon. All the company ascended through the floors of the castle until they came to the room of your king, before whom the angel bearing the crown bowed. . . . As

for this matter, the clerks say that it is not in the least probable, but it is rather a presumptuous lie, misleading and pernicious, a false statement, derogatory of the dignity of the Church and of the angels. . . .

Item: you have said that, at God's command, you have continually worn men's clothes, and that you have put on a short robe, doublet, shoes attached by points, also that you have had short hair, cut around above the ears, without retaining anything on your person which shows that you are a woman, and that several times you have received the body of Our Lord dressed in this fashion, despite having been admonished to give it up several times, the which you would not do. You have said that you would rather die than abandon the said clothing, if it were not at God's command, and that if you were wearing those clothes and were with the king, and those of your party, it would be one of the greatest benefits for the kingdom of France. You have also said that not for anything would you swear an oath not to wear the said clothing and carry arms any longer. And all these things you say you have

done for the good and at the command of God. As for these things, the clerics say that you blaspheme God and hold him in contempt in his sacraments; you transgress Divine Law, Holy Scripture, and canon law. You err in the faith. You boast in vanity. You are suspected of idolatry and you have condemned yourself in not wishing to wear clothing suitable to your sex, but you follow the custom of Gentiles and Saracens.

Source: Carolyne Larrington, ed. and trans., *Women and Writing in Medieval Europe* (New York: 1995), pp. 183–84.

Questions for Analysis

1. Paris was in the hands of the English when this condemnation was issued. Is there any evidence that its authors were coerced into making this pronouncement?

2. On what grounds was Joan condemned for heresy?

3. In what ways does Joan's behavior highlight larger trends in late medieval spirituality and popular piety?

---

the nobility, and the royal capital, Paris, to the kingdom's outlying regions. Nonetheless, the king's power was actually increased by the war's end, laying the foundations on which the power of early modern France would be built.

The Hundred Years' War also had dramatic effects on the English monarchy. When English armies in France were successful, the king rode a wave of popularity that fueled an

emerging sense of patriotism. When the war turned against the English, however, defeats abroad undermined support for the monarch at home. Of the nine English kings who ruled England between 1307 and 1485, five were deposed and murdered by aristocratic factions.

England's peculiar form of kingship depended on the king's ability to mobilize popular support through

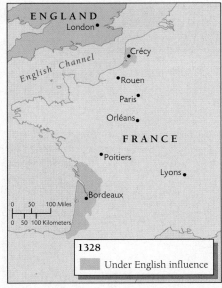

1328

Under English influence

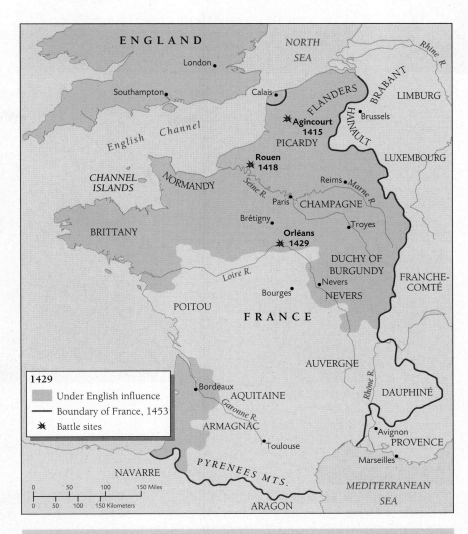

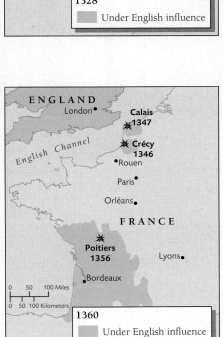

1360

Under English influence
✳ Battle sites

THE PHASES OF THE HUNDRED YEARS' WAR. Here we see three snapshots of the political geography of France during the Hundred Years' War. ▪ *In what areas of France did England make its greatest territorial gains before 1360?* ▪ *How and why did this change in the period leading up to 1429?* ▪ *What geographic and strategic advantages did the French monarchy enjoy after 1429 that might help explain its success in recapturing the French kingdom from the English?*

Parliament while maintaining the support of his nobility through successful wars. Failure to maintain this balance was even more destabilizing than it would have been elsewhere, precisely because royal power was so centralized. In France, the nobility could endure the insanity of Charles VI because his government was not powerful enough to threaten them. In England, neither the nobility nor the nation could afford the weak kingship of Henry VI. The result was an aristocratic rebellion that led to a full-blown civil war: the Wars of the Roses, so called—by the novelist Sir Walter Scott (1771–1832)—because of the floral emblems, red and white, adopted by the two com-

peting noble families, Lancaster and York. It ended only when a Lancastrian claimant, Henry Tudor (r. 1485–1509), resolved the dynastic feud by marrying Elizabeth of York, ruling as Henry VII and establishing a new Tudor dynasty whose symbol was a rose with both white and red petals (see Chapter 13).

Despite England's ultimate defeat, the Hundred Years' War strengthened the English nation in several ways. First, it equated national strength with the power of the state and its king. Second, it fomented a strong anti-French sentiment that led to the triumph of the English vernacular for the first time since the Norman conquest over 300 years

Past and Present

Replacing "Retired" Popes

When Benedict XVI decided to retire from papal office in February 2013, pundits and theologians alike struggled to find a precedent for this extraordinary decision. Most reached back to the year 1417, when Pope Martin V was elected at the Council of Constance (left) to replace the "retired" Gregory XII. But in this case, the retirement was not voluntary—and it was accompanied by the enforced resignation of an additional rival pope and the excommunication of yet another. The installation mass of Pope Francis in March 2013 (right) was much more universally celebrated and much more public than that of his medieval predecessor.

Watch related author videos on the Student Site
wwnorton.com/college/history/western-civilizationsBrief4

earlier: the first English court to speak English was that of Richard II, a patron of Geoffrey Chaucer. Third, the loss of its continental possessions made England, for the first time, a self-contained island. This would later prove to be an advantage in many ways.

Conflict in the Holy Roman Empire and Italy

Elsewhere in Europe, a new trend toward perpetual warfare was even more destructive. In the lands of the Holy Roman Empire, armed conflict among territorial princes, and between these princes and the emperor, weakened all combatants. Periodically, a powerful emperor would emerge to play a major role, but the dissolution of power continued when German princes divided their territories among their heirs while free cities and local lords strove to shake off the princes' rule. Only in the eastern regions of the empire were the rulers of Bavaria, Austria, and Brandenburg-Prussia able to strengthen their authority, mostly by supporting the efforts of the nobility to subject their peasants to serfdom and by conquering and colonizing new territories on their eastern frontiers.

In northern and central Italy, the last half of the fourteenth century was also marked by incessant conflict. With the papacy based in Avignon, the Papal States collapsed and Rome itself was riven by factional violence. Warfare among northern city-states added to the chaos. But around 1400, Venice, Milan, and Florence succeeded in stabilizing their differing forms of government. Venice was now ruled by an oligarchy of merchants; Milan by a family of despots; and Florence was a nominal republic dominated by the influence of a few wealthy clans, especially the Medici banking family. These three cities then began to expand their influence by subordinating other cities to their rule.

Eventually, almost all the towns of northern Italy were allied with one of these powers. An exception was Genoa, which had its own trading empire in the Mediterranean and Atlantic (see Chapter 10). The papacy, meanwhile, reasserted its control over central Italy when it was restored to Rome in 1377. The southern kingdom of Naples and Sicily persisted as a separate entity, though one riven by local warfare and poor government. Diplomacy and frequently shifting alliances did little to check the ambitions of any one state for further expansion, and it could not change the fact that none of these small-scale states could oppose the powers surrounded Italy.

The Growth of National Monarchies

In France and England, as well as in smaller kingdoms like Scotland and Portugal, the later Middle Ages saw the emergence of European states more cohesive than any that had existed before. The basic political patterns established in the formative twelfth and thirteenth centuries had made this possible, yet the active construction of a sense of shared identity in these territories was a new phenomenon. Forged by war and fueled by the growing cultural importance of vernacular languages, this fusion produced a new type of political organization: the national monarchy.

The advantages of these national monarchies when compared to older forms of political organization would become very evident. When the armies of France invaded the Italian peninsula at the end of the fifteenth century, neither the militias of the city-states nor the far-flung resources of Venice were a match for them. Germany and the Low Countries would suffer similar invasions and remain battlegrounds for competing armies until the middle of the nineteenth century. But the new national monarchies brought significant disadvantages, too. They guaranteed the prevalence of warfare in Europe as they continued their struggle for sovereignty and territory, and they would eventually transport their rivalry to every corner of the globe.

THE TRIALS OF THE ROMAN CHURCH

The century after the Black Death witnessed the papacy's return to Rome, as well as changes in the Church that would have far-reaching consequences.

The Great Western Schism

Calls for the papacy's return to Rome grew more insistent after the Black Death. Its return was eventually catalyzed by the letter-writing campaign of Catherine of Siena (1347–1380), a nun and influential mystic whose teasing but pious missives to Gregory XI (r. 1370–78) alternately shamed and coerced him into making the move.

But the papacy's restoration was short lived. Gregory died a year after his return to Rome, in 1377. His cardinals—many of them Frenchmen—struggled to interpret the wishes of the volatile Romans, and they would later claim to have capitulated to the Roman mob when they elected an Italian candidate, Urban VI. When Urban fell out with them soon afterward, the cardinals fled the city and, from a safe distance, declared his election invalid. They then elected a new pope, a Frenchman who took the name Clement VII. Urban retaliated by naming a new and entirely Italian College of Cardinals. The French pope and his cardinals withdrew ignominiously to the papal palace in Avignon, while the Italian pope remained in Rome.

The resulting rift is known as the Great Schism, or the Great Western Schism (to distinguish it from the ongoing schism between the Roman and Orthodox Churches). Between 1378 and 1417, the Roman Church was divided between two (and, ultimately, three) competing papacies, each claiming to be legitimate and each denouncing the heresy of the others. Europe's religious allegiances fractured along political lines: France and her allies Scotland, Castile, Aragon, and Naples recognized the pope in Avignon, whereas England, Germany, northern Italy, Scandinavia, Bohemia, Poland, and Hungary recognized the Roman pope. Nor was there any obvious way to end this embarrassing state of affairs. Finally, in 1409, some cardinals from both camps met at Pisa, where they declared the deposition of both popes and named a new one from among their number. But neither of the popes reigning in Rome and Avignon accepted that decision, so there were now three rival popes instead of two.

The Council of Constance and the Failure of the Conciliar Movement

This debacle was ultimately addressed between 1414 and 1418 at the Council of Constance, a city in southern Germany: it was the largest ecclesiastical gathering

Competing Viewpoints

Council or Pope?

The Great Schism spurred a fundamental and far-reaching debate about the nature of authority within the Church. Arguments for papal supremacy rested on traditional claims that the popes were the successors of Saint Peter, to whom Jesus Christ had delegated his own authority. Arguments for the supremacy of a general council had been advanced by many intellectuals throughout the fourteenth century, but it was only in the circumstances of the schism that these arguments found a wide audience. The following documents trace the history of the controversy, from the declaration of conciliar supremacy at the Council of Constance (Haec Sancta Synodus), to the council's efforts to guarantee regular meetings of general councils thereafter (Frequens), to the papal condemnation of appeals to the authority of general councils issued in 1460 (Execrabilis).

Haec Sancta Synodus (1415)

This holy synod of Constance . . . declares that being lawfully assembled in the Holy Spirit, constituting a general council and representing the Catholic Church Militant, it has its power directly from Christ, and that all persons of whatever rank or dignity, even a Pope, are bound to obey it in matters relating to faith and the end of the Schism and the general reformation of the church of God in head and members.

Further, it declares that any person of whatever position, rank, or dignity, even a Pope, who contumaciously refuses to obey the mandates, statutes, ordinances, or regulations enacted or to be enacted by this holy synod, or by any other general council lawfully assembled, relating to the matters aforesaid or to other matters involved with them, shall, unless he repents, be . . . duly punished. . . .

Source: R. L. Loomis, ed. and trans., *The Council of Constance* (New York: 1961), p. 229.

Frequens (1417)

The frequent holding of general councils is the best method of cultivating the field of the Lord, for they root out the briars, thorns, and thistles of heresies, errors, and schisms, correct abuses, make crooked things straight, and prepare the Lord's vineyard for fruitfulness and rich fertility. Neglect of general councils sows the seeds of these evils and encourages their growth. This truth is borne in upon us as we recall times past and survey the present.

Therefore by perpetual edict we . . . ordain that henceforth general councils shall be held as follows: the first within the five years immediately following the end of the present council, the second within seven years from the end of the council next after this, and subsequently

since the Council of Nicea, over a thousand years earlier (see Chapter 6). Its chief mission was to remove all rival claimants for papal office before electing a new pope. But many of the council's delegates had even more far-reaching plans for the reform of the Church, ambitions that stemmed from the legal doctrine that gave the council power to depose and elect popes in the first place.

This doctrine, known as conciliarism, holds that supreme authority within the Church rests not with the pope but with a representative general council: not just the council at Constance but any future council. The delegates at Constance decreed that general councils should meet regularly to oversee the governance of the Church, and to act as a check on papal power.

Had conciliarism triumphed, the Reformation of the following century might not have occurred. But, predictably, the newly elected pope Martin V did everything he could to undermine this doctrine. When the next general council met at Siena in 1423, Pope Martin duly sent representatives—who then turned around and went back to Rome. (The Council of Constance had specified frequent meetings but had not specified how long they should last.) A lengthy struggle for power ensued between the advocates of papal monarchy and the conciliarists who

every ten years forever. . . . Thus there will always be a certain continuity. Either a council will be in session or one will be expected at the end of a fixed period. . . .

Source: R. L. Loomis, ed. and trans., *The Council of Constance* (New York: 1961), pp. 246–47.

Execrabilis (1460)

An execrable abuse, unheard of in earlier times, has sprung up in our period. Some men, imbued with a spirit of rebellion and moved not by a desire for sound decisions but rather by a desire to escape the punishment for sin, suppose that they can appeal from the Pope, Vicar of Jesus Christ—from the Pope, to whom in the person of blessed Peter it was said, "Feed my sheep" and "whatever you bind on earth will be bound in heaven"—from this Pope to a future council. How harmful this is to the Christian republic, as well as how contrary to canon law, anyone who is not ignorant of the law can understand. For ... who would not consider it ridiculous to appeal to something which does not now exist anywhere nor does anyone know when it will exist? The poor are heavily oppressed by the powerful, offenses remain unpunished, rebellion against the Holy See is encouraged, license for sin is granted, and all ecclesiastical discipline and hierarchical ranking of the Church are turned upside down.

Wishing therefore to expel this deadly poison from the Church of Christ, and concerned with the salvation of the sheep committed to us . . . with the counsel and assent of our venerable brothers, the Cardinals of the Holy Roman Church, together with the counsel and assent of all those prelates who have been trained in canon and civil law who follow our Court, and with our own certain knowledge, we condemn appeals of this kind, reject them as erroneous and abominable, and declare them to be completely null and void. And we lay down that from now on, no one should dare ... to make such an appeal from our decisions, be they legal or theological, or from any commands at all from us or our successors. . . .

Source: Reprinted by permission of the publisher from Gabriel Biel, *Defensorium Obedientiae Apostolicae et Alia Documenta*, ed. and trans. Heiko A. Oberman, Daniel E. Zerfoss, and William J. Courtenay (Cambridge, MA: 1968), pp. 224–27. Copyright © 1968 by the President and Fellows of Harvard College.

Questions for Analysis

1. On what grounds does *Haec Sancta Synodus* establish the authority of a council? Why would this be considered a threat to papal power?

2. Why was it considered necessary for councils to meet regularly (*Frequens*)? What might have been the logical consequences of such regular meetings?

3. On what grounds does *Execrabilis* condemn the appeals to future councils that have no specified meeting date? Why would it not have condemned the conciliar movement altogether?

were convened at Basel. Twenty-five years later, in 1449, the Council of Basel dissolved itself—dashing the hopes of those who thought it would lead to an internal reformation of the Church.

Spiritual Challenges

We have noted that the spiritual and social lives of medieval Christians were inextricably intertwined. The parish church stood literally at the center of their lives: churchyards were communal meeting places, and church buildings were a refuge from attack and a gathering place for business. The church's holidays marked the passage of the year, and the church's bells marked the hours of the day. The church was holy, but it was also essential to daily life. Yet, in the wake of the Black Death, when many parishes ceased to exist and many communities were decimated, an increasing number of people were not satisfied with these conventional forms of worship. Many are regarded today as saints, but this was not necessarily the case in their lifetimes. As Joan of Arc's predicament reveals, medieval women found it particularly challenging to find outlets for their piety.

Many therefore internalized their devotional practices or confined them to the domestic sphere—sometimes to the inconvenience of their families and communities. For example, the young Catherine of Siena refused to help support her working-class family; instead, she took over one of the house's two rooms for her own private prayers, confining her parents and a dozen siblings to the remaining room. Juliana of Norwich (1342–1416) withdrew from the world into a small cell built next to her local church, where she spent the rest of her life in prayer and contemplation. Her younger contemporary, the housewife Margery Kempe (c. 1372–c. 1439), resented the fact that she had a husband, several children, and a household to support. In later life, she renounced her duties and devoted her life to performing acts of histrionic piety, which alienated many who came into contact with her.

The extraordinary strength of such individuals could be inspiring, but it could also threaten the Church's control over

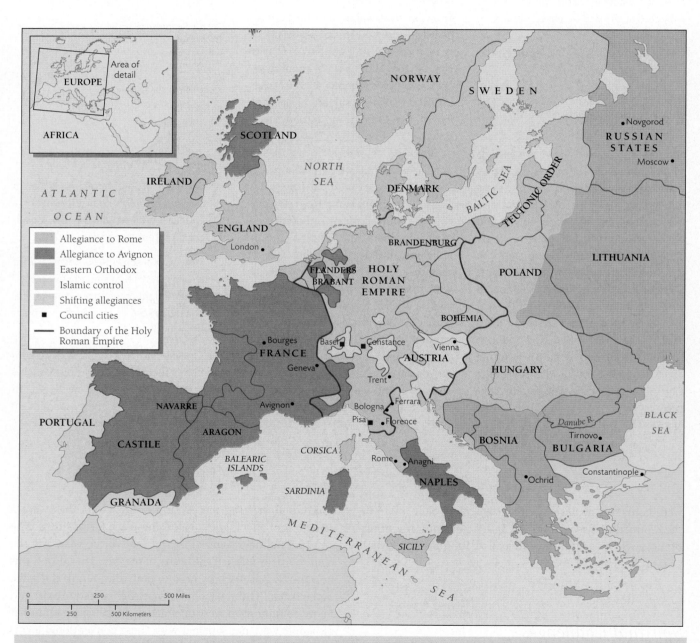

THE GREAT SCHISM, 1378–1417. During the Great Western Schism, the various territories of Europe were divided in their allegiances. ▪ *According to the map key, whom were they choosing between?* ▪ *What common interests would have united the supporters of the Avignon pope or of the Roman pope?* ▪ *Why would areas like Portugal and Austria waver in their support?*

religious life. More safely orthodox was the practical mysticism preached by Thomas à Kempis, whose *Imitation of Christ* (c. 1427) taught readers how to appreciate aspects of the divine in their everyday lives. Originally written in Latin, it was quickly translated into many languages and is now more widely read than any other Christian book except the Bible.

Popular Reform Movements

In the kingdoms of England and Bohemia (the modern Czech Republic), some popular religious movements posed serious challenges to papal authority. The key figure in both cases was John Wycliffe (c. 1330–1384), an Oxford

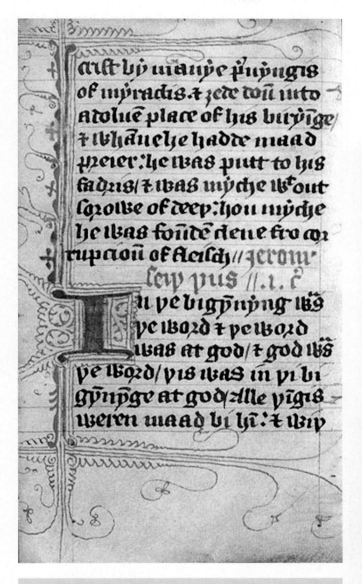

WYCLIFFE'S ENGLISH BIBLE. Although John Wycliffe was not directly responsible for this translation of the Bible, it was made in the later fourteenth century by his followers. Written in the same Middle English vernacular used by Geoffrey Chaucer for his popular works, it was designed to be accessible to lay readers who did not understand Latin. This page shows the beginning of the Gospel of John: "In ye bigynnyng was / ye word & ye word / was at god & god was the word. Yis was in ye bi / gynninge at god, all yingis weren maad bi him. . . ." ▪ *Compare this translation to a modern one. How different (or not) is this version of English?* ▪ *What might have been the impact of this language on readers and listeners in the late fifteenth century?* ▪ *How would translation have helped to further the reforming efforts of Wycliffe and his disciples?*

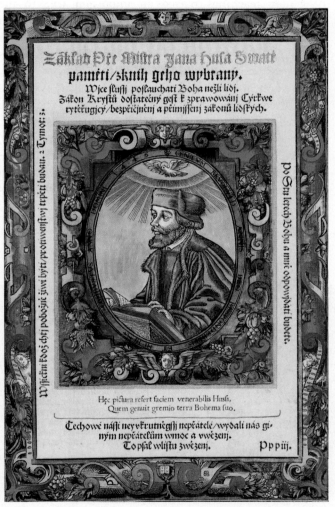

THE TEACHINGS OF JAN HUS. An eloquent religious reformer, Jan Hus was burned at the stake in 1415 after having been found guilty of heresy at the Council of Constance. This lavishly illustrated booklet of his teachings was published over a century later in his native Bohemia and includes texts in the Czech vernacular and in Latin. ▪ *What does its later publication suggest about the uses to which Hus's image and theology were put during the Protestant Reformation?*

theologian and powerful critic. Wycliffe concluded that the empty sacraments of a debased Church could not save anyone. He therefore urged the English king to confiscate the Church's wealth and to replace corrupt priests and bishops with men who would live by apostolic standards of poverty and piety.

Some of Wycliffe's followers, known to their detractors as Lollards ("mumblers" or "beggars"), went even further, dismissing the sacraments as fraudulent attempts to extort money from the faithful. Lollard preachers also promoted an English translation of the Bible sponsored by Wycliffe himself, to enable direct access to scripture. Wycliffe's teachings played an important role in the Peasants' Revolt of 1381, and the movement was even supported by a number of aristocratic families. But after a failed Lollard uprising in 1414, the movement and its supporters went underground.

In Bohemia and eastern Europe, however, Wycliffe's ideas lived on and struck even deeper roots. They were adopted by Jan Hus (c. 1373–1415), a charismatic teacher at the royal university in Prague. In contrast to the Lollards, Hus emphasized the centrality of the Eucharist. Indeed, he demanded that the laity be allowed to receive both the consecrated bread and the consecrated wine, which was usually reserved for priests. This demand became a rallying cry for the Hussite movement, which was also endorsed by influential nobles.

On behalf of his supporters, Hus traveled to the Council of Constance to urge the Church to undertake sweeping reforms. But rather than giving him a hearing, the other delegates convicted him of heresy and had him burned at the stake. Back home, Hus's supporters raised the banner of open revolt, and the aristocracy took advantage of the situation to seize Church property. Between 1420 and 1424, armed bands of fervent Hussites resoundingly defeated several armies and rallied to pursue goals of religious reform and social justice. In 1434, a more conservative arm of the Hussite movement was able to negotiate a settlement with Church officials. By the terms of this agreement, Bohemians could receive both the bread and wine of the Mass, which effectively separated the Bohemian religious establishment from Rome.

The English and Bohemian movements exhibit striking similarities. Both began in the university and then galvanized popular preaching and social activism. Both called for the clergy to live in simplicity and poverty, and both employed the vernacular (English and Czech) in opposition to the Latin of a "foreign" Church. In all these respects, they

After You Read This Chapter

 Go to **INQUIZITIVE** to see what you've learned—and learn what you've missed— with personalized feedback along the way.

REVIEWING THE OBJECTIVES

- The Black Death had short-term and long-term effects on the economy and societies of Europe. What were some of the most important changes?
- The later "Middle Ages" and "the Renaissance" are often perceived to be two different periods, but the latter was actually part of the former. Explain why.
- What were some of the intellectual, cultural, and artistic innovations of this era in Italy and elsewhere in Europe?
- How were some European kingdoms becoming stronger and more centralized during this period? What are some examples of national monarchies?
- The conciliar movement sought to limit the power of the papacy. How? Why was this movement unsuccessful?

anticipated the much larger movement of the Protestant Reformation (see Chapter 13).

CONCLUSION

The century after the Black Death was a period of tremendous creativity and revolutionary change. The effects of the plague were catastrophic, but the resulting food surpluses and opportunities encouraged experimentation and opened up broad avenues for advancement. Europe's economy diversified and expanded; increasing wealth and access to education produced new forms of art and new ways of looking at the world. Women were still excluded from formal schooling but nevertheless became active—and in many cases dominant—participants in literary endeavors, cultural life, and religious movements. Average men and women not only became more active in cultivating their own worldly goals, they also took control of their spiritual destinies at a time when the institutional Church provided little leadership.

Meanwhile, some states were growing stronger while the rise of the Ottoman Empire absorbed the venerable Muslim caliphate at Baghdad, the western portions of the former Mongol Empire, and—above all—the surviving core of the eastern Roman Empire. Greek-speaking refugees streamed into Italy, many bringing with them classics of ancient Greek literature little known in Europe. Fueled by a fervid nostalgia for the past, Italians began to experiment with new ways of reading ancient texts, advocating a return to classical models while at the same time trying to counter the political and artistic authority of the more powerful kingdoms north of the Alps.

In contrast to Italy, these emerging national monarchies cultivated a common identity through the promotion of a shared vernacular language and allegiance to a more centralized state. These tactics would allow initially smaller kingdoms like Poland and Scotland to increase their territories and influence, and would also lead France and England into an epic battle for sovereignty and hegemony. The result, in all cases, was the escalation of armed conflict made possible by new technologies and more effective administration.

The generations who survived the calamities of famine, plague, and warfare seized the opportunities their new world presented to them, and they stood on the verge of an extraordinary period of global expansion.

PEOPLE, IDEAS, AND EVENTS IN CONTEXT

- Compare and contrast the **BLACK DEATH**'s effects on rural and urban areas.
- In what ways do rebellions like the **ENGLISH PEASANTS' REVOLT** reflect the changes brought about by the plague?
- How do the works of **GIOVANNI BOCCACCIO, GEOFFREY CHAUCER**, and **CHRISTINE DE PISAN** exemplify the culture of this era?
- What was **HUMANISM**? How was it related to the artistic and intellectual movement known as the **RENAISSANCE**?
- How did the **OTTOMAN EMPIRE** come to power? What were some consequences of its rise?
- On what grounds did **MUSCOVY** claim to be "the third Rome"? What is the significance of the title **TSAR**?
- What new military technologies were in use during the **HUNDRED YEARS' WAR**? How did this conflict affect other parts of Europe, beyond England and France? What role did **JOAN OF ARC** play?
- How did the **COUNCIL OF CONSTANCE** respond to the crisis of the **GREAT SCHISM**?
- Why did **CONCILIARISM** fail? How did **JOHN WYCLIFFE** and **JAN HUS** seek to reform the Church?

THINKING ABOUT CONNECTIONS

- In the year 2000, a group of historians was asked to identify the most significant historical figure of the past millennium. Rather than selecting a person (e.g., Martin Luther, Shakespeare, Napoleon, Adolf Hitler), they chose the microbe *Yersinia pestis*, the cause of the Black Death. Do you agree with this assessment? Why or why not?
- In your view, which was more crucial to the formation of the modern state: the political and legal developments we surveyed in Chapter 9 or the emergence of national monarchies discussed in this chapter? Why?
- Was the conciliar movement doomed to failure, given what we have learned about the history of the Roman Church? How far back does one need to go in order to trace the development of disputes over ecclesiastical governance?

Before You Read This Chapter

Innovation and Exploration, 1453–1533

CORE OBJECTIVES

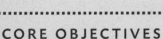

- **UNDERSTAND** the relationship between Renaissance ideals and the political and economic realities of Italy.

- **IDENTIFY** the key characteristics of Renaissance arts and learning during this period, and **EXPLAIN** their significance.

- **DEFINE** the term *Reconquista* and its meaning in Spain.

- **DESCRIBE** the methods and motives of European colonization during this period.

- **EXPLAIN** why Europeans were able to dominate the peoples of the New World.

W
hat if exact copies of an idea could circulate quickly, all over the world? What if the same could be done for the latest news, the oldest beliefs, the most beautiful poems, the most exciting—and deadly—discoveries? It would be doing for knowledge what the invention of coinage did for wealth: making it portable, easier to use and disseminate. Indeed, it's no accident that the man who developed such a technology, Johannes Gutenberg of Mainz (c. 1398–1468), was the son of a goldsmith who minted coins for the bishop of that German city. Both technologies were based on the same principle and used the same basic tools. Coins are metal disks stamped with identical words and images, impressed on them with a reusable matrix. The pages of the first printed books were stamped with ink spread on rows of movable type (lead or cast-iron letter forms and punctuation marks) slotted into frames to form lines of words. Once a set of pages was ready, a press could make hundreds of copies in a matter of hours, many hundreds of times faster than the same page could be copied by hand. Afterward, the type could be reused.

313

A major stimulus for this invention was the more widespread availability of paper. Parchment, northern Europe's chief writing material since the advent of the codex (see Chapter 6), was extremely expensive to manufacture and required special training on the part of those who used it—one reason why writing remained a specialized skill for much of the Middle Ages, while the ability to read was common. Paper, made from rags turned into pulp by mills, was both cheaper and far easier to use; accordingly, books became cheaper and written communication easier. Growing demand for books, in turn, led to experimentation with different methods of book production—and so to Gutenberg's breakthrough. By 1455, his workshop had printed multiple copies of the Latin Bible, of which forty-eight complete or partial volumes survive today. Although printing never entirely replaced traditional modes of publication via manuscript, it revolutionized the spread of information.

The printing press played a crucial role in many of the developments we study in this chapter. The artistic and intellectual experiments of the Italian Renaissance were rapidly exported to other parts of Europe; specifications for new weapons would be printed on the same presses that churned out humanist literature. News of Columbus's first voyage would spread via the same media as critiques of European imperialism. Printing not only increased the amount and rapidity of publication, it also made it more difficult for those in power to censor dissenting opinions.

But at the same time, the printing press also became an indispensable tool of power, making it possible for rulers to govern growing empires and increasingly centralized states. The "reconquest" of Spain and the extension of Spanish imperialism to the New World were both facilitated by the circulation of printed propaganda. The widespread availability of reading materials even helped to standardize national languages, by enabling governments to promote one official printed dialect over others. Hence the "king's English," the variety of the language spoken around London, was imposed as the only acceptable literary and bureaucratic language throughout the English realm. For these reasons, among others, many historians consider the advent of print to be both the defining event and the driving engine of modernity, and it coincided with another essentially modern development: the discovery of a "New World."

RENAISSANCE IDEALS— AND REALITIES

The intellectual and artistic movement that had begun in Italy during the fourteenth century (Chapter 11) was characterized by an intense interest in the classics and by a new type of curriculum: humanism. These Renaissance ideals—and the realities that undergirded them—were extended through the medium of the printing press. By the time the Ottoman conquest of Constantinople was complete, just a year before Gutenberg's Bible, hundreds of refugees from the eastern Roman Empire had been propelled into Italy. Many carried with them precious manuscripts of Greek texts: the epics of Homer, the works of Athenian dramatists, the dialogues of Plato. Prior to the invention of print, such manuscripts could be owned and studied by only a very few, very privileged men. Now printers in Venice and other European cities rushed to produce cheap editions, as well as Greek grammars and glossaries that could facilitate reading them.

In Florence, an informal "Platonic Academy" was convened. There, the work of intellectuals like Marsilio Ficino (1433–1499) and Giovanni Pico della Mirandola (1463–1494) was fostered by the patronage of the wealthy Cosimo de' Medici. Based on his reading of Plato, Ficino's philosophy moved away from the focus on civic life that had been such a feature of earlier humanist thought. He taught instead that the individual should look to free the immortal soul from its "always miserable" mortal body: a Platonic ideal compatible with much late-medieval piety. Ficino's great achievement was his translation of Plato's works into Latin. His disciple Pico also rejected the everyday world of public affairs, arguing that man (but not woman) can aspire to union with God through the exercise of his unique talents.

The Politics of Italy and the Philosophy of Machiavelli

Not all Florentines were galvanized by Platonic ideals, though. Indeed, the most influential philosopher of this era was a thoroughgoing realist who spent more time studying Roman history: Niccolò Machiavelli (1469–1527). Machiavelli's political writings reflect the unstable political situation of his home city as well as his wider aspirations for a unified Italy. We have observed that Italy had been in political disarray for centuries, a situation exacerbated by the "Babylonian Captivity" of the papacy and the controversies raging after its return to Rome (see Chapters 10 and 11). Now Italy was becoming the arena in which bloody international struggles were being played out. The monarchs of France and Spain both had imperial ambitions, and both claimed to be the rightful champions of the papacy. Both sent

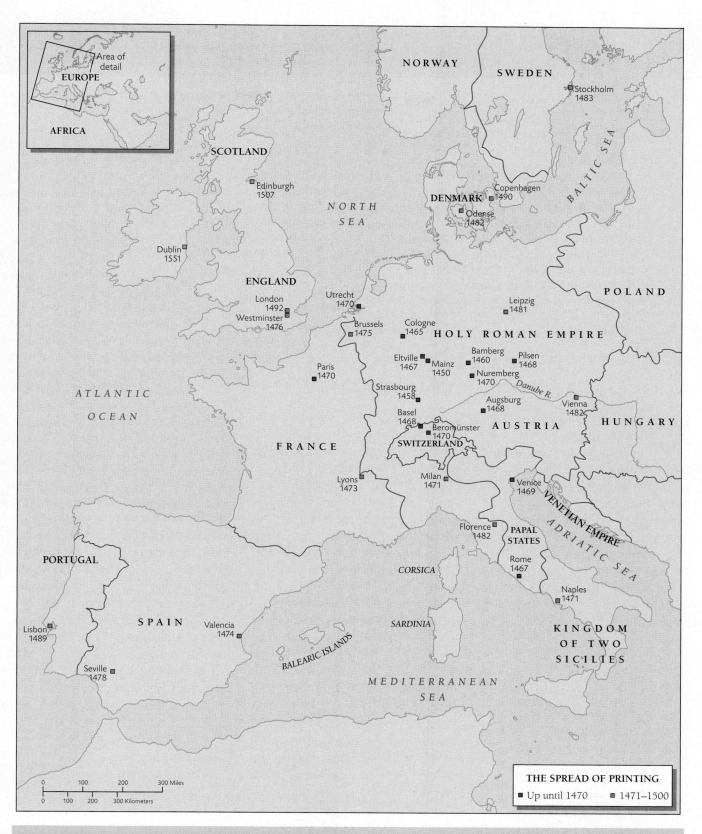

THE SPREAD OF PRINTING

■ Up until 1470	■ 1471–1500

THE SPREAD OF PRINTING. This map shows how quickly the technology of printing spread throughout Europe between 1470 and 1500.
■ *In what regions were printing presses most heavily concentrated?* ■ *What factors would have led to their proliferation in the Low Countries, northern Italy, and Germany—as compared to France, Spain, and England?*

Competing Viewpoints

Printing, Patriotism, and the Past

> *The printing press helped to create new communities of readers by standardizing national languages and even promoting patriotism. And while it enabled authors of new works to reach larger audiences, it also allowed printers to popularize older writings that had previously circulated in manuscript. The two sources presented here exemplify two aspects of this trend. The first is the preface to a version of the legend of King Arthur, which was originally written by an English soldier, Sir Thomas Malory, who completed it in 1470. It was printed for the first time in 1485, and it quickly became a best seller. The author of this preface was also the printer, William Caxton of London, who specialized in publishing books that glorified England's history and heritage. The second excerpt is from the concluding chapter of Machiavelli's treatise* The Prince. *Like the book itself, these remarks were originally addressed to Lorenzo de' Medici, head of Florence's most powerful family. But when* The Prince *was printed in 1532, five years after Machiavelli's death, the author's passionate denunciation of foreign "barbarians" and his lament for Italy's lost glory would have resonated with a wider Italian-speaking public.*

William Caxton's preface to Thomas Malory's *Le Morte d'Arthur* ("The Death of Arthur"), 1485

After I had accomplished and finished diverse histories, both of contemplation and of other historical and worldly acts of great conquerors and princes, . . . many noble and diverse gentlemen of this realm of England came and demanded why I had not made and imprinted the noble history of the Holy Grail, and of the most renowned Christian king and worthy, King Arthur, which ought most to be remembered among us Englishmen before all other Christian kings. . . . The said noble gentlemen instantly required me to imprint the history of the said noble king and conqueror King Arthur, and of his knights, with the history of the Holy Grail . . . considering that he was a man born within this realm, and king and emperor of the same: and that there be, in French, diverse and many noble volumes of his acts, and also of his knights. To whom I answered that diverse men hold opinion that there was no such Arthur, and that all such books as have been made of him be feigned and fables, because some chronicles make of him no mention. . . . Whereto they answered, and one in

special said, that in him that should say or think that there was never such a king called Arthur might well be accounted great folly and blindness. . . . For in all places, Christian and heathen, he is reputed and taken for one of the Nine Worthies, and the first of the three Christian men. And also, he is more spoken of beyond the sea, and there are more books made of his noble acts than there be in England, as well in Dutch, Italian, Spanish, and Greek, as in French. . . . Wherefore it is a marvel why he is no more renowned in his own country. . . .

Then all these things aforesaid alleged, I could not well deny but that there was such a noble king named Arthur, reputed one of the Nine Worthies, and first and chief of the Christian men. And many noble volumes be made of him and of his noble knights in French, which I have seen and read beyond the sea, which be not had in our maternal tongue. . . . Wherefore, among all such [manuscript] books as have late been drawn out briefly into English I have . . . undertaken to imprint a book of the noble histories of the said King

Arthur, and of certain of his knights, after a copy unto me delivered—which copy Sir Thomas Malory did take out of certain books of French, and reduced it into English. And I, according to my copy, have done set it in print, to the intent that noble men may see and learn the noble acts of chivalry, the gentle and virtuous deeds that some knights used in those days, by which they came to honor, and how they that were vicious were punished and oft put to shame and rebuke; humbly beseeching all noble lords and ladies (with all other estates of what estate or degree they be) that shall see and read in this said book and work, that they take the good and honest acts to their remembrance, and follow the same. . . . For herein may be seen noble chivalry, courtesy, humanity, friendliness, hardiness, love, friendship, cowardice, murder, hate, virtue, and sin. Do after the good and leave the evil, and it shall bring you to good fame and renown.

Source: Sir Thomas Malory, *Le Morte d'Arthur* (London: 1485), (text and spelling slightly modernized).

From the conclusion of Niccolò Machiavelli's *The Prince* (completed 1513, printed 1533)

Reflecting on the matters set forth above and considering within myself where the times were propitious in Italy at present to honor a new prince and whether there is at hand the matter suitable for a prudent and virtuous leader to mold in a new form, giving honor to himself and benefit to the citizens of the country, I have arrived at the opinion that all circumstances now favor such a prince, and I cannot think of a time more propitious for him than the present. If, as I said, it was necessary in order to make apparent the virtue of Moses, that the people of Israel should be enslaved in Egypt, and that the Persians should be oppressed by the Medes to provide an opportunity to illustrate the greatness and the spirit of Cyrus, and that the Athenians should be scattered in order to show the excellence of Theseus, thus at the present time, in order to reveal the valor of an Italian spirit, it was essential that Italy should fall to her present low estate, more enslaved than the Hebrews, more servile than the Persians, more disunited than the Athenians, leaderless and lawless, beaten, despoiled, lacerated, overrun and crushed under every kind of misfortune. . . . So Italy now, left almost lifeless, awaits the coming of one who will heal her wounds, putting an end to the sacking and looting in Lombardy and the spoliation and extortions in the Realm of Naples and Tuscany, and cleanse her sores that have been so long festering. Behold how she prays God to send her someone to redeem her from the cruelty and insolence of the barbarians. See how she is ready and willing to follow any banner so long as there be someone to take it up. Nor has she at present any hope of finding her redeemer save only in your illustrious house [the Medici] which has been so highly exalted both by its own merits and by fortune and which has been favored by God and the church, of which it is now ruler. . . .

This opportunity, therefore, should not be allowed to pass, and Italy, after such a long wait, must be allowed to behold her redeemer. I cannot describe the joy with which he will be received in all these provinces which have suffered so much from the foreign deluge, nor with what thirst for vengeance, nor with what firm devotion, what solemn delight, what tears! What gates could be closed to him, what people could deny him obedience, what envy could withstand him, what Italian could withhold allegiance from him? THIS BARBARIAN OCCUPATION STINKS IN THE NOSTRILS OF ALL OF US. Let your illustrious house then take up this cause with the spirit and the hope with which one undertakes a truly just enterprise. . . .

Source: Niccolò Machiavelli, *The Prince*, ed. and trans. Thomas G. Bergin (Arlington Heights, IL: 1947), pp. 75–76, 78.

Questions for Analysis

1. What do these two sources reveal about the relationship between patriotism and the awareness of a nation's past? Why do you think that Caxton looks back to a legendary medieval king, whereas Machiavelli's references are all to ancient examples? What do both excerpts reveal about the value placed on history in the popular imagination?

2. How does Caxton describe the process of printing a book? What larger conclusions can we draw from this about the market for printed books in general?

3. Why might Machiavelli's treatise have been made available in a printed version, nearly twenty years after its original appearance in manuscript? How might his new audience have responded to its message?

invading armies into the peninsula while they competed for the allegiance of the various city-states, which were torn by internal dissension.

In 1498, Machiavelli became a prominent official in the government of a new Florentine republic, set up when a French invasion had led to the expulsion of the ruling Medici family. His duties largely involved diplomatic missions to other city-states. While in Rome, he became fascinated with the attempt of Cesare Borgia, son of Pope Alexander VI, to create his own principality in central Italy. He noted Cesare's ruthlessness and his complete subordination of personal ethics to political ends. He remembered this example in 1512, when the Medici returned to overthrow the Florentine republic and Machiavelli was imprisoned, tortured, and exiled. He now devoted his energies to the articulation of a political philosophy suited to the times and to the family that had ousted him.

On the surface, Machiavelli's two great works of political analysis appear to contradict each other. In his *Discourses on Livy*, which drew on the works of that Roman historian (see Chapter 5), he praised the ancient Roman Republic as a model for his own time. There is little doubt that Machiavelli was a committed believer in the free city-state as the ideal form of human government. But Machiavelli also wrote *The Prince*, "a handbook for tyrants" in the eyes of his critics, and he dedicated this work to Lorenzo, son of Piero de' Medici, his old enemy.

Because *The Prince* has been so much more widely read than *Discourses*, it has often been interpreted as an endorsement of power for its own sake. Machiavelli's real position was quite different. In the political chaos of early-sixteenth-century Italy, he saw the likes of Cesare Borgia as the only hope for making Italy fit, eventually, for independence. Machiavelli never ceased to hope that his contemporaries would rise up, expel the French and Spanish occupying forces, and restore ancient traditions of liberty and equality. He regarded a period of despotism as a necessary step toward that end.

Yet Machiavelli continues to be a controversial figure. Some modern scholars represent him as amoral, interested solely in power. Others see him as an Italian patriot. Still others see him as a realist influenced by Saint Augustine (see Chapter 6), who understood that a ruler's good intentions do not guarantee good policies or results. Machiavelli argued that "the necessity of preserving the state will often compel a prince to take actions which are opposed to loyalty, charity, humanity, and religion." As we shall see in later chapters, many subsequent political philosophers would go even further: arguing that the preservation of the

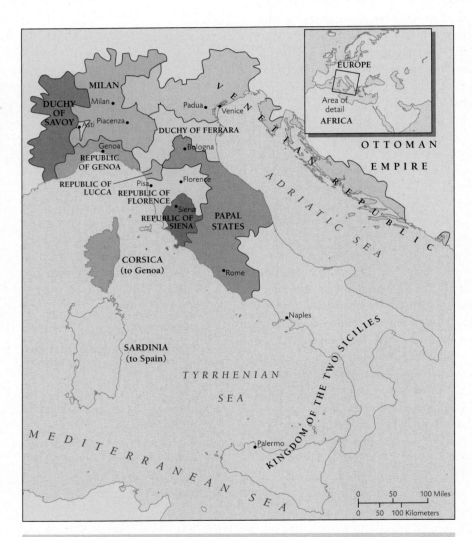

THE STATES OF ITALY, c. 1494. This map shows the divisions of Italy on the eve of the French invasion in 1494. Contemporary observers often described Italy as being divided among five great powers: Milan, Venice, Florence, the Papal States, and the united Kingdoms of Naples and Sicily. ▪ *Which of these powers would have been most capable of expanding their territories?* ▪ *Which neighboring states would have been most threatened by such attempts at expansion?* ▪ *Why would Florence and the Papal States so often find themselves in conflict with each other?*

state does indeed warrant the exercise of absolute power (see Chapters 14 and 15).

The Ideal of the Courtier

Machiavelli's political theories were informed by years of diplomatic service, and so was his engaging literary style. Indeed, he never abandoned his interest in the literary arts of the court and continued to write poems, plays, and adaptations of classical comedies. In this he resembled another poet-courtier, Ludovico Ariosto (1474–1533), who undertook diplomatic missions for the Duke of Ferrara and some of Rome's most powerful prelates. His lengthy verse narrative, *Orlando Furioso* ("The Madness of Roland"), was a comic retelling of the heroic exploits celebrated in the French *Song of Roland* (see Chapter 8)—but without the heroism. Although very different in form and tone from *The Prince*, it shared that work's skepticism of chivalric ideals. Instead, it sought to charm an audience that worshiped pleasure and beauty.

Thus a new Renaissance ideal was born, one that promoted the arts of pleasing the powerful princes who employed clever men like Machiavelli and Ariosto: the ideal of the courtier. This ideal was embodied by their contemporary, the diplomat and nobleman Baldassare Castiglione (*cah-stee-lee-OH-nay*, 1478–1529), who wrote a manual for those who wished to acquire these skills. If *The Prince* was a forerunner of modern self-help books, *The Book of the Courtier* was an early handbook of etiquette; and both stand in sharp contrast to the treatises on public virtue composed in the previous century, which taught the sober virtues of strenuous service on behalf of the city-state. Instead, Castiglione taught how to attain the elegant and seemingly effortless skills necessary for personal advancement.

Castiglione articulated and popularized the set of talents still associated with the "Renaissance man": accomplished, witty, cultured, and stylish. But in many ways, this new ideal actually represents a *rejection* of the older ideals associated with the rebirth of classical education for public men. Castiglione even rejected the misogyny of the humanists by stressing the ways in which ladies could rise to influence and prominence. Widely read throughout Europe, his *Courtier* set the standard for polite behavior until the early twentieth century.

The Dilemma of the Artist

Without question, the most enduring legacy of the Italian Renaissance has been the contributions of its artists. We have already noted (Chapter 11) the creative and economic opportunities afforded by painting on canvas or wood, which freed artists from having to work on site and on commission: such paintings are portable and can be displayed in different settings and reach different markets. We also saw that the use of oil paints, pioneered in Flanders, further revolutionized painting styles. To these benefits, the artists of Italy added an important technical ingredient: mastery of a vanishing (one-point) perspective that gave painting an illusion of three-dimensional space. They also experimented with effects of light and shade, and studied intently the anatomy and proportions of the human body. These techniques also influenced sculptors.

Behind all of the beautiful artworks created in this era—which led to the glorification of the artist as a new type of hero—lie the harsh political and economic realities within which these artists worked. Increasing private wealth and the growth of lay patronage opened up new markets and created a huge demand for buildings and objects that could increase the prestige of ambitious men. Portraiture was a direct result of this trend, since princes and merchants alike sought to glorify themselves and their families, and to compete with their neighbors and rivals.

THE IMPACT OF PERSPECTIVE. Masaccio's painting *The Trinity with the Virgin* illustrates the startling sense of depth made possible by observing the rules of one-point perspective.

An artist therefore had to study the techniques of the courtier as well as the new artistic techniques in order to succeed in winning a patron. He also had to be ready to perform other services: overseeing the building and decoration of palaces; designing tableware, furniture, fanciful liveries for servants and soldiers; and even decorating guns. Some artists, like Leonardo da Vinci, were prized as much for their capacity to invent deadly weapons as for their artworks.

New Illusions and the Career of Leonardo

For much of the fifteenth century, the majority of the great painters were Florentines who followed in the footsteps of the precocious Masaccio (1401–1428), who had died prematurely at the age of twenty-seven. His lasting legacy was the pioneering use of one-point perspective and dramatic lighting effects. Both are evident in his painting of the Trinity, where the body of the crucified Christ appears to be thrust forward by the impassive figure of God the Father, while the Virgin's gaze directly engages the viewer. Masaccio's most obvious successor was Sandro Botticelli (1445–1510), who excelled in depicting graceful motion and the sensuous pleasures of nature.

The most adventurous and versatile artist of this period was Leonardo da Vinci (1452–1519). Leonardo personifies a Renaissance ideal: he was a painter, architect, musician, mathematician, engineer, and inventor. The illegitimate son of a notary, he set up an artist's shop in Florence by the time he was twenty-five and gained the patronage of the Medici ruler, Lorenzo the Magnificent. Yet Leonardo had a weakness: he worked slowly, and he had difficulty finishing anything. This naturally displeased Lorenzo and other Florentine patrons, who regarded artists as craftsmen who worked on their patrons' time—not their own. Leonardo, however, strongly objected to this view; he considered himself to be an inspired, independent innovator. He therefore left Florence in 1482 and went to work for the Sforza dictators of Milan, whose favor he courted by emphasizing his skills as a maker of bombs, heavy ordinance, and siege engines. He remained there until the French invasion of 1499; he then wandered about, finally accepting the patronage of the French king, under whose auspices he lived and worked until his death.

THE BIRTH OF VENUS. This painting was executed by Sandro Botticelli in Florence, and represents the artist's imaginative treatment of stories from ancient mythology. Here, he depicts the moment when Aphrodite, goddess of love, was spontaneously engendered from the foam of the sea by Chronos, the god of time.

Leonardo da Vinci Applies for a Job

Few sources illuminate the tensions between Renaissance ideals and realities better than the résumé of accomplishments submitted by Leonardo da Vinci to a prospective employer, Ludovico Sforza of Milan. In the following letter, Leonardo explains why he deserves to be appointed chief architect and military engineer in the duke's household administration. He got the job and moved to Milan in 1481.

1. I have the kind of bridges that are extremely light and strong, made to be carried with great ease, and with them you may pursue, and, at any time, flee from the enemy; . . . and also methods of burning and destroying those of the enemy.

2. I know how, when a place is under attack, to eliminate the water from the trenches, and make endless variety of bridges . . . and other machines. . . .

3. . . . I have methods for destroying every rock or other fortress, even if it were built on rock, etc.

4. I also have other kinds of mortars [bombs] that are most convenient and easy to carry. . . .

5. And if it should be a sea battle, I have many kinds of machines that are most efficient for offense and defense. . . .

6. I also have means that are noiseless to reach a designated area by secret and tortuous mines. . . .

7. I will make covered chariots, safe and unattackable, which can penetrate the enemy with their artillery. . . .

8. In case of need I will make big guns, mortars, and light ordnance of fine and useful forms that are out of the ordinary.

9. If the operation of bombardment should fail, I would contrive catapults, mangonels, trabocchi [trebuchets], and other machines of marvelous efficacy and unusualness. In short, I can, according to each case in question, contrive various and endless means of offense and defense.

10. In time of peace I believe I can give perfect satisfaction that is equal to any other in the field of architecture and the construction of buildings. . . . I can execute sculpture in marble, bronze, or clay, and also in painting I do the best that can be done, and as well as any other, whoever he may be.

Having now, most illustrious Lord, sufficiently seen the specimens of all those who consider themselves master craftsmen of instruments of war, and that the invention and operation of such instruments are no different from those in common use, I shall now endeavor . . . to explain myself to your Excellency by revealing to your Lordship my secrets. . . .

Source: Excerpted from Leonardo da Vinci, *The Notebooks,* in *The Italian Renaissance Reader,* ed. Julia Conaway and Mark Mosa (Harmondsworth, UK: 1987), pp. 195–96.

Questions for Analysis

1. Based on the qualifications highlighted by Leonardo in this letter, what can you conclude about the political situation in Milan and the priorities of its duke? What can you conclude about the state of military technologies in this period and the conduct of warfare?

2. What do you make of the fact that Leonardo mentions his artistic endeavors only at the end of the letter? Does this fact alter your opinion or impression of him? Why or why not?

Paradoxically, considering his skill in fashioning weapons, Leonardo was convinced of the essential divinity of all living things. He was a vegetarian—unusual at the time—and when he went to the marketplace to buy caged birds he released them to their native habitat when he had finished observing them. His approach to painting was that it should be the most accurate possible imitation of nature. He made careful studies: blades of grass, cloud formations, a waterfall. He obtained human corpses for dissection and reconstructed in drawing the minutest features of anatomy,

THE LAST SUPPER. This fresco on the refectory wall of the monastery of Santa Maria delle Grazie in Milan is a testament to both the powers and limitations of Leonardo's artistry. It skillfully employs the techniques of one-point perspective to create the illusion that Jesus and his disciples are actually dining at the monastery's head table; but because Leonardo had not mastered the techniques of fresco painting, he applied tempera pigments to a dry wall that had been coated with a sealing agent. As a result, the painting's colors began to fade just years after its completion. By the middle of the sixteenth century, it had seriously deteriorated. Large portions of it are now invisible.

both the harmony and the differences of Platonic and Aristotelian thought (see page 90). It also includes a number of Raphael's contemporaries as models. The image of Plato is actually a portrait of Leonardo, while the architect Donato Bramante (c. 1444–1514) stands in for the geometer Euclid, and Michelangelo for the philosopher Heraclitus.

Michelangelo Buonarroti (1475–1564), who spent many decades in Rome in the service of the papacy, was another native of Florence. Like Leonardo, he was a polymath: painter, sculptor, architect, poet—and he expressed himself in all these forms with a similar power. At the center of all of his work, as at the center of Renaissance humanism, is the male figure: the embodied masculine mind.

Michelangelo's greatest achievements in painting appear in a single location, the Sistine Chapel of the Vatican palace; yet they are products of two different periods in the artist's life and consequently exemplify two different artistic styles and outlooks on the human condition. More famous are the extraordinary frescoes painted on the ceiling from 1508 to 1512, depicting scenes from the book of Genesis. All the panels in this series, including *The Creation of Adam*, exemplify the young artist's affirm the heroic qualities of humankind. But a quarter of a century later, when Michelangelo returned to work in the Sistine Chapel, both his style and mood had changed dramatically. In the enormous *Last Judgment*, a fresco completed on the chapel's altar wall in 1536, Michelangelo repudiated classical restraint and substituted a style that emphasized tension and distortion: a humanity wracked with fear, guilt, and frailty. He included himself in it—painting a grotesque self-portrait on the flayed skin of Saint Bartholomew, who was martyred by being skinned alive. Perhaps this was a metaphor for the challenges of working for the papal court.

carrying this knowledge over to his paintings. In *The Last Supper*, painted on the refectory walls of a monastery in Milan (and now in an advanced state of decay), he also displayed his keen studies of human psychology. In this image, a serene Christ has just announced to his disciples that one will betray him. The artist captures the mingled emotions of surprise, horror, and guilt on their faces as they gradually perceive the meaning of this. He also implicates the painting's viewers in this dramatic scene, since they too dined with Christ, in the very same room.

Renaissance Arts in Venice and Rome

By the end of the fifteenth century, Florentine artists had influenced a group of painters active in the wealthy city of Venice. Among them was Tiziano Vecellio, better known as Titian (c. 1490–1576). Many of Titian's paintings evoke the luxurious, pleasure-loving life of this thriving commercial center; for although they copied Florentine techniques, most Venetian painters showed little of that city's concerns for philosophical or religious allegory. They catered to patrons who wanted sumptuous portraits of the rich and powerful (see the portrait on page 347).

Rome, too, became a major artistic center in this era and a place where the Florentine school exerted a more potent influence. Among its eminent painters was Raffaello Sanzio (1483–1520), or Raphael. As we noted in Chapter 4, his fresco *The School of Athens* depicts

Michelangelo and the Renaissance of Sculpture

Although sculpture was not a new medium for artists, as oil painting was, it too became an important area of Renaissance innovation. For the first time since late antiquity, monumental statues became figures "in the round" rather than sculptural elements incorporated into buildings or featured as effigies on tombs. By freeing sculpture from

SELF-PORTRAIT OF THE ARTIST AS A YOUNG MAN: DETAIL FROM *THE SCHOOL OF ATHENS*. We have already analyzed aspects of Raphael's famous group portrait of the Greek philosophers, with Plato and Aristotle at their center (see page 90). In addition to featuring his own contemporaries as models—including the artists Leonardo, Michelangelo, and the architect Bramante—Raphael put himself in the picture, too. ▪ *What messages does this choice convey?*

an agile adolescent rather than a muscular Greek athlete like that of Michelangelo's *David*, executed in 1501, as a public expression of Florentine civic life. Michelangelo regarded sculpture as the most exalted of the arts because it allowed the artist to imitate God most fully in re-creating human forms. He also insisted on working in marble—the "noblest" sculptural material—and on creating figures twice as large as life. By sculpting a serenely confident young man at the peak of physical fitness, Michelangelo celebrated the Florentine republic's own determination to resist tyrants and uphold ideals of civic justice.

Renaissance Architecture

To a much greater extent than either sculpture or painting, Renaissance architecture had its roots in the classical past. The Gothic style pioneered in northern France (see Chapter 9) had not found a welcome reception in Italy; most of the buildings constructed there were Romanesque ("Roman-like"), and the great architects influenced by the Renaissance movement generally adopted their building plans from these structures—some of which they believed (mistakenly) to be ancient. They also copied decorative devices from the authentic ruins of ancient Rome. Above all, they derived their influence from the writings of Vitruvius (fl. c. 60–15 B.C.E.), a Roman architect and engineer whose multivolume *On Architecture* was among the humanists' rediscovered ancient texts. The governing principles laid out by Vitruvius were popularized by Leon Battista Alberti in his own book, *On the Art of Building*, which began to circulate in manuscript around 1450.

In keeping with classical models, Renaissance buildings emphasized geometrical proportion. Architectural

its bondage to architecture, the Renaissance reestablished it as a separate art form.

The first great master of Renaissance sculpture was Donatello (c. 1386–1466). His bronze statue of David, triumphant over the head of the slain Goliath, is the first freestanding nude of the period. Yet this *David* is clearly

THE CREATION OF ADAM. This is one of a series of frescoes painted on the ceiling of the Sistine Chapel of the Vatican palace in Rome, executed by Michelangelo over a period of many years and in circumstances of extreme physical hardship. It has since become an iconic image. ▪ *How might it be said to capture Renaissance ideals?*

THE GRACE AND POWER OF THE MALE BODY. Donatello's *David* (left) was the first freestanding nude executed since antiquity. It shows the Hebrew leader as an adolescent youth and is a little over five feet tall. The *David* by Michelangelo (center) stands thirteen feet high and was placed prominently in front of Florence's city hall to proclaim the city's power and humanistic values. ▪ *How does Michelangelo's representation of David—and the context in which this figure was displayed—compare to that of Donatello?*

ST. PETER'S BASILICA, ROME. This eighteenth-century painting shows the massive interior of the Renaissance building. But were it not for the perspective provided by the tiny human figures, the human eye would be fooled into thinking this a much smaller space.

values were also reinforced by the interest in Platonic philosophy, which taught that certain mathematical ratios reflect the harmony of the universe. For example, the proportions of the human body serve as the basis for the proportions of the quintessential Renaissance building: St. Peter's Basilica in Rome. Designed by some of the most celebrated architects of the time, including Bramante and Michelangelo, it is still one of the largest buildings in the world. Yet it seems smaller than a Gothic cathedral because it is built to mimic human proportions. The same artful proportions are evident in smaller-scale buildings too, as in the aristocratic country houses later designed by the northern Italian architect Andrea Palladio (1508–1580), who created secular miniatures of ancient temples (such as the Roman Pantheon) to glorify the aristocrats who dwelled within them.

THE RENAISSANCE NORTH OF THE ALPS

Despite Italian resentment of encroaching foreign monarchs, contacts between Italy and northern Europe were close throughout this period. Italian merchants and financiers were familiar figures in northern courts and cities; students from all over Europe studied at Italian universities such as Bologna or Padua; northern poets (including Geoffrey Chaucer: see Chapter 11) and their works traveled to and from Italy; and northern soldiers were frequent combattants in Italian wars. Yet only at the very end of the fifteenth century did the innovative artistry and learning of Italy begin to cross the Alps into northern Europe.

A variety of explanations have been offered for this delay. Northern European intellectual life in the later Middle Ages was dominated by universities in Paris, Oxford, Kraków, and Prague, where the curricula focused on the study of philosophical logic, Christian theology, and (to a lesser extent) medicine. In Italy, by contrast, universities were more often professional schools specializing in law and medicine and were more integrally tied to the nonacademic intellectual lives of the cities in which they were situated. As a result, a more secular, urban-oriented educational tradition took shape in Italy, as we saw in our previous discussion of humanism. In northern Europe, by contrast, those scholars who *were* influenced by Italian ideas usually worked outside the university system under the private patronage of kings and princes.

Past and Present

The Reputation of Richard III

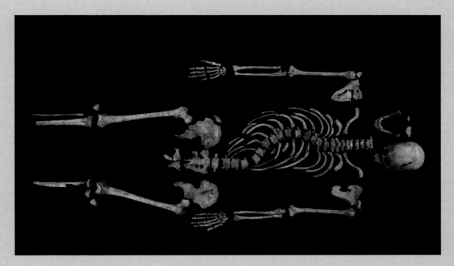

England's king Richard III (r. 1483–1485) has been a byword for villainy since the time of his death, when Sir Thomas More and other propagandists working for his successor, Henry VII, alleged that his physically deformed body was matched by the depravity of his actions. For centuries, historians have debated the truth of these claims. Was Richard really a hunchback—and a murderer, too? In 2012, the stunning discovery of Richard's body (under a parking lot near the medieval battlefield where he died) confirmed that he had indeed suffered from severe scoliosis. The other claim has yet to be proven.

Watch related author videos on the Student Site
wwnorton.com/college/history/western-civilizationsBrief4

Before the turn of the sixteenth century, northern rulers were also less committed to patronizing artists and intellectuals than were the city-states and princes of Italy. In Italy, as we have seen, such patronage was an important arena for competition between political rivals. In northern Europe, however, political units were larger and political rivals were fewer. It was therefore less necessary to use art for political purposes—a major exception being the independent duchy of Burgundy, which surpassed even the French court in its magnificence. A statue erected in a central square of Florence would be seen by all the city's residents and visitors. In Paris, such a statue would be seen by only a tiny minority of the French king's subjects. But as royal courts became showcases for royal power, kings needed to impress townspeople, courtiers, and guests—and they consequently relied more on artists and intellectuals to advertise their wealth and taste.

Christian Humanism and the Career of Erasmus

In general, then, the Renaissance movement of northern Europe differed from that of Italy because it grafted certain Italian ideals onto preexisting traditions, rather than sweeping away older forms of knowledge. This can be seen very clearly in the case of the intellectual development known as Christian humanism. Although Christian humanists shared the Italian humanists' scorn for scholasticism's limitations, northern humanists were more committed to seeking ethical guidance from biblical and religious precepts, as well as from Cicero or Virgil. Like their Italian counterparts, they embraced the wisdom of antiquity, but the antiquity they favored was Christian as well as classical—the antiquity of the New Testament and the early Church. Similarly, northern artists were inspired by the accomplishments of Italian masters and copied their techniques, but they depicted classical subjects less frequently and almost never portrayed completely nude human figures.

Any discussion of Christian humanism must begin with the career of Desiderius Erasmus (c. 1469–1536). The illegitimate son of a priest, Erasmus was born near Rotterdam in the Netherlands. Forced into a monastery against his will when he was a teenager, the young Erasmus found little formal instruction there—but plenty of freedom to read what he liked. He devoured all the classics he could get his hands on, alongside the writings of the church fathers (see Chapter 6). When he was about thirty years old, he obtained permission to leave the monastery and enroll in the University of Paris, where he completed the requirements for a bachelor's degree in theology.

***ERASMUS* BY HANS HOLBEIN THE YOUNGER.** This is generally regarded as the most evocative portrait of the preeminent Christian humanist.

But Erasmus subsequently rebelled against what he considered the arid learning of Parisian academe. Nor did he ever serve actively as a priest. Instead, he made his living from teaching and writing. Ever on the lookout for new patrons, he traveled often to England, stayed for three years in Italy, and resided in several different cities in Germany and the Low Countries before settling finally, toward the end of his life, in Basel (Switzerland). By means of a voluminous correspondence with learned friends, Erasmus became the leader of a humanist coterie.

As a Latin prose stylist, Erasmus was unequaled since the days of Cicero. Extraordinarily eloquent and witty, he reveled in tailoring his mode of discourse to fit his subject, creating dazzling verbal effects and coining puns that took on added meaning if the reader knew Greek as well as Latin. Above all, Erasmus excelled in the deft use of irony, poking fun at everything, including himself. But although Erasmus's urbane Latin style and humor earned him a wide audience on those grounds alone, he intended everything he wrote to promote what he called the "philosophy of Christ." Accordingly, he offered his contemporaries three different kinds of writings: clever satires in which people could recognize their own foibles, serious moral treatises meant to offer guidance toward proper Christian behavior, and scholarly editions of basic Christian texts.

In the first category belong the works of Erasmus that are still widely read today: *The Praise of Folly* (1509), in which he ridiculed pedantry and dogmatism, ignorance and gullibility—even within the Church; and the *Colloquies* (1518), in which he held up contemporary religious practices for examination, couching a serious message in a playful tone. In these books, Erasmus let fictional characters do the talking so his own views on any given topic can only be determined by inference. But in his second mode, Erasmus spoke clearly in his own voice. In the *Handbook of the Christian Knight* (1503), he used the popular language of chivalry as a means to encourage a life of inward piety; in the *Complaint of Peace* (1517), he argued movingly for Christian pacifism. Erasmus's pacifism was one of his most deeply held values, and he returned to it again and again in his published works.

But Erasmus considered textual scholarship his greatest achievement. Revering the authority of the earliest church fathers, he brought out reliable printed editions of works by Saints Augustine, Jerome, and Ambrose (see Chapter 6). He also used his extraordinary command of Latin and Greek to produce a more accurate edition of the New Testament. Erasmus became convinced that nothing was more imperative than divesting the Christian scriptures of myriad errors in transcription and translation that had piled up over the course of preceding centuries. He therefore spent ten years comparing all the early Greek biblical manuscripts he could find in order to establish an authoritative text. When it finally appeared in 1516, Erasmus's Greek New Testament, published together with explanatory notes and his own new Latin translation, became one of the most important scholarly landmarks of all time.

The Influence of Erasmus

One of Erasmus's closest friends was the Englishman Sir Thomas More (1478–1535). In later life, following a successful career as a lawyer and politician, More was appointed lord chancellor of England in 1529. He was not long in this position, however, before he opposed King Henry VIII's plan to establish a national church under royal control that would deny the supremacy of the pope; see Chapter 13. Much earlier, however, in 1516, More published his most famous book, *Utopia* ("*No Place*").

Purporting to describe an ideal community on an imaginary island, *Utopia* is really an Erasmian critique of its own time: disparities between poverty and wealth, heresy, and war's senseless slaughter. In contrast to Europeans, the inhabitants of the fictional Utopia hold all their goods in common, work only six hours a day (so that all may have leisure for intellectual pursuits), and practice the virtues of moderation, fortitude, and justice.

Erasmus and More head a long list of energetic and eloquent northern humanists who made signal contributions to the collective enterprise of revolutionizing the study of early Christianity, and their achievements had a direct influence on Protestant reformers—as we shall see in the next chapter. Yet very few of them were willing to join Luther and other Protestant leaders in rejecting the fundamental principles on which the power of the Roman Church was based. Most tried to remain within its fold while espousing an ideal of inward piety and scholarly inquiry. But as the leaders of the Church grew less and less tolerant, even mild criticism came to seem like heresy. Erasmus himself died early enough to escape persecution, but several of his followers did not.

The Literature of the Northern Renaissance

Although Christian humanism would be severely challenged by the Reformation, the artistic Renaissance in the north would flourish. Poets in France and England vied with one another to adapt the elegant lyric forms pioneered by Petrarch (Chapter 11) and popularized by many subsequent poets, including Michelangelo. The sonnet was particularly influential and would become one of the verse forms embraced by William Shakespeare (1554–1616; see chapter 14). Another English poet, Edmund Spenser (c. 1552–1599), drew on the literary innovation of Ariosto's *Orlando Furioso*; his *Faerie Queene* is a similarly long chivalric romance that revels in sensuous imagery. Meanwhile, the more satirical side of Renaissance humanism was embraced by the French writer François Rabelais (*RAH-beh-lay*, c. 1494–1553).

Like Erasmus, whom he greatly admired, Rabelais began his career in the Church; but he soon left the cloister to study medicine. A practicing physician, Rabelais interspersed his professional activities with literary endeavors, the most enduring of which are the twin books *Gargantua* and *Pantagruel*, a series of "chronicles" describing the lives and times of giants whose fabulous size and gross appetites serve as vehicles for much lusty humor. Also like Erasmus, Rabelais satirized religious hypocrisy, scholasticism, superstition, and bigotry. But unlike Erasmus, who wrote in a highly cultivated classical Latin style, Rabelais chose to address a different audience by writing in extremely crude French and by glorifying every human appetite as natural and healthy.

Northern Architecture and Art

Although many architects in northern Europe continued to build in the flamboyant Gothic style of the later Middle Ages, the classical values of Italian architects can be seen in some of the splendid new castles constructed in France's Loire valley—*châteaux* too elegant to be defensible—and in the royal palace (now museum) of the Louvre in Paris, which replaced an old twelfth-century fortress. The influence of Renaissance ideals are also visible in the work of the German artist Albrecht Dürer (*DIRR-er*, 1471–1528). Dürer was the first northerner to master the techniques of proportion and perspective, and he shared with contemporary Italians a fascination with nature and the human body. He also took advantage of the printing press to circulate his work to a wide audience, making his delicate pencil drawings into engravings that could be mass produced.

But Dürer never really embraced classical subjects, drawing inspiration instead from more-traditional Christian legends and from the Christian humanism of

SAINT JEROME IN HIS STUDY BY DÜRER. Jerome, the biblical translator of the fourth century (see Chapter 6), was a hero to both Dürer and Erasmus: the paragon of inspired Christian scholarship. Note how the scene exudes contentment, even down to the sleeping lion, which seems more like an overgrown tabby cat than a symbol of Christ.

Erasmus. For example, Dürer's serenely radiant engraving of Saint Jerome seems to express the scholarly absorption that Erasmus would have enjoyed while working quietly in his study.

Tradition and Innovation in Music

Like the visual arts, the gorgeous music produced during this era was nourished by patrons' desire to surround themselves with beauty. Yet unlike painting and sculpture, musical practice did not reach back to classical antiquity but drew instead on well-established medieval conventions. Even before the Black Death, a musical movement called *ars nova* ("new art") was flourishing in France, and it had spread to Italy during the lifetime of Petrarch. Its outstanding composers had been Guillaume de Machaut (c. 1300–1377) and Francesco Landini (c. 1325–1397).

The madrigals (part-songs) and ballads composed by these musicians and their successors expanded on earlier genres of secular music, but their greatest achievement was a highly complicated yet delicate contrapuntal style adapted for the liturgy of the Church. Machaut was the first-known composer to provide a polyphonic (harmonized) version of the major sections of the Mass. In the fifteenth century, the dissemination of this new musical aesthetic combined with a host of French, Flemish, and Italian elements in the multicultural courts of Europe, particularly that of Burgundy. By the beginning of the sixteenth century, Franco-Flemish composers came to dominate many important courts and cathedrals, creating a variety of new forms and styles that bear a close affinity to Renaissance art and poetry.

Throughout Europe, the general level of musical proficiency in this era was very high. The singing of part-songs was a popular pastime in homes and at social gatherings, and the ability to sight-read a part was expected of the educated elite. Aristocratic women, in particular, were expected to display mastery of the new musical instruments that had been developed to add nuance and texture to existing musical forms, including the lute, the violin, and a variety of woodwind and keyboard instruments like the harpsichord.

Although most composers of this period were men trained in the service of the Church, they rarely made sharp distinctions between sacred and secular music. Like sculpture, music was coming into its own as a serious independent art. As such, it would become an important medium for the expression of both Catholic and Protestant ideals during the Reformation.

THE POLITICS OF CHRISTIAN EUROPE

We have already observed how the intellectual and artistic activity of the Renaissance movement was fueled by the political developments of the time—within Italy and throughout Europe. In 1453 France had emerged victorious in the Hundred Years' War, while England plunged into a further three decades of bloody civil conflict that touched every corner of that kingdom. The French monarchy was therefore able to rebuild its power and prestige while at the same time extending its control over regions that had long been controlled by the English crown. In 1494, the French king Charles VIII acted on a plan to expand his reach even further, into Italy. Leading an army of 30,000 well-trained troops across the Alps, he intended to claim the duchy of Milan and the kingdom of Naples. This effort solidified

Italian opposition to French occupation, as we noted above in our discussion of Machiavelli.

The rulers of Spain, whose territorial claims on Sicily also extended to Naples, were spurred by this French challenge to forge an uneasy alliance among the Papal States, some principalities of the Holy Roman Empire, Milan, and Venice. But the respite was brief. Charles's successor, Louis XII, launched a second invasion in 1499. For over a generation, until 1529, warfare in Italy was virtually uninterrupted. Alliances and counteralliances among city-states became further catalysts for violence and made Italy a magnet for mercenaries who could barely be kept in check by the generals who employed them.

Meanwhile, northern Italian city-states' virtual monopoly of trade with Asia, which had been one of the chief economic underpinnings of artistic and intellectual patronage, was being gradually eroded by the shifting of trade routes from the Mediterranean to the Atlantic (Chapters 10 and 11). It was also hampered by the increasing power of the Ottoman Empire, and even by the imperial pretensions of a new Russian ruler.

The Imperial Power of Ivan the Great

In previous chapters, we noted that the duchy of Muscovy had become the champion of the Orthodox Church. After the fall of Constantinople to the Ottomans, the Muscovite grand duke even assumed the imperial title *tsar* (caesar) and borrowed the Byzantine ideology of the ruler's divine election. These claims would eventually undergird the sacred position later ascribed to the tsars. But ideology alone could not have built a Muscovite empire. Behind its growth lay the steadily growing power of its rulers, especially that of Grand Duke Ivan III (1462–1505), known as Ivan the Great, the first to lay down a distinctive imperial agenda.

Ivan launched a series of conquests that annexed all the independent principalities lying between Moscow and the border of Poland-Lithuania. After invading Lithuania in 1492 and 1501, Ivan even succeeded in bringing parts of that domain (portions of modern Belarus and Ukraine) under his control. Meanwhile, he married the niece of the last Byzantine emperor, giving substance to the claim that Muscovy was "New Rome." He also rebuilt his fortified Moscow residence, known as the Kremlin, in magnificent Italianate style. He would later adopt, as his imperial insignia, the double-headed eagle of Rome and its legions. By the time of his death in 1505, Muscovy was firmly established as a dominant power. Indeed, the power of the tsar was more absolute in this period than was that of any European monarch.

Papal Politics and the Growth of National Churches

As Muscovy laid claim to the mantle of Roman imperial power, the papacy was pouring resources into the glorification of the original Rome and the aggrandizement of the papal office. But neither the city nor its rulers could keep pace with their political and religious rivals. Following the Council of Constance (see Chapter 11), the papacy's victory over the conciliarists proved to be a costly one. To win the support of Europe's kings and princes, various popes negotiated a series of religious treaties known as "concordats," which granted these rulers extensive authority over churches within their domains. The papacy thus secured its theoretical supremacy at the expense of its real power. For under the terms of these concordats, kings now received many of the revenues that had previously gone to the papacy. They also acquired new powers to appoint candidates to church offices. It was, in many ways, a drastic reversal of the hard-won reforms of the eleventh and twelfth centuries that had created such a powerful papacy in the first place.

Having given away so many sources of revenue and authority, the popes of the late fifteenth century became even more dependent on their own territories in central Italy. But to tighten their hold on the Papal States, they had to rule like other Italian princes: leading armies, jockeying for alliances, and undermining their opponents by every possible means—including covert operations, murder, and assassination. Judged by the secular standards of the day, these efforts paid off: the Papal States became one of the better-governed and wealthier principalities in Italy. But such methods did nothing to increase the popes' reputation for piety, and disillusionment with the papacy as a force for the advancement of spirituality became even more widespread.

With both papal authority and Rome's spiritual prestige in decline, kings and princes became the primary figures to whom both clergy and laity looked for religious and moral guidance. Many secular rulers responded to such expectations aggressively, closing scandal-ridden monasteries, suppressing alleged heretics, and regulating vice. By these and other such measures, rulers could present themselves as champions of moral reform while also strengthening their political power. The result was an increasingly close link between national monarchies and national churches, a link that would become even stronger after the Reformation.

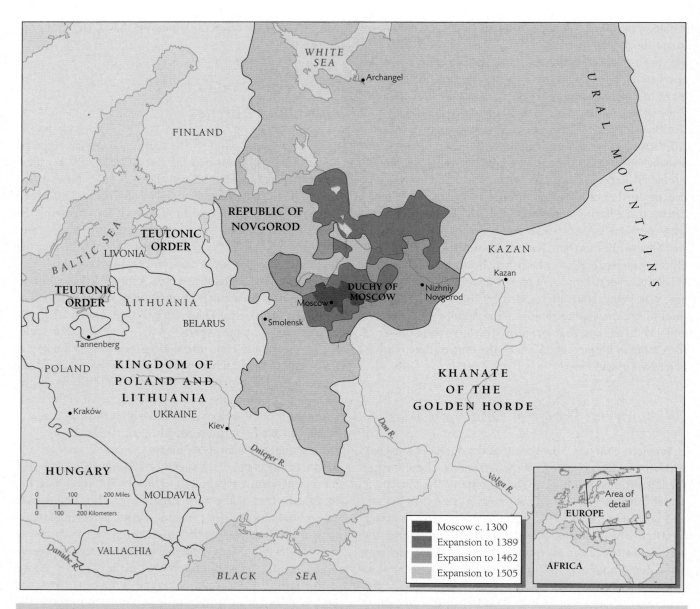

THE EXPANSION OF MUSCOVITE RUSSIA TO 1505. The grand duchy of Moscow was the heart of what would become a Russian empire. ▪ *With what other empires and polities did the Muscovites have to compete during this period of expansion?* ▪ *How did the relative isolation of Moscow, compared with early Kiev, allow for the growth of Muscovite power, on the one hand, and Moscow's distinctively non-Western culture, on the other?* ▪ *How might the natural direction of the expansion of Muscovite power until 1505 help to encourage attitudes often at odds with those of western European civilization?*

The Triumph of the "Reconquista"

The kingdoms of the Iberian Peninsula were also in constant conflict during this period. In Castile, civil war and incompetent governance allowed the Castilian nobility to gain greater control over the peasantry and greater independence from the monarchy. In Aragon, royal government benefited from the extended commercial influence of Catalonia, which was under Aragonese authority.

But after 1458, Aragon too became enmeshed in a civil war, a war in which both France and Castile were involved.

A solution to the disputed succession that had caused the war in Aragon would ultimately lie in the blending of powerful royal families. In 1469, Prince Ferdinand of Aragon was recognized as the heir to that throne and, in the same year, secured this position by marrying Isabella, the heiress to Castile. Isabella became a queen in 1474,

FERDINAND AND ISABELLA HONORING THE VIRGIN. In this Spanish painting, the royal couple are shown with two of their children and two household chaplains and in the company of the Blessed Virgin, the Christ Child, and saints from the Dominican order (the Dominicans were instrumental in conducting the affairs of the Spanish Inquisition). ▪ *How clear is the distinction between these holy figures and the royal family?* ▪ *What message is conveyed by their proximity?*

Ferdinand a king in 1479; and although Castile and Aragon continued to be ruled as separate kingdoms until 1714—there are tensions between the two former kingdoms even now—the marriage of Ferdinand and Isabella enabled the pursuit of several ambitious policies. In particular, their union allowed them to spend their combined resources on the creation of Europe's most powerful army, which was initially employed to conquer the last remaining principality of what had been al-Andalus: Muslim Spain. That principality, Granada, fell in 1492.

The End of the Convivencia and the Expulsion of the Jews

For more than seven centuries, Spain's Jewish communities had enjoyed the many privileges extended by their Muslim rulers, who were also relatively tolerant of their Christian subjects. Indeed, scholars often refer to this period of Spain's history as a time of *convivencia*—"living together" or "harmonious coexistence." While relations among various religious and ethnic groups were not always peaceful or positive, the policies of Muslim rulers in al-Andalus had enabled an extraordinary hybrid culture to flourish there.

The aims of the Spanish Reconquista were diametrically opposed to those of "living together." The crusading ideology of "reconquest" sought instead to forge a single, homogeneous community, based on the fiction that Spain had once been entirely Christian and should be restored to its former purity. The year 1492 therefore marks not only the end of Muslim rule in medieval Spain but also the culmination of a process of Jewish exclusion that had accelerated in western Europe (see Chapter 9). Within this history, the Spanish expulsion of the Jews stands out for the staggering scope of the displacements and destruction it entailed: at least 100,000 and possibly as many as 200,000 men, women, and children were deprived of their homes and livelihoods.

The Christian monarchs' motives for ordering this expulsion are still debated. Tens of thousands of Spanish Jews had converted to Christianity between 1391 and 1420, many as a result of coercion but some from sincere conviction. And for a generation or so, it seemed possible that these converts, known as *conversos*, might successfully assimilate into Christian society. But the same civil wars that led to the union of Ferdinand and Isabella made the *conversos* targets of discriminatory legislation. Conflict may also have fueled popular suspicions that these converts remained Jews in secret. To make "proper" Christians out of the *conversos*, the "Most Catholic" monarchs—as they were now called—may have concluded that they needed to remove any potentially seditious influences.

What became of the Spanish Jews? Some traveled north, to the Rhineland towns of Germany or to Poland, but most settled in Muslim regions of the Mediterranean and North Africa. Many found a haven in the Ottoman Empire. As we already noted, there were many opportunities for advancement in the Ottoman imperial bureaucracy, while the Ottoman economy benefited from the highly skilled labor of Jewish artisans and the intricate trading networks of Jewish merchants. In time, new forms and expressions of Jewish culture would emerge, and new communities would form. And although the extraordinary opportunities afforded by the *convivencia* could never be revived, the descendants of these Spanish Jews—known as Sephardic Jews, or Sephardim—still treasure the traditions and customs formed in Spain over a thousand years ago.

The Extension of the Reconquista

The victory over the Muslims of Granada and the expulsion of the Jews in 1492 were watershed events. They mark the beginning of a sweeping initiative to construct a new basis for the precariously united kingdoms of Aragon and Castile, one that could transcend rival regional affinities. Like other contemporary monarchs, Ferdinand and Isabella sought to strengthen their emerging nation-state by constructing an exclusively Christian identity for its people and by attaching that new identity to the crown and promoting a single national language, Castilian Spanish. They also succeeded in capturing and redirecting another language: the rhetoric of crusade.

The problem with the crusading ethos, as we have seen, is that it always seeks new outlets. Having created a new exclusively Christian Spanish kingdom through the defeat of all external enemies and internal threats, where were the energies harnessed by the Reconquista to be directed? The answer came from an unexpected quarter and had very unexpected consequences. Just a few months after Ferdinand and Isabella marched victoriously into Granada, the queen granted three ships to a Genoese adventurer who promised to reach India by sailing westward across the Atlantic Ocean, claiming any new lands he found for Spain. Columbus never reached India, but he did help to extend the tradition of reconquest to the New World—with far-reaching consequences.

NEW TARGETS AND TECHNOLOGIES OF CONQUEST

The Spanish monarchs' decision to underwrite a voyage of exploration was spurred by their desire to counter the successful Portuguese ventures of the past half century. For it was becoming clear that a tiny kingdom on the southwestern tip of the Iberian Peninsula would soon dominate the sea-lanes if rival entrepreneurs did not find alternate routes and establish equally lucrative colonies. This competition with its Iberian neighbor, Portugal, was another reason why Isabella turned to a Genoese sea captain—not to a Portuguese one.

Prince Henry the Navigator and Portuguese Colonial Initiatives

Although Portugal had been an independent Christian kingdom since the twelfth century (see Chapter 9), it was never able to compete effectively with its more powerful neighbors (Muslim or Christian) on land. But when the focus of European economic expansion began to shift toward the Atlantic (Chapter 10), Portuguese mariners were well placed to take advantage of the trend. A central figure in the history of Portuguese maritime imperialism is Prince Henry, later called "the Navigator" (1394–1460), a son of King João I of Portugal and his English queen, Philippa (sister of England's Henry IV).

Prince Henry was fascinated by the sciences of cartography and navigation, and he helped to ensure that Portuguese sailors had access to the latest charts and navigational instruments. He was also inspired by the stories told by John de Mandeville and Marco Polo (see Chapter 10)—particularly the legend of Prester John, a mythical Christian king dwelling somewhere at the end of the earth. More concretely, Prince Henry had ambitions to extend Portuguese control into the Atlantic, to tap into the burgeoning market for slaves in the Ottoman Empire and to establish direct links with sources of African gold.

Prince Henry played an important part in organizing the Portuguese colonization of Madeira, the Canary Islands, and the Azores—and in the process he pioneered the Portuguese slave trade, which almost entirely eradicated the population of the Canaries before targeting Africa. By the 1440s, Portuguese explorers had reached the Cape Verde Islands. In 1444, they landed on the African mainland in the area that became known as the Gold Coast, where they began to collect cargoes of gold and slaves for export back to Portugal. And in order to outflank the cross-Saharan gold trade, largely controlled by the Muslims of North Africa and mediated by the Genoese, Prince Henry decided to intercept this trade at its source by building a series of forts along the African coastline. This was also his main reason for colonizing the Canary Islands, which he saw as a staging ground for expeditions into the African interior.

From Africa to India and Beyond: An Empire of Spices

By the 1470s, Portuguese sailors had rounded the western coast of Africa and were exploring the Gulf of Guinea. In 1483, they reached the mouth of the Congo River. In 1488, the Portuguese captain Bartholomeu Dias was accidentally blown around the southern tip of Africa by a gale, after which he named the point "Cape of Storms." But King João II (r. 1481–95) took a more optimistic view of Dias's achievement: he renamed it the Cape of Good Hope and

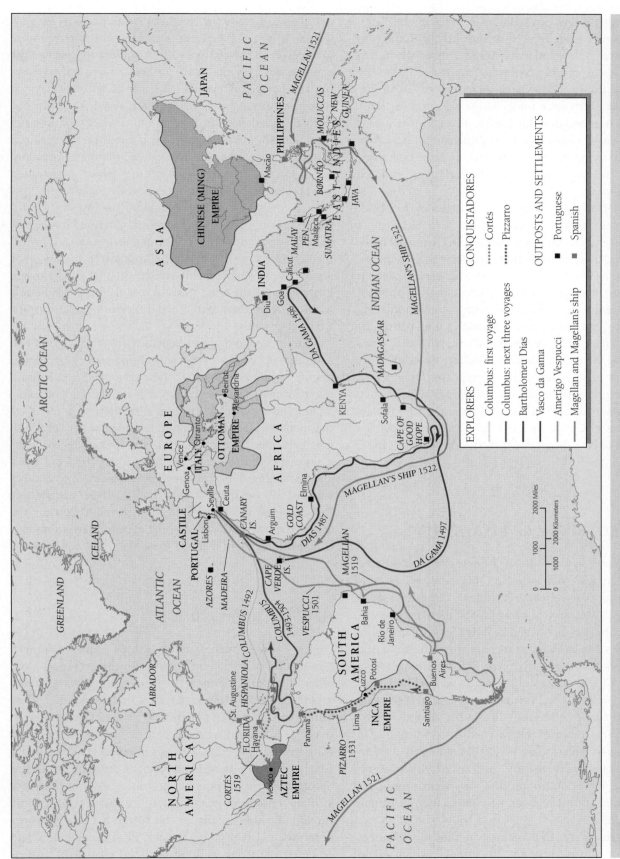

OVERSEAS EXPLORATION IN THE FIFTEENTH AND SIXTEENTH CENTURIES. ▪ *What were the major routes taken by European explorers of the fifteenth and sixteenth centuries?* ▪ *What appear to be the explorers' main goals?* ▪ *How might the establishment of outposts in Africa, America, and the East Indies have radically altered the balance of power in the Old World, and why?*

began planning a naval expedition to India. In 1497–98, Vasco da Gama rounded the cape, and then, with the help of a Muslim navigator named Ibn Majid, crossed the Indian Ocean to Calicut, on the southwestern coast of India. For the first time, this opened a viable sea route between Europe and the Far Eastern spice trade. Although Vasco da Gama lost half his fleet and one-third of his men on his two-year voyage, his cargo of spices was so valuable that his losses were deemed insignificant. His heroism became legendary, and his story became the basis for the Portuguese national epic, the *Lusiads*.

As masters of the quickest route to riches in the world, the Portuguese swiftly capitalized on their decades of accomplishment. Not only did their trading fleets sail regularly to India, there were Portuguese efforts to monopolize the entire spice trade: in 1509, the Portuguese defeated an Ottoman fleet and then blockaded the mouth of the Red Sea, attempting to cut off one of the traditional routes by which spices had traveled to Alexandria and Beirut. By 1510, Portuguese military forces had established a series of forts along the western Indian coastline, including their headquarters at Goa. In 1511, Portuguese ships seized Malacca, a center of the spice trade on the Malay Peninsula. By 1515, they had reached the Spice Islands (East Indies) and the coast of China. By the 1520s, even the Venetians were forced to buy their pepper in the Portuguese capital of Lisbon.

Naval Technology and Navigation

The Portuguese caravel—the workhorse ship of those first voyages to Africa—was based on ship and sail designs that had been in use among Portuguese fishermen since the thirteenth century. Starting in the 1440s, however, Portuguese shipwrights began building larger caravels of about 50 tons displacement and equipped with two masts, each carrying a triangular (lateen) sail. Columbus's *Niña* was a ship of this design, although it was refitted with two square sails in the Portuguese-held Canary Islands to help it sail more efficiently during the Atlantic crossing. Such ships required much smaller crews than did the multi-oared galleys that were still commonly used in the Mediterranean. By the end of the fifteenth century, still larger caravels of around 200 tons were being constructed, with a third mast and a combination of square and lateen sails.

Europeans were also making significant advances in navigation during this era. Quadrants, which could calculate latitude in the Northern Hemisphere by measuring the height of the North Star above the horizon, were in widespread use by the 1450s. As sailors approached the equator, however, the quadrant became less and less useful, and navigators instead made use of astrolabes, which reckoned latitude by the height of the sun. Like quadrants, astrolabes had been in use for centuries. But it was not until the 1480s that the astrolabe became a really practical instrument for seaborne navigation, thanks to standard tables for the calculation of latitude whose preparation was sponsored by the Portuguese crown. Compasses, too, were coming into more widespread use during the fifteenth century. Longitude, however, remained impossible to calculate accurately until the eighteenth century, when the invention of the marine chronometer finally made it possible to keep time at sea. In this age of discovery, Europeans sailing east or west across the oceans generally had to rely on their skill at dead reckoning to determine where they were.

European sailors also benefited from new maps and navigational charts. Especially important were books known as *rutters* or *routiers*. These contained detailed sailing instructions and descriptions of the coastal landmarks a pilot could expect to encounter en route to a variety of destinations. Mediterranean sailors had used similar portolan charts since the thirteenth century, mapping the ports along the coastlines, tracking prevailing winds and tides, and indicating dangerous reefs and shallow harbors (see Chapter 10). In the fifteenth century, these mapmaking techniques were extended to the Atlantic Ocean; by the end of the sixteenth century, the accumulated knowledge contained in rutters spanned the globe.

Artillery and Empire

Larger, more maneuverable ships and improved navigational aids made it possible for the Portuguese and other European mariners to reach Africa, Asia, and—eventually—the Americas. But fundamentally, these European commercial empires were military achievements that capitalized on what Europeans had learned in their wars against each other. Perhaps the most critical military advance was the increasing sophistication of artillery, a development made possible not only by gunpowder but also by improved metallurgical techniques for casting cannon. By the middle of the fifteenth century, as we observed in Chapter 11, the use of artillery pieces had rendered the stone walls of medieval castles and towns obsolete, a fact brought home in 1453 by the successful French siege of Bordeaux (which ended the Hundred Years' War), and by the Ottoman siege of Constantinople (which ended the Byzantine Empire).

The new ship designs were important in part because their larger size made it possible to mount more-effective weaponry. European vessels were now conceived as floating artillery platforms, with scores of guns mounted in fixed positions along their sides and swivel guns mounted fore and aft. These guns were vastly expensive, as were the ships that carried them. For those rulers who could afford them, such ships made it possible to back mercantile ventures with military power: Vasco da Gama had been able to sail into the Indian Ocean in 1498, but the Portuguese did not gain control of that ocean until 1509, when they defeated combined Ottoman and Indian naval forces. Portuguese trading outposts in Africa and Asia were essentially fortifications, built not so much to guard against the attacks of native peoples as to ward off assaults from other Europeans. Without this essential military component, the European maritime empires that were emerging in this period could not have existed.

Atlantic Colonization and a New Regime of Slavery

Although slavery had effectively disappeared in much of northern Europe by the early twelfth century, it continued in parts of the Mediterranean world. But this slavery existed on a very small scale. There were no slave-powered factories or large-scale agricultural systems in this period. The only major slave markets and slave economies were in the Ottoman Empire, and there slaves ran the vast Ottoman bureaucracy and staffed the army. And in all these cases, as in antiquity, no aspect of slavery was racially based. In Italy and elsewhere in the medieval Mediterranean, slaves were often captives from an array of locales. In eastern Europe, they were functionally serfs. Most Ottoman slaves were European Christians, predominantly Poles, Ukrainians, Greeks, and Bulgarians. In the early Middle Ages, Germanic and Celtic peoples had been widely enslaved. Under the Roman Empire, slaves had come from every part of the known (and unknown) world.

What was new about the slavery of the late fifteenth century was its increasing racialization—an aspect of modern slavery that has made an indelible impact on our own society. To Europeans, African slaves were visible in ways that other slaves were not, and it became convenient for those who dealt in them to justify the mass deportation of entire populations by claiming their racial inferiority and their "natural" fitness for a life of bondage.

In Lisbon, which became a significant market for enslaved Africans during Prince Henry's lifetime, something on the order of 15,000 to 20,000 African captives were sold within a twenty-year period. In the following half century, by about 1505, the numbers amounted to 150,000. For the most part, the purchasers of these slaves regarded them as status symbols; it became fashionable to have African footmen, page boys, and ladies' maids. In the Atlantic colonies—Madeira, the Canaries, and the Azores—land was still worked mainly by European settlers and sharecroppers. Slave labor, if it was employed at all, was generally used only in sugar mills. But even sugar production did not lead to the widespread introduction of slavery on these islands.

However, a new kind of slave-based sugar plantation began to emerge in Portugal's eastern Atlantic colonies in the 1460s, starting on the Cape Verde Islands and then extending southward into the Gulf of Guinea. These islands were not populated when the Portuguese began to settle them, and their climate generally discouraged most Europeans from living there. They were ideally located, however, along the routes of slave traders venturing outward from the nearby West African coast. It was this plantation model that would be exported to Brazil by the Portuguese and to the Caribbean islands of the Americas by their Spanish conquerors, with incalculable consequences for the peoples of Africa, the Americas, and Europe (see Chapter 14).

EUROPEANS IN A NEW WORLD

Like his contemporaries, Christopher Columbus (1451–1506) understood that the world was a sphere. But he also thought it was much smaller than it actually is. It had long been accepted that there were only three continents: Europe, Asia, and Africa—hence Columbus's decision to reach Asia by sailing west, a plan that seemed even more plausible after the discovery and colonization of the Canary Islands and the Azores. The existence of these islands reinforced a new hypothesis that the Atlantic was dotted with similar lands all the way to Japan. This emboldened Columbus's royal patrons, who became convinced that the Genoese mariner could reach China in about a month, after a stop for provisions in the Canaries.

This turned out to be a kind of self-fulfilling prophecy, for when Columbus reached the Bahamas and the island of Hispaniola after only a month's sailing, he reported that he had reached the outer islands of Asia.

The Shock of Discovery

Of course, Columbus was not the first European to set foot on the American continents. As we have already learned, Viking sailors briefly settled present-day Newfoundland and Labrador around the year 1000 (see Chapter 8). But knowledge of Viking explorations had been forgotten or ignored outside of Iceland for hundreds of years. It wasn't until the 1960s that the stories of these expeditions were corroborated by archaeological evidence. Moreover, the tiny Norwegian colony on Greenland—technically part of the North American landmass—had been abandoned in the fifteenth century, when the cooling of the climate (Chapter 10) destroyed the fragile ecosystems that had barely sustained the lives of Norse settlers there.

Although Columbus brought back no spices to prove that he had found an alternate route to Asia, he did return with some small samples of gold and a few indigenous people—whose existence gave promise of entire tribes that might be "saved" by conversion to Christianity and whose lands could provide homes for Spanish settlers seeking new frontiers after the Reconquista. This provided sufficient incentive for the "Most Catholic" monarchs to finance three further expeditions by Columbus.

Meanwhile, the Portuguese, who had already obtained a papal charter granting them (hypothetical) ownership of all lands south of the Canaries, rushed to establish their own claims. After two years of wrangling and conflicting papal pronouncements, the Treaty of Tordesillas (1494) sought to demarcate Spanish and Portuguese possession of as-yet-undiscovered lands by dividing the globe longitudinally. The Spanish would ultimately emerge as the big winners in this gambling match: within a decade, the coasts of two hitherto unknown continents were identified, as were clusters of new islands, most on the Spanish side of the (disputed) meridian.

Gradually, Europeans reached the conclusion that the voyages of Columbus and his immediate successors had revealed an entirely "New World." And—shockingly—this world had not been foretold either by the teachings of Christianity or the wisdom of the ancients. Among the first to champion the fact of two new continents' existence was the Italian explorer and geographer Amerigo Vespucci (1454–1512), whose name was soon adopted as a descriptor for them. Eventually, those who came to accept this fact were forced to question the reliability of the key sources of knowledge on which Western civilizations had hitherto hinged (see Chapter 14).

At first, the realization that the Americas were not an outpost of Asia came as a disappointment to the Spanish: two major land masses and two vast oceans disrupted their plans to beat the Portuguese to the Spice Islands. But new possibilities gradually became clear. In 1513, the Spanish explorer Vasco Núñez de Balboa first viewed the Pacific Ocean from the Isthmus of Panama, and news of the narrow divide between two vast oceans prompted Ferdinand and Isabella's grandson to renew their dream. This young monarch, Charles V (1500–1556), ruled not only Spain but the huge patchwork of territories encompassed by the Holy Roman Empire (see Chapter 13). In 1519, he accepted Ferdinand Magellan's proposal to see whether a route to Asia could be found by sailing around South America.

Magellan's voyage demonstrated beyond question that the world was simply too large for any such plan to be feasible at that time. Of the five ships that left Spain under his command, only one returned, three years later, having been forced to circumnavigate the globe. Out of a crew of 265 sailors, only 18 survived. Most had died of scurvy or starvation; Magellan himself had been killed in a skirmish with native peoples in the Philippines.

This fiasco ended all hope of discovering an easy southwest passage to Asia—although the deadly dream of a northwest passage survived and motivated many European explorers of North America into the twentieth century. It has been revived today: in our age of global warming, the retreat of Arctic pack ice has led to the opening of new shipping lanes, and in 2008 the first commercial voyage successfully traversed the Arctic Ocean.

The Dream of Gold and the Downfall of Empires

Although the unforeseen size of the globe made a westward passage to Asia untenable, given the technologies then available, Europeans were quick to capitalize on the sources of wealth that the New World itself could offer. What chiefly fired the imagination were those small samples of gold that Columbus had initially brought back to Spain. While rather paltry in themselves, they nurtured hopes that gold might lie piled in ingots somewhere in these vast new lands, ready to enrich any adventurer who discovered them. Rumor fed rumor, until a few freelance Spanish soldiers really did strike it rich beyond their most avaricious imaginings.

America as an Object of Desire

Under the influence of popular travel narratives that had circulated in Europe for centuries, Columbus and his fellow voyagers were prepared to find the New World full of cannibals. They also assumed that the indigenous peoples' custom of wearing little or no clothing—not to mention their "savagery"—would render their women sexually available. In a letter sent back home in 1495, one of Columbus's men recounted a notable encounter with a "cannibal girl" whom he had taken captive in his tent and whose naked body aroused his desire. He was surprised to find that she resisted his advances so fiercely that he had to tie her up—which of course made it easier for him to "subdue" her. In the end, he cheerfully reports, the girl's sexual performance was so satisfying that she might have been trained, as he put it, in a "school for whores."

The Flemish artist Jan van der Straet (1523–1605) would have heard many such reports of the encounters between (mostly male) Europeans and the peoples of the New World. This engraving, based on one of his drawings, is among the thousands of mass-produced images that circulated widely in Europe, thanks to the invention of printing. It imagines the first encounter between a male "Americus" (like Columbus or Amerigo Vespucci himself) and the New World, "America," depicted as a voluptuous, available woman. The Latin caption reads: "America rises to meet Americus; and whenever he calls her, she will always be aroused."

Questions for Analysis

1. Study the details of this image carefully. What does each symbolize, and how do they work together as an allegory of conquest and colonization?

2. On what stereotypes of indigenous peoples does this image draw? Notice, for example, the cannibalistic campfire of the group in the background or the posture of "America."

3. The New World itself—America—is imagined as female in this image. Why is this? What messages might this—and the suggestive caption—have conveyed to a European viewer?

Ioan. Stradanus invent.
Theodor. Galle sculp.
AMERICA.
Americen Americus retexit, & Semel vocauit inde semper excitam.

Their success, though, had little to do with their own efforts. Within a generation after the landing of the first ships under Columbus's command, European diseases had spread rapidly among the indigenous peoples of the Caribbean and the coastlines of the Americas. These diseases—especially measles and smallpox—were not fatal to those who carried them, because many Europeans had developed immunities to them over many generations. But to the peoples of this New World, they were deadly in the extreme. For example, there were probably 250,000 people living on Hispaniola when Columbus arrived; within thirty years—a single generation—70 percent had perished from disease.

SPANISH CONQUISTADORS IN MEXICO. This sixteenth-century drawing of conquistadors slaughtering the Aztec aristocracy emphasizes the advantages that plate armor and steel weapons gave to the Spanish soldiers.

Cape Verde Islands and St. Thomas (São Tomé) in the Gulf of Guinea, colonists began to import thousands of African slaves to labor in the new industry. Sugar production was, by its nature, a capital-intensive undertaking. The need to import slave labor added further to its costs, guaranteeing that control over the new industry would fall into the hands of a few extremely wealthy planters and financiers.

Despite the establishment of sugar production in the Caribbean and cattle ranching on the Mexican mainland—whose devastating effects on the fragile ecosystem of Central America will be discussed in Chapter 14—it was mining that would shape the Spanish colonies most fundamentally in this period. If gold was the lure that had initially inspired the conquest, silver became its most lucrative export. Even before the discovery of vast silver deposits, the Spanish crown had taken steps to assume direct control over all colonial exports. It was therefore to the Spanish crown that the profits of empire were channeled. Europe's silver shortage, which had been acute for centuries, therefore came to an abrupt end.

Yet this massive infusion of silver into the European economy created more problems than it solved, because it accelerated an inflation of wages and prices that had already begun in the late fifteenth century. Initially, inflation had been driven by the renewed growth of the European population, an expanding colonial economy, and a relatively fixed supply of food. Thereafter, thanks to the influx of New World silver, inflation was driven by the hugely increased supply of coinage. As we shall see, this abundance of coinage led to the doubling and quadrupling of prices in the course of the sixteenth century and to the

After You Read This Chapter

 Go to **INQUIZITIVE** to see what you've learned—and learn what you've missed—with personalized feedback along the way.

REVIEWING THE OBJECTIVES

- The artists of Italy were closely tied to those with political and military power. How did this relationship affect the kinds of work these artists produced?
- What aspects of Renaissance artistry and learning were adopted in northern Europe?
- What was the Reconquista, and how did it lead to a new way of thinking about Spanish identity?
- Europeans, especially the Portuguese, were developing new technologies and techniques that enabled exploration and colonial ventures in this period. What were they?
- The "discovery" of the New World had profound effects on the indigenous peoples and environment of the Americas. Describe some of these effects.

collapse of this inflated economy—paradoxically driving a wave of impoverished Europeans to settle in the New World in ever greater numbers.

CONCLUSION

The expansion of the Mediterranean world into the Atlantic, which had been ongoing since the thirteenth century, was the essential preliminary to Columbus's voyages and to the rise of European empires in Africa, India, the Caribbean, and the Americas. Other events and innovations that we have surveyed in this chapter played a key role, too: the relatively rapid communications facilitated by the printing press; the tussle for power in Italy that led to the development of ever deadlier weapons; the navigational and colonial initiatives of the Portuguese; and the success of the Spanish Reconquista, which displaced Spain's venerable Jewish community and spurred Spanish rulers and adventurers to seek their fortunes overseas.

For the indigenous peoples and empires of the Americas, the results were cataclysmic. Within a century of Europeans' arrival, between 50 and 90 percent of some native populations had perished from disease, massacre, and enslavement. Moreover, Europeans' capacity to further their imperial ambitions wherever ships could sail and guns could penetrate profoundly destabilized Europe, too, by sharpening the divisions among competing kingdoms and empires.

The ideals of the humanists and the artistry associated with the Renaissance often stand in sharp contrast to the harsh realities alongside which they coexisted and in which they were rooted. Artists could thrive in the atmosphere of competition and one-upmanship that characterized this period, but they could also find themselves reduced to the status of servants in the households of the powerful—or forced to subordinate their artistry to the demands of warfare and espionage.

Meanwhile, intellectuals and statesmen looked for inspiration to the precedents and glories of the past. But to which aspects of the past? Some humanists may have wanted to revive the principles of the Roman Republic, but many of them worked for ambitious despots who more closely resembled Rome's dictators. The theories that undergirded European politics and colonial expansion were being used to legitimize many different kinds of power, including that of the papacy. All of these trends would be carried forward in the sixteenth century and would have a role to play in the upheaval that shattered Europe's fragile religious unity. It is to this upheaval, the Reformation, that we turn in Chapter 13.

PEOPLE, IDEAS, AND EVENTS IN CONTEXT

- Why was **GUTENBERG**'s invention of the **PRINTING PRESS** such a significant development?
- How did **NICCOLÒ MACHIAVELLI** respond to Italy's political situation within Europe? In what ways do artists like **LEONARDO DA VINCI** and **MICHELANGELO BUONARROTI** exemplify the ideals and realities of the Renaissance?
- How did northern European scholars like **DESIDERIUS ERASMUS** and **THOMAS MORE** apply humanist ideas to Christianity? How were these ideas expressed in art?
- What is significant about **IVAN THE GREAT**'s use of the title **TSAR**? In what other ways did the Russian emperor claim to be the heir of Rome?
- How did **ISABELLA OF CASTILE** and **FERDINAND OF ARAGON** succeed in creating a unified Spain through the **RECONQUISTA**?
- How does **PRINCE HENRY THE NAVIGATOR** exemplify the motives for pursuing overseas expansion? Why were the Portuguese so successful in establishing colonies in this period?
- What were the expectations that launched **COLUMBUS**'s voyage? What enabled the Spanish **CONQUISTADORS** to subjugate the peoples of the **AMERICAS**?

THINKING ABOUT CONNECTIONS

- Phrases like "Renaissance man" and "a Renaissance education" are still part of our common vocabulary. Given what you have learned in this chapter, how has your understanding of such phrases changed? How would you explain their true meaning to others?
- How do the patterns of conquest and colonization discussed in this chapter compare to those of earlier periods, such as the era of the Crusades or the empires of antiquity? How many of these developments were new?
- Although the growth of the African slave trade would result in a new racialization of slavery in the Atlantic world, the justifications for slavery had very old roots. How might Europeans have used Greek and Roman precedents in defense of these new ventures? (See Chapters 4 and 5.)

Before You Read This Chapter

The Age of Dissent and Division, 1500–1564

I n 1517, on the night before the Feast of All Saints—All Hallows' Eve, or Halloween—a professor of theology at a small university in northern Germany published a series of debating points on the door of Wittenberg's All Saints' Church. (This church served as the university's chapel, and it was also called the "Castle church," because it was part of the palace recently built for the local ruler.) The act of nailing such a document to the church door was not a prank; it was the usual method of announcing a public disputation. Still, it is peculiarly appropriate that Martin Luther did this on a night associated with mischief-making. Although he cannot have anticipated the magnitude of mischief it would cause, the posting of these ninety-five theses was a subversive act. For one thing, the sheer number of propositions that Dr. Luther offered to debate was unusual. But what really caught the attention of his fellow scholars was their unifying theme: the corruption of the Church and, in particular, the office of the pope. It was a topic very much in vogue at the time, but it had seldom been dissected so clearly by a licensed theologian who was also a monk, an ordained priest, and a charismatic teacher.

Thanks to Luther's well-placed correspondents, this document and the debate it stimulated soon found audiences well beyond the university of Wittenberg. By the time the papacy formally retaliated, in 1520, dissent was widespread—and not only among academics. Many of Europe's kings and princes saw the political advantages of either defying or defending the pope, and they chose sides accordingly. Luther's own lord, Frederick III of Saxony, would spend the rest of his life shielding the man who had first expounded those theses in his own Castle church.

Martin Luther (1483–1546) had grown up in a largely peaceful Europe. After two centuries of economic, social, and political turmoil, its economy was expanding, its cities growing, and its major monarchies were secure. Europeans had also embarked on a new period of colonial expansion. Meanwhile, the Church had weathered the storms of the Avignon captivity and the Great Schism. In the struggle over conciliarism, the papacy had won the support of all major European rulers. At the local level, the devotion of ordinary Christians was strong and the parish a crucial site of community identity. To be sure, there were some problems. Reformers noted that too many priests were ignorant or neglectful of their duties. Monasticism seemed to have lost its spiritual fire, while popular religious enthusiasm sometimes led to superstition, or to movements that the Church considered heretical. Yet, on the whole, secular and ecclesiastical institutions were strong.

No one could have predicted that this coherence would be irreparably shattered in the course of a generation, or that the next century would witness an appallingly destructive series of wars. Nor could anyone have foreseen that the catalyst for these extraordinary events would be a university professor. The debate ignited by Martin Luther on that evening in 1517 would set off the chain reaction we know as the Reformation. Initially, it was intended as a call for another phase in the Church's long history of internal reforms; but Luther's teachings instead launched a revolution that would splinter western Christendom into a variety of Protestant ("dissenting") faiths, while prompting the Roman Church to reaffirm its status as the only true Catholic ("universal") religion. At the same time, these movements deepened existing divisions among peoples, rulers, and states. The result was a profound transformation that affected the lives of everyone in Europe—and everyone in the new European colonies.

MARTIN LUTHER'S CHALLENGE

To explain the impact of Martin Luther's ideas and actions, we must first ask how he arrived at his theological convictions. We then need to assess why so many Europeans were galvanized by his teachings, and why many rulers quickly adopted the Protestant faith within their territories.

As we shall see, Luther's message appealed to different types of people for different reasons. Many peasants hoped that the new religion would free them from the dominion of their lords; towns and princes thought it would allow them to consolidate their political independence; politicians thought it would liberate emerging states from the demands of foreign popes.

But what Luther's followers shared was a conviction that their new understanding of Christianity would lead to salvation, whereas the traditional religion of Rome would not. For this reason, *reformation* is a rather misleading term for the movement they initiated. Although Luther himself began as a reformer seeking to change the Church from within, he quickly developed into a committed opponent of its principles and practices. Many of his followers were even more radical. The movement that began with Luther therefore went beyond "reformation." It was a frontal assault on religious, political, and social institutions that had been in place for a thousand years.

Luther's Quest for Justice

Although Martin Luther became an inspiration to millions, he was a terrible disappointment to his father. The elder Luther was a Thuringian peasant who had prospered in business. Eager to see his clever son rise still further, he sent young Luther to the University of Erfurt to study law. In 1505, however, Martin shattered his father's hopes by becoming a monk of the Augustinian order. In some sense, though, Luther was a chip off the old block: throughout his life, he lived simply and expressed himself in the vigorous, earthy vernacular of the German peasantry.

As a monk, Luther zealously pursued all the traditional means for achieving holiness. Not only did he fast and pray continuously, but he reportedly confessed his sins so often that his exhausted confessor would sometimes jokingly suggest that he should do something really worthy of penance. Yet still Luther could find no spiritual peace; he feared that he could never perform enough good deeds to deserve salvation. But then an insight led him to a new understanding of God's justice.

For years, Luther had worried that it seemed unfair for God to issue commandments that he knew humans could not observe—and then to punish them with eternal damnation for breaking them. But after becoming a professor of

MARTIN LUTHER. This late portrait is by Lucas Cranach the Elder (1472–1553), court painter to the electors of Brandenburg and a friend of Luther.

theology at the University of Wittenberg, Luther's study of the Bible convinced him that God's justice lay in his mercy, not in the power of damnation. As Luther later wrote, "I began to understand the justice of God as that by which God makes *us* just, in his mercy and through faith . . . and at this I felt as though I had been born again, and had gone through open gates into paradise."

Lecturing at Wittenberg in the years immediately following this epiphany, which occurred around 1515, Luther pondered a passage in Paul's Letter to the Romans (1:17): "The just shall live by faith." From this, he derived his central doctrine of "justification by faith alone." By this, Luther meant that God's justice does not demand endless good works and religious rituals, because humans can never be saved entirely by their own weak efforts. Rather, humans are saved by God's grace, which God offers as an utterly undeserved gift to those whom he has selected (predestined) for salvation. Because this grace comes to humans through the gift of faith, men and women are "justified" (i.e., made worthy of salvation) by faith alone. While those whom God has justified through faith will manifest that fact by performing deeds of piety and charity, such works are not what saves them. Piety and charity are merely visible signs of each believer's invisible spiritual state, which is known to God alone.

The essence of this doctrine was not original to Luther. It had been central to the thought of Augustine (see Chapter 6), the patron saint of Luther's own monastic order. During the twelfth and thirteenth centuries, however, theologians such as Peter Lombard and Thomas Aquinas (see Chapter 9) had developed a very different understanding of salvation. They emphasized the role that the Church itself (through its sacraments) and the individual believer (through acts of piety and charity) could play in the process of salvation. Although none of these previous theologians claimed that a human being could earn his or her way to heaven by good works alone, the late medieval Church had encouraged this understanding by presenting the process of salvation in increasingly quantitative terms—declaring, for example, that by performing a specific action (such as a pilgrimage or a pious donation), a believer could reduce the amount of penance she or he owed to God by a specific number of days.

Since the fourteenth century, moreover, popes had claimed to dispense "special grace" from the so-called Treasury of Merits, a storehouse of surplus good works piled up by Christ and the saints in heaven. By the late fifteenth century, when Luther was a child, the papacy began to claim that the dead could receive this grace, too, and so speed their way through purgatory. In both cases, grace was said to be withdrawn from this "Treasury" through indulgences: special remissions of penitential obligations. When indulgences were first conceived in the eleventh and twelfth centuries, they could be earned only by demanding spiritual exercises, such as joining a crusade. By the end of the fifteenth century, however, indulgences were for sale.

To many, this looked like heresy, specifically simony: the sin of exchanging God's grace for cash. It had been a practice loudly condemned by Wycliffe and his followers (see Chapter 11), and it was even more widely criticized by reformers like Erasmus (see Chapter 12). But Luther's objection to indulgences rested on a set of theological premises that, taken to their logical conclusion, resulted in dismantling of much contemporary religious practice, including the authority and sanctity of the papacy. Luther himself does not appear to have realized these implications at first.

The Scandal of Indulgences

Luther's thinking on these issues developed in an academic setting, but in 1517 he was provoked into attacking actual practice. The worldly bishop Albert of Hohenzollern, youngest brother of the prince of Brandenburg, paid a large sum for papal permission to hold the lucrative bishoprics of Magdeburg and Halberstadt concurrently—even though, at twenty-three, he was not old enough to be a bishop at all. Moreover, when the prestigious archbishopric of Mainz fell vacant in the next year, Albert bought

SAINT PETER'S BASILICA, ROME. The construction of a new papal palace and monumental church was begun in 1506. This enormous complex replaced a modest, dilapidated Romanesque basilica that had replaced an even older church built on the site of the apostle Peter's tomb. ■ *How might this building project have been interpreted in different ways, depending on one's attitude toward the papacy?*

that, too. Obtaining the necessary funds by taking out loans from a German banking firm, he then struck a bargain with Pope Leo X (r. 1513–21): Leo would authorize the sale of indulgences in Albert's ecclesiastical territories—where Luther lived—with the understanding that half of the income would go to Rome for the building of St. Peter's Basilica, the other half to Albert.

Luther did not know the sordid details of Albert's bargain, but he did know that a Dominican friar named Tetzel was soon hawking indulgences throughout much of the region, and that Tetzel was deliberately giving people the impression that an indulgence was an automatic ticket to heaven for oneself or loved ones in purgatory. For Luther, this was doubly offensive: not only was Tetzel violating Luther's conviction that people are saved by God's grace, he was misleading people into thinking that if they purchased an indulgence, they no longer needed to confess their sins. Tetzel was putting innocent souls at risk.

Accordingly, Luther's ninety-five theses were focused on dismantling the doctrine of indulgences. He published these points for debate in Latin, but they were soon translated into German and published even more widely. Suddenly, the hitherto obscure academic gained widespread notoriety. Tetzel and his powerful allies demanded that Luther withdraw his theses. Rather than backing down, however, Luther became even bolder. In 1519, at a public disputation held in Leipzig and attended by throngs of people, Luther defiantly maintained that the pope and all clerics were merely fallible men and that the highest authority for an individual's conscience was the truth of scripture.

Luther's year of greatest activity came in 1520, when he composed a series of pamphlets setting forth his three primary premises: justification by faith, the authority of scripture, and "the priesthood of all believers." We have already examined the meaning of the first premise. By the second, he meant that the reading of scripture took precedence over Church traditions—including the teachings of all theologians—and that beliefs (such as purgatory) or practices (such as prayers to the saints) not explicitly grounded in scripture should be rejected as human inventions. Luther also declared that Christian believers were spiritually equal before God, which meant denying that priests, monks, and nuns had any special qualities by virtue of their vocations: hence "the priesthood of all believers."

From these premises, a host of practical consequences logically followed. Because works could not lead to salvation, Luther declared fasts, pilgrimages, and the veneration of relics to be spiritually valueless. He also called for the dissolution of all monasteries and convents. He advocated a demystification of religious rites, proposing the substitution of German and other vernaculars for Latin and calling for a reduction in the number of sacraments from seven to two. In his view, the only true sacraments were baptism and the Eucharist, both of which had been instituted by Christ. (Later, he included penance, too.) Although Luther continued to believe that Christ was really present in the consecrated bread and wine of the Mass, he insisted that it was only through the faith of each individual believer that this sacrament could lead anyone to God; it was not a miracle performed by a priest.

To further emphasize that those who served the Church had no supernatural authority, Luther insisted on calling them "ministers" or "pastors" rather than priests. He also proposed to abolish the entire ecclesiastical hierarchy from popes to bishops on down. Finally, on the principle that no spiritual distinction existed between clergy and laity,

Luther argued that ministers could and should marry. In 1525, he himself took a wife, Katharina von Bora, one of a dozen nuns he had helped to escape from a Cistercian convent.

The Break with Rome

Widely disseminated by means of the printing press, Luther's polemical pamphlets electrified much of Europe, gaining him passionate popular support and touching off a revolt against the papacy. In highly colloquial German, Luther declared that "the cardinals have sucked Italy dry and now turn to Germany" and that, given Rome's corruption, "the reign of Antichrist could not be worse." As word of Luther's defiance spread, his pamphlets became a publishing sensation. Whereas the average press run of a printed book before 1520 had been 1,000 copies, the first run of *To the Christian Nobility* (1520) was 4,000—and it sold out in a few days. Many thousands of copies quickly followed. Even more popular were woodcut illustrations mocking the papacy and exalting Luther. These sold in the tens of thousands and could be readily understood even by those who could not read. (See **Interpreting Visual Evidence** on page 348.)

Luther's denunciations met with this popular response in part because they expressed longstanding and widespread public dissatisfaction with the corruption of the papacy. Pope Alexander VI (r. 1492–1503) had bribed cardinals to gain his office and had then used the money raised from the papal jubilee of 1500 to support the military campaigns of his illegitimate son. Julius II (r. 1503–13) devoted his reign to enlarging the Papal States through a series of wars. Leo X (r. 1513–21), Luther's opponent, was a member of the Medici family of Florence; an able administrator, he was also a self-indulgent connoisseur. In *The Praise of Folly*, first published in 1511 and frequently reprinted (see Chapter 12), Erasmus had declared that if the popes of his day were ever forced to lead Christlike lives, as their office actually required, they would be incapable of it. In *Julius Excluded*, published anonymously in 1517, he imagined a conversation between Saint Peter and Julius II, in which Peter refuses to admit the pope to heaven.

In Germany, resentment of the papacy ran especially high because there were no special agreements (concordats) limiting papal authority in its principalities, as there were in Spain, France, Bohemia, and England (see Chapter 12). As a result, papal taxes were high, and yet Germans had almost no influence over papal policy. Frenchmen, Spaniards, and Italians dominated the College of Cardinals and the papal bureaucracy, and the popes were almost invariably Italian—as they would continue to be until 1978 and the election of the Polish cardinal Karel Wojtyla as John Paul II. As a result of these trends, graduates from the rapidly growing German universities almost never found employment in Rome. Instead, many joined the throngs of Luther's supporters to become leaders of the new religious movement.

Emperor Charles V and the Condemnation at Worms

In the year 1520, Leo X issued a papal edict condemning Luther's publications as heretical and threatening him with excommunication. This edict was of the most solemn kind, known as a *bulla,* or "bull," from the lead seal it bore. Luther's response was flagrantly defiant: rather than acquiescing to the pope's demand, he staged a public burning of the document. Thereafter, his heresy confirmed, he was formally given over for punishment to his lay overlord, Frederick III "the Wise" of Saxony.

THE EMPEROR CHARLES V. This portrait by the Venetian painter Titian depicts Europe's most powerful ruler sitting quietly in a chair, dressed in simple clothing of the kind worn by judges or bureaucrats. ■ *Why might Charles have chosen to represent himself in this way—rather than in the regalia of his many royal, imperial, and princely offices?*

Decoding Printed Propaganda

The printing press has been credited with helping to spread the teachings of Martin Luther, and so securing the success of the Protestant Reformation. But even before Luther's critiques were published, reformers were using the new technology to disseminate images that attacked the corruption of the Church. After Luther rose to prominence, both his supporters and detractors vied with one another in disseminating propaganda that appealed, visually, to a lay audience and that could be understood even by those who were unable to read.

The first pair of images below is really a single printed artifact datable to around 1500: an early example of a "pop-up" card. It shows Pope Alexander VI (r. 1492–1503) as stately pontiff (image A) whose true identity is concealed by a flap. When the flap is raised (image B), he is revealed as a devil. The Latin texts read: "Alexander VI, *pontifex maximus*" (image A) and "I am the pope" (image B).

The other two examples represent two sides of the debate as it had

A. Alexander as pontiff.

B. Alexander as a devil.

developed by 1530, and both do so with reference to the same image: the seven-headed beast mentioned in the Bible's Book of Revelation. On the left (image C), a Lutheran engraving shows the papacy as the beast, with seven heads representing seven orders of Catholic clergy. The sign on the cross (referring to the sign hung over the head of the crucified Christ) reads, in German: "For money, a sack full of indulgences." The Latin words on either side say "Reign of the Devil." On the right (image D), a Catholic engraving produced in Germany shows Luther as Revelation's beast, with its seven heads labeled:

"Doctor–Martin–Luther–Heretic–Hypocrite–Fanatic–Barabbas," the last alluding to the thief who should have been executed instead of Jesus, according to the Gospels.

Questions for Analysis

1. Given that this attack on Pope Alexander VI precedes Martin Luther's critique of the Church by nearly two decades, what can you conclude about its intended audience? To what extent can it be read as a barometer of popular disapproval? What might have been the reason(s) for the use of the concealing flap?

2. What do you make of the fact that both Catholic and Protestant propagandists were using the same imagery? What do you make of key differences: for example, the fact that the seven-headed beast representing the papacy sprouts out of an altar in which a Eucharistic chalice is displayed, while the seven-headed Martin Luther is reading a book?

3. All of these printed images also make use of words. Would the message of each image be clear without the use of texts? Why or why not?

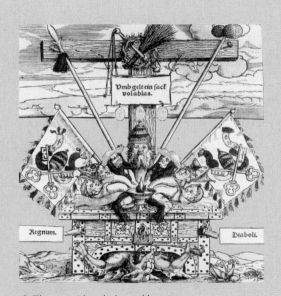

C. The seven-headed papal beast.

D. The seven-headed Martin Luther.

Frederick, however, proved a supporter of Luther and a critic of the papacy. Rather than burning Luther at the stake, Frederick declared that Luther had not yet received a fair hearing. Early in 1521, he therefore brought him to the city of Worms to be examined by a select assembly known as a "diet."

At Worms, the diet's presiding officer was the newly elected Holy Roman Emperor, Charles V. As a member of the Habsburg family, Charles had been born and bred in his ancestral holding of Flanders, then part of the Netherlands. By 1521, however, through the unpredictable workings of dynastic inheritance, marriage, election, and luck, he had

THE EUROPEAN EMPIRE OF CHARLES V, c. 1526. Charles V ruled a vast variety of widely dispersed territories in Europe and the New World, and as Holy Roman Emperor he was also the titular ruler of Germany. ▪ *What were the main territories under his control?* ▪ *Which regions would have been most threatened by Charles's extraordinary power, and where might the rulers of these regions have turned for allies?* ▪ *How might the expansion of the Ottoman Empire have complicated political and religious struggles within Christian Europe?*

become not only the ruler of the Netherlands but also king of Germany and Holy Roman emperor, duke of Austria, duke of Milan, and ruler of Burgundy's Franche-Comté. And as the grandson of Ferdinand and Isabella on his mother's side, he was also king of Spain; king of Naples, Sicily, and Sardinia; and ruler of all the Spanish possessions in the New World. Governing such an extraordinary combination of territories posed enormous challenges. Charles's empire had no capital and no centralized administrative institutions; it shared no common language, no common culture, and no geographically contiguous borders. The only thing uniting its peoples was the Church.

Charles could not, therefore, tolerate threats to the fundamental institution of Catholicism—as the religion of Rome was coming to be called. Moreover, Charles was a faithful and committed servant of the Church, and he was deeply disturbed by the prospect of heresy within his empire. There was little doubt that the Diet of Worms, held under his jurisdiction, would condemn Martin Luther. But when Luther refused to back down, his lord Frederick the Wise once more intervened, this time arranging for Luther to be "kidnapped" and hidden for a year at the castle of the Wartburg, out of harm's way.

Although the Diet of Worms proclaimed Luther an outlaw, this edict was never enforced. Instead, Charles V left Germany in order to conduct a war with France, and in 1522 Luther returned in triumph to Wittenberg and his university supporters. When several German princes formally converted to Lutheranism, they brought their territories with them. In a little over a decade, a new form of Christianity had been established.

The German Princes and the Lutheran Church

But why did some German princes, secure in their own powers, choose to establish Lutheran religious practices within their territories? This is a crucial development, because popular or academic support for Luther would not have been enough to ensure the success of his teachings had they not been embraced by a number of powerful rulers and free cities. It was only in those territories where Lutheranism was formally established that this new religion could survive. Elsewhere in Germany, Luther's sympathizers were forced to flee, face death, or conform to Catholicism.

The power of individual rulers to control the practice of religion in their own territories reflects developments we have noted in previous chapters. Rulers had long sought to control appointments to Church offices in their own realms, to restrict the flow of money to Rome and to limit the independence of ecclesiastical courts. The monarchs of Europe had already taken advantage of the continuing struggles between the papacy and the conciliarists to extract many concessions from the embattled popes during the fifteenth century (see Chapters 11 and 12). But in Germany, as noted above, neither the emperor nor the princes were strong enough to secure specially negotiated concordats.

Hence the political and economic appeal of Luther's initiatives. Luther himself had recognized that he could never hope to institute new religious practices without the strong arms of princes, so he explicitly encouraged them to confiscate the wealth of the Church as an incentive. When some princes realized that Luther had enormous public support and that Charles V could not act swiftly enough to stop them, several moved to introduce Lutheranism into their territories. Personal religious conviction surely played a role in individual cases, but considerations of power and wealth were generally more decisive. Self-proclaimed "protestant" princes could consolidate authority by naming their own religious officials, stopping the payment of fees to Rome, and curtailing the jurisdiction of Church courts. They could also guarantee that the political and religious boundaries of their territories would now coincide: no longer would a rival ecclesiastical prince (such as a bishop or abbot) be able to use his spiritual position to undermine a secular prince's sovereignty.

Similar considerations also moved a number of free cities to adopt Lutheranism. Acting independently of any prince, town councils could establish themselves as the supreme governing authorities within their jurisdictions, cutting out local bishops or powerful monasteries. Given the added fact that, under Lutheranism, monasteries and convents could be shut down and their lands appropriated by the newly sovereign Protestant authorities, the practical and economic advantages of the new faith were overwhelming.

Once safely ensconced in Wittenberg under Protestant princely protection, Luther began to express ever more vehemently his own political and social views, which tended toward the strong, conservative support of the new political order. In a treatise of 1523, *On Temporal Authority*, he even insisted that even "ungodly" Protestant princes should never be targets of dissent. In 1525, when peasants throughout Germany rebelled against their landlords, Luther therefore responded with hostility. In his vituperative pamphlet *Against the Thievish, Murderous*

Hordes of Peasants, he urged readers to hunt the rebels down as though they were mad dogs. After the ruthless suppression of this revolt, which may have cost as many as 100,000 lives, the firm alliance of Lutheranism with state power helped preserve and sanction the existing social order.

In his later years, Luther concentrated on debating with younger, more radical religious reformers who challenged his reactionary political conservatism. Never tiring in his amazingly prolific literary activity, he wrote an average of one treatise every two weeks for twenty-five years.

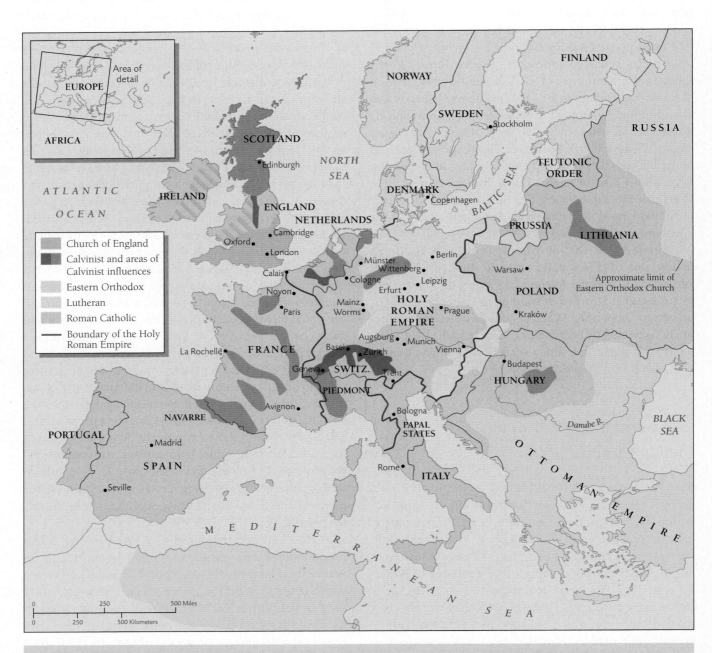

CONFESSIONAL DIFFERENCES, c. 1560. The religious affiliations (confessions) of Europe's territories had become very complicated by the year 1560, roughly a generation after the adoption of Lutheranism in some areas. ▪ *What major countries and kingdoms had embraced Protestantism by 1560?* ▪ *To what extent do these divisions conform to political boundaries, and to what extent would they have complicated the political situation?* ▪ *Why might Lutheranism have spread north into Scandinavia but not south into Bavaria?*

THE SPREAD OF PROTESTANTISM

Originating as a term applied to Lutherans who "protested" the Catholic authority of Charles V, the word *Protestant* was soon applied to a much wider range of dissenting Christianities. Lutheranism itself struck lasting roots in northern Germany and Scandinavia, where it became the state religion of Denmark, Norway, and Sweden as early as the 1520s. But some other early Lutheran successes in southern Germany, Poland, and Hungary were eventually rolled back. Elsewhere in Europe, meanwhile, competing forms of Protestantism soon emerged from the seeds that Luther had sown. By the 1550s, Protestantism had become a truly international movement and also an increasingly diverse and divisive one.

Protestantism in Switzerland

In the early sixteenth century, Switzerland was ruled neither by kings nor by territorial princes; instead, prosperous Swiss cities were either independent or on the verge of becoming so. Hence, when the leading citizens of a Swiss municipality decided to adopt Protestant reforms, no one could stop them. Although religious arrangements varied from city to city, three main forms of Protestantism emerged in Switzerland between 1520 to 1550: Zwinglianism, Anabaptism, and Calvinism.

Zwinglianism, founded by Ulrich Zwingli (*TSVING-lee*, 1484–1531) in Zürich, was the most theologically moderate form of the three. Zwingli had just begun his career as a Catholic priest when his humanist-inspired study of the Bible convinced him that Catholic theology and practice conflicted with the Gospels. His biblical studies eventually led him to condemn religious images and hierarchical authority within the Church. Yet he did not speak out publicly until Luther set a precedent. In 1522, accordingly, Zwingli began attacking the authority of the Catholic Church in Zürich. Soon, much of northern Switzerland had accepted his religious leadership.

Although Zwingli's reforms closely resembled those of the Lutherans in Germany, Zwingli differed from Luther on the theology of the Eucharist. Whereas Luther believed in the real presence of Christ's body in the sacrament, for Zwingli the Eucharist was simply a reminder and celebration of Christ's historical sacrifice. This fundamental disagreement prevented Lutherans and Zwinglians from uniting. When Zwingli died in battle against Catholic forces in 1531, his movement was absorbed by the more systematic Protestantism of John Calvin (as will be discussed later).

Before Calvinism prevailed, however, an even more radical form of Protestantism arose in Switzerland and parts of Germany. The first Anabaptists were members of Zwingli's circle in Zürich, but they broke with him around 1525 on the issue of infant baptism. Anabaptists were convinced that the sacrament of baptism was only effective if administered to willing adults who understood its significance, and so they required those who had been baptized as infants to be baptized again as adults (the term *Anabaptism* means "rebaptism"). This doctrine reflected the Anabaptists' fundamental belief that the true church was a small community of believers whose members had to make a deliberate, inspired decision to join it.

No other Protestant groups were prepared to go so far in rejecting the medieval Christian view of the Church as a single vast body to which all members of society belonged from birth. And in an age when almost everyone assumed that religious and secular authority were inextricably connected, Anabaptism was bound to be anathema to all established powers, both Protestant and Catholic. It was a movement that appealed to sincere religious piety in calling for pacifism, strict personal morality, and extreme simplicity of worship.

However, this changed when a group of Anabaptist extremists managed to gain control of the German city of Münster in 1534. These zealots were driven by millenarianism: the belief that God intends to institute a completely new order of justice and spirituality throughout the world before the end of time. Determined to help God bring about this goal, the extremists attempted to turn Münster into a new Jerusalem. A former tailor named John of Leyden assumed the title "king of the New Temple" and proclaimed himself the successor of the Hebrew king David. Under his leadership, Anabaptist religious practices were made obligatory, private property was abolished, and even polygamy was permitted on the grounds of Old Testament precedents. Such practices were deeply shocking to Protestants and Catholics alike. Accordingly, Münster was besieged and captured by Catholic forces little more than a year after the Anabaptist takeover. The new "King David," together with two of his lieutenants, was put to death by torture, and the three bodies were displayed in iron cases in the town square.

Thereafter, Anabaptists throughout Europe were ruthlessly persecuted on all sides. The few who survived banded together in the Mennonite sect, named for its founder, the Dutchman Menno Simons (c. 1496–1561). This sect, dedicated to pacifism and the simple "religion of the heart" of the original Anabaptist movement, is still particularly strong in the central United States.

John Calvin's Systematic Protestant Theology

A year after the events in Münster, a twenty-six-year-old Frenchman named John Calvin (1509–1564), published the first version of his *Institutes of the Christian Religion*, the most influential formulation of Protestant theology ever written. Born in Noyon, in northern France, Calvin had originally trained for the law; but by 1533, he was studying the Greek and Latin classics while living off the income from a priestly benefice. As he later wrote, he was "obstinately devoted to the superstitions of popery" until he experienced a miraculous conversion. He became a Protestant theologian and propagandist, eventually fleeing to the Swiss city of Basel to escape persecution.

Although some aspects of Calvin's early career resemble those of Luther's, the two men were very different. Luther was an emotionally volatile personality and a lover of controversy. He responded to theological problems as they arose or as the impulse struck him; he never attempted to systematize his beliefs. Calvin, however, had a coolly analytical legal mind and he was determined to set forth all the principles of Protestantism: comprehensively, logically, and systematically. As a result, after several revisions and enlargements (the definitive edition appeared in 1559), Calvin's *Institutes* became the Protestant equivalent of Thomas Aquinas's *Summa Theologiae* (see Chapter 9).

Calvin's austere and stoical theology started with the omnipotence of God. For Calvin, the entire universe depends utterly on the will of the Almighty, who created all things for his greater glory and who knows all things present and to come. Because of man's original fall from grace in Eden, all human beings are sinners by nature, bound to an evil inheritance they cannot escape. Yet God (for reasons of his own) has predestined some for eternal salvation and damned all the rest to the torments of hell. Nothing that individual humans may do can alter fate; all souls are stamped with God's blessing or condemnation before they are born. Nevertheless, Christians cannot be indifferent to their conduct on earth. If they are among the elect, God will implant in them the desire to live according to his laws. Upright conduct is thus a sign that an individual has been chosen for future glory. Membership in Calvin's Reformed Church was another presumptive sign of election to salvation, and Calvin charged his followers to work actively to fulfill God's commandents and stamp out sin—not because this would lead to anyone's salvation (which is predetermined by God alone), but because God's glory is diminished if sin is allowed to flourish.

Calvin always acknowledged a great debt to Luther, but his teachings diverged in several essential respects. First of all, Luther's attitude toward proper Christian conduct in the world was much more passive. For Luther, a Christian should endure the trials of life through suffering, whereas for Calvin the world was to be actively mastered through unceasing labor. Calvin's religion was also more controlling than Luther's. Luther, for example, insisted that his followers attend church on Sunday, but he did not demand that they refrain from all pleasure or work on that day. Calvin, on the other hand, forbade worldliness of any sort on the Sabbath and all sorts of minor self-indulgences even on other days.

The two men also differed on fundamental matters of church governance and worship. Although Luther had attacked the Roman church's hierarchy, Lutheran district superintendents exercised some of the same powers as bishops, including supervision of parish clergy. Luther also retained many features of traditional Christian worship, including altars, music, and ritual. Calvin, however, rejected everything that smacked of "popery." He argued that each congregation should elect its own ministers, and that assemblies of ministers and "elders" (laymen responsible for maintaining proper religious conduct) were to govern the Reformed Church as a whole. Calvin also insisted on the utmost simplicity in worship, prohibiting (among much else) rich vestments, processions, rituals, instrumental music, and religious images or any sort of church decoration. He also dispensed with all Catholic sacraments by making the sermon, rather than the Eucharist, the centerpiece of worship.

Calvinist Geneva

Calvin was intent on putting his religious teachings into practice. Sensing an opportunity in the French-speaking Swiss city of Geneva—then in the throes of political and religious upheaval—he moved there in 1536 and began preaching and organizing. In 1538, his activities caused him to be expelled by the city council, but in 1541 he returned and brought the city under his influence.

With Calvin's guidance, Geneva's government became a theocracy. Supreme authority was vested in a "consistory" composed of twelve lay elders and between ten and twenty pastors, whose weekly meetings Calvin dominated. In addition to passing legislation proposed by an assembly of ministers, the consistory's main function was to supervise morality, public and private. To this end, Geneva was divided into districts, and a committee of the consistory visited every household, without prior warning, to check on the behavior of its members. Dancing, card playing, attending the theater, and working or playing on the Sabbath: all were outlawed as works of the devil. Innkeepers were forbidden to allow anyone to consume food or drink without first saying grace, or to permit any patron to stay up after nine o'clock. Adultery, witchcraft, blasphemy, and heresy all became capital crimes. Even penalties for lesser crimes were severe. During the first four years after Calvin gained control in Geneva, there were no fewer than fifty-eight executions in this city with a total population of only 16,000.

As rigid as such a regime may seem today, Calvin's Geneva was a beacon of light to thousands of Protestants throughout Europe in the mid-sixteenth century. Calvin's disciple John Knox (c. 1514–1572), who brought the Reformed Church to Scotland, declared Geneva to be "the most perfect school of Christ that ever was on earth since the days of the Apostles." Converts flocked there for refuge or instruction and then returned home to become ardent proselytizers for the new religion. Geneva thus became the center of an international movement dedicated to spreading reformed religion to the rest of Europe through organized missionary activity and propaganda.

These efforts were remarkably successful. By the end of the sixteenth century, Calvinists were a majority in Scotland (where they were known as Presbyterians) and Holland (where they founded the Dutch Reformed Church). They were also influential in England (where they were known as Puritans), and there were substantial Calvinist minorities in France (where they were called Huguenots), Germany, Hungary, Lithuania, and Poland. By the end of the sixteenth century, Calvinism would spread to the New World.

The Beginnings of Religious Warfare

Less than a generation after Luther's challenge to the Church, wars erupted between Catholic and Protestant rulers. In Germany, Charles V attempted to reestablish Catholic unity by launching a military campaign against several German princes who had instituted Lutheran worship in their territories. But despite several notable victories, his efforts failed. In part, this was because Charles was also involved in wars against France; but primarily, it was because the Catholic princes of Germany worked against him, fearing that any suppression of Protestant princes might also diminish their own independence.

This regional warfare sputtered on and off until a compromise settlement was reached via the Peace of Augsburg in 1555. Its governing principle was *cuius regio, eius religio*: "as the ruler, so the religion." This meant that, in those principalities where Lutherans ruled, Lutheranism would be the sole state religion; but where Catholic princes ruled, the people of their territories would also be Catholic. For better and for worse, the Peace of Augsburg was a historical milestone. For the first time since Luther had been excommunicated, Catholic rulers were forced to acknowledge the legality of Protestantism. Yet the peace also set a dangerous precedent because it established the principle that no sovereign state can tolerate religious diversity. Moreover, it excluded Calvinism entirely and thus spurred German Calvinists to become aggressive opponents of the status quo. As a result, Europe would be riven by religious warfare for another century and would export sectarian violence to the New World (see Chapter 14).

THE DOMESTICATION OF REFORM

Within two decades, Protestantism had become a diverse movement whose radical claims for the spiritual equality of all Christians had the potential to undermine the political, social, and even gender hierarchies on which European society rested. Luther himself did not anticipate that his ideas might have such implications, and he was genuinely shocked when the rebellious German peasants and the radical Anabaptists at Münster interpreted his teachings in this way. And Luther was by no means the only staunchly conservative Protestant leader. None of the prominent early Protestants were social or political radicals; most depended on the support of existing elites. As a result, the Reformation movement was speedily "domesticated" in two senses. Its revolutionary potential was muffled—Luther himself rarely spoke about "the priesthood of all believers" after 1525—and there was an increasing emphasis on the patriarchal family as the central institution of reformed life.

Reform and Discipline

As we have seen, the desire to lead a more disciplined and godly life has been a frequent catalyst of religious reform movements. Since the Black Death (see Chapter 11), many of these efforts were actively promoted by princes and town councils, most famously perhaps in Florence, where the Dominican preacher Girolamo Savonarola led the city on an extraordinary but short-lived campaign of puritanism and moral reform between 1494 and 1498. And there are numerous other examples of rulers legislating against sin.

Competing Viewpoints

Marriage and Celibacy: Two Views

These two selections illustrate the strongly contrasting views of the spiritual value of marriage versus celibacy that came to be embraced by Protestant and Catholic religious authorities. The first selection is part of Martin Luther's more general attack on monasticism, which emphasizes his contention that marriage is the natural and divinely intended state for all human beings. The second selection, from the decrees of the Council of Trent (1545–63), restates traditional Catholic teaching on the holiness of marriage but also emphasizes the spiritual superiority of virginity to marriage as well as the necessity of clerical celibacy.

Luther's Views on Celibacy (1535)

Listen! In all my days I have not heard the confession of a nun, but in the light of Scripture I shall hit upon how matters fare with her and know I shall not be lying. If a girl is not sustained by great and exceptional grace, she can live without a man as little as she can without eating, drinking, sleeping, and other natural necessities.

Nor, on the other hand, can a man dispense with a wife. The reason for this is that procreating children is an urge planted as deeply in human nature as eating and drinking. That is why God has given and put into the body the organs, arteries, fluxes, and everything that serves it. Therefore what is he doing who would check this process and keep nature from running its desired and intended course? He is attempting to keep nature from being nature, fire from burning, water from wetting, and a man from eating, drinking, and sleeping.

Source: E. M. Plass, ed., *What Luther Says*, vol. 2 (St. Louis, MO: 1959), pp. 888–89.

Canons on the Sacrament of Matrimony (1563)

Canon 1. If anyone says that matrimony is not truly and properly one of the seven sacraments . . . instituted by Christ the Lord, but has been devised by men in the Church and does not confer grace, let him be anathema [cursed].

Canon 9. If anyone says that clerics constituted in sacred orders or regulars [monks and nuns] who have made solemn profession of chastity can contract marriage . . . and that all who feel that they have not the gift of chastity, even though they have made such a vow, can contract marriage, let him be anathema, since God does not refuse that gift to those who ask for it rightly, neither does *he suffer us to be tempted above that which we are able.*

Canon 10: If anyone says that the married state excels the state of virginity or celibacy, and that it is better and happier to be united in matrimony than to remain in virginity or celibacy, let him be anathema.

Source: H. J. Schroeder, *Canons and Decrees of the Council of Trent* (St. Louis, MO: 1941), pp. 181–82.

Questions for Analysis

1. On what grounds does Luther attack the practice of celibacy? Do you agree with his basic premise?

2. How do the later canons of the Catholic Church respond to Protestant views like Luther's? What appears to be at stake in this defense of marriage and celibacy?

When Desiderius Erasmus called on secular authorities to think of themselves as abbots and of their territories as giant monasteries, he was sounding an already-familiar theme.

Protestant rulers, however, took the need to enforce godly discipline with particular seriousness, because the depravity of human nature was a fundamental tenet of Protestant belief. Like Saint Augustine at the end of the fourth century, Protestants believed that people would inevitably turn out bad unless they were compelled to be good. It was therefore the responsibility of secular and religious leaders to control the behavior of their people, because otherwise their evil deeds would anger God and destroy humanity.

Protestant godliness began with the discipline of children. Luther himself wrote two catechisms (instructional tracts) designed to teach children the tenets of their faith and the obligations—toward parents, masters, and rulers—that God imposed on them. Luther also insisted that all children, boys and girls alike, be taught to read the Bible in their own languages. Schooling thus became a characteristically Protestant preoccupation and rallying cry. Even the Protestant family was designated a "school of godliness," in which fathers were expected to instruct and discipline their wives, their children, and their servants.

But private life still left much to be desired in the eyes of Protestant reformers. Drunkenness, domestic violence, illicit sex, dancing, and blasphemy were frequent topics of reforming discourse. Various methods of discipline were attempted, including private counseling, public confessions of wrongdoing, public penances and shamings, exclusion from church services, and even imprisonment. All of these efforts met with varying, but generally modest, success. Creating godly Protestant families, and enforcing godly discipline on entire communities, was going to require the active cooperation of godly authorities.

Protestantism, Government, and the Family

The domestication of the Reformation in this wider sense took place principally in the free towns of Germany, Switzerland, and the Netherlands—and from there spread westward to North America. Protestant emphasis on the depravity of the human will, and the consequent need for discipline, resonated powerfully with guilds and town governments, which were anxious to maintain and increase the control exercised by urban elites (mainly merchants and master craftsmen) over the apprentices and journeymen who made up the majority of the male population. By eliminating the competing jurisdictional authority of the Roman Church, Protestantism allowed town governments to consolidate all authority within the city into their own hands.

Protestant governments reinforced the control of individual men over their own households by emphasizing the family as the basic unit of religious education. In place of a priest, an all-powerful father figure was expected to assume responsibility for his household. At the same time, Protestantism introduced a new religious ideal for women. No longer was the virginal nun the exemplar of female holiness; in her place now stood the married and obedient Protestant "goodwife." As one Lutheran prince wrote in 1527: "Those who bear children please God better than all the monks and nuns singing and praying." By declaring the holiness of marital sex, Protestantism relieved the tensions between piety and sexuality that had long characterized Christian teachings.

Yet this did not promote a new view of women's spiritual potential, nor did it elevate their social and political status. Quite the contrary: Luther regarded women as more sexually driven than men and less capable of controlling their lusts (reflecting the fact that Luther confessed himself incapable of celibacy). His opposition to convents rested on his belief that it was impossible for women to remain chaste, so sequestering them simply made illicit behavior inevitable. To prevent sin, it was necessary that all women should be married, preferably at a young age, and so placed under the governance of a godly husband.

For the most part, Protestant town governments were happy to cooperate in shutting down female monasteries. The convent's property went to the town, after all. But conflicts did arise over marriage and sexuality, especially over the reformers' insistence that both men and women should marry young as a restraint on lust. In many towns, men were traditionally expected to delay marriage until they had achieved the status of master craftsman. In theory, then, apprentices and journeymen were not supposed to marry. Instead, they were expected to frequent brothels, a legally sanctioned outlet for extramarital sexuality long viewed as necessary to men's physical well-being, but one that Protestant reformers now deemed morally abhorrent.

Towns responded in a variety of ways to these opposing pressures. Some instituted special committees to police public morals, of the sort we have noted in Calvin's Geneva. Some abandoned Protestantism altogether. Others, like the German town of Augsburg, alternated between forms of Protestantism and Roman Catholicism for several decades. Yet regardless of a town's final choice of religious allegiance, by the end of the sixteenth century a revolution had taken place with respect to governments' attitudes toward public morality. In their competition with each other, neither Catholics nor Protestants wished to be seen as soft on sin. The result was the widespread abolition of publicly licensed brothels, the outlawing of prostitution, and far stricter governmental supervision of many other aspects of private life.

Parental Control of Marriage

Protestantism also increased parents' control over their children's choice of marital partners. The medieval Church had defined marriage as a sacrament that did not require the involvement of a priest. The mutual free consent of two individuals, even if given without witnesses or parental approval, was enough to constitute a legally valid marriage in the eyes of the Church. Opposition to this doctrine had long come from many quarters, especially from families who stood to lose from this liberal stance: because marriage involved rights of inheritance to property, it was regarded as too important a matter to be left to the choice of adolescents. Instead, parents wanted the power to prevent unsuitable matches and, in some cases, to force their children to accept the marriage arrangements their families made for them.

Protestantism offered a welcome opportunity to achieve such control. Luther had declared marriage to be a purely secular matter, not a sacrament at all, and one that could be regulated however governing authorities thought best. Calvin largely followed suit. Even the Catholic Church was eventually forced to give way. Although it never abandoned its insistence that both members of a couple must freely consent to their marriage, by the end of the sixteenth century the Church required formal public notice of intent to marry and insisted on the presence of a priest at the actual wedding ceremony. Both were efforts to prevent elopements and so to allow families time to intervene before an unsuitable marriage was formed. Individual Catholic countries sometimes went even further in trying to assert parental control over their children's choice of partners. In France, for example, although couples might still marry without parental consent, those who did so now forfeited all of their rights to inherit their families' property. In somewhat different ways, both Protestantism and Catholicism thus moved to strengthen the control that parents could exercise over their children.

THE REFORMATION OF ENGLAND

In England, the Reformation took a rather different course than it did in continental Europe. Although a long tradition of popular reform had thrived there for centuries, the number of dissidents was usually too small and their influence too limited to play a significant role. Nor was England particularly oppressed by the papal exactions and abuses that roiled Germany. When the sixteenth century began, English monarchs already exercised close control over Church appointments; they also received the lion's share of the papal taxation collected within the realm. Why, then, did England become a Protestant country at all?

The King's "Great Matter"

In 1527, King Henry VIII of England had been married to Ferdinand and Isabella's daughter, Catherine of Aragon, for eighteen years. Yet all the offspring of this union had died in infancy, with the exception of a daughter, Mary. Catherine was now past the age of childbearing. And Henry needed a male heir to preserve the fragile succession to the throne: his father, Henry VII, had come to power after a time of civil war (Chapter 11), and resentment against the new Tudor dynasty still smoldered. Henry thus had strong political reasons to propose a change of wife. He also had more personal motives, having become infatuated with a lady-in-waiting named Anne Boleyn.

Henry therefore appealed to Rome to annul his marriage to Catherine, arguing that because she had previously been married to his older brother Arthur (who had died in adolescence), their marriage had been invalid from the beginning. As Henry's representatives pointed out, the Bible pronounced it "an unclean thing" for a man to take his brother's wife and cursed such a marriage with childlessness (Leviticus 20:21). Even a papal dispensation, which Henry and Catherine had long before obtained for their marriage, could not exempt them from such a clear prohibition—as the marriage's childlessness proved.

Henry's petition put Pope Clement VII (r. 1523–34) in an awkward position. Both Henry and Clement knew that popes in the past had granted annulments to reigning monarchs on far weaker grounds than the ones Henry was alleging. If, however, the pope granted Henry's annulment, he would cast doubt on the validity of all papal dispensations. More seriously, he would provoke the wrath of Emperor Charles V, Catherine of Aragon's nephew, whose armies were in firm command of Rome and who at that moment held the pope himself in captivity. Clement was trapped; all he could do was procrastinate and hope that the matter would resolve itself. For two years, he allowed Henry's case to proceed in England without ever reaching a verdict. Then, suddenly, he transferred the case to Rome, where the legal process began all over again.

Exasperated, Henry began to take matters into his own hands. In 1531, he compelled an assembly of English clergy to declare him "protector and only supreme head" of the Church in England. In 1532, he encouraged Parliament to produce an inflammatory list of grievances against the English clergy and used this threat to force them to concede his right, as king, to approve or deny all Church legislation. In January 1533, Henry married Anne Boleyn (already pregnant) even though his marriage to Queen Catherine had still not been annulled. The new archbishop of Canterbury, Thomas Cranmer, later provided the required annulment in May, acting on his own authority.

In September, Princess Elizabeth was born; her father, disappointed again in his hopes for a son, refused to attend her christening. Nevertheless, Parliament settled the succession to the throne on the children of Henry and Anne, redirected all papal revenues from England into the king's hands, prohibited appeals to the papal court, and formally declared "the King's highness to be Supreme Head of the Church of England." In 1536, Henry executed his former tutor and chancellor Sir Thomas More (see Chapter 12) for his refusal to endorse this declaration of supremacy, and took the first steps toward dissolving England's many monasteries. By the end of 1539, the monasteries and convents were gone and their lands and wealth confiscated by the king.

These measures, largely masterminded and engineered by Henry's brilliant Protestant adviser, Thomas Cromwell (c. 1485–1540), broke the bonds that linked the English Church to Rome. But they did not make England a formally Protestant country. Although certain traditional practices (such as pilgrimages and the veneration of relics) were prohibited, the English Church remained overwhelmingly Catholic in organization, doctrine, ritual, and language. The Six Articles promulgated by Parliament in 1539 at Henry VIII's behest left no room for doubt as to official orthodoxy: confession to priests, masses for the dead, and clerical celibacy were all confirmed; the Latin Mass continued; and Catholic Eucharistic doctrine was not only confirmed but denying it was made punishable by death. To most English people, only the disappearance of the monasteries and the king's own continuing matrimonial adventures (he married six wives in all) were evidence that their Church was no longer in communion with Rome.

The Reign of Edward VI

For truly committed Protestants, and especially those who had visited Calvin's Geneva, the changes Henry VIII enforced on the English Church did not go nearly far enough. In 1547, the accession of the nine-year-old king Edward VI (Henry's son by his third wife, Jane Seymour) gave them the opportunity to finish the task of reform. Encouraged by the apparent sympathies of the young king, Edward's government moved quickly to reform the doctrine and ceremonies of the English Church. Priests were permitted to marry; English services replaced Latin ones; the veneration of images was discouraged, and the images themselves were defaced or destroyed; prayers for the dead were declared useless, and endowments for such prayers were confiscated; and new articles of belief were drawn up, repudiating all sacraments except baptism and communion and affirming the Protestant creed of justification by faith alone. Most important, *The Book of Common Prayer*, authored by Archbishop Cranmer and considered one of the great landmarks of English literature, was published to define precisely how the new English-language services of the church were to be conducted. By 1553, when the youthful Edward died, England appeared to have become a distinctly Protestant kingdom.

Mary Tudor and the Restoration of Catholicism

Edward's successor, however, was his pious and much older half sister Mary (r. 1553–58), granddaughter of "the most Catholic monarchs" of Spain. Mary speedily reversed her half-brother's religious policies, restoring the Latin Mass and requiring married priests to give up their wives. She even prevailed on Parliament to vote a return to papal allegiance. Hundreds of Protestant leaders fled abroad, many to Geneva; others, including Archbishop Thomas Cranmer, were burned at the stake for refusing to deny their Protestant faith. Yet Mary's policies could not wipe out religious resistance. Nor could they do anything to restore monastic life in England: too many leading families had profited from her father's dissolution of the monasteries.

Mary's marriage to her cousin Philip, Charles V's son and heir to the Spanish throne, was another miscalculation. Although the marriage treaty stipulated that Philip could not succeed her in the event of her death, her English subjects never trusted him. When the queen allowed herself to be drawn into a war with France on Spain's

Analyzing Primary Sources

The Six Articles of the English Church

Although Henry VIII withdrew the Church of England from obedience to the papacy, he continued to reject most Protestant theology. Some of his advisers, most notably Thomas Cromwell, were committed Protestants; and the king allowed his son and heir, Edward VI, to be raised as a Protestant. But even after several years of rapid (and mostly Protestant) change in the English Church, Henry reasserted a set of traditional Catholic doctrines in the Six Articles of 1539. These would remain binding on the Church of England until the king's death in 1547.

irst, that in the most blessed sacrament of the altar, by the strength and efficacy of Christ's mighty word, it being spoken by the priest, is present really, under the form of bread and wine, the natural body and blood of our Savior Jesus Christ, conceived of the Virgin Mary, and that after the consecration there remains no substance of bread or wine, nor any other substance but the substance of Christ, God and man;

Secondly, that communion in both kinds is not necessary for salvation, by the law of God, to all persons, and that it is to be believed and not doubted . . . that in the flesh, under the form of bread, is the very blood, and with the blood, under the form of wine, is the very flesh, as well apart as though they were both together;

Thirdly, that priests, after the order of priesthood received as afore, may not marry by the law of God;

Fourthly, that vows of chastity or widowhood by man or woman made to God advisedly ought to be observed by the law of God. . . .

Fifthly, that it is right and necessary that private masses be continued and admitted in this the king's English Church and congregation . . . whereby good Christian people . . . do receive both godly and goodly consolations and benefits; and it is agreeable also to God's law;

Sixthly, that oral, private confession is expedient and necessary to be retained and continued, used and frequented in the church of God.

Source: *Statutes of the Realm*, vol. 3 (London: 1810–28), p. 739 (modernized).

Questions for Analysis

1. Three of these six articles focus on the sacrament of the Eucharist (the Mass). Given what you have learned in this chapter, why would Henry have been so concerned about this sacrament? What does this reveal about his values and those of his contemporaries?

2. Given Henry's insistence on these articles, why might he have allowed his son to be raised a Protestant? What does this suggest about the political situation in England?

---

behalf—in which England lost Calais, its last foothold on the European continent—many people became highly disaffected. Ultimately, however, what doomed Mary's policies was the fact that she died childless, after only five years of rule. Her throne passed to her Protestant sister, Elizabeth.

The Elizabethan Compromise

As the daughter of Henry VIII and the Lutheran sympathizer Anne Boleyn, Elizabeth (r. 1558–1603) was predisposed in favor of Protestantism by the circumstances of her parents' marriage as well as by her upbringing. But Elizabeth and her advisers also recognized that supporting radical Protestantism in England might provoke bitter sectarian strife. Accordingly, she presided over what is often known as "the Elizabethan settlement." By a new Act of Supremacy (1559), Elizabeth repealed Mary's Catholic legislation, prohibiting foreign religious powers (i.e., the pope) from exercising any authority within England and declaring herself "supreme governor" of the English church—a more Protestant title than Henry VIII's "supreme head" (since most Protestants believed that Christ alone was the head of the Church). She also adopted many of the Protestant liturgical reforms instituted under

QUEEN MARY AND QUEEN ELIZABETH. The two daughters of Henry VIII were the first two queens regnant of England: the first women to rule in their own right. Despite the similar challenges they faced, they had strikingly different fates and have been treated very differently in popular histories. ■ *How do these two portraits suggest differences in their personalities and their self-representation as rulers?*

her half-brother, Edward, including the revised version of *The Book of Common Prayer*. But she retained vestiges of Catholic practice, too, including bishops, church courts, and vestments for the clergy. On most doctrinal matters, Elizabeth's Thirty-Nine Articles of Faith (approved in 1562) struck a decidedly Protestant, even Calvinist, tone. But the prayer book was more moderate and, on the critical issue of the Eucharist, deliberately ambiguous. By combining Catholic and Protestant interpretations ("This is my body. . . . Do this in remembrance of me"), the prayer book permitted there to be competing interpretations of the service by priests and parishioners alike.

Yet religious tensions persisted in Elizabeth's England, not only between Protestants and Catholics but also between moderate and more extreme Protestants, the Puritans. Ultimately, what preserved "the Elizabethan settlement" was not this artful blurring of religious doctrines and ceremonies but the extraordinary length of Queen Elizabeth's reign, combined with the fact that for much of that time England was at war with Catholic Spain. Under Elizabeth, Protestantism and nationalism gradually fused together into a potent conviction that God himself had chosen England for greatness. After 1588, when English naval forces won an improbable victory over the Spanish Armada (see Chapter 14), Protestantism and Englishness became nearly indistinguishable to most of Elizabeth's subjects. Laws against Catholic practices became increasingly severe, and although an English Catholic tradition did survive, its adherents were a persecuted minority. Significant, too, was the situation in Ireland, where the vast majority

of the population remained Catholic despite the government's efforts to impose Protestantism on them. As a result, Irishness would be as firmly identified with Catholicism as Englishness was with Protestantism; but it was the Protestants who held power in both countries.

THE REBIRTH OF THE CATHOLIC CHURCH

So far, our discussion of the Reformation has cast the spotlight on Protestant reformers. But there was also a powerful reform movement within the Roman Church in these same decades, a reform which resulted in its rebirth. For some, this movement is the "Catholic Reformation"; for others, it is the "Counter-Reformation." Those who prefer the former name emphasize that the Roman Church of the sixteenth century was actually continuing a reforming movement that can be traced back to the eleventh century (see Chapter 8) and which gained new momentum in the wake of the Great Schism (see Chapter 11): in this view, reform is just a part of Catholic tradition. Others insist that most Catholic reformers of this period were reactionary, inspired primarily by the urgent need to resist Protestantism and to strengthen the power of the Roman Church in opposition to it: hence the "Counter-Reformation." Both perspectives are valid.

Catholic Reform and the Council of Trent

Long before Luther's challenge to Rome, as we have seen, there were movements for moral and institutional reform within the medieval Church. In the fifteenth century, however, while these efforts received strong support from several secular rulers, the papacy showed little interest in them. In Spain, for example, reforming activities directed by Cardinal Francisco Ximenes de Cisneros (1436–1517) led to the imposition of strict rules of behavior and the elimination of abuses prevalent among the clergy. Ximenes (*she-MEN-ez*) also helped to regenerate the spiritual life of the Spanish Church. In Italy, meanwhile, earnest clerics labored to make the Italian Church more worthy of its prominent position. But reforming existing monastic orders was a difficult task, not least because the papal court set such a poor example. Still, Italian reformers did

Past and Present

Controlling Consumption

Although laws regulating the conspicuous consumption of expensive commodities—especially status-conscious clothing—were common during the later Middle Ages, it was not until after the Reformation that both Protestant and Catholic leaders began to criminalize formerly acceptable bodily practices and substances. New theories of sensory perception, the availability of new products like coffee and tobacco, and a new concern to internalize reform led some authorities to outlaw prostitution (hitherto legal) and to ban normal social practices like drinking and dancing. The image on the left shows the militant Catholic League founded in sixteenth-century France, which combatted Protestantism and promoted strict religious observance. The image on the right shows Czech protesters calling for the decriminalization of marijuana.

Watch related author videos on the Student Site
wwnorton.com/college/history/western-civilizationsBrief4

manage to establish several new orders dedicated to high ideals of piety and social service. In northern Europe, Christian humanists such as Erasmus and Thomas More also played a role in this Catholic reform movement, not only by criticizing abuses and editing sacred texts but also by encouraging the laity to lead lives of sincere piety (as we saw in Chapter 12).

As a response to the challenges posed by Protestantism, however, these internal reforms proved inadequate. Starting in the 1530s, therefore, a more aggressive phase of reform began to gather momentum under a new style of vigorous papal leadership. The popes of this era—Paul III (r. 1534–49), Paul IV (r. 1555–59), Pius V (r. 1566–72), and Sixtus V (r. 1585–90)—were the most zealous reformers of the Church since the eleventh century. All led upright lives; some, indeed, were so grimly ascetic that contemporaries longed for the bad old days. And these popes were not merely holy men. They were also accomplished administrators who

reorganized papal finances and filled ecclesiastical offices with bishops and abbots no less renowned for austerity and holiness than were the popes themselves.

Papal reform efforts intensified at the Council of Trent, a general council of the entire Church convened in 1545, which met at intervals thereafter until 1563. The decisions taken at Trent (a provincial capital of the Holy Roman Empire, located in modern-day Italy) provided the foundations on which a new Roman Catholic Church would be erected. Although the council began by debating some form of compromise with Protestantism, it ended by reaffirming all of the tenets challenged by Protestant critics. "Good works" were affirmed as necessary for salvation, and all seven sacraments were declared indispensable means of grace, without which salvation was impossible. Transubstantiation, Purgatory, the invocation of saints, and the rule of celibacy for the clergy were all confirmed as dogmas—essential elements—of the Catholic faith.

Analyzing Primary Sources

The Demands of Obedience

The necessity of obedience in the spiritual formation of monks and nuns can be traced back to the Rule of Saint Benedict in the early sixth century, and beyond. In keeping with the mission of its founder, Ignatius of Loyola (1491–1556), the Society of Jesus brought a new militancy to this old ideal.

Rules for Thinking with the Church

1. Always to be ready to obey with mind and heart, setting aside all judgment of one's own, the true spouse of Jesus Christ, our holy mother, our infallible and orthodox mistress, the Catholic Church, whose authority is exercised over us by the hierarchy.

2. To commend the confession of sins to a priest as it is practised in the Church; the reception of the Holy Eucharist once a year, or better still every week, or at least every month, with the necessary preparation. . . .

4. To have a great esteem for the religious orders, and to give the preference to celibacy or virginity over the married state. . . .

6. To praise relics, the veneration and invocation of Saints: also the stations, and pious pilgrimages, indulgences, jubilees, the custom of lighting candles in the churches, and other such aids to piety and devotion. . . .

9. To uphold especially all the precepts of the Church, and not censure them in any manner; but, on the contrary, to defend them promptly, with reasons drawn from all sources, against those who criticize them.

10. To be eager to commend the decrees, mandates, traditions, rites, and customs of the Fathers in the Faith or our superiors. . . .

11. That we may be altogether of the same mind and in conformity with the Church herself, if she shall have defined anything to be black which to our eyes appears to be white, we ought in like manner to pronounce it to be black. For we must undoubtingly believe, that the Spirit of our Lord Jesus Christ, and the Spirit of the Orthodox Church His Spouse, by which Spirit we are governed and directed to salvation, is the same. . . .

From the Constitutions of the Jesuit Order

Let us with the utmost pains strain every nerve of our strength to exhibit this virtue of obedience, firstly to the Highest Pontiff, then to the Superiors of the Society; so that in all things . . . we may be most ready to obey his voice, just as if it issued from Christ our Lord . . . leaving any work, even a letter, that we have begun and have not yet finished; by directing to this goal all our strength and intention in the Lord, that holy obedience may be made perfect in us in every respect, in performance, in will, in intellect; by submitting to whatever may be enjoined on us with great readiness, with spiritual joy and perseverance; by persuading ourselves that all things [commanded] are just; by rejecting with a kind of blind obedience all opposing opinion or judgment of our own. . . .

Source: Henry Bettenson, ed., *Documents of the Christian Church*, 2nd ed. (Oxford: 1967), pp. 259–61.

Questions for Analysis

1. How might Loyola's career as a soldier have inspired the language used in his "Rules for Thinking with the Church"?

2. In what ways do these Jesuit principles respond directly to the challenges of Protestant reformers?

The Bible (in its flawed Vulgate form, not the new humanist edition of Erasmus) and the tradition of apostolic teaching were held to be of equal authority as sources of Christian truth. Papal supremacy over every bishop and priest was expressly maintained, and the supremacy of the pope over any Church council was taken for granted, signaling a final defeat of the still-active conciliar movement. The Council of Trent even reaffirmed the doctrine of indulgences that had touched off the Lutheran revolt, although it condemned the worst abuses connected with their sale.

The legislation of Trent was not confined to matters of doctrine. To improve pastoral care of the laity, bishops

THE INSPIRATION OF SAINT JEROME BY GUIDO RENI (1635).
The Council of Trent declared Saint Jerome's Latin translation of the Bible, the Vulgate, to be the official version of the Catholic Church. Since biblical scholars had known since the early sixteenth century that Saint Jerome's translation contained numerous mistakes, Catholic defenders of the Vulgate insisted that even his mistakes had been divinely inspired. ▪ **How does Guido Reni's painting attempt to make this point?**

and priests were forbidden to hold more than one spiritual office. To address the problem of an ignorant priesthood, a theological seminary was to be established in every diocese. The council also suppressed a variety of local religious practices and saints' cults, replacing them with new cults authorized and approved by Rome. To prevent heretical ideas from corrupting the faithful, the council further decided to censor or suppress dangerous books. In 1564, a specially appointed commission published the first *Index of Prohibited Books* forbidden to faithful Catholics. Ironically, all of Erasmus's works were immediately placed on the *Index*, even though he had been a champion of the Church against Martin Luther only forty years before. A permanent agency known as the Congregation of the Index was later set up to revise the list, which was maintained until 1966, when it was abolished after the Second Vatican Council (1962–65). For centuries, the *Index* was symbolic of the doctrinal intolerance that characterized sixteenth-century Christianity, both in its Catholic and Protestant varieties.

Ignatius Loyola and the Society of Jesus

In addition to the concerted activities of popes and the legislation of the Council of Trent, a third main force propelling the Church's response to Protestantism was the foundation of the Society of Jesus, commonly known as the Jesuits. In 1521, in the midst of a career as a mercenary, a young Spanish nobleman called Ignatius Loyola (1491–1556) was wounded in battle. While recuperating, he turned from the reading of chivalric romances to a romantic retelling of the life of Jesus—and the impact of this experience convinced him to become a spiritual soldier of Christ. This was the same year that Luther defied papal authority at the Diet of Worms.

For ten months, Ignatius lived as a hermit in a cave near the town of Manresa, where he experienced ecstatic visions and worked out the principles of his *Spiritual Exercises*. This manual, eventually completed in 1535 and first published in 1541, offered practical advice on how to master one's will and serve God through a systematic program of meditations on sin and the life of Christ. It eventually became the basic handbook for all Jesuits and has been widely studied by Catholic laypeople as well. Indeed, Loyola's *Spiritual Exercises* ranks alongside Calvin's *Institutes* as the most influential religious text of the sixteenth century.

The Jesuit order originated as a small group of six disciples who gathered around Loyola during his belated career as a student in Paris. They vowed to serve God in poverty, chastity, and missionary work and were formally constituted as a clerical order by Pope Paul III in 1540. By the time of Loyola's death, the Society of Jesus already numbered some 1,500 members. It was by far the most militant of the religious orders fostered by the Catholic reform movements of the sixteenth century—not merely a monastic society but a company of soldiers sworn to defend the faith. Their weapons were not bullets and swords but eloquence, persuasion, and instruction in correct doctrines; as a result, the Society also became accomplished in more worldly methods of exerting influence.

The activities of the Jesuits consisted primarily of proselytizing and promoting strict educational standards. This meant that they were ideal missionaries. Accordingly, Jesuits were soon dispatched to preach to non-Christians in India, China, and Spanish America. One of Loyola's closest associates, Francis Xavier (ZAY-vyer, 1506–1552), baptized thousands of people and traveled thousands of miles in South and East Asia.

Although Loyola had not conceived of his society as a batallion of "shock troops" in the global spread of Catholicism and the fight against Protestantism, that is what it primarily became. Through preaching and diplomacy—sometimes at the risk of their lives—Jesuits in the second half of the sixteenth century helped to colonize the world. In many places, they were instrumental in keeping rulers and their subjects loyal to Catholicism; in others, they met martyrdom; and in some others, notably Poland and parts of Germany and France, they succeeded in regaining territory previously lost to followers of Luther and Calvin. Wherever they were allowed to settle, they set up schools and colleges, on the grounds that only a vigorous Catholicism nurtured by widespread literacy and learning could combat Protestant errors.

A New Catholic Christianity

The greatest achievement of these reform movements was the revitalization of the Roman Church. Had it not been for such determined efforts, Catholicism would not have swept over the globe during the seventeenth and eighteenth centuries—or reemerged in Europe as a vigorous spiritual force. There were some other consequences as well. One was the rapid advancement of lay literacy in Catholic countries, as well as in Protestant ones. Another was the growth of intense concern for acts of charity; because Catholicism continued to emphasize good works as well as faith, charitable activities took on an extremely important role.

There was also a renewed emphasis on the role of religious women. Reformed Catholicism did not exalt marriage as a route to holiness to the same degree as did Protestantism, but it did encourage the piety of a female religious elite. For example, it embraced the mysticism of women like Saint Teresa of Avila (1515–1582) and established new orders of nuns, such as the Ursulines and the Sisters of Charity. Both Protestants and Catholics continued to exclude women from the priesthood or ministry, but Catholic women could pursue religious lives with at least some degree of independence, and the convent continued to be a route toward spiritual and even political advancement in Catholic countries.

The reformed Catholic Church did not, however, perpetuate the tolerant Christianity of Erasmus. Instead, Christian humanists lost favor with the papacy, and even scientists such as Galileo Galilei (1564–1642) were regarded with suspicion (see Chapter 16). Yet contemporary Protestantism was just as intolerant, and even more hostile to the cause of rational thought. Indeed, because Catholic theologians turned for guidance to the scholasticism of Thomas Aquinas, they tended to be much more committed to the dignity of human reason than were their Protestant counterparts, who emphasized the literal interpretation of the Bible and the importance of unquestioning faith. It is no coincidence that René Descartes (1596–1650), one of the pioneers of rational philosophy ("I think, therefore I am"), was educated by Jesuits.

TERESA OF AVILA. Teresa of Avila (1515–1582) was one of many female religious figures who played an important role in the reformed Catholic Church. She was canonized in 1622. This image is dated 1576. The Latin wording on the scroll unfurled above Teresa's head reads: "I will sing forever of the mercy of the Holy Lord."

The Protestantism of this era cannot, therefore, be regarded as more progressive than Catholicism. Both were, in fact, products of the same troubled time. Each variety of Protestantism responded to specific historical conditions and to the needs of specific peoples in specific places, while carrying forward certain aspects of the Christian tradition considered valuable by those communities. The Catholic Church also responded to new spiritual, political, and social realities—to such an extent that it must be regarded as distinct from either the early Church of the later Roman Empire or even the oft-reformed Church of the Middle Ages. That is why the phrase "Roman Catholic Church" has not been used in this book prior to this chapter, because the Roman Catholic Church as we know it emerged for the first time in the sixteenth century.

CONCLUSION

The Reformation grew out of complex historical processes that we have been tracing in the last few chapters. Foremost among these was the increasing power of Europe's sovereign states. As we have seen, those German princes who embraced Protestantism were moved to do so by the desire for sovereignty. The kings of Denmark, Sweden, and England followed suit for many of the same reasons. Since Protestant leaders preached absolute obedience to godly rulers, and since the state in Protestant countries assumed direct control of its churches, Protestantism bolstered state power. Yet the power of the state had been growing for a long time prior to this, especially in such countries as France and Spain, where Catholic kings already exercised most of the same rights that were seized by Lutheran authorities, and by Henry VIII of England in the course of their own reformations. Those rulers who aligned themselves with Catholicism, then, had the same need to bolster their sovereignty and power.

Ideas of national identity, too, were already influential and thus available for manipulation by Protestants and Catholics alike. These religions, in turn, became new sources of both identity and disunity. Prior to the Reformation, peoples in the different regions of Germany spoke such different dialects that they had difficulty understanding each other. But Luther's German Bible gained such currency that it eventually became the linguistic standard for all these disparate regions, which eventually began to conceive of themselves as part of a single nation.

Elsewhere—as in the Netherlands, where Protestants fought successfully against a foreign, Catholic overlord—religion created a shared identity where politics could not. In England, membership in the Church of England became a new, but not uncontested, attribute of "Englishness." In every region of Europe, meanwhile, both Protestant and Catholic reformers called for new forms of morality, increased patriarchal control over family and

After You Read This Chapter

 Go to **INQUIZITIVE** to see what you've learned—and learn what you've missed—with personalized feedback along the way.

REVIEWING THE OBJECTIVES

- The main premises of Luther's theology had religious, political, and social implications. What were these premises, and how did they affect real change?
- Swiss cities fostered a number of different Protestant movements. Why was this the case?
- The Reformation had a profound effect on the basic structures of family life and on attitudes toward marriage and morality. Describe these changes.
- The Church of England was established in response to a specific political situation. What was this, and how did the English Church continue to evolve in the course of the sixteenth century?
- How did the Catholic Church respond to the challenge of Protestantism?

community, strict disciplinary measures, and higher educational standards.

Ideals characteristic of the Renaissance also contributed something to the Reformation and the Catholic responses to it. The criticisms of Christian humanists helped to prepare Europe for the challenges of Lutheranism, and close textual study of the Bible led to the publication of the newer, more accurate editions used by Protestant reformers. For example, Erasmus's improved edition of the Latin New Testament enabled Luther to reach some crucial conclusions concerning the meaning of penance and became the foundation for Luther's own translation of the Bible. However, Erasmus was no supporter of Lutheran principles, and most other Christian humanists followed suit, shunning Protestantism as soon as it became clear to them what Luther was actually teaching. Indeed, in certain basic respects, Protestant doctrine was completely at odds with the principles, politics, and beliefs of most humanists, who became staunch supporters of the Catholic Church.

In the New World and Asia, both Protestantism and Catholicism became forces of imperialism and new catalysts for competition. The race to secure colonies and resources now became a race for converts, too, as missionaries of both faiths fanned out over the globe. In the process, the confessional divisions of Europe were mapped onto these regions, often with violent results. Over the course of the ensuing century, newly sovereign nation-states would struggle for hegemony at home and abroad, setting off a series of religious wars that would cause as much destruction as any plague. Meanwhile, Western civilizations' extension into the Atlantic would create new kinds of ecosystems, forms of wealth, and types of bondage.

PEOPLE, IDEAS, AND EVENTS IN CONTEXT

- How did **MARTIN LUTHER**'s attack on **INDULGENCES** tap into more widespread criticism of the papacy? What role did the printing press and the German vernacular play in the dissemination of his ideas?

- Why did many German principalities and cities rally to Luther's cause? Why did his condemnation at the **DIET OF WORMS** not lead to his execution on charges of heresy?

- How did the Protestant teachings of **ULRICH ZWINGLI**, **JOHN CALVIN**, and the **ANABAPTISTS** differ from one another and from those of Luther?

- What factors made some of Europe's territories more receptive to **PROTESTANTISM** than others? What was the meaning of the principle *CUIUS REGIO, EIUS RELIGIO*, established by the Peace of Augsburg?

- How did the **REFORMATION** alter the status and lives of women in Europe? Why did it strengthen male authority in the family?

- Why did **HENRY VIII** break with Rome? How did the **CHURCH OF ENGLAND** differ from other Protestant churches in Europe?

- What decisions were made at the **COUNCIL OF TRENT**? What were the founding principles of **IGNATIUS LOYOLA**'s **SOCIETY OF JESUS**, and what was its role in the **COUNTER-REFORMATION** of the **CATHOLIC CHURCH**?

THINKING ABOUT CONNECTIONS

- Our study of Western civilizations has shown that reforming movements are nothing new: Christianity has been continuously reformed throughout its long history. What made this Reformation so different?

- Was a Protestant break with the Roman Catholic Church inevitable, in your view? Why or why not?

- The political, social, and religious structures put in place during this era continue to shape our lives in such profound ways that we scarcely notice them—or we assume them to be inevitable and natural. In your view, what is the most far-reaching consequence of this age of dissent and division, and why? In what ways has it formed your own values and assumptions?

STORY LINES

- By the middle of the sixteenth century, the Atlantic Ocean became a zone of colonization, commerce, migration, and settlement, as the peoples of this Atlantic world confronted one another.

- In the wake of the Reformation, Europe itself remained politically unstable. Devastating religious wars were waged on the Continent. In England, mounting pressures caused a crisis that resulted in civil war and the execution of the reigning king.

- At the same time, competition in the wider Atlantic world exported these political and religious conflicts to Europe's new American colonies.

- This widening world and its pervasive violence caused many to question the beliefs of earlier generations and to seek new sources of authority.

CHRONOLOGY

1555	Peace of Augsburg
1562–1598	French wars of religion
1566–1609	Dutch wars with Spain
1588	Destruction of the Spanish Armada
1598	Edict of Nantes
1607	English colony of Jamestown founded
1608	French colony in Québec founded
1611	Shakespeare's play *The Tempest* is performed in London
1618	Thirty Years' War begins
1621	Dutch West India Company founded
1642–1649	English Civil War
1648	Beginning of the *Fronde* rebellions; the Thirty Years' War ends
1649	Execution of Charles I of England
1660	Restoration of the English monarchy

Before You Read This Chapter

Europe in the Atlantic World, 1550–1660

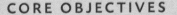
The Atlantic Ocean thrashes the shores of Europe and Africa with waves that have traveled thousands of miles from the American coasts. It links continents shaped by a wide variety of climates and diverse ecosystems. For most of human history, the limited movement of peoples on opposite sides of the ocean allowed these regions to nurture their own forms of plant and animal life, their own unique microbes and pathogens.

But in the sixteenth century, the Atlantic became an arena of cultural and economic exchange that broke down the isolation of these ecosystems. Humans, animals, and plants on once-remote shores came into intense contact. Europeans brought diseases that devastated the peoples of the Americas, along with gunpowder and a hotly divided Christianity. Meanwhile, the huge influx of silver from South America transformed (and eventually exploded) the cash-starved European economy, while the arrival of American luxury goods such as tobacco, sugar, and chocolate fostered new appetites. The need for slaves to power the plantations that supplied these consumer products created a vast industry of human trafficking, which led to the forcible removal of nearly 11 million people from Africa over the course of three centuries. Colonial settlement in North and South America also created new social hierarchies and new regimes of inequality. Indigenous peoples and newly arrived settlers confronted one another, and all were affected by the profound upheavals of Europe. In response, intellectuals and artists strove to reassess Europeans' place in this expanding Atlantic world, and to make sense of the profound changes that were occurring in daily life.

THE EMERGENCE OF THE ATLANTIC WORLD

By the middle of the sixteenth century, Spanish and Portuguese ventures into Africa, the Caribbean, and South America were galvanizing other European kingdoms to launch imperial experiments of their own. In 1585, the Englishman Walter Raleigh attempted to start a colony just north of Spanish Florida. The settlement at Roanoke Island (present-day North Carolina) was intended to solidify English claims to the territory of Virginia, which was named for the "Virgin Queen" Elizabeth and originally encompassed the North American seaboard from South Carolina to Maine, as well as Bermuda.

Raleigh's ill-fated experiment ended with the disappearance of the first colonists, but it was followed by an English expedition to the Chesapeake Bay in 1606, funded by a private London firm called the Virginia Company. These English adventurers were not being sponsored by the crown, and they probably did not intend to remain permanently in the New World. Instead, their goal was to provide agricultural goods for the European market and to make their fortunes before returning home. Nevertheless, with the Spanish model much in mind, the English reserved the right to "conquer" any peoples who proved uncooperative. So when Native Americans of the Powhatan tribe killed one-third of the settlers during a raid in 1622, the colonists responded by crushing the Powhatans and seizing their lands.

For decades thereafter, the native populations of North America both threatened and nurtured the fragile settlements that were gaining a toehold on the continent. Especially in the early years of colonization, when the number of European immigrants was small, some Native American peoples sought to take advantage of these new contacts, in order to trade for goods otherwise unavailable to them. European settlers, for their part, often exhibited a combination of paternalism and contempt for the peoples they encountered. Some hoped to convert Americans to Christianity; others sought to use them as laborers. Ultimately, however, the balance was tipped by larger environmental, biological, and demographic factors that lay outside the control of individuals.

The Columbian Exchange

The accelerating rate of global connections in the sixteenth century precipitated an extraordinary movement of peoples, plants, animals, and diseases, known as the "Columbian exchange." Yet this exchange soon encompassed lands that lay far beyond the purview of Columbus and his contemporaries, including Australia and the Pacific Islands.

Because of its far-reaching effects, the Columbian exchange is considered a fundamental turning point in both human history and the history of the earth's ecology. It put new agricultural products into circulation, introduced new domesticated species of animals, and accidentally encouraged the spread of deadly diseases and the devastation caused by invasive plants and animals. Ecosystems around the world were destroyed or transformed. For example, the introduction of pigs and dogs to islands in the Atlantic and Pacific resulted in the extinction of indigenous animals and birds. The landscapes of Central America and southwestern North America were stripped of vegetation after Spanish settlers attempted large-scale ranching operations. European honeybees displaced native insect populations and encouraged the propagation of harmful plant species. Meanwhile, gray squirrels and raccoons from North America found their way to Europe, while insects from all over the world traveled to new environments and spread unfamiliar forms of bacteria and pollen.

Obviously, the transfer of human populations in the form of settlers, soldiers, merchants, sailors, indentured servants, and slaves accelerated the process of change. Some groups were wiped out through violence, forced resettlement, and unaccustomed illnesses. As much as 90 percent of the pre-Columbian population of the Americas died from communicable diseases such as smallpox, cholera, influenza, typhoid, measles, malaria, and plague—all brought from Europe. Syphilis, on the other hand, appears to have been brought to Europe from the Americas; some scholars

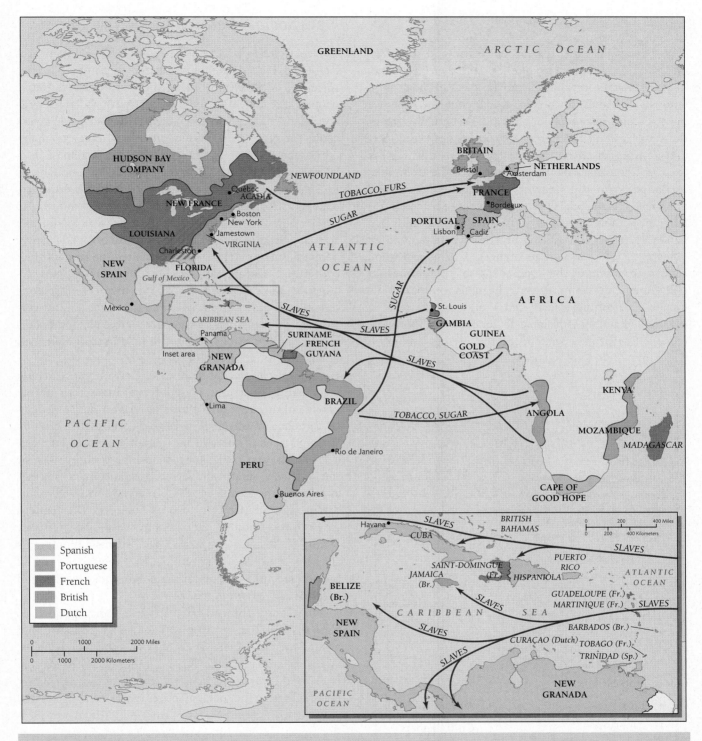

THE ATLANTIC WORLD. ▪ *Trace the routes of the triangular trade. What products did French and British colonies in North America provide to the European market?* ▪ *Which colonies would have been most dependent on slave labor?* ▪ *What did they produce, and how did these products enter into the triangle?*

have even asserted that it was Columbus's own sailors who transmitted the disease.

At the same time, the movement of foodstuffs from one part of the world to another, and their cultivation in new habitats, revolutionized the diets of local populations. The American potato, which could be grown in poor soil and stored for long periods, eventually became the staple diet of the European poor. Indeed, the foods and flavors that characterize today's iconic cuisines are, to an extraordinary degree, the result of the Columbian exchange. Who can imagine an English meal without potatoes? Italian food without tomatoes? Switzerland or Belgium without chocolate? Thai food without chili peppers? Or, on the other side of the Atlantic, Hawaii without pineapples? Florida without oranges? Colombia without coffee? Only one of the components of the quintessentially American hamburger is indigenous to America: the tomato. Everything else is Old World: beef, wheat for the bun, cucumber for the pickle, onion, lettuce. Even the name is European, a reference to the city of Hamburg in Germany.

THE COLUMBIAN EXCHANGE

The following list names just a few of the commodities and contagions that moved between the Old and New Worlds in this era.

Old World → New World	New World → Old World
• Wheat	• Corn
• Sugar	• Potatoes
• Bananas	• Beans
• Rice	• Squash
• Wine grapes	• Pumpkins
• Horses	• Tomatoes
• Pigs	• Avocados
• Chickens	• Chili peppers
• Sheep	• Pineapples
• Cattle	• Cocoa
• *Smallpox*	• Tobacco
• *Measles*	• *Syphilis*
• *Typhus*	

New Social Hierarchies in New Spain

The centralization of imperial power in New Spain was facilitated by the highly organized structure of Aztec society in Mexico and that of the Incas in Peru. Native peoples already lived, for the most part, in large, well-regulated villages and towns. The Spanish government could therefore work closely with local elites to maintain order. It did so by transplanting the system of *enco-miendas* originally set up to manage Muslim populations in Spanish territories captured by Christian crusaders (Chapter 12). The Spanish verb *encomendar* means "to trust," which means that *encomenderos* were technically agents of the crown, overseeing land still owned by native peoples. But in practice, many exploited the land for their own profit, treating native workers like serfs. Some *encomenderos* were descendants of the first conquistadors; others were drawn from Aztec and Inca elites. Many were women: the daughters of the Aztec emperor Montezuma had been given extensive lands to hold in trust after their father's capitulation to Cortés.

The *encomienda* system was effective because it built on existing structures and did not attempt to uproot native cultures. Spanish efforts to convert native peoples to Catholicism were also successful because they built on basic patterns of life and indigenous religious practices. The result was widespread cultural assimilation by the relatively small numbers of (usually male) settlers, assisted by the normalcy of intermarriage between (male) colonizers and (female) colonial subjects. This pattern gave rise to a complex and distinctive caste system in New Spain, with a few "pure-blooded" Spanish immigrants at the top; a very large number of Creoles (peoples of mixed descent) in the middle; and indigenous peoples and Africans at the bottom.

In theory, these racial categories corresponded to class distinctions, but in practice race and class did not always coincide. Racial concepts were extremely flexible, and prosperous individuals or families of mixed descent often found ways to establish their "pure" Spanish ancestry by adopting the social practices of the Spanish colonial elites. The lingering effects of this complicated stratification are still evident in Latin America today.

Patterns of English Colonial Settlement

In the early decades of the seventeenth century, the English challenge to Spanish supremacy in the Atlantic began to bear fruit. But like the colonies of New Spain, England's North American settlements were private ventures, farmed either by individual landholders (as in Maryland and Pennsylvania) or managed by groups of investors (as in Virginia and the Massachusetts Bay Colony). Many English immigrants were motivated by a desire for religious and political freedom from England—hence the name we give to the "Pilgrims" who landed at Plymouth, Massachusetts, in 1620. These radical Protestants were known in England as Puritans and were almost as unwelcome as Catholics in a country whose church was an extension of the monarchy (Chapter 13). The number of early immigrants to English territories was also swelled by indentured servitude, a practice that brought thousands of "free" laborers from overpopulated cities across the Atlantic to work under terms that made them little different from slaves. Perhaps 75–80 percent of the people who arrived in the Chesapeake colony were indentured servants, and nearly a quarter of these were women.

Strikingly, English colonists showed little interest in trying to convert Native American peoples to Christianity, another thing that set them apart from their Spanish counterparts. Still another was the fact that many English colonists tended to emigrate with their families or even as part of entire communities. Because there were many women among the first waves of settlers, intermarriage with native populations was rare, which eventually created a nearly unbridgeable social and racial divide—again in stark contrast to the colonies of South America.

Building on their experience in Ireland, where colonies had been called "plantations," English settlers established plantations—planned communities—that attempted to replicate as many features of English life as possible. Geography largely dictated the locations of these settlements, which were scattered along the northern Atlantic coast and on rivers and bays that provided good harbors. Aside from the Hudson, there were no great rivers to lead colonists very far inland, so the English colonies clung to the shoreline and to each other. Today's densely populated corridor along the Atlantic seaboard is a direct result of these early settlement patterns.

The accumulation of wealth through the control of land was a new and exciting prospect for small- and medium-scale landholders in the new English colonies; at home in the Old World, most land was owned by royal and aristocratic families, or by the Church. This helps to explain their rural, agricultural character—in contrast to the great cities of New Spain. But this focus on agriculture also resulted from the demographic catastrophe that decimated native populations in this region: by the early seventeenth century, a great deal of rich land had been abandoned because there were so few native farmers left

PLYMOUTH PLANTATION. An English settlement was established at Plymouth in the Massachusetts Bay Colony in 1620. This image shows a reconstruction of the village as it might have looked in 1627 and captures something of the plantation's diminutive fragility and isolation.

alive. As a result, indigenous peoples who had not already succumbed to European diseases were now under threat from colonists who wanted complete control over their lands.

To this end, the English soon set out to eliminate, through expulsion and massacre, the former inhabitants of the region. There were a few exceptions; in the Quaker colony of Pennsylvania, colonists and Native Americans maintained friendly relations for more than half a century. But in the Carolinas there was widespread enslavement of native peoples, either for sale to the West Indies or to work on the rice plantations along the coast. Ultimately, however, the plantation system rendered its greatest profits through the use of African slaves.

Sugar, Slaves, and the Transatlantic Triangle

In contrast to the more than 7 million African slaves who were forced to labor and die on plantations across the Atlantic, only about 1.5 million Europeans came to the Americas in the two centuries after Columbus's first voyage. Although farming and ranching were encouraged in Central and South America, and later in Florida and California, the Spanish colonial economy was dominated by intensive extraction of mineral resources, which required a constant supply of fresh workers; conditions in the mines were terrible and

Analyzing Primary Sources

Enslaved Native Laborers at Potosí

Since the Spanish crown received one-fifth of all revenues from the mines of New Spain, while maintaining a monopoly over the mercury used to refine the ore into silver, it had an important stake in ensuring the mines' productivity. To this end, the crown granted colonial mine owners the right to conscript native peoples and gave them considerable freedom when it came to the treatment of the workers. This account, dated to about 1620, describes the conditions endured by these native laborers at Potosí (also discussed in Chapter 12).

ccording to His Majesty's warrant, the mine owners on this massive range [at Potosí] have a right to the conscripted labor of 13,300 Indians in the working and exploitation of the mines, both those [mines] which have been discovered, those now discovered, and those which shall be discovered. It is the duty of the *Corregidor* [municipal governor] of Potosí to have them rounded up and to see that they come in from all the provinces between Cuzco . . . and as far as the frontiers of Tarija and Tomina. . . .

The conscripted Indians go up every Monday morning to the . . . foot of the range; the *Corregidor* arrives with all the provincial captains or chiefs who have charge of the Indians assigned him for his miner or smelter; that keeps him busy till 1 p.m., by which time the Indians are already turned over to these mine and smelter owners.

After each has eaten his ration, they climb up the hill, each to his mine, and go in, staying there from that hour until Saturday evening without coming out of the mine; their wives bring them food, but they stay constantly underground, excavating and carrying out the ore from which they get the silver. They all have tallow candles, lighted day and night; that is the light they work with, for as they are underground, they have need for it all the time. . . .

These Indians have different functions in the handling of the silver ore; some break it up with bar or pick, and dig down in, following the vein in the mine; others bring it up; others up above keep separating the good and the poor in piles; others are occupied in taking it down from the range to the mills on herds of llamas; every day they bring up more than 8,000 of these native beasts of burden for this task. These teamsters who carry the metal are not conscripted, but are hired.

Source: Antonio Vázquez de Espinosa, *Compendium and Description of the West Indies*, trans. Charles Upson Clark (Washington, DC: 1968), p. 62.

Questions for Analysis

1. From the tone of this account, what do you think was the narrator's purpose in writing? Who is his intended audience?

2. Reconstruct the conditions in which these laborers worked. What would you estimate to be the human costs of this week's labor? Why, for example, would a fresh workforce be needed every Monday?

mortality was high. In North America, plantation agriculture was also in need of a new labor supply. As we have seen, diseases and violence resulted in the deaths of millions of Native Americans in the space of only a few decades, and experiments in the use of indentured servants on plantations in tropical climates were unsuccessful. Moreover, the return of the plague in Europe, along with the devastation of religious warfare (as will be discussed later), meant that colonists could not look to Europe to satisfy their labor needs. Colonial agents thus began to import slaves from Africa to bolster the labor force and to produce the wealth they so avidly sought. And overwhelmingly, that wealth was derived from a new commodity for which there was an insatiable appetite in Europe: sugar.

Sugar was at the center of the "triangular trade" that linked markets in Africa, the Americas, and Europe—all of which were driven by slave labor. For example, ships that transported African slaves to the Caribbean might trade their human cargo for molasses made on the sugar

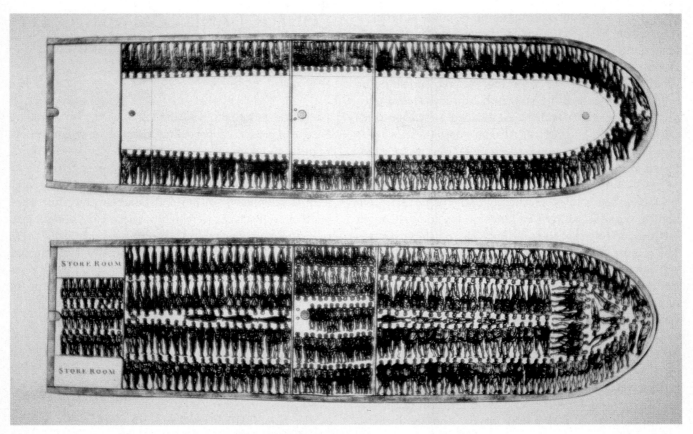

HOW SLAVES WERE STOWED ABOARD SHIP DURING THE MIDDLE PASSAGE. Men were "housed" on the right, women on the left, children in the middle. The human cargo was jammed onto platforms six feet wide without sufficient headroom to permit an adult to sit up. This diagram is from evidence gathered by English abolitionists and depicts conditions on the Liverpool slave ship *Brookes*.

plantations of the islands. These ships would then sail to New England, where the molasses would be used to make rum. Loaded with a consignment of rum, the ship would return to the African coast to repeat the process, bartering rum for human bodies. An alternative triangle might see cheap manufactured goods move from England to Africa, where they would be traded for slaves. Those slaves would then be shipped to Virginia and exchanged for tobacco, which would be shipped back to England.

Although the transatlantic slave trade was theoretically controlled by the governments of European colonial powers—Britain officially entered this trade in 1564, the year of William Shakespeare's birth—private entrepreneurs and working-class laborers were active at every stage of the supply chain: manning the ships, capturing human cargo, running the slave markets. Many other branches of the economy in Europe and the Americas were also linked to the slave trade: from the investors in Amsterdam, London, Lisbon, and Bordeaux who financed the slave trade, to the insurance brokers who protected these investments, to the

financial agents who offered credit. And this is to say nothing of the myriad ways in which the everyday lives of average people were bound to slavery. All those who bought the commodities produced by slave labor, or who manufactured the weapons that enabled enslavement, were also implicated. The slave trade was not driven by a few unscrupulous men. It was the engine of the modern globalized economy.

Counting the Human Cost of the Slave Trade

When the Portuguese began to transport African slaves to their sugarcane plantations in Brazil in the 1540s, slavery became crucial to the domestic economies of West African kingdoms. In the following decades, however, the ever-increasing demand for slaves would cause the permanent disintegration of political order in this region by creating an incentive for war and raiding among rival tribes. Moreover, the increased traffic in human beings called for more highly systematized and inhumane methods for corralling, sorting, and shipping them. At the end of the sixteenth century, accordingly, the Portuguese government established a fortified trading outpost on the central African coast (near what is now Angola). Additional trading posts were then established to assist in processing the captives.

Once on board ship, enslaved humans were shackled below decks in spaces barely wider than their own bodies, without sanitary facilities of any kind. It might seem surprising that the mortality rate on these voyages was relatively low: probably 10 or 11 percent. But this was only because the slaves chosen for the voyage were healthy to begin with, and traders were anxious to maintain their goods to sell at a profit. Those Africans who were transported were already the survivors of unimaginable hardships. In order to place the preceding statistic in a larger context, then, we need to consider how many would have died before they reached the ship. One historian has estimated that 36 out of every 100 people captured in the African interior would perish in the six-month-long forced march to the coast. Another dozen or so would die in the prisons there. Eventually, perhaps 57 of the original 100 captives would be taken on board a slave ship. Some 51 would survive the journey and be sold into slavery on arrival. If the destination was Brazil's sugar plantations, only 40 would still be alive after two years. In other words, the actual mortality rate was something like 60 percent—and this doesn't begin to account for life expectancy.

The people consigned to this fate struggled against it, and their initiatives helped to shape the emerging Atlantic world. When the opportunity presented itself, slaves banded together in revolt—a perpetual possibility that haunted slave owners and led to regimes of violence (as in ancient Rome: Chapter 5). There were other forms of resistance, among them suicide and infanticide. Above all, slaves sought to escape. Almost as soon as the slave trade escalated, there were communities of escaped slaves throughout the Americas. Many of these independent settlements were large enough to assert and defend their autonomy. One such community, founded in 1603 in the hinterlands of Brazil, persisted for over a century and had as many as 20,000 inhabitants. Others were smaller and more ephemeral, but their existence testifies to the limits of imperialism in the new American colonies.

CONFLICT AND COMPETITION IN EUROPE AND THE ATLANTIC WORLD

The colonization of the Americas seemed to guarantee European prosperity, providing an outlet for expansion and aggression. But in the second half of the sixteenth century, prolonged political, religious, and economic crises began to cripple Europe. These crises were the product of long-term developments within and between powerful states, but they were also exacerbated by these same states' imperial ambitions. Inevitably, then, European conflicts spread to European colonial holdings. Eventually, the outcome of these conflicts would determine which European powers were best positioned to enlarge their presence in the Atlantic world—and beyond.

New World Silver and Old World Economies

In the latter half of the sixteenth century, an unprecedented inflation in prices profoundly destabilized the European economy, leading to widespread financial panic. Although the twentieth century would see more dizzying inflations, skyrocketing prices were a terrifying novelty in this era, causing what some historians have termed a "price revolution."

Two developments underlay this phenomenon. The first was demographic. After the plague-induced decline of the fourteenth century (Chapter 11), Europe's population grew from roughly 50 million people in 1450 to 90 million in 1600: that is, it increased by nearly 80 percent in a relatively short span of time. Yet Europe's food supply remained nearly constant, meaning that food prices were driven sharply higher by the greater demand for basic commodities. Meanwhile, the enormous influx of silver and gold from Spanish America flooded Europe's previously cash-poor economy (Chapter 12). This sudden availability of ready coin drove prices higher still.

How? In just four years, from 1556 to 1560, about 10 million ducats' worth of silver passed through the Spanish port of Seville: roughly equivalent to 10 billion U.S. dollars in today's currency. (A single gold ducat, the standard unit of monetary exchange for long-distance trade, would be worth nearly a thousand dollars.) Consequently, the market was flooded with coins whose worth quickly

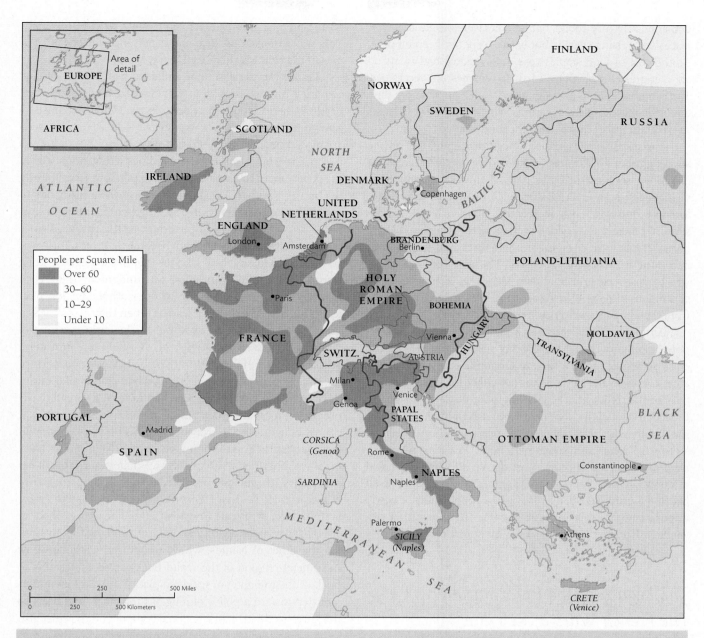

People per Square Mile

- Over 60
- 30–60
- 10–29
- Under 10

POPULATION DENSITY ▪ *What regions were most densely peopled?* ▪ *Why were many of these regions on the coasts?* ▪ *How would urbanization affect patterns of life and trade?*

became debased because there were so many of them. And still the silver poured in, cheapening the coinage even more: by 1580, the amount of imported silver had doubled; by 1595, it more than quadrupled. Because most of this money was used by the Spanish crown to pay its armies and the many creditors who had financed imperial ventures, a huge volume of coinage was put quickly into circulation through European banks, making the problem of inflation even more widespread. Since some people suddenly had more money to pay for goods and services, those who supplied these commodities could charge higher and higher prices. "I learned a proverb here," said a French traveler in Spain: "Everything costs a lot, except silver."

The New European Poor

In this economic climate, aggressive entrepreneurs profited from financial speculation, landholders from the rising prices of agricultural produce, and merchants from increasing demand for luxury goods. But laborers were caught in a vice. Prices were rising steeply, but wages were not keeping pace. As the cost of food staples rose, poor people had to spend an ever-greater percentage of their incomes on necessities. The overall cost of living in England, for example, more than doubled in Shakespeare's lifetime. When wars or bad harvests drove grain prices higher still, the poor starved to death.

The price revolution also placed new pressures on the sovereign states of Europe. Inflation depressed the real value of money, so fixed incomes derived from taxes and rents yielded less and less actual wealth. Governments were therefore forced to raise taxes merely to keep their revenues constant. Yet most states needed even more revenue than before, because they were engaging in more wars, and warfare was becoming increasingly expensive. The only recourse, then, was to raise taxes precipitously. Hence, governments faced continuous threats of defiance and even armed resistance from their citizens, who could not afford to foot these bills.

Although prices rose less rapidly after 1600, as both population growth and the flood of silver began to slow, the ensuing decades were a time of economic stagnation. A few areas—notably the Netherlands (as will be discussed later)—bucked the trend, but the laboring poor made no advances. Indeed, the lot of the poor deteriorated even further, as helpless civilians were plundered by predatory tax collectors, looting soldiers, and sometimes both. Peasants who had been dispossessed of property or driven off lands once held in common were branded as vagrants, and vagrancy itself became a criminal offense. It was this population of newly impoverished Europeans who became the indentured servants or deported criminals of the American colonies.

The Legacy of the Reformation: The French Wars of Religion

Compounding these economic problems were the wars that erupted within many European states. As we began to observe in Chapter 9, most medieval kingdoms were created through the colonization of smaller, traditionally autonomous territories—either by conquest or through marriage alliances among ruling families. Now these enlarged monarchies began to make ever-greater financial claims on their citizens while at the same time demanding religious uniformity among them. The result was regional and civil conflict, as local populations and even elites rebelled against the centralizing demands of monarchs who often embraced a different religion than that of their subjects. Although the Peace of Augsburg (1555) had established that each territory would follow the religion of its ruler (see Chapter 13), it was based on the premise that no state can tolerate religious diversity. This was a dangerous idea, and it poisoned European colonies in the New World as well.

France was the first to be enflamed by religious warfare. Calvinist missionaries from Geneva had made significant headway there in southern regions. By the 1560s, Calvinists—known as Huguenots (*HEW-guh-nohz*)—made up between 10 and 20 percent of the French population. But there was no open warfare until dynastic politics led factions within the government to break down along religious lines, pitting the (mostly southern) Huguenots against the (mostly northern) Catholic aristocracy. In 1572 the two sides almost brokered a truce: the presumptive heir to the throne, Prince Henry of Navarre—who had become a Protestant—was contracted to marry the Catholic sister of the reigning king, Henry III. But the compromise was undone by the Queen Mother, Catherine de Medici, whose Catholic faction plotted to kill all the Huguenot leaders when they assembled in Paris for her daughter's wedding. In the early morning of St. Bartholomew's Day (August 24), most of these Protestant aristocrats were murdered in their beds, and thousands of humble citizens were slaughtered when riots broke out in the city. When word of the Parisian massacre spread to the provinces, local atrocities proliferated.

Although Henry of Navarre and his bride escaped, religious warfare in France continued for more than two decades. Finally, Catherine's death in 1589 was followed by that of her son, Henry III, who had produced no heir to supplant Henry of Navarre. He became Henry IV, renouncing his Protestant faith in order to placate France's Catholic majority. Then, in 1598, Henry made a landmark effort to end conflict by issuing the Edict of Nantes, which recognized Catholicism as the official religion of the realm but enabled Protestants to practice their religion in specified places. This was an important step toward a policy of religious tolerance, and because the religious divide had a regional component, the edict also reinforced a tradition of regional autonomy in southwestern France. The success of this effort can be measured by the fact that peace was maintained in France even after Henry IV was assassinated by a Catholic in 1610.

The Revolt of the Netherlands and the Dutch Trading Empire

Warfare between Catholics and Protestants also broke out in the Netherlands during this period. Controlled for almost a century by the same Habsburg family that ruled Spain and its overseas empire, the Netherlands had prospered through intense involvement with trade in the

Atlantic world. Their inhabitants had the greatest per capita wealth in all Europe, and the metropolis of Antwerp was northern Europe's leading commercial and financial center. So when the Spanish king and emperor Philip II (r. 1556–98) attempted to tighten his hold there in the 1560s, the fiercely independent Dutch cities resented this imperial intrusion and were ready to fight it.

This conflict took on a religious dynamic because Calvinism had spread into the Netherlands from France. Philip, an ardent defender of the Catholic faith, could not tolerate this combination of political and religious disobedience. When crowds began ransacking and desecrating Catholic churches throughout the country, Philip dispatched an army of 10,000 Spanish soldiers to wipe out Protestantism in his Dutch territories. A reign of terror ensued, which further catalyzed the Protestant opposition.

In 1572, a Dutch aristocrat, William of Orange, emerged as the anti-Spanish leader and sought help from religious allies in France, Germany, and England. Organized fleets of Protestant privateers (that is, privately owned ships) began harassing the Spanish navy in the waters of the North Atlantic. William's Protestant army then seized control of the Netherlands' northern provinces. Although William was assassinated in 1584, his efforts were instrumental in forcing the Spanish crown to recognize the independence of a northern Dutch Republic in 1609. Once united, these seven northern provinces became wholly Calvinist; the southern region, still largely Catholic, remained under Spanish rule.

After gaining its independence, the new Dutch Republic began to build the most prosperous European commercial empire of the seventeenth century. Indeed, its reach extended well beyond the Atlantic world, targeting the Indian Ocean

and East Asia as well. This colonial project owed more to the strategic "fort and factory" model of expansion favored by the Portuguese than to the Spanish technique of territorial conquest and settlement. Many of its early initiatives were spurred by the establishment of the Dutch East India Company, a private mercantile corporation that came to control Sumatra, Borneo, and the Moluccas (the so-called Spice Islands). This meant that the Dutch had a lucrative monopoly on the European trade in spices. The company also secured an exclusive right to trade with Japan and maintained military and trading outposts in China and India, too.

In North America, the Dutch presence was limited to a single outpost: the colony known as New Amsterdam, until it was surrendered to the English in 1667, when it was renamed New York. The remaining Dutch territorial holdings in the Atlantic world were Dutch Guyana (present-day Suriname) on the coast of South America, and the islands of Curaçao and Tobago in the Caribbean. But if the Dutch did not match the Spanish or the English in their accumulation of land, the establishment of a second merchant enterprise, the Dutch

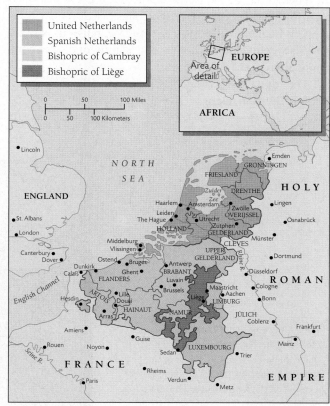

THE NETHERLANDS AFTER 1609. ■ *What were the two main divisions of the Netherlands?* ■ *Which was Protestant, and which was Catholic?* ■ *How could William of Orange and his allies use the geography of the northern Netherlands against the Spanish?*

PROTESTANTS RANSACKING A CATHOLIC CHURCH IN THE NETHERLANDS. Protestant destruction of religious images provoked a stern response from Philip II. ■ *Why would Protestants have smashed statuary and other devotional artifacts?*

West India Company, allowed them to dominate the Atlantic slave trade with Africa after 1621.

In constructing this new transoceanic empire of slaves and spices, the Dutch leveraged a new financial mechanism: the joint-stock company. The Dutch East and West India Companies were early examples, raising cash by selling shares to individual investors whose liability was limited to the sum of their investment and who were entitled to a comparable share in any profits. Originally, the Dutch East India Company intended to pay off its investors within ten years, but when the period was up, investors who wanted to realize their profits immediately were encouraged to sell their shares on the open market. The creation of a market in shares—we now call it a stock market—was an innovation that spread quickly. Stock markets now control the world's economy.

The Struggle of England and Spain

Religious strife could spark civil war, as in France, or political rebellion, as in the Netherlands. But it could also provoke warfare between sovereign states, as in the struggle between England and Spain. In this case, religious conflict was also entangled with dynastic claims and economic competition in the Atlantic world.

The dynastic strife came from the English royal family's division along confessional lines. The Catholic queen Mary (r. 1553–58), eldest daughter of Henry VIII and granddaughter of Ferdinand and Isabella of Spain (see Chapter 13), married her cousin Philip II of Spain in 1554 and ruled at a time of great tension between Catholics and Protestants in England. After Mary's death, her Protestant half-sister Elizabeth (r. 1558–1603) came to the throne, and relations with Spain rapidly declined. They deteriorated further when Catholic Ireland—an English colony—rose in rebellion in 1565, with Spain quietly supporting the Irish. Although it took almost thirty bloody years, English forces eventually suppressed the rebellion. Elizabeth then cemented the Irish defeat by encouraging extensive colonial settlement in Ireland, establishing the plantations that would provide models for those in North America. Indeed, she did so in conscious (and ironic) imitation of Spanish policy in Mexico, in the hopes of creating a colonial state with a largely English identity. Instead, these measures created the deep divisions that trouble Ireland to this day.

England's conflict with Spain, meanwhile, worsened because English economic interests were directly opposed to those of Spain. English traders were making steady inroads into Spanish commercial networks in the Atlantic, as English sea captains such as Sir Francis Drake plundered Spanish vessels on the high seas. In a particularly dramatic exploit lasting from 1577 to 1580, prevailing winds and a lust for booty propelled Drake all the way around the world, to return with stolen Spanish treasure worth twice as much as Queen Elizabeth's annual revenue.

After suffering numerous such attacks, Philip finally resolved to fight back when Elizabeth's government

THE "ARMADA PORTRAIT" OF ELIZABETH. This is one of several portraits that commemorated the defeat of the Spanish Armada in 1588. Through the window on the left (the queen's right hand), an English flotilla sails serenely on sunny seas; on the right, Spanish ships are wrecked by a "Protestant wind." Elizabeth's right hand rests protectively—and commandingly—on the globe. ▪ *How would you interpret this image?*

openly supported the Dutch rebellion against Spain in 1585. In 1588, he dispatched an enormous fleet, confidently called the "Invincible Armada," whose mission was to invade England. But the invasion never occurred. After a major battle, a fierce storm—hailed as a "Protestant wind" by the lucky English—drove the Spanish galleons off course, many of them wrecking on the Irish coast. The shattered flotilla eventually limped home and Elizabeth took credit for her country's miraculous escape. In subsequent years, continued threats from Spain nurtured a new sense of English nationalism and fueled anti-Catholic sentiment.

THE THIRTY YEARS' WAR AND THE RISE OF FRANCE

With the promulgation of the French Edict of Nantes, the end of open hostilities between England and Spain, and the truce between Spain and the Dutch Republic, religious warfare in Europe came briefly to an end. In 1618, however, a new series of conflicts broke out in some of the German-speaking lands that had felt the first divisive effects of the Reformation (Chapter 13). Not only was this period of warfare one of the longest in history, it was one of the bloodiest and most widespread, engulfing most of the European continent before it ended thirty years later, in 1648. Although it began as a religious war, it quickly became an international struggle for political dominance. In the end, some 8 million people died and entire provinces never recovered. Most of the great states involved were impoverished and weakened. The exception was France, which became a preeminent power in Europe for the first time.

The Beginnings of the Thirty Years' War

On one level, the Thirty Years' War was an outlet for tensions that had been building up since the Peace of Augsburg in 1555. On another, it grew out of even longer-standing disputes among rulers and territories (Catholic and Protestant) in the patchwork of provinces that made up the Holy Roman Empire, disputes into which allied powers were drawn. On still another, it was an opportunity for players on the fringes of power to come into prominence.

The catalyst came in 1618. In that year, the Habsburg (Catholic) prince of Austria, Ferdinand—who also ruled Hungary and Poland—was named heir to the throne of Protestant Bohemia. This prompted a rebellion among the Bohemian aristocracy. A year later, complex dynastic politics resulted in Ferdinand's election as Holy Roman Emperor. This gave him access to an imperial (Catholic) army, which he now sent in to crush the Protestant revolt. The Bohemians, meanwhile, were bolstered by the support of some Austrian elites, many of whom were also Protestant and who saw in the rebellion a way to recover power from the Habsburg ruling family.

In 1620, the war escalated further when the Ottoman Empire threw its support behind the Protestants. This touched off a war with the staunchly Catholic kingdom of Poland, whose borders the Muslim army would need to cross in order to get to Prague. The Poles won and the Ottomans retreated: a major Catholic victory. At the same time, Ferdinand's Habsburg cousin, the Spanish king and emperor Philip IV, had renewed hostilities with the Protestant Dutch Republic, so an alliance between the two Habsburg rulers made sense. This led to a major pitched battle between united Protestant forces and a Spanish-led Catholic army just outside of Prague. The Habsburgs were victorious, and Bohemia was forced to accept Ferdinand's Catholic rule.

The Tangled Politics and Terrible Price of War

The conflict, which had started in Bohemia, should have ended there. But it did not. Unrest between Catholics and Protestants now found outlets in other parts of Europe. France erupted into violence once again. Protestant Denmark, fearing that Catholic victories in neighboring parts of the Holy Roman Empire might threaten its sovereignty, was drawn into the fray—losing valuable territories before it was forced to concede defeat.

In this new phase of warfare, political expediency soon outweighed religious allegiances. When a confederation of Catholic princes seemed close to uprooting Protestantism throughout Germany, it found its way blocked by other German Catholic princes who were willing to ally with Protestants in order to preserve their own autonomy. Joining them was the (Protestant) king of Sweden, Gustavus Adolphus (r. 1611–32), who championed both the German Lutheran states and his own nation's sovereignty, but whose Protestant army was secretly subsidized by Catholic France, because France

The Devastation of the Thirty Years' War

The author of the following excerpt, Hans Jakob Christoph von Grimmelshausen (1621–1676), barely survived the horrors of the Thirty Years' War. His parents were killed, probably when he was thirteen years old, and he himself was kidnapped the following year and forced into the army. By age fifteen, he was a soldier. His darkly satiric masterpiece, Simplicissimus *("The Simpleton"), drew heavily on these experiences. Though technically a fictional memoir, it portrays with brutal accuracy the terrible realities of this era.*

lthough it was not my intention to take the peaceloving reader with these troopers to my dad's house and farm, seeing that matters will go ill therein, yet the course of my history demands that I should leave to kind posterity an account of what manner of cruelties were now and again practised in this our German war: yes, and moreover testify by my own example that such evils must often have been sent to us by the goodness of Almighty God for our profit. For, gentle reader, who would ever have taught me that there was a God in Heaven if these soldiers had not destroyed my dad's house, and by such a deed driven me out among folk who gave me all fitting instruction thereupon? . . .

The first thing these troopers did was, that they stabled their horses: thereafter each fell to his appointed task: which task was neither more nor less than ruin and destruction. For though some began to slaughter and to boil and to roast so that it looked as if there should be a merry banquet forward, yet others there were who did but storm through the house above and below stairs. Others stowed together great parcels of cloth and apparel and all manner of household stuff, as if they would set up a frippery market. All that

they had no mind to take with them they cut in pieces. Some thrust their swords through the hay and straw as if they had not enough sheep and swine to slaughter: and some shook the feathers out of the beds and in their stead stuffed in bacon and other dried meat and provisions as if such were better and softer to sleep upon. Others broke the stove and the windows as if they had a never-ending summer to promise. Houseware of copper and tin they beat flat, and packed such vessels, all bent and spoiled, in with the rest. Bedsteads, tables, chairs, and benches they burned, though there lay many cords of dry wood in the yard. Pots and pipkins must all go to pieces, either because they would eat none but roast flesh, or because their purpose was to make there but a single meal.

Our maid was so handled in the stable that she could not come out, which is a shame to tell of. Our man they laid bound upon the ground, thrust a gag into his mouth, and poured a pailful of filthy water into his body: and by this, which they called a Swedish draught, they forced him to lead a party of them to another place where they captured men and beasts, and brought them back to our farm, in which company were my dad, my mother, and our Ursula.

And now they began: first to take the flints out of their pistols and in place of

them to jam the peasants' thumbs in and so to torture the poor rogues as if they had been about the burning of witches: for one of them they had taken they thrust into the baking oven and there lit a fire under him, although he had as yet confessed no crime: as for another, they put a cord round his head and so twisted it tight with a piece of wood that the blood gushed from his mouth and nose and ears. In a word each had his own device to torture the peasants, and each peasant his several tortures.

Source: Hans Jakob Christoph von Grimmelshausen, *Simplicissimus,* trans. S. Goodrich (New York: 1995), pp. 1–3, 8–10, 32–35.

Questions for Analysis

1. The first-person narrator here recounts the atrocities committed "in this our German war," in which both perpetrators and victims are German. How believable is this description? What lends it credibility?

2. Why might Grimmelshausen have chosen to publish his account as a satirical fiction rather than as a straightforward historical narrative or autobiography? How would this choice affect a reader's response to scenes such as this?

EUROPE AT THE END OF THE THIRTY YEARS' WAR. This map shows the fragile political checkerboard that resulted from the Peace of Westphalia in 1648. ▪ *When you compare this map to the map on page 350, what are the most significant territorial changes between 1550 and 1648?* ▪ *Which regions were weakened or endangered?* ▪ *Which would be in a strong position to dominate Europe?*

wanted to avoid being surrounded by a strong (Catholic) Habsburg alliance on its northern, eastern, and southern borders.

One of the great military commanders of all time, Gustavus had become king at age seventeen. Like another young general, Alexander the Great (see Chapter 4), he was not only an expert tactician but a splendid leader. His army became the best-trained and best-equipped fighting force of the era—what some have called the first modern army. When Gustavus died in battle in 1632, a month before his thirty-eighth birthday, Sweden had become one

of Europe's great powers, rivaling Spain and Russia in size and prestige.

In 1635, with Gustavus dead, Catholic France was compelled to join Protestant Sweden in declaring open war on the Catholic Habsburgs of Austria and Spain. In the middle lay the lands of Central Europe, already weakened by seventeen years of war and now a helpless battleground. In the next thirteen years, this region suffered more from warfare than at any time until the twentieth century. Several cities were besieged and sacked nine or ten times over, while soldiers from all nations, who had to sustain themselves by plunder, gave no quarter to defenseless civilians. Most horrifying was the loss of life in the final four years of the war, when the carnage continued even after peace negotiators arrived at broad areas of agreement.

The Peace of Westphalia and the Decline of Spain

The eventual adoption of the Peace of Westphalia in 1648 was a watershed in European history. It marked the emergence of France as the predominant power on the Continent, a position it would hold for the next two centuries. The greatest losers in the conflict (aside from the millions of victims) were the Austrian Habsburgs, who were forced to surrender all the territory they had gained. The Spanish Habsburgs were also substantially weakened and were no longer able to fall back on the wealth of their Atlantic empire. While war was raging in Europe, large portions of the Atlantic trade had been infiltrated by merchants from other countries, and the expansion of local economies in Spain's colonies had made them less dependent on trade with Spain itself.

In 1600, the Spanish Empire had been the mightiest power in the world. A half century later, this empire had begun to fall apart. As we've already noted, New Spain's great wealth had begun to turn into a liability when the infusion of silver spiked inflation and slowed economic development at home. Lacking both agricultural and mineral resources of its own, Spain might have developed its own industries and a balanced trading pattern, as some of its Atlantic rivals were doing. Instead, the Spanish used imperial silver to buy manufactured goods from other parts of Europe. When the river of silver began to slow down, Spain was plunged into debt. Meanwhile, the Spanish crown's commitment to supporting the Catholic Church meant costly wars, as did attempts to maintain Spain's international dominance.

Involvement in the Thirty Years' War was the last straw. The strains of warfare drove the kingdom, with its power base in Castile, to raise more money and soldiers from other Iberian provinces. First Catalonia and then Portugal (incorporated into Spain in 1580) rose in revolt, followed by the southern Italians who rebelled against their Castilian viceroys in Naples and Sicily. It was only by chance that Spain's greatest external enemies, France and England, could not act in time to take advantage of its plight. This gave the Castilian-based government time to put down the Italian revolts and bring Catalonia to heel. But Portugal retained its independence and Spain became increasingly isolated.

French Power in Europe and North America

Like Spain, France had grown over the course of the previous centuries by absorbing formerly independent principalities whose inhabitants were not always willing to cooperate with the royal government. The fact that France became more powerful as a result of this process, while Spain did not, can be attributed in part to France's greater natural resources and the greater prestige of the French monarchy, which can be traced back to the rule of Louis IX (later canonized as Saint Louis; see Chapter 10). Most subjects of the French king, including the Protestants whose welfare had been cultivated by Henry IV, were loyal to the crown. Moreover, France had enormous economic resiliency, owing primarily to its rich and varied agricultural productivity. Unlike Spain, which had to import food, France was able to feed itself. Moreover, Henry IV's government had financed the construction of roads, bridges, and canals to facilitate the flow of goods. Royal factories manufactured luxuries such as crystal, glass, and tapestries, and Henry also supported the production of silk, linen, and wool throughout the kingdom.

France thus emerged from the crisis of the Thirty Years' War with a stronger state, a more dynamic economy, and increased influence abroad. A decade before the war, royal patronage had also allowed the explorer Samuel de Champlain to claim parts of northeastern North America as France's first foothold in the New World. In 1608, Champlain founded the colony of Québec in the Saint Lawrence river valley. But whereas the English had limited colonial settlement to regions along the Atlantic coastline, the French set out to dominate the interior of the continent. In the ensuing centuries, French traders ranged far up and down the few Canadian rivers that led inland, exchanging furs and goods with the Native American groups they encountered, while French missionaries used the same arteries to spread Catholic Christianity from Québec to Louisiana. Eventually, French imperial ventures spread via the Great Lakes and the great river systems along the Mississippi to the prairies of America's Midwest.

These far-flung French colonies were established and administered as royal enterprises like those of Spain, a fact that distinguished them from the private commercial ventures put together by the English and the Dutch. Also like New Spain, the colonies of New France were overwhelmingly populated by men. The elite of French colonial society were military officers and administrators sent from Paris. Below their ranks were fishermen, fur traders, small farmers, and common soldiers who constituted the bulk of French settlers in North America. Because the fishing and fur trades relied on cooperative relationships with native peoples, a mutual economic interdependence grew up between the French colonists and the peoples of surrounding regions. Intermarriage between French traders and native women was common.

Yet in contrast to both Spanish and English colonies, these French colonies remained very dependent on the wages and supplies sent to them from the mother country. Only rarely did they become truly self-sustaining economic enterprises. Financial rewards were modest: furs, fish, and tobacco were exported to European markets, but it was not until the late seventeenth century that some French colonies began to realize large profits by building sugar plantations in the Caribbean islands of Guadeloupe, Martinique, and Saint-Domingue (the French portion of Hispaniola, now Haiti). By 1750, 500,000 slaves on Saint-Domingue were laboring under extraordinarily harsh conditions to produce 40 percent of the world's sugar and 50 percent of its coffee (see Chapter 15).

The Policies of Cardinal Richelieu

This expansion of French power can be credited, in part, to Henry IV's de facto successor, Cardinal Richelieu (REESH-eh-lyuh). The real king of France, Henry's son Louis XIII (r. 1610–43), had come to the throne at the age of nine; and so Richelieu, as his chief advisor, dominated his reign. His aim was to centralize royal bureaucracy while exploiting opportunities to foster French influence.

Within France, Richelieu amended the Edict of Nantes so that it no longer supported the political rights of the Huguenots. He also prohibited French Protestants from settling in Québec. Yet considering that he owed his political power (in part) to his ecclesiastical position in the Catholic Church, the fact that he allowed the edict to stand speaks to his larger interest in fostering a sense of French national identity that centered on the monarchy. In keeping with this policy, he also imposed direct taxation on powerful provinces that had retained their financial autonomy up to that point. Later, to make sure that taxes were efficiently collected, Richelieu instituted a new system of local government which empowered royal officials to put down provincial resistance.

These policies made the French royal government more powerful than any in Europe. It also doubled the crown's income, allowing France to engage in the Thirty Years' War, which in turn extended its power on the continent. Yet this increased centralization would provoke challenges to royal authority from aristocratic elites in the years after Richelieu's death. Eventually, the extreme centralization of royal authority in France would lead to the French Revolution (see Chapter 18).

The Challenge of the Fronde

One more immediate response to Richelieu's policies was a series of uncoordinated revolts known collectively as the *Fronde* (from the French word for a sling used to hurl stones). In 1643, just after the death of Richelieu, Louis XIII was succeeded by his five-year-old son, Louis XIV. The young king's regents were his mother, Anne of Austria, and her alleged lover, Cardinal Mazarin. Many powerful nobles hated them and also hated the way that Richelieu's government had curtailed their own authority. Popular resentments were aroused as well, so when cliques of nobles expressed their disgust they found some support. In 1648, the levy of a new tax had protesters on the streets of Paris, armed with slings and projectiles. Years later, when Louis XIV began to rule in his own right, the memory of these early years haunted him. He resolved never to let the aristocracy or their provinces get out of hand (see Chapter 15). Over the next five years, a series of insurrections challenged the authority of the French Parlement, while factional disputes and struggles for power divided the nobility. This period of civil warfare, coinciding with an ongoing war with Spain, threatened the very existence of the French throne and the sovereignty of its child occupant.

THE CRISIS OF MONARCHY IN ENGLAND

Of all the crises that shook Europe in this era, the most radical in its consequences was the English Civil War. The causes of this conflict were similar to those that had sparked trouble in other countries: hostilities between the component parts of a composite kingdom; religious animosities; struggles for power among competing factions; and the increasing costs of war. But in England, these developments led to the unprecedented criminal trial and execution of a

Analyzing Primary Sources

Cardinal Richelieu on the Common People of France

Armand Jean du Plessis, Duke of Richelieu and cardinal of the Roman Catholic Church, was the effective ruler of France from 1624 until his death in 1642. His Political Testament was assembled after his death from historical sketches and memoranda of advice which he prepared for King Louis XIII, the ineffectual monarch whom he ostensibly served. This book was eventually published in 1688, during the reign of Louis XIV.

 ll students of politics agree that when the common people are too well off it is impossible to keep them peaceable. The explanation for this is that they are less well informed than the members of the other orders in the state, who are much more cultivated and enlightened, and so if not preoccupied with the search for the necessities of existence, find it difficult to remain within the limits imposed by both common sense and the law.

It would not be sound to relieve them of all taxation and similar charges, since in such a case they would lose the mark of their subjection and consequently the awareness of their station. Thus being free from paying tribute, they would consider themselves exempted from obedience. One should compare them with mules, which being accustomed to work, suffer more when long idle than when kept busy. But just as this work should be reasonable, with the burdens placed upon these animals proportionate to their strength, so it is likewise with the burdens placed upon the people. If they are not moderate, even when put to good public use, they are certainly unjust. I realize that when a king undertakes a program of public works it is correct to say that what the people gain from it is returned by paying the *taille* [a heavy tax imposed on the peasantry]. In the same fashion it can be maintained that what a king takes from the people returns to them, and that they advance it to him only to draw upon it for the enjoyment of their leisure and their investments, which would be impossible if they did not contribute to the support of the state.

Source: *The Political Testament of Cardinal Richelieu*, trans. Henry Bertram Hill (Madison, WI: 1961), pp. 31–32.

Questions for Analysis

1. According to Cardinal Richelieu, why should the state undertake to subjugate the common people? What assumptions about the nature and status of "common people" underlie this argument?

2. What theory of the state emerges from this argument? What are the relationships between the king and the state and between the king and the people, according to Richelieu?

---

king, an event that sent shock waves throughout Europe and the Atlantic world.

The Origins of the English Civil War

The chain of events leading to this civil war can be traced to the last decades of Queen Elizabeth's reign. The expenses of defense against Spain, rebellion in Ireland, widespread crop failures, and the inadequacies of the antiquated English taxation system drove the government deeply into debt. When Elizabeth was succeeded by her cousin, James Stuart—King James VI of Scotland, James I of England—bitter factional disputes were complicated by the financial crisis. When the English Parliament rejected James's demands for more taxes, he raised what revenues he could without parliamentary approval, imposing new tolls and selling trading monopolies on colonial imports. These measures aroused resentment and made voluntary grants of taxation from Parliament even less likely.

James also struggled with religious divisions among his subjects. His own kingdom of Scotland had been firmly Calvinist since the 1560s. England was Protestant, too, but of a very different kind because the Church of England had retained many of the rituals, hierarchies, and doctrines of the medieval Catholic Church (see Chapter 13). A significant number of English Protestants, the Puritans, wanted to bring their church more firmly into line with Calvinist principles; a particularly zealous group of these Puritans took

subjects by marrying the Catholic sister of France's Louis XIII, and he launched a new war with Spain, straining his already slender financial resources. When Parliament refused to grant him funds, he demanded forced loans from his subjects and punished those who refused by lodging soldiers in their homes. Others were imprisoned without trial. Parliament responded by imposing the Petition of Right in 1628, which declared that taxes not condoned by Parliament were illegal, condemned arbitrary imprisonment, and prohibited the quartering of soldiers in private houses. Thereafter, Charles tried to rule England without Parliament—something not attempted since the establishment of that body 400 years earlier (see Chapter 9). He also ran into trouble with his Calvinist subjects in Scotland because he began to favor the most Catholic-leaning elements in the English Church. The Scots rebelled in 1640, and a Scottish army marched south into England to demand the withdrawal of Charles's "Catholicizing" measures.

To meet the Scottish threat, Charles was forced to summon Parliament, whose members were determined to impose radical reforms on the king's government before they would even consider granting him funds to raise an army. To avoid dealing with this difficult situation, Charles tried to arrest Parliament's leaders and force his own agenda. When this failed, he withdrew from London to raise his own army. Parliament responded by mustering a separate military force and voting itself the taxation to

CHARLES I. King Charles of England was a connoisseur of the arts and a patron of artists. He was adept at using portraiture to convey the magnificence of his tastes and the grandeur of his conception of kingship. ▪ *How does this portrait by Anthony Van Dyck compare to the engravings of the "martyred" king on page 390 in* **Interpreting Visual Evidence?**

refuge in North America and founded the Massachusetts Bay Colony when their efforts were criminalized in England. James also stirred up trouble in staunchly Catholic Ireland by encouraging thousands of Scottish Calvinists to settle in the northern Irish province of Ulster, exacerbating a situation that had already become violent under Elizabeth.

Parliament versus the King

This situation became more volatile in 1625, when James was succeeded by his son Charles. Charles alarmed his Protestant

OLIVER CROMWELL AS PROTECTOR OF THE COMMONWEALTH. This coin, minted in 1658, shows the lord protector wreathed with laurel garlands like a classical hero or a Roman consul, but it also proclaims him to be "by the Grace of God Protector of the Commonwealth." ▪ *What mixed messages does this coin convey?*

Debating the English Civil War

The English Civil War raised fundamental questions about political rights and responsibilities. Many of these are addressed in the two excerpts below. The first comes from a lengthy debate held within the General Council of Cromwell's army in October of 1647. The second is taken from the speech given by King Charles, moments before his execution in 1649.

The Army Debates, 1647

Colonel Rainsborough: Really, I think that the poorest man that is in England has a life to live as the greatest man, and therefore truly, sir, I think it's clear, that every man that is to live under a government ought first by his own consent to put himself under that government, and I do think that the poorest man in England is not at all bound in a strict sense to that government that he has not had a voice to put himself under . . . insomuch that I should doubt whether I was an Englishman or not, that should doubt of these things.

General Ireton: Give me leave to tell you, that if you make this the rule, I think you must fly for refuge to an absolute natural right, and you must deny all civil right, and I am sure it will come to that in the consequence. . . . For my part, I think it is no right at all. I think that no person has a right to an interest or share in the disposing of the affairs of the kingdom, and in determining or choosing those that shall determine what laws we shall be ruled by here, no person has a right to this that has not a permanent fixed interest in this kingdom, and those persons together are properly the represented of this kingdom who, taken together, and consequently are to make up the representers of this kingdom. . . .

We talk of birthright. Truly, birthright there is. . . . Men may justly have by birthright, by their very being born in England, that we should not seclude them out of England. That we should not refuse to give them air and place and ground, and the freedom of the highways and other things, to live amongst us, not any man that is born here, though he in birth or by his birth there come nothing at all that is part of the permanent interest of this kingdom to him. That I think is due to a man by birth. But that by a man's being born here he shall have a share in that power that shall dispose of the lands here, and of all things here, I do not think it is a sufficient ground.

Source: David Wootton, ed., *Divine Right and Democracy: An Anthology of Political Writing in Stuart England* (New York: 1986), pp. 286–87 (language modernized).

---

pay for it. By the end of 1642, open warfare had erupted between the English king and the English government: something inconceivable in neighboring France, where the king and the government were inseparable.

Arrayed on the king's side were most of England's aristocrats and large landholders, many of whom owned lands in the Atlantic colonies as well. The parliamentary forces were made up of smaller landowners, tradesmen, and artisans, many of whom were Puritan sympathizers. The king's royalist supporters were commonly known by the aristocratic name of Cavaliers. Their opponents, who cut their hair short in contempt for the fashionable custom of wearing curls, were derisively called Roundheads. After 1644, when the parliamentary army was efficiently reorganized,

the royalist forces were badly beaten and the king was compelled to surrender in 1646. Soon afterward, the episcopal hierarchy of the Church of England was abolished and a Calvinist-style church was mandated throughout England and Wales.

The struggle might have ended there, but Parliament was divided on the question of the monarch's role in the new government. The majority of its members were ready to restore Charles to the throne, with limited powers, and to impose a uniform Calvinist faith. But a radical minority of Puritans insisted on religious freedom for themselves and other Protestant dissenters. Their leader was Oliver Cromwell (1599–1658), commander of the parliamentary forces, which he had reconstituted as "the

Charles I on the Scaffold, 1649

I think it is my duty, to God first, and to my country, for to clear myself both as an honest man, a good king, and a good Christian.

I shall begin first with my innocence. In truth I think it not very needful for me to insist long upon this, for all the world knows that I never did begin a war with the two Houses of Parliament, and I call God to witness, to whom I must shortly make an account, that I never did intend to incroach upon their privileges. . . .

As for the people—truly I desire their liberty and freedom as much as anybody whatsoever. But I must tell you that their liberty and freedom consists in having of government those laws by which their lives and goods may be most their own. It is not for having share in government. That is nothing pertaining to them. A subject and a sovereign are clean different things, and therefore, until they

do that—I mean that you do put the people in that liberty as I say—certainly they will never enjoy themselves.

Sirs, it was for this that now I am come here. If I would have given way to an arbitrary way, for to have all laws changed according to the power of the sword, I needed not to have come here. And therefore I tell you (and I pray God it be not laid to your charge) that I am the martyr of the people.

Source: Brian Tierney, Donald Kagan, and L. Pearce Williams, eds., *Great Issues in Western Civilization* (New York: 1967), pp. 46–47.

Questions for Analysis

1. What fundamental issues are at stake in both of these excerpts? How do the debaters within the parliamentary army (first excerpt) define "natural" and "civil" rights?

2. How does Charles defend his position? What is his theory of kingship, and how does it compare to that of Cardinal Richelieu's (page 386)? How does it conflict with the ideas expressed in the army's debate?

3. It is interesting that none of the participants in these debates seems to have recognized the implications their arguments might have for the political rights of women. Why would that have been the case?

New Model Army." Ultimately, he became the new ruler of England, too.

The Fall of Charles Stuart and Oliver Cromwell's Commonwealth

Taking advantage of the dissension within Parliament, Charles renewed the war in 1648. But his royalists were forced to surrender after a brief campaign. In order to ensure that the Puritan agenda would be carried out, Cromwell ejected all the moderates from Parliament by force. This "Rump" (remaining) Parliament then put the king on trial, finding him guilty of treason against his own subjects. Charles Stuart

was publicly beheaded on January 30, 1649: the first time in history that a reigning king had been legally deposed and executed. Europeans reacted to his death with horror, astonishment, or rejoicing, depending on their own political convictions (see **Interpreting Visual Evidence** on page 390).

After the king's execution, his son Charles and his royalist supporters fled to France. Cromwell and his faction then abolished Parliament's hereditary House of Lords and declared England a Commonwealth. Technically, Parliament was the governing body; but Cromwell, with the army at his command, possessed the real power. By 1653 the "Commonwealth" had become a thinly disguised autocracy established under legislation drafted by officers of the army. Called the *Instrument of Government*, this text is the nearest

The Execution of a King

his allegorical engraving (image A) accompanied a pamphlet called *Eikon Basilike* ("The Kingly Image"), which began to circulate in Britain just weeks after the execution of King Charles I. It purported to be an autobiographical account of the king's last days and a justification of his royal policies. It was intended to arouse widespread sympathy for the king and his exiled heir, Charles II, and it succeeded admirably: the cult of Charles "King and Martyr" became increasingly popular. Here, the Latin inscription on the shaft of light suggests that Charles's piety will beam "brighter through the shadows," while the scrolls at the left proclaim that "virtue grows beneath weight" and "unmoved, triumphant." Charles's earthly crown (on the floor at his side) is "splendid and heavy," while the crown of thorns he grasps is "bitter and light" and the heavenly crown is "blessed and eternal." Even people who could not read these and other Latin mottoes would have known that Charles's last words

were: "I shall go from a corruptible to an incorruptible Crown, where no disturbance can be."

At the same time, broadsides showing the moment of execution (image B) circulated in various European countries with

A. King Charles I as a martyr.

approximation to a written constitution England has ever had. Extensive powers were granted to Cromwell as Lord Protector, and his office was made hereditary.

The Restoration of the Monarchy

By this time, though, Cromwell's Puritan military dictatorship was growing unpopular, not least because it prohibited public recreation on Sundays and closed London's theatres. Many became nostalgic for the milder Church of England and began to hope for a restoration

of the old royalist regime. The opportunity came with Cromwell's death in 1658. His son Richard duly succeeded to the office of Lord Protector but was almost immediately removed from power by a royalist faction within the army. A new Parliament was organized, and, in April of 1660, it declared that King Charles II had been the ruler of England since his father's execution in 1649. Almost overnight, England became a monarchy again.

Charles II (r. 1660–85) revived the Church of England but was careful not to revive the contentious policies of his father. Quipping that he did not wish to "resume his travels," he agreed to respect Parliament and to observe the Petition of Right.

explanatory captions. This one was printed in Germany, and there are almost identical versions surviving from the Netherlands. It shows members of the crowd fainting and turning away at the sight of blood spurting from the king's neck while the executioner holds up the severed head.

Questions for Analysis

1. How would you interpret the message of the first image? How might it have been read differently by Catholics and Protestants within Britain and Europe?

2. What would have been the political motives underlying the publication and display of these images? For example, would you expect the depiction of the king's execution to be intended as supportive of monarchy or as antiroyalist? Why?

3. Given what you have learned about political and religious divisions in Europe at the time of the king's execution, where do you think the first image would have found the most sympathetic audiences? Why might it be significant that the second circulated more in Germany and the Netherlands rather than in France or Spain?

B. The execution of King Charles I.

He also accepted all the legislation passed by Parliament immediately before the outbreak of civil war in 1642, including the requirement that Parliament be summoned at least once every three years. England thus emerged from its civil war as a constitutional monarchy, and it remains so to this day.

The English Civil War and the Atlantic World

These tumultuous events had a significant influence on England's Atlantic colonies. While the landed aristocracy had sided with the king during this conflict, many colonists had applauded Parliament's protection of small landowners and civil liberties. Even after the restoration of the monarchy in 1660, colonial leaders retained an antimonarchist bias. Moreover, the twelve years of civil war had given the colonies a large degree of independence. As a result, efforts to re-establish royal control over colonial governance resulted in greater and greater friction (see Chapter 15). The bitter religious conflicts that had divided the more radical Puritans from the Church of England also forced the colonies to come to grips with the problem of religious diversity. Some, like Massachusetts, tried to impose their own brand of Puritanism on settlers. Others experimented with forms of tolerance that went beyond those of England.

Paradoxically, though, the spread of ideas about the protection of liberties and citizens' rights coincided with a rapid and considerable expansion of unfree labor in the colonies. The demand for workers was increasing rapidly, owing to the expansion of tobacco plantations in Virginia and sugar plantations in Barbados and Jamaica, which the British captured from the Spanish in 1655. These plantations, with their punishing conditions and high mortality rates, were insatiable in their demand for workers. Plantation owners thus sought to meet this demand by investing ever more heavily in indentured servants and African slaves. The social and political crisis unleashed by Europe's wars also led to the forced migration of paupers and political prisoners. These exiles, many without resources, swelled the ranks of the unfree and the very poor in the English colonies, creating new social hierarchies as earlier arrivals sought to distance themselves from newer immigrants regarded as inferiors. The crisis of kingship in England thus led to a substantial increase in the African slave trade and a sharpening of social and economic divisions in North America.

THE PROBLEM OF DOUBT AND THE ART OF BEING HUMAN

On the first day of November in 1611, a new play by William Shakespeare premiered in London, at the royal court. *The Tempest* takes place on a remote island, where an exiled duke has used his magical arts to subjugate the island's inhabitants. This plot drew on widespread reports from the new colonies in the Caribbean, where slaves were called Caribans—hence the name Shakespeare chose for the play's rebellious Caliban, who seeks revenge on his oppressive master. When reminded that he owes his knowledge of the English language to the civilizing influence of the magician's daughter, Caliban retorts: "You taught me language, and my profit on't is / I know how to curse." Shakespeare's audience was thus confronted with a spectacle of their own colonial ambitions gone awry.

The unrest caused by Europe's extension into the Atlantic world, and by its bitter decades of warfare, motivated many creative artists to document and critique contemporary trends. Another example of this artistic response is *Don Quixote*, which its Spanish author, Miguel de Cervantes (*sehr-VAHN-tehs*, 1547–1616), composed largely in prison.

This early novel recounts the adventures of an idealistic gentleman, Don Quixote of La Mancha, who becomes deranged by his constant reading of chivalric romances and sets off on delusional adventures of his own. His sidekick, Sancho Panza, is his exact opposite: a plain, practical man content with modest bodily pleasures. Together, they represent different facets of human nature. *Don Quixote* is both a devastating satire of Spain's decline and a sincere celebration of human optimism.

Throughout the long century between 1550 and 1660, Europeans confronted a world in which all they had once known was cast into confusion. Vast continents had been discovered, populated by millions of people whose existence challenged Western civilizations' former parameters and Europeans' most basic assumptions. Not even religion could be seen as an adequate foundation on which to build new certainties. Political allegiances were similarly under threat, as intellectuals and common people alike began to assert a right to resist princes with whom they disagreed. The foundations of morality and custom were beginning to seem arbitrary. Europeans responded to this pervasive climate of doubt by seeking new bases on which to construct some measure of certainty.

Witchcraft and the Power of the State

Contributing to the anxiety of this age was the widespread conviction that witchcraft was a new and increasing threat. Although belief in magic had always been common, it was not until the late fifteenth century that such powers were deemed to derive from some kind of satanic bargain. In 1484, papal inquisitors had been empowered to detect and eliminate witchcraft by any means. Predictably, torture increased the number of accused witches who "confessed" to their alleged crimes. And as more accused witches "confessed," more witches were "discovered," tried, and executed—even in places like England and Scotland, where torture was not legal and the Catholic Church had no influence. Both Luther and Calvin had also condoned the trial and execution of witches.

It was through this fundamental agreement between Catholics and Protestants, and with the complicity of modern secular states, that an early modern "witch craze" claimed tens of thousands of victims. The final death toll will never be known, but the vast majority were women. Accusations of witchcraft also became endemic in some colonies, as occurred in the English settlement of Salem in the Massachusetts Bay Colony. This hunt for witches resulted, in part, from fears that traditional religious remedies were no longer adequate to guard against the evils of the world. It also reflects Europeans' growing conviction that only the state had the power to protect them. In Catholic countries, where witchcraft prosecutions began in Church courts, these cases would be transferred to the state's courts for final judgment and punishment. In most Protestant countries, the entire process of detecting, prosecuting, and punishing suspected witches was carried out under state supervision.

The Search for a Source of Authority

The crisis of religious and political authority in Europe also led to more rational approaches to the problem of uncertainty. The French nobleman Michel de Montaigne (*mohn-TEHN-yeh*, 1533–1592), son of a Catholic father and a Huguenot mother of Jewish ancestry, applied a searching skepticism to all traditional ways of knowing the world and adopted instead a practice of profound introspection. His *Essays* (from the French word for "attempts" or "exercises") were composed during the wars of religion and proceed from the same basic question: "What do I know?" Their first premise is that every human perspective is limited: what may seem indisputably true to one group of people may seem absolutely false to another. From this follows Montaigne's second premise: the need for moderation. Because all people think they follow the true religion or have the best form of government, Montaigne concluded that no religion or government is really perfect, and consequently no belief is worth fighting or dying for.

Another French philosopher, Blaise Pascal (*pahs-KAHL*, 1623–1662), confronted the problem of doubt differently, by embracing an extreme form of Catholicism. Until his death, he worked on a highly ambitious philosophical-religious project meant to establish truth by appealing simultaneously to intellect and emotion. In his posthumously published work *Pensées* (*Thoughts*), Pascal argued that only faith could resolve the contradictions of the world. He argued that the awe an uncertainty we feel in the face of evil is evidence for the existence of God. Pascal's hope was that, on this foundation, some measure of confidence in the human capacity for self-knowledge could be rediscovered.

The Science of Politics

The French jurist Jean Bodin (*boh-DAN*, 1530–1596) took a more practical approach to the problem of uncertainty and found a solution in the power of the state. Like his exact contemporary Montaigne, Bodin was troubled by religious upheaval. He had witnessed the St. Bartholomew's Day Massacre of 1572 and, in response, developed a theory of absolute sovereignty that would (he surmised) put an end to such catastrophes. His monumental *Six Books of the Commonwealth* (1576) argued that the state has its origins in the needs of families and that its paramount duty is to maintain order. He defined sovereignty as "the most high, absolute, and perpetual power over all subjects," which meant that a sovereign head of state could make and enforce laws without the consent of those governed: precisely what King Charles of England later argued when he tried to dispense with Parliament—and precisely what his subjects ultimately rejected. Even if the ruler proved a tyrant, Bodin insisted that the subject had no right to resist, for any resistance would open the door to anarchy, "which is worse than the harshest tyranny in the world."

In England, the experience of civil war led Thomas Hobbes (1588–1679) to propose a different theory of state sovereignty in his treatise *Leviathan* (1651). Whereas Bodin assumed that sovereign power should be vested in a monarch, Hobbes argued that any form of government capable of protecting its subjects' lives and property might act as an all-powerful sovereign. But Hobbes's convictions arose from a similarly pessimistic view of human nature. The "state of nature" that existed before government, he wrote, was a "war of all against all." Because man naturally behaves as "a wolf" toward other men, human life without government is "solitary, poor, nasty, brutish, and short." To escape such consequences, people must surrender their liberties in exchange for the state's obligation to keep the peace.

Bodin had seen the ultimate goal of the state as the protection of property; Hobbes saw it as the preservation of people's lives, even at the expense of their liberties. Both developed such theories in response to the breakdown of traditional authorities. Their different political philosophies thus reflect a shared, practical preoccupation with the observation and analysis of actual occurrences (empirical knowledge) rather than abstract or theological arguments. Because of this, they are seen as early examples of a new kind of discipline, what we now call "political science."

A similar preoccupation with observation and results was also emerging among those who sought to understand the physical universe. Historians have often referred to the rapid scientific developments of this era as the "scientific revolution," a phenomenon that actually had its beginnings in the later Middle Ages

Analyzing Primary Sources

Montaigne on Skepticism and Faith

The Essays of Michel de Montaigne (1533–1592) reflect the sincerity of his own attempts to grapple with the contradictions of his time, even if he could not resolve those contradictions. Here, he discusses the relationship between human knowledge and the teachings of religious authorities.

Perhaps it is not without reason that we attribute facility in belief and conviction to simplicity and ignorance, for . . . the more a mind is empty and without counterpoise, the more easily it gives beneath the weight of the first persuasive argument. That is why children, common people, women, and sick people are most subject to being led by the ears. But then, on the other hand, it is foolish presumption to go around disdaining and condemning as false whatever does not seem likely to us; which is an ordinary vice in those who think they have more than common ability. I used to do so once. . . . But reason has taught me that to condemn a thing thus, dogmatically, as false and impossible, is to assume the advantage of knowing the bounds and limits of God's will and of the power of our mother Nature, and that there is no more notable folly in the world than to reduce these things to the measure of our capacity and competence. . . .

It is a dangerous and fateful presumption, besides the absurd temerity that it implies, to disdain what we do not comprehend. For after you have established, according to your fine understanding, the limits of truth and falsehood, and it turns out that you must necessarily believe things even stranger than those you deny, you are obliged from then on to abandon these limits. Now what seems to me to bring as much disorder into our consciences as anything, in these religious troubles that we are in, is this partial surrender of their beliefs by Catholics. It seems to them that they are being very moderate and understanding when they yield to their opponents some of the articles in dispute. But, besides the fact that they do not see what an advantage it is to a man charging you for you to begin to give ground and withdraw, and how much that encourages him to pursue his point, those articles which they select as the most trivial are sometimes very important. We must either submit completely to the authority of our ecclesiastical government, or do without it completely. It is not for us to decide what portion of obedience we owe it.

Source: *Montaigne: Selections from the Essays*, ed. and trans. Donald M. Frame (Arlington Heights, IL: 1971), pp. 34–38.

Questions for Analysis

1. Why does Montaigne say that human understanding is limited? How do his assumptions compare to those of Richelieu's (page 386)?

2. What does Montaigne mean by the "partial surrender" of belief? If a Catholic should place his faith in the Church, what then is the purpose of human intellect?

(see Chapters 12 and 13). It will be treated at greater length in Chapter 16.

The World of Theater

In the late sixteenth century, the construction of public playhouses—enclosed theaters—made drama an especially effective mass medium for the formation of public opinion, the dissemination of ideas, and the discussion of the rapidly changing world. This was especially so in England during the last two decades of Elizabeth's reign and the two-decade reign of her successor, James.

Christopher Marlowe (1564–1593), who may have been a spy for Elizabeth's government and who was mysteriously murdered in a tavern brawl, was extremely popular in his own day. In plays such as *Doctor Faustus* and *Tamburlaine*—about the life of the Mongolian warlord Timur the Lame (see Chapter 12)— Marlowe created vibrant heroes who

Past and Present

Shakespeare's Popular Appeal

Although the plays of William Shakespeare are frequently described as elite entertainments, their enduring appeal can hardly be explained in those terms. In fact, Shakespeare wrote for a diverse audience—and a group of actors—who would have been more likely to see the inside of a prison than a royal court. His plays combine high politics, earthy comedy, and deeply human stories that still captivate and motivate audiences at the reconstructed Globe Theatre in London (left). They also lend themselves to inventive adaptations that comment on our own contemporary world, as in the recent film of *Coriolanus* (right).

Watch related author videos on the Student Site
wwnorton.com/college/history/western-civilizationsBrief4

pursue larger-than-life ambitions only to be felled by their own human limitations. In contrast to the heroic tragedies of Marlowe, Ben Jonson's (c. 1572–1637) dark comedies expose human vices and foibles. In the *Alchemist*, he balanced an attack on pseudo-scientific quackery with admiration for resourceful lower-class characters who cleverly take advantage of their social betters.

William Shakespeare (1564–1616) was born into the family of a tradesman in the provincial town of Stratford-upon-Avon, where he attained a modest education before moving to London at around the age of twenty. There, he composed or collaborated on an unknown number of plays, of which some forty survive in whole or in part. They owe their longevity to the author's unrivaled use of langauge, humor, and psychological insight. Those written during the playwright's early years reflect the political, religious, and social upheavals of the time. These include many history plays that recount episodes from England's medieval past and the struggles that established the Tudor dynasty

of Elizabeth's grandfather, Henry VII. They also include the lyrical tragedy *Romeo and Juliet* and a number of comedies that explore fundamental problems of identity, honor, ambition, and love. The plays from Shakespeare's second period are, like other contemporary artworks, characterized by a troubled searching into the meaning of human existence. They showcase the perils of indecisive idealism (*Hamlet*) and the abuse of power (*Macbeth*, *King Lear*). The plays composed toward the end of his career emphasize the possibilities of reconciliation and peace even after years of misunderstanding and violence: *The Tempest* is one of these.

The Artists of Southern Europe

The tensions of this age were also explored in the visual arts. In Italy and Spain, painters cultivated a highly dramatic style sometimes known as "Mannerism." The most

VIEW OF TOLEDO BY EL GRECO. This is one of many landscape portraits representing the hilltop city that became the artist's home in later life. Its supple Mannerist style defies historical periodization.

THE MAIDS OF HONOR (LAS MENINAS) BY DIEGO VELÁZQUEZ. The artist himself (at left) is shown working at his easel and gazing out at the viewer—or at the subjects of his double portrait, the Spanish king and queen, depicted in a distant mirror. But the real focus of the painting is the delicate, impish princess in the center, flanked by two young ladies-in-waiting, a dwarf, and another royal child. Courtiers in the background look on.

unusual of these artists was El Greco ("the Greek," c. 1541–1614). Born Domenikos Theotokopoulos on the Greek island of Crete, El Greco absorbed the style characteristic of Byzantine icon painting (see Chapter 7) before traveling to Italy and eventually settling in Spain. Many of his paintings were too strange to be appreciated in his own day and even now appear almost surreal. His *View of Toledo*, for example, is a transfigured landscape, mysteriously lit from within. The great Spanish master Diego Velázquez (*vay-LAH-skez*, 1599–1660), who served the Habsburg court in Madrid, was also conceptually thoughtful and daring. His painting *The Maids of Honor* is a masterpiece of multiple perspectives: it shows the artist himself at work on a double portrait of the Spanish king and queen, but the scene is dominated by the children and servants of the royal family.

In architecture and sculpture, the dominant artistic style was that of the Baroque, a school whose name has become a synonym for elaborate ornamentation. This style originated in Rome during the Counter-Reformation and promoted a glorified Catholic worldview. Its most influential figure was Gianlorenzo Bernini (1598–1680), a frequent employee of the Vatican who created a magnificent celebration of papal grandeur in the sweeping colonnades leading up to St. Peter's Basilica. Breaking with the more serene classicism of Renaissance styles (Chapter 12), Bernini's work drew inspiration from the restless motion and artistic bravado of Hellenistic statuary (Chapter 4).

Dutch Painting in the Golden Age

Southern Europe's main rival in the visual arts was the Netherlands, where many painters explored the theme of man's greatness and wretchedness. Pieter Bruegel the Elder (*BROY-ghul*, c. 1525–1569) exulted in portraying the busy, elemental life of the peasantry. But later in his career, Bruegel became appalled by the intolerance and bloodshed he witnessed during the Spanish repression of the Netherlands. His work *The Massacre of the Innocents* looks, from a distance, like a snug scene of village life. In fact, however, soldiers are methodically breaking into homes and slaughtering helpless infants, as Herod's soldiers once did and as warring armies were doing in Bruegel's own day.

Another Dutch painter, Peter Paul Rubens (1577–1640), was inspired by very different politics. A native of

***THE MASSACRE OF THE INNOCENTS* BY BRUEGEL (c. 1525–1569).**
This painting shows how effectively art can be used as a means of
political and social commentary. Here, Bruegel depicts the suffering
of the Netherlands at the hands of the Spanish in his own day, with
reference to the biblical story of Herod's slaughter of Jewish children
after the birth of Jesus—thereby collapsing these two historical
incidents.

***THE HORRORS OF WAR* BY RUBENS (1577–1640).** In his old age,
Rubens took a far more critical view of war than he had done for most
of his earlier career. Here, the war-god Mars casts aside his mistress
Venus, goddess of love, and threatens humanity with death and
destruction.

SELF-PORTRAITS. Self-portraits became common during the sixteenth and seventeenth centuries, reflecting the intense introspection of the
period. Left: Rembrandt painted more than sixty self-portraits; this one, dating from around 1660, captures the artist's creativity, theatricality
(note the costume), and honesty of self-examination. Right: Judith Leyster was a contemporary of Rembrandt who pursued a successful career
during her early twenties, before she married. Respected in her own day, she was all but forgotten for centuries thereafter but is once again the
object of much attention.

Antwerp, still part of the Spanish Netherlands, Rubens was a staunch Catholic who supported the Habsburg regime. He reveled in the sumptuous extravagance of the Baroque style; he is most famous today for the pink and rounded flesh of his well-nourished nudes. But his late painting *The Horrors of War* captures what he called "the grief of unfortunate Europe."

Rembrandt van Rijn (*vahn-REEN*, 1606–1669) defies all attempts at easy characterization. Living across the border from the Spanish Netherlands in the staunchly Calvinist Dutch Republic, Rembrandt managed to put both realistic and Baroque traits to new uses. In his early career, he gained fame and fortune as a painter of biblical scenes and was also active as a portrait painter who knew how to flatter his subjects—to the great advantage of his purse. But his later portraits, including several self-portraits, are highly introspective. They can be contrasted with the frank, fearless gaze of Rembrandt's slightly younger contemporary,

Judith Leyster (1609–1660), who looks out of her own self-portrait with a refreshingly optimistic and good-humored expression.

CONCLUSION

The European states engaged in colonizing the Atlantic were riven by internal dissent and deadly competitions among themselves, all of which would be exported to the peoples of that world. Colonial initiatives, in turn, affected European politics and deepened divisions among Protestants and Catholics, causing waves of migration by persecuted minorities who replanted and propagated these rivalries across the Atlantic. Religion was not the only cause of conflict. Supporting colonial expansion in the Atlantic

After You Read This Chapter

 Go to **INQUIZITIVE** to see what you've learned—and learn what you've missed—with personalized feedback along the way.

REVIEWING THE OBJECTIVES

- How were the peoples and ecosystems of the Americas, Africa, and Europe intertwined during this period? What were some consequences of these new linkages?

- Why did the colonies of the Spanish, the English, and the Dutch differ from one another? How did these differences affect the lives and labor of colonists, both free and unfree?

- Which European powers came to dominate the Atlantic world? What factors led to the decline of Spain and to the rise of France?

- What forms did religious and political conflict take in France, the Netherlands, and Germany? What were the causes of the English Civil War, and what impact did this event have on the English colonies?

- How do the arts and political philosophies of this period reflect the turmoil of Europe and the Atlantic world?

world and fighting wars within Europe were expensive projects, and they placed strain on traditional alliances and ideas. Intellectuals and artists strove to reassess Europeans' place in this expanding Atlantic world, to process the flood of new information and commodities, and to make sense of the profound changes in daily life.

It would take centuries for Europeans to adapt themselves to the changes brought about by their integration into the Atlantic world and to process its implications. Finding new lands and cultures unknown to the ancients and unmentioned in the Bible had exposed the limitations of Western civilizations' accumulated knowledge and called for new ways of knowing and explaining the world. The Columbian exchange of people, plants, livestock, and pathogens that had previously been isolated from one another had a profound and lasting effect on populations and ecosystems throughout the Atlantic zone. The distribution of new agricultural products transformed the lives of Europe's poor and rich alike. The transatlantic slave trade, which made all of this possible, brought Africans and their cultures into a world of growing global connections under the worst possible circumstances for those who were enslaved—yet this did not prevent them from helping to shape this new world.

Meanwhile, the influx of silver from New Spain precipitated the great price inflation of the sixteenth and seventeenth centuries, which bewildered contemporary observers and contributed to the atmosphere of crisis in post-Reformation Europe, already riven by religious and civil warfare. Political and moral philosophers also struggled to redefine the role of government in a world of religious pluralism, and to articulate new ideologies that did not necessitate violence among people of different faiths. The response was a trend toward stronger centralized states, justified by theories of absolute government. Led by the French monarchy of Louis XIV, these absolutist regimes would reach their apogee in the coming century.

PEOPLE, IDEAS, AND EVENTS IN CONTEXT

- What was the **COLUMBIAN EXCHANGE**? How did it affect the relations among the peoples of the Americas, Africa, and Europe during this period?
- What circumstances led to the development of the **TRIANGULAR TRADE**?
- What were the main sources of instability in Europe during the sixteenth century? How did the **PRICE REVOLUTION** exacerbate these?
- How did **HENRY IV** of France and **PHILIP II** of Spain deal differently with the religious conflict that beset Europe during these years?
- What were the origins of the **THIRTY YEARS' WAR**? Was it primarily a religious conflict?
- How did the policies of **CARDINAL RICHELIEU** strengthen the power of the French monarchy?
- What policies of England's **CHARLES I** were most detested by his subjects? Why was his execution so momentous?
- In what ways did the **WITCH CRAZE** of early modern Europe reveal the religious and social tensions of the sixteenth and seventeenth centuries?
- What were the differences between **JEAN BODIN**'s theory of absolute sovereignty and that of **THOMAS HOBBES**?
- How did philosophers like **MONTAIGNE** and **PASCAL** respond to the uncertainties of the age? How were contemporary trends reflected in the works of **SHAKESPEARE** and in the visual arts?

THINKING ABOUT CONNECTIONS

- The emergence of the Atlantic world can be seen as a *cause* of new developments and as the *result* of historical processes. What long-term political, economic, and demographic circumstances drove the expansion of European influence into the Atlantic? What subsequent historical developments can we attribute to the creation of this interconnected world?
- The political crises of this era reveal the tensions produced by sectarian religious disputes and by a growing rift between powerful centralizing monarchies and landholding elites unwilling to surrender their authority and independence. What other periods in history display similar tensions? How do those periods compare to the one we have studied in this chapter?
- The intellectual currents of this era reveal that a new generation was challenging the assumptions of its predecessors. In what other historical eras do we find a similar phenomenon? What social and political circumstances tend to produce consensus, and which tend to produce dissent, skepticism, and doubt?

STORY LINES

- After 1660, European rulers invoked an absolutist definition of sovereignty in order to expand the power of the monarchy. The most successful absolutist kings, such as Louis XIV of France or Peter the Great of Russia, limited the power of traditional aristocratic elites and the independence of religious institutions.

- Efforts by English monarchs to create an absolutist regime in England after the civil war were resisted by political opponents in Parliament. Though they agreed with the king that a strong state was needed, they demanded a different definition of sovereignty, in which the king would rule alongside Parliament.

- Absolutism reinforced the imperial ambitions of European monarchies and led to frequent wars that were increasingly fought both in Europe and in colonial spaces in other parts of the world. The pressures of war favored dynasties capable of building strong centralized states with reliable sources of revenue from trade and taxation.

CHRONOLOGY

1643–1715	Reign of Louis XIV of France
1660	Restoration of the Stuart kings in England
1683	Ottoman siege of Vienna
1685	Revocation of the Edict of Nantes
1688	Glorious Revolution in England
1688–1697	War of the League of Augsburg
1682–1725	Reign of Peter the Great of Russia
1690	Publication of John Locke's *Two Treatises of Government*
1702–1713	War of the Spanish Succession
1713	Treaty of Utrecht

Before You Read This Chapter

European Monarchies and Absolutism, 1660–1725

CORE OBJECTIVES

- **DEFINE** *absolutism*, **UNDERSTAND** its central principles as a theory of government, and **IDENTIFY** the major absolutist rulers in Europe during this period.

- **DEFINE** *mercantilism* and its relation to absolutist rule.

- **EXPLAIN** the alternatives to absolutism that emerged, most notably in England and the Dutch Republic.

- **DESCRIBE** how the wars between 1680 and 1713 changed the balance of power in Europe and in the colonial spheres of the Atlantic world.

In the mountainous region of south-central France known as the Auvergne in the 1660s, the Marquis of Canillac had a notorious reputation. His noble title gave him the right to collect minor taxes on special occasions, but he insisted that these small privileges be converted into annual tributes. To collect these payments, he housed in his castle twelve accomplices that he called his "apostles." Their other nicknames—one was known as "Break Everything"—gave a more accurate sense of their activities in the local villages. The marquis imprisoned those who resisted and forced their families to buy their freedom. In an earlier age, the marquis might have gotten away with this profitable arrangement. In 1662, however, he ran up against the authority of a king, Louis XIV, who was determined to demonstrate that the power of the central monarch was absolute. The marquis was brought up on charges before a special court of judges from Paris. He was found guilty and forced to pay a large fine. The king confiscated his property and had the marquis's castle destroyed.

Louis XIV's special court in the Auvergne heard nearly a thousand civil cases over four months in 1662. It convicted 692 people, and many of them, like the Marquis of Canillac, were noble.

The verdicts were an extraordinary example of Louis XIV's ability to project his authority into the remote corners of his realm and to do so in a way that diminished the power of other elites. During his long reign (1643–1715), Louis XIV systematically pursued such a policy on many fronts, asserting his power over the nobility, the clergy, and the provincial courts. Increasingly, these elites were forced to look to the crown to guarantee their interests, and their own power became more closely connected with the sacred aura of the monarchy itself. Louis XIV's model of kingship was so successful that it became known as absolute monarchy. In recognition of the success and influence of Louis XIV's political system, the period from around 1660 (when the English monarchy was restored and Louis XIV began his personal rule in France) to 1789 (when the French Revolution erupted) is traditionally known as the age of absolutism. This is a crucial period in the development of modern, centralized, bureaucratic states in Europe.

Absolutism was a political theory that encouraged rulers to claim complete sovereignty within their territories. An absolute monarch could make law, dispense justice, create and direct a bureaucracy, declare war, and levy taxation, without the approval of any other governing body. Assertions of absolute authority were buttressed by claims that rulers governed by divine right, just as fathers ruled over their households. After the chaos and religious wars of the previous century, many Europeans came to believe that it was only by exalting the sovereignty of absolute rulers that order could be restored to European life.

***THE DEFENSE OF CÁDIZ AGAINST THE ENGLISH* BY FRANCISCO ZURBARAN.** The rivalry between European powers that played out over the new colonial possessions further proved the decline of Spain, which lost the island of Jamaica and ships in the harbor of Cádiz to the English in the 1650s.

European monarchs also continued to project their power abroad during this period. By 1660, as we have seen, the French, Spanish, Portuguese, English, and Dutch had all established important colonies in the Americas and in Asia. These colonies created trading networks that brought profitable new consumer goods such as sugar, tobacco, and coffee to a wide public in Europe. They also encouraged the colonies' reliance on slavery to produce these goods. Rivalry among colonial powers to control the trade in slaves and consumer goods was intense and often led to wars that were fought both in Europe and in contested colonies. These wars, in turn, increased the motivation of absolutist rulers to extract as much revenue as they could from their subjects and encouraged the development of institutions that enhanced their power: armies, navies, tax systems, tariffs, and customs controls.

Absolutism was not universally successful during this period. The English monarchy, restored in 1660 after the turbulent years of the Civil War, attempted to impose absolutist rule but met with resistance from parliamentary leaders who insisted on more-inclusive institutions of government. After 1688, England, Scotland, the Dutch Republic, Switzerland, Venice, Sweden, and Poland-Lithuania were all either limited monarchies or republics. In Russia, on the other hand, an extreme autocracy emerged that gave the tsar a degree of control over his subjects' lives and property far beyond anything imagined by western European absolutists. Even in Russia, however, absolutism was never unlimited in practice. Even the most absolute monarchs could rule effectively only with the consent of their subjects (particularly the nobility). When serious opposition erupted, even powerful kings were forced to back down. King George III of Britain discovered this when his North American colonies declared their independence in 1776, creating the United States of America. In 1789, an even more sweeping revolution began in France, and the entire structure of absolutism came crashing to the ground (see Chapter 18).

THE APPEAL AND JUSTIFICATION OF ABSOLUTISM

Absolutism's promise of stability and order was an appealing alternative to the disorder of the sixteenth and seventeenth centuries (see Chapter 14). The early theorists of absolutism such as Jean Bodin and Thomas Hobbes looked to strong royal governments as an answer to the ever-present threat of religious war and civil conflict.

Absolutist monarchs sought control of the state's armed forces and its legal system, and they demanded the right to collect and spend the state's financial resources at will.

To achieve these goals, they also needed to create an efficient, centralized bureaucracy that owed its allegiance directly to the monarch. Creating and sustaining such a bureaucracy was expensive but necessary in order to weaken the special interests that hindered the free exercise of royal power. The nobility and the clergy, with their traditional legal privileges; the political authority of semiautonomous regions; and representative assemblies such as parliaments, diets, or estates-general were all obstacles—in the eyes of absolutists—to strong, centralized monarchical government. The history of absolutism is the history of kings who attempted to bring such institutions to heel.

In most Protestant countries, the power of the church had already been subordinated to the state when the age of absolutism began. Even where Roman Catholicism remained the state religion, such as in France, Spain, and Austria, absolutist monarchs now devoted considerable attention to bringing the Church and its clergy under royal control. Louis XIV took an active role in religious matters, appointing his own bishops and encouraging the repression of religious dissidents. Unlike his predecessors, however, he rarely appointed members of the clergy to offices within his administration.

The most important potential opponents of royal absolutism were not churchmen, however, but nobles. Louis XIV deprived the French nobility of political power in the provinces but increased their social prestige by making them live at his lavish court at Versailles. Peter the Great of Russia (1689–1725) forced his nobles into lifelong government service, and successive monarchs in Brandenburg-Prussia managed to co-opt the powerful aristocracy by granting them immunity to taxation and giving them the right to enserf their peasants. In exchange, they ceded administrative control to the increasingly bureaucratized Prussian state. In most European monarchies, including Spain, France, Prussia, and England, the nobility retained their preponderant role within the military.

Struggles between monarchs and nobles frequently affected relations between local and central government. In France, the requirement that nobles live at the king's court undermined the provincial institutions that the nobility used to exercise their political power. In Spain, the monarchy, based in Castile, battled the independent-minded nobles of Aragon and Catalonia. Prussian rulers asserted control over formerly "free" cities by claiming the right to police and tax their inhabitants. The Habsburg emperors tried, unsuccessfully, to suppress the largely autonomous nobility of Hungary. Rarely, however, was the path of confrontation between crown and nobility successful in the long run. The most effective absolutist monarchies of the eighteenth century continued to trade privileges for allegiance, so that nobles came to see their own interests as tied to those of the crown. For this reason, wary cooperation between kings and nobles was more common than open conflict during the eighteenth century.

THE ABSOLUTISM OF LOUIS XIV

In Louis XIV's state portrait, it is almost impossible to discern the human being behind the facade of the absolute monarch dressed in his coronation robes and surrounded by the symbols of his authority. That facade was artfully constructed by Louis, who recognized, more fully than any other early modern ruler, the importance of theater to effective kingship. Louis and his successors deliberately staged spectacular demonstrations of their sovereignty to enhance their position as rulers endowed with godlike powers.

Performing Royalty at Versailles

Louis's most elaborate staging of his authority took place at his palace at Versailles (ver-SY), outside of Paris. The main facade of the palace was a third of a mile in length. Inside, tapestries and paintings celebrated French military victories and royal triumphs; mirrors reflected shimmering light throughout the building. In the vast gardens outside, statues of the Greek god Apollo, god of the sun, recalled Louis's claim to be the "Sun King" of France. Noblemen vied to attend him when he arose from bed, ate his meals (usually stone cold after having traveled the distance of several city blocks from kitchen to table), strolled in his gardens (even the way the king walked was choreographed by the royal dancing master), or rode to the hunt. France's leading nobles were required to reside with Louis at Versailles for a portion of the year; the splendor of Louis's court was deliberately calculated to blind them to the possibility of disobedience while raising their prestige by associating them with himself. At the same time, the almost impossibly detailed rules of etiquette at court left these privileged nobles in constant suspense, forever fearful of offending the king by committing some trivial violation of proper manners.

Of course, the nobility did not surrender social and political power entirely. The social order was still hierarchical, and noblemen retained enormous privileges and rights over local peasants within their jurisdiction. The absolutist system forced the nobility to depend on the crown, but it did not seek to undermine their superior place in society. In this sense, the relationship between Louis XIV and the nobility was more of a negotiated settlement than a complete victory of the king over other powerful elites. Louis XIV understood this, and in a memoir that he prepared for his

Absolutism and Patriarchy

These selections show how two political theorists justified royal absolutism by deriving it from the absolute authority of a father over his household. Bishop Jacques-Bénigne Bossuet (1627–1704) was a famous French preacher who served as tutor to the son of King Louis XIV of France before becoming bishop of Meaux. Sir Robert Filmer (1588–1653) was an English political theorist. Filmer's works attracted particular attention in the 1680s, when John Locke directed the first of his Two Treatises of Government *to refuting Filmer's views on the patriarchal nature of royal authority.*

Bossuet on the Nature of Monarchical Authority

There are four characteristics or qualities essential to royal authority. First, royal authority is sacred; Secondly, it is paternal; Thirdly, it is absolute; Fourthly, it is subject to reason.... All power comes from God.... Thus princes act as ministers of God, and his lieutenants on earth. It is through them that he exercises his empire.... In this way ... the royal throne is not the throne of a man, but the throne of God himself....

We have seen that kings hold the place of God, who is the true Father of the human race. We have also seen that the first idea of power that there was among men, is that of paternal power; and that kings were fashioned on the model of fathers. Moreover, all the world agrees that obedience, which is due to public power, is only found ... in the precept which obliges one to honor his parents. From all this it appears that the name "king" is a father's name, and that goodness is the most natural quality in kings....

Royal authority is absolute. In order to make this term odious and insupportable, many pretend to confuse absolute government and arbitrary government. But nothing is more distinct, as we shall make clear when we speak of justice.... The prince need account to no one for what he ordains.... Without this absolute authority, he can neither do good nor suppress evil: his power must be such that no one can hope to escape him.... The sole defense of individuals against the public power must be their innocence....

One must, then, obey princes as if they were justice itself, without which there is neither order nor justice in affairs. They are gods, and share in some way in divine independence.... It follows from this that he who does not want to obey the prince ... is condemned irremissibly to death as an enemy of public peace and of human society.... The prince can correct himself when he knows that he has done badly; but against his authority there can be no remedy....

Source: Jacques-Bénigne Bossuet, *Politics Drawn from the Very Words of Holy Scripture,* (1709) trans. Patrick Riley (Cambridge: 1990), pp. 46–69 and 81–83.

son on the art of ruling he wrote, "The deference and the respect that we receive from our subjects are not a free gift from them but payment for the justice and the protection that they expect from us. Just as they must honor us, we must protect and defend them." In their own way, absolutists depended on the consent of those they ruled.

Administration and Centralization

Louis defined his responsibilities in absolutist terms: to concentrate royal power so as to produce domestic tranquility.

In addition to convincing the nobility to cede political authority, he also recruited the upper bourgeoisie as royal intendants, administrators responsible for running the thirty-six *generalités* into which France was divided. Intendants usually served outside the region where they were born and were thus unconnected with the local elites over whom they exercised authority. They held office at the king's pleasure and were clearly his men. Other administrators, often from families newly ennobled as a reward for their service, assisted in directing affairs of state from Versailles.

Louis's administrators devoted much of their time and energy to collecting the taxes necessary to finance the

Filmer on the Patriarchal Origins of Royal Authority

The first government in the world was monarchical, in the father of all flesh, Adam being commanded to multiply, and people the earth, and to subdue it, and having dominion given him over all creatures, was thereby the monarch of the whole world; none of his posterity had any right to possess anything, but by his grant or permission, or by succession from him. . . . Adam was the father, king, and lord over his family: a son, a subject, and a servant or a slave were one and the same thing at first. . . .

I cannot find any one place or text in the Bible where any power . . . is given to a people either to govern themselves, or to choose themselves governors, or to alter the manner of government at their pleasure. The power of government is settled and fixed by the commandment of "honour thy father"; if there were a higher power than the fatherly, then this commandment could not stand and be observed. . . .

All power on earth is either derived or usurped from the fatherly power, there being no other original to be found of any power whatsoever. For if there should be granted two sorts of power without any subordination of one to the other, they would be in perpetual strife which should be the supreme, for two supremes cannot agree. If the fatherly power be supreme, then the power of the people must be subordinate and depend on it. If the power of the people be supreme, then the fatherly power must submit to it, and cannot be exercised without the licence of the people, which must quite destroy the frame and course of nature. Even the power which God himself exercises over mankind is by right of fatherhood: he is both the king and father of us all. As God has exalted the dignity of earthly kings . . . by saying they are gods, so . . . he has been pleased . . . to humble himself by assuming the title of a king to express his power, and not the title of any popular government.

Source: Robert Filmer, "Observations upon Aristotle's Politiques," in *Divine Right and Democracy: An Anthology of Political Writing in Stuart England*, ed. David Wootton (Harmondsworth, UK: 1986), pp. 110–18. First published 1652.

Questions for Analysis

1. Bossuet's definition of *absolutism* connected the sacred power of kings with the paternal authority of fathers within the household. What consequences does he draw from defining the relationship between king and subjects in this way?

2. What does Filmer mean when he says, "All power on earth is either derived or usurped from the fatherly power"? How many examples does he give of paternal or monarchical power?

3. Bossuet and Filmer make obedience the basis for order and justice in the world. What alternative political systems did they most fear?

large standing army on which his aggressive foreign policy depended. Absolutism was fundamentally an approach to government by which ambitious monarchs could increase their own power through conquest and display. As such, it was enormously expensive. In addition to the *taille*, or land tax, which increased throughout the seventeenth century, Louis's government introduced a *capitation* (a head tax) and pressed successfully for the collection of indirect taxes on salt (the *gabelle*), wine, tobacco, and other goods. Because the nobility was exempt from the taille, its burden fell most heavily on the peasantry, whose local revolts Louis easily crushed.

Regional opposition was curtailed but not eliminated during Louis's reign. By removing the provincial nobility to Versailles, Louis cut them off from their local sources of power and influence. To restrict the powers of regional parlements, Louis decreed that members of any parlement who refused to approve and enforce his laws would be summarily exiled. The Estates-General, the French representative assembly that met at the king's pleasure to act as a consultative body for the state, had last been summoned in 1614. It did not meet at all during Louis's reign and, in fact, was not convened again until 1789.

Past and Present

The Persistence of Monarchies in a Democratic Age

In the past, monarchs such as Louis XIV (left) often ran roughshod over tradition as they sought ways to increase their power. Today, twelve European states still have reigning monarchs, such as Queen Elizabeth II (right), but their popularity would probably be diminished if they sought an active role in government.

Watch related author videos on the student site
wwnorton.com/college/history/western-civilizationsBrief4

Louis XIV's Religious Policies

Both for reasons of state and of personal conscience, Louis was determined to impose religious unity on France, regardless of the economic and social costs.

Although the vast majority of the French population was Roman Catholic, French Catholics were divided among Quietists, Jansenists, Jesuits, and Gallicans. Quietists preached retreat into personal mysticism, emphasizing a direct relationship between God and the individual human heart. Such doctrine, dispensing as it did with the intermediary services of the Church, was suspect in the eyes of absolutists wedded to the doctrine of *un roi, une loi, une foi* ("one king, one law, one faith"). Jansenism—a movement named for its founder Cornelius Jansen, a seventeenth-century bishop of Ypres—emphasized that original sin could only be overcome through divine grace, and they were committed to a doctrine of predestination that sounded like a kind of Catholic Calvinism. Louis vigorously persecuted Quietists and Jansenists, offering them a choice between recanting and prison or exile. At the same time, he supported the Jesuits in their efforts to create a Counter-Reformation Catholic Church in France. Louis's support for the Jesuits upset the traditional Gallican Catholics of France, however, who desired a French church independent of papal, Jesuit, and Spanish influence. As a result of this dissension among Catholics, the religious aura of Louis's kingship diminished during the course of his reign.

Against the Protestant Huguenots, Louis waged unrelenting war. Protestant churches and schools were destroyed, and Protestants were banned from many professions. In 1685, Louis revoked the Edict of Nantes, the legal foundation of the toleration Huguenots had enjoyed since 1598. Protestant clerics were exiled, laymen were sent to the galleys as slaves, and their children were forcibly baptized as Catholics. Many families converted, but 200,000

Protestant refugees fled to England, Holland, Germany, and America, bringing with them their professional and artisanal skills. Huguenots fleeing Louis XIV's persecution established the silk industries of Berlin and London, for example. This migration was an enormous loss to France.

Colbert and Mercantilism

Louis's drive to unify France depended on a vast increase in royal revenues. Jean-Baptiste Colbert, the king's finance minister from 1664 to 1683, accomplished this by eliminating wherever possible the practice of tax farming (which permitted collection agents to retain for themselves a percentage of the taxes they gathered for the king). When Colbert assumed office, only about 25 percent of the taxes collected throughout the kingdom reached the treasury. By the time he died, that figure had risen to 80 percent. Under Colbert's direction, the state sold public offices, including judgeships and mayoralties, and guilds purchased the right to enforce trade regulations. Colbert also tried to increase the nation's income by controlling and regulating foreign trade. Colbert was a firm believer in the economic doctrine known as "mercantilism"—a theory that aimed to increase the wealth of the absolutist state by reducing imports and increasing exports (see **Analyzing Primary Sources** on page 410). He imposed tariffs on foreign goods imported into France and used state money to promote the domestic manufacture of formerly imported goods, such as silk, lace, tapestries, and glass. He was especially anxious to create domestic industries capable of producing the goods France would need for war. To encourage domestic trade, he improved France's roads, bridges, and waterways.

Despite Colbert's efforts to increase crown revenues, his policies ultimately foundered on the insatiable demands of Louis XIV's wars (see pages 413–14). Colbert himself foresaw this result when he lectured the king in 1680: "Trade is the source of public finance and public finance is the vital nerve of war. . . . I beg your Majesty to permit me only to say to him that in war as in peace he has never consulted the amount of money available in determining his expenditures." Louis, however, paid him no heed. By the end of Louis's reign, his aggressive foreign policy lay in ruins and his country's finances had been shattered by the unsustainable costs of war.

French Colonialism under Louis XIV

Finance minister Colbert regarded overseas expansion as an integral part of the French state's mercantilist economic policy, and with his guidance, Louis XIV's absolutist realm emerged as a major colonial power. Realizing the profits to be made in responding to Europe's growing demand for sugar, Colbert encouraged the development of sugar-producing colonies in the West Indies, the largest of which was Saint-Domingue (present-day Haiti). Sugar, virtually unknown in Christian Europe during the Middle Ages, became a popular luxury item in the late fifteenth century (see Chapter 14). It took the slave plantations of the Caribbean to turn sugar into a mass-market product. By 1750, slaves in Saint-Domingue produced 40 percent of the world's sugar and 50 percent of its coffee, exporting more sugar than Jamaica, Cuba, and Brazil combined. By 1700, France also dominated the interior of the North American continent, where French traders brought furs to the American Indians and missionaries preached Christianity in a vast territory that stretched from Quebec to Louisiana. The financial returns from North America were never large, however. Furs, fish, and tobacco were exported to European markets but never matched the profits from the Caribbean sugar colonies or from the trading posts that the French maintained in India.

Like the earlier Spanish colonies (see Chapter 14), the French colonies were established and administered as direct crown enterprises. French colonial settlements in North America were conceived mainly as military outposts and trading centers, and they were overwhelmingly populated by men. The elite of French colonial society were military officers and administrators sent from Paris. Below their ranks were fishermen, fur traders, small farmers, and common soldiers who constituted the bulk of French settlers in North America. Because the fishing and the fur trades relied on cooperative relationships with native peoples, a mutual economic interdependence grew up between the French colonies and the peoples of the surrounding region. Intermarriage, especially between French traders and native women, was common. These North American colonies remained dependent on the wages and supplies sent to them from the mother country. Only rarely did they become truly self-sustaining economic enterprises.

The phenomenally successful sugar plantations of the Caribbean had their own social structure, with slaves at the bottom, people of mixed African and European descent forming a middle layer, and wealthy European plantation owners at the top, controlling the lucrative trade with the outside world. Well over half of the sugar and coffee sent to France was resold and sent elsewhere to markets throughout Europe. Because the monarchy controlled the prices that colonial plantation owners

Mercantilism and War

Jean-Baptiste Colbert (1619–1683) served as Louis XIV's finance minister from 1664 until his death. He worked assiduously to promote commerce, build up French industry, and increase exports. However much Colbert may have seen his economic policies as ends in themselves, to Louis they were always means to the end of waging war. Ultimately, Louis's wars undermined the prosperity that Colbert tried so hard to create. This memorandum, written to Louis in 1670, illustrates clearly the mercantilist presumptions of self-sufficiency on which Colbert operated: every item needed to build up the French navy must ultimately be produced in France, even if it could be acquired at less cost from elsewhere.

And since Your Majesty has wanted to work diligently at reestablishing his naval forces, and since afore that it has been necessary to make very great expenditures, since all merchandise, munitions, and manufactured items formerly came from Holland and the countries of the North, it has been absolutely necessary to be especially concerned with finding within the realm, or with establishing in it, everything which might be necessary for this great plan.

To this end, the manufacture of tar was established in Médoc, Auvergne, Dauphiné, and Provence; iron cannons, in Burgundy, Nivernois, Saintonge, and Périgord; large anchors in Dauphiné, Nivernois, Brittany, and Rochefort; sailcloth for the Levant, in Dauphiné; coarse muslin, in Auvergne; all the implements for pilots and others, at Dieppe and La Rochelle; the cutting of wood suitable for vessels, in Burgundy, Dauphiné, Brittany, Normandy, Poitou, Saintonge, Provence, Guyenne, and the Pyrenees; masts, of a sort once unknown in this realm, have been found in Provence, Languedoc, Auvergne, Dauphiné, and in the Pyrenees. Iron, which was obtained from Sweden and Biscay, is currently manufactured in the realm. Fine hemp for ropes, which came from Prussia and from Piedmont, is currently obtained in Burgundy, Mâconnais, Bresse, Dauphiné; and markets for it have since been established in Berry and in Auvergne, which always provides money in these provinces and keeps it within the realm.

In a word, everything serving for the construction of vessels is currently established in the realm, so that Your Majesty can get along without foreigners for the navy and will even, in a short time, be able to supply them and gain their money in this fashion. And it is with this same objective of having everything necessary to provide abundantly for his navy and that of his subjects that he is working at the general reform of all the forests in his realm, which, being as carefully preserved as they are at present, will abundantly produce all the wood necessary for this.

Source: Charles W. Cole, *Colbert and a Century of French Mercantilism*, 2 vols. (New York: 1939), p. 320.

Questions for Analysis

1. Why would Colbert want to manufacture materials for supplying the navy within France rather than buying them from abroad?

2. From this example, does Colbert see the economy as serving any interest other than that of the state?

3. Was there a necessary connection between mercantilism and war?

---

could charge French merchants for their goods, traders in Europe who bought the goods for resale abroad could also make vast fortunes. Historians estimate that as many as 1 million of the 25 million inhabitants of France in the eighteenth century lived off the money flowing through this colonial trade, making the slave colonies of the Caribbean a powerful force for economic change in France. The wealth generated from these colonies added to the prestige of France's absolutist system of government.

ALTERNATIVES TO ABSOLUTISM

Although absolutism was the dominant model for seventeenth- and eighteenth-century European monarchs, it was by no means the only system by which Europeans governed themselves. A republican oligarchy continued to rule in Venice. In the Polish-Lithuanian commonwealth, the monarch was elected by the nobility and governed alongside a parliament that met every two years. In the Netherlands, the territories that had won their independence from Spain during the early seventeenth century combined to form the United Provinces, the only truly new country to take shape in Europe during the early modern era.

The Restoration in England and the Glorious Revolution of 1688

After the civil war of 1642–51 and the subsequent years of Oliver Cromwell's Commonwealth and Protectorate (see Chapter 14), England took a different path from that of France. By 1688, the English arrived at a constitutional settlement that gave a larger role to Parliament and admitted a degree of participation by non-nobles in the affairs of state. Arriving at this settlement was not easy, however, and two issues remained contentious between 1660 and 1688: the religious question and the relationship between Parliament and the king.

Following the Restoration of the Stuarts in 1660, Charles II (r. 1660–85) showed his affinity for Catholicism by bringing bishops back to the Church of England, but he also declared limited religious toleration for Protestant "dissenters." He comforted members of Parliament by promising to observe the Magna Carta and he accepted legislation stating that Parliament be summoned at least once every three years. England thus emerged from its civil war as a limited monarchy, with power exercised by the "king in Parliament."

During the 1670s, however, Charles began to openly model his kingship on the absolutism of Louis XIV. England's powerful elites became divided between Charles's supporters, known as "Tories" (a nickname for Irish Catholic bandits) and his opponents, called "Whigs" (a nickname for Scottish Presbyterian rebels). In fact, both sides feared both absolutism and the prospect of renewed civil war. What they could not agree on was which possibility frightened them more.

Charles's known sympathy for Roman Catholicism and his claim that he had the right to ignore parliamentary legislation worked to the advantage of his Whig opponents, who won a series of parliamentary elections between 1679 and 1681. Charles responded by moving aggressively against the Whig leadership, executing several on charges of treason. When he died in 1685, his power had been enhanced, but his divisive political and religious legacy was the undoing of his less able successor, his Roman Catholic brother, James II.

James's admiration of the French monarchy's Gallican Catholicism led him to seek ways of furthering the work of the Church by connecting it to the power of an absolutist state. His commitment to absolutism also led him to build up the English army and navy, which required increased taxation. He also took control of the country's new post office, making domestic surveillance routine and prosecutions of seditious speech frequent. For the Whigs, James's policies were

CHARLES II OF ENGLAND (r. 1660–85) IN HIS CORONATION ROBES. This full frontal portrait of the monarch, holding the symbols of his rule, seems to confront the viewer personally with the overwhelming authority of the sovereign's gaze. Compare this classic image of the absolutist monarch with the very different portraits of William and Mary, who ruled after the Glorious Revolution of 1688 (page 412). ■ *What had changed between 1660, when Charles II came to the throne, and 1688, when the more popular William and Mary became the rulers of England?*

all that they had feared. The Tories, meanwhile, remained loyal to the Church of England and were alienated by James's Catholicism. When a son was unexpectedly born to the royal couple, and it was announced that he was to be raised a Catholic, events moved swiftly to a climax. A delegation of Whigs and Tories crossed the channel to Holland to invite James's much older Protestant daughter Mary Stuart and her Protestant husband, William of Orange, to cross to England with an invading army to preserve English Protestantism and English liberties by summoning a new Parliament.

Following the invasion, James fled for exile in France. Parliament declared the throne vacant, allowing William and Mary to succeed him as joint sovereigns in 1688. Parliament passed a Bill of Rights, which reaffirmed English civil liberties such as trial by jury, habeas corpus (a guarantee that no one could be imprisoned unless charged with a crime) and the right to petition the monarch through Parliament. The Bill of Rights also declared the monarchy subject to the law. The Act of Toleration of 1689 granted Protestant dissenters the right to worship freely, and in 1701, the Act of Succession ordained that every future English monarch must be a member of the Church of England.

The English referred to the events of 1688–89 as the "Glorious Revolution" because it established England as a mixed monarchy governed by the "king in Parliament" according to the rule of law. After 1688, no English monarch ever again attempted to govern without Parliament, which has met annually ever since, while strengthening its control over taxation and expenditure. Although Parliament never codified the legal provisions of this form of monarchy into one constitutional document, historians consider 1688 as a founding moment in the development of a constitutional monarchy in Britain.

Yet the revolution of 1688 was not all glory. It was not bloodless, and it was accompanied by violence in many parts of England, Scotland, and Ireland. Also, it consolidated the position of large property holders, whose control over local government had been threatened by the centralizing absolutist policies of Charles II and James II. It thus reinforced the

power of a wealthy class of English elites who would soon become even wealthier from government patronage and the profits of war. The 1688 revolution also brought misery to the Catholic minority in Scotland and the Catholic majority in Ireland. After 1690, power in Ireland would lie firmly in the hands of a "Protestant Ascendancy," whose dominance over Irish society would last until modern times.

The Glorious Revolution nevertheless favored the growth and political power of the English commercial classes, especially the growing number of people concentrated in English cities whose livelihood depended on commerce in the Atlantic world and beyond. Whigs in Parliament became the voice of this newly influential pressure group of commercial entrepreneurs; the Whigs called for revisions to the tax code that would benefit those engaged in manufacturing and trade. In 1694, the Whigs established the Bank of England, which aimed to promote English power through the generation of wealth, inaugurating a financial revolution that would make London the center of a vast network of banking and investment in the eighteenth century.

John Locke and the Contract Theory of Government

The Glorious Revolution was the product of unique circumstances, but it also reflected antiabsolutist theories of politics that were taking shape in the late seventeenth century. Chief among these opponents of absolutism was the Englishman John Locke (1632–1704), whose *Two Treatises of Government* were written before the Glorious Revolution but published for the first time in 1690.

Locke maintained that humans had originally lived in a state of nature characterized by absolute freedom and equality, with no government of any kind. The only law was the law of nature (which Locke equated with the law of reason), by which individuals enforced for themselves their natural rights to life, liberty, and property. Soon, however, humans perceived that the inconveniences of the state of nature outweighed its advantages. Accordingly, they agreed first to establish a civil society based on absolute equality and then to set up a government to arbitrate the disputes that might arise within this civil society. But they did not make government's powers absolute. All powers not expressly surrendered to the government were reserved to the people themselves; as a result, governmental authority was both contractual and conditional. If a government exceeded or abused the authority granted to it, society had the right to dissolve that government and create another.

Locke condemned absolutism in every form. He denounced absolute monarchy, but he was also critical of

WILLIAM AND MARY. In 1688, William of Orange and his wife, Mary Stuart, became Protestant joint rulers of England in a bloodless coup that took power from her father, the Catholic James II. Compare this contemporary print with the portraits of Louis XIV (page 404) and Charles II (page 411). ▪ *What relationship does it seem to depict between the royal couple and their subjects?* ▪ *What is the significance of the gathered crowd in the public square in the background?* ▪ *How is this different from the spectacle of divine authority projected by Louis XIV or the image of Charles II looking straight at the viewer?*

claims for the sovereignty of parliaments. Government, he argued, had been instituted to protect life, liberty, and property; no political authority could infringe these natural rights. The law of nature was therefore an automatic and absolute limitation on every branch of government.

In the late eighteenth century, Locke's ideas would resurface as part of the intellectual background of both the American and French Revolutions. Between 1690 and 1720, however, they served a far less radical purpose. The landed gentry who replaced James II with William and Mary read Locke as a defense of their conservative revolution. Rather than protecting their liberty and property, James II had threatened both; hence, the magnates were entitled to overthrow the tyranny he had established and replace it with a government that would defend their interests by preserving these natural rights. English government after 1689 would be dominated by Parliament; Parliament in turn was controlled by a landed aristocracy who were firm in the defense of their common interests, and who perpetuated their control by determining that only men possessed of substantial property could vote or run for office. During the beginning of the eighteenth century, then, both France and Britain had solved the problem of political dissent and social disorder in their own way. The emergence of a limited monarchy in England after 1688 contrasted vividly with the absolutist system developed by Louis XIV, but in fact both systems worked well enough to balance the competing interests of royal authority and powerful landed nobles.

The Dutch Republic

Another exception to absolutist rule in Europe was the Dutch Republic of the United Provinces, which had gained its independence from Spanish rule in 1648 (see Chapter 14). The seven provinces of the Dutch Republic (also known as the Netherlands) preserved their autonomy with a federal legislature known as the States General. The inhabitants of the republic worked hard to prevent the reestablishment of hereditary monarchy in the Dutch Republic. They were all the more jealous of their independence because several Catholic provinces of the southern Low Countries, including present-day Belgium and Luxembourg, remained under Spanish control.

The princes of the House of Orange served the Dutch Republic with a special title, *stadtholder*, or steward. The stadtholder did not technically rule and had no power to make laws, though he did exercise some influence over the appointments of officials and military officers. Powerful merchant families in the United Provinces exercised real authority, through their dominance of the legislature. It was from the Dutch Republic that the stadtholder William

of Orange launched his successful bid to become the king of England in the Glorious Revolution of 1688.

By 1670, the prosperity of the Dutch Republic was strongly linked to trade: grains and fish from eastern Europe and the Baltic Sea; spices, silks, porcelains, and tea from the Indian Ocean and Japan; slaves, silver, coffee, sugar, and tobacco from the Atlantic world. With a population of nearly 2 million and a capital, Amsterdam, that served as an international hub for goods and finance, the Dutch Republic's commercial network was global (see Chapter 14). Trade brought with it an extraordinary diversity of peoples and religions, as Spanish and Portuguese Jews, French Huguenots, English Quakers, and Protestant dissidents from central Europe all sought to take advantage of the relative spirit of toleration that existed in the Netherlands. This toleration did have limits. Jews were not required to live in segregated neighborhoods, as in many other European capitals, but they were prohibited from joining guilds or trade associations. Tensions between Calvinists and Catholics were also a perennial issue.

The last quarter of the seventeenth century witnessed a decline in Dutch power. The turning point came in 1672, when the French king, Louis XIV, put together a coalition that quickly overran all but two of the Dutch provinces. Popular anger at the failures of Dutch leadership turned violent, and in response the panicked assemblies named William of Orange the new stadtholder of Holland, giving him the power to organize the defense of the republic and to quell internal dissent. William opened the dikes that held back the sea, and the French armies were forced to retreat in the face of rising waters. After the Glorious Revolution of 1688 in England, which brought William of Orange to the English throne, the Dutch joined an alliance with the English against the French. This alliance protected the republic against further aggression from France, but it also forced the Dutch into heavy expenditures on fortifications and defense and involved them in a series of costly wars (as will be discussed later). As a result, the flexible political institutions that had been part of the strength of the Dutch Republic became more rigid over time. Meanwhile, both the French and the British continued to pressure the Dutch commercial fleet at sea. In the eighteenth century, the Dutch no longer exercised the same influence abroad.

WAR AND THE BALANCE OF POWER, 1661–1715

By the beginning of the eighteenth century, then, Europe was being reshaped by wars whose effects were also felt far beyond Europe's borders. The initial causes of these wars lay in the French monarchy's efforts to challenge France's main European rivals, the Habsburg powers in Spain, the Spanish Netherlands, and the Holy Roman Empire. Through his continued campaigns in the Low Countries, Louis XIV expanded his territory, eventually taking Strasbourg (1681), Luxembourg (1684), and Cologne (1688). In response, William of Orange organized the League of Augsburg, which over time included Holland, England, Spain, Sweden, Bavaria, Saxony, the Rhine Palatinate, and the Austrian Habsburgs. The resulting Nine Years' War between France and the League extended from Ireland to India to North America (where it was known as King William's War), demonstrating the broadening imperial reach of European dynastic regimes and the increasing significance of French and English competition in the Atlantic world.

These wars were a sign both of the rising power of Europe's absolutist regimes and of a growing vulnerability. Financing the increasingly costly wars of the eighteenth century would prove to be one of the central challenges faced by all of Europe's absolutist regimes, and the pressure to raise revenues from royal subjects through taxation would eventually strain European society to a breaking point. By the end of the eighteenth century, popular unrest and political challenges to absolutist and imperial states were widespread, both on the European continent and in the colonies of the Atlantic world.

From the League of Augsburg to the War of the Spanish Succession

The League of Augsburg reflected the emergence of a new diplomatic goal in western and central Europe: the preservation of a balance of power. This goal would animate European diplomacy for the next 200 years, until the balance of power system collapsed with the outbreak of the First World War. The main proponents of balance of power diplomacy were England, the United Provinces (Holland), Prussia, and Austria. By 1697, the League forced Louis XIV to make peace, because France was exhausted by war and famine. Louis gave back much of his recent gains but kept his eyes on the real prize: a French claim to succeed to the throne of Spain and thus to control of the Spanish Empire in the Americas, Italy, the Netherlands, and the Philippines.

In the 1690s, it became clear that King Charles II of Spain (r. 1665–1700) would soon die without a clear heir, and both Louis XIV of France and Leopold I of Austria (r. 1658–1705) were interested in promoting their own relatives to succeed him. Either solution would have upset the balance of power in Europe, and several schemes to divide the Spanish realm between French and Austrian candidates

were discussed. Meanwhile, King Charles II's advisers sought to avoid partition by passing the entire Spanish Empire to a single heir: Louis XIV's grandson, Philip of Anjou. Philip was to renounce any claim to the French throne in becoming king of Spain, but the terms of this were kept secret. When Charles II died, Philip V (r. 1700–46) was proclaimed king of Spain and Louis XIV rushed troops into the Spanish Netherlands while also sending French merchants into the Spanish Americas to break their monopoly on trade from the region. Immediately a war broke out, known as the War of the Spanish Succession, pitting England, the United Provinces, Austria, and Prussia against France, Bavaria, and Spain. Although the English king, William of Orange, died in 1702, just as the war was beginning, his generals led an extraordinary march deep into the European continent, inflicting a devastating defeat on the French and their Bavarian allies at Blenheim in southern Germany (1704). Soon after, the English captured Gibraltar, establishing a commercial foothold in the Mediterranean. The costs of the campaign nevertheless created a chorus of complaints from English and Dutch merchants, who feared the damage that was being done to trade and commerce. Queen Anne of England (Mary's sister and William's successor) gradually grew disillusioned with the war, and her government sent out peace feelers to France.

In 1713, the war finally came to an end with the Treaty of Utrecht. Its terms were reasonably fair to all sides. Philip V, Louis XIV's grandson, remained on the throne of Spain and retained Spain's colonial empire intact. In return, Louis agreed that France and Spain would never be united under the same ruler. Austria gained territories in the Spanish Netherlands and Italy, including Milan and Naples. The Dutch were guaranteed protection of their borders against future invasions by France, but the French retained both Lille and Strasbourg. The most significant consequences of the settlement, however, were played out in the Atlantic world, as the balance of powers among Europe's colonial empires underwent a profound shift.

Imperial Rivalries after the Treaty of Utrecht

The fortunes of Europe's colonial empires changed dramatically owing to the wars of the late seventeenth and early eighteenth centuries. Habsburg Spain proved unable to defend its early monopoly over colonial trade, and by 1700, although Spain still possessed a substantial empire, it lay at the mercy of its more dynamic rivals. Portugal, too, found it impossible to prevent foreign penetration of its colonial empire. In 1703, the English signed a treaty with

Portugal allowing English merchants to export woolens duty-free into Portugal and allowing Portugal to ship its wines duty-free into England. Access to Portugal also led British merchants to trade with the Portuguese colony of Brazil, an important sugar producer and the largest of all the American markets for African slaves.

The 1713 Treaty of Utrecht opened a new era of colonial rivalries. The French retained Quebec and other territories in North America, as well as their small foothold in India. The biggest winner by far was Great Britain, as the combined kingdoms of England and Scotland were known after 1707. The British acquired large chunks of French territory in the New World, including Newfoundland, mainland Nova Scotia, the Hudson Bay, and the Caribbean island of St. Kitts. Even more valuable, however, Britain also extracted from Spain the right to transport and sell African slaves in Spanish America. As a result, the British were now poised to become the principal slave merchants and the dominant colonial and commercial power of the eighteenth-century world.

The Treaty of Utrecht thus reshaped the balance of power in the Atlantic world in fundamental ways. Spain's collapse was already precipitous; by 1713, it was complete. Spain would remain the "sick man of Europe" for the next two centuries. The Dutch decline was more gradual, but by 1713 Dutch merchants' inability to compete with the British in the slave trade diminished their economic clout. In the Atlantic, Britain and France were now the dominant powers. Although they would duel for another half century for control of North America, the balance of colonial power tilted decisively in Britain's favor after Utrecht. Within Europe, the myth of French military supremacy had been shattered. Britain's navy, not France's army, would rule the new imperial and commercial world of the eighteenth century.

THE REMAKING OF CENTRAL AND EASTERN EUROPE

The decades between 1680 and 1720 were also decisive in reshaping the balance of power in central and eastern Europe. As Ottoman power waned, the Austro-Hungarian Empire of the Habsburgs emerged as the dominant power in central and southeastern Europe. To the north, Brandenburg-Prussia was also a rising power. The most dramatic changes, however, occurred in Russia, which emerged from a long war with Sweden as the dominant power in the Baltic Sea and would soon threaten the combined kingdom of Poland-Lithuania. Within these regimes, the main tension came from ambitious monarchs who sought to increase the power of the centralized state at the expense of other elites, especially

aristocrats and the religious institutions. In Brandenburg-Prussia and in Tsarist Russia, these efforts were largely successful, whereas in Habsburg Austria, regional nobilities retained much of their influence.

The Austrian Habsburg Empire

In the second half of the seventeenth century, as Louis XIV of France demonstrated the power of absolutism in western Europe, the Austrian Habsburg Empire must have seemed increasingly like a holdover from a previous age. Habsburg Austria was the largest state within what remained of the medieval Holy Roman Empire, a complex federal association of nearly 300 nominally autonomous dynastic kingdoms, principalities, duchies, and archbishoprics that had been created to protect and defend the papacy. Some, such as the kingdom of Bavaria, were large and had their own standing armies. Each Holy Roman emperor was chosen by seven "electors" who were either of noble rank or archbishops—in practice, nevertheless, the emperor was always from the Habsburg family. Through strategic marriages with other royal lines, earlier generations of Habsburg rulers had consolidated their control over a substantial part of Europe, including Austria, Bohemia, Moravia, and Hungary in central Europe; the Netherlands and Burgundy in the west; and, if one included the Spanish branch of the Habsburg family, Spain and its vast colonial empire as well. After 1648, when the Treaty of Westphalia granted individual member states within the Holy Roman Empire the right to conduct their own foreign policy, the influence of the Austrian Habsburgs waned at precisely the moment that they faced challenges from France to the west and the Ottoman Empire to the east.

The complicated structure of the Holy Roman Empire limited the extent to which a ruler such as Leopold I of Austria could emulate the absolutist rule of Louis XIV in France. Every constituent state within the empire had its own local political institutions and its own entrenched nobilities. Each state had a strong interest in resisting attempts to centralize taxation or the raising of armies. Even if direct assertion of absolutist control was impossible, however, Habsburg rulers found ways of increasing their authority. In Bohemia and Moravia, the Habsburgs encouraged landlords to produce crops for export by forcing peasants to provide three days per week of unpaid work for their lords. In return, the landed elites of these territories permitted the emperors to reduce the political independence of their traditional legislative estates. In Hungary, however, the powerful and independent nobility resisted such compromises. When the Habsburgs began a campaign against Hungarian Protestants in 1679, an insurrection broke out that forced Leopold to

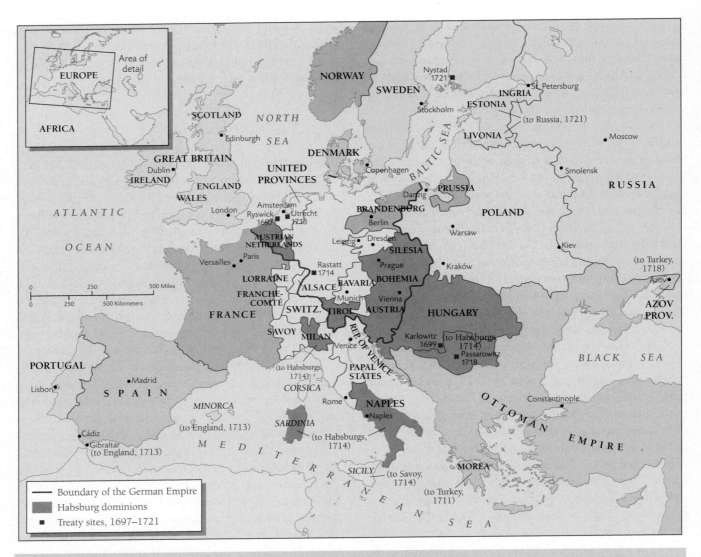

EUROPE AFTER THE TREATY OF UTRECHT (1713). ▪ *What were the major Habsburg dominions?* ▪ *What geographical disadvantage faced the kingdom of Poland as Brandenburg-Prussia grew in influence and ambition?* ▪ *How did the balance of power change in Europe as a result of the Treaty of Utrecht?*

grant concessions to Hungarian nobles in exchange for their assistance in restoring order. When the Ottoman Empire sought to take advantage of this disorder by pressing an attack against Austria from the east, the Habsburgs survived only by enlisting the help of a Catholic coalition led by the Polish king John Sobieski (r. 1674–96).

In 1683 the Ottomans launched their last assault on Vienna, but after their failure to capture the Habsburg capital, Ottoman power in southeastern Europe declined rapidly. By 1699, Austria had reconquered most of Hungary from the Ottomans; by 1718, it controlled all of Hungary and also Transylvania and Serbia. In 1722, Austria acquired the territory of Silesia from Poland. With Hungary now a buffer state between Austria and the Ottomans, Austria became one of the arbiters of the European balance of

power. The same obstacles to the development of central-ized absolutist rule persisted, however, and Austria was increasingly overshadowed in central Europe by the rise of another German-speaking state: Prussia.

The Rise of Brandenburg-Prussia

After the Ottoman collapse, the main threat to Austria came from the rising power of Brandenburg-Prussia. Like Austria, Prussia was a composite state made up of several geographically divided territories acquired through inheri-tance by a single royal family, the Hohenzollerns. Their two main holdings were Brandenburg, centered on its capital city, Berlin, and the duchy of East Prussia. Between these two territories lay Pomerania (claimed by Sweden) and an important part of the kingdom of Poland, including the port of Gdansk (Danzig). The Hohenzollerns' aim was to unite their state by acquiring these intervening territories. Over the course of more than a century of steady state building, they finally succeeded in doing so. In the process, Brandenburg-Prussia became a dominant military power and a key player in the balance-of-power diplomacy of the mid-eighteenth century.

The foundations for Prussian expansion were laid by Frederick William, the "Great Elector" (r. 1640–88). He obtained East Prussia from Poland in exchange for help in a war against Sweden. Behind the Elector's diplomatic triumphs lay his success in building an army and mobilizing the resources to pay for it. He gave the powerful nobles of his territories (known as "Junkers" [*YUN-kurs*]) the right to enserf their peasants and guaranteed them immunity from taxation. In exchange, they staffed the officer corps of his army and supported his highly autocratic taxation system. Secure in their estates and made increasingly wealthy in the grain trade, the Junkers surrendered management of the Prussian state to the Elector's newly reformed bureaucracy, which set about its main task: increasing the size and strength of the Prussian army.

By supporting Austria in the War of the Spanish Succession, the Great Elector's son, Frederick I (r. 1688–1713) earned the right to call himself king of Prussia from the Austrian emperor. He too was a crafty diplomat, but his main attention was devoted to developing the cultural life of his new royal capital, Berlin. His son, Frederick William I (r. 1713–40) focused, like his grandfather, on building the army. During his reign, the Prussian army grew from 30,000 to 83,000 men, becoming the fourth largest army in Europe, after France, Austria, and Russia. To support his army, Frederick William increased taxes and shunned the luxuries of court life. For him, the theater of absolutism was not the palace but the office, where he personally supervised his army and the growing bureaucracy that sustained it. Frederick William's son, known as Frederick the Great, would take this Prussian army and the bureaucracy that sustained it and transform the kingdom into a major power in central Europe after 1740 (see Chapter 17).

Thus, in both Prussia and Habsburg Austria, the divided nature of the respective realms and the entrenched strength of local nobilities forced the rulers in each case to grant significant concessions to noble landowners in exchange for incremental increases in the power of the centralized state. Whereas the nobility in France increasingly sought to maximize their power by participating in the system of absolutist rule at the court of Louis XIV, and wealthy landowners in England sought to exercise their influence through Parliament, the nobilities of Prussia and Habsburg Austria had more leverage to demand something in return for their cooperation. Often, what they demanded was the right to enserf or coerce labor from the peasantry in their domains. In both eastern and western Europe, therefore, the state became stronger. In eastern Europe, however, this increase in state power often came at the expense of an intensification of feudal obligations that the peasantry owed to their local lords.

AUTOCRACY IN RUSSIA

An even more dramatic transformation took place in Russia under Tsar Peter I (1672–1725). Peter's official title was "autocrat of all the Russias" but he was soon known as Peter the Great. His imposing height—he was six feet eight inches tall—and his mercurial personality—jesting one moment, raging the next—added to the outsize impression he made on his contemporaries. Peter was not the first tsar to bring his country into contact with western Europe, but his policies were decisive in making Russia a great European power.

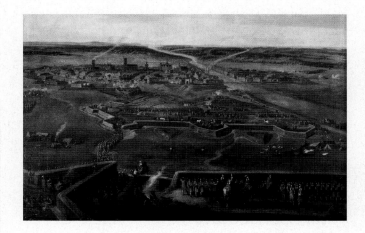

THE CITY OF STETTIN UNDER SIEGE BY THE GREAT ELECTOR FREDERICK WILLIAM IN THE WINTER OF 1677–78 (c. 1680). This painting depicts the growing sophistication and organization of military operations under the Prussian monarchy. Improvements in artillery and siege tactics forced cities to adopt new defensive strategies, especially the zone of battlements and protective walls that became ubiquitous in central Europe during this period. ▪ *How might these developments have shaped the layout of Europe's growing towns and cities?* ▪ *How might this emphasis on the military and its attendant bureaucracy have affected the relationship between the monarchy and the nobility or between the king and his subjects?*

The Early Years of Peter's Reign

Since 1613, Russia had been ruled by members of the Romanov dynasty, who had attempted to restore political stability after the chaotic "time of troubles" that followed the death of the bloodthirsty, half-mad tsar Ivan the Terrible in 1584. The Romanovs faced a severe threat to their rule between 1667 and 1671, when a Cossack leader (the Russian Cossacks were semiautonomous bands of peasant cavalrymen) named Stenka Razin led a rebellion in southeastern Russia. This uprising found widespread support, not only from oppressed serfs but also from non-Russian tribes in the lower Volga region who longed to cast off the domination of Moscow. Ultimately Tsar Alexis I (r. 1645–76) and the Russian nobility were able to defeat Razin's zealous but disorganized bands of rebels, slaughtering more than 100,000 of them in the process.

Like Louis XIV of France, Peter came to the throne as a young boy, and his minority was marked by political dissension and court intrigue. In 1689, however, at the age of seventeen, he overthrew the regency of his half sister Sophia and assumed personal control of the state. Determined to make Russia into a great military power, the young tsar traveled to Holland and England during the 1690s to study shipbuilding and to recruit skilled foreign workers to help him build a navy. While he was abroad, however, his elite palace guard (the *streltsy*) rebelled, attempting to restore Sophia to the throne. Peter quickly returned home from Vienna and crushed the rebellion with striking savagery. About 1,200 suspected conspirators were summarily executed, many of them gibbeted outside the walls of the Kremlin, where their bodies rotted for months as a graphic reminder of the fate awaiting those who dared challenge the tsar's authority.

The Transformation of the Tsarist State

Peter is most famous as the tsar who attempted to westernize Russia by imposing a series of social and cultural reforms on the traditional Russian nobility: ordering noblemen to cut off their long beards and flowing sleeves; publishing a book of manners that forbade spitting on the floor and eating with one's fingers; encouraging polite conversation between the sexes; and requiring noblewomen to appear, together with men, in Western garb at weddings, banquets, and other public occasions. The children of Russian nobles were sent to western European courts for their education. Thousands of western European experts were brought to Russia to staff the new schools and academies

Peter built; to design the new buildings he constructed; and to serve in the tsar's army, navy, and administration.

These measures were important, but the tsar was not primarily motivated by a desire to modernize or westernize Russia. Peter's policies transformed Russian life in fundamental ways, but his real goal was to make Russia a great military power, not to remake Russian society. His new taxation system (1724), for example, which assessed taxes on individuals rather than on households, rendered many of the traditional divisions of Russian peasant society obsolete. It was created, however, to raise more money for war. His Table of Ranks, imposed in 1722, had a similar impact on the nobility. By insisting that all nobles must work their way up from the (lower) landlord class to the (higher) administrative class and to the (highest) military class, Peter reversed the traditional hierarchy of Russian noble society, which had valued landlords by birth above administrators and soldiers who had risen by merit. But he also created a powerful new incentive to lure his nobility into administrative and military service to the tsar.

As "autocrat of all the Russias," Peter the Great was the absolute master of his empire to a degree unmatched elsewhere in Europe. After 1649, Russian peasants were legally the property of their landlords; by 1750, half were serfs and the other half were state peasants who lived on lands owned by the tsar himself (by comparison, many peasants in western Europe owned their own land and very few were serfs). State peasants could be conscripted to serve as soldiers in the tsar's army, as workers in his factories (whose

EXECUTION OF THE *STRELTSY* (1698). A contemporary woodcut showing how Peter the Great ordered the public hanging of guard regiments who had rebelled against his authority. How does this display of autocratic power compare with the spectacle of power so carefully orchestrated by Peter's contemporary, Louis XIV of France?

The Revolt of the Streltsy and Peter the Great

The streltsy were four regiments of Moscow guards that became involved in a conspiracy in support of Peter the Great's older sister, Sophia, who had earlier made claim to the throne while Peter was still a child. Approximately 4,000 of the rebels were defeated in June 1698 by troops loyal to Peter. Peter himself was abroad during the fighting, and although his officers had already tortured many of the streltsy to determine the involvement of other nobles, Peter ordered a more far-reaching investigation on his return. Over 1,000 of the streltsy were executed after being tortured again. Afterward, their bodies were placed on display in the capital. Johann Georg Korb, an Austrian diplomat in Moscow, recorded his observations of the power wielded by the Russian autocrat.

 ow sharp was the pain, how great the indignation to which the Czar's Majesty was mightily moved, when he knew of the rebellion of the Strelitz [*streltsy*], betrayed openly a mind panting for vengeance.... Going immediately to Lefort (the only person almost that he condescended to treat with intimate familiarity), he thus indignantly broke out: "Tell me, Francis, son of James, how I can reach Moscow, by the shortest way, in a brief space, so that I may wreak vengeance on this great perfidy of my people, with punishments worthy of their flagitious crime. Not one of them shall escape with impunity. Around my royal city, of which, with their impious efforts, they meditated the destruction, I will have gibbets and gallows set upon the walls and ramparts, and each and every of them will I put to a direful death." ...

His first anxiety, after his arrival [in Moscow] was about the rebellion. In what it consisted? What the insurgents meant? Who had dared to instigate such a crime? And as nobody could answer accurately upon all points, and some pleaded their own ignorance, others the obstinacy of the Strelitz, he began to have suspicions of everybody's loyalty, and began to cogitate about a fresh investigation. The rebels that were kept in custody ... were all brought in by four regiments of the guards, to a fresh investigation and fresh tortures. Prison, tribunal, and rack, for those that were brought in, was in Bebraschentsko. No day, holy, or profane, were the inquisitors idle; every day was deemed fit and lawful for torturing. As many as there were accused there were knouts, and every inquisitor was a butcher. Prince Feodor Jurowicz Romadonowski showed himself by so much more fitted for his inquiry, as he surpassed the rest in cruelty. He put the interrogatories, he examined the criminals, he urged those that were not confessing, he ordered such Strelitz as were more pertinaciously silent, to be subjected to more cruel tortures; those that had already confessed about many things were questioned about more; those who were bereft of strength and reason, and almost of their senses, by excess of torment, were handed over to the skill of the doctors, who were compelled to restore them to strength, in order that they might be broken down by fresh excruciations. The whole month of October was spent in butchering the backs of the culprits with knout and with flames: no day were those that were left alive exempt from scourging or scorching, or else they were broken upon the wheel, or driven to the gibbet, or slain with the axe—the penalties which were inflicted upon them as soon as their confessions had sufficiently revealed the heads of the rebellion.

Source: Johann Georg Korb, *Diary of an Austrian Secretary of Legation at the Court of Czar Peter the Great*, trans. Count MacDonnell (London: 1863), pp. 2:85–87.

Questions for Analysis

1. Why was it important for Korb to begin this description with the monarch's pain?

2. What does this episode reveal about Peter's conception of his own person and of the loyalty that his subjects owed him? Does it show that his power was fragile, immense, or both?

3. What does it mean to describe torture as an "investigation" even while it is also being described as "vengeance?"

productive capacity increased enormously during Peter's reign), or as forced laborers in his building projects. Serfs could also be taxed by the tsar and summoned for military service, as could their lords. All Russians, of whatever rank, were expected to serve the tsar, and all Russia was considered in some sense to belong to him. Russia's autocracy thus surpassed even the absolutism of Louis XIV.

To further consolidate his power, Peter replaced the Duma—the nation's rudimentary national assembly—with a handpicked senate, a group of nine administrators who supervised military and civilian affairs. In religious matters, he took direct control over the Russian Orthodox Church by appointing an imperial official to manage its affairs. To cope with the demands of war, he also fashioned a new, larger, and more efficient administration, for which he recruited both nobles and non-nobles. But rank in the new bureaucracy did not depend on birth. One of his principal advisers, Alexander Menshikov, began his career as a cook and finished as a prince. This degree of social mobility would have been impossible in any contemporary western European country. In Russia, more so than in western Europe, noble status depended on governmental service, with all nobles expected to participate in Peter's army or administration. Peter was not entirely successful in enforcing this requirement, but the administrative machinery he devised furnished Russia with its ruling class for the next 200 years.

Russian Imperial Expansion

The goal of Peter's foreign policy was to secure year-round ports for Russia on the Black Sea and the Baltic Sea. In the Black Sea, his enemy was the Ottomans. Here, however, he had little success; although he captured the port of Azov in 1696, he was forced to return it in 1711. Russia would not secure its position in the Black Sea until the end of the eighteenth century. Nevertheless, Peter continued to push against the Ottoman Empire in the North Caucasus region throughout his reign. This mountainous area on Russia's southern flank became important sites for Russia's experiments in colonial expansion into central Asia, which began during the sixteenth century and would later mirror the process of colonial conquest undertaken by European powers and the United States in North and South America. Like France and Britain, the Russian state bureaucracy was built during a period of ambitious colonialism; and like Spain, the monarchy's identity was shaped by a long contest with Muslim power on its borders.

Since the late sixteenth century, successive Russian leaders had extended their control over bordering territories of central Asia to the south and east. Although merchants

PETER THE GREAT CUTS THE BEARD OF AN OLD BELIEVER. This woodcut depicts the Russian emperor's enthusiastic policy of westernization, as he pushed everybody in Russia who was not a peasant to adopt Western styles of clothes and grooming. The Old Believer (a member of a religious sect in Russia) protests that he has paid the beard tax and should therefore be exempt. ■ *Why would an individual's choices about personal appearance be so politically significant in Peter's Russia?* ■ *What customs were the target of Peter's reforms?*

helped fund early expeditions into Siberia, this expansion was primarily motivated by geopolitical concerns; the tsar sought to gain access to the populations of Russia's border areas and bring them into the service of the expanding Russian state. In this sense, Russian colonialism during this period differed from western European expansion into the Atlantic world, which had primarily been motivated by hopes of commercial gain. Nevertheless, tsarist Russia's colonization of central Asia was similar to the process of European colonial expansion elsewhere in some respects. Like European colonizers in the Americas, Russian expansion brought Russian troops into contact with a variety of peoples with different religious beliefs and their own political structures. Some, such as the Muslim Kumyks of northern Dagestan, had a highly centralized government. Others, such as the Kabardinians or the Chechens, were more fragmented politically.

THE GROWTH OF THE RUSSIAN EMPIRE. ■ *How did Peter the Great expand the territory controlled by Russia?* ■ *What neighboring dynasties would have been the most affected by Russian expansion?* ■ *How did the emergence of a bigger, more powerful Russia affect the European balance of power?*

In its early stages, as successive Russian emperors moved Russian troops into the region, they relied on a process of indirect rule, often seeking to co-opt local elites. Later in the eighteenth century, they had more success settling Russians in border regions who ruled over local populations directly. Religion also provided a cover for expansion, and Peter and his successors funded missionary work by Georgian Christians among Muslims in the Caucasus. Efforts to convert Muslim populations to Orthodox Christianity had little effect, and in fact the opposite occurred: the region's commitment to Islam was continuously renewed through contact with different strains of Islamic practice coming from neighboring Ottoman lands and Persia.

Peter could point to more concrete success to the north. In 1700, he began what would become a twenty-one-year war with Sweden, then the dominant power in the Baltic Sea. By 1703, Peter had secured a foothold on the Gulf of Finland and immediately began to build a new capital city there, which he named St. Petersburg. After 1709, when Russian armies, supported by Prussia, decisively defeated the Swedes at the battle of Poltava, work on Peter's new

capital city accelerated. An army of serfs was now conscripted to build the new city, whose centerpiece was a royal palace designed to imitate and rival Louis XIV's Versailles.

The Great Northern War with Sweden ended in 1721 with the Peace of Nystad. This treaty marks a realignment of power in eastern Europe comparable to that effected by the Treaty of Utrecht in the West. Sweden lost its North Sea territories to Hanover and its Baltic German territories to Prussia. Its eastern territories, including the entire Gulf of Finland, Livonia, and Estonia, passed to Russia. Sweden was now a second-rank power in the northern European world. Poland-Lithuania survived but it too was a declining power; by the end of the eighteenth century, the kingdom would disappear altogether, its territories swallowed up by its more powerful neighbors (see Chapter 17).

The victors at Nystad were the Prussians and the Russians. These two powers secured their position along the Baltic coast, positioning themselves to take advantage of the lucrative eastern European grain trade with western Europe. Peter's accomplishments came at enormous cost. Direct taxation in Russia increased 500 percent during his reign, and his army in the 1720s numbered more than 300,000 men. Peter made Russia a force to be reckoned with on the European scene; but in so doing, he also aroused great resentment, especially among his nobility. Peter's only son and heir, Alexis, became the focus for conspiracies against the tsar, until finally Peter had him arrested and executed in 1718. As a result, when Peter died in 1725, he left no son to succeed him. A series of ineffective tsars followed, mostly creatures of the palace guard, under whom the resentful nobles reversed many of Peter the Great's reforms. In 1762, however, the crown passed to Catherine the Great, a ruler whose ambitions and determination were equal to those of her great predecessor (see Chapter 17).

CONCLUSION

By the time of Peter the Great's death in Russia in 1725, the power of Europe's absolutist regimes to reinvigorate European political institutions was visible to all. Government had become more bureaucratic, state service had been more professionalized, administrators loyal to the king had become more numerous, more efficient, and more demanding. Despite the increasing scope of government, however, the structure and principles of government changed relatively little. Apart from Great Britain and the Dutch Republic, the great powers of eighteenth-century Europe were still governed by rulers who styled themselves as absolutist monarchs in the mold of Louis XIV, who claimed an authority that came directly from God and who ruled over a society where social hierarchies based on birth were taken for granted.

These absolutist regimes could not hide the fact, however, that their rule depended on a kind of negotiated settlement with other powerful elites within European society, in particular with landed aristocrats and with religious leaders. Louis XIV used his power to curb the worst excesses of nobles who abused their position, and he defended Catholic orthodoxy against dissident Catholics and Protestants. However, his power depended on a delicate exchange of favors—French aristocrats would surrender their political authority to the state in exchange for social and legal privileges and immunity from many (but not all) forms of taxation. The Church made a similar bargain. Peter the Great's autocratic rule in Russia worked out a slightly different balance of powers between his state and the Russian aristocracy, one that tied aristocrats more closely to an ideal of state service, a model that also worked well for the rulers of Brandenburg-Prussia. Even in England, the establishment of a limited constitutional monarchy and a king who

After You Read This Chapter

 Go to **INQUIZITIVE** to see what you've learned—and learn what you've missed— with personalized feedback along the way.

REVIEWING THE OBJECTIVES

- Absolutist rulers claimed a monopoly of power and authority within their realms. Who were the most important absolutist rulers, how did they justify their innovations, and what did they do to achieve their goals?
- Mercantilism was an economic doctrine that guided the policies of absolutist rulers. What did mercantilists believe?
- Between 1660 and 1688, political leaders in England continued to debate the nature of the state, the role of Parliament, and religious divisions. What was the significance of these dates, and what was the outcome of these debates?
- What circumstances led to the decline of the Dutch Republic's power in this period?
- The wars begun by Louis XIV after 1680 drove his opponents to ally with one another to achieve a balance of power. What was the result of these conflicts in Europe and in the Atlantic world?

ruled alongside Parliament was not really a radical departure from the European absolutist model. It was merely a different institutional answer to the same problem—what relationship should the monarchical state have with other elites within society?

The demands of state building during this period required that kings raise enormous revenues—for the sumptuous displays of their sovereignty in royal residences like Louis XIV's palace at Versailles, for the sponsorship of royal academies and the patronage of artists, but most of all, for war. Territorial expansion within Europe and holding on to colonial empires in the Atlantic world was costly. Distributing the burden of taxation to pay for these endeavors became an intensely fought political issue for European monarchs during this period, and the financing of royal debt became an increasingly sophisticated art. Colbert's mercantilist policy was an attempt to harness the full power of the economy for the benefit of royal government, and the competition among Spain, Holland, England, and France to control the revenue flows coming from the Atlantic world forced Europe's monarchs to recognize that the "balance of powers" was increasingly being played out on a global stage.

These themes—the expansion of state powers; conflicts between the monarchy and the aristocracy or with religious dissidents; the intensification of the tax burden on the population; and the opening up of Europe to ever more frequent interactions with other peoples in the Atlantic world, the Indian Ocean, and eventually, the Pacific—prompted many in eighteenth-century Europe to reflect on the consequences of these developments. What were the limits to state power, and by what criteria were the actions of rulers to be judged? What was the proper measure of economic prosperity, and who was it for? Could a well-ordered society tolerate religious diversity? Given Europe's growing awareness of cultures in other parts of the world with different religions, different political systems, and different ways of expressing their moral and ethical values, how might Europeans justify or take the measure of their own beliefs and customs? The intellectuals who looked for answers to these questions were similar to earlier generations of scientific researchers in their respect for reason and rational thought, but they turned their attention beyond problems of natural philosophy and science to the messy world of politics and culture. Their movement—known as the Enlightenment—reached its peak in the middle decades of the eighteenth century, and created the basis for a powerful critique of Europe's absolutist regimes. The Enlightenment itself emerged slowly from a revolution in scientific thinking that had begun earlier in the early modern period, and it is to this history that we now turn.

PEOPLE, IDEAS, AND EVENTS IN CONTEXT

- What did **LOUIS XIV** of France and **PETER THE GREAT** of Russia have in common? How did they deal with those who resisted their attempts to impose absolutist rule?

- Compare the religious policies of **LOUIS XIV** of France with the religious policies of the English Stuart kings **CHARLES II** and **JAMES II**. In what way did religious disagreements limit their ability to rule effectively?

- How did European monarchies use the economic theory known as **MERCANTILISM** to strengthen the power and wealth of their kingdoms, and how did this theory influence **FRENCH COLONIALISM**?

- What was the **CONTRACT THEORY OF GOVERNMENT** according to the English political thinker **JOHN LOCKE**?

- What limits to royal power were recognized in Great Britain as a result of the **GLORIOUS REVOLUTION**?

- What was significant about the new **BALANCE OF POWERS** that developed in Europe as a result of **LOUIS XIV**'s wars?

- What does the **TREATY OF UTRECHT** (1713) tell us about the diminished influence of Spain and the corresponding rise of Britain and France as European and colonial powers?

- What was different about the attempts by rulers in Habsburg Austria and Brandenburg-Prussia to impose **ABSOLUTISM** in central Europe?

- What innovations did **PETER THE GREAT** bring to Russia?

THINKING ABOUT CONNECTIONS

- What makes absolutism different from earlier models of kingship in earlier periods?

- Was the absolutist monarchs' emphasis on sumptuous displays of their authority something new? Is it different from the way that political power is represented today in democratic societies?

STORY LINES

- After c. 1550, new sciences in Europe questioned older beliefs about the physical universe. New methods of inquiry led to the development of astronomy, physics, biology, and chemistry, as well as new institutions that supported scientific research and education.

- The scientific revolution entailed both theoretical breakthroughs in explaining the physical universe and advances in the practical knowledge of artisans who built mechanical devices such as telescopes. This combination of scientific inquisitiveness and craft techniques encouraged technological developments that would later be useful in industrialization.

- The new sciences did not mark a clean rupture with older traditions of religious thinking. Most scientists in the 1600s remained essentially religious in their worldview, and in any case, their work was only accessible to a small, literate minority who had access to books.

CHRONOLOGY

1543	Nicolaus Copernicus (1473–1543) publishes *On the Revolutions of the Heavenly Spheres*
1576	Tycho Brahe sets up Uraniborg observatory
1609	Johannes Kepler (1571–1643) publishes *Astronomia nova*
1610	Galileo (1564–1642) publishes *Starry Messenger*
1620	Francis Bacon (1561–1626) publishes *Novum Organum*
1632	Galileo publishes *Dialogue Concerning the Two Chief World Systems*
1633	Galileo's trial
1637	René Descartes (1596–1650) publishes *Discourse on Method*
1660	Royal Society of London founded
1666	French Academy of Sciences founded
1687	Isaac Newton (1642–1727) publishes *Principia Mathematica*

The New Science of the Seventeenth Century

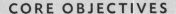

CORE OBJECTIVES

- **DEFINE** *scientific revolution* and **EXPLAIN** what is meant by *science* in this historical context.

- **UNDERSTAND** the older philosophical traditions that were important for the development of new methods of scientific investigation in the seventeenth century.

- **IDENTIFY** the sciences that made important advances during this period and **UNDERSTAND** what technological innovations encouraged a new spirit of investigation.

- **EXPLAIN** the differences between the Ptolemaic view of the universe and the new vision of the universe proposed by Nicolaus Copernicus.

- **UNDERSTAND** the different definitions of *scientific method* that emerged from the work of Francis Bacon and René Descartes.

Doubt thou the stars are fire,
Doubt that the sun doth move,
Doubt truth to be a liar,
But never doubt I love.

SHAKESPEARE, HAMLET, II.2

Doubt thou the stars are fire" and "that the sun doth move." Was Shakespeare alluding to controversial ideas about the cosmos that contradicted the teachings of medieval scholars? *Hamlet* (c. 1600) was written more than fifty years after Copernicus had suggested, in his treatise *On the Revolutions of the Heavenly Spheres* (1543), that the sun did not move and that the earth did, revolving around the sun. Shakespeare probably knew of such theories, although they circulated only among small groups of learned Europeans. As Hamlet's love-torn speech to Ophelia makes clear, they were considered conjecture—or strange mathematical hypotheses. These theories were not exactly new—a heliocentric (sun-centered) universe had been proposed as early as the second century B.C.E. by ancient Greek astronomers. But they flatly contradicted the consensus that had

425

set in after Ptolemy proposed a geocentric (earth-centered) universe in the second century C.E., and to Shakespeare's contemporaries they defied common sense and observation. Learned philosophers, young lovers, shepherds, and sailors alike could watch the sun and the stars move from one horizon to the other each day and night, or so they thought.

Still, a small handful of thinkers did doubt. Shakespeare was born in 1564, the same year as Galileo Galilei. By the time the English playwright and the Italian natural philosopher were working, the long process of revising knowledge about the universe, and discovering a new set of rules that explained how the universe worked, was under way. By the end of the seventeenth century a hundred years later, the building blocks of the new view had been put in place. This intellectual transformation brought sweeping changes to European philosophy and to Western views of the natural world and of humans' place in it.

Science entails at least three things: a body of knowledge, a method or system of inquiry, and a community of practitioners and the institutions that support them and their work. The *scientific revolution* of the seventeenth century (usually understood to have begun in the mid-sixteenth century and to have culminated in 1687 with Newton's *Principia*) involved each of these three realms. As far as the content of knowledge is concerned, the scientific revolution saw the emergence and confirmation of a heliocentric view of the planetary system, which displaced the earth—and humans—from the center of the universe. Even more fundamental, it brought a new mathematical physics that described and confirmed such a view. Second, the scientific revolution established a method of inquiry for understanding the natural world: a method that emphasized the role of observation, experiment, and the testing of hypotheses. Third, *science* emerged as a distinctive branch of knowledge. During the period covered in this chapter, people referred to the study of matter, motion, optics, or the circulation of blood variously as natural philosophy, experimental philosophy, medicine, and—increasingly—science. The growth of societies and institutions dedicated to what we now commonly call scientific research was central to the changes at issue here. Science required not only brilliant thinkers but patrons, states, and communities of researchers; the scientific revolution was thus embedded in other social, religious, and cultural transformations.

The scientific revolution was not an organized effort. Brilliant theories sometimes led to dead ends, discoveries were often accidental, and artisans grinding lenses for telescopes played a role in the advance of knowledge just as surely as did great abstract thinkers. Educated women also claimed the right to participate in scientific debate, but their efforts were met with opposition or indifference.

Old and new worldviews often overlapped as individual thinkers struggled to reconcile their discoveries with their faith or to make their theories (about the earth's movements, for instance) fit with received wisdom. Science was slow to work its way into popular understanding. It did not necessarily undermine religion, and it certainly did not intend to; figures like Isaac Newton thought their work confirmed and deepened their religious beliefs. In short, change came slowly and fitfully. But as the new scientific method began to produce radical new insights into the workings of nature, it eventually came to be accepted well beyond the small circles of experimenters, theologians, and philosophers with whom it began.

THE INTELLECTUAL ORIGINS OF THE SCIENTIFIC REVOLUTION

The scientific revolution marks one of the decisive breaks between the Middle Ages and the modern world. For all its novelty, however, it was rooted in earlier developments. Medieval artists and intellectuals had been observing and illustrating the natural world with great precision since at least the twelfth century. Medieval sculptors carved plants and vines with extraordinary accuracy, and fifteenth-century painters and sculptors devoted the same careful attention to the human face and form. Nor was the link among observation, experiment, and invention new to the sixteenth century. The magnetic compass had been known in Europe since the thirteenth century; gunpowder since the early fourteenth; printing, which permeated the intellectual life of the period and opened new possibilities—disseminating ideas quickly, collaborating more easily, buying books, and building libraries—since the middle of the fifteenth. "Printing, firearms, and the compass," wrote Francis Bacon, "no empire, sect, or star appears to have exercised a greater power and influence on human affairs than these three mechanical discoveries." A fascination with light, which was a powerful symbol of divine illumination for medieval thinkers, encouraged the study of optics and, in turn, new techniques for grinding lenses. Lens grinders laid the groundwork for the seventeenth-century inventions of the telescope and microscope, creating reading glasses along the way. Astrologers were also active in the later Middle Ages, charting the heavens in the firm belief that the stars controlled the fates of human beings.

Behind these efforts to understand the natural world lay a nearly universal conviction that the natural world had been created by God. Religious belief spurred scientific study.

One school of thinkers (the Neoplatonists) argued that nature was a book written by its creator to reveal the ways of God to humanity. Convinced that God's perfection must be reflected in nature, Neoplatonists searched for the ideal and perfect structures they believed must lie behind the "shadows" of the everyday world. Mathematics, particularly geometry, were important tools in this quest.

Renaissance humanism also helped prepare the grounds for the scientific revolution. Humanists revered the authority of the ancients. Yet the energies the humanists poured into recovering, translating, and understanding classical texts (the source of conceptions of the natural world) made many of those important works available for the first time, and to a wider audience. Previously, Arabic sources had provided Europeans with the main route to ancient Greek learning; Greek classics were translated into Arabic by Islamic scholars who often knew them better than Europeans. Later they returned to Europe through the work of medieval scholars in Spain and Sicily. The humanists' return to the texts themselves—and the fact that the new texts could be more easily printed and circulated—encouraged new study and debate. The humanist rediscovery of works by Archimedes—the great Greek mathematician who had proposed that the natural world operated on the basis of mechanical forces, like a great machine, and that these forces could be described mathematically—profoundly impressed important late-sixteenth- and seventeenth-century thinkers, including the Italian scientist Galileo, and shaped mechanical philosophy in the 1600s.

The Renaissance also encouraged collaboration between artisans and intellectuals. Twelfth- and thirteenth-century thinkers had observed the natural world, but they rarely tinkered with mechanical devices and they had little contact with artisans who constructed machines for practical use. During the fifteenth century, however, these two worlds began to come together. Renaissance artists such as Leonardo da Vinci were accomplished craftsmen; they investigated the laws of perspective and optics, they worked out geometric methods for supporting the weight of enormous architectural domes, they studied the human body, and they devised new and more effective weapons for war. The Renaissance brought a vogue for alchemy and astrology; wealthy amateurs built observatories and measured the courses of the stars. These social and intellectual developments laid the groundwork for the scientific revolution.

What of the voyages of discovery? Sixteenth-century observers often linked the exploration of the globe to new knowledge of the cosmos. An admirer wrote to Galileo that he had kept the spirit of exploration alive: "The memory of Columbus and Vespucci will be renewed through you, and with even greater nobility, as the sky is more worthy than the earth." In truth, Columbus had not been driven by an interest in science, and the links between the voyages of discovery and breakthroughs in science were largely indirect and slow to develop. The discoveries made the most immediate impact in the field of natural history, which was vastly enriched by travelers' detailed accounts of the flora and fauna of the Americas. Finding new lands and cultures in Africa and Asia and the revelation of the Americas, a world unknown to the ancients and unmentioned in the Bible, also laid bare gaps in Europeans' inherited body of knowledge. In this sense, the exploration of the New World dealt a blow to the authority of the ancients.

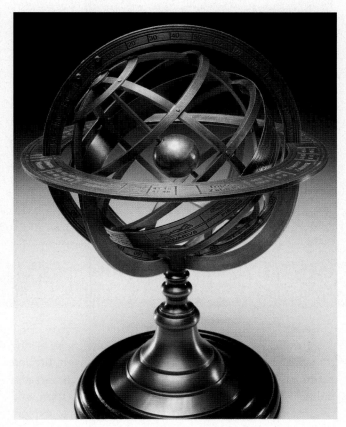

PTOLEMAIC ASTRONOMICAL INSTRUMENTS. Pictured here is an armillary sphere, 1560s, built to facilitate the observation of planetary positions relative to the earth, in support of Ptolemy's theory of an earth-centered universe. In the sphere, seven concentric rings rotated about different axes. When the outermost ring was set to align with a north–south meridian, and the next ring was set to align with the celestial pole (the North Star, or the point around which the stars seem to rotate), one could determine the latitude of the place where the instrument was placed. The inner rings were used to track the angular movements of the planets, key measurements in validating the Ptolemaic system. ▪ *What forms of knowledge were necessary to construct such an instrument?* ▪ *How do they relate to the breakthrough that is known as the scientific revolution?*

Past and Present

Has Science Replaced Religion?

Galileo recanted his claims about the movement of heavenly bodies when challenged by the Church (left); but physicists persisted in their research, leading eventually to the development of modern particle accelerators like the one located in this lab in Grenoble, France (right). Few would say, however, that science has replaced religion in the modern world.

Watch related author videos on the student site
wwnorton.com/college/history/western-civilizationsBrief4

In sum, the late-medieval recovery of ancient texts long thought to have been lost, the expansion of print culture and reading, the turmoil in the Church and the fierce wars and political maneuvering that followed the Reformation, and the discovery of a new world across the oceans to explore and exploit all shook the authority of older ways of thinking. What we call the scientific revolution was part of the intellectual excitement that surrounded these challenges, and, in retrospect, the scientific revolution enhanced and confirmed the importance of these other developments.

THE COPERNICAN REVOLUTION

Medieval cosmologists, like their ancient counterparts and their successors during the scientific revolution, wrestled with the contradictions between ancient texts and the evidence of their own observations. Their view of a geocentric universe was particularly influenced by the teachings of Aristotle (384–322 B.C.E.), especially as they were systematized by Ptolemy of Alexandria (100–178 C.E.). In fact, Ptolemy's vision of an earth-centered universe contradicted an earlier proposal by Aristarchus of Samos (310–230 B.C.E.), who had deduced that the earth and other planets revolve around the sun. Like the ancient Greeks, Ptolemy's medieval followers used astronomical observations to support their theory, but the persuasiveness of the model for medieval scholars also derived from the ways that it fit with their Christian beliefs (see Chapter 4). According to Ptolemy, the heavens orbited the earth in a carefully organized hierarchy of spheres. Earth and the heavens were fundamentally different, made of different matter and subject to different laws of motion. The sun, moon, stars, and planets were formed of an unchanging (and perfect) quintessence or ether. The earth, by contrast, was composed of four elements (earth, water, fire, and air), and each of these elements had its natural place: the heavy elements (earth and water) toward the center and the lighter ones farther out. The heavens—first the planets, then the stars—traced perfect circular paths around the stationary earth. The motion of these celestial bodies was produced by a prime mover, whom Christians identified as God. The view fit Aristotelian physics, according to which objects could move only if acted on by an external force, and it fit with a belief that each fundamental element of the universe had a natural place. Moreover, the view both followed from and confirmed belief in the purposefulness of God's universe.

By the late Middle Ages astronomers knew that this cosmology, called the "Ptolemaic system," did not correspond exactly to what many had observed. Orbits did not conform to the Aristotelian ideal of perfect circles. By the early fifteenth century, the efforts to make the observed motions of the planets fit into the model of perfect circles in a geocentric cosmos had produced astronomical charts that were mazes of complexity. Finally, the Ptolemaic system proved unable to solve serious difficulties with the calendar. That practical crisis precipitated Copernicus's intellectual leap forward.

Realizing that the old Roman calendar was significantly out of alignment with the movement of the heavenly bodies, Catholic authorities consulted mathematicians and astronomers all over Europe. One of these was a Polish church official and astronomer, Nicolaus Copernicus (1473–1543). Educated in Poland and northern Italy, he was a man of diverse talents. He was trained in astronomy, canon law, and medicine. He read Greek. He was well versed in ancient philosophy. He was also a careful mathematician and a devout Catholic who did not believe that God's universe could be as messy as the one in Ptolemy's model. His proposed solution, based on mathematical calculations, was simple and radical: Ptolemy was mistaken; the earth was neither stationary nor at the center of the planetary system; the earth rotated on its axis and orbited with the other planets around the sun. Reordering the Ptolemaic system simplified the geometry of astronomy and made the orbits of the planets comprehensible.

Copernicus was in many ways a conservative thinker. He did not consider his work to be a break with either the Church or with the authority of ancient texts. He believed, rather, that he had restored a pure understanding of God's design, one that had been lost over the centuries. Still, the implications of his theory troubled him. His ideas contradicted centuries of astronomical thought, and they were hard to reconcile with the observed behavior of objects on earth. If the earth moved, why was that movement imperceptible? How did people and objects remain standing?

NICOLAUS COPERNICUS. This anonymous portrait of Copernicus characteristically blends his devotion and his scientific achievements. His scholarly work (behind him in the form of an early planetarium) is driven by his faith (as he turns toward the image of Christ triumphant over death). ■ *What relationship between science and religion is evoked by this image?*

Copernicus was not a physicist. He tried to refine, rather than overturn, traditional Aristotelian physics, but his effort to reconcile that physics with his new model of a sun-centered universe created new problems and inconsistencies that he could not resolve. These frustrations and complications dogged Copernicus's later years, and he hesitated to publish his findings. Just before his death, he consented to the release of his major treatise, *On the Revolutions of the Heavenly Spheres* (*De Revolutionibus*), in 1543. To fend off scandal, the Lutheran scholar who saw his manuscript through the press added an introduction to the book declaring that Copernicus's system should be understood as an abstraction, a set of mathematical tools for doing astronomy and not a dangerous claim about the nature of heaven and earth. For decades after 1543, Copernicus's ideas were taken in just that sense—as useful but not realistic mathematical hypotheses. In the long run, however, as one historian puts it, Copernicanism represented the first "serious and systematic" challenge to the Ptolemaic conception of the universe.

TYCHO'S OBSERVATIONS AND KEPLER'S LAWS

Within fifty years, Copernicus's cosmology was revived and modified by two astronomers also critical of the Ptolemaic model of the universe: Tycho Brahe (*TI-koh BRAH-hee*, 1546–1601) and Johannes Kepler (1571–1630). Each was considered the greatest astronomer of his day. Tycho was born into the Danish nobility, but he abandoned his family's military and political legacy to pursue his passion for astronomy. Like Copernicus, he sought to correct the contradictions in traditional astronomy. Unlike Copernicus, who was a theoretician, Tycho championed observation and believed careful study of the heavens would unlock the secrets of the universe. He first made a name for himself by observing a completely new star, a "nova," that flared into sight in 1572. The Danish king Friedrich II, impressed by Tycho's work, granted him the use of a small island, where he built a castle specially designed to house an observatory. For over twenty years, Tycho meticulously charted the movements of each significant object in the night sky, compiling the finest set of astronomical data in Europe.

Tycho was not a Copernican. He suggested that the planets orbited the sun and the whole system then orbited a stationary earth. This picture of cosmic order, though clumsy, seemed to fit the observed evidence better than the Ptolemaic system, and it avoided the upsetting theological implications of the Copernican model. In the late 1590s, Tycho moved his work and his huge collection of data to Prague, where he became court astronomer to the Holy Roman emperor Rudolph II. In Prague, he was assisted by a young mathematician from a troubled family, Johannes Kepler. Kepler was more impressed with the Copernican model than was Tycho, and Kepler combined study of Copernicus's work with his own interest in mysticism, astrology, and the religious power of mathematics.

Kepler believed that everything in creation, from human souls to the orbits of the planets, had been created according to mathematical laws. Understanding those laws would thus allow humans to share God's wisdom and penetrate the inner secrets of the universe. For Kepler, then, mathematics was God's language. His search for patterns of mathematical perfection took him through musical harmonies, nested geometric shapes inside the planets' orbits, and

numerical formulas. After Tycho's death, Kepler inherited Tycho's position in Prague, as well as his trove of observations and calculations. That data demonstrated to Kepler that two of Copernicus's assumptions about planetary motion simply did not match observations. Copernicus, in keeping with Aristotelian notions of perfection, had believed that planetary orbits were circular. Kepler calculated that the planets traveled in elliptical orbits around the sun; this finding became his First Law. Copernicus held that planetary motion was uniform; Kepler's Second Law stated that the speed of the planets varied with their distance from the sun. Kepler also argued that magnetic forces between the sun and the planets kept the planets in orbital motion, an insight that paved the way for Newton's law of universal gravitation formulated nearly eighty years later, at the end of the seventeenth century.

Kepler's version of Copernicanism fit with remarkable accuracy the best observations of the time (which were Tycho's). Kepler's search for rules of motion that could account for the earth's movements in its new position was also significant. Even more than Copernicus, Kepler broke down the distinction between the heavens and the earth that had been at the heart of Aristotelian physics.

NEW HEAVENS, NEW EARTH, AND WORLDLY POLITICS: GALILEO

Kepler had a friend deliver a copy of his *Cosmographic Mystery* to the "mathematician named Galileus Galileus," then teaching mathematics and astronomy at Padua, near Venice. Galileo (1564–1642) thanked Kepler in a letter that nicely illustrates the Italian's views at the time (1597).

> So far I have only perused the preface of your work, but from this I gained some notion of its intent, and I indeed congratulate myself of having an associate in the study of Truth who is a friend of Truth. . . . I adopted the teaching of Copernicus many years ago, and his point of view enables me to explain many phenomena of nature which certainly remain inexplicable according to the more current hypotheses. I have written many arguments in support of him and in refutation of the opposite view—which, however, so far I have not dared to bring into the public light. . . . I would certainly dare to publish my reflections at once if more people like you existed; as they don't, I shall refrain from doing so.

Kepler replied, urging Galileo to "come forward!" Galileo did not answer.

At Padua, Galileo couldn't teach what he believed; Ptolemaic astronomy and Aristotelian cosmology were the established curriculum. By the end of his career, however, Galileo had provided powerful evidence in support of the Copernican model and laid the foundation for a new physics. What was more, he wrote in the vernacular (Italian) as well as in Latin. Kepler's work was abstruse and bafflingly mathematical. (So was Copernicus's.) By contrast, Galileo's writings were widely translated and widely read, raising awareness of changes in natural philosophy across Europe. Ultimately, Galileo made the case for a new relationship between religion and science, challenging in the process some of the most powerful churchmen of his day.

Galileo became famous by way of discoveries with the telescope. In 1609, he heard reports from Holland of a lens grinder who had made a spyglass that could magnify very distant objects. Excited, Galileo quickly devised his own telescope; trained it first on earthly objects to demonstrate that it worked; and then, momentously, pointed it at the night sky. Galileo studied the moon, finding on it mountains, plains, and other features of an earthlike landscape. His observations suggested that celestial bodies resembled the earth, a view at odds with the conception of the heavens as an unchanging sphere of heavenly perfection, inherently and necessarily different from the earth. He saw moons orbiting Jupiter, evidence that earth was not at the center of all orbits. He saw spots on the sun. Galileo published these results, first in *The Starry Messenger* (1610) and then in *Letters on Sunspots* in 1613, a work that declared his Copernicanism openly.

A seventeenth-century scientist needed powerful and wealthy patrons. As a professor of mathematics, Galileo chafed at the power of university authorities who were subject to Church control. Princely courts offered an inviting alternative. The Medici family of Tuscany, like others, burnished its reputation and bolstered its power by surrounding itself with intellectuals as well as artists. Persuaded he would be freer at its court than in Padua, Galileo took a position as tutor to the Medicis and flattered and successfully cultivated the family. He was rewarded with the title of chief mathematician and philosopher to Cosimo de' Medici, the grand duke of Tuscany. Now well positioned in Italy's networks of power and patronage, Galileo was able to pursue

his goal of demonstrating that Copernicus's heliocentric (sun-centered) model of the planetary system was correct.

In 1614, however, an ambitious and outspoken Dominican friar denounced Galileo's ideas as dangerous deviations from biblical teachings. Other philosophers and churchmen began to ask Galileo's patrons, the Medicis, whether their court mathematician was teaching heresy.

Disturbed by the murmurings against Copernicanism, Galileo penned a series of letters to defend himself, arguing that one could be a sincere Copernican and a sincere Catholic (see **Analyzing Primary Sources** on page 434). The Church, Galileo said, did the sacred work of teaching scripture and saving souls. Accounting for the workings of the physical world was a task better left to natural philosophy, grounded in observation and mathematics. For the Church to take a side in controversies over natural science might compromise the Church's spiritual authority and credibility. Galileo envisioned natural philosophers and theologians as partners in a search for truth, but with very different roles. In a brilliant rhetorical moment, he quoted Cardinal Baronius in support of his own argument: the purpose of the Bible was to "teach us how to go to heaven, not how heaven goes."

Nevertheless, in 1616, the Church moved against Galileo. The Inquisition ruled that Copernicanism was "foolish and absurd in philosophy and formally heretical." Copernicus's *De Revolutionibus* was placed on the Index

GALILEO GALILEI BEFORE THE INQUISITION BY FRANÇOIS FLEURY-RICHARD. This nineteenth-century painting of Galileo before the Holy Office dramatizes the conflict between science and religion and depicts the Italian natural philosopher as defiant. In fact, Galileo submitted to the Church but continued his work under house arrest and published, secretly, in the Netherlands. ▪ *Would Galileo himself have subscribed to the message of this much later painting, that religion and science were opposed to one another?*

Interpreting Visual Evidence

Astronomical Observations and the Mapping of the Heavens

 ne (often-repeated) narrative about the scientific revolution is that it marked a crucial break separating modern science from an earlier period permeated by an atmosphere of superstition and theological speculation. In fact, medieval scholars tried hard to come up with empirical evidence for beliefs that their faith told them must be true, and without these traditions of observation, scientists like Copernicus would never have been led to propose alternative cosmologies (see "Ptolemaic Astronomical Instruments" on page 427).

The assumption, therefore, that the "new" sciences of the seventeenth century marked an extraordinary rupture with a more ignorant or superstitious past is thus not entirely correct. It would be closer to the truth to suggest that works such as that of Copernicus or Galileo provided a new context for assessing the relationship between observations and knowledge that came from other sources. Printed materials provided opportunities for early modern scientists to learn as much from each other as from more ancient sources.

The illustrations here are from scientific works on astronomy both before and after the appearance of

A. The Ptolemaic universe, as depicted in Peter Apian, *Cosmographia* (1540).

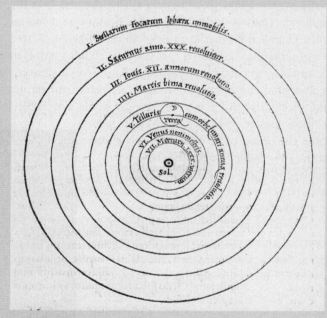

B. The Copernican universe (1543).

of Prohibited Books, and Galileo was warned not to teach Copernicanism.

For a while, he did as he was asked. But when his Florentine friend and admirer Maffeo Barberini was elected pope as Urban VIII in 1623, Galileo believed the door to Copernicanism was (at least half) open. He drafted one of his most famous works, *A Dialogue Concerning the Two Chief World* *Systems*, published in 1632. The *Dialogue* was a hypothetical debate between supporters of the old Ptolemaic system, represented by a character he named Simplicio (simpleton), on the one hand, and proponents of the new astronomy, on the other. Throughout, Galileo gave the best lines to the Copernicans. At the very end, however, to satisfy the letter of the Inquisition's decree, he had them capitulate to Simplicio.

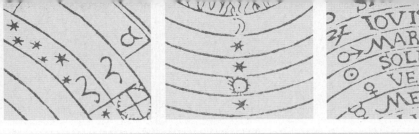

Copernicus's work. All of them were based on some form of observation and claimed to be descriptive of the existing universe. Compare the abstract illustrations of the Ptolemaic (image A) and Copernican (image B) universes with Tycho Brahe's (image C) attempt to reconcile heliocentric observations with geocentric assumptions or with Galileo's illustration of sunspots (image D) observed through a telescope.

Questions for Analysis

1. What do these illustrations tell us about the relationship between knowledge and observation in sixteenth- and seventeenth-century science? What kinds of knowledge were necessary to produce these images?

2. Are the illustrations A and B intended to be visually accurate, in the sense that they represent what the eye sees?

Can one say the same of D? What makes Galileo's illustration of the sunspots different from the others?

3. Are the assumptions about observation contained in Galileo's drawing of sunspots (D) applicable to other sciences such as biology or chemistry? How so?

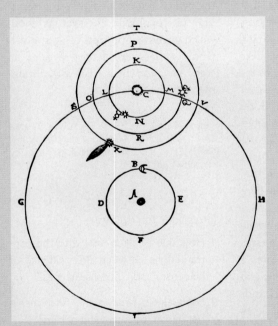

C. Brahe's universe (c. 1572). A, earth; B, moon; C, sun.

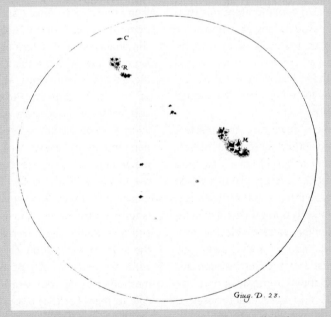

D. Galileo's sunspots, as observed through a telescope (1612).

The Inquisition banned the *Dialogue* and ordered Galileo to stand trial in 1633. Pope Urban, provoked by Galileo's scorn and needing support from Church conservatives during a difficult stretch of the Thirty Years' War, refused to protect his former friend. The verdict of the secret trial shocked Europe. The Inquisition forced Galileo to repent his Copernican position, banned him from working on or even discussing Copernican ideas, and placed him under house arrest for life. According to a story that began to circulate shortly afterward, as he left the court for house arrest he stamped his foot and muttered defiantly, looking down at the earth: "Still, it moves."

The Inquisition could not put Galileo off his life's work. He refined the theories of motion he had begun to

Galileo on Nature, Scripture, and Truth

One of the clearest statements of Galileo's convictions about religion and science comes from his 1615 letter to the Grand Duchess Christina, mother of Galileo's patron, Cosimo de' Medici, and a powerful figure in her own right. Galileo knew that others objected to his work. The Church had warned him that Copernicanism was inaccurate and impious; it could be disproved scientifically, and it contradicted the authority of those who interpreted the Bible. Thoroughly dependent on the Medicis for support, he wrote to the Grand Duchess to explain his position. In this section of the letter, Galileo sets out his understanding of the parallel but distinct roles of the Church and natural philosophers. He walks a fine line between acknowledging the authority of the Church and standing firm in his convictions.

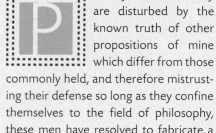

Possibly because they are disturbed by the known truth of other propositions of mine which differ from those commonly held, and therefore mistrusting their defense so long as they confine themselves to the field of philosophy, these men have resolved to fabricate a shield for their fallacies out of the mantle of pretended religion and the authority of the Bible. . . .

Copernicus never discusses matters of religion or faith, nor does he use arguments that depend in any way upon the authority of sacred writings which he might have interpreted erroneously. He stands always upon physical conclusions pertaining to the celestial motions, and deals with them by astronomical and geometrical demonstrations, founded primarily upon sense experiences and very exact observations. He did not ignore the Bible, but he knew very well that if his doctrine were proved, then it could not contradict the Scriptures when they were rightly understood. . . .

I think that in discussions of physical problems we ought to begin not from the authority of scriptural passages, but from sense-experiences and necessary demonstrations; for the holy Bible and the phenomena of nature proceed alike from the divine Word, the former as the dictate of the Holy Ghost and the latter as the observant executrix of God's commands. It is necessary for the Bible, in order to be accommodated to the understanding of every man, to speak many things which appear to differ from the absolute truth so far as the bare meaning of the words is concerned. But Nature, on the other hand, is inexorable and immutable; she never transgresses the laws imposed upon her, or cares a whit whether her abstruse reasons and methods of operation are understandable to men. For that reason it appears that nothing physical which sense-experience sets before our eyes, or which necessary demonstrations prove to us, ought to be called in question (much less condemned) upon the testimony of biblical passages which may have some different meaning beneath their words. For the Bible is not chained in every expression to conditions as strict as those which govern all physical effects; nor is God any less excellently revealed in Nature's actions than in the sacred statements of the Bible. . . .

Source: Galileo, "Letter to the Grand Duchess Christina," in *The Discoveries and Opinions of Galileo Galilei*, ed. Stillman Drake (Garden City, NY: 1957), pp. 177–83.

Questions for Analysis

1. How does Galileo deal with the contradictions between the evidence of his senses and biblical teachings?

2. For Galileo, what is the relationship between God, man, and nature?

3. Why did Galileo need to defend his views in a letter to Christina de' Medici?

develop early in his career. He proposed an early version of the theory of inertia, which held that an object's motion stays the same until an outside force changes it. He calculated that objects of different weights fall at almost the same speed and with a uniform acceleration. He argued that the motion of objects follows regular mathematical laws. The same laws that govern the motions of objects on earth (which could be observed in experiments) could also be observed in the heavens—again a direct contradiction of Aristotelian principles and an important step toward a coherent physics based on a sun-centered model of the universe. Compiled under the title *Two New Sciences* (1638), this work was smuggled out of Italy and published in Protestant Holland.

Among Galileo's legacies, however, was exactly the rift between religion and science that he had hoped to avoid. Galileo believed that Copernicanism and natural philosophy in general need not subvert theological truths, religious belief, or the authority of the Church. But his trial seemed to show the contrary, that natural philosophy and Church authority could not coexist. Galileo's trial silenced Copernican voices in southern Europe, and the Church's leadership retreated into conservative reaction. It was therefore in northwest Europe that the new philosophy Galileo had championed would flourish.

METHODS FOR A NEW PHILOSOPHY: BACON AND DESCARTES

As the practice of the new sciences became concentrated in Protestant northwest Europe, new thinkers began to spell out standards of practice and evidence. Sir Francis Bacon and René Descartes (*deh-KAHRT*) loomed especially large in this development, setting out the methods or rules that should govern modern science. Bacon (1561–1626) lived at roughly the same time as Kepler and Galileo—and Shakespeare; Descartes (1596–1650) was a generation younger. Both Bacon and Descartes came to believe that theirs was an age of profound change, open to the possibility of astonishing discovery. Both were persuaded that knowledge could take the European moderns beyond the ancient authorities. Both set out to formulate a philosophy to encompass the learning of their age.

"Knowledge is power." The phrase is Bacon's and captures the changing perspective of the seventeenth century and its new confidence in the potential of human thinking. Bacon trained as a lawyer, served in Parliament and, briefly, as lord chancellor to James I of England. His abiding concern was with the assumptions, methods, and practices that he believed should guide natural philosophers and the progress of knowledge. The authority of the ancients should not constrain the ambition of modern thinkers. Deferring to accepted doctrines could block innovation or obstruct understanding. "There is but one course left . . . to try the whole thing anew upon a better plan, and to commence a total reconstruction of sciences, arts, and all human knowledge, raised upon the proper foundations." To pursue knowledge did not mean to think abstractly and leap to conclusions; it meant observing, experimenting, confirming ideas, or demonstrating points. If thinkers will

FRONTISPIECE TO BACON'S *NOVUM ORGANUM* (1620). The illustration suggests that scientific work is like a voyage of discovery, similar to a ship setting out through uncharted waters. Is it a voyage of conquest? ▪ *What metaphors and allegorical imagery did scientists use during this period to characterize the significance of their work?*

be "content to begin with doubts," Bacon wrote, "they shall end with certainties." We thus associate Bacon with the gradual separation of scientific investigation from philosophical argument.

Bacon advocated an *inductive* approach to knowledge: amassing evidence from specific observations to draw general conclusions. In Bacon's view, many philosophical errors arose from beginning with assumed first principles. The traditional view of the cosmos, for instance, rested on the principles of a prime mover and the perfection of circular motion for planets and stars. The inductive method required accumulating data (just as Tycho had done) and then, after careful review and experiment, drawing appropriate conclusions. Bacon argued that scientific knowledge was best tested through the cooperative efforts of researchers performing experiments that could be repeated and verified. The knowledge thus gained would be predictable and useful to philosophers and artisans alike, contributing to a wide range of endeavors, from astronomy to shipbuilding.

René Descartes was French, though he lived all over Europe. Descartes's *Discourse on Method* (1637), for which he is best known, began simply as a preface to three essays on optics, geometry, and meteorology. It is personal, recounting Descartes's dismay at the "strange and unbelievable" theories he encountered in his traditional education. His first response, as he described it, was to systematically doubt everything he had ever known or been taught. Better to clear the slate, he believed, than to build an edifice of knowledge on received assumptions. His first rule was "never to receive anything as a truth which [he] did not clearly know to be such." He took the human ability to think as his point of departure, summed up in his famous and enigmatic *Je pense, donc je suis*, later translated into Latin as *cogito ergo sum* and into English as "I think, therefore I am." As the phrase suggests, Descartes's doubting led (quickly, by our standards) to self-assurance and truth: the thinking individual existed, reason existed, God existed. For Descartes, then, doubt was a ploy, or a piece that he used in an intellectual chess game to defeat skepticism. Certainty, not doubt, was the centerpiece of the philosophy he bequeathed to his followers.

Descartes, like Bacon, sought a "fresh start for knowledge" or the rules for understanding of the world as it was. Unlike Bacon, Descartes emphasized *deductive* reasoning, proceeding logically from one certainty to another. "So long as we avoid accepting as true what is not so," he wrote in *Discourse on Method*, "and always preserve the right order of deduction of one thing from another, there can be nothing too remote to be reached in the end, or too well hidden to be discovered." For Descartes, mathematical thought expressed the highest standards of reason, and his work contributed greatly to the authority of mathematics as a model for scientific reasoning.

Descartes made a particularly forceful statement for *mechanism*, a view of the world shared by Bacon and Galileo and one that came to dominate seventeenth-century scientific thought. As the name suggested, mechanical philosophy proposed to consider nature as a machine. It rejected the traditional Aristotelian distinction between the works of humans and those of nature and the view that nature, as God's creation, necessarily

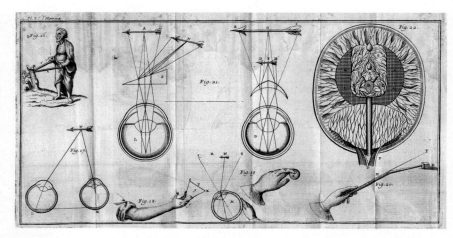

FROM RENÉ DESCARTES, *L'HOMME* **(1729; ORIGINALLY PUBLISHED AS** *DE HOMINI,* **1662).** Descartes's interest in the body as a mechanism led him to suppose that physics and mathematics could be used to understand all aspects of human physiology, and his work had an important influence on subsequent generations of medical researchers. In this illustration, Descartes depicts the optical properties of the human eye. ▪ *How might such a mechanistic approach to human perception have been received by proponents of Baconian science, who depended so much on the reliability of human observations?*

belonged to a different—and higher—order. In the new picture of the universe that was emerging from the discoveries and writings of the early seventeenth century, it seemed that all matter was composed of the same material and all motion obeyed the same laws. Descartes sought to explain everything, including the human body, mechanically. As he put it firmly, "There is no difference between the machines built by artisans and the diverse bodies that nature alone composes." Nature operated according to regular and predictable laws and was thus accessible to human reason. This belief guided, indeed inspired, much of the scientific experiment and argument of the seventeenth century.

The Power of Method and the Force of Curiosity: Seventeenth-Century Experimenters

For nearly a century after Bacon and Descartes, most of England's natural philosophers were Baconian, and most of their colleagues in France, Holland, and elsewhere in northern Europe were Cartesians (followers of Descartes). The English Baconians concentrated on performing experiments in many different fields, producing results that could then be debated and discussed. The Cartesians turned instead toward mathematics and logic. Descartes himself pioneered analytical geometry. Blaise Pascal (1623–1662) worked on probability theory and invented a calculating machine before applying his intellectual skills to theology. The Cartesian thinker Christian Huygens (1629–1695) from Holland combined mathematics with experiments to understand problems of impact and orbital motion. The Dutch Cartesian Baruch Spinoza (1632–1677) applied geometry to ethics and believed he had gone beyond Descartes by proving that the universe was composed of a single substance that was both God and nature.

English experimenters pursued a different course. They began with practical research, putting the alchemist's tool, the laboratory, to new uses. They also sought a different kind of conclusion: empirical laws or provisional generalizations, based on evidence, rather than absolute statements of deductive truth. Among the many English laboratory scientists of the era were the physician William Harvey (1578–1657), the chemist Robert Boyle (1627–1691), and the inventor and experimenter Robert Hooke (1635–1703).

Harvey's contribution was enormous: he observed and explained that blood circulated through the arteries, heart, and veins. To do this, he was willing to dissect living animals (vivisection) and experiment on himself. Boyle performed experiments and established a law (known as Boyle's law) showing that at a constant temperature the volume of a gas decreases in proportion to the pressure placed on it. Hooke introduced the microscope to the experimenter's tool kit. The compound microscope had been invented in Holland early in the seventeenth century. But it was not until the 1660s that Hooke and others demonstrated its potential by using it to study the cellular structure of plants. Like the telescope before it, the microscope revealed an unexpected dimension of material phenomena. Examining even the most ordinary objects revealed detailed structures of perfectly connected smaller parts and persuaded many that with improved instruments they would uncover even more of the world's intricacies.

The microscope also provided what many regarded as new evidence of God's existence. The way each minute structure of a living organism, when viewed under a microscope, corresponded to its purpose testified not only to God's existence but to God's wisdom as well. The mechanical philosophy did not exclude God but rather could be used to confirm his presence. If the universe was a clock, after all, there must be a clockmaker. Hooke himself declared that only imbeciles would believe that what they saw under the microscope was "the production of chance" rather than of God's creation.

The State, Scientific Academies, and Women Scientists

Seventeenth-century state building (see Chapter 14) helped secure the rise of science. In 1660, England's monarchy was restored after two decades of revolution and civil war. The newly crowned King Charles II granted a group of natural philosophers and mathematicians a royal charter (1662) to establish the Royal Society of London, for the "improvement of natural knowledge" through experimentation and collaborative work among natural philosophers. The founders of the Royal Society, in particular Boyle, believed it could serve a political as well as an intellectual purpose. The Royal Society would pursue Bacon's goal of collective research in which members would conduct formal experiments, record the results, and share them with other members. These members would in turn study the methods,

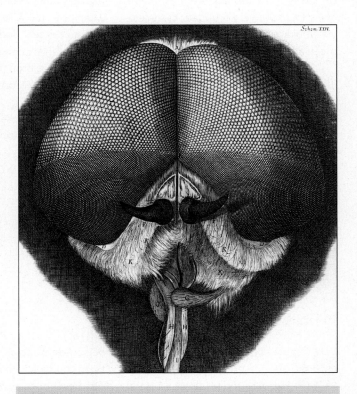

ROBERT HOOKE'S *MICROGRAPHIA*. Hooke's diagram of a fly's eye as seen through a microscope seemed to reveal just the sort of intricate universe the mechanists predicted. ▪ *Compare this image with that of Galileo's sunspots (page 433). What do these two images have in common?*

The New Science and The Foundations of Certainty

> *Francis Bacon (1561–1626) and René Descartes (1596–1650) were both enthusiastic supporters of science in the seventeenth century, but they differed in their opinions regarding the basis for certainty in scientific argumentation. Bacon's inductive method emphasized the gathering of particular observations about natural phenomena, which he believed could be used as evidence to support more general conclusions about causes, regularity, and order in the natural world. Descartes, on the other hand, defended a deductive method: he believed that certainty could be built only by reasoning from first principles that one knew to be true and was less certain of the value of evidence that came from the senses alone.*

Aphorisms from Francis Bacon's *Novum Organum*

XXXI

It is idle to expect any advancement in science from the super-inducing and engrafting of new things upon old. We must begin anew from the very foundations, unless we would revolve forever in a circle with mean and contemptible progress....

XXXVI

One method of delivery alone remains to us which is simply this: we must lead men to the particulars themselves, and their series and order; while men on their side must force themselves for a while to lay their notions by and begin to familiarize themselves with facts....

XLV

The human understanding of its own nature is prone to suppose the existence of more order and regularity in the world than it finds. And though there be many things in nature which are singular and unmatched, yet it devises for them parallels and conjugates and relatives which do not exist. Hence the fiction that all celestial bodies move in perfect circles.... Hence too the element of fire with its orb is brought in, to make up the square with the other three which the sense perceives.... And so on of other dreams. And these fancies affect not dogmas only, but simple notions also....

XCV

Those who have handled sciences have been either men of experiment or men of dogmas. The men of experiment are like the ant, they only collect and use; the reasoners resemble spiders, who make cobwebs out of their own substance. But the bee takes a middle course: it gathers its material from the flowers of the garden and of the field, but transforms and digests it by a power of its own. Not unlike this is the true business of philosophy; for it neither relies solely or chiefly on the powers of the mind, nor does it take the matter which it gathers from natural history and mechanical experiments and lay it up in the memory whole ... but lays it up in the understanding altered and digested. Therefore, from a closer and purer league between these two faculties, the experimental and the rational (such as has never yet been made), much may be hoped....

Source: Michael R. Matthews, ed., *The Scientific Background to Modern Philosophy: Selected Readings* (Indianapolis, IN: 1989), pp. 47–48, 50–52.

From *A Discourse on Method*

Just as a great number of laws is often a pretext for wrongdoing, with the result that a state is much better governed when, having only a few, they are strictly observed; so also I came to believe that in the place of the great number of precepts that go to make up logic, the following four would be sufficient for my purposes, provided that I took a firm but unshakeable decision never once to depart from them.

The first was never to accept anything as true that I did not *incontrovertibly* know to be so; that is to say, carefully to avoid both *prejudice* and premature conclusions; and to include nothing in my judgments other than that which presented itself to my mind so *clearly* and *distinctly*, that I would have no occasion to doubt it.

The second was to divide all the difficulties under examination into as many parts as possible, and as many as were required to solve them in the best way.

The third was to conduct my thoughts in a given order, beginning with the *simplest* and most easily understood objects, and gradually ascending, as it were step by step, to the knowledge of the most *complex*; and *positing* an order even on those which do not have a natural order of precedence.

The last was to undertake such complete enumerations and such general surveys that I would be sure to have left nothing out.

The long chain of reasonings, every one simple and easy, which geometers habitually employ to reach their most difficult proofs had given me cause to suppose that all those things which fall within the domain of human understanding follow on from each other in the same way, and that as long as one stops oneself taking anything to be true that is not true and sticks to the right order so as to deduce one thing from another, there can be nothing so remote that one cannot eventually reach it, nor so hidden that one cannot discover it. . . .

Because I wished . . . to concentrate on the pursuit of truth, I came to think that I should . . . reject as completely false everything in which I could detect the least doubt, in order to see if anything thereafter remained in my belief that was completely indubitable. And so, because our senses sometimes deceive us, I decided to suppose that nothing was such as they lead us to imagine it to be. And because there are men who make mistakes in reasoning, even about the simplest elements of geometry, and commit logical fallacies, I judged that I was as prone to error as anyone else, and I rejected as false all the reasoning I had hitherto accepted as valid proof. Finally, considering that all the same thoughts which we have while awake can come to us while asleep without any one of them then being true, I resolved to pretend that everything that had ever entered my head was no more true than the illusions of my dreams. But immediately afterwards I noted that, while I was trying to think of all things being false in this way, it was necessarily the case that I, who was thinking them, had to be something; and observing this truth: *I am thinking therefore I exist*, was so secure and certain that it could not be shaken by any of the most extravagant suppositions of the sceptics, I judged that I could accept it without scruple, as the first principle of the philosophy I was seeking.

Source: René Descartes, *A Discourse on the Method*, trans. Ian Maclean (New York: 2006), pp. 17–18, 28.

Questions for Analysis

1. Descartes's idea of certainty depended on a "long chain of reasonings" that departed from certain axioms that could not be doubted and rejected evidence from the senses. What science provided him with the model for this idea of certainty? What was the first thing that he felt he could be certain about? Did he trust his senses?

2. Bacon's idea of certainty pragmatically sought to combine the benefits of sensory knowledge and experience (gathered by "ants") with the understandings arrived at through reason (cobwebs constructed by "spiders"). How would Descartes have responded to Bacon's claims? According to Bacon, was Descartes an ant or a spider?

3. What do these two thinkers have in common?

reproduce the experiment, and assess the outcome. The enterprise would give England's natural philosophers a common sense of purpose and a system to reach reasoned, gentlemanly agreement on "matters of fact." By separating systematic scientific research from the dangerous language of politics and religion that had marked the civil war, the Royal Society could also help restore a sense of order and consensus to English intellectual life.

The society's journal, *Philosophical Transactions*, reached out to professional scholars and experimenters throughout Europe. Similar societies began to appear elsewhere.

The French Academy of Sciences was founded in 1666 and was also tied to seventeenth-century state building, in this case French absolutism (see Chapter 15). Scientific societies reached rough agreement about what constituted legitimate research. They established the modern scientific custom of crediting discoveries to those who were first to publish results. They enabled information and theories to be exchanged more easily across national boundaries, although philosophical differences among Cartesians, Baconians, and traditional Aristotelians remained very difficult to bridge. Science began to take shape as a discipline.

Gassendi on the Science of Observation and the Human Soul

Pierre Gassendi (1592–1655) was a seventeenth-century French Catholic priest and philosopher. A contemporary of Descartes's, Gassendi was part of a group of intellectuals in France who sought a new philosophy of nature that could replace the traditional teachings of Aristotle that had been so severely criticized by Copernicus and his followers. Gassendi had no doubt that his faith as a Christian was compatible with his enthusiasm for the new sciences of observation, but in order to demonstrate this to his contemporaries he had to show that the mechanical explanations of the universe and the natural world did not necessarily lead to a heretical materialism or atheism. In the following passage, taken from his posthumously published work Syntagma Philosophicum *(1658), Gassendi attempted to demonstrate that one might infer the existence of the human soul, even if it was not accessible to the senses.*

There are many such things for which with the passage of time helpful appliances are being found that will make them visible to the senses. For example, take the little animal the mite, which is born under the skin; the senses perceived it as a certain unitary little point without parts; but since, however, the senses saw that it moved by itself, reason had deduced from this motion as from a perceptible sign that this little body was an animal and because its forward motion was somewhat like a turtle's, reason added that it must get about by the use of certain tiny legs and feet. And although this truth would have been hidden to the senses, which never perceived these limbs, the microscope was recently invented by which sight could perceive that matters were actually as predicted. Likewise, the question had been raised what the galaxy in the sky with the name of the Milky Way was. Democritus, concerning whom it was said that even when he did not know something he was knowing, had deduced from the perceptible sign of its filmy whiteness that it was nothing more than an innumerable multitude of closely packed little stars which could not be seen separately, but produced that effect of spilt milk when many of them were joined together. This truth had become known to him, and yet had remained undisclosed to the senses until our day and age, until the moment that the telescope, recently discovered, made it clear that things were in fact what he had said. But there are many such things which, though they were hidden from the ancients, have now been made manifest for our eyes. And who knows but a great many of those which are concealed in our time, which we perceive only through the intelligence, will one day also be clearly perceived by the senses through the agency of some helpful appliance thought up by our descendants? . . .

Secondly, if someone wonders whether a certain body is endowed with a soul or not, the senses are not at all capable of determining that by taking a look as it were at the soul itself; yet there are operations which when they come to the senses' notice, lead the intellect to deduce as from a sign that there is some soul beneath them. You will say that this sign belongs to the empirical type, but it is not at all of that type, for it is not even one of the indicative signs since it does not inform us of something that the senses have ever perceived in conjunction with the sign, as they have seen fire with smoke, but informs us instead of something that has always been impenetrable to the senses themselves, like our skin's pores or the mite's feet before the microscope.

You will persist with the objection that we should not ask so much whether there is a soul in a body as what its nature is, if it is the cause of such operations, just as there is no question that there is a force attracting iron in a magnet or that there is a tide in the sea, but there are questions over what their nature is or what they are caused by. But let me omit these matters which are to be fully treated elsewhere, and let it be enough if we say that not every truth can be known by the mind, but at least some can concerning something otherwise hidden, or not obvious to the senses themselves. And we bring up the example of the soul both because vital action is proposed by Sextus Empiricus as an example of an indicative sign and because even though it pertains not so much to the nature of the soul as to its existence, still a truth of existence of such magnitude as this, which it is most valuable for us to know, is made indisputable. For when among other questions we hear it asked if God is or exists in the universe, that is a truth of existence which it would be a great service to establish firmly even if it is not proven at the same time what he is or what his nature is. Although God is such that he can no more come under the perusal of the senses than the soul can, still we infer that the soul exists in the body from the actions that occur before the senses and are so peculiarly appropriate to a soul that if one were not present, they would not be, either. In the same way we deduce that God exists in the universe from his effects perceived by the senses, which could not be produced by anything but God and which therefore would not be observed unless God were present in the world, such as the great order of the universe, its great beauty, its grandeur, its harmony, which are so great that they can only result from a sovereignly wise, good, powerful, and inexhaustible cause. But these things will be treated elsewhere at greater length.

Source: Craig B. Brush, ed., *The Selected Works of Pierre Gassendi* (New York: 1972), pp. 334–36.

Questions for Analysis

1. What is the relationship between new knowledge and new scientific tools (the microscope and the telescope) in Gassendi's examples of the mite and the Milky Way? Is he a Baconian or a Cartesian?

2. What are the limitations of the senses when it comes to questions of the human soul, according to Gassendi?

3. Given these limitations, does Gassendi conclude that science will never be able to say anything about his religious faith?

The early scientific academies did not have explicit rules barring women, but with few exceptions they contained only male members. This did not mean that women did not practice science, though their participation in scientific research and debate remained controversial. In some cases, the new science could itself become a justification for women's inclusion, as when the Cartesian philosopher François Poullain de la Barre used anatomy to declare in 1673 that "the mind has no sex." Since women possessed the same physical senses as men and the same nervous systems and brains, Poullain asked, why should they not equally occupy the same roles in society? In fact, historians have discovered more than a few women who taught at European universities in the sixteenth and seventeenth centuries, especially in Italy. Elena Cornaro Piscopia received her doctorate of philosophy in Padua in 1678, the first woman to do so. Laura Bassi became a professor of physics at the University of Bologna after receiving her doctorate there in 1733, and based on her exceptional contributions to mathematics she became a member of the Academy of Science in Bologna. Her papers—including titles such as "On the Compression of Air" (1746), "On the Bubbles Observed in Freely Flowing Fluid" (1747), "On Bubbles of Air That Escape from Fluids" (1748)—gained her a stipend from the academy.

Italy appears to have been an exception in allowing women to get formal recognition for their education and research in established institutions. Elsewhere, elite women could educate themselves by associating with learned men. The aristocratic Margaret Cavendish (1623–1673), a natural philosopher in England, gleaned the information necessary to start her career from her family and their friends, a network that included Thomas Hobbes and, while she was in exile in France in the 1640s, René Descartes. These connections were not enough to overcome the isolation she felt working in a world of letters that was still largely the preserve of men, but this did not prevent her from developing her own speculative natural philosophy and using it to critique those who would exclude her from scientific debate. The "tyrannical government" of men over women, she wrote, "hath so dejected our spirits, that we are become so stupid, that beasts being but a degree below us, men use us but a degree above beasts. Whereas in nature we have as clear an understanding as men, if we are bred in schools to mature our brains."

The construction of observatories in private residences enabled some women living in such homes to work their way into the growing field of astronomy. Between 1650 and 1710, 14 percent of German astronomers were women, the most famous of whom was Maria Winkelmann (1670–1720). Winkelmann had worked with her husband, Gottfried Kirch, in his observatory, and when he died she had already done significant work, discovering a comet and preparing calendars for the Berlin Academy of Sciences. When Kirch died, she petitioned the academy to be granted her husband's place in the prestigious body but was rejected. Gottfried Leibniz, the academy's president, explained, "Already during her husband's lifetime the society was burdened with ridicule because its calendar was prepared by a woman. If she were now to be kept on in such capacity, mouths would gape even wider." In spite of this rejection, Winkelmann continued to work as an

FROM MARIA SYBILLA MERIAN, *METAMORPHOSIS OF THE INSECTS OF SURINAM* (1705). Merian, the daughter of a Frankfurt engraver, learned in her father's workshop the skills necessary to become an important early entomologist and scientific illustrator who conducted her research on two continents.

astronomer, training both her son and two daughters in the discipline.

Like Winkelmann, the entomologist Maria Sibylla Merian (1647–1717) also made a career based on observation. And like Winkelmann, Merian was able to carve out a space for her scientific work by exploiting the precedent of guild women who learned their trade in family workshops. Merian was the daughter of an engraver and illustrator in Frankfurt, and she served as an informal apprentice to her father before beginning her own career as a scientific illustrator, specializing in detailed engravings of insects and plants. Traveling to the Dutch colony of Surinam, Merian supported herself and her two daughters by selling exotic insects and animals she collected and brought back to Europe. She endured the colony's sweltering climate and overcame malaria to publish her most important scientific work, *Metamorphosis of the Insects of Surinam*, which detailed the life cycles of Surinam's insects in sixty ornate

illustrations. Merian's *Metamorphosis* was well received in her time; in fact, Peter I of Russia proudly displayed Merian's portrait and books in his study.

"AND ALL WAS LIGHT": ISAAC NEWTON

Sir Isaac Newton's work marks the culmination of the scientific revolution. Galileo, peering through his telescope in the early 1600s, had come to believe that the earth and the heavens were made of the same material. And Galileo's experiments with pendulums aimed to discover the laws of motion, and he proposed theories of inertia. But it was Newton who articulated those laws and presented a coherent, unified vision of how the universe worked. All bodies in the universe, Newton said, whether on earth or in the heavens, obeyed the same basic laws. One set of forces and one pattern, which could be expressed mathematically, explained why planets orbited in ellipses and why (and at what speed) apples fell from trees. An Italian mathematician later commented that Newton was the "greatest and most fortunate of mortals"—because there was only one universe, and he had discovered its laws.

Isaac Newton (1642–1727) was born on Christmas Day to a family of small landowners. His father died before his birth, and it fell to a succession of relatives, family friends, and schoolmasters to spot, and then encourage, his genius. In 1661, he entered Trinity College in Cambridge University, where he would remain for the next thirty-five years, first as a student, then as the Lucasian Professor of Mathematics.

Newton's first great burst of creativity came at Cambridge in the years from 1664 to 1666, "the prime of my age for invention." During these years, Newton broke new ground in three areas. The first was optics. Descartes believed that color was a secondary quality produced by the rotational speed of particles but that light itself was white. Newton, using prisms he had purchased at a local fair, showed that white light was composed of different-colored rays (see image on page 443). The second area in which Newton produced innovative work during these years was in mathematics. In a series of brilliant insights, he invented both integral calculus and differential calculus, providing mathematical tools to model motion in space. The third area of his creative genius involved his early works on gravity. Newton later told different versions of the same story: the idea about gravity had come to him when he was in a "contemplative mood" and was "occasioned by the fall of an apple." Why did the apple "not go sideways or upwards, but constantly to the earth's

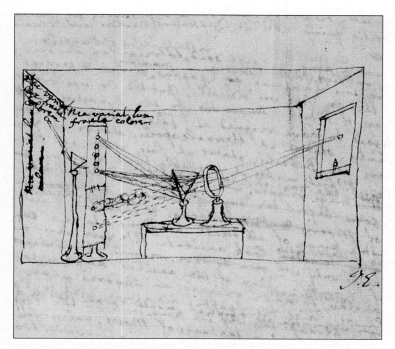

NEWTON'S EXPERIMENTS WITH LIGHT (1672). Newton's own sketch (left) elegantly displays the way he proved that white light was made up of differently colored light rays. Earlier scientists had explained the color spectrum produced by shining sunlight through a prism by insisting that the colors were a by-product of contaminating elements within the prism's glass. Newton disproved this theory by shining the sunlight through two consecutive prisms. The first produced the characteristic division of light into a color spectrum. When one of these colored beams passed through a second prism, however, it emerged on the other side unchanged, demonstrating that the glass itself was not the cause of the dispersal. He was not yet thirty when he published the results of this experiment.

center? . . . Assuredly the reason is, that the earth draws it. There must be a drawing power in matter." Voltaire, the eighteenth-century French essayist, retold the story to dramatize Newton's simple brilliance. But the theory of gravity rested on mathematical formulations, it was far from simple, and it would not be fully worked out until Newton published his *Principia*, more than twenty years later.

Newton's work on the composite nature of white light led him to make a reflecting telescope, which used a curved mirror rather than lenses. The telescope earned him election to the Royal Society (in 1672) and drew him out of his sheltered obscurity at Cambridge. Encouraged by the Royal Society's support, he wrote a paper describing his theory of optics and allowed it to be published in *Philosophical Transactions*. Astronomers and scientists across Europe applauded the work. Robert Hooke, the Royal Society's curator of experiments, did not. Hooke was not persuaded by Newton's mode of argument; he found Newton's claims that science had to be mathematical both dogmatic and high-handed; and he objected—in a series of sharp exchanges with the reclusive genius—that Newton had not provided any physical explanation for his results. Stung by the conflict with Hooke and persuaded that few natural philosophers could understand his theories, Newton

withdrew to Cambridge and long refused to share his work. Only the patient effort of friends and fellow scientists like the astronomer Edmond Halley (1656–1742), already well known for his astronomical observations in the Southern Hemisphere (and the person for whom Halley's Comet is named), convinced Newton to publish again.

Newton's *Principia Mathematica* (Mathematical Principles of Natural Philosophy) was published in 1687. It was prompted by a visit from Halley, in which the astronomer asked Newton for his ideas on a question being discussed at the Royal Society: was there a mathematical basis for the elliptical orbits of the planets? Halley's question inspired Newton to expand calculations he had made earlier into an all-encompassing theory of celestial—and terrestrial—dynamics. Halley not only encouraged Newton's work but supervised and financed its publication (though he had less money than Newton); and on several occasions he had to persuade Newton, enraged again by reports of criticism from Hooke and others, to continue with the project and to commit his findings to print.

Principia was long and difficult—purposefully so, for Newton said he did not want to be "baited by little smatterers in mathematics." Its central proposition was that gravitation was a universal force and one that could be expressed mathematically. Newton built on Galileo's work on inertia, Kepler's findings concerning the elliptical orbits of planets, the work of Boyle and Descartes, and even his rival Hooke's work on gravity. He once said, "If I have seen further, it is by standing on the shoulders of giants." But Newton's universal theory of gravity, although it drew on work of others before him, formulated something entirely new. His synthesis offered a single, descriptive account of mass and motion. "All bodies whatsoever are endowed with a principle of mutual gravitation." The law of gravitation was stated in a mathematical formula and supported by observation and experience; it was, literally, universal.

The scientific elite of Newton's time were not uniformly persuaded. Many mechanical philosophers, particularly Cartesians, objected to the prominence in Newton's theory of forces acting across empty space. Such attractions smacked of mysticism (or the occult); they seemed to lack any driving mechanism. Newton responded to these criticisms in a note entitled *General Scholium*, added to the next edition of the *Principia* in 1713. He did not know what *caused* gravity, he said, and he did not "feign hypotheses." "For whatever is not deduced from the phenomena must be called hypothesis," he wrote, and has "no place in the experimental philosophy." For Newton, certainty and objectivity lay in the precise mathematical characterization of phenomena—"the mathematization of the universe," as one historian puts it. Science could not, and need not, always uncover causes. It did describe natural phenomena and accurately predict the behavior of objects as confirmed by experimentation.

Other natural philosophers immediately acclaimed Newton's work for solving long-standing puzzles. Thinkers persuaded that the Copernican version of the universe was right had been unable to piece together the physics of a revolving earth. Newton made it possible to do so. Halley provided a poem to accompany the first edition of *Principia*. "No closer to the gods can any mortal rise," he wrote of the man with whom he had worked so patiently. Halley did have a financial as well as an intellectual interest in the book, and he also arranged for it to be publicized and reviewed in influential journals. John Locke (whose own *Essay Concerning Human Understanding* was written at virtually the same time, in 1690) read *Principia* twice and summarized it in French for readers across the Channel. By 1713, pirated editions of *Principia* were being published in Amsterdam for distribution throughout Europe. By the time Newton died, in 1727, he had become an English national hero and was given a funeral at Westminster Abbey. The poet Alexander Pope expressed the awe that Newton inspired in some of his contemporaries in a famous couplet:

> Nature and nature's law lay hid in night;
> God said, "Let Newton be!" and all was light.

Voltaire, the French champion of the Enlightenment (discussed in the next chapter), was largely responsible for Newton's reputation in France. In this, he was helped by a woman who was a brilliant mathematician in her own right, Emilie du Châtelet. Du Châtelet coauthored a book with Voltaire introducing Newton to a French audience; and she translated *Principia*, a daunting scientific and mathematical task and one well beyond Voltaire's mathematical abilities. Newton's French admirers and publicists disseminated Newton's findings. In their eyes, Newton also represented a cultural transformation, a turning point in the history of knowledge.

NEWTON AND SATIRE. The English artist and satirist William Hogarth mocking both philosophy and "Newton worship" in 1763. The philosophers' heads are being weighed on a scale that runs from "absolute gravity" to "absolute levity" or "stark fool."

Science and Cultural Change

From the seventeenth century on, science stood at the heart of what it meant to be "modern." It grew increasingly central to the self-understanding of Western culture, and scientific and technological power became one of the justifications for the expansion of Western empires and the subjugation of other peoples. For all these reasons, the scientific revolution was and often still is presented as a thoroughgoing break with the past, a moment when Western culture was recast. But, as one historian has written, "no house is ever built of entirely virgin materials, according to a plan bearing no resemblance to old patterns, and no body of culture is able to wholly reject its past. Historical change is not like that, and most 'revolutions' effect less sweeping changes than they advertise or than are advertised for them."

To begin with, the transformation we have canvassed in this chapter involved elite knowledge. Ordinary people inhabited a very different cultural world. Second, natural philosophers' discoveries—Tycho's mathematics and Galileo's observations, for instance—did not undo the authority of the ancients in one blow, nor did they seek to do so. Third, science did not subvert religion. Even when traditional concepts collapsed in the face of new discoveries, natural philosophers seldom gave up on the project of restoring a picture of a divinely ordered universe. Mechanists argued that the intricate universe revealed by the discoveries of Copernicus, Kepler, Galileo, Newton, and others was evidence of God's guiding presence. Robert Boyle's will provided the funds for a lecture series on the "confutation of atheism" by scientific means. Isaac Newton was happy to have his work contribute to that project. "Nothing," he wrote to one of the lecturers in 1692, "can rejoice me more than to find [*Principia*] usefull for that purpose." The creation of "the Sun and Fixt stars," "the motion which the Planets now have could not spring from any naturall cause alone but were imprest with a divine Agent." Science was thoroughly compatible with belief in God's providential design, at least through the seventeenth century.

The greatest scientific minds were deeply committed to beliefs that do not fit present-day notions of science. Newton, again, is the most striking case in point. The great twentieth-century economist John Maynard Keynes was one of the first to read through Newton's private manuscripts. On the three hundredth anniversary of Newton's birth (the celebration of which was delayed because of the Second World War), Keynes offered the following reappraisal of the great scientist:

> I believe that Newton was different from the conventional picture of him. . . .
>
> In the eighteenth century and since, Newton came to be thought of as the first and greatest of the modern age of scientists, a rationalist, one who taught us to think on the lines of cold and untinctured reason.
>
> I do not see him in this light. I do not think that any one who has pored over the contents of that box which he packed up when he finally left Cambridge in 1696 and which, though partly dispersed, have come down to us, can see him like that. Newton was not the first of the age of reason. He was the last of the magicians, the last of the Babylonians and Sumerians, the last great mind which looked out on the visible and intellectual world with the same eyes as those who began to build our intellectual inheritance rather less than 10,000 years ago.

Like his predecessors, Newton saw the world as God's message to humanity, a text to be deciphered. Close reading and study would unlock its mysteries. This same impulse led Newton to read accounts of magic, investigate

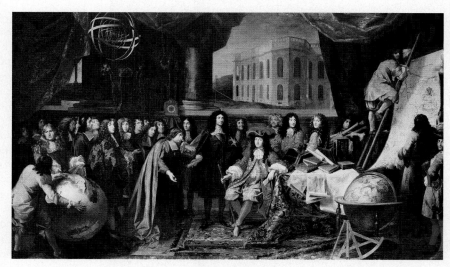

ESTABLISHMENT OF THE ACADEMY OF SCIENCES AND FOUNDATION OF THE OBSERVATORY, 1667. The 1666 founding of the Academy of Sciences was a measure of the new prestige of science and the potential value of research. Louis XIV sits at the center, surrounded by the religious and scholarly figures who offer the fruits of their knowledge to the French state. ▪ *What was the value of science for absolutist rulers like Louis?*

alchemist's claims that base metals could be turned into gold, and to immerse himself in the writings of the Church Fathers and in the Bible, which he knew in intimate detail. If these activities sound unscientific from the perspective of the present, it is because the strict distinction between rational inquiry and belief in the occult or religious traditions simply did not exist in his time. Such a distinction is a product of the long history of scientific developments after the eighteenth century. Newton, then, was the last representative of an older tradition, and also, quite unintentionally, the first of a new one.

What, then, did the scientific revolution change? Seventeenth-century natural philosophers had produced new answers to fundamental questions about the physical world. Age-old questions about astronomy and physics had been recast and, to some extent (although it was not yet clear to what extent), answered. In the process, there had developed a new approach to amassing and integrating information in a systematic way, an approach that helped

yield more insights into the workings of nature as time went on. In this period, too, the most innovative scientific work moved out of the restrictive environment of the Church and the universities. Natural philosophers began talking to and working with each other in lay organizations that developed standards of research. England's Royal Society spawned imitators in Florence and Berlin and later in Russia. The French Royal Academy of Sciences had a particularly direct relationship with the monarchy and the French state. France's statesmen exerted control over the academy and sought to share in the rewards of any discoveries its members made.

New, too, were beliefs about the purpose and methods of science. The practice of breaking a complex problem down into parts made it possible to tackle more and different questions in the physical sciences. Mathematics assumed a more central role in the new science. Finally, rather than simply confirming established truths, the new methods were designed to explore the unknown and provide

After You Read This Chapter

 Go to **INQUIZITIVE** to see what you've learned—and learn what you've missed— with personalized feedback along the way.

REVIEWING THE OBJECTIVES

- The scientific revolution marked a shift toward new forms of explanation in descriptions of the natural world. What made the work of scientists during this period different from earlier forms of knowledge or research?

- The scientific revolution nevertheless depended on earlier traditions of philosophical thought. What earlier traditions proved important in fostering a spirit of scientific investigation?

- Astronomical observations played a central role in the scientific revolution. What technological innovations made new astronomical work possible, and what conclusions did astronomers reach using these new technologies?

- Central to the scientific revolution was the rejection of the Ptolemaic view of the universe and its replacement by the Copernican model. What was this controversy about?

- Francis Bacon and René Descartes had contrasting ideas about scientific method. What approach to science did each of these natural philosophers defend?

means to discover new truths. As Kepler wrote to Galileo, "How great a difference there is between theoretical speculation and visual experience, between Ptolemy's discussion of the Antipodes and Columbus's discovery of the New World." Knowledge itself was reconceived. In the older model, to learn was to read: to reason logically, to argue, to compare classical texts, and to absorb a finite body of knowledge. In the newer one, to learn was to discover, and what could be discovered was boundless.

CONCLUSION

The pioneering natural philosophers remained circumspect about their abilities. Some sought to lay bare the workings of the universe; others believed humans could only catalog and describe the regularities observed in nature. By unspoken but seemingly mutual agreement, the question of first causes was left aside. The new science did not say *why*, but *how*. Newton, for one, worked toward explanations that would reveal the logic of creation laid out in mathematics. Yet, in the end, he settled for theories explaining motions and relationships that could be observed and tested.

The eighteenth-century heirs to Newton were much more daring. Laboratory science and the work of the scientific societies largely stayed true to the experimenters' rules and limitations. But as we will see in the next chapter, the natural philosophers who began investigating the human sciences cast aside some of their predecessors' caution. Society, technology, government, religion, even the individual human mind seemed to be mechanisms or parts of a larger nature waiting for study. The scientific revolution overturned the natural world as it had been understood for a millennium; it also inspired thinkers more interested in revolutions in society.

PEOPLE, IDEAS, AND EVENTS IN CONTEXT

- How did the traditions of **NEOPLATONISM, RENAISSANCE,** and **HUMANISM** contribute to a vision of the physical world that encouraged scientific investigation and explanation?
- In what way did the work of **NICOLAUS COPERNICUS, TYCHO BRAHE, JOHANNES KEPLER,** and **GALILEO GALILEI** serve to undermine the intellectual foundations of the **PTOLEMAIC SYSTEM**? Why did their work largely take place outside of the traditional centers of learning in Europe, such as universities?
- What differences in scientific practice arose from **FRANCIS BACON**'s emphasis on observation and **RENÉ DESCARTES**'s insistence that knowledge could only be derived from unquestionable first principles?
- What were **ISAAC NEWTON**'s major contributions to the scientific revolution? Why have some suggested that Newton's interests and thinking were not all compatible with modern conceptions of scientific understanding?
- What was important about the establishment of institutions such as the British **ROYAL SOCIETY** or the French **ACADEMY OF SCIENCES** for the development of scientific methods and research?
- What prevented women from entering most of Europe's scientific academies? How did educated women such as **LAURA BASSI, MARGARET CAVENDISH, MARIA WINKELMANN,** and **MARIA SYBILLA MERIAN** gain the skills necessary to participate in scientific work?

THINKING ABOUT CONNECTIONS

- How did ideas about the value of ancient scholarship and philosophy change after the development of new sciences of observation in the seventeenth century?
- What possible connections might be made between the intellectual developments in scientific thinking during the seventeenth century and the Reformation of the sixteenth century? Was the new science incompatible with religious faith?

Before
You
Read
This
Chapter

STORY LINES

- In the eighteenth century, intellectuals in Europe sought to answer questions about the nature of good government, morality, and the social order by applying principles of rational argument. They questioned the value of traditional institutions and insisted that "enlightened" reason could solve social problems better than age-old customs.

- Population growth, economic development, and colonial expansion to other continents created new sources of prosperity in western Europe, fostering a new kind of consumer culture and a new awareness of the world's diversity of peoples and customs.

- Absolutist rulers used Enlightenment ideals to justify the centralization of authority and the establishment of rationalized bureaucracies. Enlightenment ideas also helped establish a radical critique of the eighteenth-century social and political order.

CHRONOLOGY

1734	Voltaire (1694–1778), *Philosophical Letters*
1740–80	Maria Theresa of Austria
1740–86	Reign of Frederick II of Prussia
1748	Baron Montesquieu (1689–1755), *The Spirit of Laws*
1748	David Hume (1711–1776), *An Enquiry Concerning Human Understanding*
1751–72	Denis Diderot (1713–1784), *Encyclopedia*
1756–63	The Seven Years' War
1762–96	Catherine the Great of Russia
1762	Jean-Jacques Rousseau (1712–1778), *The Social Contract*
1776	The American Revolution begins
1776	Adam Smith (1723–1790), *An Inquiry into the Nature and Causes of the Wealth of Nations*
1792	Mary Wollstonecraft (1759–1797), *A Vindication of the Rights of Woman*

Europe during the Enlightenment

CORE OBJECTIVES

- **DEFINE** the term *Enlightenment* as eighteenth-century thinkers used it, and **IDENTIFY** the figures most closely associated with this intellectual movement.

- **DESCRIBE** the eighteenth-century consumer revolution in Europe and its relationship to the Enlightenment.

- **EXPLAIN** how the ideas associated with the Enlightenment spread and the consequences of this expanded world of public discussion.

- **EXPLORE** the ways that the Enlightenment was linked to imperial expansion as larger numbers of Europeans became more aware of the globe's diverse cultures and peoples.

- **UNDERSTAND** how Enlightenment thought challenged central tenets of eighteenth-century culture and politics.

I n 1762, the *Parlement* (law court) of Toulouse, in France, convicted Jean Calas, a Protestant, of murdering his son. Witnesses claimed that the young Calas had wanted to convert to Catholicism, and the father had killed him to prevent this conversion. The court tortured Jean Calas twice before executing him. His arms and legs were slowly pulled apart, gallons of water were poured down his throat, his body was publicly broken on the wheel, and each of his limbs smashed with an iron bar. Then the executioner cut off his head. Throughout the trial, torture, and execution, Calas maintained his innocence. Two years later, the Parlement reversed its verdict, declared Calas not guilty, and offered the family a payment in compensation.

François Marie Arouet, also known as Voltaire, was appalled by the verdict and punishment. Voltaire was the most famous personality in the European intellectual movement known as the Enlightenment. Prolific and well connected, Voltaire took up his pen to clear Calas's name. He hired lawyers for the family and wrote briefs, letters, and essays to bring the case to the public eye. These essays circulated widely among an increasingly literate middle-class audience. For Voltaire, Calas's case exemplified nearly everything he found backward in European culture. Intolerance, ignorance, and religious "fanaticism" had made a travesty of justice. "Shout everywhere, I beg you, for Calas and against fanaticism, for it is this infamy that has caused their misery." Torture demonstrated the power of the courts but could not uncover the truth. Secret interrogations, trials behind closed doors, summary judgment (Calas was executed the day after being convicted, with no review by a higher court), and barbaric punishments defied reason, morality, and human dignity. Any criminal, however wretched, "is a man," wrote Voltaire, "and you are accountable for his blood."

Voltaire's writings on the Calas case illustrate the classic concerns of the Enlightenment: the dangers of arbitrary and unchecked authority, the value of religious toleration, and the overriding importance of law, reason, and human dignity in all affairs. He borrowed most of his arguments from others—from his predecessor the Baron de Montesquieu and from the Italian writer Cesare Beccaria, whose *On Crimes and Punishments* appeared in 1764. Voltaire's reputation did not rest on his originality as a philosopher. It came from his effectiveness as a writer and advocate, his desire and ability to reach a wide audience in print.

THE CRUEL DEATH OF CALAS. This print, reproduced in a pamphlet that circulated in Britain in the late eighteenth century, portrayed the French Protestant Jean Calas as a martyr to his beliefs and directly implicated the Roman Catholic Church in the cruelty of his execution by prominently placing an enthusiastic priest at the scene. The pamphlet may also have sought to reinforce anti-French sentiments among an increasingly nationalistic British population. ▪ *How might Enlightenment authors have used such a scene to promote their message of toleration?* ▪ *How might Church officials have responded to such attacks?*

The emergence of this wide audience for Voltaire's writings was just as significant as the arguments that he made. The growth of European cities, the spread of literacy, and new forms of social interaction at all levels of society helped fuel the Enlightenment's atmosphere of critical reflection about religion, law, the power of the state, and the dignity of the individual. The fact that a writer such as Voltaire could become a celebrity showed that a new kind of literate reading public had developed in Europe. Enough people who could read and had income to spare for printed material created a market for newspapers and novels, which in turn showed the emergence of a new kind of consumer society. The works of writers like Voltaire and his peers were discussed over sweetened caffeinated drinks in coffeehouses and cafes where ordinary people gathered to smoke and debate the issues of the day. (Coffee, sugar, and tobacco all came from the Atlantic colonial trade.) Similar scenes took place in the homes of aristocrats. The Enlightenment was thus not only an intellectual movement—it was a cultural phenomenon, which exposed an increasingly broad part of the population to new forms of consumption, of goods as well as ideas.

PROSPERITY, COMMERCE, AND CONSUMPTION

The Enlightenment's audience consisted of urban readers and consumers who were receptive to new cultural forms: the essay, the political tract, the satirical engraving, the novel, the newspaper, theatrical spectacles, and even musical performances. Clearly, such developments could only occur in a society where significant numbers of people had achieved a level of wealth that freed them from the immediate cares of daily sustenance. By the beginning of the eighteenth century, this level of wealth had been achieved in the cities of northwestern Europe, particularly in France, the Low Countries, and Britain.

Economic Growth in Eighteenth-Century Europe

Rapid economic and demographic growth in northwestern Europe was made possible by cheaper food and declines in mortality from infectious disease. In Britain and Holland, better farming methods produced more food per acre, resulting in fewer famines and a better-nourished population. New crops, especially maize and potatoes from the

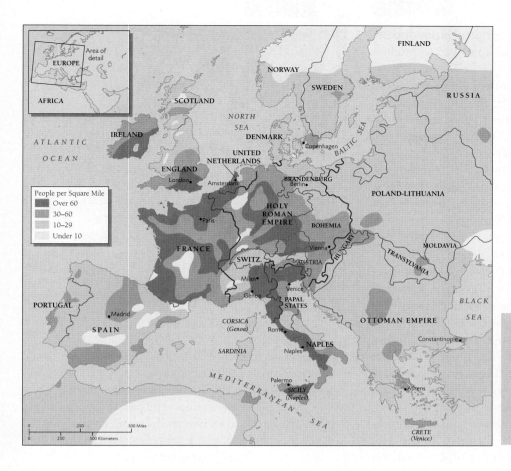

POPULATION GROWTH BEFORE THE ENLIGHTENMENT c. 1600.
• *Where was the population density greatest?* • *Did population density always correspond to economic growth?* • *How did urbanization affect patterns of life and trade?*

Americas, also increased the supply of food. Infectious disease continued to kill half of all Europeans before the age of twenty, but plague was ceasing to be a major killer, as a degree of immunity (perhaps the result of a genetic mutation) began to emerge within the European population. Better diet and improved sanitation may also have reduced infection rates.

Northwestern Europe was also increasingly urbanized. The total number of urban dwellers in Europe did not change much between 1600 and 1800. At both dates, approximately 200 cities in Europe had a population of over 10,000. These cities were increasingly concentrated in northern and western Europe, however, and the largest experienced extraordinary growth, especially those connected with Atlantic trade. Hamburg, Liverpool, Toulon, and Cádiz grew by about 250 percent between 1600 and 1750. Amsterdam increased in population from 30,000 in 1530 to 200,000 by 1800. Naples went from a population of 300,000 in 1600 to nearly 500,000 by the late eighteenth century. Spectacular population growth also occurred in London, Paris, and Berlin, the administrative capitals of Europe.

The rising prosperity of northwestern Europe also depended on developments in trade and manufacturing.

Improvements in transportation led entrepreneurs to produce textiles in the countryside. They distributed, or "put out," wool and flax to rural workers who spun it and wove it into cloth on a piece-rate basis. The entrepreneur sold the finished cloth in a market that extended from local towns to international exporters. For country dwellers, this system provided welcome employment during slack seasons of the agricultural year. The system also allowed merchants to avoid expensive guild restrictions in the towns and reduced their production costs. Urban cloth workers suffered, but the system led to increased employment and to higher levels of industrial production, not only for textiles but also for iron, metalworking, and even toy and clock making.

Some cities also became manufacturing centers during the eighteenth century. In northern France, many of the million or so men and women employed in the textile trade lived and worked in Amiens, Lille, and Rheims. The rulers of Prussia made it their policy to develop Berlin as a manufacturing center, taking advantage of an influx of French Protestants to establish a silk-weaving industry there. Most urban manufacturing took place in small shops employing from five to twenty journeymen, but the scale of such enterprise was growing. In some manufacturing districts several thousand workers might be employed to produce the same product.

New inventions changed the pattern of work as well as the nature of the product. Knitting frames, simple devices to speed the manufacture of textile goods, made their appearance in Britain and Holland. Wire-drawing machines and slitting mills, which allowed nail makers to convert iron bars into rods, spread from Germany into Britain. Techniques for printing colored designs directly on calico cloth were imported from Asia. New and more efficient printing presses appeared, first in Holland and then elsewhere.

Workers did not readily accept innovations of this kind. Labor-saving machines threw people out of work. Artisans, especially those organized into guilds, were by nature conservative, anxious to protect not only their rights but also the secrets of their trade. Governments would often intervene to block the use of machines if they threatened to increase unemployment or create unrest. States might also act to protect the interests of their powerful commercial and financial backers. Both Britain and France outlawed calico printing for a time, to protect local textile manufacturers and importers of Indian goods. Mercantilist doctrines could also impede innovation. In both Paris and Lyons, for example, the use of indigo dyes was banned because they were manufactured abroad. But the pressures for economic innovation were irresistible, because behind them lay an insatiable eighteenth-century appetite for goods.

A World of Goods

In the eighteenth century, a mass market for consumer goods emerged, concentrated at first in northwestern Europe. Houses of middling ranks were now stocked with hitherto uncommon luxuries such as sugar, tobacco, tea, coffee, chocolate, newspapers, books, pictures, clocks, toys, china, glassware, pewter, silver plate, soap, razors, furniture (including beds with mattresses, chairs, and chests of drawers), shoes, cotton cloth, and spare clothing. Demand for such products consistently outstripped the supply, causing prices for these items to rise faster than the price of foodstuffs throughout the century. But the demand for them continued unabated.

The exploding consumer economy of the eighteenth century also encouraged the provision of services. In eighteenth-century Britain, the service sector was the fastest-growing part of the economy, outstripping both agriculture and manufacturing. Almost everywhere in urban

***TOPSY-TURVY WORLD* BY JAN STEEN.** This Dutch painting depicts a household in the throes of the exploding consumer economy that hit Europe by the end of the seventeenth century. Consumer goods ranging from silver and china to clothing and furniture cluttered the houses of ordinary people as never before.

Europe, the eighteenth century was the golden age of the small shopkeeper. People bought more prepared foods and more ready-made (as opposed to personally tailored) clothing. Advertising became an important part of doing business, helping create demand for new products and shaping popular taste for changing fashions. Even political allegiances could be expressed through consumption when people purchased plates and glasses commemorating favorite rulers or causes.

The result of all these developments was a European economy vastly more complex, more specialized, more integrated, more commercialized, and more productive than anything the world had seen before. These developments necessarily affected the way people thought of the world and their place in it—above all, people in the Enlightenment shared a sense of living in a time marked by change. Many Enlightenment thinkers defended such changes as "progress." Others were more critical, fearing that valued traditions were being lost. Such debates lay at the heart of Enlightenment thought.

The Foundations of the Enlightenment

Enlightenment thinkers did not agree on everything, but most shared a sense that they lived in an exciting moment in history in which human reason would prevail over the accumulated superstitions and traditions of the past. Enlightenment authors believed themselves to be the defenders of a new ideal, "the party of humanity."

The confidence that Enlightenment thinkers placed in the powers of human reason stemmed from the accomplishments of the scientific revolution. Even when the details of Newton's physics were poorly understood, his methods provided a model for scientific inquiry into other phenomena. Nature operated according to laws that could be grasped by study, observation, and thought. The work of the Scottish writer David Hume (*A Treatise of Human Nature*, 1739–40, and *An Enquiry Concerning Human Understanding*, 1748) provided the most direct bridge from science to the Enlightenment. Newton had refused speculation about ultimate causes, arguing instead for a precise description of natural phenomena (see Chapter 16). Hume took this same rigor and skepticism to the study of morality, the mind, and government, often drawing analogies to scientific laws. Hume criticized the "passion for hypotheses and systems" that dominated earlier philosophical thinking. Experience and careful observation, he argued, usually did not support the premises on which those systems rested.

Embracing human reason also required confronting the power of Europe's traditional monarchies and the religious institutions that supported them. "Dare to know!" the German philosopher Immanuel Kant challenged his contemporaries in his classic 1784 essay "What Is Enlightenment?" For Kant, the Enlightenment represented a declaration of intellectual independence. Kant compared the intellectual history of humanity to the growth of a child. Enlightenment, in this view, was an escape from humanity's "self-imposed immaturity" and a long overdue break with humanity's self-imposed parental figure, the Catholic Church. Coming of age meant the "determination and courage to think without the guidance of someone else"—as an individual. Reason required autonomy, and freedom from tradition.

Enlightenment thinkers nevertheless recognized a great debt to their predecessors, especially John Locke, Francis Bacon, and Isaac Newton. Enlightenment thinkers drew heavily on Locke's studies of human knowledge, especially his *Essay Concerning Human Understanding* (1690). Locke's theories of how humans acquire knowledge gave education and environment a critical role in shaping human character. All knowledge, he argued, originates from sense perception. The human mind at birth is a "blank tablet" (in Latin, *tabula rasa*). Only when an infant begins to perceive the external world with its senses, does anything register in its mind. Education, then, was essential to the creation of a good and moral individual. Locke's starting point, which became a central premise for those who followed, was the goodness and perfectibility of humanity. Building on Locke, eighteenth-century thinkers made education central to their project, because education promised that social progress could be achieved through individual moral improvement. Locke's theories had potentially

DIVINE LIGHT. The frontispiece for Voltaire's book on the science of Isaac Newton portrays Newton as the source of a divine light that is reflected onto Voltaire's desk from a mirror held by Émilie du Châtelet, the French translator of Newton who also was Voltaire's lover. Newton's throne of clouds and the adoring angels holding du Châtelet aloft were familiar motifs from earlier generations of religious paintings, but the significance of the carefully portrayed ray of light is recast by the books, inkwell, and precise scientific measuring tools surrounding Voltaire. ■ *What does this image say about the relationship between religious thought and Enlightenment science?*

radical implications for eighteenth-century society: if all humans were capable of reason, education might also level hierarchies of status, sex, or race. As we will see, only a few Enlightenment thinkers made such egalitarian arguments. Still, optimism and a belief in universal human progress constituted a second defining feature of nearly all Enlightenment thinking.

Enlightenment thinkers sought nothing less than the organization of all knowledge. The *scientific method*, by which they meant the empirical observation of particular phenomena in order to arrive at general laws, offered a way to pursue research in all areas—to study human affairs as well as natural ones. Thus they collected evidence to learn the laws governing the rise and fall of nations, and they compared governmental constitutions to deduce an ideal and universally applicable political system. Enlightenment thinkers took up a strikingly wide array of subjects in this systematic manner: knowledge and the mind, natural history, economics, government, religious beliefs, customs of indigenous peoples in the New World, human nature, and sexual (or what we would call gender) and racial differences.

As one can see from these examples, the culture of the *philosophes*, or Enlightenment thinkers, was international. French became the lingua franca of much Enlightenment discussion, but "French" books were often published in Switzerland, Germany, and Russia. Enlightenment thinkers admired British institutions and British scholarship, and Great Britain produced important ones: the historian Edward Gibbon and the Scottish philosophers David Hume and Adam Smith. The philosophes considered the Americans Thomas Jefferson and Benjamin Franklin to be a part of their group. Despite stiffer resistance from religious authorities, stricter state censors, and smaller networks of educated elites, the Enlightenment also flourished across central and southern Europe. Frederick II of Prussia hosted Voltaire during one of his exiles from France, and he also patronized a small but unusually productive group of Enlightenment thinkers. Northern Italy was also an important center of Enlightenment thought.

THE WORLD OF THE PHILOSOPHES

France nevertheless provided the stage for some of the most widely followed Enlightenment projects. For this reason, Enlightenment thinkers, regardless of where they lived, are often called by the French word *philosophes*. *Philosophe*, as used in the Enlightenment, simply meant "a freethinker," a person whose reflections were unhampered by the constraints of religion or dogma in any form.

Voltaire

The best known of the philosophes was Voltaire, born François Marie Arouet (1694–1778). As Erasmus two centuries earlier had embodied Christian humanism, Voltaire personified the Enlightenment, commenting on an enormous range of subjects in a wide variety of literary forms. Educated by the Jesuits, he became a gifted and sharp-tongued writer. His gusto for provocation landed him in the Bastille (a notorious prison in Paris) for libel and

soon afterward in temporary exile in England. In his three years there, Voltaire became an admirer of British political institutions, British culture, and the ideas of Newton, Bacon, and Locke. His single greatest accomplishment may have been popularizing Newton's work in France and more generally championing the cause of British empiricism and the scientific method against the more Cartesian French.

Voltaire's themes were religious and political liberty, and his weapons were comparisons. His admiration for British culture and politics became a stinging critique of France—and other absolutist countries on the Continent. He praised British open-minded empiricism, respect for scientists, and support for research. He considered the relative weakness of the British aristocracy a sign of Britain's political health. Unlike the French, the British respected commerce and people who engage in it, Voltaire wrote. The British tax system was rational, free of the complicated exemptions for the privileged that were ruining French finances. The British House of Commons represented the middle classes and, in contrast with French absolutism, brought balance to British government and checked arbitrary power. In his "Letters on the English Nation," Voltaire argued that violent revolution had actually produced political moderation and stability in Britain: "The idol of arbitrary power was drowned in seas of blood. . . . The English nation is the only nation in the world that has succeeded in moderating the power of its kings by resisting them."

Of all Britain's reputed virtues, religious toleration loomed largest of all. Britain, Voltaire argued, brought together citizens of different religions in a harmonious and productive culture. In this and other instances, Voltaire oversimplified: British Catholics, Dissenters, and Jews did not have equal civil rights. Yet the British policy of "toleration" did contrast with Louis XIV's intolerance of Protestants. Revoking the Edict of Nantes (1685) had stripped French Protestants of civil rights and had helped create the atmosphere in which Jean Calas—and others—were persecuted.

Of all forms of intolerance, Voltaire opposed religious bigotry most, and with real passion he denounced religious fraud, faith in miracles, and superstition. His most famous battle cry was "*Écrasez l'infâme!*" ("Crush this infamous thing"), by which he meant all forms of repression, fanaticism, and bigotry. "The less superstition, the less fanaticism; and the less fanaticism, the less misery." He did not oppose religion per se; rather, he sought to rescue morality, which he believed to come from God, from dogma—elaborate ritual, dietary laws, formulaic prayers—and from a powerful Church bureaucracy. He argued for common sense and simplicity, certain that these would bring out the goodness in humanity and establish stable authority.

Voltaire relished his position as a critic, and he was regularly exiled from France and other countries, his books banned and burned. As long as his plays attracted large audiences, however, the French king felt he had to tolerate their author. Voltaire had an attentive international public, including Frederick of Prussia, who invited him to his court at Berlin, and Catherine of Russia, with whom he corresponded about reforms she might introduce in Russia. When he died in 1778, a few months after a triumphant return to Paris, he was possibly the best-known writer in Europe.

Montesquieu

The Baron de Montesquieu (*mahn-tuhs-KYOO,* 1689–1755) was a very different kind of Enlightenment figure. Montesquieu was born to a noble family. He was not a stylist or a provocateur like Voltaire but a relatively cautious jurist, though he did write a satirical novel, *The Persian Letters* (1721), as a young man. The novel, which he published anonymously in Amsterdam, was composed as letters from two Persian visitors to France. The visitors detailed the odd religious superstitions they witnessed, compared manners at the French court with those in Turkish harems, and likened French absolutism to their own brands of *despotism,* or the abuse of government authority. *The Persian Letters* was an immediate best seller, which inspired many imitators, as other authors used the formula of a foreign observer to criticize contemporary French society.

Montesquieu's treatise, *The Spirit of Laws* (1748), may have been the most influential work of the Enlightenment. It was a groundbreaking study in what we would call comparative historical sociology and very Newtonian in its careful, empirical approach. Montesquieu asked about the structures that shaped law. How had different environments, histories, and religious traditions combined to create the variety of governmental institutions observable in the world? Why were there so many different forms of government: what spirit characterized each, and what were their respective virtues and shortcomings?

Montesquieu suggested that there were three basic forms of government: republics, monarchies, and despotisms. A republic was governed by many individuals—either an elite aristocracy of citizens or the people as a whole. The soul of a republic was virtue, which allowed individual citizens to transcend their particular interests and rule in accordance with the common good. In a monarchy, on the other hand, one person ruled in accordance with the law. The soul of a monarchy, wrote Montesquieu,

was honor, which gave individuals an incentive to behave with loyalty toward their sovereign. The third form of government, despotism, was rule by a single person unchecked by law or other powers. The soul of despotism was fear, since no citizen could feel secure and punishment took the place of education. Lest this seem abstract, Montesquieu devoted two chapters to the French monarchy, in which he spelled out what he saw as a dangerous drift toward despotism in his own land. Like other Enlightenment thinkers, Montesquieu admired the British system and its separation of the executive, legislative, and judicial functions of government. Such a balance of powers preserved liberty by avoiding a concentration of authority in a single individual or group. His idealization of "checks and balances" had a formative influence on Enlightenment political theorists and helped to guide the authors of the U.S. Constitution in 1787.

Diderot and the Encyclopedia

The most remarkable and ambitious Enlightenment project was a collective one: the *Encyclopedia.* The *Encyclopedia* claimed to summarize all the most advanced contemporary philosophical, scientific, and technical knowledge, making it available to any reader. It demonstrated how scientific analysis could be applied in nearly all realms of thought, and it further aimed to encourage critical reflection of an enormous range of traditions and institutions. The guiding spirit behind the venture was another Frenchman, Denis Diderot (1713–1784). Diderot was helped by the mathematician Jean Le Rond d'Alembert (1717–1783) and other leading men of letters, including Voltaire and Montesquieu. Published in installments between 1751 and 1772, the *Encyclopedia* ran to seventeen large volumes of text and eleven more of illustrations, with over 71,000 articles.

Diderot commissioned articles on science and technology, showing how machines worked and illustrating new industrial processes. The point was to demonstrate how science could promote progress and alleviate human misery. Diderot turned the same methods to politics and the social order, including articles on economics, taxes, and the slave trade. Censorship made it difficult to write openly antireligious articles. Diderot thumbed his nose at religion in oblique ways; at the entry on the Eucharist, the reader found a terse cross-reference: "See *cannibalism.*" At one point, the French government revoked the publishing permit for the *Encyclopedia,* declaring in 1759 that the encyclopedists were trying to "propagate materialism" (by which they meant atheism), "to destroy Religion, to inspire a spirit of independence, and to nourish the corruption of morals." The volumes sold remarkably well despite such bans and their hefty price. Purchasers belonged to the elite: aristocrats, government officials, prosperous merchants, and a scattering of members of the higher clergy. That elite stretched across Europe, including its overseas colonies.

Although the French philosophes sparred with the state and the church, they sought political stability and reform. Montesquieu hoped that an enlightened aristocracy would press for reforms and defend liberty against a despotic king. Voltaire, persuaded that aristocrats would represent only their particular narrow interests, looked to an enlightened monarch for leadership. Neither was a democrat, and neither conceived of reform from below. Still, their widely read critiques of arbitrary power stung. By the 1760s, the French critique of despotism provided the language in which many people across Europe articulated their opposition to existing regimes.

MAJOR THEMES OF ENLIGHTENMENT THOUGHT

Enlightenment thinkers across Europe raised similar themes: humanitarianism, or the dignity and worth of all individuals; religious toleration; and liberty. These ideals inspired important debates about three issues in particular: law and punishment, the place of religious minorities, and the state's relationship to society and the economy.

Law and Punishment

Enlightenment beliefs about education and the perfectibility of human society led many thinkers to question the harsh treatment of criminals by European courts. An influential work by the Italian jurist Cesare Beccaria (1738–1794), *On Crimes and Punishments* (1764), provided Voltaire with most of his arguments in the Calas case. Beccaria criticized the use of arbitrary power and attacked the prevalent view that punishments should represent society's vengeance on the criminal. Instead, he insisted, the only legitimate rationale for punishment was to maintain social order and to prevent other crimes. Beccaria argued that respect for individual dignity dictated that humans should punish other humans no more than is absolutely necessary.

Above all, Beccaria's book eloquently opposed torture and the death penalty. Public execution, he argued, was

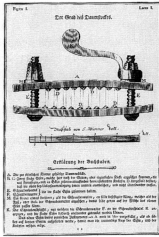

INSTRUMENTS OF TORTURE. A man being stretched on the rack (left), and a thumbscrew (right), both from an official Austrian government handbook. By 1800, Beccaria's influence had helped phase out the use of such instruments.

intended to dramatize the power of the state and the horrors of hell, but it dehumanized the victim, judge, and spectators. In 1766, a few years after the Calas case, another French trial provided an example of what horrified Beccaria and the philosophes. A nineteen-year-old French nobleman, convicted of blasphemy, had his tongue cut out and his hand cut off before he was burned at the stake. The court discovered the blasphemer had read Voltaire, and it ordered his *Philosophical Dictionary* burned along with the body. Sensational cases such as this helped publicize Beccaria's work. *On Crimes and Punishments* was quickly translated into a dozen languages. Owing primarily to its influence, most European countries by around 1800 abolished torture, branding, whipping, and mutilation, and reserved the death penalty for capital crimes.

Humanitarianism and Religious Toleration

Humanitarianism and reason also counseled religious toleration. Enlightenment thinkers spoke almost as one on the need to end religious warfare and the persecution of heretics and religious minorities. Most Enlightenment authors distinguished between religious belief, which they accepted, and the Church as an institution and as dogma, which they rebelled against. It was in this sense that Voltaire opposed the Church's influence over society. Few Enlightenment authors were atheists—a notable exception was Paul-Henri d'Holbach (1723–1789)—and only a few more were agnostics. Many, including Voltaire, were deists, believing in a God that acted as a "divine watchmaker" who at the beginning of time constructed a perfect universe and left it to run with predictable regularity. Enlightenment inquiry proved compatible with very different stances on religion.

Nevertheless, Enlightenment support for toleration was sometimes limited. Most Christians of the era saw Jews as heretics and Christ killers. Although Enlightenment thinkers deplored persecution, they commonly viewed Judaism and Islam as backward, superstitious religions. One of the few Enlightenment figures to treat Jews sympathetically was the German philosophe Gotthold Lessing (1729–1781). Lessing's play *Nathan the Wise* (1779) takes place in Jerusalem during the Fourth Crusade and begins with a pogrom—a violent, orchestrated attack—in which the wife and children of Nathan, a Jewish merchant, are murdered. Nathan survives to become a sympathetic and wise father figure. He adopts a Christian-born daughter

and raises her with three religions: Christianity, Islam, and Judaism. At several points, authorities ask him to choose the single true religion. Nathan shows none exists. The three great monotheistic religions are three versions of the truth. Religion is authentic, or true, only insofar as it makes the believer virtuous.

Lessing modeled his hero on his friend Moses Mendelssohn (1729–1786), a self-educated rabbi and bookkeeper (and the grandfather of the composer Felix Mendelssohn). Moses Mendelssohn moved—though with some difficulty—between the Enlightenment circles of Frederick II and the Jewish community of Berlin. Repeatedly attacked and pressured to convert to Christianity, he defended Jewish communities against anti-Semitic policies and Judaism against Enlightenment criticism. At the same time, he also promoted reform within the Jewish community, arguing that his community had special reason to embrace the broad Enlightenment project: religious faith should be voluntary, states should promote tolerance, humanitarianism would bring progress to all.

Government, Administration, and the Economy

Enlightenment ideas had a very real influence over affairs of state. The philosophes defended reason and knowledge for humanitarian reasons. But they also promised to make nations stronger, more efficient, and more prosperous. Beccaria's proposed legal reforms were a good case in point; he sought to make laws not simply more just but also more effective. In other words, the Enlightenment spoke to individuals but also to states. The philosophes addressed issues of liberty and rights but also took up matters of administration, tax collection, and economic policy.

The rising fiscal demands of eighteenth-century states and empires made these issues newly urgent. Which economic resources were most valuable to states? In the seventeenth century, mercantilists had argued that regulation of trade was necessary to maximize government revenues (see Chapter 15). In the eighteenth century, Enlightenment economic thinkers known as the physiocrats argued that real wealth came from the land and agricultural production, which prospered with less government interference. They advocated simplifying the tax system and following a policy of laissez-faire, which comes from the French expression *laissez faire la nature* ("let nature take its course"), letting wealth and goods circulate without government interference.

The classic expression of laissez-faire economics, however, came from the Scottish economist Adam Smith

LESSING AND MENDELSSOHN. This painting of a meeting between the philosophe Gotthold Lessing (standing) and his friend Moses Mendelssohn (seated right) emphasizes the personal nature of their intellectual relationship, which transcended their religious backgrounds (Christian and Jewish, respectively). The Enlightenment's atmosphere of earnest discussion is invoked both by the open book before them and the shelf of reading material behind Lessing. Compare this image of masculine discussion (note the role of the one woman in the painting) with the image of the aristocratic salon on page 467 and the coffeehouse on page 468. ■ *What similarities and differences might one point to in these various illustrations of the Enlightenment public sphere?*

(1723–1790) and his landmark treatise, *An Inquiry into the Nature and Causes of the Wealth of Nations* (1776). Smith disagreed with the physiocrats on the value of agriculture, but he shared their opposition to mercantilism. For Smith, the central issues were the productivity of labor and how labor was used in different sectors of the economy. Mercantile restrictions—such as high taxes on imported goods, one of the grievances of the colonists throughout Europe's American empires—did not encourage the productive deployment of labor and thus did not create real economic health. For Smith, general prosperity would only result by allowing individuals to pursue their own interests by buying and selling goods and labor freely on the open market. Producers who charged too much for their goods, or laborers who demanded more than their neighbor in wages, would be driven by the force of competition to either lower their prices or face ruin and unemployment. Competition, in his formulation, was the "invisible hand" that made markets efficient.

The Wealth of Nations spelled out, in more technical and historical detail, the different stages of economic development, how the invisible hand actually worked, and the beneficial aspects of competition. Its perspective owed much to Newton and to the Enlightenment's idealization of both nature and human nature. Smith thought of himself as the champion of liberty against state-sponsored economic privilege and monopolies. And he became the most influential of the new eighteenth-century economic thinkers. In the following century, his work and his followers became the target of reformers and critics who had less faith in the power of markets to generate wealth and prosperity for all.

EMPIRE AND ENLIGHTENMENT

The colonial world loomed large in Enlightenment thinking. Many Enlightenment thinkers saw the Americas as an uncorrupted territory where humanity's natural simplicity was expressed in the lives of native peoples. In comparison, Europe and Europeans appeared decadent or corrupt. European colonial activities—especially the slave trade—raised pressing issues about humanitarianism, individual rights, and natural law. The effects of colonialism on Europe were a central Enlightenment theme.

Smith wrote in *The Wealth of Nations* that the "discovery of America, and that of a passage to the East Indies by the Cape of Good Hope are the two greatest and most important events recorded in the history of mankind." At roughly the same moment, a French writer, the abbé Guillaume Thomas François Raynal published the massive *Philosophical and Political History of European Settlements and Trade in the Two Indies* (1770). This work, a coauthored collection like the *Encyclopedia*, was one of the most widely read works of the Enlightenment, going through twenty printings and at least forty pirated editions. Raynal drew his inspiration from the *Encyclopedia* and aimed at nothing less than a total history of colonization: customs and civilizations of indigenous peoples, natural history, exploration, and commerce in the Atlantic world and India.

Raynal asked whether colonization had made humanity happier, more peaceful, or better. The question was fully in the spirit of the Enlightenment. So was the answer: Raynal believed that industry and trade brought improvement and progress. Like other Enlightenment writers, however, he and his coauthors considered natural simplicity an antidote to the corruptions of civilized culture. They sought out and idealized what they considered examples of "natural" humanity, many of them in the New World. What Europeans considered savage life might be "a hundred times preferable to that of societies corrupted by despotism," and they lamented the loss of humanity's "natural liberty." They condemned the tactics of the Spanish in Mexico and Peru, of the Portuguese in Brazil, and of the British in North America. In the New World, they argued, Europeans found themselves with virtually unlimited power, which encouraged them to be arrogant, cruel, and despotic. In a later edition, after the outbreak of the American Revolution, the book went even further, drawing parallels between exploitation in the colonial world and inequality at home: "We are mad in the way we act with our colonies, and inhuman and mad in our conduct toward our peasants," asserted one author.

Such critiques did little, however, to check the growing importance of colonial commerce in the eighteenth century. The wealth generated by colonial trade tied the interests of governments and transoceanic merchants in an increasingly tight embrace. As this colonial trade grew in importance, no issue challenged Enlightenment thinkers as much as the institution of slavery.

Slavery and the Atlantic World

The Atlantic slave trade (see Chapter 14) reached its peak in the eighteenth century. European slave traders sent at least 1 million Africans into New World slavery in the late seventeenth century, and at least 6 million in the eighteenth century. Control of the slave trade became fundamental to great-power politics in Europe during this period, as the British used their dominance of the trade to their advantage in their long-running competition with France.

Analyzing Primary Sources

Slavery and the Enlightenment

The encyclopedists made an exhaustive and deliberate effort to comment on every institution, trade, and custom in Western culture. The project was conceived as an effort to catalog, analyze, and improve each facet of society. Writing in an age of burgeoning maritime trade and expanding overseas empires, they could not, and did not wish to, avoid the subject of slavery. These were their thoughts on plantation slavery, the African slaves who bore its brunt, and broader questions of law and liberty posed by the whole system.

 hus there is not a single one of these hapless souls—who, we maintain, are but slaves—who does not have the right to be declared free, since he has never lost his freedom; since it was impossible for him to lose it; and since neither his ruler nor his father nor anyone else had the right to dispose of his freedom; consequently, the sale of his person is null and void in and of itself: this Negro does not divest himself, indeed cannot under any condition divest himself of his natural rights; he carries them everywhere with him, and he has the right to demand that others allow him to enjoy those rights. Therefore, it is a clear case of inhumanity on the part of the judges in those free countries to which the slave is shipped, not to free the slave instantly by legal declaration, since he is their brother, having a soul like theirs.

Source: From *Encyclopédie*, vol. 16 (1765), as cited in David Brion Davis, *The Problem of Slavery in Western Culture* (Ithaca, NY: 1966), p.416.

Questions for Analysis

1. What arguments against slavery does this *Encyclopedia* article present? What "natural rights" were violated by the practice, according to this view?

2. Historically, the enslavement of conquered peoples was an ancient and well-established custom, approved by civil and religious authorities. Even some Enlightenment figures, such as Thomas Jefferson, were slave owners. How did some Enlightenment philosophes use universal ideas of freedom to argue against custom in regard to slavery and other questions?

Enlightenment thinking began with the premise that individuals could reason for and govern themselves. Individual moral freedom lay at the heart of what the Enlightenment considered to be a just, stable, and harmonious society. Slavery defied natural law and natural freedom. Montesquieu, for instance, wrote that civil law created chains, but natural law would always break them. Nearly all Enlightenment thinkers condemned slavery in the metaphorical sense. That the "mind should break free of its chains" and that "despotism enslaved the king's subjects" were phrases that echoed through much eighteenth-century writing.

Enlightenment thinkers dealt more gingerly, however, with the actual enslavement and slave labor of Africans. Smith condemned slavery as uneconomical. Voltaire, quick to expose his contemporaries' hypocrisy, wondered whether Europeans would look away if Europeans—rather than Africans—were enslaved. Voltaire, however, did not question his belief that Africans were inferior peoples. Montesquieu (who came from Bordeaux, one of the central ports for the Atlantic trade) believed that slavery debased master and slave alike. But he also argued that all societies balanced their systems of labor in accordance with their different needs, and slave labor was one such system. Finally, like many Enlightenment thinkers, Montesquieu defended property rights, including those of slaveholders.

The *Encyclopedia*'s article on the slave trade did condemn the slave trade in the clearest possible terms as a violation of self-government. Humanitarian antislavery movements, which emerged in the 1760s, advanced similar arguments. From deploring slavery to imagining freedom for slaves, however, proved a very long step, and one that few were willing to take. In the end, the Enlightenment's environmental determinism—the belief that environment shaped character—provided a

The Europeans Encounter the Peoples of the Pacific in the Eighteenth Century

When European explorers set out to map the Pacific, they brought with them artists to paint the landscapes and peoples they encountered. Later, other artists produced engravings of the original paintings and these engravings were made available to a wider public. In this way, even people of modest means or only limited literacy could learn something about the different cultures and peoples now in more regular contact with European commerce elsewhere in the world.

These artists documented what they saw, but their vision was also shaped by the ideas that they brought with them and by the classical European styles of portraiture and landscape painting that they had been trained to produce. On the one hand, their images sometimes emphasized the exotic or essentially different quality of life in the Pacific. At the same time, the use of conventional poses in the portraiture or in the depiction of human forms suggested hints of a developing understanding of the extent to which Europeans and people elsewhere in the world shared essential

A. *Portrait of Omai* by Joshua Reynolds (c. 1774).

B. "Omiah [*sic*] the Indian from Otaheite, presented to their Majesties at Kew," 1774.

common means of postponing the entire issue. Slavery corrupted its victims, destroyed their natural virtue, and crushed their natural love of liberty. Enslaved people, by this logic, were not ready for freedom. This belief explains why Warville de Brissot's Society of the Friends of Blacks could both call for abolition of the slave trade and invite Thomas Jefferson, a slaveholder, to join the organization. In fact, only a very few advocated abolishing slavery, and they insisted that emancipation be gradual. The debate about slavery demonstrated that different currents in Enlightenment thought could lead to very different conclusions.

Exploration and the Pacific World

The Pacific world also figured prominently in Enlightenment thinking. Systematically mapping new sections of the Pacific was among the crucial developments of the age and had tremendous impact on the public imagination. These explorations were also scientific missions, sponsored as part of the Enlightenment project of expanding scientific knowledge. In 1767, the French government sent Louis-Antoine de Bougainville (1729–1811) to the South Pacific in search of a new route to China, new lands suitable for colonization, and new spices for the ever-lucrative trade.

C. *View of the Inside of a House in the Island of Ulietea, with the Representation of a Dance to the Music of the Country*, engraving after Sydney Parkinson, 1773.

voyage to the Pacific in 1768 (image C). The two artists had never visited the South Pacific, and their image is noteworthy for the way that the bodies of the islanders were rendered according to the classical styles of European art.

Questions for Analysis

1. Does the Reynolds portrait, in its choice of posture and expression, imply that Europeans and the peoples of the Pacific might share essential traits? What uses might Enlightenment thinkers have made of such a universalist implication?

2. How might a contemporary person in Britain have reacted to the portrait of Omai kneeling before the king?

3. Do you think image C is an accurate representation of life in the South Pacific? What purpose did such imaginary and idyllic scenes serve for their audience in Europe?

human characteristics. This ambiguity was typical of Enlightenment political and social thought, which sought to uncover universal human truths, while at the same time remaining deeply interested and invested in exploring the differences they observed in peoples from various parts of the globe.

The first two images depict a Tahitian named Omai, who came to Britain as a crew member on a naval vessel in July 1774. Taken three days later to meet King George III and Queen Charlotte at Kew (image B), he became a celebrity in England and had his portrait drawn by Joshua Reynolds, a famous painter of the period (image A). The third image is an engraving by two Florentine artists after a drawing by Sydney Parkinson, who was with James Cook on his first

Bougainville found none of what he sought, but his travel accounts—above all his fabulously lush descriptions of the earthly paradise of Tahiti—captured the imaginations of many at home. The British captain James Cook (1728–1779), who followed Bougainville, made two trips into the South Pacific (1768–1771 and 1772–1775), with impressive results. He charted the coasts of New Zealand and New Holland and added the New Hebrides and Hawaii to European maps. He explored the outer limits of the Antarctic continent, the shores of the Bering Sea, and the Arctic Ocean. A misguided attempt to communicate with Polynesian islanders, perhaps with the intention of conveying them to Europe, ended in the grisly deaths of Cook and four royal marines on Hawaii in late January 1779. Large numbers of people in Europe avidly read travel accounts of these voyages.

The Impact of the Scientific Missions

Back in Europe, Enlightenment thinkers drew freely on reports of scientific missions. Since they were already committed to understanding human nature and the origins of society and to studying the effects of the environment on character and culture, stories of new peoples and cultures were immediately fascinating. In 1772, Diderot, one of many eager readers of Bougainville's accounts, published his own reflections on the cultural significance of those accounts, the *Supplément au Voyage de Bougainville*. For Diderot, the Tahitians were the original human beings and, unlike the inhabitants of the New World, were virtually free of European influence. They represented humanity in its natural state, Diderot believed, uninhibited about sexuality and free of religious dogma. Their simplicity exposed the hypocrisy and rigidity of overcivilized Europeans.

Such views said more about Europe and European utopias than about indigenous cultures in the Pacific. Enlightenment thinkers found it impossible to see other peoples as anything other than primitive versions of Europeans. Even these views, however, marked a change from former times. In earlier periods, Europeans had understood the world as divided between Christendom and heathen others. Now all peoples were seen to be part of a shared humanity, with cultures and beliefs that reflected their own experiences. In sum, during the eighteenth century a religious understanding of Western identity was giving way to more secular and historical explanations of human diversity.

One of the most important scientific explorers of the period was the German scientist Alexander von Humboldt (1769–1859). Humboldt spent five years in Spanish America, aiming to do nothing less than assess the civilization and natural resources of the entire continent. He went equipped with the most advanced scientific instruments Europe could provide. Humboldt, in good Enlightenment fashion, attempted to demonstrate that climate and physical environment determined which forms of life would survive in any given region. These investigations inspired nineteenth-century discussions of evolutionary change. Charles Darwin referred to Humboldt as "the greatest scientific traveler who ever lived," and the German scientist's writing would inspire Darwin's voyage to the Galápagos Islands off the coast of Ecuador.

For some Enlightenment thinkers and rulers, scientific reports from overseas fit into a broad inquiry about civilization and human nature. That inquiry at times encouraged self-criticism and at others simply shored up Europeans' sense of their superiority. These themes reemerged during the nineteenth century, when new empires were built and the West's place in the world was reassessed.

The Radical Enlightenment

How revolutionary was the Enlightenment? Enlightenment thought did undermine central tenets of eighteenth-century culture and politics. Nevertheless, even the most radical eighteenth-century thinkers disagreed on the implications of their thought. Jean-Jacques Rousseau and Mary Wollstonecraft provide good examples both of the radical nature of the Enlightenment, and of its central disagreements.

The World of Rousseau

Jean-Jacques Rousseau (*roo-SOH,* 1712–1778) was an "outsider" who quarreled with the other philosophes. He shared their search for intellectual and political freedom, yet he introduced other strains into Enlightenment thought, especially what was then called "sensibility," or the cult of feeling. Rousseau's interest in emotions led him to develop a more complicated portrait of human psychology than that of most Enlightenment writers, who emphasized reason as the most important human attribute. He was also considerably more radical than his counterparts, one of the first to talk about popular sovereignty and democracy.

Rousseau's milestone treatise on politics, *The Social Contract*, began with a now famous paradox: "Man was born free, and everywhere he is in chains." How had humans freely forged these chains? What were the origins of government? Was government's authority legitimate? If not, Rousseau asked, how could it become so?

Rousseau argued that in the state of nature all men had been equal. (On women, men, and nature, see **Competing Viewpoints** on pages 464.) Social inequality, anchored in private property, profoundly corrupted "the social contract," or the formation of government. Under conditions of inequality, governments and laws represented only the rich and privileged. They became instruments of repression and enslavement. Nevertheless, legitimate governments could be formed, Rousseau argued. "The problem is to find a form of association . . . in which each, while uniting himself with all, may still obey himself alone, and remain as free as before." Freedom did not mean the absence of restraint; it meant that equal citizens obeyed laws they had made themselves. Rousseau hardly imagined any social leveling, and by *equality* he meant only that no one would be "rich enough to buy another, nor poor enough to have to sell oneself."

Rousseau's argument about legitimate authority has three parts. First, sovereignty belonged to the people alone. This meant sovereignty should not be divided among different branches of government (as suggested by Montesquieu), and it could not be usurped by a king. Second, exercising sovereignty transformed the nation. Rousseau argued that when individual citizens formed a "body politic," that body became more than just the sum of its parts. He offered what

Analyzing Primary Sources

Rousseau's Social Contract (1762)

Jean-Jacques Rousseau (1712–1778) was one of the most radical Enlightenment thinkers. In his works, he suggested that humans needed not only a clearer understanding of natural laws but also a much closer relationship with nature itself and a thorough reorganization of society. He believed that a sovereign society, formed by free association of equal citizens without patrons or factions, was the clearest expression of natural law. This society would make laws and order itself by the genuinely collective wisdom of its citizens. Rousseau sets out the definition of his sovereign society and its authority in the passages reprinted here.

Book I, Chapter 6

"To find a form of association that defends and protects the person and possessions of each associate with all the common strength, and by means of which each person, joining forces with all, nevertheless obeys only himself, and remains as free as before." Such is the fundamental problem to which the social contract furnishes the solution.

Book II, Chapter 4

What in fact is an act of sovereignty? It is not an agreement between a superior and an inferior, but an agreement between the body and each of its members, a legitimate agreement, because it is based upon the social contract; equitable, because it is common to all; useful, because it can have no other purpose than the general good; and reliable, because it is guaranteed by the public force and the supreme power. As long as the subjects are only bound by agreements of this sort, they obey no one but their own will, and to ask how far the respective rights of the sovereign and citizens extend is to ask to what point the latter can commit themselves to each other, one towards all and all towards one.

Source: Jean-Jacques Rousseau, *Rousseau's Political Writings*, trans. Julia Conaway Bondanella, ed. Allan Ritter and Julia Conaway Bondanella (New York: 1988), pp. 92–103.

Questions for Analysis

1. What was the goal of political association, according to Rousseau?

2. How did Rousseau claim to overcome the tension between the need for some form of social constraint and the desire to preserve liberty?

3. What is more important for Rousseau: equality or liberty?

was to many an appealing image of a regenerated and more powerful nation, in which citizens were bound by mutual obligation rather than coercive laws and united in equality rather than divided and weakened by privilege. Third, the national community would be united by what Rousseau called the "general will." This term is notoriously difficult. Rousseau proposed it as a way to understand the common interest, which rose above particular individual demands. The general will favored equality; that made it general, and in principle at least equality guaranteed that citizens' common interests would be represented in the whole. These radical arguments were widely cited during the French Revolution.

Rousseau was also well known for his writing on education and moral virtue. His widely read novel *Emile* (1762) tells the story of a young man who learns virtue and moral autonomy in the school of nature rather than in the academy. Rousseau disagreed with other philosophes' emphasis on reason, insisting instead that "the first impulses of nature are always right." Children should not be forced to reason early

in life. Books, which "teach us only to talk about things we do not know," should not be central to learning until adolescence. Emile's tutor thus walked him through the woods, studying nature and its simple precepts, cultivating his conscience, and above all, his sense of independence.

Such an education aimed to give men moral autonomy and make them good citizens. Rousseau argued that women should have very different educations. "All education of women must be relative to men, pleasing them, being useful to them, raising them when they are young and caring for them when they are old, advising them, consoling them, making their lives pleasant and agreeable; these have been the duties of women since time began." Women were to be useful socially as mothers and wives. In *Emile*, Rousseau laid out just such an education for Emile's wife-to-be, Sophie. At times, Rousseau seemed convinced that women "naturally" sought out such a role: "Dependence is a natural state for women, girls feel themselves made to obey." At other moments he insisted that girls needed to be disciplined and weaned from their "natural" vices.

Competing Viewpoints

Rousseau and His Readers

Jean-Jacques Rousseau's writings provoked very different responses from eighteenth-century readers—women as well as men. Many women readers loved his fiction and found his views about women's character and prescriptions for their education inspiring. Other women disagreed vehemently with his conclusions. In the first excerpt here, from Rousseau's novel Emile *(1762), the author sets out his views on a woman's education. He argues that her education should fit with what he considers her intellectual capacity and her social role. It should also complement the education and role of a man. The second selection is an admiring response to* Emile *from Anne-Louise-Germaine Necker, or Madame de Staël (1766–1817), a well-known French writer and literary critic. While she acknowledged that Rousseau sought to keep women from participating in political discussion, she also thought that he had granted women a new role in matters of emotion and domesticity. The third excerpt is from Mary Wollstonecraft, who shared many of Rousseau's philosophical principles but sharply disagreed with his assertion that women and men should have different virtues and values. She believed that women like Madame de Staël were misguided in embracing Rousseau's ideas.*

Rousseau's *Emile*

Researches into abstract and speculative truths, the principles and axioms of sciences—in short, everything which tends to generalize our ideas—is not the proper province of women; their studies should be relative to points of practice; it belongs to them to apply those principles which men have discovered. . . . All the ideas of women, which have not the immediate tendency to points of duty, should be directed to the study of men, and to the attainment of those agreeable accomplishments which have taste for their object; for as to works of genius, they are beyond their capacity; neither have they sufficient precision or power of attention to succeed in sciences which require accuracy; and as to physical knowledge, it belongs to those only who are most active, most inquisitive, who comprehend the greatest variety of objects. . . .

She must have the skill to incline us to do everything which her sex will not enable her to do herself, and which is necessary or agreeable to her; therefore she ought to study the mind of man thoroughly, not the mind of man in general, abstractedly, but the dispositions of those men to whom she is subject either by the laws of her country or by the force of opinion. She should learn to penetrate into the real sentiments from their conversation, their actions, their looks and gestures. She should also have the art, by her own conversation, actions, looks, and gestures, to communicate those sentiments which are agreeable to them without seeming to intend it. Men will argue more philosophically about the human heart; but women will read the heart of men better than they. . . . Women have most wit, men have most genius; women observe, men reason. From the concurrence of both we derive the clearest light and the most perfect knowledge which the human mind is of itself capable of attaining.

Source: Jean-Jacques Rousseau, *Emile* (1762), as cited in Mary Wollstonecraft, *A Vindication of the Rights of Woman* (New York: 1992), pp. 124–25.

Rousseau's conflicting views on female nature provide a good example of the shifting meaning of *nature*, a central preoccupation of Enlightenment thought. Enlightenment thinkers used nature as a yardstick against which to measure society's shortcomings. "Natural" was better, simpler, uncorrupted. What, though, was *nature*? It could refer to the physical world. It could refer to allegedly primitive societies. Often, it was a useful invention.

The World of Wollstonecraft

Rousseau's sharpest critic was the British writer Mary Wollstonecraft (1759–1797). Wollstonecraft published her best-known work, *A Vindication of the Rights of Woman*, in 1792, during the French Revolution. Her argument, however, was anchored in Enlightenment debates and needs to be understood here. Wollstonecraft was a republican

Madame de Staël

Though Rousseau has endeavoured to prevent women from interfering in public affairs, and acting a brilliant part in the theatre of politics; yet in speaking of them, how much has he done it to their satisfaction! If he wished to deprive them of some rights foreign to their sex, how has he for ever restored to them all those to which it has a claim! And in attempting to diminish their influence over the deliberations of men, how sacredly has he established the empire they have over their happiness! In aiding them to descend from an usurped throne, he has firmly seated them upon that to which they were destined by nature; and though he be full of indignation against them when they endeavour to resemble men, yet when they come before him with all the *charms*, *weaknesses*, *virtues*, and *errors* of their sex, his respect for their *persons* amounts almost to adoration.

Source: Cited in Mary Wollstonecraft, *A Vindication of the Rights of Woman* (New York: 1992), pp. 203–4.

Mary Wollstonecraft

Rousseau declares that a woman should never, for a moment, feel herself independent, that she should be governed by fear to exercise her *natural* cunning, and made a coquettish slave in order to render her a more alluring object of desire, a *sweeter* companion to man, whenever he chooses to relax himself. He carries the arguments, which he pretends to draw from the indications of nature, still further, and insinuates that truth and fortitude, the corner stones of all human virtue, should be cultivated with certain restrictions, because, with respect to the female character, obedience is the grand lesson which ought to be impressed with unrelenting rigour.

What nonsense! When will a great man arise with sufficient strength of mind to puff away the fumes which pride and sensuality have thus spread over the subject! If women are by nature inferior to men, their virtues must be the same in quality, if not in degree, or virtue is a relative idea; consequently, their conduct should be founded on the same principles, and have the same aim.

Source: Cited in Susan Bell and Karen Offen, eds., *Women, the Family, and Freedom: The Debate in Documents*, vol. 1, 1750–1880 (Stanford, CA: 1983), p. 58.

Questions for Analysis

1. Why did Rousseau seek to limit the sphere of activities open to women in society? What capacities did he feel they lacked? What areas of social life did he feel women were most suited for?

2. Did Madame de Staël agree with Rousseau that women's social roles were essentially different from men's roles in society?

3. What is the basis for Mary Wollstonecraft's disagreement with Rousseau?

4. Why did gender matter to Enlightenment figures such as Rousseau, de Staël, and Wollstonecraft?

who admired many of Rousseau's writings. She called monarchy "the pestiferous purple which renders the progress of civilization a curse, and warps the understanding." She spoke even more forcefully than Rousseau against inequality and the artificial distinctions of rank, birth, or wealth. Believing that equality laid the basis for virtue, she contended, in classic Enlightenment language, that the society should seek "the perfection of our nature and capability of happiness." She argued more forcefully than any other Enlightenment thinker that (1) women had the same innate capacity for reason and self-government as men, (2) *virtue* should mean the same thing for men and women, and (3) relations between the sexes should be based on equality.

Wollstonecraft did what few of her contemporaries even imagined. She applied the radical Enlightenment critique of

MARY WOLLSTONECRAFT. The British writer and radical suggested that Enlightenment critiques of monarchy could also be applied to the power of fathers within the family.

monarchy and inequality to the family. The legal inequalities of marriage law, which among other things deprived married women of property rights, gave husbands "despotic" power over their wives. Just as kings cultivated their subjects' deference, so culture, she argued, cultivated women's weakness. "Civilized women are . . . so weakened by false refinement, that, respecting morals, their condition is much below what it would be were they left in a state nearer to nature." Middle-class girls learned manners, grace, and seductiveness to win a husband; they were trained to be dependent creatures. "My own sex, I hope, will excuse me, if I treat them like rational creatures instead of flattering their *fascinating* graces, and viewing them as if they were in a state of perpetual childhood, unable to stand alone. I earnestly wish to point out in what true dignity and human happiness consists—I wish to persuade women to endeavor to acquire strength, both of mind and body." In contrast to Rousseau's prescriptions for female education, Wollstonecraft argued that education for women should promote liberty and self-reliance. She was considered scandalously radical for merely hinting that women might have political rights.

The Enlightenment as a whole left a mixed legacy on gender, one that closely paralleled that on slavery. Enlightenment writers developed and popularized arguments about natural rights. They also elevated natural differences to a higher plane by suggesting that nature should dictate different, and quite possibly unequal, social roles for Africans or women. Mary Wollstonecraft and Jean-Jacques

Rousseau shared a radical opposition to despotism and slavery, a moralist's vision of a corrupt society, and a concern with virtue and community. Their divergence on gender is characteristic of Enlightenment disagreements about nature and is a good example of the way that Enlightenment thinking could lead to different conclusions.

THE ENLIGHTENMENT AND EIGHTEENTH-CENTURY CULTURE

The Book Trade

What about the social structures that produced these debates and received these ideas? To begin with, the Enlightenment was bound up in a much larger expansion of printing and print culture. From the early eighteenth century on, book publishing and selling flourished, especially in Britain, France, the Netherlands, and Switzerland. Much of the book trade was both international and clandestine. Readers bought books from stores, by subscription, and by special mail order from book distributors abroad. Cheaper printing and better distribution also helped multiply the numbers of journals, and made daily newspapers, which first appeared in London in 1702, possible for the first time. These changes have been called a "revolution in communication," and they form a crucial part of the larger picture of the Enlightenment.

Governments did little to check this revolutionary transformation. In Britain, the press encountered few restrictions, although the government did use a stamp tax on printed goods to raise the price of newspapers or books and thereby discourage buyers. Elsewhere, laws required publishers to apply in advance for the license or privilege (in the sense of "private right") to print and sell any given work. In practice, publishers frequently printed books without advance permission, hoping that the regime would not notice. Russian, Prussian, and Austrian censors tolerated much less dissent, but those governments also sought to stimulate publishing and, to a certain degree, permitted public discussion. That governments were patrons as well as censors of new scholarship illustrates the complex relationship between the age of absolutism and the Enlightenment.

As one historian puts it, censorship only made banned books expensive, keeping them out of the hands of the poor. Clandestine booksellers, most near the French border in Switzerland and the Rhineland, smuggled thousands of books across the border to bookstores, distributors, and private customers. What did readers want, and what does this tell us about the reception of the Enlightenment? Many clandestine dealers specialized in what they called "philosophical books," which meant subversive literature of all kinds: stories of languishing in prison, gossipy memoirs of life at the court, pornographic fantasies (often about religious and political figures), and tales of crime and criminals. Much of this flourishing eighteenth-century "literary underground" echoed the radical Enlightenment's themes, especially the corruption of the aristocracy and the monarchy's degeneration into despotism.

High Culture, New Elites, and the Public Sphere

The Enlightenment was not simply embodied in books; it was produced in networks of readers and new forms of sociability and discussion. These networks included people of diverse backgrounds. Eighteenth-century elite, or "high," culture was small in scale but cosmopolitan and very literate, and it took literary and scientific discussion seriously. Middleclass men and women also became consumers of literature. Meanwhile, popular discussions of Enlightenment themes developed in the coffeehouses and taverns of European cities, where printed material might be read aloud, allowing even illiterate people to have access to the news and debates of the day. Together, this permissive atmosphere of frequent discussion among people of different social position led to the development of a new idea: "public opinion."

Among the institutions that produced a new elite were learned societies such as the American Philosophical Society of Philadelphia, or the Select Society of Edinburgh. Such groups organized intellectual life outside of the universities, and they provided libraries and meeting places for discussion. Elites also met in "academies," financed by governments to advance knowledge, whether through research into the natural sciences (the Royal Society of London, and the French Academy of Science, both founded in 1660, and the Berlin Royal Academy in 1701), promoting the national language (the Académie Française, or French Academy of Literature), or safeguarding traditions in the arts (the various academies of painting). In smaller cities in the countryside, provincial academies played much the same role, providing a way for Enlightenment discussions to spread beyond European capitals.

Salons provided an alternative venue for discussion but operated informally. Usually they were organized by well-connected and learned aristocratic women who invited local personalities to their homes to meet with authors and discuss their latest works. The prominent role of women distinguished the salons from the academies and universities. Salons brought together men and women of letters with members of the aristocracy for conversation, debate, drink, and food. Rousseau loathed this kind of ritual and viewed salons as a sign of superficiality and vacuity in a privileged and overcivilized world. Thomas Jefferson thought the influence of women in salons had put France in a "desperate state." Madame Marie-Thérèse Geoffrin, a celebrated French *salonière*, nevertheless became an important patron of the *Encyclopedia* and exercised influence in placing scholars in academies. Salons in London, Vienna, Rome, and Berlin worked the same way, and, like academies, they promoted among their participants a sense of belonging to an active, learned elite.

Scores of similar societies emerged in the eighteenth century, eventually breaking the hold of elites over public debate and literate discussion. Masonic lodges, organizations with elaborate secret rituals whose members pledged themselves to the regeneration of society, attracted a remarkable array of aristocrats and middle-class men. The composer Wolfgang Amadeus Mozart, Emperor Frederick II, and Montesquieu were Masons. Behind their closed doors, the lodges were egalitarian. They pledged themselves to a common project of rational thought and benevolent action and to banishing religion and social distinction—at least from their ranks. Other networks

A READING IN THE SALON OF MADAME GEOFFRIN, 1755. Enlightenment salons encouraged a spirit of intellectual inquiry and civil debate, at least among educated elites. Such salon discussions were notable for the extent to which women helped organize and participate in the conversations. This fact led Rousseau to attack the salons for encouraging unseemly posturing and promiscuity between the sexes, which he believed were the antithesis of rational pursuits. In this painting, Madame Geoffrin, a famed hostess (at left in gray), presides over a discussion of a learned work. Note the bust of Voltaire in the background, the patron saint of rationalist discourse. ▪ *What developments were required for this notion of free public discussion among elites to become more general in society?* ▪ *Would Enlightenment thinkers favor such developments? (Compare with images on pages 457 and 468).*

of sociability were even less exclusive. Coffeehouses multiplied with the colonial trade in sugar, coffee, and tea, and they occupied a central spot in the circulation of ideas. A group of merchants gathering to discuss trade, for instance, could turn to politics; and the many newspapers lying about the cafe tables provided a ready-to-hand link between their smaller discussions and news and debates elsewhere.

Eighteenth-century cultural changes—the expanding networks of sociability, the flourishing book trade, the new genres of literature, and the circulation of Enlightenment ideas—widened the circles of reading and discussion, expanding what some historians and political theorists call the "public sphere." That, in turn, began to change politics. Informal deliberations, debates about how to regenerate the nation, discussions of civic virtue, and efforts to forge a consensus played a crucial role in moving politics beyond the confines of the court.

Middle-Class Culture and Reading

Enlightenment fare constituted only part of the new cultural interests of the eighteenth-century middle classes. Lower on the social scale, shopkeepers, small merchants, lawyers, and professionals read more and more different kinds of books. Instead of owning one well-thumbed Bible to read aloud, a middle-class family would buy and borrow books to read casually, pass along, and discuss. This literature consisted of science, history, biography, travel literature, and fiction. A great deal of it was aimed at middle-class women, among the fastest-growing groups of readers in the eighteenth century. Etiquette books sold very well; so did how-to manuals for the household. Scores of books about the manners, morals, and education of daughters, popular versions of Enlightenment treatises on education and the mind, illustrate close parallels between the intellectual life of the high Enlightenment and everyday middle-class reading matter.

The rise of a middle-class reading public, much of it female, helps account for the soaring popularity and production of novels, especially in Britain. Novels were the single most popular new form of literature in the eighteenth century. A survey of library borrowing in late-eighteenth-century Britain, Germany, and North America showed that 70 percent of books taken out were novels. For centuries, Europeans had read romances such as tales of the Knights of the Round Table. The setting of popular eighteenth-century novels was closer to home. The novel's more recognizable, nonaristocratic characters seemed more relevant to common middle-class experience. Moreover, examining emotion and inner feeling also linked novel writing with a larger eighteenth-century concern with personhood and humanity. Classic Enlightenment

A COFFEEHOUSE IN LONDON, 1798. Coffeehouses served as centers of social networks and hubs of opinion, contributing to a public consciousness that was new to the Enlightenment. This coffeehouse scene illustrates a mixing of classes, lively debate, and a burgeoning culture of reading. Compare this image with that of the aristocratic salon on page 467 and the meeting of Lessing and Mendelssohn on page 457. ▪ *How were coffeehouses different from aristocratic salons or the middle-class drawing-room discussion between the two German thinkers?* ▪ *Can they all be seen as expressions of a new kind of "public sphere" in eighteenth-century Europe?*

writers like Voltaire, Goethe, and Rousseau wrote very successful novels, and those should be understood alongside *Pamela* and *Clarissa* by Samuel Richardson (1689–1761), *Moll Flanders* and *Robinson Crusoe* by Daniel Defoe (1660–1731), and *Tom Jones* by Henry Fielding (1707–1754).

Many historians have noted that women figured prominently among fiction writers. The works of Jane Austen (1775–1817), especially *Pride and Prejudice* and *Emma* are to many readers the height of a novelist's craft. Women writers did not confine their attention to the domestic or private sphere. Best-selling authors such as Fanny Burney and later, Mary Shelley took up central eighteenth-century themes of human nature, morality, virtue, and reputation. Their novels, like much of the nonfiction of the period, explored those themes in both domestic and public settings.

Popular Culture: Urban and Rural

How much did books and print culture touch the lives of the common people? Literacy rates varied dramatically by gender, social class, and region, but were generally higher in northern than in southern and eastern Europe. It is not surprising

The Internet and the Enlightenment Public Sphere

In many ways, today's Internet is simply a technologically sophisticated version of the public sphere of literate readers that was created and celebrated by the philosophes of the Enlightenment. It contains the same confusing mix of the educational, the commercial, the pleasurable . . . and the perverse.

Watch related author videos on the student site
wwnorton.com/college/history/western-civilizationsBrief4

that literacy ran highest in cities and towns—higher, in fact, than we might expect. In early eighteenth-century Paris, 85 percent of men and 60 percent of women could read. Well over half the residents of poorer Parisian neighborhoods, especially small shopkeepers, domestic servants and valets, and artisans, could read and sign their names. Even the illiterate lived in a culture of print, and although they had few books on their own shelves, they saw one-page newspapers and broadsides or fly sheets posted on streets and tavern walls and regularly heard them read aloud. Moreover, visual material—inexpensive woodcuts, especially, but also prints, drawings, and satirical cartoons—figured as prominently as text in much popular reading material. By many measures, then, the circles of reading and discussion were even larger than literacy rates might suggest, especially in cities.

In neither England nor France was any primary schooling made compulsory, leaving education to haphazard local initiatives. In central Europe, some regimes made efforts to develop state-sponsored education. Catherine of Russia summoned an Austrian consultant to set up a system of primary schools, but by the end of the eighteenth century only 22,000 of a population of 40 million had attended any kind of school. In the absence of primary schooling, most Europeans were self-taught. The varied texts in the peddler's cart—whether religious, political propaganda, or entertainment—attest to a widespread and rapidly growing popular interest in books and reading.

Like its middle-class counterpart, popular culture rested on networks of sociability. Guild organizations offered discussion and companionship. Street theater and singers mocking local political figures offered culture to people from different social classes. The difficulties of deciphering popular culture are considerable. Most testimony comes to us from outsiders who regarded the common people as hopelessly superstitious and ignorant. Still, historical research has begun to reveal new insights. It has shown, first, that popular culture did not exist in isolation. Particularly in the countryside, market days and village festivals brought social classes together, and popular entertainments reached a wide social audience. Folktales and traditional songs resist pigeonholing as elite, middle-class, or popular culture, for they passed from one cultural world to another, being revised and reinterpreted in the process. Second, oral and literate culture overlapped. In other words, even people who could not read often had a great deal of "book knowledge": they argued seriously about points from books and believed that books conferred authority. A group of villagers, for instance, wrote this eulogy to a deceased friend: "He read his life long, and died without ever knowing how to read." The logic and worldview of popular culture needs to be understood on its own terms.

It remains true that the countryside, especially in less economically developed regions, was desperately poor. Life there was far more isolated than in towns. A yawning chasm separated peasants from the world of the high Enlightenment. The philosophes, well established in the summits of European society, looked at popular culture with mistrust and ignorance. They saw the common people of Europe much as they did indigenous peoples of other continents. They were humanitarians, critical thinkers, and reformers; they were not democrats. The Enlightenment, while well entrenched in eighteenth-century elite culture, nonetheless involved changes that reached well beyond elite society.

WAR AND POLITICS IN ENLIGHTENMENT EUROPE

War and Empire in the Eighteenth-Century World

After 1713, western Europe remained largely at peace for a generation. In 1740, however, that peace was shattered when Frederick the Great of Prussia seized the Austrian province of Silesia (to be discussed later). In the resulting War of the Austrian Succession, France and Spain fought on the side of Prussia, hoping to reverse some of the losses they had suffered in the Treaty of Utrecht. As they had done since the 1690s, Britain and the Dutch Republic sided with Austria. Like those earlier wars, this war quickly spread beyond the frontiers of Europe. In India, the British East India Company lost control over the coastal area of Madras to its French rival; but in North America, British colonists from New England captured the important French fortress of Louisbourg on Cape Breton Island, hoping to put a stop to French interference with their fishing

and shipping. When the war finally ended in 1748, Britain recovered Madras and returned Louisbourg to France.

Eight years later, these colonial conflicts reignited when Prussia once again attacked Austria. This time, however, Prussia allied itself with Great Britain. Austria found support from both France and Russia. In Europe, the Seven Years' War (1756–63) ended in stalemate. In India and North America, however, the war had decisive consequences. In India, mercenary troops employed by the British East India Company joined with native allies to eliminate their French competitors. In North America (where the conflict was known as the French and Indian War), British troops captured both Louisbourg and Québec and also drove French forces from the Ohio River Valley and the Great Lakes. By the Treaty of Paris in 1763, which brought the Seven Years' War to an end, France formally surrendered both Canada and its possessions in India to the British. Six years later, the French East India Company was dissolved.

Enlightened Absolutism in Eastern Europe

The rulers of Prussia, Austria, and Russia who initiated these wars on the continent were among the pioneers of a new style of "enlightened absolutism" within their realms. They demonstrated their commitment to absolutist rule by centralizing their administrations, increasing taxation, creating a professional army, and tightening their control of the Church. They justified this expansion of powers, however, in the name of the enlightenment ideal of reason—as rational solutions to the problems of government.

Rulers influenced by the spirit of enlightened absolutism included Empress Maria Theresa (r. 1740–80) of Austria and her son Joseph II (r. 1765–90; from 1765 until 1780 the two were co-rulers). The two rulers relaxed censorship, created statewide systems of primary education, and instituted a more liberal criminal code for the Habsburg Empire. Joseph II was particularly energetic in challenging the power of the Church: he closed hundreds of monasteries, drastically limited the number of monks and nuns permitted to live in contemplative orders, and ordered that the education of priests be placed under government supervision (see Chapter 15).

The most emblematic enlightened absolutist, however, was Frederick II (r. 1740–86) of Prussia. As a young man, Frederick devoted himself to the flute and admired French culture, exasperating his military-minded father, Frederick William I. When Frederick rebelled by running away from court with a friend, his father had them apprehended and the friend was executed before Frederick's eyes. The grisly

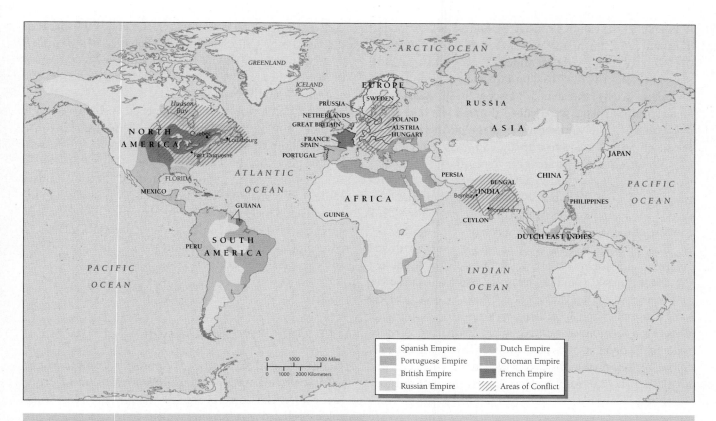

THE SEVEN YEARS' WAR, 1756–1763. ▪ *What continents were involved in the Seven Years' War?* ▪ *What was the impact of naval power on the outcome of the war?* ▪ *What were the consequences for the colonies involved in the conflict?*

lesson took. Although Frederick never gave up his love of music and literature, he applied himself energetically to his royal duties, earning himself the title of Frederick the Great.

Frederick raised Prussia to the status of a major power. In 1740, as soon as he became king, he mobilized his army and occupied the Austrian province of Silesia, with French support. Empress Maria Theresa, also new to the throne, counterattacked; but, despite the support of Britain and Hungary, she could not recover Silesia. Eventually Frederick consolidated his gains over all the Polish territories that lay between East Prussia and Brandenburg, transforming Prussia by 1786 into a powerful, contiguous kingdom. Frederick was careful to cultivate support from the Prussian nobility, known as the Junkers. His father had recruited civil servants according to merit rather than birth, but Frederick relied on the Junkers to staff the army and his expanding administration. Frederick's strategy worked. His nobility remained loyal, and he fashioned the most professional and efficient bureaucracy in Europe.

Frederick supervised a series of "enlightened" social reforms: he prohibited the judicial torture of accused criminals, abolished the bribing of judges, and established a system of elementary schools. Although strongly anti-Semitic,

he encouraged religious toleration toward Jews and declared that he would happily build a mosque in Berlin if he could find enough Muslims to fill it. On his own royal estates, he abolished capital punishment, curtailed the forced labor services of his peasantry, and granted these peasants long leases on the land they worked. He encouraged scientific forestry and the cultivation of new crops. He cleared new lands in Silesia and brought in thousands of immigrants to cultivate them. When wars ruined their farms, he supplied his peasants with new livestock and tools. But he never attempted to extend these reforms to the estates of the Prussian nobility. To have done so would have alienated the very group on whom Frederick's rule depended.

Like Frederick, Catherine the Great of Russia (r. 1762–96) thought of herself as an enlightened ruler and she corresponded with French philosophers. Also like Frederick, she could not afford to lose the support of the Russian nobility, who had placed her on the throne after executing her husband, the weak and possibly mad Peter III. Catherine's efforts at enlightened reform were limited: she founded hospitals and orphanages, created an elementary school system for the children of the provincial nobility, and called a commission to examine the possibility of codifying

Russian law. The commission's radical proposals—abolition of capital punishment and judicial torture, prohibitions on the selling of serfs—were set aside, however, after a massive peasant revolt in 1773–75 led by a Cossack named Emelyan Pugachev briefly threatened Moscow itself. Catherine's greatest achievements were gained through war and diplomacy. In 1774, she won control over the northern coast of the Black Sea after a war with the Ottoman Empire, and she also took several Ottoman provinces along the Danube River. Russia thus obtained a long-sought goal: a warm-water port for the Russian navy. In addition, Catherine succeeded in expanding Russian territory in the west, at the expense of the weaker kingdom of Poland.

The plan for Russia, Austria, and Prussia to divide Poland among them was originally proposed by Frederick the Great: Russia would abandon its Danubian provinces and receive in exchange the grain fields of eastern Poland (and between 1 and 2 million Poles); Austria would take Galicia (population 2.5 million); while Prussia would consolidate the divided lands of its kingdom by taking Poland's coastal regions on the Baltic coast. When the agreement was finalized in 1772, Poland had lost 30 percent of its territory and half of its population. After a second war between Russia and the Ottomans in 1788, Poland tried to reassert itself, but it was no match for the three major powers—Russia, Austria, and Prussia—and by 1795 Poland had disappeared from the map altogether.

As a political program, enlightened absolutism clearly had its limits. On the one hand, Catherine the Great, Frederick the Great, and Joseph II in Austria were personally inspired by the literary culture of the philosophes, and their political programs reflected Enlightenment ideas about the rational organization of state institutions. On the other hand, they were ready to abandon the humanitarian impulse of Enlightenment thought and the ideal of self-government when it came to preserving their own power and the social hierarchies that sustained it.

The American Revolution

The American Revolution of 1776 provided a more fruitful opportunity for putting Enlightenment ideals into practice. Along the Atlantic seaboard, the rapidly growing British colonies chafed at rule from London. To recover some of the costs of the Seven Years' War and to pay for the continuing costs of protecting its colonial subjects, the British Parliament imposed a series of new taxes on its American colonies. These taxes were immediately unpopular. Colonists complained that because they had no representatives in Parliament, they were being taxed without their consent—a fundamental violation of their rights as British subjects. They also complained that British restrictions on colonial trade, particularly the requirement that certain goods pass first through British ports before being shipped to the Continent, were strangling American livelihoods and making it impossible to pay even the king's legitimate taxes.

The British government, led since 1760 by the young and inexperienced King George III, responded to these complaints with a badly calculated mixture of vacillation and force. Various taxes were imposed and then withdrawn in the face of colonial resistance. In 1773, however, when East India Company tea was dumped in Boston Harbor by rebellious colonials objecting to the customs duties that had been imposed on it, the British government closed the port of Boston and curtailed the colony's representative institutions. These "Coercive Acts" galvanized the support of the other American colonies for Massachusetts. In 1774, representatives from all the American colonies met at Philadelphia to form the Continental Congress to negotiate with the Crown over their grievances. In April 1775, however, local militiamen at Lexington and Concord clashed with regular British

MARIA THERESA OF AUSTRIA AND HER FAMILY. A formidable and capable ruler who fought to maintain Austria's dominance in central Europe against the claims of Frederick the Great of Prussia, Maria Theresa had sixteen children, including Marie Antoinette, later queen of France as wife of Louis XVI. ▪ *Why did she emphasize her role as mother in a royal portrait such as this one rather than her other undeniable political skills?* ▪ *How does this compare to the portraits of Louis XIV or of William and Mary in Chapter 15, pages 404 and 412?*

Analyzing Primary Sources

The American Declaration of Independence

The Declaration of Independence, issued from Philadelphia on July 4, 1776, is perhaps the most famous single document of American history. Written by Thomas Jefferson with contributions from Benjamin Franklin, John Adams, and others, its familiarity does not lessen its interest as a piece of political philosophy. Its debt to the ideas of John Locke will be obvious from the selections here. But Locke, in turn, drew many of his ideas about the contractual and conditional nature of human government from the conciliarist thinkers of the fifteenth and early sixteenth centuries. The appeal of absolutism notwithstanding, the Declaration shows how vigorous the medieval tradition of contractual, limited government remained at the end of the eighteenth century.

When in the course of human events, it becomes necessary for one people to dissolve the political bonds which have connected them with another, and to assume among the powers of the earth the separate and equal station to which the Laws of Nature and of Nature's God entitle them, a decent respect to the opinions of mankind requires that they should declare the causes which impel them to the separation. . . . We hold these truths to be self-evident, that all men are created equal, that they are endowed by their Creator with certain unalienable rights, that among these are Life, Liberty and the pursuit of Happiness. . . . That to secure these rights, Governments are instituted among men, deriving their just powers from the consent of the governed. . . . That whenever any form of Government becomes destructive of these ends, it is the Right of the People to alter or to abolish it, and to institute new Government, laying its foundation upon such principles and organizing its power in such form, as to them shall seem most likely to effect their Safety and Happiness. Prudence, indeed, will dictate that Governments long established should not be changed for light and transient causes; and accordingly all experience has shown, that mankind are more disposed to suffer, while evils are sufferable, than to right themselves by abolishing the forms to which they are accustomed. But when a long train of abuses and usurpations, pursuing invariably the same Object, evinces a design to reduce them under absolute despotism, it is their right, it is their duty, to throw off such Government, and to provide new Guards for their future security. . . . Such has been the patient sufferance of these Colonies; and such is now the necessity which constrains them to alter their former Systems of Government. . . .

Questions for Analysis

1. Who are "the people" mentioned in the first sentence of this selection? Are the rights of "the people" the same as individual rights? How did the authors of this document come to think of themselves as the representatives of such a body?

2. What is the purpose of government, according to this document? Who gets to decide if the government is doing its job?

3. How does this document's use of the term *political bonds* compare with Rousseau's "form of association" in *The Social Contract*? What is similar about these two texts? What is different?

---

troops sent to disarm them. Soon thereafter, the Continental Congress began raising an army, and an outright rebellion erupted against the British government.

On July 4, 1776, the thirteen colonies formally declared their independence from Great Britain, in language that showed their debt to Enlightenment writers (see **Analyzing Primary Sources**). During the first two years of the war, it seemed unlikely that such independence would ever become a reality. In 1778, however, France, anxious to undermine the colonial hegemony that Great Britain had

established since 1713, joined the war on the side of the Americans. Spain entered the war in support of France, hoping to recover Gibraltar and Florida (the latter lost to Britain in 1763). In 1780, Britain also declared war on the Dutch Republic for continuing to trade with the rebellious colonies. Now facing a coalition of its colonial rivals, Great Britain saw the war turn against it. In 1781, combined land and sea operations by French and American troops forced the surrender of the main British army at Yorktown in Virginia. As the defeated British soldiers surrendered their weapons, their band played a song titled "The World Turned Upside Down."

Negotiations for peace began soon after the defeat at Yorktown but were not concluded until September 1783. The Treaty of Paris left Great Britain in control of Canada and Gibraltar. Spain retained its possessions west of the Mississippi River and recovered Florida. The United States gained its independence; its western border was fixed on the Mississippi River, and it secured valuable fishing rights off the eastern coast of Canada. France gained only the satisfaction of defeating its colonial rival, but even that satisfaction was short lived. Six years later, the massive debts France had incurred in supporting the American Revolution helped bring about another, very different kind of revolution in France that would permanently alter the history of Europe.

CONCLUSION

The Enlightenment arose from the scientific revolution, from the new sense of power and possibility that rational thinking made possible, and from the rush of enthusiasm for new forms of inquiry. Enlightenment thinkers scrutinized a remarkably wide range of topics: human nature, reason, understanding, religion, belief, law, the origins of government, economics, new forms of technology, and social practices—such as marriage, child rearing, and education. Enlightenment ideas about social improvement and progress could and did occasionally serve the interests of European rulers, who saw in them a means to both rationalize their administrations and to challenge social groups or institutions that resisted the centralization of authority. Maria Theresa in Austria, Frederick the Great in Prussia, and Catherine the Great in Russia all found ways to harness aspects of Enlightenment thought to their strategies of government.

At the same time, however, the radical implications of the Enlightenment critique of tradition made many people uncomfortable. Ideas with subversive implications circulated in popular forms from pamphlets and newspapers to plays and operas. The intellectual movement that lay behind the Enlightenment thus had broad consequences for the creation of a new kind of elite based not on birth but on the acquisition of knowledge and the encouragement of open expression and debate. A new sphere of public opinion had come into existence, one which was difficult for the state to monitor and to control, and one which would have profound consequences in the nineteenth and twentieth centuries.

After You Read This Chapter

 Go to **INQUIZITIVE** to see what you've learned—and learn what you've missed—with personalized feedback along the way.

REVIEWING THE OBJECTIVES

- Many eighteenth-century thinkers used the term *Enlightenment* to describe what their work offered to European society. Who were they, and what did they mean by the term?

- Enlightenment ideas spread rapidly throughout Europe and in European colonies. How did this expanded arena for public discussion shape the development of Enlightenment thought?

- Enlightenment debates were shaped by the availability of new information about peoples and cultures in different parts of the globe. How did Enlightenment thinkers incorporate this new information into their thought?

- Enlightenment thinkers were often critical of widely held cultural and political beliefs. What was radical about the Enlightenment?

The prosperity that had made the Enlightenment possible remained very unevenly distributed in late-eighteenth-century Europe. In the cities, rich and poor lived separate lives in separate neighborhoods. In the countryside, regions bypassed by the developing commercial economy of the period continued to suffer from hunger and famine, just as they had done in the sixteenth and seventeenth centuries. In eastern Europe, the contrasts between rich and poor were even more extreme, as many peasants fell into a new kind of serfdom that would last until the end of the nineteenth century. War, too, remained a fact of European life, bringing death and destruction to hundreds of thousands of people across the Continent and around the world—yet another consequence of the worldwide reach of these European colonial empires.

Finally, the Atlantic revolutions (the American Revolution of 1776, the French Revolution of 1789, and the Latin American upheavals of the 1830s) were steeped in the language of the Enlightenment. The constitutions of the new nations formed by these revolutions made reference to the fundamental assumptions of Enlightenment liberalism: on the liberty of the individual conscience and the freedom from the constraints imposed by religious or government institutions. Government authority could not be arbitrary; equality and freedom were natural; and humans sought happiness, prosperity, and the expansion of their potential. These arguments had been made earlier, though tentatively, and even after the Atlantic revolutions, their aspirations were only partially realized. But when the North American colonists declared their independence from Britain in 1776, they called such ideas "self-evident truths." That bold declaration marked both the distance traveled since the late seventeenth century and the self-confidence that was the Enlightenment's hallmark.

SEVENTEENTH- AND EIGHTEENTH-CENTURY WARS

Glorious Revolution	1688–1689
War of the League of Augsburg	1689–1697
War of the Spanish Succession	1702–1713
Seven Years' War	1756–1763
American Revolution	1775–1783
The Russo-Turkish War	1787–1792

PEOPLE, IDEAS, AND EVENTS IN CONTEXT

- How did the **COMMERCIAL REVOLUTION** change social life in Europe?
- Who were the **PHILOSOPHES**? What gave them such confidence in **REASON**?
- What did **DAVID HUME** owe to **ISAAC NEWTON**? What made his work different from that of the famous physicist?
- What did **VOLTAIRE** admire about the work of **FRANCIS BACON** and **JOHN LOCKE**? What irritated Voltaire about French society?
- What was **MONTESQUIEU**'s contribution to theories of government?
- What made **DENIS DIDEROT**'s *ENCYCLOPEDIA* such a definitive statement of the Enlightenment's goals?
- What influence did **CESARE BECCARIA** have over legal practices in Europe?
- What contributions did **ADAM SMITH** make to economic theory?
- What was radical about **JEAN-JACQUES ROUSSEAU**'s views on education and politics?
- What does the expansion of the **PUBLIC SPHERE** in the eighteenth century tell us about the effects of the Enlightenment?

THINKING ABOUT CONNECTIONS

- Compare the Enlightenment as an intellectual movement to the Reformation of the sixteenth century. What is similar about the two movements? How are they distinct?
- Did increases in literacy, the rise of print culture, and the emergence of new forms of intellectual sociability such as salons, reading societies, and coffeehouses really make public opinion more rational? How has our understanding of public opinion changed since the eighteenth century?

Before
You
Read
This
Chapter

STORY LINES

- The French Revolution of 1798–99 overthrew Louis XVI and created a government committed in principle to the rule of law, the liberty of the individual, and an idea of the nation as a sovereign body of citizens. These political changes also opened the way for the expression of a wide range of social grievances by peasants, laborers, women, and other social groups in Europe.

- The French Revolution encouraged the spread of democratic ideas, but it also led to an increase in the power of centralized nation-states in Europe. The pressures of the revolutionary wars led governments to develop larger national bureaucracies, modern professional armies, new legal codes, and new tax structures.

- The French Revolution was part of a broader set of changes that rocked the Atlantic world at the end of the eighteenth century. Along with the American Revolution and the Haitian Revolution, this wave of cataclysmic change reshaped the political order of Europe and the Americas.

CHRONOLOGY

May 1789	The Estates General meets
June 1789	The Tennis Court Oath
July 1789	The Fall of the Bastille
September 1792	First French Republic
January 1793	Execution of King Louis XVI
September 1793– July 1794	The Terror
1798–1799	Napoleon's invasion of Egypt
January 1804	Haitian independence
1804	Napoleon crowned emperor
1804	Civil code
1808	Invasion of Spain
1812	Invasion of Russia
1814–1815	Napoleon's abdication and defeat

The French Revolution

When a crowd of Parisians attacked the antiquated and nearly empty royal prison known as the Bastille on July 14, 1789, they were doing several things all at once. On the one hand, the revolt was a popular expression of support for the newly created National Assembly. This representative body had only weeks earlier declared an intention to put an end to absolutism in France by writing a constitution that made the nation, rather than the king, the sovereign authority in the land. But the Parisians in the street on July 14 did not express themselves like members of the National Assembly, who spoke the language of the Enlightenment. The actions of the revolutionary crowd were an expression of violent anger at the king's soldiers, who they feared might turn their guns on the city in a royal attempt to restore order by force. When the troops guarding the Bastille prison opened fire on the attackers, killing as many as a hundred, the crowd responded with redoubled fury. By the end of the day, the prison had fallen, and its governor's battered body was dragged to the square before the city hall, where he was beheaded. Among the first to meet such an end as a consequence of revolution in France, he would not

be the last. This tension between noble political aspirations and cruel violence lies at the heart of the French Revolution.

Other kingdoms were not immune to the same social and political tensions that divided the French. Aristocrats across Europe and the colonies resented monarchical inroads on their ancient freedoms. Members of the middle classes chafed under a system of official privilege that they increasingly saw as unjust and outmoded. Peasants fiercely resented the endless demands of central government on their limited resources. Nor were resentments focused exclusively on absolutist monarchs. Bitter resentments and tensions existed between country and city dwellers, between rich and poor, overprivileged and underprivileged, slave and free. The French Revolution was the most dramatic and tumultuous expression of all of these conflicts.

This age of revolution had opened on the other side of the Atlantic ocean. The American Revolution of 1776 was a crisis of the British Empire, linked to a long series of conflicts between England and France over colonial control of North America. It led to a major crisis of the Old Regime in France. Among "enlightened" Europeans, the success with which citizens of the United States had thrown off British rule and formed a republic based on Enlightenment principles was a source of tremendous optimism.

By any measure, the accomplishments of the revolutionary decade were extraordinary: it proved that the residents of an old monarchy in the heart of Europe could come together to constitute themselves as citizens of a new political idea, the nation. Freed from the shackles of tradition, revolutionaries in France posed new questions about the

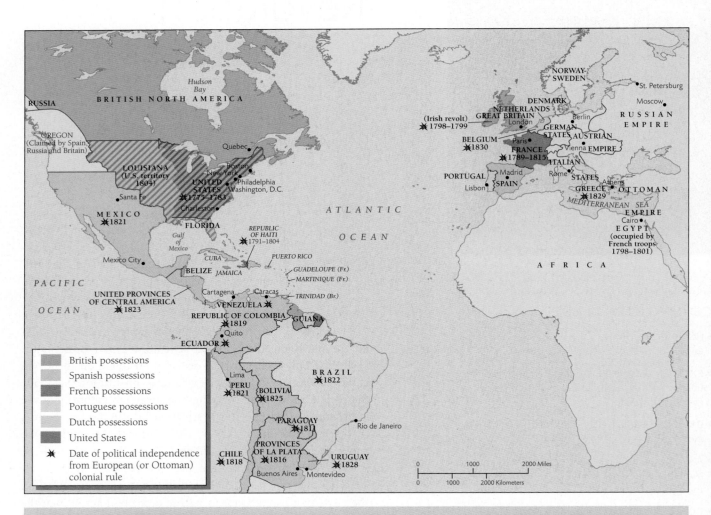

THE ATLANTIC REVOLUTIONS. The Atlantic revolutions shook nations and empires on both sides of the ocean, challenging the legitimacy of Europe's dynastic realms, lending further support to notions of popular sovereignty, and forcing contemporaries to rethink the meanings of citizenship in a context of intense political and economic struggle. ▪ *How many of these struggles took place within Europe?* ▪ *How many appear to have taken place on the periphery of the Atlantic world?* ▪ *What circumstances may have made it more difficult for such revolutionary movements to develop within Europe itself?*

role of women in public life, about the separation of church and state, about the rights of Jews and other minorities. A slave revolt in the French colonies convinced the revolutionaries that the new liberties they defended so ardently also belonged to African slaves, though few had suggested such a thing at the outset. Meanwhile, the European wars precipitated by the revolution marked the first time that entire populations were mobilized as part of a new kind of devastating international conflict, the first "total wars." In other words, in spite of the optimism of those who began the revolution in 1789, it quickly became something much more costly, complex, and violent. Its effects were to resonate throughout Europe for the next half century.

THE FRENCH REVOLUTION: AN OVERVIEW

The term *French Revolution* is a shorthand for a complex series of events between 1789 and 1799. Some historians also include the period of Napoleon's rule, 1799–1814. To simplify, the period from 1789–1814 can be divided into four stages. In the first stage, running from 1788 to 1792, the struggle was constitutional and relatively peaceful. An increasingly bold elite articulated its grievances against the king. Like the American revolutionaries, French elites refused taxation without representation; attacked despotism, or arbitrary authority; and offered an Enlightenment-inspired program to rejuvenate the nation. Reforms, many of them breathtakingly wide-ranging, were instituted—some accepted or even offered by the king, and others enacted over his objections. This peaceful, constitutional phase did not last.

The threat of dramatic change within one of the most powerful countries in Europe created international tensions. In 1792 these tensions exploded into war, and the crises of war, in turn, spelled the end of the Bourbon monarchy and the beginning of the republic. The second stage of the revolution, which lasted from 1792 to 1794, was one of acute crisis, consolidation, and repression. A ruthlessly centralized government mobilized all the country's resources to fight the foreign enemy as well as counterrevolutionaries at home, to destroy traitors and the vestiges of the Old Regime.

The Terror, as this policy was called, did save the republic, but it exhausted itself in factions and recriminations and collapsed in 1794. In the third phase, from 1794 to 1799, the government drifted. France remained a republic. It continued to fight with Europe. Undermined by corruption and division, the state fell prey to the ambitions of a military leader, Napoleon Bonaparte. Napoleon's rule, punctuated

by astonishing victories and catastrophes, stretched from 1799 to 1815, and constitutes the end of the revolution. It began as a republic, became an empire, and ended—after a last hurrah—in the muddy fields outside the Belgian village of Waterloo. After Napoleon's final defeat, the other European monarchs restored the Bourbons to the throne. That restoration, however, would be short-lived, and the cycle of revolution and reaction continued into the nineteenth century.

THE COMING OF THE REVOLUTION

What were the long-term causes of the revolution in France? Historians long ago argued that the causes and outcomes should be understood in terms of class conflict. According to this interpretation, a rising bourgeoisie, or middle class, inspired by Enlightenment ideas and by its own self-interest, overthrew what was left of the aristocratic order.

Historians have substantially modified this bold thesis. French society was not simply divided between a bourgeois class and the aristocracy. Instead, it was increasingly dominated by a new elite or social group that brought together aristocrats, officeholders, professionals, and—to a lesser degree—merchants and businessmen. To understand the revolution, we need to understand this new social group and its conflicts with the government of Louis XVI.

French society was divided legally into Three Estates. (An individual's *estate*, or status, determined legal rights, taxes, and so on.) The First Estate comprised all the clergy; the Second Estate, the nobility. The Third Estate, by far the largest, included everyone else, from wealthy lawyers and businessmen to urban laborers and poor peasants. These legal distinctions often seemed artificial. To begin with, the social boundaries between nobles and wealthy commoners were ill-defined. Noble title was accessible to those who could afford to buy an ennobling office. Fifty thousand new nobles were created between 1700 and 1789. The nobility depended on a constant infusion of talent and economic power from the wealthy social groups of the Third Estate.

Most noble wealth was proprietary—that is, tied to land, urban properties, purchased offices, and the like. Yet noble families did not disdain trade or commerce, as historians long thought. In fact, noblemen financed most industry, and they also invested heavily in banking and such enterprises as shipping, the slave trade, mining, and metallurgy. Moreover, the very wealthy members of the Third Estate also preferred to invest in secure, proprietary holdings. Thus, throughout the century, much middle-class

PREREVOLUTIONARY PROPAGANDA. Political cartoons in late-eighteenth-century France commonly portrayed the Third Estate as bearing the burden of taxation while performing the bulk of the nation's productive work. ■ *Would one expect the nobility or the clergy to defend their status on the basis of their usefulness to society?* ■ *Can one detect the power of certain Enlightenment ideas behind these forms of social critique?* ■ *Which ones?* ■ *How might an opponent of Enlightenment thought have confronted such arguments?*

Less wealthy nobles resented the success of rich, upstart commoners whose income allowed them to live in luxury. In sum, several fault lines ran through the elite and the middle classes. All these social groups could nonetheless join in attacking a government and an economy that were not serving their interests.

The Enlightenment had changed public debate (see Chapter 17). Ideas did not cause the revolution, but they played a critical role in articulating grievances. The political theories of Locke, Voltaire, and Montesquieu could appeal to both discontented nobles and members of the middle class. Voltaire was popular because of his attacks on noble privileges; Locke and Montesquieu gained widespread followings because of their defense of private property and limited sovereignty. Montesquieu's ideas appealed to the noble lawyers and officeholders who dominated France's powerful law courts, the *parlements*. They read his doctrine of checks and balances as support for their argument that *parlements* could provide a check to the despotism of the king's government. When conflicts arose, noble leaders presented themselves as defenders of the nation threatened by the king and his ministers.

The campaign for change was also fueled by economic reformers. The "physiocrats" urged the government to simplify the tax system and free the economy from mercantilist regulations. They advocated an end to price controls in the grain trade, which had been imposed to keep the cost of bread low. Such interventions, they argued, interfered with the natural workings of the market.

In the countryside, peasants were caught in a web of obligations to landlords, church, and state: a tithe, or levy, on farm produce owed to the church; fees for the use of a landlord's mill or wine press; rents to the landlord; and fees when land changed hands. In addition, peasants paid a disproportionate share of both direct and indirect taxes—the most onerous of which was the salt tax—levied by the government. Further grievances stemmed from the requirement to maintain public roads (the *corvée*) and from the hunting privileges that nobles for centuries had regarded as the distinctive badge of their order.

Social and economic conditions deteriorated on the eve of the revolution. A general price increase during much of the eighteenth century, which permitted the French economy to expand by providing capital for investment, created hardship for the peasantry and for urban tradesmen and laborers. Their plight deteriorated further at the end of the 1780s, when poor harvests sent bread prices sharply higher. In 1788 families found themselves spending more than 50 percent of their income on bread, which made up the bulk of their diet. The following year the figure rose to as much as 80 percent. Poor harvests reduced demand for manufactured goods, and

wealth was transformed into noble wealth, and a significant number of rich bourgeois became noblemen. Wealthy members of the bourgeoisie themselves did not see themselves as a separate class. They thought of themselves as different from—and often opposed to—the common people, who worked with their hands, and they identified with the values of a nobility to which they frequently aspired.

There were, nonetheless, important social tensions. Less prosperous lawyers—and there were an increasing number of them—were jealous of the privileged position of a favored few in their profession. Over the course of the century the price of offices rose, making it more difficult to buy one's way into the nobility, and creating tensions between middling members of the Third Estate and the very rich in trade and commerce who, by and large, were the only group able to afford to climb the social ladder.

contracting markets in turn created unemployment. Many peasants left the countryside for the cities, hoping to find work there—only to discover that urban unemployment was far worse than that in rural areas. Evidence indicates that between 1787 and 1789 the unemployment rate in many parts of urban France was as high as 50 percent.

Failure and Reform

An inefficient tax system further weakened the country's financial position. Taxation was tied to differing social standings and varied from region to region—some areas were subject to a much higher rate than others. The financial system, already burdened by debts incurred under Louis XIV, all but broke down completely under the increased expenses brought on by French participation in the American Revolution.

Problems with the economy reflected weaknesses in France's administrative structure, ultimately the responsibility of the country's absolutist monarch, Louis XVI (r. 1774–92). Louis wished to improve the lot of the poor, abolish torture, and shift the burden of taxation onto the richer classes, but he lacked the ability to accomplish these tasks. When he pressed for new taxes to be paid by the nobility, he was defeated by the provincial *parlements*, who defended the aristocracy's immunity from taxation. By 1788, a weak monarch, together with a chaotic financial situation and severe social tensions, brought absolutist France to the edge of political disaster.

LOUIS XVI. The last prerevolutionary French king, who was to lose his life in the Terror, combined in his person a strong attachment to the monarchy's absolutist doctrine with an inability to find workable solutions to the financial crisis facing his government. His royal portrait mimicked the forms of spectacular display that proved so useful to his ancestor Louis XIV in shoring up the power of the monarchy. ■ *What made this display so much less potent in the late eighteenth century?* ■ *What caused the monarchy to lose its aura?*

THE DESTRUCTION OF THE OLD REGIME

The fiscal crisis precipitated the revolution. In 1787 and 1788 the king's ministers proposed new taxes to meet the growing deficit, notably a stamp duty and a direct tax on the annual produce of the land.

Hoping to persuade the nobility to agree to these reforms, the king summoned an Assembly of Notables from among the aristocracy and clergy. This group insisted that any new tax scheme must be approved by the Estates General, the representative body of the Three Estates of the realm, and that the king had no legal authority to arrest and imprison arbitrarily. These proposed constitutional changes echoed the English aristocrats of 1688 and the American revolutionaries of 1776.

Faced with economic crisis and financial chaos, Louis XVI summoned the Estates General (which had not met since 1614) to meet in 1789. His action appeared to many as the only solution to France's deepening problems. Long-term grievances and short-term hardships produced bread riots across the country in the spring of 1789. Fear that the forces of law and order were collapsing and that the common people might take matters into their own hands spurred the Estates General. Each of the three orders elected its own deputies—the Third Estate indirectly through local assemblies. These assemblies were charged as well with the responsibility of drawing up lists of grievances (*cahiers des doléances*), further heightening expectations for fundamental reform.

By tradition, each estate met and voted as a body. In the past, this had generally meant that the First Estate (the clergy) had combined with the Second (the nobility) to defeat the Third. The king's finance minister, Jacques Necker, feared that this would place the government at

THE TENNIS COURT OATH BY JACQUES LOUIS DAVID (1748–1825). In June 1789, the members of the Third Estate, now calling themselves the National Assembly, swear an oath not to disband until France has a constitution. In the center stands Jean Bailly, president of the new assembly. The Abbé Sieyès is seated at the table. In the foreground, a clergyman, an aristocrat, and a member of the Third Estate embrace in a symbol of national unity. The single deputy who has refused to take the oath sits at right, his hands clasped against his chest. ■ *What is the significance of this near unanimity expressed in defiance of the king?* ■ *What options were available to those who did not support this move?*

the mercy of the most conservative nobles and so prevent financial reform. Members of the Third Estate, meanwhile, argued that the representatives of the Three Estates should sit together and vote as individuals, and that the Third Estate delegation should be doubled in size, so as to give the commoners an equal voice. Necker convinced the king to go along with this plan in December 1788. When the nobility predictably protested against what they saw as a royal betrayal, a radical priest named Abbé Sieyès penned an incendiary pamphlet, "What Is the Third Estate?" His answer: everything. Comparing the nobility to parasites, he argued that they were not even a part of the body politic.

The king, alarmed by this violent language, backed away from his support of the Third Estate when the Estates General convened in May 1789. Angered by the king's attitude, the Third Estate's representatives took the revolutionary step of leaving the body and declaring themselves the National Assembly. The king tried to prevent the National Assembly from meeting, but when the delegates found themselves locked out of their meeting hall on June 20, the representatives moved to a nearby tennis court, along with a handful of sympathetic nobles and clergymen. Here, under the leadership of the volatile, maverick aristocrat Mirabeau and the radical clergyman Sieyès, they swore an oath not to disband until France had a constitution.

This Tennis Court Oath, sworn on June 20, 1789, can be seen as the beginning of the French Revolution. By claiming the authority to remake the government in the name of the people, the National Assembly was asserting its right to act as the highest sovereign power in the nation. On June 27 the king virtually conceded this right by ordering all the delegates to join the National Assembly.

First Stages of the French Revolution

The first stage of the French Revolution extended from June 1789 to August 1792. In the main, this stage was moderate, its actions dominated by the leadership of liberal nobles and men of the Third Estate. Yet three events in the summer and fall of 1789 furnished evidence that their leadership would be challenged.

WOMEN OF PARIS LEAVING FOR VERSAILLES, OCTOBER 1789. A crowd of women, accompanied by Lafayette and the National Guard, marched to Versailles to confront the king about shortages and rising prices in Paris. ▪ *Did the existence of the National Assembly change the meaning of such popular protests?*

POPULAR REVOLTS

From the beginning of the political crisis, the public paid close attention. Many believed that the aristocracy and the king were conspiring to punish the Third Estate by encouraging scarcity and high prices. Rumors circulated in Paris during the latter days of June 1789 that the king's troops were mobilizing to march on the city. The electors of Paris (those who had voted for the Third Estate) feared not only the king but also the Parisian poor, who had been parading through the streets and threatening violence. The common people would soon be referred to as *sans-culottes* (*sahn koo-LAWTS*). The term, which translates to "without breeches," was an antiaristocratic badge of pride: a man of the people wore full-length trousers rather than aristocratic breeches with stockings and gold-buckled shoes. Led by the electors, the people formed a provisional municipal government and organized a militia of volunteers to maintain order. Determined to obtain arms, they made their way on July 14 to the Bastille, an ancient fortress and symbol of royal authority where guns and ammunition were stored. When crowds demanded arms from its governor, he procrastinated and then, fearing a frontal assault, ordered his troops to open fire, killing ninety-eight of the attackers. The crowd took revenge, capturing the fortress and decapitating the governor. Similar groups took control in other cities across France. The fall of the Bastille was the first instance of the people's role in revolutionary change.

The second popular revolt occurred in the countryside. Peasants, too, feared a counterrevolution. Rumors flew that the king's armies were on their way, that Austrians, Prussians, or "brigands" were invading. Frightened and uncertain, peasants and villagers organized militias; others attacked and burned manor houses, sometimes to look for grain but usually to find and destroy records of manorial dues. This "Great Fear," as historians have labeled it, compounded the confusion in rural areas in July and August 1789. The news, when it reached Paris, convinced deputies at Versailles that the administration of rural France had simply collapsed.

The third instance of popular uprising, the "October Days of 1789," was brought on by economic crisis. This time Parisian women from the market district, angered by the soaring price of bread and fired by rumors of the king's continuing unwillingness to cooperate with the assembly, marched to Versailles on October 5 and demanded to be heard. Not satisfied with its reception by the assembly, the crowd broke through the gates to the palace and demanded that the king return to Paris from Versailles. On the afternoon of the following day the king yielded and returned to Paris, accompanied by the crowd and the National Guard.

Each of these popular uprisings shaped the political events unfolding at Versailles. The storming of the Bastille persuaded the king and nobles to agree to the creation of the National Assembly. The Great Fear compelled the most sweeping changes of the entire revolutionary period. In an effort to quell rural disorder, on the night of August 4 the assembly took a giant step toward abolishing all forms of privilege. It eliminated the church tithe (tax on the harvest), the labor requirement known as the *corvée*, the nobility's hunting privileges, and a wide variety of tax exemptions and monopolies. In effect, these reforms obliterated the remnants of feudalism. One week later, the assembly abolished the sale of offices, thereby sweeping away one of the fundamental institutions of the Old Regime. The king's return to Paris during the October Days of 1789 undercut his ability to resist further changes.

THE NATIONAL ASSEMBLY AND THE RIGHTS OF MAN

The assembly issued its charter of liberties, the Declaration of the Rights of Man and of the Citizen, in August 1789. It declared rights to property, liberty, security, and "resistance to oppression," as well as freedom of speech, religious toleration, and liberty of the press. All (male) citizens were to

Analyzing Primary Sources

What Is the Third Estate? (1789)

The Abbé Emmanuel-Joseph Sieyès (1748–1836) was, by virtue of his office in the church, a member of the First Estate of the Estates General. Nevertheless, his political savvy led him to be elected as a representative of the Third Estate from the district of Chartres. Sieyès was a formidable politician as well as a writer. His career during the revolution, which he ended by assisting Napoleon's seizure of power, began with one of the most important radical pamphlets of 1789. In What Is the Third Estate?, *Sieyès posed fundamental questions about the rights of the estate that represented the great majority of the population, thereby helping to provoke its secession from the Estates General.*

he plan of this book is fairly simple. We must ask ourselves three questions.

1. What is the Third Estate? *Everything.*

2. What has it been until now in the political order? *Nothing.*

3. What does it want to be? *Something.*

It suffices to have made the point that the so-called usefulness of a privileged order to the public service is a fallacy; that without help from this order, all the arduous tasks in the service are performed by the Third Estate; that without this order the higher posts could be infinitely better filled; that they ought to be the natural prize and reward of recognized ability and service; and that if the privileged have succeeded in usurping all well-paid and honorific posts, this is both a hateful iniquity towards the generality of citizens and an act of treason to the commonwealth.

Who is bold enough to maintain that the Third Estate does not contain within itself everything needful to constitute a complete nation? It is like a strong and robust man with one arm still in chains. If the privileged order were removed, the nation would not be something less but something more. What then is the Third Estate? All; but an "all" that is fettered and oppressed. What would it be without the privileged order? It would be all; but free and flourishing. Nothing will go well without the Third Estate; everything would go considerably better without the two others.

Source: Emmanuel-Joseph Sieyès, *What Is the Third Estate?*, trans. M. Blondel, ed. S. E. Finer (London: 1964), pp. 53–63.

Questions for Analysis

1. How might contemporaries have viewed Sieyès's argument that the Three Estates should be evaluated according to their usefulness to the "commonwealth"?

2. Was Sieyès's language—accusing the privileged orders of "treason" and arguing for their "removal"—an incitement to violence?

3. What did Sieyès mean by the term *nation*? Could one speak of France as a nation in these terms before 1789?

---

be treated equally before the law. No one was to be imprisoned or punished without due process of law. Sovereignty resided in the people, who could depose officers of the government if they abused their powers. The Declaration became the preamble to the new constitution, which the assembly finished in 1791.

Whom did the Declaration mean by "man and the citizen"? The constitution distinguished between "passive" citizens, who were guaranteed rights under law, and "active" citizens, who paid a certain amount in taxes and could thus vote and hold office. About half the adult males in France qualified as active citizens. Even their power was curtailed, because they could vote only for "electors," men whose property ownership qualified them to hold office. Later in

the revolution, the more radical republic abolished the distinction between active and passive, and the conservative regimes reinstated it.

Which men could be trusted to participate in politics and on what terms was a hotly contested issue. The revolution gave full civil rights to Protestants and, hesitantly, to Jews. Religious toleration, a central theme of the Enlightenment, meant ending persecution; it did not mean that the regime was prepared to accommodate religious difference. The assembly abolished serfdom and banned slavery in continental France. It remained silent on colonial slavery, however, and the assembly exempted the colonies from the constitution's provisions. Events in the Caribbean, as we will see, later forced the issue.

The rights and roles of women became the focus of sharp debate, as revolutionaries confronted demands that working women participate in guilds or trade organizations, and laws on marriage, divorce, poor relief, and education were reconsidered. Only a handful of thinkers broached the subject of women in politics: among them were the aristocratic Enlightenment thinker the Marquis de Condorcet and Marie Gouze, the self-educated daughter of a butcher. Gouze became an intellectual and playwright and renamed herself Olympe de Gouges. Like many "ordinary" people, she found in the explosion of revolutionary activity an opportunity to address the public by writing speeches and by publishing pamphlets and newspaper articles. She composed her own manifesto, the *Declaration of the Rights of Woman and the Citizen* (1791). Beginning with the proposition that "social distinctions can only be based on the common utility," she declared that women had the same rights as men, including resistance to authority and participation in government. She also insisted that women had unique rights, including naming the fathers of illegitimate children. This last demand offers a glimpse of the shame, isolation, and hardship faced by an unmarried woman.

De Gouges's demand for equal rights was unusual, but many women nevertheless participated in the everyday activities of the revolution, joining clubs, demonstrations, and debates and making their presence known, sometimes forcefully. Women artisans' organizations used the revolution as an opportunity to assert their rights to produce and sell goods. Market women were often central to circulating the news and sparking spontaneous popular demonstrations (the October Days are a good example). When the revolution became more radical, however, some revolutionaries saw autonomous political activity by women's organizations as a threat to public order, and in 1793 the revolutionaries shut down the women's political clubs. Even so, many ordinary women were able to make use of the revolution's new legislation on marriage (divorce was legalized in 1792) and inheritance to support claims for relief from abusive husbands or absent fathers, claims that would have been impossible under the prerevolutionary *Ancien Régime* (Old Regime).

THE NATIONAL ASSEMBLY AND THE CHURCH

In November 1789, the National Assembly decided to confiscate all church lands to use them as collateral for issuing interest-bearing notes known as *assignats*. The assembly hoped that this action would resolve the economy's inflationary crisis, and eventually these notes circulated widely as paper money. In July 1790, the assembly enacted the Civil Constitution of the Clergy, bringing the church under state authority. The new law forced all bishops and priests to swear allegiance to the state, which henceforth paid their salaries. The aim was to make the Catholic Church of France a national institution, free from interference from Rome.

These reforms were bitterly divisive. For centuries the parish church had been a central institution in small towns and villages, providing poor relief and other services, in addition to baptisms and marriages. When the pope threatened to excommunicate priests who signed the Civil Constitution, he raised the stakes: allegiance to the new French state meant damnation. Many people, especially peasants in the deeply Catholic areas of western France, were driven into open revolt.

The National Assembly made a series of economic and governmental changes with lasting effects. To raise money, it sold off church lands, although few of the genuinely needy could afford to buy them. To encourage the growth of economic enterprise, it abolished guilds. To rid the country of local aristocratic power, it reorganized local governments, dividing France into eighty-three equal departments. These measures aimed to defend individual liberty and freedom from customary privilege. Their principal beneficiaries were, for the most part, members of the elite, people on their way up under the previous regime who were able to take advantage of the opportunities that the new one offered. In this realm as elsewhere, the social changes of the revolution endorsed changes already under way in the eighteenth century.

A NEW STAGE: POPULAR REVOLUTION

In the summer of 1792, the revolution's moderate leaders were toppled and replaced by republicans, who repudiated the monarchy and claimed to rule on behalf of a sovereign people. Historians have focused on three factors to explain the revolution's radical turn: changes in popular politics, a crisis of leadership, and international polarization.

First, the revolution politicized the common people, especially in cities. Newspapers filled with political and social commentary multiplied, freed from censorship. From 1789 forward, a wide variety of political clubs became part of daily political life. Some were formal, almost like political parties, gathering members of the elite to debate issues facing the country and influence decisions in the assembly. Other clubs opened their doors to those excluded from formal politics. Members read aloud from newspapers and discussed the options facing the country. Shortages and high prices particularly exasperated the working people of Paris who had eagerly awaited change since their street demonstrations of 1789. Urban demonstrations, often led

Analyzing Primary Sources

Declaration of the Rights of Man and of the Citizen

One of the first important pronouncements of the National Assembly after the Tennis Court Oath was the Declaration of the Rights of Man and of the Citizen. *The authors drew inspiration from the American Declaration of Independence, but the language is even more heavily influenced by the ideals of French Enlightenment philosophes, particularly Rousseau. Following are the* Declaration's *preamble and some of its most important principles.*

he representatives of the French people, constituted as the National Assembly, considering that ignorance, disregard, or contempt for the rights of man are the sole causes of public misfortunes and the corruption of governments, have resolved to set forth, in a solemn declaration, the natural, inalienable, and sacred rights of man, so that the constant presence of this declaration may ceaselessly remind all members of the social body of their rights and duties; so that the acts of legislative power and those of the executive power may be more respected . . . and so that the demands of the citizens, grounded henceforth on simple and incontestable principles, may always be directed to the maintenance of the constitution and to the welfare of all. . . .

Article 1. Men are born and remain free and equal in rights. Social distinctions can be based only on public utility.

Article 2. The aim of every political association is the preservation of the natural and imprescriptible rights of man.

These rights are liberty, property, security, and resistance to oppression.

Article 3. The source of all sovereignty resides essentially in the nation. No body, no individual can exercise authority that does not explicitly proceed from it.

Article 4. Liberty consists in being able to do anything that does not injure another; thus the only limits upon each man's exercise of his natural laws are those that guarantee enjoyment of these same rights to the other members of society.

Article 5. The law has the right to forbid only actions harmful to society. No action may be prevented that is not forbidden by law, and no one may be constrained to do what the law does not order.

Article 6. The law is the expression of the general will. All citizens have the right to participate personally, or through representatives, in its formation. It must be the same for all, whether it protects or punishes. All citizens, being equal in its eyes, are equally admissable to all public dignities, positions, and employments, according to their ability, and on the basis of no other distinction than that of their virtues and talents. . . .

Article 16. A society in which the guarantee of rights is not secured, or the separation of powers is not clearly established, has no constitution.

Source: *Declaration of the Rights of Man and of the Citizen,* as cited in K. M. Baker, ed., *The Old Regime and the French Revolution* (Chicago: 1987), pp. 238–39.

Questions for Analysis

1. Whom is the Declaration addressed to? Is it just about the rights of the French or do these ideas apply to all people?

2. What gave a group of deputies elected to advise Louis XVI on constitutional reforms the right to proclaim themselves a National Assembly? What was revolutionary about this claim to represent the French nation?

3. Article 6, which states that "law is the expression of general will," is adapted from Rousseau's *Social Contract.* Does the Declaration give any indication of how the "general will" can be known?

---

by women, demanded cheaper bread; political leaders in clubs and newspapers called for the government to control rising inflation.

A second major reason for the revolution's change of course was a lack of effective national leadership. Louis XVI remained a weak monarch. He was forced to support measures personally distasteful to him, and he was sympathetic to the plottings of the queen, Marie Antoinette, who was in contact with her brother Leopold II of Austria. Urged on by his wife, Louis agreed to attempt an escape from France in June 1791, hoping to rally foreign support for counterrevolution. The members of the royal family were apprehended near the border at Varennes and brought back to the capital. The constitution of 1791 declared France a monarchy, but after the escape to Varennes, Louis was little more than a prisoner of the assembly.

The Counterrevolution

The third major reason for the dramatic turn of affairs was war. From the outset of the revolution, men and women across Europe had been compelled, by the very intensity of the events in France, to take sides in the conflict. In the years immediately after 1789, the revolution in France won the enthusiastic support of a wide range of thinkers, including the English poet William Wordsworth and the German writer Johann Gottfried von Herder, who declared the revolution the most important historical moment since the Reformation. In Britain, the Low Countries, western Germany, and Italy, "patriots" proclaimed their allegiance to the new revolution.

Others opposed the revolution from the start. Exiled nobles, who fled France for sympathetic royal courts in Germany and elsewhere, did all they could to stir up counterrevolutionary sentiment. In Britain the conservative cause was strengthened by the publication in 1790 of Edmund Burke's *Reflections on the Revolution in France*, which attacked the revolution as a monstrous crime against the social order (see **Competing Viewpoints** on page 490).

The first European states to express public concern about events in revolutionary France were Austria and Prussia, declaring in 1791 that order and the rights of the monarch of France were matters of "common interest to all sovereigns of Europe." The leaders of the French assembly pronounced the declaration an affront to the principle of national sovereignty. Nobles who had fled France played into their hands with plots and pronouncements against the new government. Oddly, perhaps, both supporters and opponents of the revolution in France believed war would serve their cause. The National Assembly's leaders expected that an aggressive policy would shore up the people's loyalty and bring freedom to the rest of Europe. Counterrevolutionaries hoped the intervention of Austria and Prussia would undo all that had happened since 1789. Radicals, suspicious of aristocratic leaders and the king, believed that war would expose traitors with misgivings about the revolution and flush out those who sympathized with the king and European tyrants. On April 20, 1792, the assembly declared war against Austria and Prussia. Thus began the war that would keep the Continent in arms for a generation.

As the radicals expected, the French forces met serious reverses. By August 1792 the allied armies of Austria and Prussia had crossed the frontier and were threatening to capture Paris. Many, including soldiers, believed that the military disasters were evidence of the king's treason. On August 10, Parisian crowds, organized by their radical leaders, attacked the royal palace. The king was imprisoned and a second and far more radical revolution began.

The French Republic

From this point, the country's leadership passed into the hands of the more egalitarian leaders of the former Third Estate. These new leaders were known as Jacobins, the name of a political club to which many of them belonged. Although their headquarters were in Paris, their membership extended throughout France. Their members included large numbers of professionals, government officeholders, and lawyers; but an increasing number of artisans joined Jacobin clubs as the movement grew, and other, more democratic, clubs expanded as well.

The National Convention, elected by free white men, became the effective governing body of the country for the next three years. It was elected in September 1792, at a time when enemy troops were advancing, spreading panic. Rumors flew that prisoners in Paris were plotting to aid the enemy. They were hauled from their cells, dragged before hastily convened tribunals, and killed. The "September Massacres" killed more than a thousand "enemies of the Revolution" in less than a week. Similar riots engulfed Lyons, Orléans, and other French cities.

The newly elected convention was far more radical than its predecessor, and its leadership was determined to end the monarchy. On September 21, the convention declared France a republic. In December it placed the king on trial, and in January 1793 he was condemned to death by a narrow margin. The heir to the grand tradition of French absolutism met his end bravely as "citizen Louis Capet," beheaded by the guillotine. Introduced as a swifter and more humane form of execution, the frightful mechanical headsman came to symbolize revolutionary fervor.

The convention took other radical measures. It confiscated the property of enemies of the revolution, and it canceled the policy of compensating nobles for their lost privileges. It repealed primogeniture, so that property would be divided in substantially equal portions among all immediate heirs. It abolished slavery in French colonies (as will be discussed later). It set maximum prices for grain and other necessities. In an astonishing effort to root out Christianity from everyday life, the convention adopted a new calendar, with the calendar year to begin with the birth of the republic (September 22, 1792) and months to be divided in such a way as to eliminate the Catholic Sunday.

The convention also reorganized its armies, with astonishing success. By February 1793, Britain, Holland, Spain, and Austria were in the field against the French.

Britain came into the war for strategic and economic reasons: they feared a French threat to Britain's growing global power. The revolution flung fourteen hastily drafted armies into battle under the leadership of newly promoted, young, and inexperienced officers. What they lacked in training and discipline they made up for in organization, mobility, flexibility, courage, and morale. In 1793–94, the French armies preserved their homeland. In 1794–95, they occupied the Low Countries; the Rhineland; and parts of Spain, Switzerland, and Savoy. In 1796, they invaded and occupied key parts of Italy and broke the coalition that had arrayed itself against them.

The Reign of Terror

In 1793, however, those victories lay in a hard-to-imagine future. France was in crisis. In 1793, the convention drafted a new democratic constitution based on male suffrage. That constitution never took effect—suspended indefinitely by wartime emergency. Instead, the convention delegated its responsibilities to a group of twelve leaders, the Committee of Public Safety. The committee had two purposes: to seize control of the revolution and to prosecute all the revolution's enemies—"to make terror the order of the day." The Terror proper lasted from September 1793 to July 1794, but this was only the climax of a two-year period between the summer of 1792 and the summer of 1794 that saw repeated episodes of war and civil conflict. The Terror left a bloody and authoritarian legacy.

Perhaps the three best-known leaders of the radical revolution were Jean Paul Marat, Georges Jacques Danton, and Maximilien Robespierre, the latter two members of the Committee of Public Safety. Marat, educated as a physician, opposed nearly all of his moderate colleagues' assumptions. Persecuted by powerful factions in the constituent assembly who feared his radicalism, he was forced to take refuge in unsanitary sewers and dungeons. He persevered as the editor of the popular news sheet *The Friend of the People*. In the summer of 1793, at the height of the crisis of the revolution, he was stabbed in his bath by Charlotte Corday, a young royalist, and thus became a revolutionary martyr.

Danton, like Marat, was a popular political leader, well known in the more plebian clubs of Paris. Elected a member of the Committee of Public Safety in 1793, he had much to do with organizing the Terror. As time went on, however, he wearied of ruthlessness and displayed a tendency to compromise, which gave his opponents in the convention their opportunity. In April 1794, Danton was sent to the guillotine.

The most famous of the radical leaders was Maximilien Robespierre. Robespierre trained in law and quickly became a modestly successful lawyer. His eloquence and his consistent, or ruthless, insistence that leaders respect the "will of the people" eventually won him a following in the Jacobin club. Later, he became president of the National Convention and a member of the Committee of Public Safety. Though he had little to do with starting the Terror, he was nevertheless responsible for enlarging its scope. Popularly known as "The Incorruptible," he came to represent ruthlessness justified as virtue and as necessary to revolutionary progress.

The two years of the radical Republic (August 1792–July 1794) brought dictatorship, centralization, suspension of any liberties, and war. The committee faced foreign enemies and opposition from both the political right and left at home. In June 1793, responding to an escalating crisis, leaders of the "Mountain," a party of radicals allied with Parisian artisans, purged moderates from the convention. Rebellions broke out in the provincial cities of Lyons, Bordeaux, and Marseilles, mercilessly repressed by the committee and its local representatives. The government also faced counterrevolution in the western region known as the Vendée, where movements enlisted peasants and artisans, who believed their local areas were being invaded and who fought for their local priest or against the summons from the revolutionaries' conscription boards. Determined to stabilize France, whatever the cost, the committee launched murderous campaigns of pacification—torching villages, farms, and fields and killing all who dared oppose them as well as many who did not.

During the period of the Terror, from September 1793 to July 1794, the most reliable estimates place the number of deaths at close to 40,000—about 16,500 from actual death sentences, with the rest resulting from extrajudicial killings and deaths in prison. Approximately 300,000 were incarcerated between March 1793 and August 1794. These numbers, however, do not include the pacification of the Vendée and rebellious cities in the Rhone Valley, which took more than 100,000 lives. Few victims of the Terror were aristocrats. Many more were peasants or laborers accused of hoarding, treason, or counterrevolutionary activity. Anyone who appeared to threaten the republic, no matter what his or her social or economic position, was at risk.

The Legacy of the Second French Revolution

The "second" French Revolution affected the everyday life of French men, women, and children in a remarkably direct way. Workers' trousers replaced the breeches that had been

THE EXECUTION OF LOUIS XVI. The execution of Louis XVI shocked Europe, and even committed revolutionaries in France debated the necessity of such a dramatic act. The entire National Convention (a body of over seven hundred members) acted as jury, and although the assembly was nearly unanimous in finding the king guilty of treason, a majority of only one approved the final death sentence. Those who voted for Louis XVI's execution were known forever after as "regicides." ▪ *What made this act necessary from the point of view of the most radical of revolutionaries?* ▪ *What made it repugnant from the point of view of the revolution's most heated enemies?*

a badge of the middle classes and the nobility. A red cap, said to symbolize freedom from slavery, became popular headgear, while wigs vanished. Men and women addressed each other as "citizen" or "citizeness." Public life was marked by ceremonies designed to dramatize the break with the Old Regime and celebrate new forms of fraternity. In the early stages of the revolution, these festivals seem to have captured genuine popular enthusiasm. Under the Committee of Public Safety, they became didactic and hollow.

The radical revolution of 1792–93 also dramatically reversed the trend toward decentralization and democracy. The assembly replaced local officials with "deputies on mission," whose task was to conscript troops and generate patriotic fervor. When these deputies appeared too eager to act independently, they were replaced by "national agents," with instructions to report directly to the committee.

In another effort to stabilize authority, the assembly closed down all the women's political clubs, decreeing them a political and social danger. Ironically, those who claimed to govern in the name of the people found the popular movement threatening.

Finally, the revolution eroded the strength of those traditional institutions—church, guild, parish—that had for centuries given people a common bond. In their place now stood patriotic organizations and a culture that insisted on loyalty to one national cause. Those organizations had first emerged with the election campaigns, meetings, and pamphlet wars of 1788 and the interest they heightened. They included the political clubs and local assemblies, which at the height of the revolution (1792–93) met every day of the week and offered an apprenticeship in politics. The army of the republic become the premier national institution.

Debating the French Revolution: Edmund Burke and Thomas Paine

The best known debate in English on the French Revolution set the Irish-born conservative Edmund Burke against the British radical Thomas Paine, who participated in both the American and French revolutions and became an American citizen. Burke opposed the French Revolution from the beginning because he believed that "rights" were not natural, but rather the product of specific historical traditions. In Reflections on the Revolution in France (1790), *he argued that the revolutionaries had undermined the fabric of French civilization by attempting to remodel the state without reference to tradition and custom.*

Thomas Paine responded to Burke in The Rights of Man (1791–92) *with a defense of the revolutionary concept of universal and natural rights. In the polarized atmosphere of the revolutionary period in Britain, simply possessing Paine's pamphlet was grounds for imprisonment.*

Edmund Burke

You will observe, that from the Magna Carta to the Declaration of Right, it has been the uniform policy of our constitution to claim and assert our liberties, as an entailed inheritance derived to us from our forefathers.... We have an inheritable crown; an inheritable peerage; and a house of commons and a people inheriting privileges, franchises, and liberties, from a long line of ancestors....

You had all these advantages in your ancient states, but you chose to act as if you had never been moulded into civil society, and had every thing to begin anew. You began ill, because you began by despising every thing that belonged to you.... If the last generations of your country appeared without much luster in your eyes, you might have passed them by, and derived your claims from a more early race of ancestors.... Respecting your forefathers, you would have been taught to respect yourselves. You would not have chosen to consider the French as a people of yesterday, as a nation of low-born servile wretches until the emancipating year of 1789.... You would not have been content to be represented as a gang of Maroon slaves, suddenly broke loose from the house of bondage, and therefore to be pardoned for your abuse of liberty to which you were not accustomed and ill fitted....

... The fresh ruins of France, which shock our feelings wherever we can turn our eyes, are not the devastation of civil war; they are the sad but instructive monuments of rash and ignorant counsel in time of profound peace. They are the display of inconsiderate and presumptuous, because unresisted and irresistible, authority....

Nothing is more certain, than that of our manners, our civilization, and all the good things which are connected with manners, and with civilization, have, in this European world of ours, depended upon two principles; and were indeed the result of both combined; I mean the spirit of a gentleman, and the spirit of religion. The nobility and the clergy, the one by profession, the other by patronage, kept learning in existence,

On the one hand, the revolution divided France, mobilizing counterrevolutionaries as well as revolutionaries. At the same time, the revolution, war, and the culture of sacrifice forged new bonds. The sense that the rest of Europe sought to crush the new nation and its citizens unquestionably strengthened French national identity.

FROM THE TERROR TO BONAPARTE: THE DIRECTORY

The Committee of Public Safety might have saved France from enemy armies but could not save itself. Inflation became catastrophic. The long string of military victories

even in the midst of arms and confusions. . . . Learning paid back what it received to nobility and priesthood. . . . Happy if they had all continued to know their indissoluble union, and their proper place. Happy if learning, not debauched by ambition, had been satisified to continue the instructor, and not aspired to be the master! Along with its natural protectors and guardians, learning will be cast into the mire, and trodden down under the hoofs of a swinish multitude.

Source: Edmund Burke, *Reflections on the Revolution in France (1790)* (New York: 1973), pp. 45, 48, 49, 52, 92.

Thomas Paine

Mr. Burke, with his usual outrage, abuses the *Declaration of the Rights of Man*. . . . Does Mr. Burke mean to deny that man has any rights? If he does, then he must mean that there are no such things as rights anywhere, and that he has none himself; for who is there in the world but man? But if Mr. Burke means to admit that man has rights, the question will then be, what are those rights, and how came man by them originally?

The error of those who reason by precedents drawn from antiquity, respecting the rights of man, is that they do not go far enough into antiquity. They stop in some of the intermediate stages of an hundred or a thousand years, and produce what was then a rule for the present day. This is no authority at all. . . .

To possess ourselves of a clear idea of what government is, or ought to be, we must trace its origin. In doing this, we shall easily discover that governments must have arisen either *out* of the people, or *over* the people. Mr. Burke has made no distinction. . . .

What were formerly called revolutions, were little more than a change of persons, or an alteration of local circumstances. They rose and fell like things of course, and had nothing in their existence or their fate that could influence beyond the spot that produced them. But what we now see in the world, from the revolutions of America and France, is a renovation of the natural order of things, a system of principles as universal as truth and the existence of man, and combining moral with political happiness and national prosperity.

Source: Thomas Paine, *The Rights of Man* (New York: 1973), pp. 302, 308, 383.

Questions for Analysis

1. How does Burke define *liberty*? Why does he criticize the revolutionaries for representing themselves as slaves freed from bondage?

2. What does Paine criticize about Burke's emphasis on history? According to Paine, what makes the French Revolution different from previous changes of regime in Europe?

3. How do these two authors' attitudes about the origins of human freedoms shape their respective understanding of the revolution?

---

convinced growing numbers that the committee's demands for continuing self-sacrifice and terror were no longer justified. By July 1794, the committee was virtually without allies. On July 27 (9 Thermidor, according to the new calendar), Robespierre was shouted down while attempting to speak on the floor of the convention. The following day, along with twenty-one associates, he met his death by guillotine.

Ending the Terror did not immediately bring moderation. Vigilante groups of royalists hunted down Jacobins. The repeal of price controls, combined with the worst winter in a century, caused widespread misery. Other measures that had constituted the Terror were gradually repealed. In 1795 the National Convention adopted a new and more conservative constitution. It granted suffrage to all adult male citizens who could read and write. Yet it set up indirect

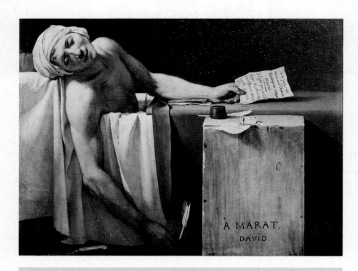

THE DEATH OF MARAT. This painting by the French artist David immortalized Marat. The note in the slain leader's hand is from Charlotte Corday, his assassin. ■ *Why was it important to represent Marat as a martyr?*

elections: citizens voted for electors, who in turn chose the legislative body. Wealthy citizens thus held authority. Eager to avoid personal dictatorship, the new constitution vested executive authority in a board of five men known as the Directory, chosen by the legislative body. The constitution included not only a bill of rights but also a declaration of the duties of the citizen.

The Directory lasted longer than its revolutionary predecessors. It still faced discontent on both the radical left and the conservative right. On the left, the Directory repressed radical movements to abolish private property and parliamentary-style government. Dispatching threats from the right proved more challenging. In 1797 the first free elections held in France as a republic returned a large number of monarchists to the councils of government, alarming politicians who had voted to execute Louis XVI. Backed by the army, the Directory annulled most of the election results. After two years of more uprisings and purges, and with the country still plagued by severe inflation, the Directors grew desperate. This time they called for help from a brilliant young general named Napoleon Bonaparte.

Bonaparte's first military victory had come in 1793, with the recapture of Toulon from royalist and British forces, and had earned him promotion from captain to brigadier general at the age of twenty-four. After the Terror, he was briefly arrested for his Jacobin associations. But he proved his usefulness to the Directory in October 1795 when he put down an uprising with "a whiff of grapeshot," saving the new regime from its opponents. Promoted, he won a string

of victories in Italy, forcing Austria to withdraw (temporarily) from the war. He attempted to defeat Britain by attacking British forces in Egypt and the Near East, a campaign that went well on land but ran into trouble at sea, where the French fleet was defeated by Admiral Horatio Nelson (Aboukir Bay, 1798). Bonaparte found himself trapped in Egypt by the British and unable to win a decisive victory.

It was at this point that the call came from the Directory. Bonaparte slipped away from Egypt and appeared in Paris, already having agreed to participate in a coup d'état with the leading Director, that former revolutionary champion of the Third Estate, the Abbé Sieyès. On November 9, 1799 (18 Brumaire), Bonaparte was declared a "temporary consul." He was the answer to the Directory's prayers: a strong, popular leader who was not a king. Sieyès declared that Bonaparte would provide "confidence from below, authority from above." With those words Sieyès pronounced the end of the revolutionary period.

NAPOLEON AND IMPERIAL FRANCE

Few figures in Western history have compelled the attention of the world as Napoleon Bonaparte did during the fifteen years of his rule in France. Few men have lived on with such persistence as myth, not just in their own countries, but across the West. Why? For the great majority of ordinary Europeans, memories of the French Revolution were dominated by those of the Napoleonic wars, which devastated Europe, convulsed its politics, and traumatized its peoples for a generation.

And yet Bonaparte's relationship to the revolution was not simple. His regime consolidated some of the revolution's political and social changes but sharply repudiated others. He presented himself as a son of the revolution, but he also borrowed freely from very different regimes, fashioning himself as the heir to Charlemagne or to the Roman Empire. His regime remade revolutionary politics and the French state; offered stunning examples of the new kinds of warfare; and left a legacy of conflict and legends of French glory that lingered in the dreams, or nightmares, of Europe's statesmen and citizens for more than a century.

Consolidating Authority: 1799–1804

Bonaparte owed his career to the revolution. The son of a provincial Corsican nobleman, he would have been unable to rise beyond the rank of major in prerevolutionary

***NAPOLEON ON HORSEBACK AT THE ST. BERNARD PASS* BY JACQUES-LOUIS DAVID, 1801, AND *LITTLE BONEY GONE TO POT* BY GEORGE CRUIKSHANK, 1814.** The depth of Napoleon's celebrity in Europe can be measured in the equal shares of adulation and hatred that he stirred up within Europe among his supporters and his enemies. David's portrait, painted before he became emperor of France, captures the ardent hopes that many attached to his person. The painting explicitly compared Napoleon to two previous European conquerors, Charlemagne and Hannibal, by evoking their names in the stones at the base of the painting. In George Cruikshanks's bitter caricature, published after Napoleon's exile to Elba, the devil offers him a pistol to commit suicide, and the former emperor, seated on a chamber pot, says he might, but only if the firing mechanism is disabled. Both images use assumptions about virility and masculine authority to make their point. ▪ *Who are the intended audiences for these images, and how do they convey their respective arguments?*

under the monarchy, acquired under Napoleon the character that they have preserved to this day: centralized, meritocratic, and geared to serving the state.

To win support for these ambitious reforms, Bonaparte made allies without regard for their past political affiliations. He admitted back into the country exiles of all political stripes. His two fellow consuls were a regicide of the Terror and a bureaucrat of the Old Regime. His minister of police had been an extreme radical republican; his minister of foreign affairs was the aristocrat and opportunist Charles Talleyrand. The most remarkable act of political reconciliation came in 1801, with Bonaparte's concordat with the pope, an agreement that put an end to more than a decade of hostility between the French state and the Catholic Church. Although it shocked anticlerical revolutionaries, Napoleon, ever the pragmatist, believed that reconciliation would create domestic harmony and international solidarity. The agreement gave the pope the right to depose French bishops and to discipline the French clergy. In return, the Vatican agreed to forgo any claims to

church lands expropriated by the revolution. That property would remain in the hands of its new middle-class rural and urban proprietors. The concordat did not revoke the principle of religious freedom established by the revolution, but it did win Napoleon the support of conservatives who had feared for France's future as a godless state.

Such political balancing acts increased Bonaparte's general popularity. Combined with early military successes (peace with Austria in 1801 and with Britain in 1802), they muffled any opposition to his personal ambitions. He had married Josephine de Beauharnais, a Creole from Martinique who had been the mistress of several revolutionary leaders after the execution of her first husband in the Terror. Josephine had given the Corsican soldier-politician legitimacy and access among the revolutionary elite early in his career. Neither Bonaparte nor his ambitious wife were content to be first among equals, however; and in December of 1804, he finally cast aside any traces of republicanism. In a ceremony that evoked the splendor of medieval kingship and Bourbon absolutism, he crowned himself Emperor Napoleon I in the Cathedral of Notre Dame in Paris. Napoleon did much to create the modern state, but he did not hesitate to proclaim his links to the past.

In Europe as in France: Napoleon's Empire

The nations of Europe had looked on—some in admiration, others in horror, all in astonishment—at the phenomenon that was Napoleon. Austria, Prussia, and Britain led two coalitions against revolutionary France in 1792–95 and in 1798, and both were defeated. After Napoleon came to power in 1799, the alliance split. Russia and Austria withdrew from the fray in 1801, and even the intransigent British were forced to make peace the following year.

By 1805 the Russians, Prussians, Austrians, and Swedes had joined the British in an attempt to contain France. Their efforts were to no avail. Napoleon's military superiority led to defeats, in turn, of all the continental allies. Napoleon was a master of well-timed, well-directed shock attacks on the battlefield: fast, fully engaged assaults designed to surprise and terrify enemy troops. He led an army that had transformed European warfare; first raised as a revolutionary militia, it was now a trained conscript army, loyal, well supplied by a nation whose economy was committed to serving the war effort, and led by generals promoted largely on the basis of talent. This new kind of army inflicted crushing defeats on his enemies. The battle of Austerlitz, in December 1805, was a triumph for the French against the combined forces of Austria and Russia and became a symbol of the emperor's apparent invincibility. His subsequent victory against the Russians at Friedland in 1807 only added to his reputation.

Out of these victories Napoleon created his new empire and affiliated states. To the southeast, the empire included Rome and the pope's dominions, Tuscany, and the Dalmatian territories of Austria (now the coastline of Croatia). To the east Napoleon's rule extended over a federation of German states known as the Confederation of the Rhine and a section of Poland. These new states served as a military buffer against renewed expansion by Austria. The empire itself was ringed by the allied kingdoms of Italy, Naples, Spain, and Holland. Napoleon himself was the king of Italy, and his brothers, brothers-in-law, and trusted generals ruled in the other kingdoms.

The empire brought the French Revolution's practical consequences—a powerful, centralizing state and an end to old systems of privilege—to Europe's doorstep, applying to the empire principles that had already transformed France. Administrative modernization, which meant overhauling the procedures, codes, and practices of the state, was the most powerful feature of the changes introduced. The empire changed the terms of government service ("careers open to talent"), handing out new titles and recruiting new men for the civil service and the judiciary. It ended the nobility's monopoly on the officer corps. The new branches of government hired engineers, mapmakers, surveyors, and legal consultants. Public works and education were reorganized. Prefects in the outer reaches of the empire, as in France, built roads, bridges, dikes (in Holland), hospitals, and prisons; they reorganized universities and built observatories. In the empire and some of the satellite kingdoms, tariffs were eliminated, feudal dues abolished, new tax districts formed, and plentiful new taxes collected to support the new state.

In the realm of liberty and law, Napoleon's rule eliminated feudal and church courts and created a single legal system. The Napoleonic Code was often introduced, but not always or entirely. Reforms eliminated many inequalities and legal privileges. In most areas, the empire gave civil rights to Protestants and Jews. In some areas, Catholic monasteries, convents, and other landholdings were broken up and sold, almost always to wealthy buyers. In the empire as in France, and under Napoleon as during the revolution, many who benefited were the elite: people and groups already on their way up and with the resources to take advantage of opportunities.

In government, the regime sought a combination of legal equality (for men) and stronger state authority. The French and local authorities created new electoral districts, expanded suffrage, and wrote constitutions, but newly elected representative bodies were dismissed if they failed to cooperate, few constitutions were ever fully applied, and political freedoms were often fleeting. Napoleon's regime referred to revolutionary principles to anchor its legitimacy, but authority remained its guiding light. All governmental direction emanated from Paris and therefore from Napoleon.

Finally, in the empire as in France, Napoleon displayed his signature passions. The first of these was an Enlightenment zeal for accumulating useful knowledge. The empire gathered statistics as never before, for it was important to know the resources—including population—that a state had at its disposal. Napoleon's second passion was cultivating his relationship to imperial glories of the past. He poured time and energy into (literally) cementing his image for posterity. The Arc de Triomphe in Paris, designed to imitate the Arch of Constantine in Rome, is the best example; but Napoleon also ordered work to be undertaken to restore ruins in Rome, to make the Prado Palace in Madrid a museum, and to renovate and preserve the Alhambra in Granada.

Such were Napoleon's visions of his legacy and himself. How did others see him? Europe offered no single reaction. Some countries and social groups collaborated enthusiastically, some negotiated, some resisted. Napoleon's image as a military hero genuinely inspired young men from the elite, raised in a culture that prized military honor. Yet the Napoleonic presence proved a mixed blessing. Vassal states contributed heavily to the maintenance of the emperor's military power. The French levied taxes, drafted men, and required states to support occupying armies. In Italy, the policy was called "liberty and requisitions"; and the Italians, Germans, and Dutch paid an especially high price for reforms—in terms of economic cost and numbers of men recruited. From the point of view of the common people, the local lord and priest had been replaced by the French tax collector and army recruiting board.

THE RETURN TO WAR AND NAPOLEON'S DEFEAT, 1806–1815

Napoleon's boldest attempt at consolidation, a policy banning British goods from the Continent, was a dangerous failure. Britain had bitterly opposed each of France's revolutionary regimes since the death of Louis XVI; now it tried to rally Europe against Napoleon with promises of generous financial loans and trade. Napoleon's Continental System, established in 1806, sought to starve Britain's trade and force its surrender. The system failed for several reasons. Throughout the war Britain retained control of the seas, and the British naval blockade of the Continent, begun in 1807, effectively countered Napoleon's system. While the French Empire strained to transport goods and raw materials overland to avoid the British blockade, the British successfully developed a lively trade with South America. A second reason for the failure of the system was its internal tariffs. Europe divided into economic camps, at odds with each other as they tried to subsist on what the Continent alone could produce and manufacture. Finally, the system hurt the Continent more than Britain. Stagnant trade in Europe's ports and unemployment in its manufacturing centers eroded public faith in Napoleon's dream of a working European empire.

The Continental System was Napoleon's first serious mistake. His ambition to create a European empire, modeled on Rome and ruled from Paris, was to become a second cause of his decline. The symbols of his empire—reflected in painting, architecture, and the design of furniture and clothing—were deliberately Roman in origin. Where early revolutionaries referred to the Roman Republic for their imagery, Napoleon looked to the more ostentatious style of the Roman emperors. In 1809 he divorced the empress Josephine and ensured himself a successor of royal blood by marrying a Habsburg princess, Marie Louise—the great-niece of Marie-Antionette. Such actions lost Napoleon the support of revolutionaries, former Enlightenment thinkers, and liberals across the Continent.

Over time, the bitter tonic of defeat began to have an effect on Napoleon's enemies, who changed their own approach to waging war. After the Prussian army was humiliated at Jena in 1806 and forced out of the war, a whole generation of younger Prussian officers reformed their military and their state by demanding rigorous practical training for commanders and a genuinely national army made up of patriotic Prussian citizens rather than well-drilled mercenaries.

The myth of Napoleon's invincibility worked against him as well, as he took ever-greater risks with France's military and national fortunes. Russian troops and Austrian artillery inflicted horrendous losses on the French at Wagram in 1809, although these difficulties were forgotten in the glow of victory. Napoleon's allies and supporters shrugged off the British admiral Horatio Nelson's victory at Trafalgar in 1805 as no more than a temporary check to the emperor's ambitions. But Trafalgar broke French naval power in the Mediterranean and led to a rift with Spain, which had been France's equal partner in the battle and suffered equally in the defeat. In the Caribbean, too, Napoleon was forced to cut growing losses (see page 502).

A crucial moment in Napoleon's undoing came with his invasion of Spain in 1808. Napoleon overthrew the Spanish king, installed his own brother on the throne, and then imposed a series of reforms similar to those he had instituted elsewhere in Europe. Napoleon's blow against the Spanish monarchy weakened its hold on its colonies across the Atlantic, and the Spanish crown never fully regained its grip (see Chapter 20). But in Spain itself, Napoleon reckoned with two factors that led to the ultimate failure of his mission: the presence of British forces and the determined resistance of the Spanish people, who detested Napoleon's interference in the affairs of the church. The Peninsular Wars, as the Spanish conflicts were called, were long and bitter. The smaller British force laid siege to French garrison towns, and the Spanish quickly began to wear down the French invaders through guerrilla warfare. Terrible atrocities were committed by both sides; the French military's torture and execution of Spanish guerrillas and civilians was immortalized by the Spanish artist Francisco Goya (1746–1828) with sickening realism in his prints and paintings. The Spanish campaign was the first indication that Napoleon could be beaten, and it encouraged resistance elsewhere.

The second, and most dramatic stage in Napoleon's downfall began with the disruption of his alliance with Russia. In 1811, Napoleon grew tired of Russia's violations of the Continental System. Tsar Alexander I had turned a blind eye toward trade with Britain because it provided important

Past and Present

The Atlantic Revolutions and Human Rights

The eighteenth-century revolutions in the Atlantic world, such as the slave revolt in Saint-Domingue (left), were based on the idea that individual rights were universal—they applied to everybody. Since the world is divided into autonomous nation-states, however, it has been challenging for defenders of universal human rights, like the organization Amnesty International (right), to ensure their enforcement globally.

Watch related author videos on the Student Site
wwnorton.com/college/history/western-civilizationsBrief4

outlets for Russian grain. To punish Russia, Napoleon collected the largest army ever assembled on the continent: the six-hundred-thousand-strong "Grande Armée." The invasion began in the spring of 1812. The Russians, vastly outmanned, refused to meet Napoleon's army and withdrew deep into the countryside. After an inconsequential victory over Russian forces at Borodino, Napoleon reached Moscow only to find that partisans had burned the Russian capital before departing. Unable to force the tsar to surrender, Napoleon was forced to retreat as the Russian winter set in, with devastating effects on his remaining soldiers. Frostbite, disease, starvation, and almost continuous harrassment by mounted Cossacks reduced Napoleon's army to a few thousand survivors when the emperor arrived in Germany in December, 1812.

After the retreat from Russia, the anti-Napoleonic forces took renewed hope. United by a belief that they might finally succeed in defeating the emperor, Prussia, Russia, Austria, Sweden, and Britain renewed their attack. Citizens of many German states in particular saw this as a war of liberation,

and indeed most of the fighting took place in Germany. The climax of the campaign occurred in October 1813 when, at what was thereafter known as the Battle of the Nations, fought near Leipzig, the allies dealt the French a resounding defeat. Meanwhile, allied armies won significant victories in the Low Countries and Spain. By the beginning of 1814, they had crossed the Rhine into France. Left with an army of inexperienced youths, Napoleon retreated to Paris, urging the French people to resist despite constant setbacks at the hands of the larger invading armies. On March 31, Tsar Alexander I of Russia and King Frederick William III of Prussia made their triumphant entry into Paris. Napoleon was forced to abdicate unconditionally and was sent into exile on the island of Elba, off the Italian coast.

Napoleon was back on French soil in less than a year. In the interim the allies had restored the Bourbon dynasty to the throne, in the person of Louis XVIII, brother of Louis XVI. Despite his administrative abilities, Louis could not fill the void left by Napoleon's abdication. It was no surprise that, when the former emperor staged his escape from Elba, his fellow countrymen once more rallied to his side. By the time Napoleon reached Paris, he had generated enough support to cause Louis to flee the country. The allies, meeting in Vienna to conclude peace treaties with the French, were stunned by the news of Napoleon's return. They dispatched a hastily organized army to meet the emperor's characteristically bold offensive push into Belgium. At the battle of Waterloo, fought over three bloody days from June 15 to 18, 1815, Napoleon was stopped by the forces of his two most persistent enemies, Britain and Prussia, and suffered his final defeat. This time the allies took no chances and shipped their prisoner off to the bleak island of St. Helena in the South Atlantic. The once-mighty emperor, now the exile Bonaparte, lived out a dreary existence writing self-serving memoirs until his death in 1821.

Liberty, Politics, and Slavery: The Haitian Revolution

In the French colonies across the Atlantic, the revolution took a different course, with wide-ranging ramifications. The Caribbean islands of Guadeloupe, Martinique, and Saint-Domingue occupied a central role in the eighteenth-century French economy because of the sugar trade. Their planter elites had powerful influence in Paris. The French National Assembly (like its American counterpart) declined to discuss the matter of slavery in the colonies, unwilling to encroach on the property rights of slave owners and fearful of losing the lucrative sugar islands to their British or Spanish rivals should disgruntled slave owners talk of independence from France. (Competition between the European powers for the islands of the Caribbean was intense; that islands would change hands was a real possibility.) French men in the National Assembly also had to consider the question of rights for free men of color, a group that included a significant number of wealthy owners of property (and slaves).

Saint-Domingue had about 40,000 whites of different social classes, 30,000 free people of color, and 500,000 slaves, most of them recently enslaved in West Africa. In 1790, free people of color from Saint-Domingue sent a delegation to Paris, asking to be seated by the assembly, underscoring that they were men of property and, in many cases, of European ancestry. The assembly refused. Their refusal sparked a rebellion among free people of color in Saint-Domingue. The French colonial authorities repressed the movement quickly—and brutally. They captured Vincent Ogé, a member of the delegation to Paris and one of the leaders of the rebellion, and publicly executed him and his allies by breaking on the wheel and decapitation. Radical deputies in Paris, including Robespierre, expressed outrage but could do little to change the assembly's policy.

In August 1791 the largest slave rebellion in history broke out in Saint-Domingue. How much that rebellion owed to revolutionary propaganda is unclear; like many rebellions during the period, it had its own roots. The British and the Spanish invaded, confident they could crush the rebellion and take the island. In the spring of 1792, the French government, on the verge of collapse and war with Europe, scrambled to win allies in Saint-Domingue by making free men of color citizens. A few months later (after the revolution of August 1792), the new French Republic dispatched commissioners to Saint-Domingue with troops and instructions to hold the island. There they faced a combination of different forces: Spanish and British troops, defiant Saint-Domingue planters, and slaves in rebellion. In this context, the local French commissioners reconsidered their commitment to slavery; in 1793 they promised freedom to slaves who would join the French. A year later, the assembly in Paris extended to slaves in all the colonies a liberty that had already been accomplished in Saint-Domingue, by the slave rebellion.

Emancipation and war brought new leaders to the fore, chief among them a former slave, Toussaint Bréda, later Toussaint L'Ouverture (*too-SAN LOO-vehr-tur*), meaning "the one who opened the way." Over the course of the next five

TOUSSAINT L'OUVERTURE. A portrait of L'Ouverture, leader of what would become the Haitian Revolution, as a general.

years, Toussaint and his soldiers, now allied with the French army, emerged victorious over the French planters, the British (in 1798), and the Spanish (in 1801). Toussaint also broke the power of his rival generals in both the mulatto and former slave armies, becoming the statesman of the revolution. In 1801, Toussaint set up a constitution, swearing allegiance to France but denying France any right to interfere in Saint-Domingue affairs. The constitution abolished slavery, reorganized the military, established Christianity as the state religion (this entailed a rejection of Vodou, a blend of Christian and various West and Central African traditions), and made Toussaint governor for life. It was an extraordinary moment in the revolutionary period: the formation of an authoritarian society but also an utterly unexpected symbol of the universal potential of revolutionary ideas.

Toussaint's accomplishments, however, put him on a collision course with the other French general he admired and whose career was remarkably like his own: Napoleon Bonaparte. Saint-Domingue stood at the center of Bonaparte's vision of an expanded empire in the New World, an empire that would recoup North American territories France had lost under the Old Regime and pivot around the lucrative combination of the Mississippi, French Louisiana, and the sugar and slave colonies of the Caribbean. In January 1802, Bonaparte dispatched 20,000 troops to bring the island under control. Toussaint, captured when he arrived for discussions with the French, was shipped under heavy guard to a prison in the mountains of eastern France, where he died in 1803. Fighting continued in Saint-Domingue, however, with fires now fueled by Bonaparte's decree reestablishing slavery where the convention had abolished it. The war turned into a nightmare for the French. Yellow fever killed thousands of French troops, including Napoleon's brother-in-law, one of his best generals. Armies on both sides committed atrocities. By December 1803 the French army had collapsed. Napoleon scaled back his vision of an American empire and sold the Louisiana territories to Thomas Jefferson. In Saint-Domingue, a general in the army of former slaves, Jean-Jacques Dessalines, declared the independent state of Haiti in 1804.

The Haitian Revolution remained, in significant ways, an anomaly. It was the only successful slave revolution in history and by far the most radical of the revolutions that occurred in this age. It suggested that the emancipatory ideas of the revolution and Enlightenment might apply to non-Europeans and enslaved peoples—a suggestion that residents of Europe attempted to ignore but one that struck home with planter elites in North and South America. Combined with later rebellions in the British colonies, it contributed to the British decision to end slavery in 1838. And it cast a long shadow over nineteenth-century slave societies from the southern United States to Brazil. The Napoleonic episode, then, had wide-ranging effects across

After You Read This Chapter

 Go to **INQUIZITIVE** to see what you've learned—and learn what you've missed—with personalized feedback along the way.

REVIEWING THE OBJECTIVES

- The French Revolution resulted both from an immediate political crisis and long-term social tensions. What was this crisis, and how did it lead to popular revolt against the monarchy?

- The revolutionaries in the National Assembly in 1789 set out to produce a constitution for France. What were their political goals, and what was the reaction of monarchs and peoples elsewhere in Europe?

- After 1792, a more radical group of revolutionaries seized control of the French state. How did they come to power, and how were their political goals different from their predecessors?

- Napoleon's career began during the revolution. What did he owe to the revolution, and what was different about his regime?

- Three major revolutions took place in the Atlantic world at the end of the eighteenth century: the American Revolution, the French Revolution, and the Haitian Revolution. What was similar about these revolutions? What was different?

the Atlantic: in North America, the Louisiana purchase; in the Caribbean, the Haitian Revolution; in Latin America, the weakening of Spain and Portugal's colonial empires.

CONCLUSION

The tumultuous events in France formed part of a broad pattern of late-eighteenth-century democratic upheaval. The French Revolution was the most violent, protracted, and contentious of the revolutions of the era; but the dynamics of revolution were much the same everywhere. One of the most important developments of the French Revolution was the emergence of a popular movement, which included political clubs representing people previously excluded from politics, newspapers read by and to the common people, and political leaders who spoke for the sans-culottes. In the French Revolution as in other revolutions, the popular movement challenged the early and moderate revolutionary leadership, pressing for more radical and democratic measures. And as in other revolutions, the popular movement in France was defeated, and authority was reestablished by a quasi-military figure. Likewise, the revolutionary ideas of liberty, equality, and fraternity were not specifically French; their roots lay in the social structures of the eighteenth century and in the ideas

and culture of the Enlightenment. Yet French armies brought them, literally, to the doorsteps of many Europeans.

What was the larger impact of the revolution and the Napoleonic era? Its legacy is partly summed up in three key concepts: liberty, equality, and nation. *Liberty* meant individual rights and responsibilities and, more specifically, freedom from arbitrary authority. By *equality*, as we have seen, the revolutionaries meant the abolition of legal distinctions of rank among European men. Though their concept of equality was limited, it became a powerful mobilizing force in the nineteenth century. The most important legacy of the revolution may have been the new term *nation*. Nationhood was a political concept. A nation was formed of citizens, not a king's subjects; it was ruled by law and treated citizens as equal before the law; sovereignty did not lie in dynasties or historic fiefdoms but in the nation of citizens. This new form of nation gained legitimacy when citizen armies repelled attacks against their newly won freedoms; the victories of "citizens in arms" lived on in myth and history and provided the most powerful images of the period. As the war continued, military nationhood began to overshadow its political cousin. By the Napoleonic period, this shift became decisive; a new political body of freely associated citizens was most powerfully embodied in a centralized state, its army, and a kind of citizenship defined by individual commitment to the needs of the nation at war. This understanding of national identity spread throughout Europe in the coming decades.

PEOPLE, IDEAS, AND EVENTS IN CONTEXT

- Why was **LOUIS XVI** forced to convene the **ESTATES GENERAL** in 1789?
- What argument did **ABBÉ SIEYÈS** make about the role of the **THIRD ESTATE**?
- What made the **TENNIS COURT OATH** a revolutionary act?
- What was the role of popular revolt (the attack on the **BASTILLE**, the **GREAT FEAR**, the **OCTOBER DAYS**) in the revolutionary movements of 1789?
- What was the connection between the French Revolution and the **SLAVE REVOLT IN SAINT-DOMINGUE** that began in 1791?
- What was the **DECLARATION OF THE RIGHTS OF MAN AND OF THE CITIZEN**?
- What was the **CIVIL CONSTITUTION OF THE CLERGY**?
- What circumstances led to the abolition of the monarchy in 1792?
- Why did the **JACOBINS** in the **NATIONAL CONVENTION** support a policy of **TERROR**?
- What were **NAPOLEON'S** most significant domestic accomplishments in France? What significance did **NAPOLEON'S MILITARY CAMPAIGNS** have for other parts of Europe and for the French Empire?
- What was the significance of the **HAITIAN REVOLUTION** of 1804?

THINKING ABOUT CONNECTIONS

- Was the French Revolution a success? Why or why not?
- Who benefited from the French Revolution? Who suffered the most from its consequences?
- In what ways do you think the French Revolution would have an impact on nineteenth-century history?

STORY LINES

- Industrialization put Europe on the path to a new form of economic development, based on the concentration of labor and production in areas with easy access to new sources of energy. This led to rapid growth of new industrial cities and the development of new transportation links to connect industrial centers to growing markets.

- Industrialization created new social groups in society, defined by their place in the new economy. Workers faced new kinds of discipline in the workplace, and women and children entered the industrial workforce in large numbers. A new elite, made up of entrepreneurs, bankers, engineers, and merchants emerged as the primary beneficiaries of industrialization.

- Population growth spurred migration to cities where laborers and the middle classes did not mix socially. They adopted different forms of dress, speech, and leisure activities, and had significantly different opportunities when it came to marriage, sex, family life, and the raising of children.

CHRONOLOGY

1780s	Industrialization begins in Britain
1825	First railroad in Britain
1830s	Industrialization begins in France and Belgium
1845–1849	Irish Potato Famine
1850s	Industrialization begins in Prussia and the German states of central Europe
1861	Russian tsar emancipates the serfs

Before You Read This Chapter

The Industrial Revolution and Nineteenth-Century Society

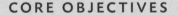

CORE OBJECTIVES

- **UNDERSTAND** the circumstances that allowed for industrialization to begin in Great Britain.

- **IDENTIFY** the regions in Europe that industrialized first and the industries located there.

- **DESCRIBE** changes in production and employment that occurred as a result of the mechanization of industry.

- **EXPLAIN** the effects of industrialization on social life in Europe, especially in the new urban centers associated with industrial development.

- **IDENTIFY** the essential characteristics of the new "middle classes" in nineteenth-century Europe and their differences from property-owning groups prior to the Industrial Revolution.

The French Revolution transformed the political landscape of Europe suddenly and dramatically. More gradual, but just as consequential for the modern world, was the economic transformation that began in Europe in the 1780s. Following the development of mechanized industry and the emergence of large-scale manufacturing in the British textile trade, industrialization spread to the European Continent and eventually to North America. This "Industrial Revolution" led to the proliferation of more capital-intensive enterprises, new ways of organizing human labor, and the rapid growth of cities. It was accompanied by population growth and made possible by new sources of energy and power, which led to faster forms of mechanized transportation, higher productivity, and the emergence of large consumer markets for manufactured goods. In turn, these interrelated developments triggered social and cultural changes with revolutionary consequences for Europeans and their relationship to the rest of the world.

Of all the changes, perhaps the most revolutionary came at the very root of human endeavor: new forms of energy. Over the space of two or three generations, a society and an economy

505

that had drawn on water, wind, and wood for most of its energy needs came to depend on machines driven by steam engines and coal. In 1800, the world produced 10 million tons of coal. In 1900, it produced 1 billion: a hundred times more. The Industrial Revolution brought the beginning of the fossil-fuel age, altering as it did so the balance of humanity and the environment.

Mechanization made possible enormous gains in productivity in some sectors of the economy, but to focus only on mechanization can be misleading. The new machines were limited to a few sectors of the economy, especially at the outset, and did not always lead to a dramatic break with older techniques. Above all, technology did not dispense with human toil. Historians emphasize that the Industrial Revolution intensified human labor—constructing and maintaining railway tracks, digging trenches, harvesting cotton, sewing by hand, or pounding hides—much more often than it eased it. One historian has suggested that we would do better to speak of the "industrious revolution." This revolution did not lie solely in machines but in a new economic system based on mobilizing capital and labor on a much larger scale. The "industrious" economy redistributed wealth and power, creating new social classes and producing new social tensions.

It also prompted deep-seated cultural shifts. The English critic Raymond Williams has pointed out that in the eighteenth century, *industry* referred to a human quality: a hardworking woman was "industrious," an ambitious clerk showed "industry." By the middle of the nineteenth century, industry had come to mean an economic system, one that followed its own logic and worked on its own—seemingly independent of humans. This is our modern understanding of the term, and it was born in the early nineteenth century. As the Industrial Revolution altered the foundations of the economy, it also changed the very assumptions with which people approached economics and the ways in which they regarded the role of human beings in the economy. These new assumptions could foster a sense of power but also anxieties about powerlessness. The new economy created both opportunity and a new kind of vulnerability for those whose livelihoods were threatened by industrialization. This dynamic ensured that the industrial era would be marked by new forms of social conflict, as well as new forms of wealth.

THE INDUSTRIAL REVOLUTION IN BRITAIN, 1760–1850

Industrialization began in the north of Britain in the late 1700s. In part this was due to a set of fortunate circumstances: Britain was a secure island nation with a robust empire, profitable overseas trade networks, and established credit institutions. Perhaps even more important, Britain had ample supplies of coal lying close to the surface, and a well-developed transportation network in its many rivers and canals.

In addition to these advantages, British agriculture was already thoroughly commercialized. British farming had been transformed by a combination of new techniques and new crops, as well as by the "enclosure" of fields and pastures, which turned small holdings, and in many cases commonly held lands, into large fenced tracts that were privately owned by commercial landlords. The British Parliament encouraged enclosure with a series of bills in the second half of the eighteenth century. Commercialized agriculture was more productive and yielded more food for a growing and increasingly urban population. The concentration of property in fewer hands drove small farmers off the land, sending them to look for work in other sectors of the economy. Finally, commercialized agriculture produced higher profits, wealth that could be invested in industry.

A key precondition for industrialization, therefore, was Britain's growing supply of available capital, in the forms of private wealth and well-developed banking and credit institutions. London had become the leading center for international trade, and the city was

ENCLOSED FIELDS IN CENTRAL BRITAIN. The large, uniform, square fields in the background of this photograph are fields that were enclosed from smaller holdings and common lands in the 1830s. They contrast with the smaller and older strip fields in the foreground. The larger enclosed fields were more profitable for their owners, who benefited from legislation that encouraged enclosure, but the process created hardship for the village communities that depended on the use of these lands for their survival. ▪ *What circumstances made enclosure possible?* ▪ *What connection have historians made between enclosure and early industrialization?*

a headquarters for the transfer of raw material, capital, and manufactured products throughout the world. This capital was readily available to underwrite new economic enterprises and eased the transfer of money and goods—importing, for instance, silks from Asia or Egyptian and North American cotton.

Social and cultural conditions also encouraged investment in enterprises. In Britain far more than on the Continent, the pursuit of wealth was perceived to be a worthy goal. Unlike European nobility, British aristocrats respected commoners with a talent for making money and did not hesitate to invest themselves. Their scramble to enclose their lands reflected a keen interest in commercialization and investment. Outside the aristocracy, an even lower barrier separated merchants from the rural gentry. Many of the entrepreneurs of the early Industrial Revolution came from the small gentry or independent farmer class. Eighteenth-century Britain was not by any means free of social snobbery, but a lord's disdain for a merchant might well be tempered by the fact that his own grandfather had worked in the counting house.

Growing domestic and international markets increased demand for goods and made eighteenth-century Britain prosperous. The British were voracious consumers. The court elite followed and bought up yearly fashions, and so did most of Britain's landed and professional society. The country's small size and the fact that it was an island encouraged the development of a well-integrated domestic market. Unlike continental Europe, Britain did not have a system of internal tolls and tariffs, so goods could be moved freely to wherever they might fetch the best price. A constantly improving transportation system boosted that freedom of movement. So did a favorable political climate. Some members of Parliament were businessmen themselves; others were investors.

Foreign markets promised even greater returns than domestic ones, though with greater risks. British foreign policy responded to its commercial needs. At the end of every major eighteenth-century war, Britain wrested overseas territories from its enemies. At the same time, Britain penetrated hitherto unexploited territories such as India and South America. In 1759, over one-third of all British exports went to the colonies; by 1784, if we include the former colonies in North America, that figure had increased to one-half. Production for export rose by 80 percent between 1750 and 1770; production for domestic consumption gained just 7 percent over the same period. The British possessed a merchant marine capable of transporting goods around the world and a navy practiced in the art of protecting its commercial

fleets. By the 1780s, Britain's markets, together with its fleet and its established position at the center of world commerce, gave its entrepreneurs unrivaled opportunities for trade and profit.

Innovation in the Textile Industries

The Industrial Revolution began with dramatic technological leaps in a few industries, the first of which was cotton textiles. The industry was already long established. British textile manufacturers imported raw cotton from India and the American South and borrowed patterns from Indian spinners and weavers. What were the revolutionary breakthroughs?

In 1733, John Kay's invention of the flying shuttle speeded the process of weaving. The spinning jenny, invented by James Hargreaves in 1764, could produce sixteen threads at once. The invention of the water frame by Richard Arkwright, a barber, in 1769, made it possible to produce stronger threads in great quantity. In 1799 Samuel Compton invented the spinning mule, which combined the features of both the jenny and the water frame. All of these important technological changes were accomplished by the end of the eighteenth century.

These machines revolutionized production across the textile industry. A jenny could spin from six to twenty-four times more yarn than a hand spinner. By the end of the eighteenth century, a spinning mule could produce two to three hundred times more. The cotton gin, invented by the American Eli Whitney in 1793, mechanized the process of separating cotton seeds from the fiber, thereby speeding up the production of cotton and reducing its price. The supply of cotton fibers expanded to keep pace with rising demand from cotton cloth manufacturers. The cotton gin had many effects, including, paradoxically, making slavery more profitable in the United States. The cotton-producing slave plantations in the American South became enmeshed in the lucrative trade with manufacturers who produced cotton textiles in the northern United States and England.

The first textile machines were inexpensive enough to be used by spinners in their own cottages. But as machines grew in size and complexity, they were housed instead in workshops or mills located near water that could be used to power the machines. Eventually, the further development of steam-driven equipment allowed manufacturers to build mills wherever they could be used. Frequently, those mills went up in towns and cities in the north of England, away from the older commercial and seafaring centers, but nearer to the coal fields that provided fuel for new machines.

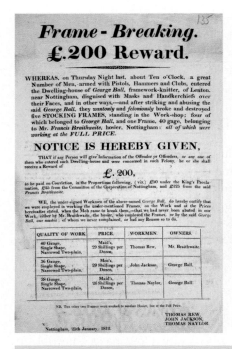

NED LUDD AND THE LUDDITES. In 1811 and 1812, in northern England, bands of working men who resented the adoption of new mechanical devices in the weaving industries attacked several establishments and destroyed the frames used to weave cloth. The movement took the name Luddites from Ned Ludd, a man who in 1779 had broken the frames belonging to his employer. His mythological presence in the movement is depicted in the illustration at the right. Although their anger was directed at the machines, the real target of their resentment may have been a new pricing scheme imposed on them by the merchants who bought finished work. The debate about prices underlies the message of the poster on the left, which offers a reward for information leading to the conviction of frame breakers. The poster is signed by several workers of the establishment, who published the price they received for each piece of clothing and their lack of complaints about their employer. ▪ *How might the need to adjust to the price fluctuations of a market economy have been perceived by weavers accustomed to getting fixed prices for their goods?*

From 1780 on, British cotton textiles flooded the world market. In 1760, Britain imported 2.5 million pounds of raw cotton; in 1787, 22 million pounds; in 1837, 366 million pounds. Although the price of manufactured cotton goods fell dramatically, the market expanded so rapidly that profits continued to increase.

The explosive growth of textiles also prompted a debate about the benefits and tyranny of the new industries. By the 1830s, the British House of Commons was holding hearings on employment and working conditions in factories, recording testimony about working days that stretched from 3:00 A.M. to 10:00 P.M., the employment of very small children, and workers who lost hair and fingers in the mills' machinery. Women and children counted for roughly two-thirds of the labor force in textiles. The principle of regulating any labor (and emphatically that of adult men), however, was controversial. Only gradually did a series of factory acts prohibit hiring children under age nine and limit the labor of workers under age eighteen to ten hours a day.

Coal and Iron

Meanwhile, decisive changes were transforming the production of iron. As in the textile industry, many important technological changes came during the eighteenth century. A series of innovations (coke smelting, rolling, and puddling) enabled the British to substitute coal (which they had in abundance) for wood (which was scarce and inefficient) to heat molten metal and make iron. The new "pig iron" was higher quality and could be used in building an enormous variety of iron products: machines, engines, railway tracks, agricultural implements, and hardware. Those iron products became, literally, the infrastructure of industrialization. Britain found itself able to export both coal and iron to rapidly expanding markets around the industrializing regions of the world. Between 1814 and 1852, exports of British iron doubled, rising to over 1 million tons of iron, more than half of the world's total production.

Rising demand for coal required mining deeper veins. In 1711, Thomas Newcomen had devised a cumbersome but remarkably effective steam engine for pumping water from mines. Though it was immensely valuable to the coal industry, its usefulness in other industries was limited by the amount of fuel it consumed. In 1763, James Watt improved on Newcomen's machine, and by 1800, Watt and his partner, Matthew Boulton, had sold 289 engines for use in factories and mines.

Steam power was still energy consuming and expensive, and so it only slowly replaced traditional water power. Even in its early form, however, the steam engine

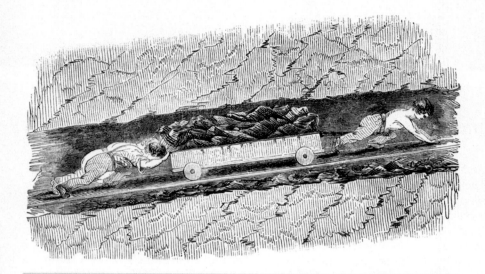

CHILD LABOR IN THE MINES. This engraving of young workers hauling a coal cart up through the narrow shaft of a mine accompanied a British parliamentary report on child labor. ▪ *What attitudes about government and the economy made it difficult for legislatures to regulate working conditions in the new industries?*

decisively transformed the nineteenth-century world with one application: the steam-driven locomotive. Railroads revolutionized industry, markets, public and private financing, and ordinary people's conceptions of space and time.

THE COMING OF RAILWAYS

Transportation had improved during the years before 1830, but moving heavy materials, particularly coal, remained a problem. It is significant that the first modern railway, built in England in 1825, ran from the Durham coal field of Stockton to Darlington, near the coast. The locomotives on the Stockton-Darlington line traveled at fifteen miles per hour, the fastest rate at which machines had yet moved goods overland. Soon they would move people as well, transforming transportation in the process.

Building railways became a massive enterprise and a risky but potentially profitable opportunity for investment. No sooner did the first combined passenger and goods service open in 1830, operating between Liverpool and Manchester, England, than plans were formulated and money pledged to extend rail systems throughout Europe, the Americas, and beyond. In 1830, there were no more than a few dozen miles of railway in the world. By 1840, there were over forty-five hundred miles; by 1850, over twenty-three thousand.

Throughout the world, a veritable army of construction workers built the railways. In Britain, they were called "navvies," derived from *navigator*, a term first used for the construction workers on Britain's eighteenth-century canals. Navvies were a rough lot, living with a few women in temporary encampments as they migrated across the countryside. Often they were immigrant workers and faced local hostility. Later in the century, railway building projects in Africa and the Americas were lined with camps of immigrant Indian and Chinese laborers, who became targets of nativist (a term that means "opposed to foreigners") anger.

The magnitude of the navvies' accomplishment was extraordinary. In Britain and in much of the rest of the world, mid-nineteenth-century railways were constructed almost entirely without the aid of machinery. An assistant engineer on the London-to-Birmingham line calculated that the labor involved was the equivalent of lifting 25 billion cubic feet of earth and stone one foot high. He compared this feat with building the Great Pyramid, which had required over 200,000 men and had taken twenty years. The construction of the London-to-Birmingham railway was accomplished by 20,000 men in less than five years. Railways were produced by toil as much as by technology, by human labor as much as by engineering; they illustrate why some historians prefer to use the term *industrious* revolution.

Steam engines, textile machines, new ways of making iron, and railways—all these were interconnected. Changes in one area amplified changes in another. Pumps run by steam engines made it possible to mine deeper veins of coal; steam-powered railways made it possible to transport coal. Mechanization fueled the production of iron for machines and the mining of coal to run steam engines. The railway boom multiplied the demand for iron products: rails, locomotives, carriages, signals, and switches. The scale of production expanded and the tempo of economic activity quickened, spurring the search for more coal, the production of more iron, the mobilization of more capital, and the recruitment of more labor. Steam and speed were becoming the foundation of the economy and of a new way of life.

The Factory System, Science, and Morality: Two Views

Reactions to the Industrial Revolution and the factory system it produced ranged from celebration to horror. Dr. Andrew Ure (1778–1857), a Scottish professor of chemistry, was fascinated with these nineteenth-century applications of Enlightenment science. He believed that the new machinery and its products would create a new society of wealth, abundance, and, ultimately, stability through the useful regimentation of production.

Friedrich Engels (1820–1895) was one of the many socialists to criticize Dr. Ure as shortsighted and complacent in his outlook. Engels was himself part of a factory-owning family and so was able to examine the new industrial cities at close range. He provides a classic nineteenth-century analysis of industrialization. The Condition of the Working Class in England *is compellingly written, angry, and revealing about middle-class concerns of the time, including female labor.*

Dr. Andrew Ure (1835)

This island [Britain] is preeminent among civilized nations for the prodigious development of its factory wealth, and has been therefore long viewed with a jealous admiration by foreign powers. This very pre-eminence, however, has been contemplated in a very different light by many influential members of our own community, and has even been denounced by them as the certain origin of innumerable evils to the people, and of revolutionary convulsions to the state. . . .

The blessings which physico-mechanical science has bestowed on society, and the means it has still in store for ameliorating the lot of mankind, has been too little dwelt upon; while, on the other hand, it has been accused of lending itself to the rich capitalists as an instrument for harassing the poor, and of exacting from the operative an accelerated rate of work. It has been said, for example, that the steam-engine now drives the power-looms with such velocity as to urge on their attendant weavers at the same rapid pace; but that the hand-weaver, not being subjected to this restless agent, can throw his shuttle and move his treddles at his convenience. There is, however, this difference in the two cases, that in the factory, every member of the loom is so adjusted, that the driving force leaves the attendant nearly nothing at all to do, certainly no muscular fatigue to sustain, while it produces for him good, unfailing wages, besides a healthy workshop *gratis*: whereas the non-factory weaver, having everything to execute by muscular exertion, finds the labour irksome, makes in consequence innumerable short pauses, separately of little account, but great when added together; earns therefore proportionally low wages, while he loses his health by poor diet and the dampness of his hovel.

Source: Andrew Ure, *The Philosophy of Manufacturers: Or, An Exposition of the Scientific, Moral, and Commercial Economy of the Factory System of Great Britain, 1835,* as cited in J. T. Ward, *The Factory System,* vol. 1 (New York: 1970), pp. 140–41.

THE INDUSTRIAL REVOLUTION ON THE CONTINENT

Continental Europe followed a different path. Eighteenth-century France, Belgium, and Germany did have manufacturing districts in regions with raw materials, access to markets, and long-standing traditions of craft and skill. Yet for a variety of reasons, changes along the lines seen in Britain did not occur until the 1830s. Britain's transportation system was highly developed; those of France and Germany were not. France was far larger than England: its rivers more difficult to navigate; its seaports, cities, and coal deposits farther apart. Much of central Europe was divided into small principalities, each with its own tolls and tariffs, which complicated the transportation of goods over any considerable distance. The Continent had fewer raw materials, coal in particular, than Britain. The abundance and cheapness of wood discouraged exploration that might

Friedrich Engels (1844)

Histories of the modern development of the cotton industry, such as those of Ure, Baines, and others, tell on every page of technical innovations.... In a well-ordered society such improvements would indeed be welcome, but social war rages unchecked and the benefits derived from these improvements are ruthlessly monopolized by a few persons.... Every improvement in machinery leads to unemployment, and the greater the technical improvement the greater the unemployment. Every improvement in machinery affects a number of workers in the same way as a commercial crisis and leads to want, distress, and crime....

Let us examine a little more closely the process whereby machine-labour continually supersedes hand-labour. When spinning or weaving machinery is installed practically all that is left to be done by the hand is the piecing together of broken threads, and the machine does the rest. This task calls for nimble fingers rather than muscular strength. The labour of grown men is not merely unnecessary but actually unsuitable.... The greater the degree to which physical labour is displaced by the introduction of machines worked by water- or steam-power, the fewer grown men need be employed. In any case women and children will work for lower wages than men and, as has already been observed, they are more skillful at piecing than grown men. Consequently it is women and children who are employed to do this work.... When women work in factories, the most important result is the dissolution of family ties. If a woman works for twelve or thirteen hours a day in a factory and her husband is employed either in the same establishment or in some other works, what is the fate of the children? They lack parental care and control.... It is not difficult to imagine that they are left to run wild.

Source: Friedrich Engels, *The Condition of the Working Class in England in 1844*, trans. and ed. W. O. Henderson and W. H. Chaloner (New York: 1958), pp. 150–51, 158, 160.

Questions for Analysis

1. According to Andrew Ure, why was industrialization good for Britain? How can the blessings of "physico-mechanical science" lead to the improvement of humanity?

2. What criticism did Engels level at Ure and other optimists on industrialization? Why did Engels think conditions for workers were getting worse instead of better?

3. What consequences do these two writers see for society in the wake of technological change? What assumptions do they make about the relationship between economic development and the social order?

---

have resulted in new discoveries of coal. It also meant that coal-run steam engines were less economical on the Continent. Capital, too, was less readily available. Early British industrialization was underwritten by private wealth; this was less feasible elsewhere. Different patterns of landholding formed obstacles to the commercialization of agriculture. In the East, serfdom was a powerful disincentive to labor-saving innovations. In the West, especially in France, the large number of peasants, or small farmers, stayed put on the land.

The wars of the French Revolution and Napoleon disrupted economies. During the eighteenth century, the population had grown and mechanization had begun in a few key industries. The ensuing political upheaval and the financial strains of warfare did virtually nothing to help economic development. Napoleon's Continental System and British destruction of French merchant shipping hurt commerce badly. Probably the revolutionary change most beneficial to industrial advance in Europe was the removal of previous restraints on the movement of capital and labor—for example, the abolition of craft guilds and the reduction of tariff barriers across the Continent.

After 1815, a number of factors combined to change the economic climate. In those regions with a well-established commercial and industrial base—the northeast of France, Belgium, and swaths of territory across the Rhineland, Saxony, Silesia, and northern Bohemia (see map on page 513)—population growth further boosted economic development. Rising population did not by itself produce industrialization, however: in Ireland, where other necessary factors were absent, more people meant less food.

Transportation improved. The Austrian Empire added over 30,000 miles of roads between 1830 and 1847; Belgium almost doubled its road network in the same period; France built not only new roads but 2,000 miles of canals. These improvements, combined with the construction of railroads in the 1830s and 1840s, opened up new markets and encouraged new methods of manufacturing. In many of the Continent's manufacturing regions, however, industrialists continued to tap large pools of skilled but inexpensive labor. Thus older methods of putting-out industry and handwork persisted alongside new-model factories longer than in Britain.

In what other ways was the continental model of industrialization different? Governments played a considerably more direct role in industrialization. France and Prussia granted subsidies to private companies that built railroads. After 1849, the Prussian state took on the task itself, as did Belgium and, later, Russia. In Prussia, the state also operated a large proportion of that country's mines. Governments on the Continent provided incentives for industrialization. Limited-liability laws, to take the most important example, allowed investors to own shares in a corporation or company without becoming liable for the company's debts—and they enabled enterprises to recruit investors to put together the capital for railroads, other forms of industry, and commerce. In this way, latecomers to industrialization could use state policies to catch up with nations that had industrialized earlier.

Mobilizing capital for industry was one of the challenges of the century. In Great Britain, overseas trade had created well-organized financial markets; on the Continent, capital was dispersed and in short supply. New joint-stock investment banks, unlike private banks, could sell bonds to and take deposits from individuals and smaller companies. They could offer start-up capital in the form of long-term, low-interest commercial loans to aspiring entrepreneurs. The French Crédit Mobilier, for instance, founded in 1852 by the wealthy and well-connected Péreire brothers, assembled enough capital to finance a wide range of infrastructure projects, including a massive railroad-building spree in the 1850s. The Crédit Mobilier collapsed in scandal, but the revolution in banking was well under way.

Finally, continental Europeans actively promoted invention and technological development. They were willing for the state to establish educational systems whose aim, among others, was to produce a well-trained elite capable of assisting in the development of industrial technology. In sum, what Britain had produced almost by chance, the Europeans began to reproduce by design.

Industrialization after 1850

Until 1850 Britain remained the preeminent industrial power. Between 1850 and 1870, however, France, Germany, Belgium, and the United States emerged as challengers to the power of British manufacturers. The British iron industry remained the largest in the world, but it grew more slowly than did its counterparts in France and Germany. Most of continental Europe's gains came as a result of continuing changes in those areas we recognize as important for sustained industrial growth: transport, commerce, and government policy. The spread of railways encouraged the free movement of goods. International monetary unions were established and restrictions removed on international waterways. Free trade went hand in hand with removing guild barriers to entering trades and ending restrictions on practicing business. Guild control over artisanal production was abolished in Austria and most of Germany by the mid-1860s. Laws against usury, most of which had ceased to be enforced, were officially abandoned in Britain, Holland, Belgium, and in many parts of Germany. Investment banks continued to form, encouraged by an increase in the money supply and an easing of credit after the California gold fields opened in 1849.

The first phase of the Industrial Revolution, one economic historian reminds us, was confined to a narrow set of industries and can be summed up rather simply: "cheaper and better clothes (mainly made of cotton), cheaper and better metals (pig iron, wrought iron, and steel), and faster travel (mainly by rail)." The second half of the century brought changes further afield and in areas where Great Britain's early advantages were no longer decisive. Transatlantic cable (starting in 1865) and the telephone (invented in 1876) laid the ground for a revolution in communications. New chemical processes, dyestuffs, and pharmaceuticals emerged. So did new sources of energy: electricity, in which the United States and Germany led both invention and commercial

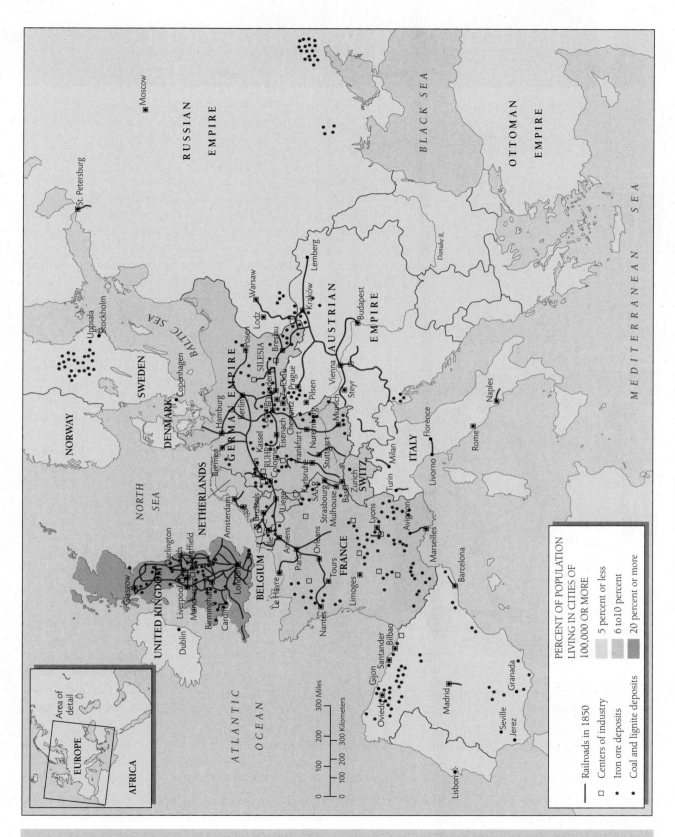

THE INDUSTRIAL REVOLUTION. Rapid industrial growth depended on a circular network of relationships between population, transport, and natural resources. ▪ *How were these elements connected, and how might they have reinforced one another, contributing to rapid growth?* ▪ *Why do you think the percentage of populations living in cities was so much greater in the United Kingdom?*

Interpreting Visual Evidence

Learning to Live in a Global Economy

The commercial networks of the Atlantic world were already well established before the Industrial Revolution, and Europeans were also trading widely with South and East Asia before the end of the eighteenth century. Nevertheless, the advent of an industrial economy in Europe at the beginning of the nineteenth century created such a demand for raw materials and such a need for new markets abroad that it became profitable for manufacturers and merchants to ship much larger amounts of goods over longer distances than ever before. As different industrialized regions in Europe became more and more dependent on overseas markets, people in Europe became aware of the extent to which their own activities were linked to other parts of the world. Awareness of these linkages did not always mean that they possessed complete or accurate information about the people who produced the cotton that they wore, or who purchased the manufactured goods that they made, but the linkages stimulated their imagination and changed their consciousness of their place in the world.

This awareness is well illustrated in the cartoons shown here, which come from the British paper *Punch* in the 1850s and 1860s. The first (image A) depicts John Bull (representing British textile manufacturers) looking on as U.S. cotton suppliers fight one another during the Civil War in the United States. He remarks, "Oh! If you two like fighting better than business, I shall deal at the other shop." In the background, an Indian cotton merchant is happy to have him as a customer.

The second cartoon (image B) depicts the ways that the increasingly interconnected global economy might

A. John Bull and cotton merchants.

development; and oil, which was being refined in the 1850s and widely used by 1900 (see Chapter 23).

In eastern Europe, the nineteenth century brought different patterns of economic development. Spurred by the ever-growing demand for food and grain, large sections of eastern Europe developed into concentrated, commercialized agriculture regions that played the specific role of exporting food to the West. Many of those large agricultural enterprises were based on serfdom and remained so, in the face of increasing pressure for reform, until 1850. Peasant protest and liberal demands for reform only gradually chipped away at the nobility's determination to hold on to its privilege and system of labor.

stimulate a new kind of political awareness. Emperor Napoleon III has placed a French worker in irons for participating in a revolutionary movement. The worker compares his situation to an African slave seated next to him, saying, "Courage, my friend! Am I not a man and a brother?" On the wall behind the two men a poster refers to the Portuguese slave trade—Napoleon III himself came to power by overthrowing the Second Republic in France, a government that had abolished the slave trade in French territories.

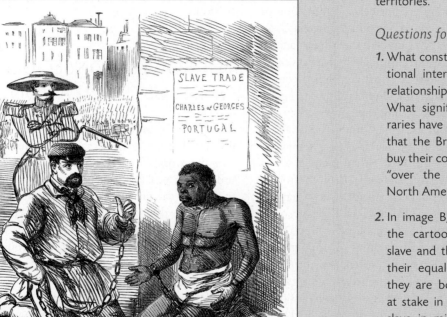

POOR CONSOLATION.

Parisian. "COURAGE, MON AMI; 'AM I NOT A MAN AND A BROTHER?'"

B. Increasing global awarness in France.

Questions for Analysis

1. What constellation of private and national interests were at play in the relationships portrayed in image A? What significance might contemporaries have attached to the possibility that the British may have chosen to buy their cotton from an Asian source "over the way" rather than from North America?

2. In image B, what is the message of the cartoon's suggestion that the slave and the worker might discover their equality only in the fact that they are both in chains? What was at stake in comparing a worker to a slave in mid-nineteenth-century Europe? Why does the caption read "Poor Consolation?"

3. How does the racial imagery of these images relate to their intended message?

Serfdom was abolished in most parts of eastern and southern Europe by 1850 and in Poland and Russia in the 1860s.

By 1870, then, the core industrial nations of Europe included Great Britain, France, Germany, Italy, the Netherlands, and Switzerland. Austria stood at the margins. Russia, Spain, Bulgaria, Greece, Hungary, Romania, and Serbia formed the industrial periphery—and some regions of these nations seemed virtually untouched by the advance of industry. What was more, even in Great Britain, the most fully industrialized nation, agricultural laborers still constituted the single largest occupational category in 1860 (although they formed only 9 percent of the overall population). In Belgium, the Netherlands, Switzerland, Germany, France, Scandinavia, and Ireland, 25 to 50 percent of the population still worked on the land. In Russia, the number was 80 percent. *Industrial*, moreover, did not mean automation or machine production, which long remained confined to a few sectors of the economy. As machines were introduced in some sectors to do specific tasks, they usually intensified the tempo of hand work in other sectors. Thus even in the industrialized regions, much work was still accomplished in tiny workshops—or at home.

Industry and Empire

From an international perspective, nineteenth-century Europe was the most industrial region of the world. Europeans, particularly the British, jealously guarded their international advantages. They preferred to do so through financial leverage. Britain, France, and other European nations gained control of the national debts of China, the Ottoman Empire, Egypt, Brazil, Argentina, and other non-European powers. They also supplied large loans to other states, which bound those nations to their European investors. If the debtor nations expressed discontent, as Egypt did in the 1830s when it attempted to establish its own cotton textile industry, they confronted financial pressure and shows of force. Coercion, however, was not always necessary or even one-sided. Social change in other empires—China, Persia, and the Mughal Empire of India, for example—made those empires newly vulnerable and created new opportunities for the European powers and their local partners. Ambitious local elites often reached agreements with Western governments or groups such as the British East India Company. These trade agreements transformed regional economies on terms that sent the greatest profits to Europe after a substantial gratuity to the Europeans' local partners. Where agreements could not be made, force prevailed, and Europe took territory and trade by conquest (see Chapter 22).

Industrialization tightened global links between Europe and the rest of the world, creating new networks of trade and interdependence. To a certain extent, the world economy divided between the producers of manufactured goods—Europe itself—and suppliers of the necessary raw materials and buyers of finished goods—everyone else. Cotton growers in the southern United States, sugar growers in the Caribbean, and wheat growers in Ukraine accepted their arrangements with the industrialized West and typically profited by them. If there were disputes, however, those suppliers often found that Europe could look elsewhere for the same goods or dictate the terms of trade down the business end of a bank ledger or a cannon barrel.

In 1811 Britain imported 3 percent of the wheat it consumed. By 1891 that portion had risen to 79 percent. Why? In an increasingly urban society, fewer people lived off the land. The commercialization of agriculture, which began early in Britain, had taken even firmer hold elsewhere, turning new regions—Australia, Argentina, and North America—into centers of grain and wheat production. New forms of transportation, finance, and communication made it easier to shuttle commodities and capital through international networks. Those simple percentages, in other words, dramatize the new interdependence of the nineteenth century; they illustrate as well as any statistics can how ordinary Britons' lives—like their counterparts' in other nations—were embedded in an increasingly global economy.

THE SOCIAL CONSEQUENCES OF INDUSTRIALIZATION

The effects of industrialization in Europe were soon visible in all aspects of social life. Changes in production and the workplace created new centers of employment, unleashing a cascading sequence of population movements that led to the growth of new cities in regions that a short time before had been largely agricultural. The development of these new cities and the sudden growth of older ones strained the infrastructure of Europe's urban centers, creating a demand for new housing, and forcing many to crowd into neighborhoods where newcomers could find short-term rentals as they looked for employment. Growth in these new cities was often uneven, with new and prosperous middle-class neighborhoods developing alongside more densely populated working-class districts. The concentration of new populations in cities that had been built for smaller numbers of people led in turn to environmental degradation, declining air quality, and fears of contagion. Traditional elites watched these developments with some dismay, fearing that the growth of urban populations would be accompanied by increases in crime and disease, or worse, revolution.

Population

By any measure, the nineteenth century was a turning point in European demographic history. In 1800 the population of Europe was roughly 205 million. By 1914 the figure had jumped to 480 million. (Over the same span of time, the world population went from about 900 million to 1.6 billion.) Britain, with its comparatively high standard of living, saw its population rise from 16 to 27 million. Throughout Europe, increases came in both urban and rural areas. In Russia, which did not begin the process of industrialization until the 1890s, the population rose from 39 million in 1800 to 60 million in 1914.

This population explosion did not occur because people were living longer—declines in mortality were not observable on a large scale until late in the nineteenth century, when improvements in hygiene and medicine had significant impact on the number of people who survived childhood to reach adulthood. Even in 1880, the average male life expectancy at birth in Berlin was no more than thirty years (in rural districts nearby it was forty-three). Population growth in the nineteenth century resulted from increasing fertility—there were simply more babies being born. Men and women married earlier, which raised the average number of children born to each woman and increased the size of families. Peasants tended to set up households at a younger age. The spread of rural manufacturing allowed couples in the countryside to marry and set up households—even before they inherited any land. Not only did the age of marriage fall but more people married. And because population growth increased the proportion of young and fertile people, the process reinforced itself in the next generation, setting the stage for a period of prolonged growth. It is important to note, however, that this growth did not occur evenly in all regions of Europe: England, the Netherlands, and Germany witnessed population growth that was much higher than average in the nineteenth century, while the French and Spanish populations grew much more slowly.

Life on the Land: The Peasantry

Even as the West grew more industrial, the majority of people continued to live on the land. Conditions in the countryside were harsh. Peasants still farmed largely by hand. Millions of tiny farms produced, at most, a bare subsistence living. The average daily diet for an entire family in a good year might amount to no more than two or three pounds of bread—a total per family of about 3,000 calories daily. By many measures, living conditions for rural inhabitants of many areas in Europe grew worse in the first half of the nineteenth century, a fact of considerable political importance in the 1840s. Rising population put more pressure on the land. Over the course of the century some 37 million people—most of them peasants—left Europe,

eloquent testimony to the bleakness of rural life. They settled in the United States, South America, northern Africa, New Zealand, Australia, and Siberia. In many cases, governments encouraged emigration to ease overcrowding.

The most tragic combination of famine, poverty, and population in the nineteenth century came to Ireland in the Great Famine of 1845–49. Potatoes, which had come to Europe from the New World, fundamentally transformed the diets of European peasants, providing much more nutrition for less money than corn and other grains. They also grew more densely, an enormous advantage for peasants scraping a living from small plots of land. Nowhere did they become more important than in Ireland, where the climate and soil made growing grain difficult and where both overpopulation and poverty were rising. When a fungus hit the potato crop—first in 1845 and again, fatally, in 1846 and 1847—no alternate foods were at hand. At least a million Irish died of starvation; of dysentery from spoiled foods; or of fever, which spread through villages and the overcrowded poorhouses. Before the famine, tens of thousands of Irish were already crossing the Atlantic to North America. In the ten years after 1845, 1.5 million people left Ireland for good. The Irish famine illustrated just how vulnerable the nineteenth-century countryside remained to bad harvests and shortages.

Changes in the land depended partly on particular governments. States sympathetic to commercial agriculture

IRISH POTATO FAMINE, 1845–49. The Irish potato famine was widely held by many in Ireland to have human as well as natural causes. Historians have noted that food exports from Ireland continued and may have even increased for some products during the famine, as merchants sought higher prices abroad. This cartoon depicts armed soldiers keeping starving Irish Catholic families at bay as sacks of potatoes are loaded onto a ship owned by a prosperous Irish Protestant trader.

Past and Present

Are There Limits to Economic Growth?

Even in its infancy, industrial society had its critics—those who regretted the changes that the new forms of manufacture brought to work, to the social order, and to the environment (left). The current concern about climate change caused by the burning of fossil fuels (right) is thus the latest chapter in a long history of debate and controversy over the consequences of industrialization.

Watch related author videos on the Student Site
wwnorton.com/college/history/western-civilizationsBrief4

made it easier to transfer land, eliminate small farms, and create larger estates. In Britain, over half the total area of the country, excluding wasteland, was composed of estates of a thousand acres or more. In Russia some of the largest landowners possessed over half a million acres. Until the emancipation of the serfs in the 1860s, landowners claimed the labor of dependent peasant populations for as much as several days per week. But the system of serfdom gave neither landowners nor serfs much incentive to improve farming techniques.

European serfdom, which bound hundreds of thousands of men, women, and children to particular estates for generations, made it difficult to buy and sell land freely and created an obstacle to the commercialization of agriculture. Yet the opposite was also sometimes the case. In France, peasant landholders who had benefited from the French Revolution's sale of lands and laws on inheritance stayed in the countryside, continuing to work their small farms. Although French peasants were poor, they could sustain

themselves on the land. This had important consequences. France suffered less agricultural distress, even in the 1840s, than did other European countries; migration from country to city was slower than in the other nations; far fewer peasants left France for other countries.

Industrialization came to the countryside in other forms. Improved communication networks not only afforded rural populations a keener sense of events and opportunities elsewhere but also made it possible for governments to intrude into the lives of these men and women to a degree previously impossible. Central bureaucracies now found it easier to collect taxes from the peasantry and to conscript sons of peasant families into armies. Some rural cottage industries faced direct competition from factory-produced goods, which meant less work or lower piece rates and falling incomes for families, especially during winter months. In other sectors of the economy, industry spread out into the countryside, making whole regions producers of shoes, shirts, ribbons, cutlery, and so on in small shops and workers' homes. Changes in the market could usher in prosperity, or they could bring entire regions to the verge of starvation.

Many onlookers considered the nineteenth-century cities dangerous seedbeds of sedition. Yet conditions in the countryside and frequent flareups of rural protest remained the greatest source of trouble for governments. In England in the 1820s, small farmers marched under the banner of the mythical "Captain Swing" to protest the introduction of threshing machines, a symbol of agricultural capitalism. In southwest France, peasants attacked authorities who tried to prevent them from gathering wood in forests. Similar disturbances broke out elsewhere in Europe, and rural politics exploded, as we will see, in the 1840s. Peasants were land poor, deep in debt, and precariously dependent on markets. More important, however, a government's inability to contend with rural misery made it look autocratic, indifferent, or inept—all political failings.

Industrialization and the Urban Landscape

The growth of cities was one of the most important facts of nineteenth-century social history, and one with significant cultural reverberations. Over the course of the nineteenth century, as we have seen, the overall population of Europe doubled. The percentage of that population living in cities tripled—that is, urban populations rose sixfold. Cities like Manchester, Birmingham, and Essen seemed to spring up from nowhere. Between 1750 and 1850, London (Europe's largest city) grew from 676,000 to 2.3 million. The population of Paris went from 560,000 to 1.3 million, and Berlin nearly tripled in size during the first

VIEW OF LONDON WITH SAINT PAUL'S CATHEDRAL IN THE DISTANCE BY WILLIAM HENRY CROME. Despite the smog-filled skies and intense pollution, many entrepreneurs and politicians celebrated the new prosperity of the Industrial Revolution. As W. P. Rend, a Chicago businessman, wrote in 1892, "Smoke is the incense burning on the altars of industry. It is beautiful to me. It shows that men are changing the merely potential forces of nature into articles of comfort for humanity."

half of the century. Such rapid expansion brought in its wake new social problems.

Almost all nineteenth-century cities were overcrowded and unhealthy, their largely medieval infrastructures strained by the burden of new population and the demands of industry. Construction lagged far behind population growth, and the poorest workers dwelt in wretched basement or attic rooms, often without any light or drainage. Such conditions bred misery and epidemic disease.

Dickens's description of the choking air and polluted water of "Coketown," the fictional city in *Hard Times* (1854) is deservedly well known:

> It was a town of red brick, or of brick that would have been red if the smoke and ashes had allowed it. . . . It was a town of machines and tall chimneys, out of which interminable serpents of smoke trailed themselves forever and ever, and never got uncoiled. It had a black canal in it, and a river that ran purple with ill-smelling dye, and vast piles of building full of windows where there was a rattling and a trembling all day long.

Wood-fired manufacturing and heating for homes had long spewed smoke across the skies, but the new concentration of industrial activity and the transition to coal made the air measurably worse. In London especially, where even homes switched to coal early, smoke from factories, railroads, and domestic chimneys hung heavily over the city; and the last third of the century brought the most intense pollution in its history. Over all of England, air pollution took an enormous toll on health, contributing to the bronchitis and tuberculosis that accounted for 25 percent of British deaths. The coal-rich and industrial regions of North America (especially Pittsburgh) and central Europe were other concentrations of pollution; the Ruhr in particular by the end of the century had the most polluted air in Europe.

Toxic water—produced by industrial pollution and human waste—posed the second critical environmental hazard in urban areas. London and Paris led the way in building municipal sewage systems, though those emptied into the Thames and the Seine. Cholera, typhus, and tuberculosis were natural predators in areas without adequate sewage facilities or fresh water. The Rhine River, which flowed through central Europe's industrial heartland and intersected with the Ruhr, was thick with detritus from coal mining, iron processing, and the chemical industry. Spurred by several epidemics of cholera, in the late nineteenth century the major cities began to purify their water supplies; but conditions in the air, rivers, and land continued to worsen until at least the mid-twentieth century.

Governments gradually adopted measures in an attempt to cure the worst of these ills, if only to prevent the spread of catastrophic epidemics. Yet by 1850, these projects had only just begun. Paris, perhaps better supplied with water than any other European city, had enough for no more than two baths per person per year; in London, human waste remained uncollected in 250,000 domestic cesspools; in Manchester, fewer than one-third of the dwellings were equipped with toilets of any sort.

The Social Question

Against the backdrop of the French Revolution of 1789 and subsequent revolutions in the nineteenth century (as we will see in the following chapters), the new "shock" cities of the nineteenth century and their swelling multitudes posed urgent questions. Political leaders, social scientists, and public health officials across all of Europe issued thousands of reports—many of them several volumes long—on criminality, water supply, sewers, prostitution, tuberculosis and cholera, alcoholism, wet nursing, wages, and unemployment. Radicals and reformers grouped all these issues under a broad heading known as "the social question." Governments, pressed by reformers and by the omnipresent rumblings of unrest, felt they had to address these issues before complaints swelled into revolution. They did so, in the first social engineering: police forces, public health, sewers and new water supplies, inoculations, elementary schools, Factory Acts (regulating work hours), poor laws (outlining the conditions of receiving relief), and new urban regulation and city planning. Central Paris, for instance, would be almost entirely redesigned in the nineteenth century—the crowded, medieval, and revolutionary poor neighborhoods gutted; markets rebuilt; streets widened and lit (see Chapter 21). From the 1820s on, the social question hung over Europe like a cloud, and it formed part of the backdrop to the revolutions of 1848 (discussed in Chapter 21).

THE MIDDLE CLASSES

Nineteenth-century novelists such as Charles Dickens and William Thackeray in Britain, Victor Hugo and Honoré de Balzac in France, and Theodor Fontane in Germany painted a sweeping portrait of middle-class society in the nineteenth century. The plots of these stories explore the ways

when a woman might become pregnant eight or nine times in her life, this was a sobering prospect. Those dangers varied with social class, but even among wealthy and better-cared-for women, they took a real toll. It is not surprising that middle-class women's diaries and letters are full of their anticipations of childbirth, both joyful and anxious. Queen Victoria, who bore nine children, declared that childbirth was the "shadow side" of marriage—and she was a pioneer in using anesthesia!

Middle-Class Life in Public

As cities grew, they became increasingly segregated. Middle-class people lived far from the unpleasant sights and smells of industrialization. Their homes, usually built out of the path of the prevailing breeze and therefore of industrial pollution, were havens from congestion. Solidly built, heavily decorated, they proclaimed the financial worth and social respectability of those who dwelt within. In provincial cities they were often freestanding villas. In London, Paris, Berlin, and Vienna, they might be in rows of five- or six-story townhouses or large apartments.

The public buildings in the civic center, many constructed during the nineteenth century, were celebrated as signs of development and prosperity. The middle classes increasingly managed their cities' affairs, although members of the aristocracy retained considerable power, especially in central Europe. And it was these new middle-class civic leaders who provided new industrial cities with many of their architectural landmarks: city halls, stock exchanges, museums, opera houses, concert halls, and department stores. One historian has called these buildings the new cathedrals of the industrial age; projects intended to express the community's values and represent public culture, they were monuments to social change.

THE WORKING CLASSES

Like the middle class, the working class was divided into various subgroups and categories, determined in this case by skill, wages, gender, and workplace. Workers'

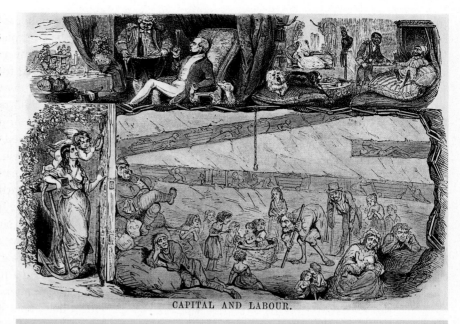

CAPITAL AND LABOUR.

CAPITAL AND LABOUR. In its earliest years, the British magazine *Punch,* though primarily a humorous weekly, manifested a strong social conscience. This 1843 cartoon shows the capitalists enjoying the rewards of their investments while the workers shiver in cold and hunger. ▪ *How would a defender of the new industrial order respond to this cartoon?* ▪ *What is the significance of the image on the top right, showing a scene from the British Empire?*

experiences varied, depending on where they worked, where they lived, and, above all, how much they earned. A skilled textile worker lived a life far different from that of a ditch digger, the former able to afford the food, shelter, and clothing necessary for a decent existence, the latter barely able to scrape by.

Some movement from the ranks of the unskilled to the skilled was possible, if children were provided, or provided themselves, with at least a rudimentary education. Yet education was considered by many parents a luxury, especially since children could be put to work at an early age to supplement a family's meager earnings. Downward mobility from skilled to unskilled was also possible, as technological change—the introduction of the power loom, for example—drove highly paid workers into the ranks of the unskilled and destitute.

Working-class housing was unhealthy and unregulated. In older cities, single-family dwellings were broken up into apartments, often of no more than one room per family. In new manufacturing centers, rows of tiny houses, located close by smoking factories, were built back to back, thereby eliminating any cross-ventilation or space for gardens. Crowding was commonplace.

Household routines, demanding in the middle classes, were grinding for the poor. The family remained a survival network, in which everyone played a crucial role.

In addition to working for wages, wives were expected to house, feed, and clothe the family on the very little money that all the members of the family earned. A good wife was able to make ends meet even in bad times. Working women's daily lives involved constant rounds of carrying and boiling water, cleaning, cooking, and doing laundry. Families could not rely on their own gardens to help supply them with food. City markets catered to their needs for cheap foods, but these were regularly stale, nearly rotten, or dangerously adulterated. Formaldehyde was added to milk to prevent spoilage. Pounded rice was mixed into sugar. Fine brown earth was introduced into cocoa. Only much later did governmental authorities try to protect consumers from such dangerous practices.

Working Women in the Industrial Landscape

Few figures raised more public anxiety and outcry in the nineteenth century than the working woman. Contemporaries worried out loud about the "promiscuous mixing of the sexes" in crowded and humid workshops. Nineteenth-century writers, starting in England and France, chronicled what they considered to be the economic and moral horrors of female labor: unattended children running in the streets, small children caught in accidents at the mills or the mines, pregnant women hauling coal, or women laboring alongside men in shops.

Women's work was not new, but industrialization made it more visible. Both before and after the Industrial Revolution labor was divided by gender, but as employers implemented new manufacturing processes, ideas about which jobs were appropriate for women shifted. In traditional textile production, for example, women spun and men operated the looms. In industrial textile factories, on the other hand, employers preferred women and children, both because they were considered more docile and less likely to make trouble and because it was believed that their smaller hands were better suited to the intricate job of tying threads on the power looms. Manufacturers sought to recruit women from neighboring villages as mill hands, paying good wages by comparison with other jobs open to women. Most began to work at the age of ten or eleven, and when they had children they either put their children out to a wet nurse, brought them to the mills, or continued to work doing piecework at home. This transformation of the gendered structure of work caused intense anxiety in the first half of the nineteenth century and is one of the reasons that the emerging labor movement began to include calls for excluding women from the workplace in their programs.

Most women did not work in factories, however, and continued to labor at home or in small workshops—"sweatshops," as they came to be called—for notoriously low wages paid not by the hour but by the piece for each shirt stitched or each matchbox glued. The greatest number of unmarried working-class women worked less visibly in domestic service, a job that brought low wages and, to judge by the testimony of many women, coercive sexual relationships with male employers or their sons. Domestic service, however, provided room and board. In a time when a single woman simply could not survive on her own wages, a young woman who had just arrived in the city had few choices: marriage, which was unlikely to happen right away; renting a room in a boardinghouse, many of which were often centers of prostitution; domestic service; or sharing a household with someone. How women balanced the demands for money and the time for household work varied with the number and age of their children. Mothers were actually more likely to work when their children were very small, for there were more mouths to feed and the children were not yet old enough to earn wages.

Poverty, the absence of privacy, and the particular vulnerabilities of working-class women made working-class sexuality very different from its middle-class counterpart. Illegitimacy rose dramatically between 1750 and 1850. In Frankfurt, Germany, for example, where the illegitimacy rate had been a mere 2 percent in the early 1700s, it reached 25 percent in 1850. In Bordeaux, France, in 1840, one-third of the recorded births were illegitimate. Reasons for this increase are difficult to establish. Greater mobility and urbanization meant weaker family ties, more opportunities for young men and women, and more vulnerabilities. Premarital sex was an accepted practice in preindustrial villages, but because of the social controls that dominated village life, it was almost always followed by marriage. These controls were weaker in the far more anonymous setting of a factory town or commercial city. The economic uncertainties of the early industrial age meant that a young workingman's promise of marriage based on his expectation of a job might frequently be difficult to fulfill. Economic vulnerability drove many single women into temporary relationships that produced children and a continuing cycle of poverty and abandonment. Historians have shown, however, that in the city as in the countryside, many of these temporary relationships became enduring ones: the parents of illegitimate children would marry later. Prostitution flourished in nineteenth-century cities. At mid-century, the number of prostitutes in Vienna was estimated at 15,000; in Paris, where prostitution was a licensed trade, 50,000; in London, 80,000. London newspaper reports of the 1850s cataloged the elaborate hierarchies of the underworld of prostitutes and their customers. These included entrepreneurs who ran lodging houses, the pimps and "fancy men" who managed the trade of prostitutes on the street; and the relatively few "prima donnas" or courtesans who enjoyed the protection of rich, upper-middle-class lovers, and whose wealth allowed them to entertain lavishly and move on the fringes of more respectable high society.

Yet the vast majority of prostitutes were young women (and some men) who worked long and dangerous hours in port districts of cities or at lodging houses in the overwhelmingly male working-class neighborhoods. Most prostitutes were young women who had just arrived in the city or working women trying to manage during a period of unemployment. Single women in the cities were very vulnerable to sexual exploitation. Many were abandoned by their partners if they became pregnant, others faced the danger of rape by their employers. Such experiences—abandonment and rape—could often lead to prostitution, since women in these circumstances were unlikely to secure "respectable" employment.

Nineteenth-century writers dramatized what they considered the disreputable sexuality of the "dangerous classes" in the cities. Some of them attributed illegitimacy, prostitution, and so on to the moral weakness of working-class people, others to the systematic changes wrought by industrialization. Both sides, however, overstated the collapse of the family and the destruction of traditional morality. Working-class families transmitted expectations about gender roles and sexual behavior: girls should expect to work, daughters were responsible for caring for their younger siblings as well as for earning wages, sexuality was a fact of life, midwives could help desperate pregnant girls, marriage was an avenue to respectability, and so on. The gulf that separated these expectations and codes from those of middle-class women was one of the most important factors in the development of nineteenth-century class identity.

A Life Apart: "Class Consciousness"

The new demands of life in an industrial economy created common experiences and difficulties. The factory system denied skilled workers the pride in craft they had previously enjoyed. Stripped of the protections of guilds and apprenticeships and prevented from organizing by legislation in France, Germany, and Britain in the first half of the nineteenth century, workers felt vulnerable in the face of their socially and politically powerful employers. Factory hours were long—usually twelve to fourteen hours. Textile mills were unventilated, and minute particles of lint lodged in workers' lungs. Machines were unfenced and posed dangers to child workers. British physicians cataloged the toll that long hours tending machines took on children, including spinal curvature and bone malformations. Children were also employed in large numbers in mines—over 50,000 worked in British mines in 1841.

Factories also imposed new routines and disciplines. Artisans in earlier times worked long hours for little pay, but they set their own schedules and controlled the pace of work, moving from their home workshops to their small garden plots as they wished. In a factory all hands learned the discipline of the clock. To increase production, the factory system encouraged the breaking down of the manufacturing process into specialized steps, each with its own time. Workers began to see machinery itself as the tyrant that changed their lives and bound them to industrial slavery.

Yet the defining feature of working-class life was vulnerability—to unemployment, sickness, accidents in dangerous jobs, family problems, and spikes in the prices of food. Seasonal unemployment, high in almost all trades, made it impossible to collect regular wages. Markets for manufactured goods were small and unstable, producing cyclical economic depressions; when those came, thousands of workers found themselves laid off with no system of unemployment insurance to sustain them. The early decades of industrialization were also marked by several severe agricultural depressions and economic crises. During the crisis years of the 1840s, half the working population of Britain's industrial cities was unemployed. In Paris, 85,000 went on relief in 1840. Families survived by working several small jobs, pawning their possessions, and getting credit from local wineshops and grocery stores. The chronic insecurity of working-class life helped fuel the creation of workers' self-help societies, fraternal associations, and early socialist organizations. It also meant that economic crises could have explosive consequences (see Chapter 20).

By mid-century, various experiences were beginning to make working people conscious of themselves as different from and in opposition to the middle classes. Changes in the workplace—whether the introduction of machines and factory labor, speedups, subcontracting to cheap labor, or the loss of guild protections—were part of the picture. The social segregation of the rapidly expanding nineteenth-century cities also contributed to the sense that working people lived a life apart. Class differences seemed embedded in a very wide array of everyday experiences and beliefs: work, private life, expectations for children, the roles of men and women, and definitions of respectability. Over the course of the nineteenth century all of these different experiences gave concrete, specific meaning to the word *class*.

CONCLUSION

Why did the Industrial Revolution occur at this moment in human history? Why did it begin in Europe? Why did it not occur in other regions in the world with large populations and advanced technologies, such as China or India? These fundamental questions remain subject to serious debate among historians. One school of explanations focuses on the fact that the mechanization of industry occurred first in northern Europe, and seeks to explain the Industrial Revolution's origins in terms of this region's vibrant towns, its well-developed commercial markets, and the presence of a prosperous land-owning elite that had few prejudices against entrepreneurial activity. These historians have suggested that industrialization is best understood as a process rooted in European culture and history.

More recently, however, historians with a more global approach have argued that it may be incorrect to assert that industrialization developed as it did because of the advantages enjoyed by a central, European, core. Instead, they have explored the possibility that the world's economies constituted a larger interlocking system that had no definitive center until *after* the take-off of European industrialization. Before that period, when it came to agricultural practices, ecological constraints,

After You Read This Chapter

 Go to **INQUIZITIVE** see what you've learned—and learn what you've missed—with personalized feedback along the way.

REVIEWING THE OBJECTIVES

- The Industrial Revolution in Europe began in northern Great Britain. What circumstances made this process of economic development begin there?
- Certain regions in Europe industrialized earlier than others. Where were these regions, and what factors favored early industrial development?
- Industrial development changed the nature of work and production in significant ways. What were these changes, and how did they change the relations between laborers and their employers, or local producers and wider markets?
- Industrialization had social effects far beyond the factories. What larger changes in European society were associated with the Industrial Revolution?
- A large and diverse group of middle-class people emerged in Europe as a result of the social changes brought on by industrialization. What kinds of people qualified as middle-class during the nineteenth century and how were they different from other social groups?

population densities, urbanization, and technological development, *many* global regions were not so different from the western European model. In the end, suggest these historians, Europe was able to move more quickly to industrial production because its economies were better positioned to mobilize new sources of energy and the resources available to them on the periphery of their trading sphere. The access enjoyed by European traders to agricultural products from slave-owning societies in the Americas helped them escape the ecological constraints imposed by their own intensely farmed lands, and made the move to an industrial economy possible. Contingent factors—such as patterns of disease and epidemic or the location of coal fields—may have also played a role.

There is less debate about the consequences of the Industrial Revolution within Europe. New forms of industrial production created a new economy and changed the nature of work for both men and women. Industrialization changed the landscape of Europe and changed the structures of families and the private lives of people in both the cities and the countryside. Industrialization created new forms of wealth along with new kinds of poverty. It also fostered an acute awareness of the disparity between social groups. In the eighteenth century, that disparity would have been described in terms of birth, rank, or privilege. In the nineteenth century, it was increasingly seen in terms of class. Both champions and critics of the new industrial order spoke of a "class society." The identities associated with class were formed in the crowded working-class districts of the new cities, in experiences of work, and in the new conditions of respectability that determined life in middle-class homes. These new identities would be sharpened in the political events to which we now turn.

PEOPLE, IDEAS, AND EVENTS IN CONTEXT

- Why was **ENCLOSURE** an important factor in the Industrial Revolution?
- What was the **FLY SHUTTLE** or the **SPINNING JENNY**? What was the **COTTON GIN**? What effect did these machines have on industrial development?
- What was the significance of **EUROPEAN EMPIRE** and overseas expansion for industrialization?
- How did industrialization affect **POPULATION GROWTH** in Europe? What effects did it have on the **PEASANTRY**?
- What **ENVIRONMENTAL CHANGES** were associated with the use of new sources of fuel such as coal or the construction of large and concentrated centers of industrial manufacture?
- How did people in Europe come to see the differences between the new **MIDDLE CLASSES** and the **WORKING CLASSES** after industrialization? Did the new economy affect men and women differently?

THINKING ABOUT CONNECTIONS

- What might the changes associated with the Industrial Revolution have done to people's conceptions of time and space? How might they have perceived their lives against what they knew of the experience of their parents' generation or what they anticipated for their children?
- What did the Industrial Revolution do for European nation-states?

STORY LINES

- The conservative regimes that defeated Napoleon in 1815 set out to reverse the changes in Europe prompted by the French Revolution. They aimed for a balance of forces between European powers so that no single ruler could dominate Europe.

- Conservative rulers in Europe remained on the defensive. Liberalism, republicanism, and nationalism continued to fuel resistance to the conservative order. Socialism provided Europe's laborers with a new vocabulary to express their unhappiness with industrialization.

- The conservative political reaction after 1815 found its cultural counterpart in Romanticism. This movement rejected the Enlightenment's rationalism and emphasized instead the power of nature and human emotions.

CHRONOLOGY

1808	Slave trade, but not slavery itself, prohibited by Britain and United States
1810–1825	South American revolutions
1814–1815	Congress of Vienna
1821–1827	Greek war for independence
1823	France restores King Ferdinand of Spain
1825	Decembrist Revolt in Russia
1830	Revolutions in France and Belgium
1832	British Reform Bill
1833	British Empire abolishes slavery
1840s	Chartist movement in Britain
1846	Corn Laws repealed
1848	Karl Marx's *Communist Manifesto* published

Before You Read This Chapter

The Age of Ideologies: Europe in the Aftermath of Revolution, 1815–1848

CORE OBJECTIVES

- **UNDERSTAND** the goals of the Congress of Vienna in 1815 and the challenges to the Concert of Europe in the decades between 1815 and 1848.

- **TRACE** the evolution of the debate about slavery after the French Revolution, and **UNDERSTAND** the reasons why an abolition movement developed even as slavery persisted in the United States and Latin America, particularly Cuba.

- **IDENTIFY** the core principles of conservatism, liberalism, republicanism, and socialism in Europe after 1815.

- **DEFINE** *nationalism* and **UNDERSTAND** how conservatives, liberals, republicans, and socialists were forced to grapple with this powerful political idea.

- **EXPLAIN** the ideas contained in the cultural movement known as Romanticism and its relationship to the Enlightenment.

hen the defeated Napoleon left the field of battle at Waterloo on June 18, 1815, headed eventually to exile on the rocky island of St. Helena in the South Atlantic, his victorious opponents hoped the age of revolution had ended. The Austrian foreign minister, Klemens von Metternich, perhaps the most influential conservative diplomat of the early nineteenth century, called revolution a "sickness," "plague," and "cancer," and with his allies he set out to inoculate Europe against any further outbreaks. In their view, revolution produced war and disorder. Peace depended on reinforcing the power of conservative monarchies in all corners of Europe. Bolstering the legitimacy of such monarchies was Metternich's primary goal in the post-Napoleonic decades.

The decades between 1815 and 1848 saw the legitimacy of these monarchies challenged on multiple fronts. Conservative efforts to restore the old order succeeded only in part. Why? To begin with, the developments of the eighteenth century proved impossible to reverse. The expansion of an informed public, begun in the Enlightenment, continued. The word *citizen* (and the liberal political ideas contained within it) was controversial in the aftermath of the French Revolution, but it was difficult to banish the term from political debates. Liberalism's fundamental principles—equality before the law, freedom of expression, and the consent of the governed—were still a potent threat to Europe's dynastic rulers, especially when coupled with the emotions stirred up by popular nationalism. Liberal nationalists believed that legitimate sovereignty could only be exercised by citizens acting collectively as a nation. Such a conception of sovereignty was diametrically opposed to conservative monarchs who believed their authority came not from the people but from God.

At the same time, the political opposition to the conservative order in Europe began to be infused with new and more-radical political ideologies. Some liberals were comfortable living under a constitutional monarch—one who agreed to rule in accordance with the law. Others accepted the idea of representation but believed that voting was a privilege that should be extended only to wealthy property owners. Much more radical were republicans who called for universal (male) suffrage and an end to monarchy altogether. Socialists, disturbed by the inequalities produced in the new market economy of industrial society, went even further and argued that political reform was not enough to free the people from want and exploitation. To socialists, justice was possible only with a radical reordering of society that redistributed property equitably. Between 1815 and 1848, none of these more-radical oppositional movements succeeded in carrying the day, but their ideas circulated widely and occupied the attention of conservative monarchs (and their police spies) throughout Europe.

In culture as well as in politics, imagination and a sense of possibility were among the defining characteristics of the first half of the century. Romanticism broke with what many artists considered the cold Classicism and formality of eighteenth-century art. The Enlightenment had championed reason; the Romantics prized subjectivity, feeling, and spontaneity. Their revolt against eighteenth-century conventions had ramifications far beyond literature and painting. The Romantics had no single political creed: some were fervent revolutionaries and others fervent traditionalists who looked to the past, to religion or history, for inspiration. Their sensibility, however, infused politics and culture. And to look ahead, their collective search for new means of expression sent nineteenth-century art off in a new direction.

THE SEARCH FOR ORDER IN EUROPE, 1815–1830

In 1814, the European powers met at the Congress of Vienna to settle pressing questions about the post-Napoleonic political order. The lavish celebrations of Louis XVIII's return to the throne in France could not hide the fact that twenty years of war, revolution, and political experimentation had changed Europe in fundamental ways. The task of the Congress of Vienna was to reinforce Europe's monarchical regimes against the powerful social and political forces that had been unleashed after 1789.

The Congress of Vienna and the Restoration

The Russian tsar Alexander I (r. 1801–25) and the Austrian diplomat Klemens von Metternich (1773–1859) dominated the Congress of Vienna. After Napoleon's fall, Russia became the most powerful continental state. Alexander I presented himself during the Napoleonic Wars as the "liberator" of Europe, and many feared that he would substitute an all-powerful Russia for an all-powerful France. The French were represented by prince Charles Maurice de Talleyrand (1754–1838), a canny survivor who been a bishop and a revolutionary before becoming Napoleon's foreign minister.

Metternich's central concerns at the Congress of Vienna were checking Russian expansionism and preventing political change in Europe. As a student in Strasbourg in 1789 he had witnessed the violence of the French Revolution, and the memory fueled a lifelong hatred of radical political movements. He favored treating the defeated French with moderation but he remained an archconservative who readily resorted to harsh repressive tactics, including secret police and spying. Nevertheless, the peace he crafted was enormously significant and helped prevent a major European war until 1914.

The Congress sought to restore order by insisting that Europe's dynastic rulers were the only legitimate political authority. It recognized Louis XVIII as the legitimate sovereign of France and confirmed the restoration of Bourbon rulers in Spain and the Two Sicilies. Other European monarchs had no interest in undermining the French restoration: Louis XVIII was a bulwark against revolution. After Napoleon's Hundred Days, the allies imposed an indemnity of 700 million francs and an occupying army for five years. France's borders

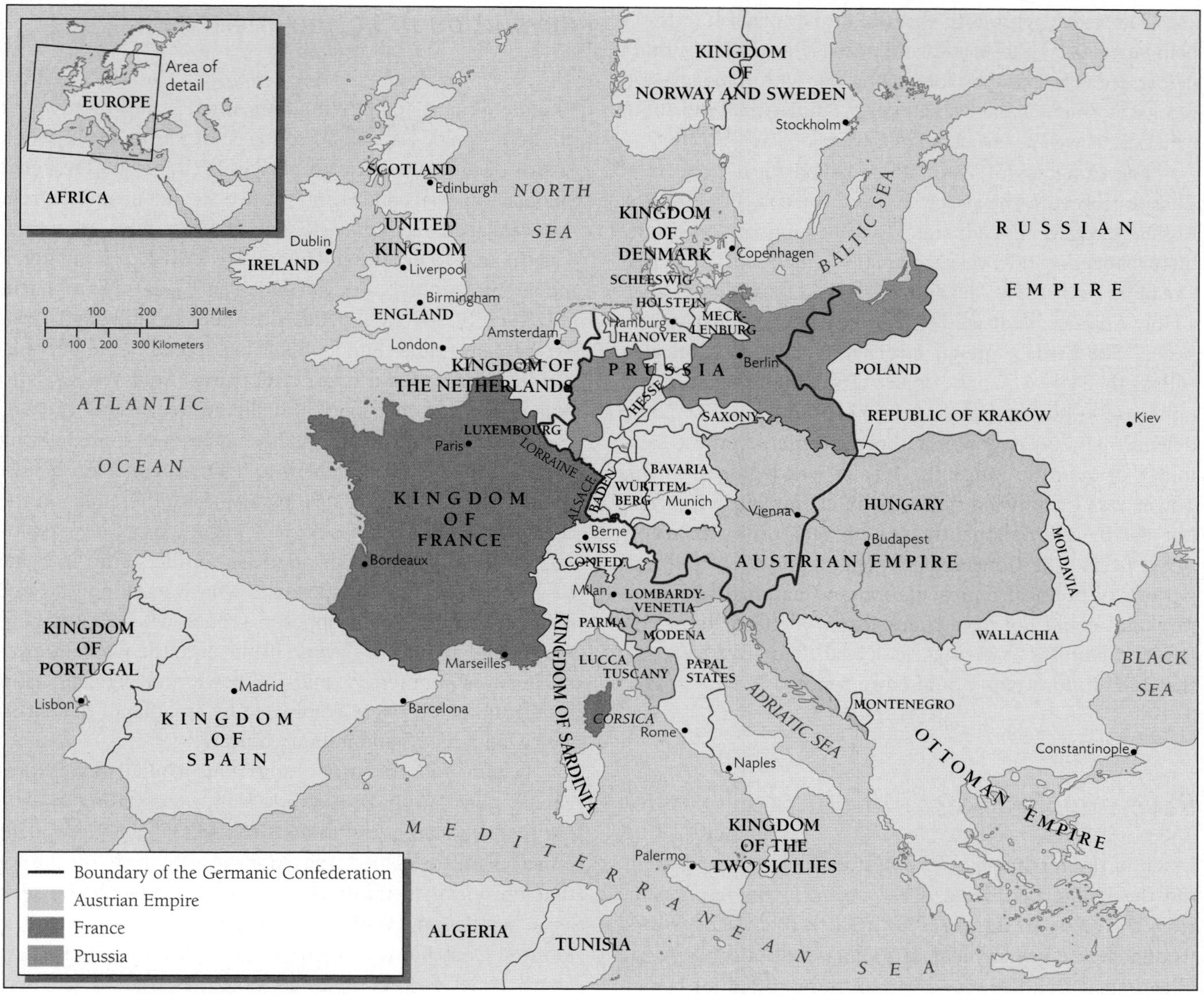

Area of detail
EUROPE
AFRICA
KINGDOM OF NORWAY AND SWEDEN
Stockholm
SCOTLAND
Edinburgh
NORTH SEA
UNITED KINGDOM
Dublin
IRELAND
Liverpool
Birmingham
ENGLAND
London
Amsterdam
KINGDOM OF DENMARK
Copenhagen
BALTIC SEA
RUSSIAN EMPIRE
SCHLESWIG
HOLSTEIN
Hamburg
MECKLENBURG
HANOVER
PRUSSIA
Berlin
POLAND
KINGDOM OF THE NETHERLANDS
HESSE
SAXONY
REPUBLIC OF KRAKÓW
Kiev
LUXEMBOURG
Paris
LORRAINE
ATLANTIC OCEAN
0 100 200 300 Miles
0 100 200 300 Kilometers
BAVARIA
WÜRTTEMBERG
BADEN
ALSACE
Munich
Vienna
HUNGARY
KINGDOM OF FRANCE
Berne
SWISS CONFED.
Budapest
AUSTRIAN EMPIRE
MOLDAVIA
Bordeaux
Milan
LOMBARDY-VENETIA
PARMA
MODENA
WALLACHIA
KINGDOM OF PORTUGAL
LUCCA
TUSCANY
PAPAL STATES
BLACK SEA
Marseilles
Madrid
Lisbon
Barcelona
KINGDOM OF SPAIN
KINGDOM OF SARDINIA
CORSICA
Rome
ADRIATIC SEA
MONTENEGRO
Constantinople
Naples
OTTOMAN EMPIRE
MEDITERRANEAN SEA
KINGDOM OF THE TWO SICILIES
Palermo
ALGERIA
TUNISIA
Boundary of the Germanic Confederation
Austrian Empire
France
Prussia

THE CONGRESS OF VIENNA. Note how the borders of European nations were established after the final defeat of Napoleon in 1815, and compare these boundaries to Europe in 1713 after the Peace of Utrecht (page 416). ▪ ***What major changes had occurred in the intervening years in central Europe?*** ▪ ***Which territorial powers played an active role in determining the balance of power at the Congress of Vienna?*** ▪ ***What social or political developments might disrupt this balance?***

remained the same as in 1789—less than the revolution's "greater France" but not as punitive as they might have been.

The guiding principle of the peace was the balance of power, according to which no country should be powerful enough to destabilize international relations. Metternich's immediate goal, therefore, was to build a barrier against renewed French expansion. The Dutch Republic, conquered by the French in 1795, was restored as the kingdom of the Netherlands, securing France's northern border. The Congress also ceded the left bank of the Rhine to Prussia, and Austria expanded into northern Italy.

In central Europe, the allied powers reduced the number of German states from over 300 in number to 39. Prussia and Habsburg Austria joined these German states in a loosely structured German Confederation, with Austria careful to reserve for itself the presidency of this new body, as a check against Prussia. Eventually, this confederation became the basis for German unification, but this was not the intention in Vienna in 1815. Bavaria, Württemburg, and Saxony remained independent kingdoms. Poland became a particular bone of contention, and the final compromise saw a nominally independent kingdom of Poland placed under the control of

Tsar Alexander, with large slices of formerly Polish territory being handed over to Austria and Prussia. Meanwhile, Britain demanded compensation for its long war with Napoleon and received formerly French territories in South Africa and South America, as well as the island of Ceylon.

The Congress of Vienna also called for a Concert of Europe to secure the peace. Britain, Austria, Prussia, and Russia pledged to cooperate in the suppression of any disturbances—and France officially joined this conservative alliance in 1818. Alexander I pushed for what he called a Holy Alliance, dedicated to justice, Christian charity, and peace. The British foreign minister remained skeptical—calling the Holy Alliance "a piece of sublime mysticism and nonsense"—but agreed that the European powers should defend their conception of authority, centered on the legitimacy of dynastic kingship. A ruler was legitimate if his power was guaranteed not only by claims of divine right but also by international treaties and support by his recognized peers. The Concert of Europe's opposition to liberal notions of political representation and national self-determination could not have been clearer. Metternich and his fellow diplomats at Vienna dedicated their lives to seeing that such innovations would never succeed.

Revolt against Restoration

Much of the resistance to the Restoration was clandestine. On the Italian peninsula, the Carbonari (the name came from the charcoal they used to blacken their faces) vowed to oppose the government in Vienna and its conservative allies. Their political views varied: some called for constitutions and representative government and others praised Bonaparte. The Carbonari's influence spread through southern Europe and France in the 1820s, with members meeting in secret and identifying one another with closely guarded rituals. Veterans of Napoleon's armies and military officers were prominent in their ranks.

In Naples and Piedmont, and especially in Spain and the Spanish Empire, opposition to Metternich's Concert of Europe turned to revolt when monarchs restored by the Congress of Vienna betrayed their promises of reform. Metternich responded by spurring Austria, Prussia, and Russia to take a strong stand against revolution. In the Troppau Memorandum (1820), the conservative regimes pledged to assist one another in suppressing revolt. Austria dealt firmly with the Italian revolts, and France sent 200,000 troops to the Iberian Peninsula in 1823, crushing the Spanish revolutionaries and restoring King Ferdinand's authority.

Revolution in Latin America

King Ferdinand's empire in Latin America, however, would not be restored. Napoleon's conquest of Spain (1807) shook Spain's once-vast empire. Local elites in the colonies resented Spanish imperial control and pushed for independence from the weakened monarchy. Rio de la Plata (now Argentina) was the first to declare independence in 1816. Soon after, a monarchist general from Rio de la Plata, José de San Martin (1778–1850), led an expedition to liberate Chile and Peru. At the same time, Simón Bolívar (1783–1830), a republican leader, sparked a series of uprisings from Venezuela to Bolivia. Bolívar envisioned mobilizing free people of color and slaves (who made up roughly a quarter of those fighting the Spanish) as well as Indians to fight against Spanish rule. Bolívar's goal was to create a pan-American republic on the continent, along the lines of the United States. These political revolts unleashed violent social conflicts and, in some cases, civil war. Elite landowners who wanted only to free themselves from Spain opposed groups who wanted land reform and an end to slavery. In the end, the radical movements were suppressed, and the newly independent Latin American nations were dominated by an alliance of conservative landowners and military officers.

Britain and the newly ambitious United States prevented the European powers from intervening in the Latin American revolutions. In 1823, U.S. president James Monroe issued the Monroe Doctrine, declaring that European meddling in the Americas would be seen as a hostile act. Without British support, however, the Monroe Doctrine was unenforceable. Britain saw the new South American republics as potential trading partners and used its navy to prevent Spain from intervening. By the 1820s, the Spanish Empire had vanished, ending an age that had begun in 1492. Brazil's independence in 1823 similarly ended the era of Portuguese colonialism in South America. The Latin American revolutionaries that created these new nations had been inspired in part by the French Revolution and Napoleon, and their success would in turn inspire nationalists in Europe who sought to overthrow Metternich's conservative Concert of Europe.

Russia: The Decembrists

Revolt also broke out in conservative Russia, but it did not succeed. In 1825, Tsar Alexander died, and a group of army officers known as the Decembrists led an uprising to push the pace of reform. Many were veterans of the Napoleonic

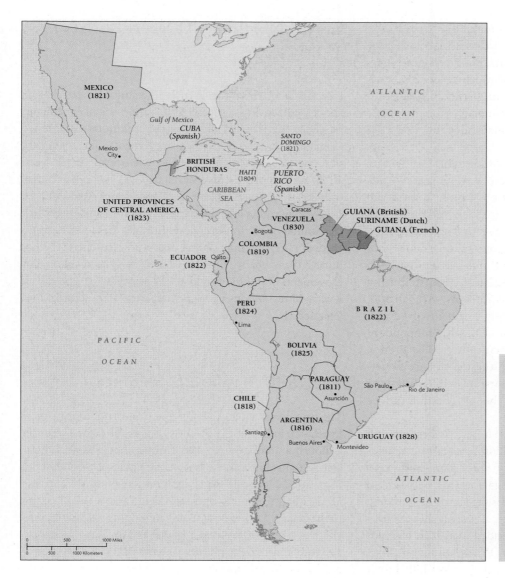

Wars, and they feared that Russia could not live up to its promise to be the "liberator of Europe" without change in its social and political order.

The officers failed to gain support from the rank-and-file soldiers, and without that support their revolt was doomed. The new tsar, Nicholas I (r. 1825–55), interrogated hundreds of mutinous soldiers, sentencing many to hard labor and exile. The five leaders—all young and leading members of the aristocratic elite—were sentenced to death. Fearing they would be seen as martyrs, the tsar had them hung at dawn behind the walls of a fortress in St. Petersburg and buried in secret graves.

Nicholas went on to rule in the manner of his predecessor, becoming Europe's most uncompromising conservative. Still, Russia was not immune to change. Bureaucracy became more centralized, more efficient, and less dependent on the nobility. Accomplishing this task required making Russia's complex legal system more systematic and uniform. Nicholas oversaw the publication of a new Code of Law, which reviewed every law passed since 1648 and published them in forty-eight volumes, a measure comparable to Napoleon's Civil Code of 1804. Meanwhile, landowners responded to increased demand for Russian grain by reorganizing their estates to increase productivity, and the state began to build railroads to transport the grain to Western markets. In spite of the failure of the Decembrists, Russia could not avoid the pressing need to adapt to Europe's changing political and economic realities.

Southeastern Europe: Greece and Serbia

When the Greeks and Serbians revolted against the once-powerful Ottoman Empire, European powers showed themselves to be more tolerant of rebellion. Serbs in the Balkans rebelled against the Ottomans as early as 1804 and, with the help of the Russians, succeeded in establishing hereditary rule by a Serbian prince in 1817. This Serbian quasi-state persisted as an Orthodox Christian principality with a significant minority Muslim population until finally achieving formal independence from the Ottoman Empire in 1878.

The Serb revolt and the subsequent Greek war for independence (1821–27) were part of a new pattern in Ottoman history in which groups within the empire's border regions began to seek independence from Ottoman rule. Eighteenth-century revolts against Ottoman control in these regions had usually not sought outright separation and had generally been resolved within the imperial system, by redistributing tax burdens or instituting legal reforms. After 1800, European powers were more likely to get involved and the result was the establishment of newly independent states and a weakening of Ottoman power. The French and the British hoped to expand their commercial networks in the eastern Mediterranean while Russians sought greater influence over the Ottoman Empire's Balkan territories.

Sympathy for the Greek revolt was widespread in Europe. Christians cast the rebellion as part of an ongoing struggle between Christianity and Islam, and secular observers interpreted the struggle as one between an ancient pre-Christian European heritage and the Ottoman Empire. On the ground in Greece, the struggle was brutal. In March 1822, the Greeks invaded the island of Chios and proclaimed its independence. When Ottoman troops arrived to retake the island, the Greek invaders killed their prisoners and fled. The Ottoman armies took revenge by slaughtering thousands of Greeks and selling 40,000 more into slavery.

In the end, Greek independence depended on great-power politics, as it did in Serbia. In 1827, British, French, and Russian troops sided with the Greeks against the Ottomans, who were forced to concede and grant Greek independence. The new nations of Serbia and Greece were small and fragile. Only 800,000 Greeks actually lived in the new Greek state. Serbia, meanwhile, could not survive without Russian protection. Moreover, neither of the new nations broke their close links with the Ottomans, and Greek and Serbian merchants, bankers, and administrators were still very present in the Ottoman Empire. The region remained a borderland of Europe, a region where peoples alternated between tolerant coexistence and bitter conflict.

CITIZENSHIP AND SOVEREIGNTY, 1830–1848

In the aftermath of the French Revolution, then, debates about citizenship, sovereignty, and social inequality remained divisive in many parts of Europe. In France, Belgium, and Poland, political movements challenging the post-Napoleonic settlement led to open revolt in the years 1830–32. A similar threat developed in the 1840s. During these same decades, many in Britain feared that conflicts over voting rights and the treatment of the poor might lead to a similar crisis. In the end, political leaders in Britain succeeded in negotiating reforms that prevented open rebellion during these years. On the Continent, the revolutionary movements of the 1830s and 1840s proved to be a prelude to a wave of revolutions in 1848 that swept across Europe (see Chapter 21).

The 1830 Revolution in France

The first decisive blow against the Concert of Europe came in 1830 in France. In 1815, the Congress of Vienna returned a Bourbon monarch to the throne, Louis XVIII. Louis claimed absolute power, but in the name of reconciliation he granted a "charter" and conceded some important rights: legal equality, careers open to talent, and a two-chamber parliamentary government. Voting rights excluded most citizens from government. Louis XVIII's narrow base of support, combined with the sting of military defeat, nostalgia for the Napoleonic empire, and memories of the revolution undermined the Restoration in France.

In 1824, Louis XVIII was succeeded by his far more conservative brother, Charles X (r. 1824–30). Charles antagonized property holders by pushing the assembly to compensate nobles whose land had been confiscated and sold during the revolution. He restored the Catholic Church to its traditional place in French schools, provoking discontent among French liberals, who began to organize an oppositional movement in Parliament. Economic troubles encouraged the opposition. In Paris and the provinces, police reports documented widespread unemployment, hunger, and anger. Confronted with alarming evidence of the regime's unpopularity, Charles called for new elections; when they went against him, he tried to overthrow the parliament with his so-called July Ordinances of 1830: he dissolved the new assembly before it had met, restricted suffrage even further, and announced strict press censorship.

In return, Charles got revolution. Parisian workers, artisans, and students took to the streets in three days of intense street battles. Crucial to the spread of the movement was the press, which defied the censors and quickly spread the news of the initial confrontations between protesters and the forces of order. In the end, the army was unwilling to fire into the crowd, and Charles was forced to abdicate, his support evaporating. Although many revolutionaries who had fought in the streets wanted another republic, the leaders of the movement opted for stability by crowning the former king's cousin, the Duke of Orléans, Louis-Philippe (r. 1830–48), as a constitutional monarch. The July Monarchy, as it was called, doubled the number of voters, though voting was still based on steep property requirements. The properties classes benefited most from the revolution of 1830, but it also brought the common people back into politics, reviving memories of 1789, and spurring movements elsewhere in Europe. For opponents of the Restoration, the year 1830 suggested that history was moving in a new direction and that the political landscape had changed since the Congress of Vienna.

Belgium and Poland in 1830

In 1815, the Congress of Vienna joined Belgium (then called the Austrian Netherlands) to Holland to form a buffer against France known as the United Provinces. The Belgians had never accepted this arrangement, and the 1830 revolution in France energized the Belgian opposition. The city of Brussels rebelled and forced Dutch troops to withdraw. Unwilling to intervene, the great powers agreed to guarantee Belgian independence and neutrality—a provision that remained in force until 1914. Although the economy of Belgian cities suffered by being separated from the Atlantic trade of the Dutch ports, religious divisions between the largely Catholic provinces of Belgium and Protestant Holland reinforced the division. French-speaking elites in Belgium also supported independence, though Flemish-speaking Belgians continue to cultivate a sense of cultural distinctiveness that persists today.

The years 1830–32 thus became full-fledged crisis for the Concert of Europe. After France and Belgium, revolt also spread to Poland, governed by the Russian tsar's brother, Constantine. Poland had its own parliament (or *diet*), a relatively broad electorate, a constitution, and basic liberties of speech and the press. The Russian head of state increasingly ignored these liberties, however, and news of the French Revolution of 1830 tipped Poland into revolt. The revolutionaries—including aristocrats, students, military officers, and middle-class people—drove out Constantine. Within less than a year, Russian forces retook Warsaw, and the conservative tsar Nicholas crushed the revolt and put Poland under military rule.

Analyzing Primary Sources

Women in the Anti–Corn Law League, 1842

Members of the Anti–Corn Law League sought to repeal the protectionist laws that prohibited foreign grain from entering the British market. The laws were seen as an interference with trade that kept bread prices artificially high, benefiting British landowners and grain producers at the expense of the working population. The campaign to repeal the Corn Laws enlisted many middle-class women in its ranks, and some later campaigned for woman suffrage. This article, hostile to the reform, deplored women's participation in the reform movement.

e find that the council of the Manchester Anti–Corn Law Association had invited the inhabitants to "an *anti-Corn-law tea-party*, to be held on the 20th of May, 1841—gentlemen's tickets, 2s.; ladies 1s. 6d." . . . Ladies were advertised as *stewardesses* of this assembly. So now the names of about 300 Ladies were pompously advertised as the *Patroness* and *Committee* of the *National Bazaar*. We exceedingly wonder and regret that the members of the Association . . . and still more that anybody else, should have chosen to exhibit their wives and daughters in the character of political agitators; and we most regret that so many ladies—modest, excellent, and amiable persons we have no doubt in their domestic circles—should have been persuaded to allow their names to be *placarded* on such occasions—for be it remembered, this Bazaar and these *Tea-parties* did not even pretend to be for any *charitable* object, but entirely for the purposes of *political agitation*. . . .

We have before us a letter from Mrs. Secretary *Woolley* to one body of workmen. . . . She "appeals to them to stand forth and denounce as *unholy*, unjust, and cruel all restrictions on the food of the people." She acquaints them that "the ladies are resolved to perform *their* arduous part in the attempt to *destroy a monopoly* which, for *selfishness* and its *deadly* effects, has no parallel in the history of the world." "We therefore," she adds, "ask you for contributions. . . ." Now surely . . . not only should the *poorer classes* have been exempt from such unreasonable solicitations, but whatever subscriptions might be obtainable from the wealthier orders should have been applied, not to *political agitation* throughout England, but to charitable relief at home.

Source: J. Croker, "Anti–Corn Law Legislation," *Quarterly Review* (December 1842), as cited in Patricia Hollis, ed., *Women in Public: The Women's Movement 1850–1900* (London: 1979), p. 287.

Questions for Analysis

1. Why does the article highlight the participation of women in the Anti–Corn Law Association? What does this argument tell us about attitudes toward women's political activity?

2. Does the article actually mention any of the arguments in favor of repealing the Corn Laws? What alternative to repeal does the article appear to support?

Reform in Great Britain

Why was there no revolution in England between 1815 and 1848? One answer is that there almost was.

The end of the Napoleonic Wars brought a major agricultural depression to Britain. Low wages, unemployment, and bad harvests provoked regular social unrest. In the new industrial towns of the north, radical members of the middle class joined with workers to demand increased representation in Parliament. When 60,000 people gathered in 1819 to demonstrate for political reform at St. Peter's Field in Manchester, the militia and soldiers on horseback charged the crowd, killing 11 and injuring 400. Following the "Peterloo" massacre—a domestic Waterloo—the conservative Parliament quickly passed the Six Acts (1819), outlawing "seditious" literature, increasing the stamp tax on newspapers, allowing house searches, and restricting rights of assembly.

British political leaders reversed their opposition to reform in response to pressure from below. The crucial issue was parliamentary representation. About two-thirds of the members of the House of Commons owed their seats to the patronage of the richest titled landowners in the country. In districts known as "rotten" or "pocket" boroughs, landowners used their power to return members of Parliament who would serve their interests. Defenders of this system argued that the interests of landed property coincided with the nation at large.

Liberals in the Whig Party, the new industrial middle class, and radical artisans argued passionately for reform. They were not necessarily democrats—liberals in particular wanted only to enfranchise responsible citizens—but they made common cause with organized middle-class and working-class radicals to push for reform. By July 1830, reform groups arose in several cities, and some clashed with the army and police. Middle-class shopkeepers announced they would withhold taxes and form a national guard. The country appeared to be on the verge of serious general disorder, if not outright revolution. Lord Grey, head of the Whig Party, seized the opportunity to push through reform.

The Reform Bill of 1832 eliminated the rotten boroughs and reallocated 143 parliamentary seats, mostly from the rural south, to the industrial north. The bill expanded the franchise, but only one in six men could vote. Landed aristocrats had their influence reduced but not destroyed. This modest reform nevertheless brought British liberals and members of the middle class into a junior partnership with a landed elite that had ruled Britain for centuries.

What changes did this more liberal parliament produce? It abolished slavery in the British colonies in 1838 (see Chapter 21). The most significant example of middle-class power came in the repeal of the Corn Laws in 1846. The Corn Laws (the British term for grain is *corn*) protected British landowners and farmers from foreign competition by establishing tariffs for imports, thus keeping bread prices high. The middle class increasingly saw this as an unfair protection of the aristocracy and pushed for their repeal in the name of free trade. The Anti–Corn Law League held meetings throughout the north of England and lobbied Parliament, eventually resulting in a repeal of the law and a free-trade policy that lasted until the 1920s.

British Radicalism and the Chartist Movement

Reformers disappointed with the narrow gains of 1832 pushed for expanded political reforms. Their attention focused on a petition known as the "People's Charter," which contained six demands: universal white male suffrage, a secret ballot, an end to property qualifications as a condition of public office, annual parliamentary elections, salaries for members of the House of Commons, and equal electoral districts. The Chartists organized committees across the country, and the charter was eventually signed by millions, its appeal strengthened by a climate of economic hardship in the 1840s.

The Chartists presented massive petitions to Parliament in 1839 and 1842, but the Parliament rejected them both times. Members of the movement resorted to strikes, trade union demonstrations, and attacks on factories and manufacturers who imposed low wages and long hours or who harassed unionists. The movement peaked in April 1848. Inspired by revolutions in continental Europe (see Chapter 21), the Chartists' leaders planned a major demonstration in London. Twenty-five thousand workers carried to Parliament a petition with 6 million signatures. Confronted with the specter of class conflict, special constables and regular army units were marshaled by the aged Duke of Wellington to resist any threat to public order. In the end, only a small delegation presented the petition, and rain and an unwillingness to do battle with the constabulary put an end to the Chartist movement. A relieved liberal observer, Harriet Martineau, observed, "From that day it was a settled matter that England was safe from revolution."

THE GREAT CHARTIST RALLY OF APRIL 10, 1848. The year 1848 brought revolution to continental Europe and militant protest to England. This photo shows the April rally in support of the Chartists' six points, which included expanding the voting franchise, abolishing property qualifications for representatives, and instituting a secret ballot.

THE POLITICS OF SLAVERY AFTER 1815

These political conflicts within nations about citizenship, sovereignty, and equality were also linked to a transnational debate about slavery and its legitimacy, which was taking place at the same time. When the age of revolution opened in the 1770s, slavery was legal everywhere in the Atlantic world. By 1848, slavery remained legal only in the southern United States, Brazil, and Cuba. (It endured, too, in most of Africa and parts of India and the Islamic world.) Given the importance of slavery to the Atlantic economy, this was a remarkable shift. The debate about slavery was fundamental, because it challenged the defenders of citizenship rights to live up to the claims of universality that had been a central part of Enlightenment political thought. If "all men" were "created equal," how could some be enslaved?

Slavery, Enlightenment, and Revolution

In fact, the revolutions of the eighteenth century by no means brought emancipation in their wake. Eighteenth-century Enlightenment thinkers had persuaded many Europeans that slavery contradicted natural law and natural freedom (see Chapter 17). As one historian trenchantly puts it, however, "Slavery became a metaphor for everything that was bad—except the institution of slavery itself." Thus, Virginia planters who helped lead the American Revolution angrily refused to be "slaves" to the English king while at the same time defending plantation slavery. The planters' success in throwing off the British king expanded their power and strengthened slavery.

Likewise, French revolutionaries denounced the tyranny of a king who would "enslave" them but refused to admit free people of color to the revolutionary assembly for fear of alienating the planters in the lucrative colonies of Martinique, Guadeloupe, and Saint-Domingue. Only a slave rebellion in Saint-Domingue in 1791 forced the French revolutionaries to contend with the contradictions of revolutionary policy. Napoleon's failure to repress that rebellion allowed for the emergence of Haiti in 1804 (see Chapter 18). The Haitian Revolution sent shock waves through the Americas, alarming slave owners and offering hope to slaves and former slaves. In the words of a free black sailmaker in Philadelphia, the Haitian nation signaled that black people "could not always be detained in their present bondage."

Yet the revolution in Haiti had other, contradictory consequences. The "loss" of slave-based sugar production in the former Saint-Domingue created an opportunity for its expansion elsewhere: in Brazil, where slavery expanded in the production of sugar, gold, and coffee, and in the American South. Slavery remained intact in the French, British, and Spanish colonial islands in the Caribbean, backed by the Congress of Vienna in 1815.

The Slow Path to Abolition

An abolitionist movement did emerge, in England. From the 1780s on, pamphlets and books (the best known is *The Interesting Narrative of the Life of Olaudah Equiano*, 1789) detailed the horrors of the slave ships to an increasingly sympathetic audience. Abolitionist leaders like William Wilberforce believed that the slave trade was immoral and hoped that banning it would improve conditions for the enslaved, though like most abolitionists Wilberforce did not want to foment revolt. In 1807, the reform movement compelled Parliament to pass a bill declaring the "African Slave Trade to be contrary to the principles of justice, humanity, and sound policy" and prohibiting British ships from participating in it, effective 1808. The United States joined in the agreement; ten years later the Portuguese agreed to a limited ban on traffic north of the equator. More treaties followed, which slowed but did not stop the trade.

What roots did abolitionism tap? Some historians argue that slavery was becoming less profitable and that its decline made humanitarian concern easier to accept. Others argue that slavery was expanding: among other things, ships carried 2.5 million slaves to markets in the Americas in the four decades *after* the abolition of the slave trade.

In England, and especially in the United States, religious revivals supplied much of the energy for the abolitionist movement. The hymn "Amazing Grace" was written by a former slave trader turned minister, John Newton, to describe his conversion experience and salvation. The moral and religious dimensions of the struggle made it acceptable for women, who would move from antislavery to the Anti–Corn Law League and, later, to woman suffrage. Finally, the issue spoke to laborers whose sometimes brutal working conditions and sharply limited political rights we have discussed in previous chapters. To oppose slavery and to insist that labor should be dignified, honorable, and minimally free resonated broadly in the social classes accustomed to being treated as "servile." The issue, then, cut across material interests and class politics, and antislavery petitions were signed by millions in the 1820s and 1830s.

Slave rebellions and conspiracies to rebel also shook opinion, especially after the success of the Haitian Revolution (see Chapter 19). In 1800, slaves rebelled in Virginia; in 1811, there was an uprising in Louisiana; and in 1822, an alleged conspiracy took hold in South Carolina. The British colonies saw significant rebellions in the Barbados (1816); Demerara, just east of Venezuela (1823); and, most important, a month-long insurrection in Jamaica (1831). All of these were ferociously repressed. Slave rebellions had virtually no chance of succeeding and usually erupted only when some crack in the system opened up: divisions within the white elite or the (perceived) presence of a sympathetic outsider. Still, these rebellions had important consequences. They increased slaveholders' sense of vulnerability and isolation. They polarized debate. Outsiders (in England or New England) often recoiled at the brutality of repression.

In Great Britain, the force of abolitionism wore down the defense of slavery. In the aftermath of the Great Reform Bill of 1832, Great Britain emancipated 800,000 slaves in its colonies—effective in 1838, after four years of "apprenticeship." In France, republicans took the strongest antislavery stance, and emancipation came to the French colonies when the revolution of 1848 brought republicans, however briefly, to power (see Chapter 21).

FEAR OF SLAVE VIOLENCE. This cartoon, published in Britain in 1789 in opposition to the movement to end slavery, played on public fears of the consequences of abolition. The former slaves, dressed in the fashionable attire of the landed gentry, dine at their former master's table, and beat the master in retaliation for what they have suffered. In the background, other former slave owners are stooped in labor in the cane fields. By the logic of this cartoon, such a reversal was intolerable, and given the choice between "Abolition" and "Regulation" (the two heads at the bottom) the cartoonist chose "Regulation" as the wiser course.

In Latin America, slavery's fate was determined by demographics, economics, and the politics of breaking away from the Spanish and Portuguese empires. In most of mainland Spanish America (in other words, not Cuba or Brazil), slavery had been of secondary importance, owing to the relative ease of escape and the presence of other sources of labor. As the struggles for independence escalated, nationalist leaders recruited slaves and free people of color to fight against the Spanish, promising emancipation in return. Simón Bolívar's 1817 campaign to liberate Venezuela was fought in part by slaves, ex-slaves, and 6,000 troops from Haiti. The new nations in Spanish America passed emancipation measures in stages but had eliminated slavery by the middle of the century.

Cuba was starkly different: with 40 percent of its population enslaved, the Spanish island colony had almost as many slaves as all of mainland Spanish America together. A Cuban independence movement would have detonated a slave revolution, a fact that provided a powerful incentive for Cuba to remain under the Spanish crown. Spain, for its part, needed the immensely profitable sugar industry and could not afford to alienate Cuban planters by pushing for an end to slavery. Only a combination of slave rebellion in Cuba and liberal revolution in Spain brought abolition, beginning in the 1870s. Brazil too was 40 percent enslaved and, like Cuba, had a large population of free people of color. Unlike Cuba, Brazil won national independence, breaking away from Portugal with relative ease (1822). Like the American South, Brazil came through the revolution for independence with slavery not only intact but expanding, and slavery endured in Brazil until 1888.

TAKING SIDES: NEW IDEOLOGIES IN POLITICS

Debates about citizenship, sovereignty, and slavery made it clear that issues raised by the French Revolution were very much alive in Europe after 1815. The Congress of Vienna was able to place the Bourbon family back on the throne in France, but it could not make debates about popular sovereignty, national independence, or the authority of conservative dynastic regimes go away. Throughout Europe, political actors increasingly understood themselves to be facing a choice between extremist positions—attempting to defeat political opponents definitively using all means necessary—and more moderate positions that sought a compromise or middle way between seemingly incompatible worldviews.

It was within this context that modern political ideologies of conservatism, liberalism, socialism, and nationalism began to come into clearer focus.

Early nineteenth-century politics did not have parties as we know them today. But more clearly defined political doctrines, or ideologies, took shape during this time. An ideology may be defined as a coherent system of thought that claims to represent the workings and structure of the social order and its relationship to political institutions. Ideologies consciously compete with other views of how the world is or should be, and their defenders seek to establish their views as dominant. The roots of conservatism, liberalism, and nationalism lay in earlier times, but ongoing political battles about the legacy of the French Revolution brought them to the fore. The Industrial Revolution (see Chapter 19) and the social changes that accompanied it also proved a tremendous spur to political and social thought.

Principles of Conservatism

At the Congress of Vienna and in the Restoration generally, the most important guiding concept was legitimacy. It might be best understood as a code word for the anti-revolutionary political order that the Congress sought to impose. Conservatives aimed to make legitimate—and thus to solidify—both the monarchy's authority and the hierarchical social order undermined by the French Revolution. They believed that the monarchy guaranteed political stability, that the nobility were the rightful leaders of the nation, and that both needed to play active and effective roles in public life. Conservatives believed that change had to be slow, incremental, and managed so as to strengthen rather than weaken the structures of authority. Conserving the past and cultivating tradition would ensure an orderly future.

Edmund Burke's *Reflections on the Revolution in France* was more influential in this new context than it had been during the 1790s, when it was first published. Burke did not oppose all change; he had argued, for instance, that the British should let the North American colonies go. But he opposed talk of natural rights, which he considered dangerous abstractions. He believed enthusiasm for constitutions to be misguided and the Enlightenment's emphasis on what he called the "conquering power of reason" to be dangerous. Instead, Burke counseled deference to experience, tradition, and history. Burke and other conservatives, such as the French writers Joseph de Maistre (1753–1821) and Louis-Gabriel-Ambroise

Bonald (1754–1840) believed that the monarchy, the aristocracy, and the Church were the mainstays of the social and political order. Those institutions needed to stand together in face of the challenges of the new century.

Liberalism

Liberalism's core was a commitment to individual liberties, or rights. Liberals believed that the most important function of government was to protect liberties and that doing so would benefit all, promoting justice, knowledge, progress, and prosperity. Liberalism had three components. First, liberalism called for equality before the law, which meant ending traditional privileges and the restrictive power of rank and hereditary authority. Second, liberalism held that government needed to be based on political rights and the consent of the governed. Third, with respect to economics, liberals believed that individuals should be free to engage in economic activities without interference from the state or their community.

The roots of legal and political liberalism lay in the seventeenth and eighteenth centuries, in the work of John Locke and in the Enlightenment writers who influenced the founding texts of the American and French Revolutions (the Declaration of Independence and the Declaration of the Rights of Man). Freedom from arbitrary authority, imprisonment, and censorship; freedom of the press; the right to assemble and deliberate—these principles were the starting points for nineteenth-century liberalism. Most liberals called for constitutional as opposed to hereditary monarchy; all agreed that a monarch who abused power could legitimately be overthrown.

Liberals advocated direct representation in government but did not always insist on democracy. In the July Monarchy in France, established after the 1830 revolution, the property qualifications were so high that only 2 percent of the population could vote. Even after the Reform Bill of 1832 in England, only 18 percent of the population could vote for parliamentary representatives. Nineteenth-century liberals, with fresh memories of the French Revolution of 1789, were torn between their belief in rights and their fears of political turmoil. They considered property and education essential prerequisites for participation in politics. Wealthy liberals opposed extending the vote to the common people. To demand universal male suffrage was too radical, and to speak of enfranchising women or people of color even more so. As far as slavery was concerned, nineteenth-century liberalism inherited the contradictions

Analyzing Primary Sources

Edmund Burke, *Reflections on the Revolution in France*

Edmund Burke's Reflections on the Revolution in France *was first published in 1790, while the French Revolution was still under way. Burke's opposition to revolutionary change had a profound influence on conservatives in the decades after the Congress of Vienna in 1815. The following passages contain Burke's defense of hereditary elites, his insistence on the power of tradition—here referred to as "convention"—and his criticism of the doctrine of natural rights.*

 he power of perpetuating our property in our families is one of the most valuable and interesting circumstances belonging to it, and that which tends the most to the perpetuation of society itself. It makes our weakness subservient to our virtue; it grafts benevolence even upon avarice. The possessors of family wealth, and of the distinction which attends hereditary possession . . . are the natural securities for this transmission. With us, the house of peers is formed upon this principle. It is wholly composed of hereditary property and hereditary distinction; and made therefore the third of the legislature; and in the last event, the sole judge of all property in all its subdivisions. The house of commons too, though not necessarily, yet in fact, is always so composed in the far greater part. Let those large proprietors be what they will, and they have their chance of being amongst the best, they are at the very worst, the ballast in the vessel of the commonwealth. [. . .]

If civil society be the offspring of convention, that convention must be its law. That convention must limit and modify the descriptions of constitution which are formed under it. Every sort of legislative, judicial, or executor power are its creatures. They can have no being in any other state of things; and how can any man claim, under the conventions of civil society, rights which do not so much as suppose its existence? Rights which are absolutely repugnant to it? One of the first motives to civil society, and which becomes one of its fundamental rules, is *that no man should be judge in his own cause*. By this each person has at once divested himself of the first fundamental right of uncovenanted man, that is, to judge for himself, and to assert his own cause. He abdicates all right to be his own governor. He inclusively, in a great measure, abandons the right of self-defense, the first law of nature. Men cannot enjoy the rights of an uncivil and of a civil state together. That he may obtain justice he gives up his right of determining what it is in points the most essential to him. That he may secure some liberty, he makes a surrender in trust of the whole of it. [. . .]

Government is not made in virtue of natural rights, which may and do exist in total independence of it; and in a much greater degree of abstract perfection; but their abstract perfection is their practical defect. . . . The moment you abate anything from the full rights of men, each to govern himself, and suffer any artificial positive limitation upon those rights, from that moment the whole organization of government becomes a consideration of convenience. That is which makes the constitution of a state, and the due distribution of its powers, a matter of the most delicate and complicated skill. It requires a deep knowledge of human nature and human necessities, and of the things which facilitate or obstruct the various ends which are to be pursued by the mechanism of civil institutions. The state is to have recruits to its strength and remedies to its distempers. What is the use of discussing a man's abstract right to food or to medicine? The question is upon the method of procuring and administering them. In that deliberation I shall always advise to call in the aid of the farmer and the physician, rather than the professor of metaphysics.

Source: Edmund Burke, *Reflections on the Revolution in France* (London: J. Dodsley, 1791, 9th ed.), pp. 75–76, 86–88, 89–90.

Questions for Analysis

1. Note that Burke does not defend hereditary elites with reference to God or a divinely inspired order. How does he justify the authority of the hereditary aristocracy?

2. What power does Burke grant to "convention" in the construction of the state and its laws?

3. What is Burke's principal complaint about revolutionaries who base their programs on "natural rights"?

of the Enlightenment. Belief in individual liberty collided with vested economic interests, determination to preserve order and property, and increasingly "scientific" theories of racial inequality (see Chapter 23).

Economic liberalism was newer. Its founding text was Adam Smith's *Wealth of Nations* (1776), which attacked mercantilism (the government practice of regulating manufacturing and trade to raise revenues) in the name of free markets. The economists (or political economists, as they were called) sought to identify basic economic laws: the law of supply and demand, the balance of trade, the law of diminishing returns, and so on. They argued that economic policy had to begin by recognizing these laws. David Ricardo (1772–1823) of Britain, for example, set out laws of wages and of rents, trying to determine the long-run outcomes of fluctuations in each.

Liberal political economists such as Smith and Ricardo believed that economic activity should be unregulated. Labor should be contracted freely, unhampered by guilds or unions, or state interference. Property should be unencumbered by feudal restrictions. Goods should circulate freely, which meant, concretely, an end to government-granted monopolies, trade barriers, import tariffs, and traditional practices of regulating markets, especially in valuable commodities such as grain, flour, or corn. Liberal economists believed that the functions of the state should be kept to a minimum, though they also argued that markets could not function without states to preserve the rule of law. The belief that government's role was to preserve order and protect property but not to interfere with the natural play of economic forces became known as *laissez-faire*, which translates, roughly, as "leave things to take their own course." This strict opposition to government intervention makes nineteenth-century liberalism different from common understandings of "liberalism" in the United States today.

One of the most influential British liberals was Jeremy Bentham (1748–1832). Bentham's major work, *The Principles of Morals and Legislation* (1789), illustrates how nineteenth-century liberalism continued the Enlightenment legacy and also transformed it. Unlike, for instance, Smith, Bentham did not believe that human interests were naturally harmonious or that a stable social order could emerge naturally from a body of self-interested individuals. Instead he proposed that society adopt the organizing principle of utilitarianism. Social institutions and laws (an electoral system, for instance, or a tariff) should be measured according to their social usefulness—according to whether they produced the "greatest happiness of the greatest number." If a law passed this test, it could remain on the books; if it failed, it

should be jettisoned. Utilitarians acknowledged the importance of the individual. Each individual best understood his or her own interests and was, therefore, best left free, whenever possible, to pursue those interests as he or she saw fit. Only when an individual's interests conflicted with the interests—the happiness—of the greatest number was individual freedom to be curtailed. The intensely practical spirit of utilitarianism enhanced its influence as a creed for reform. In his personal political views, Bentham went further than many liberals—he befriended Jacobins and believed in granting equal rights for women. Nevertheless, his rationalist approach to measuring the "utility" of laws and reforms nevertheless was an essential contribution to the liberal tradition.

Radicalism, Republicanism, and Early Socialism

The liberals were flanked on their left by two radical groups: republicans and socialists. Whereas liberals advocated a constitutional monarchy (in the name of stability and keeping power in the hands of men of property), republicans, as their name implies, pressed further, demanding a government by the people, an expanded franchise, and democratic participation in politics. The crucial distinction between the more moderate liberals and radical republicans, therefore, depended on the criteria they used for defining citizenship. Both groups believed that government should have the consent of citizens, but liberals were more likely to support restricted qualifications for citizenship, such as property ownership or the amount of taxes paid. Republicans were more committed to political equality and advocated more open definitions of citizenship, regardless of wealth or social standing. In thinking about the legacy of the French Revolution, therefore, liberals were likely to look favorably on the attempts by the National Assembly to create a constitution between 1789 and 1791. Republicans sympathized more openly with the Jacobins of the French Republic after 1792. Likewise, liberals remained suspicious of direct democracy and "mob rule" and sought constitutional measures that would allow propertied elites to exert their control over the political process and maintain social order. Radical republicans, on the other hand, were more likely to support civil militias, free public education, and civic liberties such as a free press and the right to assemble. In the debates between liberals and republicans, however, a general consensus about gender remained uncontroversial: only a very few liberals or republicans supported allowing

QUADRILLE DANCING AT NEW LANARK, ROBERT OWEN'S MODEL COMMUNITY. Owen's Scottish experiment with cooperative production and community building, including schooling for infants, was only one of many utopian ventures in early-nineteenth-century Europe and North America.

women to vote. The virtues necessary for citizenship—rationality, sobriety, and independence of mind—were assumed by nearly all political thinkers of the period to be essentially masculine traits.

Socialism was a nineteenth-century system of thought and a response in large measure to the visible problems ushered in by industrialization: the intensification of labor, the poverty of working-class neighborhoods in industrial cities, and the widespread perception that a hierarchy based on rank and privilege had been replaced by one based on social class. Socialists believed that these problems could not be solved simply by giving more people the right to vote. The problems of industrial society were not incidental; they arose from the core principles of competition, individualism, and private property. Socialists offered varied solutions: redistribution of economic and political power, collective ownership of industrial establishments, and new methods for organizing everyday life. The socialists did not oppose industry and economic development. On the contrary, what they took from the Enlightenment was a commitment to reason and human progress. They believed society could be both industrial and humane.

These radical thinkers were often explicitly utopian. Robert Owen, a wealthy industrialist turned reformer, bought a large cotton factory at New Lanark in Scotland and proceeded to organize the mill and the surrounding town according to the principles of cooperation rather than those of profitability. New Lanark organized decent housing and sanitation, good working conditions, child care, free schooling, and a system of social security for the factory's workers. The Frenchman Charles Fourier, too, tried to organize utopian communities based on the abolition of the wage system, the division of work according to people's natural inclinations, the complete equality of the sexes, and collectively organized child care and household labor. The charismatic

socialist Flora Tristan (1803–1844) toured France speaking to workers about the principles of cooperation and the equality of men and women. Thousands followed like-minded leaders into experimental communities. That so many took utopian visions seriously is a measure of people's unhappiness with early industrialization and of their conviction that society could be organized along radically different lines.

Other socialists proposed simpler, practical reforms. Louis Blanc, a French politician and journalist, campaigned for universal male suffrage with an eye to giving working-class men control of the state. Instead of protecting private property and the manufacturing class, the transformed state would become "banker of the poor," extending credit to those who needed it and establishing "associations of production," a series of workshops governed by laborers that would guarantee jobs and security for all. Such workshops were established, fleetingly, during the French Revolution of 1848. So were clubs promoting women's rights. Pierre-Joseph Proudhon (1809–1865) also proposed establishing producers' cooperatives, which would sell goods at a price workers could afford; working-class credit unions; and so on. Proudhon's "What Is Property?"—to which the famous answer was "Property is theft"—became one of the most widely read socialist pamphlets, familiar to artisans, laborers, and middle-class intellectuals, including Karl Marx. As we will see, a period of economic depression and widespread impoverishment in the 1840s brought the socialists many more working-class followers.

Karl Marx's Socialism

After 1848, a wave of violent revolutions in Europe seemed to make the earlier socialists' emphasis on cooperation,

the properties of light but aimed to capture the "poetry" of a rainbow. Turner's intensely subjective paintings were even more unconventional. His experiments with brushstroke and color produced remarkable images. Critics assailed the paintings, calling them incomprehensible, but Turner merely responded, "I did not paint it to be understood." In France, Théodore Géricault (1791–1824) and Eugène Delacroix (1799–1863) produced very different paintings from Turner's, but like the English painter, they too were preoccupied by subjectivity and the creative process. The poet Charles Baudelaire credited Delacroix with showing him new ways to see: "The whole visible universe is but a storehouse of images and signs. . . . All the faculties of the human soul must be subordinated to the imagination." These Romantic experiments prepared the way for the later development of modernism in the arts.

Romantic Politics: Liberty, History, and Nation

Victor Hugo (1802–1885) wrote that "Romanticism is only . . . liberalism in literature." Hugo's plays, poetry, and historical novels focused sympathetically on the experience of common people, especially *Notre-Dame de Paris* (1831) and *Les Misérables* (1862). Delacroix's painting *Liberty Leading the People* gave a revolutionary face to Romanticism, as did Shelley's and Byron's poetry. In works such as these, political life was no longer the preserve of social elites, and the commoners in the street could embrace new freedoms with a violent passion that would have surprised the philosophes, with their emphasis on reasoned debate.

Yet Romantics could also be ardently conservative. French conservative François Chateaubriand's *Genius of Christianity* (1802) emphasized the primacy of religious emotions and feeling in his claim that religion was woven into the national past and could not be ignored without threatening the culture as a whole. The period, in fact, witnessed a broad and popular religious revival and a renewed interest in medieval literature, art, and architecture, all of which drew heavily on religious themes.

Early-nineteenth-century nationalism took the Romantic emphasis on individuality and turned it into a faith in the uniqueness of individual cultures. Johann von Herder, among the most influential of nationalist thinkers, argued that civilization sprang from the culture of the common people, not from a learned or cultivated elite, as the philosophes had argued in the Enlightenment. Herder extolled the special creative genius of the German people, the *Volk*, and

insisted that each nation must be true to its own particular heritage and history.

The Romantics' keen interest in history and the lives of ordinary people led to new kinds of literary and historical works. The brothers Grimm, editors of the famous collection of fairy tales (1812–15), traveled across Germany to study native dialects and folktales. The poet Friedrich Schiller retold the story of William Tell (1804) to promote German national consciousness, but the Italian composer Gioacchino Rossini turned Schiller's poem into an opera that promoted Italian nationalism. In Britain, Sir Walter Scott retold the popular history of Scotland and the Pole Adam Mickiewicz wrote a national epic *Pan Tadeusz* ("*Lord Thaddeus*") as a vision of a Polish past that had been lost. After 1848, these nationalist enthusiasms would overwhelm the political debates that divided conservatives from liberals and socialists in the first half of the nineteenth century (see Chapter 21).

Orientalism

This passion for theories and histories of distinctive cultures also created broad interest in what contemporary Europeans called the "Orient"—a catch-all term used rather indiscriminately and confusingly to refer to the non-European cultures of North Africa, the eastern Mediterranean, the Arabian Peninsula, and eventually to the vast and densely populated lands of southern and eastern Asia. Napoleon wrote, "This Europe of ours is a molehill. Only in the East, where 600 million human beings live, is it possible to found great empires and realize great revolutions." The dozens of scholars who accompanied Napoleon on his invasion of Egypt in 1798 collected information on Egyptian history and culture. Among the artifacts the French took from Egypt was the Rosetta Stone, with versions of the same text in three different languages: hieroglyphic writing (pictorial script), demotic (an early alphabetic writing), and Greek, which scholars used to decode and translate the first two. The twenty-three-volume, lavishly illustrated *Description of Egypt*, published in French between 1809 and 1828, was a major event, heightening the soaring interest in Eastern languages and history. "We are now all Orientalists," wrote Victor Hugo in 1829. The political echoes to this cultural fascination with the "Orient" could be seen in great-power rivalries that surfaced in the British incursion into India, in the Greek war for independence, and in the French invasion of Algeria in 1830.

Nineteenth-century Europeans cast the East as a contrasting mirror for their own civilization, a process that did more to create a sense of their own identity as Europeans than it did

***WOMEN OF ALGIERS* BY EUGÈNE DELACROIX.** This is one of many paintings done during Delacroix's trips through North Africa and a good example of the Romantics' Orientalism.

to promote an accurate understanding of the diversity of cultures that lay beyond Europe's uncertain eastern and southern frontiers. During the Greek war for independence, Europeans identified with Greek heritage against Eastern despotism. Romantic painters such as Delacroix depicted the landscapes of the East in bold and sensuous colors and emphasized the sensuality, mystery, and irrationality of Eastern peoples. The fascination with medieval history and religion shared by many Romantic writers also bred interest in the medieval crusades in the Holy Lands of the Middle East—important subjects for Romantics such as Scott and Chateaubriand. These habits of mind, encouraged by Romantic literature and art, helped to crystallize a sense of what were felt to be essential differences between the East and the West.

Goethe and Beethoven

Two important artists of the period are especially difficult to classify. Johann Wolfgang von Goethe (1749–1832) had an enormous influence on the Romantic movement with his early novel *The Passions of Young Werther* (1774), which told the story of a young man's failure in love and eventual suicide. The novel brought international fame to its young author, though many who sympathized with the main character perhaps missed the point about the self-destructiveness of the "cult of feeling." Rumors spread that some in his audience identified so strongly with Werther's alienation that they killed themselves in imitation. Though scholars now doubt that such suicides actually occurred, the rumor itself indicates the fascination that Goethe's emotionally complex character exerted over the reading public. The significance of the novel lay in Goethe's ability to capture in prose the longing that many middle-class readers felt for something more meaningful than a life lived in strict conformity with social expectations. It also revealed that a new sense of self and aspirations for self-fulfillment might be emerging in Europe alongside the narrower definitions of individualism that one might find in liberal political or economic theory. In his masterpiece, *Faust*, published in part in 1790 and finished just before his death in 1832, Goethe retold the German story of a man who sold his soul to the devil for eternal youth and universal knowledge. Written in dramatic verse, *Faust* was more Classical in its tone, though it still expressed a Romantic concern with spiritual freedom and human courage in probing life's divine mysteries.

The composer Ludwig van Beethoven (1770–1827) was steeped in the principles of Classical music composition, but his insistence that instrumental music without vocal accompaniment could be more expressive of emotion made him a key figure for later Romantic composers. The glorification of nature and Romantic individuality rang clearly throughout his work. Like many of his contemporaries, Beethoven was enthusiastic about the French Revolution in 1789, but he became disillusioned with Napoleon. At the age of thirty-two he began to lose his hearing, and by 1819 he was completely deaf—the intensely personal crisis that this catastrophe produced in the young musician drove him to retreat into the interior of his own musical imagination, and the compositions of his later life expressed his powerfully felt alienation and his extraordinary and heroic creativity in the face of enormous hardship.

Beethoven and Goethe marked the transition from eighteenth-century artistic movements that prized order and harmony to the turbulent and disruptive emotions of the nineteenth-century artists and writers. Their work embraced the cult of individual heroism, sympathized with the Romantics' quasi-mystical view of nature, and represented different aspects of a shared search for new ways of seeing and hearing. The many shapes of Romanticism make a simple definition of the movement elusive, but at the core, the Romantics sought to find a new way of expressing emotion, and in doing so, they sent nineteenth-century art in a new direction.

Interpreting Visual Evidence

Romantic Painting

Romantic painters shared with Romantic poets a fascination with the power of nature. To convey this vision of nature as both an overwhelming power and source of creative energy, Romantic painters created new and poetic visions of the natural world, where human beings and their activities were reduced in significance, sometimes nearly disappearing altogether. At times, these visions also were linked to a backward-looking perspective, as if the dramatic changes associated with industrialization provoked a longing for a premodern past, where Europeans sought and found their sense of place in the world from an awareness of a quasi-divine natural setting invested with powerful mysteries. John Martin's *The Bard* (image A) shows a highly romanticized vision of a medieval subject: a single Welsh bard strides across rocky peaks above a mountain river, after escaping a massacre ordered by the English king Edward I. Across the river, Edward's troops can barely be seen leaving the scene of the crime, which still glows with destructive fires. The emotional qualities of this early expression of Romantic nationalism are reinforced by the forbidding and dynamic sky above, where the clouds merge into the Welsh mountaintops as if they were stirred by the hand of God himself.

Other Romantic painters minimized the significance of human activity in their landscapes, though without reference to history. John Constable's *Weymouth Bay* (image B) contains a tiny, almost imperceptible human figure in the middle ground, a man walking on the beach, near a thin stone wall that snakes up a hill in the background. These passing references to human lives are completely dominated, however, by Constable's sky and the movement of the clouds in particular, which seem to be the real subject of the painting.

Of all the Romantic painters, J. M. W. Turner (image C) may have tackled the tricky subject of the new industrialized landscape in the most novel way. His painting *Rain, Steam, Speed—The Great Western Railway* (1844) boldly places the most modern technology of the period,

A. John Martin, *The Bard*, 1817.

B. John Constable, *Weymouth Bay*, 1816.

the steam train on an arched bridge, into a glowing and radiant painting where both nature's forces and the tremendous new power unleashed by human activity seem to merge into one continuous burst of energy. To the left of the train, on the river's edge, a fire of indeterminate but evidently industrial origin burns, illuminating several small but ecstatic figures with its light. Most enigmatic of all, a tiny rabbit (unfortunately invisible in this reproduction) sprints ahead of the train between the rails, highlighting the painting's complex message about nature and human creation. Are they heading in the same direction? Will one overtake the other and destroy it in the process?

C. J. M. W. Turner, *Rain, Steam, Speed—The Great Western Railway*, 1844.

Questions for Analysis

1. In Martin's *Bard*, what vision of the individual emerges from this painting, and how is it different from the rational, rights-bearing individual that political liberalism sought to protect?

2. Is Constable's painting concerned with nature as a source of nourishment for humans, or is it presented as a value in itself?

3. How is one to interpret Turner's explicit connection between the power of nature and the new force of industrial societies? Is he suggesting that contemplating the industrial landscape can be just as moving to a human observer as is the sight of nature's magnificence?

CONCLUSION

With the fizzling of the Chartist movement, the British monarchy avoided an outbreak of revolution in 1848. Monarchs on the Continent were not so lucky. As we will see in the next chapter, a wave of revolutionary activity unprecedented since the 1790s spread to nearly every capital in Europe in 1848. This resurgence of rebellion and revolt pointed to the powerful ways that the French Revolution of 1789 polarized Europe in the first half of the nineteenth century. In its aftermath, the Congress of Vienna aimed to establish a new conservative, international system and to prevent further revolutions. It succeeded in the first aim but only partially in the second. A combination of new political movements and economic hardship undermined the conservative order. Social grievances and political disappointments created powerful movements for change, first in Latin America and the Balkans and then in western Europe and Great Britain.

All of the contesting ideologies of these postrevolutionary decades could point to a longer history: conservatives could point to traditional religious justifications for royal authority and the absolutist's conception of indivisible monarchical power; liberals could point to the debates about the rule of law in the English revolution of the seventeenth century; even socialists could point to age-old collective traditions among rural communities as precedents for their defense of communal property and egalitarianism. Nevertheless, all of these ideologies were shaped and brought into clearer focus during these decades by the combined effects of the French Revolution and industrialization. Conservatives may have differed among themselves as to why they preferred a government of monarchs and landed aristocrats, but they were united by their horror of revolutionary violence and dismayed by the social disruptions

After You Read This Chapter

 Go to **INQUIZITIVE** to see what you've learned—and learn what you've missed— with personalized feedback along the way.

REVIEWING THE OBJECTIVES

- The European leaders who met at the Congress of Vienna possessed a conservative vision for post-Napoleonic Europe. What were their goals and what challenges did their political system face between 1815 and 1848?

- Slavery persisted long after the French Revolution. What accounts for the development of an abolition movement, and why did it persist in the United States and in Latin America, especially Cuba?

- Conservatives, liberals, and republicans differed from one another about the lessons to be learned from the French Revolution, while socialists sought to address the inequalities produced by the Industrial Revolution. What were the core principles of conservatism, liberalism, republicanism, and socialism?

- Nationalism reshaped the political landscape in Europe between 1815 and 1848. How did conservatives, liberals, republicans, and socialists view the claims of nationalists?

- Romanticism was a cultural movement defined in opposition to the Enlightenment. Who were the Romantics and what did they believe?

that attended industrialization. Liberals may have disagreed with each other about who qualified for citizenship, but they defended the revolutionary's insistence that the only legitimate government was one whose institutions and laws reflected the consent of at least some, if not all, of the governed. Many socialists, Marx included, celebrated the insurrectionary tradition of the French revolutionaries, even as they demanded a reordering of society that went far beyond the granting of new political rights to include a redistribution of society's wealth. Meanwhile, nationalists throughout Europe remained inspired by the collective achievements of the French nation that was forged in revolution in the 1790s.

The reemergence of social and political conflict in 1848 pit the defenders of these ideologies against one another under the most dramatic of circumstances, making the revolutions of 1848 the opening act of a much larger drama. In France, as in 1792 and 1830, revolutionaries rallied around an expanded notion of representative government and the question of suffrage, though they were divided on how much responsibility their new government had for remedying social problems. In southern and central Europe, as we will see in the next chapter, the issues were framed differently, around new struggles for national identity. The eventual failure of these revolutions set a pattern that was also observed elsewhere: exhilarating revolutionary successes were followed by a breakdown of revolutionary unity and the emergence of new forms of conservative government. The crisis of 1848 became a turning point for all of Europe. The broad revolutionary alliances that had pushed for revolutionary change since 1789 were broken apart by class politics, and earlier forms of utopian socialism gave way to Marxism. In culture as in politics, Romanticism lost its appeal, its expansive sense of possibility replaced by the more biting viewpoint of realism. No nationalist, conservative, liberal, or socialist was exempt from this bitter truth after the violent conflicts of 1848.

PEOPLE, IDEAS, AND EVENTS IN CONTEXT

- Who was **KLEMENS VON METTERNICH** and what was the **CONCERT OF EUROPE**?
- How did the **CARBONARI** in Italy, the **DECEMBRISTS** in Russia, and **GREEK NATIONALISTS** in the Balkans in the 1820s disturb the conservative order in Europe after Napoleon's defeat?
- Where did revolutions occur in 1830–32, and what was their outcome?
- What political changes did movements such as the **CHARTISTS** or the **ANTI–CORN LAW LEAGUE** accomplish in Britain? Why was there no revolution in Britain?
- What beliefs made **EDMUND BURKE** a conservative?
- What beliefs made **ADAM SMITH** and **JEREMY BENTHAM** liberals? What was **UTILITARIANISM**?
- What beliefs did **UTOPIAN SOCIALISTS** such as **ROBERT OWEN** and **CHARLES FOURIER** share? What made **KARL MARX**'s brand of socialism different from that of his predecessors?
- How did the values of **ROMANTICISM** challenge Europeans to reconsider their assumptions about the differences between men and women?
- What beliefs led Romantic writers such as **WILLIAM WORDSWORTH**, **WILLIAM BLAKE**, and **LORD BYRON** to reject the rationalism of the Enlightenment and embrace emotion and imagination as the most essential and vital aspects of human experience?

THINKING ABOUT CONNECTIONS

- What new ideas about historical change made it possible to think in terms of a political conflict between "conservatives" and "revolutionaries" during the decades immediately before and after 1800? Would such an opposition have been conceivable in earlier periods of history?
- Terms such as *conservative*, *liberal*, and *socialist* are still used today in contemporary political debates. Do they still mean the same thing as they did between 1815 and 1848?

Before You Read This Chapter

STORY LINES

■ In 1848, a wave of liberal and national revolutions demanded but failed to achieve lasting constitutions and elected parliaments in many European kingdoms. Instead, Europe's conservative monarchs found ways to harness the popular nationalism expressed in the 1848 revolutions to their own ends.

■ The emergence of Germany and Italy as unified nation-states upset the European balance of power, as did the increasing weakness of the Ottoman Empire. The resulting wars benefited Germany and diminished the power of Austria-Hungary in central Europe.

■ Russia, the United States, and Canada also went through an intense phase of nation building after 1850. Common to all three were the conquest of native peoples, the acquisition of new territories, and economic development. As in Europe, the process of nation building unleashed sectional conflicts and intense debates about citizenship, slavery (or serfdom, in Russia), and the power of the nation-state.

CHRONOLOGY

1834–1870	Unification of Germany
1848	Revolutions of 1848
1848	France and Denmark abolish slavery
1848–1870	Unification of Italy
1853–1856	Crimean War
1861	Emancipation of the serfs, Russia
1861–1865	American Civil War
1871–1888	Brazilian emancipation

Revolutions and Nation Building, 1848–1871

CORE OBJECTIVES

■ **EXPLAIN** why so many revolutions occurred nearly simultaneously in Europe in 1848.

■ **UNDERSTAND** the causes and failure of the revolutions of 1848 in France.

■ **DESCRIBE** the goals of revolutionaries in the German-speaking lands of central Europe and their relationship to the monarchies of Prussia and Austria.

■ **IDENTIFY** the social groups in Italy and Germany that supported a process of national unification from below, by the people, and those that favored a process of national unification directed from the top, by the state.

■ **DESCRIBE** the process of nation building in Russia and the United States in the nineteenth century and the ensuing debates about slavery, serfdom, and citizenship.

■ **IDENTIFY** the powers involved in the Crimean War, the Austro-Prussian War, and the Franco-Prussian War, and **UNDERSTAND** how these wars changed the balance of power in Europe.

The year 1848 was a tumultuous one. From Paris to Berlin, and Budapest to Rome, insurgents rushed to hastily built barricades, forcing kings and princes to beat an equally hasty—though only temporary—retreat. Perhaps the most highly symbolic moment came on March 13, 1848, when Klemens von Metternich, the primary architect of the Concert of Europe, was forced to resign as minister of state in the Austrian capital of Vienna while a revolutionary crowd outside celebrated his departure. Metternich's balance of powers between traditional dynastic rulers was swept aside in a wave of enthusiasm for liberal political ideals mixed with popular anger. Metternich himself was forced to flee to England less than one month after another revolution in France had swept aside King Louis-Philippe.

Metternich's downfall and the collapse of the French monarchy made clear that the 1848 revolutions were strongly linked to the forces for change unleashed by the French Revolution of 1789. At the same time, however, this was also the year that Karl Marx and Friedrich Engels published *The Communist Manifesto*, which announced as its goal an even more sweeping

561

transformation of society. If 1848 was the last wave of the political movements that began in Europe and the Atlantic world at the end of the eighteenth century, it was also the first chapter in a new revolutionary movement that sought to challenge the emerging industrial order of the modern world.

Revolutionary regime change, territorial expansion, economic development, and debates about who deserved citizenship: all of these were issues in 1848, and all were related to the spread of nationalism and nation building in Europe and the Americas. As we saw in the last chapter, the term *nation* had taken on a new meaning at the end of the eighteenth century and had come to mean "a sovereign people." *Nationalism* was a related political ideal, based on the assumption that governments could be legitimate only if they reflected the character, history, and customs of the nation—that is, the common people. This idea undermined the assumptions of Europe's dynastic rulers, as hereditary monarchs had emphasized the differences between themselves and the people they ruled. Kings and aristocrats often did not even speak the same language as their subjects. Nobody would have thought this odd before 1789, since peasants often spoke regional dialects that were different from the language spoken in cities. But once the notion of national sovereignty emanating from the people became widespread, such discrepancies between the language and culture of elites and of the common people loomed larger as political questions that needed to be solved. Intellectuals, revolutionaries, and governments all propagated the radical new idea that nations of like peoples and the states that ruled over them should be congruent with one another. This simple idea lay at the heart of all forms of nationalism, but there was often bitter debate about who best represented the nation and what the goals of a unified nationalist government should be.

Between 1789 and 1848, Europeans commonly associated nationalism with liberalism. Liberals saw constitutions, the rule of law, and elected assemblies as necessary expressions of the people's will, and they sought to use popular enthusiasm for liberal forms of nationalism against the conservative monarchs of Europe. The upheavals of 1848 marked the high point of this period of liberal revolution, and their failure marked the end of that age. By the end of the nineteenth century, conservative governments also found ways to mobilize popular support by invoking nationalist themes. The only political movement to swim against the tide of nationalism was that of the socialists, who stressed the importance of class unity across national boundaries: Marx and his followers believed that German, French, and British workers had more in common with each other than with their middle-class employers.

Even so, however, socialist movements in Europe developed in distinctly different nationalist political contexts, making traditions of French socialism, for example, different from German socialism or from Italian socialism.

The years following the 1848 revolutions witnessed a shift in the connections between liberalism, nationalism, and nation building. In the United States, territorial changes transformed the boundaries of North American nations; equally significant was the American Civil War, which resulted in wrenching political change. The unification of Germany and Italy in the years after 1848 also involved the conquest of territory, but the process could not have been completed without political reforms and new state structures that changed how governments worked and how they related to their citizens. The governments of France, Britain, Russia, and Austria undertook vast projects of administrative reform during this period: they overhauled their bureaucracies, expanded their electorates, and reorganized relations among ethnic groups. The Russian tsar abolished serfdom, and Abraham Lincoln, an American president, abolished slavery, decades after the French and British had prohibited slavery in their territories. All of these developments helped shape an emerging consensus that the world was naturally organized into "nations" defined in terms of people, states, and territory.

As the process of nation building continued, the balance of power in Europe shifted toward the states that were the earliest to industrialize and most successful in building strong, centralized states. Older imperial powers such as the Habsburg Empire in Austria-Hungary or the Ottoman Empire found their influence waning, in spite of their long history of successful rule over vast territories with diverse populations. At the heart of this nineteenth-century period of nation building lay changing relations between states and those they governed, and these changes were hastened by reactions to the revolutionary upheavals of 1848.

THE REVOLUTIONS OF 1848

Throughout Europe, the spring of 1848 brought a dizzying sequence of revolution and repression. The roots of revolution lay in economic crisis, social antagonisms, and political grievances. But these revolutions were also shaped decisively by nationalism, especially in southern, central, and eastern Europe. Many reformers and revolutionaries had liberal goals: representative government, an end to privilege, economic development, and so on. They also sought some form of national unity. The fate of the

GERMAN CONFEDERATION, 1815. Compare this map with the one on page 583. ■ *What major areas were left out of the German Confederation?* ■ *Why do you think they were left out?* ■ *What obstacles made it difficult to establish a unified German nation during this period?*

Map legend:

— Boundary of the Germanic Confederation, 1815
Austrian Empire
France
Prussia
The Zollverein, 1834

1848 revolutions in these regions demonstrated nationalism's power to mobilize opponents of the regime but also its potential to splinter revolutionary alliances and to override other allegiances and values entirely.

The Hungry Forties

A deteriorating economic situation throughout Europe contributed to the outbreak of revolution in 1848, and helps to explain why revolutions occurred in so many places nearly simultaneously. Poor harvests in the early 1840s were followed by two years in 1845–46 when the grain harvest failed completely. A potato blight brought starvation in Ireland and hunger in Germany. Food prices doubled in 1846–47, and bread riots broke out across Europe. Villagers attacked carts carrying grain, refusing to let merchants take it to other markets. Compounding the problem was a cyclical industrial slowdown that spread across Europe, throwing thousands into unemployment. Starving peasants and unemployed laborers swamped public-relief organizations in many European cities. The years 1846 and 1847 were "probably the worst of the entire century in terms of want and human suffering," and the decade came to be known as the Hungry Forties.

Hunger itself cannot cause revolution. It does, however, test governments' abilities to manage a crisis, and failure can make a ruler seem illegitimate. When public relief foundered in France and troops repressed potato riots in Berlin, when regimes armed middle-class citizens to protect themselves against the poor, governments looked both authoritarian and inept. In the 1840s, European

Competing Viewpoints

Two Views of the June Days, France, 1848

These two passages make for an interesting comparison. The socialist Karl Marx reported on the events of 1848 in France as a journalist for a German newspaper. For Marx, the bloodshed of the June Days shattered the "fraternal illusions" of February 1848, when the king had been overthrown and the provisional government established. That bloodshed also symbolized a new stage in history: one of acute class conflict.

The French liberal politician Alexis de Tocqueville also wrote about his impressions of the revolution. (Tocqueville's account, however, is retrospective, for he wrote his memoirs well after 1848.) For Marx, a socialist observer, the June Days represented a turning point: "The working class was knocking on the gates of history." For Tocqueville, a member of the government, the actions of the crowd sparked fear and conservative reaction.

Karl Marx's Journalism

The last official remnant of the February Revolution, the Executive Commission, has melted away, like an apparition, before the seriousness of events. The fireworks of Lamartine [French Romantic poet and member of the provisional government] have turned into the war rockets of Cavaignac [French general, in charge of putting down the workers' insurrection]. *Fraternité,* the fraternity of antagonistic classes of which one exploits the other, this *fraternité,* proclaimed in February, on every prison, on every barracks— its true, unadulterated, its prosaic expression is civil war, civil war in its most fearful form, the war of labor and capital. This fraternity flamed in front of all the windows of Paris on the evening of June 25, when the Paris of the bourgeoisie was illuminated, whilst the Paris of the proletariat [Marxist term for the working people] burnt, bled, moaned. . . . The February Revolution was the beautiful revolution, the revolution of universal sympathy, because the antagonisms, which had flared up in it against the monarchy, slumbered peacefully side by side, still undeveloped, because the social struggle which formed its background had won only a joyous existence, an existence of phrases, of words. The June revolution is the ugly revolution, the repulsive revolution, because things have taken the place of phrases, because the republic uncovered the head of the monster itself, by striking off the crown that shielded and concealed it.—Order! was the battle cry of Guizot . . . Order! shouts Cavaignac, the brutal echo of the French National Assembly and of the republican bourgeoisie. Order! thundered his grape-shot, as it ripped up the body of the proletariat. None of

states already faced a host of political challenges: from liberals who sought constitutional government and limits on royal power, from republicans who campaigned for universal male suffrage, from nationalists who challenged the legitimacy of their hereditary rulers, and from socialists whose appeal lay in their claim to speak for laborers and the poor. These political challenges were reinforced by the economic crisis of the 1840s, and the result was a wave of revolution that swept across Europe as one government after another lost the confidence of its people. The first of these revolutions came in France, and as elsewhere in 1848, it did not have the outcome that revolutionaries had hoped for.

The French Revolution of 1848: A Republican Experiment

The French monarchy after the revolution of 1830 (see Chapter 20) seemed little different from its predecessor. King Louis Philippe gathered around him members of

the numerous revolutions of the French bourgeoisie since 1789 was an attack on order; for they allowed the rule of the class, they allowed the slavery of the workers, they allowed the bourgeois order to endure, however often the political form of this rule and of this slavery changed. June has attacked this order. Woe to June!

Source: *Neue Rheinische Zeitung (New Rhineland Gazette)*, June 29, 1848, as cited in Karl Marx, *The Class Struggles in France* (New York: 1964), pp. 57–58.

Alexis de Tocqueville Remembers the June Days (1893)

Now at last I have come to that insurrection in June which was the greatest and the strangest that had ever taken place in our history, or perhaps in that of any other nation: the greatest because for four days more than a hundred thousand men took part in it, and there were five generals killed; the strangest, because the insurgents were fighting without a battle cry, leaders, or flag, and yet they showed wonderful powers of coordination and a military expertise that astonished the most experienced officers.

Another point that distinguished it from all other events of the same type during the last sixty years was that its object was not to change the form of government, but to alter the organization of society. In truth it was not a political struggle (in the sense in which we have used the word "political" up to now), but a class struggle, a sort of "Servile War." . . . One should not see it only as a brutal and a blind, but as a powerful effort of the workers to escape from the necessities of their condition, which had been depicted to them as an illegitimate depression, and by the sword to open up a road towards that imaginary well-being that had been shown to them in the distance as a right. It was this mixture of greedy desires and false theories that engendered the insurrection and made it so formidable. These poor people had been assured that the goods of the wealthy were in some way the result of a theft committed against themselves. They had been assured that inequalities of fortune were as much opposed to morality and the interests of society as to nature. This obscure and mistaken conception of right, combined with brute force, imparted to it an energy, tenacity and strength it would never have had on its own.

Source: From Alexis de Tocqueville, *Recollections: The French Revolution of 1848*, ed. J. P. Mayer and A. P. Kerr, trans. George Lawrence (New Brunswick, NJ: 1987), pp. 436–37.

Questions for Analysis

1. Was Tocqueville sympathetic to the revolutionaries of June?

2. Did Tocqueville think the events were historically significant?

3. Where did Tocqueville agree and disagree with Marx?

the banking and industrial elite and refused demands to enlarge the franchise. Building projects, especially the railway, presented ample opportunities for graft, and the reputation of the government suffered. Republican associations proliferated in French cities, and in 1834 the government declared these organizations illegal. Rebellions broke out in Paris and Lyon, bringing a harsh repression that resulted in deaths and arrests. The government's refusal to compromise drove even moderates into opposition. In 1847, the opposition organized a campaign for electoral reform around repeated political "banquets"—an attempt to get around the laws against assembly. When they called for a giant banquet on February 22, 1848, the king responded by banning the meeting. A sudden and surprising popular revolution in the streets caused Louis Philippe to abdicate his throne only days later. A hastily assembled group of French political figures declared France a republic, for the first time since 1792.

The provisional government of the new French republic consisted of liberals, republicans, and—for the first time— socialists. They produced a new constitution, with elections based on universal male suffrage. Among their first acts was the abolition of slavery in France and French colonies (slavery had been abolished in 1794 during the revolution but reestablished by Napoleon in 1802). In spite of these accomplishments, tensions between propertied republicans and socialists shattered the unity of the coalition that toppled Louis Philippe. Suffering because of the economic crisis, working men and women demanded the "right to work," the right to earn a living wage. The provisional government responded by creating the National Workshops, a program of public works, to give jobs to the unemployed, headed by the socialist Louis Blanc. Initial plans were made to employ 10,000–12,000 workers, but unemployment was so high that 120,000 job-seekers had gathered in the city by June 1848. Meanwhile, voters in rural areas resented the increase in taxation that was required to pay for the public works program. When elections for parliament were held—France's first elections ever to take place under a regime of universal male suffrage—the conservative voices won out, and a majority of moderate republicans and monarchists were elected.

A majority in the new assembly believed the National Workshops were a financial drain and a threat to order. In May, they closed the workshops to new enrollment, excluded recent arrivals to Paris, and sent members between the ages of eighteen and twenty-five into the army. On June 21, they abolished the workshops altogether. In defense of this social program, the workers of Paris—laborers, journeymen, the unemployed—rose in revolt, building barricades across Paris. For four days, June 23–26, they fought a hopeless battle against armed forces recruited from the provinces. The repression of the June Days shocked many observers. About 3,000 were killed and 12,000 arrested. Many of the

prisoners were deported to Algerian labor camps. After this repression, support for the republic among the workers in Paris declined rapidly.

In the aftermath, the government moved quickly to restore order. The parliament hoped for a strong leader in the presidential election and found one in the eventual victor, Louis Napoleon Bonaparte, the nephew of the former emperor, who had spent his life in exile. Buoyed by enthusiastic support from rural voters, the upstart Louis Napoleon polled more than twice as many votes as the other three candidates combined. Louis Napoleon used his position to consolidate his power. He rallied the Catholics by restoring the Church to its former role in education and by sending an expedition to Rome to rescue the pope from revolutionaries (see Chapter 22). He banned radical activities, workers' associations, and suspended press freedoms. In 1851, he called for a plebiscite to give him the authority to change the constitution, and one year later another plebiscite allowed him to establish the Second Empire, ending the Republican experiment. He assumed the title of Napoleon III (r. 1852–70), emperor of the French.

The dynamics of the French Revolution of 1848—initial success, followed by divisions among the supporters of revolution, followed by a reassertion of authoritarian

BARRICADE IN THE RUE DE LA MORTELLERIE, JUNE, 1848 BY ERNEST MEISSONIER (1815–1891). A very different view of 1848, a depiction of the June Days.

THE BURNING OF THE THRONE (1848). A contemporary print shows revolutionaries burning the king's throne. Note the man with a top hat and the man in a worker's smock. Delacroix used similar images to depict cooperation between workers and middle-class revolutionaries (see page 537).

control—would be repeated elsewhere, especially evidenced in the pivotal role of the propertied middle classes. Louis Philippe's reign had been proudly bourgeois but alienated many of its supporters. Key groups in the middle class joined the opposition, allying with radicals who could not topple the regime alone. Yet demands for reform soon led to fears of disorder and the desire for a strong state. This dynamic led to the collapse of the republic and to the rule of Napoleon III. The abandonment of the revolution's social goals—most visibly evident in the National Workshops—led to a stark polarization along class lines, with middle-class and working-class people demanding different things from the state. This political conflict would grow even more intense as socialism came into its own as an independent political force.

Nationalism, Revolution, and the German Question in 1848

The revolutions of 1848 in the German-speaking lands of Europe shared some similarities with the revolutions in France. Like liberals in France, liberal Germans wanted a ruler who would abide by a constitution, allow for greater press freedoms, and accept some form of representative government, though not necessarily universal suffrage. As in France, artisans and urban laborers in German cities gravitated toward more radical ideologies of republicanism and socialism, and protested against new methods of industrial production. The great difference between France and Germany in 1848, however, was that France already had a centralized state and a unified territory. In central Europe, a unified Germany did not exist in 1848. In 1815, the Congress of Vienna had created the German Confederation, a loose organization of thirty-nine states, including the German-speaking lands of Habsburg Austria with its Catholic monarchy, and the German territories of Prussia, ruled by a Protestant king. Because Prussia and Austria competed with one another to occupy the dominant position in German politics, revolutionaries in the German states were forced to reckon with these two conservative powers as they struggled to find a path to national unity.

In 1806, Prussia had been defeated by the French under Napoleon. In response Prussian reformers passed a series of aggressive reforms, imposed from above. They reconstituted the army, imitating Napoleon's policy of recruiting and promoting officers on the basis of merit rather than birth. In 1807, serfdom and the estate system were abolished. A year later, in a conscious attempt to increase middle-class Germans' sense of themselves as citizens,

cities and towns were allowed to elect their councilmen and handle their own finances. (Justice and security continued to be administered by the central government in Berlin.) The Prussian reformers expanded facilities for both primary and secondary education and founded the University of Berlin, which numbered among its faculty several ardent nationalists.

Prussia aimed to establish itself as the leading German state and a counter to Austrian power in the region. Prussia's most significant victory in this respect came with the *Zollverein*, or customs union, in 1834, which established free trade among the German states and a uniform tariff against the rest of the world—an openly protectionist policy advocated by the economist Friedrich List. By the 1840s, the union included almost all of the German states except German Austria and offered manufacturers

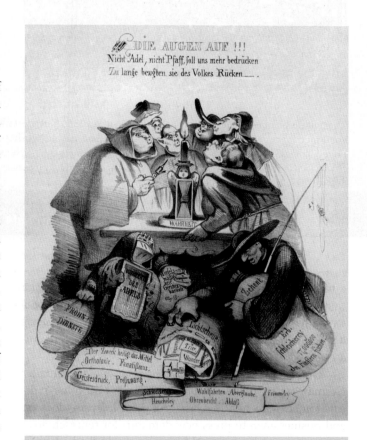

"EYES OPEN!" (c. 1845). This German cartoon from just before the 1848 revolution warns that aristocrats and clergy are conspiring to deny the German people their rights. The caption reads "Eyes Open! Neither the nobility nor the clergy shall oppress us any longer. For too long they have broken the backs of the people." ■ *Did supporters of the revolution consider the aristocracy or the clergy to be legitimate members of the nation? Compare the cartoon with the pamphlet of Abbé Sieyès in the French Revolution (see page 484).*

those of the workers and artisans who had led the street protests against the king. The delegates assumed that the Frankfurt Assembly would draft a constitution for a liberal, unified Germany, much as an assembly of Frenchmen had done for their country in 1789. The comparison was mistaken. In 1789, a French nation-state and a centralized sovereign power already existed, to be reformed and redirected by the assembled French delegates. By contrast, the Frankfurt Assembly had no resources, no sovereign power to take, no single legal code, and, of course, no army.

On the assembly floor, questions of nationality proved contentious and destructive. Which Germans would be in the new state? At first, a majority of the assembly's delegates supported a "Great German" position, arguing that the new nation should include as many Germans as possible. This was countered by a minority who called for a "Small Germany," one that left out all lands of the Habsburg Empire, including German Austria. After a long and difficult debate, the Austrian emperor withdrew his support, and the assembly retreated to the Small German solution. In April 1849, the Frankfurt Assembly offered the crown of a new German nation to the Prussian king, Frederick William IV.

By this time, however, Frederick William was negotiating from a position of greater strength. He used the military to repress radical revolutionaries in Berlin while the delegates debated the constitutional question in Frankfurt. He was also encouraged by a backlash against revolutionary movements in Europe after the bloody repression during the June Days in Paris. He therefore refused to become a constitutional monarch on the terms offered by the Frankfurt Assembly. The Prussian monarch wanted both the crown and a larger German state, but on his own terms, and he therefore dissolved the assembly before they could approve it with an official vote. The Frankfurt delegates went home, disillusioned by their experience and convinced that their liberal and nationalist goals were incompatible. Some fled repression by emigrating to the United States. Others convinced themselves to sacrifice their liberal views for the seemingly realistic goal of nationhood. In Prussia itself, the army dispatched what remained of the revolutionary forces.

Elsewhere in the German-speaking states as popular revolution was taking its own course, many moderate liberals began to have second thoughts about the pace of change. Peasants ransacked tax offices and burned castles; workers smashed machines in protests against industrialization. Citizen militias formed in towns and cities, threatening the power of established elites. New daily newspapers multiplied. So did political clubs. For the first time, many of these clubs admitted women (although they denied them the right to speak), and newly founded

THE FRANKFURT PREPARLIAMENT MEETS AT ST. PAUL'S CHURCH, 1848. This assembly brought together 500 delegates from the various German states to establish a constitution for a new German nation. An armed militia lined the square, and lines of student gymnasts (dressed in white with wide-brimmed hats) escorted the delegates. Their presence was a sign that the organizers of the preparliament feared violence. The black, red, and gold banners were also associated with republicanism.

■ *What image did the organizers mean to convey with this pageantry, the disciplined lines of students and delegates, their forms of dress, and their use of republican symbols?*

women's clubs demanded political rights. This torrent of popular unrest made moderate reformers uneasy; they now considered universal male suffrage too radical. Throughout the German states, rulers took advantage of this shift in middle-class opinion to undo the concessions that they had granted in 1848 and to push through counterrevolutionary measures in the name of order.

For German liberals, national unification was now seen as necessary to maintain political stability. "In order to realize our ideas of freedom and equality, we want above all a strong and powerful government," claimed one candidate during the election campaigns for the Frankfurt Assembly. Popular sovereignty, he continued, "strengthened by the authority of a hereditary monarchy, will be able to repress with an iron hand any disorder and any violation of the law." In this context, nationhood stood for a new constitution and political community but also for a sternly enforced rule of law. After the failure of the Frankfurt Assembly, therefore, German liberals increasingly looked to a strong Prussian state as the only possible route toward national unification.

Peoples against Empire: The Habsburg Lands

In the sprawling Habsburg (Austrian) Empire, nationalism played a different role. On the one hand, the Habsburg emperors could point to a remarkable record of political success: as heir to the medieval Holy Roman Empire, Habsburg kings had ruled for centuries over a diverse array of central European ethnicities and language groups that included Germans, Czechs, Magyars, Poles, Slovaks, Serbs, and Italians, to name only the most prominent. In the sixteenth century, under Charles V, the empire had included Spain, parts of Burgundy, and the Netherlands. In the nineteenth century, however, the Habsburgs found it increasingly difficult to hold their empire together as the national demands of the different peoples in the realm escalated after 1815. Whereas the greater ethnic and linguistic homogeneity of the northern and western German-speaking lands allowed for a convergence between liberal ideas of popular sovereignty and national unification, no such program was possible in the Habsburg Empire. Popular sovereignty for peoples defined in terms of their ethnic identity implied a breakup of the Habsburg lands.

At the same time, however, the existence of nationalist movements did not imply unity, even within territories that spoke the same language. In the Polish territories of the empire, nationalist sentiment was strongest among aristocrats, who were especially conscious of their historic role as leaders of the Polish nation. Here, the Habsburg Empire successfully set Polish serfs against Polish lords, ensuring that social grievances dampened ethnic nationalism. In the Hungarian region, national claims were likewise advanced by the relatively small Magyar aristocracy. (*Hungarian* is a political term; *Magyar,* which was often used, refers to the Hungarians' non-Slavic language.) Yet they gained an audience under the gifted and influential leadership of Lajos (Louis) Kossuth (*KAW-shut*). A member of the lower nobility, Kossuth was by turns a lawyer, publicist, newspaper editor, and political leader. To protest the closed-door policy of the empire's barely representative Diet (parliament), Kossuth published transcripts of parliamentary debates and distributed them to a broader public. He campaigned for independence and a separate Hungarian parliament, but he

"NO PIECE OF PAPER WILL COME BETWEEN MYSELF AND MY PEOPLE" (1848). In this cartoon, Frederick William IV and a military officer refuse to accept the constitution for a new Germany offered to him by the Frankfurt Assembly. Note that the caption refers to a conservative definition of the relationship between a monarch and "his people." Compare this autocratic vision of the nation-state with the liberal nationalist's demand for a government that reflects the people's will. ▪ *What contrasting visions of the nation and its relation to the state are contained in this cartoon?*

HUNGARIAN REVOLUTIONARY LAJOS KOSSUTH, 1851. A leader of the Hungarian nationalist movement who combined aristocratic style with rabble-rousing politics, Kossuth almost succeeded in an attempt to separate Hungary from Austria in 1849.

also (and more influentially) brought politics to the people. Kossuth staged political "banquets" like those in France, at which local and national personalities made speeches in the form of toasts and interested citizens could eat, drink, and participate in politics. The Hungarian political leader combined aristocratic style with rabble-rousing politics: a delicate balancing act but one that, when it worked, catapulted him to the center of Habsburg politics.

The other major nationalist movement that troubled the Habsburg Empire was pan-Slavism. Slavs included Russians, Poles, Ukrainians, Czechs, Slovaks, Slovenes, Croats, Serbs, Macedonians, and Bulgarians. Before 1848, pan-Slavism was primarily a cultural movement united by a general pro-Slavic sentiment. It was internally divided, however, by the competing claims of different Slavic languages and traditions. Pan-Slavism inspired the works of the Czech historian and political leader, František Palacký, author of the *History of the Bohemian People*, and the Slovak Jan Kollár, whose book *Slávy Dcera* ("Slava's Daughter") mourned the loss of identity among Slavs in the Germanic world. The movement also influenced the Polish Romantic poet Adam Mickiewicz (*mihtz-KYAY-vihch*), who sought to rekindle Polish nationhood against foreign oppression.

The fact that Russia and Austria were rivals in eastern Europe made pan-Slavism a volatile and unpredictable political force in the regions of eastern Europe where the two nations vied for power and influence. Tsar Nicholas of Russia sought to use pan-Slavism to his advantage, making arguments about "Slavic" uniqueness part of his "autocracy, orthodoxy, nationality" ideology after 1825. Yet the tsar's Russian-sponsored pan-Slavism alienated Western-oriented Slavs who resented Russia's ambitions. Here, as elsewhere, nationalism created a tangled web of alliances and antagonisms.

Austria and Hungary in 1848: Springtime of Peoples and the Autumn of Empire

The empire's combination of political, social, and ethnic tensions came to the point of explosion in 1848. The opening salvo came from Kossuth who stepped up his Hungarian reform campaign, pillorying the "Metternich system" of Habsburg autocracy and control, demanding representative institutions throughout the empire and autonomy for the Hungarian Magyar nation. The Hungarian Diet prepared to draft its own constitution. In Vienna, the seat of Habsburg power, a popular movement of students and artisans demanding political and social reforms built barricades and attacked the imperial palace. A Central Committee of Citizens took shape, as did a middle-class

militia, or national guard, determined at once to maintain order and to press demands for reform. The Habsburg regime tried to shut the movement down by closing the university, but that only unleashed more popular anger. The regime found itself forced to retreat almost entirely. Metternich, whose political system had weathered so many storms, fled to Britain in disguise—a good indication of the political turmoil—leaving the emperor Ferdinand I in Vienna. The government acceded to radical demands for male suffrage and a single house of representatives. It agreed to withdraw troops from Vienna and to put forced labor and serfdom on a path to abolition. The government also yielded to Czech demands in Bohemia, granting that kingdom its own constitution. To the south, Italian liberals and nationalists attacked the empire's territories in Naples and Venice. As what would be called "the springtime of peoples" unfolded, Habsburg control of its various provinces seemed to be coming apart.

Yet the explosion of national sentiment that shook the empire later allowed it to recoup its fortunes. The paradox of nationalism in central Europe was that no cultural

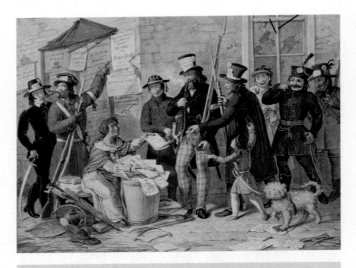

THE FIRST UNCENSORED NEWSPAPER AFTER THE REVOLUTION IN VIENNA, JANUARY 1848. This watercolor illustrates the power of public information during the 1848 revolution in the Austrian capital. An uncensored newspaper, wall posters, caps with political insignia and slogans, and an armed citizenry all are evidence of a vibrant and impassioned public discussion on the events of the day. Note, too, the modest dress of the woman selling the papers, the top hat and fashionable dress of the middle-class man smoking a pipe, and the presence of military uniforms, all of which illustrate support for the revolution among a broad portion of the population. ▪ *How does this vision of the public sphere in action compare with previous depictions of public debate during the Enlightenment (see page 468) or in the French Revolution (see page 493), or elsewhere in Europe in 1848 (see page 577)?*

or ethnic majority could declare independence in a given region without prompting rebellion from other minority groups that inhabited the same area. In Bohemia, for instance, Czechs and Germans who lived side by side had worked together to pass reforms scuttling feudalism. Within a month, however, nationalism began to fracture their alliance. German Bohemians set off to attend the all-important Frankfurt Assembly, but the Czech majority refused to send representatives and countered by convening a confederation of Slavs in Prague. What did the delegates at the Slav confederation want? Some were hostile to what the Russian anarchist Mikhail Bakunin called the "monstrous Austrian Empire." But the majority of delegates preferred to be ruled by the Habsburgs (though with some autonomy) than to be dominated by either the Germans or the Russians.

This bundle of animosities allowed the Austrians to divide and conquer. In May 1848, during the Slav Congress, a student- and worker-led insurrection broke out in Prague. On the orders of the newly installed liberal government, Austrian troops entered the city to restore order, sent the Slav Congress packing, and reasserted control in Bohemia.

For economic as well as political reasons, the new government was determined to keep the empire intact. The regime also sent troops to regain control in the Italian provinces of Lombardy and Venetia, and quarrels among the Italians helped the Austrians succeed.

Nationalism and counter-nationalism in Hungary set the stage for the final act of the drama. The Hungarian parliament had passed a series of laws including new provisions for the union of Hungary and Austria. In the heat of 1848, Ferdinand I had little choice but to accept them. The Hungarian parliament abolished serfdom and ended noble privilege to prevent a peasant insurrection. It also established freedom of the press and of religion and changed the suffrage requirements, enfranchising small property holders. Many of these measures (called the March laws) were hailed by Hungarian peasants, Jewish communities, and liberals. But other provisions—particularly the extension of Magyar control—provoked opposition from the Croats, Serbs, and Romanians within Hungary. On April 14, 1848, Kossuth upped the ante, severing all ties between Hungary and Austria. The new

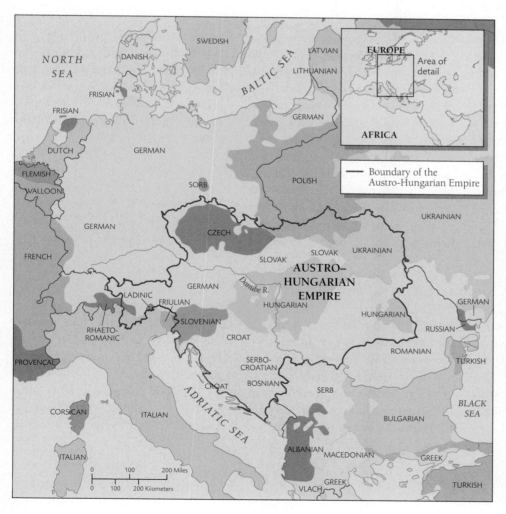

LANGUAGES OF CENTRAL AND EASTERN EUROPE. In Habsburg Austria-Hungary, ethnic/linguistic boundaries did not conform to political boundaries between states.
▪ *How many different language groups can you count in the Austrian Empire?* ▪ *Why was it ultimately easier for the German states to unify, as suggested by this map?* ▪ *How did the diversity of peoples in the Habsburg Empire make a convergence between liberal revolution and nationalism more difficult to achieve?*

Building the Italian Nation: Three Views

The charismatic revolutionary Giuseppe Mazzini left more than fifty volumes of memoirs and writings. In the first excerpt, he sets out his vision of the "regeneration" of the Italian nation and the three Romes: ancient Rome, the Rome of the popes, and (in the future) the Rome of the people, which would emancipate the peoples of Europe. Mazzini's conception of Italian nationalism was Romantic in its interpretation of Italy's distinctive history and destiny, and revolutionary in its emphasis on the Italian people rather than on statesmen.

The National Society was formed in 1857 to support Italian unification. By the 1860s, the society had over 5,000 members. It was especially strong in the Piedmont, where it was formed, and in central Italy. Giuseppe la Farina was a tenacious organizer; he drafted the society's political creed and had it printed and sold throughout Italy.

The unification of Italy owed as much to Cavour's hard-nosed diplomacy as it did to middle-class movements for unification. In 1862, one of Cavour's contemporaries offered an assessment of the count and how he had found "an opening in the complicated fabric of European politics," reprinted in the third piece here.

Mazzini and Romantic Nationalism

I saw regenerate Italy becoming at one bound the missionary of a religion of progress and fraternity. . . .

The worship of Rome was a part of my being. The great Unity, the One Life of the world, had twice been elaborated within her walls. Other peoples—their brief mission fulfilled—disappeared for ever. To none save to her had it been given twice to guide and direct the world. . . . There, upon the vestiges of an epoch of civilization anterior to the Grecian, which had had its seat in Italy . . . the Rome of the Republic, concluded by the Caesars, had arisen to consign the former world to oblivion, and borne her eagles over the known world, carrying with them the idea of right, the source of liberty.

In later days . . . she had again arisen, greater than before, and at once constituted herself, through her Popes—the accepted center of a new Unity. . . .

Why should not a new Rome, the Rome of the Italian people . . . arise to create a third and still vaster Unity; to link together and harmonize earth and heaven, right [law] and duty; and utter, not to individuals but to peoples, the great word Association—to make known to free men and equal their mission here below?

Source: Giuseppe Mazzini, *The Life and Writings of Joseph Mazzini* (London: 1964), as cited in Denis Mack Smith, *The Making of Italy, 1796–1870* (New York: 1968), pp. 48–49.

The Political Creed of the National Society, February 1858

Italian independence should be the aim of every man of spirit and intelligence. Neither our educational system in Italy, nor our commerce and industry, can ever be flourishing or properly modernized while Austria keeps one foot on our neck. . . . What good is it to be born in the most fertile and beautiful country in the world, to lie midway between East and West with magnificent ports in both the Adriatic and Mediterranean, to be descended from the Genoese, the Pisans, the men of Amalfi, Sicily, and Venice? What use is it to have invented the compass, to have discovered the New World and been the progenitor of two civilizations? . . .

To obtain political liberty we must expel the Austrians who keep us enslaved. To win freedom of conscience

we must expel the Austrians who keep us slaves of the Pope. To create a national literature we must chase away the Austrians who keep us uneducated....

Italy must become not only independent but politically united. Political unity alone can reconcile various interests and laws, can mobilize credit and put out collective energies to speeding up communications. Only thus will we find sufficient capital for large-scale industry. Only thus will we create new markets, suppress internal obstacles to the free flow of commerce, and find the strength and reputation needed for traffic in distant lands....

Everything points irresistibly to political unification. Science, industry, commerce, and the arts all need it. No great enterprise is possible any longer if we do not first put together the skill, knowledge, capital, and labor of the whole of our great nation. The spirit of the age is moving toward concentration, and woe betide any nation that holds back!

Source: A. Franchi, ed., *Scritti politici di Giuseppe La Farina,* vol. 2 (Milan: 1870), as cited in Denis Mack Smith, *The Making of Italy, 1796–1870* (New York: 1968), pp. 224–25.

Count Cavour as a Leader

Count Cavour undeniably ranks as third among European statesmen after Lord Palmerston [British prime minister 1855–1858, 1859–1865] and the Emperor Napoleon. ... Count Cavour's strength does not lie in his principles; for he has none that are altogether inflexible. But he has a clear, precise aim, one whose greatness would—ten years ago—have made any other man reel: that of creating a unified and independent Italy. Men, means, circumstances were and still are matters of indifference to him. He walks straight ahead, always firm, often alone, sacrificing his friends, his sympathies, sometimes his heart, and often his conscience. Nothing is too difficult for him....

Count Cavour ... always has the talent to assess a situation and the possibilities of exploiting it. And it is this wonderful faculty that has contributed to form the Italy of today. As minister of a fourth-rate power, he could not create situations like Napoleon III, nor has he possessed the support of a great nation like Palmerston.

Count Cavour had to seek out an opening in the complicated fabric of European politics; he had to wriggle his way in, conceal himself, lay a mine, and cause an explosion. And it was by these means that he defeated Austria and won the help of France and England. Where other statesmen would have drawn back, Cavour plunged in headlong—as soon as he had sounded the precipice and calculated the possible profit and loss. The Crimean expeditionary force ... the cession of Nice, the invasion of the Papal States last autumn [i.e., in 1860], were all the outcome of his vigorous stamina of mind.

There in brief you have the man of foreign affairs. He is strong; he is a match for the situation, for the politicians of his time or indeed of any time.

Source: F. Petruccelli della Gattina, *I moribundi del Palazzo Carignano* (Milan: 1862), as cited in Denis Mack Smith, *The Making of Italy, 1796–1870* (New York: 1968), pp. 181–82.

Questions for Analysis

1. Compare Mazzini's romantic vision of Italian history with the more pragmatic arguments for political unity coming from the liberal supporters of the National Society. Are there any points of overlap?

2. How would a supporter of Mazzini or a member of the National Society react to the third document's claim that an individual, Cavour, deserved primary credit for Italian unification?

3. Why should history and claims about "the spirit of the age" be so important to Italian nationalists?

Austrian emperor, Franz Josef, now played his last card: he asked for military support from Nicholas I of Russia. By mid-August 1849, with the help of 300,000 Russian troops, the Hungarian revolt was crushed.

In the Habsburg capital of Vienna, the revolutionary movement also lost ground. When economic crisis and unemployment helped spark a second popular uprising, the emperor's forces, with Russian support, descended on the capital. On October 31, the liberal government capitulated. The regime reestablished censorship, disbanded the national guard and student organizations, and put twenty-five revolutionary leaders to death in front of a firing squad. Kossuth went into hiding and lived the rest of his life in exile.

Paradoxically, then, the Habsburg Empire of Austria was in part saved during the revolutions of 1848 by the very nationalist movements that threatened to tear it apart. Although nationalists in Habsburg lands, especially in Hungary, gained the support of significant numbers of people, the fact that different nationalist movements found it impossible to cooperate with one another allowed the new emperor, Franz Josef, to defeat the most-significant challenges to his authority one by one and consolidate his rule (with Russian help). Franz Josef would survive these crises, and many others, until his death in 1916 during World War I, a much larger conflict that would finally overwhelm and destroy the Habsburg Empire for good.

The Early Stages of Italian Unification in 1848

The Italian peninsula had not been united since the Roman Empire. In 1800, like the German-speaking lands of central Europe, the area that is now Italy was a patchwork of small states (see map on page 533). Austria occupied the northern states of Lombardy and Venetia, which were also the most urban and industrial. Habsburg dependents also ruled Tuscany, Parma, and Modena. The independent Italian states included the southern kingdom of the Two Sicilies, governed by members of the Bourbon family; the Papal States, ruled by Pope Gregory XVI (r. 1831–46); and most important, Piedmont-Sardinia, ruled by the reform-minded monarch Charles Albert (r. 1831–49) of the House of Savoy. Charles Albert was not a nationalist himself, but Piedmont-Sardinia's economic power, geographical location, and opposition to Austrian influence gave it a central role in the development of Italian nationalism.

The leading Italian nationalist in this period was Giuseppe Mazzini (1805–1872) from the city of Genoa, in Piedmont. Mazzini began his political career as a member of the Carbonari (see Chapter 20), an underground society pledged to resisting Austrian control of the region and establishing constitutional rule. In 1831, Mazzini founded his own society, Young Italy, which was anti-Austrian and in favor of constitutional reforms but also dedicated to Italian unification. Charismatic and persuasive, Mazzini was one of the best-known nationalists of his time. Under his leadership, Young Italy clubs multiplied. Yet the organization's favored tactics, plotting mutinies and armed rebellions, proved ineffective. In 1834, Mazzini launched an invasion of the kingdom of Sardinia. Without sufficient support, it fizzled, driving Mazzini into exile in England.

Mazzini's republican vision of a united Italy clashed with the goals of his potential allies. Many liberals shared his commitment to creating a single Italian state but not his enthusiasm for the people and popular movements. They hoped instead to merge existing governments into some form of constitutional monarchy; a few wanted to establish a government under the pope. Mazzini's insistence on a democratic republic committed to social and political transformation struck pragmatic liberals as utopian and well-to-do members of the middle classes as dangerous.

The turmoil that swept across Europe in 1848 raised hopes for political and social change and put Italian unification on the agenda. In March 1848, only a few weeks after revolution had toppled the French monarchy, popular revolts broke out in the northern provinces of Venetia and Lombardy, fueled by anger at the Austrian occupation. In Milan, the capital of Lombardy, thousands of people marched on the palace of the Austrian governor general calling for reforms, leading to pitched battles in the streets. In Venice, the revolutionaries forced the Austrian troops out of the city and declared a republic. Charles Albert of Piedmont-Sardinia provided the rebels with military support and took up the banner of Italian nationalism, although many charged that he was primarily interested in expanding his own power. At the same time, Charles Albert pleased Italian liberals by creating an elected legislature and relaxing press censorship in his kingdom.

In August 1848, an insurrection of laborers broke out in Bologna, challenging the authority of the pope in the Papal States. Soon after, a popular uprising in Rome confronted the pope directly, and by February 1849 a new government in Rome had declared itself a republic. The next month, Mazzini arrived from exile to join the revolutionary movement in Rome. These movements were neither coordinated nor ultimately successful. Charles Albert hesitated to confront the Austrians directly, and over the next few months the Austrians regained the upper hand in the north. French forces under Louis Napoleon intervened in Rome and the Papal States; and although they met fierce

SIEGE OF VENICE, 1848. This image, designed to provoke an anti-Austrian and nationalist sentiment among Italians, shows Venetian women and children donating their jewels to support their city while it was besieged by the Austrian army in 1848.
■ *What makes the image of women and children sacrificing their possessions for the larger good so powerful?* ■ *What does it say about the connections between nationalism and social obligations associated with gender?* ■ *Did nationalism depend on a vision of the family as well as a vision of the nation?*

GIUSEPPE MAZZINI (1805–1872). Born in Genoa when it was ruled by Napoleon's France, Mazzini devoted his life to the cause of Italian unification and independence. As a young man, Mazzini was a member of the underground revolutionary organization known as the Carbonari, and in 1831 he founded a new group, Young Italy, which soon attracted many adherents. Early attempts at insurrection resulted in political exile, but he returned during the 1848 revolutions to help lead the Roman Republic. Although his hopes for a Republican Italy were blocked by Cavour's plans for unification under the leadership of Piedmont-Sardinia, Mazzini remained a hero to many Italians, and his description of a "United States of Europe" anticipated the European Union.

resistance from the Roman republicans joined by Giuseppe Garibaldi (to be discussed later), they nonetheless restored the pope's power and defeated the Roman Republic. The Venetian Republic was the last of the Italian revolutions to fall after a blockade and an artillery bombardment from the Austrian army in August 1849. Like most of the radical movements of 1848, these Italian uprisings all failed. Still, they raised the hopes of nationalists who spoke of a *risorgimento*, or Italian resurgence, that would restore the nation to the position of leadership it had held in Roman times and during the Renaissance.

BUILDING THE NATION-STATE

In the wake of the revolutions of 1848, new nation-states were built or consolidated—often by former critics of nationalism. Since the French Revolution of 1789, conservative politicians had associated nationhood with liberalism: constitutions, reforms, new political communities. During the second half of the century, however, the political ground shifted dramatically. States and governments took the national initiative. Alarmed by revolutionary ferment,

they promoted economic development, pressed social and political reforms, and sought to shore up their base of support. Rather than allow popular nationalist movements to emerge from below, statesmen consolidated their governments' powers and built nations from above.

France under Napoleon III

Napoleon III, like his uncle, believed in personal rule and a centralized state. As emperor, he controlled the nation's finances, the army, and foreign affairs. The assembly, elected by universal male suffrage, could approve only legislation drafted at the emperor's direction. Napoleon's regime aimed to undermine France's traditional elites by expanding the bureaucracy and cultivating a new relationship with the people. "The confidence of our rough peasants can be won by an energetic authority," asserted one of the emperor's representatives. In the cities, an efficient system of police informers rooted out revolutionary groups.

Napoleon III also took steps to develop the economy, believing that industrial expansion would bring prosperity and national glory. His government encouraged new forms of financing, passed new limited-liability laws, and signed a free-trade treaty with Britain in 1860. The government also created the Crédit Mobilier, an investment banking institution that sold shares and financed railroads, insurance and gas companies, coal and construction companies, and the building of the Suez Canal (see Chapter 22). Napoleon reluctantly permitted the existence of trade unions and legalized strikes. By appealing to both workers and the middle class, he sought to gain support for his goal of reestablishing France as a leading world power.

Most emblematic of the emperor's ambition was his transformation of the nation's capital. Paris's medieval infrastructure was buckling under the weight of population growth and economic development. Cholera epidemics in 1832 and 1849 killed tens of thousands. In 1850, only one house in five had running water. Official concerns about public health were reinforced by political fears of crime and revolutionary militancy in working-class neighborhoods. A massive rebuilding project razed much of the medieval center of the city and erected 34,000 new buildings, including elegant hotels with the first elevators. The construction installed new water pipes and sewer lines, laid out 200 kilometers of new streets, and rationalized the traffic flow. The renovation did not benefit everyone. Although the regime built model worker residences, rising rents drove

PARIS REBUILT. Baron Haussmann, prefect of Paris under Napoleon III, presided over the wholesale rebuilding of the city, with effects we still see today. The Arc de Triomphe, seen here in a photograph from the 1960s, became the center of an *étoile* (star) pattern, with the wide boulevards named after Napoleon I's famous generals.

working people from the city's center into increasingly segregated suburbs. Baron Haussmann, the prefect of Paris who presided over the project, considered the city a monument to "cleanliness and order." Others called Haussmann an "artist of demolition."

Victorian Britain and the Second Reform Bill (1867)

Less affected by the revolutionary wave of 1848, Great Britain under Queen Victoria (r. 1837–1901) continued the social and political changes that had begun in 1832 with the First Reform Bill. The government faced mounting demands to extend the franchise beyond the middle classes. Industrial expansion sustained a growing stratum of highly skilled and relatively well-paid workers (almost exclusively male). These workers turned away from the tradition of militant radicalism that had characterized the Hungry Forties. Instead, they favored collective self-help through cooperative societies or trade unions, whose major role was to accumulate funds for insurance against old age and unemployment. These associations saw education as a tool for advancement and their activities created real pressure for electoral reform.

Some argued for the vote in the name of democracy. Others borrowed arguments from earlier middle-class campaigns for electoral reform: they were responsible workers, respectable and upstanding members of society, with strong religious convictions and patriotic feelings. Unquestionably loyal to the state, they deserved the vote and direct representation just as much as the middle class. These workers were joined in their campaign by many middle-class dissenting reformers in the Liberal party, whose religious beliefs (as dissenters from the Church of England) linked them to the workers' campaigns for reform. Dissenters had long faced discrimination. They were denied posts in the civil service and the military and for centuries had been excluded from the nation's premier universities, Oxford and Cambridge. Moreover, they resented paying taxes to support the Church of England. The fact that the community of dissent crossed class lines was vital to Liberal party politics and the campaign for reforming the vote.

Working-class leaders and middle-class dissidents joined in a countrywide campaign for a new reform bill to expand the vote. They were backed by some shrewd Conservatives, such as Benjamin Disraeli (1804–1881), who argued that political life would be improved, not disrupted, by including the "aristocrats of labor." In actuality, Disraeli was betting that the newly enfranchised demographic would vote Conservative; and in 1867, he steered through

Parliament a bill that reached further than anything proposed by his political opponents. The 1867 Reform Bill doubled the franchise by extending the vote to any men who paid poor rates or rent of £10 or more a year in urban areas (this meant, in general, skilled workers) and to rural tenants paying rent of £12 or more. The bill also redistributed seats, with large northern cities gaining representation at the expense of the rural south. Although the Chartists' goal of universal male suffrage remained unfulfilled (see Chapter 20), the 1867 law allowed the responsible working class to participate in the affairs of state.

The 1867 reform bill was silent on women, but an important minority insisted that liberalism should include women's enfranchisement. These advocates mobilized a woman suffrage movement, building on women's remarkable participation in earlier reform campaigns, especially the Anti-Corn Law League and the movement to abolish slavery. Their cause found a passionate supporter in John Stuart Mill, perhaps the century's most brilliant, committed, and influential defender of personal liberty. Mill's father had worked closely with the utilitarian philosopher Jeremy Bentham, and the young Mill had been a convinced utilitarian himself (see Chapter 20). He went on, however, to develop much more expansive notions of human freedom. In 1859, Mill wrote *On Liberty*, which many consider the classic defense of individual freedom in the face of the state and the "tyranny of the majority." During the same period he coauthored—with his lover and eventual wife, Harriet Taylor—essays on women's political rights, the law of marriage, and divorce. At the time, Taylor was trapped in an unhappy marriage, and divorce required an act of Parliament. Taylor's relationship with Mill thus added a measure of personal scandal to their political views, which contemporaries considered scandalous enough. His *Subjection of Women* (1869), published after Harriet died, argued what few could even contemplate: that women had to be considered individuals on the same plane as men and that women's freedom was a measure of social progress. *Subjection* was an international success and, with *On Liberty*, became one of the defining texts of Western liberalism. Mill's arguments, however, did not carry the day. Only militant suffrage movements and the crisis of the First World War brought women the vote.

The decade or so following the passage of the Reform Bill of 1867 marked the high point of British liberalism. By opening the doors to political participation, liberalism had accomplished a peaceful restructuring of political institutions and social life. It did so under considerable pressure from below, however, and in Britain, as elsewhere, liberal leaders made it unquestionably clear that these doors were not open to everyone. Their opposition to woman

MILL'S LOGIC, OR FRANCHISE FOR FEMALES
"Pray clear the way, there, for these—ah—persons."

JOHN STUART MILL AND VOTES FOR WOMEN. By 1860, when this cartoon was published, Mill had established a reputation as a liberal political philosopher and a supporter of women's right to vote. Mill argued that women's enfranchisement was essential both from the standpoint of individual liberty and for the good of society as a whole. ■ *What was amusing about Mill's assertion that women be considered persons in their own right?*

suffrage is interesting for what it reveals about their views on male and female nature. They insisted that female individuality (expressed in voting, education, or wage earning) would destabilize family life. Yet their opposition to woman suffrage also reflected their conception of the vote: casting a ballot was a privilege granted only to specific social groups in return for their contributions to and vested interest in society. Men of property might champion the rule of law and representative government, but they balked at the prospect of a truly democratic politics and did not shy away from heavy-handed law-and-order politics. Expanding the franchise created new constituencies with new ambitions and paved the way for socialist and labor politics in the last quarter of the century. Tensions within liberalism remained and prefigured conflicts in the future.

Italian Unification: Cavour and Garibaldi

After the failure of Italian unification in 1848, nationalists in Italy faced a choice between two strategies for achieving statehood. Mazzini and his follower Giuseppe Garibaldi, a former guerilla fighter who had been exiled to Latin America for his political beliefs, envisioned a republican

Italy built from below by a popular uprising. A second group of more moderate nationalists were mistrustful of democracy and sought to unify Italy as a constitutional monarchy from above, under the leadership of the kingdom of Piedmont-Sardinia.

The king of Piedmont-Sardinia, Charles Albert, had drawn the attention of Italian nationalists in 1848 when he took up the anti-Austrian cause. Though he later died in exile, his son Victor Emmanuel II (r. 1849–61) brought a man into his government who would embody the conservative vision of nationhood: the shrewd Sardinian nobleman Count Camillo Benso di Cavour (1810–1861). "In Italy a democratic movement has almost no chance of success," Cavour declared. He instead pursued ambitious but pragmatic reforms guided by the state. As prime minister, he promoted economic expansion, encouraged the construction of a modern transportation infrastructure, reformed the currency, and sought to raise Piedmont-Sardinia's profile in international relations.

GIUSEPPE GARIBALDI. Note the simple uniform Garibaldi wears in this commemorative portrait, with its iconic symbols of his nationalist movement: the red shirt and the flag of Italy in the background. Compare this with the official portraits of absolutist rulers in previous chapters. ▪ *What was significant about the absence of finery and precious materials in this painting?* ▪ *What does it say about images of masculine leadership in the mid-nineteenth-century nationalist imagination?*

Cavour's plan depended on diplomacy. Since Piedmont-Sardinia did not have the military capacity to counter the Austrians in northern Italy, Cavour enlisted the help of the French emperor, Napoleon III, who agreed to cooperate in driving the Austrians from Italy if Piedmont would cede Savoy and Nice to France. A war with Austria was duly provoked in 1859, and for a time all went well for the Franco-Italian allies. After the conquest of Lombardy, however, Napoleon III suddenly withdrew, concerned that he might either lose the battle or antagonize French Catholics, who were alienated by Cavour's hostility to the pope. Deserted by the French, Piedmont could not expel the Austrians from Venetia. Yet the campaign had made extensive gains: with the addition of Lombardy, Tuscany, Parma, and Modena, Piedmont-Sardinia had grown to more than twice its original size and was by far the most powerful state in Italy.

As Cavour consolidated the northern and central states, events in the southern states seemed to put those areas up for grabs as well. The unpopular Bourbon king of the Two Sicilies, Francis II (r. 1859–60), faced a fast-spreading peasant revolt that rekindled the hopes of earlier insurrections of the 1820s and 1840s. That revolt, in turn, got a much-needed boost from Garibaldi, who landed in Sicily in May of 1860. "The Thousand," as Garibaldi's volunteer fighters called themselves, embodied the widespread support for Italian unification: they came from the north as well as from the south and counted among them members of the middle class as well as workers and artisans. Garibaldi's troops took Sicily and continued on to the mainland. By November 1860, Garibaldi's forces, alongside local insurgents, had taken Naples and toppled the kingdom of Francis II. Emboldened by success, Garibaldi looked to Rome, where French troops guarded the pope.

Garibaldi's rising popularity put him on a collision course with Cavour. Cavour worried that Garibaldi's forces would bring French or Austrian intervention, with unknown consequences. He dispatched Victor Emmanuel to Rome with an army, and the king ordered Garibaldi to cede him military authority. Garibaldi obeyed. Most of the peninsula was united under a single rule, and Victor Emmanuel assumed the title of king of Italy (r. 1861–78). Cavour's vision of Italian nationhood had won the day.

The final steps of Italy's territorial nation building came indirectly. Venetia remained in the hands of the Austrians until 1866, when Austria was defeated by Prussia and forced to relinquish their last Italian stronghold. Rome had resisted conquest largely because of the military protection that Napoleon III accorded the pope. But in 1870, the

Route of Garibaldi's Campaign, 1860

The Kingdom of Sardinia at the time of the Congress of Vienna, 1815

Territories acquired, 1859–1860

Territories acquired, 1861–1870

THE UNIFICATION OF ITALY. ▪ *How many phases were involved in Italian unification, according to the map key?* ▪ *Why did it take an extra decade to incorporate Rome and Venetia into the Italian state?* ▪ *Why was Italian unification incomplete until the early twentieth century?*

outbreak of the Franco-Prussian War compelled Napoleon to withdraw his troops. That September, Italian soldiers occupied Rome, and in July 1871 Rome became capital of the united Italian kingdom.

What of the pope's authority? The Italian parliament passed the Law of Papal Guarantees to define and limit the pope's status—an act promptly defied by the reigning pontiff, Pius IX, who refused to have anything to do with a disrespectful secular government. His successors continued to close themselves off in the Vatican until 1929, when a series of agreements between the Italian government and Pius XI settled the dispute.

By 1871 Italy was a state, but nation building was hardly over. Only a minority of the "Italian" population spoke Italian; the rest used local and regional dialects so diverse that schoolteachers sent from Rome to Sicily were mistaken for foreigners. As one politician remarked, "We have made Italy; now we must make Italians." The task did not prove easy. The gap between an increasingly industrialized north and a poor and rural south remained wide. Banditry in the territory of the former kingdom of the Two Sicilies

compelled the central administration to dispatch troops to quell serious uprisings, killing more people than in the war of unification. Regional differences and social tensions made building the Italian nation an ongoing process.

The Unification of Germany: Realpolitik

After the failure of the 1848 revolutions, many political observers in German-speaking lands rejected the more utopian goals of the German liberal tradition in favor a more pragmatic attention to the problem of political power: how to achieve it, and how to preserve it. This attitude—summed up in the expression *Realpolitik*, or practical, realistic policies—held that Enlightenment visions of rights or constitutions were less important than a cold-eyed assessment of power and interests. Realpolitik became the watchword of Prussian diplomacy in the 1850s and 1860s and was most closely associated with the deeply conservative and pragmatic Otto von Bismarck, whose skillful leadership played an important role in German unification.

King Frederick William granted a Prussian constitution in 1850. The constitution established a two-house parliament, with the lower house elected by universal male suffrage, but the king preserved the power of traditional elites by dividing voters into three classes based on the amount of taxes they paid. In this way, a large landowner or a wealthy industrialist exercised perhaps seventeen times the voting power of a working man. Furthermore, voting took place in public, orally, so a secret ballot was impossible.

In 1861, William I became king of Prussia. Under his rule, Prussia remained a notoriously conservative state, but a decade of industrial growth had also expanded the size and confidence of the middle classes. By the late 1850s, Prussia had an active liberal intelligentsia, a thoughtful and engaged press, and a liberal civil service dedicated to political and economic modernization. These changes helped forge a liberal political movement that won a majority in elections to the lower house and could confidently confront the king.

Liberals in Prussia were especially opposed to the king's high levels of military spending. William wanted to expand the standing army, reduce the role of reserve forces (a more middle-class group), and ensure that military matters were not subject to parliamentary control. Opponents in Parliament suspected the king of making the military his own private force or a state within a state. Between 1859 and 1862, relations deteriorated; and when liberals' protests went unanswered, they refused to approve the regular budget. Faced with a crisis, in 1862 William named Otto von Bismarck (1815–1898) minister-president of Prussia. (A prime minister answers to Parliament; Bismarck did not.) This crucial moment in Prussian domestic politics became a decisive turning point in the history of German nationhood.

Born into the Junker class of conservative, land-owning aristocrats, Bismarck had fiercely opposed the liberal movement of 1848–49. He was not a nationalist. He was before all else a Prussian. He did not institute domestic reforms because he favored the rights of a particular group but because he thought that these policies would unify and strengthen Prussia. When he maneuvered to bring other German states under Prussian domination, he did so not in pursuit of a grand German design but because he believed that union in some form was inevitable and that Prussia had to seize the initiative.

In Prussia, Bismarck defied parliamentary opposition. When the liberal majority refused to pass a budget because of disagreements about spending for the army, he

dissolved Parliament, claiming that the constitution, whatever its purposes, had not been designed to subvert the state. His most decisive actions, however, were in foreign policy. Bismarck skillfully played the national card to preempt his liberal opponents at home and to make German nation building an accomplishment—and an extension—of Prussian authority.

The other "German" power was Austria, which wielded considerable influence within the German Confederation and especially over the largely Catholic regions in the south. Bismarck saw a stark contrast between Austrian and Prussian interests and skillfully exploited Austria's economic disadvantages and the Habsburgs' internal ethnic struggles. He inflamed a long-smoldering dispute with Denmark over Schleswig (*SHLAYS-vihg*) and Holstein, two provinces peopled by Germans and Danes and claimed by both the German Confederation and Denmark. In 1864, the Danish king attempted to annex the provinces, prompting a German nationalist outcry. Bismarck cast the conflict as a Prussian matter and persuaded Austria to join Prussia in a war against Denmark. The war was short, and it forced the Danish ruler to cede the two provinces to Austria and Prussia. As Bismarck hoped, Prussia and Austria disputed the spoils of their victory, and in 1866, he declared war on Austria, claiming that Prussia was the defender of larger German interests. The conflict, known as the Seven Weeks' War, ended in Prussian victory. Austria gave up all claims to Schleswig and Holstein, surrendered Venetia to the Italians, and agreed to dissolve the German Confederation. In its place, Bismarck created the North German Confederation, a union of all the German states north of the Main River.

Both wars had strong public support, and Prussian victories weakened liberal opposition to the king and his president-minister. In the aftermath of the Austrian defeat, Prussian liberals gave up their battle over budgets, the military, and constitutional provisions. Bismarck also sought support among the masses. He understood that Germans did not necessarily support business elites, the bureaucracies of their own small states, or the Austrian Habsburgs. The constitution of the North German Confederation gave the appearance of a more liberal political body, with a bicameral legislature, freedom of the press, and universal male suffrage in the lower house. Its structure, however, gave Prussia and the conservative emperor a decisive position in German politics.

The final step in the completion of German unity was the Franco-Prussian War of 1870–71. Bismarck hoped that a conflict with France would arouse German nationalism in Bavaria, Württemberg, and other southern states still outside the confederation. A diplomatic tempest concerning the right of the Hohenzollerns (Prussia's ruling

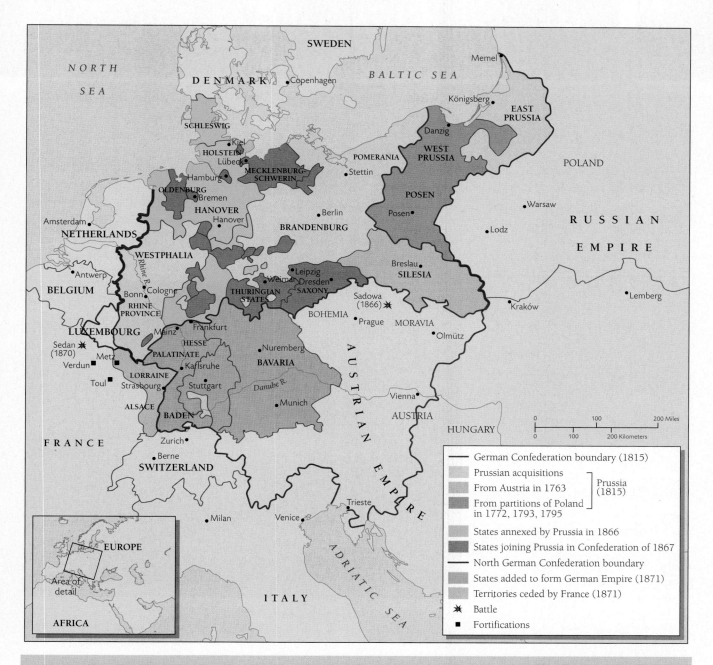

TOWARD THE UNIFICATION OF GERMANY. Note the many elements that made up a unified Germany and the stages that brought them together. ▪ *Did this new nation have any resemblance to the unified Germany envisioned by the liberal revolutionaries of the Frankfurt Preparliament in 1848? (See page 570.)* ▪ *How many stages were involved in the unification of Germany, and how many years did it take?* ▪ *What region filled with German-speaking peoples was not included in the new unified Germany, and why?*

family) to occupy the Spanish throne created an opportunity to foment a Franco-German misunderstanding. King William agreed to meet with the French ambassador at the resort spa of Ems in Prussia to discuss the Spanish succession. William initially acquiesced to French demands, but when the French blundered by asking for "perpetual exclusion" of the Hohenzollern family from the Spanish throne, Bismarck seized his opportunity. He edited a telegraph from King William so as to make it appear that the Prussian king had rebuffed the French ambassador. Once the redacted report reached France, the nation reacted with calls for war. Prussia echoed the call, and Bismarck published evidence that he claimed proved French designs on the Rhineland.

The New German Nation

In order to silence their critics at home and abroad, nationalists in Germany sought to create a vision of German history that made unification the natural outcome of a deep historical process that had begun hundreds of years before. In image A, the family of a cavalry officer prepares to hang a portrait of Kaiser Wilhelm on the wall, next to portraits of Martin Luther, Frederick the Great, and Field Marshal von Blücher, who commanded the Prussian forces at Waterloo. In the lower left corner, two boys roll up a portrait of the defeated French emperor, Napoleon III. The implication, of course, was that the unification of Germany was the inevitable culmination of generations of German heroes who all worked toward the same goal.

This unity was itself controversial among German people. Image B, a pro-Bismarck cartoon, shows the German minister-president dragging the unwilling liberal members of the Prussian parliament along with him as he pulls a triumphal chariot toward his military confrontation with Austria in 1866. The caption reads: "And in this sense, too, we are in agreement with Count Bismarck, and we have pulled the same rope as him." Image C, on the other hand, expresses reservations about Prussian dominance in the new empire. The title "Germany's Future" and the caption:

A. *Homage to Kaiser Wilhelm I* by Paul Bürde, 1871.

As soon as war was declared, the south German states rallied to Prussia's side. The conflict was quickly over. No European powers came to France's aid. Austria, the most likely candidate, remained weakened by its recent war with Prussia. On the battlefield, France could not match Prussia's professionally trained and superbly equipped forces. The war began in July and ended in September with the defeat of the French and the capture of Napoleon III at Sedan in France. Insurrectionary forces in Paris continued to hold out against the Germans through the winter of 1870–71, but the French imperial government collapsed.

On January 18, 1871, in the Hall of Mirrors at Versailles, symbol of the powerful past of French absolutism, the German Empire was proclaimed. All the German states that had not already been absorbed into the Prussian fold, except Austria, declared their allegiance to William I, henceforth emperor or kaiser. Four months later, at Frankfurt, a treaty between the French and the Germans ceded the border region of Alsace to the new German Empire and forced

"Will it fit under one hat? I think it will only fit under a [Prussian] Pickelhaube." The Pickelhaube—the characteristic spike-topped helmet of the Prussian army—had already become a much-feared symbol of Prussian military force. Such an image may well have struck a chord with residents of the non-Prussian German states who now paid taxes to the Prussian monarchy and served in an army dominated by Prussian officers.

Questions for Analysis

1. What is the significance of the familial setting in image A? Why was it important for nationalists to emphasize a multigenerational family as the repository of German national spirit?

2. How do images B and C treat the question of Prussia's role within the new German nation? Was German national identity seen as something built from below or defined from above by a strong monarchy?

3. What is the place of the individual citizen in these representations of the German nation?

B. Prussian liberals and Bismarck after Königgrätz (1866).

C. "Germany's Future" (1870).

the French to pay an indemnity of 5 billion francs. Prussia accounted for 60 percent of the new state's territory and population. The Prussian kaiser, prime minister, army, and most of the bureaucracy remained intact, now reconfigured as the German nation-state. This was not the new nation for which Prussian liberals had hoped. It marked a "revolution from above" rather than from below. Still, the more optimistic believed that the German Empire would evolve in a different political direction and that they could eventually "extend freedom through unity."

The State and Nationality: Centrifugal Forces in the Austrian Empire

Germany emerged from the 1860s a stronger, unified nation. The Habsburg Empire faced a very different situation, with different resources, and emerged a weakened, precariously balanced, multiethnic dual monarchy, also called Austria-Hungary.

As we have seen, ethnic nationalism was a powerful force in the Habsburg monarchy in 1848. Yet the

Habsburg state, with a combination of military repression and tactics that divided its enemies, had proved more powerful. It abolished serfdom but made few other concessions to its opponents. The Hungarians, who had nearly won independence in the spring of 1848, were essentially reconquered. Administrative reforms created a new and more uniform legal system, rationalized taxation, and imposed a single-language policy that favored German. The issue of managing ethnic relations, however, only grew more difficult. Through the 1850s and 1860s, the subject nationalities, as they were often called, bitterly protested military repression, cultural disenfranchisement, and the powerlessness of their local diets. The Czechs in Bohemia, for instance, grew increasingly alienated by policies that favored the German minority of the province. In response, they became more insistent on their Slavic identity—a movement welcomed by Russia, which became the sponsor of a broad pan-Slavism. The Hungarians, or Magyars, the most powerful of the subject nationalities, sought to reclaim the autonomy they had glimpsed in 1848.

In this context, Austria's defeats at the hands of Piedmont-Sardinia in 1859 and Prussia in 1866 became especially significant. The 1866 war forced the emperor Franz Josef to renegotiate the very structure of the empire. To stave off a revolution by the Hungarians, Francis Joseph agreed to a new federal structure in the form of the Dual Monarchy. Austria-Hungary had a common system of taxation, a common army, and made foreign and military policy together. Francis Joseph was emperor of Austria and king of Hungary. But internal and constitutional affairs were separated. The *Ausgleich*, or Settlement, allowed the Hungarians to establish their own constitution; their own legislature; and their own capital, combining the cities of Buda and Pest.

What of the other nationalities? The official policy of the Dual Monarchy stated that they were not to be discriminated against and that they could use their own languages. Official policy was only loosely enforced. More important, elevating the Hungarians and conferring on them alone the benefits of political nationhood could only worsen relations with other groups. On the Austrian side of the Dual Monarchy, minority nationalities such as the Poles, Czechs, and Slovenes resented their second-class status. On the Hungarian side, the regime embarked on a project of Magyarization, attempting to make the state, the civil service, and the schools more thoroughly Hungarian—an effort that did not sit well with Serbs and Croats.

In spite of these divisions, however, the Austro-Hungarian Empire succeeded for a time in creating a different kind of political and culture space within a Europe that was increasingly given over to nation-states that perceived their interests to be irrevocably opposed. The Austrian capital of Vienna developed a reputation for intellectual and cultural refinement that was in part a product of the many different peoples who made up the Habsburg lands, including Germans, Jews, Hungarians, Italians, Czechs, Poles, Serbs, Croats, and Balkan Muslims from lands that formerly belonged to the Ottoman Empire. This polyglot culture produced Béla Bartók (1881–1945), the great Hungarian composer and admirer of folk musical traditions; Gustav Mahler (1860–1911), a German-Austrian composer whose romantic symphonies and conducting prowess made him a global celebrity by the time of his death. From the same intellectual milieu came Sigmund Freud (1856–1939), a German-speaking Jewish doctor from Vienna whose writings helped shape modern psychology; and Gustav Klimt (1862–1918), a painter and founding member of the Viennese Secession movement, which rejected the reigning classicism of the Austrian art world and made the Austrian capital an important center for the birth of modern art.

The Austrian emperor's deep opposition to nationalism was not just geopolitical, therefore, but also a defense of a different relationship between the nation-state and culture. Unlike the governments of France, England, Italy, or Germany, the Habsburgs did not seek to build a nation-state based on a common cultural identity. It tried instead to build a state and administrative structure strong enough to keep the pieces from spinning off, at times playing different minorities off against each other, but also conceding greater autonomy to different groups when it seemed necessary. As the nineteenth century unfolded, however, discontented subject nationalities would appeal to other powers—Serbia, Russia, the Ottomans—and this balancing act would become more difficult.

NATION AND STATE BUILDING IN RUSSIA AND THE UNITED STATES

The challenges of nationalism and nation building also occupied Russia, the United States, and Canada. In all three countries, nation building entailed territorial and economic expansion, the incorporation of new peoples, and—in Russia and the United States—contending with the enormous problems of slavery and serfdom.

Territory, the State, and Serfdom: Russia

Serfdom in Russia, which had been legally formalized in 1649, had begun to draw significant protest from the intelligentsia under the reign of Catherine the Great (r. 1762–96). After the European revolutions of 1789 and 1848, the abolition of serfdom became part of the larger and controversial project of building Russia as a modern nation. Two schools of thought emerged. The "Slavophiles," or Romantic nationalists, sought to preserve Russia's distinctive features. They idealized traditional Russian culture and the peasant commune, rejecting Western secularism, urban commercialism, and bourgeois culture. In contrast, the "westernizers" wished to see Russia adopt European developments in science, technology, and education, which they believed to be the foundation for Western liberalism. Both groups agreed that serfdom must be abolished. The Russian nobility, however, tenaciously opposed emancipation. Tangled debates about how lords would be compensated for the loss of "their" serfs, and how emancipated serfs would survive without full-scale land redistribution, also checked progress on the issue. The Crimean War (to be discussed later) broke the impasse. In its aftermath, Alexander II (r. 1855–81) forced the issue. Worried that the persistence of serfdom had sapped Russian strength and contributed to its defeat in the war, and persuaded that serfdom would only continue to prompt violent conflict, he ended serfdom by decree in 1861.

The emancipation decree of 1861 granted legal rights to some 22 million serfs and authorized their entitlement to a portion of the land they had worked. It also required the state to compensate landowners for the properties they relinquished. Large-scale landowners vastly inflated their compensation claims, however, and managed to retain much of the most profitable acreage for themselves. As a result, the land granted to peasants was often of poor quality and insufficient to sustain themselves and their families. Moreover, the newly liberated serfs had to pay in installments for their land, which was not granted to them individually but rather to a village commune, which collected their payments. As a result, the pattern of rural life in Russia did not change drastically. The system of payment kept peasants in the villages—not as freestanding farmers but as agricultural laborers for their former masters.

While the Russian state undertook reforms, it also expanded its territory. After midcentury, the Russians pressed east and south. They invaded and conquered several independent Islamic kingdoms along the former Silk Road and expanded into Siberia in search of natural

THE EMANCIPATION OF THE SERFS. This engraving depicts officials delivering the formal decree liberating serfs. A massive reform granting legal rights to millions of people, emancipation was undermined by the payments serfs owed to their former owners.

resources. Russian diplomacy wrung various commercial concessions from the Chinese that led to the founding of the Siberian city of Vladivostok in 1860. Racial, ethnic, and religious differences made governing a daunting task. In most cases, the Russian state did not try to assimilate the populations of the new territories: an acceptance of ethnic particularity was a pragmatic response to the difficulties of governing such a heterogeneous population. When the state did attempt to impose Russian culture, the results were disastrous. Whether power was wielded by the nineteenth-century tsars or, later, by the Soviet Union, powerful centrifugal forces pulled against genuine unification. Expansion helped Russia create a vast empire that was geographically of one piece but by no means one nation.

Territory and the Nation: The United States

The American Revolution had bequeathed to the United States a loose union of slave and free states, tied together in part by a commitment to territorial expansion. The so-called Jeffersonian Revolution combined democratic aspirations with a drive to expand the nation's boundaries. Leaders of the movement, under the Democratic-Republican presidency of Thomas Jefferson (1801–9), campaigned to add the Bill of Rights to the Constitution and were almost exclusively responsible for its success. Though they supported, in principle, the separation of powers, they believed in the supremacy of the people's representatives and viewed with alarm attempts of the

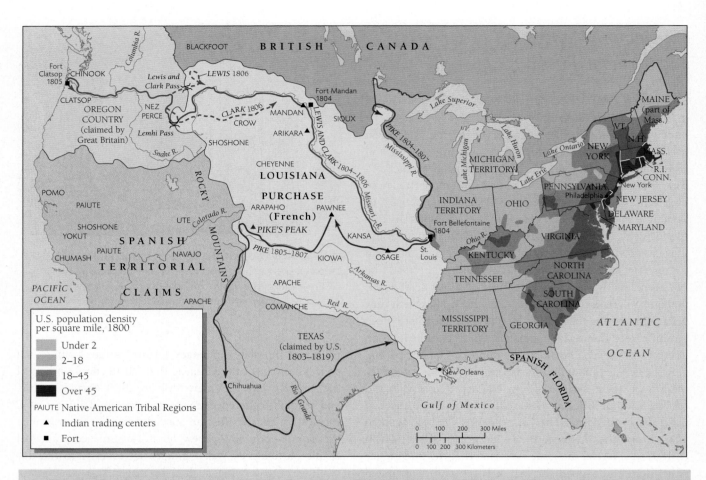

AMERICAN EXPANSION IN THE EARLY NINETEENTH CENTURY. ▪ *What three European powers had a substantial role to play in American expansion?* ▪ *What events enabled the United States to acquire all lands west of the Mississippi River?* ▪ *How did the loss of these lands affect European powers?*

executive and judicial branches to increase their power. They supported a political system based on an aristocracy of "virtue and talent," in which respect for personal liberty would be the guiding principle. They opposed the establishment of a national religion and special privilege, whether of birth or of wealth. Yet the Jeffersonian vision of the republic rested on the independence of yeoman farmers, and the independence and prosperity of those farmers depended on the availability of new lands. This made territorial expansion, as exemplified by the Louisiana Purchase in 1803, central to Jeffersonian America. Expansion brought complications. While it did provide land for many yeoman farmers in the north and south, it also added millions of acres of prime cotton land, thus extending the empire of slavery. The purchase of the port of New Orleans made lands in the south well worth developing but led the American republic forcibly to resettle Native Americans from the Old South to areas west of the Mississippi River. This process of expansion

and expropriation stretched from Jefferson's administration through the age of Jackson, or the 1840s.

Under Andrew Jackson, the Democrats (as some of the Democratic-Republicans were now called) transformed the circumscribed liberalism of the Jeffersonians. They campaigned to extend the suffrage to all white males; they argued that all officeholders should be elected rather than appointed; and they sought the frequent rotation of men in positions of political power—a doctrine that permitted politicians to use patronage to build national political parties. Moreover, the Jacksonian vision of democracy and nationhood carried over into a crusade to incorporate more territories into the republic. It was the United States' "Manifest Destiny," wrote a New York editor, "to overspread the continent allotted by Providence for the free development of our yearly multiplying millions." That "overspreading" brought Oregon and Washington into the Union through a compromise with the British and brought Arizona, Texas, New Mexico, Utah, Nevada, and California

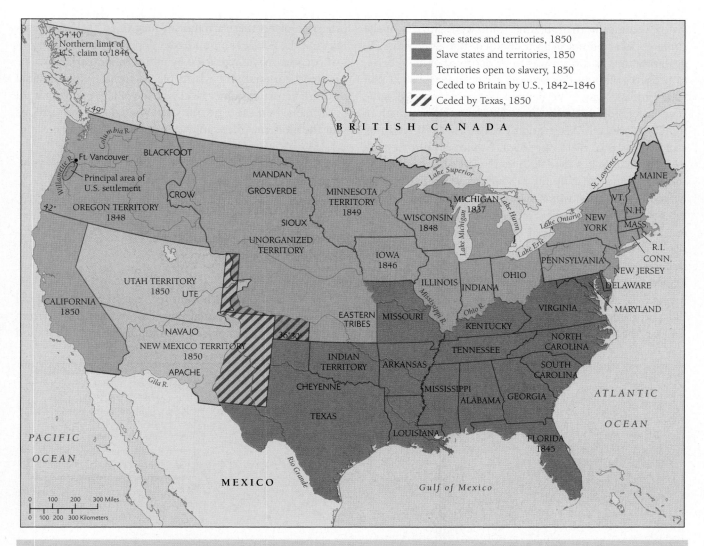

AMERICAN EXPANSION IN THE LATE NINETEENTH CENTURY. Note the stages of American settlement across the North American continent and the dates for the extension of slavery into new territories. ▪ *How did the question of slavery shape the way that new territories were absorbed into the republic?* ▪ *How does American expansion compare with European colonialism?*

through war with Mexico—all of which led to the wholesale expropriation of Native American lands. Territorial expansion was key to nation building, but it was built on increasingly impossible conflict over slavery.

The American Civil War, 1861–1865

The politics of slavery had already led to its abolition in France and Britain (see Chapter 20), but in the United States the combination of a growing abolitionist movement, a slave-owning class that feared the economic power of the north, and territorial expansion created deadlock and crisis. As the country expanded westward,

the North and South engaged in a protracted tug of war about whether new states were to be "free" or "slave." In the North, territorial expansion heightened calls for free labor; in the South, it deepened whites' commitment to an economy and society based on plantation slavery. Ultimately, the changes pushed southern political leaders toward secession. The failure of a series of elaborate compromises led to the outbreak of the Civil War in 1861.

The protracted and costly struggle proved a first experience of the horrors of modern war and prefigured the First World War. It also decisively transformed the nation. First, it resulted in the abolition of slavery. Second, it established the preeminence of the national government over states' rights. The Fourteenth Amendment to the Constitution stated specifically that all Americans were citizens of the United States and not of an individual state or territory. In declaring that no citizen was to be deprived of life, liberty, or property without due process of law, it established that "due process" was to be defined by the national, not the state or territorial, government. Third, in the aftermath of the Civil War, the U.S. economy expanded with stunning rapidity. In 1865, there were 35,000 miles of railroad track in the United States; by 1900, there were almost 200,000. Industrial and agricultural production rose, putting the United States in a position to compete with Great Britain. As we will see later on, American industrialists, bankers, and retailers introduced innovations in assembly-line manufacturing, corporate organization, and advertising that startled their European counterparts and gave the United States new power in world politics. These developments were all part of the process of nation building. They did not overcome deep racial, regional, or class divides. Though the war brought the South back into the Union,

the rise of northern capitalism magnified the backwardness of the South as an underdeveloped agricultural region whose wealth was extracted by northern industrialists. The railroad corporations, which pieced together the national infrastructure, became the classic foe of labor and agrarian reformers. In these ways, the Civil War laid the foundations for the modern American nation-state.

"EASTERN QUESTIONS": INTERNATIONAL RELATIONS AND THE DECLINE OF OTTOMAN POWER

During the nineteenth century, questions of national identity and international power were inextricable from contests over territory. War and diplomacy drew and

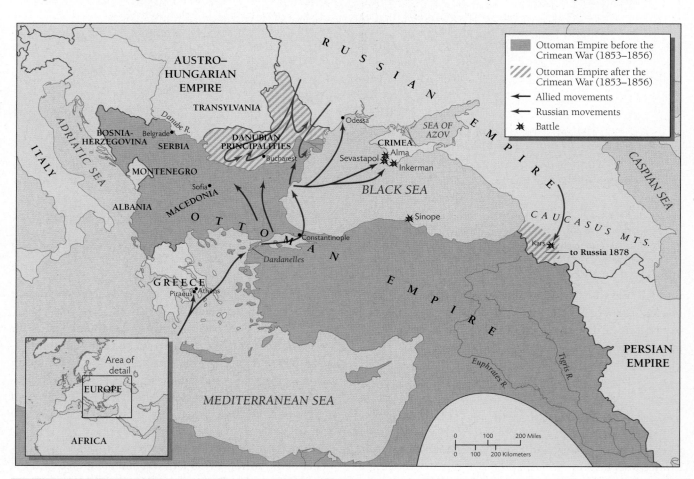

THE CRIMEAN WAR. Note the theater of operations and the major assaults of the Crimean War. ■ *Which empires and nations were in a position to take advantage of Ottoman weakness?* ■ *Who benefited from the outcome, and who was most harmed?* ■ *In what ways was the Crimean War the first modern war?*

redrew boundaries as European nations groped toward a sustainable balance of power. The rise of new powers, principally the German Empire, posed one set of challenges to continental order. The waning power of older regimes posed another. The Crimean War, which lasted from 1853 to 1856, was a particularly gruesome attempt to cope with the most serious such collapse. As the Ottoman Empire lost its grip on its provinces in southeastern Europe, the "Eastern Question" of who would benefit from Ottoman weakness drew Europe into war. At stake were not only territorial gains but also strategic interests, alliances, and the balance of power in Europe. And though the war occurred before the unification of the German and Italian states, it structured the system of Great Power politics that guided Europe until (and indeed toward) the First World War.

The Crimean War, 1853–1856

The root causes of the war lay in the Eastern Question and the decline of the Ottoman Empire. The crisis that provoked it, however, involved religion—namely French and Russian claims to protect religious minorities and the holy places of Jerusalem within the Muslim Ottoman Empire. In 1853, a three-way quarrel among France (on behalf of Roman Catholics), Russia (representing Eastern Orthodox Christians), and Turkey devolved into a Russian confrontation with the Turkish sultan. Confident that Turkey would be unable to resist, concerned that other powers might take advantage of Turkish weakness, and persuaded (mistakenly) that they had British support, the Russians moved troops into the Ottoman-governed territories of Moldavia and Walachia (see the map on page 590). In October 1853, Turkey, also persuaded they would be supported by the British, declared war on Russia. The war became a disaster for the Turks, who lost their fleet at the battle of Sinope in November. But Russia's success alarmed the British and the French, who considered Russian expansion a threat to their interests in the Balkans, the eastern Mediterranean, and, for the British, the route to India. Determined to check that expansion, France and Britain each declared war on Russia in March 1854. In September, they landed on the Russian peninsula of Crimea and headed for the Russian naval base at Sevastopol, to which they laid siege. France, Britain, and the Ottomans were joined in 1855 by the small but ambitious Italian state of Piedmont-Sardinia, all fighting against the Russians. This was the closest Europe had come to a general war since 1815.

Conditions on the Crimean peninsula were dire, and the disastrous mismanagement of supplies and hygiene by the British and French led to epidemics among the troops. At least as many soldiers died from typhus or cholera as in combat. Despite the disciplined toughness of the British and French troops, and despite their nations' dominance of the seas around Crimea, the Russians denied them a clear victory. Sevastopol, under siege for nearly a year, did not fall until September 1855. The bitter, unsatisfying conflict was ended by treaty in 1856.

The peace settlement dealt a blow to Russia, whose influence in the Balkans was drastically curbed. The provinces of Moldavia and Walachia were united as Romania and became an independent nation. Austria's refusal to come to the aid of Russia cost Russia the support of its powerful former ally. The Crimean War embarrassed France and left Russia and Austria considerably weaker, opening an advantage for Bismarck in the 1860s, as we saw earlier.

CAPTAIN DAMES OF THE ROYAL ARTILLERY, 1855. Roger Fenton studied painting in London and then Paris, where he learned about and started to experiment with photography. He developed a mobile darkroom and ventured into the English countryside. In 1855, he went to the Crimea, subsidized by the British government. Photographs of movement and troops in battle were still impossible, and political restraint kept him from photographing the horrors of the increasingly unpopular Crimean War. Still, his were the first war photographs.

The Crimean war was covered by the first modern war correspondents and photojournalists, making it the most public war to date. Reports from the theater of war were sent "live" by telegraph to Britain and France with objective and sobering detail. The care and supply of the troops became national scandals in the popular press, prompting dramatic changes in the military's administrative and logistical systems and making heroes of individual doctors and nurses such as Florence Nightingale. The British government and commercial publishers both sent photographers to document the war's progress and perhaps also to counter charges that troops were undersupplied and malnourished. These photographs introduced a new level of realism and immediacy to the European public's conception of war.

CONCLUSION

The decades between 1848 and 1870 brought intense nation building in the Western world. The unification of Germany and Italy changed the map of Europe, with important consequences for the balance of power. The emergence of the United States as a major power also had international ramifications. For old as well as new nation-states, economic development and political transformation—often on a very large scale—were important means of increasing and securing the state's power. Even though the liberal revolutionaries of 1848 had not achieved the goals they sought, their demands for more-representative government, the abolition of privilege, and land reform still had to be reckoned with, as did the systems of slavery and serfdom. Trailing

After You Read This Chapter

 Go to **INQUIZITIVE** to see what you've learned—and learn what you've missed— with personalized feedback along the way.

REVIEWING THE OBJECTIVES

- Revolutions broke out in 1848 in almost every capital of Europe except for London and St. Petersburg. What accounts for this wave of simultaneous revolutionary movements?
- Liberal revolutionaries in France in 1848 did not have the same goals as their socialist allies. What were their goals and why did they fail to achieve them?
- Liberal revolutionaries in the German-speaking lands of central Europe in 1848 were forced to reckon with Austrian and Prussian states in their bid for national unification. What did they want, and why did they fail?
- Nationalists in both Germany and Italy were divided between those who supported the creation of a new nation from below, through popular movements, and those who preferred nation building from above. How did these divisions work themselves out in the process of national unification?
- Creating a modern nation in Russia entailed the end of serfdom, whereas in the United States, political leaders from the North and South debated the place of slavery in the modern nation-state. In what ways were national debates about citizenship in these countries shaped by the widespread practices of bondage?
- The three major European wars of this period were of relatively short duration, but they had profound effects on the international balance of power in Europe. Which countries emerged stronger from these conflicts, and which found their interests most damaged?

the banner of nationhood was an explosive set of questions about how to balance the power and interests of minorities and majorities, of the wealthy and poor, of the powerful and the dispossessed. Nation building not only changed states, it transformed relations between states and their citizens.

These transformations were anything but predictable. Nationalism showed itself to be a volatile, erratic, and malleable force during the mid-nineteenth century. It provided much of the fuel for revolutionary movements in 1848, but it also helped tear their movements apart, undermining revolutionary gains. Those who had linked their democratic goals to the rise of new nation-states were sorely disappointed. In the aftermath of the defeated revolutions, most nation building took a conservative tack. Nationalism came to serve the needs of statesmen and bureaucrats who did not seek an "awakening of peoples" and who had serious reservations about popular sovereignty. For them, nations simply represented more modern, better organized, and stronger states.

The result of these many tensions was an age that seemed a contradictory mix of the old and the new, of monarchies beset with debates about nationality and citizenship, of land-owning aristocratic elites rubbing elbows with newly wealthy industrialists, and of artisan handworkers meeting up with factory laborers in worker's associations that debated the proper path toward realizing their socialist goals. Remarkably, the result of this period of intense nation building was a period of unusual stability on the Continent, which ushered in an era of unprecedented capitalist and imperial expansion. The antagonisms unleashed by German unification and the crumbling of the Ottoman Empire would reemerge, however, in the Great Power politics that precipitated the First World War.

PEOPLE, IDEAS, AND EVENTS IN CONTEXT

- What circumstances led to the downfall of **LOUIS PHILIPPE**'s government in France? What divisions between supporters of the revolution led to the **JUNE DAYS** in Paris in 1848?
- What role did the **ZOLLVEREIN** and the **FRANKFURT PARLIAMENT** play in the creation of a unified Germany?
- How and why did **OTTO VON BISMARCK** aim for a policy of German national unification during his time in office?
- How did **GIUSEPPE GARIBALDI** and **CAMILLO BENSO DI CAVOUR** initially see the process of Italian unification? Whose vision came closest to reality?
- Who was **NAPOLEON III**, and how did his policies contribute to nation building in France?
- What was the contribution of **JOHN STUART MILL** to debates about citizenship in Britain?
- Why were nationalist movements such as **PAN-SLAVISM** or **MAGYAR NATIONALISM** such a danger to the Austro-Hungarian Empire?
- Why did **TSAR ALEXANDER II** decide to **EMANCIPATE THE SERFS**?
- What made the **CRIMEAN WAR** different from previous conflicts and more like the wars of the twentieth century?

THINKING ABOUT CONNECTIONS

- Revolutionaries in 1848, whether they were in Paris, Rome, Berlin, or Vienna, must have been aware of connections between their own struggles and the historical example of the French Revolution of 1789–99. Did revolutionaries in 1848 have goals that were similar to the goals of French revolutionaries at the end of the eighteenth century?
- How might the failure of the 1848 revolutions have shaped the beliefs of European conservatives and liberals or the beliefs of supporters of more radical ideologies such as republicanism and socialism?

STORY LINES

■ Industrialization, rapid technological development, and the concentration of economic wealth gave western European nations great power during this period, along with the confidence to use this power to extend their control to other parts of the world.

■ Colonial expansion occurred simultaneously with the development of mass politics and the spread of consumer culture in Europe, a combination that made colonies and the power to control them an important part of national identity for many people in Europe, especially in Britain, France, and Germany.

■ The new imperialism ushered in a new era of conflict: between European powers and newly colonized peoples in Africa and Asia, and between the colonizing nations themselves, as they competed with one another for global influence and resources.

Before You Read This Chapter

Imperialism and Colonialism, 1870–1914

CORE OBJECTIVES

- **DEFINE** *imperialism* and **LOCATE** the major colonies established by European powers in Africa and Asia in the nineteenth century.

- **UNDERSTAND** the differences between direct rule, indirect rule, and informal imperialism, and **PROVIDE** examples of each type of colony.

- **DESCRIBE** the choices faced by colonized peoples in the face of European power and culture.

- **EXPLAIN** how imperialism shaped the culture of European nations at home.

- **UNDERSTAND** the nature of the crisis faced by European imperial powers at the end of the nineteenth century.

I n 1869, the Suez Canal opened with a grand celebration. The imperial yacht *Eagle*, with Empress Eugénie of France on board, entered the canal on November 17, followed by sixty-eight steamships carrying the emperor of Austria, the crown prince of Prussia, the grand duke of Russia, and scores of other dignitaries. Flowery speeches flowed freely, as did the champagne. The ceremony cost a staggering £1.3 million (about $132 million today). Even so, the size of the celebration paled in comparison to the canal itself. The largest project of its kind, the canal sliced through a hundred miles of Egyptian desert to link the Mediterranean and Red seas, cutting the trip from London to Bombay in half. The canal dramatically showcased the abilities of Western power and technology to transform the globe, but the human cost was high: 30,000 Egyptians worked on the canal as forced laborers, and thousands died during cholera epidemics in the work camps.

The building of the canal was the result of decades of European involvement in Egypt. French troops under Napoleon had led the way, but Britain's bankers soon followed. European financial interests developed a close relationship with those who governed Egypt as a semi-independent state inside the Ottoman Empire.

By 1875, the British controlled the canal after purchasing 44 percent of the canal's shares from the Egyptian khedive (viceroy) when he was threatened with bankruptcy. By the late 1870s, these economic and political relationships had produced debt and instability in Egypt. In a bid for national independence, a group of Egyptian army officers led by 'Urabi Pasha took control of Egypt's government in 1882.

The British government, determined to protect their investments, decided to intervene. The Royal Navy shelled Egyptian forts along the canal into rubble, and a British task force landed near 'Urabi Pasha's central base, overwhelming the Egyptian lines. This striking success rallied popular support at home, and the political consequences lasted for seventy years. Britain took effective control of Egypt. A British lord, Evelyn Baring, assumed the role of proconsul in a power-sharing relationship with Egyptian authorities, but real power rested with Britain. Britain demanded the repayment of loans and regulated the trade in Egyptian cotton that helped supply Britain's textile mills. Most important, the intervention secured the route to India and the markets of the East.

The Suez Canal and the conquest of Egypt was made possible by the convergence of technology, money, politics, and a global strategy of imperial control. A similar interplay between economics and colonialism produced the stunning expansion of European empires in the late nineteenth century. The years 1870 to 1914 brought both rapid industrialization throughout the West and an intense push to expand the power and influence of Western power abroad. The "new imperialism" of the late nineteenth century was distinguished by its scope, intensity, and long-range consequences. It transformed cultures and states in Europe, Africa, and Asia. Projects such as the Suez Canal changed—literally—the landscape and map of the world. They also represented an ideology: the belief in technology and Western superiority. In the minds of imperialists, the elimination of geographic barriers had opened the entire world, its lands and its peoples, to the administrative power of the West.

The new imperialism, however, was not a one-way street. Europeans could not simply conquer vast territories and dictate their terms to the rest of the world. The new political and economic relationships between colonies and dependent states on the one hand and the "metropole" (the colonizing power) on the other ran both ways, bringing changes to both parties. Fierce competition among nations upset the balance of power. The new imperialism was an expression of European strength, but it was also profoundly destabilizing.

IMPERIALISM

Imperialism is the process of extending one state's control over another—a process that takes many forms. Sometimes this control was exercised by *direct rule*, by which the colonizing nation annexed territories outright and subjugated the peoples who lived there. At times colonialism worked through *indirect rule*, by which conquering European nations reached agreements with local leaders and governed through them. Finally, *informal imperialism* could be a less visible exercise of state power, where stronger states allowed weaker states to maintain their independence while reducing their sovereignty. Informal imperialism took the form of carving out zones of European influence and privilege, such as treaty ports, within other states. There was no single technique of colonial control; as we will see, resistance forced colonial powers to shift strategies frequently. At times European powers chose to delegate authority over colonial lands and trade to private companies, effectively blurring the line between direct and indirect rule.

Both formal and informal imperialism expanded dramatically in the nineteenth century. The "scramble for Africa" was the most startling case of formal imperialism: from 1875 to 1902 Europeans seized up to 90 percent of the continent. The overall picture is no less remarkable: between 1870 and 1900, a small group of states (France, Britain, Germany, the Netherlands, Russia, and the United States) colonized about one quarter of the world's land surface. In addition, these same states extended informal

THE INAUGURATION OF THE SUEZ CANAL. This allegory illustrates the union of the Mediterranean and Red Seas attended by Ismail Pasha, the khedive of Egypt, Abdul Aziz, sultan of the Ottoman Empire, Ferdinand de Lesseps, president of the Suez Canal Company, Empress Eugénie of France, and several mermaids. It also represents the nineteenth-century vision of imperialism as a bearer of global progress, promoting technological advance and breaking down barriers between the Orient and the West. ▪ *Who was the audience for this image?*

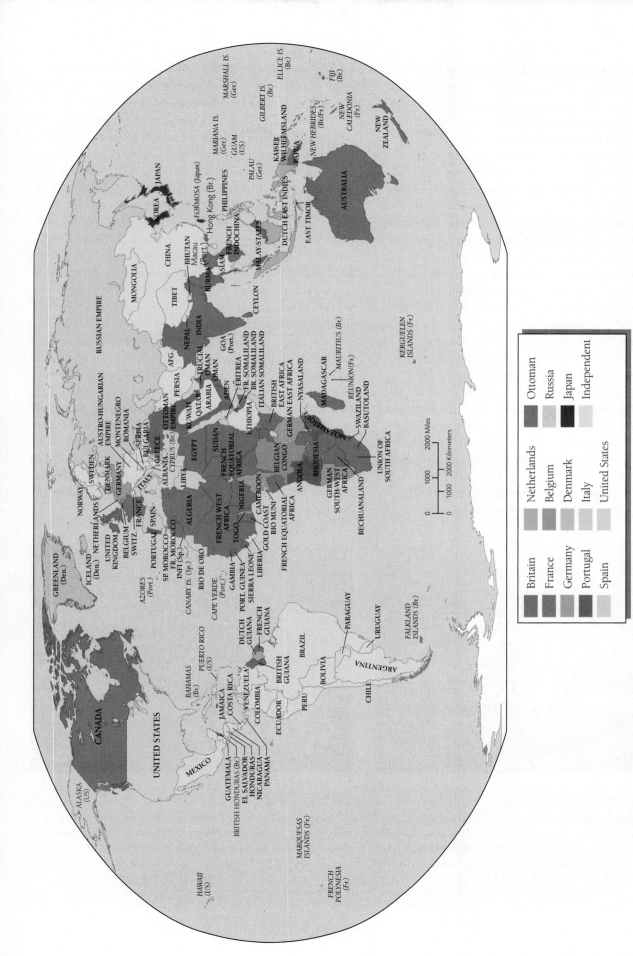

EUROPEAN EMPIRES IN 1900. ■ *Where were Britain's major imperial interests, and what trade routes did they have most incentive to protect?* ■ *Where were France's most important imperial holdings and who was their major competitor?* ■ *How substantial were German, Dutch, Portuguese, or U.S. colonies in comparison to British and French holdings?*

empire in China and Turkey, across South and East Asia, and into Central and South America. So striking was this expansion of European power that contemporaries spoke of the "new imperialism." Nevertheless, imperialism was not new. It is more helpful to think of these nineteenth-century developments as a new stage of European empire building, after the collapse of Europe's early modern empires in North and South America at the end of the eighteenth century.

The nineteenth-century empires rose against the backdrop of industrialization, liberal revolution, and the rise of nation-states. Industrialization produced greater demand for raw materials from distant locations. At the same time, many Europeans became convinced in the nineteenth century that their economic development, science, and technology would inevitably bring progress to the rest of the world. Finally, especially in Britain and France, nineteenth-century imperial powers were in principle democratic nations, where government authority relied on consent and on notions of civic equality. This made conquest difficult to justify and raised thorny questions about the status of colonized peoples. Earlier European conquerors had claimed a missionary zeal to convert people to Christianity as a justification for their actions. Nineteenth-century imperialists justified their projects by saying that their investment in infrastructure—railroads, harbors, and roads—and their social reforms would fulfill Europe's secular mission to bring civilization to the rest of the world. This vision of the "white man's

burden"—the phrase is Rudyard Kipling's—became a powerful argument in favor of imperial expansion throughout Europe (see **Competing Viewpoints** on page 600).

In spite of these ambitious goals, the resistance of colonized peoples did as much to shape the history of colonialism as did the ambitious plans of the colonizers. The Haitian revolution of 1804 compelled the British and the French to end the slave trade and slavery in their colonies in the 1830s and the 1840s, though new systems of forced labor cropped up to take their places. The American Revolution encouraged the British to grant self-government to white settler states in Canada (1867), Australia (1901), and New Zealand (1912). Rebellion in India in 1857 caused the British to place the colony under the direct control of the crown, rather than the East India Company. In general, nineteenth-century imperialism involved less independent entrepreneurial activity by merchants and traders and more "settlement and discipline." This required legal distinctions made on racial or religious grounds in order to organize relationships between Europeans and different indigenous groups, and an administration to enforce such distinctions. (The apartheid system in South Africa developed out of such practices.) Defending such empires thus became a vast project, involving legions of government officials, schoolteachers, and engineers. Nineteenth-century imperialism produced new forms of government and management in the colonies, and as it did so, it forged new interactions between Europeans and indigenous peoples.

IMAGES OF WOMEN IN THE COLONIES. Photographs and engravings of women in Africa and Asia circulated widely in Europe during the nineteenth century, and these images shaped attitudes toward colonization. Many images—some openly pornographic—portrayed African or Asian women as attractive, exotic, and in postures that invited European fantasies of domination. "Reclining Jewess" (left) is a typical example of such imagery, from French Algeria. Other images portrayed colonial women as victims of barbaric customs, as in the depiction of *sati*, a Hindu practice in which a widow would immolate herself on her husband's funeral pyre (right). This image, which first appeared in a work by a missionary who had been to Calcutta, was widely reproduced later as an illustration of the need for British intervention in Indian culture, to bring "civilization" to India. ▪ *Could these images have had the same impact without the emphasis on the gender of the subject?*

Past and Present

The Legacy of Colonialism

Decolonization in the 1950s and 1960s brought an end to the era of European imperialism (left), but the colonial past continues to shape the relations among European nations and former colonies elsewhere in the world. These links are reinforced by the large number of people from former colonies who now live in Europe, including the diverse neighborhood of Southall, London (right).

Watch related author videos on the Student Site
wwnorton.com/college/history/western-civilizationsBrief4

IMPERIALISM IN SOUTH ASIA

India was the center of the British Empire, the jewel of the British crown, secured well before the period of the new imperialism. The conquest of most of the subcontinent began in the 1750s and quickened during the age of revolution. Conquering India helped compensate for "losing" North America. By the mid-nineteenth century, India was the focal point of Britain's newly expanded global power, which reached from southern Africa across South Asia and to Australia. Keeping this region involved changing tactics and forms of rule.

Until the mid-nineteenth century, British territories in India were under the control of the British East India Company. The company had its own military, divided into European and (far larger) Indian divisions. The company held the right to collect taxes on land from Indian peasants. Until the early nineteenth century, the company had legal monopolies over trade in all goods, including indigo, textiles, salt, minerals, and—most lucrative of all—opium. Unlike North America, India never became a settler state. In the 1830s Europeans were a tiny minority, numbering 45,000 in an Indian population of 150 million. The company's rule was repressive and enforced by the military. Soldiers collected taxes; civil servants wore military uniforms; British troops brashly commandeered peasants' oxen and carts for their own purposes. Typically, though, the company could not enforce its rule uniformly. It governed

Rudyard Kipling and His Critics

Rudyard Kipling (1865–1936) remains one of the most famous propagandists of empire. His novels, short stories, and poetry about the British imperial experience in India were defining texts for the cause in which he believed wholeheartedly. Kipling's poem "The White Man's Burden" was—and continues to be—widely read, analyzed, attacked, and praised. Some scholars have asserted that this poem was intended to influence American public opinion during the Spanish-American War, and that it should be read as a celebration of the moral and religious values of European imperialism in general. Others read the poem as a subtle satire of the colonial project and claim that it should be read as irony.

Rudyard Kipling, "The White Man's Burden"

Take up the White Man's burden—
    Send forth the best ye breed—
Go, bind your sons to exile
    To serve your captives' need;
To wait, in heavy harness,
    On fluttered folk and wild—
Your new-caught sullen peoples,
    Half devil and half child.

Take up the White Man's burden—
    In patience to abide,
To veil the threat of terror
    And check the show of pride;
By open speech and simple,
    An hundred times made plain,
To seek another's profit
    And work another's gain.

Take up the White Man's burden—
    The savage wars of peace—
Fill full the mouth of Famine,
    And bid the sickness cease;

And when your goal is nearest
    (The end for others sought)
Watch sloth and heathen folly
    Bring all your hope to nought.
Take up the White Man's burden—
    No iron rule of kings,
But toil of serf and sweeper—
    The tale of common things.
The ports ye shall not enter,
    The roads ye shall not tread,
Go, make them with your living
    And mark them with your dead.

Take up the White Man's burden,
    And reap his old reward—
The blame of those ye better
    The hate of those ye guard—
The cry of hosts ye humour
    (Ah, slowly!) toward the light:—
"Why brought ye us from bondage,
    Our loved Egyptian night?"

Take up the White Man's burden—
    Ye dare not stoop to less—
Nor call too loud on Freedom
    To cloak your weariness.
By all ye will or whisper,
    By all ye leave or do,
The silent sullen peoples
    Shall weigh your God and you.

Take up the White Man's burden!
    Have done with childish days—
The lightly-proffered laurel,
    The easy ungrudged praise:
Comes now, to search your manhood
    Through all the thankless years,
Cold, edged with dear-bought wisdom,
    The judgment of your peers.

Source: Rudyard Kipling, "The White Man's Burden," *McClure's Magazine* 12 (Feb. 1899).

Alfred Webb, To the Editor of *The Nation*

Sir: The cable informs us that "Kipling's stirring verses, the 'Call to America,' have created a . . . profound impression" on your side. What that impression may be, we can only conjecture. There is something almost sickening in this "imperial" talk of assuming and bearing burdens for the good of others. They are never assumed or held where they are not found to be of material advantage or ministering to honor or glory. Wherever empire (I speak of the United Kingdom) is extended, and the climate suits the white man, the aborigines are, for the benefit of the white man, cleared off or held in degradation for his benefit. . . .

Taking India as a test, no one moves a foot in her government that is not well paid and pensioned at her cost. No appointments are more eagerly contended

for than those in the Indian service. A young man is made for life when he secures one. The tone of that service is by no means one "bound to exile," "to serve . . . captives' need," "to wait in heavy harness," or in any degree as expressed in Mr. Kipling's highfalutin lines. It is entirely the contrary: "You are requested not to beat the servants" is a not uncommon notice in Indian hotels. . . . So anxious are we, where good pay is concerned, to save Indians the heavy burden of enjoying them, that, while our sons can study and pass at home for Indian appointments, her sons must study and pass in England; and even in India itself whites are afforded chances closed to natives. . . .

There never was a fostered trade and revenue in more disastrous consequences to humanity than the opium trade and revenue. There never was a more grinding and debilitating tax than that on salt. . . .

Source: Alfred Webb, "Mr. Kipling's Call to America," *The Nation* 68 (Feb. 23, 1899).

Questions for Analysis

1. What benefits did Kipling think imperialism brought, and to whom?

2. What, exactly, was the "burden"? Are there any indications that Kipling's language is meant to be read as satire?

3. What were Webb's arguments against Kipling? Why did he think that imperial talk was "almost sickening"? Did Europeans really suffer in their colonial outposts? In British India, with its well-established civil service, Webb thought not. Why did he mention the opium trade and the salt tax?

some areas directly, others through making alliances with local leaders, and still others by simply controlling goods and money. Indirect rule, here as in other empires, meant finding indigenous collaborators and maintaining their good will. They offered economic privileges, state offices, or military posts to groups or nations that agreed to ally with the British against others.

British policy shifted between two poles: one group wanted to "Westernize" India, another believed it safer, and more practical, to defer to local culture. Christian missionaries, whose numbers rose as occupation expanded, were determined to replace "blind superstition" with the "genial influence of Christian light and truth." Indignant at such practices as child marriage and *sati* (in which a widow immolated herself on her husband's funeral pyre), missionaries sought support in England for a wide-ranging assault on Hindu culture. Secular reformers, many of them liberal, considered "Hindoos" and "Mahommedans" susceptible to forms of despotism—both in the family and in the state. They turned their reforming zeal to legal and political change. But other British administrators warned their countrymen not to meddle with Indian institutions. Indirect rule, they argued, would work only with the cooperation of local powers. Conflicts such as these meant that the British never agreed on any single cultural policy.

From Mutiny to Rebellion

The East India Company's rule often met resistance and protest. In 1857–58, it was badly shaken by a revolt of Indian soldiers in the British army, now known in India as the Great Mutiny of 1857. The uprising began near Delhi, when the military disciplined a regiment of *sepoys* (the traditional term for Indian soldiers employed by the British) for refusing to use rifle cartridges greased with pork fat—unacceptable to either Hindus or Muslims. The causes of the mutiny were deeper, however, and involved social, economic, and political grievances. Indian peasants attacked law courts and burned tax rolls, protesting debt and corruption. In areas that had recently been annexed, rebels defended their traditional leaders, who had been ousted by the British. The mutiny spread through large areas of northwest India. European troops, which counted for fewer than one-fifth of those in arms, found themselves losing control. Religious leaders, both Hindu and Muslim, seized the occasion to denounce Christian missionaries sent in by the British and their assault on local traditions.

At first the British were faced with a desperate situation, with areas under British control cut off from one another and pro-British cities under siege. Loyal Indian troops were brought south from the frontiers, and British troops, fresh from the Crimean War, were shipped directly from Britain to suppress the rebellion. The fighting lasted more than a year, and the British matched the rebels' early massacres with a systematic campaign of repression. Whole rebel units were killed rather than being allowed to surrender, or they were tried on the spot and executed. Towns and villages that supported the rebels were burned, just as the rebels had burned European homes and outposts. Yet the defeat of the rebellion caught the British public's imagination. After the bloody, inconclusive mess of the Crimean War, the terrifying threat to British India and the heroic rescue of European hostages and British territory by British troops were electrifying news. At a political level, British leaders were stunned by how close the revolt had brought them to disaster and were determined never to repeat the same mistakes.

After the mutiny, the British were compelled to reorganize their Indian empire, developing new strategies of rule. The East India Company was abolished, replaced by the British crown. The British *raj* (or rule) was governed directly, though the British also sought out collaborators and cooperative interest groups. Princely India was left to the local princes, who were subject to British advisers. The British also reorganized the military and tried to change relations among soldiers. Indigenous troops were separated from each other to avoid the kind of fraternization that proved subversive. Even more than before, the British sought to rule through the Indian upper classes rather than in opposition to them. Civil-service reform opened new positions to members of the Indian upper classes. The British had to reconsider their relationship to Indian cultures. Missionary activity was no longer encouraged, and the British channeled their reforming impulses into the more secular projects of economic development, railways, roads, irrigation, and so on. Still, consensus on effective colonial strategies was lacking. Some administrators counseled more reform; others sought to support the princes. The British tried both policies, in fits and starts, until the end of British rule in 1947.

What did India do for Great Britain? By the eve of the First World War, India was Britain's largest export market. One-tenth of all the British Empire's trade passed through India's port cities of Madras, Bombay, and Calcutta. India mattered enormously to Britain's balance of payments; surpluses earned there compensated for deficits with Europe and the United States. Equally important to Great Britain were the human resources of India. Indian laborers worked on tea plantations in Assam, near Burma, and they built railways and dams in southern Africa and Egypt. Over a million indentured Indian servants left their country in the second half of the century to work elsewhere in the empire. India also provided the British Empire with highly trained engineers, land surveyors, clerks, bureaucrats, schoolteachers, and merchants. The nationalist leader Mohandas Gandhi, for instance, first came into the public eye as a young lawyer in Pretoria, South Africa, where he worked for an Indian law

THE EXECUTION OF INDIANS WHO PARTICIPATED IN THE REBELLION OF 1857. The British were determined to make an example of rebel Indian soldiers after the Great Mutiny. The engraving on the left shows executions in which the condemned were blown apart by cannons. The cartoon on the right, "The Execution of 'John Company,'" shows the same cannons destroying the British East India Company, which was abolished by the British government as a result of the rebellion. ■ *What do these images tell us about public awareness of the rebellion's violence and its suppression?*

firm. The British deployed Indian troops across the empire. (They would later call up roughly 1.2 million troops in the First World War.) Many British leaders found it impossible to imagine their empire, or even their nation, without India.

How did the British raj shape Indian society? The British practice of indirect rule sought to create an Indian elite that would serve British interests, a group "who may be the interpreters between us and the millions whom we govern—a class of persons Indian in colour and blood, but English in tastes, in opinion, in morals, and in intellect," as one British writer put it. Eventually, this practice created a class of British-educated and English-speaking Indian civil servants and businessmen, well trained for government and skeptical about British claims that the empire brought progress to the subcontinent. This group provided the leadership for the nationalist movement that challenged British rule in India. At the same time, this group became increasingly distant from the rest of the nation. The overwhelming majority of Indians remained desperately poor peasants struggling to subsist on diminishing plots of land and, in many cases, in debt to British landlords.

IMPERIALISM IN CHINA

In China, too, European imperialism began early, well before the period of the new imperialism. Yet there it took a different form. Europeans did not conquer and annex whole regions. Instead, they forced favorable trade agreements at gunpoint, set up treaty ports where Europeans lived and worked under their own jurisdiction, and established outposts of European missionary activity.

Since the seventeenth century, European trade with China had focused on coveted luxuries such as silk, porcelain, art objects, and tea. The Chinese government, however, was determined to keep foreign traders, and foreign influence in general, at bay. By the early nineteenth century, Britain's global ambitions and rising power were setting the stage for a confrontation. Freed from the task of fighting Napoleon, the British set their sights on improving the terms of the China trade, demanding the rights to come into open harbors and to have special trading privileges. The other source of constant friction involved the harsh treatment of British subjects

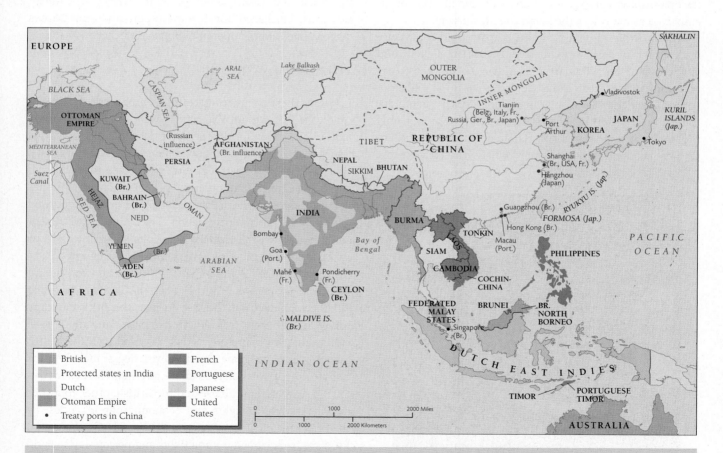

IMPERIALISM IN SOUTH AND EAST ASIA, c. 1914. ■ *Which imperial powers were most present in Asia and where were their primary zones of control and influence?* ■ *Why were European nations and the United States interested in establishing treaty ports in China?* ■ *How were the Chinese treaty ports different from the territorial conquest pursued by the British, French, and Dutch in their respective Asian colonies?*

by Chinese law courts—including the summary execution of several Britons convicted of crimes. By the 1830s, these diplomatic conflicts had been intensified by the opium trade.

The Opium Trade

Opium provided a direct connection linking Britain, British India, and China. Since the sixteenth century, the drug had been produced in India and carried by Dutch and, later, British traders. In fact, opium (derived from the poppy plant) was one of the very few commodities that Europeans could sell in China. For this reason it became crucial to the balance of East-West trade. When the British conquered northeast India, they also annexed one of the world's richest opium-growing areas and became deeply involved in the trade—so much so that modern-day historians have called the East India Company's rule a "narco-military empire." British agencies designated specific poppy-growing regions and gave cash advances to Indian peasants who cultivated the crop. Producing opium was a labor-intensive process: in the opium-producing areas northwest of Calcutta, "factories" employed as many as a thousand Indian workers.

From India, the East India Company sold the opium to "country traders"—small fleets of British, Dutch, and Chinese shippers who carried the drug to Southeast Asia and China. The East India Company used the silver it earned from the sale of opium to buy Chinese goods for the European market. The trade, therefore, was not only profitable, it was key to a triangular European-Indian-Chinese economic relationship. Production and export rose

AN OPIUM FACTORY IN PATNA, INDIA, c. 1851. Balls of opium dry in a huge warehouse before being shipped to Calcutta for export to China and elsewhere.

dramatically in the early nineteenth century, in spite of the Chinese emperor's attempts to discourage the trade. By the 1830s, when the British-Chinese confrontation was taking shape, opium provided British India with more revenue than any other source except taxes on land.

People all over the world consumed opium, for medicinal reasons as well as for pleasure. The Chinese market was especially lucrative. Eighteenth-century China witnessed a craze for tobacco smoking that taught users how to smoke opium. A large, wealthy Chinese elite of merchants and government officials provided much of the market, but opium smoking also became popular among soldiers, students, and Chinese laborers. In the nineteenth century opium imports followed Chinese labor all over the world—to Southeast Asia and San Francisco. In 1799, in an effort to control the problem, the Chinese government banned opium imports, prohibited domestic production, criminalized smoking, and in the 1830s began a full-scale campaign to purge the drug from China. That campaign set the Chinese emperor on a collision course with British opium traders. In one confrontation the Chinese drug commissioner Lin confiscated three million pounds of raw opium from the British and washed it out to sea. In another the Chinese authorities blockaded British ships in port, and local citizens demonstrated angrily in front of British residences.

THE OPIUM WARS

In 1839, these simmering conflicts broke into what was called the first Opium War. Drugs were not the core of the matter. The dispute over the drug trade highlighted larger issues of sovereignty and economic status. The Europeans claimed the right to trade with whomever they pleased, bypassing Chinese monopolies. They wished to set up zones of European residence in defiance of Chinese sovereignty and to proselytize and to open schools. The Chinese government could not accept these challenges to its authority, and war flared up several times over the course of the century. After the first war of 1839–42, in which British steam vessels and guns overpowered the Chinese fleet, the Treaty of Nanking (1842) compelled the Chinese to give the British trading privileges, the right to reside in five cities, and the port of Hong Kong "in perpetuity." After a second war, the British secured yet more treaty ports and privileges, including the right to send in missionaries. In the aftermath of those agreements between the Chinese and the British, other countries demanded similar rights and economic opportunities. By the end of the nineteenth century the French, Germans, and Russians had claimed mining rights and permission to build railroads, to begin manufacturing with cheap Chinese labor, and to arm and police European communities in Chinese cities. The United States, not wanting to be shouldered aside,

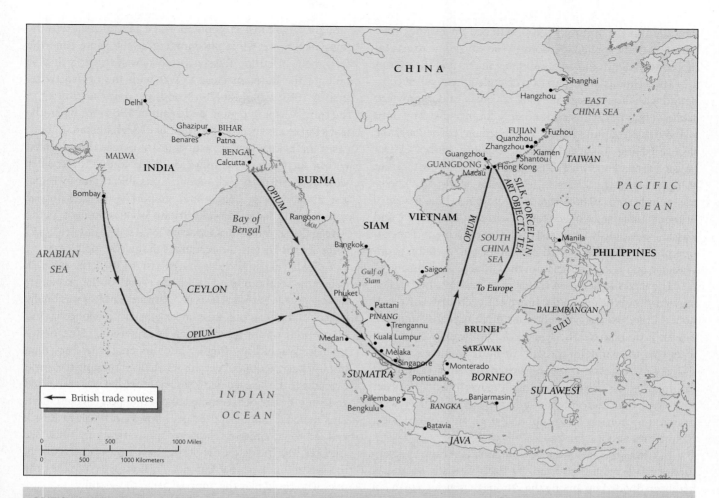

BRITISH OPIUM TRADE. Note the way that the British trade in opium linked the economies of India, China, and Europe. ▪ *What were the major products involved in trade among East Asia, South Asia, and Europe during this period?* ▪ *In what ways did the opium trade destabilize East Asia?* ▪ *What efforts did the Chinese government make to restrict the sale of opium?* ▪ *What was the response of European nations involved in this trade?*

demanded its own Open Door Policy. Japan was an equally active imperialist power in the Pacific, and the Sino-Japanese War of 1894–95 was a decisive moment in the history of the region. The Japanese victory forced China to concede trading privileges, the independence of Korea, and the Liaotung Peninsula in Manchuria. It opened a scramble for spheres of influence and for mining and railway concessions.

Surrendering privileges to Europeans and the Japanese seriously undermined the authority of the Chinese Qing (Ching) emperor at home and heightened popular hostility to foreign intruders. Authority at the imperial center had been eroding for more than a century by 1900, hastened by the Opium Wars and by the vast Taiping Rebellion (1852–64), an enormous, bitter, and deadly conflict in which radical Christian rebels in south-central China challenged the authority of the emperors. On the defensive against the rebels, the dynasty hired foreign generals, including the British commander Charles Gordon, to lead

its forces. The war devastated China's agricultural heartland; and the death toll, never confirmed, may have reached 20 million. This ruinous disorder and the increasing inability of the emperor to keep order and collect the taxes necessary to repay foreign loans led European countries to take more and more direct control of the China trade.

The Boxer Rebellion

From a Western perspective, the most important of the nineteenth-century rebellions against the corruptions of foreign rule was the Boxer Rebellion of 1900. The Boxers were a secret society of young men trained in Chinese martial arts and believed to have spiritual powers. Antiforeign and antimissionary, they provided the spark for a loosely organized but widespread uprising in northern China. Bands of Boxers attacked foreign engineers, tore up railway lines, and in the spring of 1900 marched on Beijing. They laid siege to the foreign legations in the city, home to several thousand Western diplomats and merchants and their families. The legations' small garrison defended their walled compound with little more than rifles, bayonets, and improvised artillery; but they withstood the siege for fifty-five days until a large relief column arrived. The rebellion, particularly the siege at Beijing, mobilized a global response. Europe's Great Powers, rivals everywhere else in the world, drew together in response to this crisis to tear China apart. An expedition numbering 20,000 troops—combining the forces of Britain, France, the United States, Germany, Italy, Japan, and Russia—ferociously repressed the Boxer movement. The outside powers then demanded indemnities, new trading concessions, and reassurances from the Chinese government.

The Boxer Rebellion was one of several anti-imperialist movements at the end of the nineteenth century. The rebellion testified to the vulnerability of Europeans' imperial power. It dramatized the resources Europeans would have to devote to maintaining their far-flung influence. In the process of repression, the Europeans became committed to propping up corrupt and fragile governments in order to protect their agreements and interests, and they were drawn into putting down popular uprisings against local inequalities and foreign rule.

In China the age of the new imperialism capped a century of conflict and expansion. By 1900, virtually all of Asia had been divided up among the European powers. Japan, an active imperial power in its own right, maintained its independence. British rule extended from India across Burma, Malaya, Australia, and New Zealand. The Dutch, Britain's longstanding trade rivals, secured Indonesia. Siam (Thailand) remained independent. During the 1880s, the French moved into Indochina. Imperial rivalries (among Britain, France, and Russia, China and Japan, Russia and Japan) drove European powers to press for influence and economic advantage in Asia; that struggle, in turn, encouraged the development of nationalist feeling among local populations. Imperial expansion was showing its destabilizing effects.

Russian Imperialism

Russia championed a policy of annexation—by conquest, treaty, or both—of lands bordering on the existing Russian state throughout the nineteenth century. Beginning in 1801 with the acquisition of Georgia after a war with Persia, the tsars continued to pursue their expansionist dream. Bessarabia and Turkestan (taken from the Turks) and Armenia (from the Persians) vastly increased the empire's size. The colonization of Kazakhstan in the same period

brought large Muslim populations in central Asia into the Russian Empire while encouraging at the same time the settlement of ethnic Russians into new territories. It also brought the Russians close to war with the British twice: first in 1881, when Russian troops occupied territories in the trans-Caspian region, and again in 1884–87, when the tsar's forces advanced to the frontier of Afghanistan. In both cases the British feared incursions into areas they deemed within their sphere of influence in the Middle East. They were concerned, as well, about a possible threat to India. The maneuvering, spying, and support of friendly puppet governments by Russia and Britain became known as the "Great Game" and foreshadowed Western countries' jockeying for the region's oil resources in the twentieth century.

Russian expansion also moved east. In 1875, the Japanese traded the southern half of Sakhalin Island for the previously Russian Kurile Islands. The tsars' eastward advance was finally halted in 1904, when Russian expansion in Mongolia and Manchuria came up against Japanese expansion. In the Russo-Japanese War of 1904, Russia's huge imperial army more than met its match. Russia's navy was sent halfway around the world to reinforce the beleaguered Russian troops but was ambushed and sunk by the better-trained and -equipped Japanese fleet. This national humiliation helped provoke a revolt in Russia and led to an American-brokered peace treaty in 1905 (see Chapter 23). The defeat shook the already unsteady regime of the tsar and proved that European nations were not the only ones who could play the imperial game successfully.

THE FRENCH EMPIRE AND THE CIVILIZING MISSION

Like British expansion into India, French colonialism in northern Africa began before the new imperialism of the late nineteenth century. France invaded Algeria in 1830, a conquest that would take nearly two decades to complete. From the outset the Algerian conquest was different from most other colonial ventures: Algeria became a settler state, one of the few apart from South Africa. The settlers were by no means all French; they included Italian, Spanish, and Maltese merchants and shopkeepers of modest means, laborers, and peasants. By the 1870s, in several of the coastal cities, this new creole community outnumbered indigenous Algerians, and within it, other Europeans outnumbered the French. With the French military's help, the settlers appropriated land, and French business concerns took cork forests and established mines to extract copper, lead, and iron. Economic activity was for European benefit. The first railroads, for instance, did not even carry

Legend:
- Russian Empire, 1795
- Russian acquisitions, 1795–1855
- Russian acquisitions, 1855–1914
- Russian sphere of influence
- Occupied by Russia

BUILDING THE RUSSIAN EMPIRE. ▪ *In what directions did the Russian Empire primarily expand after 1795?* ▪ *What drove Russian expansion?* ▪ *Which areas were most contentious, and why?*

passengers; they took iron ore to the coast for export to France, where it could be smelted and sold.

The settlers and the French government did not necessarily pursue common goals. In the 1870s, the new and still fragile Third Republic (founded after Napoleon III was defeated in 1870; see Chapter 21), in an effort to ensure the settlers' loyalty, made the colony a department of France. This gave the French settlers the full rights of republican citizenship. It also gave them the power to pass laws in Algeria that consolidated their privileges and community (naturalizing all Europeans, for instance) and further disenfranchised indigenous Muslim populations, who had no voting rights at all. France's divide-and-rule strategy, which treated European settlers, Arabs, Berbers, and Jews very differently, illustrates the contradictions of "the civilizing mission" in action.

Before the 1870s, colonial activities aroused relatively little interest among the French at home. But after France's humiliating defeat in the Franco-Prussian War (1870–71) and the establishment of the Third Republic, colonial lobby groups and politicians became increasingly adamant about

the benefits of colonialism. These benefits were not simply economic. Taking on the "civilizing mission" would reinforce the international influence of the French republic and the prestige of the French people. Jules Ferry, a republican leader, argued that "the superior races have a right vis-à-vis the inferior races. . . . They have a right to civilize them."

Under Ferry, the French acquired Tunisia (1881), northern and central Vietnam (Tonkin and Annam; 1883), and Laos and Cambodia (1893). They also carried this civilizing mission into their colonies in West Africa. European and Atlantic trade with the west coast of Africa—in slaves, gold, and ivory—had been well established for centuries. In the late nineteenth century, trade gave way to formal administration. The year 1895 saw the establishment of a Federation of French West Africa, a loosely organized administration to govern an area nine times the size of France, including Guinea, Senegal, the Ivory Coast, and vast stretches of the western Sahara. Even with reforms and centralization in 1902, French control remained uneven. Despite military campaigns of pacification, resistance persisted. The French dealt gingerly with tribal leaders, at times deferring to their authority and at others trying to break their power. They established French courts and law only in cities, ceding authority to Islamic or tribal courts in other areas. The federation aimed to rationalize the economic exploitation of the area and to replace "booty capitalism" with a more careful management and development of resources. They embarked on ambitious public works projects including the construction of railroads, harbors, and sanitation systems. The French called this "enhancing the value" of the region, which was part of the "civilizing mission" of the modern republic.

Such programs plainly served French interests. "Officially this process is called civilizing, and after all, the term is apt, since the undertaking serves to increase the degree of prosperity of our civilization," remarked one Frenchman who opposed the colonial enterprise. None of these measures aimed to give indigenous peoples political rights. As one historian puts it, "the French Government General was in the business not of making citizens, but of civilizing its subjects." More telling, however, the French project was seldom successful. The French government did not have the resources to carry out its plans, which proved much more expensive and complicated than anyone imagined. Transportation costs ran very high. Labor posed the largest problems. Here as elsewhere, Europeans faced massive resistance from the indigenous peasants, whom they wanted to do everything from building railroads to working mines and carrying rubber. The Europeans resorted to forced labor, signing agreements with local tribal leaders to deliver workers, and they turned a blind eye to the continuing use of slave labor in the interior. For all of these reasons, the colonial project did not produce the profits some expected.

SLAVES IN CHAINS, 1896. In Africa, native labor was exploited by Europeans and by other Africans, as here.

THE "SCRAMBLE FOR AFRICA" AND THE CONGO

French expansion into West Africa was only one instance of Europe's voracity on the African continent. The scope and speed with which the major European powers conquered and asserted formal control was astonishing. The effects were profound. In 1875, 11 percent of the continent was in European hands. By 1902, the figure was 90 percent. European powers mastered logistical problems of transport and communication; they learned how to keep diseases at bay. They also had new weapons. The Maxim gun, adopted by the British army in 1889 and first used by British colonial troops, pelted out as many as five hundred rounds a minute; it turned encounters with indigenous forces into bloodbaths and made armed resistance virtually impossible.

The Congo Free State

In the 1870s, the British had formed new imperial relationships in the north and west of Africa and along the southern and eastern coasts. A new phase of European involvement struck right at the heart of the continent. Until the latter part of the nineteenth century this territory had been out of bounds for Europeans. The rapids upstream on such strategic rivers as the Congo and the Zambezi made it difficult to move inland, and tropical diseases were lethal to most European explorers. But during the 1870s, a new drive into central Africa produced results. The target was the fertile valleys around the Congo River, and the European colonizers were a group of Belgians privately financed by their king, Leopold II (r. 1865–1909). They followed in the footsteps of Henry Morton Stanley, an American newspaperman and explorer who later became a British subject and a knight of the realm. Stanley hacked his way through thick canopy jungle into territory where no European had previously set foot. His "scientific" journeys inspired the creation of a society of researchers and students of African culture in Brussels, in reality a front organization for the commercial company set up by Leopold. The ambitiously named International Association for the Exploration and Civilization of the Congo was set up in 1876 and soon set about signing treaties with local elites, which opened the whole Congo River basin to commercial exploitation. The vast resources of palm oil and natural rubber and the promise of minerals (including diamonds) were now within Europeans' reach.

The strongest resistance that Leopold's company faced came from other colonial powers, particularly Portugal,

Analyzing Primary Sources

Atrocities in the Congo

George Washington Williams (1849–1891), an African American pastor, journalist, and historian, was among a handful of international observers who went to the Congo in the 1890s to explore and report back on conditions. He wrote several reports: one for the U.S. government, another that he presented at an international antislavery conference, several newspaper columns, and an open letter to King Leopold, from which the following is excerpted.

 ood and Great Friend,

I have the honour to submit for your Majesty's consideration some reflections respecting the Independent State of Congo, based upon a careful study and inspection of the country and character of the personal Government you have established upon the African Continent. . . .

I was led to regard your enterprise as the rising of the Star of Hope for the Dark Continent, so long the habitation of cruelties. . . . When I arrived in the Congo, I naturally sought for the results of the brilliant programme:—*"fostering care," "benevolent enterprise,"* an *"honest and practical effort"* to increase the knowledge of the natives *"and secure their welfare."* . . .

I was doomed to bitter disappointment. Instead of the natives of the Congo *"adopting the fostering care"* of your Majesty's Government, they everywhere complain that their land has been taken from them by force; that the Government is cruel and arbitrary, and declare that they neither love nor respect the Government and its flag. Your Majesty's Government has sequestered their land, burned their towns, stolen their property, enslaved their women and children, and committed other crimes too numerous to mention in detail. It is natural that they everywhere shrink from *"the fostering care"* your Majesty's Government so eagerly proffers them.

There has been, to my absolute knowledge, no *"honest and practical effort made to increase their knowledge and secure their welfare."* Your Majesty's Government has never spent one franc for educational purposes, nor instituted any practical system of industrialism. Indeed the most unpractical measures have been adopted *against* the natives in nearly every respect; and in the capital of your Majesty's Government at Boma there is not a native employed. The labour system is radically unpractical. . . . Recruits are transported under circumstances more cruel than cattle in European countries. They eat their rice twice a day by the use of their fingers; they often thirst for water when the season is dry; they are exposed to the heat and rain, and sleep upon the damp and filthy decks of the vessels often so closely crowded as to lie in human ordure. And, of course, many die. . . .

All the crimes perpetrated in the Congo have been done in *your* name, and *you* must answer at the bar of Public Sentiment for the misgovernment of a people, whose lives and fortunes were entrusted to you by the august Conference of Berlin, 1884–1885. . . .

Source: George Washington Williams, "An Open Letter to His Serene Majesty Leopold II, King of the Belgians, and Sovereign of the Independent State of Congo, July 1890," in *George Washington Williams: A Biography*, ed. John Hope Franklin (Chicago: 1985), pp. 243–54.

Questions for Analysis

1. What expectations did Williams have on arriving in the Congo and how did he think of Africa in relation to Europe?

2. What promises had the Belgian monarch made as justification for European expansion into the Congo?

3. What evidence did Williams look for in order to evaluate the reality of these commitments?

which objected to this new drive for occupation. In 1884, a conference was called in Berlin to settle the matter of control over the Congo River basin. It was chaired by the master of European power politics, German chancellor Otto von Bismarck, and attended by all the leading colonial nations as well as by the United States. The conference established ground rules for a new phase of European economic and political expansion. Europe's two great overseas empires, Britain and France, and the strongest emerging power inside Europe, Germany, agreed to a settlement that seemed to be perfectly in line with nineteenth-century liberalism. The Congo valleys would

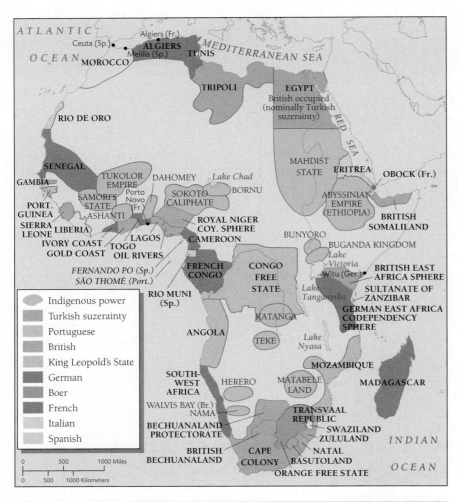

AFRICA, c. 1886.

the different cycle of seasons in central Africa, whole crop years were lost, leading to famines. Laborers working in the heat of the dry season often carried on their backs individual loads that would have been handled by heavy machinery in a European factory. Thousands of Africans were pressed into work harvesting the goods that Europe wanted. They did so for little or no pay, under the threat of beatings and mutilation for dozens of petty offenses against the plantation companies, which made the laws of the Free State. Eventually the scandal of the Congo became too great to go on unchallenged. A whole generation of authors and journalists, most famously Joseph Conrad in his *Heart of Darkness,* publicized the arbitrary brutality and the vast scale of suffering. In 1908 Belgium was forced to take direct control of the Congo, turning it into a Belgian colony. A few restrictions at least were imposed on the activities of the great plantation companies that had brought a vast new store of raw materials to European industry by using slavery in all but name.

The Partition of Africa

The occupation of the Congo, and its promise of great material wealth, pressured other colonial powers into expanding their holdings. By the 1880s, the "scramble for Africa" was well under way. The guarantees made at the 1884 Berlin conference allowed the Europeans to take further steps. The French and Portugese increased their holdings. Italy moved into territories along the Red Sea, beside British-held land and the independent kingdom of Ethiopia.

Germany came relatively late to empire overseas. Bismarck was reluctant to engage in an enterprise that he believed would yield few economic or political advantages. Yet he did not want either Britain or France to dominate Africa, and Germany seized colonies in Cameroon and Tanzania. Though the Germans were not the most enthusiastic colonialists, they were fascinated by the imperial adventure and jealous of their territories. When the Herero people of German Southwest Africa (now Namibia) rebelled in the early 1900s, the Germans responded with a vicious campaign of village

be open to free trade and commerce; a slave trade still run by some of the Islamic kingdoms in the region would be suppressed in favor of free labor; and a Congo Free State would be set up, denying the region to the formal control of any single European country.

In reality the Congo Free State was run by Leopold's private company, and the region was opened up to unrestricted exploitation by a series of large European corporations. The older slave trade was suppressed, but the European companies took the "free" African labor guaranteed in Berlin and placed workers in equally bad conditions. Huge tracts of land, larger than whole European countries, became diamond mines or plantations for the extraction of palm oil, rubber, or cocoa. African workers labored in appalling conditions, with no real medicine or sanitation, too little food, and according to production schedules that made European factory labor look mild by comparison. Hundreds of thousands of African workers died from disease and overwork. Because European managers did not comprehend or respect burning and ethnic killing that nearly annihilated the Herero.

Great Britain and France had their own ambitions. The French aimed to move west to east across the continent, an important reason for the French expedition to Fashoda (in the Sudan) in 1898 (as will be discussed later). Britain's part in the scramble took place largely in southern and eastern Africa and was encapsulated in the dreams and career of one man: the diamond tycoon, colonial politician, and imperial visionary Cecil Rhodes. Rhodes, who made a fortune from the South African diamond mines in the 1870s and 1880s and founded the diamond-mining company DeBeers, became prime minister of Britain's Cape Colony in 1890. (He left part of this fortune for the creation of the Rhodes Scholarships to educate future leaders of the empire at Oxford.) In an uneasy alliance with the Boer settlers in their independent southern African republics and with varying levels of support from London, Rhodes pursued two great personal and imperial goals. The personal goal was to build a southern African empire that was founded on diamonds. "Rhodesia" would fly the Union Jack out of pride but send its profits into Rhodes's own companies. Through bribery, double dealing, careful coalition politics with the British and Boer settlers, warfare, and outright theft, Rhodes helped carve out territories occupying the modern nations of Zambia, Zimbabwe, Malawi, and Botswana—most of the savannah of southern Africa. Rhodes's second goal was a British presence along the whole of eastern Africa, symbolized by the goal of a Cape-to-Cairo railway. He believed that the empire should make Britain self-sufficient, with British industry able to run on the goods and raw materials shipped in from its colonies, then exporting many finished products back to those lands. Once the territories of Zambeziland and Rhodesia were taken, Rhodes found himself turning against the Boer settlers in the region, a conflict that led to the Boer war in 1899 (to be discussed later in this chapter).

As each European power sought its "place in the sun," in the famous phrase of the German kaiser Wilhelm II,

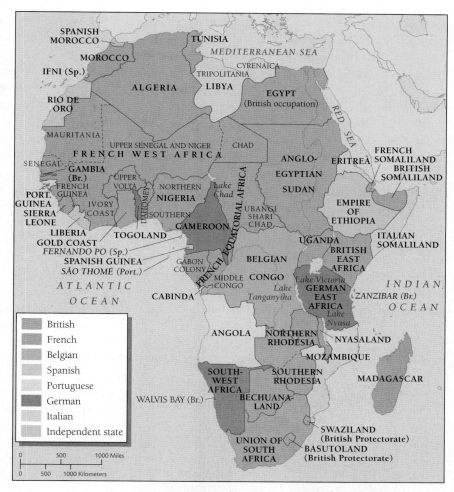

AFRICA, c. 1914. ■ *What is the single biggest difference in terms of rulership between the two maps?* ■ *Who were the winners and losers in the scramble for Africa before the First World War?* ■ *What does the result of the scramble for Africa suggest about how European powers regarded each other?*

they brought more and more of Africa under direct colonial control. African peoples thus faced a combination of direct European control and indirect rule, which allowed local elites friendly to European interests to lord over those who resisted. The partition of Africa was the most striking instance of the new imperialism, with broad consequences for the subject peoples of European colonies and for the international order as a whole.

IMPERIAL CULTURE

Imperialism was thoroughly anchored in the culture of late-nineteenth-century Europe and the United States. Images of empire were everywhere. Not just in the propagandist literature of colonialism's supporters, but on tins of tea and boxes of cocoa, as background themes in posters advertising everything from dance halls to sewing machines. Museums and world's fairs displayed the products of empire and introduced spectators to "exotic peoples." Music halls rang to the sound of imperialist songs. Empire was present in novels of the period, sometimes appearing as a faraway setting for fantasy, adventure, or stories of self-discovery. The popular literature of empire showed a particular fascination with sexual practices in faraway places—photos and postcards of North African harems and unveiled Arab women were common in European pornography, as were colonial memoirs that chronicled the sexual adventures of their authors.

Empire thus played an important part in establishing European identity during these years. In France, the "civilizing mission" demonstrated to French citizens the grandeur of their nation; building railroads and "bringing progress to other lands" illustrated the vigor of the French republic. Many British writers spoke in similar tones. One author

THE WHITE MAN'S BURDEN AND PEARS' SOAP. The presence of imperialist themes in advertising is well illustrated by this advertisement, which appeared in 1899 in the American magazine *McClure's*. The ad connects the theme of cleanliness and personal hygiene to racial superiority and the necessity of bringing civilization to "the dark corners of the earth." The goal of the ad, of course, was to sell soap—but the fact that such themes could work for advertisers reveals the extent to which imperialist ideas were widespread within the culture.

wrote, "The British race may safely be called a missionary race. The command to go and teach all nations is one that the British people have, whether rightly or wrongly, regarded as specially laid upon themselves."

This sense of high moral purpose was not restricted to male writers or to figures of authority. In England, the United States, Germany, and France, the speeches and projects of women's reform movements were full of references to empire and the "civilizing mission." Britain's woman suffrage movement, for example, was fiercely critical of the government but was also nationalist and imperialist. For these militants, women's participation in politics also meant the right to participate in imperial projects. British women reformers wrote about the oppression of Indian women by child marriage and *sati*, and saw themselves shouldering the "white women's burden" of reform. In France, suffragist Hubertine Auclert criticized the colonial government in Algeria for their indifference to the condition of Muslim women in their domains, and she used an image of women suffering in polygamous marriages abroad to dramatize the need for reform. Arguments such as these enabled European women in their home countries to see themselves as bearers of progress, as participants in a superior civilization. Similarly, John Stuart Mill often used Hindu or Muslim culture as a foil when he wanted to make a point of freedom of speech and religion. This contrast between colonial backwardness and European civility and cultural superiority shaped Western culture and political debate about liberal ideas in particular.

Imperialism and Racial Thought

Imperial culture gave new prominence to racial thinking. Count Arthur de Gobineau (*GOH-bih-noh*, 1816–1882) wrote a massive work, *The Inequality of the Races*, in the 1850s, but it sparked little interest until the period of the new imperialism, when it was translated from French into English and widely discussed. For Gobineau, race offered the "master key" for understanding human societies in the modern world. Gobineau's work followed from Enlightenment investigations of different cultures in the world, but unlike Enlightenment authors who attributed these differences largely to environmental factors, Gobineau argued that "blood" was the determining factor in human history. Gobineau claimed that humans were originally divided into three races, "black," "white," and "yellow," and that the peoples of the present day were variously mixed from these original components. The white race, he argued, had preserved purer bloodlines, and was therefore superior. The others suffered "adulteration" and were therefore degenerate and no longer capable of civilization. Gobineau's readers included some defenders of the Confederacy during the American Civil War and Adolf Hitler in the twentieth century.

Followers of Gobineau's racial thinking looked increasingly to science to legitimate their theories. The natural scientist Charles Darwin, no racist himself, attracted wide attention with a theory of evolution that sought to explain the variety of species observable in the natural world. Darwin suggested that only the most "fit" individuals in a species survived to bear viable offspring, and that this process of "natural selection" explained how species diverged from one another: variations that made certain individuals better able to secure food and mates were likely to be passed on to future generations. Social scientists such as Herbert Spencer sought to use Darwin's logic of competition among individuals for scarce resources to explain the evolution of social groups, suggesting that inequalities of wealth or ability could also be explained as the result of a process of "natural selection." Racial theorists and followers of Gobineau such as Houston Stewart Chamberlain (1855–1927) wasted little time in harnessing such scientific arguments to the claim that human "races" evolved over time. Chamberlain's books sold tens of thousands of copies in England and Germany.

Francis Galton (1822–1911), a half-cousin of Charles Darwin and a scientist who studied evolution, went so far as to advocate improving the population's racial characteristics by selective breeding of "superior types." Galton and others feared that improvements in health care and hygiene might allow individuals with inferior traits to survive to reproductive age, and his system of racial management, which he called *eugenics*, would save European populations from a decline in their vitality and biological fitness. Theories such as Galton's or Gobineau's did not cause imperialism, and they were closely linked with other developments in European culture, in particular renewed anxieties about social class and a fresh wave of European anti-Semitism. Yet the increasingly scientific racism of late-nineteenth-century Europe made it easier for many to reconcile the rhetoric of progress, individual freedom, and the "civilizing mission" with contempt for other peoples.

Opposition to Imperialism

Support for imperialism was not unanimous. John A. Hobson and Vladimir Lenin condemned the entire enterprise for being rooted in greed and arrogance. Polish-born Joseph Conrad, a British novelist, shared many of the racial attitudes of his contemporaries, but he nevertheless believed that imperialism was an expression of deeply rooted pathologies in European culture. Other anti-imperialists were men and women from the colonies themselves who brought their case to the metropole. The British Committee of the Indian National Congress gathered together many members of London's Indian community to educate British public opinion about the exploitation of Indian peoples and resources.

Perhaps the most defiant anti-imperialist action was the London Pan-African conference of 1900, staged at the height of the scramble for Africa and during the Boer War (discussed on page 614). The conference grew out of an international tradition of African American, British, and American antislavery movements and brought the rhetoric used earlier to abolish slavery to bear on the tactics of European imperialism. They protested forced labor in the mining compounds of South Africa as akin to slavery and asked in very moderate tones for some autonomy and representation for African peoples. The Pan-African Conference of 1900 was small, but it drew delegates from the Caribbean, West Africa, and North America, including the thirty-two-year-old Harvard PhD and leading African American intellectual, W. E. B. Du Bois (1868–1963). The conference issued a proclamation "To the Nations of the World," with a famous introduction written by Du Bois. "The problem of the Twentieth Century is the problem of the color line. . . . In the metropolis of the modern world, in this closing year of the nineteenth century," the proclamation read, "there has been assembled a congress of men and women of African blood, to deliberate solemnly the present situation and outlook of the darker races of mankind." The British government ignored the conference, but Pan-Africanism, like Indian nationalism, grew rapidly after the First World War.

Colonial Cultures

Imperialism also created new colonial cultures in other parts of the world. Cities such as Bombay, Calcutta, and Shanghai boomed, more than tripling in size. Treaty ports like Hong Kong were transformed as Europeans built banks, shipping enterprises, schools, and religious missions. As Europeans and indigenous peoples encountered and transformed one another, new hybrid cultures emerged. Elsewhere, new social instabilities were produced as European demands for labor brought men out of their villages, away from their families, and crowded them into shantytowns bordering sprawling new cities. Hopes that European rule would create a well-disciplined labor force were quickly dashed.

People on both sides of the colonial divide worried about preserving national traditions and identity in the face of these hybrid and changing colonial cultures. In Africa and the Middle East, Islamic scholars debated the proper response to European control. In China and India, suggestions that local populations adopt European models of education set off fierce controversies. Chinese elites, already divided over such customs as footbinding and concubinage (the legal practice of maintaining formal sexual partners for men outside their marriage), found their dilemmas heightened as imperialism became a more powerful force. Should they defend such practices as integral to their culture? Should they argue for a Chinese path to reform? Proponents of change in China or India thus had to sort through their stances toward both Western culture and traditional popular culture.

For their part, British, French, and Dutch authorities fretted that too much familiarity between colonized and colonizer would weaken European prestige and authority. In Phnom Penh, Cambodia (part of French Indochina), French citizens lived separated from the rest of the city by a moat, and authorities required "dressing appropriately and keeping a distance from the natives." Sexual relations provoked the most anxiety and the most contradictory responses. "In this hot climate, passions run higher," wrote a French administrator in Algeria. "French soldiers seek out Arab women due to their strangeness and newness." "It was common practice for unmarried Englishmen resident in China to keep a Chinese girl, and I did as the others did," reported a British man stationed in Shanghai. He married an Englishwoman, however, and sent his Chinese mistress and their three children to England to avoid awkwardness. European administrators fitfully tried to prohibit liaisons between European men and local women, labeling such affairs as "corrupting." Such prohibitions only drove these relations underground, increasing the gap between the public facade of colonial rule and the private reality of colonial lives.

CRISES OF EMPIRE AT THE TURN OF THE TWENTIETH CENTURY

The turn of the twentieth century brought a series of crises to the Western empires. Those crises did not end European rule. They did, however, shake Western confidence and create sharp tensions among Western nations. The crises also drove imperial nations to expand their economic and military commitments in territories overseas. In all of these ways, they became central to Western culture in the years before the First World War.

Fashoda

In the fall of 1898, British and French armies nearly went to war at Fashoda, in the Egyptian Sudan. The crisis had complex causes: in the early 1880s the British had used a local uprising in the Sudan as an excuse to move southward from Egypt in an attempt to control the headwaters of the Nile River. This project began with grandiose dreams of connecting Cairo to the Cape of Good Hope, but it ran into catastrophe when an army led by Britain's most flamboyant general, Charles Gordon, was massacred in Khartoum in 1885 by the forces of the Mahdi, a Sufi religious leader who claimed to be the successor to the prophet Muhammad. Avenging Gordon's death preoccupied the British for more than a decade, and in 1898 a second large-scale rebellion gave them the opportunity. An Anglo-Egyptian army commanded by General Horatio Kitchener and armed with modern machine guns and artillery attacked Khartoum and defeated the Mahdi's army.

The victory brought complications, however. France, which held territories in central Africa adjacent to the Sudan, saw the British victory as a threat. A French expedition was sent to the Sudanese town of Fashoda (now Kodok) to challenge British claims in the area. The French faced off with troops from Kitchener's army, and for a few weeks in September 1898 the situation teetered on the brink of war. The matter was resolved diplomatically, however, and France ceded the southern Sudan to Britain in exchange for a stop to further expansion. The incident was a sobering reminder of the extent to which imperial competition could lead to international tensions between European powers.

Ethiopia

During the 1880s and 1890s Italy had been developing a small empire on the shores of the Red Sea. Italy annexed Eritrea and parts of Somalia, and shortly after the death of Gordon at Khartoum, the Italians defeated an invasion of their territories by the Mahdi's forces. Bolstered by this success, the Italians set out to conquer Ethiopia in 1896. Ethiopia was the last major independent African kingdom, ruled by a shrewd and capable emperor, Menelik II. His largely Christian subjects engaged in profitable trade on the East African coast, and revenues from this trade allowed Menelik to invest in the latest European artillery. When the Italian army—mostly Somali conscripts and a few thousand Italian troops—arrived, Menelik allowed them to penetrate into the mountain passes of Ethiopia. To keep to the roads, the Italians were forced to divide their forces into separate columns. Meanwhile, the Ethiopians moved over the mountains themselves, and at Adowa, in March 1896, Menelik's army attacked, destroyed the Italian armies completely, and killed six thousand. Adowa was a national humiliation for Italy and an important symbol for African political radicals during the early twentieth century.

Interpreting Visual Evidence

Displays of Imperial Culture: The Paris Exposition of 1889

The French colonies were very visible during the celebration of the centenary of the French Revolution in 1889. In that year, the French government organized a "Universal Exposition" in the capital that attracted over 6 million visitors to a broad esplanade covered with exhibitions of French industry and culture, including the newly constructed Eiffel Tower, a symbol of modern French engineering.

At the base of the Eiffel Tower (image A), a colonial pavilion displayed objects from France's overseas empire, and a collection of temporary architectural exhibits featured reproductions of buildings from French colonies in Asia and Africa as well as samples of architecture from other parts of the world. The photographs here show a reproduction of a Cairo street (image B); the Pagoda of Angkor, modeled after a Khmer temple in

A. The Eiffel Tower in 1889.

Cambodia, a French protectorate (image C); and examples of West African dwellings (image D). The Cairo street was the second-most popular tourist destination at the fair, after the Eiffel Tower. It contained twenty-five shops and restaurants,

and employed dozens of Egyptian servers, shopkeepers, and artisans who had been brought to Paris to add authenticity to the exhibit. Other people on display in the colonial pavilion included Senegalese villagers and a Vietnamese theater troupe.

Questions for Analysis

1. What vision of history and social progress is celebrated in this linkage between France's colonial holdings and the industrial power on display in the Eiffel Tower?

2. What might account for the popularity of the Cairo street exhibit among the public?

3. Why was it so important for the exposition to place people from European colonies on display for a French audience?

B. Reproduction of a Cairo street at the Paris World's Fair, 1889.

C. Pagoda of Angkor at the Paris World's Fair, 1889.

D. West African houses at the Paris World's Fair, 1889.

South Africa: The Boer War

In the late 1800s, competition between Dutch settlers in South Africa—known as Afrikaners or Boers ("farmers")—and the British led to a shooting war between Europeans. The Boers arrived in South Africa in the mid-seventeenth century and had long had a troubled relationship with their British neighbors in the colony. In the 1830s the Boers trekked inland from the Cape, setting up two republics away from British influence: the Transvaal and the Orange Free State. Gold reserves were found in the Transvaal in the 1880s, and Cecil Rhodes, the diamond magnate, tried to provoke war between Britain and the Boers in order to gain control of the Afrikaners' diamond mines. The war finally broke out in 1899, but the British were unprepared for the ferocity of Boer resistance. British columns were shot to pieces by Afrikaner forces who knew the territory, and the British towns of Ladysmith and Mafeking were besieged. Angered by these early failures, the British replaced their commanders and began to fight in deadly earnest, using the railroads built to service the diamond mines to bring in modern military hardware.

The Afrikaners responded by taking to the hills, fighting a costly guerrilla war that lasted another three years. The British tactics became more brutal as the campaign went on, setting up concentration camps—the first use of the term—where Afrikaner civilians were rounded up and forced to live in appalling conditions so that they would not be able to help the guerrillas. Nearly 20,000 civilians died in the camps due to disease and poor sanitation over the course of two years.

Black Africans, despised by both sides, also suffered the effects of famine and disease as the war destroyed valuable farmland.

Meanwhile, the concentration camps aroused opposition in Britain and internationally, and protesters campaigned against these violations of "European" rights, without saying anything about the fate of Africans in the conflict. In the end, the Afrikaners ceded control of their republics to a new British Union of South Africa that gave them a share of political power. In the aftermath of the war, both the British and the Afrikaners preserved their high standards of living by relying on cheap African labor and, eventually, a system of racial segregation known as apartheid.

U.S. Imperialism: The Spanish-American War of 1898

Imperialism also brought Spain and the United States to war in 1898. American imperialism in the nineteenth century was closely bound up with nation building, the conquest of new territories, and the defeat of the North American Indians (see Chapter 21). In the 1840s the United States provoked Mexico into war over Texas and California after unsuccessfully trying to purchase the territories. Mexico's defeat, and the treaty of Guadalupe Hidalgo that followed in 1848, gave the American Southwest to the United States, an enormous territorial gain that made the question of slavery more acute in the years before the American Civil War.

After You Read This Chapter

 Go to **INQUIZITIVE** to see what you've learned—and learn what you've missed—with personalized feedback along the way.

REVIEWING THE OBJECTIVES

- European imperialism in the nineteenth century differed from earlier phases of colonial expansion. How was it different, and which parts of the globe were singled out for special attention by European imperial powers?
- Colonial control took a variety of forms. What are the differences between direct rule, indirect rule, and informal colonialism?
- The subjugated peoples of European colonies faced a choice between resistance and accommodation, though these choices were rarely exclusive of one another. What examples of resistance to colonialism can you identify? Of accommodation?
- Imperialism also shaped cultural developments within Europe in the nineteenth century. How did imperialism change the lives of Europeans and their sense of their place in the world?
- Imperialism unleashed destabilizing competitive forces that, by the end of the nineteenth century, drove European colonial powers into conflict with one another. Where were the flashpoints of these conflicts?

The conflict with Spain followed a similar pattern. In the 1880s and 1890s, Spain was considerably weakened as an imperial power, and they faced rebellion in their colonies in the Caribbean and the Pacific. American economic interests had considerable investments in Cuba, and when an American battleship accidentally exploded while at anchor in Havana, advocates of empire and the press in general clamored for revenge. President William McKinley gave in to political necessity, in spite of his misgivings, and the United States declared war on Spain in 1898, determined to protect its economic interests in the Americas and the Pacific. The United States swiftly won.

In Spain, the Spanish-American War provoked an entire generation of writers, politicians, and intellectuals to national soul searching. The defeat undermined the Spanish monarchy, which fell in 1912. The ensuing political tensions resurfaced in the Spanish Civil War of the 1930s, an important episode in the origins of the Second World War.

In the United States, this "splendid little war" was followed by the annexation of Puerto Rico, the establishment of a protectorate over Cuba, and a short but brutal war against Philippine rebels who liked American colonialism no better than the Spanish variety. Elsewhere in the Americas, the United States intervened in a rebellion in Panama in 1903, quickly backing the rebels and helping establish a republic while building the Panama Canal on land leased from the new government. The Panama Canal opened in 1914, and like Britain's canal at Suez, it cemented U.S. dominance of the seas in the Western Hemisphere and the eastern Pacific. Later interventions in Hawaii and Santo Domingo gave further evidence of U.S. imperial power and committed the former colony to a broad role in its new and greater sphere of influence.

CONCLUSION

In the last quarter of the nineteenth century, the long-standing relationship between Western nations and the rest of the world entered a new stage. That stage was distinguished by the stunningly rapid extension of formal Western control, by new forms of economic exploitation, and by new patterns of social discipline and settlement. It was driven by the rising economic needs of the industrial West; by territorial conflict; and by nationalism, which by the late nineteenth century linked nationhood to empire. Among its immediate results was the creation of a self-consciously imperial culture in the West. At the same time, however, it plainly created unease and contributed powerfully to the sense of crisis that swept through the late-nineteenth-century West.

For all its force, this Western expansion never went unchallenged. Imperialism provoked resistance and required constantly changing strategies of rule. During the First World War, mobilizing the resources of empire would become crucial to victory. In the aftermath, reimposing the conditions of the late nineteenth century would become nearly impossible. And over the longer term, the political structures, economic developments, and racial ideologies established during this period would be contested throughout the twentieth century.

PEOPLE, IDEAS, AND EVENTS IN CONTEXT

- What was the **EAST INDIA COMPANY**? How did the British reorganize their rule in India after the **SEPOY MUTINY**?
- What did the French mean when they justified colonial expansion in the name of the **CIVILIZING MISSION**?
- How did the **OPIUM WARS** change the economic and political relationships between Europe and China?
- How did the **BERLIN CONFERENCE** of 1884 shape the subsequent colonization of Africa?
- What limits to the exercise of colonial power were revealed by the **BOXER REBELLION**, the failed **ITALIAN INVASION OF ETHIOPIA**, or the **RUSSO-JAPANESE WAR**?
- What expressions of anti-imperialism emerged from the **LONDON PAN-AFRICAN CONFERENCE**?
- How did the **BOER WAR** and the **FASHODA INCIDENT** contribute to a sense of crisis among European colonial powers?
- What effects did the **SPANISH-AMERICAN WAR** have on attitudes toward imperialism in the United States, itself a former European colony?

THINKING ABOUT CONNECTIONS

- Compare the consequences of late-nineteenth-century European colonial conquest with earlier episodes of imperial expansion such as the Roman Empire or early modernization in the Atlantic world. What was similar? What was different?
- What challenges were faced by colonial regimes such as France and Britain, which during the nineteenth century expanded their institutions of representative and elected government at home even as they subjugated the conquered peoples in their new colonies?
- The histories of colonial conquest in the nineteenth century helped to establish a network of political and cultural connections that shaped the history of the world in the twentieth century. What was the legacy of these connections forged during the period of decolonization?

Before
You
Read
This
Chapter

Modern Industry and Mass Politics, 1870–1914

CORE OBJECTIVES

- **UNDERSTAND** what made the second industrial revolution and its consequences different from the first industrial revolution.

- **DEFINE** *mass politics* and **EXPLAIN** how the expansion of voting rights in European nations led to the development of organized political parties that sought the support of the working classes.

- **UNDERSTAND** the arguments both for and against women's suffrage during this period.

- **IDENTIFY** the ways that European liberalism and conservatism evolved with the advent of mass politics and intensifying industrial development.

- **EXPLAIN** the contributions of scientists and other cultural figures who came to prominence in the final decades of the nineteenth century, and their views on human nature, modern society, and the natural world.

"We are on the extreme promontory of ages!" decreed the Italian poet and literary editor F. T. Marinetti in 1909. In a bombastic manifesto—a self-described "inflammatory declaration" printed on the front page of a Paris newspaper—Marinetti introduced Europe to an aggressive art movement called *futurism*. Rebelling against what he considered the tired and impotent conservatism of Italian culture, Marinetti called for a radical renewal of civilization through "courage, audacity, and revolt." Enamored with the raw power of modern machinery, with the dynamic bustle of urban life, he trumpeted "a new form of beauty, the beauty of speed." Most notably, Marinetti celebrated the heroic violence of warfare and disparaged the moral and cultural traditions that formed the bedrock of nineteenth-century liberalism.

Few Europeans embraced the modern era with the unflinching abandon of the futurists, but many would have agreed with Marinetti in his claim that modern life was characterized above all by flux, movement, and an accelerating rate of change. In the last decades of the nineteenth century, a second

619

industrial revolution produced new techniques for manufacturing and new sources of power, including electricity and petroleum-based fuels. These developments transformed the infrastructure of European towns and cities, and immediately people felt the effects of these changes in their daily lives.

At the same time, European nation-states faced new political realities as their electorates expanded and new blocs of voters began participating directly in shaping both parliamentary bodies and their legislative agendas. New mass-based political parties brought new demands to the political arena, and national governments struggled to maintain order and legitimacy in the face of these challenges. Socialists mobilized growing numbers of industrial workers, while suffragists demanded the franchise for women. The ability of traditional elites to control political life was sorely tested, even in nations that continued to be governed by hereditary monarchs.

In the arts and sciences, new theories challenged older notions of nature, society, truth, and beauty. Since the eighteenth century at least, science had been a frequent ally of political liberalism, as both liberals and scientists shared a common faith in human reason and an openness to rational inquiry into the laws of society and nature. In the late nineteenth century, however, this common agenda was strained by scientific investigations in new fields such as biology and psychology that challenged liberal assumptions about human nature. Meanwhile, in the arts, a new generation of artists and writers embraced innovation and rejected the established conventions in painting, sculpture, poetry, and literature.

A period of intense experimentation in the arts followed, leading artists and writers to develop radically new forms of expression.

The nineteenth century, then, ended in a burst of energy as many Europeans embraced a vision of their society racing headlong into what they hoped was a more promising and better future. Behind this self-confidence, however, lay significant uncertainty about the eventual destination. What aspects of the European past would continue to be relevant in the modern age? In politics and social life and in the culture as a whole, such questions produced more conflict than consensus.

NEW TECHNOLOGIES AND GLOBAL TRANSFORMATIONS

In the last third of the nineteenth century, new technologies transformed the face of manufacturing in Europe, leading to new levels of economic growth and complex realignments among industry, labor, and national governments. This second industrial revolution relied on innovation in three key areas: steel, electricity, and chemicals.

Steel had long been prized as a construction material. But until the mid-nineteenth century, producing steel cheaply and in large quantities was impossible. Between the 1850s and 1870s, different processes for mass-producing alloy steel revolutionized the metallurgical industry. Britain's shipbuilders switched to steel construction and thus kept their lead in the industry. Germany and

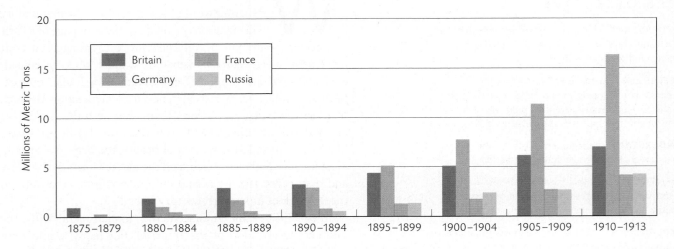

FIGURE 23.1 ANNUAL OUTPUT OF STEEL (IN MILLIONS OF METRIC TONS).
Source: Carlo Cipolla, *The Fontana Economic History of Europe*, vol. 3(2) (London: 1976), p. 775.

THE SECOND INDUSTRIAL REVOLUTION. A German electrical engineering works illustrates the scale of production during the second industrial revolution. ▪ *What changes in business practices and labor management made factories of this size possible?*

America dominated the rest of the steel industry. By 1901 Germany was producing almost half again as much steel as Britain, allowing Germany to build a massive national and industrial infrastructure.

Electricity was made available for commercial and domestic use in the 1880s, after the development of alternators and transformers capable of producing high-voltage alternating current. By century's end, large power stations, which often used cheap water power, could send electric current over vast distances. In 1879 Thomas Edison and his associates invented the light bulb and changed electricity into light. The demand for electricity skyrocketed, and soon entire metropolitan areas were electrified. Electrification powered subways, tramways, and, eventually, long-distance railroads; it made possible new techniques in the chemical and metallurgical industries, and dramatically altered living habits in ordinary households.

Advances in the chemical industry transformed the manufacture of such consumer goods as paper, soaps, textiles, and fertilizer. Britain and particularly Germany became leaders in the field. Heightened concerns for household hygiene and new techniques in mass marketing enabled the British entrepreneur Harold Lever to market his soaps and cleansers around the world. German production, on the other hand, focused on industrial uses, such as developing synthetic dyes and methods for refining petroleum, and came to control roughly 90 percent of the world's chemical market.

Other innovations contributed to the second industrial revolution. The growing demand for efficient power spurred the invention of the liquid-fuel internal combustion engine. By 1914 most navies had converted from coal to oil, as had domestic steamship companies. The new engines' dependence on crude petroleum and distilled gasoline at

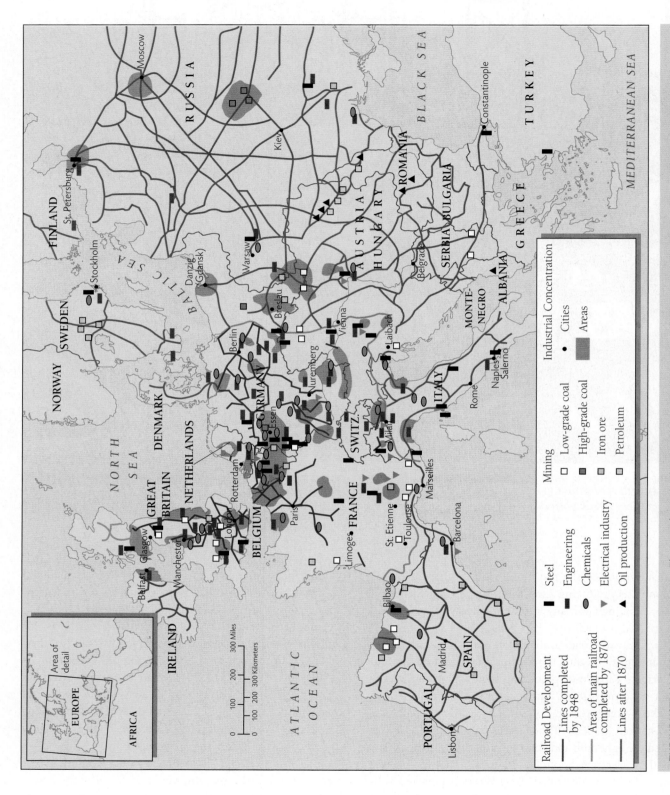

THE INDUSTRIAL REGIONS OF EUROPE. This map shows the distribution of mineral resources, rail lines, and industrial activity. ■ *What nations enjoyed advantages in the development of industry and why?* ■ *What resources were most important for industrial growth in the second half of the nineteenth century?* ■ *What resources in England became dominant as a result of industrialization?*

first threatened their general application, but the discovery of oil fields in Russia, Borneo, Persia, and Texas around 1900 allayed fears. Protecting these oil reserves thus became a vital state obligation. The adoption of oil-powered machinery had another important consequence: industrialists who had previously depended on nearby rivers or coal mines for power were free to take their enterprises to regions bereft of natural resources. The potential for worldwide industrialization was in place.

Changes in Scope and Scale

These technological changes were part of a much larger process—impressive increases in the scope and scale of industry. At the end of the nineteenth century, size mattered. The rise of heavy industry and mass marketing had factories and cities growing hand in hand, while advances in media and mobility spurred the creation of national mass cultures. For the first time, ordinary people followed the news on national and global levels. They watched as European powers divided the globe, enlarging their empires with prodigious feats of engineering mastery; railroads, dams, canals, and harbors grew to monumental proportions. Such projects embodied the ideals of modern European industry. They also generated enormous income for builders, investors, bankers, entrepreneurs, and, of course, makers of steel and concrete. Canals in central Europe, railroads in the Andes, and telegraph cables spanning the ocean floors: these "tentacles of empire," as one historian dubs them, stretched across the globe.

Industrialization was also accompanied by broader social changes. The population grew constantly, particularly in central and eastern Europe. Russia's population increased by nearly a quarter and Germany's by half in the space of a generation. Britain's population, too, grew by nearly one-third between 1881 and 1911. Thanks to improvements in both crop yields and shipping, food shortages declined, which rendered entire populations less susceptible to illness and high infant mortality. Advances in medicine, nutrition, and personal hygiene diminished the prevalence of dangerous diseases such as cholera and typhus, and improved conditions in housing and public sanitation helped relieve the pressure on Europe's growing cities.

Credit and Consumerism

Changes in scope and scale not only transformed production but also altered consumption. The era in which economists would worry about consumer confidence and experts could systematically track the public's buying habits did not begin until the middle of the twentieth century, but late-nineteenth-century developments pointed toward that horizon. Department stores offering both practical and luxury goods to the middle class were one mark of the times—of urbanization, economic expansion, and the new importance attached to merchandising. Advertising took off as well. Even more significant, by the 1880s new stores sought to attract working-class people by introducing the all-important innovation of credit payment. In earlier times, working-class families pawned watches, mattresses, or furniture to borrow money; now they began to buy on credit, a change that would eventually have seismic effects on both households and national economies.

These new, late-nineteenth-century patterns of consumption, however, were largely urban. In the countryside, peasants continued to save money under mattresses and to make, launder, and mend their own clothes and linens. Only slowly did retailers whittle away at these traditional habits. Mass consumption remained difficult to imagine in what was still a deeply stratified society.

The Rise of the Corporation

Economic growth and the demands of mass consumption spurred the reorganization, consolidation, and regulation of capitalist institutions. Businesses had sold shares to investors in joint-stock companies since the sixteenth century, but it was during the late nineteenth century that the modern corporation came into its own. To provide protection for investors, most European countries enacted or improved their limited-liability laws, which ensured that stockholders could lose only the value of their shares in the event of bankruptcy. Prior to such laws, investors could be held liable for company debts. Insured in this way, many thousands of middle-class men and women now considered corporate investment a promising venture. After 1870, stock markets ceased to be primarily a clearinghouse for state paper and railroad bonds, and instead attracted new commercial and industrial ventures.

Limited liability was one part of a larger trend of incorporation. Whereas most firms had been small or middle size, companies now incorporated to attain the necessary size for survival. In doing so, they tended to shift control from company founders and local directors to distant bankers and financiers whose concern for the bottom line encouraged a more impersonal style of financial management.

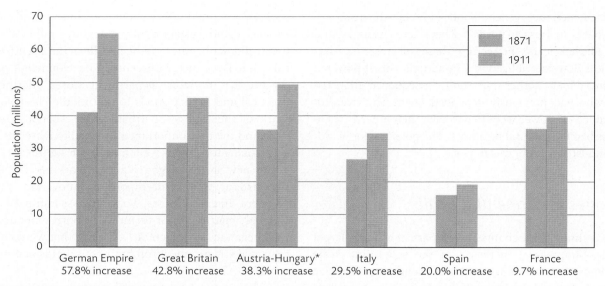

FIGURE 23.2 POPULATION GROWTH IN MAJOR STATES BETWEEN 1871 AND 1911 (POPULATION IN MILLIONS).
*Not including Bosnia-Herzegovina.
Source: Colin Dyer, *Population and Society in Twentieth-Century France* (New York: 1978), p. 5.

Equally important, the second industrial revolution created a strong demand for technical expertise, which undercut traditional forms of family management. University degrees in engineering and chemistry became more valuable than on-the-job apprenticeships. The emergence of a white-collar class (middle-level salaried managers who were neither owners nor laborers) marked a significant change in work life and for society's evolving class structure.

The drive toward larger business enterprises was encouraged by a belief that consolidation protected society against the hazards of boom-and-bust economic fluctuations. Some industries combined vertically, attempting to control every step of production, from the acquisition of raw materials to the distribution of finished products. A second form of corporate self-protection was horizontal alignment. Organizing into cartels, companies in the same industry would band together to fix prices and control competition, if not eliminate it outright. Coal, oil, and steel companies were especially suited to the organization of cartels, since only a few major players could afford the huge expense of building, equipping, and running mines, refineries, and foundries. Cartels were particularly strong in Germany and America but less so in Britain, where dedication to free-trade policies made price fixing more difficult, and in France, where family firms and laborers alike opposed cartels and where there was also less heavy industry.

Though governments sometimes tried to stem the burgeoning power of cartels, the dominant trend of this period was increased cooperation between governments and industry. Contrary to the laissez-faire mentality of early capitalism, corporations developed close relationships with the states in the West—most noticeably in colonial industrial projects, such as the construction of railroads, harbors, and seafaring steamships. These efforts were so costly, or so unprofitable, that private enterprise would not have undertaken them alone. But because they served larger political and strategic interests, governments funded them willingly.

Global Economics

From the 1870s on, the rapid spread of industrialization heightened competition among nations. The search for markets, goods, and influence fueled much of the imperial expansion and, consequently, often put countries at odds with each other. Trade barriers arose again to protect home markets. All nations except Britain raised tariffs, arguing that the needs of the nation-state trumped laissez-faire doctrine. Yet changes in international economics fueled the continuing growth of an interlocking, worldwide system of manufacturing, trade, and finance. For example, the near universal adoption of the gold standard in currency exchange greatly facilitated world trade. Pegging the value of currencies, particularly Britain's powerful pound sterling, against the value of gold meant that currencies could be readily exchanged. The common standard also allowed nations to use a third country to mediate trade and exchange to mitigate trade imbalances—a common problem for the industrializing West. Almost all European countries, dependent on vast supplies of raw materials to sustain their rate of industrial production, imported more than they exported. To avoid the mounting deficits that this practice would otherwise incur, European economies relied on "invisible" exports: shipping, insurance, and banking services. The extent of Britain's exports in these areas was far greater than that of any other country. London was the money market of the world, to which would-be borrowers looked for assistance before turning elsewhere.

During this period the relationship between European manufacturing nations and the overseas sources of their materials—whether colonies or not—was transformed, as detailed in the last chapter. Those changes, in turn, reshaped economies and cultures on both sides of the imperial divide. Europeans came to expect certain foods on their tables; whole regions of Africa, Latin America, and Asia geared toward producing for the European market. This international push toward mass manufacturing and commodity production necessarily involved changes in deep-seated patterns in consumption and in production. It altered the landscape and habits of India as well as those of Britain. It brought new rhythms of life to women working in clothing factories in Germany, to porters carrying supplies to build railways in Senegal, to workers dredging the harbor of Dakar.

LABOR POLITICS, MASS MOVEMENTS

The rapid expansion of late-nineteenth-century industry brought a parallel growth in the size, cohesion, and activism of Europe's working classes. The men and women who worked as wage laborers resented corporate power—resentment fostered not only by the exploitation and inequalities they experienced on the job but also by living "a life apart" in Europe's expanding cities (see Chapter 19). Corporations had devised new methods of protecting and promoting their interests, and workers did the same. Labor unions, which were traditionally limited to skilled male workers in small-scale enterprises, grew during the late nineteenth century into mass, centralized, nationwide organizations. This "new unionism" emphasized organization across entire industries and, for the first time, brought unskilled workers into the ranks, increasing their power to negotiate wages and job conditions. More important, though, the creation of national

unions provided a framework for a new type of political movement: the socialist mass party.

Why did socialism find increased support in Europe after 1870? Changing national political structures provide part of the answer. Parliamentary constitutional governments opened the political process to new participants, including socialists. Now part of the legislative process, socialists in national assemblies led efforts to expand voting rights in the 1860s and 1870s. Their success created new constituencies of working-class men. At the same time, traditional struggles between labor and management moved up to the national level; governments aligned with business interests, and legislators countered working-class agitation with antilabor and antisocialist laws. To radical leaders, the organization of national mass political movements seemed the only effective way to counter industrialists' political strength. Thus, during this period, socialist movements abandoned their earlier revolutionary traditions (exemplified by the romantic image of barricaded streets) in favor of legal, public competition within Europe's parliamentary systems.

The Spread of Socialist Parties— and Alternatives

The emergence of labor movements in Europe owed as much to ideas as to social changes. The most influential radical thinker was Karl Marx, whose early career was discussed in Chapter 20. Since the 1840s, Marx and his collaborator Friedrich Engels had been intellectuals and activists, participating in the organization of fledgling socialist movements. Marx's three-volume study, *Capital*, attacked capitalism using the tools of economic analysis, allowing Marx to claim a scientific validity for his work. Marx's work claimed to offer a systematic analysis of how capitalism forced workers to exchange their labor for subsistence wages while enabling their employers to amass both wealth and power. Followers of Marx called for workers everywhere to ally with one another to create an independent political force, and few other groups pushed so strongly to secure civil liberties, expand conceptions of citizenship, or build a welfare state. Marxists also made powerful claims for gender equality, though in practice women's suffrage took a backseat to class politics.

Not all working-class movements were Marxist, however. Differences among various left-wing groups remained strong, and the most divisive issues were the role of violence and whether socialists should cooperate with liberal governments—and if so, to what end. Some "gradualists" were willing to work with liberals for piecemeal reform, while anarchists and syndicalists rejected parliamentary politics altogether. When European labor leaders met in 1864 at the first meeting of the International Working Men's Association, Marx argued strongly in favor of political mass movements that would prepare the working classes for revolution. He was strongly opposed by the anarchist Mikhail Bakunin, who rejected any form of state or party organization, and called instead for terror and violence to destabilize society.

Between 1875 and 1905, Marxist socialists founded political parties in Germany, Belgium, France, Austria, and Russia. These parties were disciplined workers' organizations that aimed to seize control of the state to make revolutionary changes in the social order. The most successful was the German Social Democratic Party (SPD). Initially intending to work for political change within the parliamentary political system, the SPD became more radical in the face of Bismarck's oppressive antisocialist laws. By the outbreak of the First World War, the German Social Democrats were the largest, best-organized workers' party in the world. Rapid and extensive industrialization, a large urban working class, and a national government hostile to organized labor all made German workers particularly receptive to the goals and ideals of social democracy.

In Britain—the world's first and most industrialized economy—the socialist presence was much smaller and more moderate. Why? The answer lies in the fact that much of the socialist agenda was advanced by radical liberals in Britain, which forestalled the growth of an independent socialist party. Even when a separate Labour party was formed in 1901 it remained moderate, committed to reforming capitalism with measures such as support for public housing or welfare benefits, rather than a complete overhaul of the economy. For the Labour party, and for Britain's many trade unions, Parliament remained a legitimate vehicle for achieving social change, limiting the appeal of revolutionary Marxism.

Militant workers seeking to organize themselves for political action found alternatives to Marxism in the ideas of anarchists and syndicalists. Anarchists were opposed to centrally organized economies and to the very existence of the state. They aimed to establish small-scale, localized, and self-sufficient democratic communities that could guarantee a maximum of individual sovereignty. Renouncing any form of modern mass organization, the anarchists fell back on the tradition of conspiratorial violence, which Marx had denounced. Anarchists assassinated Tsar Alexander II in

SOCIALIST PARTY PAMPHLET, c. 1895. Socialism emerged as a powerful political force throughout Europe in the late nineteenth century, although appearing in different forms depending on the region. This German pamphlet quotes from Marx's *Communist Manifesto* of 1848, calling for workers of the world to unite under the banners of equality and brotherhood. ▪ *Were nationalism and socialism compatible with one another?*

1881 and five other heads of state in the following years, believing that such "exemplary terror" would spark a popular revolt. Syndicalists, on the other hand, embraced a strategy of strikes and sabotage by workers. Their hope was that a general strike of all workers would bring down the capitalist state and replace it with workers' syndicates or trade associations. Anarchism's opposition to any form of organization kept it from making substantial gains as a movement. Likewise, the syndicalists' refusal to participate in politics limited their ability to command wide influence.

By 1895, popular socialist movements had made impressive gains in Europe: seven socialist parties had captured between a quarter and third of the votes in their countries. But just as socialists gained a permanent foothold in national politics, they were also straining under limitations and internal conflicts. Working-class movements, in fact, had never gained full worker support. Some workers remained loyal to older liberal traditions or to religious parties, and many others were excluded from socialist politics by its narrow definition of who constituted the working class—male industrial workers.

Furthermore, some committed socialists began to question Marx's core assumptions about the inevitability of workers' impoverishment and the collapse of the capitalist order. A German group of so-called revisionists, led by Eduard Bernstein, challenged Marxist doctrine and called for a shift to moderate and gradual reform, accomplished through electoral politics. Radical supporters of direct action were incensed at Bernstein's betrayal of Marxist theory of revolution, because they feared that the official reforms that favored workers might make the working class more accepting of the status quo. The radicals within the labor movement called for mass strikes, hoping to ignite a widespread proletarian revolution.

Conflicts over strategy peaked just before the First World War. On the eve of the war, governments discreetly consulted with labor leaders about workers' willingness to enlist and fight. Having built impressive organizational and political strength since the 1870s, working-class parties now affected the ability of nation-states to wage war. Much to the disappointment of socialist leaders, however, European laborers—many of whom had voted for socialist candidates in previous elections—nevertheless donned the uniforms of their respective nations and marched off to war in 1914, proving that national identities and class identities were not necessarily incompatible with one another.

DEMANDING EQUALITY: SUFFRAGE AND THE WOMEN'S MOVEMENT

After the 1860s, working-class activism and liberal constitutionalism expanded male suffrage rights across Europe, and by 1884 most men could vote in Germany, France, and Britain. But nowhere could women vote. Excluded from parliamentary politics, women pressed their interests through independent organizations and direct action. This new women's movement won some crucial legal reforms, as British, French, and German women gained access to education and won the rights to control their own property and to initiate divorce. The next step was the vote.

To the suffragists, the enfranchisement of women meant not merely political progress but economic, spiritual,

and moral advancement as well. Throughout western Europe, middle-class women founded clubs, published journals, organized petitions, and sponsored assemblies to press for the vote. To the left of middle-class movements were movements of feminist socialists, women such as Clara Zetkin and Lily Braun who believed that only a socialist revolution would free women from economic as well as political exploitation. Meanwhile, the French celebrity journalist and novelist Gyp (the pseudonym of Sibylle de Riguetti de Mirabeau) carved out a name for herself on the nationalist and anti-Semitic right with her acerbic commentary on current events.

In Britain, campaigns for women's suffrage exploded in violence. Millicent Fawcett brought together sixteen different organizations into the National Union of Women's Suffrage Societies in 1897, a group that was committed to peaceful reform. When the major political parties rejected their proposals, however, many members became exasperated and in 1903 Emmeline Pankhurst founded a new group, the Women's Social and Political Union (WSPU), which adopted militant tactics and civil disobedience. WSPU women chained themselves to the visitors' gallery in Parliament, slashed paintings in museums, burned politicians' houses and smashed department-store windows. The government countered with repression. When arrested women went on hunger strikes in prisons, they were tied down and force-fed through tubes inserted in their throats. The intensity of the suffragists' moral claims was embodied by the 1913 martyrdom of Emily Wilding Davison, who, wearing a "Votes for Women" sash, threw herself in front of the king's horse on Derby day and was trampled to death.

Redefining Womanhood

The campaign for women's suffrage was perhaps the most visible and inflammatory aspect of a larger cultural shift in which traditional Victorian gender roles were redefined. In the last third of the nineteenth century, economic, political, and social changes were undermining the view that men and women should occupy distinctly different spheres. Women became increasingly visible in the workforce as growing numbers of them took up a greater variety of jobs. Many working-class women joined the new factories and workshops in an effort to stave off their families' poverty, in spite of many working-class men's insistence that stable families required women at home. In addition, the expansion of government as well as business, health care, and education brought middle-class women to the workforce as social workers, clerks, nurses, and teachers. A shortage of

CHANGES IN WHITE-COLLAR WORK. Clerical work was primarily male until the end of the nineteenth century, when cadres of women workers and the emergence of new industries and bureaucracies transformed employment. ▪ *How might these changing patterns of employment have affected family life or attitudes toward marriage and child-rearing?*

male workers and a need to fill so many new jobs as cheaply as possible made women a logical choice. Thus women, who had campaigned vigorously for access to education, began to see doors opening to them. These changes in women's employment began to deflate the myth of female domesticity.

Women became more active in politics—an area previously considered off-limits. This is not to say that female political activity was unprecedented; reform movements of the early nineteenth century depended on women and raised women's standing in public. First with charity work in religious associations and later with hundreds of secular associations, women throughout Europe directed their energies toward poor relief, prison reform, Sunday school, temperance, ending slavery and prostitution, and expanding educational opportunities for women. Reform groups brought women together outside the home, encouraging them to speak their minds as freethinking equals and to pursue political goals—a right denied them as individual females.

These changes in women's roles were paralleled by the emergence of a new social type, dubbed the "new woman." A new woman demanded education and a job; she refused to be escorted by chaperones when she went out; she rejected the restrictive corsets of mid-century fashion. In other words, she claimed the right to a physically and intellectually active life and refused to conform to the norms that defined nineteenth-century womanhood. The new woman was an image—in part the creation of artists and journalists, who filled newspapers, magazines, and advertising billboards with pictures of women riding bicycles, smoking cigarettes, and enjoying other emblems of consumerism. Very few women actually fit this image: among other things, most were too poor. Still, middle- and working-class women demanded more social freedom and redefined gender norms in the process. For some onlookers, women's newfound independence amounted to shirking domestic responsibilities, and they attacked women who defied convention as ugly "half-men," unfit and unable to marry. For supporters, though, these new women symbolized a welcome era of social emancipation.

Opposition to these changes was intense, sometimes violent, and not exclusively male. Men scorned the women who threatened their elite preserves in universities, clubs, and public offices; but a wide array of female antisuffragists also denounced the movement. Conservatives such as Mrs. Humphrey Ward maintained that bringing women into the political arena would sap the virility of the British Empire. Christian commentators criticized suffragists for bringing moral decay through selfish individualism. Still others believed feminism would dissolve the family, a theme that fed into a larger discussion on the decline of the West amid a growing sense of cultural crisis. Indeed, the struggle for women's rights provided a flashpoint for an array of European anxieties over labor, politics, gender, and biology—all of which suggested that an orderly political consensus, so ardently desired by middle-class society, was slipping from reach.

LIBERALISM AND ITS DISCONTENTS: NATIONAL POLITICS AT THE TURN OF THE CENTURY

Having championed doctrines of individual rights throughout the nineteenth century, middle-class liberals found themselves on the defensive after 1870. Previously, political power had rested on a balance between middle-class interests and traditional elites. The landed aristocracy shared power with industrial magnates; monarchical rule coexisted with constitutional freedoms. During the late nineteenth century, the rise of mass politics upset this balance. An expanding franchise and rising expectations brought newcomers to the political stage. As we have seen, trade unions, socialists, and feminists all challenged Europe's governing classes by demanding that political participation be open to all. Governments responded, in turn, with a mix of conciliatory and repressive measures. As the twentieth century approached, political struggles became increasingly fierce, and by the First World War, the foundation of traditional parliamentary politics was crumbling. For both the left and the right, for both insiders and outsiders, negotiating this unfamiliar terrain required the creation of new and distinctly modern forms of mass politics.

France: The Third Republic and the Paris Commune

The Franco-Prussian War of 1870 resulted in a bruising defeat for France. The Second Empire collapsed and a republic, France's third, was declared in its wake. Profound divisions among political leaders and among social classes meant that the early years of the republic were extremely volatile.

Even before its first year was complete, the republic faced a revolutionary challenge from militants in Paris. During the war of 1870, the city had appointed its own municipal government, the Commune, which broke with the politicians who negotiated the armistice with Germany, and refused to surrender to the German troops who besieged the city. In March 1871 the national government sent troops into Paris to disarm the Commune and its working-class supporters. The Communards responded by declaring a revolutionary socialist movement in the city, and the struggle quickly took on aspects of a violent class war. After holding out for over fifty days, the Commune was finally defeated in a week of bloody street fighting in which over 20,000 Parisians were killed and much of the city burned. Thousands of Commune supporters were deported to penal colonies in the South Pacific. Paris's working-class populations did not forget the repression of the Commune, and socialist leaders such as Karl Marx argued that it showed the futility of the older insurrectionary tradition. Instead, Marx argued in favor of organizing

mass-based democratic movements founded on the principle of working-class unity.

The Dreyfus Affair and Anti-Semitism as Politics

On the other side of the French political spectrum, new forms of radical right-wing politics emerged that would foreshadow developments elsewhere. As the age-old foundations of conservative politics, the Catholic Church and the landed nobility, weakened, more radical right-wing politics took shape. Stung by the defeat of 1870 and critical of the republic and its premises, the new right was nationalist, antiparliamentary, and antiliberal (in the sense of commitment to individual liberties). During the first half of the nineteenth century, nationalism had been associated with the left (see Chapter 20). Now it was more often invoked by the right and linked to xenophobia (fear of foreigners) in general and anti-Semitism in particular.

The power of popular anti-Semitism in France was made clear by a public controversy that erupted in the 1890s known as the Dreyfus Affair. In 1894 a group of monarchist officers in the army accused Alfred Dreyfus, a Jewish captain on the general staff, of selling military secrets to Germany. Dreyfus was convicted and deported for life to Devil's Island, a ghastly South American prison colony in French Guiana. Two years later, an intelligence officer named Georges Picquart discovered that the documents used to convict Dreyfus were forgeries. The War Department refused to grant Dreyfus a new trial, and the case became an enormous public scandal, fanned on both sides by the involvement of prominent intellectual figures. Republicans, some socialists, liberals, and intellectuals such as the writer Émile Zola backed Dreyfus, claiming that the case was about individual rights and the legitimacy of the republic and its laws. Nationalists, prominent Catholics, and other socialists who believed that the case was a distraction from economic issues, opposed Dreyfus and refused to question the military's judgment. One Catholic newspaper insisted that the question was not whether Dreyfus was guilty or innocent but whether Jews and unbelievers were not the "secret masters of France."

The anti-Semitism of the anti-Dreyfus camp was a combination of three strands of anti-Jewish thinking in Europe: (1) long-standing currents of anti-Semitism within Christianity, which damned the Jewish people as Christ-killers; (2) economic anti-Semitism, which insisted that a wealthy banking family, the Rothschilds, were representative of all Jews; and (3) late-nineteenth-century racial thinking,

Anti-Semitism in Late-Nineteenth-Century France

Over the course of the nineteenth century, European (though not Russian) Jewish people slowly gained more legal and political rights: access to occupations from which they had been barred, the right to vote and hold political office, the right to marry non-Jews, and so on. France, the land of the Revolution of 1789, appeared to many European Jews as the beacon of liberty. But in the late nineteenth century, France also proved the birthplace of new forms of anti-Semitism. This excerpt from Édouard Drumont's best-selling Jewish France *(1885) illustrates some themes of that ideology: the effort to displace economic grievances; conservative hatred of the republic and parliamentary government; the legacy of 1789; and conservative nationalism.*

he only one who has benefitted from the Revolution [of 1789] is the Jew. Everything comes from the Jew; everything returns to the Jew.

We have here a veritable conquest, an entire nation returned to serfdom by a minute but cohesive minority, just as the Saxons were forced into serfdom by William the Conqueror's 60,000 Normans.

The methods are different, the result is the same. One can recognize all the characteristics of a conquest: an entire population working for another population, which appropriates, through a vast system of financial exploitation, all of the profits of the other. Immense Jewish fortunes, castles, Jewish townhouses, are not the fruit of any actual labor, of any production: they are the booty taken from an enslaved race by a dominant race.

It is certain, for example, that the Rothschild family, whose French branch alone possesses a declared fortune of three billion [francs], did not have that money when it arrived in France; it has invented nothing, it has discovered no mine, it has tilled no ground. It has therefore appropriated these three billion francs from the French without giving them anything in exchange. . . .

Thanks to the Jews' cunning exploitation of the principles of '89, France was collapsing into dissolution. Jews had monopolized all of the public wealth, had invaded everything, except the army. The representatives of the old [French] families, whether noble or bourgeois . . . gave themselves up to pleasure, and were corrupted by the Jewish prostitutes they had taken as mistresses or were ruined by the horse-sellers and money-lenders, also Jews, who aided the prostitutes. . . .

The *fatherland*, in the sense that we attach to that word, has no meaning for the Semite. The Jew . . . is characterized by an *inexorable universalism*.

I can see no reason for reproaching the Jews for thinking this way. What does the word "Fatherland" mean? Land of the fathers. One's feelings for the Fatherland are engraved in one's heart in the same way that a name carved in a tree is driven deeper into the bark with each passing year, so that the tree and the name eventually become one. You can't become a patriot through improvisation; you are a patriot in your blood, in your marrow.

Can the Semite, a perpetual nomad, ever experience such enduring impressions? . . .

Source: Édouard Drumont, *La France Juive. Essai d'histoire contemporaine* (Paris: 1885), excerpt trans. Cat Nilan, 1997.

Questions for Analysis

1. What historical changes does Drumont blame on the Jews over the course of the nineteenth century? Why?

2. Drumont tries to elicit several anxieties. What does he think his readers should fear, and why? What does he mean by "inexorable universalism"?

3. In what ways was anti-Semitism an ideology?

---

which opposed a so-called Aryan (Indo-European) race to an inferior Semitic race. Anti-Dreyfus propagandists whipped these ideas into a potent form of propaganda in anti-Semitic newspapers such as Édouard Drumont's *La Libre Parole* (Free Speech), a French daily that claimed a circulation of 200,000 during the height of the Dreyfus affair.

In 1899 Dreyfus was pardoned and freed by executive order. In 1906 the French Supreme Court declared him free of all guilt, and he was reinstated in the army as a major. A major consequence of the controversy was passage of laws between 1901 and 1905 that separated church and state in France. Convinced that the church and the army were hostile to the republic, the republican legislature passed new laws that prohibited any religious orders in France that were not authorized by the state and forbade clerics to teach in public schools.

The French Republic withstood the attacks of radical anti-Semites in the first decade of the twentieth century, but the same right-wing and nationalist forces made their voices known elsewhere in Europe. The mayor of Vienna in 1897 was elected on an anti-Semitic platform. The Russian secret police forged and published a book called *The Protocols of the Learned Elders of Zion* (1903 and 1905), which imagined a Jewish plot to dominate the world and held Jews responsible for the French Revolution and the dislocating effects of industrialization. Political anti-Semitism remained popular among a substantial number of Europeans who accepted its insistence that social and political problems could be understood in racial terms.

Zionism

Among the many people who watched with alarm as the Dreyfus Affair unfolded was Theodor Herzl (1860–1904), a Hungarian-born journalist working in Paris. The rise of virulent anti-Semitism in the land of the French Revolution troubled Herzl deeply. He considered the Dreyfus Affair "only the dramatic expression of a much more fundamental malaise." Despite Jewish emancipation, or the granting of civil rights, Herzl came to believe that Jewish people might never be assimilated into Western culture and that staking the Jewish community's hopes on acceptance and tolerance was dangerous folly. Herzl endorsed the different strategy of Zionism, the building of a separate Jewish homeland outside of Europe (though not necessarily in Palestine). A small movement of Jewish settlers, mainly refugees from Russia, had already begun to establish settlements outside of Europe. Herzl was not the first to voice these goals, but he was the most effective advocate of political Zionism. He argued that Zionism should be recognized as a modern nationalist movement, capable of negotiating with other states. Although Herzl's writings met with much skepticism, they received an enthusiastic reception among Jews who lived in areas of eastern Europe where anti-Semitism was especially violent. During the turmoil of the First World War, specific wartime needs prompted the British to become involved in the issue, embroiling Zionism in international diplomacy (see Chapter 24).

Germany's Search for Imperial Unity

Through deft foreign policy, three short wars, and a groundswell of national sentiment, Otto von Bismarck united Germany under the banner of Prussian conservatism during the years 1864 to 1871. In constructing a federal political system, Bismarck sought to create the centralizing institutions of a modern nation-state while safeguarding the privileges of Germany's traditional elites, including a dominant role for Prussia. Bismarck's constitution gave the emperor full control of foreign and military affairs, and the power of the Reichstag's (parliament's) lower house was checked by a conservative upper house whose members were appointed by the emperor.

Under a government that was neither genuinely federal nor democratic, building a nation with a sense of common purpose was no easy task. Three fault lines in Germany's political landscape especially threatened to crack the national framework: the divide between Catholics and Protestants; the growing Social Democratic Party; and the potentially contentious economic interests of agriculture and industry.

Between 1871 and 1878, Bismarck governed principally with liberal factions interested in promoting free trade and economic growth. To strengthen ties with these liberal coalitions, Bismarck unleashed an anti-Catholic campaign in Prussia. In what is known as the *Kulturkampf*, or "cultural struggle," Bismarck passed laws that imprisoned priests for political sermons, banned Jesuits from Prussia, and curbed the church's control over education and marriage. The campaign backfired, however, and public sympathy for the persecuted clergy helped the Catholic Center party win fully one-quarter of the seats in the Reichstag in 1874.

Bismarck responded by fashioning a new coalition that would bring socially conservative Catholics into an alliance with agricultural and industrial interests. This alliance passed protectionist legislation (tariffs on grain, iron, and steel) that satisfied German producers but alienated free-trade liberals and the social democrats whose constituents faced higher prices as a result of the tariffs. Bismarck responded by declaring that the Social Democrats were enemies of the empire, and he passed laws that prevented them from meeting or distributing their literature. The Social Democrats became a clandestine party, and many of its members increasingly viewed socialism as the sole answer to their political persecution.

To woo the working classes away from their militant leadership, Bismarck offered a package of social reforms: old-age pensions, health and accident insurance, factory inspections, limited working hours for women and children, and a maximum workday for men. By 1890 Germany's social legislation was unrivaled in Europe and it became a prototype for the majority of Western nations in the decades to come. The reforms failed to win workers' loyalty, however, and by 1912 the Social Democrats were the largest bloc in the Reichstag. The standoff between the German government and its increasingly well-organized

Competing Viewpoints

Toward the First World War: Diplomacy in the Summer of 1914

The assassination of Franz Ferdinand in Sarajevo on June 28, 1914, set off an increasingly desperate round of diplomatic negotiations. As the following exchanges show, diplomats and political leaders on both sides swung from trying to provoke war to attempting to avert or, at least, contain it. A week after his nephew, the heir to the throne, was shot, Franz Joseph set out his interpretation of the long-standing conflict with Serbia and its larger implications—reprinted here.

The second selection comes from an account of a meeting of the Council of Ministers of the Austro-Hungarian Empire on July 7, 1914. The ministers disagreed sharply about diplomatic strategies and about how crucial decisions should be made.

British foreign secretary Sir Edward Grey, for one, was shocked by Austria's demands, especially its insistence that Austrian officials would participate in Serbian judicial proceedings. The Serbian government's response was more conciliatory than most diplomats expected, but diplomatic efforts to avert war still failed. The Austrians' ultimatum to Serbia included the demands given in the final extract here.

Emperor Franz Joseph of Austria-Hungary to Kaiser William II of Germany, July 5, 1914

The plot against my poor nephew was the direct result of an agitation carried on by the Russian and Serb Pan-Slavs, an agitation whose sole object is the weakening of the Triple Alliance and the destruction of my realm.

So far, all investigations have shown that the Sarajevo murder was not perpetrated by one individual, but grew out of a well-organized conspiracy, the threads of which can be traced to Belgrade. Even though it will probably be impossible to prove the complicity of the Serb government, there can be no doubt that its policy, aiming as it does at the unification of all Southern Slavs under the Serb banner, encourages such crimes, and that the continuation of such conditions constitutes a permanent threat to my dynasty and my lands. . . .

This will only be possible if Serbia, which is at present the pivot of Pan-Slav policies, is put out of action as a factor of political power in the Balkans.

You too are [surely] convinced after the recent frightful occurrence in Bosnia that it is no longer possible to contemplate a reconciliation of the antagonism between us and Serbia and that the [efforts] of all European monarchs to pursue policies that preserve the peace will be threatened if the nest of criminal activity in Belgrade remains unpunished.

Austro-Hungarian Disagreements over Strategy

Count Leopold Berchtold, foreign minister of Austria-Hungary] . . . both Emperor Wilhelm and [Chancellor] Bethmann Hollweg had assured us emphatically of Germany's unconditional support in the event of military complications with Serbia. . . . It was clear to him that a military conflict with Serbia might bring about war with Russia. . . .

[Count Istvan Tisza, prime minister of Hungary] . . . We should decide what our demands on Serbia will be [but] should only present an ultimatum if Serbia rejected them. These demands must be hard but not so that they cannot be complied with. If Serbia accepted them, we could register a noteworthy diplomatic success and our prestige in the Balkans would be enhanced. If Serbia rejected our demands, then he too would favor military action. But he would already now go on record that we could aim at the downsizing but not the complete annihilation of Serbia because, first, this would provoke Russia to fight to the death and, second, he—as Hungarian premier—could never consent to the monarchy's annexation of a part of Serbia. Whether or not we ought to go to war with Serbia was not a matter for Germany to decide. . . .

[Count Berchtold] remarked that the history of the past years showed that diplomatic successes against Serbia might enhance the prestige of the monarchy temporarily, but that in reality the tension in our relations with Serbia had only increased.

[Count Karl Stürgkh, prime minister of Austria] . . . agreed with the Royal Hungarian Prime Minister that we and not the German government had to determine whether a war was necessary or not . . . [but] Count Tisza should take into account that in pursuing a hesitant and weak policy, we run the risk of not being so sure of Germany's unconditional support. . . .

[Leo von Bilinsky, Austro-Hungarian finance minister] . . . The Serb understands only force, a diplomatic success would make no impression at all in Bosnia and would be harmful rather than beneficial. . . .

Austro-Hungary's Ultimatum to Serbia

The Royal Serb Government will publish the following declaration on the first page of its official journal of 26/13 July:

"The Royal Serb Government condemns the propaganda directed against Austria-Hungary, and regrets sincerely the horrible consequences of these criminal ambitions.

"The Royal Serb Government regrets that Serb officers and officials have taken part in the propaganda above-mentioned and thereby imperiled friendly and neighbourly relations.

"The Royal Government . . . considers it a duty to warn officers, officials, and indeed all the inhabitants of the kingdom [of Serbia], that it will in future use great severity against such persons who may be guilty of similar doings.

The Royal Serb Government will moreover pledge itself to the following.

1. to suppress every publication likely to inspire hatred and contempt against the Monarchy;

2. to begin immediately dissolving the society called Narodna Odbrana,* to seize all its means of propaganda and to act in the same way against all the societies and associations in Serbia, which are busy with the propaganda against Austria-Hungary;

3. to eliminate without delay from public instruction everything that serves or might serve the propaganda against Austria-Hungary, both where teachers or books are concerned;

4. to remove from military service and from the administration all officers and officials who are guilty of having taken part in the propaganda against Austria-Hungary, whose names and proof of whose guilt the I. and R. Government [Imperial and Royal, that is, the Austro-Hungarian Empire] will communicate to the Royal Government;

5. to consent to the cooperation of I. and R. officials in Serbia in suppressing the subversive movement directed against the territorial integrity of the Monarchy;

6. to open a judicial inquest [enquête judiciaire] against all those who took part in the plot of 28 June, if they are to be found on Serbian territory; the I. and R. Government will delegate officials who will take an active part in these and associated inquiries;

The I. and R. Government expects the answer of the Royal government to reach it not later than Saturday, the 25th, at six in the afternoon. . . .

---

*Narodna Odbrana, or National Defense, was pro-Serbian and anti-Austrian but nonviolent. The Society of the Black Hand, to which Franz Ferdinand's assassin belonged, considered Narodna Odbrana too moderate.

Source (for all three excerpts): Ralph Menning, *The Art of the Possible: Documents on Great Power Diplomacy, 1814–1914* (New York: 1996), pp. 400, 402–3, and 414–15.

Questions for Analysis

1. Emperor Franz Joseph's letter to Kaiser Wilhelm II tells of the Austrian investigation into the assassination of Archduke Franz Ferdinand. What did Franz seek from his German ally? What did the emperors understand by the phrase, "if Serbia . . . is put out of action as a factor of political power in the Balkans"? Why might the Germans support a war against Serb-sponsored terrorism?

2. Could the Serbians have accepted the Austrian ultimatum without total loss of face and sacrifice of their independence? British and Russian foreign ministers were shocked by the demands on Serbia. Others thought the Austrians were justified, and that Britain would act similarly if threatened by terrorism. If, as Leo von Bilinsky said, "The Serb understands only force," why didn't Austria declare war without an ultimatum?

on August 1 and declared war on Russia—and two days later, on France. The next day, the German army invaded Belgium on its way to take Paris.

The invasion of neutral Belgium gave Britain the reason it needed to honor its treaty with France and enter the war against Germany. Other nations were quickly drawn into the struggle. On August 7 the Montenegrins joined the Serbs against Austria. Two weeks later the Japanese declared war on Germany, mainly to attack German possessions in the Far East. On August 1 Turkey allied with Germany, and in October began the bombardment of Russian ports on the Black Sea. Italy had been allied with Germany and Austria before the war, but at the outbreak of hostilities, the Italians declared neutrality, insisting that since Germany had invaded neutral Belgium, they owed Germany no protection.

The diplomatic maneuvers during the five weeks that followed the assassination at Sarajevo have been called a "tragedy of miscalculation." Austria's determination to punish Serbia, Germany's unwillingness to restrain their Austrian allies, and Russia's desire to use Serbia as an excuse to extend their influence in the Balkans all played a part in making the war more likely. Diplomats were further constrained by the strategic thinking and rigid timetables set by military leaders, and all sides clearly felt that it was important to make a show of force during the period of negotiation that preceded the outbreak of war. It is clear, however, that powerful German officials were arguing that war was inevitable. They insisted that Germany should fight before Russia recovered from their 1905 loss to Japan and before the French army could benefit from its new three-year conscription law, which would put more men in uniform. This sense of urgency characterized the strategies of all combatant countries. The lure of a bold, successful strike against one's enemies, and the fear that too much was at stake to risk losing the advantage, created a rolling tide of military mobilization that carried Europe into battle.

THE MARNE AND ITS CONSEQUENCES

Declarations of war were met with a mix of public fanfare and private concern. Nationalists hoped the war would bring glory and spiritual renewal, while others recognized that a general war put decades of prosperity at risk. Bankers and financiers were among those most opposed to war, correctly predicting that the conflict would create financial crisis. Many young men, however, enlisted with excitement, swelling Europe's conscript armies with volunteers (Britain did not introduce conscription until 1916). Like the military commanders, these volunteers thought they would be finished by Christmas—the general consensus was that modern weaponry made protracted war impossible.

The German high command had long foreseen the danger of a two-front war against France and Russia. Their offensive strategy, developed earlier by General Alfred von Schlieffen, was to attack France first, in the hopes that a quick victory would allow them to turn and face the slower Russian army in turn. Schlieffen's plan almost worked—the German army swept through Belgium and northern France and nearly attained its goal, the city of Paris. Early attempts by the French to counterattack failed, but at the crucial moment the French commander, Jules Joffre, drew the German attackers into a trap on the very outskirts of Paris. The French counterattack on the Marne river in September stopped the German advance for good. The Germans retreated to the Aisne river, both sides dug deeper in their trenches, and what remained of the Schlieffen plan was dead.

The Marne was the most strategically important battle of the entire war, and it dashed the hopes of those who hoped for a rapid end to the fighting. The war of movement was stopped in its tracks, and the Western Front moved little between 1914 and 1918. Politicians and military commanders sought for ways to break the stalemate in the trenches by seeking new allies, new theaters of conflict, and new weapons. They also remained committed to offensive tactics, and in a combination of stubbornness, callousness, and desperation, military leaders continued to order their troops to go "over the top."

Allied sucess at the Marne resulted in part from an unexpectedly strong Russian assault in eastern Prussia, which pulled some German units away from the attack on the west. But Russia's initial gains were obliterated at the battle of Tannenberg, August 26–30. Plagued with an array of problems, the Russian army was tired and half-starved; the Germans devastated it, taking nearly 100,000 prisoners and virtually destroying the Russian Second Army. The Russian general killed himself on the battlefield. Two weeks later, the Germans won another decisive victory at the battle of the Masurian Lakes, forcing the Russians to retreat from German territory. Despite this, Russian forces were able to defeat Austrian attacks to their south, inflicting terrible losses and thereby forcing the Germans to commit more troops to Russia. Through 1915 and 1916, the Eastern Front remained bloody and indecisive, with neither side able to capitalize on its gains.

STALEMATE, 1915

In the search for new points of attack, both the Allies and the Central Powers added new partners. The Ottoman Empire (Turkey) joined Germany and Austria at the end of 1914. In May 1915, Italy joined the Allies, lured by promises of financial reparations, parts of Austrian territory, and pieces of Germany's African colonies. Bulgaria joined the war on the side of the Central Powers a few months later. The entry of these new belligerents introduced the possibility of breaking the stalemate in the west by waging offensives on other fronts.

Gallipoli and Naval Warfare

Turkey's involvement, in particular, altered the dynamics of the war, for it threatened Russia's supply lines and endangered Britain's control of the Suez Canal. To defeat Turkey quickly—and in hopes of bypassing the Western Front—the British first lord of the admiralty, Winston Churchill, argued for a naval offensive in the Dardanelles, the narrow strait separating Europe and Asia Minor. Under particularly incompetent leadership, however, the Royal Navy lacked adequate planning, supply lines, and even maps to mount a successful campaign, and quickly lost six ships. The Allies then attempted a land invasion of the Gallipoli peninsula, in April 1915, with a combined force of French, British, Australian, and New Zealand troops. The Turks defended the narrow coast from positions high on fortified cliffs, and the shores were covered with nearly impenetrable barbed wire. During the disastrous landing, a British officer recalled, "the sea behind was absolutely crimson, and you could hear the groans through the rattle of musketry." The battle became entrenched on the beaches at Gallipoli, and the casualties mounted for seven months before the Allied commanders admitted defeat and ordered a withdrawal in December. The Gallipoli campaign—the first large-scale amphibious attack in history—brought death into London's neighborhoods and the cities of Britain's industrial north. Casualties were particularly devastating to the "white dominions"—practically every town and hamlet in Australia, New Zealand, and Canada lost young men, sometimes all the sons of a single family. The defeat cost the Allies 200,000 soldiers and did little to shift the war's focus away from the deadlocked Western Front.

By 1915, both sides realized that fighting this prolonged war of attrition would require countries to mobilize all of their resources. Accordingly, the Allies started to wage war on the economic front. Germany was vulnerable, dependent as it was on imports for at least one-third of its food supply. The Allies' naval blockade against all of central Europe aimed to slowly drain their opponents of food and raw materials. Germany responded with a submarine blockade, threatening to attack any vessel in the seas around Great Britain. On May 7, 1915, the German submarine *U-20*, without warning, torpedoed the passenger liner *Lusitania*, which was secretly carrying war supplies. The attack killed 1,198 people, including 128 Americans. The attack provoked the animosity of the United States, and Germany was forced to promise that it would no longer fire without warning. (This promise proved only temporary: in 1917 Germany would again declare unrestricted submarine warfare, drawing America into the war.) Although the German blockade against Britain destroyed more tonnage, the blockade against Germany was more devastating in the long run, as the continued war effort placed unsustainable demands on the national economy.

Trench Warfare

While the war escalated economically and politically, life in the trenches—the "lousy scratch holes," as one soldier called them—remained largely the same: a cramped and miserable existence of daily routines and continual killing. Some 25,000 miles of trenches snaked along the Western Front. Behind the front lay a maze of connecting trenches and lines, leading to a complex of ammunition

WAR: OLD AND NEW. Chlorine gas entered the war at the first battle of Ypres in 1915; mustard gas, which burned eyes and skin, came soon after. Gas did not tilt the military balance, but it was frightening, and pictures like this added to the surreal image of the First World War.

Interpreting Visual Evidence

War Propaganda

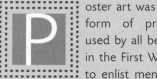

Poster art was a leading form of propaganda used by all belligerents in the First World War to enlist men, sell war bonds, and sustain morale on the home front. Posters also demonized the enemy and glorified the sacrifices of soldiers in order to better rationalize the unprecedented loss of life and national wealth. The posters shown here, from a wide range of combatant nations during the war, share a common desire to link the war effort to a set of assumptions about the different roles assigned to men and women in the national struggle.

A. British Poster: "Women of Britain say 'Go!'"

B. Russian Poster: "Women Workers! Take Up the Rifle!"

Questions for Analysis

1. Why would nationalists resort to such gendered images in a time of crisis?

2. What do these images tell us about the way that feelings of national belonging are created and sustained in times of urgency?

3. How might the changes that the war brought about—an increase in the number of women working in industry or outside the home, increased autonomy for women in regard to their wages or management of their household affairs—have affected the way that individuals responded to such images?

C. German Poster: "Collect women's hair that has been combed out. Our industry needs it for drive belts."

D. American Poster: "Destroy This Mad Brute. Enlist." The mad beast, meant to represent Germany, with *militarism* on his helmet, threatens American civilization with a club of *Kultur* (culture).

dumps, telephone exchanges, water points, field hospitals, and command posts. These logistical centers were supposed to allow an army to project its power forward, but just as often, they acted as a tether, making it difficult to advance.

The common assertion that railroads, the central symbol of an industrial age, made war more mobile, is misleading. Trains might take men to the front, but mobility ended there. Machine guns and barbed wire gave well-supplied and entrenched defenders an enormous advantage even against a larger attacking force, and logistics stymied generals' efforts to regain a war of movement.

The British and French trenches were wet, cold, and filthy. Rain turned the dusty corridors into squalid mud pits and flooded the floors up to waist level. Soldiers lived with lice and large black rats, which fed on the dead soldiers and horses that cast their stench over everything. Cadavers could go unburied for months and were often just embedded in the trench walls. Meanwhile the threat of enemy fire was constant: 7,000 British men were killed or wounded daily. This "wastage," as it was called, was part of the routine, along with the inspections, rotations, and mundane duties of life on the Western Front.

As the war progressed, new weapons added to the frightening dimensions of daily warfare. Besides artillery, machine guns, and barbed wire, the instruments of war now included exploding bullets, liquid fire, and poison gas. Gas, in particular, brought visible change to the battlefront. First used effectively by the Germans in April 1915 at the second battle of Ypres, poison gas was not only physically devastating—especially in its later forms—but also psychologically unnerving. The deadly cloud frequently hung over the trenches, although the quick appearance of gas masks limited its effectiveness. Like other new weapons, poison gas solidified the lines and took more lives but could not end the stalemate. The war dragged through its second year, bloody and stagnant.

SLAUGHTER IN THE TRENCHES: THE GREAT BATTLES, 1916–1917

The bloodiest battles of all—those that epitomize the First World War—occurred in 1916–17, when first the Germans and later the British and French launched major offensives in attempts to end the stalemate. Massive campaigns in the war of attrition, these assaults produced hundreds of thousands of casualties and only minor territorial gains.

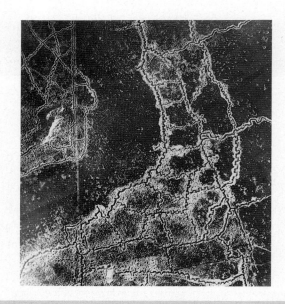

THE LINES OF BATTLE ON THE WESTERN FRONT. A British reconnaissance photo showing three lines of German trenches (right), No Man's Land (the black strip in the center), and the British trenches (partially visible to the left). The upper right hand quadrant of the photo shows communications trenches linking the front to the safe area. ▪ *What technologies gave these defenses such decisive advantages?*

These battles encapsulated the military tragedy of the war: a strategy of soldiers in cloth uniforms marching against machine guns.

Verdun

The first of these major battles began with a German attack on the French stronghold of Verdun, near France's eastern border, in February 1916. Verdun had little strategic importance, but it quickly became a symbol of France's strength and was defended at all costs. Germany's goal was not necessarily to take the city but rather to break French morale. As the German general Erich von Falkenhayn said, the offensive would "compel the French to throw in every man they have. If they do so the forces of France will bleed to death." One million shells were fired on the first day of battle, inaugurating a ten-month struggle of back-and-forth fighting—offensives and counteroffensives of intense ferocity at enormous cost and zero gain. Led by General Henri Pétain, the French pounded the Germans with artillery and received heavy bombardment in return. The Germans relied on large teams of horses, 7,000 of which were killed in a single day, to drag their guns through the muddy, cratered terrain. The French moved supplies and troops into Verdun continually. Approximately

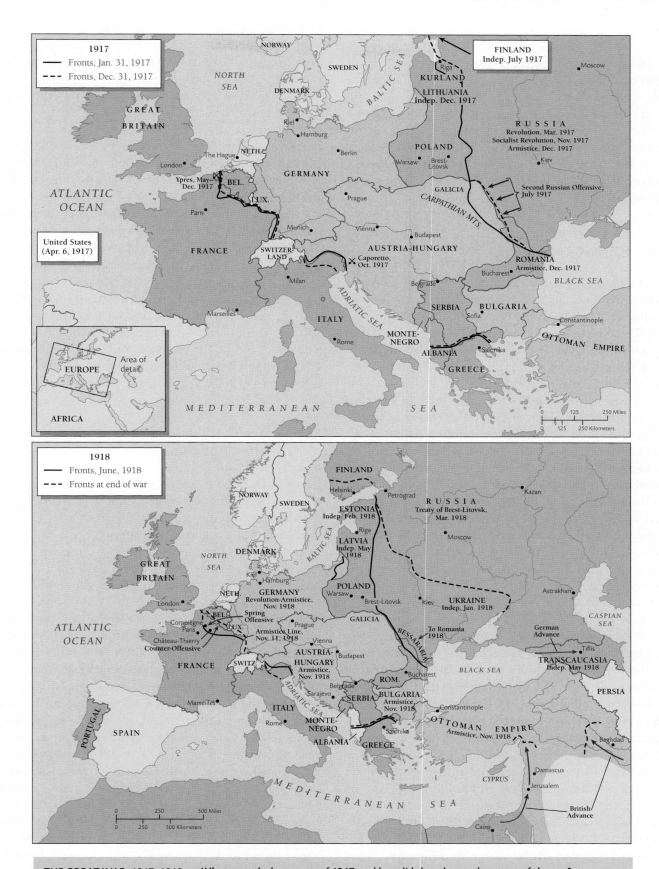

1917
— Fronts, Jan. 31, 1917
- - - Fronts, Dec. 31, 1917

United States
(Apr. 6, 1917)

FINLAND
Indep. July 1917

RUSSIA
Revolution, Mar. 1917
Socialist Revolution, Nov. 1917
Armistice, Dec. 1917

Second Russian Offensive,
July 1917

Ypres, May–
Dec. 1917

Caporetto,
Oct. 1917

ROMANIA
Armistice, Dec. 1917

EUROPE   Area of detail

AFRICA

1918
— Fronts, June, 1918
- - - Fronts at end of war

FINLAND

ESTONIA
Indep. Feb. 1918

RUSSIA
Treaty of Brest-Litovsk,
Mar. 1918

LATVIA
Indep. May
1918

UKRAINE
Indep. Jan. 1918

German
Advance

GERMANY
Revolution–Armistice,
Nov. 1918

Spring
Offensive

To Romania
1918

Armistice Line,
Nov. 11, 1918

TRANSCAUCASIA
Indep. May 1918

Château-Thierry
Counter-Offensive

AUSTRIA-
HUNGARY
Armistice,
Nov. 1918

BULGARIA
Armistice,
Nov. 1918

OTTOMAN EMPIRE
Armistice, Nov. 1918

British
Advance

THE GREAT WAR, 1917–1918. ▪ *What were the key events of 1917, and how did they change the course of the war?*
▪ *Consider the map of 1918. Why might many German people have believed they nearly won the war?* ▪ *Why were developments in the Middle East significant in the war's aftermath?*

12,000 delivery trucks were employed for service. So were 259 out of the 330 regiments of the French army. Neither side could gain a real advantage—one small village on the front changed hands thirteen times in one month alone—but both sides incurred devastating losses of life. By the end of June, over 400,000 French and German soldiers were dead. In the end, the advantage fell to the French, who survived and who bled the Germans as badly as they suffered themselves.

The Somme

Meanwhile, the British opened their own offensive against Germany farther west, beginning the battle of the Somme on June 24, 1916. The Allied attack began with a fierce bombardment, blasting the German lines with 1,400 guns. The blasts could be heard all the way across the English Channel. The British assumed that this preliminary attack would break the mesh of German wire, destroy Germany's trenches, and clear the way for Allied troops to advance forward. They were tragically wrong. On the first day of battle alone, a stunning 20,000 British soldiers died, and another 40,000 were wounded. The carnage continued from July until mid-November, resulting in massive casualties on both sides: 500,000 German, 400,000 British, and 200,000 French. The losses were unimaginable, and the outcome was equally hard to fathom: for all their sacrifices, neither side made any real gains. The futility of offensive war was not lost on the soldiers, yet morale remained surprisingly strong. Mutinies and desertions were rare before 1917; and surrenders became an important factor only in the final months of the war.

With willing armies and fresh recruits, military commanders maintained their strategy and pushed for victories on the Western Front again in 1917. The French general Robert Nivelle promised to break through the German lines with overwhelming manpower, but the "Nivelle Offensive" (April–May 1917) failed immediately, with first-day casualties like those at the Somme. The British also reprised the Somme at the third battle of Ypres (July–October 1917), in which a half million casualties earned Great Britain only insignificant gains—and no breakthrough. The one weapon with the potential to break the stalemate, the tank, was finally introduced into battle in 1916, but with such reluctance by tradition-bound commanders that its half-hearted deployment made almost no difference. Other innovations were equally indecisive. Airplanes were used almost exclusively for reconnaissance, though occasional "dogfights" did occur between German and Allied pilots.

And though the Germans sent airships to raid London, they did little significant damage.

Off the Western Front, fighting produced further stalemate. The Austrians continued to fend off attacks in Italy and Macedonia, while the Russians mounted a successful offensive against them on the Eastern Front. The initial Russian success brought Romania into the war on Russia's side, but the Central Powers quickly retaliated and knocked the Romanians out of the war within a few months.

The war at sea was equally indecisive, with neither side willing to risk the loss of enormously expensive battleships. The British and German navies fought only one major naval battle early in 1916, which ended in stalemate. Afterward they used their fleets primarily in the economic war of blockades.

As a year of great bloodshed and growing disillusionment, 1916 showed that not even the superbly organized Germans had the mobility or fast-paced communications to win the western ground war. Increasingly, warfare would be turned against entire nations, including civilian populations on the home front and in the far reaches of the European empires.

WAR OF EMPIRES

Coming as it did at the height of European imperialism, the Great War quickly became a war of empires, with far-reaching repercussions. As the demands of warfare rose, Europe's colonies provided soldiers and material support. Britain, in particular, benefited from its vast network of colonial dominions and dependencies, bringing in soldiers from Canada, Australia, New Zealand, India, and South Africa. Nearly 1.5 million Indian troops served as British forces, some on the Western Front and many more in the Middle East. The French Empire, especially North and West Africa, sent 607,000 soldiers to fight with the Allies; 31,000 of them died in Europe. Colonial recruits from China, Vietnam, Egypt, India, the West Indies, and Madagascar were also employed in industry.

As the war stalled in Europe, colonial areas also became strategically important theaters for armed engagement. In 1916 Allied forces won a series of battles in the Middle East, pushing the Turks out of Egypt and eventually capturing Baghdad, Jerusalem, Beirut, and other cities. The British sought and gained the support of different Arab peoples who sought independence from the Turks, resulting in a successful revolt of Bedouin tribes (nomadic peoples of the Arabian Peninsula) that split the Ottoman Empire. When one of the senior Bedouin aristocrats, the emir Abdullah, captured the strategic port of Aqaba in July 1917, a British officer, T. E. Lawrence, took credit and entered popular mythology as "Lawrence of Arabia."

BRITISH REPRESSION OF EASTER REBELLION, DUBLIN, 1916. British troops line up behind a moveable barricade made up of household furniture during their repression of the Irish revolt. The military action did not prevent further conflict.

Britain encouraged Arab nationalism for its own strategic purposes, offering a qualified acknowledgment of Arab political aspirations. At the same time, for similar but conflicting strategic reasons, the British declared their support of "the establishment in Palestine of a national home for the Jewish people." Britain's foreign secretary, Arthur Balfour, made the pledge. European Zionists, who were seeking a Jewish homeland, took the Balfour Declaration very seriously. The conflicting pledges to Bedouin leaders and Zionists sowed the seeds of the future Arab-Israeli conflict. First the war and then the promise of oil drew Europe more deeply into the Middle East, where conflicting dependencies and commitments created numerous postwar problems.

Irish Revolt

The Ottoman Empire was vulnerable; so was the British. The demands of war strained precarious bonds to the breaking point. Before the war, long-standing tensions between Irish Catholics and the Protestant British government had reached fever pitch, and some feared civil war. The Sinn Féin ("We Ourselves") party had been formed in 1900 to fight for Irish independence, and a home rule bill had passed Parliament in 1912. But with the outbreak of war in 1914, the "Irish question" was tabled, and 200,000 Irishmen volunteered for the British army. The problem festered, however; and on Easter Sunday 1916, a group of nationalists revolted in Dublin. The insurgents' plan to smuggle in arms from Germany failed, and they had few delusions of achieving victory. The British army arrived with artillery and

machine guns; they shelled parts of Dublin and crushed the uprising within a week.

The revolt was a military disaster but a striking political success. Britain shocked the Irish public by executing the rebel leaders. Even the British prime minister David Lloyd George thought the military governor in Dublin exceeded his authority with these executions. The martyrdom of the "Easter Rebels" seriously damaged Britain's relationship with its Irish Catholic subjects. The deaths galvanized the cause of Irish nationalism and touched off guerrilla violence that kept Ireland in turmoil for years. Finally, a new home rule bill was enacted in 1920, establishing separate parliaments for the Catholic south of Ireland and for Ulster, the northeastern counties where the majority population was Protestant. The leaders of the so-called Dáil Éireann (Irish Assembly), which had proclaimed an Irish Republic in 1918 and therefore been outlawed by Britain, rejected the bill but accepted a treaty that granted dominion status to Catholic Ireland in 1921. Dominion was followed almost immediately by civil war between those who abided by the treaty and those who wanted to absorb Ulster, but the conflict ended in an uneasy compromise. The Irish Free State was established, and British sovereignty was partially abolished in 1937. Full status as a republic came, with some American pressure and Britain's exhausted acquiescence, in 1945.

THE HOME FRONT

When the war of attrition began in 1915, the belligerent governments were unprepared for the strains of sustained warfare. The costs of war—in both money and manpower—were staggering. In 1914 the war cost Germany 36 million marks per day (five times the cost of the war of 1870), and by 1918 the cost had skyrocketed to 146 million marks per day. Great Britain had estimated it would need a hundred thousand soldiers but ended up mobilizing 3 million. The enormous task of feeding, clothing, and equipping the army became as much of a challenge as breaking through enemy lines; civilian populations were increasingly asked—or forced—to support these efforts. Bureaucrats and industrialists led the effort to mobilize the home front, focusing all parts of society on the single goal of military victory. The term *total war* was introduced to describe this intense mobilization of society. Government propagandists insisted that civilians were as important to the war effort as soldiers, and in many ways they were. As workers, taxpayers, and consumers, civilians were vital parts of the war economy. They produced munitions; purchased war bonds; and shouldered the burden of tax hikes, inflation, and material privations.

The demands of industrial warfare led first to a transition from general industrial manufacturing to munitions production and then to increased state control of all aspects of production and distribution. The governments of Britain and France managed to direct the economy without serious detriment to the standard of living in their countries. Germany, meanwhile, put its economy in the hands of army and industry; under the Hindenburg Plan, named for Paul von Hindenburg, the chief of the imperial staff of the German army, pricing and profit margins were set by individual industrialists.

Largely because of the immediate postwar collapse of the German economy, historians have characterized Germany's wartime economy as a chaotic, ultimately disastrous system governed by personal interest. New research, however, suggests that this was not the case: Germany's systems of war finance and commodity distribution, however flawed, were not decisively worse than those of Britain or France.

Women in the War

As Europe's adult men left farms and factories to become soldiers, the composition of the workforce changed: thousands of women were recruited into fields that had previously excluded them. Young people, foreigners, and unskilled workers were also pressed into newly important tasks; in the case of colonial workers, their experiences had equally critical repercussions. But because they were more visible, it was women who became symbolic of many of the changes brought on by the Great War. In Germany, one-third of the labor force in heavy industry was female by the end of the war; and in France, 684,000 women worked in the munitions industry alone. In England the "munition-ettes," as they were dubbed, numbered nearly a million. Women also entered the clerical and service sectors. In the villages of France, England, and Germany, women became mayors, school principals, and mail carriers. Hundreds of thousands of women worked with the army as nurses and ambulance drivers, jobs that brought them very close to the front lines. With minimal supplies and under squalid conditions, they worked to save lives and patch bodies together.

In some cases, war offered new opportunities. Middle-class women often said that the war broke down the restrictions on their lives; those in nursing learned to drive and acquired rudimentary medical knowledge. At home they could now ride the train, walk the street, or go out to dinner without an older woman present to chaperone them. In terms of gender roles, an enormous gulf sometimes seemed to separate the wartime world from nineteenth-century Victorian society. In one of the most famous autobiographies of the war, *Testament of Youth*, author Vera Brittain (1896–1970) recorded the dramatic new social norms that she and others forged during the rapid changes of wartime. "As a generation of women we were now sophisticated to an extent which was revolutionary when compared with the romantic

WOMEN AT WORK. The all-out war effort combined with a manpower shortage at home brought women into factories across Europe in unparalleled numbers. In this photo men and women work side by side in a British shell factory. ▪ *How might the increased participation of women in the industrial workforce have changed attitudes toward women's labor?* ▪ *What tensions might this participation have created within families or between male and female workers?*

ignorance of 1914. Where we had once spoken with polite evasion of 'a certain condition,' or 'a certain profession,' we now unblushingly used the words 'pregnancy' and 'prostitution.'" For every Vera Brittain who celebrated the changes, however, there were journalists, novelists, and other observers who grumbled that women were now smoking, refusing to wear the corsets that gave Victorian dresses their hourglass shape, or cutting their hair into the fashionable new bobs. The "new woman" became a symbol of profound and disconcerting cultural transformation.

How long lasting were these changes? In the aftermath of the war, governments and employers scurried to send women workers home, in part to give jobs to veterans, in part to deal with male workers' complaints that women were undercutting their wages. Efforts to demobilize women faced real barriers. Many women wage earners—widowed, charged with caring for relatives, or faced with inflation and soaring costs—needed their earnings more than ever. It was also difficult to persuade women workers who had grown accustomed to the relatively higher wages in heavy industry to return to their poorly paid traditional sectors of employment: the textile and garment industries and domestic service. The demobilization of women after the war, in other words, created as many dilemmas as had their mobilization. Governments passed "natalist" policies to encourage women to go home, marry, and—most important—have children. These policies did make maternity benefits—time off, medical care, and some allowances for the poor—available to women for the first time. Nonetheless, birth rates had been falling across Europe by the early twentieth century, and they continued to do so after the war. One upshot of the war was the increased availability of birth control—Marie Stopes (1880–1958) opened a birth-control clinic in London in 1921—and a combination of economic hardship, increased knowledge, and the demand for freedom made men and women more likely to use it. Universal suffrage, and the vote for all adult men and women, and for women in particular, had been one of the most controversial issues in European politics before the war. At the end of the fighting it came in a legislative rush. Britain was first off the mark, granting the vote to all men and women over thirty with the Representation of the People Act in 1918; the United States gave women the vote with the Nineteenth Amendment the following year. Germany's new republic and the Soviet Union did likewise. France was much slower to offer woman suffrage (1945) because the persistent antifeminism of conservatives was reinforced by fears among anticlerical republicans that women would vote for candidates close to the Catholic church.

Mobilizing Resources

Along with mobilizing the labor front, the wartime governments had to mobilize men and money. All the belligerent countries except for Great Britain had conscription laws before the war. Military service was seen as a duty, not an option. Bolstered by widespread public support for the war, this belief brought millions of young Europeans into recruitment offices in 1914. The French began the war with about 4.5 million trained soldiers, but by the end of 1914—just four months into the war—300,000 were dead and 600,000 injured. Conscripting citizens and mustering colonial troops became increasingly important. Eventually, France called up 8 million citizens: almost two-thirds of Frenchmen aged eighteen to forty. In 1916 the British finally introduced conscription, dealing a serious blow to civilian morale; by the summer of 1918, half its army was under the age of nineteen.

Government propaganda, while part of a larger effort to sustain both military and civilian morale, was also important to the recruitment effort. From the outset, the war had been sold to the people on both sides of the conflict as a moral and righteous crusade. In 1914, the French president Raymond Poincaré assured his fellow citizens that France had no other purpose than to stand "before the universe for Liberty, Justice, and Reason." Germans were presented with the task of defending their superior *Kultur* (culture) against the wicked encirclement policy of the Allied nations. By the middle of the war, massive propaganda campaigns were under way. Film, posters, postcards, newspapers—all forms of media proclaimed the strength of the cause, the evil of the enemy, and the absolute necessity of total victory. The success of these campaigns is difficult to determine, but it is clear that they had at least one painful effect—they made it more difficult for any country to accept a fair, non-punitive peace settlement.

Financing the war was another heavy obstacle. Military spending accounted for 3–5 percent of government expenditure in the combatant countries before 1914 but soared to perhaps half of each nation's budget during the war. Governments had to borrow money or print more of it. The Allied nations borrowed heavily from the British, who borrowed even more from the United States. American capital flowed across the Atlantic long before the United States entered the war. And though economic aid from the United States was a decisive factor in the Allies' victory, it left Britain with a $4.2 billion debt and hobbled the United Kingdom as a financial power after the war. The situation was far worse for Germany, which faced a total blockade of money and goods. In an effort to get around this predicament, and lacking an outside source of cash, the German government funded its war effort largely by increasing the money supply. The amount of paper money in circulation increased by over 1,000 percent during the war, triggering a dramatic rise in inflation. During the war, prices in Germany rose about 400 percent, double the inflation in Britain and France. For middle-class people living on pensions or fixed incomes, these price hikes were a push into poverty.

The Strains of War, 1917

The demands of total war worsened as the conflict dragged into 1917. After the debacle of the Nivelle Offensive, the French army recorded acts of mutiny in two-thirds of its divisions; similar resistance arose in nearly all major armies in 1917. Military leaders portrayed the mutineers as part of a dangerous pacifist movement, but most were non-political. Resistance within the German army was never organized or widespread but existed in subtler forms. Self-mutilation rescued some soldiers from the horror of the trenches; many more were released because of various emotional disorders.

The war's toll also mounted for civilians, who often suffered from the same shortages of basic supplies that afflicted the men at the front. In 1916–17, the lack of

DESPERATION ON THE GERMAN HOME FRONT, 1918. A German photograph of women digging through garbage in search of food. The last year of the war brought starvation to cities in Germany and Austria-Hungary, sending many people into the countryside to forage for provisions. Such foraging was often illegal, a violation of rationing rules. ▪ *How might the need to break the law in this way have affected support for the war effort and the state?*

clothing, food, and fuel was aggravated in central Europe by abnormally cold, wet weather. These strains provoked rising discontent on the home front. Although governments attempted to solve the problem with tighter controls on the economy, their policies often provoked further hostility from civilians.

In urban areas, where undernourishment was worst, people stood in lines for hours to get food and fuel rations that scarcely met their most basic needs. The price of bread and potatoes—still the central staples of working-class meals—soared. Prices were even higher in the thriving black market that emerged in cities. Consumers worried aloud that speculators were hoarding supplies and creating artificial shortages, selling tainted goods, and profiting from others' miseries. Governments, meanwhile, concentrated on the war effort and faced difficult decisions about who needed supplies the most—soldiers at the front, workers in the munitions industry, or hungry and cold families.

Like other nations, Germany moved from encouraging citizens to restrain themselves—"those who stuff themselves full, those who push out their paunches in all directions, are traitors to the Fatherland"—to direct control, issuing ration cards in 1915. Britain was the last to institute control, rationing bread only in 1917 when Germany's submarines sank an average of 630,000 tons per month and brought British food reserves within two weeks of starvation level. But rations indicated only what was allowed, not what was available. Hunger continued despite mass bureaucratic control. Governments regulated not only food but also working hours and wages; and unhappy workers directed their anger at the state, adding a political dimension to labor disputes and household needs. The bread lines, filled mainly by women, were flash points of political dissent, petty violence, even large-scale riots. Likewise, the class conflicts of prewar Europe had been briefly muffled by the outbreak of war and mobilization along patriotic lines, but as the war ground on, political tensions reemerged with new intensity. Thousands of strikes erupted throughout Europe, involving millions of frustrated workers. In April 1917, 300,000 in Berlin went on strike to protest ration cuts. In May, a strike of Parisian seamstresses touched off a massive work stoppage that included even white-collar employees and munitions workers. Shipbuilders and steelworkers in Glasgow went on strike as well, and the British government replied by sending armored cars to "Red Glasgow." Stagnation had given way to crisis on both sides. The strains of total war and the resulting social upheavals threatened political regimes throughout Europe. The Russian Revolution, which resulted in the overthrow of the tsar and the rise of Bolshevism, was only the most dramatic response to widespread social problems.

Total War

As early as 1915 contemporaries were speaking of "the Great War"; the transformations were there for all to see. This was modern, industrialized warfare, first glimpsed in the American Civil War but now more advanced and on a much larger scale. It still deployed cloth-uniformed men, heartbreakingly unprotected against the newly destructive weapons. And it still required human intelligence, speed, brute force—or courage—on a massive scale. The statistics and what they imply still strain the imagination: 74 million soldiers were mobilized on both sides; 6,000 people were killed each day for more than 1,500 days.

The warring nations, Europe's new industrial powerhouses, were also empires, and this "world" war consumed resources and soldiers from all over the globe. Mobilization also reached more deeply into civilian society. Economies bent to military priorities. Propaganda escalated to sustain the effort, fanning old hatreds and creating new ones. Atrocities against civilians came in its wake. Europe had known brutal wars against civilians before, and guerilla war during the time of Napoleon, but the First World War vastly magnified the violence and multiplied the streams of refugees. Minorities who lived in the crumbling Russian, Austro-Hungarian, or Ottoman empires were especially vulnerable. Jewish populations in Russia had lived in fear of pogroms before 1914; now they were attacked by Russian soldiers who accused them of encouraging the enemy. Austria-Hungary, likewise, summarily executed minorities suspected of Russian sympathies. The worst atrocities came against the Armenian community in Turkey. Attacked by the Allies at Gallipoli and at war with the Russians to the north, the Turkish government turned on its Armenian subjects, labeling them a security risk. Orders came down for "relocation," and relocation became genocide. Armenian leaders were arrested; Armenian men were shot; and entire Armenian villages were forcibly marched to the south, robbed, and beaten to death along the way. Over the course of the war, a million Armenians died.

All of these developments—military, economic, and psychological mobilization; a war that tested the powers of a state and its economy; violence against civilians—were the component parts of total war and foreshadowed the conflict to be unleashed in 1939.

THE RUSSIAN REVOLUTIONS OF 1917

The first country to break under the strain of total war was tsarist Russia. The outbreak of war temporarily united Russian society against a common enemy, but Russia's military effort quickly turned sour. All levels of Russian society became disillusioned with Tsar Nicholas II, who was unable to provide effective leadership but was nonetheless unwilling to open government to those who could. The political and social strains of war brought two revolutions in 1917. The first, in February, overthrew the tsar and established a transitional government. The second, in October, was a communist revolution that marked the emergence of the Soviet Union.

The First World War and the February Revolution

Like the other participants in the First World War, Russia entered the war with the assumption that it would be over quickly. Autocratic Russia, plagued by internal difficulties before 1914 (see Chapter 23), could not sustain the political strains of extended warfare. Tsar Nicholas II's political authority had been shaky since the October Revolution of 1905, and corruption in the royal court further tarnished the tsar's image. Once war broke out the tsar insisted on personally commanding Russian troops, leaving the government in the hands of his court, especially his wife, Alexandra, and her eccentric spiritual mentor and faith healer, Grigorii Rasputin (1869–1916). Rasputin won the tsarina's sympathy by treating her hemophiliac son, and he used his influence to operate corrupt and self-aggrandizing schemes. His presence only added to the image of a court mired in decadence, incompetent to face the modern world.

In 1914 and 1915 Russia suffered terrible defeats. All of Poland and substantial territory in the Baltics fell to the Germans at the cost of a million Russian casualties. Although the Russian army was the largest in Europe, it was poorly trained and, at the beginning of the war, undersupplied and inadequately equipped. In the first battles of 1914, generals sent soldiers to the front without rifles or shoes, instructing them to scavenge supplies from fallen comrades. By 1915, to the surprise of many, Russia was producing enough food, clothing, and ammunition, but political problems blocked the supply effort. Another major

Toward the October Revolution: Lenin to the Bolsheviks

In the fall of 1917, Lenin was virtually the only Bolshevik leader who believed that an insurrection should be launched immediately. As the provisional government faltered, he attempted to convince his fellow Bolsheviks that the time for revolution had arrived.

aving obtained a majority in the Soviets of Workers' and Soldiers' Deputies of both capitals, the Bolsheviks can and *must* take power into their hands.

They can do so because the active majority of the revolutionary elements of the people of both capitals is sufficient to attract the masses, to overcome the resistance of the adversary, to vanquish him, to conquer power and to retain it. For, in offering immediately a democratic peace, in giving the land immediately to the peasants, in re-establishing the democratic institutions and liberties which have been mangled and crushed by Kerensky [leader of the provisional government], the Bolsheviks will form a government which *nobody* will overthrow. . . .

The majority of the people is *with* us. . . . The majority in the Soviets of the capitals is the *result* of the people's progress *to our side*. The vacillation of the Socialist-Revolutionaries and Mensheviks . . . is proof of the same thing. . . .

To "wait" for the Constituent Assembly would be wrong. . . . Only our party, having assumed power, can secure the convocation of the Constituent Assembly, and, after assuming power, it could blame the other parties for delaying it and could substantiate its accusations. . . .

It would be naive to wait for a "formal" majority on the side of the Bolsheviks; no revolution ever waits for *this*. . . . History will not forgive us if we do not assume power now.

No apparatus? There is an apparatus: the Soviets and democratic organisations. The international situation *just now*, on the *eve* of a separate peace between the English and the Germans, is *in our favour*. It is precisely now that to offer peace to the peoples means to *win*.

Assume power *at once* in Moscow and in Petrograd . . . ; we will win *absolutely and unquestionably*.

Source: Vladimir Ilyich Lenin, *Bol'sheviki dolzhny vzyat'vlast'* (*The Bolsheviks must seize power*), cited in Richard Sakwa, *The Rise and Fall of the Soviet Union, 1917–1991* (New York and London: 1999), p. 45.

Questions for Analysis

1. Lenin was surprised by the sudden collapse of the tsarist regime in the February revolution of 1917. Why did he think the Bolsheviks could seize power? What were the key elements of his strategy for winning the necessary popular support?

2. Convinced he was right, Lenin returned to Petrograd in disguise and personally presented his arguments for an armed takeover to the Bolshevik Central Committee. What did he mean by saying that "it would be naive to wait for a 'formal' majority on the side of the Bolsheviks; no revolution ever waits for *this*"?

---

offensive in the summer of 1916 brought hope for success but turned into a humiliating retreat. When word came that the government was requisitioning grain from the countryside to feed the cities, peasants in the army began to desert en masse, returning to their farms to guard their families' holdings. By the end of 1916, a combination of political ineptitude and military defeat brought the Russian state to the verge of collapse.

The same problems that hampered the Russian war effort also crippled the tsar's ability to override domestic discontent and resistance. As the war dragged on, the government faced not only liberal opposition in the Duma, soldiers unwilling to fight, and an increasingly militant labor movement, but also a rebellious urban population. City dwellers were impatient with inflation and shortages of food and fuel. In February 1917, these forces came together in Petrograd (now St. Petersburg). The revolt began on International Women's Day, February 23, an occasion for a loosely organized march of women—workers, mothers, wives, and consumers—demanding food, fuel, and political reform. The march was the latest in a wave of demonstrations and strikes that had swept through the country during the winter months. This time, within a few days the unrest spiraled into a mass strike of 300,000 people. Nicholas II sent in police and military forces to quell the disorder. When nearly 60,000 troops in Petrograd mutinied and joined the revolt, what was left of the tsar's power evaporated. Nicholas II abdicated the throne on March 2. This abrupt decision brought a century-long struggle over Russian autocracy to a sudden end.

After the collapse of the monarchy, two parallel centers of power emerged, each with its own objectives and policies. The first was the provisional government, organized by leaders in the Duma and composed mainly of middle-class liberals. The new government hoped to establish a democratic system under constitutional rule. Its main task was to set up a national election for a constituent assembly, and it also acted to grant and secure civil liberties, release political prisoners, and redirect power into the hands of local officials. The other center of power lay with the *soviets*, a Russian term for local councils elected by workers and soldiers. Since 1905 socialists had been active in organizing these councils, which claimed to be the true democratic representatives of the people. A soviet, organized during the 1905 revolution and led by the well-known socialist Leon Trotsky, reemerged after February 1917 and asserted its claim to be the legitimate political power in Russia. The increasingly powerful soviets pressed for social reform, the redistribution of land, and a negotiated settlement with Germany and Austria. Yet the provisional government refused to concede military defeat. Continuing the war effort made domestic reform impossible and cost valuable popular support. More fighting during 1917 was just as disastrous as before, and this time the provisional government paid the price. By autumn, desertion in the army was rampant, administering the country was nearly impossible, and Russian politics teetered on the edge of chaos.

The Bolsheviks and the October Revolution

The Bolsheviks, a branch of the Russian socialist movement, had little to do with the events of February 1917. Over the course of the next seven months, however, they became enough of a force to overthrow the provisional government. The chain of events leading to the October Revolution surprised most contemporary observers, including the Bolsheviks themselves. Marxism had been quite weak in late-nineteenth-century Russia, although it made small but rapid inroads during the 1880s and 1890s. In 1903 the leadership of the Russian Social

VLADIMIR ILYICH LENIN. Lenin speaking in Moscow in 1918, at the first anniversary of the October Revolution. A forceful speaker and personality, Lenin was the single most powerful politician in Russia between October 1917 and his death in 1924.

Democrats split over revolutionary strategy and the steps to socialism. One group, which won a temporary majority (and chose to call itself the Bolsheviks, or "members of the majority"), favored a centralized party of active revolutionaries. They believed that revolution alone would lead directly to a socialist regime. The Mensheviks ("members of the minority"), like most European socialists, wanted to move toward socialism gradually, supporting bourgeois or liberal revolution in the short term. Because peasants constituted 80 to 85 percent of the population, the Mensheviks also reasoned that a proletarian revolution was premature and that Russia needed to complete its capitalist development first. The Mensheviks regained control of the party, but the Bolshevik splinter party survived under the leadership of the young, dedicated revolutionary Vladimir Ilyich Ulyanov, who adopted the pseudonym Lenin.

Lenin was a member of the middle class; his father had been an inspector of schools and a minor political functionary. Lenin himself had been expelled from university for engaging in radical activity after his elder brother was executed for involvement in a plot to assassinate Tsar Alexander III. Lenin spent three years as a political prisoner in Siberia. After that, from 1900 until 1917, he lived and wrote as an exile in western Europe.

Lenin believed that the development of Russian capitalism made socialist revolution possible. To bring revolution, he argued, the Bolsheviks needed to organize on behalf of the new class of industrial workers. Without the party's disciplined leadership, Russia's factory workers could not accomplish change on the necessary scale.

Lenin's Bolsheviks remained a minority among Social Democrats well into 1917, and industrial workers were a small part of the population. But the Bolsheviks' dedication to the singular goal of revolution and their tight, almost conspiratorial organization gave them tactical advantages over larger and more loosely organized opposition parties. The Bolsheviks merged a peculiarly Russian tradition of revolutionary zeal with western European Marxism, creating a party capable of seizing the moment when the tsar left the scene.

Throughout 1917 the Bolsheviks consistently demanded an end to the war, improvement in working and living conditions for workers, and redistribution of aristocratic land to the peasantry. While the provisional government struggled to hold together the Russian war effort, Lenin led the Bolsheviks on a bolder course, shunning any collaboration with the "bourgeois" government and condemning its imperialist war policies. Even most Bolsheviks considered Lenin's approach too radical. Yet as conditions in Russia deteriorated, his uncompromising calls for "Peace, Land, and Bread, Now" and "All Power to the Soviets" won the Bolsheviks support from workers, soldiers, and peasants. As many ordinary people saw it, the other parties could not govern, win the war, or achieve an honorable peace. While unemployment continued to climb and starvation and chaos reigned in the cities, the Bolsheviks' power and credibility were rising fast.

In October 1917, Lenin convinced his party to act. He goaded Trotsky, who was better known among workers, into organizing a Bolshevik attack on the provisional government on October 24–25, 1917. On October 25, Lenin appeared from hiding to announce to a stunned meeting of soviet representatives that "all power had passed to the Soviets." The head of the provisional government fled to rally support at the front lines, and the Bolsheviks took over the Winter Palace, the seat of the provisional government. The initial stage of the revolution was quick and relatively bloodless. In fact, many observers believed they had seen nothing more than a coup d'état, one that might quickly be reversed. Life in Petrograd went on as normal.

The Bolsheviks took the opportunity to rapidly consolidate their position. First, they moved against all political competition, beginning with the soviets. They immediately expelled parties that disagreed with their actions, creating a new government in the soviets composed entirely of Bolsheviks. The Bolsheviks did follow through on the provisional government's promise to elect a Constituent Assembly. But when they did not win a majority in the elections, they refused to let the assembly reconvene. From that point on, Lenin's Bolsheviks ruled socialist Russia, and later the Soviet Union, as a one-party dictatorship.

In the countryside, the new Bolshevik regime did little more than ratify a revolution that had been going on since the summer of 1917. When peasant soldiers at the front heard that a revolution had occurred, they streamed home to take land they had worked for generations and believed was rightfully theirs. The provisional government had set up commissions to deal methodically with the legal issues surrounding the redistribution of land, a process that threatened to become as complex as the emancipation of the serfs in 1861. The Bolsheviks simply approved the spontaneous redistribution of the nobles' land to peasants without compensation to former owners. They nationalized banks and gave workers control of factories.

Most important, the new government sought to take Russia out of the war. It eventually negotiated a separate treaty with Germany, signed at Brest-Litovsk in March 1918. The Bolsheviks surrendered vast Russian territories: the rich agricultural region of Ukraine, Georgia, Finland, Russia's Polish territories, the Baltic states, and more. However humiliating, the treaty ended Russia's role in the fighting and saved the fledgling communist regime from almost certain military defeat at the hands of the Germans. The treaty enraged Lenin's political enemies, both moderates and reactionaries, who were still a force to be reckoned with—and who were prepared to wage a civil war rather than accept the revolution. Withdrawing from Europe's war only plunged the country into a vicious civil conflict (see Chapter 28).

THE ROAD TO GERMAN DEFEAT, 1918

Russia's withdrawal dealt an immediate strategic and psychological blow to the Allies. Germany could soothe domestic discontent by claiming victory on the Eastern Front, and it could now concentrate its entire army in the west. The Allies feared that Germany would win the war before the United States, which entered the conflict in April 1917, could make a difference. It almost happened. With striking results, Germany shifted its offensive strategy to infiltration by small groups under flexible command. On March 21, 1918, Germany initiated a major assault on the west and quickly broke through the Allied lines. The British were hit hardest. Some units, surrounded, fought to the death with bayonets and grenades, but most recognized their plight and surrendered, putting tens of thousands of prisoners in German hands. The British were in retreat everywhere and their commander, Sir Douglas Haig, issued a famous order warning that British troops "now fight with our backs to the wall." The Germans advanced to within fifty miles of Paris by early April. Yet the British—and especially troops from the overseas empire—did just as they were asked and stemmed the tide. As German forces turned southeast instead, the French, who had refused to participate in the foolish attacks over the top, showed stubborn courage on the defensive, slowing and ultimately halting the advance after many casualties. It had been a last great try by the well-organized German army; exhausted, it now waited for the Allies to mount their own attack.

The final turning point of the war was the entry of the United States in April 1917. Although America had supported the Allies financially throughout the war, its official intervention undeniably tipped the scales. The United States created a fast and efficient wartime bureaucracy, instituting conscription in May 1917. About 10 million men were registered, and by the next year, 300,000 soldiers a month were being shipped "over there." Large amounts of food and supplies also crossed the Atlantic under the armed protection of the U.S. Navy. This system of convoys effectively neutralized the threat of German submarines to Allied merchant ships: the number of ships sunk fell from 25 to 4 percent. America's entry—though not immediately decisive—gave a quick, colossal boost to British and French morale, while severely undermining Germany's.

When it came in July and August, the Allied counterattack was devastating and quickly gathered steam. New offensive techniques had finally materialized. The Allies improved their use of tanks and the "creeping barrage," in which infantry marched close behind a rolling wall of shells to overwhelm their targets. In another of the war's ironies, these new tactics were pioneered by the conservative British, who launched a crushing counterattack in July, relying on the survivors of the armies of the Somme reinforced by troops from Australia, Canada, and India. The French made use of American troops, whose generals attacked the Germans with the same harrowing indifference to casualties shown in 1914. Despite their lack of experience, the American troops were tough and resilient. When combined with more-experienced French and Australian forces, they punched several large holes through German lines, crossing into the "lost provinces" of Alsace and Lorraine by October. At the beginning of November, the sweeping British offensive had joined up with the small Belgian army and was pressing toward Brussels.

The Allies finally brought their material advantage to bear on the Germans, who were suffering acutely by the spring of 1918. This was not only because of the continued effectiveness of the Allied blockade but also because of growing domestic conflict over war aims. On the front lines, German soldiers were exhausted. Following the lead

CASUALTY OF WAR. A German soldier killed during the Allies' October 1917 offensive.

of their distraught generals, the troops let morale sink, and many surrendered. Faced with one shattering blow after another, the German army was pushed deep into Belgium. Popular discontent mounted, and the government, which was now largely in the hands of the military, seemed unable either to win the war or to meet basic household needs.

Germany's network of allies was also coming undone. By the end of September, the Central Powers were headed for defeat. In the Middle East, the British army, which combined Bedouin guerrillas, Indian sepoys, Scottish highlanders, and Australian light cavalry, decisively defeated Ottoman forces in Syria and Iraq. In the Balkans, the French brought Greece into the war on the side of the Allies and knocked Bulgaria out of the war in September 1918. Meanwhile Austria-Hungary faced disaster on all sides, collapsing in Italy as well as the Balkans. Czech and Polish representatives in the Austrian government began pressing for self-government. Croat and Serb politicians proposed a "kingdom of Southern Slavs" (soon known as Yugoslavia). When Hungary joined the chorus for independence, the emperor, Karl I, accepted reality and sued for peace. The empire that had started the conflict surrendered on November 3, 1918, and disintegrated soon after.

Germany was now left with the impossible task of carrying on the struggle alone. By the fall of 1918, the country was starving and on the verge of civil war. When German sailors mutinied in early November, the kaiser's government collapsed. On November 8 a republic was proclaimed in Bavaria, and the next day nearly all of Germany was in the throes of revolution. The kaiser's abdication was announced in Berlin on November 9; he fled to Holland early the next morning. Control of the German government fell to a provisional council headed by Friedrich Ebert, the socialist leader in the Reichstag. Ebert and his colleagues immediately took steps to negotiate an armistice.

The Germans could do nothing but accept the Allies' terms, so at five o'clock in the morning of November 11, 1918, two German delegates met with the Allied army commander in the Compiègne forest and signed papers officially ending the war. Six hours later the order for cease fire was given across the Western Front. That night thousands of people danced through the streets of London, Paris, and Rome, engulfed in a different delirium from that of four years before, a joyous burst of exhausted relief.

The Peace Settlement

The Paris Peace Conference, which opened in January 1919, was an extraordinary moment, one that dramatized just how much the world had been transformed by the war and the decades that preceded it. Gone were the Russian, Austro-Hungarian, and German empires. That the American president Woodrow Wilson played such a prominent role marked the emergence of the United States as a world power. The United States' new status was rooted in the economic development of the second industrial revolution during the nineteenth century. In mass production and technological innovation, it had rivaled the largest European powers (England and Germany) before the war. During the war, American intervention (although it came late) had decisively broken the military-economic deadlock. And in the war's aftermath American industrial culture, engineering, and financial networks loomed very large on the European continent. Wilson and his entourage spent several months in Paris at the conference—a first for an

American president while in office and European leaders' first extended encounter with an American head of state.

American prominence was far from the only sign of global change. Some thirty nations sent delegates to the peace conference, a reflection of three factors: the scope of the war, heightened national sentiments and aspirations, and the tightening of international communication and economic ties in the latter part of the nineteenth century. The world in 1900 was vastly more globalized than it had been fifty years earlier. Many more countries had political, economic, and human investments in the war and its settlement. A belief that peace would secure and be secured by free peoples in sovereign nations represented the full flowering of nineteenth-century liberal nationalism. Delegates came to work for Irish home rule, for a Jewish state in Palestine, and for nations in Poland, Ukraine, and Yugoslavia. Europe's colonies, which had been key to the war effort and were increasingly impatient with their status, sent delegates to negotiate for self-determination. They discovered, however, that the western European leaders' commitment to the principle of national self-determination was hedged by their imperial assumptions. Non-state actors—in other words, international groups asking for women's suffrage, civil rights, minimum wages, or maximum hours—came to the Paris Peace Conference as well, for these were now seen as international issues. Finally, reporters from all over the world wired news home from Paris, a sign of vastly improved communications, transatlantic cables, and the mushrooming of the mass press.

Although many attended, the conference was largely controlled by the so-called Big Four: U.S. president Woodrow Wilson, British prime minister David Lloyd George, French premier Georges Clemenceau, and Italian premier Vittorio Orlando. The debates among these four personalities were fierce, as they all had conflicting ambitions and interests. In total, five separate treaties were signed, one with each of the defeated nations: Germany, Austria, Hungary, Turkey, and Bulgaria. The settlement with Germany was called the Treaty of Versailles, after the France town in which it was signed.

Wilson's widely publicized Fourteen Points represented the spirit of idealism. Wilson had proposed the Fourteen Points, even before the war ended, as the foundation of a permanent peace. Based on the principle of "open covenants of peace, openly arrived at," they called for freedom of the seas, an end to secret diplomacy, removal of international tariffs, and reduction of national armaments "to the lowest point consistent with safety." They also called for the "self-determination of peoples" and for the establishment of a League of Nations to settle international conflicts. Thousands of copies of the

"LONG LIVE WILSON!" Paris crowds greet President Wilson after the war. Despite public demonstrations of this sort, Wilson's attempt to shape the peace was a failure.

The Legacy of World War I

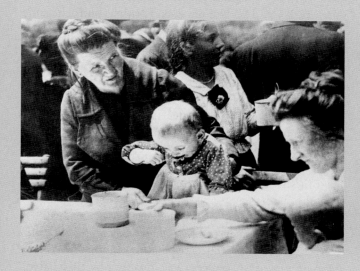

World War I had severe consequences for civilian populations, resulting not only from military conflict but also from economic dislocation, food shortages, and disease (see photo of a feeding station in Vienna for hungry families in 1918, on left). Recognizing the contribution of civilians to the war effort, states involved in World War I intervened massively in the economy, paying separation allowances to the families of soldiers, unemployment benefits to those thrown out of work, and regulating the sale and production of consumer goods. This example of the ways a government could play a role in the economy set a precedent for later in the twentieth century, and it is part of the history of current debates about the role the state can play in remedying inequality (see photo of protesters demonstrating against cuts in social security, on right).

Watch related author videos on the Student Site
wwnorton.com/college/history/western-civilizationsBrief4

Fourteen Points had been scattered by Allied planes over the German trenches and behind the lines in an attempt to convince both soldiers and civilians that the Allied nations were striving for a just and durable peace. Wilson's Fourteen Points thus shaped the expectations that Germans brought to the peace talks. When Wilson said, "The day of conquest and aggrandizement is gone by," many Germans expected that the treaty would not single Germany out for punishment.

Idealism, however, was undermined by other imperatives. Throughout the war, Allied propaganda led soldiers and civilians to believe that their sacrifices to the war effort would be compensated by payments extracted from the enemy. Total war demanded total victory. Lloyd George had campaigned during the British election of 1918

on the slogan "Hang the Kaiser!" Clemenceau had twice in his long lifetime seen France invaded and its existence imperiled. With the tables turned, he believed that the French should take full advantage of their opportunity to place Germany under strict control. The devastation of the war and the fiction that Germany could be made to pay for it made compromise impossible. The settlement with Germany was shaped more by this desire for punishment than by Wilson's idealism.

The Versailles treaty required Germany to surrender the "lost provinces" of Alsace and Lorraine to France and to give up other territories to Denmark and the new state of Poland. Germany's province of East Prussia was cut off from the rest of its territory. The port of Danzig, where the majority of the population was German, was put under the administrative control of the League of Nations and the economic domination of Poland. The treaty disarmed Germany, forbade a German air force, and reduced its navy to a token force to match an army capped at a hundred thousand volunteers. To protect France and Belgium, all German soldiers and fortifications were to be removed from the Rhine Valley.

The most important part of the Versailles treaty, and one of the parts at odds with Wilson's original plan, was the "war-guilt" provision in Article 231. Versailles held Germany and its allies responsible for the loss and damage suffered by the Allied governments and their citizens "as a consequence of the war imposed upon them by the aggression of Germany and her allies." Germany would be forced to pay massive reparations. The exact amount was left to a Reparations Commission, which set the total at $33 billion in 1921 (over $430 billion today). The Germans deeply resented these harsh demands, but others outside of Germany also warned of the dangers of punitive reparations. In *The Economic Consequences of the Peace*, the noted British economist John Maynard Keynes (1883–1946) argued that reparations would undermine Europe's most important task: repairing the world economy.

The other treaties at the Paris Peace Conference were based partly on the Allies' strategic interests, partly on the principle of national self-determination. The experience of the prewar years convinced leaders that they should draw nations' boundaries to conform to the ethnic, linguistic, and historical traditions of the people they were to contain. Wilson's idealism about freedom and equal representation confirmed these aims. Thus representatives of Yugoslavia were granted a state. Czechoslovakia was created, Poland reestablished, Hungary separated from Austria, and the Baltic states made independent (see the map on page 671). These national boundaries did not, indeed in most cases could not, follow ethnic divisions; they were created according to facts on the ground, hasty compromises, and political dictates—such as insulating western Europe from the communist threat of the Soviet Union. The peacemakers carved new nations from older, multiethnic empires, especially the Austro-Hungarian Empire, whose fragility had helped spark the war and whose structure had collapsed with the conflict. Creating nations, however, almost invariably created new minorities within those nations. The architects of the new Europe wrestled, briefly, with the problem of minorities, but did not resolve it. The issue would return to undermine European stability in the 1930s.

The Ottoman Empire ended as well, with two results: the creation of the modern Turkish state and a new structure for British and French colonial rule. As territories were taken from the Ottomans, Greece chose to seize some by force. The effort was successful at first, but the Turks counterattacked, driving out Greek forces by 1923 and creating the modern state of Turkey under the charismatic leadership of General Mustafa Kemal Attaturk. Ottoman territories placed under French and British control became part of the colonial "mandate system," which legitimized Europe's dominance over territories in the Middle East, Africa, and the Pacific. Territories were divided into groups on the basis of their location and their "level of development," or how far, in European eyes, they would have to travel to earn self-government. Choice pieces of land became mandates held, in principle, by the League of Nations but administered by Britain (Transjordan, Iraq, and Palestine) and France (Lebanon and Syria). The British and French empires, then, expanded after the war, although those territories held trouble ahead—the British faced revolt in Iraq and escalating tensions in Palestine, where they tried to juggle the promises made to Zionist settlers as well as the claims of indigenous Arab communities. Arab leaders, accompanied by their advocate T. E. Lawrence, attended the Versailles conference and listened as their hopes for independence were strictly circumscribed.

The peoples of the Allies' existing colonies were also disappointed. Ho Chi Minh, a young student from French Indochina attending a Parisian university, was one of many colonial activists who attended the conference to protest conditions in the colonies and to ask that the rights of nations be extended to their homelands. Well-organized delegations from French West Africa and from the Congress Party of India, which favored dominion status in return for the wartime efforts of millions of Indian soldiers who had fought for the British Empire, were also snubbed. The peacemakers' belief in democracy and self-determination collided with their baseline assumptions—inherited from the nineteenth century—about Western superiority; those assumptions justified imperial rule. Although the European powers spoke about reforming colonialism, little was done. Many nationalists in the colonies who had favored moderate legislative change decided that active struggle might be the only answer to the injustices of colonialism.

Each of the five peace treaties incorporated the Covenant of the League of Nations, an organization envisioned as the arbiter of world peace, but it never achieved the idealistic aims of its founders. The League was handicapped from the

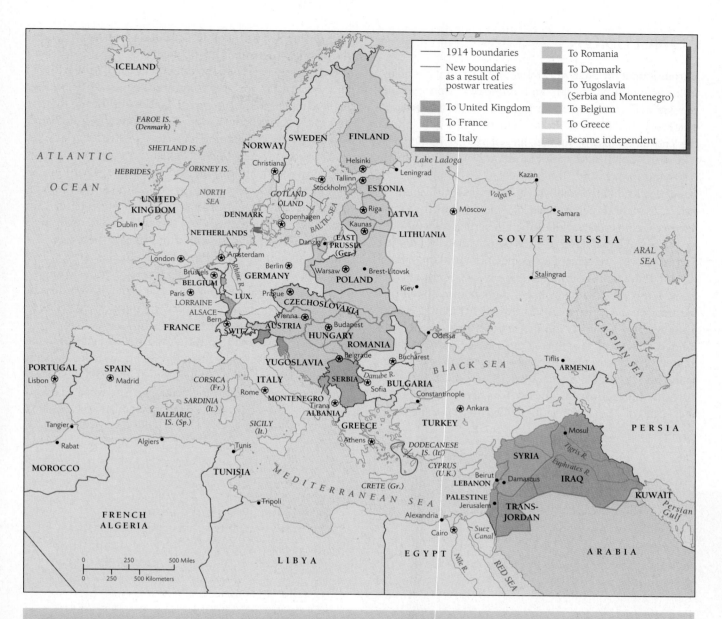

TERRITORIAL CHANGES IN EUROPE AND THE NEAR EAST AFTER THE FIRST WORLD WAR. Note the changes in geography as a result of the First World War. ▪ *What areas were most affected by the changes within Europe, and why?* ▪ *Can you see any obvious difficulties created by the redrawing of the map of Europe?* ▪ *What historical circumstances and/or new threats guided the victors to create such geopolitical anomalies?*

start by a number of changes to its original design. The arms-reduction requirement was watered down, and the League's power to enforce it was rendered almost nonexistent. Japan would not join unless it was allowed to keep former German concessions in China. France demanded that both Germany and Russia be excluded from the League. This contradicted Wilson's goals but had already been legitimized in Paris, where neither Soviet Russia nor the defeated Central Powers were allowed at the talks. The League received an even more debilitating blow when the U.S. Congress, citing the long-standing national preference for isolation, refused to approve U.S. membership in the League. Hobbled from the start, the international organization had little potential to avert conflicts.

The League began as a utopian response to global conflict and registered the urgency of reorganizing world governance. Its history, however, reflected the larger problems of power politics that emerged after the war.

CONCLUSION

Europe fought the First World War on every front possible—military, political, social, and economic. Consequently, the war's effects extended far beyond the devastated landscapes of the Western Front. Statistics can only hint at the enormous loss of human life: of the 70 million men who were mobilized, nearly 9 million were killed. Russia, Germany, France, and Hungary recorded the highest number of deaths, but the smaller countries of southeast Europe had the highest percentages of soldiers killed. Almost 40 percent of Serbia's soldiers died in battle. With the addition of war-related deaths caused by privation and disease, Serbia lost 15 percent of its population. In comparison, Britain, France, and Germany lost only 2–3 percent of their populations. But the percentages are much more telling if we focus on the young men of the war generation. Germany lost one-third of men aged nineteen to twenty-two in 1914. France and Britain sustained similar losses, with mortality among young men reaching eight to ten times the normal rate. This was the "lost generation."

The breakdown of the prewar treaty system and the scale of the diplomatic failure that produced the war discredited the political classes in many countries. Meanwhile, the war itself planted seeds of political and social discontent around the globe. Relations between Russia and western Europe grew sour and suspicious. The Allies had attempted to overthrow the Bolsheviks during the war and had excluded them from the negotiations afterward; these actions instilled in the Soviets a mistrust of the West that lasted for generations. The Allied nations feared that Russia would dominate the new states of eastern Europe, building a "Red Bridge" across the continent. Elsewhere, the conflicting demands of colonialism and nationalism struck only a temporary balance, while the redrawn maps left ethnic and linguistic minorities in every country. The fires of discontent raged most fiercely in Germany, where the Treaty of Versailles was decried as outrageously unjust. Nearly all national governments agreed that it would eventually have to be revised. Neither war nor peace had ended the rivalries that caused the Great War.

The war also had powerful and permanent economic consequences. Beset by inflation, debt, and the difficult task of industrial rebuilding, Europe found itself displaced from the center of the world economy. The war had accelerated the decentralization of money and markets. Many

After You Read This Chapter

 Go to **INQUIZITIVE** to see what you've learned—and learn what you've missed—with personalized feedback along the way.

REVIEWING THE OBJECTIVES

- The First World War broke out as a result of conflicts in the Balkans. Why?
- The Western Front was seen by all sides as a crucial theater of the conflict. What technologies led to a stalemate on the Western Front, and how did military leaders hope to achieve a breakthrough?
- European governments intervened in extraordinary ways in the economy to ensure the production of material for the war effort and to remedy the social crisis caused by mobilization. How did governments intervene in the economy?
- The war led European nations to mobilize people and resources from their colonies. How did colonial subjects participate in the war effort, and what did many of them expect in return?
- Russia was devastated by the war, and the population lost confidence in the tsar's government. What circumstances allowed the Bolsheviks to seize power in 1917 and what were their goals?
- The Versailles Peace Treaty blamed the Germans for the war. Who were the most important participants in the peace conference, and who shaped the terms of the treaty the most?

Asian, African, and South American nations benefited financially as their economies became less dependent on Europe, and they were better able to profit from Europe's need for their natural resources. The United States and Japan reaped the biggest gains and emerged as leaders in the new world economy.

The war's most powerful cultural legacy was disillusionment. A generation of men had been sacrificed to no apparent end. Surviving soldiers—many of them permanently injured, both physically and psychologically—were sickened by their participation in such useless slaughter. Women and other civilians had also made extraordinary sacrifices on the home front, for little apparent gain. Both veterans and civilians were disgusted by the greedy abandonment of principles by the politicians at Versailles. In the postwar period many younger men and women mistrusted the "old men" who had dragged the world into the war. These feelings of loss and alienation were voiced in the vastly popular genre of war literature—memoirs and fiction that commemorated the experience of soldiers on the front lines. The German writer and ex-soldier Erich Maria Remarque captured the disillusion of a generation in his novel *All Quiet on the*

Western Front: "Through the years our business has been killing;—it was our first calling in life. Our knowledge of life is limited to death. What will happen afterwards? And what shall come out of us?"

That was the main question facing postwar Europe. The German novelist Thomas Mann recognized that 1918 had brought "an end of an epoch, revolution, and the dawn of a new age," and that he and his fellow Germans were "living in a new and unfamiliar world." The struggle to define this new world would increasingly be conceived in terms of rival ideologies—democracy, communism, and fascism—competing for the future of Europe. The eastern autocracies had fallen with the war, but liberal democracy was soon on the decline as well. While militarism and nationalism remained strong, calls for major social reforms gained force during worldwide depression. Entire populations had been mobilized during the war, and they would remain so afterward—active participants in the age of mass politics. Europe was about to embark on two turbulent decades of rejecting and reinventing its social and political institutions. As Tomas Masaryk, the first president of newly formed Czechoslovakia, described it, postwar Europe was "a laboratory atop a graveyard."

PEOPLE, IDEAS, AND EVENTS IN CONTEXT

- Why was **FRANZ FERDINAND** assassinated and how did his death contribute to the outbreak of the war?
- What was the **SCHLIEFFEN PLAN** and how was it related to the outbreak of the war?
- What was the significance of the first **BATTLE OF THE MARNE** in 1914?
- Why did the British attempt to attack the Ottoman Empire at **GALLIPOLI**?
- What was the goal of the attacking forces at **VERDUN** and the **SOMME** in 1916? What was accomplished?
- Why did many people in Russia, and especially soldiers in the Russian army, lose faith in **NICHOLAS II** of Russia?
- Who were the **BOLSHEVIKS** and the **MENSHEVIKS** and what were their disagreements?
- How did **LENIN** make use of the **SOVIETS** in challenging the **PROVISIONAL GOVERNMENT** in Russia after the fall of the tsar?
- What policies did the **BOLSHEVIKS** follow after seizing power in Russia?
- What were **WOODROW WILSON'S GOALS** at the negotiations for the Versailles Treaty?
- What treatment did Germany receive under the terms of the **TREATY OF VERSAILLES**?

THINKING ABOUT CONNECTIONS

- What made World War I different from previous military conflicts in Europe that had involved large numbers of states, such as the Napoleonic Wars of the early nineteenth century (see Chapter 18), or the Thirty Years' War of the seventeenth century (see Chapter 15)?
- In what way might the effects and consequences of World War I have shaped the lives of Europeans in the decades to come? How did it change the lives of various peoples from other parts of the world who were drawn into the conflict?

STORY LINES

- With the exception of Bolshevik Russia, European states attempted to find stability in the traumatic aftermath of the First World War by reinforcing representative institutions and focusing on an orderly transition from wartime production to a peacetime economy.

- The Bolsheviks won the civil war that followed the Russian Revolution in 1917, and by the late 1920s Joseph Stalin embarked on an unprecedented revolution from above, industrializing the nation and transforming rural life through the collectivization of agriculture. The human costs were enormous, as millions died of hunger and millions more were arrested and deported to labor camps in the Soviet East.

- The Great Depression undermined political support for Europe's democracies in the 1930s, and the decade saw the consolidation of fascist regimes in Italy and Germany and an anti-capitalist communist regime in the Soviet Union.

CHRONOLOGY

1918	The November Revolution establishes the Weimar Republic
1918–1920	Russian Civil War
1920	National Socialist Workers' party founded in Germany
1922	Mussolini comes to power in Italy
1923	Hitler's Beer Hall Putsch in Munich
1928	First Soviet Five-Year Plan
1928–1929	Stalin gains power in Russia
1929–1933	Collectivization and famine in Soviet Union
1933	Hitler becomes chancellor of Germany
1937–1938	The Great Terror in Soviet Union

Before
You
Read
This
Chapter

Turmoil between the Wars

K äthe Kollwitz, a Berlin painter and sculptor, understood as well as anybody in Europe the terrible costs and futility of the First World War. Her youngest son, Peter, was killed on October 22, 1914, in Germany's failed attack on France. Her diary recorded the last moments she spent with him, an evening walk from the barracks on October 12, the day before his departure for the front: "It was dark, and we went arm in arm through the wood. He pointed out constellations to me, as he had done so often before." Her entry for October 30 was more succinct, a quotation from the postcard she had received from his commanding officer: "Your son has fallen." Kollwitz's pain at this loss found expression in her later work, which explored in naked terms the grief and powerlessness that she and her family had felt during the war years. Her suffering found expression, too, in a commitment to socialism, a political ideology that provided her with an antidote to the nationalism that pervaded German society during the war years and after. Kollwitz's socialism drew her to the attention of the Gestapo (state police) after the Nazis came to power in 1933, and she was fired from her position at the Academy of Art. She put up with house searches and harrassment, but refused invitations from friends abroad to go into exile. She died in Germany in 1945, having survived long enough to see her cherished grandson, also named Peter, killed in a second war while fighting as a German soldier on the Eastern Front in Russia in 1942.

The story of Käthe Kollwitz and her family between 1914 and 1945 is only unusual for the fact that she was a well-known artist. The suffering was all too familiar to others, as was the search for new political ideologies that might save Europeans from their past. The Great War left 9 million dead in its wake, and shattered the confidence that had been such a characteristic of nineteenth-century European culture. It led tragically to another world war, even more horrific than the first. Many in the interwar years shared Kollwitz's hope for a socialist or communist future, and many others turned to extremisms of the right. The result was a near collapse of democracy. By the late 1930s, few Western democracies remained. Even in those that did, most notably Britain, France, and the United States, regimes were frayed by the same pressures and strains that wrecked democratic governments elsewhere.

The foremost cause of democracy's decline in this period was a series of continuing disruptions in the world economy, caused first by the First World War and later, by the Great Depression of 1929–33. A second source of crisis lay in increased social conflict, exacerbated by the war. Although many hoped that these conflicts would be resolved by the peace and a renewed commitment to democratic institutions, the opposite occurred. Broad swaths of the electorate rallied to extremist political parties that promised radical transformations of nations and their cultures. Nationalism, sharpened by the war, proved a key source of discontent in its aftermath, and in Italy and Germany, frustrated nationalist sentiment turned against their governments.

The most dramatic instance of democracy's decline came with the rise of new authoritarian dictatorships, especially in the Soviet Union, Italy, and Germany. The experiences of these three nations differed significantly as a result of varying historical circumstances and personalities. In each case, however, many citizens allowed themselves to be persuaded that only drastic measures could bring order from chaos. Those measures, including the elimination of parliamentary government, strict restrictions on political freedom, and increasingly virulent repression of "enemies" of the state, were implemented with a combination of violence, intimidation, and propaganda. That so

***WIDOWS AND ORPHANS* BY KÄTHE KOLLWITZ, 1919.** Kollwitz (1867–1945), a German artist and socialist active in Berlin, lost a son in the First World War and a grandson in the Second World War. Her work poignantly displayed the effects of poverty and war on the lives of ordinary people.

many citizens seemed willing to sacrifice their freedoms—or those of others—was a measure of their alienation, impatience, or desperation.

THE RUSSIAN REVOLUTION UNDER LENIN AND STALIN

The Russian Civil War

The Bolsheviks seized power in October 1917. They signed a separate peace with Germany in March 1918 (the Treaty of Brest-Litovsk), but Russia collapsed into civil war soon after. Fury at the terms of Brest-Litovsk mobilized the Bolsheviks' enemies. Known collectively as "Whites," the Bolsheviks' opponents included supporters of the old regime, the former nobility, and liberal supporters of the provisional government. They were joined by anti-Bolshevik dissident groups and peasant bands who opposed all central state power. The Bolsheviks, or "Reds," also faced insurrections from strong nationalist movements in the Ukraine, Georgia, and the north Caucasus. Finally, several foreign powers, including the United States, Great Britain, and Japan, landed troops on the periphery of the old empire. These interventions were only a minor threat, but they heightened Bolshevik mistrust of the capitalist world which, in the Marxists' view, would naturally oppose the existence of the world's first "socialist" state.

The Bolsheviks eventually won the civil war because they gained greater support—or at least tacit acceptance—from the majority of the population and because they were better organized for the war effort itself. Leon Trotsky, the revolutionary hero of 1905 and 1917, became the new commissar of war and created a hierarchical, disciplined military machine that grew to some 5 million men by 1920. Trotsky's Red Army triumphed over the White armies by the end of 1920, although fighting continued into 1922. The Bolsheviks also invaded Poland and nearly reached Warsaw before being thrown back. During this period, the Bolsheviks consolidated their control over the Russian Empire of the Tsars, now divided into four federated socialist republics: Russia, the Transcaucus, Ukraine, and Belorussia. In 1922 these republics were officially consolidated into the Union of Soviet Socialist Republics (USSR), or the Soviet Union.

The costs of the civil war were even greater than Russia's losses in the First World War: 1 million combat casualties, several million deaths from famine caused by the war, and 100,000–300,000 executions of noncombatants as part of Red and White terror. The barbarism of the war engendered lasting hatreds within the emerging Soviet nation, especially among ethnic minorities, and it brutalized the fledgling society that came into existence under the new Bolshevik regime.

The civil war also shaped the Bolsheviks' approach to the economy. On taking power in 1917, Lenin expected to create, for the short term at least, a state-capitalist system that resembled the successful European wartime economies. The new government took control of large-scale industry, banking, and all other major capitalist concerns while allowing small-scale private economic activity, including agriculture, to continue. The civil war pushed the new government toward a more radical economic stance known as "war communism." The Bolsheviks began to requisition grain from the peasantry, and they outlawed private trade in consumer goods as "speculation," militarized production facilities, and abolished money. Many believed that war communism would replace the capitalist system that had collapsed in 1917.

Such hopes were largely unfounded. War communism sustained the Bolshevik military effort, but further disrupted the already war-ravaged economy. The civil war

LENIN AND STALIN. Under Stalin this picture was used to show his close relationship with Lenin. In fact, the photograph was a fabrication. ▪ *What opportunities for propaganda and manipulation were offered by new technologies of photography and film?*

devastated Russian industry and emptied major cities. The population of Moscow fell by 50 percent between 1917 and 1920. The masses of urban workers who had strongly supported the Bolshevik revolution melted back into the countryside, and industrial output in 1920–21 fell to only 20 percent of prewar levels. Most devastating were the effects of war communism on agriculture. The peasants had initially benefited from the revolution when they spontaneously seized and redistributed lands held by the former nobility. Nonetheless, the agricultural system was severely disrupted by the civil war, by the grain requisitioning of war communism, and by the outlawing of all private trade in grain. Large-scale famine resulted in 1921 and claimed some 5 million lives.

As the civil war came to a close, urban workers and soldiers became increasingly impatient with the Bolshevik regime, which had promised socialism and workers' control but had delivered something more akin to a military dictatorship. Large-scale strikes and protests broke out in late 1920, but the Bolsheviks moved swiftly and effectively to subdue the "popular revolts." In crushing dissent, the Bolshevik regime that emerged from the civil war made a clear statement that public opposition would not be tolerated.

The NEP Period

In response to these political and economic difficulties, the Bolsheviks abandoned war communism and in March 1921 embarked on a radically different course known as the New Economic Policy (NEP). The state continued to own all major industry and financial concerns, while individuals were allowed to own private property, trade freely within limits, and—most important—farm their land for their own benefit. Fixed taxes on the peasantry replaced grain requisitioning; what peasants grew beyond the tax requirements was theirs to do with as they saw fit. The Bolshevik most identified with the NEP was Nikolai Bukharin (1888–1938), who argued that the Bolsheviks could best industrialize the lands under their control by taxing private peasant economic activity.

The NEP was undeniably successful in allowing Soviet agriculture to recover from the civil war; by 1924 agricultural harvests had returned to prewar levels. Peasants were largely left alone to do as they pleased, and they responded by producing enough grain to feed the country, though they continued to use very primitive farming methods to do so. The NEP was less successful, however, in encouraging peasants to participate in markets to benefit urban areas. The result was a series of shortages in grain deliveries to cities, a situation that prompted many Bolsheviks to call for revival of the radical economic practices of war communism. The fate of these radical proposals, however, was tied to the fate of the man who would, contrary to all expectations, replace Lenin as the leader of the USSR and become one of the most notorious dictators of all time: Joseph Stalin.

Stalin and the "Revolution from Above"

Stalin's rise was swift and unpredicted. His political success was rooted in intraparty conflicts in the 1920s, but it was also closely tied to the abrupt end of the NEP period in the late 1920s and to the beginning of a massive program of social and economic modernization. This "revolution from above" was the most rapid social and economic transformation any nation has seen in modern history. It was carried out, however, at unprecedented human cost.

Stalin (1879–1953), the son of a poor shoemaker, was a Bolshevik from the Caucasus nation of Georgia. His real name was Iosep Jughashvili. Receiving his early education in an Orthodox seminary, he participated in revolutionary activity in the Caucasus and spent many years in Siberian exile before the revolution. He was an important member

WINTER DEPORTATIONS, 1929–30. Ukrainian families charged with being *kulaks* were deported from their homes because of their refusal to join Stalin's collective farming plan. Many of the evicted families were shipped north by train to the Arctic, where they perished due to the lack of adequate food and shelter.

of the Bolshevik party during the Russian Revolution, but he was not one of the central figures and was certainly not a front runner for party leadership. After Lenin's death in 1924, the civil war hero Leon Trotsky was widely assumed to be the best candidate to succeed him.

Stalin shrewdly played the game of internal party politics after Lenin's death. He sidelined his opponents within the Bolshevik party by isolating and expelling each of them successively. Trotsky was the first to go, driven out by a coalition of Stalin and others who feared Trotsky's desire to take control of the party himself. Stalin then turned on his former allies and removed them in turn, culminating in the removal of Bukharin from the Politburo (short for political bureau, which governed the Communist party and state) in 1928–29.

Stalin's campaign against Bukharin was connected to his desire to discard the NEP system and to launch an all-out industrialization drive. By the late 1920s, Stalin believed that the Soviet Union could not hope to industrialize by relying on taxes generated from small-scale peasant agriculture. He began to push for an increase in the tempo of industrialization as early as 1927, prompted by fears of falling behind the West and by the perceived threat of another world war. Almost all of the Bolshevik leaders supported Stalin's plan to step up the tempo of industrialization. But hardly anybody supported what happened next: an abrupt turn toward forced industrialization and collectivization of agriculture.

COLLECTIVIZATION

In late 1929 Stalin embarked on collectivization of agriculture by force. Peasants would either pool their resources and join collective farms or work on state farms as paid laborers. Within a few months, the Politburo began to issue orders to use force against peasants who resisted collectivization. The process that ensued was brutal and chaotic. Local party and police officials forced peasants to give up their private land, farming implements, and livestock and to join collective farms. Peasants resisted, often violently. There were some 1,600 large-scale rebellions in the Soviet Union between 1929 and 1933; some involved several thousand people, and quelling them required military intervention, including the use of artillery. By 1935 collectivization of agriculture was complete in most areas of the Soviet Union.

To facilitate collectivization, Stalin also launched an all-out attack on peasants designated as *kulaks* (a derogatory term for well-to-do farmers, literally meaning "tight-fisted ones"). Most kulaks, though, were not any better off than their neighbors, and the word became one of many terms for peasants hostile to collectivization. Between 1929 and 1933, some 1.5 million peasants were uprooted, dispossessed of their property, and resettled from their farmlands to either inhospitable reaches of the Soviet east and north or to poor farmland closer to their original homes. The liquidation of kulaks as a class magnified the disruptive effects of agricultural collectivization, and the two together produced one of the most devastating famines in modern European history. Peasants who were forced into collective farms had little incentive to produce extra food, and exiling many of the most productive peasants not surprisingly weakened the agricultural system. In 1932–33, famine spread across the southern region of the Soviet Union. This was the most productive agricultural area in the country, and the famine that struck there was thus particularly senseless. The 1933 famine cost some 3–5 million lives. During the famine, the Bolsheviks maintained substantial grain reserves in other parts of the country, enough to save many hundreds of thousands of lives at a minimum, but they refused to send this grain to the affected areas, preferring instead to seal off famine-stricken regions and allow people to starve. Grain reserves were instead sold overseas for hard currency and stockpiled in case of war. After 1935 there would never again be any large-scale resistance to Soviet power in the countryside.

The Five-Year Plans

In Stalin's view, collectivization provided the resources for the other major aspect of his revolution from above: a rapid campaign of forced industrialization. The road map for this industrialization process was the first Five-Year Plan (1928–32), an ambitious set of goals that Stalin and his cohorts drew up in 1927. The results rank as one of the most stunning periods of economic growth the modern world has ever seen. Soviet statistics boasted of annual growth rates of 20 percent a year. Even the more cautious Western estimates of 14 percent annual growth were remarkable, given the worldwide depression elsewhere. The Bolsheviks built entirely new industries in entirely new cities. In 1926, only one-fifth of the population lived in towns. Fifteen years later, in 1939, roughly a third did. The urban population had grown from 26 million to 56 million in under fifteen years. The Soviet Union was well on its way to becoming an urban, industrial society.

This rapid industrialization came, however, at enormous human cost. Many large-scale projects were carried out with prison labor, especially in the timber and mining industries. The labor camp system, known as the *gulag*,

"IMPERIALISTS CANNOT STOP THE SUCCESS OF THE FIVE-YEAR PLAN!" ▪ *Did propaganda like this also appeal to Russian nationalist pride?*

Stalin's Industrialization of the Soviet Union

> How did the Soviet people experience Stalin's industrialization drive? New archives have helped historians glimpse what the common people lived through and how they responded. The first excerpt is a speech that Stalin gave at The Conference of Managers of Socialist Industry in 1931. In his usual style, he invoked fears of Soviet backwardness and Russian nationalism while summoning all to take up the task of industrial production.
>
> The letters in the second selection come from several hundred that workers and peasants sent to Soviet newspapers and authorities recounting their experiences and offering their opinions. Both of the ones printed here were sent to the Soviet newspaper Pravda ("Truth").

"The Tasks of Business Executives"

It is sometimes asked whether it is not possible to slow down the tempo somewhat, to put a check on the movement. No, comrades, it is not possible! The tempo must not be reduced! On the contrary, we must increase it as much as is within our powers and possibilities. This is dictated to us by our obligations to the workers and peasants of the USSR. This is dictated to us by our obligations to the working class of the whole world.

To slacken the tempo would mean falling behind. And those who fall behind get beaten. But we do not want to be beaten. No, we refuse to be beaten. One feature of the history of old Russia was the continual beatings she suffered because of her backwardness. She was beaten by the Mongol khans. She was beaten by the Turkish beys. . . . She was beaten by the British and French capitalists. She was beaten by the Japanese barons. All beat her—for her backwardness: for military backwardness, for cultural backwardness, for political backwardness, for industrial backwardness, for agricultural backwardness. . . .

We are fifty or a hundred years behind the advanced countries. We must make good this distance in ten years. Either we do it, or we shall be crushed. . . .

In ten years at most we must make good the distance which separates us from the advanced capitalist countries. We have all the "objective" possibilities for this. The only thing lacking is the ability to take proper advantage of these possibilities. And that depends on us. *Only* on us! . . . It is time to put an end to the rotten policy of noninterference in production. It is time to adopt a new policy, a policy adapted to the present times—the policy of interfering in everything. If you are a factory manager, then interfere in all the affairs of the factory, look into everything, let nothing escape you, learn and learn again. Bolsheviks must master technique. It is time Bolsheviks themselves became experts. . . .

became a central part of the Stalinist economic system. People were arrested and sent to camps on a bewildering array of charges, ranging from petty criminal infractions to contact with foreigners to having the ill fortune to be born of bourgeois or kulak parents. The camp system spread throughout the Soviet Union in the 1930s: by the end of the decade, roughly 3.6 million people were incarcerated by the regime. This army of prisoners was used to complete the most arduous and dangerous industrialization tasks.

The economic system created during this revolution from above was also fraught with structural problems that would plague the Soviet Union for its entire history. The command economy, with each year's production levels entirely planned in advance in Moscow, never functioned in a rational way. Heavy industry was favored over light industry, and uncertainty about future orders encouraged factory directors to hoard raw materials and keep extra workers on staff so as to be able to meet their quotas quickly when ordered to do so. A factory that was charged with producing a certain number of pairs of shoes could cut costs by producing all one style and size. Periods of slow production would alternate with intense activity, and shortages would be followed by excess production

There are no fortresses which Bolsheviks cannot capture. We have assumed power. We have built up a huge socialist industry. We have swung the middle peasants to the path of socialism. . . . What remains to be done is not so much: to study technique, to master science. And when we have done that we will develop a tempo of which we dare not even dream at present.

Source: Joseph Stalin, "The Tasks of Business Executives" [speech given at the First All-Union Conference of Managers of Socialist Industry, February 4, 1931], cited in Richard Sakwa, *The Rise and Fall of the Soviet Union, 1917–1991* (New York: 1999), pp. 187–88.

Stalin's Industrial Development: The View from Below

It should not be forgotten that many millions of workers are participating in the building of socialism. A horse with its own strength can drag seventy-five poods,* but its owner has loaded it with a hundred poods, and in addition he's fed it poorly. No matter how much he uses the whip, it still won't be able to move the cart.

This is also true for the working class. They've loaded it with socialist competition, shock work, over-fulfilling the industrial and financial plan, and so forth. A worker toils seven hours, not ever leaving his post, and this is not all he does. Afterward he sits in meetings or else attends classes for an hour and a half or two in order to increase his skill level, and if he doesn't do these things, then he's doing things at home. And what does he live on? One hundred fifty grams of salted mutton, he will make soup without any of the usual additives, neither carrots, beets, flour, nor salt pork. What kind of soup do you get from this? Mere "dishwater."

—B. N. Kniazev, Tula, Sept. 1930

Comrade Editor, Please give me an answer. Do the local authorities have the right to forcibly take away the only cow of industrial and office workers? What is more, they demand a receipt showing that the cow was handed over voluntarily and they threaten you by saying if you don't do this, they will put you in prison for failure to fulfill the meat procurement. How can you live when the cooperative distributes only black bread, and at the market goods have the prices of 1919 and 1920? Lice have eaten us to death, and soap is given only to railroad workers. From hunger and filth we have a massive outbreak of spotted fever.

—Anonymous, from Aktybinsk, Kazakhstan

*A pood is a Russian unit of weight, equal to 36.11 pounds.

Source: Lewis Siegelbaum and Andrei Sokolov, *Stalinism as a Way of Life: A Narrative in Documents* (New Haven, CT: 2000), pp. 39–41.

Questions for Analysis

1. What are Stalin's priorities?

2. What images does Stalin use to capture his audience's attention?

3. How did the Soviet people experience Stalin's industrialization drive?

of unnecessary goods. Stalin's industrialization drive did transform the country from an agrarian nation to a world industrial power in the space of a few short years, but in the longer run, the system would prove to be an economic disaster.

The Stalin revolution also produced fundamental cultural and economic changes. The revolution from above altered the face of Soviet cities and the working class populating them. New cities were largely made up of first-generation peasants who brought their rural traditions to the cities with them, changing the fragile urban culture that had existed during the 1920s. Women, too, entered the urban workforce in increasing numbers in the 1930s—women went from 20 percent to almost 40 percent of the workforce in one decade, and in light industry they made up two-thirds of the labor force by 1940.

At the same time, Stalin promoted a sharply conservative shift in all areas of culture and society. In art, the radical modernism of the 1920s was crushed by socialist realism, a deadening aesthetic that celebrated the drive toward socialism and left no room for experimentation. Family policy and gender roles underwent a similar reversal. Early Bolshevik activists had promoted a utopian attempt to rebuild one of the basic structures of prerevolutionary society—the family—and to create a genuinely new proletarian social structure. The Bolsheviks in the 1920s legalized divorce, expelled the Orthodox Church from marriage ceremonies, and legalized abortion. Stalin abandoned these ideas of communist familial relations in favor of efforts to strengthen traditional family ties: divorce became more difficult, abortion was outlawed in 1936 except in cases that threatened the life of the mother, and homosexuality was declared a criminal offense. State subsidies and support for mothers, which were progressive for the time, could not change the reality that Soviet women were increasingly forced to carry the double burden of familial and wage labor in order to support Stalin's version of Soviet society. All areas of Soviet cultural and social policy experienced similar reversals.

The Great Terror

The "Great Terror" of 1937–38 left nearly a million people dead and as many as 1.5 million more in labor camps. As Stalin consolidated his personal dictatorship over the country, he eliminated enemies—real and imagined—along with individuals and groups he considered superfluous to the new Soviet society.

The Terror was aimed at various categories of internal "enemies," from the top to the very bottom of Soviet society. The top level of the Bolshevik party itself was purged almost completely; some 100,000 party members were removed, most facing prison sentences or execution. The purge also struck—with particular ferocity—nonparty elites, industrial managers, and intellectuals. In 1937 and 1938 Stalin purged the military, arresting some 40,000 officers and shooting at least 10,000. These purges disrupted the government and the economy but allowed Stalin to promote a new, young cadre of officials who owed their careers, if not their lives, to Stalin personally. Whole ethnic groups were viewed with suspicion, including Poles, Ukrainians, Lithuanians, Latvians, Koreans, and others. From the bottom, some 200,000–300,000 "dekulakized" peasants, petty criminals, and other social misfits were arrested, and many shot.

The Great Terror remains one of the most puzzling aspects of Stalin's path to dictatorial power. The Terror succeeded, with a certain paranoid logic, in solidifying Stalin's personal control over all aspects of social and political life in the Soviet Union, but it did so by destroying the most talented elements in Soviet society.

The results of the Stalin revolution were profound. No other regime in the history of Europe had ever attempted to reorder completely the politics, economy, and society

of a major nation. The Soviets had done so in a mere ten years. By 1939, private manufacturing and trade had been almost entirely abolished. Factories, mines, railroads, and public utilities were exclusively owned by the state. Stores were either government enterprises or cooperatives in which consumers owned shares. Agriculture had been almost completely socialized. The society that emerged from this terrible decade was industrial, more urban than rural, and more modern than traditional. But the USSR that emerged from this tumultuous period would barely be able to withstand the immense strains placed on it when the Germans struck less than three years after the end of the Terror.

THE EMERGENCE OF FASCISM IN ITALY

Like many European nations, Italy emerged from the First World War as a democracy in distress. Italy was on the winning side but the war had cost nearly 700,000 Italian lives and over $15 billion. Moreover, during the war Italy had received secret promises of specific territorial gains, only to find those promises withdrawn when they conflicted with principles of self-determination. Italian claims to the west coast of the Adriatic, for instance, were denied by Yugoslavia. At first the nationalists blamed the "mutilated victory" on President Wilson, but after a short time they turned on their own rulers and what they considered the weaknesses of parliamentary democracy.

Italy had long-standing problems that were made worse by the war. Since unification, the Italian nation had been rent by an unhealthy economic split—divided into a prosperous industrialized north and a poor agrarian south. Social conflict over land, wages, and local power caused friction in the countryside as well as in urban centers. Governments were often seen as corrupt, indecisive, and defeatist. This was the background for the more immediate problems that Italy faced after the war.

Inflation and unemployment were perhaps the most destructive effects of the war. Inflation produced high prices, speculation, and profiteering. And though normally wages would have risen also, the postwar labor market was glutted by returning soldiers. Furthermore, business elites were shaken by strikes, which became increasingly large and frequent, and by the closing of foreign markets. The parliamentary government that was set up after the war failed to ease these dire conditions, and Italians wanted radical reforms. For the working class, this meant socialism. The movement grew increasingly radical: in 1920, the socialist and anarchist workers seized scores of factories, most in the metallurgy sector, and tried to run them for the benefit of the workers themselves. In some rural areas, so-called Red Leagues tried to break up large estates and force landlords to reduce their rents. In all these actions, the model of the Russian Revolution, although it was only vaguely understood, encouraged the development of local radicalism.

The rising radical tide, especially seen against the backdrop of the Bolshevik revolution, worried other social groups. Industrialists and landowners feared for their property. Small shopkeepers and white-collar workers—social groups that did not think the working-class movement supported their interests—found themselves alienated by business elites on the one hand and by apparently revolutionary radicals on the other. The threat from the left provoked a strong surge to the right. Fascism appeared in the form of vigilante groups breaking up strikes, fighting with workers in the streets, or ousting the Red Leagues from lands occupied in the countryside.

The Rise of Mussolini

"I am fascism," said Benito Mussolini, and indeed, the success of the Italian fascist movement depended heavily on his leadership. Mussolini (1883–1945) was the son of a socialist blacksmith and a schoolteacher. He studied to become a teacher, but settled on journalism as a career, writing for socialist newspapers. After a brief period in Switzerland he was expelled from the country for fomenting strikes. He returned to Italy, where he became the editor of *Avanti* ("Forward"), the leading socialist daily.

When war broke out in August 1914, Mussolini broke with the socialists and became an ardent nationalist, urging Italy to join the Allies. Deprived of his position as the editor of *Avanti*, he founded a new paper, *Il Popolo d'Italia* ("The People of Italy"), and dedicated its columns to arousing enthusiasm for war.

As early as October 1914, Mussolini had organized groups, called *fasci*, to help drum up support for the war. Members of the fasci were young idealists, fanatical nationalists. After the war, these groups formed the base of Mussolini's fascist movement. (The word *fascism* derives from the Latin *fasces*: an ax surrounded by a bundle of sticks that represented the authority of the ancient Roman state. The Italian *fascio* means "group" or "band.") In 1919 Mussolini drafted the original platform of the Fascist party. It had several surprising elements, including universal suffrage (including woman), an eight-hour work day, and a tax on inheritances. A new platform, adopted in 1920, abandoned all references to economic reforms. Neither platform earned the fascists many followers.

What the fascists lacked in political support, they made up for in aggressive determination. They gained the respect of the middle class and landowners, and intimidated many others, by forcefully repressing radical movements of industrial workers and peasants. They attacked socialists, often physically, and succeeded in taking over some local governments. As the national regime weakened, Mussolini's coercive politics made him look like a solution to the absence of leadership, and the number of his supporters grew. In September 1922 he began to negotiate with other parties and the king for fascist participation in government. On October 28 an army of about 50,000 fascist militiamen, in black-shirted uniforms, marched into Rome and occupied the capital. The premier resigned, and the following day the king, Victor Emmanuel III, reluctantly invited Mussolini to form a cabinet. Without firing a shot, the Black Shirts had gained control of the Italian government. The explanation of their success is to be found less in the strength of the fascist movement itself than in the Italian disappointments after the war and the weakness of the older governing classes.

The parliamentary system had folded under pressure. And though Mussolini had "legally" been granted his power, he immediately began to establish a one-party dictatorship. The doctrines of Italian fascism had three components. The first was statism. The state was declared to incorporate every interest and every loyalty of its members. There was to be "nothing above the state, nothing outside the state, nothing against the state." The second was nationalism. Nationhood was the highest form of society, with a life and a soul of its own, transcending the individuals who composed it. The third was militarism. Nations that did not expand would eventually wither and die. Fascists believed that war ennobled man and regenerated sluggish and decadent peoples.

Mussolini began to rebuild Italy in accordance with these principles. The first step was to change electoral laws so they granted his party solid parliamentary majorities and to intimidate the opposition. He then moved to close down parliamentary government and other parties entirely. He abolished the cabinet system and all but extinguished the powers of the parliament. He made the Fascist party an integral part of the Italian constitution. Mussolini assumed the dual position of prime minister and party leader (*duce*), and he used the party's militia to eliminate his enemies by intimidation and violence. Mussolini's government also controlled the police, muzzled the press, and censored academic activity.

Meanwhile, Mussolini preached the end of class conflict and its replacement by national unity. He began to reorganize the economy and labor, taking away the power of the country's labor movement. The Italian economy was placed under the management of twenty-two corporations, each responsible for a major industrial enterprise. In each corporation were representatives of trade unions, whose members were organized by the Fascist party, the employers, and the government. Together, the members of these corporations were given the task of determining working conditions, wages, and prices. It is not surprising, however, that the decisions of these bodies were closely supervised by the government and favored the position of management. Indeed, the government quickly aligned with big business, creating more of a corrupt bureaucracy than a revolutionary economy.

Mussolini secured some working-class assent with state-sponsored programs, including massive public-works projects, library building, paid vacations for

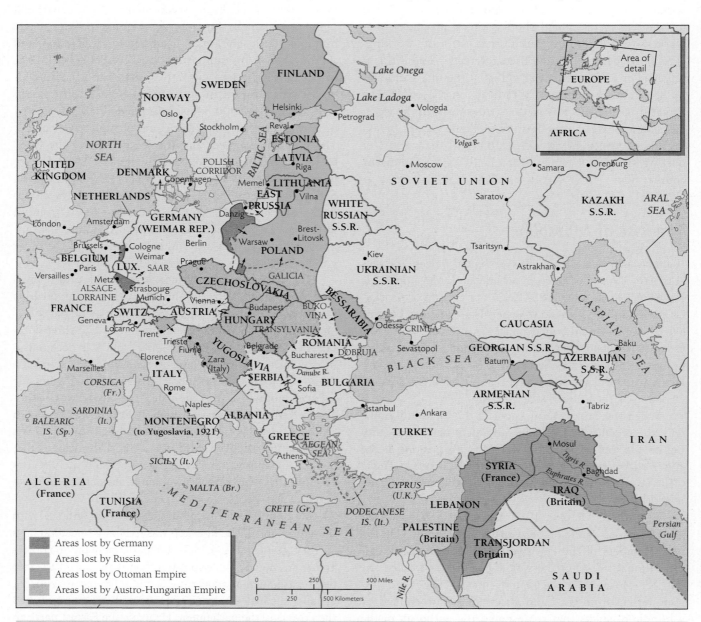

EUROPE IN 1923. ■ *Which countries and empires lost territories after the First World War, and with what consequences?* ■ *How did the Russian Revolution change European politics?* ■ *What problems arose in the central and eastern European nations created after the First World War?*

workers, and social security. In 1929, he settled Italy's sixty-year-old conflict with the Roman Catholic Church. He signed a treaty that granted independence to the papal residence in the Vatican City and established Roman Catholicism as the official religion of the state. The treaty also guaranteed religious education in the nation's schools and made religious marriage ceremonies mandatory.

In fact, Mussolini's regime did much to maintain the status quo. Party officers exercised some political supervision over bureaucrats, yet did not infiltrate the bureaucracy in significant numbers. Moreover, Mussolini remained on friendly terms with the elites who had assisted his rise to power. Whatever he proclaimed about the distinctions between fascism and capitalism, the economy of Italy remained dependent on private enterprise. Fascism, however, did little to lessen Italy's plight during the worldwide depression of the 1930s.

Like Nazism later, fascism had contradictory elements. It sought to restore traditional authority and, at the same time, mobilize all of Italian society for economic and nationalist purposes—a process that inevitably undercut older authorities. It created new authoritarian organizations and activities that comported with these goals: exercise programs to make the young fit and mobilized, youth camps, awards to mothers of large families, political rallies, and parades in small towns in the countryside. Activities like these offered people a feeling of political involvement though they no longer enjoyed political rights. This mobilized but essentially passive citizenship was a hallmark of fascism.

WEIMAR GERMANY

On November 9, 1918—two days before the armistice ending the First World War—a massive and largely unexpected uprising in Berlin resulted in the kaiser's abdication and the birth of a new German republic. The leader of the new government was Friedrich Ebert, a member of the Social Democratic party (SPD) in the Reichstag. The revolution spread quickly. By the end of the month, councils of workers and soldiers controlled hundreds of German cities. The "November Revolution" was fast and far reaching, though not as revolutionary as many middle- and upper-class conservatives feared. The majority of socialists steered a cautious, democratic course: they wanted reforms but were willing to leave much of the existing imperial bureaucracy intact. Above all,

they wanted a popularly elected national assembly to draft a constitution for the new republic.

Two months passed, however, before elections could be held—a period of crisis that verged on civil war. The revolutionary movement that had brought the SPD to power now threatened it. Independent socialists and a nascent Communist party wanted radical reforms, and in December 1918 and January 1919 they staged armed uprisings in the streets of Berlin. Fearful of a Bolshevik-style revolution, the Social Democratic government turned against its former allies and sent militant bands of workers and volunteers to crush the uprisings. During the conflict, the government's fighters murdered Rosa Luxemburg and Karl Liebknecht—two German communist leaders who became instant martyrs. Violence continued into 1920, creating a lasting bitterness among groups on the left.

More important, the revolutionary aftermath of the war gave rise to bands of militant counterrevolutionaries. Veterans and other young nationalists joined so-called *Freikorps* (free corps). Such groups developed throughout the country, drawing as many as several hundred thousand members. Former army officers who led these militias continued their war experience by fighting against Bolsheviks, Poles, and communists. The politics of the Freikorps were fiercely right-wing. Anti-Marxist, anti-Semitic, and antiliberal, they openly opposed the new German republic and its parliamentary democracy. Many of the early Nazi leaders had fought in the First World War and participated in Freikorps units.

Germany's new government—known as the Weimar Republic (*VY-mahr*) for the city in which its constitution was drafted—rested on a coalition of socialists, Catholic centrists, and liberal democrats, a necessary compromise since no single party won a majority of the votes in the January 1919 election. The Weimar constitution was based on the values of parliamentary liberalism and set up an open, pluralistic framework for German democracy. Through a series of compromises, the constitution established universal suffrage (for both women and men) and a bill of rights that guaranteed not only civil liberties but also a range of social entitlements. On paper, at least, the revolutionary movement had succeeded.

Yet the Weimar government lasted just over a decade. By 1930 it was in crisis, and in 1933 it collapsed. What happened? Many of Weimar's problems were born from Germany's defeat in the First World War, which was not only devastating but also humiliating. Many Germans soon latched onto rumors that the army hadn't actually been defeated in battle but instead had been stabbed in the back by socialists and Jewish leaders in the German government. Army officers cultivated this story even before the war was

Between 1924 and 1933, the Nazis persisted in their attempts to win seats in the German parliament through elections. At first this strategy brought meager results—after a high of 6.6 percent of the vote in the "inflation election" of 1924, the Nazis made little progress as the economy stabilized. After 1928, however, political polarization in the Weimar Republic worked to Hitler's advantage, and the unemployment crisis brought about by the beginning of the depression proved to be the decisive factor. Hitler stopped in his attempts to attract votes from workers (who tended to vote on the left) and switched instead to a campaign designed to win support from rural voters and members of the middle classes.

The Nazi electoral campaigns focused on a few themes: the dangers of communism, the "degenerate" and "decadent" culture of the postwar years, the weakness of parliamentary government, and the influence of "cosmopolitan" (a code word for Jewish or insufficiently nationalist) movies such as *All Quiet on the Western Front*. In 1930 the Nazis received 18.3 percent of the vote and won 107 of 577 seats in the parliament, second only to the Social Democrats. Hitler ran for president in 1932 and lost, but the results showed Hitler drawing support across class lines, among all age groups, and in all regions of Germany. Later that year, the Nazis polled 37.4 percent of the vote in parliamentary elections, a significant plurality.

In January 1933, therefore, President Hindenburg invited Hitler to be chancellor of Germany, hoping to create a conservative coalition that would bring the Nazis into line with less radical parties. Once legally installed in power, however, Hitler made the most of it. When a Dutch anarchist with links to the Communist party set fire to the Reichstag on the night of Feburary 27, Hitler seized the opportunity to suspend civil rights "as a defensive measure against communist acts of violence." He convinced Hindenburg to dissolve the Reichstag and to order a new election on March 5, 1933. Under Hitler's sway, the new parliament granted him unlimited powers for the next four years. Hitler proclaimed his government the "Third Reich"—the first was the realm of Charlemagne in the Middle Ages, and the second was the German Empire of 1870–1918.

Nazi Germany

By the fall of 1933, Germany had become a one-party state. The socialist and communist left was crushed by the new regime. Almost all non-Nazi organizations had been either abolished or forced to become part of the Nazi system. Party propaganda sought to impress citizens with the regime's "monolithic efficiency." But in fact, the Nazi government was a tangled bureaucratic maze, with both agencies and individuals vying fiercely for Hitler's favor.

Ironically, at the end of the party's first year in power, the most serious challenges to Hitler came from within the party. Hitler's paramilitary Nazi storm troopers (the SA) had been formed to maintain discipline within the party and impose order in society. SA membership soared after 1933, and many in the SA hailed Hitler's appointment as the beginning of a genuinely Nazi revolution. Such radicalism was alarming to the more traditional conservative groups that had helped make Hitler chancellor. If Hitler was to maintain power, then, he needed to tame the SA. On the night of June 30, 1934, more than a thousand high-ranking SA officials, including several of Hitler's oldest associates, were executed in a bloody purge known as the Night of the Long Knives.

The purge was accomplished by a second paramilitary organization, the *Schutzstaffel* ("Protection Squad"), or SS. Headed by the fanatical Heinrich Himmler, the SS became the most dreaded arm of Nazi terror. As Himmler saw it, the mission of the SS was to fight political and racial enemies of the regime, which included building the system of concentration camps. The first camp, at Dachau, opened in March 1933. The secret state police, known as the Gestapo, were responsible for the arrest, incarceration in camps, and murder of thousands of Germans. But the police force was generally understaffed and deluged with paperwork—as one historian has shown, the Gestapo was not "omniscient, omnipotent, and omnipresent." In fact, the majority of arrests was based on voluntary denunciations made by ordinary citizens against each other, often as petty personal attacks. It was not lost on the Gestapo leadership that these denunciations created a level of control that the Gestapo itself could never achieve.

Hitler and the Nazis enjoyed a sizable degree of popular support. Many Germans approved of Hitler's use of violence against the left. The Nazis could play on deep-seated fears of communism, and they spoke a language of intense national pride and unity that had broad appeal. Many Germans saw Hitler as a symbol of a strong, revitalized Germany. Propagandists fostered a Führer ("Leader") cult, depicting Hitler as a charismatic leader endowed with magnetic energy. Hitler's appeal also rested on his ability to give the German people what they wanted: jobs for workers, a productive economy for industrialists, a bulwark against communism for those who feared the wave of revolution. His appeal lay not so much in the programs he championed, many of which were ill-conceived or contradictory, but in his revolt against politics as they had been practiced in Germany. Finally, he promised to lead Germany back to national greatness and to "overthrow" the Versailles settlement.

Hitler's plans for national recovery called for full-scale rearmament and economic self-sufficiency. With policies similar to those of other Western nations, the Nazis made massive public investments, set strict market controls to stop inflation and stabilize the currency, and sealed Germany off from the world economy. The regime launched state-financed construction projects—highways, public housing, reforestation. Late in the decade, as the Nazis rebuilt the entire German military complex, unemployment dropped from over 6 million to under 200,000. The German economy looked better than any other in Europe. Hitler claimed this as his "economic miracle." Such improvements were significant, especially in the eyes of Germans who had lived through the continual turmoil of war, inflation, political instability, and economic crisis.

Like Mussolini, Hitler moved to abolish class conflict by stripping working-class institutions of their power. He outlawed trade unions and strikes, froze wages, and organized workers and employers into a National Labor Front. At the same time, the Nazis increased workers' welfare benefits, generally in line with those of the other Western nations. Class distinctions were somewhat blurred by the regime's attempts to infuse a new national "spirit" into the entire society. Popular organizations cut across class lines, especially among the youth. The Hitler Youth, a club modeled on the Boy Scouts, was highly successful at teaching children the values of Hitler's Reich; the National Labor Service drafted students for a term to work on state-sponsored building and reclamation projects. Government policy encouraged women to withdraw from the labor force, both to ease unemployment and to conform to Nazi notions of a woman's proper role. "Can woman," one propagandist asked, "conceive of anything more beautiful than to sit with her husband in her cozy home and listen inwardly to the loom of time weaving the weft and warp of motherhood?"

NAZI RACISM

At the core of Nazi ideology lay a particularly virulent racism. Much of this racism was not new. Hitler and the Nazis drew on a revived and especially violent form of nineteenth-century social Darwinism, according to which nations and people struggled for survival, with the superior peoples strengthening themselves in the process. By the early twentieth century, the rise of the social sciences had taken nineteenth-century prejudices and racial thinking into new terrain. Just as medical science had cured bodily ills, criminologists and social workers sought ways to cure social ills. Across the West, scientists and intellectuals worked to purify the body politic, improve the human race, and eliminate the "unfit." Even progressive-minded individuals sometimes subscribed to eugenics, a program of racial engineering to improve either personal or public fitness. Eugenic policies in the Third Reich began with a 1933 law for the compulsory sterilization of "innumerable inferior and hereditarily tainted" people. This "social-hygienic racism" later became the systematic murder of mentally and physically ill individuals. Social policy was governed by a basic division between those who possessed "value" and those who did not, with the aim of creating a racial utopia.

The centerpiece of Nazi racism was anti-Semitism. This centuries-old phenomenon had been part of Christian society from the Middle Ages on. By the nineteenth century, traditional Christian anti-Semitism was joined by a current of nationalist anti-Jewish theory. A great many of the theorists of European nationalism saw the Jewish people as permanent outsiders who could only be assimilated and become citizens if they denied their Jewish identity. At the end of the nineteenth century, during the Dreyfus affair in France (see Chapter 23), French and other European anti-Semites launched a barrage of propaganda against Jews—scores of books, pamphlets, and magazines blamed Jews for all the troubles of modernity, from socialism to international banks and mass culture. The late nineteenth century also brought a wave of pogroms—violent assaults on Jewish communities—especially in Russia. Racial anti-Semitism drew the line between Jews and non-Jews on the basis of erroneous biology. Religious conversion, which traditional Christian anti-Semites encouraged, would not change biology. Nor would assimilation, which was counseled by more-secular nationalist thinkers.

Anti-Semitism in these different forms was a well-established and open political force in most of the West. By attacking Jews, anti-Semites attacked modern institutions—from socialist parties and the mass press to international banking—as part of an "international Jewish conspiracy" to undermine traditional authority and nationality. Conservative party leaders told shopkeepers and workers that "Jewish capitalists" were responsible for the demise of small businesses, for the rise of giant department stores, and for precarious economic swings that threatened their livelihoods.

Analyzing Primary Sources

Nazi Propaganda

The Nazis promised many things to many people. As the document by Goebbels shows, anti-Semitism allowed them to blend their racial nationalism, vaguely defined (and anti-Marxist) socialism, and disgust with the current state of German culture and politics. Joseph Goebbels, one of the early members of the party, became director of propaganda for the party in 1928. Later Hitler appointed him head of the National Ministry for Public Enlightenment and Propaganda. The Nazis worked hard to win the rural vote, as evidenced by the Nazi campaign pamphlet reprinted in the second excerpt. The Nazis tried to appeal to farmers' economic grievances, their fears of socialism on the one hand and big business on the other, and their more general hostility to urban life and culture.

Joseph Goebbels, "Why Are We Enemies of the Jews?"

 We are NATIONALISTS because we see in the NATION the only possibility for the protection and the furtherance of our existence.

The NATION is the organic bond of a people for the protection and defense of their lives. He is nationally minded who understands this IN WORD AND IN DEED. . . .

Young nationalism has its unconditional demands, BELIEF IN THE NATION is a matter of all the people, not for individuals of rank, a class, or an industrial clique. The eternal must be separated from the contemporary. The maintenance of a rotten industrial system has nothing to do with nationalism. I can love Germany and hate capitalism; not only CAN I do it, I also MUST do it. The germ of the rebirth of our people LIES ONLY IN THE DESTRUCTION OF THE SYSTEM OF PLUNDERING THE HEALTHY POWER OF THE PEOPLE.

WE ARE NATIONALISTS BECAUSE WE, AS GERMANS, LOVE GERMANY. And because we love Germany, we demand the protection of its national spirit and we battle against its destroyers.

WHY ARE WE SOCIALISTS?

We are SOCIALISTS because we see in SOCIALISM the only possibility for maintaining our racial existence and through it the reconquest of our political freedom and the rebirth of the German state. SOCIALISM has its peculiar form first of all through its comradeship in arms with the forward-driving energy of a newly awakened nationalism. Without nationalism it is nothing, a phantom, a theory, a vision of air, a book. With it, it is everything, THE FUTURE, FREEDOM, FATHERLAND! . . .

WHY DO WE OPPOSE THE JEWS?

We are ENEMIES OF THE JEWS, because we are fighters for the freedom of the German people. THE JEW IS THE CAUSE AND THE BENEFICIARY OF OUR MISERY. He has used the social difficulties of the broad masses of our people to deepen the unholy split between Right and Left among our people. He has made two halves of Germany. He is the real cause for our loss of the Great War.

The Jew has no interest in the solution of Germany's fateful problems. He CANNOT have any. FOR HE LIVES ON THE FACT THAT THERE HAS BEEN NO SOLUTION. If we would make the German people a unified community and give them freedom before the world, then the Jew can have no place among us. He has the best trumps in his hands when a people lives in inner and outer slavery. THE JEW IS RESPONSIBLE FOR OUR MISERY AND HE LIVES ON IT.

That is the reason why we, AS NATIONALISTS and AS SOCIALISTS, oppose the Jew. HE HAS CORRUPTED OUR RACE, FOULED OUR MORALS, UNDERMINED OUR CUSTOMS, AND BROKEN OUR POWER.

In Vienna, middle-class voters supported the openly anti-Semitic Christian Democrats. In Germany, sixteen avowed anti-Semites were elected to the Reichstag in 1893, and the Conservative party made anti-Semitism part of its official program. Hitler gave this anti-Semitism an especially murderous twist by tying it to doctrines of war and biological racism.

To what extent was the Nazis' virulent anti-Semitism shared? Although the "Jewish Question" was clearly Hitler's primary obsession during the early 1920s, he made the theme less central in campaign appearances as the Nazi movement entered mainstream politics, shifting instead to attacks on Marxism and the Weimar democracy. Moreover,

National Socialist Campaign Pamphlet, 1932

 ERMAN FARMER, YOU BELONG TO HITLER! WHY?

The German farmer stands between two great dangers today:

The one danger is the American economic system—Big capitalism!

it means "world economic crisis"

it means "eternal interest slavery" . . .

it means that the world is nothing more than a bag of booty for Jewish finance in Wall Street, New York, and Paris

it enslaves man under the slogans of progress, technology, rationalization, standardization, etc.

it knows only profit and dividends

it wants to make the world into a giant trust

it puts the machine over man

it annihilates the independent, earth-rooted farmer, and its final aim is the world dictatorship of Jewry [. . .]

it achieves this in the political sphere through parliament and the swindle of democracy. In the economic sphere, through the control of credit, the mortgaging of land, the stock exchange, and the market principle [. . .]

The farmer's leagues, the Landvolk and the Bavarian Farmers' League, all pay homage to this system.

The other danger is the Marxist economic system of bolshevism:

it knows only the state economy

it knows only one class, the proletariat

it brings in the controlled economy

it doesn't just annihilate the self-sufficient farmer economically—it roots him out [. . .]

it brings the rule of the tractor

it nationalizes the land and creates mammoth factory-farms

it uproots and destroys man's soul, making him the powerless tool of the communist idea—or kills him

it destroys the family, belief, and customs [. . .]

it is anti-Christ, it desecrates the churches [. . .]

its final aim is the world dictatorship of the proletariat, that means ultimately the world dictatorship of Jewry, for the Jew controls this powerless proletariat and uses it for his dark plans

Big capitalism and bolshevism work hand in hand; they are born of Jewish thought and serve the master plan of world Jewry.

Who alone can rescue the farmer from these dangers?

NATIONAL SOCIALISM!

Source (for both documents): Anton Kaes, Martin Jay, and Edward Dimendberg, *The Weimar Republic Sourcebook* (Los Angeles: 1994), pp. 137–38, 142.

Questions for Analysis

1. How did Goebbels use metaphors of illness and health, growth and decay? Do the metaphors suggest what the Nazis would try to do to cure the ills of Germany if they took power?

2. How did Goebbels's anti-Semitism differ from the nineteenth-century French anti-Semitism documented on page 633?

3. The Nazi campaign pamphlet of 1932 targeted German farmers. How did the pamphlet play on their fears of market manipulation by American big business and Bolshevik demands for collectivization and seizure of private land? How did the Nazis identify themselves with Christianity and traditional values, sincerely or not?

4. How, specifically, does the party propose to deal with the "two great dangers of today"?

anti-Semitic beliefs would not have distinguished the Nazi from any other party on the political right; it was likely of only secondary importance to people's opinions of the Nazis. Soon after Hitler came to power, though, German Jews faced discrimination, exclusion from rights as citizens, and violence. Racial laws excluded Jews from public office as early as April 1933. The Nazis encouraged a boycott of Jewish merchants, while the SA created a constant threat of random violence. In 1935 the Nuremberg Decrees deprived Jews (defined by bloodline) of their German citizenship and prohibited marriage between Jews and other Germans. Violence escalated. In November 1938 the SA attacked some 7,500 Jewish stores, burned nearly 200 synagogues, killed ninety-one Jews, and beat up thousands more in a campaign of terror known as *Kristallnacht*, "the Night of Broken Glass." Violence like this did raise some opposition from ordinary Germans. Legal persecution, however, met only silent acquiescence. And from the perspective of Jewish people, *Kristallnacht* made it plain that there was no safe place for them in Germany. Unfortunately, only one year remained before the outbreak of war made it impossible for Jews to escape.

What did national socialism and fascism have in common? Both arose in the interwar period as responses to the First World War and the Russian Revolution. Both were violently antisocialist and anticommunist, determined to "rescue" their nations from the threat of Bolshevism. Both were intensely nationalistic; they believed that national solidarity came before all other allegiances and superseded all other rights. Both opposed parliamentary government and democracy as cumbersome and divisive. Both found their power in mass-based authoritarian politics. Similar movements existed in all the countries of the West, but only in a few cases did they actually form regimes. Nazism, however, distinguished itself by making a racially pure state central to its vision, a vision that would lead to global struggle and mass murder.

NAZI BOYCOTT OF JEWISH SHOPS IN BERLIN, 1933. Nazis stand in front of a Jewish-owned clothing store. "Germans! Buy nothing from the Jews!"

THE GREAT DEPRESSION IN THE DEMOCRACIES

The histories of the three major Western democracies—Great Britain, France, and the United States—run roughly parallel during the years after the First World War. In all three countries governments put their trust in prewar policies and assumptions until the Great Depression forced them to make major social and economic reforms, reforms that would lay the foundations of the modern welfare state. These nations weathered the upheavals of the interwar years, but they did not do so easily.

In the 1920s both France and Britain sought to keep the price of manufactured goods low in order to stimulate demand in the world markets. This policy of deflation kept businessmen happy but placed a great burden on French and British workers, whose wages and living standards remained low. Class conflict boiled just below the surface in both countries as successive governments refused to raise taxes to pay for social reforms. Workers' resentment in Britain helped elect the first Labour party

government in 1924 and another in 1929. A general strike in Britain in 1926 succeeded only in increasing middle-class antipathy toward workers. In France a period of strikes immediately after the war subsided and was followed by a period in which employers refused to bargain with labor unions. When the French government passed a modified social insurance program in 1930—insuring against sickness, old age, and death—French workers remained unsatisfied.

Among the democracies, the United States was a bastion of conservatism. Presidents Warren G. Harding, Calvin Coolidge, and Herbert Hoover upheld a social philosophy formulated by the barons of big business in the nineteenth century. The Supreme Court used its power of judicial review to nullify progressive legislation enacted by state governments and occasionally by Congress.

Nevertheless, the conservative economic and social policies of the prewar period were dealt their deathblow by the Great Depression of 1929. This worldwide depression peaked during the years 1929–33, but its effects lasted a decade. For those who went through it, the depression was perhaps the formative experience of their lives and the decisive crisis of the interwar period. In Germany, the depression was an important factor in the rise of Nazism; in fact, though, it forced every country to forge new economic policies and to deal with unprecedented economic turmoil.

The Origins of the Great Depression

What caused the Great Depression? Its deepest roots lay in the instability of national currencies and in the interdependence of national economies. Throughout the 1920s Europeans had seen a sluggish growth rate. A major drop in world agricultural prices hurt the countries of southern and eastern Europe, where agriculture was small in scale and high in cost. Unable to make a profit on the international market, these agricultural countries bought fewer manufactured goods from the more industrial sectors of northern Europe, causing a widespread drop in industrial productivity. Restrictions on free trade crippled the economy even more. Although debtor nations needed open markets in order to sell their goods, most nations were raising high trade barriers to protect domestic manufacturers from foreign competition.

Then in October of 1929, prices on the New York Stock Exchange collapsed. On October 24, "Black Thursday," 12 million shares were traded amid unprecedented chaos. Even more surprising, the market kept falling. Black Thursday was followed by Black Monday and then Black Tuesday: falling prices, combined with an enormously high number of trades, made for the worst day in the history of the stock exchange to that point. The rise of the United States as an international creditor during the Great War meant that the crash had immediate, disastrous consequences in Europe. When the value of stocks dropped, banks found themselves short of capital and then, when not rescued by the government, forced to close. The financial effects of bank closures rippled through the economy: firms closed their factories, workers lost their jobs—indeed, manufacturers laid off virtually entire workforces. In 1930, 4 million Americans were unemployed; in 1933, 13 million—nearly a third of the workforce. By then, per capita income in the United States had fallen 48 percent. In Germany, too, the drop was brutal. In 1929, 2 million were unemployed; in 1932, 6 million.

The governments of the West initially responded to the depression with monetary measures. In 1931 Great Britain abandoned the gold standard; the United States followed suit in 1933. By no longer pegging their currencies to the price of gold, these countries hoped to make money cheaper and thus more available for economic recovery programs. This action was the forerunner of a broad program of currency management, which became an important element in a general policy of economic nationalism. In another important move, Great Britain abandoned its time-honored policy of free trade in 1932, raising protective tariffs as high as 100 percent. But monetary policy alone could not end the hardships of ordinary families. Governments were increasingly forced to address their concerns with a wide range of social reforms.

Britain was the most cautious in its relief efforts. A national government composed of Conservative, Liberal, and Labour party members came to power in 1931. To underwrite effective programs of public assistance, however, the government would have to spend beyond its income—something it was reluctant to do. France, on the other hand, adopted the most advanced set of policies to combat the effects of the depression. In 1936, responding to a threat from ultraconservatives to overthrow the republic, a Popular Front government under the leadership of the socialist Léon Blum was formed by the Radical, Socialist, and Communist parties, and lasted for two years. The Popular Front nationalized the munitions industry and reorganized the Bank of France to break the largest stockholders' monopolistic control over credit. The government also decreed a forty-hour week for all urban workers and initiated a program of public works. For the benefit of the farmers it established a wheat office to fix the price and regulate the distribution of grain. Although the Popular Front temporarily quelled the threat from the political right, conservatives were generally uncooperative and unimpressed by the attempts to aid the French working class. Both a socialist and Jewish, Blum faced fierce anti-Semitism in France. Fearing that Blum was the forerunner of a French Lenin, conservatives declared, "Better Hitler than Blum." They got their wish before the decade was out.

The most dramatic response to the depression came in the United States, where its effects were most severe. In 1933 Franklin D. Roosevelt succeeded Herbert Hoover as president and announced the New Deal, a program of reform and reconstruction to rescue the country. The New Deal aimed to get the country back on its feet without destroying the capitalist system. The government would manage the economy, sponsor relief programs, and fund public-works projects to increase mass purchasing power. These policies were shaped by the theories of the British economist John Maynard Keynes, who had already proved influential during the 1919 treaty meetings at Paris. Keynes argued that capitalism could create a just and efficient society if governments played a part in its management. First, Keynes abandoned the sacred cow of balanced budgets. Without advocating continuous deficit financing, he would have the government deliberately operate in the red whenever private investments were insufficient. Keynes also favored the creation of large amounts of venture capital—money for high-risk, high-reward investments—which he saw as the only socially productive form of capital. Finally, he recommended monetary control to promote prosperity and full employment.

ARCHITECTURAL STYLE IN GERMANY BETWEEN THE WARS.
The Bauhaus, by Walter Gropius (1883–1969). This school in Dessau, Germany, is a starkly functional prototype of the interwar "international style."

sought an unflinching portrayal of human reality in all its emotional complexity. The "dadaists" went further, rebelling against any and all aesthetic principles. They pulled their name at random from a dictionary and preferred random combinations, including cutouts and collages, to formal compositions.

Architects also rejected tradition. Charles Edouard Jeanneret (Le Corbusier) in France, Otto Wagner in Austria, and Frank Lloyd Wright in the United States pioneered a new "functionalist" style that minimized decorative elements and explored the use of new materials—chrome, glass, steel, and concrete. In 1919 the German functionalist Walter Gropius established a school—the Bauhaus—to serve as a center of what became known as the international style, literally creating the blueprints for what became the familiar twentieth-century cityscape, from New York to Brazil to Tokyo.

Scientists in the interwar period also contributed to this sense of bewildering rejection of past assumptions. In 1915 German physicist Albert Einstein proposed his general theory of relativity, a new way of thinking about space, matter, time, and gravity. Einstein's theories, based on the understanding that mass and energy could be converted into one another, paved the way for the splitting of the atom by German physicists in 1939, and led to an arms race during the Second World War, as both Germany and the United States competed to produce an atomic weapon. Einstein himself devoted his life to pacifism and social justice, but the weapons that emerged from interwar physics were the most destructive ever created by humans.

Mass Culture and Its Possibilities

Cultural change, however, extended far beyond circles of artistic and intellectual elites. The explosive rise of mass media in the interwar years transformed popular culture and the lives of ordinary people. New mass media—especially radio and films—reached audiences of unprecedented size. Political life incorporated many of these new media, prompting worries that the common people, increasingly referred to as the "masses," could be manipulated by demagogues and propaganda. In 1918 mass politics was rapidly becoming a fact of life: it meant nearly universal suffrage (varying by country), well-organized political parties reaching out to voters, and in general, more participation in political life. Mass politics was accompanied by the rise of mass culture: books, newspapers, films, and fashions were produced in large numbers and standardized formats that were less expensive and more accessible, appealing not only to more people but to more kinds of people. Older forms of popular culture were often local and class specific; mass culture, at least in principle, cut across lines of class and ethnicity, and even nationality. The term, however, can easily become misleading. The world of culture did not suddenly

***VOICE OF THE PEOPLE, VOICE OF GOD* BY GEORGE GROSZ (1920).** Industrialization, the First World War, and political change combined to make early-twentieth-century Berlin a center of mass culture and communication. In this drawing, the radical artist and social critic George Grosz deplores the newspapers' power over public opinion. That public opinion could be manipulated was a common theme for many who wrote about early-twentieth-century democracy. ▪ *How does this cynicism about the public sphere compare with earlier defenders of free speech, such as John Stuart Mill?*

become homogeneous. No more than half the population read newspapers regularly. Not everyone listened to the radio, and those who did certainly did not believe everything they heard. The pace of cultural change, however, did quicken perceptibly. And in the interwar years, mass culture showed that it held both democratic and authoritarian potential.

The expansion of mass culture rested on widespread applications of existing technologies. Wireless communication, for instance, was invented before the turn of the twentieth century and saw limited use in the First World War. With major financial investment in the 1920s, though, the radio industry boomed. Three out of four British families had a radio by the end of the 1930s, and in Germany the ratio was even higher. In every European country, broadcasting rights were controlled by the government; in the United States, radio was managed by corporations. The radio broadcast soon became the national soapbox for politicians, and it played no small role in creating new kinds of political language. President Franklin Roosevelt's reassuring "fireside chats" took advantage of the way that radio bridged the public world of politics with the private world of the home. Hitler cultivated a different kind of radio personality, barking his fierce invectives; he made some fifty addresses in 1933 alone. In Germany, Nazi propagandists beamed their messages into homes or blared them through loudspeakers in town squares, constant and repetitive. Broadcasting created new rituals of political life—and new means of communication and persuasion.

So did advertising. Advertising was not new, but it was newly prominent. Businesses spent vastly more on advertising than they had before. Hard-hitting visual images replaced older ads that simply announced products, prices, and brand names. Many observers considered advertising the most "modern" of art forms. Why? It was efficient communication, streamlined and standardized, producing images that would appeal to all. It was scientific, drawing on modern psychology; advertising agencies claimed to have created a science of selling to people. In a world remade by mass politics, and at a moment when the purchasing power of the common people was beginning to rise, however slowly, the high stakes in advertising (as in much of mass culture) were apparent to many.

The most dramatic changes came on movie screens. The technology of moving pictures had come earlier; the 1890s were the era of nickelodeons and short action pictures. And in that period, France and Italy had strong film industries. Further popularized by news shorts during the war, film boomed in the war's aftermath throughout Europe. When sound was added to movies in 1927, costs

FRITZ LANG'S *M* (1931). In this film Peter Lorre, a Jewish actor, played the role of a child murderer who maintains that he should not be punished for his crimes. Lorre's speech at the end of the film was used in the Nazi propaganda film *The Eternal Jew* as proof that Jews were innate criminals who showed no remorse for their actions.

soared, competition intensified, and audiences grew rapidly. By the 1930s, an estimated 40 percent of British adults went to the movies once a week, a strikingly high figure. Many went more often than that.

Many found the new mass culture disturbing. As they perceived it, the threat came straight from the United States, which deluged Europe with cultural exports after the war. Hollywood westerns, cheap dime novels, and jazz music—which became increasingly popular in the 1920s—introduced Europe to new ways of life. Advertising, comedies, and romances disseminated new and often disconcerting images of femininity. With bobbed haircuts and short dresses, "new women" seemed assertive, flirtatious, capricious, and materialistic. The Wild West genre was popular with teenage boys, much to the dismay of their parents and teachers, who saw westerns as an inappropriate, lower-class form of entertainment. In Europe, the cross-class appeal of American popular culture grated against long-standing social hierarchies. Conservative critics abhorred the fact that "the parson's wife sat nearby his maid at Sunday matinees, equally rapt in the gaze of Hollywood stars."

Authoritarian governments, in particular, decried these developments as decadent threats to national culture. Fascist, communist, and Nazi governments alike tried to control not only popular culture but also high culture and modernism, which were typically out of line with the designs of the dictators. Stalin much preferred socialist realism—art depicting heroic workers struggling to play their part in the revolution—to the new Soviet avant-garde. Mussolini had a penchant for classical kitsch, though he was far more accepting of modern art than Hitler, who despised it as decadent. Nazism had its own cultural aesthetic, promoting "Aryan" art and architecture and rejecting the modern, international style they associated with the "international Jewish conspiracy." This led them to condemn jazz, modern art, and the new architecture, and to encourage the development of artistic movements that celebrated the accomplishments of "Aryan" culture.

The Nazis, like other authoritarian governments, used mass media as efficient means of indoctrination and control. Movies became part of the Nazis' pioneering use of "spectacular politics." Media campaigns, mass rallies, parades, and ceremonies: all were designed to display the strength and glory of the Reich and to impress and intimidate spectators. In 1934 Hitler commissioned the filmmaker Leni Riefenstahl to record a political rally staged by herself and Albert Speer in Nuremberg. The film, titled *Triumph of the Will*, was a visual hymn to the Nordic race and the Nazi regime. Everything in the film was on a huge scale: masses of bodies stood in parade formation, flags rose and fell in unison; the film invited viewers to surrender to the power of grand ritual and symbolism. The comedian Charlie Chaplin lampooned it in his celebrated *The Great Dictator* (1940), an enormously successful parody of Nazi pomposities.

After You Read This Chapter

 Go to **INQUIZITIVE** to see what you've learned—and learn what you've missed— with personalized feedback along the way.

REVIEWING THE OBJECTIVES

- After 1917 the Bolsheviks in Russia debated how fast they should move to reorganize society along the lines demanded by their revolutionary ideology. What circumstances determined the outcome of this debate and what were the consequences of Stalin's revolution from above in the 1930s?

- Mussolini's Fascist party offered an alternative to Italian voters disappointed with their government in the aftermath of the First World War. What was fascism and how did Mussolini come to power?

- The Weimar Republic failed in its attempt to establish a stable democracy in Germany, while other democracies in France, Britain, and the United States underwent severe strain. What challenges did democratic regimes face during the interwar period?

- Hitler came to power legally in 1933 through the German electoral system. What did he stand for, and why did so many Germans support his cause?

- Artists, writers, and other intellectuals in the interwar period could not help but reflect the atmosphere of social and political crisis in their work. How did artists and writers react to the crisis of the interwar period?

CONCLUSION

The strains of the First World War created a world that few recognized—transformed by revolution, mass mobilization, and loss. In retrospect, it is hard not to see the period that followed as a succession of failures. Capitalism foundered in the Great Depression, democracies collapsed in the face of authoritarianism, and the Treaty of Versailles proved hollow. Stalin's Soviet Union paid a terrible price for the creation of a modern industrial economy in the years of famine, political repression, and state terror. Hitler's Germany and Mussolini's Italy offered a vision of the future that held no comfort for those committed to basic human freedoms and equality under the law. Yet we better understand the experiences and outlooks of ordinary people if we do not treat the failures of the interwar period as inevitable. By the late 1920s, many were cautiously optimistic that the Great War's legacy could be overcome and that problems were being solved. The Great Depression wrecked these hopes, bringing economic chaos and political paralysis. Paralysis and chaos, in turn, created new audiences for political leaders offering authoritarian solutions and brought more voters to their political parties. Finally, economic troubles and political turmoil made contending with rising international tensions, to which we now turn, vastly more difficult. By the 1930s, even cautious optimism about international relations had given way to apprehension and dread.

PEOPLE, IDEAS, AND EVENTS IN CONTEXT

- What is the difference between the Bolshevik policies of **WAR COMMUNISM** and the **NEW ECONOMIC POLICY (NEP)**?
- What were **JOSEPH STALIN**'s goals in implementing his catastrophic plan for **COLLECTIVIZATION** of agriculture, and what did he hope to accomplish with his purging of an entire generation of Bolshevik leaders, along with millions of other Soviet citizens, in the **GREAT TERROR**?
- What was the basis of **BENITO MUSSOLINI**'s rejection of liberal democracy? What kinds of changes in Italian society followed from the adoption of **FASCISM** as the official state ideology?
- How important was **ANTI-SEMITISM** to **ADOLF HITLER**'s political career? What do events like *KRISTALLNACHT* tell us about the depth of German anti-Semitism?
- What effects did the **GREAT DEPRESSION** have on the European economy, and how did this economic crisis affect the political developments of the 1930s?
- How did the **NEW DEAL** attempt to deal with the economic crisis in the United States?

THINKING ABOUT CONNECTIONS

- What did Soviet communism, national socialism in Germany, and Italian fascism have in common during the years 1919–39? What made them different from one another?
- How much of the crisis of the interwar period can be attributed to the effects of World War I? To the economic upheaval of the Great Depression? Is it possible to see the ideological conflicts of these years as the result of a much longer history?

STORY LINES

- In the 1930s, Hitler's Germany and Mussolini's Italy allied with imperial Japan to form the Axis. The Axis provoked a Second World War, confronting the Allied powers that included Britain, the United States, Canada, Australia, and the Soviet Union.

- The Nazi regime's military successes in 1939–41 brought almost all of Europe under German control. The Russian victory at Stalingrad in 1942 proved to be a turning point, and from 1942 to 1945 the Allies progressively rolled back the German and Japanese armies, leading to Allied victory in 1945.

- The Nazi state embarked on a genocidal project of mass murder to exterminate Europe's Jews, homosexuals, and the Roma.

- Attacks on civilian populations and the plundering of resources by occupying armies made the Second World War a "total war" in which the distinction between military and home front meant little for many Europeans. Even in the United States, rationing and the constraints of the wartime economy had profound effects on civilian life.

CHRONOLOGY

1931	Japanese invasion of Manchuria
1936–1939	Spanish Civil War
September 1938	Sudeten Crisis and Munich Conference
August 1939	Nazi-Soviet Pact
September 1939	German invasion of Poland
May 1940	German invasion of the Low Countries and France
June 1941	German invasion of the Soviet Union
December 1941	Japanese attack on Pearl Harbor
September 1942– January 1943	Battle of Stalingrad
June 1944	D-Day invasion
May 1945	German surrender
August 1945	The United States drops atomic bombs on Hiroshima and Nagasaki
August 1945	Japanese surrender

Before
You
Read
This
Chapter

The Second World War

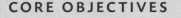
I n September 1939, Europe was consumed by another world war. Like the First World War, the Second World War was triggered by threats to the European balance of power. Yet even more than the Great War, the Second World War was a conflict among nations, whole peoples, and fiercely opposing ideals. Adolf Hitler and his supporters in Germany and abroad cast the conflict as a racial war against the twin enemies of national socialism: the democracies in western Europe and the United States on the one hand, and the communist order of the Soviet Union on the other. Hitler's opponents in the West and the East believed just as fervently that they were defending a way of life and a vision of justice that was bigger than narrow definitions of national interest.

Belief that the world was now characterized by ideologies and worldviews that were necessarily in mortal combat with one another meant that the scale of the killing overtook even that of the First World War. In 1914, military firepower outmatched mobility, resulting in four years of static, mud-sodden slaughter. In 1939, mobility was joined to firepower on a massive scale, with terrifying results. On the battlefield, the tactics of high-speed armored warfare (*Blitzkrieg*), aircraft carriers sinking ships far beyond the horizon, and submarines used in vast numbers to dominate shipping lanes all changed the scope and the pace of fighting. This was not a war of trenches and barbed wire but a war of motion, dramatic conquests, and terrible destructive power. The devastation of 1914–18 paled in comparison to this new global conflict.

The other great change involved not tactics, but targets. Much of the unprecedented killing power now available was aimed directly at civilians. Cities were laid waste by artillery and aerial bombing. Whole regions were put to the torch, while towns and villages were systematically cordoned off and leveled. Whole populations were targeted as well, in ways that continue to appall. The Nazi regime's systematic murder of Roma, homosexuals, and other "deviants," along with its effort to exterminate the Jewish people completely, made the Second World War a horrifyingly unique event. So did the United States' use of a weapon whose existence would dominate politics and society for the next fifty years: the atomic bomb. The naive enthusiasm that had marked the outbreak of war in 1914 was absent from the start. Terrible memories of the First World War lingered. Yet those who fought against the Axis Powers (and many of those who fought for them) found that their determination to fight and win grew as the war went on. Unlike the seemingly meaningless killing of the Great War, the Second World War was cast as a war of absolutes, of good and evil, of national and global survival. Nevertheless, the scale of destruction brought with it a profound weariness. It also provoked deep-seated questions about the value of Western "civilization" and the terms on which the West, and the rest of the world, might live peaceably in the future.

THE CAUSES OF THE WAR: UNSETTLED QUARRELS, ECONOMIC FALLOUT, AND NATIONALISM

Historians have isolated four main causes for the Second World War: the punishing terms of the Versailles peace settlement, the failure to create international guarantees for peace and security after 1918, the successive economic crises of the interwar years, and the violent forms of nationalism that emerged in Europe in the 1930s.

The peace settlement of 1919–20 created as many problems as it solved. The Versailles treaty created new nations out of the ruins of the eastern European empires and proclaimed the principle of self-determination for the peoples of eastern and southern Europe. In doing so, the peacemakers

sowed fresh bitterness and conflict. The treaty created new states that crossed ethnic boundaries, and it created new minorities without protecting them. Many of these boundaries would be redrawn by force in the 1930s. The Allied powers also imposed harsh terms in the treaty, saddling the German economy with a heavy bill for reparations and forcing the Weimar Republic to accept a humiliating reduction in the size of the German military. Most galling to the German public was the Versailles treaty's "war guilt" clause, which blamed the Germans for starting the war. Since the Allied powers refused to lift the naval blockade of Germany until the treaty was signed, the new German government had no choice but to accept the terms. As a consequence, many Germans saw the treaty as illegitimate and unjust. The fact that the victors used the peace settlement to lay claim to German colonies reinforced their impression that the peace was fundamentally an alliance of the victors against the vanquished.

Another cause of the outbreak of another world war was the victors' failure to create binding standards for peace and security. Some diplomats put their faith in the legal and moral authority of the League of Nations. Others pursued disarmament as a means of securing peace. In 1928, the Kellogg-Briand Pact declared war an international crime, but such measures carried little weight. The League of Nations was hampered by the absence of key players. Germany and the Soviet Union were excluded for most of the interwar period and the United States never joined.

Economic conditions were a third cause of the Second World War. The reparations imposed on Germany and France's occupation of Germany's industrial heartland slowed Germany's recovery. Disagreements about the reparations led to the German hyperinflation of the early 1920s, making German money nearly worthless. The stability and credibility of the fragile new German republic were damaged almost beyond repair. The German economy had barely emerged from this catastrophe when the world economy collapsed in 1929.

The Great Depression of the 1930s contributed to the outbreak of war by weakening Europe's democracies at a moment when they were under siege by political extremists on the left and the right. The depression intensified economic nationalism and inflamed tensions between labor and management. The collapse of the economy caused mass unemployment and business failure throughout Europe, and this crisis was the last blow to the Weimar Republic. In 1933, with unemployment peaking at nearly 6 million (roughly one out of every three workers), power passed to the Nazis.

Despite the misgivings of many inside the governments of Britain and France, Germany was allowed to ignore the terms of the peace treaties and rearm. Armaments expansion on a large scale first began in Germany in 1935, with the result that unemployment was reduced and the effects of the depression eased. Other nations followed the German example, not simply as a way to boost their economies but in response to growing Nazi military power.

While Hitler was rearming Germany, other nations were also pushing against the League of Nations and the international order set up after World War I. In the Pacific, Japan's military regime had embarked on a program of imperial expansion aimed at China. They began in 1931 with the invasion of Manchuria. Meanwhile, in Italy, Mussolini tried to distract his public with overseas conquests, culminating in the invasion of Ethiopia in 1935.

In sum, the tremendous economic hardship of the depression, a contested peace treaty, and political weakness all undermined international stability. But the decisive factor in the crises of the 1930s and the trigger for another world war lay in a blend of violent nationalism and modern ideologies that glorified the nation and national destiny. This blend, particularly in the forms of fascism and militarism, appeared around the world in many countries. By the middle of the 1930s, recognizing common interests, fascist Italy and Nazi Germany formed an Axis, an alliance binding their goals of national glory and international power. They were later joined by Japan's military regime. In the 1930s these regimes tested the resolve of their opponents. The Japanese invaded Manchuria in 1931, and Nazi Germany and fascist Italy supported the nationalists in the Spanish Civil War (1936–39). After 1939 the Axis embarked on a much more ambitious set of conquests, initiating a second global war even more destructive than the first.

ANTIFASCIST PROPAGANDA, SPANISH CIVIL WAR. This poster, produced by a left-wing labor organization affiliated with the international anarchist movement, shows a worker about to deliver a killing blow to a fascist snake.

THE 1930s: CHALLENGES TO THE PEACE

The 1930s brought the tensions and failures caused by the treaties of 1919–20 to a head, creating a global crisis. Fascists, Nazis, and other nationalist governments flouted the League of Nations by launching new conquests and other aggressive efforts at national expansion. With the memories of 1914–18 still fresh, these new crises created an atmosphere of deepening fear and apprehension. Each new conflict seemed to warn that another, much wider war would follow unless it could somehow be averted. Ordinary people, particularly in Britain, France, and the United States, were divided. Some saw the actions of the aggressors as a direct challenge to civilization, one that had to be met with force if necessary. Others hoped to avoid premature or unnecessary conflict. Their governments tried instead at several points to negotiate with the fascists and keep a

tenuous peace. Writers, intellectuals, and politicians on the left vilified these efforts. Many saw the period as a series of missed opportunities to prevent renewed warfare.

Most controversial was the policy of "appeasement" pursued by Western governments in the face of German, Italian, and Japanese aggression. Appeasement was neither simple power politics nor pure cowardice. It was grounded in three deeply held assumptions. The first was that doing anything to provoke another war was unthinkable. With the memory of the slaughter of 1914–18 fresh in their minds, many in the West embraced pacifism, or did not want to deal with the uncompromising aggression of the fascist governments, especially Nazi Germany. Second, many in Britain and the United States argued that Germany had been mistreated by the Versailles treaty and harbored legitimate grievances that should be acknowledged and resolved. Finally, many appeasers were staunch anticommunists. They believed that the fascist states in Germany and Italy were an essential bulwark against the advance of Soviet communism and that division among the major European states only played into the hands of the USSR. It took most of the 1930s for the debate among appeasers to come to a head. Meanwhile, the League of Nations faced more immediate and pressing challenges.

The 1930s brought three crucial tests for the League: crises in China, Ethiopia, and Spain. In China, the Japanese invasion of Manchuria in 1931 turned into an invasion of the whole country. Chinese forces were driven before the Japanese advance, and the Japanese deliberately targeted civilians in order to break the Chinese will to fight. In 1937 the Japanese laid siege to the strategic city of Nanjing. More than 200,000 Chinese citizens were slaughtered in what came to be known as the "Rape of Nanjing." The League voiced shock and disapproval but did nothing. In 1935 Mussolini began his efforts to make the Mediterranean an Italian empire by returning to Ethiopia to avenge the defeat of 1896. This time the Italians came with tanks, bombers, and poison gas. The Ethiopians fought bravely but hopelessly, and this imperial massacre aroused world opinion. The League attempted to impose sanctions on Italy and condemned Japan. But for two reasons, no enforcement followed. The first was British and French fear of communism and their hope that Italy and Japan would act as counterweights to the Soviets. The second reason was practical. Enforcing sanctions would involve challenging Japan's powerful fleet or Mussolini's newly built battleships.

Britain and France were unwilling, and dangerously close to unable, to use their navies to achieve those ends.

The Spanish Civil War

The third challenge came closer to home. In 1936 civil war broke out in Spain. A series of weak republican governments, committed to large-scale social reforms, could not overcome opposition to those measures and political polarization. War broke out as extreme right-wing military officers rebelled. Hitler and Mussolini both sent troops and equipment to assist the rebel commander, Francisco Franco (1892–1975). The Soviet Union countered with aid to communist troops serving under the banner of the Spanish Republic. Again Britain and France failed to act decisively. Thousands of volunteers from England, France, and the United States—including many working-class socialists and writers such as George Orwell and Ernest Hemingway—took up arms as private soldiers for the Republican government. Their governments were much more hesitant. For the British, Franco was at least anticommunist, just like Mussolini and the Japanese. French prime minister Léon Blum, a committed antifascist, stood at the head of a Popular Front government—an alliance of socialists, communists, and republicans. The Popular Front had been elected on a program of social reform and opposition to Hitler abroad

GUERNICA BY PABLO PICASSO (1937). One of Picasso's most influential works, *Guernica* was painted as a mural for the Spanish republican government as it fought for survival in the Spanish Civil War. The Basque town of Guernica had been bombed by German warplanes just a few months earlier, in April 1937. Near the center a horse writhes in agony; to the left a distraught woman holds her dead child. Compare Picasso's image to the antifascist propaganda poster reproduced on page 703. ■ *What is different about the way that the two images deliver their political messages?* ■ *Does Picasso's rejection of realism diminish the power of his political message?* ■ *Does the antifascist poster seek any outcome other than the annihilation of the enemy?*

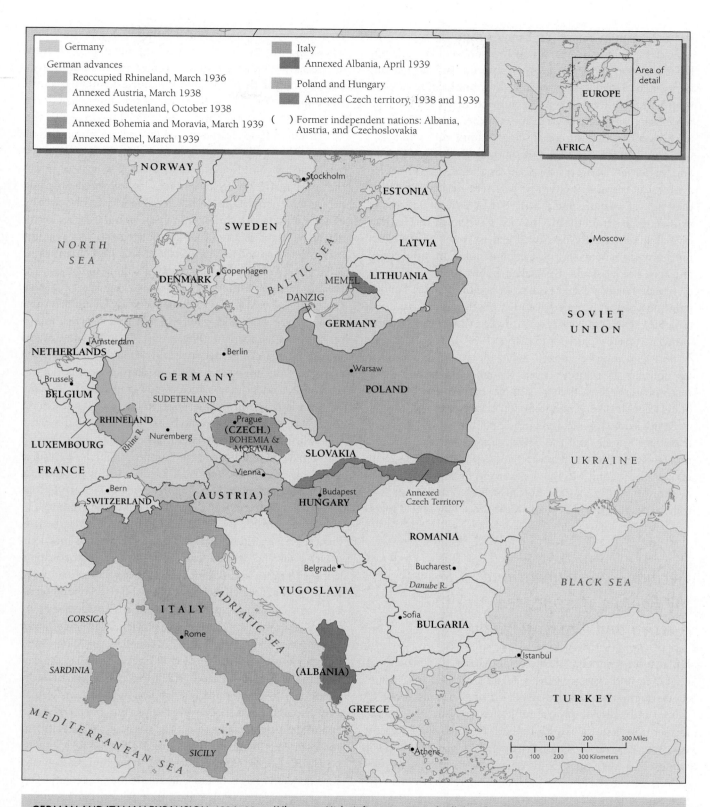

Legend:
- Germany
- German advances
  - Reoccupied Rhineland, March 1936
  - Annexed Austria, March 1938
  - Annexed Sudetenland, October 1938
  - Annexed Bohemia and Moravia, March 1939
  - Annexed Memel, March 1939
- Italy
  - Annexed Albania, April 1939
- Poland and Hungary
  - Annexed Czech territory, 1938 and 1939
- ( ) Former independent nations: Albania, Austria, and Czechoslovakia

EUROPE
AFRICA
Area of detail

GERMAN AND ITALIAN EXPANSION, 1936–39. ▪ *What were Hitler's first steps to unify all the ethnic Germans in Europe?* ▪ *How did he use these initial gains to annex territory from the Czechs?* ▪ *What were the official reactions from Britain, France, and the Soviet Union?*

and to fascism in France. Yet Blum's margin of support was limited. He feared that intervening in Spain would further polarize his country, bring down his government, and make it impossible to follow through on any commitment to helping resolve the conflict. In Spain, despite some heroic fighting, the republican camp degenerated into a hornet's nest of competing factions: republican, socialist, communist, and anarchist.

The Spanish Civil War was brutal. Both the German and the Soviet "advisers" saw Spain as a "dress rehearsal" for a later war between the two powers. They each brought in their newest weapons and practiced their skills in destroying civilian targets from the air. In April 1937, a raid by German dive bombers utterly destroyed the town of Guernica in northern Spain in an effort to cut off Republican supply lines and terrorize civilians. It shocked public opinion and was commemorated by Pablo Picasso in one of the most famous paintings of the twentieth century. Both sides committed atrocities. The Spanish Civil War lasted three years, ending with a complete victory for Franco in 1939. In the aftermath, Britain and France proved reluctant to admit Spanish Republicans as refugees, even though Republicans faced recriminations from Franco's regime. Franco sent 1 million of his Republican enemies to prison or concentration camps.

Hitler drew two lessons from Spain. The first was that if Britain, France, and the Soviet Union ever tried to contain fascism, they would have a hard time coordinating their efforts. The second was that Britain and France were deeply averse to fighting another European war. This meant that the Nazis could use almost any means to achieve their goals.

German Rearmament and the Politics of Appeasement in Austria and Czechoslovakia

Hitler took advantage of this combination of international tolerance and war weariness to advance his ambitions. As Germany rearmed, Hitler played on Germans' sense of shame and betrayal, proclaiming their right to regain their former power in the world. In 1933 he removed Germany from the League of Nations, to which it had finally been admitted in 1926. In 1935 he defied the disarmament provisions of the Treaty of Versailles and revived conscription and universal military training. Hitler's stated goals were the restoration of Germany's power and dignity inside Europe and the unification of all ethnic Germans inside his Third German Reich. As the first step in this process, Germany reoccupied the Rhineland in 1936. It was a risky move, chancing war with the much more powerful

French army. But France and Britain did not mount a military response. In retrospect, this was an important turning point; the balance of power tipped in Germany's favor. Only as long as the Rhineland remained demilitarized and German industry in the Ruhr valley was unprotected, did France hold the upper hand. After 1936, it no longer did so.

In March 1938 Hitler annexed Austria, reaffirming his intention to bring all Germans into his Reich. Once more, no official reaction came from the West. The Nazis' next target was the Sudetenland in Czechoslovakia, a region with a large ethnic German population. With Austria now a part of Germany, Czechoslovakia was almost entirely surrounded by its hostile neighbor. Hitler declared that the Sudetenland was a natural part of the Reich and that he intended to occupy it. Many in the French and Polish governments were willing to come to the Czechs' aid. According to plans already being laid for a wider European war, Germany would not be ready for another three to four years. But Hitler gambled, and British prime minister Neville Chamberlain obliged him. Chamberlain decided to take charge of international talks about the Sudetenland and agreed to Hitler's terms. Chamberlain's logic was that this dispute was about the balance of power in Europe. If Hitler were allowed to unify all Germans in one state, he reasoned, then German ambitions would be satisfied. Chamberlain also believed that his country could not commit to a sustained war. Finally, defending eastern European boundaries against Germany ranked low on Great Britain's list of priorities, at least in comparison to ensuring free trade in western Europe and protecting the strategic centers of the British Empire.

On September 29, 1938, Hitler met with Chamberlain, French premier Édouard Daladier, and Mussolini in a four-power conference in Munich. The result was another capitulation by France and Britain. The four negotiators bargained away a major slice of Czechoslovakia, while Czech representatives were left to await their fate outside the conference room. Chamberlain returned to London proclaiming "peace in our time." Hitler soon proved that boast hollow. In March 1939 Germany invaded what was left of Czechoslovakia, annexed Bohemia and Moravia, and established a puppet regime in Slovakia. This was Germany's first conquest of non-German territory, and it sent shock waves across Europe. It convinced public and political opinion outside Germany of the futility of appeasement. Chamberlain was forced to shift his policies completely. British and French rearmament sped up dramatically. Together with France, Britain guaranteed the sovereignty of the two states now directly in Hitler's path, Poland and Romania.

Meanwhile, the politics of appeasement had fueled Stalin's fears that the Western democracies might strike a deal with Germany at Soviet expense, thus diverting Nazi expansion eastward. The Soviet Union had not been invited to the Munich conference, and, suspicious that Britain and

France were unreliable allies, Stalin became convinced that he should look elsewhere for security. Tempted by the traditional Russian desire for territory in Poland, Stalin was promised a share of Poland, Finland, the Baltic states, and Bessarabia by Hitler's representatives. In a reversal of their anti-Nazi proclamations that stunned many, the Soviets signed a nonaggression pact with the Nazis in August 1939. By going to Munich, Britain and France had put their interests first; the Soviet Union would now look after its own.

THE OUTBREAK OF HOSTILITIES AND THE FALL OF FRANCE

After his success in Czechoslovakia, Hitler turned his attention to Poland. With the Soviets now in his camp, he expected that the Western allies would back down again. On September 1, 1939, German troops crossed the Polish border. Britain and France sent a joint warning to Germany to withdraw. There was no reply. On September 3, Britain and France declared war.

The conquest of Poland was shockingly quick. It demanded great resources—Germany committed nearly all of its combat troops and planes to the invasion—but the results were remarkable. Well-coordinated attacks by German panzers (tanks) and armored vehicles, supported by devastating air power, cut the large but slow-moving Polish army to pieces. The Poles fought doggedly but were so stunned and disorganized that they had little hope of mounting an effective defense. The "lightning war" (Blitzkrieg, blitz-KREEG) for which the German officer corps had trained so long was a complete success. Poland, a large country with a large army, was dismembered in four weeks.

In accordance with its agreement with Nazi Germany, the Soviet Union also invaded Poland from the east, taking their share of Polish territory and using Stalin's signature methods to deal with the enemy: rounding up millions to be deported, imprisoned, or executed. Shortly after the invasion of Poland, the Soviets also attacked Finland in an attempt to secure their northern border. Despite the Soviets' overwhelming superiority in numbers and material, the Finns fought back tenaciously. The Soviets faced a very difficult campaign—an alarming demonstration of the damaging effects of Stalin's terror on the Soviet military. Although the Soviet Union concluded the undeclared four-month Winter War with a precarious victory in March 1940, Hitler and the rest of the world had made note of Stalin's weaknesses.

The fighting in Poland was followed by a winter of anxious nonactivity in western Europe, known as the "phony war." In the spring of 1940 that calm was broken by a terrible storm. The Germans struck first in Scandinavia, taking Denmark in a day and invading Norway. On May 10, German forces swarmed through Belgium and the Netherlands on their way to France. The two nations were conquered in short order. When the Dutch succeeded in flooding canals that protected their major cities and defended that line with hard-fighting marines, Hitler ordered his air force to bomb the city of Rotterdam. More than 800 Dutch civilians died, and the Netherlands surrendered the next day. The Belgians' stubborn and effective defense of their nation was cut short when King Leopold III suddenly surrendered after two weeks of fighting, fearing similar destruction. Leopold stayed on as a figurehead for the Nazis, reviled by Belgians who found other ways to carry on the fight against Germany.

The large French army was carved up by the Blitzkrieg. Its divisions were isolated, outflanked, and overwhelmed by German aircraft and armored columns working according to an exacting plan. The French army and French artillery (much of it better built than its German equivalent) were poorly organized and rendered useless in the face of rapid German maneuvers. The defeat turned quickly into a rout. Hundreds of thousands of civilians, each carrying a few precious possessions loaded onto carts, fled south. They were joined by thousands of Allied soldiers without weapons, and these columns of refugees were attacked constantly by German dive bombers. The disorganized British made a desperate retreat to the port of Dunkirk on the English Channel, where many of Britain's best troops were sacrificed holding off the panzers. At the beginning of June 1940, despite heavy German air attacks, Britain's Royal Navy evacuated more than 300,000 British and French troops, with the help of commercial and pleasure boats that had been pressed into emergency service.

After Dunkirk, the conflict was bitter but the outcome inevitable. French reservists fought, as their commanders asked, "to the last cartridge," killing thousands of Germans. The Germans nevertheless swept through the northwest and the heart of the country, reaching Paris in mid-June 1940. The political will of France's government collapsed along with its armies, and the French surrendered on June 22. The armistice cut the country in two. The Germans occupied all of northern France, including Paris and the Channel ports. The south, and French territories in North Africa, lay under the jurisdiction of a deeply conservative government formed at the spa town of Vichy (VIH-shee) under the leadership of an elderly First World War hero, Marshal Henri Philippe Pétain. France had fallen. One of Germany's historic enemies, the victor of the previous war, an imperial power and nation of almost 60 million citizens, was reduced to chaos and enemy occupation in forty days.

The penalties exacted on France did not end with defeat. Many liberals within France, and most of the Free

French movement quickly established in London, soon felt they had two enemies to fight: Germany and Pétain's regime. The Vichy government proposed to collaborate with the Germans in return for retaining a small measure of sovereignty, or so it believed. The regime also instituted its own National Revolution, which came very close to fascism. Vichy repudiated the republic, accusing it of sapping France's strength. The state proceeded to reorganize French life and political institutions, strengthening the authority of the Catholic Church and the family, and helping the Germans crush any resistance. "Work, Family, and Country"—this was Vichy's call to order.

NOT ALONE: THE BATTLE OF BRITAIN AND THE BEGINNINGS OF A GLOBAL WAR

Before launching an invasion across the Channel, the Nazis attempted to establish superiority in the air. From July 1940 to June 1941, in the Battle of Britain, thousands of German planes dropped millions of tons of bombs on British targets: first aircraft and airfields and then, as the focus shifted to breaking Britain's will, civilian targets such as London. More than 40,000 British civilians died. Yet the British stood firm. This was possible in part because of a German mistake. After a daring British bombing raid on Berlin, Hitler angrily told his generals to concentrate on civilian targets. This spared the Royal Air Force, whose bases had been steadily devastated up to that point. Given the chance to keep fighting, the R.A.F. forced a costly stalemate in the air. Hitler scrapped the invasion plans, turning his attention east toward Russia.

Another important reason for the determined British resistance was a change of political leadership. In May 1940 Chamberlain's catalog of failures finished his career. He was toppled by a coalition government that brought together Conservative, Liberal, and Labour politicians under Winston Churchill. Churchill was a political maverick who had changed parties more than once. He was extremely talented, but also arrogant. He had a sharp temper and sometimes seemed unstable, and before 1939 his political career had been judged to be over. As prime minister he was not much of an administrator, constantly proposing wild schemes, but he had two genuine strengths. The first was a gift for language. Churchill spoke extraordinary words of courage and defiance just when the British public wanted and needed to hear them. He was utterly committed to winning the war. "You ask what is our policy," Churchill said in his first speech as prime minister in May of 1940, before the Battle of Britain began. "I will say, it is to wage war with all our might, with all the strength that God

LONDON DURING THE BATTLE OF BRITAIN. German air raids that lasted from August 1940 to June 1941 wrought destruction but did not achieve Hitler's goal of breaking the British. The Holland House Library in London lost its roof but managed to engage in business as usual.

can give us, to wage war against a monstrous tyranny never surpassed in the dark, lamentable catalogue of human crime."

Churchill's other strength was personal diplomacy. He convinced the American president, Franklin Roosevelt, who supported the Allies, to break with American neutrality and send massive amounts of aid and weapons to Britain, free of charge, under a program called Lend-Lease. Churchill also allowed the new government coalition to work to best effect. The ablest Conservative ministers stayed, but Labour politicians were also allowed to take positions of genuine power. Most of the Labour representatives turned out to be excellent administrators and were directly in touch with Britain's huge working class, which now felt fully included in the war effort.

With Britain's survival, the war moved into different theaters: the Atlantic (a battle over sea lanes and supplies), North Africa (strategically important for the Suez Canal and access to oil), the Pacific (the war with Japan), and the Soviet Union (where Hitler's determination to annihilate Stalin merged with his murderous campaign against the Jewish populations of Europe).

The Atlantic and North Africa

German submarines in the Atlantic Ocean were a dire threat to the Allies, with Britain's supply of weapons, raw materials, and food hanging in the balance. The British devoted a huge naval effort to saving their convoys, developing modern sonar and new systems of aerial reconnaissance. They also broke the German code for communicating with the submarine "wolf

THE SECOND WORLD WAR IN EUROPE. ▪ *What parts of the European theater were controlled by the Allies?* ▪ *The Axis?* ▪ *What countries were neutral in 1941?* ▪ *In what parts of the European theater did the major Axis and Allied campaigns occur?* ▪ *What was Germany's greatest geographical challenge during the Second World War?*

packs" roving the shipping lanes. When the United States entered the war in December 1941, the British shared their technology and experience, and many more U-boats (German submarines) were sunk. By late 1942 the threat receded.

The British defense of the Suez Canal made North Africa an important area of conflict, but the stakes soon grew as both the Germans and the Italians sought to end British dominance in this region and the Middle East. The

Soviets and the British invaded Iran to keep that country's oil from falling into the hands of the Germans, and in Egypt a small British army humiliated a much larger Italian force. The British nearly succeeded in taking Libya from the Italians in 1941, but Hitler responded by sending his most daring tank commander, Erwin Rommel, at the head of an invasion force. Rommel's Afrika Korps gradually drove the British back, but when the German commander tried to follow up by invading Egypt in the autumn of 1942, his army was stopped near the town of El Alamein. Meanwhile, the United States intervened in November 1942, landing in the French territories of Morocco and Algeria. The Vichy French commanders surrendered peacefully, and the combined Allied forces finally broke through Rommel's line in March 1943, ending the fighting in Africa.

The Allies and Japan in the Pacific

The war became truly global when Japan struck the American naval base at Pearl Harbor, Hawaii, on the morning of December 7, 1941. To establish a Japanese empire in Asia, they would have to destroy America's Pacific fleet and seize the colonies of the British, Dutch, and French empires. The attack on Pearl Harbor was a brilliant act of surprise that devastated the American fleet and shocked the American public. It was not, however, the success that the Japanese wanted. Eight U.S. battleships were sunk and more than 2,000 lives lost; but much of the American fleet was safely at sea on the day of the strike. The unprovoked attack galvanized American public opinion in a way the war in Europe had not. When Germany rashly declared war on the United States as well, America declared itself ready to take on all comers and joined the Allies.

Despite the mixed results at Pearl Harbor, the Japanese enjoyed a number of stunning successes elsewhere. Japanese troops swept through the British protectorate of Malaya in weeks, sinking the Pacific squadrons of both the British and Dutch navies in the swift attacks. Britain's fortified island port at Singapore, the keystone of British defenses in the Pacific, fell at the end of December 1941. Thousands of British and Australian troops were captured and sent off to four years of torture, forced labor, and starvation in Japanese prison camps. The Japanese also invaded the Philippines in December; and while American soldiers and marines held out on the island of Corregidor for some time, they too were eventually forced to surrender. Some took to the hills to fight as guerrillas; the rest were forced on a death march to Japanese labor camps. The Dutch East Indies fell next, and it seemed there would be no stopping Japanese ships and soldiers before they reached Australia.

Reeling from Japan's blows, the Allies finally reorganized during 1942. After taking Singapore, Japanese troops pressed on into Burma, threatening India. The British defense of Burma failed, but they were able to regroup, and a joint force of British and Indian troops defeated an attempted Japanese invasion of India at the border near the end of 1942. After that, with an army drawn from around the world, the British began to push the Japanese back.

"A DATE WHICH WILL LIVE IN INFAMY"—DECEMBER 7, 1941. The USS *West Virginia* was one of eight battleships sunk during the Japanese surprise attack targeting "Battleship Row" at the American naval base at Pearl Harbor. More than 2,000 people were killed, but most of the American fleet, en route to or from other locations in the Pacific, was spared.

At sea, America's navy benefited from a rapidly increased production schedule that turned out enough new ships and planes to outnumber the Japanese. In 1942 the United States won crucial victories in the Coral Sea and at Midway, battles fought by aircraft flown from each side's carriers. American marines landed on the island of Guadalcanal in early 1942 and captured this strategic Japanese base after months of bitter fighting. Their success began a campaign of "island hopping" as the marines destroyed Japan's network of island bases throughout the Pacific. This was brutal warfare, often settled with grenades and bayonets. Each side considered the other racially inferior. The Japanese often refused to surrender; the Americans and Australians were able to take few prisoners. By 1943 the Japanese advance had been halted, the Japanese navy had lost most of its capital ships, and the Allies began a slow march to Singapore and the Philippines.

THE RISE AND RUIN OF NATIONS: GERMANY'S WAR IN THE EAST AND THE OCCUPATION OF EUROPE

While battles ebbed and flowed in the Atlantic and the North African desert, Germany moved southeast into the Balkans. In 1941 Germany took over Yugoslavia almost without a fight. The Germans split Yugoslavia's ethnic patchwork by establishing a Croatian puppet state, pitting Croats against their Serb neighbors, who were ruled directly by the Nazis. Romania, Hungary, and Bulgaria joined the Nazis' cause as allies. The Greeks, who had dealt a crushing defeat to an Italian invasion, were suddenly confronted with a massive German force that overran the country. The Greeks stubbornly refused to surrender. An unexpected combination of Greek, British, and New Zealand troops nearly defeated the German paratroopers sent to capture the island of Crete in June of 1941. Many Greeks also took to the mountains as guerrillas, but in the end the country fell. By the summer of 1941, the whole European continent, with the exceptions of Spain, Portugal, Sweden, and Switzerland, was either allied with the Nazis or subject to their rule. These victories, and the economy of plunder that enriched Germany with forced labor and other nations' wealth, won Hitler considerable popularity at home. But these were only the first steps in a larger plan.

Hitler's ultimate goals, and his conception of Germany's national destiny, lay to the east. Hitler had always seen the nonaggression pact with the Soviet Union as an act of convenience, to last only until Germany was prepared for this final conflict. By the summer of 1941, it seemed Germany was ready. On June 22, 1941, Hitler began Operation Barbarossa, the invasion of the Soviet Union. The elite of the German army led the way, defeating all the forces the Russians could put in front of them. Stalin's purges of the 1930s had exiled or executed many of his most capable army officers, and the effects showed in Russian disorganization and disaffection in the face of the panzers. Hundreds of thousands of prisoners were taken as German forces pressed deep into Byelorussia (modern Belarus), the Baltic states, and Ukraine. Like Napoleon, the Germans led a multinational army; it included Italians, Hungarians, most of the Romanian army, and freelance soldiers from the Baltics and Ukraine who bore grudges against Stalin's authoritarian regime. During the fall of 1941 the Nazis destroyed much of the Red Army's fighting strength and vigorously pursued their two goals: the destruction of communism and racial purification.

The war against the Soviets was a war of ideologies and of racial hatred. The advancing Nazi forces left burning fields and towns in their wake and methodically wiped

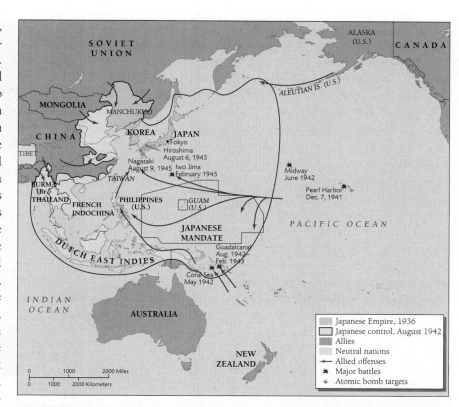

WORLD WAR II IN THE PACIFIC. ▪ *What areas did the Japanese and Allies each control in the Pacific theater during the Second World War?* ▪ *Based on tracing the route of the Allied offense of the map, what did the main Allied strategy appear to be?* ▪ *What factors led the Americans to decide that the dropping of atomic bombs on Hiroshima and Nagasaki was the most expeditious way to end the war, rather than invading Japan?*

the occupied territories clean of "undesirable elements." When Russian guerrillas counterattacked with sniping and sabotage, German forces shot or hanged hundreds of innocent hostages at a time in reprisal, often torturing their victims first. The Russian guerrillas quickly chose to deliver the same punishment to any captured Germans. By the end of 1941 it was clear that the war in the East was a war of destruction and that both sides believed that only one side would be allowed to survive. In 1941, it seemed the victors would be German: their forces were on the march toward the capital at Moscow. On orders from Berlin, however, some of the German forces pushing toward Moscow were diverted southward to attack Russia's industrial heartland in an effort to destroy the Soviets' ability to resist before the Russian winter set in. Moscow was never taken, and the Russian population, its leaders, and its armies, began to organize a much more determined resistance.

Hitler nonetheless managed to piece together an empire that stretched across the entire continent of Europe. "We come as the heralds of a New Order and a new justice," his regime announced. Hitler specifically compared his rule to a "new Indian empire," and claimed to have studied British imperial techniques. Much of the "New Order" was improvised and rested on a patchwork of provisional regimes: military government in Poland and Ukraine, collaborators in France, allied fascists in Hungary, and so on. The clearest principle was German supremacy. The empire was meant to feed German citizens and maintain their morale and support for the war, which would prevent the "stab in the back" that Hitler believed had thwarted a German victory in 1914–18. Occupied countries paid inflated "occupation costs" in taxes, food, industrial production, and manpower. More than 2 million foreign workers were brought into Germany in 1942–43 from France, Belgium, Holland, and the Soviet Union.

The demands of enemy occupation, and the political and moral questions of collaboration and resistance, were issues across occupied Europe. The Nazis set up puppet regimes in a number of occupied territories. Both Norway and the Netherlands were deeply divided by the occupation. In each country a relatively small but dedicated party of Nazis governed in the name of the Germans, while at the same time well-organized and determined resistance movements gathered information for the Allies and carried out acts of sabotage. In Denmark, the population was much more united against their German occupiers, engaging in regular acts of passive resistance that infuriated German administrators. They also banded together as private citizens to smuggle most of the country's Jewish population out to safety in neutral Sweden.

Elsewhere the relationship between collaboration, resistance, and self-interested neutrality was more complex. In France, collaboration ranged from simple survival tactics under occupation to active support for Nazi ideals and goals. The worst example of this was the Vichy regime's active anti-Semitism and the aid given by French authorities in isolating and criminalizing French Jews and deporting them to the concentration camps. Living with the German conquerors forced citizens in France (and elsewhere) to make choices. Many chose to protect their own interests by sacrificing those of others, particularly such "undesirables" as Jews and communists. At the same time, communist activists, some members of the defeated French military, and ordinary citizens—such as the people of France's central mountains, who had a long tradition of smuggling and resisting government—became active guerrillas and saboteurs. They established links with the Free French movement in London, led by the charismatic, stiff-necked general Charles de Gaulle, and supplied important intelligence to the Allies. In eastern Europe, resistance movements provoked both open warfare against the fascists and civil war within their own countries. The Germans' system

"CULTURAL TERROR," 1944. Produced in Nazi-occupied Holland, this cultural Frankenstein's monster warns of the looming destruction of European identity with the advance of American troops who will bring American culture with them. The terror of this culture is embodied in a long list of references: aerial bombardment, the violence of lynching and the Ku Klux Klan, African American jazz, Jewish racial threats, sexual license, common criminality, and financial manipulation. ▪ *What image of European culture was this image designed to defend?*

of occupation in Yugoslavia pitted a fascist Croat regime against most Serbs; the Croatian fascist guard, the Ustasha, massacred hundreds of thousands of Orthodox Christian Serbs. Josip Broz (Tito), born in Croatia to a Croatian father and a Slovene mother, emerged as the leader of the most powerful Yugoslavian resistance movement—militarily the most significant resistance in the war. Tito's troops were communists and strong enough to form a guerrilla army. They fought Germans, Italians, and Croat fascists, gaining support and supplies from the Allies.

Perhaps the most important moral issue facing citizens of occupied Europe was not their national allegiance but rather their personal attitude to the fate of the Nazis' sworn enemies: Jews, communists, Roma, homosexuals, and political "undesirables." Some French Jews along the Riviera found the Italian Catholic army officers who occupied the area more willing to save them from deportation than their fellow Frenchmen. This deeply personal choice—whether to risk family, friends, and careers to aid the deportees or simply to look the other way and allow mass murder—was one of the most powerful dilemmas of the war.

RACIAL WAR, ETHNIC CLEANSING, AND THE HOLOCAUST

From the beginning, the Nazis had seen the conflict as a racial war. In *Mein Kampf* Hitler had already outlined his view that war against the *Untermenschen*, or "subhuman" Jews, Roma, and Slavs, was natural and necessary. Not only would it purify the German people, but it would also conquer territory for their expansion. Thus as soon as the war broke out, the Nazis began to implement the Reich's ambitious plans for redrawing the racial map—what is now called ethnic cleansing. In the fall of 1939, with Poland conquered, Heinrich Himmler directed the SS to begin massive population transfers. Ethnic Germans were moved from elsewhere into the borders of the Reich, while Poles and Jews were deported to specially designated areas in the east. Over 200,000 ethnic Germans from the Baltic states were resettled in Western Prussia. Welcoming these ethnic Germans went hand in hand with a brutal campaign of terror against the Poles, especially Polish Jews. The Nazis sought to root out all sources of potential resistance. Professors at the University of Kraków, considered dangerous intellectuals, were deported to concentration camps, where they died. The SS shot "undesirables," such as the inmates of Polish mental asylums, partly to allow SS troops to occupy the asylums' barracks. Poles were deported to forced labor camps. The Nazis began to transport Jews by the thousands to the region of Lublin, south of Warsaw. Special death squads also began to shoot Jews in the streets and in front of synagogues. These Polish campaigns took 100,000 Jewish lives in 1940.

The elimination of European Jewry stood at the center of the Nazis' *Rassenkampf*, or "racial struggle." We have seen the role of anti-Semitism in Hitler's rise to power and the escalating campaign of terror against the Jewish community inside Germany in the 1930s, including the Night of Broken Glass (see Chapter 25). Most historians now agree that although Hitler and other Nazis verbally announced "war" against the Jews early on, such a policy was not possible until the conquest of territory in the east after 1941 suddenly brought millions of Jews under Nazi control. Until the organized pogroms of 1938 the Nazis' anti-Jewish policy aimed not at extermination but at emigration, and until 1941 the Nazi leadership continued to consider plans to deport Europe's Jews to Madagascar, a French colony off the eastern coast of Africa. These schemes took shape against the background of daily terror and frequent massacres, especially in Poland. The invasion of the Soviet Union turned these atrocities into something much more deadly. Operation Barbarossa was animated by the Nazis' intense ideological and racial hatreds, directed against Slavs, Jews, and Marxists. The campaign's initial success also created pressing practical problems for the German army in the newly conquered territories as officials debated how to control the millions of people, including military prisoners, eastern European Jews, and other civilians, who had now fallen into Nazi hands. Although Hitler had certainly prepared the way for what followed in his long-nurtured campaigns against Jews, historians now believe that much of the driving force for the Holocaust came from rivalries within the Nazi bureaucracy that led to a radicalization of persecution and murder on a scale few could have imagined.

OPENING THE CONCENTRATION CAMPS. Many Allied soldiers documented the liberation of the concentration camps at the end of the war, recording in photographs and films the appalling scenes they encountered. In many cases, German civilians were brought into the camps and compelled to witness the countless bodies of camp prisoners that remained unburied, before being conscripted to help with the disposal of the corpses in order to prevent the spread of disease. In this photograph, local residents view the victims of Nazi crimes at Landesburg camp near Dachau in 1945. ■ *What complications faced the Allies in the task of assigning responsibility for these crimes?*

As the Nazi army swept into the Soviet Union in 1941, captured communist officials, political agitators, and any hostile civilians were imprisoned, tortured, or shot. About 5.5 million military prisoners were taken and marched to camps. Over half of them died of starvation or were executed. Poles from regions that had been under Soviet rule, Jews, and Russians were deported to Germany to work as slave labor in German factories. On the heels of the army came special battalions of *Einsatzgruppen*—special-operations troops working as death squads. Joined by 11,000 extra SS troops, they stormed through Jewish villages and towns with Russian or Polish populations identified as "difficult." The men of the villages were shot; the women and children either deported to labor camps or massacred along with the men. By September 1941 the *Einsatzgruppen* reported that in their efforts at pacification they had killed 85,000 people, most of them Jews. By April 1942, the number was 500,000. This killing began before the gas chambers had gone into operation and continued through the campaigns on the Eastern Front. As of 1943, the death squads had killed roughly 2.2 million Jews.

As Operation Barbarossa progressed, German administrations of occupied areas herded local Jewish populations even more tightly into the ghettos that some Jewish communities had occupied for centuries; Warsaw and Lodz in Poland were the largest. There, Nazi administrators, accusing Jewish people in the ghettos of hoarding supplies, refused to allow food to go in. The ghettos became centers of starvation and disease. Those who left the ghetto were shot rather than returned. A German doctor summarized the regime's logic about killing this way: "One must, I can say it quite openly in this circle, be clear about it. There are only two ways. We sentence the Jews in the ghetto to death by hunger or we shoot them. Even if the end result is the same, the latter is more intimidating." In other words, the point was not simply death, but terror.

Through the late summer and fall of 1941, Nazi officials formulated plans for mass killings in death camps. The ghettos had already been sealed; now orders came down that no Jews were to leave any occupied areas. That summer the Nazis had experimented with vans equipped with poison gas, which could kill thirty to fifty people at a time. Those experiments and the gas chambers were designed with the help of scientists from the T-4 euthanasia program, which had already killed 80,000 racially, mentally, or physically "unfit" individuals in Germany. By October 1941 the SS was building camps with gas chambers and deporting people to them. Auschwitz-Birkenau (*OWSH-vihts BIHR-kuh-now*), which had been built to hold Polish prisoners, was expanded to be the largest of the camps. Auschwitz eventually held many different types of prisoners—"undesirables" like Jehovah's Witnesses and homosexuals, Poles, Russians, and even some British POWs—but Jews and Roma were the ones systematically annihilated there. Between the spring of 1942 and the fall of 1944 over one million people were killed at Auschwitz-Birkenau alone. The creation of the death camps set off the greatest wave of slaughter, from 1942 to 1943. Freight cars were used to haul Jewish people to the camps, first from the ghettos of Poland, then from France, Holland, Belgium, Austria, the Balkans, and later from Hungary and Greece. Bodies were buried in pits dug by prisoners or burned in crematoria.

The death camps have come to symbolize the horrors of Nazism as a system of modern mass murder. Yet it is worth emphasizing that the slaughter was not all anonymous, industrialized, or routine, and that much of it took place in face-to-face encounters outside the camps. Jews and other victims were not simply killed. They were tortured, beaten, and executed publicly while soldiers and other onlookers recorded the executions with cameras—and sent photos home to their families. During the last phases of the war, inmates still in the concentration camps were taken on death marches whose sole purpose was suffering and death. Nor was the killing done by the specially indoctrinated troops of the SS and *Einsatzgruppen*. The Nazi regime called up groups of conscripts such as Reserve Police Battalion 101 from duty in its home city of Hamburg and sent it into occupied territories. Once there, the unit of middle-aged policemen received and obeyed orders to kill, in one day, 1,500 Jewish men, women, and children in one village. The commander offered to excuse men who did not feel they could carry out this assignment; only a few asked for a different task.

"JEWISH COUPLE IN BUDAPEST," EVGENY KHALDEI (1945). Khaldei, a Soviet photographer and journalist who traveled with the Red Army, left a remarkable and moving account of his encounter with this woman and man. "There was a Jewish couple wearing Stars of David. They were afraid of me. There was still fighting going on in the city, and they thought I might be an SS soldier. So I said *Shalom Aleichem* [hello] to them, and the woman began to cry. After I'd taken the picture, I pulled their stars off and said, 'The fascists are beaten. It's terrible to be marked like that.'"

HITLER'S "FINAL SOLUTION": JEWS MARKED FOR DEATH

Country or Region	Jewish Population
Soviet Union	5 million
Ukraine	2,994,684
Poland	3,104,000
Hungary	742,800
France (Unoccupied Zone including French North Africa)	700,000
White Russia	446,484
Romania	342,000
France (Occupied Zone)	165,000
Netherlands	160,800
Germany	131,800
Slovakia	88,000
Bohemia & Moravia	74,200
Greece	69,600
Italy	58,000
Balkans	50,200
Bulgaria	48,000
Austria	43,700
Belgium	43,000
Baltic States	37,500

HITLER'S "FINAL SOLUTION": JEWS MARKED FOR DEATH. On January 20, 1942, German officials met at Wannsee (just outside Berlin) to discuss the "final solution" to the "Jewish problem." They also discussed what they believed to be the remaining number of Jewish people in territories they controlled or soon hoped to control. Examine these figures closely. ▪ *How many millions of innocent people did the Nazis propose to slaughter?* ▪ *Based on your reading, what percentage of the Jews did they actually kill?* ▪ *What two countries were scheduled for the most executions?*

In one Polish town, occupied first by the Soviets and then retaken by the Nazis, the Polish villagers themselves, with minimal guidance or help from German soldiers, turned on their Jewish neighbors and killed hundreds in a day.

How many people knew of the extent of the Holocaust? No operation of this scale could be carried out without the cooperation or knowledge of many: the Nazi hierarchy; architects who helped build the camps; engineers who designed the gas chambers and crematoria; municipal officials of cities from which people were deported; train drivers; residents of villages near the camps, who reported the smell of bodies burning; and so on. It is not surprising that most who suspected the worst were terrified and powerless. It is also not surprising that many people did not want to know and did their best to ignore evidence and carry on with their lives. Many who continued to support the Nazis did so for other reasons, out of personal opportunism or because they opposed communism and wanted order restored. Yet mere popular indifference does not provide a satisfactory explanation for the Nazis' ability to accomplish the murder of so many people. Many Europeans—German, French, Dutch, Polish, Swiss, and Russian—had come to believe that there was a "Jewish problem" that had to be "solved." The Nazis tried to conceal the death camps. Yet they knew they could count on vocal support for requiring Jews to be specially identified, for restrictions on marriage and property ownership, and for other kinds of discrimination. For reasons that had to do with both traditional Christian anti-Semitism and modern, racialized nationalism, many Europeans had come to see Jewish Europeans as "foreign," no longer members of their national communities.

What of other governments? Their level of collaboration with the Nazis' plans varied. The French Vichy regime, on its own initiative, passed laws that required Jews to wear identifying stars and strictly limited their movements and activities. When the German government demanded roundups and deportations of Jews, Vichy cooperated. On the other hand, Italy, though a fascist country, participated less actively. Not until the Germans occupied the north of Italy in 1943 were drastic anti-Semitic measures implemented. The Hungarian government, also fascist and allied with the Nazis, persecuted Jews but dragged its heels about deportations. Thus the Hungarian Jewish community survived—until March 1944, when Germans, disgusted with their Hungarian collaborators, took direct control and immediately began mass deportations. So determined were the Nazis to carry out their "final solution" that they killed up to 12,000 Hungarian Jews a day at Auschwitz in May 1944, contributing to a total death toll of 600,000 Jews from Hungary.

In the face of this Nazi determination, little resistance was possible. The concentration camps were designed to numb and incapacitate their inmates, making them acquiesce in their own slow deaths even if they were not killed right away. In his famous account, the survivor Primo Levi, an Italian Jew, writes: "Our language lacks words to express this offense, the demolition of a man. . . . It is not possible to sink lower than this; no human condition is more their aircraft, and huge stores of supplies were destroyed or captured. Nazi forces penetrated deep into European Russia. The Soviets fought regardless. By late 1941 German and Finnish forces had cut off and besieged Leningrad (St. Petersburg). Yet the city held out for 844 days—through three winters, massive destruction by artillery and aircraft, and periods of starvation—until a large relief force broke the siege. Russian partisans stepped up their campaigns of ambush and terrorism, and many of the Germans' former allies in Ukraine and elsewhere turned against them in reaction to Nazi pacification efforts.

The Eastern Front

In the East, the character of the war changed as Russians rallied to defend the *rodina*—the Russian motherland. Stalin's efforts were aided by the weather: successive winters took a heavy toll in German lives. At the same time, Soviet industry made an astonishing recovery during the war years. Whole industries were rebuilt behind the safety of the Ural mountains and entire urban populations were sent to work in them, turning out tanks, fighter planes, machine guns, and ammunition. Finally, the Germans were the victims of their own success with their *Blitzkrieg* tactics, as their lines extended deep into Russian territory, spreading their forces more thinly and opening them up to attack from unexpected angles.

The turning point came in 1942–43, when the Germans attempted to take Stalingrad, an industrial city in southwestern Russia, in an effort to break the back of Soviet industry. The Russians drew the invading army into the city, where they were bogged down in house-to-house fighting that neutralized the German tanks and gave the outnumbered Soviet forces greater chances of success, despite their lack of equipment. The Germans found their supplies running low as winter set in, and in November 1942 large Russian armies encircled the city and besieged the invaders in a battle that continued through a cruel winter. At the end of January 1943, the German commander defied his orders and surrendered. More than half a million German, Italian, and Romanian soldiers had been killed; Russian casualties were over a million, including a hundred thousand civilians.

After Stalingrad, a series of Soviet attacks drove the Germans back toward the frontier and beyond. In what may have been the largest land battle ever fought, Soviet armies destroyed a German force at Kursk in the summer of 1943—the battle involved over 6,000 tanks and 2 million men. Following this victory, the Russians launched a major offensive into Ukraine, and by the spring of 1944 Ukraine was back in Soviet hands. Meanwhile, Leningrad was liberated and Romania forced to capitulate. Soviet armies entered the Balkans, where they met up with Tito's partisans in Yugoslavia. In Poland, successive German armies collapsed, and the Soviets, joined by communist partisans from eastern Europe, retook large parts of Czechoslovakia. Hitler's ambitious goal of conquest in the East had brought

STORMING "FORTRESS EUROPE." American troops landing on Omaha Beach in Normandy, France on June 6, 1944. In the three months that followed, the Allies poured more than 2 million men, almost half a million vehicles, and 4 million tons of supplies onto the Continent—a measure of how firmly the Germans were established.

"RAISING THE RED FLAG OVER THE REICHSTAG," EVGENY KHALDEI, MAY 1, 1945. Khaldei was one of several Soviet Jewish photographers to document Nazi atrocities and (in this case) Soviet heroism on the Eastern Front. In this photograph, which became the best-known image of Soviet victory, a Soviet soldier raises a flag over the Reichstag in Berlin. ■ *How was the Soviet occupation of the German capital seen from the perspective of the other Allied governments?*

the downfall of the Nazi regime and death to another generation of German soldiers.

The Western Front

When the Nazis invaded Russia, Stalin called on the Allies to open a second front in the West. In response, the Americans led an attack on Italy in 1943, beginning with an invasion of Sicily in July. Italy's government deposed Mussolini and surrendered in the summer of 1943, while the nation collapsed into civil war. Italian partisans, especially the communists, sided with the Americans, while dedicated fascists fought on. The Germans occupied Italy with more than a dozen elite divisions, and the hard-fought and bitter campaign with American and British forces lasted eighteen months.

The most important Western European front was opened on June 6, 1944, with the massive Allied landings on the French coast of Normandy. Casualties were high, but careful planning and deception allowed the Allied invasion to gain a foothold in northern Europe, eventually leading to breakthrough of the German lines. A second landing in southern France also succeeded, aided by the resistance. By August,

THE ATOM BOMB. A mushroom cloud hovers over Nagasaki after the city was bombed on August 9, 1945. Hiroshima had been bombed three days earlier.

these Allied armies had liberated Paris and pushed into Belgium. In the fall, the Germans managed to defeat a British airborne invasion in the Netherlands and an American thrust into the Rhineland forests before mounting a devastating attack in December 1944, in the Battle of the Bulge. The Allied lines nearly broke, but the American forces held long enough for a crushing counterattack. In April 1945 the Allies crossed the Rhine into Germany, and the last defenders of the German Reich were swiftly overwhelmed. This military success was helped by the fact that most Germans preferred to surrender to Americans or Britons than face the Russians to the east.

Those Soviet troops were approaching fast. The Russian Army took Prague and Vienna, and by late April they reached the suburbs of Berlin. In the savage ten-day battle to take the German capital more than a hundred thousand Russians and Germans died. Adolf Hitler killed himself in a bunker beneath the Chancellery on April 30. On May 2 the heart of the city was captured, and the Soviets' red banner flew from the Brandenburg Gate. On May 7 the German high command signed a document of unconditional surrender. The war in Europe was over.

The War in the Pacific

The war in the Pacific ended four months later. The British pushed the Japanese out of Burma while the Germans were surrendering in the West, and soon afterwards Australian forces recaptured the Dutch East Indies. In the fall of 1944, the U.S. Navy had destroyed most of Japan's surface ships in the gulfs of the Philippine Islands, and American troops took Manila house by house in bloody fighting. The remaining battles—amphibious assaults on a series of islands running toward the Japanese mainland—were just as brutal. Japanese pilots mounted suicide attacks on American ships, while American marines and Japanese soldiers fought over every inch of the shell-blasted rocks in the Pacific. The Japanese island of Okinawa fell to the Americans after eighty-two days of desperate fighting, giving the United States a foothold less than 500 miles from the Japanese home islands. At the same time, the Soviet Union marched an army into Manchuria and the Japanese colonial territory of Korea. The government in Tokyo called on its citizens to defend the nation against an invasion.

On July 26, the U.S., British, and Chinese governments jointly called on Japan to surrender or be destroyed. The United States had already been using long-range B-29 bombers in systematic attacks on Japanese cities, killing hundreds of thousands of Japanese civilians in firestorms produced by incendiary bombs. When the Japanese

The Cold War: Soviet and Western Views

> The first excerpt is from a speech titled "The Sinews of Peace" that was delivered by Winston Churchill at Westminster College in Fulton, Missouri, in early 1946. In it, he coined the phrase Iron Curtain, warning of the rising power of the Soviet Union in Eastern Europe.
> The next excerpt is from an address by Nikita Khrushchev, who became first secretary of the Communist party in 1953. Three years later, his power secure, he began publicly to repudiate the crimes of Joseph Stalin. Khrushchev presided over a short-lived thaw in Soviet–Western relations. Yet, as can be seen in his address, Khrushchev shared Churchill's conception of the world divided into two mutually antagonistic camps.

Winston Churchill's "Iron Curtain" Speech

A shadow has fallen upon the scenes so lately lighted by the Allied victory. Nobody knows what Soviet Russia and its Communist international organization intend to do in the immediate future, or what are the limits, if any, to their expansive and proselytizing tendencies. I have a strong admiration and regard for the valiant Russian people and for my wartime comrade, Marshal Stalin. There is deep sympathy and goodwill in Britain . . . towards the people of all the Russias and a resolve to persevere through many differences and rebuffs in establishing lasting friendships. We understand the Russian need to be secure on her western frontiers by the removal of all possibility of German aggression. We welcome Russia

to her rightful place among the leading nations of the world. We welcome her flag upon the seas. Above all, we welcome constant, frequent, and growing contacts between the Russian people and our own people on both sides of the Atlantic. It is my duty, however . . . to place before you certain facts about the present position in Europe.

From Stettin in the Baltic to Trieste in the Adriatic, an iron curtain has descended across the Continent. Behind that line lie all the capitals of the ancient states of Central and Eastern Europe. Warsaw, Berlin, Prague, Vienna, Budapest, Belgrade, Bucharest, and Sofia, all these famous cities and the populations around them lie in what I must call the Soviet sphere, and all are subject in

one form or another, not only to Soviet influence but to a very high and, in many cases, increasing measure of control from Moscow. . . .

From what I have seen of our Russian friends and Allies during the war, I am convinced that there is nothing they admire so much as strength, and there is nothing for which they have less respect than for weakness, especially military weakness. For that reason the old doctrine of a balance of power is unsound. We cannot afford, if we can help it, to work on narrow margins, offering temptations to a triad of strength. If the Western Democracies stand together in strict adherence to the principles of the United Nations Charter, their influences for furthering those principles

Krushchev's accusations were widely discussed. The harshness of Stalin's regime had generated popular discontent and demands for a shift from the production of heavy machinery and armaments to the manufacture of consumer goods, for a measure of freedom in the arts, and for an end to police repression. How, under these circumstances, could the regime keep de-Stalinization within safe limits? The thaw did unleash forces that proved difficult to control. Between 1956 and 1958 the Soviet prison camps released thousands of prisoners. Soviet citizens besieged the regime with

requests to rehabilitate relatives who had been executed or imprisoned under Stalin, partly to make themselves again eligible for certain privileges of citizenship, such as housing.

The thaw provided a brief window of opportunity for some of the Soviet Union's most important writers. In 1957 Boris Pasternak's novel *Doctor Zhivago* could not be published in the Soviet Union, and in 1958 Pasternak was barred from receiving the Nobel Prize in Literature. That Aleksandr Solzhenitsyn's (*suhl-zhih-NYEE-tsihn*) first novel, *One Day in the Life of Ivan Denisovich*, could be published in

will be immense and no one is likely to molest them. If, however, they become divided or falter in their duty and if these all-important years are allowed to slip away, then indeed catastrophe may overwhelm us all.

Source: Winston Churchill, *Winston S. Churchill: His Complete Speeches, 1897–1963,* vol. 7, 1943–1949, ed. Robert Rhodes James (New York: 1983), pp. 7290–91.

Nikita Khrushchev, "Report to the Communist Party Congress" (1961)

Comrades! The competition of the two world social systems, the socialist and the capitalist, has been the chief content of the period since the 20th party Congress. It has become the pivot, the foundation of world development at the present historical stage. Two lines, two historical trends, have manifested themselves more and more clearly in social development. One is the line of social progress, peace, and constructive activity. The other is the line of reaction, oppression, and war.

In the course of the peaceful competition of the two systems capitalism has suffered a profound moral defeat in the eyes of all peoples. The common people are daily convinced that capitalism is incapable of solving a single one of the urgent problems confronting mankind. It becomes more and more obvious that only on the paths to socialism can a solution to these problems be found. Faith in the capitalist system and the capitalist path of development is dwindling. Monopoly capital, losing its influence, resorts more and more to intimidating and suppressing the masses of the people, to methods of open dictatorship in carrying out its domestic policy, and to aggressive acts against other countries. But the masses of the people offer increasing resistance to reaction's acts.

It is no secret to anyone that the methods of intimidation and threat are not a sign of strength but evidence of the weakening of capitalism, the deepening of its general crisis. As the saying goes, if you can't hang on by the mane, you won't hang on by the tail! Reaction is still capable of dissolving parliaments in some countries in violation of their constitutions, of casting the best representatives of the people into prison, of sending cruisers and marines to subdue the "unruly." All this can put off for a time the approach of the fatal hour for the rule of capitalism. The imperialists are sawing away at the branch on which they sit. There is no force in the world capable of stopping man's advance along the road of progress.

Source: *Current Soviet Policies IV,* ed. Charlotte Saikowski and Leo Gruliow, from trans. *Current Digest of the Soviet Press,* Joint Committee on Slavic Studies (1962), pp. 42–45.

Questions for Analysis

1. Whom did Churchill blame for building the Iron Curtain between the Soviet sphere and the Western sphere?

2. Was the Soviet Union actively trying to create international communism? Was the United States trying to spread the Western way of life on a global scale?

1962 marked the relative cultural freedom of the thaw. *Ivan Denisovich* was based on Solzhenitsyn's own experiences in the labor camps, where he had spent eight years for criticizing Stalin in a letter, and was a powerful literary testimony to the repression Khrushchev had acknowledged. By 1964, however, Khrushchev had fallen and the thaw ended, driving criticism and writers such as Solzhenitsyn underground. Solzhenitsyn kept working on what would become *The Gulag Archipelago,* the first massive historical and literary study of the Stalinist camps (gulags).

Repression in Eastern Europe

Stalin's death in 1953 coincided with mounting tensions in Eastern Europe. The East German government, burdened by reparations payments to the Soviet Union, faced an economic crisis. The illegal exodus of East German citizens to the West rose sharply: 58,000 left in March 1953 alone. In June, when the government demanded hefty increases in industrial productivity, strikes broke out in East Berlin. Unrest spread throughout the country. The Soviet army put down the uprising, and hundreds were executed in the subsequent purge. In the aftermath, the East German government, under the leadership of Walter Ulbricht, used fears of disorder to solidify one-party rule.

In 1956, emboldened by Khrushchev's de-Stalinization, Poland and Hungary rebelled, demanding more independence in the management of their domestic affairs. Striking workers led the opposition in Poland. The government wavered, responding first with military repression and then with a promise of liberalization. Eventually the anti-Stalinist Polish leader Wladyslaw Gomulka won Soviet permission for his country to pursue its own "ways of Socialist development" by pledging Poland's loyalty to the terms of the Warsaw Pact.

Events in Hungary turned out very differently. The charismatic leader of Hungary's communist government, Imre Nagy, was as much a Hungarian nationalist as a communist. Under his government, protests against Moscow's policies developed into a much broader anticommunist struggle and, even more important, attempted secession from the Warsaw Pact. Khrushchev might contemplate looser ties between Eastern Europe and Moscow, but he would not tolerate an end to the pact. On November 4, 1956, Soviet troops occupied Budapest, arresting and executing leaders of the Hungarian rebellion. The Hungarians took up arms, and street fighting continued for several weeks. The Hungarians had hoped for Western aid, but Dwight Eisenhower, newly elected to a second term as U.S. president, steered clear of giving support. Soviet forces installed a new government under the staunchly communist Janos Kadar, the repression continued, and tens of thousands of Hungarian refugees fled for the West. Khrushchev's efforts at presenting a gentler, more conciliatory Soviet Union to the West had been shattered by revolt and repression.

What was more, East Germans continued to flee the country via West Berlin. Between 1949 and 1961, 2.7 million East Germans left, blunt evidence of the unpopularity of the regime. Attempting to stem the tide, Khrushchev demanded that the West recognize the permanent division of Germany with a free city in Berlin. When that demand was refused, in 1961 the East German government built a ten-foot wall separating the two sectors of the city. For almost thirty years, until 1989, the Berlin Wall remained a monument to how the hot war had gone cold, and mirrored, darkly, the division of Germany and Europe as a whole.

ECONOMIC RENAISSANCE

Despite the ongoing tensions of a global superpower rivalry, the postwar period brought a remarkable recovery in Western Europe: the economic "miracle." The war

THE BERLIN WALL, 1961. Thirteen years after the blockade, the East German government built a wall between East and West Berlin to stop the flow of escapees to the West. This manifestation of the Iron Curtain was dismantled in 1989.

encouraged a variety of technological innovations that could be applied in peacetime: improved communications (the invention of radar, for example), the development of synthetic materials, the increasing use of aluminum and alloy steels, and advances in the techniques of prefabrication. Wartime manufacturing had added significantly to nations' productive capacity. The Marshall Plan seems to have been less central than many claimed at the time, but it solved immediate problems having to do with the balance of payments and a shortage of American dollars to buy American goods. The boom was fueled by high consumer demand and, consequently, very high levels of employment throughout the 1950s and 1960s. Brisk domestic and foreign consumption encouraged expansion, continued capital investment, and technological innovation. Rising demand for Europe's goods hastened agreements that encouraged the free flow of international trade and currencies (as will be discussed later).

It was now assumed that states would do much more economic management—directing investment, making decisions about what to modernize, coordinating policies between industries and countries—than before. This, too, was a legacy of wartime. As one British official observed, "We are all planners now." The result was a series of "mixed" economies combining public and private ownership. In France, where public ownership was already well advanced in the 1930s, railways, electricity and gas, banking, radio and television, and a large segment of the automobile industry were brought under state management. In Britain the list was equally long: coal and utilities; road, railroad, and air transport; and banking. Though nationalization was less common in West Germany, the railway system (state owned since the late nineteenth century); some electrical, chemical, and metallurgical concerns; and the Volkswagen company—the remnant of Hitler's attempt to produce a "people's car"—were all in state hands, though the latter was largely returned to the private sector in 1963.

These government policies and programs contributed to astonishing growth rates. Between 1945 and 1963 the average yearly growth of West Germany's gross domestic product (gross national product [GNP] minus income received from abroad) was 7.6 percent; in Austria, 5.8 percent; in Italy, 6 percent; in the Netherlands, 4.7 percent; and so on. Not only did the economies recover from the war but they reversed prewar economic patterns of slack demand, overproduction, and insufficient investment. Production facilities were hard pressed to keep up with soaring demand.

West Germany's recovery was particularly spectacular, and particularly important to the rest of Europe. Production increased sixfold between 1948 and 1964. Unemployment fell to record lows, reaching 0.4 percent in 1965, when there were six unfilled jobs for every unemployed person. The contrast with the catastrophic unemployment of the Great Depression heightened the impression of a miracle. In the 1950s, the state and private industry built half a million new housing units each year to accommodate citizens whose homes had been destroyed, new resident refugees from East Germany and Eastern Europe, and transient workers from Italy, Spain, Greece, and elsewhere drawn by West Germany's high demand for labor.

European nations with little in common in terms of political traditions or industrial patterns all shared in the general prosperity. Economic growth, however, did not level the differences among and within states. In southern Italy, illiteracy remained high and land continued to be held by a few rich families; the per capita GNP in Sweden was almost ten times that of Turkey. Britain remained a special case. British growth was respectable when compared with past performance. Yet the British economy remained sluggish. The country was burdened with obsolete factories and methods, the legacy of its early industrialization, and by an unwillingness to adopt new techniques in old industries or invest in more-successful new ones. It was plagued as well by a series of balance-of-payments crises precipitated by an inability to sell more goods abroad than it imported.

European Economic Integration

The Western European renaissance was a collective effort. From the Marshall Plan on, a series of international economic organizations began to bind the Western European countries together. The first of these was the European Coal and Steel Community (ECSC), founded in 1951 to coordinate trade in, and the management of, Europe's most crucial resources. Coal was still king in mid-twentieth-century Europe; it fueled everything from steel manufacturing and trains to household heating, and counted for 82 percent of Europe's primary energy consumption. It was also key to relations between West Germany, with abundant coal mines, and France, with its coal-hungry steel mills. The ECSC was soon followed by a broader agreement. In 1957, the Treaty of Rome transformed France, West Germany, Italy, Belgium, Holland, and Luxembourg into the European Economic Community (EEC), or Common Market. The EEC aimed to abolish trade barriers among its members. Moreover, the organization pledged itself to common external tariffs, to the free movement of labor and capital among the member nations, and to building uniform wage structures and social security systems to create similar working conditions throughout the Common Market.

Integration did not proceed smoothly. Great Britain stayed away, fearing the effects of the ECSC on its declining coal industry and on its longtime trading relationship with Australia, New Zealand, and Canada. Britain did not share France's need for raw materials and the others' need for markets; it continued to rely on its economic relations with the Empire and Commonwealth. One of the few victors in the Second World War, Britain assumed that it could hold its global economic position in the postwar world.

The European Economic Community was a remarkable success. By 1963, it had become the world's largest importer. Its steel production was second only to that of the United States, and total industrial production was over 70 percent higher than it had been in 1950. It also established a new long-term political trend: individual countries sought to Europeanize solutions to their problems.

European integration was also shaped by crucial agreements reached in Bretton Woods, New Hampshire, in July 1944 aimed to coordinate the movements of the global economy and to internationalize solutions to economic crises, avoiding catastrophes such as those that plagued the 1930s. The Bretton Woods conference created the International Monetary Fund and the World Bank, both designed to establish predictable and stable exchange rates, prevent speculation, and enable currencies—and consequently trade—to move freely. All other currencies were pegged to the dollar, which both reflected and enhanced the United States' role as the foremost financial power. The new international system was formed with the American–European sphere in mind, but these organizations soon began to play a role in economic development in what came to be known as the Third World. The postwar period, then, quickened global economic integration, largely on American terms.

Economic Development in the East

Although economic development in Eastern Europe was not nearly so dramatic as that in the West, significant advances occurred there as well. National incomes rose and output increased. Poland and Hungary, in particular, strengthened their economic connections with the West, primarily with France and West Germany. By the late 1970s, about 30 percent of Eastern Europe's trade was conducted outside the Soviet bloc. Nevertheless, the Soviet Union required its satellites to design their economic policies to serve more than their own national interests. Regulations governing Comecon, the Eastern European equivalent of the Common Market, ensured that the Soviet Union could sell its exports at prices well above the world level and compelled other members to trade with the Soviet Union to their own disadvantage. Emphasis initially was on heavy industry and collectivized agriculture, though political tension in countries such as Hungary and Poland forced the Soviets eventually to moderate their policies so as to permit the manufacture of more consumer goods and the development of a modest trade with the West.

The Welfare State

Economic growth became one of the watchwords of the postwar era. Social welfare was another. The roots of the new legislation extended back to the insurance plans for old age,

EUROPE DURING THE COLD WAR. Examine the membership of NATO and the Warsaw Pact, respectively. ▪ *What were the member states in NATO?* ▪ *Why do you think some countries did not join NATO?* ▪ *Why did the membership of each alliance stay relatively stable for nearly half a century?*

sickness, and disability introduced by Bismarck in Germany in the late 1880s. But economic expansion allowed postwar European states to fund more comprehensive social programs, and commitments to putting democracy on a stronger footing provided the political motivation. Clement Atlee, a socialist and the leader of the British Labour party, coined the term *welfare state*; his government, in power until 1951, led the way in enacting legislation that provided free medical care to all through the National Health Service, as well as assistance to families and guaranteed secondary education of some kind. The welfare state also rested on the assumption that governments could and should try to support popular purchasing power, generate demand, and provide either employment or unemployment insurance, assumptions spelled out earlier by John Maynard Keynes (*General Theory*, 1936) or William Beveridge's important 1943 report on full employment. Although the British Labour party and continental socialist parties pressed these measures, welfare was a consensus issue, backed by the moderate coalitions that governed most postwar Western European states. Understood in this way, welfare was not poor relief, but an entitlement. Thus it marked a break with centuries-old ways of thinking about both poverty and citizenship.

European Politics

Postwar political leaders were overwhelmingly pragmatic. Konrad Adenauer, the West German chancellor from 1949 to 1963, despised German militarism and blamed that tradition for Hitler's rise to power. Still, he was apprehensive about German parliamentary democracy and governed in a paternalistic, sometimes authoritarian, manner. His determination to end the centuries-old hostility between France and Germany contributed significantly to the movement toward economic union. Alcide De Gasperi, the Italian premier from 1948 to 1953, was also centrist. Among postwar French leaders, the most colorful was the Resistance hero General Charles de Gaulle. De Gaulle had retired from politics in 1946 when French voters refused to accept his proposals for strengthening the executive branch of the government. In 1958, faced with civil turmoil caused by the Algerian war (see page 747) and an abortive coup attempt by a group of right-wing army officers, France's government collapsed and de Gaulle was invited to return. De Gaulle accepted but insisted on a new constitution. That constitution, which created the Fifth Republic in 1958, strengthened the executive branch of the government in an effort to avoid the parliamentary deadlocks that had weakened the country earlier. De Gaulle used his new authority to restore France's

power and prestige. Resisting U.S. influence in Europe, he pulled French forces out of NATO in 1966. He cultivated better relations with the Soviet Union and with West Germany, and presided over the decolonization of Algeria. Finally, he accelerated French economic and industrial expansion by building a modern military establishment, complete with atomic weapons. Like his counterparts, de Gaulle was not, by nature, a democrat. He steered a centrist course, working hard to produce practical solutions to political problems and thereby undermine radicalism in any form. Most other Western European nations did the same.

REVOLUTION, ANTICOLONIALISM, AND THE COLD WAR

In the colonial world as in Europe, the end of war unleashed new conflicts. Those conflicts became closely bound up with Europe's political and economic recovery, they had an enormous if delayed effect on Western culture, and they complicated the Cold War. The Cold War, as we have seen, created two powerful centers of gravity for world politics. But the wave of anticolonial independence movements that swept through postwar Asia and Africa created a new group of nations that would attempt to avoid aligning with one bloc or the other, and would call itself the "Third World."

The Chinese Revolution

The Chinese Revolution was the single most radical change in the developing world after the Second World War. A civil war had raged in China since 1926, with Mao Zedong's (*mow zeh-DOONG*, 1893–1976) communist insurgents in the north in revolt against the Nationalist forces of Jiang Jeishi (Chiang Kai-shek, 1887–1975). Though they agreed on a truce in order to face the Japanese during the war years, the civil war resumed after the Japanese defeat, and in 1949, Mao's insurgents took control of the Chinese government and drove the Nationalists into exile.

The Chinese Revolution was above all a peasant revolution, even more so than the Russian Revolution. Mao adapted Marxism to conditions very different from those imagined by Marx himself, emphasizing radical reform in the countryside (reducing rents, providing health care and education, and reforming marriage) and autonomy from Western colonial powers. The leaders of the revolution set about turning China into a modern industrial nation within a generation, at huge human cost and with very mixed results.

To anticolonial activists in many parts of the world, the Chinese Revolution stood as a model. To colonial powers, it represented the dangers inherent in decolonization. The "loss of China" provoked fear and consternation in the West, particularly in the United States. Although Mao and Stalin distrusted each other and relations between the two regimes were extremely difficult, the United States considered both nations a communist bloc until the early 1970s, and the Chinese Revolution intensified Western military and diplomatic anxiety about governments in Asia.

The Korean War

Anxiety about China turned Korea into a hot spot in the Cold War. Korea, a former Japanese colony, was divided into two states after World War II: communist North Korea, run by the Soviet client Kim Il Sung, and South Korea, led by the anticommunist autocrat Syngman Rhee, who was backed by the United States. When North Korean troops attacked the South in 1950, the United Nations Security Council gave permission for the United States to defend South Korea.

U.S. General Douglas MacArthur, a Second World War hero, drove the Korean communists to the Chinese border, but was relieved of his command by President Harry Truman after calling for attacks on Chinese territory. More than a million Chinese troops flooded across the border in support of the North Koreans, forcing the international troops into a bloody retreat. The war became a stalemate, pitting Chinese and North Korean troops against UN forces—made up largely of American and South Korean forces but also containing contingents from Britain, Australia, Ethiopia, the Netherlands, Turkey, and elsewhere. Two years later, the war ended inconclusively, with Korea divided roughly along the original line. South Korea had not been "lost," but with over 53,000 Americans and over a million Koreans and Chinese dead, neither side could claim a decisive victory. As in Germany, the inability of major powers to achieve their goals resulted in a divided nation.

Decolonization

The Chinese Revolution proved to be the start of a larger wave. Between 1947 and 1960, the sprawling European empires built during the nineteenth century disintegrated. Opposition to colonial rule had stiffened after the First World War, forcing war-weakened European states to renegotiate the terms of empire. After the Second World War, older forms of empire quickly became untenable. In some regions, European states simply sought to cut their losses and withdraw. In others, well-organized and tenacious nationalist movements successfully demanded new constitutional arrangements and independence. In a third set of cases, European powers were drawn into complicated, multifaceted, and extremely violent struggles between different movements of indigenous peoples and European settler communities—conflicts the European states had helped create.

The British Empire Unravels

India was the first and largest of the colonies to win self-government after the war. As we have seen, rebellions such as the Sepoy Mutiny challenged the representatives of Britain in India throughout the nineteenth century (see Chapter 25). During the early stages of the Second World War, the Indian National Congress (founded in 1885), the umbrella party for the independence movement, called on Britain to "quit India." The extraordinary Indian nationalist Mohandas K. (Mahatma) Gandhi (1869–1948) had been at work in India since the 1920s and had pioneered anticolonial ideas and tactics that echoed the world over. In the face of colonial domination, Gandhi advocated not violence but *swaraj*, or self-rule, urging Indians individually and collectively to develop their own resources and to withdraw from the imperial economy—by going on strike, refusing to pay taxes, or boycotting imported textiles and wearing homespun. By 1947 Gandhi and his fellow nationalist Jawaharlal Nehru (1889–1964, prime minister 1947–64), the leader of the pro-independence Congress party, had gained such widespread support that the British found it impossible to continue to hold power. The Labour party government elected in Britain in 1945 had always favored Indian independence. Now that independence became a British political necessity.

While talks established the procedures for independence, however, India was torn by ethnic and religious conflict. A Muslim League, led by Mohammed Ali Jinnah (1876–1948), wanted autonomy in largely Muslim areas and feared the predominantly Hindu Congress party's authority in a single united state. Cycles of rioting broke out between the two religious communities. In June 1947, British India was partitioned into the nations of India (majority Hindu) and Pakistan (majority Muslim). The process of partition brought brutal religious and ethnic warfare. More than 1 million Hindus and Muslims died, and an estimated 12 million became refugees, evicted from their lands or fleeing the fighting. Throughout the chaos

Mohandas Gandhi and Nonviolent Anticolonialism

After leading a campaign for Indian rights in South Africa between 1894 and 1914, Mohandas K. Gandhi (1869–1948), known as Mahatma ("great-souled") Gandhi, became a leader in the long battle for home rule in India. This battle was finally won in 1947 and brought with it the partition of India and the creation of Pakistan. Gandhi's insistence on the power of nonviolent noncooperation brought him to the forefront of Indian politics and provided a model for many later liberation struggles, including the American civil rights movement. Gandhi argued that only nonviolent resistance, which dramatized the injustice of colonial rule and colonial law, had the spiritual force to unite a community and end colonialism.

Passive resistance is a method of securing rights by personal suffering; it is the reverse of resistance by arms. When I refuse to do a thing that is repugnant to my conscience, I use soul-force. For instance, the Government of the day has passed a law which is applicable to me. I do not like it. If by using violence I force the Government to repeal the law, I am employing what may be termed body-force. If I do not obey the law and accept the penalty for its breach, I use soul-force. It involves sacrifice of self.

Everybody admits that sacrifice of self is infinitely superior to sacrifice of others. Moreover, if this kind of force is used in a cause that is unjust, only the person using it suffers. He does not make others suffer for his mistakes.

Men have before now done many things which were subsequently found to have been wrong. . . . It is therefore meet that he should not do that which he knows to be wrong, and suffer the consequence whatever it may be. This is the key to the use of soul-force. . . .

It is contrary to our manhood if we obey laws repugnant to our conscience. Such teaching is opposed to religion and means slavery. If the Government were to ask us to go about without any clothing, should we do so? If I were a passive resister, I would say to them that I would have nothing to do with their law. But we have so forgotten ourselves and become so compliant that we do not mind any degrading law.

A man who has realized his manhood, who fears only God, will fear no one else. Man-made laws are not necessarily binding on him. Even the Government does not expect any such thing from us. They do not say: "You must do such and such a thing." But they say: "If you do not do it, we will punish you." We are sunk so low that we fancy that it is our duty and our religion to do what the law lays down. If man will only realize that it is unmanly to obey laws that are unjust, no man's tyranny will enslave him. This is the key to self-rule or home-rule.

Source: M. K. Gandhi, "Indian Home Rule (1909)," in *The Gandhi Reader: A Source Book of His Life and Writings*, ed. Homer A. Jack (Bloomington, IN: 1956), pp. 104–21.

Questions for Analysis

1. Why did Gandhi believe that "sacrifice of self" was superior to "sacrifice of others"?

2. What did Gandhi mean when he said that "it is contrary to our manhood if we obey laws repugnant to our conscience"?

Gandhi, now eighty, continued to protest violence and to focus attention on overcoming the legacy of colonialism. He argued that "real freedom will come when we free ourselves of the dominance of western education, western culture, and western way of living which have been ingrained in us." In January 1948, he was assassinated by a Hindu zealot. Conflict continued between the independent states of India and Pakistan. Nehru, who became first prime minister of India, embarked on a program of industrialization and modernization—not at all what Gandhi would have counseled. Nehru proved particularly adept

at maneuvering in the Cold War world, steering a course of nonalignment with either of the blocs, getting aid for industry from the Soviet Union and food imports from the United States.

PALESTINE

The year 1948 brought more crises for the British Empire, including an end to the British mandate in Palestine. During the First World War, British diplomats had encouraged Arab nationalist revolts against the Ottoman Empire. With the

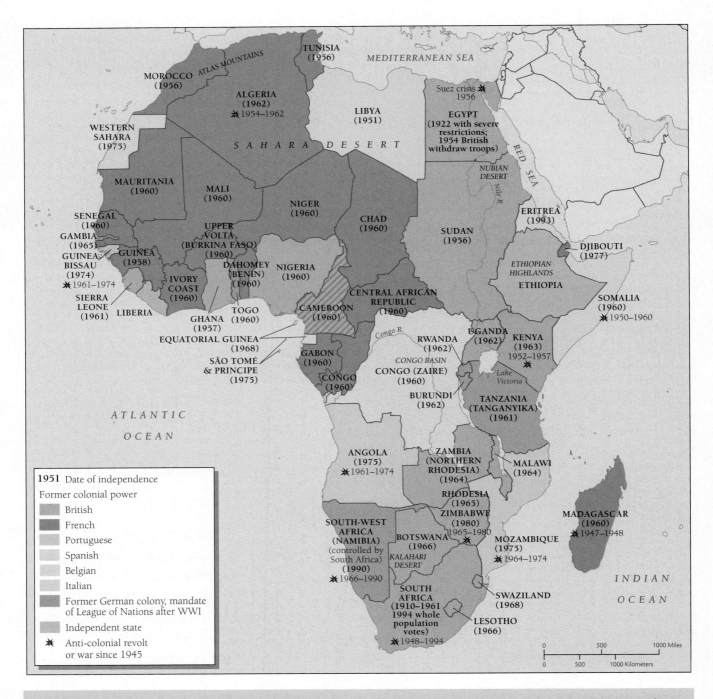

MEDITERRANEAN SEA

TUNISIA
(1956)

MOROCCO
(1956)

ATLAS MOUNTAINS

ALGERIA
(1962)
✳ 1954–1962

LIBYA
(1951)

Suez crisis ✳
1956

EGYPT
(1922 with severe
restrictions;
1954 British
withdraw troops)

WESTERN
SAHARA
(1975)

S A H A R A   D E S E R T

NUBIAN
DESERT

RED SEA

Nile R.

MAURITANIA
(1960)

MALI
(1960)

NIGER
(1960)

CHAD
(1960)

SUDAN
(1956)

ERITREA
(1993)

SENEGAL
(1960)

GAMBIA
(1965)

GUINEA
BISSAU
(1974)
✳ 1961–1974

GUINEA
(1958)

UPPER
VOLTA
(BURKINA FASO)
(1960)

DAHOMEY
(BENIN)
(1960)

NIGERIA
(1960)

CENTRAL AFRICAN
REPUBLIC
(1960)

DJIBOUTI
(1977)

ETHIOPIAN
HIGHLANDS

ETHIOPIA

SIERRA
LEONE
(1961)

LIBERIA

IVORY
COAST
(1960)

GHANA
(1957)

TOGO
(1960)

CAMEROON
(1960)

Congo R.

RWANDA
(1962)

UGANDA
(1962)

KENYA
(1963)
1952–1957
✳

SOMALIA
(1960)
✳ 1950–1960

EQUATORIAL GUINEA
(1968)

SÃO TOMÉ
& PRINCIPE
(1975)

GABON
(1960)

CONGO
(1960)

CONGO BASIN

CONGO (ZAIRE)
(1960)

BURUNDI
(1962)

Lake
Victoria

TANZANIA
(TANGANYIKA)
(1961)

ATLANTIC

OCEAN

ANGOLA
(1975)
✳ 1961–1974

ZAMBIA
(NORTHERN
RHODESIA)
(1964)

MALAWI
(1964)

RHODESIA
(1965)

ZIMBABWE
(1980)
1965–1980
✳

MADAGASCAR
(1960)
✳ 1947–1948

SOUTH-WEST
AFRICA
(NAMIBIA)
(controlled by
South Africa)
(1990)
✳ 1966–1990

BOTSWANA
(1966)

KALAHARI
DESERT

MOZAMBIQUE
(1975)
✳ 1964–1974

INDIAN

OCEAN

SOUTH
AFRICA
(1910–1961
1994 whole
population
votes)
✳ 1948–1994

SWAZILAND
(1968)

LESOTHO
(1966)

1951 Date of independence

Former colonial power

British

French

Portuguese

Spanish

Belgian

Italian

Former German colony, mandate
of League of Nations after WWI

Independent state

✳ Anti-colonial revolt
or war since 1945

0   500   1000 Miles

0   500   1000 Kilometers

DECOLONIZATION OF AFRICA. ■ *Who were the biggest imperial losers in the decolonization of Africa?* ■ *By what decade had most African countries achieved their independence?* ■ *What were the forces behind decolonization in Africa?*

1917 Balfour Declaration, they had also promised a "Jewish homeland" in Palestine for European Zionists. Contradictory promises and the flight of European Jews from Nazi Germany contributed to rising conflict between Jewish settlers and Arabs in Palestine during the 1930s and provoked an Arab revolt that was bloodily suppressed by the British. At the same time, the newly important oil concessions in the Middle East were multiplying Britain's strategic interests in the Suez

Canal, Egypt, and the Arab nations generally. Mediating local conflicts and balancing their own interests proved an impossible task. In 1939, in the name of regional stability, the British strictly limited further Jewish immigration. They tried to maintain that limit after the war, but now they faced pressure from tens of thousands of Jewish refugees from Europe. The conflict quickly became a three-way war: among Palestinian Arabs fighting for what they considered their land

and their independence, Jewish settlers and Zionist militants determined to defy British restrictions, and British administrators with divided sympathies, embarrassed and shocked by the plight of Jewish refugees and committed to maintaining good Anglo-Arab relations. The British responded militarily. By 1947, there was one British soldier for every eighteen inhabitants of the Mandate. The years of fighting, however, with terrorist tactics on all sides, persuaded the British to leave. The United Nations voted (by a narrow margin) to partition the territory into two states. Neither Jewish settlers nor Palestinian Arabs found the partition satisfactory and both began to fight for territory even before British troops withdrew. No sooner did Israel declare its independence in May 1948 than five neighboring states invaded. The new but well-organized Israeli nation survived the war and extended its boundaries. On the losing side, a million Palestinian Arabs who fled or were expelled found themselves clustered in refugee camps in the Gaza Strip and on the West Bank of the Jordan River, which the armistice granted to an enlarged state of Jordan. It is remarkable that the conflict did not become a Cold War confrontation at the start. For their own reasons, both Soviets and Americans recognized Israel. The new nation, however, marked a permanent change to the culture and balance of power in the region.

AFRICA

A number of West African colonies established assertive independence movements before and during the 1950s, and the British government moved hesitantly to meet their demands. By the middle of the 1950s, Britain agreed to a variety of terms for independence in these territories, leaving them with written constitutions and a British legal system but little else in terms of modern infrastructure or economic support. Defenders of British colonialism claimed that these formal institutions would give advantages to the independent states, but without other resources, even the most promising foundered. Ghana, known formerly as the Gold Coast and the first of these colonies to gain independence, was seen in the early 1960s as a model for free African nations. Its politics soon degenerated, however, and its president, Kwame Nkrumah, became the first of several African leaders driven from office for corruption and autocratic behavior.

Belgium and France also withdrew from their holdings. By 1965 virtually all of the former African colonies had become independent, and virtually none of them possessed the means to redress losses from colonialism in order to make that independence work. As Belgian authorities raced out of the Congo in 1960, they left crumbling railways and fewer than two dozen indigenous people with college educations.

The process of decolonization was relatively peaceful—except where large populations of European settlers complicated European withdrawal. In the north, settler resistance made the French exit from Algeria wrenching and complex (as will be discussed later). In the east, in Kenya, the majority Kikuyu population revolted against British rule and against a small group of settlers. The uprising, which came to be known as the Mau Mau rebellion, soon turned bloody. British troops fired freely at targets in rebel-occupied areas, sometimes killing civilians. Internment camps set up by colonial security forces became sites of atrocities that drew public investigations and condemnation by even the most conservative British politicians and army officers. In 1963, a decade after the rebellion began, the British conceded Kenyan independence.

In the late 1950s, the British prime minister Harold Macmillan endorsed independence for a number of Britain's African colonies as a response to powerful winds of change. In southern Africa, the exceptionally large and wealthy population of European settlers set their sails against those winds, a resistance that continued for decades. These settlers, a mixture of English migrants and the Franco-Dutch Afrikaners who traced their arrival to the seventeenth and eighteenth centuries, controlled huge tracts of fertile farmland along with some of the most lucrative gold and diamond mines on earth. This was especially true in South Africa. There, during the late 1940s, Britain's Labour government set aside its deep dislike of Afrikaner racism in a fateful political bargain. In return for guarantees that South African gold would be used carefully to support Britain's global financial power, Britain tolerated the introduction of the apartheid system in South Africa. Even by other standards of segregation, apartheid was especially harsh. Under its terms, Africans, Indians, and "colored persons" of mixed descent lost all political rights. All the institutions of social life, including marriage and schools, were segregated. What was more, the government tried to block the dramatic social consequences of the expansion of mining and industrialization in general, especially African migration to cities and a new wave of labor militancy in the mines. Apartheid required Africans to live in designated "homelands," forbade them to travel without specific permits, and created elaborate government bureaus to manage the labor essential to the economy. The government also banned any political protest. These measures made Western powers uncomfortable with the segregationist regime, but white South Africans held on to American support by presenting themselves as a bulwark against communism.

To the north, in the territories of Rhodesia, the British government encouraged a large federation, controlled by white settlers but with the opportunity for majority rule in the future. By the early 1960s, however, the federation was

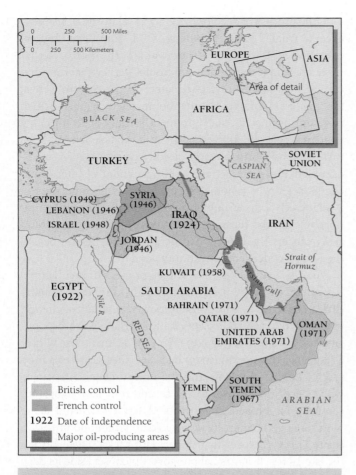

0 ————— 250 ————— 500 Miles
0 ————— 250 ————— 500 Kilometers

EUROPE   ASIA
        Area of detail
AFRICA

BLACK SEA

TURKEY

SOVIET UNION

CASPIAN SEA

CYPRUS (1949)
LEBANON (1946)
SYRIA (1946)
ISRAEL (1948)
IRAQ (1924)
IRAN
JORDAN (1946)

Strait of Hormuz

KUWAIT (1958)

EGYPT (1922)

Nile R.

SAUDI ARABIA
BAHRAIN (1971)
QATAR (1971)
UNITED ARAB EMIRATES (1971)
OMAN (1971)

RED SEA

Persian Gulf

British control
French control
1922 Date of independence
Major oil-producing areas

YEMEN
SOUTH YEMEN (1967)

ARABIAN SEA

DECOLONIZATION IN THE MIDDLE EAST. ▪ *What were the colonial possessions of the British and French in the Middle East?* ▪ *What were the three stages of decolonization in the Middle East?* ▪ *Why did the British hold on to the small states bordering the Persian Gulf and Arabian Sea until 1971?*

on the verge of collapse; the majority-rule state of Malawi was allowed to exit the federation in 1964, and Rhodesia split on northern and southern lines. In the north, the premier relented and accepted majority government under the black populist Kenneth Kaunda. In the south, angry Afrikaners backed by 200,000 right-wing English migrants who had arrived since 1945 refused to accept majority rule. When the British government attempted to force their hand, the settlers unilaterally declared independence in 1965 and began a bloody civil war against southern Rhodesia's black population that lasted half a generation.

CRISIS IN SUEZ AND THE END OF AN ERA

For postwar Britain, empire was not only politically complicated but too costly. Britain began to withdraw from naval and air bases around the world because they had become too expensive to maintain. Still, the Labour government did try

to maintain British power and prestige in the postwar world. In Malaya, British forces repressed a revolt by ethnic Chinese communists and then helped support the independent states of Singapore and Malaysia, maintaining British companies' and banks' ties with Malaysia's lucrative rubber and oil reserves. Labour also launched carefully targeted efforts at "colonial development" to tap local natural resources that Britain hoped to sell on world markets. "Development," however, was underfunded and largely disregarded in favor of fulfilling Cold War commitments elsewhere. In the Middle East, the British government protected several oil-rich states with its military and helped overthrow a nationalist government in Iran to ensure that the oil states invested their money in British financial markets.

In Egypt, however, the British refused to yield a traditional point of imperial pride. In 1951 nationalists compelled the British to agree to withdraw their troops from Egyptian territory within three years. In 1952 a group of nationalist army officers deposed Egypt's King Farouk, who had close ties to Britain, and proclaimed a republic. Shortly after the final British withdrawal, an Egyptian colonel, Gamal Abdel Nasser (1918–1970), became president of the country (1956–70). His first major public act as president was to nationalize the Suez Canal Company. So doing would help finance the construction of the Aswan Dam on the Nile, and both the dam and nationalizing the canal represented economic independence and Egyptian national pride. Nasser also helped develop the anticolonial ideology of pan-Arabism, proposing that Arab nationalists throughout the Islamic world should create an alliance of modern nations, no longer beholden to the West. Finally, Nasser was also willing to accept aid and support from the Soviets to achieve that goal, which made the canal a Cold War issue.

Three nations found Nasser and his pan-Arab ideals threatening. Israel, surrounded on all sides by unfriendly neighbors, was looking for an opportunity to seize the strategic Sinai Peninsula and create a buffer between itself and Egypt. France, already fighting a war against Algerian nationalists, hoped to destroy what it considered the Egyptian source of Arab nationalism. Britain depended on the canal as a route to its strategic bases and was stung by this blow to imperial dignity. Though the British were reluctant to intervene, they were urged on by their prime minister, Sir Anthony Eden, who had developed a deep personal hatred of Nasser. In the autumn of 1956, the three nations colluded in an attack on Egypt. Israel occupied the Sinai while British and French jets destroyed Egypt's air force on the ground. The former colonial powers landed troops at the mouth of the canal but lacked the resources to push on in strength toward Cairo. As a result, the war left Nasser in power and made him a hero to the Egyptian public for

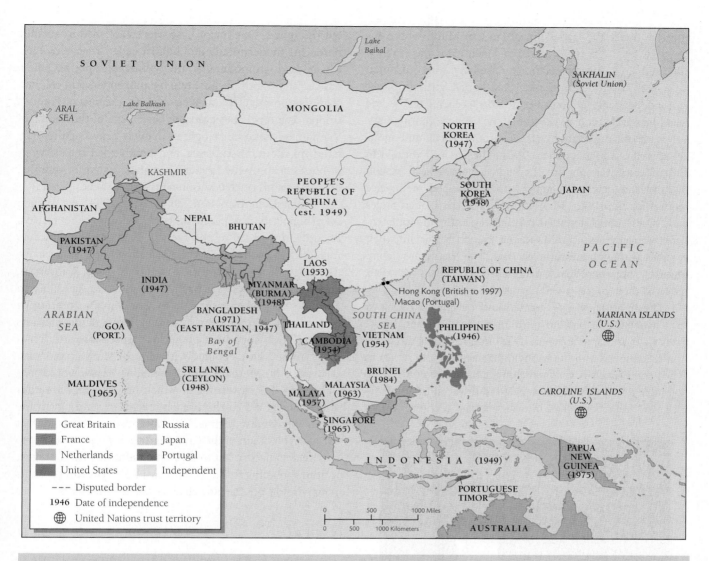

DECOLONIZATION IN ASIA. ▪ *Among colonial powers, who were the biggest losers post–World War II?* ▪ *What was the single most important geopolitical change in Asia during this period?* ▪ *What role did the Soviet Union and the United States play in Asia during this period?*

holding the imperialists at bay. The attack was condemned around the world. The United States angrily called its allies' bluff, inflicting severe financial penalties on Britain and France. Both countries were forced to withdraw their expeditions. For policy makers in Great Britain and France, the failure at Suez marked the end of an era.

French Decolonization

In two particular cases, France's experience of decolonization was bloodier, more difficult, and more damaging to French prestige and domestic politics than any in Britain's experience, with the possible exception of Northern Ireland. The first was Indochina, where French efforts to

restore imperial authority after losing it in the Second World War only resulted in military defeat and further humiliation. The second case, Algeria, became not only a violent colonial war but also a struggle with serious political ramifications at home.

THE FIRST VIETNAM WAR, 1946–1954

Indochina was one of France's last major imperial acquisitions in the nineteenth century. Here, as elsewhere, the two world wars had helped galvanize first nationalist and then, also, communist independence movements. In Indonesia, nationalist forces rebelled against Dutch efforts to restore colonialism, and the country became independent in 1949. In Indochina, the communist resistance became particularly effective under the leadership of Ho Chi Minh, who campaigned for Vietnamese independence. Ho was French educated and, his expectations raised by the Wilsonian principles of self-determination, had hoped Vietnam might win independence at Versailles in 1919 (see Chapter 24). He read Marx and Lenin and absorbed the Chinese communists' lessons about organizing peasants around social and agrarian as well as national issues. During the Second World War, Ho's movement fought first the Vichy government of the colony and later Japanese occupiers; it also provided intelligence reports for the Allies. In 1945, however, the United States and Britain repudiated their relationship with Ho's independence movement and allowed the French to reclaim their colonies throughout Southeast Asia. The Vietnamese communists, who were fierce nationalists as well as Marxists, renewed their guerrilla war against the French.

The fighting was protracted and bloody; France saw in it a chance to redeem its national pride. After one of France's most capable generals, Jean de Lattre de Tassigny, finally achieved a military advantage against the rebels in 1951, the French government might have decolonized on favorable terms. Instead, it decided to press on for total victory, sending troops deep into Vietnamese territory to root out the rebels. One major base was established in a valley bordering modern Laos, at a hamlet called Dien Bien Phu. Ringed by high mountains, this vulnerable spot became a base for thousands of elite French paratroopers and colonial soldiers from Algeria and West Africa—the best of France's troops. The rebels besieged the base. Tens of thousands of Vietnamese nationalist fighters hauled heavy artillery by hand up the mountainsides and bombarded the network of forts set up by the French. The siege lasted for months, becoming a protracted national crisis in France.

When Dien Bien Phu fell in May 1954, the French government began peace talks in Geneva. The Geneva Accords, drawn up by the French, Vietnamese politicians including the communists, the British, and the Americans, divided Indochina into three countries: Laos, Cambodia, and Vietnam, which was partitioned into two states. North Vietnam was taken over by Ho Chi Minh's Communist party; South Vietnam by a succession of Vietnamese leaders with Western support. Corruption, repression, and instability in the south, coupled with Ho Chi Minh's nationalist desire to unite Vietnam, guaranteed that the war would continue. The U.S. government, which had provided military and financial aid to the French, began to send aid to the South Vietnamese regime. The Americans saw the conflict through the prism of the Cold War: their project was not to restore colonialism but to contain communism and prevent it from spreading through Southeast Asia. The limits of this policy would not become clear until the mid-1960s.

ALGERIA

The French faced a complex colonial problem closer to home—in Algeria, the North African colony that they had first conquered in the 1830s. By the 1950s, there were close to a million European settlers in Algeria, and their representatives dominated both the political establishment and the economy of the colony. The rest of the diverse population consisted of Berbers and Arabs who had few political rights and scarce opportunities for education or economic advancement.

At the end of the Second World War, Algerian nationalists called for the Allies to recognize Algerian independence. Public demonstrations turned violent, and when settlers were attacked in the town of Sétif in May 1945, the French responded with a harsh repression that killed thousands of Algerians. These events convinced a younger generation of nationalists that independence could only be achieved by force. On November 1, 1954, the Algerian National Liberation Front (FLN) announced their rebellion with a series of attacks on military and police targets.

"DIEN-BIEN-PHU: . . . THEY SACRIFICED THEMSELVES FOR LIBERTY." The sentiments expressed in this poster, which was intended to commemorate the French soldiers who died at Dien Bien Phu in May 1954, helped to deepen French commitments to colonial control in Algeria.

Analyzing Primary Sources

Anticolonialism and Violence

Born in the French Caribbean colony of Martinique, Frantz Fanon (1925–1961) studied psychiatry in France before moving on to work in Algeria in the early 1950s. Fanon became a member of the Algerian revolutionary National Liberation Front (FLN) and an ardent advocate of decolonization. Black Skin, White Masks, *published in 1952 with a preface by Jean-Paul Sartre, was a study of the psychological effects of colonialism and racism on black culture and individuals.* The Wretched of the Earth *(1961) was a revolutionary manifesto, one of the most influential of the period. Fanon attacked nationalist leaders for their ambition and corruption. He believed that revolutionary change could come only from poor peasants, those who "have found no bone to gnaw in the colonial system." Diagnosed with leukemia, Fanon sought treatment in the Soviet Union and then in Washington, D.C., where he died.*

n decolonization, there is therefore the need of a complete calling in question of the colonial situation. If we wish to describe it precisely, we might find it in the well-known words: "The last shall be first and the first last." Decolonization is the putting into practice of this sentence. . . .

The naked truth of decolonization evokes for us the searing bullets and bloodstained knives which emanate from it. For if the last shall be first, this will only come to pass after a murderous and decisive struggle between the two protagonists. That affirmed intention to place the last at the head of things, and to make them climb at a pace (too quickly, some say) the well-known steps which characterize an organized society, can only triumph if we use all means to turn the scale, including, of course, that of violence.

You do not turn any society, however primitive it may be, upside down with such a program if you have not decided from the very beginning, that is to say from the actual formation of that program, to overcome all the obstacles that you will come across in so doing. The native who decides to put the program into practice, and to become its moving force, is ready for violence at all times. From birth it is clear to him that this narrow world, strewn with prohibitions, can only be called in question by absolute violence.

Source: Frantz Fanon, *The Wretched of the Earth*, trans. Constance Farrington (New York: 1963), pp. 35–37.

Questions for Analysis

1. Why did Fanon believe that violence lay at the heart of both the colonial relationship and anticolonial movements?

2. What arguments would he offer to counter Gandhi's philosophy of nonviolent resistance?

The war in Algeria was fought on several fronts. The struggle between the French and the Algerian nationalists was fought first as a guerrilla war between the French army and the FLN in the countryside. In 1956, the FLN launched an urban campaign of terror bombings against the settler population, and the French army responded with the systematic use of torture against thousands of suspected FLN members. At the same time, however, the war also had elements of civil conflict on both sides. In both France and Algeria, rival groups of Algerian nationalists fought with one another, and as the strains of the war dragged on, increasingly bitter splits opened up within the French side as well, as radical elements in the settler population turned violently against French politicians who were seen to be too moderate in their defense of French Algeria.

The Algerian crisis brought Charles de Gaulle back to power in France in 1958, and although the settlers in Algeria saw his return favorably, he disappointed them by engaging in negotiations that led to a referendum on independence in July 1962. The FLN entered the capital in triumph, and nearly a million settlers and thousands of Algerians who had fought on the French side fled into exile in France.

The war cut deep divides through French society and left much of Algeria scarred and in ruins. Withdrawing from Algeria meant recasting French views of what it meant to be a modern power. In France and other imperial powers, the conclusions seemed clear. Traditional forms of colonial rule could not withstand the demands of postwar politics and culture; the leading European nations, once distinguished by their empires, would have to look for new forms of influence.

Past and Present

The Divisions of the Cold War

The Cold War conflict between the United States and the Soviet Union (captured in the image of the Berlin Wall, left) was largely seen as a split between the East and the West, though global competition between the two powers also had profound effects on other regions of the world. The movement of the "Non-Aligned Nations" (represented here by Prime Minister Jawaharlal Nehru of India, President Kwame Nkrumah of Ghana, President Gamal Abdel Nasser of Egypt, President Sukarno of Indonesia, and President Tito of Yugoslavia) was an attempt to provide an alternative to this division.

Watch related author videos on the Student Site
wwnorton.com/college/history/western-civilizationsBrief4

POSTWAR CULTURE AND THOUGHT

The devastation of the Second World War, followed by the looming confrontation between superpowers armed with nuclear weapons, set the stage for a remarkable burst of cultural production in the postwar decades. Writers and artists did not hesitate to tackle the big issues: freedom, civilization, and the human condition. The process of decolonization, meanwhile, ensured that these issues could not be seen as the property of Europeans alone.

Black Voices

A generation of intellectuals from European colonies achieved new prominence in the late 1940s. Writers Aimé Césaire (1913–2008) of Martinique and Léopold Senghor from Senegal were elected to the French National Assembly and were prominent voices associated with the *Négritude* movement, which asserted that people of African descent could and should retain a sense of black identity (a rough translation of *Négritude*), even as they sought to participate in the civic life of European nations. Both asserted that colonialism damaged the colonizers as much as the colonized peoples of Africa and Asia.

Frantz Fanon, a student of Césaire's who was also from Martinique, went further, arguing that the promotion of *Négritude* was not an effective response to racism. People of color, he argued, needed a theory of radical social change. Fanon's manifesto, *The Wretched of the Earth* (1961) bluntly rejected Gandhi's prescriptions for change, arguing that colonialism was inherently violent, and had to be overcome with force. Fanon worked in Algeria as a psychiatrist, and eventually joined the National Liberation Front.

The provocative arguments of these writers complicated efforts by European intellectuals to promote humanism and democratic values after the atrocities of the Second World War, since the European powers who were victorious over the Nazis proved to be capable of brutality themselves in defending their colonial empires. Writers such as Fanon pointed to the ironies of Europe's civilizing mission and forced Europeans to reevaluate the universal claims of their culture.

Existentialism, Amnesia, and the Aftermath of War

Existentialism was a postwar intellectual movement in Europe that posed challenging questions about the possibility of individual choice and moral commitment—questions that seemed especially urgent in this period of intense ideological competition. The existentialist writers, most prominently Jean-Paul Sartre (SAHR-truh, 1905–1980) and Albert Camus (KAM-oo, 1913–1960) shared a common pessimism about European "civilization." Most radically, they declared that human lives had no meaning that could be learned or understood through the study of traditional morality, religion, or science. Instead,

they argued that "existence precedes essence," by which they meant that there was no predetermined meaning for human lives. Humans exist—and they create their own meanings by making choices and accepting responsibility for what follows. To deny this freedom to choose was to live in "bad faith." It is no accident that this vision of human ethics emerged from writers who had lived through the moral ambiguities of the German occupation of France, when even the quiet pursuit of a "normal" life could be seen as accepting or abetting a great evil.

Existentialist insights opened other doors. Black writers of African descent, such as Frantz Fanon, used existentialist claims about the absence of predetermined "essences" to insist that skin color had no significance, and that identity could only emerge from a lived experience. Simone de Beauvoir (duh bohv-WAHR, 1908–1986) made a similar claim about gender, arguing that "One is not born a woman, one becomes one." In *The Second Sex* (1949), de Beauvoir questioned the tendency of women to accept a secondary status in society, insisting that they should become the authors of their own lives rather than accept unquestioningly the roles of wife or mother that society had prepared for them.

The theme of individual helplessness in the face of state power and empty moral teachings pervaded the literature of the period. George Orwell's *Animal Farm* (1946) explored the fearsome capacities of the Stalinist state in a barnyard allegory, while his novel *1984* (1949) imagined a future in which the state—"Big Brother"—was omnipresent and all-powerful. Hannah Arendt (1906–1975) was the first to propose that both Nazism and Stalinism should be understood as forms of a new twentieth-century form of government: totalitarianism (*The Origins of Totalitarianism*, 1951). Unlike earlier forms of tyranny, totalitarianism worked by mobilizing mass support and using terror to crush resistance. In such a world, a collective response was impossible—social and political institutions were broken down, the public realm disappeared, and individuals were reduced to powerlessness, becoming atomized beings with no meaningful connection to one another.

Discussions of the war itself were limited. Few memoirs received wide attention in the immediate aftermath, though an exception was Anne Frank's *Diary of a Young Girl* (1947), a posthumously published diary by a child who had died at Auschwitz. The main current in postwar culture ran more toward forgetting than exploring the painful memories of the war years. Postwar governments did not purge all those implicated in war crimes. In France, the courts sentenced 2,640 to death and executed 791; in Austria, 13,000 were convicted of war crimes and 30 executed. Many who called for justice grew demoralized and cynical, as it was also clear that Cold War politics favored forgetting rather than punishing

THE COLD WAR IN EVERYDAY LIFE. A Soviet matchbook label, 1960, depicts a Soviet fist destroying a U.S. plane. Soviet nationalism had been a potent force since the Second World War. ▪ *Could the Soviet leadership sustain this nationalist sentiment without an external threat?*

the guilty. The eagerness of the United States, Britain, and France to embrace West Germany as an ally, the preoccupation with economic rebuilding, and anticommunism all worked to discourage the difficult task of investigating who in Germany had actively supported the Nazi regime and who had been responsible for their murderous policies.

THE CUBAN MISSILE CRISIS

One of the last serious and most dramatic confrontations of the Cold War came in 1962, in Cuba. A revolution in 1958 had brought the charismatic communist Fidel Castro to power. Immediately after, the United States began to work with exiled Cubans, supporting among other ventures a bungled attempt to invade via the Bay of Pigs in 1961. Castro not only aligned himself with the Soviets but invited them to base nuclear missiles on Cuban soil, just a few minutes' flying time from Florida. When American spy planes identified the missiles and related military equipment in 1962, Kennedy confronted Khrushchev. After deliberating about the repercussions of

an air strike, Kennedy ordered a naval blockade of Cuba. On October 22, he appeared on television, visibly tired and without makeup, announced the grave situation to the public, and challenged Khrushchev to withdraw the weapons and "move the world back from the abyss of destruction." Terrified of the looming threat of nuclear war, Americans fled urban areas, prepared for a cramped and uncomfortable existence in fallout shelters, and bought firearms. After three nerve-wracking weeks, the Soviets agreed to withdraw and to remove the bombers and missiles already on Cuban soil. But citizens of both countries spent many anxious hours in their bomb shelters, and onlookers the world over wrestled with their rising fears that a nuclear Armageddon was upon them.

CONCLUSION

The Cold War reached deep into postwar culture and dominated postwar politics. It decisively shaped the development of both the Soviet and American states. Fearful of losing control of territory they had conquered at such cost in the

After You Read This Chapter

 Go to **INQUIZITIVE** to see what you've learned—and learn what you've missed—with personalized feedback along the way.

REVIEWING THE OBJECTIVES

- The Cold War between the United States and the Soviet Union began as the Second World War ended. How did these two nations seek to influence the postwar political order in Europe?

- Postwar economic growth was accompanied by greater economic integration among Western European nations. What were the goals of those who sought to create the unified European market, and which nations played key roles in its development?

- Between the late 1940s and the mid-1960s, almost all the European colonies in Asia and Africa demanded and received their independence, either peacefully or through armed conflict. What combination of events made Europeans less able to defend their colonial empires against the claims of nationalists who sought independence from Europe?

- Decolonization and the Cold War reinforced a sense that Europe's place in the world needed to be rethought. How did intellectuals, writers, and artists react to the loss of European influence in the world?

Second World War, the Soviets intervened repeatedly in the politics of their Eastern European allies in the 1940s and 1950s, ensuring the creation of hard-line governments in East Germany, Czechoslovakia, Poland, Hungary, and elsewhere in the Eastern bloc. In the United States, anti-communism became a powerful political force, shaping foreign policy and preparations for military confrontation with the Soviet Union to such an extent that President Eisenhower warned in his farewell address that a "military-industrial complex" had taken shape in the U.S. and that its "total influence— economic, political, even spiritual—is felt in every city, every statehouse, every office of the federal government."

In Western Europe, rebuilding the economy and creating a new political order in the aftermath of the Second World War meant accepting the new power and influence of the United States, but Europeans also searched for ways to create and express a European identity that would retain some independence and freedom of action. Led by the efforts of France and Germany, Western Europeans eventually found elements of this freedom in increasing integration and economic cooperation. In Eastern Europe, on the other hand, the political leadership found fewer opportunities for independent action, and the threat of military intervention by the Soviet Union made any innovations or experimentation difficult or impossible.

The sense that Europeans were no longer in a position to act independently or to exert their influence in other parts of the world was compounded by the loss of colonies abroad. Former European colonies in Africa and Asia became independent nations, and this loss of influence may have further encouraged the former European imperial powers in their attempts to create a more integrated Europe. The consensus in the West about the new role that the state should take in economic planning, education, and social welfare helped lay the groundwork for a Europe that was dedicated to ensuring equal opportunities to its citizens. These commitments were driven by the search for stable forms of democratic government—the memories of the violent ideological conflicts of the 1920s and 1930s were still fresh, and the achievement of an integrated Western Europe (under U.S. sponsorship) on the hinge of Franco-German cooperation must be seen as one of the major victories of the postwar decades. The hard-won stability of this period was to be temporary, however, and beginning in the 1960s a new series of political conflicts and economic crises would test the limits of consensus in Cold War Europe.

PEOPLE, IDEAS, AND EVENTS IN CONTEXT

- When Allied leaders met to discuss the postwar order at **YALTA** in 1945, what were the major issues they discussed?
- What were the goals of the U.S. **MARSHALL PLAN**? How did **STALIN** react to its implementation?
- What was the **TRUMAN DOCTRINE** and how was it related to the creation of **NATO**?
- How did the Soviet Union's successful explosion of an **ATOMIC BOMB** in 1949 change the dynamic of the **COLD WAR**?
- How did the political climate in the Soviet Union and Eastern Europe change under **NIKITA KHRUSHCHEV** during the so-called **THAW** that followed Stalin's death?
- What nations were key to the plans for the **EUROPEAN COMMON MARKET**?
- Why was the **DECOLONIZATION** of settler colonies in Africa such as Algeria, Kenya, and Rhodesia more violent than in other colonies on the continent?
- What was **APARTHEID** and why was it adopted by the settler government in South Africa?

THINKING ABOUT CONNECTIONS

- Insofar as one can determine from today's perspective, what were the long-term consequences of the Cold War for people in both Western and Eastern Europe?
- What challenges did the process of decolonization pose to those who believed that European traditions of democratic rule and individual rights—ideas associated with the Enlightenment and the French Revolution—were universal?

STORY LINES

- The postwar economy in Western Europe saw record growth that lasted until the 1970s. Labor shortages led many nations to recruit workers from abroad, causing tensions when unemployment rates went up as the postwar boom came to an end.

- Radio, television, and film combined to create a new kind of global mass culture that contributed to a spirit of novelty and rebellion among young people. More-open discussion of sexual matters and an end to restrictions on contraception led some to speak of a "sexual revolution."

- Movements for national independence found an echo in the Civil Rights Movement in the United States and in student protests in Europe and the Americas in the 1960s. These protest movements peaked in 1968, provoking a conservative backlash in the 1970s and 1980s.

- Support for the Soviet Union waned in the 1980s as its economy stagnated and its political system failed to adapt. The Eastern bloc collapsed suddenly in 1989, ending the Cold War.

CHRONOLOGY

1957	Treaty of Rome forms European Common Market
1961	Berlin Wall built
1963	Betty Friedan, *The Feminine Mystique*
1964–1975	Vietnam War
mid-1960s	Birth control pill becomes available
1968	Czech revolt, Prague spring
1968	Student protests in Europe and the Americas
1970s	Détente between Soviet Union and Western powers
1973–1980s	Rising oil prices and worldwide recession
1980	Polish Solidarity workers movement
1989	Berlin Wall falls
1990	Reunification of Germany
1991–1995	Yugoslavian civil wars
1992	Soviet Union dissolved
1993	European Union

Before
You
Read
This
Chapter

Red Flags and Velvet Revolutions: The End of the Cold War, 1960s–1990s

In 1964, a photograph of a Portuguese laborer named Armando Rodriguez appeared on the cover of the German newsmagazine *Der Spiegel*. Rodriguez had been met at the border by an official delegation and celebrated as the one millionth "guest worker" to arrive in Germany. As a prize, he received the gift of a motorcycle. The moment reflected the confidence of the West German government that their postwar economic recovery would continue, and that material prosperity would bring a new stability to Europe. In fact, the early 1960s seemed golden and full of promise for many in Western Europe. Despite nearly constant international tension, everyday life seemed to be improving. Full employment drove increases in living standards, the mass availability of consumer items and modern appliances transformed daily life, and a life of relative prosperity and ample leisure now seemed accessible to many. Television, radio, and film promoted images of American middle-class life, and Europeans looked across the Atlantic and saw their own aspirations reflected back at them. Even amid the uncertainties of the Cold War, a new spirit of cooperation animated European governments, party divisions had given way to a broad consensus in favor of an expanded welfare state, and the future looked good.

By the 1990s, however, most of that confidence was gone, and the European landscape had been dramatically transformed. Western Europeans could no longer be so certain of their prosperity or of their leaders' ability to provide the sort of life they took for granted. Already in the late 1960s, the economic boom had come to an end, and movements of social protest, especially among young people, shattered the postwar consensus. The material comforts of a consumer society proved less satisfying than they had once seemed, and environmentalists, feminists, and other cultural critics criticized the assumptions of the older generation. These problems were compounded after 1975 by a continuing economic crisis that threatened the security that the postwar generation had labored so hard to achieve. European societies began to fragment in unexpected ways, well before the epochal transformations that accompanied the end of the Cold War.

The challenges of these decades proved even more fundamental in the Soviet sphere. Economic decay combined with political and social stagnation to produce another wave of revolt. The year 1989 marked the beginning of an extraordinarily rapid and surprising series of events: Communist rule collapsed in Eastern Europe. Hopes for peace were soon replaced by fears of conflict from unexpected quarters. Immigrants were no longer celebrated in Germany and elsewhere—instead they became targets of suspicion or even violence. In 1991, shortly after the reunification of Germany, a wave of attacks against immigrants and refugees in Eastern Germany by right-wing extremists took the lives of seventeen foreigners, including two Turkish women and a Turkish girl who died in an arson attack by neo-Nazi skinheads in Schleswig-Holstein. Similar attacks took place in France, Britain, Italy, and elsewhere. When postsocialist Yugoslavia collapsed into a brutal civil war in the early 1990s, Europeans faced once again the spectacle of mass political movements motivated by hatred and fear, leading to ethnic violence and mass murder in a European land.

The startlingly sudden dissolution of the Soviet bloc brought an end to the postwar era of superpower confrontation, and observers of European society were forced to confront the uncomfortable fact that the Cold War had provided its own form of stability. Seen from the early 1990s, the future looked much less certain. Could the emerging institutions of an integrated Europe absorb *all* the peoples of the former Soviet sphere? What would such a Europe look like, and who would determine its larger boundaries? What these changes meant for the future of democracy, the stability of the European economy, and definitions of European identity, remained an open question.

SOCIAL CHANGE AND CULTURAL DYNAMISM, 1945–1968

The economic "boom" of the 1950s, made especially striking by contrast with the bleak years immediately after the Second World War, had profound and far-reaching effects on social life. Both West Germany and France found it necessary to import workers to sustain their production booms. Most came from the south, particularly from the agrarian areas of southern Italy, where unemployment remained high. Workers from former colonies emigrated to Britain, often to take low-paid, menial jobs and encounter pervasive discrimination at work and in the community. Migrations of this sort, in addition to the vast movement of political and ethnic refugees that occurred during and immediately after the war, contributed to the breakdown of national barriers that was accelerated by the creation of the Common Market.

The most dramatic changes were encapsulated in the transformation of the land and agriculture. Agricultural productivity had barely changed over the first half of the century. After mid-century it soared. Common Market policy, state-sponsored programs of modernization, new agricultural machinery, and new kinds of fertilizer, seed, and animal feed helped produce the transformation. In Poland and the Eastern bloc, socialist regimes replaced small peasant holdings with large-scale agriculture. The effects reached across the economic and social landscape. Abundance meant lower food prices. Families spent a smaller proportion of their budgets on food, freeing up money for other forms of consumption and fueling economic growth. Peasants with large holdings or valuable specialized crops (dairy products or wine), who could withstand debt, adjusted. Others lost ground. Many farmers resorted to protest movements in an attempt to protect their standard of living.

Change also came in the workplace. Many commentators noted the striking growth in the number of middle-class, white-collar employees—the result, in part, of the dramatic bureaucratic expansion of the state. By 1964, the total number of men and women employed in government service in most European states exceeded 40 percent of the labor force, significantly higher than the number in the 1920s and 1930s. In business and industry, the number of middle-management employees grew as well. And industrial labor meant something far different from what it had meant in the nineteenth century. Skills were more specialized, based on technological expertise rather than custom and routine. *Skill* came to mean the ability to monitor automatic controls; to interpret abstract signals; and to make precise, mathematically calculated adjustments. More women entered the workforce, meeting less resistance than they had in the past, and their jobs were less starkly differentiated from men's.

Nineteenth-century society had been marked by clearly defined class cultures. In 1900, no one would have mistaken a peasant for a worker, and middle-class people had their own schools, recreations, and stores. But economic changes after 1950 chipped away at those distinctive cultures. Trade unions remained powerful institutions and workers still identified themselves as such, but *class* had a less rigidly defined meaning.

The expansion of education helped shift social hierarchies. All Western nations passed laws providing for the extension of compulsory secondary education. New legislation combined with rising birthrates to boost school populations dramatically. Education did not automatically produce social mobility, but when combined with economic prosperity, new structures of labor, and the consumerist boom, it began to lay the foundation for what would be called "postindustrial" society.

How did patterns differ in the Eastern bloc? Soviet workers were not noted for their specialized skills—in fact, a major factor in the slowdown of the Soviet economy was its failure to innovate. Factory workers in the "workers' state" commonly enjoyed higher wages than people in middle-class positions (with the exception of managers), but they had far less status. Their relatively high wages owed little to independent trade unions, which had been effectively abolished under Stalin; they were the product of persistent labor shortages and the accompanying fear of labor unrest. As far as the middle classes were concerned, two wars and state

socialism devastated traditional, insular bourgeois culture throughout Eastern Europe, though the regimes also created new ways of gaining privilege and status. Commentators spoke of a new class of bureaucrats and party members. Soviet education also aimed to unify a nation that remained culturally and ethnically heterogeneous. Afraid that the pull of ethnic nationality might tear at the none-too-solid fabric of the Soviet "union" increased the government's desire to impose one unifying culture by means of education, though not always with success.

Mass Consumption

Rising employment, higher earnings, and lower agricultural prices combined to give households and individuals more purchasing power. Household appliances and cars were the most striking emblems of what was virtually a new world of everyday objects. In 1956, 8 percent of British households had refrigerators. By 1979 that figure had skyrocketed to 69 percent. Vacuum cleaners, washing machines, and telephones all became common features of everyday life. They did not simply save labor or create free time, for household appliances came packaged with more demanding standards of housekeeping and new investments in domesticity—"more work for mother," in the words of one historian.

In 1948, 5 million Western Europeans had cars; in 1965, 40 million did. Cars captured imaginations throughout the world; in magazines, advertisements, and countless films, the car was central to new images of romance, movement, freedom, and vacation. Of course, automobiles alone did not allow workers to take inexpensive holidays; reducing the workweek from forty-eight hours to about forty-two was more important, as was the institution of annual vacations—in most countries workers received over thirty days of paid vacation per year.

These changes marked a new culture of mass consumption. They were boosted by new industries devoted to marketing, advertising, and credit payment. They also entailed shifts in values. In the nineteenth century, a responsible middle-class family did not go into debt; discipline and thrift were hallmarks of respectability. By the second half of the twentieth century, banks and retailers, in the name of mass consumption and economic growth, were persuading middle- and working-class people alike not to be ashamed of debt. *Abundance*, *credit*, *consumer spending*, and *standards of living*—all these terms became part of the vocabulary of everyday economic life. This new vocabulary gradually came to reshape how citizens thought about their needs, desires, and entitlements. Standards of living, for instance,

MORNING CALISTHENICS AT RUSSIAN FACTORY, 1961. The growing number of industrial workers and of women in the workforce in the latter half of the twentieth century was reflected in this Soviet factory. The workers' state still bestowed little status on its workers, however—a factor that contributed to weakening the Russian economy.

A CAR FOR THE PEOPLE. Volkswagen Beetle in Germany.

created a yardstick for measuring—and protesting—glaring social inequalities.

In Eastern Europe and the Soviet Union, consumption was organized differently. Governments rather than markets determined how consumer goods would be distributed. Economic policy channeled resources into heavy indus-try at the expense of consumer durables. This resulted in general scarcity, erratic shortages of even basic necessities, and often poor-quality goods. Women in particular often waited for hours in store lines after finishing a full day of wage work. Though numbers of household appliances increased dramati-cally in the Soviet Union and in Eastern Europe, the inefficiencies of the Soviet Union's consumer economy meant that women's double burden of work and house-work remained especially heavy. Citizens' growing unhappiness with scarcities and seemingly irrational policies posed serious problems. As one historian puts it, the failure of policies on consumption was "one of the major dead ends of communism," and it contributed to the downfall of communist regimes.

Mass Culture

New patterns of consumption spurred wide-ranging changes in mass culture. The origins of "mass" culture lay in the 1890s, in the expansion of the popular press, music halls, organized sports, and "nickelodeons," all of which started the long process of displacing traditional, class-based forms of entertainment: village dances, boulevard theater, middle-class concerts, and so on. Mass culture quickened in the 1920s, its importance heightened by mass politics (see Chapter 25). The social transformations of the 1950s, which we have traced above, meant that families had both more spending money and more leisure time. The combi-nation created a golden opportunity for the growing culture industry. The postwar desire to break with the past created further impetus for change. The result can fairly be called a cultural revolution: a transformation of culture, of its role in the lives of ordinary men and women, and of the power wielded by the media.

MUSIC AND YOUTH CULTURE

Much of the new mass culture of the 1960s depended on the spending habits and desires of the new generation. That new generation stayed in school longer, prolonging their adoles-cent years. Young people had more distance from their par-ents and the workforce and more time to be with each other. In the countryside especially, schooling began to break down the barriers that had separated the activities of boys and girls, creating one factor in the "sexual revolution" (as will be discussed later). From the late 1950s on, music became *the* cultural expression of this new generation. The transistor radio came out at the time of the Berlin airlift; by the mid-1950s these portable radios began to sell in the United States and Europe. Radio sets gave birth to new radio programs

MUSIC MEETS TELEVISION. The Beatles' Paul McCartney instructs popular variety show host Ed Sullivan on the electric bass, 1964.

and, later, to new magazines reporting on popular singers and movie stars. All of these helped create new communities of interest. As one historian puts it, these radio programs were the "capillaries of youth culture." Social changes also affected the content of music: its themes and lyrics aimed to reach the young. Technological changes made records more than twice as long-playing as the old 78s and less expensive. The price of record players fell, multiplying the number of potential buyers. Combined, these developments changed how music was produced, distributed, and consumed. It was no longer confined to the concert hall or café but instead reverberated through people's homes or cars and teenagers' rooms—providing a soundtrack for everyday life.

Postwar youth culture owed much to the hybrid musical style known as rock and roll. During the 1930s and 1940s, the synthesis of music produced by whites and African Americans in the American South found its way into northern cities. After the Second World War, black rhythm and blues musicians and white Southern rockabilly performers found much wider audiences through the use of new technology—electric guitars, better equipment for studio recording, and wide-band radio stations in large cities. The blend of styles and sounds and the cultural daring of white teenagers who listened to what recording studios at the time called "race music" came together to create rock and roll. The music was exciting, sometimes aggressive, and full of energy.

In Europe, rock and roll found its way into working-class neighborhoods, particularly in Britain and Ireland. There, local youths took American sounds, echoed the inflections of poverty and defiance, and added touches of music-hall showmanship to produce many successful artists and bands, who went on to dominate the U.S. charts in what became known as the "British invasion." As the music's popularity spread, music culture came loose from its national moorings. The Beatles managed to get their own music on the hit lists in France, Germany, and the United States. By the time a half a million young people gathered near Woodstock, New York, for "Three Days of Peace and Music" in 1969, youth music culture was international. Rock became the sound of worldwide youth culture, providing a bridge across the Cold War divide. Despite Eastern bloc limits on importing "capitalist" music, pirated songs circulated—sometimes even on X-ray plates salvaged from hospitals. Recording studios latched onto the earning potential of the music and became corporations as powerful as car manufacturers or steel companies.

Art and Painting

The cultural revolution we have been tracing changed high as well as popular art. Record companies' influence reached well beyond rock. New recording techniques made it possible to reissue favorites in classical music, and companies marketed them more aggressively. Record companies buoyed the careers of internationally acclaimed stars, such as the soprano Maria Callas and (much later) the tenor Luciano Pavarotti, staging concerts, using their influence on orchestras, and offering new recordings of their art.

Painting and other visual arts, too, were changed by the rise of mass and consumer culture. The art market boomed. The power of the dollar was one factor in the rise of New York as a center of modern art, one of the most striking developments of the period. Immigration was another: a slow stream of immigrants from Europe nourished American art as well as social and political thought (see Chapter 27), and New York proved hospitable to European artists. The creative work of the school of abstract expressionism sealed New York's postwar reputation. The abstract expressionists—William de Kooning (from the Netherlands), Mark Rothko (from Russia), Franz Kline, Jackson Pollock, Helen Frankenthaler, and Robert Motherwell—followed trends established by the cubists and surrealists, experimenting with color, texture, and

MASS CULTURE IN A MEDIA AGE. When John Lennon declared the Beatles were "more popular than Jesus," he raised a storm of protest. Here an American teenager tosses the album *Meet the Beatles* into a bonfire. ■ *What was different about this kind of celebrity when compared with earlier generations of popular entertainers?*

ACTION PAINTING. Photographer Martha Holmes reveals the dynamic technique of abstract expressionist Jackson Pollock as he paints, 1950.

technique to find new forms of expression. Many of them emphasized the physical aspects of paint and the act of painting. Pollock is a good example: he poured and even threw paint on the canvas, creating powerful images of personal and physical expressiveness that some dubbed "action painting." Critics called the drip paintings "unpredictable, undisciplined, and explosive" and saw in them the youthful exuberance of postwar American culture.

But abstract expressionism also produced its opposite, sometimes called pop art. Pop artists distanced themselves from the moody and elusive meditations of abstract expressionism. They refused to distinguish between avant garde and popular art, or between the artistic and the commercial. They lavished attention on commonplace, instantly recognizable, often commercial images; they borrowed techniques from graphic design; they were interested in the immediacy of everyday art and ordinary people's visual experience. Jasper Johns's paintings of the American flag formed part of this trend. So did the works of Andy Warhol and Roy Lichtenstein, who took objects such as soup cans and images of comic-strip heroes as their subjects. Treating popular culture with this tongue-in-cheek seriousness became one of the central themes of 1960s art.

Film

Mass culture made its most powerful impact in the visual world, especially through film. Film flourished after the

Second World War, developing along several different lines. The Italian neorealists of the late 1940s and 1950s, antifascists and socialists, set out to capture authenticity, or "life as it was lived," by which they usually meant working-class existence. They dealt with the same themes that marked the literature of the period: loneliness, war, and corruption. They shot on location, using natural light and little-known actors, deliberately steering away from the artifice and high production values they associated with the tainted cinema of fascist and wartime Europe. Not strictly realists, they played with nonlinear plots as well as unpredictable characters and motivations. Roberto Rossellini's *Rome: Open City* (1945) was a loving portrait of Rome under Nazi occupation. Vittorio de Sica's *Bicycle Thief* (1948) tells a story of a man struggling against unemployment and poverty, who desperately needs his bicycle to keep his job as a poster hanger. Federico Fellini came out of the neorealist school and began his career writing for Rossellini. Fellini's breakout film *La Dolce Vita* (1959, starring Marcello Mastroianni) took Italian film to screens throughout Europe and the United States, and it also marked Fellini's transition to his signature surrealist and carnivalesque style, developed further in *8½* (1963).

The French directors of the new wave continued to develop this unsentimental, naturalistic, and enigmatic social vision. New wave directors worked closely with each other, casting each other (and their wives and lovers) in their films, encouraging improvisation, and experimenting with disjointed narrative. François Truffaut's (1932–1984) *The 400 Blows* (1959) and *The Wild Child* (1969), and Jean-Luc Godard's (b. 1930) *Breathless* (1959) and *Contempt* (1963, with Brigitte Bardot), are leading examples. *Closely Watched Trains* (1966) was the Czech director Jiří Menzel's (b. 1938) contribution to the new wave. The new wave raised the status of the director, insisting that the film's camera work and vision (rather than the acting) constituted the real art—part, again, of the new value accorded to the visual. France made other contributions to international film by sponsoring the Cannes Film Festival. The first Cannes Festival was held before the Second World War, but the city opened its gates again in 1946 under the banner of artistic internationalism. Placing itself at the center of an international film industry became part of France's ongoing recovery from the war, and Cannes became one of the world's largest marketplaces for film.

HOLLYWOOD AND THE AMERICANIZATION OF CULTURE

The American film industry, however, had considerable advantages, and the devastating aftereffects of the Second World War in Europe allowed Hollywood to consolidate its earlier gains (see Chapter 27). The United States' huge domestic market gave Hollywood its biggest advantage. By the 1950s Hollywood was making 500 films a year and accounted for between 40 and 75 percent of the films shown in Europe. The same period brought important innovations in filmmaking: the conversion to color and new optical formats, including widescreen.

The Cold War also weighed heavily on the film industry in the United States. Between 1947 and 1951, the House Un-American Activities Committee called before it hundreds of actors, directors, and writers in their investigation of Hollywood's political allegiances. The major studios blacklisted many, fearing their associations with communism or left-wing political activity. Paradoxically, this occurred as the American censorship system was breaking down. Since the 1930s, the Motion Picture Production Code had refused to approve "scenes of passion" (including married couples sharing a bed), immorality, realistic violence, and profanity. In the mid-1950s, popular films such as *Rebel without a Cause* (1955) challenged these standards, dealing frankly with teenage rebellion, sexual themes, or other previously taboo subjects. By the 1960s the Production Code had been scuttled—the extremely graphic violence at the end of Arthur Penn's *Bonnie and Clyde* (1967) marked the scope of the transformation.

Gender Roles and Sexual Revolution

What some called the sexual revolution of the 1960s had several aspects. The first was less censorship, which we have already seen in film, and fewer taboos regarding discussion of sexuality in public. In the United States, the notorious Kinsey Reports on male and female sexuality (in 1948 and 1953, respectively) made morality and sexual behavior front-page news. Alfred Kinsey was a zoologist turned social scientist, and the way in which he applied science and statistics to sex attracted considerable attention. Kinsey showed that moral codes and private behaviors did not line up neatly. For instance, 80 to 90 percent of the women he interviewed disapproved of premarital sex, but 50 percent of the women he interviewed had had it. *Time* magazine warned that publicizing disparities between beliefs and behavior might prove subversive—that women and men would decide there was "morality in numbers."

Was the family crumbling? Transformations in agriculture and life in the countryside did mean that the peasant family was no longer the institution that governed birth, work, courtship, marriage, and death. Yet the family became newly important as the center of consumption, spending, and leisure time, for television took people (usually men)

out of bars, cafés, and music halls. It became the focus of government attention in the form of family allowances, health care, and Cold War appeals to family values. People brought higher expectations to marriage, which raised rates of divorce, and they paid more attention to children, which brought smaller families. Despite a postwar spike in the birthrate that produced the "baby boom," over the long term, fertility declined, even in countries that outlawed contraception. The family assumed new meanings as its traditional structures of authority—namely paternal control over wives and children—eroded under the pressure of social change.

A second aspect of the revolution was the growing centrality of sex and eroticism to mass consumer culture. Magazines, which flourished in this period, offered advice on how to succeed in love and how to be attractive. Cultivating one's looks, including sexiness, fit with the new accent on consumption; indeed, health and personal hygiene was the fastest-rising category of family spending. Advertising, advice columns, TV, and film blurred boundaries between buying consumer goods, seeking personal fulfillment, and sexual desire. There was nothing new about appeals to eroticism. But the fact that sexuality was now widely considered a form of self-expression—perhaps even the core of one's self—was new to the twentieth century. These developments helped propel change, and they also made the sexual revolution prominent in the politics of the time.

The third aspect of the revolution came with legal and medical or scientific changes in contraception. Oral contraceptives, first approved for development in 1959, became mainstream in the next decade. "The Pill" did not have revolutionary effects on birthrates, which were already falling. It marked a dramatic change, however, because it was simple (though expensive) and could be used by women themselves. By 1975, two-thirds of British women between fifteen and forty-four said they were taking the Pill. Numbers like these marked a long, drawn-out end to centuries-old views that even to discuss birth control was pornographic, an affront to religion, and an invitation to indulgence and promiscuity. By and large, Western countries legalized contraception in the 1960s and abortion in the 1970s. In 1965, for instance, the U.S. Supreme Court struck down laws banning the use of contraception, though selling contraceptives remained illegal in Massachusetts until 1972. The Soviet Union legalized abortion in 1950, after banning it during most of Stalin's regime. Throughout Eastern Europe, abortion rates were extremely high. Why? Contraceptives proved as difficult to obtain as other consumer goods; men often refused to use them; and women—doubly burdened with long hours of work and housework, and facing, in addition, chronic housing shortages—had little choice but to resort to abortion.

Legal changes would not have occurred without the women's movements of the time. For nineteenth-century feminists, winning the right to vote was the most difficult practical and symbolic struggle (see Chapter 23). For the revived feminism of the 1960s and 1970s, the family, work, and sexuality—all put on the agenda by the social changes of the period—were central. Since the Second World War the assumption that middle-class women belonged in the home had been challenged by the steadily rising demand for workers, especially in education and the service sector. Thus many more married women and many more mothers were part of the labor force. Moreover, across the West young middle-class women, like men, were part of the rising number of university students. But in the United States, to take just one example, only 37 percent of women who enrolled in college in the 1950s finished their degrees, believing they should marry instead. As one of them explained, "We married what we wanted to be": doctor, professor, manager, and so on. Women found it difficult to get non-secretarial jobs; they received less pay for the same work; and, even when employed, they had to rely on their husbands to establish credit.

The tension between rising expectations that stemmed, on the one hand, from abundance, growth, and the emphasis on self-expression, and, on the other, the reality of narrow horizons, created quiet waves of discontent. Betty Friedan's *The Feminine Mystique* (1963) brought much of this discontent into the open, contrasting the cultural myths of the fulfilled and happy housewife with the realities of economic inequality, hard work, and narrowed horizons. In 1949, Simone de Beauvoir had asked how Western culture (myth, literature, and psychology) had created an image of woman as the second and lesser sex; Friedan, using a more journalistic style and writing at a time when social change had made readers more receptive to her ideas, showed how the media, the social sciences, and advertising at once exalted femininity and also lowered women's expectations and possibilities. Friedan co-founded NOW (the National Organization of Women) in the United States in 1966; smaller and often more radical women's movements multiplied across Europe in the following decades. For this generation of feminists, reproductive freedom was both a private matter and a basic right—a key to women's control over their lives. Outlawing contraception and abortion made women alone bear responsibility for the consequences of sweeping changes in Western sexual life. Such measures were ineffective as well as unjust, they argued. Mass consumption, mass culture, and startlingly rapid transformations in public and private life were all intimately related.

SOCIAL MOVEMENTS DURING THE 1960s

The social unrest of the 1960s was international. Its roots lay in the political struggles and social transformations of the postwar period. Of these, the most important were anticolonial and civil rights movements. The successful anticolonial movements (see Chapter 27) reflected a growing racial consciousness and also helped encourage that consciousness. Newly independent African and Caribbean nations remained wary about revivals of colonialism and the continuing economic hegemony of Western Europe and America. Black and Asian immigration into those nations produced tension and frequent violence. In the West, particularly in the United States, people of color identified with these social and economic grievances.

The Civil Rights Movement in the United States Seen from Europe

Increasingly vocal demands by African Americans for equal rights and an end to segregation in the United States paralleled the emergence of new black nations in Africa and the Caribbean following decolonization. The American Civil Rights Movement had its origins in local organizing by prewar organizations such as the National Association for the Advancement of Colored People (NAACP). By 1960 a

MARTIN LUTHER KING, JR., 1964. The African American civil rights leader is welcomed in Oslo, Norway, on a trip to accept the Nobel Peace Prize. He would be assassinated four years later. ▪ *How might Europeans have viewed King's campaign?* ▪ *Would it affect their vision of the United States?*

new generation of civil rights activists, led by the Congress of Racial Equality (CORE), sought a more confrontational approach to end segregation, organizing boycotts and demonstrations against private businesses and public services that discriminated against blacks in the South.

Martin Luther King, Jr. (1929–1968), a Baptist minister who embraced the philosophy of nonviolence promoted by the Indian social and political activist Mohandas K. Gandhi, emerged as the most visible and effective leader of the movement until his assassination in 1968. Other African American leaders, such as Malcolm X (1925–1965), rejected King's goal of integration and called instead for African Americans to develop a nationalist consciousness of their own, emphasizing their own heritage and rejecting white domination. Although the Civil Rights Movement in the United States could point to real successes—voting rights and school desegregation among them—the visible and violent resistance to civil rights organizers in the South and persistent racism in housing and job opportunities hurt the image of the United States in Europe.

Many Europeans watched the U.S. Civil Rights Movement—and the vocal resistance it faced from American defenders of segregation—with real discomfort. American troops had been stationed in Western European nations since the Second World War as part of their Cold War defense system, and for many people in Europe, the persistence of racial discrimination in the United States undermined American claims to be the defenders of liberty in Europe. At the same time, the U.S. civil rights campaign served as a reminder of the injustices of European colonial empires. West Indian, Indian, and Pakistani immigrants faced racial discrimination in Britain, as did Algerian immigrants in France and Turkish "guest workers" in Germany.

The root causes of these enduring problems lay in the long and different histories of American slavery and European imperial expansion, but whatever the cause, the question of racial equality proved challenging to democracies on both sides of the Atlantic in the postwar decades and after. In Western Europe, as in the United States, struggles for racial and ethnic integration became central to the postcolonial world.

The Antiwar Movement

By the late 1960s the United States' escalating war in Vietnam had become a lightning rod for discontent. In 1961, President John F. Kennedy had promised to "bear any burden" necessary to fight communism and to ensure the victory of American models of representative government and free-market economics in the developing nations.

Kennedy's plan entailed massive increases in foreign aid, much of it in weapons. It provided the impetus for humanitarian institutions such as the Peace Corps, intended to improve local conditions and show Americans' benevolence and good intentions. Bearing burdens, however, also meant fighting guerrillas who turned to the Soviets for aid. This commitment led to covert interventions in Latin America, the Congo, and, most important, Vietnam.

By the time of Kennedy's death in 1963, nearly 15,000 American "advisers" were on the ground alongside South Vietnamese troops. Kennedy's successor, Lyndon Johnson, began the strategic bombing of North Vietnam and rapidly drew hundreds of thousands of American troops into combat in South Vietnam. The rebels in the south, known as the Viet Cong, were solidly entrenched, highly experienced guerrilla fighters, and were backed by the professional, well-equipped North Vietnamese army under Ho Chi Minh, who also received support from the Soviet Union. The South Vietnamese government resisted efforts at reform, losing popular support. Massive efforts by the United States produced only stalemate, mounting American casualties, and rising discontent.

Opposition to the Vietnam War helped to galvanize a broad protest movement in the United States and in other countries. In the United States, protesters focused on the military draft, which, when combined with deferments for educational purposes, ended up conscripting a disproportionate number of African Americans. The failure to achieve military victory in spite of escalating numbers of troops discredited the U.S. government's policy, and by the late 1960s the Vietnam War was seen by many people in the world as a tragedy and a folly: the wealthiest, most powerful nation in the world seemed intent on destroying a land of poor peasants in the name of anticommunism, democracy, and freedom. This tarnished image of Western values stood at the center of the 1960s protest movements in the United States and Western Europe.

The Student Movement in 1968

Nineteen sixty-eight was an extraordinary year, quite similar to 1848 with its wave of revolution (see Chapter 20). International youth culture fostered a sense of collective identity. The new media relayed images of civil rights protests in the United States to Europe, and broadcast news footage of the Vietnam War on television screens from West Virginia to West Germany. The wave of unrest shook both the Eastern and Western blocs.

The student movement itself can be seen as a consequence of postwar developments: a rapidly growing cohort

The "Woman Question" on Both Sides of the Atlantic

How did Western culture define femininity, and how did women internalize those definitions? These questions were central to postwar feminist thought, and they were sharply posed in two classic texts: Simone de Beauvoir's The Second Sex *(1949) and Betty Friedan's* The Feminine Mystique *(1963). Beauvoir (1908–1986) started from the existentialist premise that humans were "condemned to be free"—and condemned as well to give their own lives meaning. Why, then, did women accept the limitations imposed on them and, in Beauvoir's words, "dream the dreams of men"? Although dense and philosophical,* The Second Sex *was read throughout the world. Betty Friedan's equally influential bestseller drew heavily on Beauvoir. Friedan sought the origins of the "feminine mystique," her term for the model of femininity promoted by experts, advertised in women's magazines, and seemingly embraced by middle-class housewives throughout the postwar United States. As Friedan points out in the excerpt here, the new postwar mystique was in many ways more conservative than prewar ideals had been, despite continuing social change, a greater range of careers opening up to women, the expansion of women's education, and so on. Friedan (1921–2006) co-founded the National Organization for Women in 1966 and served as its president until 1970.*

Simone de Beauvoir, *The Second Sex* (1949)

But first, what is a woman? . . . Everyone agrees there are females in the human species; today, as in the past, they make up about half of humanity; and yet we are told that "femininity is in jeopardy"; we are urged. "Be women, stay women, become women." . . . Although some women zealously strive to embody it, the model has never been patented. It is typically described in vague and shimmering terms borrowed from a clairvoyant's vocabulary. . . .

If the female function is not enough to define woman, and if we also reject the explanation of the "eternal feminine," but if we accept, even temporarily, that there are women on the earth, we then have to ask: what is a woman?

Merely stating the problem suggests an immediate answer to me. It is significant that I pose it. It would never occur to a man to write a book on the singular situation of males in humanity. If I want to define myself, I first have to say, "I am a woman;" all other assertions will arise from this basic truth. A man never begins by positing himself as an individual of a certain sex: that he is a man is obvious. The categories "masculine" and "feminine" appear as symmetrical in a formal way on town hall records or identification papers. The relation of the two sexes is not that of two electrical poles: the man represents both the positive and the neuter. . . . Woman is the negative, to such a point that any determination is imputed to her as a limitation, without reciprocity. . . . A man is in his right by virtue of being man; it is the woman who is in the wrong. . . . Woman has ovaries and a uterus; such are the particular conditions that lock her in her subjectivity; some even say she thinks with her hormones. Man vainly forgets that his anatomy also includes hormones and testicles. He grasps his body as a direct and normal link with the world that he believes he apprehends in all objectivity, whereas he considers woman's body an obstacle, a prison, burdened by everything that particularises it. "The female is female by virtue of a certain *lack* of qualities," Aristotle said. "We should regard women's nature as suffering from natural defectiveness." And St. Thomas in his turn decreed that woman was an "incomplete man," an "incidental" being. This is what the Genesis story symbolises, where Eve appears as if drawn from Adam's "supernumerary" bone, in Bossuet's words. Humanity is male, and man defines woman, not in herself, but in relation to himself; she is not considered an autonomous being. . . . And she is nothing other than what man decides; she is thus called "the sex," meaning that the male sees her essentially as a sexed being; for him she is sex, so she is it in the absolute. She determines and differentiates herself in relation to man, and he does not in relation to her; she is the inessential in front of the essential. He is the Subject, he is the Absolute. She is the Other.

Source: Simone de Beauvoir, *The Second Sex*, trans. Constance Borde and Sheila Malovany-Chevallier (London: 2009), pp. 3–6.

Betty Friedan, *The Feminine Mystique* (1963)

"In 1939, the heroines of women's magazine stories were not always young, but in a certain sense they were younger than their fictional counterparts today. They were young in the same way that the American hero has always been young: they were New Women, creating with a gay determined spirit a new identity for women—a life of their own. There was an aura about them of becoming, of moving into a future that was going to be different from the past. . . .

These stories may not have been great literature. But the identity of their heroines seemed to say something about the housewives who, then as now, read the women's magazines. These magazines were not written for career women. The New Woman heroines were the ideal of yesterday's housewives; they reflected the dreams, mirrored the yearning for identity and the sense of possibility that existed for women then. . . .

In 1949 . . . the feminine mystique began to spread through the land. . . .

The feminine mystique says that the highest value and the only commitment for women is the fulfillment of their own femininity. It says that the great mistake of Western culture, through most of its history, has been the undervaluation of this femininity. . . . The mistake, says the mystique, the root of women's troubles in the past, is that women envied men, women tried to be like men, instead of accepting their own nature, which can find fulfillment only in sexual passivity, male domination, and nurturing maternal love.

But the new image this mystique gives to American women is the old image: "Occupation: housewife." The new mystique makes the housewife-mothers, who never had a chance to be anything else, the model for all women; it presupposes that history has reached a final and glorious end in the here and now, as far as women are concerned. . . .

It is more than a strange paradox that as all professions are finally open to women in America, "career woman" has become a dirty word; that as higher

education becomes available to any woman with the capacity for it, education for women has become so suspect that more and more drop out of high school and college to marry and have babies; that as so many roles in modern society become theirs for the taking, women so insistently confine themselves to one role. Why . . . should she accept this new image which insists she is not a person but a "woman," by definition barred from the freedom of human existence and a voice in human destiny?

Source: Betty Friedan, *The Feminine Mystique* (New York: 2001), pp. 38, 40, 42–43, 67–68.

Questions for Analysis

1. Why does Beauvoir ask, "What is a woman?"

2. Why does Friedan think that a "feminine mystique" emerged after the Second World War?

of young people with more time and wealth than in the past; generational consciousness heightened, in part, by the marketing of mass youth culture; and educational institutions unable to deal with rising numbers and expectations. By 1969, universities and high schools in Western Europe had five times as many students as in 1949. Lecture halls were packed, university bureaucracies did not respond to requests, and thousands of students took exams at the same time. More philosophically, students raised questions about the role and meaning of elite education in a democratic society and about relations between universities, state-funded scientific research, and the Cold War military intervention in Vietnam. In addition, student demands for fewer restrictions on personal life—for instance, permission to have a member of the opposite sex in a dormitory room—provoked authoritarian reactions from university officials. Waves of student protest were not confined to the United States and Western Europe. They also swept across Poland and Czechoslovakia, where students protested one-party bureaucratic rule, a stifled intellectual life, and authoritarianism; they also helped sustain networks of dissidents. By the mid-1960s, simmering anger in Eastern Europe had once again reached a dangerous point.

PARIS

The most serious outbreak of student unrest in Europe came in Paris in the spring of 1968. The French Republic had been shaken by conflicts over the Algerian war in the early 1960s. Even more important, the economic boom had undermined the foundations of the regime and de Gaulle's traditional style of rule. French students at the University of Paris demanded reforms that would modernize their university. In the face of growing disorder, the entire University of Paris shut down—sending students into the streets and into ugly confrontations with the police. The police reacted with repression and violence, which startled onlookers and television audiences and backfired on the regime. Sympathy with the students' cause expanded rapidly, bringing in other opponents of President de Gaulle's regime. Massive trade-union strikes broke out. Workers in the automobile industry, technical workers, and public-sector employees—from gas and electricity utilities to the mail system to radio and television—went on strike. By mid-May, an astonishing 10 million French workers had walked off their jobs. At one point, it looked as if the government would fall. The regime, however, was able to satisfy the strikers with wage increases and to appeal to public demand for order. Isolated, the student movements gradually petered out and students agreed to resume university life. The regime did recover, but the events of 1968 helped weaken de Gaulle's position as president and contributed to his retirement from office the following year.

Paris was not the only city to explode in 1968. Student protest broke out in West Berlin, targeting the government's close ties to the autocratic shah of Iran and the power of media corporations. Clashes with the police turned violent. In Italian cities, undergraduates staged several demonstrations to draw attention to university overcrowding. Twenty-six universities were closed. The London School of Economics was nearly shut down by protest. In the United States, antiwar demonstrations and student rebellions spread across the country after the North Vietnamese and Viet Cong launched the Tet offensive. President Johnson, battered by the effects of Tet and already worn down by the war, chose not to run for reelection. The year 1968 also saw damage and trauma for the country's political future because of the assassinations of Martin Luther King, Jr.

(April 4), and presidential candidate Robert F. Kennedy (June 5). King's assassination was followed by a wave of rioting in more than fifty cities across the United States, followed in late summer by street battles between police and student protesters at the 1968 Democratic National Convention in Chicago. Some saw the flowering of protest as another "springtime of peoples." Others saw it as a long nightmare.

"PRAGUE SPRING"

The student movement in the United States and Western Europe also took inspiration from one of the most significant challenges to Soviet authority since the Hungarian revolt of 1956 (see Chapter 27): the "Prague spring" of 1968. The events began with the emergence of a liberal communist government in Czechoslovakia, led by the Slovak Alexander Dubček (*DOOB-chehk*). Dubček had outmaneuvered the more traditional, authoritarian party leaders. He advocated "socialism with a human face," encouraging debate within the party, academic and artistic freedom, and less censorship. As was often the case, party members were divided between proponents of reform and those fearful that reform would unleash revolution. The reformers, however, also gained support from outside the party, from student organizations, the press, and networks of dissidents. As in Western Europe and the United States, the protest movement overflowed the bounds of traditional party politics.

In the Soviet Union, Khrushchev had fallen in 1964, and the reins of Soviet power passed to Leonid Brezhnev as secretary of the Communist party. Brezhnev was more conservative than Khrushchev, less inclined to bargain

A RUSSIAN TANK ATTACKED BY DEMONSTRATORS FOLLOWING THE PRAGUE SPRING, 1968.

Ludvík Vaculík, "Two Thousand Words" (1968)

During the Prague spring of 1968, a group of Czech intellectuals published a document titled "Two Thousand Words That Belong to Workers, Farmers, Officials, Scientists, Artists, and Everybody"; it has become known simply as "Two Thousand Words." This manifesto called for further reform, including increased freedom of the press. Seen by Moscow as a direct affront, the manifesto heightened Soviet-Czech tensions. In August 1968 Warsaw Pact tanks rolled into Prague, overthrowing the reformist government of Alexander Dubček.

ost of the nation welcomed the socialist program with high hopes. But it fell into the hands of the wrong people. It would not have mattered so much that they lacked adequate experience in affairs of state, factual knowledge, or philosophical education, if only they had enough common prudence and decency to listen to the opinion of others and agree to being gradually replaced by more able people. . . .

The chief sin and deception of these rulers was to have explained their own whims as the "will of the workers." Were we to accept this pretense, we would have to blame the workers today for the decline of our economy, for crimes committed against the innocent, and for the introduction of censorship to prevent anyone writing about these things. The workers would be to blame for misconceived investments, for losses suffered in foreign trade, and for the housing shortage. Obviously no sensible person will hold the working class responsible for such things. We all know, and every worker knows especially, that they had virtually no say in deciding anything. . . .

Since the beginning of this year we have been experiencing a regenerative process of democratization. . . .

Let us demand the departure of people who abused their power, damaged public property, and acted dishonorably or brutally. Ways must be found to compel them to resign. To mention a few: public criticism, resolutions, demonstrations, demonstrative work brigades, collections to buy presents for them on their retirement, strikes, and picketing at their front doors. But we should reject any illegal, indecent, or boorish methods. . . . Let us convert the district and local newspapers, which have mostly degenerated to the level of official mouthpieces, into a platform for all the forward-looking elements in politics; let us demand that editorial boards be formed of National Front representatives, or else let us start new papers. Let us form committees for the defense of free speech. . . .

There has been great alarm recently over the possibility that foreign forces will intervene in our development. Whatever superior forces may face us, all we can do is stick to our own positions, behave decently, and initiate nothing ourselves. We can show our government that we will stand by it, with weapons if need be, if it will do what we give it a mandate to do. . . .

The spring is over and will never return. By winter we will know all.

Source: Jaromir Navratil, *The Prague Spring 1968,* trans. Mark Kramer, Joy Moss, and Ruth Tosek (Budapest: 1998), pp. 177–81.

Questions for Analysis

1. Where, according to the authors of this document, did socialism go wrong?

2. What specific reforms do they demand?

with the West, and prone to defensive actions to safeguard the Soviet sphere of influence. Initially, the Soviets tolerated Dubček as a political eccentric. The events of 1968 raised their fears. Most Eastern European communist leaders denounced Czech reformism, but student demonstrations of support broke out in Poland and Yugoslavia, calling for an end to one-party rule, less censorship, and reform of the judicial system. In addition, Josip Broz Tito of Yugoslavia and Nicolae Ceausescu (*chow-SHEHS-koo*) of Romania—two of the more stubbornly independent communists in Eastern Europe—visited Dubček. To Soviet eyes these activities looked as if they were directed against the Warsaw Pact and Soviet security; they also saw American intervention in Vietnam as evidence of heightened anticommunist activities around the world. When Dubček attempted to democratize the Communist party and did not attend a meeting of members of the Warsaw Pact, in August 1968 the Soviets sent tanks and troops into Prague. Again the world watched as streams of Czech refugees left the country and a repressive government, installed by Soviet security forces, took charge. Dubček and his allies were subjected to imprisonment or "internal exile." Twenty percent of the members of the Czech Communist party were expelled in a series of purges. After the destruction of the Prague spring, Soviet diplomats consolidated their position according to the new Brezhnev Doctrine, which stated that no socialist state could adopt policies endangering the interests of international socialism, and that the Soviet Union could intervene in the domestic affairs of any Soviet bloc nation if communist rule was threatened. In other words, the repressive rules that had been applied to Hungary in 1956 would not change.

What were the effects of 1968? De Gaulle's government recovered. The Republican Richard M. Nixon won the U.S. presidential election of 1968. From 1972 to 1975 the United States withdrew from Vietnam; in the wake of that war came a refugee crisis and a new series of horrific regional conflicts. In Prague, Warsaw Pact tanks put down the uprising, and in the Brezhnev Doctrine the Soviet regime reasserted its right to control its satellites. Serious Cold War confrontations rippled along Czechoslovakia's western border as refugees fled west, and in the Korean peninsula after North Korea's seizure of a U.S. Navy eavesdropping ship, the *Pueblo*. Over the long term, however, the protesters' and dissidents' demands proved more difficult to contain. In Eastern Europe and the Soviet Union, dissent was defeated but not eliminated. The crushing of the Czech rebellion proved thoroughly disillusioning, and in important respects the events of 1968 prefigured the collapse of Soviet control in 1989. In Western Europe and the United States, the student movement subsided but its issues and the kinds of politics that it pioneered proved more enduring. Feminism (or, more accurately, second-wave feminism) really came into its own after 1968 with an influx of women a generation younger than Simone de Beauvoir and Betty Friedan. Finally, the environmental movement took hold—concerned not only with pollution and the world's dwindling resources but also with mushrooming urbanization and the kind of unrestrained economic growth that had characterized the 1960s. Over the long term, in both Europe and the United States, voters' loyalties to traditional political parties became less reliable and smaller parties multiplied; in this way, new social movements eventually became part of a very different political landscape.

ECONOMIC STAGNATION: THE PRICE OF SUCCESS

Economic as well as social problems plagued Europe during the 1970s and 1980s, but these problems had begun earlier. By the middle of the 1960s, for example, the postwar economic boom had slowed. Demand for manufactured goods fell, and unemployment crept up. Though new industries continued to prosper, the basic industries—coal, steel, and railways—began to run up deficits. The Common Market—expanded in 1973 to include Britain, Ireland, and Denmark, and again in the early 1980s to admit Greece, Spain, and Portugal—struggled to overcome problems stemming from the conflict between the domestic economic regulations characteristic of many European states and the free-market policies that prevailed within what would become the European Economic Community (EEC) countries.

Oil prices spiked for the first time in the early 1970s, compounding these difficulties. In 1973, the Arab-dominated Organization of the Petroleum Exporting Countries (OPEC) instituted an oil embargo against the Western powers. In 1973, a barrel of oil cost $1.73; in 1975, it cost $10.46; by the early 1980s, the price had risen to over $30. This increase produced an inflationary spiral; interest rates rose and with them the price of almost everything else Western consumers were used to buying. Rising costs at a time of economic slowdown produced wage demands and strikes. The calm industrial relations of the 1950s and early 1960s were a thing of the past. At the same time, European manufacturers encountered serious competition, not only from such highly developed countries as Japan but also from the increasingly active economies of Asia and Africa, in which the West had eagerly invested capital in the previous decades. By 1980 Japan had captured 10 percent of the automobile market in West Germany and 25 percent in Belgium. In 1984 unemployment in Western Europe reached about 19 million. The lean years had arrived.

Economies in the Soviet bloc also stalled. The expansion of heavy industry had helped recovery in the postwar period, but by the 1970s those sectors no longer provided growth or innovation. The Soviet Communist party proclaimed in 1961 that by 1970 the USSR would exceed the United States in per capita production. By the end of the 1970s, however, Soviet per capita production was not much higher than in the less industrialized countries of southern Europe. The Soviets were also overcommitted to military defense industries that had become inefficient, though lucrative for the party members who ran them. The Soviet economy did get a boost from the OPEC oil price hikes of

1973 and 1979. (OPEC was founded in 1961; the Soviet Union did not belong, but as the world's largest producer of oil, it benefited from rising prices.) Without this boost, the situation would have been far grimmer.

Western governments struggled for effective reactions to the abrupt change in their economic circumstances. The new leader of the British Conservative party, Margaret Thatcher, was elected prime minister in 1979—and reelected in 1983 and 1987—on a program of curbing trade-union power, cutting taxes to stimulate the economy, and privatizing publicly owned enterprises. The economy remained weak, with close to 15 percent of the workforce unemployed by 1986. In West Germany, a series of Social Democratic governments attempted to combat economic recession with job-training programs and tax incentives, both financed by higher taxes. These programs did little to assist economic recovery, and the country shifted to the right.

The fact that governments of right and left were unable to recreate Europe's unprecedented postwar prosperity suggests the degree to which economic forces remained outside the control of individual states. The continuing economic malaise renewed efforts to Europeanize common problems. By the end of the 1980s, the EEC embarked on an ambitious program of integration. Long-term goals, agreed on when the EU (European Union) was formed in 1991, included a monetary union—with a central European bank and a single currency—and unified social policies to reduce poverty and unemployment.

Solidarity in Poland

In 1980, unrest again peaked in Eastern Europe, this time with the Polish labor movement Solidarity. Polish workers organized strikes that brought the government of the country to a standstill. The workers objected to laboring conditions, high prices, and especially shortages, all of which had roots in government policy. Above all, though, the Polish workers in Solidarity demanded truly independent labor unions instead of labor organizations sponsored by the government. Their belief that society had the right to organize itself and, by implication, to create its own government, stood at the core of the movement. The strikers were led by an electrician from the Gdansk shipyards, Lech Walesa, whose charismatic personality appealed not only to the Polish citizenry but to sympathizers in the West. Again, however, the Soviets assisted a military regime in reimposing authoritarian rule. The Polish president, General Wojciech Jaruzelski, had learned from Hungary and Czechoslovakia and played a delicate game

of diplomacy to maintain the Polish government's freedom of action while repressing Solidarity itself. But the implied Soviet threat remained.

EUROPE RECAST: THE COLLAPSE OF COMMUNISM AND THE END OF THE SOVIET UNION

The sudden collapse of the Eastern European communist regimes in 1989 led to the dramatic end of the Cold War and the subsequent disintegration of the once-powerful Soviet Union.

Gorbachev and Soviet Reform

This collapse flowed, unintended, from a new wave of reform begun in the mid-1980s. In 1985 a new generation of officials began taking charge of the Soviet Communist party, a change heralded by Mikhail Gorbachev's appointment to the party leadership. In his mid-fifties, Gorbachev was significantly younger than his immediate predecessors and less subject to the habits of mind that had shaped Soviet domestic

GORBACHEV IN POLAND AT THE HEIGHT OF HIS POWER IN 1986. His policy of *perestroika* undermined the privileges of the political elite and would eventually lead to his own fall from power.

and foreign affairs. He was frankly critical of the repressive aspects of communist society as well as its sluggish economy, and he did not hesitate to voice those criticisms openly. His twin policies of *glasnost* (intellectual openness) and *perestroika* (economic restructuring) held out hope for a freer, more prosperous Soviet Union.

The policies of glasnost took aim at the privileges of the political elite and the immobility of the state bureaucracy by allowing greater freedom of speech, instituting competitive elections to official positions, and limiting terms of office. Gorbachev's program of perestroika called for a shift from the centrally planned economy instituted by Stalin to a mixed economy combining state planning with the operation of market forces. In agriculture, perestroika accelerated the move away from cooperative production and instituted incentives for the achievement of production targets. Gorbachev planned to integrate the Soviet Union into the international economy by participating in organizations such as the International Monetary Fund.

Even these dramatic reforms, however, were too little, too late. Ethnic unrest, a legacy of Russia's nineteenth-century imperialism, threatened to split the Soviet Union apart, while secession movements gathered steam in the Baltic republics and elsewhere. From 1988 onward, fighting between Armenians and Azerbaijanis over Nagorno-Karabakh, an ethnically Azerbaijani region located inside Armenia, threatened to escalate into a border dispute with Iran. Only Soviet troops patrolling the border, and Gorbachev's willingness to suppress a separatist revolt in Azerbaijan by force, temporarily quelled the conflict.

Spurred on by these events in the Soviet Union, the countries of Eastern Europe began to agitate for independence from Moscow. Gorbachev encouraged open discussion—glasnost—not only in his own country but also in the satellite nations. He revoked the Brezhnev Doctrine's insistence on single-party socialist governments and made frequent and inspiring trips to the capitals of neighboring satellites.

Glasnost rekindled the flame of opposition in Poland, where Solidarity had been defeated but not destroyed by the government in 1981. In 1988 the union launched a new series of strikes. These disturbances culminated in an agreement between the government and Solidarity that legalized the union and promised open elections. The results, in June 1989, astonished the world: virtually all of the government's candidates lost; the Citizen's Committee, affiliated with Solidarity, won a sizable majority in the Polish parliament.

In Hungary and Czechoslovakia, events followed a similar course during 1988 and 1989. Janos Kadar, the Hungarian leader since the Soviet crackdown of 1956, resigned in the face of continuing demonstrations in May 1988 and was replaced by the reformist government of the Hungarian Socialist Workers' party. By the spring of 1989 the Hungarian regime had been purged of Communist party supporters. The government also began to dismantle its security fences along the Austrian border.

The Czechs, too, staged demonstrations against Soviet domination in late 1988. Brutal beatings of student demonstrators by the police in 1989 radicalized the nation's workers and provoked mass demonstrations. Civic Forum, an opposition coalition, called for the installation of a coalition government to include noncommunists, for free elections, and for the resignation of the country's communist leadership. It reinforced its demands with continuing mass demonstrations and threats of a general strike that resulted in the toppling of the old regime and the election of the playwright and Civic Forum leader Václav Havel as president.

Fall of the Berlin Wall

The most significant political change in Eastern Europe during the late 1980s was the collapse of communism in East Germany and the unification of East and West Germany. Although long considered the most prosperous of the Soviet satellite countries, East Germany suffered from severe economic stagnation and environmental degradation. Waves of East Germans registered their discontent with worsening conditions by massive illegal emigration to the West. This exodus combined with evidence of widespread official corruption to force the resignation of East Germany's long-time, hard-line premier, Erich Honecker. His successor, Egon Krenz, promised reforms, but he was nevertheless faced with continuing protests and mass emigration.

U.S. PRESIDENT RONALD REAGAN AT BERLIN'S BRANDENBURG GATE, JUNE 12, 1987.

Past and Present

Shock Therapy in Post-Soviet Russia

The transition from a command economy to open markets in Russia after 1991 (on left, the banner reads "Privatization Yes") proved destabilizing in Russia, and for many ordinary people the first experience of the new order was profoundly unsettling. When Vladimir Putin came to power after 2000, he moved against the independence of this new business class, imprisoning some (including Mikhail Khodorkovsky, right, who awaits the verdict in his 2005 trial for fraud) and forcing others into exile. Khodorkovsky was imprisoned in 2005 and pardoned by Putin in 2013. He now lives in exile in Switzerland.

Watch related author videos on the Student Site
wwnorton.com/college/history/western-civilizationsBrief4

On November 4, 1989, in a move that acknowledged its powerlessness to hold its citizens captive, the government opened its border with Czechoslovakia. This move effectively freed East Germans to travel to the West. In a matter of days, the Berlin Wall—the embodiment of the Cold War, the Iron Curtain, and the division of East from West—was demolished, first by groups of ordinary citizens and later by the East German government. Jubilant throngs from both sides walked through the gaping holes that now permitted men, women, and children to take the few steps that symbolized the return to freedom and a chance for national unity. Free elections were held throughout Germany in March 1990, resulting in a victory for the Alliance for Germany, a coalition allied with the West

German chancellor Helmut Kohl's Christian Democratic Union. With heavy emigration continuing, reunification talks quickly culminated in the formal proclamation of a united Germany on October 3, 1990.

The public mood, in Eastern Europe and worldwide, was swept up with the jubilation of these peaceful "velvet revolutions" during the autumn of 1989. Yet the end of one-party rule in Eastern Europe was not accomplished without violence. The single most repressive government in the old Eastern bloc, Nicolae Ceaucescu's outright dictatorship in Romania, came apart with much more bloodshed. By December, faced with the wave of popular revolts in surrounding countries and riots by the ethnic Hungarian minority in Transylvania, a number of party officials and army officers in Romania tried to hold on to their own positions by deposing Ceaucescu. His extensive secret police, however, organized resistance to the coup; the result was nearly two weeks of bloody street fighting in the capital Bucharest. Ceaucescu himself and his wife were seized by populist army units and executed; images of their bloodstained bodies flashed worldwide by satellite television.

Throughout the rest of Eastern Europe, single-party governments in the countries behind what was left of the tattered Iron Curtain—Albania, Bulgaria, and Yugoslavia—collapsed in the face of democratic pressure for change. Meanwhile, in the Soviet Union itself, inspired by events in Eastern Europe, the Baltic republics of Lithuania and Latvia strained to free themselves from Soviet rule. In 1990 they unilaterally proclaimed their independence from the Soviet Union, throwing into sharp relief the tension between "union" and "republics." Gorbachev reacted with an uncertain mixture of armed intervention and promises of greater local autonomy. In the fall of 1991 Lithuania and Latvia, along with the third Baltic state of Estonia, won international recognition as independent republics.

The Collapse of the Soviet Union

While Soviet influence eroded in Eastern Europe, at home the unproductive Soviet economy continued to fuel widespread ire. With the failure of perestroika—largely the result of a lack of resources and an inability to increase production—came the rise of a powerful political rival to Gorbachev, his erstwhile ally Boris Yeltsin. The reforming mayor of Moscow, Yeltsin was elected president of the Russian Federation—the largest Soviet republic—on an anti-Gorbachev platform in 1990. Pressure from the Yeltsin camp weakened Gorbachev's ability to maneuver independent of reactionary factions in the Politburo and the military, undermining his reform program and his ability to remain in power.

The Soviet Union's increasingly severe domestic problems led to mounting protests in 1991, when Gorbachev's policies failed to improve—and indeed diminished—the living standards of the Soviet people. Demands increased that the bloated government bureaucracy respond with a dramatic cure for the country's continuing economic stagnation. Gorbachev appeared to lose his political nerve, having first ordered and then canceled a radical "500-day" economic reform plan, at the same time agreeing to negotiations with the increasingly disaffected republics within the union, now clamoring for independence. Sensing their political lives to be in jeopardy, a group of highly placed hard-line Communist party officials staged an abortive coup in August 1991. They made Gorbachev and his wife prisoners in their summer villa, then declared a return to party-line orthodoxy in an effort to salvage what remained of the Soviet Union's global leverage and the Communist party's domestic power. The Soviet citizenry, especially in large cities like Moscow and Leningrad, defied their self-proclaimed saviors. Led by Boris Yeltsin, who at one point climbed atop a tank in a Moscow street to rally the people, they gathered support among the Soviet republics and the military and successfully called the plotters' bluff. Within two weeks, Gorbachev was back in power and the coup leaders were in prison.

Ironically, this people's counterrevolution returned Gorbachev to office while destroying the power of the Soviet state he led. Throughout the fall of 1991, as Gorbachev struggled to hold the union together, Yeltsin joined the presidents of the other large republics to capitalize on the discontent. On December 8, 1991, the presidents of the republics of Russia, Ukraine, and Byelorussia (now called Belarus) declared that the Soviet Union was no more: "The USSR as a subject of international law and geopolitical reality is ceasing to exist." Though the prose was flat, the message was momentous. The once-mighty Soviet Union, founded seventy-five years before in a burst of revolutionary fervor and violence, had evaporated nearly overnight, leaving in its wake a collection of eleven far from powerful nations loosely joined together as the Commonwealth of Independent States. On December 25, 1991, Gorbachev resigned and left political life, not pushed from office in the usual way but made irrelevant as other actors dismantled the state. The Soviet flag—the hammer and sickle symbolizing the nation that for fifty years had kept half of Europe in thrall—was lowered for the last time over the Kremlin.

The dramatic collapse of the Soviet Union left enormous problems in its wake. Boris Yeltsin pleaded for and received economic assistance from the West, but the Russian economy was soon in severe crisis. The sudden establishment of a market economy caused a dramatic increase in unemployment and created opportunities for profiteering and corruption as state assets were sold off to a new class of oligarchs, many with ties to the former leadership. Conservative politicians allied with military officers attempted a coup against Yeltsin in September 1993, claiming that the reforms had gone too quickly. Yeltsin's administration shelled the rebel-held parliament building in response. The government's show of force succeeded, but Yeltsin faced discontented voters in the elections that followed. Meanwhile, ethnic and religious conflict plagued the former Soviet republics, with war breaking out in Georgia, Armenia, Azerbaijan, and Chechnya. The worst of these conflicts, in Chechnya, dragged on into the new century, a brutal war that overshadowed the optimism that

The map legend reads:

Soviet Union
Eastern Bloc countries
✳ Sites of popular demonstrations
⊛ Capital cities

EASTERN EUROPE IN 1989. ■ *What political changes in the Soviet Union allowed for the spread of demonstrations throughout Eastern Europe?* ■ *Why did the first political upheavals of 1989 occur in Poland and East Germany?* ■ *In what countries were demonstrations the most widespread, and why?*

diplomatic uncertainty about both the new Russian government and single-superpower domination, sometimes called American unilateralism. Within Russia and several of the other former Soviet republics there emerged a new era that some called the Russian "Wild West." Capitalist market relations began to develop without clearly defined property relations or a stable legal framework. Former government officials profited from their positions of power to take over whole sectors of the economy. Corruption ran rampant. Organized crime controlled entire industries, stock exchanges, a thriving trade in illegal drugs, and even some local governments. Even the most energetic central governments in the large republics such as Russia, Ukraine, and Kazakhstan found themselves faced with enormous problems. Post-Soviet openness could lay the groundwork for a new democratic Russia; it could also set in motion the resurgence of older forms of tyranny.

Postrevolutionary Troubles: Eastern Europe after 1989

The velvet revolutions of Central and Eastern Europe raised high hopes: local hopes that an end to authoritarian government would produce economic prosperity and cultural pluralism, and Western hopes that these countries would join them as capitalist partners in an enlarged European Community. The reality has been slower and harder than the optimists of 1989 foresaw. The reunification of Germany produced new and unexpected political challenges. The euphoria of reunification masked uncertainty even among Germans themselves. The foundering East German economy has remained a problem. Piled onto other economic difficulties in the

many in Russia and the West had felt at the downfall of the Soviet regime.

The Iron Curtain had established one of the most rigid borders in European history. The collapse of the Soviet Union opened up both Russia and its former imperial dominions, bringing the Cold War to an end. It also created a host of unforeseen problems throughout Eastern Europe and the advanced industrial world: ethnic conflict,

Trade Center in 2001 gave the term *globalization* a new and frightening meaning as well. It shattered many Americans' sense of relative isolation and security. Globalization, then, conjures up new possibilities—but also new vulnerabilities.

What, precisely, does the term mean? What causes or drives globalization, and what are its effects? To begin simply, globalization means integration. It is the process of creating a rising number of networks—political, social, economic, and cultural—that span larger sections of the globe. Information, ideas, goods, and people now move rapidly and easily across national boundaries. Yet *globalization* is not synonymous with *internationalization*, and the distinction is important. International relations are established between nation-states. Global exchange can be quite independent of national control: today trade, politics, and cultural exchange often happen "underneath the radar of the nation-state," in the words of one historian.

Globalization has radically altered the distribution of industry and patterns of trade around the world. Supranational economic institutions such as the International Monetary Fund are examples of globalization and also work to quicken its pace. Likewise, the International Criminal Court represents an important trend in law: the globalization of judicial power. New, rapid, and surprisingly intimate forms of mass communication (blogs, social media sites, Internet-based political campaigns, and so on) have spawned new forms of politics. Perhaps most interesting, the sovereignty of nation-states and the clear boundaries of national communities seem to be eroded by many globalizing trends.

All these developments seem to be characteristic of our time. But are they new? For centuries, religion, empire, commerce, and industry have had globalizing impulses and effects. The East India Companies (Dutch and English), for instance, were to the seventeenth century what Google is to the early twenty-first: the premier global enterprises of the time. The economic development of Europe in general was thoroughly enmeshed in global networks that supplied raw materials, markets, and labor. It has always been hard to strip the "West" of its global dimensions.

For another striking example, consider migration and immigration. We think of the contemporary world as fluid, characterized by vast movements of people. Mass, long-distance migration and immigration, however, peaked during the nineteenth century. Between 1846 (when the first reliable statistics were kept) and 1940, 55–58 million people left Europe for the Americas, especially for the United States, Canada, Argentina, and Brazil. During that same period, 48–52 million Indians and southern Chinese migrated to Southeast Asia, the Southern Pacific, and the areas surrounding the Indian Ocean (many of the Indian migrants going to other parts of the British Empire). Roughly another 50 million people left

northeastern Asia and Russia for Manchuria, Siberia, central Asia, and Japan. Faster long-distance transportation (railways and steamships) made these long journeys possible; the industrialization of the receiving regions provided the economic dynamics. The demographic, social, economic, and cultural effects of these migrations were transformative. After the First World War, governments set out to close their gates; from the 1920s on, laborers (and refugees) found it much harder to move. If migration is the measure of globalization, our world is less "globalized" than it was a century ago.

What is more, to equate globalization with integration may be misleading. Globalizing trends do not necessarily produce peace, equality, or homogeneity. Their effects are hard to predict. During the early 1900s many Europeans firmly believed that the world, at least the part of the world dominated by Western empires, would become harmonious, that Western culture would be exported, and that Western standards would become universal. History defied those expectations. Some scholars argue that the term *globalization* should be jettisoned because it suggests a uniform, leveling process, one that operates similarly everywhere. Globalization has very different and very disparate effects, effects shaped by vast asymmetries of power and wealth among nations or regions. In the last several decades, worldwide inequality has increased. Global processes encounter obstacles and resistance; they sow division as well as unity.

In this chapter we explore three subjects crucial to our early efforts to understand globalization, especially as it relates to the post–Cold War world of the twenty-first century. The first subject is the set of global changes that have accelerated the free flow of money, people, products, and ideas. The second subject is what we have come to call postcolonial politics—the varied trajectories that mark the contemporary experience of former colonies. Finally, we will consider in greater depth the complex and important role of Middle Eastern politics in contemporary global affairs. Throughout, we hope to suggest ways in which recent developments relate to familiar historical issues we have already examined in other contexts.

LIQUID MODERNITY? THE FLOW OF MONEY, IDEAS, AND PEOPLES

A key feature of late-twentieth-century globalization has been the transformation of the world economy, highlighted by the rapid integration of markets since 1970. In a series of historic changes, the international agreements that had regulated the movement of people, goods, and money since

"CHECKERBOARD OF POVERTY AND AFFLUENCE." Scenes of slums confronting towering skylines, such as this one from Argentina in 2000, are visible around the world as one of the side effects of development.

the Second World War were overturned. To begin with, the postwar economic arrangements sealed at Bretton Woods (see Chapter 27) steadily eroded in the late 1960s, as Western industrial nations faced a double burden of inflation and economic stagnation. A crucial shift in monetary policy occurred in 1971, when the United States abandoned the postwar gold standard and allowed the dollar—the keystone of the system—to range freely. As a result, formal regulations on currencies, international banking, and lending among states faded away. They were replaced with an informal network of arrangements managed autonomously by large private lenders, their political friends in leading Western states, and independent financial agencies such as the International Monetary Fund and the World Bank. The economists and administrators who dominated these new networks steered away from the interventionist policies that shaped postwar planning and recovery. Instead they relied on a broad range of market-driven models dubbed "neoliberalism." In a variation on classic liberal economics, neoliberal economists stressed the value of free markets, profit incentives, and sharp restraints on both budget deficits and social welfare programs, whether run by governments or corporations. The new systems of lending they backed had mixed results, funding breakneck growth in some cases and bringing catastrophic debt in others. Industrial development in the globalized economy has created jarring juxtapositions of development and deterioration across entire continents and even within single cities—a phenomenon described as a "checkerboard of poverty and affluence."

At the same time, the world's local, national, and regional economies became far more connected and interdependent. Export trade flourished and, with the technological advances of the 1960s, 1970s, and 1980s, came to include an increasing proportion of high-technology goods. The boom in export commerce was tied to important changes in the division of labor worldwide. More industrial jobs were

created in the postcolonial world, not just among Japan, China, and South Korea but also in India, Latin America, and elsewhere. Although such steady, skilled manual employment started to disappear in Western nations—often replaced by lower-paying menial work—financial and service sector employment leaped ahead. The exchange and use of goods became much more complex. Goods were designed by companies in one country, manufactured in another, and tied into a broader interchange of cultures. Taken together, these global economic changes had deep political effects, forcing painful debates about the nature of citizenship and entitlement inside national borders, about the power and accountability of transnational corporations, and about the human and environmental costs of global capitalism.

Another crucial change involved not only the widespread flow of information but also the new commercial and cultural importance attached to information itself. Electronic systems and devices designed to create, store, and share information multiplied, becoming staggeringly more powerful and accessible—none with so great an impact on the everyday lives of men and women around the world as the personal computer. By the early 1990s, increasingly sophisticated computers brought people into instant communication with each other across continents, not only by new means but also in new cultural and political settings. Electronic communications over the Internet gave a compelling new meaning to the phrase *global village*, Marshall McLuhan's term for the new global audience for mass media in the 1960s. The Internet revolution shared features of earlier print revolutions. It was pioneered by entrepreneurs with utopian ambitions and driven by the new network's ability to deliver personal or commercial messages as well as culturally illicit and politically scandalous material that could be published easily and informally. It offered new possibilities to the social and political groups that constituted new "publics." And it attracted large, established corporate interests, eager to cash in on new channels of culture and business.

However commonplace their use now seems, the Internet and similar technologies have had wide-ranging effects on political struggles around the globe. Embattled ethnic minorities have found worldwide audiences through online campaign sites. Satellite television arguably sped the sequence of popular revolts in Eastern Europe in 1989. That same year, fax machines brought Chinese demonstrators at Tiananmen Square news of international support for their efforts. More recently, Facebook and Twitter allowed Egyptians to express their unhappiness with Hosni Mubarak in early 2011, ultimately leading to his resignation as the president of Egypt. Meanwhile, leaps forward in electronic technologies provided new worldwide platforms for commercial interests. Companies such as

AN AFGHAN GIRL WEEDS A POPPY FIELD, 2004. Though Afghanistan was historically a center for the silk trade, opium (derived from poppies) is its most important cash crop today.
- *How is this development related to globalization?*

Sony and RCA produced entertainment content, including music, motion pictures, and television shows, as well as the electronic equipment needed to play that content. Bill Gates's Microsoft emerged as the world's major producer of computer software—with corporate profits that surpassed Spain's gross domestic product. At the level of production, marketing, and management, information industries are global, spread widely across the United States, India, Western Europe, and parts of the developing world. Their corporate headquarters, however, typically remain in the West and support neoliberal politics. The international media, news, and entertainment conglomerates run by the Australian Rupert Murdoch or by Time Warner, for example, are firmly allied to U.S. institutions and world-views, edging aside state-run companies.

Like the movement of money, goods, and ideas, the flow of labor has become a central aspect of globalization. Since 1945, the widespread migration of peoples, particularly between former colonies and imperial powers, has changed everyday life around the world. Groups of immigrant workers have filled the lower rungs of expanding economies not only in Europe but also in oil-rich Arab states that have attracted Asian and Filipino laborers, and in the United States, where both permanent and seasonal migrations from Mexico and other Latin American nations have spread across the continent. This fusion of peoples and cultures has produced striking new blends of music, food, language, and other forms of popular culture and sociability. It has also raised tensions over the definition of citizenship and the boundaries of political and cultural communities—familiar themes from modern history. As a result, cycles of violent

xenophobic backlash, bigotry, and political extremism have appeared in host countries and regions, but so too have new conceptions of civil rights and cultural belonging.

As suggested earlier, sharp divides exist between the most successful global players and the poorer, disadvantaged, sometimes embattled states and cultures. In one particular area of manufacture, however, poorer postcolonial regions have been able to respond to a steady and immensely profitable market in the West. The production of illegal drugs like opium, heroin, and cocaine is a thriving industry in countries such as Colombia, Myanmar (formerly Burma), and Malaysia. Though the trade in such substances is banned, the fragile economies of the countries where they are produced have encouraged public and private powers to turn a blind eye to their production—or even to intervene for their own profit. Other, similar forms of illegal commerce have also grown far beyond the old label of "organized crime" in their structure and political importance. Trafficking in illegal immigrants, the management of corrupt financial dealings, trade in illicit animal products, and "conflict" diamonds from several brutal postcolonial civil wars are all indicative of this trend. The organizations behind these criminal trades grew out of the political violence and economic breakdown of failing postcolonial states or from the human and commercial traffic between these parts of the world and leading Western economic powers. They have exploited cracks, loopholes, and unsupervised opportunities in the less regulated system of global trade and carved out centers of power not directly subject to the laws of any single state.

Demographics and Global Health

The developments of globalization are tied in complex ways to the evolving size and health of the world's population. Between 1800 and the middle of the twentieth century, the worldwide population roughly tripled, rising from 1 to 3 billion. Between 1960 and 2010, however, the growth rate soared and population more than doubled again, to almost 7 billion. Huge, if uneven, improvements in basic standards of health, particularly for young children and childbearing women, contributed to the increase—as did local efforts to improve the urban-industrial environment. Asia's population as a whole has increased nearly fourfold since 1900. Such growth has strained underdeveloped social services, public-health facilities, and urban infrastructures, increasing the potential for epidemic disease as well as for cycles of ethnic and ideological violence nursed by poverty and dislocation.

A different type of demographic crisis confronts parts of the West, where steadily shrinking populations erode social welfare systems. Longer life spans, broadened welfare programs, and rising health-care costs have contributed to the challenge. Populations in the United States and Great Britain have been stable or have been slowly expanded by immigration; in Italy, Scandinavia, and, recently, Russia, sharp drops in the birthrate have led to population decline. Declining birthrates have been accompanied by growing populations of older adults, whose health and vitality resulted from decades of improved medical standards and state-run entitlement programs. Maintaining the long-term solvency of such programs poses difficult choices for European countries in particular, as they struggle to balance guarantees of social well-being with fiscal and political realities.

Globalization has also changed public health and medicine, creating dangerous new threats as well as promising new treatments. Better and more comprehensive health care has generally accompanied other kinds of prosperity and has thus been more accessible in the West. In Africa, Latin America, and elsewhere, political chaos, imbalances of trade, and the practices of some large pharmaceutical companies have often resulted in shortages of medicine and a rickety medical infrastructure, making it difficult to combat deadly new waves of disease. Indeed, the worldwide risk of exposure to epidemic diseases is a new reality of globalization—a product of increased cultural interaction, exposure of new ecosystems to human development, and the speed of intercontinental transportation. By the 1970s, the acceleration of airplane travel led to fears that an epidemic would leapfrog the globe much faster than the pandemics of the Middle Ages. Such fears were confirmed by the worldwide spread of infection by the human immunodeficiency virus (HIV), whose final stage is acquired immunodeficiency syndrome (AIDS), which first appeared at the end of the 1970s. As HIV-AIDS became a global health crisis—particularly in Africa, where the disease spread catastrophically—international organizations recognized the need for an early, swift, and comprehensive response to future outbreaks of disease, as evidenced by the successful global containment of severe acute respiratory syndrome (SARS) in 2003. The slow international response to the deadly outbreak of Ebola virus in West Africa in 2014 demonstrates that much remains to be done to prevent the spread of disease in a globalized and interconnected world.

Meanwhile, recent advances in genetic engineering have opened up new possibilities for preventing and treating diseases. Genetic engineers developed—and patented— new strains of laboratory animals that contained cells or even organs of other species. During the 1990s scientists successfully mapped the complete human genome—that is, the entire architecture of human chromosomes. This

GOVERNMENT EFFORTS TO CURTAIL THE SPREAD OF SEVERE ACUTE RESPIRATORY SYNDROME (SARS). In May 2003, migrant workers at a Beijing railway station line up to have their temperatures checked before boarding the trains.

new knowledge allowed scientists to experiment with altering human biology itself. Infertile couples could now conceive through out-of-body medical procedures. It is now possible to determine the genetic makeup of any human being and measure their chances of developing cancer, schizophrenia, or many other diseases. The new field of epigenetics can trace the effects of behaviors such as smoking through more than one generation, demonstrating that choices made by a grandparent can affect the genes of their grandchildren. These developments raise provocative questions about individual responsibility and public health, about how we should understand biological "defects" and diversions from genetic norms, and about the privacy of medical information. At present, the debate continues about who should establish the ground rules for dealing with the consequences of this new knowledge— should it be nations, international bodies, or local cultural and religious communities? Once again, scientific progress has raised fundamental questions about ethics, citizenship, and the measure of humanity.

The question of climate change has also raised thorny questions about scientific knowledge, economic development, and the health of populations. Climate scientists now largely agree that the average temperature of the planet is rising steadily as a result of increases in carbon dioxide in the atmosphere produced by burning fossil fuels. Every year of the twenty-first century has ranked among the fifteen hottest since records were first kept in 1980. The consequences of this warming could include: a rise in sea levels as polar ice caps melt; an increase in the frequency of heat waves, droughts, and coastal flooding; and possibly, increases in the frequency and severity of storms, including tornados and tropical cyclones.

Government first sounded the alarm about climate change in the early 1990s. It proved hard to establish a coordinated policy, however, because individual nations worried that limits to the burning of fossil fuels would make them less competitive economically. Energy producers were resistant to pollution limits or requirements that they develop "clean" technologies. It is also very hard to change consumer behavior in developed countries where people have long depended on easy access to electric power produced by the burning of coal, manufactured goods imported from distant places, cheap air travel, and the extensive use of automobiles. Finding solutions is doubly difficult because the parts of the world most closely associated with pollution from fossil fuels are not necessarily those that will feel the worst effects of climate change in the near term. Rather, the most severely impacted will be poorer countries in the global south that have few resources for coping with the effects of climate change.

Since 1990s, international efforts to coordinate a response to climate change have focused on a UN-sponsored agreement known as the Kyoto Protocol, which the United States never signed. Current efforts are aimed at reducing fossil-fuel pollution through a plan that will allow market forces to generate economic incentives through emissions trading. Under this "cap and trade" system, a central authority will allocate permits to pollute at a certain level (the "cap") and demand that industries hold the necessary permits to maintain their operations. Industries that manage to reduce their emissions can sell the permits that they do not need on the open market to other firms (the "trade"), thus allowing for a reduction of emissions that is compatible with economic development.

AFTER EMPIRE: POSTCOLONIAL POLITICS IN THE GLOBAL ERA

Even after the superpower rivalry of the Cold War collapsed, another legacy of the postwar era continued to shape international relations into the twenty-first century. The so-called postcolonial relationships between former colonies and Western powers emerged from the decolonization struggles detailed in Chapter 27. Former colonies, as well as other nations that had fallen under the political and economic sway of imperial powers, gained formal independence at the least, along with new kinds of cultural and political authority. In other respects, however, very little changed for people in the former colonies. In some cases the former colonizers or their local allies retained so much power that formal independence actually meant very little,

leading some to speak of a "neo-colonialism." In others, bloody independence struggles poisoned the political culture. The emergence of new states and new kinds of politics was sometimes propelled by economic goals, sometimes by the revival of cultural identities that preceded colonization, and in other cases by ethnic conflict. The results ranged from breakneck industrial success to ethnic slaughter, from democratization to new local models of absolutism. During the Cold War, these postcolonial regions were often the turf on which the superpower struggle was waged. They benefited from superpower patronage but also became the staging ground for proxy wars funded by the West in the fight against communism. Their various trajectories since 1989 point to the complex legacy of the imperial past in the post–Cold War world of globalization.

Emancipation and Ethnic Conflict in Africa

The legacies of colonialism have weighed heavily on sub-Saharan Africa. Most of the continent's former colonies came into their independence after the Second World War with their basic infrastructures deteriorating after decades of imperial negligence (see map on page 742 in Chapter 27). The Cold War decades brought scant improvement, as governments across the continent were plagued by both homegrown and externally imposed corruption, poverty, and civil war. In sub-Saharan Africa, two very different trends began to emerge around 1989, each shaped by a combination of the end of the Cold War and volatile local conditions.

The first trend can be seen in South Africa, where politics had revolved for decades around the brutal racial policies of apartheid, sponsored by the white minority government. The most prominent opponent of apartheid, Nelson Mandela, who led the African National Congress (ANC), had been imprisoned since 1962. Intense repression and violent conflict continued into the 1980s and reached a dangerous impasse by the end of the decade. Then the South African government chose a daring new tack: in early 1990 it released Mandela from prison. He resumed active leadership of the ANC and turned the party toward a combination of renewed public demonstrations and plans for negotiation. Politics changed within the Afrikaner-dominated white regime as well when F. W. de Klerk succeeded P. W. Botha as prime minister. A pragmatist who feared civil war and national collapse over the issue of apartheid, de Klerk was well matched to Mandela. In March 1992 the two men began direct talks to establish majority rule. Legal and constitutional reforms followed, and in May 1994, during

NELSON MANDELA VOTES IN SOUTH AFRICA'S FIRST FULLY DEMO-CRATIC ELECTIONS, 1994. He would be elected the country's president.

elections in which all South Africans took part, Nelson Mandela was chosen as the country's first black president. Although many of his government's efforts to reform housing, the economy, and public health foundered, Mandela defused the climate of organized racial violence. He also gained and kept tremendous personal popularity among black and white South Africans alike as a living symbol of a new political culture. Mandela's popularity extended to all of sub-Saharan Africa and worldwide. In a number of smaller postcolonial states such as Benin, Malawi, and Mozambique, the early 1990s brought political reforms that ended one-party or one-man rule in favor of parliamentary democracy and economic reform.

The other major trend ran in a different, less encouraging direction. Even as some former autocracies gave way to calls for pluralism, other states across the continent collapsed into ruthless ethnic conflict. In Rwanda, a former Belgian colony, conflicts between the Hutu and Tutsi populations erupted into a highly organized campaign of genocide against the Tutsis after the country's president was assassinated. Carried out by ordinary Hutus of all backgrounds, the ethnic slaughter left over 800,000 Tutsi dead in a matter of weeks. International pressure eventually turned local Rwandan politics against the perpetrators. Many of them fled to neighboring Zaire and became hired mercenaries in the many-sided civil war that followed the overthrow of Mobutu Sese Seko,

the country's long-time dictator, infamous for diverting billions of dollars in foreign aid into his personal bank accounts. A number of ambitious neighboring countries intervened in Zaire, hoping not only to secure its valuable resources but also to settle conflicts with their own ethnic minorities that spilled over the border. Fighting continued through the late 1990s into the new century, dubbed "Africa's world war" by many observers. Public services, normal trade, even basic health and safety inside Zaire—renamed the Democratic Republic of Congo by an ineffective government in Kinshasa—collapsed. With a death toll that reached into the millions from combat, massacre, and disease, the fighting remained unresolved in the next decade.

Economic Power on the Pacific Rim

By the end of the twentieth century, East Asia had become a center of industrial and manufacturing production. China, whose communist government began to establish commercial ties with the West in the 1970s, had become the world's leading heavy industrial producer by the year 2000. Its state-owned companies acquired contracts from Western firms to produce products cheaply and in bulk, for sale back to home markets in the United States and Europe. In a deliberate reversal of Europe's nineteenth-century intrusions on the China trade, Beijing established semicapitalist commercial zones around major port cities like Shanghai, a policy whose centerpiece was the transfer of sovereignty over Hong Kong from Britain to China in 1997. The commercial zones were intended to encourage massive foreign investment on terms that left China a favorable balance of trade for its huge volume of cheap exports.

Other Asian nations emerged as global commercial powers as well. Industry flourished in a string of countries, starting with Japan and extending along Asia's Pacific coastline into Southeast Asia and Oceania, during the decades after the Second World War. By the 1980s their robust industrial expansion and their apparent staying power earned them the collective nickname of "the Asian tigers," taken from the ambitious, forward-looking tiger in Chinese mythology. These Pacific Rim states collectively formed the most important industrial region in the world outside the United States and Europe. Among them, Japan not only led the way but also became the most influential model of success, with a postwar revival that eventually surpassed West Germany's economic miracle (see Chapter 28). Other East Asian nations, newer or less stable than Japan, tried to mimic its success.

Interpreting Visual Evidence

Media Representations of Globalization

Because the set of historical developments collectively known as *globalization* are so complex and because the local effects of these developments have often been felt as disruptions of well-entrenched habits or ways of life, debates about globalization are particularly open to manipulation through the presentation of charged imagery. Since the end of the Cold War, provocative images that capture certain aspects of the world's new interconnectedness—and the accompanying need for new kinds of boundaries—have become ubiquitous in the media. The movement of peoples and goods are variously defined as necessary to maintaining standards of living or as a threat to local jobs and local production. Globalization is defended as good for the economy, good for the consumer, and good for competition—but is also blamed for hurting workers, damaging the environment, destroying local cultures, and eroding long-standing definitions of national identity.

The images here all illustrate essential aspects of globalization. Image A shows ships waiting for loading and unloading at one of the largest container terminals in the world, in Hong Kong. Most of the shipping from China comes through this terminal. Image B shows family members separated by the border fence between the United States and Mexico in Mexicali, Mexico. In the twentieth century, Mexicali grew to be a city of 1.5 million people, in large part due to the prosperity generated

A. Cargo ships in Hong Kong's Kowloon Bay, 2002.

Some, such as South Korea and the Chinese Nationalist stronghold of Taiwan, treated the creation of prosperity as a fundamental patriotic duty. In postcolonial nations such as Malaysia and Indonesia, governments parlayed their natural resources and large local labor pools (which had made them attractive to imperial powers in earlier times) into investment for industrialization. As in China, the factories that emerged were either run as subsidiaries of Western companies or operated on their behalf in new multinational versions of the putting-out system of early industrialization.

The Pacific Rim's boom, however, also contained the makings of a first postwar "bust." During the 1990s a confluence of factors resulted in an enormous slowdown of growth and the near collapse of several currencies. Japan experienced rising production costs, overvalued stocks, rampant speculation on its high-priced real estate market, and the customary kickbacks that rewarded staunch corporate loyalty. Responses to the economic downturn varied widely. Japan launched programs of monetary austerity to cope with its first serious spike in unemployment in two generations. In South

B. Mexican family members talk through border fence, 2003.

C. Filipino protester on Labor Day, 2003.

by sending field workers across the border to the United States. Image C shows a Labor Day protester in Manila, Philippines, at a demonstration in which globalization was blamed for amendments to the labor code favorable to employers, a ban on strikes, and antiterrorist measures that were perceived to be an infringement on personal liberties. The medical mask is a reference to the SARS epidemic.

Questions for Analysis

1. Image A is typical of images that emphasize the economic consequences of globalization. Does globalization appear to be a force subject to human control in this image? How do such images shape perceptions of China's place in the global economy?

2. Compare images A and B. Is there a connection between the accelerating flows of money and goods between different parts of the world and restrictions on the movements of people?

3. In image C, the woman's medical mask names globalization as the enemy of Filipino workers. Who is being targeted by this protest? What does this say about the local contest over the conditions of labor in the Philippines?

Korea, an older generation that remembered economic catastrophe after the Korean War responded to national calls for sacrifice, frequently by investing their own savings to prop up ailing companies. In Indonesia, inflation and unemployment reignited sharp ethnic conflicts that prosperity and violent state repression had dampened in earlier times. This predominantly Muslim country, with a long tradition of tolerance and pluralism inside the faith, also saw outbursts of violent religious fundamentalism popularly associated with another region—the Middle East.

A NEW CENTER OF GRAVITY: ISRAEL, OIL, AND POLITICAL ISLAM IN THE MIDDLE EAST

Perhaps no other region has drawn more of the West's attention in the age of globalization than the Middle East, where a volatile combination of Western military, political, and economic interests converged with deep-seated regional conflicts and transnational Islamic politics. The results of this ongoing confrontation promise to shape the twenty-first century. Here we consider three of the most important aspects of recent history in the region. First is the unfolding of the Arab-Israeli conflict. Second is the region's development as the vital global center of oil production. The third emerges from inside the Arab world, largely as a reaction against the region's recent relations with the West. This is the development of a specific, modern brand of Islamic radicalism that challenges the legacies of imperialism and promises revolutionary and sometimes apocalyptic change in postcolonial nations, and whose most violent elements generate a cycle of fear, anger, and ultimately direct conflict with Western governments.

The Arab-Israeli Conflict

As we saw in Chapter 27, Israel's existence has been fraught from the start. The national aspirations of Jewish immigrants from Europe fleeing the Holocaust and violent postwar anti-Semitism clashed with the motives of pan-Arabists—secular, anticolonial nationalists who urged Arab pride and self-reliance against European domination. The 1967 war between Israel and its Arab neighbors led to Israeli occupation of the West Bank, the Golan Heights (near Syria), and the densely populated Gaza Strip on the border with Egypt. By the late 1990s, despite another war in 1973, it appeared that a generation of fighting might come to an end. American mediators began sponsoring talks to prevent further, sudden outbursts of conflict, while Soviet leaders remained neutral but did not discourage peace efforts. Most notably, the Egyptian president Anwar Sadat, who authorized and directed the 1973 war against Israel, decided that coexistence rather than the destruction of Israel was the long-term answer to regional conflict. Aided by the American president, Jimmy Carter, Sadat brokered a peace between Egypt and Israel's staunchly conservative leader, Menachem Begin, in 1978. Leaders on both sides of the conflict believed the potential rewards were greater than the obvious risks.

Hopes for a lasting peace were soon dashed. Hostilities escalated between Israel and the Palestinian Arabs displaced by Arab-Israeli warfare, a confrontation that increasingly polarized a much larger group of people. On each side of the Israeli-Palestinian conflict, a potent blend of ethnic and religious nationalism began to control both debate and action. Conservatives in Israel played to a public sentiment that put security ahead of other priorities, particularly among the most recent Jewish immigrants, many from the former Soviet Union. On the other side, younger Palestinians, angered by their elders' failures to provoke revolution, turned against the secular radicalism of the Palestinian Liberation Organization (PLO) and toward radical Islam.

In this combustible political environment, the Palestinians living on the West Bank and in the desperately overcrowded Gaza Strip revolted in an outburst of street rioting in 1987. This rebellion—called the *intifada* (literally, a "throwing off" or uprising)—continued for years in daily battles between stone-throwing Palestinian youths and armed Israeli security forces. The street fights escalated into cycles of Palestinian terrorism, particularly suicide bombings of civilian targets, and reprisals from the Israeli military. International efforts to broker a peace produced the Oslo Accords of 1993, which established an autonomous Palestinian Authority led by the PLO chief, Yasser Arafat. Yet the peace was always fragile at best—suffering perhaps fatal damage from the assassination of Israel's reformist prime minister Yitzhak Rabin in 1995 by a reactionary Israeli, and from continued attacks by Islamist terrorists. By the turn of the twenty-first century the cycle of violence flared again, with a "second intifada" launched by Palestinians in late 2000. Thus continued the war of riots and bombings fought by next-door neighbors.

In the first decade of the twenty-first century, the Israeli-Palestinian conflict has remained unresolved. The second *intifada* came to an end after Arafat's death in 2004 and the election of Mahmoud Abbas as the president of the Palestinian Authority in 2005. The electoral victory of a more militant Palestinian organization, Hamas, in the parliamentary elections of 2006, however, limited Abbas's power to negotiate with Israel. Meanwhile, continued attacks on Israel by Hamas—labeled a terrorist organization by the United States and the European Union—led to Israeli military operations in Gaza against Hamas in 2008–2009 and again in the summer of 2014, resulting in the deaths of over 3,000 Palestinian civilians in the two operations. In 2013 the UN General Assembly recognized the state of Palestine and granted it nonmember observer status, but an end to the crisis is still not in sight.

Oil, Power, and Economics

The struggles between the state of Israel and its neighbors have been important in their own right. Yet one of the most compelling reasons that this conflict mattered to outside powers was material: oil. The global demand for oil skyrocketed during the postwar era and has accelerated since. Starting with the consumer boom in the Cold War West, ordinary citizens bought cars and other petroleum-powered consumer durable goods, while industrial plastics made from petroleum by-products were used to manufacture a wealth of basic household items. Those needs, and the desires for profit and power that went with them, drew Western corporations and

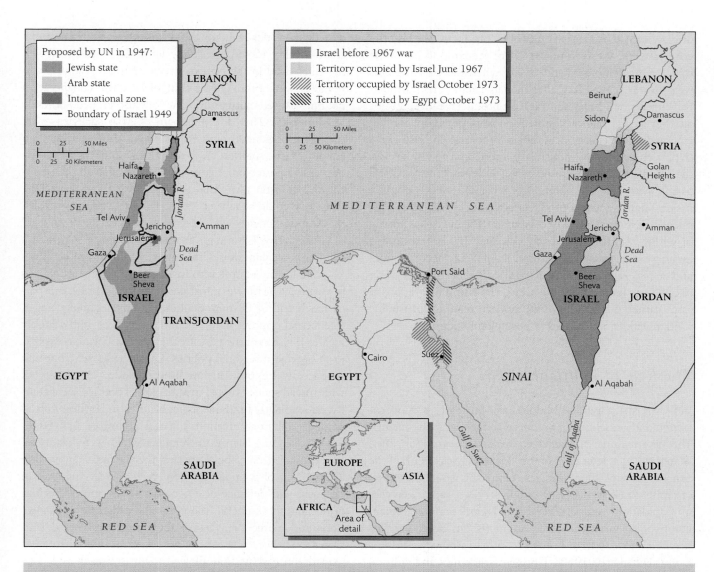

THE ARAB-ISRAELI WARS OF 1967 AND 1973. ▪ *What were the major changes in the political geography of the Middle East as a result of the Arab-Israeli conflict of 1967?* ▪ *Why did the Israelis wish to occupy the Sinai and West Bank regions at the end of the 1967 war?* ▪ *What problems did this create, and how might it have led to the conflict in 1973?*

governments steadily toward the oil-rich states of the Middle East, whose vast reserves were discovered in the 1930s and 1940s. Large corporations conducted joint diplomacy with Middle Eastern states and their own home governments to design concessions for drilling, refining, and shipping the oil. Pipelines were laid by contractors based around the world, from California to Rome to Russia.

The enormous long-term economic value of the Middle Eastern oil reserves made oil a fundamental tool in new struggles over political power. Many producer states sought to turn their resources into leverage with the West's former imperial powers. In 1960, the leading Middle Eastern, African, and Latin American producers banded together in a cartel to take advantage of this vital resource, forming the Organization of the Petroleum Exporting Countries (OPEC) to regulate the production and pricing of crude oil. During the 1970s, OPEC played a leading role in the global economy. Its policies reflected not only the desire to draw maximum profits out of bottlenecks in oil production but also the militant politics of some OPEC leaders who wanted to use oil as a weapon against the West in the Arab-Israeli conflict. After the 1973 Arab-Israeli war, an embargo inspired by the hard-liners sparked spiraling inflation and economic troubles in Western nations, triggering a cycle of dangerous recession that lasted nearly a decade.

In response, Western governments treated the Middle Eastern oil regions as a vital strategic center of gravity, the subject of constant Great Power diplomacy. If conflict directly threatened the stability of oil production or friendly governments, Western powers were prepared to intervene by force, as demonstrated in 1991 when the United States went to war against Iraq after the latter nation had invaded Kuwait, a small but important oil producer. By the 1990s another new front of competition and potential conflict emerged as the energy demands of other nations also grew. In particular, the new industrial giants China and India eyed the Middle Eastern oil reserves with the same nervousness as the West. The oil boom also generated violent conflict inside Middle Eastern producer states as oil revenues produced uneven economic development. The huge gaps among or within Middle Eastern societies that divided oil's haves and have-nots caused deep resentments, official corruption, and a new wave of radical politics. With the pan-Arab nationalists fading from the scene, the rising revolutionary force gathered instead around modern readings of Islamic fundamentalism, now tied to postcolonial politics.

The Rise of Political Islam

In North Africa and the Middle East, processes of modernization and globalization produced tremendous discontents. The new nations that emerged from decolonization often shared the characteristics of the "kleptocracies" south of the Sahara: corrupt state agencies, cronyism based on ethnic or family kinship, decaying public services, rapid increases in population, and constant state repression of dissent. Disappointment with these conditions ran deep, perhaps nowhere more so than in the seat of pan-Arabism, Nasser's Egypt. During the 1960s, Egyptian academics and cultural critics leveled charges against Nasser's regime that became the core of a powerful new political movement. Their critique offered modern interpretations of certain legal and political currents in Islamic thought, ideas linked loosely across centuries by their association with revolt against foreign interference and official corruption. They denounced Egypt's nationalist government as greedy, brutal, and corrupt.

There was a twist to their claims, however: that the roots of the Arab world's moral failure lay in centuries of colonial contact with the West. The most influential of these Islamist critics, Sayyid Qutb (*KUH-tub*, 1906–1966), presented these ideas in a series of essays for which he was arrested several times by Egyptian authorities and ultimately executed. His argument ran as follows. As a result of corrupting outside influences, the ruling elites of the new Arab states pursued policies that frayed local and family bonds, deepening economic divides while abandoning the government's responsibility for charity and stability. What was more, the nation's elites were morally bankrupt—their lives defied codes of morality, self-discipline, and communal responsibility rooted in Islamic faith. To maintain power, the elites lived in the pockets of Western imperial and corporate powers. From Qutb's point of view, this collaboration not only caused cultural impurity but also eroded authentic Muslim faith. This dire judgment of Arab societies—that they were poisoned from without and within—required an equally drastic solution. Arab societies should reject not only oppressive postcolonial governments but also all the political and cultural ideas that traveled with them, especially those that could be labeled "Western." After popular revolts, the Arab autocracies would be replaced by an idealized form of conservative Islamic government—a system in which a rigid form of Islam would link law, government, and culture.

In a formula familiar to historians of European politics throughout the nineteenth and twentieth centuries, this particular brand of Islamist politics combined popular anger, intellectual opposition to "foreign" influences, and a highly idealized vision of the past. By the 1970s it began to express itself openly in regional politics. Qutb's ideas were put into practice by Egypt's Muslim Brotherhood, a secretive but widespread society rooted in anticolonial politics, local charity, and violently fundamentalist Islam. Similar ideas spread among similar organizations in other urbanized Arab countries and leading Islamic universities, which were historically centers of debate about political theory and religious law. These forms of political Islam emerged as a driving force in criticism and defiance of autocratic Arab regimes. Secular critics and more-liberal Islamists, who called for open elections and a free press, were more fragmented and thus easier to silence, whereas the new wave of fundamentalists gained concessions that allowed them to preach and publish in public so long as they did not launch actual revolts. In Egypt, where an Islamic militant assassinated President Anwar Sadat in 1981, the Muslim Brotherhood eventually renounced violence. Meanwhile, political Islam's defining moment came in an unexpected place: Iran.

IRAN'S ISLAMIC REVOLUTION

Iran offered one of the most dramatic examples of modernization gone sour in the Middle East. Despite tremendous economic growth in the 1960s and 1970s, Iranians labored with legacies of foreign intervention and corrupt rule at the hands of the shah, Reza Pahlavi, a Western-friendly leader installed during a 1953 military coup supported by Britain and the United States. In exchange for the shah's role as a friend to the West during the Cold War and for providing a steady source of reasonably priced oil, the Iranian government received vast sums in oil contracts, weapons, and development aid. Thousands of Westerners, especially Americans,

GAMAL ABDEL NASSER AND SOVIET MINISTER ALEKSEY KOSYGIN, 1966. As the most prominent spokesman for secular pan-Arabism, Nasser became a target for Islamist critics, such as Sayyid Qutb and the Muslim Brotherhood, angered by the Western-influenced policies of his regime.

came to Iran, introducing foreign influences that not only challenged traditional values but also offered economic and political alternatives. The shah, however, kept these alternatives out of reach, consistently denying democratic representation to Westernizing middle-class Iranian workers and deeply religious university students alike. He governed through a small aristocracy riven by constant infighting. His army and secret police conducted regular and brutal campaigns of repression. Despite all this, and the public protests it spurred in the West, governments such as the conservative Nixon administration embraced the shah as a strategically vital ally: a key to anti-Soviet alliances and a safe source of oil.

Twenty-five years after the 1953 coup, the shah's autocratic route to an industrial state ended. After a lengthy economic downturn, public unrest, and personal illness, the shah realized he could not continue in power. He retired from public life under popular pressure in February 1979. Eight months of uncertainty followed, most Westerners fled the country, and the provisional government appointed by the shah collapsed. The strongest political coalition among Iran's revolutionaries surged into the vacuum—a broad-based Islamic movement centered on the ayatollah Ruhollah Khomeini (1902–1989), Iran's senior cleric and leading Shi'ite theologian, returned from exile in France. Other senior clerics and the country's large population of unemployed, deeply religious university students provided the movement's energy. Disenfranchised secular protesters joined the radical Islamists in condemning decades of Western indifference and the shah's oppression. Under the new regime, some limited economic and political populism

combined with strict constructions of Islamic law, restrictions on women's public life, and the prohibition of many ideas or activities linked to Western influence.

The new Iranian government also defined itself against its enemies: as Shi'ites, they criticized the Sunni religious establishment of neighboring Muslim nations; they also criticized "atheistic" Soviet communism, and were especially critical of Israel and the United States. Iranians feared that the United States would try to overthrow Khomeini as it had other leaders. Violence in the streets of Tehran reached a peak when militant students stormed the American embassy in November 1979 and seized fifty-two hostages. The act quickly became an international crisis that heralded a new kind of confrontation between Western powers and postcolonial Islamic radicals. Democratic president Jimmy Carter's administration ultimately gained the hostages' release, but not before the catalog of earlier failures led to the election of the Republican Ronald Reagan.

Iran, Iraq, and Unintended Consequences of the Cold War

Iran's victory in the hostage crisis was fleeting. During the later part of 1980, Iran's Arab neighbor and traditional rival Iraq invaded, hoping to seize Iran's southern oil fields during the revolutionary confusion. Iran counterattacked. The result was a murderous eight-year conflict marked by the use of chemical weapons and human waves of young Iranian radicals fighting the Soviet-armed Iraqis. The war ended in stalemate with Iran's theocratic regime intact. In the short term, their long defense of Iranian nationalism left the clerics more entrenched at home, while abroad they used oil revenues to back grass-roots radicals in Lebanon and elsewhere who engaged in anti-Western terrorism. The strongest threats to the Iranian regime ultimately came from within, from a new generation of young students and disenfranchised service workers who found their prospects for prosperity and active citizenship had not changed much since the days of the shah.

The Iran-Iraq conflict created another problem for Western interests and the governments of leading OPEC states: Iraq. Various governments—including an unlikely alliance of France, Saudi Arabia, the Soviet Union, and the United States—supported Iraq during the war in an effort to bring down Iran's clerics. Their patronage went to one of the most violent governments in the region, Saddam Hussein's dictatorship. Iraq exhausted itself in the war, politically and economically. To shore up his regime and restore Iraq's influence, Hussein looked elsewhere in the region. In 1990 Iraq invaded its small, oil-rich neighbor Kuwait. With the Cold War on the wane, Iraq's Soviet supporters would not condone

The Place of Islam in Modern Societies

The end of the colonial era and the impact of postcolonial migrations provided the backdrop for a renewed discussion in Europe and the Middle East about the presence of Muslim peoples in European nations and the relationship of religion to politics in traditionally Muslim societies. Among Muslim scholars and clerics, a wide range of opinions has been expressed about the place of Islam in the modern world, and the two figures here represent two distinct voices within this discussion.

Born into a family of Shi'ite Muslim religious leaders, Ruhollah Khomeini (1902–1989) was recognized as the leading Iranian religious authority in the 1950s. He represented a highly conservative Islamic fundamentalism intended to unite Iranian Muslims in violent opposition to the Western-supported government of the shah of Iran, and he continues to have a powerful influence on Muslims seeking an alternative to Western cultural, political, and economic domination.

Tariq Ramadan (born in 1962 in Geneva, Switzerland) is a professor of religion and philosophy, and a leading voice speaking for the increasingly large number of Muslims who live in Europe and North America—members of a religious minority in non-Muslim societies. He has taught at the University of Fribourg, the College de Saussure in Geneva, and St. Antony's College, Oxford. In 2004 he was forced to decline an offer to become a professor at the University of Notre Dame in the United States when the State Department denied him a visa. Ramadan argues that Muslims can and should be productive and active citizens in Western societies while remaining true to their religious beliefs.

Ruhollah Khomeini, *Islamic Government* (1979)

The Islamic government is not similar to the well-known systems of government. It is not a despotic government in which the head of state dictates his opinion and tampers with the lives and property of the people. The prophet, may God's prayers be upon him, and 'Ali, the amir of the faithful, and the other imams had no power to tamper with people's property or with their lives.[1] The Islamic government is not despotic but constitutional. However, it is not constitutional in the well-known sense of the word, which is represented in the parliamentary system or in the people's councils. It is constitutional in the sense that those in charge of affairs observe a number of conditions and rules underlined in the Koran and in the Sunna and represented in the necessity of observing the system and of applying the dictates and laws of Islam.[2] This is why the Islamic government is the government of the divine law. The difference between the Islamic government and the constitutional governments, both monarchic and republican, lies in the fact that the people's representatives or the king's representatives are the ones who codify and legislate, whereas the power of legislation is confined to God, may He be praised, and nobody else has the right to legislate and nobody may rule by that which has not been given power by God. . . .

The government of Islam is not monarchic, . . . and not an empire, because Islam is above squandering and unjustly undermining the lives and property of people. This is why the government of Islam does not have the many big palaces, the servants, the royal courts, the crown prince courts, and other trivial requirements that consume half or most of the country's resources and that the sultans and the emperors have. The life of the great prophet was a life of utter simplicity, even though the prophet was the head of the state, who ran and ruled it by himself. . . . Had this course continued until the present, people would have known the taste of happiness and the country's treasury would not have been plundered to be spent on fornication, abomination, and the court's costs and expenditures. You know that most of the corrupt aspects of our society are due to the corruption of the ruling dynasty and the royal family. What is the legitimacy of these rulers who build houses of entertainment, corruption, fornication, and abomination and who destroy houses which God ordered be raised and in which His name is mentioned? Were it not for what the court wastes and what it embezzles, the country's budget would not experience any deficit that forces the state to borrow from America and England, with all the humiliation and insult that accompany such borrowing. Has our oil decreased or have our minerals that are stored under this good earth run out? We possess everything and we would not need the help of America or of others if it were not for the costs of the court and for its wasteful use of the people's money.

[1] "The prophet" refers to Muhammed; 'Ali was Muhammed's son-in-law and, according to the Shi'ite tradition, his legitimate heir; an amir is a high military official; and an imam, in the Shi'ite tradition, is an important spiritual leader with the sole power to make decisions about doctrine.

[2] The Koran (Qu'ran) is the book of the holy scriptures of Islam; the Sunna is the body of customary Islamic law second only to the Koran in authority.

Source: Ruhollah Khomeini, *Islamic Government*, trans. Joint Publications Research Service (New York: 1979).

Tariq Ramadan, Western Muslims and the Future of Islam (2002)

... With the emergence of the young Muslim generation ... it has been deemed necessary to reanalyze the main Islamic sources (Qu'ran and Sunnah) when it comes to interpreting legal issues (*fiqh*) in the European context. Many of these young people intend to stay permanently in a European country, and a large number have already received their citizenship. New forms of interpretation (known as *ijtihad*) have made it possible for the younger generation to practice their faith in a coherent manner in a new context. It is important to note that this has been a very recent phenomenon. Only within the past few years have Muslim scholars and intellectuals felt obliged to take a closer look at the European laws, and at the same time, to think about the changes that have been taking place within the diverse Muslim communities. ... Five main points ... have been agreed upon by those working on the basis of the Islamic sources and by the great majority of Muslims living in Europe:

1. Muslims who are residents or citizens of a non-Islamic state should understand that they are under a moral and social contract with the country in which they reside. In other words, they should respect the laws of the country.
2. Both the spirit and the letter of the secular model permit Muslims to practice their faith without requiring a complete assimilation into the new culture and, thereby, partial disconnection from their Muslim identity.
3. The ancient division of the world into denominations of *dar al-harb* (abode of war) and *dar al-Islam* (abode of Islam), used by the jurists during a specific geopolitical context, namely the ninth-century Muslim world, is

invalid and does not take into account the realities of modern life. Other concepts have been identified as exemplifying more positively the presence of Muslims in Europe.

4. Muslims should consider themselves full citizens of the nations in which they reside and can participate with conscience in the organizational, economic, and political affairs of the country without compromising their own values.
5. With regard to the possibilities offered by European legislation, nothing stops Muslims, like any other citizens, from making choices that respond to the requirements of their own consciences and faith. If any obligations should be in contradiction to the Islamic principles (a situation that is quite rare), the specific case must be studied in order to identify the priorities and the possibility of adaptation (which should be developed at the national level). ...

For some Muslims, the idea of an "Islamic culture," similar to the concepts of identity and community, connotes the necessity of Muslim isolation from and rejection of European culture. Such an understanding suggests that Muslims are not genuine in their desire to integrate into the society in which they live. They play the citizenship card, while trying to maintain such cultural particularities as dress code, management of space when it comes to men and women, concern about music, and other issues. For them, real integration means becoming European in every aspect of one's character and behavior. This is, in fact, a very narrow vision of integration, almost resembling the notion of assimilation.

One admits theoretically that Muslims have the right to practice their religion but revokes these rights when expression of faith becomes too *visible*.

In actuality, the future of Muslim presence in Europe must entail a truly "European Islamic culture" disengaged from the cultures of North Africa, Turkey, and Indo-Pakistan, while naturally referring to them for inspiration. This new culture is just in the process of being born and molded. By giving careful consideration to everything from appropriate dress to the artistic and creative expression of Islam, Muslims are mobilizing a whole new culture. The formation of such a culture is a pioneering endeavor, making use of European energy while taking into account various national customs and simultaneously respecting Islamic values and guidelines.

Source: Tariq Ramadan, "Islam and Muslims in Europe: A Silent Revolution toward Rediscovery," in *Muslims in the West: From Sojourners to Citizens*, ed. Yvonne Yazbeck Haddad (New York: 2002), pp. 160–63.

Questions for Analysis

1. What prevents Islamic government from being despotic, according to Khomeini? Why is there no legislative branch in an Islamic government, in his view?

2. What criticism does Ramadan make of those Muslims who seek to isolate themselves from European culture while living in Europe? What does he mean by "European Islamic culture"?

3. In what ways do these two Muslim thinkers show an engagement with European traditions of political thought?

Iraqi aggression. A coalition of nations led by the United States reacted forcefully. Within months Iraq faced the full weight of the United States military—trained intensively since Vietnam to face much more capable Soviet-armed forces than Iraq's—along with forces from several OPEC states, French troops, and armored divisions from Britain, Egypt, and Syria. This coalition pummeled Iraqi troops from the air for six weeks, then routed them and retook Kuwait in a brief, well-executed ground campaign. This changed the tenor of relations between the United States and Arab oil producers, encouraging not only closeness between governments but also the anti-Americanism of radicals angry at a newly expanded Western presence. It was also the beginning rather than the end of Western confrontation with Iraq in response to Hussein's efforts to develop nuclear and biological weapons.

Elsewhere in the region, the proxy conflicts of the Cold War snared both superpowers in the new and growing networks of Islamic radicalism. In 1979 the socialist government of Afghanistan turned against its Soviet patrons. Fearing a result like Iran, with a spread of fundamentalism into the Muslim regions of Soviet Central Asia, Moscow responded by overthrowing the Afghan president and installing a pro-Soviet faction. The new government, backed by more than a hundred thousand Soviet troops, found itself immediately at war with fighters who combined local conservatism with militant Islam and who attracted volunteers from radical Islamic movements in Egypt, Lebanon, Saudi Arabia, and elsewhere. These fighters, who called themselves *mujahidin*—Arabic for "holy warriors"—benefited from advanced weapons and training, supplied by Western powers led by the United States. Those who provided the aid saw the conflict in Cold War terms, as a chance to sap Soviet resources in a fruitless imperial war. On those terms the aid worked; the war dragged on for nearly ten years, taking thousands of Russian lives and damaging the Soviet government's credibility at home. Soviet troops withdrew in 1989. After five years of clan warfare, hard-line Islamic factions tied to the foreign elements in the mujahidin took over the country. Their experiment in theocracy would make Iran's seem mild by comparison.

VIOLENCE BEYOND BOUNDS: WAR AND TERRORISM IN THE TWENTY-FIRST CENTURY

The global networks of communication, finance, and mobility discussed at the beginning of this chapter gave radical political violence a disturbing new character at the end of the twentieth century. In the 1960s, organized,

sectarian terrorist tactics had become an important part of political conflict in the Middle East, Europe, and Latin America. Most of these early terrorist organizations (including the Irish Republican Army, the Italian Red Brigades, and the different Palestinian revolutionary organizations) had specific goals, such as ethnic separatism or the establishment of revolutionary governments. By the 1980s and increasingly during the 1990s, such groups were complemented and then supplanted by a different brand of terrorist organization, one that ranged freely across territory and local legal systems. These newer, apocalyptic terrorist groups called for decisive conflict to eliminate their enemies and gain themselves martyrdom. Some such groups emerged from the social dislocations of the postwar boom, while others were linked directly to brands of radical religion. They often divorced themselves from the local crises that first spurred their anger, roaming widely among countries in search of recruits to their cause.

A leading example of such groups, and soon the most famous, was the radical Islamist umbrella organization al Qaeda. It was created by leaders of the foreign mujahidin who had fought against the Soviet Union in Afghanistan. Its official leader and financial supporter was the Saudi-born multimillionaire Osama bin Laden. Among its operational chiefs was the famous Egyptian radical Ayman al-Zawahiri, whose political career linked him directly to Sayyid Qutb and other founding thinkers in modern revolutionary Islam. These leaders organized broad networks of largely self-contained terrorist cells around the world, from the Islamic regions of Southeast Asia to Europe, East Africa, and the United States, funded by myriad private accounts, front companies, illegal trades, and corporate kickbacks throughout the global economy. Their organization defied borders, and so did their goals. They did not seek to negotiate for territory, or to change the government of a specific state. Instead, they spoke of the destruction of the state of Israel and American, European, and other non-Islamic systems of government worldwide and called for a united, apocalyptic revolt by fundamentalist Muslims to create an Islamic community bounded only by faith. During the 1990s they involved themselves in a variety of local terrorist campaigns in Islamic countries and organized large-scale suicide attacks against American targets, notably the American embassies in Kenya and Tanzania in 1998.

At the beginning of the twenty-first century, al Qaeda's organizers struck again at their most obvious political enemy, the symbolic seat of globalization: the United States. Small teams of suicidal radicals, aided by al Qaeda's organization, planned to hijack airliners and use them as flying bombs to strike the most strategically important symbols of America's global power. On September 11, 2001, they

TWENTY-FIRST CENTURY TERRORISM. New York's World Trade Center Towers under attack on September 11, 2001.

carried out this mission in the deadliest series of terrorist attacks ever to occur on American soil. In the space of an hour, hijacked planes struck the Pentagon, the headquarters of the U.S. military, and the World Trade Center towers in New York City. A fourth plane, possibly aimed at the U.S. Capitol, crashed in open farmland in Pennsylvania, its attack thwarted when the passengers fought back against their captors. The World Trade Center towers, among the tallest buildings in the world, crumbled into ash and wreckage in front of hundreds of millions of viewers on satellite television and the Internet. In these several simultaneous attacks more than 3,000 people died.

The attacks were at once a new brand of terror, deeply indebted to globalization in both its outlook and its method, and something older: the extreme, opportunistic violence of marginal groups against national cultures during a period of general dislocation and uncertainty. The immediate American response was action against al Qaeda's central haven in Afghanistan, a state in near collapse after the warfare of the previous thirty years. The United States' versatile professional soldiers and unmatched equipment, along with armed Afghan militias angry at the country's disarray quickly routed al Qaeda's Taliban sponsors and scattered the terrorists. The search for Osama bin Laden took a decade, during which time the United States and its allies in the war in Afghanistan faced a renewed insurrection by the Taliban that began in 2003. U.S. forces killed Osama bin Laden at his sanctuary in nearby Pakistan in 2011.

During the intervening years, the United States succeeded in disrupting, though not completely eliminating, many of the hidden networks of leadership, finance, and information that made al Qaeda's apocalyptic terrorism possible. Meanwhile, the economic and political rebuilding of Afghanistan, a necessary consequence of American and European military action, began from almost nothing in terms of administration and infrastructure. These efforts were hampered by challenging political circumstances within the country, which made it difficult for the Afghan government to position itself between its U.S. ally and a population with a long tradition of mistrusting foreign powers intervening in their land. At the beginning of 2015, thousands of foreign troops remained in Afghanistan, including 10,000 soldiers. In spite of their presence, the stability of the nation after more than three decades of war remains an open question.

One reason for the persistent fears about groups such as al Qaeda has to do with the increasing power and availability of the weapons that they might use: chemical substances, biological agents that could kill millions, even portable nuclear weapons. With the end of the Cold War, methods and technologies that the superpowers employed to maintain their nuclear balance of power became available to displaced groups with the financial or political leverage to seek them out. Arms races in other contested areas, such as Israel/Palestine or India/Pakistan have helped spread the development of production sites and resources for weapons of horrific power beyond the control of superpowers.

Fear that the Iraqi government of Saddam Hussein was reaching for biological and nuclear capabilities helped propel the Gulf War of 1991 and efforts to disarm Iraq thereafter. Fear that Iraq had been involved with the terrorists who perpetrated the 9/11 attacks on New York City and Washington, D.C., provided the rationale for an American-led invasion of Iraq in 2003. The campaign, which used a remarkably small force both on the ground and in the air, quickly seized Iraq and deposed Saddam Hussein. No evidence of recent, active, weapons development programs was found, however, and in the process the United States inherited the complex reconstruction of a broken state that was further fractured by guerrilla violence and anti-Western terrorism. The last U.S. troops left Iraq in 2011, but ongoing civil conflict there has led to thousands of deaths. In August 2014, President Obama sent military advisors and ordered airstrikes to prevent further territorial gains from a new Islamist movement that threatens the Iraqi government, known as the Islamic State of Iraq and al-Sham (ISIS), that seeks to unify radical Islamists across the Middle East.

for twentieth-century Indians, Vietnamese, and Algerians—to name just a few—fighting for national independence was the way to secure the rights of citizens. National sovereignty, once achieved, was tightly woven into the fabric of politics and international relations and would not be easily relinquished.

The world wars marked a turning point. The First World War, an unprecedented global conflict, almost inevitably fostered dreams of global peace under the auspices of international organizations. The Peace of Paris aimed for more than a territorial settlement: with the League of Nations it tried, tentatively, to establish an organization that would transcend the power of individual nations and uphold the (ill-defined) principles of "civilization." (Despite this commitment, the League bowed to British and American objections to a statement condemning racial discrimination.) The experiment failed: the fragile League was swept aside by the surge of extreme nationalism and aggression in the 1930s. The shock and revulsion at the atrocities of the war that followed, however, brought forth more decisive efforts. The Second World War's aftermath saw the establishment of the United Nations, an International Court of Justice at the Hague (Netherlands), and the UN's High Commission on Human Rights. Unlike anything attempted after the First World War, the Commission on Human Rights set out to establish the rights of individuals—against the nation-state.

This Universal Declaration of Human Rights, published by the High Commission in 1948, became the touchstone of our modern notion of human rights. It was very much a product of its time. Its authors included Eleanor Roosevelt and the French jurist René Cassin, who had been wounded in the First World War (and held his intestines together during a nearly 400-mile train ride to medical treatment), lost his family in the Holocaust, and had seen his nation collaborate with the Nazis. The High Commission argued that the war and the "barbarous acts which have outraged the conscience of mankind" showed that no state should have absolute power over its citizens. The Universal Declaration prohibited torture, cruel punishment, and slavery. A separate convention, also passed in 1948, dealt with the newly defined crime of genocide. The Universal Declaration of 1948 built on earlier declarations that universalized the rights to legal equality, freedom of religion and speech, and the right to participate in government. Finally, it reflected the postwar period's effort to put democracy on a more solid footing by establishing *social* rights—to education, work, a "just and favorable remuneration," a "standard of living," and social security, among others.

Few nations were willing to ratify the Universal Declaration of Human Rights. For decades after the war, its idealistic principles could not be reconciled with British and French colonialism, American racial segregation, or Soviet dictatorship. For as long as wars to end colonialism continued, declarations of universal principles rang hollow. For as long as the Cold War persisted, human rights seemed only a thinly veiled weapon in the sparring between the superpowers. After decolonization and the end of the Cold War, however, the legitimacy and luster of human rights seemed enhanced. Global communications and media dramatically expanded the membership and influence of organizations that, like Amnesty International (founded in 1961), operated outside the economic or political boundaries of the nation-state. Memories of the Second World War, long buried by the Cold War, helped to drive the creation of the International Criminal Tribunals for Yugoslavia and Rwanda in 1993, providing a context for protecting human rights in ways that nation-states themselves could not.

It is nevertheless the case that the troubled era that began with the 9/11 attacks on the United States in 2001 has seen many challenges to the notion of universal human rights. Terrorism, no matter what the ideology of the perpetrator, is a fundamental violation of every human's right to safety and security. In their zeal to deter terrorists, meanwhile, many nations in the world have tacitly turned away from the emerging international legal structures that attempted to defend the rights of all individuals everywhere. The struggle that the United States and its allies waged against al Qaeda and the Taliban leadership has raised difficult questions about the tactics used, which included torture, indefinite detention without trial, and the use of pilotless drones to kill suspected militant leaders in distant countries. The use of drone technologies makes it easier to avoid U.S. casualties in operations against a dangerous enemy, but many in the United States and abroad have expressed concern about the government's right to identify, target, and execute individuals, including in some cases U.S. citizens, based on criteria that are never subject to independent legal review. Public support for torture has actually increased significantly in the United States since 2005, but public anger in Afghanistan and Pakistan has focused on cases of mistaken identity and the deaths of family members and bystanders in drone attacks. Even within the U.S. government and military, some have expressed concern that these methods could be counterproductive in the long term.

As the U.S. and European government pursue their interests abroad, debates about the use of military power in other parts of the world and the form that this power takes have become pressing concerns, and the issues turn on questions that have been a central part of the liberal democratic political tradition ever since it emerged in opposition to monarchist forms of government in the seventeenth century. How should a nation determine the balance between individual freedoms and national security? What forms of force or violence can the state legitimately use against its enemies at home or abroad? What kinds of information about its citizenry should a government be allowed to keep? Are the terrorist threats that democratic regimes routinely face today so serious that they justify the suspension of internationally recognized human rights? No easy answers to these questions exist—but the answers that governments and societies in Europe and the United States give to them will shape how people everywhere perceive the legitimacy of the democratic political institutions that they claim to represent.

EUROPE AND THE UNITED STATES IN THE TWENTY-FIRST CENTURY

As the first decade of the twenty-first century drew to a close, the initial confidence that Europeans felt in the aftermath of the revolutions of 1989 seemed badly shaken. The process of European integration, which had contributed so much to the political stability of Europe in the decades after the Second World War, seemed to have reached its limits in the East. Although a few independent nations that were formerly a part of the Soviet Union, such as Ukraine, might be interested in joining the European Union, it is unlikely that Russia would be comfortable with this realignment toward the West. Even the future membership of Turkey, an official candidate for entry into the EU since 1999 and an associate member of the European Union since 1963, remains uncertain because of growing discomfort in many European nations about admitting a historically Muslim nation into Europe. Turkey is a modern industrial nation that participated in the Marshall Plan after the Second World War, was a member of the Council of Europe in 1949, and became a member of NATO in 1952. A 2010 poll carried out in five European countries nevertheless found that 52 percent of respondents were opposed to Turkish membership in the European Union, and only 41 percent in favor.

In the economic realm, the global financial crisis of 2007–10 caused many in Europe and North America to rethink the central assumptions of late-twentieth-century neoliberalism, especially the belief that markets were by definition self-regulating. The crisis had its origins in a classic bubble in global housing prices, which encouraged banks to make ever-riskier bets in the real estate market, while also experimenting with the sale of complicated securities whose risk became impossible to gauge with accuracy. When housing prices fell, many key banks in different parts of the world found themselves unable to state clearly the value of their plummeting investments tied to real estate. Since nobody knew how much money the largest financial institutions had, banks simply stopped lending money to one another, and in the resulting liquidity crisis many businesses failed and trillions of dollars of consumer savings were wiped out. Massive government bailouts of the largest banks with taxpayer money were required to stabilize the global financial system, and popular resentment against the financial industry stimulated many nations to consider widespread reform and government regulation of banks as a result.

Contemporary debates about political integration in Europe or the benefits of free-market capitalism are closely connected with the developments that followed the end of the Cold War in the early 1990s and the period of economic globalization that followed, but they can also be seen as a continuation of debates within the traditions of political and economic liberalism that go back to the eighteenth century. In its classic formulation as put forth by liberal theorists such as Adam Smith, political and economic liberties were best defended in a nation that possessed a small and limited government. The closely related traditions of social democracy that developed in Europe in the nineteenth and twentieth century, on the other hand, arose out of a concern that limited governments in the classic liberal mold could not do enough to remedy the inequalities that emerged from modern industrial societies, and the result was the creation of welfare-state institutions that aimed to use the power of the state to maintain a base level of social and economic equality. This tension between the goals of liberty and equality is a constant one within the liberal tradition, and the different trajectories of Europe and the United States in the twentieth century reflect the respective priorities of successive governments in both places.

Many Europeans, therefore, watched the election of Barack Obama to the presidency of the United States in 2008 with great interest. Since the election of Ronald Reagan in 1980, the divergences between governments in the United States and Europe in their attitudes toward the role that the state might play in remedying social problems had become even wider. With few exceptions, European governments were much more willing to use the power of the state to assist the unemployed or the aged, to support families, and to provide subsidies for education, public transportation, and national programs for health care. As we have seen, this consensus emerged in part because of a belief that the economic dislocations of the 1920s and 1930s had led directly to the emergence of destabilizing and antidemocratic extremist political movements. In the United States, on the other hand, widespread discontent with attempts by the Johnson administration in the 1960s to use the power of the federal government to end racial segregation and address broad problems such as urban poverty and environmental pollution contributed to a conservative backlash in the 1980s and 1990s. Throughout those years, conservatives in the United States called for an end to welfare programs, repeal of environmental regulations, and reduced government oversight in the marketplace.

Obama's election in 2008, following on the heels of the financial meltdown earlier the same year, seemed to mark a turning point of sorts in American politics, as his pragmatic campaign was predicated on a claim that government itself was not the problem facing industrial democracies at the outset of the twenty-first century. The Obama administration's ambitious plan to overhaul the health care system faced stiff opposition from many quarters, but a compromise package succeeded in passing the Congress and was signed into law in 2010. Obama's reelection in 2012 led to the implementation of the law's first measures. The fierceness of the health care debate—which revolved around questions about the power of the state, the responsibilities of elected officials, the nature of the public good, and the balance between liberty and equality—should not obscure the fact that partisans on both sides of these controversies use a vocabulary and a set of references that are part of the same liberal democratic political traditions that emerged in Europe and North America in the previous two centuries.

If Obama's two-term presidency has given some hope to those who see an important role for the state in solving persistent social problems, the situation in Europe in the aftermath of the 2008 financial crisis has been less comforting. The European postwar welfare state was based on a combination of Marshall Plan investment, European economic integration, and cooperation among representatives of labor, employers, and the state. Trade unions agreed to limit their wage demands in exchange for social protections from the state. Business leaders agreed to higher taxes in exchange for labor peace. Government officials convinced their electorates to pay higher taxes in exchange for universal health care, unemployment payments, and old-age pensions.

This system worked well as long as the economy kept growing. When the economy flattened out in the 1970s, however, businesses reduced their investments, unemployment went up, workers expressed discontent with their former restraint on wage demands, and European states had less revenue to pay for social protections. They resorted to deficit spending in the 1980s and 1990s to maintain the welfare state, and this system worked well enough—as long as banks were confident that the loans they extended to the European governments would be repaid. Faith in the system led to the creation of the Eurozone as a single-currency area in 2002.

After the financial crisis of 2008, however, the delicate balance in Europe between banks and governments began to crumble. European banks that were already fragile from losses in the real estate bubble demanded extraordinarily high interest rates before they would loan money to governments that were in financial trouble. The crisis was most acute in Greece, Spain, Italy, Ireland, and Portugal, where government debt reached threatening levels.

So far, the solution has been for the stronger economies in the Eurozone to bail out the weaker economies by providing emergency funds. To receive these funds, however, the indebted governments are forced to accept steep cuts in state spending, which are deeply unpopular with their populations. The ensuing political crisis has led some to think that the Eurozone might not survive in its present form. If that happens, it will mark a significant turning point in the history of European integration, which has provided a template for thinking about the European future since the years after the Second World War.

THE ARAB SPRING OF 2011

The dramatic events that began in Tunisia in December 2010 brought a wave of protest and popular insurrection to much of the Arab Middle East, overthrowing powerful dictators and presidents-for-life in Tunisia, Egypt, and Libya in 2011. The speed of these momentous changes surprised people living in these countries as much as they astonished foreign observers—many had long assumed that political change, when it came to these regimes, would proceed at a glacial pace. Zine Al-Abidine Ben Ali of Tunisia, Hosni Mubarak of Egypt, and Muammar Qadhafi of Libya had governed for decades. Ben Ali and Mubarak were establishment figures in the international world, regularly meeting with European leaders and U.S. presidents, who were among their most loyal supporters. How had this happened so suddenly? Did it mean that a wave of democratic revolution was sweeping through the Middle East?

In order to explain these events, many observers in Europe and the United States looked to their own histories. Some people suggested that these revolts were comparable to the movements to overthrow the dictatorial regimes of Eastern Europe that culminated in the fall of the Berlin Wall in 1989 and the collapse of the Soviet Union in 1991. The very name "Arab Spring" recalled the "Prague Spring" of 1968, when young people in Czechoslovakia attempted (and ultimately failed) to create a different and more democratic form of socialism in that country. Others feared that these revolts might turn out like the Tiananmen Square protests in China of 1989, which ended up in a violent repression of a democratic movement. And finally, there was considerable unease in many quarters about the possibility that these states could simply collapse, leaving an opening for armed militants with ties to international

Past and Present

The Arab Spring in Historical Perspective

With the collapse of the Berlin Wall in 1989 still a relatively fresh memory, many people in Europe and North America sought to compare the protests in the Middle East against authoritarian governments to these recent European events. Comparisons with 1968 (see left, the Prague Spring), 1989, or 1848 may be instructive, but it is also likely that the forms of democracy that protesters in Tunisia, Egypt (see right, protesters in Tahrir Square, Cairo), and most recently, Turkey, are striving to create will reflect their own values, rather than conform to political models borrowed from elsewhere.

Watch related author videos on the Student Site
wwnorton.com/college/history/western-civilizationsBrief4

terrorist organizations. The civil war in Syria, continued violence in Libya, and the emergence of ISIS in 2014 are reminders of the reality behind such fears.

The comparisons with Europe's past might be instructive, but they also reveal something significant about the way that many people think about movements for democratic revolutions: there is a tendency to assume that movements for democracy all want the same thing. History shows that these aspirations are usually much more complicated than that. Great coalitions can be assembled at a moment of crisis to challenge established regimes, but success brings on new challenges. The revolution of February 2011 succeeded in removing Hosni Mubarak from power in Egypt, but the activists who were united in opposition to Mubarak's regime were deeply divided when it came to the future of Egypt. In the first round of voting in the presidential elections of June 2012, over 50 percent of the votes were split between liberal, non-fundamentalist candidates of various political or religiously affiliated parties,

but the two top vote-getters were Mohamed Morsi, from the illiberal Muslim Brotherhood (25 percent), and a figure from the former regime, Ahmed Shafiq (23 percent). This polarizing choice was offered to voters in the second round, and Mohamed Morsi won a narrow victory with 53 percent of the vote. In this way, the more secular or democratic currents in Egyptian politics were sidelined in the presidential elections, though they showed their relevance just over a year later in a protest movement that accused Morsi of refusing to share power with other groups. He was also widely reviled for his authoritarian style of rule and his mismanagement of Egypt's economy. When the protest movements threatened to overwhelm the country once again in July 2013, the military staged a coup, overthrowing Morsi. The Muslim Brotherhood organized their own protests in response, but the military responded with violent repression, killing hundreds. Egypt's democratic future is uncertain at present, as the revolutions of 2011–13 seem only to have further polarized an already deeply divided society.

Nevertheless, if the short term remains uncertain, there may be reason for hope in the long term. As the protests in the Middle East and North Africa unfolded in 2011, observers frequently noted how new technologies such as cell phones, or new social media such as Facebook and Twitter, allowed people to make their voices heard in a new way and to coordinate mass actions almost instantaneously. The mass participation of young people in the revolutions in Tunisia, Libya, and Egypt revealed an aspiration for political and cultural openness and a desire to break with older political and religious traditions that surprised many observers in the West. Whereas the older generation in these countries had been convinced by their political leaders that democratic openness could only come after economic development that would free the former colonies from dependence on Europe, the new generation insisted that they would not tolerate the persistence of authoritarian regimes. The revolutions produced an active and unprecedented civil society—with debates about politics unfolding in newspapers, pamphlets, and social media. Whatever happens in the next years and decades, the new regimes in the Middle East will not be able to function in the same way as their predecessors. For this reason alone, the movements of 2011 deserve to be called "revolutions."

CONCLUSION

Globalization—defined loosely as the process by which the economies, societies, and cultures of different parts of the world become increasingly interconnected—has been hailed as a solution to old problems even as it has been criticized as a source of new ones. Although some thought that the end of the Cold War in 1989 meant that economic liberalism—that is, a global free-market capitalist system unfettered by government regulations—had finally triumphed in the world, continued political instability in many parts of the globe and the global economic crisis of 2008 have called into question such optimistic interpretations of world events. In the economic realm, national states have looked for ways to reassert their control over the flow of currencies and goods and protect their populations against decisions made elsewhere by financial speculators and investors. Meanwhile, the danger of radical forms of terrorism, both foreign and domestic, has caused even strongly democratic governments in the West to create new and pervasive surveillance bureaucracies, demonstrating that global threats can have real and seemingly permanent local effects on definitions of citizenship, the permeability of borders, and extensions of state power.

After You Read This Chapter

 Go to **INQUIZITIVE** to see what you've learned—and learn what you've missed—with personalized feedback along the way.

REVIEWING THE OBJECTIVES

- Globalization in the second half of the twentieth century was not new. What does *globalization* mean, and what was similar or different about the most recent phase of globalization in human history?
- The burden of the colonial past continued to weigh heavily on many former colonies after the 1960s. What accounts for the success of some former colonies in the global economy and the continued social and political challenges facing others?
- Since the end of the Second World War, conflicts and events in the Middle East have taken on a global significance far beyond the region's borders. What are the crucial conflicts that occupied the attention of other nations, and what events have proved to be crucial turning points in the emergence of the Middle East as a region that drives developments elsewhere?

In such uncertain times, it is difficult to remain consistent or to determine national priorities: is the threat of terrorism greater than the threat of a loss of liberty stemming from extensions in government power? Is it fair of the International Monetary Fund to ask developing nations to adhere to austere cuts to their social welfare spending when wealthy private investment banks receive billion-dollar bailouts after making bad bets in the financial markets because they are "too big to fail"? The complexity of the world's interconnections makes it difficult to determine definitive answers to such questions, and even if one could, any ensuing policy decisions would create winners and losers, ensuring that the political struggles implicit in such questions will endure. Globalization, therefore, is not a final destination—it is the new complex reality of human existence, the context for future struggles about the goals of political association, the meanings of liberty or equality, and the possibility of shared values.

The loss of familiar moorings makes fundamental questions about human behavior and political community difficult to answer. History offers no quick solutions, and historians are reluctant to offer what historian Peter Novick calls "pithy lessons that fit on a bumper sticker." As Novick puts it:

If there is, to use a pretentious word, any wisdom to be acquired from contemplating an historical event, I would think it would derive from confronting it in all its complexity and its contradictions; the ways in which it resembles other events to which it might be compared as well as the ways it differs from them. . . . If there are lessons to be extracted from encountering the past, that encounter has to be with the past in all its messiness; they're not likely to come from an encounter with a past that's been shaped so that inspiring lessons will emerge.

The untidy and contradictory evidence that historians discover in the archives rarely yields unblemished heroes or irredeemable villains. Good history reveals the complex processes and dynamics of change over time. It helps us understand the many layers of the past that have formed and that constrain us in our present world. At the same time, it shows again and again that these constraints do not preordain what happens next or how we can make the history of the future.

PEOPLE, IDEAS, AND EVENTS IN CONTEXT

- What were the policy goals of **NEOLIBERALISM** after the 1970s, as exemplified by the activities of institutions such as the **INTERNATIONAL MONETARY FUND** and the **WORLD BANK**?
- How do the **HIV EPIDEMIC** of the 1980s or the **SARS EPIDEMIC** of 2003 illustrate the new realities of public health in a globalized world?
- What was the significance of **NELSON MANDELA**'s election as president of South Africa in 1994?
- How was the **1973 OIL EMBARGO** related to the **ARAB-ISRAELI CONFLICT**, and what were its effects on the global economy?
- What did radical critics dislike about secular forms of **ARAB NATIONALISM** such as that represented by **GAMAL ABDEL NASSER** in Egypt?
- What led the United States and Britain to support the regime of **REZA PAHLAVI** in Iran, and what events brought **RUHOLLAH KHOMEINI** to power in Iran in 1979?
- What circumstances link the Soviet invasion of Afghanistan in 1979, at the height of the Cold War, with the origins of **AL QAEDA?**
- How did the **UN'S UNIVERSAL DECLARATION OF HUMAN RIGHTS** challenge older assumptions about political rights?
- What was revolutionary about the events of the **ARAB SPRING** of 2011?

THINKING ABOUT CONNECTIONS

- Many of the global linkages between Europe and the United States, on the one hand, and the independent nations of Asia, Africa, and Latin America, on the other, were first forged during earlier periods of imperial expansion. How does this history continue to be felt in the present?
- Global networks of transport, trade, and communication have long been significant vectors for cultural change, by bringing different peoples into contact and conversation with one another. How have recent developments in technology changed the nature of this global conversation?

Rulers of Principal States

THE CAROLINGIAN DYNASTY

Pepin of Heristal, Mayor of the Palace, 687–714
Charles Martel, Mayor of the Palace, 715–741
Pepin III, Mayor of the Palace, 741–751; King, 751–768
Charlemagne, King, 768–814; Emperor, 800–814
Louis the Pious, Emperor, 814–840

West Francia

Charles the Bald, King, 840–877; Emperor, 875–877
Louis II, King, 877–879
Louis III, King, 879–882
Carloman, King, 879–884

Middle Kingdoms

Lothair, Emperor, 840–855
Louis (Italy), Emperor, 855–875
Charles (Provence), King, 855–863
Lothair II (Lorraine), King, 855–869

East Francia

Ludwig, King, 840–876
Carloman, King, 876–880
Ludwig, King, 876–882
Charles the Fat, Emperor, 876–887

HOLY ROMAN EMPERORS

Saxon Dynasty

Otto I, 962–973
Otto II, 973–983
Otto III, 983–1002
Henry II, 1002–1024

Franconian Dynasty

Conrad II, 1024–1039
Henry III, 1039–1056
Henry IV, 1056–1106
Henry V, 1106–1125
Lothair II (Saxony), 1125–1137

Hohenstaufen Dynasty

Conrad III, 1138–1152
Frederick I (Barbarossa), 1152–1190
Henry VI, 1190–1197
Philip of Swabia, 1198–1208 ⎫
Otto IV (Welf), 1198–1215 ⎬ Rivals

Frederick II, 1220–1250
Conrad IV, 1250–1254

Interregnum, 1254–1273

Emperors from Various Dynasties

Rudolf I (Habsburg), 1273–1291
Adolf (Nassau), 1292–1298
Albert I (Habsburg), 1298–1308
Henry VII (Luxemburg), 1308–1313
Ludwig IV (Wittelsbach), 1314–1347
Charles IV (Luxemburg), 1347–1378
Wenceslas (Luxemburg), 1378–1400
Rupert (Wittelsbach), 1400–1410
Sigismund (Luxemburg), 1410–1437

Habsburg Dynasty

Albert II, 1438–1439
Frederick III, 1440–1493

Maximilian I, 1493–1519
Charles V, 1519–1556
Ferdinand I, 1556–1564
Maximilian II, 1564–1576
Rudolf II, 1576–1612
Matthias, 1612–1619
Ferdinand II, 1619–1637
Ferdinand III, 1637–1657

Leopold I, 1658–1705
Joseph I, 1705–1711
Charles VI, 1711–1740
Charles VII (not a Habsburg), 1742–1745
Francis I, 1745–1765
Joseph II, 1765–1790
Leopold II, 1790–1792
Francis II, 1792–1806

RULERS OF FRANCE FROM HUGH CAPET

Capetian Dynasty

Hugh Capet, 987–996
Robert II, 996–1031
Henry I, 1031–1060
Philip I, 1060–1108
Louis VI, 1108–1137
Louis VII, 1137–1180
Philip II (Augustus), 1180–1223
Louis VIII, 1223–1226
Louis IX (St. Louis), 1226–1270
Philip III, 1270–1285
Philip IV, 1285–1314
Louis X, 1314–1316
Philip V, 1316–1322
Charles IV, 1322–1328

Valois Dynasty

Philip VI, 1328–1350
John, 1350–1364
Charles V, 1364–1380
Charles VI, 1380–1422
Charles VII, 1422–1461
Louis XI, 1461–1483
Charles VIII, 1483–1498
Louis XII, 1498–1515
Francis I, 1515–1547

Henry II, 1547–1559
Francis II, 1559–1560
Charles IX, 1560–1574
Henry III, 1574–1589

Bourbon Dynasty

Henry IV, 1589–1610
Louis XIII, 1610–1643
Louis XIV, 1643–1715
Louis XV, 1715–1774
Louis XVI, 1774–1792

After 1792

First Republic, 1792–1799
Napoleon Bonaparte, First Consul, 1799–1804
Napoleon I, Emperor, 1804–1814
Louis XVIII (Bourbon dynasty), 1814–1824
Charles X (Bourbon dynasty), 1824–1830
Louis Philippe, 1830–1848
Second Republic, 1848–1852
Napoleon III, Emperor, 1852–1870
Third Republic, 1870–1940
Pétain regime, 1940–1944
Provisional government, 1944–1946
Fourth Republic, 1946–1958
Fifth Republic, 1958–

RULERS OF ENGLAND

Anglo-Saxon Dynasty

Alfred the Great, 871–899
Edward the Elder, 899–924
Ethelstan, 924–939
Edmund I, 939–946
Edred, 946–955
Edwy, 955–959
Edgar, 959–975

Edward the Martyr, 975–978
Ethelred the Unready, 978–1016
Canute, 1016–1035 (Danish Nationality)
Harold I, 1035–1040
Hardicanute, 1040–1042
Edward the Confessor, 1042–1066
Harold II, 1066

House of Normandy

William I (the Conqueror), 1066–1087
William II, 1087–1100
Henry I, 1100–1135
Stephen, 1135–1154

House of Plantagenet

Henry II, 1154–1189
Richard I, 1189–1199
John, 1199–1216
Henry III, 1216–1272
Edward I, 1272–1307
Edward II, 1307–1327
Edward III, 1327–1377
Richard II, 1377–1399

House of Lancaster

Henry IV, 1399–1413
Henry V, 1413–1422
Henry VI, 1422–1461

House of York

Edward IV, 1461–1483
Edward V, 1483
Richard III, 1483–1485

House of Tudor

Henry VII, 1485–1509
Henry VIII, 1509–1547
Edward VI, 1547–1553
Mary, 1553–1558
Elizabeth I, 1558–1603

House of Stuart

James I, 1603–1625
Charles I, 1625–1649

Commonwealth and Protectorate, 1649–1659

House of Stuart Restored

Charles II, 1660–1685
James II, 1685–1688
William III and Mary II, 1689–1694
William III alone, 1694–1702
Anne, 1702–1714

House of Hanover

George I, 1714–1727
George II, 1727–1760
George III, 1760–1820
George IV, 1820–1830
William IV, 1830–1837
Victoria, 1837–1901

House of Saxe-Coburg-Gotha

Edward VII, 1901–1910
George V, 1910–1917

House of Windsor

George V, 1917–1936
Edward VIII, 1936
George VI, 1936–1952
Elizabeth II, 1952–

RULERS OF AUSTRIA AND AUSTRIA-HUNGARY

*Maximilian I (Archduke), 1493–1519
*Charles V, 1519–1556
*Ferdinand I, 1556–1564
*Maximilian II, 1564–1576
*Rudolf II, 1576–1612
*Matthias, 1612–1619
*Ferdinand II, 1619–1637
*Ferdinand III, 1637–1657
*Leopold I, 1658–1705
*Joseph I, 1705–1711
*Charles VI, 1711–1740
Maria Theresa, 1740–1780

*Joseph II, 1780–1790
*Leopold II, 1790–1792
*Francis II, 1792–1835 (Emperor of Austria as Francis I after 1804)
Ferdinand I, 1835–1848
Francis Joseph, 1848–1916 (after 1867 Emperor of Austria and King of Hungary)
Charles I, 1916–1918 (Emperor of Austria and King of Hungary)
Republic of Austria, 1918–1938 (dictatorship after 1934)
Republic restored, under Allied occupation, 1945–1956
Free Republic, 1956–

*Also bore title of Holy Roman Emperor

RULERS OF PRUSSIA AND GERMANY

*Frederick I, 1701–1713
*Frederick William I, 1713–1740
*Frederick II (the Great), 1740–1786
*Frederick William II, 1786–1797
*Frederick William III,1797–1840
*Frederick William IV, 1840–1861
*William I, 1861–1888 (German Emperor after 1871)
Frederick III, 1888

*Kings of Prussia

*William II, 1888–1918
Weimar Republic, 1918–1933
Third Reich (Nazi Dictatorship), 1933–1945
Allied occupation, 1945–1952
Division into Federal Republic of Germany in west and
    German Democratic Republic in east, 1949–1991
Federal Republic of Germany (united), 1991–

RULERS OF RUSSIA

Ivan III, 1462–1505
Vasily III, 1505–1533
Ivan IV, 1533–1584
Theodore I, 1534–1598
Boris Godunov, 1598–1605
Theodore II,1605
Vasily IV, 1606–1610
Michael, 1613–1645
Alexius, 1645–1676
Theodore III, 1676–1682
Ivan V and Peter I, 1682–1689
Peter I (the Great), 1689–1725
Catherine I, 1725–1727
Peter II, 1727–1730

Anna, 1730–1740
Ivan VI, 1740–1741
Elizabeth, 1741–1762
Peter III, 1762
Catherine II (the Great), 1762–1796
Paul, 1796–1801
Alexander I,1801–1825
Nicholas I, 1825–1855
Alexander II,1855–1881
Alexander III, 1881–1894
Nicholas II, 1894–1917
Soviet Republic, 1917–1991
Russian Federation, 1991–

RULERS OF UNIFIED SPAIN

Ferdinand { and Isabella, 1479–1504
           { and Philip I, 1504–1506
           { and Charles I, 1506–1516
Charles I (Holy Roman Emperor Charles V), 1516–1556
Philip II, 1556–1598
Philip III, 1598–1621
Philip IV, 1621–1665
Charles II, 1665–1700
Philip V, 1700–1746
Ferdinand VI, 1746–1759
Charles III, 1759–1788
Charles IV, 1788–1808

Ferdinand VII, 1808
Joseph Bonaparte, 1808–1813
Ferdinand VII (restored), 1814–1833
Isabella II, 1833–1868
Republic, 1868–1870
Amadeo, 1870–1873
Republic, 1873–1874
Alfonso XII, 1874–1885
Alfonso XIII, 1886–1931
Republic, 1931–1939
Fascist Dictatorship, 1939–1975
Juan Carlos I, 1975–

RULERS OF ITALY

Victor Emmanuel II, 1861–1878
Humbert I, 1878–1900
Victor Emmanuel III, 1900–1946

Fascist Dictatorship, 1922-1943 (maintained in northern Italy until 1945)
Humbert II, May 9–June 13, 1946
Republic, 1946–

PROMINENT POPES

Silvester I, 314–335
Leo I, 440–461
Gelasius I, 492–496
Gregory I, 590–604
Nicholas I, 858–867
Silvester II, 999–1003
Leo IX, 1049–1054
Nicholas II, 1058–1061
Gregory VII, 1073–1085
Urban II, 1088–1099
Paschal II, 1099–1118
Alexander III, 1159–1181
Innocent III, 1198–1216
Gregory IX, 1227–1241
Innocent IV, 1243–1254
Boniface VIII, 1294–1303
John XXII, 1316–1334
Nicholas V, 1447–1455
Pius II, 1458–1464

Alexander VI, 1492–1503
Julius II, 1503–1513
Leo X, 1513–1521
Paul III, 1534–1549
Paul IV, 1555–1559
Sixtus V, 1585–1590
Urban VIII, 1623–1644
Gregory XVI, 1831–1846
Pius IX, 1846–1878
Leo XIII, 1878–1903
Pius X, 1903–1914
Benedict XV, 1914–1922
Pius XI, 1922–1939
Pius XII, 1939–1958
John XXIII, 1958–1963
Paul VI, 1963–1978
John Paul I, 1978
John Paul II, 1978–2005
Benedict XVI, 2005–2013
Francis, 2013–

Further Readings

CHAPTER 1

Aldred, Cyril. *The Egyptians*. 3d ed. London, 1998. An indispensable, lively overview of Egyptian culture and history by one of the great masters of Egyptology.

Baines, J., and J. Málek. *Atlas of Ancient Egypt*. Rev. ed. New York, 2000. A reliable, well-illustrated survey, with excellent maps.

Bottéro, Jean. *Everyday Life in Ancient Mesopotamia*. Trans. Antonia Nevill. Baltimore, MD, 2001. A wide-ranging, interdisciplinary account.

Bottéro, Jean. *Religion in Ancient Mesopotamia*. Chicago, 2001. An accessible, engaging survey.

Dodson, Aidan. *Amarna Sunset: Nefertiti, Tutankhamun, Ay, Horemheb, and the Egyptian Counter-Reformation*. Cairo, 2009. A provocative study of the resistance to Akhenaten's religious "reformation," this book argues that Nefertiti was not only queen but also a kind of "joint-pharaoh," the mother of Tutankhamun, and the leader of the movement toward a return to traditional forms of worship.

Foster, Benjamin R. and Karen Polinger Foster. *Civilizations of Ancient Iraq*. Princeton, 2011. A critically-acclaimed survey that charts the history of this region from the earliest Sumerian civilization to the Arab conquests of the seventh C. C.E.

Geller, Markham J. *Ancient Babylonian Medicine: Theory and Practice*. Malden, MA, 2010. Makes use of previously unstudied cuneiform sources to tell a new story about the relationship between medicine and magic.

George, Andrew, trans. *The Epic of Gilgamesh: A New Translation. The Babylonian Epic Poem and Other Texts in Akkadian and Sumerian*. New York and London, 1999. A reliable translation which carefully distinguishes the chronological "layers" of this famous text; also includes many related texts.

Hodder, Ian. *The Leopard's Tale:Revealing the Mysteries of Çatalhöyük*. London and New York, 2006. The most up-to-date account of this fascinating archaeological site, written for general readers by the director of the excavation.

Kemp, Barry. *The City of Akhenaten and Nefertiti: Armana and Its People*. London, 2012. A cutting-edge study of this ancient site, based on decades of archeological research.

Leick, Gwendolyn. *The Babylonians: An Introduction*. London and New York, 2002. A wide-ranging survey of Babylonian civilization across the centuries.

McDowell, A. G. *Village Life in Ancient Egypt: Laundry Lists and Love Songs*. Oxford, 1999. A fascinating collection of translated texts recovered from an Egyptian peasant village, dating from 1539 to 1075 B.C.E.

McGregor, Neil. *A History of the World in 100 Objects*. London, 2011. Based on an acclaimed BBC Radio program, this book features a range of artifacts from the collections British Museum, embeds them in their historical contexts, and explores the ways that that still hold meaning today.

Pollock, Susan. *Ancient Mesopotamia*. Cambridge, 1999. An advanced textbook that draws on theoretical anthropology to interpret Mesopotamian civilization up to 2100 B.C.E.

Redford, Donald B., ed. *The Oxford Encyclopedia of Ancient Egypt*. 3 vols. New York, 2001. An indispensible reference work, intended for both specialists and beginners.

Roaf, Michael. *Cultural Atlas of Mesopotamia and the Ancient Near East*. New York, 1990. An informative, authoritative, and lavishly illustrated guide, with excellent maps.

Robins, Gay. *The Art of Ancient Egypt*. London, 1997. An excellent survey, now the standard account.

Shafer, Byron E., ed. *Religion in Ancient Egypt: Gods, Myths, and Personal Practice*. London, 1991. A scholarly examination of Egyptian belief and ritual, with contributions from leading authorities.

Shaw, Ian, ed. *The Oxford History of Ancient Egypt*. Oxford, 2000. An outstanding collaborative survey of Egyptian history from the Stone Age to c. 300 C.E., with excellent bibliographical essays.

Shryock, Andrew and Daniel Lord Smail. Berkeley, 2012. *Deep History: The Architecture of Past and Present*. A fascinating fusion of historical, anthropological, and scientific research on what it means to be human.

Smail, Daniel Lord. *On Deep History and the Brain*. Berkeley, 2008. A pioneering introduction to the historical uses of neuroscience and evolutionary biology.

Snell, Daniel C., ed. *A Companion to the Ancient Near East*. Oxford, 2005. A topical survey of recent scholarly work, particularly strong on society, economy, and culture.

Wengrow, David. *The Archaeology of Early Egypt: Social Transformations in North-East Africa, 10,000 to 2650 B.C.* Cambridge, 2006. An authoritative account of archeological evidence and its interpretation.

CHAPTER 2

Aubet, Maria Eugenia. *Phoenicia and the West: Politics, Colonies, and Trade*. Trans. Mary Turton. Cambridge, 1993. An intelligent and thought-provoking examination of Phoenician civilization and its influence.

Boardman, John. *Assyrian and Babylonian Empires and Other States of the Near East from the Eighth to the Sixth Centuries B.C.* New York, 1991. Scholarly and authoritative.

———. *Persia and the West.* London, 2000. A great book by a distinguished scholar, with a particular focus on art and architecture as projections of Persian imperial ideologies.

Boyce, Mary. *Textual Sources for the Study of Zoroastrianism.* Totowa, NJ, 1984. An invaluable collection of documents.

Bryce, Trevor. *The Kingdom of the Hittites.* Oxford, 1998. And *Life and Society in the Hittite World.* Oxford, 2002. An extraordinary synthesis, now the standard account of Hittite political, military, and daily life.

Curtis, John. *Ancient Persia.* Cambridge, MA, 1990. Concise, solid, reliable.

Dever, William. *Who Were the Early Israelites and Where Did They Come From?* Grand Rapids, MI, 2003. A balanced, fair-minded account with excellent bibliographical guidance to recent work.

Dickinson, O. T. P. K. *The Aegean Bronze Age.* Cambridge, 1994. An excellent summary of archaeological evidence and scholarly argument concerning Minoan, Mycenaean, and other cultures of the Bronze Age Aegean basin.

Dothan, Trude, and Moshe Dothan. *Peoples of the Sea: The Search for the Philistines.* New York, 1992. The essential starting point for understanding Philistine culture and its links to the Aegean basin.

Drews, Robert. *The End of the Bronze Age: Changes in Warfare and the Catastrophe ca. 1200 B.C.* Princeton, NJ, 1993. A stimulating analysis and survey, with excellent bibliographies.

Finkelstein, Israel, and Nadav Na'aman, eds. *From Nomadism to Monarchy: Archaeological and Historical Aspects of Early Israel.* Jerusalem, 1994. Scholarly articles on the Hebrews' transformation from pastoralists to a sedentary society focused on the worship of Yahweh.

Fitton, J. Lesley. *Minoans: Peoples of the Past* (British Museum Publications). London, 2002. A careful, reliable debunking of myths about the Minoans, written for nonspecialists.

Kamm, Antony. *The Israelites: An Introduction.* New York, 1999. A short, accessible history of the land and people of Israel up to 135 C.E., aimed at students and general readers.

Kuhrt, Amélie. *The Ancient Near East, c. 3000–330 B.C.* 2 vols. London and New York, 1995. An outstanding survey, written for students, that includes Egypt and Israel as well as Mesopotamia, Babylonia, Assyria, and Persia.

Marinatos, Nannos. *Minoan Kingship and the Solar Goddess: A Near Eastern Koine.* Champaign, IL, 2010. A rich new interpretation of Minoan culture and its wider connections and influence within the world of the late Bronze Age.

Metzger, Bruce M., and Michael D. Coogan, eds. *The Oxford Companion to the Bible.* New York, 1993. An outstanding reference work, with contributions by leading authorities.

Niditch, Susan. *Ancient Israelite Religion.* New York, 1997. A short introduction designed for students, emphasizing the diversity of Hebrew religious practices.

Prezioso, Donald and Louise A. Hitchcock. *Aegean Art and Architecture.* Oxford, 2000. Archaic Greek artistic forms in their broader geographic and cultural context, from the fourth millennium to 1000 B.C.E.

Redford, Donald B. *Egypt, Canaan, and Israel in Ancient Times.* Princeton, NJ, 1992. An overview of the interactions between these peoples from about 1200 B.C.E. to the beginning of the Common Era.

Renfrew, Colin. *Archaeology and Language: The Puzzle of Indo-European Origins.* Cambridge, 1987. A masterful but controversial work by one of the most creative archaeologists of the twentieth century.

Sandars, Nancy K. *The Sea Peoples: Warriors of the Ancient Mediterranean.* Rev. ed. London, 1985. An introductory account for students and scholars.

Tubb, Jonathan N., and Rupert L. Chapman. *Archaeology and the Bible.* London, 1990. A good starting point for students that clearly illustrates the difficulties in linking archeological evidence to biblical accounts of early Hebrew history and society.

Wood, Michael. *In Search of the Trojan War.* New York, 1985. Aimed at a general audience, this carefully researched and engagingly written book is an excellent introduction to the late–Bronze Age context of the Trojan War.

CHAPTER 3

Penguin Classics and the Loeb Classical Library both offer reliable translations of Greek literary, philosophical, and historical texts.

Beard, Mary. *The Parthenon.* Cambridge, MA, 2003. A book that traces the successive stages of this monument's construction, deconstruction, reconstruction, and restoration.

Boardman, John, Jaspar Griffin, and Oswyn Murray, eds. *Greece and the Hellenistic World.* Oxford, 1988. A reprint of the Greek and Hellenistic chapters from *The Oxford History of the Classical World,* originally published in 1986. Excellent, stimulating surveys, accessible to a general audience.

Brunschwig, Jacques, and Geoffrey E. R. Lloyd. *Greek Thought: A Guide to Classical Knowledge.* Translated by Catherine Porter. Cambridge, MA, 2000. An outstanding work of reference.

Buckley, Terry, ed. *Aspects of Greek History, 750–323 B.C.: A Source-Based Approach.* London, 1999. An outstanding collection of source materials.

Cartledge, Paul A. *The Spartans: An Epic History.* New York, 2003. A lively and authoritative history of Sparta from its origins to the Roman conquest.

Dover, Kenneth J. *Greek Homosexuality.* Cambridge, MA, 1978. The standard account of an important subject.

Fantham, Elaine, Helene Foley, Natalie Kampen, Sarah B. Pomeroy, and H. A. Shapiro. *Women in the Classical World: Image and Text.* Oxford, 1994. Wide-ranging analysis drawing on both visual and written sources, covering both the Greek and the Roman periods.

Fornara, Charles W., and Loren J. Samons II. *Athens from Cleisthenes to Pericles.* Berkeley, CA, 1991. An excellent narrative history of Athenian politics during the first half of the fifth century B.C.E.

Garlan, Yvon. *Slavery in Ancient Greece*. Ithaca, NY, 1988. Now the standard account.

Hanson, Victor Davis. *The Other Greeks: The Family Farm and the Agrarian Roots of Western Civilization*. New York, 1995. Polemical and idiosyncratic, but convincing in its emphasis on smallholding farmers as the backbone of Greek urban society.

Havelock, Eric A. *The Literate Revolution in Greece and Its Cultural Consequences*. Princeton, 1982. A now-classic account of the wide-ranging effects of writing on Greek society.

Jones, Nicholas F. *Ancient Greece: State and Society*. Upper Saddle River, NJ, 1997. A concise survey from the Minoans up to the end of the Classical Period that emphasizes the connections between the social order and politics.

Krentz, Peter. *The Battle of Marathon*. New Haven, 2011. A fresh analysis of this landmark battle, paying special attention to the conditions in which hoplite warriors fought.

Lefkowitz, Mary, and Maureen Fant. *Women's Life in Greece and Rome: A Source Book in Translation*. 3rd ed. Baltimore, MD, 2005. A remarkably wide-ranging collection, topically arranged, invaluable to students.

Nevett, Lisa C. *Domestic Space in Classical Antiquity*. Cambridge, 2010. Reassesses what we can know about the architecture of households in antiquity through a fresh assessment of archeological evidence and material culture.

Pomeroy, Sarah B., Stanley M. Burstein, Walter Donlan, and Jennifer Tolbert Roberts. *Ancient Greece: A Political, Social, and Cultural History*. Oxford, 1999. An outstanding textbook; clear and lively.

Pomeroy, Sarah. *Goddesses, Whores, Wives, and Slaves: Women in Classical Antiquity*. New York, 1995. The first historical survey of antiquity to place women at the center of the narrative, and still unrivaled in scope.

Price, Simon. *Religions of the Ancient Greeks*. Cambridge, 1999. Concise and authoritative, this survey extends from the Archaic Period up to the fifth century C.E.

Seaford, Richard. *Money and the Greek Mind: Homer, Philosophy, Tragedy*. Cambridge, 2004. A provocative study of portable wealth and its far-reaching effects.

Strassler, Robert B., ed. *The Landmark Thucydides*. New York, 1996. Reprints the classic Richard Crawley translation with maps, commentary, notes, and appendices by leading scholars.

Thomas, Carol G., and Craig Conant. *Citadel to City-State: The Transformation of Greece, 1200–700 B.C.E.* Bloomington, IN, 1999. A lucid and accessible study that examines developments at a number of different Dark Age sites.

Thomas, Rosalind. *Oral Tradition and Written Record in Classical Athens*. Cambridge, 1989. A fascinating look at how oral epic, lyric, and drama were transmitted over time.

CHAPTER 4

Penguin Classics and the Loeb Classical Library both offer reliable translations of scores of literary and historical texts from this period. Particularly important are historical works by Arrian (*Anabasis of Alexander*), Plutarch (*Life of Alexander*), and Polybius (*The Histories*).

Austin, M. M. *The Hellenistic World from Alexander to the Roman Conquest: A Selection of Ancient Sources in Translation*. Cambridge, 1981. A good collection of primary documents.

Bagnall, R. S., and P. Derow. *Greek Historical Documents: The Hellenistic Period*. Chico, CA, 1981. Another useful collection.

Borza, Eugene N. *In the Shadow of Olympus: The Emergence of Macedon*. Princeton, NJ, 1990. The standard account of the rise of Macedon up to the accession of Philip II.

Bosworth, A. B. *Conquest and Empire: The Reign of Alexander the Great*. Cambridge, 1988. A political and military analysis of Alexander's career that strips away the romance, maintaining a clear vision of the ruthlessness and human cost of his conquests.

———. *The Legacy of Alexander: Politics, Warfare, and Propaganda under the Successors*. Oxford, 2002. The most recent survey of the half century following Alexander's death and of the people who created the Hellenistic kingdoms of Egypt, Persia, and Macedon.

Burstein, Stanley M., ed. and trans. *The Hellenistic Age from the Battle of Ipsos to the Death of Kleopatra VII*. Cambridge, 1985. An excellent collection, with sources not found elsewhere.

Cartledge, Paul. *Agesilaus and the Crisis of Sparta*. Baltimore, MD, 1987. A thorough but readable analysis of the social and political challenges besetting Sparta in the fourth century B.C.E.

———. *Alexander the Great: The Hunt for a New Past*. Woodstock, NY, 2004. A compelling account of Alexander's life, times, and influences.

Green, Peter. *Alexander to Actium: The Historical Evolution of the Hellenistic Age*. Berkeley, CA. 1990. An outstanding, comprehensive, and wide-ranging history of the period.

———. *Alexander of Macedon, 356–323 B.C.* Berkeley, CA, 1991. Revised edition of the author's earlier biography; entertainingly written, rich in detail and insight.

———. *The Hellenistic Age: A Short History*. New York, 2007. An authoritative synthesis that carries the history of Greek influence into the fourth century C.E.

Hansen, Mogens H. *The Athenian Democracy in the Age of Demosthenes*. Oxford, 1991. An examination of the political institutions of Athens in the fourth century B.C.E.

Holt, Frank. L. *Into the Land of Bones: Alexander the Great in Afghanistan*. Berkeley, 2012 repr. ed. A vivid, charged narrative that places the beginning of a current war in the distant past.

Lloyd, Geoffrey, and Nathan Sivin. *The Way and the Word: Science and Medicine in Early China and Greece*. New Haven, CT, 2002. An extraordinary comparative study.

McGing, Brian. *Polybius' Histories*. Oxford, 2010. A critical dissection of this influential ancient historian's techniques and historical philosophy.

Nicholas, G. L. *The Genius of Alexander the Great*. Chapel Hill, NC, 1998. A clear, authoritative, admiring account, distilling a lifetime of research on the subject.

Ober, Josiah. *Mass and Elite in Democratic Athens: Rhetoric, Ideology, and the Power of the People*. Princeton, NJ, 1989. An excellent study of the ideology of democracy in Athens that borrows from the insights of modern social science.

Pollitt, Jerome J. *Art in the Hellenistic Age*. New York, 1986. The standard account, blending cultural history with art history.

Sherwin-White, Susan, and Amélie Kuhrt. *From Samarkhand to Sardis: A New Approach to the Seleucid Empire*. London, 1993. A stimulating examination of the relationship between rulers and ruled in the vast expanses of the Seleucid Empire.

Shipley, Graham. *The Greek World after Alexander, 323–30 B.C.* New York and London, 2000. A study of the social, intellectual, and artistic changes in the Hellenistic era.

Thomas, Carol G. *Alexander the Great in His World*. Oxford and Malden, MA, 2007. A study of the contexts—familial, political, and social—that shaped Alexander's career.

Tripolitis, Antonia. *Religions of the Hellenistic-Roman Age*. Grand Rapids, MI, 2002. Survey of the variety of religious experience, ritual, and belief in the centuries before the emergence of Christianity.

Tritle, Lawrence A., ed. *The Greek World in the Fourth Century: From the Fall of the Athenian Empire to the Successors of Alexander*. New York, 1997. A wide-ranging collection of scholarly essays.

CHAPTER 5

Translations of Roman authors are available in both the Penguin Classics series and in the Loeb Classical Library.

Arnason, Johann P. and Kurt A. Raaflaub, eds. *The Roman Empire in Context: Historical and Comparative Perspectives*. Malden, MA, 2011. One of the few books to place the formation of the Roman Empire in a comparative, global perspective.

Barker, Graeme, and Tom Rasmussen. *The Etruscans*. Oxford and Malden, MA, 1998. A fine survey, from the Blackwell *Peoples of Europe* series.

Beard, Mary. *Pompeii: The Life of a Roman Town*. A fascinating, cutting-edge study of daily life.

Boardman, John, Jasper Griffin, and Oswyn Murray. *The Oxford History of the Roman World*. Oxford, 1990. Reprint of relevant portions of the excellent *Oxford History of the Classical World* (1986). Stimulating, accessible topical chapters by British specialists.

Cornell, T. J. *The Beginnings of Rome: Italy and Rome from the Bronze Age to the Punic Wars (c. 1000–264 B.C.)*. London, 1995. An ambitious survey of the archaeological and historical evidence for early Rome.

Crawford, Michael. *The Roman Republic*, 2d ed. Cambridge, MA, 1993. A lively, fast-paced survey of republican Rome. An excellent place to start.

Fantham, Elaine, Helene Peet Foley, Natalie Boymel Kampen, Sarah B. Pomeroy, and H. Alan Shapiro. *Women in the Classical World*. Oxford, 1994. An expert survey of both Greece and Rome.

Garnsey, Peter, and Richard Saller. *The Roman Empire: Economy, Society, and Culture*. Berkeley, CA, 1987. A straightforward short survey.

Gruen, Erich S. *The Hellenistic World and the Coming of Rome*. 2 vols. Berkeley, CA, 1984. A massive survey, focused on the unpre-dictable rise of Rome to a position of dominance within the Mediterranean world.

Harris, William V. *War and Imperialism in Republican Rome, 327–70 B.C.* Oxford, 1979. A challenging study arguing that Rome's need for military conquest and expansion was deeply embedded in the fabric of Roman life.

Krebs, Christopher. *A Most Dangerous Book: Tacitus's "Germania" from the Roman Empire to the Third Reich*. A history of this ancient ethnography's transmission and reception, and especially the political uses to which was put in Nazi Germany.

Lancel, Serge. *Carthage: A History*. Trans. Antonia Nevill. Oxford, 1995. An account of Rome's great rival for control of the Mediterranean world.

Millar, Fergus G. B. *The Emperor in the Roman World, 31 B.C.–A.D. 337*. London, 1977. A classic work that showed (among much else) the importance of emperor worship to the religious outlook of the Roman Empire.

———. *The Crowd in Rome in the Late Republic*. Ann Arbor, MI, 1999. A revisionist account that emphasizes the reality of Roman democracy in the late republic, against those who would see the period's politics as entirely under the control of aristocratic families.

Ward, Allen M., Fritz Heichelheim, and Cedric A. Yeo. *A History of the Roman People*, 3d ed. Upper Saddle River, NJ, 1999. An informative, well-organized textbook covering Roman history from its beginnings to the end of the sixth century C.E.

Watkin, David. *The Roman Forum*. London, 2009. A history of the successive buildings and archeological excavations of this central Roman space.

Wells, Colin. *The Roman Empire*, 2d ed. Cambridge, MA, 1992. An easily readable survey from the reign of Augustus to the mid-third century C.E., particularly useful for its treatment of the relationship between the Roman central government and its Italian provinces.

Wiseman, T. P. *Remembering the Roman People*. Oxford, 2009. A collection of studies devoted to popular politics in the late republic.

Woolf, Greg. *Becoming Roman: The Origins of Provincial Civilization in Gaul*. Cambridge, 1998. An exemplary study of how provincial elites made themselves "Roman."

———. *Rome: An Empire's Story*. Oxford, 2012. A masterful account of Rome's reconfiguration of the ancient world and enduring impact; critically acclaimed by scholars and general readers.

———. *Tales of the Barbarians: Ethnography and Empire in the Roman West*. Malden, MA, 2011. Applies modern ethnographic methodologies to a dissection of Romans applied their own ethnographic theories to contemporary "others."

CHAPTER 6

Augustine. *The City of God*. Trans. Henry Bettenson. Baltimore, MD, 1972.

———. *Confessions*. Trans. Henry M. Chadwick. Oxford, 1991.

———. *On Christian Doctrine*. Trans. D. W. Robertson Jr. New York, 1958.

Boethius. *The Consolation of Philosophy*. Trans. R. Green. Indianapolis, IN, 1962.

Bowersock, G. W., Peter Brown, and Oleg Grabar. *Late Antiquity: A Guide to the Postclassical World*. Cambridge, MA, 1999. An authoritative compilation. The first half is devoted to essays on the cultural features of the period; the second half is organized as an encyclopedia.

Brown, Peter. *Augustine of Hippo*. Berkeley, CA, 1967. A great biography by the great scholar of late antiquity.

———. *The Body and Society: Men, Women and Sexual Renunciation in Early Christianity*. New York, 1988. A revealing study of the fundamental transformations wrought by Christianity in the late antique world.

———. *Power and Persuasion in Late Antiquity: Toward a Christian Empire*. Madison, WI, 1992. An important account of Christianity's effects on the political culture of the later Roman Empire.

———. *The Rise of Western Christendom: Triumph and Diversity, 200–1000*, 2d ed. Oxford, 2002. An evocative picture of Christianity's spread eastward and northward from the Mediterranean world.

———. *The World of Late Antiquity*. New York, 1971. Still the best short survey of the period, with excellent illustrations.

———. *Through the Eye of a Needle: Wealth, the Fall of Rome, and the Making of Christianity in the West, 350–550 AD*. Princeton, NJ, 2012. The most recent of this historian's magisterial dissections of late antiquity, focused on the relationship between religion, culture, power, and wealth (or its lack).

Cameron, Averil. *The Later Roman Empire, A.D. 284–430*. London, 1993. Now the standard account of its period, with an emphasis on imperial politics.

———. *The Mediterranean World in Late Antiquity, A.D. 395–600*. London, 1993. Masterful, with excellent, succinct bibliographical essays.

Cassiodorus. *An Introduction to Divine and Human Readings*. Trans. L. W. Jones. New York, 1946.

Chadwick, Henry M. *Augustine*. Oxford, 1986. A short introduction to Augustine's thought.

———. *Boethius*. Oxford, 1981. An intellectual biography of this important thinker.

Clark, Gillian. *Christianity and Roman Society*. Cambridge, 2004. A short, stimulating survey that places early Christianity firmly in its Roman social context.

———. *Women in Late Antiquity*. Oxford, 1993. A clear, compact account of an important subject.

Coogan, Michael, ed. *The Oxford History of the Biblical World*. Oxford, 1998. A reliable but rather traditional account of the historical events recounted in the Hebrew Bible and the New Testament.

Ehrman, Bart D. *The New Testament: A Historical Introduction to the Early Christian Writings*, 4th ed. Oxford, 2008. The standard textbook by a leading authority.

Ehrman, Bart D. and Zlatko Pleše, eds. *The Aprocryphal Gospels: Texts and Translations* Oxford, 2011. The first scholarly edition and translation of all the apocryphal gospels, including Latin, Greek, and Coptic texts.

Eusebius. *The History of the Church*. Trans. G. A. Williamson. Baltimore, MD, 1965. A contemporary account of Constantine's reign, written by one of his courtier-bishops.

———. *Eusebius' Life of Constantine*. Trans. Averil Cameron and Stuart Hall. Oxford, 1999. An admiring biography that reflects Constantine's own vision of his religious authority.

Hopkins, Keith. *A World Full of Gods: The Strange Triumph of Christianity*. New York, 1999. An imaginative study of religious pluralism in the Roman world and the context in which Christianity emerged.

Kulikowski, Michael. *Rome's Gothic Wars: From the Third Century to Alaric*. Cambridge, 2007. An authoritative and critical account.

Lawrence, Clifford Hugh. *Medieval Monasticism*, 3d ed. London, 2000. Concise, perceptive survey of monasticism from its beginnings to the end of the Middle Ages.

Pagels, Elaine. *The Gnostic Gospels*. New York, 1979. A pathbreaking study of the noncanonical gospels and the history of their exclusion from the Bible.

Potter, David. *The Roman Empire at Bay, A.D. 180–395*. London and New York, 2004. The most up-to-date account of the empire's reorganization and transformation in this era.

Rebillard, Éric. *Christians and Their Many Identities in Late Antiquity, North Africa, 200–450 ce*. Ithaca, 2012. In this book, as in his earlier works, the author argues that there was no special importance attached to being a "Christian" in late antiquity, and that religious identities are better understood as fluid and hybrid.

Sanders, E. P. *The Historical Figure of Jesus*. London and New York, 1993. A fine study of Jesus in his first-century Jewish context.

Shanks, Hershel, ed. *Christianity and Rabbinic Judaism: A Parallel History of Their Origins and Early Development*. Washington, DC, 1992. Accessible chapters written by top authorities, describing both Jewish and Christian developments from the first to the sixth centuries C.E.

Sherwin-White, A. N. *Roman Society and Roman Law in the New Testament*. Oxford, 1963. A fascinating reading of the New Testament in its historical context.

Traina, Giusto. *428 AD: An Ordinary Year at the End of the Roman Empire*. Princeton, NJ, 2011. An enlightening glimpse into the world of late antiquity, from the vantage point of a single "average" year.

Wallace-Hadrill, John Michael. *The Barbarian West*, 3d ed. London, 1966. A classic analysis of the hybrid culture of the late Roman West.

Whittaker, C. R. *Frontiers of the Roman Empire: A Social and Economic Study*. Baltimore, MD, 1994. A convincing picture of the frontiers of the Roman Empire as zones of intensive cultural interaction.

Williams, Stephen. *Diocletian and the Roman Recovery*. New York, 1997. Thorough and authoritative.

CHAPTER 7

Bede. *A History of the English Church and People*. Trans. Leo Sherley-Price. Baltimore, MD., 1955. The fundamental source for early Anglo-Saxon history.

Campbell, James, ed. *The Anglo-Saxons*. Oxford, 1982. An authoritative and splendidly illustrated volume.

Collins, Roger. *Early Medieval Europe, 300–1000*. 2d ed. New York, 1999. Dry and detailed, but a useful textbook nonetheless.

Conant, Jonathan. *Staying Roman: Conquest and Identity in Africa and the Mediterranean, 439–700*. Cambridge, 2012. An exploration of what it meant to be "Roman" and the sources of identity in this tumultuous period.

Donner, Fred. *The Early Islamic Conquests*. Princeton, NJ, 1981. A scholarly but readable narrative and analysis.

Einhard and Notker the Stammerer. *Two Lives of Charlemagne*. Trans. Lewis Thorpe. Baltimore, MD, 1969. Lively and entertaining works of contemporary biography.

Fletcher, Richard A. *The Barbarian Conversion: From Paganism to Christianity*. Berkeley, CA, 1999. Slow paced but informative and perceptive.

———. *Moorish Spain*. Berkeley, CA, 1993. The best short survey in English.

Geanakoplos, Deno John, ed. *Byzantium: Church, Society and Civilization Seen through Contemporary Eyes*. Chicago, 1984. An outstanding source book.

Gregory, Timothy E. A *History of Byzantium*. Malden, MA, and Oxford, 2005. The most accessible of the recent textbooks on Byzantium. An excellent place to start.

Herrin, Judith. *Byzantium: The Surprising Life of a Medieval Empire*. Princeton, 2009. An accessible and comprehensive history of the eastern Roman Empire.

———. *The Formation of Christendom*. Princeton, NJ, 1987. A synthetic history of the Christian civilizations of Byzantium and western Europe from 500 to 800, written by a prominent historian.

Hodges, Richard, and David Whitehouse. *Mohammed, Charlemagne and the Origins of Europe*. London, 1983. A critical analysis of the "Pirenne thesis," reexaming the relationship between the Mediterranean world and northern Europe.

Hourani, Albert. *A History of the Arab Peoples*. New York, 1992. A sympathetic and clear survey written for nonspecialists.

Kazhdan, Alexander P., ed. *The Oxford Dictionary of Byzantium*. 3 vols. Oxford, 1991. An authoritative reference work.

Kennedy, Hugh. *The Prophet and the Age of the Caliphates*. 2d ed. Harlow, UK, 2004. A lucid introduction to the political history of the Islamic world from the sixth through the eleventh centuries.

Krautheimer, Richard. *Early Christian and Byzantine Architecture*. 4th ed. New York, 1986. A classic work by one of the greatest Byzantine art historians of the twentieth century.

Little, Lester K., ed., *Plague and the End of Antiquity: The Pandemic of 541–750*. Cambridge, 2006. The first full-length scholarly history of the first global pandemic.

Mango, Cyril, ed. *The Oxford History of Byzantium*. Oxford and New York, 2002. Full of sharp judgments and attractively illustrated.

McCormick, Michael. *The Origins of the European Economy: Communications and Commerce A.D. 300–900*. Cambridge, 2002. An astonishing reinterpretation of the evidence for the myriad contacts between Christian Europe and Islam.

McKitterick, Rosamond. *Charlemagne: The Formation of a European Identity*. Cambridge, 2008. A history of Charlemagne's career and its lasting impact by an eminent scholar of the Carolingian world.

———, ed. *The Uses of Literacy in Early Medieval Europe*. New York, 1990. A superb collection of essays.

McNamara, Jo Ann, and John E. Halborg, eds. *Sainted Women of the Dark Ages*. Durham, NC, 1992. Translated saints' lives from Merovingian and Carolingian Europe.

Murray, A. C., ed. *From Roman to Merovingian Gaul: A Reader*. Toronto, 2000. An excellent collection of sources.

Pelikan, Jaroslav. *The Christian Tradition*. Vol. II, *The Spirit of Eastern Christendom*. Chicago, 1974. An outstanding synthetic treatment of the doctrines of Byzantine Christianity.

Procopius. *The Secret History*. Trans. G. A. Williamson. Baltimore, MD, 1966. An "unauthorized" account of Justinian's reign, written by the emperor's offical historian.

Reuter, Timothy. *Germany in the Early Middle Ages, 800–1056*. New York, 1991. The best survey in English.

Treadgold, Warren. *A History of the Byzantine State and Society*. Stanford, CA, 1997. A massive, encyclopedic narrative of the political, economic, and military history of Byzantium from 284 until 1461.

Wallace-Hadrill, John Michael. *Early Germanic Kingship in England and on the Continent*. Oxford, 1971. A classic analysis of changing ideas about kingship in early medieval Europe, emphasizing the links between Anglo-Saxon and Carolingian cultures.

———. *The Frankish Church*. Oxford, 1983. A masterful account that links the Merovingian and Carolingian churches.

Watt, W. Montgomery. *Islamic Philosophy and Theology*, 2d ed. Edinburgh, UK, 1985. The standard English account.

Wemple, Suzanne Fonay. *Women in Frankish Society: Marriage and the Cloister, 500–900*. Philadelphia, PA, 1981. An influential account of changing attitudes toward marriage among the early Franks.

Whittow, Mark. *The Making of Orthodox Byzantium, 600–1025*. London, 1996. Emphasizes the centrality of orthodoxy in shaping Byzantine history. Particularly good on Byzantine relations with the peoples outside the empire.

Wickham, Chris. *Framing the Middle Ages: Europe and the Mediterranean, 400–800*. Oxford, 2007. An eye-opening history that spans the transitional periods of late antiquity and the early Middle Ages, paying careful attention to regional differences.

Wood, Ian. *The Merovingian Kingdoms, 450–751*. New York, 1994. A detailed study, but difficult for beginners.

CHAPTER 8

Amt, Emily, ed. *Women's Lives in Medieval Europe: A Sourcebook*. New York, 1993. An excellent collection of primary texts.

The Song of Roland. Trans. Robert Harrison. Penguin, 1970. A lively translation.

Arnold, Benjamin. *Princes and Territories in Medieval Germany*. Cambridge and New York, 1991. The best such survey in English.

Blumenthal, Uta-Renate. *The Investiture Controversy*. Philadelphia, 1988. A clear review of a complicated subject.

Boswell, John E. *Christianity, Social Tolerance, and Homosexuality: Gay People in Western Europe from the Beginning of the Christian Era to the Fourteenth Century*. Chicago, 1980. A pioneering account, hotly debated but highly respected.

Burman, Thomas E. *Reading the Qur'ān in Latin Christendom, 1140–1560*. Philadelphia, 2007. A fascinating account of the Qu'ran's reception in medieval Europe.

Colish, Marcia. *Medieval Foundations of the Western Intellectual Tradition, 400–1400*. New Haven, CT, 1997. An encyclopedic work, best used as a reference.

Dunbabin, Jean. *France in the Making, 843–1180,* 2d ed. Oxford and New York, 2000. An authoritative survey of the disparate territories that came to make up the medieval French kingdom.

Dyer, Christopher. *Making a Living in the Middle Ages: The People of Britain 850–1520*. New Haven, 2002. A splendid new synthesis that combines social, economic, and archaeological evidence.

Fossier, Robert. *The Ax and the Oath: Ordinary Life in the Middle Ages*. Princeton, 2010. A quirky, personal, and often insightful look at the daily lives and worldview of this era by a leading French historian.

Frankopan, Peter. *The First Crusade: The Call from the East*. Cambridge, MA, 2012. Analyzes the causes and catalysts of the crusading movement.

Hicks, Carola. *The Bayeux Tapestry: The Life Story of Masterpiece*. London, 2006. An art historian's engrossing account of the making, reception, and interpretation of this amazing artifact.

Horden, Peregrine and Nicholas Purcell. *The Corrupting Sea: A Study of Mediterranean History*. Malden, MA, 2000. An extraordinary attempt to encompass the history of the Mediterranean World over a span of three millennia.

Leyser, Henrietta. *Medieval Women: A Social History of Women in England, 440–1500*. New York, 1995. Although limited to one country, this is the best of the recent surveys treating medieval women.

McLaughlin, Megan. *Sex, Gender, and Episcopal Authority in an Age of Reform, 1000–1122*. Cambridge, 2010. A new interpretation of gendered discourse and politics during the Investiture Controversy.

Miller, Maureen C. *Power and the Holy in the Age of the Investiture Conflict. A Brief History with Documents*. Boston, 2005. A stimulating approach to the eleventh-century conflicts over temporal and spiritual power, with many newly translated sources.

Moore, Robert I. *The First European Revolution, c. 970–1215*. Oxford and Cambridge, MA, 2000. A remarkable description of the ways in which European society was fundamentally reshaped during the eleventh and twelfth centuries.

Peters, F. E. *Aristotle and the Arabs*. New York, 1968. Well written and engaging.

Raffensperger, Christian. *Reimagining Europe: Kievan Rus' in the Medieval World*. Cambridge, MA, 2012. An exciting new study of early Rus' and its neighbors.

Reilly, Bernard F. *The Medieval Spains*. New York, 1993. A succinct account that covers the entire Iberian peninsula from 500 to 1500.

Reynolds, Susan. *Fiefs and Vassals: The Medieval Evidence Reinterpreted*. Oxford and New York, 1994. A detailed revisionist history of "feudalism."

Rubenstein, Jay. *Armies of Heaven: The First Crusade and the Quest for Apocalypse*. New York, 2011. An accessible narrative of the First Crusade, written for a general audience and arguing for a new interpretation of crusaders' motives.

Sawyer, Peter, ed. *The Oxford Illustrated History of the Vikings*. Oxford, 1997. The best one-volume account, lavishly illustrated.

Sheingorn, Pamela, trans. *The Book of Sainte Foy*. Philadelphia, 1995.

Stillman, Norman A. *The Jews of Arab Lands: A History and Source Book*. Philadelphia, PA, 1979. An essential resource.

Stow, Kenneth R. *Alienated Minority: The Jews of Medieval Latin Europe*. Cambridge, MA, 1992. An excellent survey.

Tierney, Brian. *The Crisis of Church and State, 1050–1300*. Toronto, 1988. An indispensable collection for both teachers and students.

Winroth, Anders. *The Conversion of Scandinavia: Vikings, Merchants, and Missionaries in the Remaking of Northern Europe*. New Haven, 2012. Argues that the peoples of Scandinavia were active participants in the cultural, economic, and political processes that accompanied their conversion to Christianity.

CHAPTER 9

Abelard and Heloise. *The Letters and Other Writings*. Trans. William Levitan. Indianapolis, 2007. A beautiful and accurate translation of the correspondence and related documents, with a full introduction and notes.

Abulafia, David. *Frederick II: A Medieval Emperor*. London and New York, 1988. A reliable biography that strips away much of the legend that has hitherto surrounded this monarch.

Baldwin, John W. *The Government of Philip Augustus*. Berkeley and Los Angeles, CA, 1986. A landmark scholarly account.

Barber, Malcolm. *The Crusader States*. New Haven, 2012. A new and comprehensive history by an esteemed historian.

Bartlett, Robert. *The Making of Europe: Conquest, Colonization and Cultural Change, 950–1350*. Princeton, NJ, 1993. A wide-ranging examination of the economic, social, and religious expansion of Europe, full of stimulating insights.

Bisson, Thomas N. *The Crisis of the Twelfth Century: Power, Lordship, and the Origins of European Government*. Princeton, NJ, 2009. A new interpretation of the evidence.

Bynum, Caroline Walker. *Holy Feast and Holy Fast: The Religious Significance of Food to Medieval Women*. Berkeley and Los Angeles, 1988. One of the most influential and important works of scholarship published in the late twentieth century.

Camille, Michael. *Gothic Art: Glorious Visions*. New York, 1996. A succinct and beautifully illustrated introduction.

Chrétien de Troyes. *Arthurian Romances*. Trans. W. W. Kibler. New York, 1991.

Clanchy, Michael T. *Abelard: A Medieval Life*. Oxford and Cambridge, MA, 1997. A great biography.

———. *From Memory to Written Record: England, 1066–1307*. Oxford, 1992. A fascinating and hugely influential account of this revolutionary shift.

Cobban, Alan B. *The Medieval Universities*. London, 1975. The best short treatment in English.

Fassler, Margot. *Gothic Song: Victorine Seqeunces and Augustinian Reform in Twelfth-Century Paris*. Cambridge, UK, 1993. The emergence of new musical genres and their cultural context.

Gillingham, John. *The Angevin Empire*, 2d ed. Oxford and New York, 2001. The best treatment by far of its subject, brief but full of ideas.

Gottfried von Strassburg. *Tristan*. Trans. A. T. Hatto. Baltimore, MD, 1960.

Hallam, Elizabeth, and Judith Everard. *Capetian France, 987–1328*, 2d ed. New York, 2001. A clear and well-organized account.

Haskins, Charles Homer. *The Renaissance of the Twelfth Century*. Cambridge, MA, 1927. A classic and influential study.

Jones, P. J. *The Italian City-State: From Commune to Signoria*. Oxford and New York, 1997. A fundamental reinterpretation of the evidence.

Jordan, William C. *Europe in the High Middle Ages: The Penguin History of Europe*. Vol. III. New York and London, 2003. An outstanding new survey.

Kaeuper, Richard W. *Chivalry and Violence in Medieval Europe*. Oxford and New York, 1999. A darker view of chivalry than Keen's.

Keen, Maurice. *Chivalry*. New Haven, CT, 1984. A comprehensive treatment of chivalry from its origins to the sixteenth century.

Lawrence, Clifford Hugh. *The Friars: The Impact of the Early Mendicant Movement on Western Society*. London and New York, 1994. The best short introduction to the early history of the Franciscans and the Dominicans.

Leclerq, Jean. *The Love of Learning and the Desire for God*, 3d ed. New York, 1982. A beautiful interpretation of twelfth-century monastic culture and the influence of Bernard of Clairvaux.

Little, Lester. *Religious Poverty and Profit Economy in Medieval Europe*. Ithaca, 1978. A fascinating study of the relationship between religious practice and economic reality.

Lopez, Robert S., and Irving W. Raymond, eds. *Medieval Trade in the Mediterranean World*. New York, 1990. A pathbreaking collection of source material.

Madden, Thomas F. *The New Concise History of the Crusades*. New York, 2005. An acclaimed and accessible survey for students.

Marie de France. *Lais*. Trans. Glyn S. Burgess and Keith Busby. Harmondsworth, UK, 1999. A compelling and entertaining prose translation.

Moore, R. I. *The War on Heresy*. Cambridge, MA, 2012. A courageous and searching revisionist history, based on decades of research and reflection. Moore argues for a radical reassessment of what "heresy" consisted of, and why those branded as "heretics" were persecuted during the Middle Ages.

Morris, Colin. *The Papal Monarchy: The Western Church from 1050 to 1250*. Oxford, 1989. An excellent scholarly survey; part of the Oxford History of the Christian Church series.

Newman, Barbara, ed. *Voice of the Living Light: Hildegard of Bingen and Her World*. Berkeley and Los Angeles, CA, 1998. An introduction to Hildegard's life and work.

Otto, Bishop of Freising. *The Deeds of Frederick Barbarossa*. Trans. C. C. Mierow. New York, 1953. A contemporary chronicle interesting enough to read from start to finish.

Smalley, Beryl. *The Study of the Bible in the Middle Ages*, 3d ed. Oxford, 1983. The standard work, gracefully written and illuminating.

Strayer, Joseph R. *On the Medieval Origins of the Modern State*. With new forewords by Charles Tilly and William Chester Jordan. Princeton, 2005. This new edition of Strayer's series of lectures places them in their scholarly context.

Swanson, R. N. *The Twelfth-Century Renaissance*. Manchester, UK, 1999. An updated survey of the intellectual developments of the twelfth century.

Symes, Carol. *A Common Stage: Theater and Public Life in Medieval Arras*. Ithaca, NY, 2007. A study of a vibrant cultural hub.

Wakefield, Walter, and Austin P. Evans, eds. and trans. *Heresies of the High Middle Ages*. New York, 1969, 1991. A comprehensive collection of sources.

Wilhelm, James J., ed. and trans. *Medieval Song: An Anthology of Hymns and Lyrics*. New York, 1971. An excellent collection of sacred and secular poetry that illustrates the connections between them.

Wolfram von Eschenbach. *Parzival*. Trans. H. M. Mustard and C. E. Passage. New York, 1961.

CHAPTER 10

Abu-Lughod, Janet L. *Before European Hegemony: The World System* A.D. *1250–1350*. Oxford and New York, 1989. A study of the trading links among Europe, the Middle East, India, and China, with special attention to the role of the Mongol Empire; extensive bibliography.

Allsen, Thomas T. *Culture and Conquest in Mongol Eurasia*. Cambridge and New York, 2001. A synthesis of the author's earlier studies, emphasizing Mongol involvement in the cultural and commercial exchanges that linked China, Central Asia, and Europe.

Christian, David. *A History of Russia, Central Asia and Mongolia*. Vol. 1, *Inner Eurasia from Prehistory to the Mongol Empire*. Oxford, 1998. The authoritative English-language work on the subject.

Cole, Bruce. *Giotto and Florentine Painting, 1280–1375*. New York, 1976. A clear and stimulating introduction.

Crummey, Robert O. *The Formation of Muscovy, 1304–1613*. New York, 1987. The standard account.

Dante Alighieri. *The Divine Comedy*. Trans. Mark Musa. 3 vols. Baltimore, MD, 1984–86.

Dunn, Ross E. *The Adventures of Ibn Battuta: A Muslim Traveler of the Fourteenth Century*. Berkeley, rev. ed. 2005. Places the writings and experiences of this far-reaching Muslim traveler in their historical and geographical contexts.

Dyer, Christopher. *Standards of Living in the Later Middle Ages: Social Change in England, c. 1200–1520*. Cambridge and New York, 1989. Detailed but highly rewarding.

Foltz, Richard. *Religions of the Silk Road: Premodern Patterns of Globalization*. New York, 2nd ed. 2010. A compelling and thought-provoking study of the varieties of religious experience and cross-cultural interaction in medieval Eurasia.

The History and the Life of Chinggis Khan: The Secret History of the Mongols. Trans. Urgunge Onon. Leiden, 1997. A newer version of *The Secret History*, now the standard English version of this important Mongol source.

Horrox, Rosemary, ed. *The Black Death*. New York, 1994. A fine collection of documents reflecting the impact of the Black Death, especially in England.

Jackson, Peter. *The Mongols and the West, 1221–1410*. Harlow, UK, 2005. A well-written survey that emphasizes the interactions among the Mongol, Latin Christian, and Muslim worlds.

Jordan, William Chester. *The Great Famine: Northern Europe in the Early Fourteenth Century.* Princeton, NJ, 1996. An outstanding social and economic study.

Keen, Maurice, ed. *Medieval Warfare: A History.* Oxford and New York, 1999. The most attractive introduction to this important subject. Lively and well illustrated.

Kitsikopoulos, Harry, ed. *Agrarian Change and Crisis in Europe, 1200–1500.* London, 2011. An up-to-date collection of scholarly essays that addresses a classic and complicated set of historical questions.

Komaroff, Linda and Stefano Carboni, eds. *The Legacy of Ghenghis Khan: Courtly Art and Culture in Western Asia, 1256–1353.* New York, 2002. An informative and lavishly illustrated catalog of an acclaimed exhibition.

Larner, John. *Marco Polo and the Discovery of the World.* New Haven, CT, 1999. A study of the influence of Marco Polo's *Travels* on Europeans.

Mandeville's Travels. Ed. M. C. Seymour. Oxford, 1968. An edition of the *Book of Marvels* based on the Middle English version popular in the fifteenth century.

Memoirs of a Renaissance Pope: The Commentaries of Pius II. Abridged ed. Trans. F. A. Gragg, New York, 1959. Remarkable insights into the mind of a particularly well-educated mid-fifteenth-century pope.

Nicholas, David. *The Transformation of Europe, 1300–1600.* Oxford and New York, 1999. The best textbook presently available.

Rossabi, M. *Khubilai Khan: His Life and Times.* Berkeley, CA, 1988. The standard English biography.

Swanson, R. N. *Religion and Devotion in Europe, c. 1215–c. 1515.* Cambridge and New York, 1995. An excellent study of late-medieval popular piety; an excellent complement to Oakley.

The Travels of Marco Polo. Ed. Peter Harris. London, 2008 repr. A new edition of a classic translation.

Vaughan, Richard. *Valois Burgundy.* London, 1975. A summation of the author's four-volume study of the Burgundian dukes.

CHAPTER 11

Alberti, Leon Battista. *The Family in Renaissance Florence (Della Famiglia).* Trans. Renée Neu Watkins. Columbia, SC, 1969.

Allmand, Christopher T., ed. *Society at War: The Experience of England and France During the Hundred Years' War.* Edinburgh, 1973. An outstanding collection of documents.

———. *The Hundred Years' War: England and France at War, c. 1300–c. 1450.* Cambridge and New York, 1988. Still the best analytic account of the war; after a short narrative, the book is organized topically.

Boccaccio, Giovanni. *The Decameron.* Trans. Mark Musa and P. E. Bondanella. New York, 1977.

Brucker, Gene. *Florence, the Golden Age, 1138–1737.* Berkeley and Los Angeles, CA, 1998. The standard account.

Bruni, Leonardo. *The Humanism of Leonardo Bruni: Selected Texts.* Trans. Gordon Griffiths, James Hankins, and David Thompson. Binghamton, NY, 1987. Excellent translations, with introductions, to the Latin works of a key Renaissance humanist.

Burke, Peter. *The Renaissance.* New York, 1997. A brief introduction by an influential modern historian.

Burkhardt, Jacob. *The Civilization of the Renaissance in Italy.* Many editions. The nineteenth-century work that first crystallized an image of the Italian Renaissance, and with which scholars have been wrestling ever since.

Canning, Joseph. *Ideas of Power in the Late Middle Ages, 1296–1417.* Cambridge, 2011. An old fashioned but nonetheless original synthesis.

Cassirer, Ernst, et al., eds. *The Renaissance Philosophy of Man.* Chicago, 1948. Important original works by Petrarch, Ficino, and Pico della Mirandola, among others.

Chaucer, Geoffrey. *The Canterbury Tales.* Trans. Nevill Coghill. New York, 1951. A modern English verse translation, lightly annotated.

Cohn, Samuel K., Jr. *Lust for Liberty: The Politics of Social Revolt in Medieval Europe, 1200–1425. Italy, France, and Flanders.* Cambridge, MA, 2006. An important new study.

Coles, Paul. *The Ottoman Impact on Europe.* London, 1968. An excellent introductory text, still valuable despite its age.

Dobson, R. Barrie. *The Peasants' Revolt of 1381,* 2d ed. London, 1983. A comprehensive source collection, with excellent introductions to the documents.

Fernández-Armesto, Felipe. *Before Columbus: Exploration and Colonisation from the Mediterranean to the Atlantic, 1229–1492.* London, 1987. An indispensible study of the medieval background to the sixteenth-century European colonial empires.

Froissart, Jean. *Chronicles.* Trans. Geoffrey Brereton. Baltimore, MD, 1968. A selection from the most famous contemporary account of the Hundred Years' War to about 1400.

Goffman, Daniel. *The Ottoman Empire and Early Modern Europe.* Cambridge and New York, 2002. A revisionist account that presents the Ottoman Empire as a European state.

Hankins, James. *Plato in the Italian Renaissance.* Leiden and New York, 1990. A definitive study of the reception and influence of Plato on Renaissance intellectuals.

———, ed. *Renaissance Civic Humanism: Reappraisals and Reflections.* Cambridge and New York, 2000. An excellent collection of scholarly essays reassessing republicanism in the Renaissance.

Hobbins, Daniel, ed. and trans. *The Trial of Joan of Arc.* Cambridge, MA, 2007. A new and excellent translation of the transcripts of Joan's trial.

Inalcik, Halil. *The Ottoman Empire: The Classical Age, 1300–1600.* London, 1973. The standard history by the dean of Turkish historians.

———, ed. *An Economic and Social History of the Ottoman Empire, 1300–1914.* Cambridge, 1994. An important collection of essays, spanning the full range of Ottoman history.

John Hus at the Council of Constance. Trans. M. Spinka, New York, 1965. The translation of a Czech chronicle with an expert introduction and appended documents.

Kafadar, Cemal. *Between Two Worlds: The Construction of the Ottoman State.* Berkeley and Los Angeles, 1995. An important study of Ottoman origins in the border regions between Byzantium, the Seljuk Turks, and the Mongols.

Kempe, Margery. *The Book of Margery Kempe*. Trans. Barry Windeatt. New York, 1985. A fascinating personal narrative by an early-fifteenth-century Englishwoman who hoped she might be a saint.

Lane, Frederic C. *Venice: A Maritime Republic*. Baltimore, MD, 1973. An authoritative account.

Morgan, David. *The Mongols*. 2d ed. Oxford, 2007. An accessible introduction to Mongol history and its sources, written by a noted expert on medieval Persia.

Ormrod, W. Mark. *Edward III*. New Haven, 2012. A new biography of this English monarch by a leading social historian.

Saunders, J. J. *The History of the Mongol Conquests*. London, 1971. Still the standard English-language introduction; somewhat more positive about the Mongols' accomplishments than is Morgan.

Shirley, Janet, trans. *A Parisian Journal, 1405–1449*. Oxford, 1968. A marvelous panorama of Parisian life recorded by an eyewitness.

Sumption, Jonathan. *The Hundred Years' War*. Vol. 1: *Trial by Battle*. Vol. 2: *Trial by Fire*. Philadelphia, 1999. The first two volumes of a massive narrative history of the war, carrying the story up to 1369.

The Four Voyages: Christopher Columbus. Trans. J. M. Cohen. New York, 1992. Columbus's own self-serving account of his four voyages to the Indies.

CHAPTER 12

Baxandall, Michael. *Painting and Experience in Fifteenth-Century Italy*. Oxford, 1972. A classic study of the perceptual world of the Renaissance.

Castiglione, Baldassare. *The Book of the Courtier*. Many editions. The translations by C. S. Singleton (New York, 1959) and by George Bull (New York, 1967) are both excellent.

Cellini, Benvenuto. *Autobiography*. Trans. George Bull. Baltimore, MD, 1956. This Florentine goldsmith (1500–1571) is the source for many of the most famous stories about the artists of the Florentine Renaissance.

Erasmus, Desiderius. *The Praise of Folly*. Trans. J. Wilson. Ann Arbor, MI, 1958.

Fernández-Armesto, Felipe. *1492: The Year the World Began*. London, 2010. A panoramic view of the world in a pivotal year, putting the voyage of Columbus in a broad historical perspective.

Flint, Valerie I. J. *The Imaginative Landscape of Christopher Columbus*. Princeton, NJ, 1992. A short, suggestive analysis of the intellectual influences that shaped Columbus's geographical ideas.

Fox, Alistair. *Thomas More: History and Providence*. Oxford, 1982. A balanced account of a man too easily idealized.

Grafton, Anthony, and Lisa Jardine. *From Humanism to the Humanities: Education and the Liberal Arts in Fifteenth- and Sixteenth-Century Europe*. London, 1986. An account that presents Renaissance humanism as the elitist cultural program of a self-interested group of pedagogues.

Grendler, Paul, ed. *Encyclopedia of the Renaissance*. New York, 1999. A valuable reference work.

Jardine, Lisa. *Worldly Goods*. London, 1996. A revisionist account that emphasizes the acquisitive materialism of Italian Renaissance society and culture.

Kanter, Laurence, Hilliard T. Goldfarb, and James Hankins. *Botticelli's Witness: Changing Style in a Changing Florence*. Boston, 1997. This catalog for an exhibition of Botticelli's works, at the Gardner Museum in Boston, offers an excellent introduction to the painter and his world.

King, Margaret L. *Women of the Renaissance*. Chicago, 1991. Deals with women in all walks of life and in a variety of roles.

Kristeller, Paul O. *Renaissance Thought: The Classic, Scholastic, and Humanistic Strains*. New York, 1961. Very helpful in defining the main trends of Renaissance thought.

Machiavelli, Niccolò. *The Discourses* and *The Prince*. Many editions. These two books must be read together if one is to understand Machiavelli's political ideas properly.

Mallett, Michael and Christine Shaw. *The Italian Wars, 1494–1559: War, State, and Society in Early Modern Europe*. Boston, 2012. Argues that the endemic warfare of this period within Italy revolutionized European military tactics and technologies.

Mann, Charles. C. *1491: New Revelations of the Americas Before Columbus*. New York, 2006.

———. *1493: Uncovering the New World Columbus Created*. New York, 2012. Written for a popular audience, these are also engaging and well-informed syntheses of historical research.

Martines, Lauro. *Power and Imagination: City-States in Renaissance Italy*. New York, 1979. Insightful account of the connections among politics, society, culture, and art.

More, Thomas. *Utopia*. Many editions.

Olson, Roberta, *Italian Renaissance Sculpture*. New York, 1992. The most accessible introduction to the subject.

Parker, Geoffrey. *The Military Revolution: Military Innovation and the Rise of the West (1500–1800)*. 2d ed. Cambridge and New York, 1996. A work of fundamental importance for understanding the global dominance achieved by early modern Europeans.

Perkins, Leeman L. *Music in the Age of the Renaissance*. New York, 1999. A massive new study that needs to be read in conjunction with Reese.

Phillips, J. R. S. *The Medieval Expansion of Europe*. 2d ed. Oxford, 1998. An outstanding study of the thirteenth- and fourteenth-century background to the fifteenth-century expansion of Europe. Important synthetic treatment of European relations with the Mongols, China, Africa, and North America. The second edition includes a new introduction and a bibliographical essay; the text is the same as in the first edition (1988).

Phillips, William D., Jr., and Carla R. Phillips. *The Worlds of Christopher Columbus*. Cambridge and New York, 1991. The first book to read on Columbus: accessible, engaging, and scholarly. Then read Fernández-Armesto's biography.

Rabelais, François. *Gargantua and Pantagruel*. Trans. J. M. Cohen. Baltimore, MD, 1955. A robust modern translation.

Reese, Gustave. *Music in the Renaissance*, rev. ed. New York, 1959. A great book; still authoritative, despite the more recent work by Perkins, which supplements but does not replace it.

Rice, Eugene F., Jr., and Anthony Grafton. *The Foundations of Early Modern Europe, 1460–1559*, 2d ed. New York, 1994. The best textbook account of its period.

Rowland, Ingrid D. *The Culture of the High Renaissance: Ancients and Moderns in Sixteenth-Century Rome*. Cambridge and New York, 2000. Beautifully written examination of the social, intellectual, and economic foundations of the Renaissance in Rome.

Russell, Peter. *Prince Henry "The Navigator": A Life*. New Haven, CT, 2000. A masterly biography by a great historian who has spent a lifetime on the subject. The only book one now needs to read on Prince Henry.

Scammell, Geoffrey V. *The First Imperial Age: European Overseas Expansion, 1400–1715*. London, 1989. A useful introductory survey, with a particular focus on English and French colonization.

CHAPTER 13

Bainton, Roland. *Erasmus of Christendom*. New York, 1969. Still the best biography in English of the Dutch reformer and intellectual.

Benedict, Philip. *Christ's Churches Purely Reformed: A Social History of Calvinism*. New Haven, CT, 2002. A wide-ranging recent survey of Calvinism in both western and eastern Europe.

Bossy, John. *Christianity in the West, 1400–1700*. Oxford and New York, 1985. A brilliant, challenging picture of the changes that took place in Christian piety and practice as a result of the sixteenth-century reformations.

Bouwsma, William J. *John Calvin: A Sixteenth-Century Portrait*. Oxford and New York, 1988. The best biography of the magisterial reformer.

Dixon, C. Scott, ed. *The German Reformation: The Essential Readings*. Oxford, 1999. A collection of important recent articles.

Duffy, Eamon. *The Stripping of the Altars: Traditional Religion in England, c. 1400–c. 1550*. A brilliant study of religious exchange at the parish level.

———. *The Voices of Morebath: Reformation and Rebellion in an English Village*. New Haven, 2003. How the crises of this period affected and are reflected in the history of a single parish.

Hart, D. G. *Calvinism: A History*. New Haven, 2013. A new survey of this leading Protestant movement from its beginnings to the present day.

John Calvin: Selections from His Writings, ed. John Dillenberger. Garden City, NY, 1971. A judicious selection, drawn mainly from Calvin's *Institutes*.

Koslofksy, Craig. *The Reformation of the Dead: Death and Ritual in Early Modern Germany*. Basingstoke, 2000. How essential rituals and responses to death were reshaped in this period.

Loyola, Ignatius. *Personal Writings*. Trans. by Joseph A. Munitiz and Philip Endean. London and New York, 1996. An excellent collection that includes Loyola's autobiography, his spiritual diary, and some of his letters, as well as his *Spiritual Exercises*.

Luebke, David, ed. *The Counter-Reformation: The Essential Readings*. Oxford, 1999. A collection of nine important recent essays.

MacCulloch, Diarmaid. *Reformation: Europe's House Divided, 1490–1700*. London and New York, 2003. A definitive new survey; the best single-volume history of its subject in a generation.

Martin Luther: Selections from His Writings, ed. John Dillenberger. Garden City, NY, 1961. The standard selection, especially good on Luther's theological ideas.

McGrath, Alister E. *Reformation Thought: An Introduction*. Oxford, 1993. A useful explanation, accessible to non-Christians, of the theological ideas of the major Protestant reformers.

Mullett, Michael A. *The Catholic Reformation*. London, 2000. A sympathetic survey of Catholicism from the mid-sixteenth to the eighteenth century that presents the mid-sixteenth-century Council of Trent as a continuation of earlier reform efforts.

Murray, Linda. *High Renaissance and Mannerism*. London, 1985. The place to begin a study of fifteenth- and sixteenth-century Italian art.

Oberman, Heiko A. *Luther: Man between God and the Devil*. Trans. by Eileen Walliser-Schwarzbart. New Haven, CT, 1989. A biography stressing Luther's preoccupations with sin, death, and the devil.

O'Malley, John W. *The First Jesuits*. Cambridge, MA, 1993. A scholarly account of the origins and early years of the Society of Jesus.

———. *Trent and All That: Renaming Catholicism in the Early Modern Era*. Cambridge, MA, 2000. Short, lively, and with a full bibliography.

———. *Trent: What Happened at the Council*. Cambridge, MA, 2012. A clear and comprehensive narrative of the Church council that gave birth to the modern Catholic Church.

Pettegree, Andrew, ed. *The Reformation World*. New York, 2000. An exhaustive multi-author work representing the most recent thinking about the Reformation.

Pelikan, Jaroslav. *Reformation of Church and Dogma, 1300–1700*. Vol. 4 of *A History of Christian Dogma*. Chicago, 1984. A masterful synthesis of Reformation theology in its late-medieval context.

Roper, Lyndal. *The Holy Household: Women and Morals in Reformation Augsburg*. Oxford, 1989. A pathbreaking study of Protestantism's effects on a single town, with special attention to its impact on attitudes toward women, the family, and marriage.

Shagan, Ethan H. *Popular Politics and the English Reformation*. Cambridge, 2002. Argues that the English Reformation reflects an ongoing process of negotiation, resistance, and response.

Tracy, James D. *Europe's Reformations, 1450–1650*. 2d ed. Lanham, MD, 2006. An outstanding survey, especially strong on Dutch and Swiss developments, but excellent throughout.

Williams, George H. *The Radical Reformation*. 3d ed. Kirksville, MO, 1992. Originally published in 1962, this is still the best book on Anabaptism and its offshoots.

CHAPTER 14

Bonney, Richard. *The European Dynastic States, 1494–1660*. Oxford and New York, 1991. An excellent survey of continental Europe during the "long" sixteenth century.

Briggs, Robin. *Early Modern France, 1560–1715*, 2d ed. Oxford and New York, 1997. Updated and authoritative, with new bibliographies.

———. *Witches and Neighbors: The Social and Cultural Context of European Witchcraft*. New York, 1996. An influential recent account of Continental witchcraft.

Cervantes, Miguel de. *Don Quixote*. Trans. Edith Grossman. New York, 2003. A splendid new translation.

Clarke, Stuart. *Thinking with Demons: The Idea of Witchcraft in Early Modern Europe*. Oxford and New York, 1999. By placing demonology into the context of sixteenth- and seventeenth-century intellectual history, Clarke makes sense of it in new and exciting ways.

Cochrane, Eric, Charles M. Gray, and Mark A. Kishlansky. *Early Modern Europe: Crisis of Authority*. Chicago, 1987. An outstanding source collection from the University of Chicago Readings in Western Civilization series.

Elliot, J. H. *The Old World and the New, 1492–1650*. Cambridge, 1992 repr. A brilliant and brief set of essays on the ways that the discovery of the Americas challenged European perspectives on the world and themselves.

———. *Empires of the Atlantic World: Britain and Spain in America, 1492–1830*. An illuminating comparative study. New Haven, 2007.

Hibbard, Howard. *Bernini*. Baltimore, MD, 1965. The basic study in English of this central figure of Baroque artistic activity.

Hirst, Derek. *England in Conflict, 1603–1660: Kingdom, Community, Commonwealth*. Oxford and New York, 1999. A complete revision of the author's *Authority and Conflict* (1986), this is an up-to-date and balanced account of a period that has been a historical battleground over the past twenty years.

Hobbes, Thomas. *Leviathan*. Ed. Richard Tuck. 2d ed. Cambridge and New York, 1996. The most recent edition, containing the entirety of *Leviathan*, not just the first two parts.

Holt, Mack P. *The French Wars of Religion, 1562–1629*. Cambridge and New York, 1995. A clear account of a confusing time.

Kors, Alan Charles, and Edward Peters. *Witchcraft in Europe, 400–1700: A Documentary History*, 2d ed. Philadelphia, 2000. A superb collection of documents, significantly expanded in the second edition, with up-to-date commentary.

Kingdon, Robert. *Myths about the St. Bartholomew's Day Massacres, 1572–1576*. Cambridge, MA, 1988. A detailed account of this pivotal moment in the history of France.

Levack, Brian P. *The Witch-Hunt in Early Modern Europe*, 2d ed. London and New York, 1995. The best account of the persecution of suspected witches; coverage extends from Europe in 1450 to America in 1750.

Levin, Carole. *The Heart and Stomach of a King: Elizabeth I and the Politics of Sex and Power*. Philadelphia, PA, 1994. A provocative argument for the importance of Elizabeth's gender for understanding her reign.

Limm, Peter, ed. *The Thirty Years' War*. London, 1984. An outstanding short survey, followed by a selection of primary-source documents.

Lynch, John. *Spain, 1516–1598: From Nation-State to World Empire*. Oxford and Cambridge, MA, 1991. The best book in English on Spain at the pinnacle of its sixteenth-century power.

MacCaffrey, Wallace. *Elizabeth I*. New York, 1993. An outstanding traditional biography by an excellent scholar.

Martin, Colin, and Geoffrey Parker. *The Spanish Armada*. London, 1988. Incorporates recent discoveries from undersea archaeology with more traditional historical sources.

Mattingly, Garrett. *The Armada*. Boston, 1959. A great narrative history that reads like a novel; for more recent work, however, see Martin and Parker.

McGregor, Neil. *Shakespeare's Restless World*. London, 2013. Based on an acclaimed BBC Radio program, this book illuminates Shakespeare's life, times, and plays with reference to specific objects in the British Museum.

Newson, Linda A. and Susie Minchin. *From Capture to Sale: The Portuguese Slave Trade to Spanish South America in the Early Seventeenth Century*. London, 2007. Makes use of slave traders' own rich archives to track the process of human trafficking.

Parker, Geoffrey. *The Dutch Revolt*, 2d ed. Ithaca, NY, 1989. The standard survey in English on the revolt of the Netherlands.

———. *Philip II*. Boston, 1978. A fine biography by an expert in both the Spanish and the Dutch sources.

———, ed. *The Thirty Years' War*, rev. ed. London and New York, 1987. A wide-ranging collection of essays by scholarly experts.

Pascal, Blaise. *Pensées* (French-English edition). Ed. H. F. Stewart. London, 1950.

Pestana, Carla. *Protestant Empire: Religion and the Making of the British Atlantic World*. Philadelphia, 2010. How the Reformation helped to drive British imperial expansion.

Roberts, Michael. *Gustavus Adolphus and the Rise of Sweden*. London, 1973. Still the authoritative English-language account.

Russell, Conrad. *The Causes of the English Civil War*. Oxford, 1990. A penetrating and provocative analysis by one of the leading "revisionist" historians of the period.

Schmidt, Benjamin. *Innocence Abroad: The Dutch Imagination and the New World, 1570–1670*. Cambridge, 2006. A cultural history of Europeans' encounter with the Americas that highlights the perspective and experience of Dutch merchants, colonists, and artists.

Tracy, James D. *Holland under Habsburg Rule, 1506–1566: The Formation of a Body Politic*. Berkeley and Los Angeles, CA, 1990. A political history and analysis of the formative years of the Dutch state.

CHAPTER 15

Beik, William. *A Social and Cultural History of Early Modern France*. Cambridge, UK, 2009. A broad synthesis of French history from the end of the Middle Ages to the French Revolution, by one of the world's foremost authorities on absolutism.

Clark, Christopher, *Iron Kingdom: The Rise and Downfall of Prussia, 1600–1947*. Cambridge, MA, 2009. A definitive account of Prussian history over nearly four centuries.

Jones, Colin. *The Great Nation: France From Louis XV to Napoleon*. New York, 2002. An excellent and readable scholarly account that argues that the France of Louis XV in the eighteenth century was even more dominant than the kingdom of Louis XIV in the preceding century.

Kishlansky, Mark A. *A Monarchy Transformed: Britain, 1603–1714.* London, 1996. An excellent survey that takes seriously its claims to be a "British" rather than merely an "English" history.

Klein, Herbert S. *The Atlantic Slave Trade.* Cambridge and New York, 1999. An accessible survey by a leading quantitative historian.

Lewis, William Roger, gen. ed. *The Oxford History of the British Empire.* Vol. I: *The Origins of Empire: British Overseas Enterprise to the Close of the Seventeenth Century*, ed. Nicholas Canny. Vol. II: *The Eighteenth Century*, ed. Peter J. Marshall. Oxford and New York, 1998. A definitive, multiauthor account.

Locke, John. *Two Treatises of Government.* Ed. Peter Laslett. Rev. ed. Cambridge and New York, 1963. Laslett has revolutionized our understanding of the historical and ideological context of Locke's political writings.

Massie, Robert. *Peter the Great, His Life and World.* New York, 1980. Prize-winning and readable narrative account of the Russian tsar's life.

Monod, Paul K. *The Power of Kings: Monarchy and Religion in Europe, 1589–1715.* New Haven, CT, 1999. A study of the seventeenth century's declining confidence in the divinity of kings.

Quataert, Donald. *The Ottoman Empire, 1700–1822.* Cambridge and New York, 2000. Well balanced and intended to be read by students.

Riasanovsky, Nicholas V., and Steinberg, Mark D. *A History of Russia.* 7th ed. Oxford and New York, 2005. Far and away the best single-volume textbook on Russian history: balanced, comprehensive, intelligent, and with full bibliographies.

Saint-Simon, Louis. *Historical Memoirs.* Many editions. The classic source for life at Louis XIV's Versailles.

Snyder, Timothy, *The Reconstruction of Nations: Poland, Ukraine, Lithuania, Belarus, 1569–1999.* New Haven, CT, 2004. Essential account of nation building and state-collapse in Eastern Europe with significant relevance to the region's contemporary situation.

Thomas, Hugh. *The Slave Trade: The History of the Atlantic Slave Trade, 1440–1870.* London and New York, 1997. A survey notable for its breadth and depth of coverage and for its attractive prose style.

Tracy, James D. *The Rise of Merchant Empires: Long-Distance Trade in the Early Modern World, 1350–1750.* Cambridge and New York, 1990. Important collection of essays by leading authorities.

White, Richard. *The Middle Ground: Indians, Empires and Republics in the Great Lakes Region, 1650–1815.* Cambridge, UK, 1991. A path-breaking account of interactions between Europeans and Native Americans during the colonial period.

CHAPTER 16

Biagioli, Mario. *Galileo, Courtier.* Chicago, 1993. Emphasizes the importance of patronage and court politics in Galileo's science and career.

Cohen, I. B. *The Birth of a New Physics.* New York, 1985. Emphasizes the mathematical nature of the revolution; unmatched at making the mathematics understandable.

Daston, Lorraine, and Elizabeth Lunbeck, eds. *Histories of Scientific Observation.* Chicago, IL, 2011. Field-defining collection of essays on the history of scientific observation from the seventeenth to the twentieth centuries.

Daston, Lorraine. *Wonders and the Order of Nature, 1150–1750.* Cambridge, MA, 2001. Erudite sweeping account of the history of science in the early modern period, emphasizing the natural philosopher's awe and wonder at the marvelous, the unfamiliar, and the counter-intuitive.

Dear, Peter. *Revolutionizing the Sciences: European Knowledge and Its Ambitions, 1500–1700.* Princeton, NJ, 2001. Among the best short histories.

Drake, Stillman. *Discoveries and Opinions of Galileo.* Garden City, NY, 1957. The classic translation of Galileo's most important papers by his most admiring modern biographer.

Feingold, Mardechai, *The Newtonian Moment: Isaac Newton and the Making of Modern Culture.* New York, 2004. An engaging essay on the dissemination of Newton's thought, with excellent visual material.

Gaukroger, Stephen. *Descartes: An Intellectual Biography.* Oxford, 1995. Detailed and sympathetic study of the philosopher.

Gleick, James. *Isaac Newton.* New York, 2003. A vivid and well-documented brief biography.

Grafton, Anthony. *New Worlds, Ancient Texts: The Power of Tradition and the Shock of Discovery.* Cambridge, MA, 1992. Accessible essay by one of the leading scholars of early modern European thought.

Jacob, Margaret. *Scientific Culture and the Making of the Industrial West.* Oxford, 1997. A concise examination of the connections between developments in science and the Industrial Revolution.

Kuhn, Thomas. *The Structure of Scientific Revolutions.* Chicago, 1962. A classic and much-debated study of how scientific thought changes.

Pagden, Anthony, *European Encounters with the New World.* New Haven, CT, and London, 1993. Subtle and detailed on how European intellectuals thought about the lands they saw for the first time.

Scheibinger, Londa. *The Mind Has No Sex? Women in the Origins of Modern Science.* Cambridge, MA, 1989. A lively and important recovery of the lost role played by women mathematicians and experimenters.

Shapin, Steven. *The Scientific Revolution.* Chicago, 1996. Engaging, accessible, and brief—organized thematically.

Shapin, Steven, and Simon Schaffer. *Leviathan and the Air Pump.* Princeton, NJ, 1985. A modern classic, on one of the most famous philosophical conflicts in seventeenth-century science.

Stephenson, Bruce. *The Music of the Heavens: Kepler's Harmonic Astronomy.* Princeton, NJ, 1994. An engaging and important explanation of Kepler's otherworldly perspective.

Thoren, Victor. *The Lord of Uranibourg: A Biography of Tycho Brahe.* Cambridge, 1990. A vivid reconstruction of the scientific revolution's most flamboyant astronomer.

Westfall, Richard. *The Construction of Modern Science.* Cambridge, 1977.

———. *Never at Rest: A Biography of Isaac Newton.* Cambridge, 1980. The standard work.

Wilson, Catherine. *The Invisible World: Early Modern Philosophy and the Invention of the Microscope.* Princeton, NJ, 1995. An important study of how the "microcosmic" world revealed by technology reshaped scientific philosophy and practice.

Zinsser, Judith P. *La Dame d'Esprit: A Biography of the Marquise Du Châtelet*. New York, 2006. An excellent cultural history. To be issued in paper as *Emilie du Châtelet: Daring Genius of the Enlightenment* (2007).

CHAPTER 17

Baker, Keith. *Condorcet: From Natural Philosophy to Social Mathematics*. Chicago, 1975. An important reinterpretation of Condorcet as a social scientist.

Blum, Carol. *Rousseau and the Republic of Virtue: The Language of Politics in the French Revolution*. Ithaca and London, 1986. Fascinating account of how eighteenth-century readers interpreted Rousseau.

Buchan, James. *The Authentic Adam Smith: His Life and Ideas*. New York, 2006.

Calhoun, Craig, ed. *Habermas and the Public Sphere*. Cambridge, MA, 1992. Calhoun's introduction is a good starting point for Habermas's argument.

Cassirer, E. *The Philosophy of the Enlightenment*. Princeton, NJ, 1951.

Chartier, Roger. *The Cultural Origins of the French Revolution*. Durham, NC, 1991. Looks at topics from religion to violence in everyday life and culture.

Darnton, Robert. *The Business of Enlightenment: A Publishing History of the* Encyclopédie, *1775–1800*. Cambridge, MA, 1979. Darnton's work on the Enlightenment offers a fascinating blend of intellectual, social, and economic history. See his other books as well: *The Literary Underground of the Old Regime* (Cambridge, MA, 1982); *The Great Cat Massacre and Other Episodes in French Cultural History* (New York, 1984); and *The Forbidden Best Sellers of Revolutionary France* (New York and London, 1996).

Davis, David Brion. *The Problem of Slavery in Western Culture*. New York, 1988. A Pulitzer Prize–winning examination of a central issue as well as a brilliant analysis of different strands of Enlightenment thought.

Gay, Peter. *The Enlightenment: An Interpretation*. Vol. 1, *The Rise of Modern Paganism*. Vol. 2, *The Science of Freedom*. New York, 1966–1969. Combines an overview with an interpretation. Emphasizes the *philosophes'* sense of identification with the classical world and takes a generally positive view of their accomplishments. Includes extensive annotated bibliographies.

Gray, Peter. *Mozart*. New York, 1999. Brilliant short study.

Goodman, Dena. *The Republic of Letters: A Cultural History of the French Enlightenment*. Ithaca, NY, 1994. Important in its attention to the role of literary women.

Hazard, Paul. *The European Mind: The Critical Years (1680–1715)*. New Haven, CT, 1953. A basic and indispensable account of the changing climate of opinion that preceded the Enlightenment.

Hunt, Lynn, Margaret C. Jacob, and Wijnand Mijnhardt. *The Book That Changed Europe: Picart and Bernard's Religious Ceremonies of the World*. Cambridge, MA, 2010. Lively study of a book on global religions that came out of the fertile world of the Dutch Enlightenment in the eighteenth century.

Israel, Jonathan Irvine. *Radical Enlightenment: Philosophy and the Making of Modernity, 1650–1750*. New York, 2001. Massive and erudite, a fresh look at the international movement of ideas.

———. *Enlightenment Contested: Philosophy, Modernity, and the Emancipation of Man, 1670–1752*. New York, 2006. Massive and erudite, a fresh look at the international movement of ideas.

Munck, Thomas. *The Enlightenment: A Comparative Social History 1721–1794*. London, 2000. An excellent recent survey, especially good on social history.

Outram, Dorinda. *The Enlightenment*. Cambridge, 1995. An excellent short introduction and a good example of new historical approaches.

Pagden, Anthony. *The Enlightenment: And Why It Still Matters*. New York, 2013. Spirited history of the Enlightenment and a defense of its continued relevance.

Porter, Roy. *The Creation of the Modern World: The Untold Story of the British Enlightenment*. New York, 2000.

Sapiro, Virginia. *A Vindication of Political Virtue: The Political Theory of Mary Wollstonecraft*. Chicago, 1992. A subtle and intelligent analysis for more advanced readers.

Shklar, Judith. *Men and Citizens: A Study of Rousseau's Social Theory*. London, 1969.

———. *Montesquieu*. Oxford, 1987. Shklar's studies are brilliant and accessible.

Taylor, Barbara. *Mary Wollstonecraft and the Feminist Imagination*. Cambridge and New York, 2003. Fascinating study that sets Wollstonecraft in the radical circles of eighteenth-century England.

Taylor, Barbara and Sarah Knott, eds. *Women, Gender, and Enlightenment*. New York, 2007. Multi-author collection examining the significance of sex, gender, and politics across a wide swath of the Enlightenment world, from Europe to the American colonies.

Venturi, Franco. *The End of the Old Regime in Europe, 1768–1776: The First Crisis*. Trans. R. Burr Litchfield. Princeton, NJ, 1989.

———. *The End of the Old Regime in Europe, 1776–1789*. Princeton, NJ, 1991. Both detailed and wide-ranging, particularly important on international developments.

Watt, Ian P. *The Rise of the Novel*. London, 1957. The basic work on the innovative qualities of the novel in eighteenth-century England.

Wolff, Larry. *Inventing Eastern Europe: The Map of Civilization on the Mind of the Enlightenment*. Stanford, CA, 1994. The place of Eastern Europe in the imagination of Enlightenment thinkers interested in the origins and destiny of the civilizing process.

CHAPTER 18

Applewhite, Harriet B., and Darline G. Levy, eds. *Women and Politics in the Age of the Democratic Revolution*. Ann Arbor, MI, 1990. Essays on France, Britain, the Netherlands, and the United States.

Bell, David A. *The First Total War: Napoleon's Europe and the Birth of Warfare as We Know It*. Boston and New York, 2007. Lively and concise study of the "cataclysmic intensification" of warfare.

Blackburn, Robin. *The Overthrow of Colonial Slavery*. London and New York, 1988. A longer view of slavery and its abolition.

Blanning, T. C. W. *The French Revolutionary Wars, 1787–1802*. Oxford, 1996. On the revolution and war.

Blum, Carol. *Rousseau and the Republic of Virtue: The Language of Politics in the French Revolution*. Ithaca, NY, 1986. Excellent on how Rousseau was read by the revolutionaries.

Cobb, Richard. *The People's Armies*. New Haven, CT, 1987. Brilliant and detailed analysis of the popular militias.

Cole, Juan. *Napoleon's Egypt: Invading the Middle East*. New York, 2007. Readable history by a scholar familiar with sources in Arabic as well as European languages.

Connelly, Owen. *The French Revolution and Napoleonic Era*. 3rd ed. New York, 2000. Accessible, lively, one-volume survey.

Darnton, Robert, *The Forbidden Best-Sellers of Pre-Revolutionary France*. New York, 1995. One of Darnton's many imaginative studies of subversive opinion and books on the eve of the revolution.

Desan, Suzanne. *The Family on Trial in Revolutionary France*. Berkeley, CA, 2006. Persuasive study of the ways that women in France were able to take advantage of the revolution and defend their interests in debates about marriage, divorce, parenthood, and the care of children.

Desan, Suzanne, Lynn Hunt, and William Max Nelson, eds. *The French Revolution in Global Perspective*. Ithaca, NY, 2013. Multi-author exploration of the French Revolution's global resonance.

Doyle, William. *Origins of the French Revolution*. New York, 1988. A revisionist historian surveys recent research on the political and social origins of the revolution and identifies a new consensus.

———. *Oxford History of the French Revolution*. New York, 1989.

Dubois, Laurent. *Avengers of the New World. The Story of the Haitian Revolution*. Cambridge, MA, 2004. Now the best and most accessible study.

———, and John D. Garrigus. *Slave Revolution in the Caribbean, 1789–1804: A Brief History with Documents*. New York, 2006. A particularly good collection.

Englund, Steven. *Napoleon, A Political Life*. Cambridge, MA, 2004. Prize-winning biography, both dramatic and insightful.

Forrest, Alan. *The French Revolution and the Poor*. New York, 1981. A moving and detailed social history of the poor, who fared little better under revolutionary governments than under the Old Regime.

Furet, Francois. *Revolutionary France, 1770–1880*. Trans. Antonia Nerill. Cambridge, MA, 1992. Overview by the leading revisionist.

Hunt, Lynn. *The French Revolution and Human Rights*. Boston, 1996. A collection of documents.

———. *Politics, Culture, and Class in the French Revolution*. Berkeley, CA, 1984. An analysis of the new culture of democracy and republicanism.

Hunt, Lynn, and Jack R. Censer. *Liberty, Equality, Fraternity: Exploring the French Revolution*. University Park, PA, 2001. Two leading historians of the revolution have written a lively, accessible study, with excellent documents and visual material.

Landes, Joan B. *Women and the Public Sphere in the Age of the French Revolution*. Ithaca, NY, 1988. On gender and politics.

Lefebvre, Georges. *The Coming of the French Revolution*. Princeton, NJ, 1947. The classic Marxist analysis.

Lewis, G., and C. Lucas. *Beyond the Terror: Essays in French Regional and Social History, 1794–1815*. New York, 1983. Shifts focus to the understudied period after the Terror.

O'Brien, Connor Cruise. *The Great Melody: A Thematic Biography of Edmund Burke*. Chicago, 1992. Passionate, partisan, and brilliant study of Burke's thoughts about Ireland, India, America, and France.

Palmer, R. R. *The Age of the Democratic Revolution: A Political History of Europe and America, 1760–1800*. 2 vols. Princeton, NJ, 1964. Impressive for its scope; places the French Revolution in the larger context of a worldwide revolutionary movement.

———, and Isser Woloch. *Twelve Who Ruled: The Year of the Terror in the French Revolution*. Princeton, NJ, 2005. The terrific collective biography of the Committee of Public Safety, now updated.

Schama, Simon. *Citizens: A Chronicle of the French Revolution*. New York, 1989. Particularly good on art, culture, and politics.

Scott, Joan. *Only Paradoxes to Offer: French Feminists and the Rights of Man*. Cambridge, MA, 1997. A history of feminist engagement with a revolutionary ideology that promised universal liberties while simultaneously excluding women from citizenship.

Soboul, Albert. *The Sans-Culottes: The Popular Movement and Revolutionary Government, 1793–1794*. Garden City, NY, 1972. Dated, but a classic.

Sutherland, D. M. G. *France, 1789–1815: Revolution and Counterrevolution*. Oxford, 1986. An important synthesis of work on the revolution, especially in social history.

Tocqueville, Alexis de. *The Old Regime and the French Revolution*. Garden City, NY, 1955. Originally written in 1856, this remains a provocative analysis of the revolution's legacy.

Trouillot, Michel Rolph. *Silencing the Past*. Boston, 1995. Essays on the Haitian revolution.

Woloch, Isser. *The New Regime: Transformations of the French Civic Order, 1789–1820*. New York, 1994. The fate of revolutionary civic reform.

Woolf, Stuart. *Napoleon's Integration of Europe*. New York, 1991. Technical but very thorough.

CHAPTER 19

Bridenthal, Renate, Claudia Koonz, and Susan Stuard, eds. *Becoming Visible: Women in European History*. 2d ed. Boston, 1987. Excellent, wide-ranging introduction.

Briggs, Asa. *Victorian Cities*. New York, 1963. A survey of British cities, stressing middle-class attitudes toward the new urban environment.

Chevalier, Louis. *Laboring Classes and Dangerous Classes during the First Half of the Nineteenth Century*. New York, 1973. An important, though controversial, account of crime, class, and middle-class perceptions of life in Paris.

Cipolla, Carlo M., ed. *The Industrial Revolution, 1700–1914*. New York, 1976. A collection of essays that emphasizes the wide range of industrializing experiences in Europe.

Clark, Anna. *The Struggle for the Breeches: Gender and the Making of the British Working Class*. Berkeley, CA, 1997. Examines the process of class formation during the industrial revolution in Britain through the lens of gender.

Cott, Nancy. *The Bonds of Womanhood: "Woman's Sphere" in New England, 1780–1935*. New Haven, CT, and London, 1977. One of the most influential studies of the paradoxes of domesticity.

Davidoff, Leonore, and Catherine Hall. *Family Fortunes: Men and Women of the English Middle Class, 1780–1850*. Chicago, 1985. A brilliant and detailed study of the lives and ambitions of several English families.

Ferguson, Niall. "The European Economy, 1815–1914." In *The Nine-teenth Century*, ed. T. C. W. Blanning. Oxford and New York, 2000. A very useful short essay.

Gay, Peter. *The Bourgeois Experience: Victoria to Freud*. New York, 1984. A multivolume, path-breaking study of middle-class life in all its dimensions.

———. *Schnitzler's Century: The Making of Middle-Class Culture, 1815–1914*. New York and London, 2002. A synthesis of some of the arguments presented in *The Bourgeois Experience*.

Hellerstein, Erna, Leslie Hume, and Karen Offen, eds. *Victorian Women: A Documentary Account*. Stanford, CA, 1981. Good collection of documents, with excellent introductory essays.

Hobsbawm, Eric J. *The Age of Revolution, 1789–1848*. London, 1962.

———, and George Rudé. *Captain Swing: A Social History of the Great English Agricultural Uprising of 1830*. New York, 1975. Analyzes rural protest and politics.

Horn, Jeff. *The Path Not Taken: French Industrialization in the Age of Revolution, 1750–1830*. Cambridge, 2006. Argues that industrialization in France succeeded in ways that other historians have not appreciated, and was much more than a failed attempt to imitate the British model.

Jones, Eric. *The European Miracle: Environments, Economies and Geopolitics in the History of Europe and Asia*. Cambridge, 2003. Argues that the Industrial Revolution is best understood as a European phenomenon.

Kemp, Tom. *Industrialization in Nineteenth-Century Europe*. London, 1985. Good general study.

Kindelberger, Charles. *A Financial History of Western Europe*. London, 1984. Emphasis on finance.

Landes, David S. *The Unbound Prometheus: Technological Change and Industrial Development in Western Europe from 1750 to the Present*. London, 1969. Excellent and thorough on technological change and its social and economic context.

McNeill, J. R. *Something New under the Sun: An Environmental History of the Twentieth-Century World*. New York and London, 2000. Short section on the nineteenth century.

Mokyr, Joel. *The Lever of Riches: Technological Creativity and Economic Progress*. New York, 1992. A world history, from antiquity through the nineteenth century

O'Gráda, Cormac. *Black '47 and Beyond: The Great Irish Famine*. Princeton, NJ, 1999.

———. *The Great Irish Famine*. Cambridge, 1989. A fascinating and recent assessment of scholarship on the famine.

Kenneth Pomeranz. *The Great Divergence: China, Europe, and the Making of the Modern World Economy*. Princeton, NJ, 2000. Path-breaking global history of the Industrial Revolution that argues that Europe was not as different from other parts of the world as scholars have previously thought.

Rendall, Jane. *The Origins of Modern Feminism: Women in Britain, France and the United States, 1780–1860*. New York, 1984. Helpful overview.

Rose, Sonya O. *Limited Livelihoods: Gender and Class in Nineteenth-Century England*. Berkeley, CA, 1992. On the intersection of culture and economics.

Sabean, David Warren. *Property, Production, and Family Neckarhausen, 1700–1870*. New York, 1990. Brilliant and very detailed study of gender roles and family.

Sabel, Charles, and Jonathan Zeitlin. "Historical Alternatives to Mass Production." *Past and Present* 108 (August 1985): 133–176. On the many forms of modern industry.

Schivelbusch, Wolfgang. *Disenchanted Night: The Instrialization of Light in the Nineteenth Century*. Berkeley, CA, 1988.

———. *The Railway Journey*. Berkeley, 1986. Schivelbusch's imaginative studies are among the best ways to understand how the transformations of the nineteenth century changed daily experiences.

Thompson, E. P. *The Making of the English Working Class*. London, 1963. Shows how the French and Industrial Revolutions fostered the growth of working-class consciousness. A brilliant and important work.

Tilly, Louise, and Joan Scott. *Women, Work and the Family*. New York, 1978. Now the classic study.

Valenze, Deborah. *The First Industrial Woman*. New York, 1995. Excellent and readable on industrialization and economic change in general.

Williams, Raymond. *Keywords: A Vocabulary of Culture and Society*. New York, 1976. Brilliant and indispensable for students of culture, and now updated as *New Keywords: A Revised Vocabulary of Culture and Society* (2005), by Lawrence Grossberg and Meaghan Morris.

Zeldin, Theodore. *France, 1848–1945*, 2 vols. Oxford, 1973–1977. Eclectic and wide-ranging social history.

CHAPTER 20

Anderson, Benedict. *Imagined Communities: Reflections on the Origin and Spread of Nationalism*. London, 1983. The most influential recent study of the subject, highly recommended for further reading.

Barzun, Jacques. *Classic, Romantic, and Modern*. Chicago, 1943. An enduring and penetrating mid-twentieth-century defense of the Romantic sensibility by a humane and influential cultural historian.

Berlin, Isaiah. *Karl Marx: His Life and Environment*. 4th ed. New York, 1996. An excellent short account.

Briggs, Asa. *The Age of Improvement, 1783–1867*. New York, 1979. A survey of England from 1780 to 1870, particularly strong on Victorian attitudes.

Colley, Linda. *Britons: Forging the Nation, 1707–1837*. New Haven, CT, 1992. An important analysis of Britain's emerging national consciousness in the eighteenth and early nineteenth centuries.

Furet, François. *Revolutionary France, 1770–1880*. New York, 1970. An excellent and fresh overview by one of the preeminent historians of the revolution of 1789.

Gilbert, Sandra M., and Susan Gubar. *The Madwoman in the Attic: The Woman Writer and the Nineteenth-Century Literary Imagination*. New Haven, CT, and London, 1970. A study of the history of women writers and on examination of women writers as historians of their time.

Kramer, Lloyd. *Nationalism: Political Cultures in Europe and America, 1775–1865.* London, 1998. Excellent recent overview.

Langer, William. *Political and Social Upheaval, 1832–1851.* New York, 1969. Long the standard and still the most comprehensive survey.

Laven, David, and Lucy Riall. *Napoleon's Legacy: Problems of Government in Restoration Europe.* London, 2002. A recent collection of essays.

Levinger, Matthew. *Enlightened Nationalism: The Transformation of Prussian Political Culture 1806–1848.* New York, 2000. A nuanced study of Prussian conservatism, with implications for the rest of Europe.

Macfie, A. L. *Orientalism.* London, 2002. Introductory but very clear.

Merriman, John M., ed. *1830 in France.* New York, 1975. Emphasizes the nature of revolution and examines events outside Paris.

Pinkney, David. *The French Revolution of 1830.* Princeton, NJ, 1972. A reinterpretation, now the best history of the revolution.

Porter, Roy, and Mikulas Teich, eds. *Romanticism in National Context.* Cambridge, 1988.

Raeff, Marc. *The Decembrist Movement.* New York, 1966. A study of the Russian uprising with documents.

Sahlins, Peter. *Forest Rites: The War of the Demoiselles in Nineteenth-Century France.* Cambridge, MA, 1994. A fascinating study of relations among peasant communities, the forests, and the state.

Said, Edward W. *Orientalism.* New York, 1979. A brilliant and biting study of the imaginative hold of the Orient on European intellectuals.

Saville, John. *1848: The British State and the Chartist Movement.* New York, 1987. A detailed account of the movement's limited successes and ultimate failure.

Schroeder, Paul. *The Transformation of European Politics, 1763–1848.* Oxford and New York, 1994. For those interested in international relations and diplomacy; massively researched and a fresh look at the period. Especially good on the Congress of Vienna.

Sewell, William H. *Work and Revolution in France: The Language of Labor from the Old Regime to 1848.* Cambridge, 1980. A very influential study of French radicalism and its larger implications.

Smith, Bonnie. *The Gender of History: Men, Women, and Historical Practice.* Cambridge, MA, 1998. On Romanticism and the historical imagination.

Sperber, Jonathan. *Karl Marx: A Nineteenth-Century Life.* New York, 2013. A detailed biography examining Marx's public and private engagements, setting him in the context of his time.

Wordsworth, Jonathan, Michael C. Jaye, and Robert Woof. *William Wordsworth and the Age of English Romanticism.* New Brunswick, NJ, 1987. Wide ranging and beautifully illustrated, a good picture of the age.

CHAPTER 21

Agulhon, Maurice. *The Republican Experiment, 1848–1852.* New York, 1983. A full treatment of the revolution in France.

Beales, Derek. *The Risorgimento and the Unification of Italy.* New York, 1971. Objective, concise survey of Italian unification.

Blackbourn, David. *The Long Nineteenth Century: A History of Germany, 1780–1918.* New York, 1998.

Blackbourn, David, and Geoff Eley. *The Peculiarities of German History: Bourgeois Society and Politics in Nineteenth-Century Germany.* Oxford, 1984. Critical essays on the course of German history during the age of national unification and after.

Blackburn, Robin. *The Overthrow of Colonial Slavery.* London, 1988. Brilliant and detailed overview of the social history of slavery and antislavery movements.

Brophy, James M. *Capitalism, Politics, and Railroads in Prussia, 1830–1870.* Columbus, Ohio, 1998. Important, clear, and helpful.

Coppa, Frank. *The Origins of the Italian Wars of Independence.* London, 1992. Lively narrative.

Craig, Gordon. *Germany, 1866–1945.* New York, 1978. An excellent and thorough synthesis.

Davis, David Brian. *Inhuman Bondage: The Rise and Fall of Slavery in the New World.* New York, 2006. As one reviewer aptly puts it, "A gracefully fashioned masterpiece."

Deak, Istvan. *The Lawful Revolution: Louis Kossuth and the Hungarians, 1848–1849.* New York, 1979. The best on the subject.

Eyck, Erich. *Bismarck and the German Empire.* 3d ed. London, 1968. The best one-volume study of Bismarck.

Hamerow, Theodore S. *The Birth of a New Europe: State and Society in the Nineteenth Century.* Chapel Hill, NC, 1983. A discussion of political and social change, and their relationship to industrialization and the increase in state power.

———. *The Social Foundations of German Unification, 1858–1871.* 2 vols. Princeton, NJ, 1969–1972. Concentrates on economic factors that determined the solution to the unification question. An impressive synthesis.

Higonnet, Patrice. *Paris: Capital of the World.* London, 2002. Fascinating and imaginative study of Paris as "capital of the nineteenth century."

Hobsbawm, Eric J. *The Age of Capital, 1848–1875.* London, 1975. Among the best introductions.

———. *Nations and Nationalism since 1870: Programme, Myth, Reality.* 2d ed. Cambridge, 1992. A clear, concise analysis of the historical and cultural manifestations of nationalism.

Howard, Michael. *The Franco-Prussian War.* New York, 1981. The war's effect on society.

Hutchinson, John, and Anthony Smith, eds. *Nationalism.* New York, 1994. A collection of articles, not particularly historical, but with the merit of discussing non-European nationalisms.

Johnson, Susan. *Roaring Camp.* New York, 2000. A history of one mining camp in California and a micro-history of the larger forces changing the West and the world.

Kolchin, Peter. *Unfree Labor: American Slavery and Russian Serfdom.* Cambridge, MA, 1987. Pioneering comparative study.

Mack Smith, Denis. *Cavour and Garibaldi.* New York, 1968.

———. *The Making of Italy, 1796–1870.* New York, 1968. A narrative with documents.

McPherson, James. *Battle Cry of Freedom: The Civil War Era.* New York, 1988. Universally acclaimed and prize-winning book on the politics of slavery and the conflicts entailed in nation building in mid-nineteenth-century United States.

Pflanze, Otto. *Bismarck and the Development of Germany.* 2d ed. 3 vols. Princeton, NJ, 1990. Extremely detailed analysis of Bismarck's aims and policies.

Pinkney, David. *Napoleon III and the Rebuilding of Paris.* Princeton, NJ, 1972. An interesting account of the creation of modern Paris during the Second Empire.

Robertson, Priscilla. *Revolutions of 1848: A Social History.* Princeton, NJ, 1952. Old-fashioned narrative, but very readable.

Sammons, Jeffrey L. *Heinrich Heine: A Modern Biography.* Princeton, NJ, 1979. An excellent historical biography as well as a study of culture and politics.

Scott, Rebecca J. *Degrees of Freedom: Louisiana and Cuba after Slavery.* Cambridge, MA, 2008. Brings the lives of slaves and their owners to life during the era of emancipation in a comparative history that places the southern United States in the context of the Atlantic world.

Sheehan, James J. *German Liberalism in the Nineteenth Century.* Chicago, 1978. Fresh and important synthesis.

Sperber, Jonathan. *The European Revolutions, 1848–1851.* Cambridge, 2005. An excellent synthesis and the best one-volume treatment of the 1848 revolutions, describing the reasons for their failure.

——. *Rhineland Radicals: The Democratic Movement and the Revolution of 1848–1849.* Princeton, NJ, 1993. A detailed study of Germany, by the author of an overview of the revolutions of 1848.

Stearns, Peter N. *1848: The Revolutionary Tide in Europe.* New York, 1974. Stresses the social background of the revolutions.

Zeldin, Theodore. *The Political System of Napoleon III.* New York, 1958. Compact and readable, by one of the major scholars of the period.

CHAPTER 22

Achebe, Chinua. *Things Fall Apart.* Expanded edition with notes. Portsmouth, NH, 1996. An annotated edition of the now classic novel about colonial Africa.

Adas, Michael. *Machines as the Measure of Man: Science, Technology, and Ideologies of Western Dominance.* Ithaca, NY, and London, 1989. An important study of Europeans' changing perceptions of themselves and others during the period of industrialization.

Bayly, C. A. *Indian Society and the Making of the British Empire.* Cambridge, 1988. A good introduction, and one that bridges eighteenth- and nineteenth-century imperialisms.

Burbank, Jane, and Frederick Cooper. *Empires in World History: Power and the Politics of Difference.* Princeton, NJ, 2010. Powerful synthesis that sets European empires in the broader context of world history.

Burton, Antoinette. *Burdens of History: British Feminists, Indian Women, and Imperial Culture, 1865–1915.* Chapel Hill, NC, 1994. On the ways in which women and feminists came to support British imperialism.

Cain, P. J., and A. G. Hopkins. *British Imperialism, 1688–2000.* London, 2002. One of the most influential studies. Excellent overview and exceptionally good on economics.

Chakrabarty, Dipesh. *Provincializing Europe: Postcolonial Thought and Historical Difference.* Princeton, 2000. Sophisticated theoretical challenge to European narratives of social and political progress.

Clancy Smith, Julia, and Frances Gouda. *Domesticating the Empire: Race, Gender, and Family Life in French and Dutch Colonialism.* Charlottesville, VA., and London, 1998. A particularly good collection of essays that both breaks new historical ground and is accessible to nonspecialists. Essays cover daily life and private life in new colonial cultures.

Cohn, Bernard S. *Colonialism and its Forms of Knowledge.* Princeton, 1996. Argues that new forms of cultural knowledge were essential to the project of British imperialism in India.

Conklin, Alice. *A Mission to Civilize: The Republican idea of Empire in France and West Africa, 1895–1930.* Stanford, CA, 1997. One of the best studies of how the French reconciled imperialism with their vision of the Republic.

Cooper, Frederick. *Colonialism in Question: Theory, Knowledge, History.* Berkeley, 2005. Crucial collection of path-breaking essays on the history of colonialism.

Cooper, Frederick, and Ann Laura Stoler. *Tensions of Empire: Colonial Cultures in a Bourgeois World.* Berkeley, CA, 1997. New approaches, combining anthropology and history, with an excellent bibliography.

Darwin, John. *The Empire Project: The Rise and Fall of the British World System.* Cambridge, 2009.

Headrick, Daniel R. *The Tools of Empire: Technology and European Imperialism in the Nineteenth Century.* Oxford, 1981. A study of the relationship between technological innovation and imperialism.

Hobsbawm, Eric. *The Age of Empire, 1875–1914.* New York, 1987. Surveys the European scene at a time of apparent stability and real decline.

Hochschild, Adam. *King Leopold's Ghost: A Story of Greed, Terror, and Heroism in Colonial Africa.* Boston, 1998. Reads like a great novel.

Hull, Isabell. *Absolute Destruction: Military Culture and the Practices of War in Imperial Germany.* Ithaca, 2005. A study of the German military and its role in imperial expansion in Africa, arguing that the experience was crucial in shaping the institution as it entered the twentieth century.

Lorcin, Patricia. *Imperial Identities: Stereotyping, Prejudice and Race in Colonial Algeria.* New York, 1999.

Louis, William Roger. *The Oxford History of the British Empire.* 5 vols. Oxford, 1998. Excellent and wide-ranging collection of the latest research.

Metcalf, Thomas. *Ideologies of the Raj.* Cambridge, 1995.

Pakenham, Thomas. *The Scramble for Africa, 1876–1912.* London, 1991. A well-written narrative of the European scramble for Africa in the late nineteenth century.

Prochaska, David. *Making Algeria French: Colonialism in Bône, 1870–1920.* Cambridge, 1990. One of the few social histories of European settlement in Algeria in English.

Robinson, Ronald, and J. Gallagher. *Africa and the Victorians: The Official Mind of Imperialism.* London, 1961. A classic.

Said, Edward. *Culture and Imperialism.* New York, 1993. A collection of brilliant, sometimes controversial, essays.

Sangari, Kumkum, and Sudesh Vaid. *Recasting Women: Essays in Colonial History.* New Delhi, 1989. A collection of essays on women in India.

Schneer, Jonathan. *London 1900: The Imperial Metropolis.* New Haven, CT, 1999. Excellent study of the empire—and opposition to empire—in the metropole.

Spence, Jonathan. *The Search for Modern China.* New York, 1990. An excellent and readable introduction to modern Chinese history.

CHAPTER 23

Berghahn, Volker. *Imperial Germany, 1871–1914: Economy, Society, Culture, and Politics.* Providence, 1994. Inclusive history that seeks to go beyond standard political accounts.

Berlanstein, Lenard. *The Working People of Paris, 1871–1914.* Baltimore, MD. 1984. A social history of the workplace and its impact on working men and women.

Blackbourn, David. *The Long Nineteenth Century: A History of Germany, 1780–1918.* New York, 1998. Among the best surveys of German society and politics.

Bowler, Peter J. *Evolution: The History of an Idea.* Berkeley, CA, 1984. One of the author's several excellent studies of evolution of Darwinism.

Burns, Michael. *Dreyfus: A Family Affair.* New York, 1992. Follows the story Dreyfus through the next generations.

Clark, T. J. *The Painting of Modern Life: Paris in the Art of Manet and His Followers.* New York, 1985. Argues for seeing impressionism as a critique of French society.

Eley, Geoff. *Forging Democracy.* Oxford, 2002. Wide-ranging and multinational account of European radicalism from 1848 to the present.

Engelstein, Laura. *Slavophile Empire: Imperial Russia's Illiberal Path.* Ithaca, 2009. An examination of Russia's political culture before World War 1, with an eye toward later evolution in the twentieth century.

Frank, Stephen. *Crime, Cultural Conflict, and Justice in Rural Russia, 1856–1914.* Berkeley, CA, 1999. A revealing study of social relations from the ground up.

Gay, Peter. *The Bourgeois Experience: Victoria to Freud,* 5 vols. New York, 1984–2000. Imaginative and brilliant study of private life and middle class culture.

———. *Freud: A Life of Our Time.* New York, 1988. Beautifully written and lucid about difficult concepts; now the best biography.

Harris, Ruth. *Dreyfus: Politics, Emotion, and the Scandal of the Century.* London, 2011. A reassessment of the politics of the Dreyfus affair, with a eye toward its resonance in the culture as a whole.

Herbert, Robert L. *Impressionism: Art, Leisure, and Parisian Society.* New Haven, CT, 1988. An accessible and important study of the impressionists and the world they painted.

Hughes, H. Stuart. *Consciousness and Society.* New York, 1958. A classic study on late-nineteenth-century European thought.

Jelavich, Peter. *Munich and Theatrical Modernism: Politics, Playwriting, and Performance, 1890–1914.* Cambridge, MA, 1985. On modernism as a revolt against nineteenth-century conventions.

Jones, Gareth Stedman. *Outcast London.* Oxford, 1971. Studies the breakdown in class relationships during the second half of the nineteenth century.

Joyce, Patrick. *Visions of the People: Industrial England and the Question of Class, 1848–1914.* New York, 1991. A social history of the workplace.

Kelly, Alfred. *The German Worker: Autobiographies from the Age of Industrialization.* Berkeley, CA, 1987. Excerpts from workers' autobiographies provide fresh perspective on labor history.

Kern, Stephen. *The Culture of Time and Space.* Cambridge, MA, 1983. A cultural history of the late nineteenth century.

Lidtke, Vernon. *The Alternative Culture: Socialist Labor in Imperial Germany.* New York, 1985. A probing study of working-class culture.

Marrus, Michael Robert. *The Politics of Assimilation: A Study of the French Jewish Community at the Time of the Dreyfus Affair.* Oxford, 1971. Excellent social history.

Micale, Mark S. *Approaching Hysteria: Disease and Its Interpretations.* Princeton, NJ, 1995. Important study of the history of psychiatry before Freud.

Rupp, Leila J. *Worlds of Women: The Making of an International Women's Movement.* Princeton, NJ, 1997.

Schivelbusch, Wolfgang. *Disenchanted Night: The Industrialization of Light in the Nineteenth Century.* Berkeley, CA, 1995. Imaginative study of how electricity transformed everyday life.

Schorske, Carl E. *Fin-de-Siècle Vienna: Politics and Culture.* New York, 1980. Classic account of avant-garde art, music, and intellectual culture set against the background of mass politics in the Austrian capital.

Schwartz, Vanessa. *Spectacular Realities: Early Mass Culture in Fin-de-Siècle Paris.* Berkeley, 1998. Innovative approach to the emergence of mass culture in modern France.

Showalter, Elaine. *The Female Malady: Women, Madness, and English Culture, 1890–1980.* New York, 1985. Brilliant and readable on Darwin, Freud, gender, and the First World War.

Silverman, Deborah L. *Art Nouveau in Fin-de-Siècle France: Politics, Psychology, and Style.* Berkeley, CA, 1989. A study of the relationship between psychological and artistic change.

Smith, Bonnie. *Changing Lives: Women in European History since 1700.* New York, 1988. A useful overview of European women's history.

Stern, Fritz. *The Politics of Cultural Despair: A Study of the Rise of the Germanic Ideology.* Berkeley, 1974. Classic account of the rise of nationalist and populist politics in German-speaking lands of central Europe before World War I.

Tickner, Lisa. *The Spectacle of Women: Imagery of the Suffrage Campaign, 1907–14.* Chicago, 1988. A very engaging study of British suffragism.

Verner, Andrew. *The Crisis of Russian Autocracy: Nicholas II and the 1905 Revolution.* Princeton, NJ, 1990. A detailed study of this important event.

Vital, David. *A People Apart: A Political History of the Jews in Europe, 1789-1939.* Oxford and New York, 1999. Comprehensive and extremely helpful.

Walkowitz, Judith. *City of Dreadful Delight: Narratives of Sexual Danger in Late-Victorian London.* Chicago, 1992. Cultural history of the English capital at the end of the nineteenth century.

Weber, Eugen. *Peasants into Frenchmen: The Modernization of Rural France, 1870–1914.* Stanford, CA, 1976. A study of how France's peasantry was assimilated into the Third Republic.

Wehler, Hans-Ulrich. *The German Empire, 1871–1918*. Dover, 1997. Standard account by respected German historian.

CHAPTER 24

Aksakal, Mustapha. *The Ottoman Road to War in 1914: The Ottoman Empire and the First World War*. Cambridge, 2009. A compelling look at Ottoman involvement in the First World War.

Bourke, Joanna. *Dismembering the Male: Men's Bodies, Britain, and the Great War*. Chicago, 1996. A cultural history of the war's effects on male bodies and codes of masculinity.

Chickering, Roger. *Imperial Germany and the Great War, 1914–1918*. New York, 1998. An excellent synthesis.

Clark, Christopher. *The Sleepwalkers: How Europe Went to War in 1914*. New York, 2013. Comprehensive reassessment of the war's origins.

Eksteins, Modris. *Rites of Spring: The Great War and the Birth of the Modern Age*. New York, 1989. Fascinating, though impressionistic, on war, art, and culture.

Ferguson, Niall. *The Pity of War*. London, 1998. A fresh look at the war, including strategic issues, international relations, and economics.

Ferro, Marc. *The Great War, 1914–1918*. London, 1973. Very concise overview.

Figes, Orlando. *A People's Tragedy: A History of the Russian Revolution*. New York, 1997. Excellent, detailed narrative.

Fischer, Fritz. *War of Illusions*. New York, 1975. Deals with Germany within the context of internal social and economic trends.

Fitzpatrick, Sheila. *The Russian Revolution, 1917–1932*. New York and Oxford, 1982. Concise overview.

Fussell, Paul. *The Great War and Modern Memory*. New York, 1975. A brilliant examination of British intellectuals' attitudes toward the war.

Hynes, Samuel. *A War Imagined: The First World War and English Culture*. New York, 1991. The war as perceived on the home front.

Jelavich, Barbara. *History of the Balkans: Twentieth Century*. New York, 1983. Useful for an understanding of the continuing conflict in eastern Europe.

Joll, James. *The Origins of the First World War*. London, 1984. Comprehensive and very useful.

Keegan, John. *The First World War*. London, 1998. The best overall military history.

Macmillan, Margaret, and Richard Holbrooke. *Paris 1919: Six Months That Changed the World*. New York, 2003. Fascinating fresh look at the peace conference.

Mazower, Mark. *Dark Continent: Europe's Twentieth Century*. New York, 1999. An excellent survey, particularly good on nations and minorities in the Balkans and eastern Europe.

Rabinowitch, Alexander. *The Bolsheviks Come to Power*. New York, 1976. A well-researched and carefully documented account.

Roberts, Mary Louise. *Civilization without Sexes: Reconstructing Gender in Postwar France, 1917–1927*. Chicago, 1994. A prize-winning study of the issues raised by the "new woman."

Schivelbusch, Wolfgang. *The Culture of Defeat: On National Trauma, Mourning, and Recovery*. New York, 2001. Fascinating if impressionistic comparative study.

Smith, Leonard. *Between Mutiny and Obedience: The Case of the French Fifth Infantry Division during World War I*. Princeton, NJ, 1994. An account of mutiny and the reasons behind it.

Stevenson, David. *Cataclysm: The First World War as Political Tragedy*. New York, 2003. Detailed and comprehensive, now one of the best single-volume studies.

Stites, Richard. *Revolutionary Dreams: Utopian Visions and Experimental Life in the Russian Revolution*. New York, 1989. The influence of utopian thinking on the revolution.

Suny, Ronald Grigor, Fatma Muge Gocek, and Norman Naimark, eds. *A Question of Genocide: Armenians and Turks at the End of the Ottoman Empire*. Oxford, 2011. Multi-author work offering a comprehensive summary of research on the Armenian genocide.

Williams, John. *The Home Fronts: Britain, France and Germany, 1914–1918*. London, 1972. A survey of life away from the battlefield and the impact of the war on domestic life.

Winter, Jay. *Sites of Memory, Sites of Mourning: The Great War in European Cultural History*. Cambridge, 1998. An essential reference on the legacy of World War I in European cultural history.

Winter, Jay and Jean-Louis Robert. *Capital Cities at War: Paris, London, Berlin, 1914–1919*. Cambridge, 1997 (vol. 1), 2007 (vol. 2). Multi-author work on the demographic, social, and cultural effects of the war on civilian populations of three European capitals.

CHAPTER 25

Bosworth, R. J. B. *Mussolini's Italy: Life under the Fascist Dictatorship, 1915–1945*. New York, 2007. Comprehensive account of "everyday" fascism in Italy.

Conquest, Robert. *The Great Terror: A Reassessment*. New York, 1990. One of the first histories of the Terror, should be read in conjunction with others in this list.

Crew, David F., ed. *Nazism and German Society, 1933–1945*. New York, 1994. An excellent and accessible collection of essays.

de Grazia, Victoria. *How Fascism Ruled Women: Italy, 1922–1945*. Berkeley, 1993. The contradictions between fascism's vision of modernity and its commitment to patriarchal instutions, seen from the point of view of Italian women.

Figes, Orlando. *Peasant Russia Civil War: The Volga Countryside in Revolution, 1917–1921*. Oxford, 1989. Detailed and sophisticated but readable. Study of the region from the eve of the revolution through the civil war.

Fitzpatrick, Shelia. *Everyday Stalinism: Ordinary Life in Extraordinary Times: Soviet Russia in the 1930s*. Oxford and New York, 1999. Gripping on how ordinary people dealt with famine, repression, and chaos.

Friedlander, Saul. *Nazi Germany and the Jews: The Years of Persecution. 1933–1939*. Rev. ed. New York, 2007. Excellent; the first of a two-volume study.

Gay, Peter. *Weimar Culture*. New York, 1968. Concise and elegant overview.

Getty, J. Arch, and Oleg V. Naumov. *The Road to Terror: Stalin and the Self-Destruction of the Bolsheviks, 1932–1939*. New Haven, CT, 1999. Combines analysis with documents made public for the first time.

Goldman, Wendy Z. *Women, the State, and Revolution: Soviet Family Policy and Social Life, 1917–1936*. New York, 1993. On the Bolshevik attempts to transform gender and family.

Kershaw, Ian. *Hitler*. 2 vols: *1889–1936 Hubris*, New York, 1999; *1936–1945: Nemesis*, New York, 2001. The best biography: insightful about politics, culture, and society as well as the man.

———. *The Hitler Myth: Image and Reality in the Third Reich*. New York, 1987. Brilliant study of how Nazi propagandists sold the myth of the Fuhrer and why many Germans bought it.

Klemperer, Victor. *I Will Bear Witness: A Diary of the Nazi Years, 1933–1941*. New York, 1999. *I Will Bear Witness: A Diary of the Nazi Years, 1942–1945*. New York, 2001. Certain to be a classic.

Lewin, Moshe. *The Making of the Soviet System: Essays in the Social History of Interwar Russia*. New York, 1985. One of the best to offer a view from below.

Maier, Charles. *Recasting Bourgeois Europe*. Princeton, 1975. Now classic account of the political and social adjustments made between state and society in the interwar years throughout Europe.

McDermott, Kevin. *Stalin: Revolutionary in an Era of War*. Basingstoke, UK, and New York, 2006. Useful, short, and recent.

Montefior, Simon Sebag. *Stalin: The Court of the Red Tsar*. London, 2004. On the relations among the top Bolsheviks, an interesting personal portrait. Takes you inside the inner circle.

Orwell, George. *The Road to Wigan Pier*. London, 1937. On unemployment and life in the coal mining districts of England, by one of the great British writers of the twentieth century.

———. *Homage to Catalonia*. London, 1938. A firsthand account of the Spanish Civil War.

Payne, Stanley G., *A History of Fascism, 1914–1945*. Madison, WI, 1996. Thorough account of the origins and evolution of fascism in Europe through the end of World War II.

Paxton, Robert O. *The Anatomy of Fascism*. New York, 2004. Excellent introduction to a complex subject by a foremost historian of twentieth century Europe.

Peukert, Detlev. *The Weimar Republic*. New York, 1993. Useful and concise history of Weimar by respected German historian of the period.

Rentschler, Eric. *The Ministry of Illusion: Nazi Cinema and Its Afterlife*. Cambridge, MA, 1996. For the more advanced student.

Service, Robert. *Stalin: A Biography*. London, 2004. Updates Tucker.

Suny, Ronald Grigor. *The Revenge of the Past: Nationalism, Revolution, and the Collapse of the Soviet Union*. Stanford, CA, 1993. Path-breaking study of the issues of nationalism and ethnicity form the revolution to the end of the Soviet Union.

Tucker, Robert C. *Stalin as Revolutionary, 1879–1929*. New York, 1973.

———. *Stalin in Power: The Revolution from Above, 1928–1941*. New York, 1990. With *Stalin as Revolutionary* emphasizes Stalin's purpose and method and sets him in the tradition of Russian dictators.

Weitz, Eric D. *Weimar Germany: Promise and Tragedy*. Princeton, NJ, 2009. A valuable and thorough account that ties together the complex connections between Weimar culture and politics in this transformational period.

CHAPTER 26

The U.S. Holocaust Memorial Museum has an extraordinary collection of articles, photographs, and maps. See www.ushmm.org.

Bartov, Omer. *Hitler's Army: Soldiers, Nazis, and War in the Third Reich*. New York, 1991. A Study of the radicalization of the German army on the Russian front.

Braithwaite, Rodric. *Moscow. 1941: A City and Its People at War*. London, 2006. Readable account of one of the turning points of the war.

Browning, Christopher R. *The Path to Genocide: Essays on Launching the Final Solution*. Cambridge, 1992. Discusses changing interpretations and case studies. See also the author's *Ordinary Men: Reserve Police Battalion 101 and the Final Solution in Poland*.

Burrin, Philippe. *France under the Germans: Collaboration and Compromise*. New York, 1996. Comprehensive on occupation and collaboration.

Carr, Raymond. *The Spanish Tragedy: The Civil War in Perspective*. London, 1977. A thoughtful introduction to the Spanish Civil War and the evolution of Franco's Spain.

Davies, Norman. *Heart of Europe: The Past in Poland's Present*. Oxford, 2001. Revised edition of a classic account of Poland's place in European history, with special attention to the second half of the twentieth century.

Dawidowicz, Lucy S. *The War against the Jews, 1933–1945*. New York, 1975. A full account of the Holocaust.

Divine, Robert A. *Roosevelt and World War II*. Baltimore, MD, 1969. A diplomatic history.

Djilas, Milovan. *Wartime*. New York, 1977. An insider's account of the partisans' fighting in Yugoslavia and a good example of civil war within the war.

Fritzsche, Peter. *Life and Death in the Third Reich*. Cambridge, MA, 2009. A compelling account of the appeal of Nazi ideology and the extent to which it was embraced by ordinary people in Germany.

Gellately, Robert, and Ben Kiernan, eds. *The Specter of Genocide: Mass Murder in Historical Perspective*. New York, 2003. A particularly thoughtful collection of essays.

Graham, Helen. *The Spanish Civil War: A Very Short Introduction*. Oxford and New York, 2005. Excellent and very concise, based on the author's new interpretation in the more detailed *The Spanish Republic at War, 1936–1939*. Cambridge, 2002.

Hilberg, Raul. *The Destruction of the European Jews*. 2nd ed. 3 vols. New York, 1985. An excellent treatment of the Holocaust, its origins, and its consequences.

Hitchcock, William I. *The Bitter Road to Freedom: A New History of the Liberation of Europe*. New York, 2008. The story of Europe's liberation from Hitler's control, seen from the point of view of civilian populations.

Kedward, Roderick. *In Search of the Maquis: Rural Resistance in Southern France, 1942–1944*. Oxford, 1993. An engaging study of French guerilla resistance.

Keegan, John. *The Second World War*. New York, 1990. By one of the great military historians of our time.

Marrus, Michael R. *The Holocaust in History*. Hanover, NH, 1987. Thoughtful analysis of central issues.

Mawdsley, Evan. *Thunder in the East: The Nazi-Soviet War, 1941–1945.* New York, 2005.

Megargee, Geoffrey. *War of Annihilation: Combat and Genocide on the Eastern War, 1941.* Lanham, MD, 2006. Represents some of the new historical work on the eastern front.

Merridale, Catherine. *Ivan's War: Life and Death in the Red Army, 1939–1945.* New York, 2006. Raised many questions and insights.

Michel, Henri. *The Shadow War: The European Resistance, 1939–1945.* New York, 1972. Compelling reading.

Milward, Alan S. *War, Economy, and Society, 1939–1945.* Berkeley, CA, 1977. On the economic impact of the war and the strategic impact of the economy.

Noakes, Jeremy, and Geoffrey Pridham. *Nazism: A History in Documents and Eyewitness Accounts, 1919–1945.* New York, 1975. An excellent combination of analysis and documentation.

Overy, Richard. *Russia's War.* New York, 1998. A very readable account that accompanies the PBS series by the same title.

————. *Why the Allies Won.* New York, 1995. Excellent analysis; succinct.

Paxton, Robert O. *Vichy France: Old Guard and New Order, 1940–1944.* New York, 1982. Brilliant on collaboration and Vichy's National Revolution.

Roberts, Mary Louise. *What Soldiers Do: Sex and the American GI in World War II France.* Chicago, 2013. Critical reappraisal of how sex between GIs and civilians became an issue for French and U.S. military personnel after the D-Day invasion.

Snyder, Timothy. *Bloodlands: Europe between Hitler and Stalin.* New York, 2010. Thorough and penetrating account of the methods and motives of Hitler's and Stalin's regimes.

Stoff, Michael B. *The Manhattan Project: A Documentary Introduction to the Atomic Age.* New York, 1991. Political, scientific, and historical; excellent documents and commentary.

Weinberg, Gerhard L. *A World At Arms: A Global History of World War II.* Cambridge, 2005. Second edition of a comprehensive and respected global account of the Second World War.

Wilkinson, James D. *The Intellectual Resistance in Europe.* Cambridge, MA, 1981. A comparative study of the movement throughout Europe.

CHAPTER 27

Aron, Raymond. *The Imperial Republic: The United States and the World, 1945–1973.* Lanham, MD, 1974. An early analysis by a leading French political theorist.

Carter, Erica. *How German Is She? Postwar West German Reconstruction and the Consuming Woman.* Ann Arbor, MI, 1997. A thoughtful examination of gender and the reconstruction of the family in West Germany during the 1950s.

Clayton, Anthony. *The Wars of French Decolonization.* London, 1994. Good survey.

Connelly, Matthew. *A Diplomatic Revolution: Algeria's Fight for Independence and the Origins of the Post–Cold War Era.* New York and Oxford, 2003. An international history.

Cooper, Frederick, and Ann Laura Stoler, eds. *Tensions of Empire: Colonial Cultures in a Bourgeois World.* Berkeley, CA, 1997. Collection of new essays, among the best.

Darwin, John. *Britain and Decolonization: The Retreat from Empire in the Postwar World.* New York, 1988. Best overall survey.

Deák, István, Jan T. Gross, and Tony Judt, eds. *The Politics of Retribution in Europe: World War II and Its Aftermath.* Princeton, NJ, 2000. Collection focusing on the attempt to come to terms with the Second World War in Eastern and Western Europe.

Farmer, Sarah. *Martyred Village: Commemorating the 1944 Massacre at Oradour-sur-Glane.* Berkeley, CA, 1999. Gripping story of French attempts to come to terms with collaboration and complicity in atrocities.

Holland, R. F. *European Decolonization 1918–1981: An Introductory Survey.* New York, 1985. Sprightly narrative and analysis.

Jarausch, Konrad Hugo, ed. *Dictatorship as Experience: Towards a Socio-Cultural History of the GDR.* Trans. Eve Duffy. New York, 1999. Surveys recent research on the former East Germany.

Judt, Tony. *The Burden of Responsibility: Blum, Camus, and the French Twentieth Century.* Chicago and London, 1998. Also on French intellectuals.

————. *A Grand Illusion? An Essay on Europe.* New York, 1996. Short and brilliant.

————. *Past Imperfect: French Intellectuals, 1944–1956.* Berkeley, CA, 1992. Very readable, on French intellectuals, who loomed large during this period.

————. *Postwar. A History of Europe Since 1945.* London, 2005. Detailed, comprehensive, and ground breaking, this single volume surpasses any other account of the entire postwar period.

Koven, Seth, and Sonya Michel. *Mothers of a New World: Maternalist Politics and the Origins of Welfare States.* New York, 1993. Excellent essays on the long history of welfare politics.

LaFeber, Walter. *America, Russia, and the Cold War.* New York, 1967. A classic, now in its ninth edition.

Large, David Clay. *Berlin.* New York, 2000. Accessible and engaging.

Leffler, Melvyn P. *A Preponderance of Power: National Security, the Truman Administration, and the Cold War.* Stanford, CA, 1992. Solid political study.

Louis, William Roger. *The Ends of British Imperialism: The Scramble for Empire, Suez, and Decolonization.* London, 2006. Comprehensive and wide ranging.

Macey, David. *Frantz Fanon.* New York, 2000. Comprehensive recent biography.

Medvedev, Roy. *Khrushchev.* New York, 1983. A perceptive biography of the Soviet leader by a Soviet historian.

Milward, Alan S. *The Reconstruction of Western Europe, 1945–1951.* Berkeley, CA, 1984. A good discussion of the "economic miracle."

Moeller, Robert G. *War Stories: The Search for a Usable Past in the Federal Republic of Germany.* Berkeley, CA, 2001. Revealing analyses of postwar culture and politics.

Reynolds, David. *One World Divisible: A Global History Since 1945.* New York, 2000. Fresh approach, comprehensive, and very readable survey.

Rousso, Henri. *The Vichy Syndrome: History and Memory in France since 1944.* Cambridge, MA, 1991. First in a series of books by one of the preeminent French historians.

Schissler, Hanna, ed. *The Miracle Years: A Cultural History of West Germany, 1949–1968.* Princeton, NJ, 2001. The cultural effects of the economic miracle.

Schneider, Peter. *The Wall Jumper: A Berlin Story*. Chicago, 1998. A fascinating novel about life in divided Berlin.

Shepard, Todd. *The Invention of Decolonization: The Algerian War and the Remaking of France*. Ithaca, NY, 2006. Excellent and original: a study of the deeply wrenching war's many ramifications.

Shipway, Martin. *Decolonization and Its Impact: A Comparative Approach to the End of the Colonial Empires*. Malden, MA, 2008. Accessible account emphasizing the unintended consequences of decolonization.

Trachtenberg, Mark. *A Constructed Peace: The Making of the European Settlement, 1945–1963*. Princeton, NJ, 1999. A detailed study of international relations that moves beyond the Cold War framework.

Tessler, Mark. *A History of the Israeli-Palestinian Conflict*. 2nd ed. Bloomington, IN, 2009. Updated edition of the definitive account from the 1990s.

Westad, Odd Arne. *The Global Cold War*. New York, 2005. An international history that sees the roots of the world's present conflict in the history of the Cold War.

Wilder, Gary. *The French Imperial Nation-State: Negritude and Colonial Humanism between the Two World Wars*. Chicago, 2005. Fascinating new study of the Negritude thinkers in their context.

Yergin, Daniel. *Shattered Peace: The Origins of the Cold War*. New York, 1977. Rev. ed. 1990. Dramatic and readable.

Young, Marilyn B. *The Vietnam Wars, 1945–1990*. New York, 1991. Excellent account of the different stages of the war and its repercussions.

CHAPTER 28

Bailey, Beth. *From Front Porch to Back Seat: Courtship in Twentieth-Century America*. Baltimore, MD, 1988. Good historical perspective on the sexual revolution.

Beschloss, Michael, and Strobe Talbott. *At the Highest Levels: The Inside Story of the End of the Cold War*. Boston, 1993. An analysis of the relationship between presidents Gorbachev and George H. W. Bush and their determination to ignore hard-liners.

Brown, Archie. *The Gorbachev Factor*. Oxford and New York, 1996. One of the first serious studies of Gorbachev, by an Oxford scholar of politics.

Caute, David. *The Year of the Barricades: A Journey through 1968*. New York, 1988. A well-written global history of 1968.

Charney, Leo, and Vanessa R. Schwartz, eds. *Cinema and the Invention of Modern Life*. Berkeley, CA, 1995. Collection of essays.

Dallin, Alexander, and Gail Lapidus. *The Soviet System: From Crisis to Collapse*. Boulder, CO, 1995.

de Grazia, Victoria. *Irresistable Empire: America's Advance through Twentieth-Century Europe*. Cambridge, MA, 2006. Thorough exploration of the history of consumer culture in Europe and its links to relations with the United States.

Echols, Alice. *Daring to Be Bad: Radical Feminism in America, 1967–1975*. Minneapolis, Minn., 1989. Good narrative and analysis.

Eley, Geoff. *Forging Democracy: The History of the Left in Europe, 1850–2000*. Oxford and New York, 2002. Among its other qualities, one of the best historical perspectives on the 1960s.

Fink, Carole, Phillipp Gassert, and Detlef Junker, eds. *1968: The World Transformed*. Cambridge, 1998. A transatlantic history of 1968.

Fulbrook, Mary, ed. *Europe since 1945* (The Short Oxford History of Europe). Oxford, 2001. Particularly good articles on economics and political economy. Structural analysis.

Garton Ash, Timothy. *In Europe's Name: Germany and the Divided Continent*. New York, 1993. An analysis of the effect of German reunification on the future of Europe.

Glenny, Misha. *The Balkans, 1804–1999: Nationalism, War and the Great Powers*. London, 1999. Good account by a journalist who covered the fighting.

Horowitz, Daniel. *Betty Friedan and the Making of the Feminine Mystique: The American Left, the Cold War, and Modern Feminism*. Amherst, MA, 1998. A reconsideration.

Hosking, Geoffrey. *The Awakening of the Soviet Union*. Cambridge, MA, 1990. The factors that led to the end of the Soviet era.

Hughes, H. Stuart. *Sophisticated Rebels: The Political Culture of European Dissent, 1968–1987*. Cambridge, MA, 1990. The nature of dissent on both sides of the disintegrating Iron Curtain in the years 1988–1989.

Hulsberg, Werner. *The German Greens: A Social and Political Profile*. New York, 1988. The origins, politics, and impact of environmental politics.

Jarausch, Konrad. *The Rush to German Unity*. New York, 1994. The problems of reunification analyzed.

Judah, Tim. *The Serbs: History, Myth, and the Destruction of Yugoslavia*. New Haven, CT, 1997. Overview of Serbian history by journalist who covered the war.

Kaplan, Robert D. *Balkan Ghosts: A Journey through History*. New York, 1993. More a political travelogue than a history, but very readable.

Kotkin, Stephen. *Armegeddon Averted: The Soviet Collapse, 1970–2000*. Oxford, 2001. Excellent short account.

Kurlansky, Mark. *1968: The Year that Rocked the World*. New York, 2005. An accessible introduction for nonspecialists.

Lewin, Moshe. *The Gorbachev Phenomenon*. Expanded ed. Berkeley, CA, 1991. Written as a firsthand account, tracing the roots of Gorbachev's successes and failures.

Lieven, Anatol. *Chechnya, Tomb of Russia Power*. New Haven, CT, and London, 1998. Longer view of the region, by a journalist.

Maier, Charles S. *Dissolution: The Crisis of Communism and the End of East Germany*. Princeton, NJ, 1997. Detailed and sophisticated.

Mann, Michael. *The Dark Side of Democracy: Explaining Ethnic Cleansing*. New York, 2005. Brilliant essay on different episodes from Armenia to Rwanda.

Marwick, Arthur. *The Sixties*. Oxford and New York, 1998. An international history.

Pells, Richard. *Not Like Us: How Europeans Have Loved, Hated, and Transformed American Culture since World War II*. New York, 1997. From the point of view of an American historian.

Poiger, Uta G. *Jazz, Rock, and Rebels: Cold War Politics and American Culture in a Divided Germany*. Berkeley, CA, 2000. Pioneering cultural history.

Sheehan, Neil. *A Bright Shining Lie: John Paul Vann and America in Vietnam.* New York, 1988. A study of the war and its escalation through one of the U.S. Army's field advisers.

Strayer, Robert. *Why Did the Soviet Union Collapse? Understanding Historical Change.* Armonk, NY, and London, 1998. A good introduction, with bibliography.

Suri, Jeremi. *Power and Protest.* New ed. Cambridge, MA, 2005. One of the best of the new global histories of the 1960s, looking at relations between social movements and international relations.

Wright, Patrick. *On Living in an Old Country: The National Past in Contemporary Britain.* New York, 1986. The culture of Britain in the 1980s.

CHAPTER 29

Bowen, John R. *Why the French Don't Like Headscarves: Islam, the State, and Public Space.* Princeton, NJ, 2008. An ethnographic account of this volatile debate in France.

Coetzee, J. M. *Waiting for the Barbarians.* London, 1980. A searing critique of apartheid-era South Africa by a leading Afrikaner novelist.

Epstein, Helen. *The Invisible Cure: Africa, the West, and the Fight Against AIDS.* New York, 2007. One of the best recent studies.

Frieden, Jeffrey H. *Global Capitalism: Its Rise and Fall in the Twentieth Century.* New York, 2007. Broad-ranging history for the advanced student.

Geyer, Michael, and Charles Bright. "World History in a Global Age." *American Historical Review* (October 1995). An excellent short discussion.

Glendon, Mary Ann. *A World Made New: Eleanor Roosevelt and the Universal Declaration of Human Rights.* New York, 2001. A fascinating study of the High Commission in its time by a legal scholar.

Harvey, David. *A Brief History of Neoliberalism.* New York, 2007, A critical account of the history of neoliberalism that encompasses the U.S., Europe, and Asia.

Held, David, et al. *Global Transformations: Politics, Economics, and Culture.* Stanford, CA, 1999. Major survey of the globalization of culture, finance, criminality, and politics.

Hopkins, A. G., ed. *Globalization in World History.* New York, 2002. Excellent introduction, written by one of the first historians to engage the issue.

Hunt, Lynn. *Inventing Human Rights: A History.* New York, 2007. A short study of the continuities and paradoxes in the West's human rights tradition, by one of the foremost historians of the French Revolution. On 1776, 1789, and 1948.

Keddie, Nikki. *Modern Iran: Roots and Results of Revolution.* New Haven, CT, 2003. A revised edition of her major study of Iran's 1979 revolution, with added perspective on Iran's Islamic government.

Lacqueur, Walter. *The Age of Terrorism.* Boston, 1987. An important study of the first wave of post-1960s terrorism.

Landes, David. *The Wealth and Poverty of Nations: Why Some Are So Rich and Some So Poor.* New York, 1998. Leading economic historian's account of globalization's effects on the international economy.

Lewis, Bernard. *The Crisis of Islam: Holy War and Unholy Terror.* New York, 2003. Conservative scholar of the Arab world discussing the political crises that fueled terrorism.

Mckeown, Adam. "Global Migration, 1846–1940." *Journal of World History* 15.2 (2004). Includes references to more work on the subject.

McNeill, J. R. *Something New under the Sun: An Environmental History of the Twentieth-Century World.* New York and London, 2000. Fascinating new approach to environmental history.

Merlini, Cesare, and Olivier Roy, eds. *Arab Society in Revolt: The West's Mediterranean Challenge.* Washington DC, 2012. A multi-author attempt to understand the Arab Spring of 2011

Novick, Peter. *The Holocaust in American Life.* Boston, 1999.

Power, Samantha. *The Problem from Hell: America in the Age of Genocide.* A prize-winning survey of the entire twentieth century, its genocides, and the different human rights movements that responded to them.

Reynolds, David. *One World Divisible: A Global History since 1945.* New York and London, 2000. Excellent study of the different dimensions of globalization.

Roy, Olivier. *Globalized Islam: The Search for a New Ummah.* New York, 2006. Examines changes in religious belief and practice as Islam has spread from its historic centers in the Middle East to other areas of the world, including Europe and North America.

Scott, Joan. *The Politics of the Veil.* Princeton, NJ, 2010. A leading feminist scholar analyzes the debate about the veil and the Islamic headscarf in Europe.

Shilts, Randy. *And the Band Played On: Politics, People, and the AIDS Epidemic.* New York, 1987. An impassioned attack on the individuals and governments that failed to come to grips with the early spread of the disease.

Shlaim, Avi. *The Iron Wall: Israel and the Arab World.* New York, 2000. Leading Israeli historian on the evolution of Israel's defensive foreign policy.

Stiglitz, Joseph E. *Globalization and Its Discontents.* New York, 2002. A recent and important consideration of contemporary globalization's character and the conflicts it creates, particularly over commerce and culture.

————. *Freefall: America, Free Markets, and the Sinking of the World Economy.* New York, 2010. Nobel-prize-winning economist gives account of the financial crisis of 2008.

Turkle, Sherry. *Life on the Screen: Identity in the Age of the Internet.* New York, 1995. An important early study of Web culture and the fluid possibilities of electronic communication.

Winter, Jay. *Dreams of Peace and Freedom: Utopian Moments in the Twentieth Century.* New Haven, CT, 2006. One of the leading historians of war and atrocity turns here to twentieth-century hopes for peace and human rights.

Glossary

1973 OPEC oil embargo Some leaders in the Arab-dominated Organization of the Petroleum Exporting Countries (OPEC) wanted to use oil as a weapon against the West in the Arab-Israeli conflict. After the 1972 Arab-Israeli war, OPEC instituted an oil embargo against Western powers. The embargo increased the price of oil and sparked spiraling inflation and economic troubles in Western nations, triggering in turn a cycle of dangerous recession that lasted nearly a decade. In response, Western governments began viewing the Middle Eastern oil regions as areas of strategic importance.

Abbasid Caliphate (750–930) The Abbasid family claimed to be descendants of Muhammad, and in 750 they successfully led a rebellion against the Umayyads, seizing control of Muslim territories in Arabia, Persia, North Africa, and the Near East. Establishing a new capital at Baghdad, the Abbasids modeled their behavior and administration on that of the Persian princes and their rule on that of the Persian Empire.

Peter Abelard (1079–1142) Highly influential philosopher, theologian, and teacher, often considered the founder of the University of Paris.

absolutism Form of government in which one body, usually the monarch, controls the right to make war, tax, judge, and coin money. The term was often used to refer to the state monarchies in seventeenth- and eighteenth-century Europe. In other countries the end of feudalism is often associated with the legal abolition of serfdom, as in Russia in 1861.

abstract expressionism Mid-twentieth-century school of art based in New York that included Jackson Pollock, Willem de Kooning, and Franz Kline. It emphasized form, color, gesture, and feeling instead of figurative subjects.

Academy of Sciences French institute of scientific inquiry founded in 1666 by Louis XIV. France's statesmen exerted control over the academy and sought to share in the rewards of any discoveries its members made.

Aeneas Mythical founder of Rome, Aeneas was a refugee from the city of Troy whose adventures were described by the poet Virgil in the *Aeneid*, which mimicked the oral epics of Homer.

Aetolian and Achaean Leagues Two alliances among Greek poleis formed during the Hellenistic period in opposition to the Antigonids of Macedonia. Unlike the earlier defensive alliances of the classic period, each league represented a real attempt to form a political federation.

African National Congress (ANC) Multiracial organization founded in 1912 whose goal was to end racial discrimination in South Africa.

Afrikaners Descendants of the original Dutch settlers of South Africa; formerly referred to as Boers.

agricultural revolution Numerous agricultural revolutions have occurred in the history of Western civilizations. One of the most significant began in the tenth century C.E., and increased the amount of land under cultivation as well as the productivity of the land. This revolution was made possible through the use of new technology, an increase in global temperatures, and more-efficient methods of cultivation.

AIDS Acquired Immunodeficiency Syndrome. AIDS first appeared in the 1970s and has developed into a global health catastrophe; it is spreading most quickly in developing nations in Africa and Asia.

Akhenaten (r. 1352–1336 B.C.E.) Pharaoh whose attempt to promote the worship of the sun god, Aten, ultimately weakened his dynasty's position in Egypt.

Alexander the Great (356–323 B.C.E.) Macedonian king whose conquests of the Persian Empire and Egypt created a new Hellenistic world.

Tsar Alexander II (1818–1881) After the Crimean War, Tsar Alexander embarked on a program of reform and modernization, which included the emancipation of the serfs. A radical assassin killed him in 1881.

Alexius Comnenus (1057–1118) Byzantine emperor who requested Pope Urban II's help in raising an army to recapture Anatolia from the Seljuk Turks. Instead, Pope Urban II called for knights to go to the Holy Land and liberate it from its Muslim captors, which launched the First Crusade.

Algerian War (1954–1962) War between France and Algerians seeking independence. Led by the National Liberation Front (FLN), guerrillas fought the French army in the mountains and desert of Algeria. The FLN also initiated a campaign of bombing and terrorism in Algerian cities that led French soldiers to torture many Algerians, attracting world attention and international scandal.

Dante Alighieri (c. 1265–1321) Florentine poet and intellectual whose *Divine Comedy* was a pioneering work in the Italian vernacular and a vehicle for political and religious critique.

Allied Powers First World War coalition of Great Britain, Ireland, Belgium, France, Italy, Russia, Portugal, Greece, Serbia, Montenegro, Albania, and Romania.

al Qaeda Radical Islamic organization founded in the late 1980s by former mujahidin who had fought against the Soviet Union in Afghanistan. Al Qaeda carried out the 9/11 terrorist attacks and is responsible as well for attacks in Africa, Southeast Asia, Europe, and the Middle East.

Ambrose (c. 340–397) One of the early "Fathers" of the Church, he helped to define the relationship between the sacred authority of bishops and other Church leaders and the secular authority of worldly rulers. He believed that secular rulers were a part of the Church and therefore subject to it.

Americanization The fear of many Europeans, since the 1920s, that U.S. cultural products, such as film, television, and music, exerted too much influence. Many of the criticisms centered on America's emphasis on mass production and organization. The fears about Americanization were not limited to culture. They extended to corporations, business techniques, global trade, and marketing.

Americas The name given to the two great landmasses of the New World, derived from the name of the Italian geographer Amerigo Vespucci. In 1492, Christopher Columbus reached the Bahamas and the island of Hispaniola, which began an era of Spanish conquest in North and South America. Originally, the Spanish sought a route to Asia. Instead they discovered two continents whose wealth they decided to exploit. They were especially interested in gold and silver, which they either stole from indigenous peoples or mined using the labor of indigenous peoples. Silver became Spain's most lucrative export from the New World.

Amnesty International Nongovernmental organization formed in 1961 to defend "prisoners of conscience"—those detained for their beliefs, color, sex, ethnic origin, language, or religion.

Anabaptists Protestant movement that emerged in Switzerland in 1521; its adherents insisted that only adults could be baptized Christians.

anarchists Nineteenth-century political movement with the aim of establishing small-scale, localized, and self-sufficient democratic communities that could guarantee a maximum of individual sovereignty. Renouncing parties, unions, and any form of modern mass organization, the anarchists fell back on the tradition of conspiratorial violence.

Anti–Corn Law League Organization that successfully lobbied Parliament to repeal Britain's Corn Laws in 1846. The Corn Laws of 1815 had protected British landowners and farmers from foreign competition by establishing high tariffs, which kept bread prices artificially high for British consumers. The league saw these laws as unfair protection of the aristocracy and pushed for their repeal in the name of free trade.

anti-Semitism Hostility toward Jewish people. Religious forms of anti-Semitism have a long history in Europe, but in the nineteenth century anti-Semitism emerged as a potent ideology for mobilizing new constituencies in the era of mass politics. Playing on popular conspiracy theories about alleged Jewish influence in society, anti-Semites effectively rallied large bodies of supporters in France during the Dreyfus Affair, and then again during the rise of National Socialism in Germany after the First World War. The Holocaust would not have been possible without the acquiescence or cooperation of many thousands of people who shared anti-Semitic views.

apartheid The racial segregation policy of the Afrikaner-dominated South African government. Legislated in 1948 by the Afrikaner National Party, it existed in South Africa for many decades.

appeasement Policy pursued by Western governments in the face of German, Italian, and Japanese aggression leading up to the Second World War. The policy, which attempted to accommodate and negotiate peace with the aggressive nations, was based on the belief that another global war like the First World War was unimaginable, a belief that Germany and its allies had been mistreated by the terms of the Treaty of Versailles, and a belief that fascist Germany and its allies protected the West from the spread of Soviet communism.

Thomas Aquinas (1225–1274) Dominican friar and theologian whose systematic approach to Christian doctrine was influenced by Aristotle.

Arab-Israeli conflict Between the founding of the state of Israel in 1948 and the present, a series of wars has been fought between Israel and neighboring Arab nations: the war of 1948 when Israel defeated attempts by Egypt, Jordon, Iraq, Syria, and Lebanon to prevent the creation of the new state; the 1956 war between Israel and Egypt over the Sinai peninsula; the 1967 war, when Israel gained control of additional land in the Golan Heights, the West Bank, the Gaza strip, and the Sinai; and the Yom Kippur War of 1973, when Israel once again fought with forces from Egypt and Syria. A particularly difficult issue in all of these conflicts has been the situation of the 950,000 Palestinian refugees made homeless by the first war in 1948 and the movement of Israeli settlers into the occupied territories (outside of Israel's original borders). In the late 1970s, peace talks between Israel and Egypt inspired some hope of peace, but an ongoing cycle of violence between Palestinians and the Israeli military has made a final settlement elusive.

Arab nationalism During the period of decolonization, secular forms of Arab nationalism, or pan-Arabism, found a wide following in many countries of the Middle East, especially in Egypt, Syria, and Iraq.

Arianism Variety of Christianity condemned as a heresy by the Roman Church; it derives from the teaching of a fourth-century priest called Arius, who rejected the idea that Jesus could be the divine equal of God.

aristocracy From the Greek word meaning "rule of the best." By 1000 B.C.E., the accumulated wealth of successful traders in Greece had created a new type of social class, which was based on wealth rather than warfare or birth. These men saw their wealth as a reflection of their superior qualities and aspired to emulate the heroes of old.

Aristotle (384–322 B.C.E.) Student of Plato whose philosophy was based on the rational analysis of the material world. In contrast to his teacher, he stressed the rigorous investigation of real phenomena, rather than the development of universal ethics. He was, in turn, the teacher of Alexander the Great.

Asiatic Society Cultural organization founded in 1784 by British Orientalists who lauded native cultures but believed in colonial rule.

Assyrians Semitic-speaking people who moved into northern Mesopotamia around 2400 B.C.E.

Athens Athens emerged as the Greek polis with the most markedly democratic form of government through a series of political struggles during the sixth century B.C.E. After its key role in the defeat of two invading Persian forces, Athens became the preeminent naval power of ancient Greece and the exemplar of Greek culture. But it antagonized many other poleis and became embroiled in a war with Sparta and her allies in 431 B.C.E. Called the Peloponnesian War, this bloody conflict lasted until Athens was defeated in 404 B.C.E.

atomic bomb In 1945, the United States dropped atomic bombs on Hiroshima and Nagasaki in Japan, ending the Second World War. In 1949, the Soviet Union tested its first atomic bomb, and in 1953 both superpowers demonstrated their new hydrogen bombs. Strategically, the nuclearization of warfare polarized the world. Countries without nuclear weapons found it difficult to avoid joining either the Soviet or American military pacts. The nuclearization of warfare encouraged "proxy wars" between client nations of the superpowers. Culturally, the hydrogen bomb came to symbolize the age as well as humanity's power and vulnerability.

Augustine (c. 354–397) One of the most influential theologians of all time, Augustine described his conversion to Christianity in his autobiographical *Confessions* and articulated a new Christian worldview in *The City of God*, among other works.

Augustus (63 B.C.E.–14 C.E.) Born Gaius Octavius, this grandnephew and adopted son of Julius Caesar came to power in 27 B.C.E. His reign signals the end of the Roman Republic and the beginning of the Principate, the period when Rome was dominated by autocratic emperors.

Auschwitz-Birkenau Nazi concentration camp in Poland designed to systematically murder Jews and Gypsies. Between 1942 and 1944 over 1 million people were killed in Auschwitz-Birkenau.

Austro-Hungarian Empire Dual monarchy established by the Habsburg family in 1867; it collapsed at the end of the First World War.

authoritarianism Centralized and dictatorial form of government, proclaimed by its adherents to be superior to parliamentary democracy. Authoritarian governments claim to be above the law, do not respect individual rights, and do not tolerate political opposition. Authoritarian regimes that have developed a central ideology such as fascism or communism are sometimes termed "totalitarian."

Avignon City in southeastern France that became the seat of the papacy between 1305 and 1377, a period known as the "Babylonian Captivity" of the Roman Church.

Aztecs An indigenous people of central Mexico; their empire was conquered by Spanish conquistadors in the sixteenth century.

baby boom (1950s), The post–Second World War upswing in U.S. birth rates it reversed a century of decline.

Babylon Ancient city between the Tigris and Euphrates Rivers, which became the capital of Hammurabi's empire in the eighteenth century B.C.E. and continued to be an important administrative and commercial capital under many subsequent imperial powers, including the Neo-Assyrians, Chaldeans, Persians, and Romans. It was here that Alexander the Great died in 323 B.C.E.

Babylonian captivity Reference to both the Jews' exile in Babylon during the sixth century B.C.E. and the period from 1309 to 1378, when papal authority of the Roman Catholic Church was subjugated to the French crown and the papal court was moved from Rome to the French city of Avignon.

Francis Bacon (1561–1626) British philosopher and scientist who pioneered the scientific method and the systematic use of inductive reasoning. In other words, he argued that thinkers should amass many observations and then draw general conclusions or propose theories on the basis of these data.

balance of powers Principle that no single country should be powerful enough to destabilize international relations. Starting in the seventeenth century, this goal of maintaining balance influenced diplomacy in western and central Europe for two centuries until the system collapsed with the onset of the First World War.

Balfour Declaration Letter of November 2, 1917, by Lord Arthur J. Balfour, British foreign secretary, promising a homeland for the Jews in Palestine.

Laura Bassi (1711–1778) Italian mathematician; her acceptance into the Academy of Science in Bologna for her work in mathematics made her one of the few women to be welcomed into a scientific academy in the seventeenth century.

Bastille Royal fortress and prison in Paris. In June 1789, a revolutionary crowd attacked the Bastille to show support for the newly created National Assembly. The fall of the Bastille was the first instance of the people's role in revolutionary change in France.

Bay of Pigs (1961) Site of the unsuccessful invasion of Cuba by Cuban exiles, supported by the U.S. government. The rebels intended to incite an insurrection in Cuba and overthrow the communist regime of Fidel Castro.

Cesare Beccaria (1738–1794) Influential Enlightenment-era writer who advocated for legal reforms. Beccaria believed that the only legitimate rationale for punishments was to maintain social order and to prevent other crimes. He argued for the greatest-possible leniency compatible with deterrence and opposed the use of torture and the death penalty.

Beer Hall Putsch (1923) Early attempt by the Nazi party to seize power, in Munich; Adolf Hitler was imprisoned for a year after the incident.

Benedict of Nursia (c. 480–c. 547) Italian abbot regarded as the patron saint of Europe; his "rule" for monks formed the basis of western monasticism and is still observed in monasteries all over the world.

Benedictine Monasticism Form of monasticism developed by Benedict of Nursia; its followers adhere to a defined cycle of daily prayers, lessons, communal worship, and manual labor.

Berlin airlift (1948) Transport of vital supplies to West Berlin by air, primarily under U.S. auspices, in response to a blockade of the city that had been instituted by the Soviet Union to force the Allies to abandon West Berlin.

Berlin Conference (1884) Conference of the leading colonial powers that met and established ground rules for the partition of

Africa by European nations. By 1914, 90 percent of African territory was under European control. The Berlin Conference ceded control of the Congo region to a private company run by King Leopold II of Belgium. They agreed to make the Congo valleys open to free trade and commerce, to end the slave trade in the region, and to establish a Congo Free State. In reality, King Leopold II's company established a regime so brutal in its treatment of local populations that in 1908 an international scandal forced the Belgian state to take over the colony.

Berlin Wall Wall built in 1961 by East German communists to prevent citizens of East Germany from fleeing to West Germany; it was torn down in 1989.

birth control pill Oral contraceptive that became widely available in the mid-1960s. For the first time, women had a simple method of birth control that they could take themselves.

Otto von Bismarck (1815–1898) Prime minister of Prussia and later first chancellor of a unified Germany: Bismarck was the architect of German unification and helped to consolidate the new nation's economic and military power.

Black Death Epidemic of bubonic plague that ravaged Europe, Asia, and North Africa in the fourteenth century, killing one third to one half of the population.

Black Jacobins Nickname for the rebels in Saint-Domingue, including Toussaint L'Ouverture, a former slave who in 1791 led the slaves of this French colony in the largest and most successful slave insurrection.

Blackshirts Troops of Mussolini's fascist regime; the squads received money from Italian landowners to attack socialist leaders.

Black Tuesday (October 29, 1929) Day on which the U.S. stock market crashed, plunging U.S. and international trading systems into crisis and leading the world into the Great Depression.

William Blake (1757–1827) English writer who criticized industrial society and factories; Blake championed the imagination and poetic vision, seeing both as transcending the limits of the material world.

Blitzkrieg German "lightning war" strategy used during the Second World War; the Germans invaded Poland, France, Russia, and other countries with fast-moving and well-coordinated attacks using aircraft, tanks, and other armored vehicles, followed by infantry.

Bloody Sunday On January 22, 1905, the Russian tsar's guards killed 130 demonstrators who were protesting the tsar's mistreatment of workers and the middle class.

Giovanni Boccaccio (1313–1375) Florentine author best known for his *Decameron*, a collection of prose tales about sex, adventure, and trickery, written in the Italian vernacular after the Black Death.

Jean Bodin (1530–1596) French political philosopher whose *Six Books of the Commonwealth* advanced a theory of absolute sovereignty, on the grounds that the state's paramount duty is to maintain order and that monarchs should therefore exercise unlimited power.

Boer War (1898–1902) Conflict between the British army and ethnically European Afrikaners in South Africa, with terrible casualties on both sides.

Boethius (c. 480–524) Roman scholar who sought to preserve aspects of ancient learning by compiling a series of handbooks and anthologies appropriate for Christian readers. His translations of Greek philosophers provided a crucial link between classical Greek thought and the early intellectual culture of Christianity.

Bolsheviks Former members of the Russian Social Democratic Party who advocated the destruction of capitalist political and economic institutions and started the Russian Revolution. In 1918, the Bolsheviks changed their name to the Russian Communist Party. Prominent Bolsheviks included Vladimir Lenin, Joseph Stalin, and Leon Trotsky.

Napoleon Bonaparte (1769–1821) Corsican-born French general who seized power and ruled as dictator from 1799 to 1814. After the successful conquest of much of Europe, he was defeated by Russian, British, and Prussian forces and died in exile.

Boniface VIII Pope (r.1294–1303) whose repeated claims to papal authority were challenged by King Philip IV of France. When Boniface died in 1309 (at the hands of Philip's thugs), the French king moved the papal court from Rome to the French city of Avignon, where it remained until 1378.

Sandro Botticelli (1445–1510) Italian painter devoted to the blending of classical and Christian motifs by using ideas associated with the pagan past to illuminate sacred stories.

bourgeoisie Term for the middle class, derived from the French word for a town-dweller, *bourgeois*.

Boxer Rebellion (1899–1900) Chinese peasant movement that opposed foreign influence, especially that of Christian missionaries; it was finally put down after the Boxers were defeated by a foreign army composed mostly of Japanese, Russian, British, French, and American soldiers.

Tycho Brahe (1546–1601) Danish astronomer who believed that the careful study of the heavens would unlock the secrets of the universe. For over twenty years, he charted the movements of significant objects in the night sky, compiling the finest set of astronomical data in Europe.

British Commonwealth of Nations Formed in 1926, the Commonwealth conferred "dominion status" on Britain's white settler colonies in Canada, Australia, and New Zealand.

Bronze Age (3200–1200 B.C.E.) Name given to the era characterized by the discovery of techniques for smelting bronze (an alloy of copper and tin), which was then the strongest known metal.

Brownshirts German paramilitary troops who dedicated themselves to the Nazi cause in the early 1930s, holding street marches and mass rallies. They engaged in beatings of Jews and confronted anyone who opposed the Nazis.

Lord Byron (1788–1824) Writer and poet whose life helped give the Romantics their reputation as rebels against conformity; Byron was known for his love affairs, his defense of working-class movements, and his passionate engagement in politics, which led to his death in the war for Greek independence.

Byzantium Originally a small settlement located at the mouth of the Black Sea and at the crossroads between Europe and Asia, it was chosen by Constantine as the site for his new imperial capital of Constantinople in 324. Modern historians use this name to refer to the eastern Roman Empire that persisted in this region until 1453, but the inhabitants of that empire referred to themselves as Romans.

Julius Caesar (100–44 B.C.E.) Roman general who conquered the Gauls, invaded Britain, and expanded Rome's territory in Asia Minor. He became the dictator of Rome in 46 B.C.E. His assassination led to the rise of his grandnephew and adopted son, Gaius Octavius Caesar, who ruled the Roman Empire as Caesar Augustus.

caliphs Islamic rulers who claim descent from the prophet Muhammad.

John Calvin (1509–1564) French-born theologian and reformer whose radical form of Protestantism was adopted in many Swiss cities, notably Geneva.

Canary Islands Islands off the western coast of Africa that were colonized by Portugal and Spain in the mid-fifteenth century, after which they became bases for further expeditions around the African coast and across the Atlantic.

Carbonari Underground organization that opposed the Concert of Europe's restoration of monarchies. They flourished in southern Europe during the 1820s, especially in Italy.

Carolingian Derived from the Latin name Carolus (Charles), this term refers to the Frankish dynasty that began with the rise to power of Charles Martel (r. 718–41). At its height under his grandson, Charlemagne (Charles the Great), the dynasty controlled what is now France, Germany, northern Italy, Catalonia, and portions of central Europe. The Carolingian Empire collapsed under the combined weight of Viking raids, economic disintegration, and the growing power of local lords.

Carolingian Renaissance Cultural and intellectual flowering that took place around the court of Charlemagne in the late eighth and early ninth centuries.

Carthage Great maritime empire that grew out of Phoenician trading colonies in North Africa and eventually rivaled the power of Rome. Its wars with Rome, collectively known as the Punic Wars, ended in the destruction of Carthage in 146 B.C.E.

Cassiodorus (c. 490–c. 583) Member of an old Roman family, he was largely responsible for introducing classical learning into the monastic curriculum and for turning monasteries into centers for the collection, preservation, and transmission of knowledge. His *Institutes*, an influential handbook of classical literature for Christian readers, was intended as a preface to more-intensive study of theology and the Bible.

Catholic Church The "universal" (catholic) Christian church based in Rome; it was redefined in the sixteenth century when the Counter-Reformation resulted in the rebirth of the Catholic faith at the Council of Trent.

Margaret Cavendish (1623–1673) English aristocrat and scientist who developed her own speculative natural philosophy and critiqued those who sought to exclude her from scientific debate.

Camillo Benso di Cavour (1810–1861) Prime minister of Piedmont-Sardinia and founder of the Italian Liberal party; he played a key role in the movement for Italian unification under the Piedmontese king, Victor Emmanuel II.

Central Powers First World War alliance between Germany, Austria-Hungary, Bulgaria, and Turkey.

Charlemagne (742–814) As king of the Franks (767–813), Charles "the Great" consolidated much of western Europe under his rule. In 800, he was crowned emperor by the pope in Rome, establishing a problematic precedent that would have wide-ranging consequences for western Europe's relationship with the eastern Roman Empire in Byzantium and for the relationship between the papacy and secular rulers.

Charles I (r. 1625–49) The second Stuart king of England, Charles attempted to rule without the support of Parliament, sparking a controversy that erupted into civil war in 1642. The king's forces were ultimately defeated and Charles himself was executed by act of Parliament, the first time in history that a reigning king was legally deposed and executed by his own government.

Charles II (1630–1685) Nominally King of England, Ireland, and Scotland after his father Charles I's execution in 1649, Charles II lived in exile until he was restored to the throne in 1660. Influenced by his cousin, King Louis XIV of France, he presided over an opulent royal court until his death.

Chartists Working-class movement in Britain that called for reform of the British political system during the 1840s. They were supporters of the "People's Charter," which had six demands: universal white male suffrage, secret ballots, an end to property qualifications as a condition of public office, annual parliamentary elections, salaries for members of the House of Commons, and equal electoral districts.

Geoffrey Chaucer (1340–1400) English poet whose collection of versified stories, *The Canterbury Tales*, features characters from a variety of different classes.

Christine de Pisan (c. 1364–c. 1431) Born in Italy, Christine spent her adult life attached to the French court and, after her husband's death, became the first laywoman to earn her living by writing. She is the author of treatises on warfare and chivalry as well as of books and pamphlets that challenge long-standing misogynistic claims.

Church of England Protestant denomination founded by Henry VIII in the 1530s as a consequence of his break with the authority of the Roman pope.

Winston Churchill (1874–1965) British prime minister who led the country during the Second World War. He also coined the phrase "Iron Curtain" in a speech at Missouri's Westminster College in 1946.

Cicero (106–43 B.C.E.) Influential Roman senator, orator, Stoic philosopher, and prose stylist; his published writings still form the basis of instruction in classical Latin grammar and usage.

Cincinnatus (519–c. 430 B.C.E.) Legendary citizen-farmer of Rome who reluctantly accepted an appointment as dictator. After defeating Rome's enemies, he is said to have left his political office and returned to his farm.

Civil Constitution of the Clergy Charter issued by the French National Assembly in 1790. It decreed that all bishops and priests should be subject to the authority of the state. Their salaries were to be paid out of the public treasury, and they were required to swear allegiance to the new state, making it clear they served France rather than Rome. The Assembly's aim was to make the Catholic Church of France a truly national and civil institution.

civilizing mission Argument made by Europeans to justify colonial expansion in the nineteenth century. Supporters of this idea believed that Europeans had a duty to impose Western ideas of economic and political progress on the indigenous peoples they ruled over in their colonies. In practice, the colonial powers often found that ambitious plans to impose European practices on colonial subjects led to unrest that threatened the stability of colonial rule, and by the early twentieth century most colonial powers were more cautious in their plans for political or cultural transformation.

Civil Rights Movement The Second World War increased African American migration from the American South to northern cities, intensifying a drive for rights, dignity, and independence. By 1960, civil rights groups had started organizing boycotts and demonstrations directed at discrimination against blacks in the South. During the 1960s, civil rights laws passed under President Lyndon B. Johnson did bring African Americans some equality with regard to voting rights and, to a much lesser degree, school desegregation. However, racism continued in areas such as housing, job opportunities, and the economic development of African American communities.

Civil War (1861–1865) Conflict between the northern and southern states of America that cost over 600,000 lives; this struggle led to the abolition of slavery in the United States.

classical learning Study of ancient Greek and Latin texts. After Christianity became the only legal religion of the Roman Empire, scholars needed to find a way to make classical learning applicable to a Christian way of life. Christian monks played a significant role in resolving this problem by reinterpreting the classics for a Christian audience.

Cluny Powerful Benedictine monastery, founded in 910, whose enormous wealth and prestige would derive from its independence from secular authorities as well as from its wide network of daughter houses (priories).

Cold War (1945–1991) Ideological, political, and economic conflict in which the USSR and Eastern Europe opposed the United States and Western Europe in the decades after the Second World War. The Cold War's origins lay in the breakup of the wartime alliance between the United States and the Soviet Union in 1945 and resulted in a division of Europe into two spheres: the West, committed to market capitalism, and the East, which sought to build socialist republics in areas under Soviet Control. The Cold War ended with the collapse of the Soviet Union in 1991.

collectivization Stalin's plan for nationalizing agricultural production in the USSR, begun in 1929. Twenty-five million peasants were forced to give up their land and join 250,000 large collective farms. Many who resisted were deported to labor camps in the Far East, and Stalin's government cut off food rations to those areas most resistant to collectivization. In the ensuing man-made famines, millions of people starved to death.

Columbian Exchange The widespread exchange of peoples, plants, animals, diseases, goods, and culture between the African and Eurasian landmass (on the one hand) and the region that encompasses the Americas, Australia, and the Pacific Islands (on the other); precipitated by the first voyage of Columbus in 1492.

Christopher Columbus (1451–1506) Genoese sailor who persuaded King Ferdinand and Queen Isabella of Spain to fund his expedition across the Atlantic, with the purpose of discovering a new trade route to Asia. His miscalculations landed him in the Bahamas and the island of Hispaniola in 1492.

Commercial Revolution A period of economic development in Europe lasting from c. 1500 to c. 1800. Advances in agriculture and handicraft production, combined with the expansion of trade networks in the Atlantic world, brought new wealth and new kinds of commercial activity to Europe. The commercial revolution prepared the way for the industrial revolution of the 1800s.

Committee of Public Safety Political body during the French Revolution that was controlled by the Jacobins, who defended the revolution by executing thousands during the Reign of Terror (September 1793–July 1794).

commune Community of individuals who have banded together in a sworn association, with the aim of establishing their independence and setting up their own form of representative government. Many medieval towns originally founded by lords or monasteries gained their independence through such methods.

The Communist Manifesto Radical pamphlet by Karl Marx (1818–1883) and Friedrich Engels (1820–1895) that predicted the downfall of the capitalist system and its replacement by a classless egalitarian society. Marx and Engels believed that this revolution would be accomplished by industrial and agricultural workers (the proletariat).

Compromise of 1867 Agreement between the Habsburgs and the peoples living in Hungarian parts of the empire that re-established Hungarian sovereignty, thus creating the Austro-Hungarian Empire.

Concert of Europe (1814–1815) Series of diplomatic agreements, designed primarily by Austrian minister Klemens von Metternich between 1814 and 1848 and supported by other European powers until 1914, to maintain a balance of power on the Continent and to prevent destabilizing social and political change in Europe.

conciliarism Doctrine developed in the thirteenth and fourteenth centuries to counter the growing power of the papacy; conciliarism holds that papal authority should be subject to a council of the Church at large. Conciliarists emerged as a dominant force after the Council of Constance (1414–18) but were eventually outmatched by a rejuvenated papacy.

Congress of Vienna (1814–15) International conference to reorganize Europe after the downfall of Napoleon and the French Revolution. European monarchies restored the Bourbon family to the French throne, and agreed to respect each other's borders and to cooperate in guarding against future revolutions and wars.

conquistador Spanish term for "conqueror," applied to the mercenaries and adventurers who campaigned against indigenous peoples in central and southern America.

conservatives In the nineteenth century, European conservatives aimed to legitimize and solidify the monarchy's authority and the hierarchical social order. They believed that change had to be slow, incremental, and managed so that the structures of authority were strengthened.

Constantine (275–337) The first emperor of Rome to convert to Christianity, Constantine came to power in 312. In 324, he founded a new imperial capital, Constantinople, on the site of a maritime settlement in Asia Minor known as Byzantium.

Constantinople City founded by the emperor Constantine on the site of a village called Byzantium; it became the new capital of the Roman Empire in 324 and continued to be the seat of imperial power after its capture by the Ottoman Turks in 1453. It is now known as Istanbul.

contract theory of government Theory developed by Englishman John Locke (1632–1704) which posits that government authority is both contractual and conditional; therefore, if a government has abused its given authority, society has the right to dissolve it and create another.

Nicholaus Copernicus (1473–1543) Polish astronomer who advanced the idea that the earth revolves around the sun.

cosmopolitanism Stemming from the Greek word meaning "universal city," the culture characteristic of the Hellenistic world challenged and transformed the more narrow worldview of the Greek polis.

cotton gin Invented by Eli Whitney in 1793, this device mechanized the process of separating cotton seeds from the cotton fiber, which sped up the production of cotton and reduced its price. This change made slavery profitable in the United States.

Council of Constance (1417–20) A meeting of clergy and theologians in an effort to resolve the Great Schism within the Roman Church. The council deposed all rival papal candidates and elected a new pope, Martin V, but it also adopted the doctrine of conciliarism, which holds that the supreme authority within the Church rests with a representative general council and not with the pope. However, Martin V himself was an opponent of this doctrine and refused to be bound by it.

Council of Trent Name given to a series of meetings held in the Italian city of Trent (Trento) between 1545 and 1563, when leaders of the Roman Church reaffirmed Catholic doctrine and instituted internal reforms.

Counter-Reformation Movement to counter the Protestant Reformation, initiated by the Catholic Church at the Council of Trent in 1545.

coup d'état French term for the overthrow of an established government by a group of conspirators, usually with military support.

Crimean War (1854–56) War waged by Russia against Great Britain and France. Spurred by Russia's encroachment on Ottoman territories, the conflict revealed Russia's military weakness when Russian forces fell to British and French troops.

Cuban missile crisis (1962) Diplomatic standoff between the United States and the Soviet Union that was provoked by the Soviet Union's attempt to base nuclear missiles in Cuba; it brought the world closer to nuclear war than ever before or since.

Cuius regio, eius religio A Latin phrase meaning "as the ruler, so the religion." Adopted as a part of the settlement of the Peace of Augsburg in 1555, it meant that those principalities ruled by Lutherans would have Lutheranism as their official religion and those ruled by Catholics would practice Catholicism.

cult of domesticity Concept associated with Victorian England that idealized women as nurturing wives and mothers.

cult of the Virgin Beliefs and practices associated with the veneration of Mary, the mother of Jesus, which became increasingly popular in the twelfth century.

cuneiform Early writing system that began to develop in Mesopotamia in the fourth millennium B.C.E. By 3100 B.C.E., its distinctive markings were impressed on clay tablets using a wedge-shaped stylus.

Cyrus the Great (c. 585–529 B.C.E.) As architect of the Persian Empire, Cyrus extended his dominion over a vast territory stretching from the Persian Gulf to the Mediterranean and incorporating the ancient civilizations of Mesopotamia. His successors ruled this Persian Empire as "Great Kings."

Darius (521–486 B.C.E.) The Persian emperor whose conflict with Aristagoras, the Greek ruler of Miletus, ignited the Persian Wars. In 490 B.C.E., Darius sent a large army to punish the Athenians for their intervention in Persian imperial affairs, but this force was defeated by Athenian hoplites on the plain of Marathon.

Charles Darwin (1809–1882) British naturalist who wrote *On the Origin of Species* (1859) and developed the theory of natural selection to explain the evolution of living organisms.

D-Day (June 6, 1944) Date of the Allied invasion of Normandy, under General Dwight Eisenhower, to liberate Western Europe from German occupation.

Decembrists Russian army officers who were influenced by events in France and formed secret societies that espoused liberal governance. They were put down by Tsar Nicholas I in December 1825.

Declaration of Independence (1776) Historic document stating the principles of government on which the United States was founded.

Declaration of the Rights of Man and of the Citizen (1789) French charter of liberties formulated by the National Assembly during the French Revolution. The seventeen articles later became the preamble to the new constitution, which the assembly finished in 1791.

democracy In ancient Greece, the form of government that allowed a class of propertied male citizens to participate in the governance of their polis, but excluded women, slaves, and citizens without property from the political process. As a result, the ruling class amounted to only a small percentage of the entire population.

René Descartes (1596–1650) French philosopher and mathematician who emphasized the use of deductive reasoning.

Denis Diderot (1713–1784) French philosophe and author who was the guiding force behind the publication of the *Encyclopedia,* which showed how reason could be applied to nearly all realms of thought; it aimed to be a compendium of all human knowledge.

Dien Bien Phu (1954) Defining battle in the war between French colonialists and the Viet Minh that secured North Vietnam for Ho Chi Minh and his army and left the south to form its own government, to be supported by France and the United States.

Diet of Worms The select council of the Roman Catholic Church that convened in the German city of Worms and condemned Martin Luther on a charge of heresy in 1521.

Diocletian (245–316) As emperor of Rome from 284 to 305, Diocletian recognized that the empire could not be governed by one man in one place. His solution was to divide the empire into four parts, each with its own imperial ruler, but he himself remained the dominant ruler of the resulting tetrarchy (rule of four). He also initiated the Great Persecution, a time when many Christians became martyrs to their faith.

Directory (1795–1799) Executive committee that governed revolutionary France after the fall of Robespierre and held control until the coup of Napoleon Bonaparte.

Discourse on Method Philosophical treatise by René Descartes (1596–1650) proposing that the path to knowledge was through logical deduction, beginning with one's own self: "I think, therefore I am."

Dominican Order Also called the Order of Preachers, it was founded by Dominic of Osma (1170–1221), a Castilian preacher and theologian, and approved by Innocent III in 1216. The order was dedicated to the rooting out of heresy and the conversion of Jews and Muslims. Many of its members held teaching positions in European universities and contributed to the development of medieval philosophy and theology. Others became the leading administrators of the Inquisition.

Dominion in the British Commonwealth Canadian promise to maintain their fealty to the British crown, even after their independence in 1867; later applied to Australia and New Zealand.

Dreyfus Affair The 1894 French scandal surrounding accusations that a Jewish captain, Alfred Dreyfus, had sold military secrets to the Germans. Convicted, Dreyfus was sentenced to solitary confinement for life. However, after public outcry, it was revealed that the trial documents were forgeries, and Dreyfus was pardoned after a second trial in 1899. In 1906, he was fully exonerated and reinstated in the army. The affair revealed the depths of popular anti-Semitism in France.

Alexander Dubček (1921–1992) Communist leader of the Czechoslovakian government who advocated for "socialism with a human face." He encouraged debate within the party, academic and artistic freedom, and less censorship, which led to the "Prague spring" of 1968. People in other parts of Eastern Europe began to demonstrate in support of Dubček and to demand their own reforms. When Dubček tried to democratize the Communist party and failed to attend a meeting of the Warsaw Pact, the Soviets sent tanks and troops into Prague and ousted Dubček and his allies.

Duma The Russian parliament, created in response to the revolution of 1905.

Dunkirk French port on the English Channel where the British and French forces retreated after sustaining heavy losses against the German military early in World War II. Between May 27 and June 4, 1940, the Royal Navy evacuated over 300,000 troops using commercial and pleasure boats.

Eastern Front Battlefront between Germany and the Soviet Union during the First and Second World Wars.

East India Company (1600–1858) British charter company created to outperform Portuguese and Spanish traders in the Far East; in the eighteenth century the company became, in effect, the ruler of a large part of India. There was also a Dutch East India Company.

Edict of Nantes (1598) Proclamation issued by Henry IV of France in an effort to end religious violence; it declared France to be a Catholic country but tolerated some forms of Protestant worship.

Edward I of England King of England from 1272 to his death in 1307, Edward presided over the creation of new legal and bureaucratic institutions in his realm, violently subjugated the Welsh, and attempted to colonize Scotland. He expelled English Jews from his domain in 1290.

Eleanor of Aquitaine (1122–1204) Ruler of the wealthy province of Aquitaine and wife of Louis VII of France, Eleanor had her marriage annulled in order to marry the young count of Anjou, Henry Plantagenet, who became King Henry of England a year later. Mother of two future kings of England, she was an important patron of the arts.

Elizabeth I (1533–1603) Protestant daughter of Henry VIII and his second wife, Anne Boleyn, Elizabeth succeeded her sister Mary as the second queen regnant of England (r. 1558–1603).

emancipation of the serfs (1861) The abolition of serfdom was central to Tsar Alexander II's program of modernization and reform, but it produced a limited amount of change. Former serfs now had legal rights. However, farmland was granted to the village communes instead of to individuals. Most of this land was of poor quality and the former serfs had to pay for it in installments to the village commune.

emperor Originally the term for any conquering commander of the Roman army whose victories merited celebration in an official triumph; after Augustus seized power in 27 B.C.E., it was the title born by the sole ruler of the Roman Empire.

empire Centralized political entity consolidated through the conquest and colonization of other nations or peoples in order to benefit the ruler and/or his homeland.

Enabling Act (1933) Emergency act passed by the Reichstag (German parliament) that helped transform Hitler from Germany's chancellor, or prime minister, into a dictator, following the suspicious burning of the Reichstag building and a suspension of civil liberties.

enclosure Long process of privatizing what had been public agricultural land in eighteenth-century Britain; it helped to stimulate the development of commercial agriculture and forced many people in rural areas to seek work in cities during the early stages of industrialization.

The Encyclopedia Joint venture of French philosophe writers, led by Denis Diderot (1713–1784), which proposed to summarize all modern knowledge in a multivolume, illustrated work with over 70,000 articles.

Friedrich Engels (1820–1895) German social and political philosopher who collaborated with Karl Marx on *The Communist Manifesto* and many other publications.

English Civil War (1642–49) Conflicts between the English Parliament and King Charles I erupted into civil war, which ended in the defeat of the royalists and the execution of Charles on charges of high treason. A short time later, Parliament abolished the monarchy and hereditary House of Lords, and England was declared a Commonwealth.

English Navigation Act of 1651 English law stipulating that only English ships could carry goods between the mother country and its colonies.

Enlightenment Intellectual movement in eighteenth-century Europe marked by a belief in human betterment through the application of reason to solve social, economic, and political problems.

Epicureanism Philosophical position articulated by Epicurus of Athens (c. 342–270 B.C.E.), who rejected the idea of an ordered universe governed by divine forces; instead, he emphasized individual agency and proposed that the highest good is the pursuit of pleasure.

Desiderius Erasmus (c. 1469–1536) Dutch-born scholar, social commentator, and Catholic humanist whose new translation of the Bible influenced the theology of Martin Luther.

Estates-General Representative body of the three estates in France. In 1789, King Louis XVI summoned the Estates-General to meet for the first time since 1614 because it seemed to be the only solution to France's worsening economic crisis and financial chaos.

Etruscans Settlers of the Italian peninsula who dominated the region from the late Bronze Age until the rise of the Roman Republic in the sixth century B.C.E.

Euclid (fl. 300 B.C.E.) Hellenistic mathematician whose *Elements of Geometry* forms the basis of modern geometry.

eugenics Greek term, meaning "good birth," referring to the project of "breeding" a superior human race. Eugenics was popularly championed by scientists, politicians, and social critics in the late nineteenth and early twentieth centuries.

European Common Market (1957) The Treaty of Rome created the European Economic Community (EEC), or Common Market. The original members were France, West Germany, Italy, Belgium, Holland, and Luxembourg. The EEC sought to abolish trade barriers between its members and it pledged itself to common external tariffs, the free movement of labor and capital among the member nations, and uniform wage structures and social security systems to create similar working conditions in all member countries.

European Union (EU) Successor organization to the European Economic Community or European Common Market, formed by the Maastricht Treaty, which took effect in 1993. Currently twenty-eight member states compose the EU, which has a governing council, an international court, and a parliament. Over time, member states of the EU have relinquished some of their sovereignty, and cooperation has evolved into a community with a single currency, the euro.

Exclusion Act of 1882 U.S. congressional act prohibiting nearly all immigration from China to the United States; it was fueled by animosity toward Chinese workers in the American West.

existentialism Philosophical movement that arose out of the Second World War and emphasized the absurdity of the human condition. Led by Jean-Paul Sartre and Albert Camus, existen-

tialists encouraged humans to take responsibility for their own decisions and dilemmas.

expulsion of the Jews European rulers began to expel their Jewish subjects from their kingdoms beginning in the 1280s, mostly due to their inability to repay the money they had extorted from Jewish money-lenders but also as a result of escalating anti-Semitism in the wake of the Crusades. Jews were also expelled from the Rhineland in the fourteenth century and from Spain in 1492.

fascism Doctrine propounded by Italian dictator Benito Mussolini, which emphasized three main ideas: statism ("nothing above the state, nothing outside the state, nothing against the state"), nationalism, and militarism. Its name derives from the Latin *fasces*, a symbol of Roman imperial power adopted by Mussolini.

Fashoda Incident (1898) Disagreements between the French and the British over land claims in North Africa led to a standoff between armies of the two nations at the Sudanese town of Fashoda. The crisis was resolved diplomatically. France ceded southern Sudan to Britain in exchange for a stop to further expansion by the British.

The Feminine Mystique Groundbreaking book by feminist Betty Friedan (1921–2006), which offered various definitions of *femininity* and explored how women internalized those definitions.

Franz Ferdinand (1863–1914) Archduke of Austria and heir to the Austro-Hungarian Empire; his assassination led to the beginning of the First World War.

Ferdinand (1452–1516) **and Isabella** (1451–1504) In 1469, Ferdinand of Aragon married the heiress to Castile, Isabella. Their union allowed them to pursue several ambitious policies, including the conquest of Granada, the last Muslim principality in Spain, and the expulsion of Spain's large Jewish community. In 1492, Isabella granted three ships to Christopher Columbus of Genoa (Italy), who went on to claim portions of the New World for Spain.

Fertile Crescent Region of fertile land in what is now Syria, Israel, Turkey, eastern Iraq, and western Iran that was able to sustain settlements due to its wetter climate and its suitability for agriculture. Some of the earliest known civilizations emerged there between 9000 and 4500 B.C.E.

feudalism Problematic modern term that attempts to explain the diffusion of power in medieval Europe and the many different kinds of political, social, and economic relationships that were forged through the giving and receiving of fiefs (*feoda*). But because it is anachronistic and inadequate, this term has been rejected by most historians of the medieval period.

First Crusade (1095–1099) Campaign launched by Pope Urban II in response to a request from the Byzantine emperor Alexius Comnenus, who had asked for a small contingent of knights to assist him in fighting Turkish forces in Anatolia; Urban instead directed the crusaders' energies toward the Holy Land and the recapture of Jerusalem, promising those who took up the cross (*crux*) that they would merit eternal salvation if they died in the attempt. This crusade prompted attacks against Jews throughout Europe and resulted in six subsequent—and ultimately unsuccessful—military campaigns.

First World War A total war from August 1914 to November 1918, involving the armies of Britain, France, and Russia (the Allies), who eventually prevailed against Germany, Austria-Hungary, and the Ottoman Empire (the Central Powers). Italy joined the Allies in 1915, and the United States joined them in 1917, helping to tip the balance in favor of the Allies, who also drew upon the populations and raw materials of their colonial possessions. Also known as the Great War and World War I.

Five Pillars of Islam Muslim doctrine that salvation is only assured through observance of five basic precepts: submission to God's will as described in the teachings of Muhammad (the Qur'an), frequent prayer, ritual fasting, the giving of alms, and an annual pilgrimage to Mecca (the Hajj).

Five-Year Plan Soviet effort launched under Stalin in 1928 to replace the free-market economy with a state-owned and state-managed economy in order to promote rapid economic development over a five-year period and thereby "catch and overtake" the leading capitalist countries. The First Five-Year Plan was followed by the Second Five-Year Plan (1933–37) and so on, until the collapse of the Soviet Union in 1991.

fly-shuttle Invented by John Kay in 1733, this device sped up the process of weaving.

Fourteen Points President Woodrow Wilson's proposal for a diplomatic foundation on which to build peace in the world after the First World War. The Fourteen Points called for an end to secret treaties, "open covenants, openly arrived at," freedom of the seas, the removal of international tariffs, the reduction of arms, the "self-determination of peoples," and the establishment of a League of Nations to settle international conflicts.

Franciscan Order Also known as the Order of the Friars Minor. The earliest Franciscans were followers of Francis of Assisi (1182–1226) and strove, like him, to imitate the life and example of Jesus. The clerical order was formally established by Pope Innocent III in 1209. Its special mission was the care and instruction of the urban poor.

Frankfurt Parliament (1848–49) Failed attempt to create a unified Germany under constitutional principles. In 1849, the assembly offered the crown of a new German nation to Frederick William IV of Prussia, but he refused the offer and suppressed a brief protest. The delegates went home disillusioned.

Frederick the Great (1712–1786) Prussian ruler (r. 1740–86) who engaged the nobility in maintaining a strong military and bureaucracy and led Prussian armies to notable military victories. He also encouraged Enlightenment rationalism and artistic endeavors.

French Revolution of 1789 In 1788, a severe financial crisis forced the French monarchy to convene an assembly known as the Estates General, representing the three estates of the realm: the clergy, the nobility, and the commons (known as the Third Estate). When the Estates General met in 1789, representatives of the Third Estate demanded major constitutional changes, and when the king and his government proved uncooperative, these delegates broke with the other two estates and renamed themselves the National Assembly, demanding a written constitution. The position of the National Assembly was confirmed by a popular uprising in Paris, and the king was forced to accept the transformation of France into a constitutional monarchy. This constitutional phase of the revolution lasted until 1792, when the pressures of foreign invasion and the emergence of a more-radical revolutionary movement led to the collapse of the monarchy and the establishment of a republic.

French Revolution of 1830 French popular revolt against Charles X's July Ordinances of 1830, which dissolved the French Chamber of Deputies and restricted suffrage to exclude almost everyone except the nobility. After several days of violence, Charles abdicated the throne and was replaced by a constitutional monarch, Louis Philippe.

French Revolution of 1848 Revolution overthrowing Louis-Philippe in February, 1848, leading to the formation of the Second Republic (1848–52). Initially enjoying broad support from both the middle classes and laborers in Paris, the new government became more conservative after elections in which the French peasantry participated for the first time. A workers' revolt was violently repressed in June 1848, and in December 1848, Napoleon Bonaparte's nephew, Louis-Napoleon Bonaparte, was elected president. In 1852, Louis-Napoleon declared himself emperor and abolished the republic.

Sigmund Freud (1856–1939) Austrian physician who founded the discipline of psychoanalysis and suggested that human behavior was largely motivated by unconscious and irrational forces.

Galileo Galilei (1564–1642) Italian physicist and inventor; the implications of his ideas raised the ire of the Catholic Church, and he was forced to retract most of his findings.

Gallipoli (1915) In the First World War, a combined force of French, British, Australian and New Zealand troops tried to invade Turkey's Gallipoli Peninsula, in the first large-scale amphibious attack in history, and seize it from the Turks. After seven months of fighting, the Allies had lost 200,000 soldiers. Defeated, they withdrew.

Mohandas K. (Mahatma) Gandhi (1869–1948) Indian leader who advocated nonviolent noncooperation to protest colonial rule and helped win home rule for India in 1947.

Giuseppe Garibaldi (1807–1882) Italian revolutionary leader who led the fight to free Sicily and Naples from the Habsburg Empire; the lands were then peaceably annexed by Sardinia to produce a unified Italy.

Gaul Region of the Roman Empire that was home to the Celtic people of that name, comprising modern France, Belgium, and western Germany.

Geneva Conference (1954) International conference to restore peace in Korea and Indochina. The chief participants were the United States, the Soviet Union, Great Britain, France, the People's Republic of China, North Korea, South Korea, Vietnam, the Viet Minh party, Laos, and Cambodia. The conference resulted in the division of North and South Vietnam.

Genoa Maritime city on Italy's northwestern coast; the Genoese were active in trading ventures along the Silk Road and in the establishment of trading colonies in the Mediterranean. They were also involved in the world of finance and backed the commercial ventures of other powers, especially Spain's.

German Democratic Republic Communist nation founded from the Soviet zone of occupation of Germany after the Second World War; also known as East Germany.

German Social Democratic party Founded in 1875, it was the most powerful socialist party in Europe before 1917.

Gilgamesh Sumerian ruler of the city of Uruk around 2700 B.C.E.; Gilgamesh became the hero of one of the world's oldest epics, which circulated orally for nearly a millennium before being written down.

Giotto (c. 1266–1337) Florentine painter and architect who is often considered a forerunner of the Renaissance.

glasnost Introduced by Soviet leader Mikhail Gorbachev in June 1987, *glasnost* was one of the five major policies that constituted *perestroika* ("Restructuring"). Often translated into English as "openness," *glasnost* called for transparency in Soviet government and institutional activities by reducing censorship in mass media and lifting significant bans on the political, intellectual, and cultural lives of Soviet civilians.

globalization Term used to describe political, social, and economic networks that span the globe. Such global exchanges are not limited to nation-states and in recent decades are associated with new technologies such as the Internet. Globalization is not new, however, as human cultures and economies have been in contact with one another for centuries.

Glorious Revolution The overthrow of King James II of England and the installation of his Protestant daughter, Mary Stuart, and her husband, William of Orange, to the throne in 1688 and 1689. It is widely regarded as the founding moment in the development of a constitutional monarchy in Britain, while also establishing a more favorable climate for the economic and political growth of the English commercial classes.

Gold Coast Name that European mariners and merchants gave to that part of West Equatorial Africa from which gold and slaves were exported. Originally controlled by the Portuguese, this area later became the British colony of the Gold Coast (present-day Ghana).

Mikhail Gorbachev (b. 1931) Soviet leader who attempted to reform the Soviet Union through his programs of glasnost and perestroika in the late 1980s. He encouraged open discussions in other countries in the Soviet bloc, which helped inspire "velvet" revolutions throughout Eastern Europe. Eventually the political, social, and economic upheaval he had unleashed would lead to the breakup of the Soviet Union.

Gothic style Type of graceful architecture emerging in twelfth- and thirteenth-century England and France. The style is characterized by pointed arches, delicate decoration, and large windows.

Olympe de Gouges (1748–1793) French political radical and feminist whose *Declaration of the Rights of Woman and the Female Citizen* demanded an equal place for women in France.

Great Depression Global economic crisis following the U.S. stock market crash on October 29, 1929, and ending with the onset of the Second World War.

Great Famine Period of terrible hunger and deprivation in Europe that peaked between 1315 and 1317, caused by a cooling of the climate and by environmental degradation due to over-farming. It is estimated to have reduced the population of Europe by 10–15 percent.

Great Fear (1789) Following the outbreak of revolution in Paris, fear spread throughout the French countryside, as rumors circulated that armies of brigands or royal troops were coming. The peasants and villagers organized into militias, while others attacked and burned the manor houses in order to destroy the records of manorial dues.

Great Schism (1378–1417) Also known as the Great Western Schism, to distinguish it from the longstanding rupture between the Greek East and Latin West. During the schism, the Roman Church was divided between two (and, ultimately, three) competing popes. Each pope claimed to be legitimate and each denounced the heresy of the others.

Great Terror (1936–38) The systematic murder of nearly a million people and the deportation of another million and a half to labor camps by Stalin's regime in an attempt to consolidate power and eliminate perceived enemies.

Greek East After the founding of Constantinople, the eastern Greek-speaking half of the Roman Empire grew more populous, prosperous, and central to imperial policy. Its inhabitants considered themselves to be the true heirs of Rome, and their own Orthodox Church to be the true manifestation of Jesus's ministry.

Greek independence Nationalists in Greece revolted against the Ottoman Empire and fought a war that ended with Greek independence in 1827. They received crucial help from British, French, and Russian troops as well as widespread sympathy throughout Europe.

Pope Gregory I (r. 590–604) Also known as Gregory the Great, he was the first bishop of Rome to successfully negotiate a more universal role for the papacy. His political and theological agenda widened the rift between the western Latin (Catholic) Church and the eastern Greek (Orthodox) Church in Byzantium. He also articulated the Church's official position on the status of Jews, promoted affective approaches to religious worship, encouraged the Benedictine monastic movement, and sponsored missionary expeditions.

Guernica Basque town bombed by German planes in April 1937 during the Spanish Civil War. Guernica is also the subject of Pablo Picasso's famous painting from the same year.

guilds Professional organizations in commercial towns that regulated business and safeguarded the privileges of those practicing a particular craft. Often identical to confraternities ("brotherhoods").

Gulag Vast system of forced labor camps under the Soviet regime; it originated in 1919 in a small monastery near the Arctic Circle and spread throughout the Soviet Union. Penal labor was required of both ordinary criminals and those accused of political crimes. Tens of millions of people were sent to the camps between 1928 and 1953; the exact figure is unknown.

Gulf War (1991) Armed conflict between Iraq and a coalition of thirty-two nations, including the United States, Britain, Egypt, France, and Saudi Arabia. The war was prompted Iraq's invasion of Kuwait on August 2, 1990.

Johannes Gutenberg (c. 1398–1468) European inventor of the printing press; his shop in Mainz produced the first printed book—a Bible—between the years 1453 and 1455.

Habsburg Dynasty Powerful European dynasty that first came to power in the eleventh century in a region now part of Switzerland. Early generations of Habsburgs consolidated their control over neighboring German-speaking lands; through strategic marriages with other royal lines, later rulers eventually controlled a substantial part of Europe—including much of central Europe, the Netherlands, and even Spain and all its colonies for a time. In practice, the Holy Roman Emperor was chosen from a member of the Habsburg lineage. By the latter half of the seventeenth century, the Austrian Habsburg Empire was made of up nearly 300 nominally autonomous dynastic kingdoms, principalities, duchies, and archbishoprics.

Hagia Sophia Enormous church dedicated to "Holy Wisdom," built in Constantinople at the behest of the emperor Justinian in the sixth century C.E. When Constantinople fell to Ottoman forces in 1453, it became an important mosque.

Haitian Revolution (1802–4) In 1802, Napoleon sought to reassert French control of the colony of Saint-Domingue, but stiff resistance and yellow fever crushed the French army. In 1804, Jean-Jacques Dessalines, a general in the army of former slaves, declared the independent state of Haiti. (See **slave revolt in Saint-Domingue**.)

Hajj The annual pilgrimage to Mecca; an obligation for Muslims.

Hammurabi Ruler of Babylon from 1792 to 1750 B.C.E.; Hammurabi issued a collection of laws that were greatly influential in the Near East and which constitute the world's oldest surviving legal code.

Harlem Renaissance Cultural movement in the 1920s that was based in Harlem, a part of New York City with a large African American population. The movement gave voice to black novelists, poets, painters, and musicians, many of whom used their art to protest racial subordination.

Hatshepsut (r. 1479–1458 C.E.) As Egyptian pharaoh during the New Kingdom, she launched several successful military campaigns and extended trade and diplomacy. She was an ambitious builder who probably constructed the first tomb in the Valley of the Kings. Though she never pretended to be a man, she was routinely portrayed with a masculine figure and a ceremonial beard.

Hebrews Originally a pastoral people divided among several tribes, the Hebrews were briefly united under the rule of David and his son, Solomon, who promoted the worship of a single god, Yahweh, and constructed the first temple at the new capital city of Jerusalem. After Solomon's death, the Hebrew tribes were divided between the two kingdoms of Israel and Judah, which were eventually conquered by the Neo-Assyrian and Chaldean empires. It was in captivity that the Hebrews came to define themselves through worship of Yahweh and to develop a religion, Judaism, that could exist outside of Judea. They were liberated by the Persian king Cyrus the Great in 539 B.C.E.

Hellenistic art The art of the Hellenistic period bridged the tastes, ideals, and customs of classical Greece and those that would be more characteristic of Rome. Striving to emulate Hellenistic city planning and civic culture, the Romans thereby exported Hellenistic culture to their own far-flung colonies in western Europe.

Hellenistic culture The "Greek-like" culture that dominated the ancient world in the wake of Alexander's conquests.

Hellenistic kingdoms Following the death of Alexander the Great, his vast empire was divided into three separate states: Ptolemaic Egypt (under the rule of the general Ptolemy and his successors), Seleucid Asia (ruled by the general Seleucus and his heirs) and Antigonid Greece (governed by Antigonus of Macedonia). Each state maintained its independence, but the shared characteristics of Greco-Macedonian rule and a shared Greek culture and heritage bound them together in a united cosmopolitan world.

Hellenistic world The various Western civilizations of antiquity that were loosely united by shared Greek language and culture, especially around the eastern Mediterranean.

Heloise of Argentevil (c. 1090–1164) One of the foremost scholars of her time, she became the pupil and the wife of the philosopher and teacher Peter Abelard. In later life, she was the founder of a new religious order for women.

Henry IV of Germany King of Germany and Holy Roman Emperor from 1056—when he ascended the throne at the age of six years old—until his death in 1106. Henry's reign was first weakened by conflict with the Saxon nobility and later marked by the Investiture Controversy with Pope Gregory VII.

Henry VIII (1491–1547) King of England from 1509 until his death, Henry rejected the authority of the Roman Church in 1534 when the pope refused to annul his marriage to his queen, Catherine of Aragon; he became the founder of the Church of England.

Henry of Navarre (1553–1610) Crowned King Henry IV of France, he renounced his Protestantism but granted limited toleration for Huguenots (French Protestants) by the Edict of Nantes in 1598.

Prince Henry the Navigator (1394–1460) A brother of the king of Portugal, Henry encouraged the exploration and conquest of western Africa and the trade in gold and slaves.

hieroglyphs Writing system of ancient Egypt, based on a complicated series of pictorial symbols. It fell out of use when Egypt was absorbed into the Roman Empire and was only deciphered after the discovery of the Rosetta Stone in the early nineteenth century.

Hildegard of Bingen (1098–1179) A powerful German abbess, theologian, scientist, musician, and visionary who claimed to receive regular revelations from God. Although highly influential in her own day, she was never officially canonized by the Church, in part because her strong personality no longer accorded with the shifting ideal of female piety.

Hiroshima Japanese port devastated by an atomic bomb on August 6, 1945.

Adolf Hitler (1889–1945) Author of *Mein Kampf* and leader of the National Socialists (Nazis) who became chancellor of Germany in 1933. Hitler and his National Socialists Nazi regime started the Second World War and orchestrated the systematic murder of over 6 million Jews.

Hitler-Stalin Pact (1939) Treaty between Nazi Germany and the Soviet Union, which promised the USSR a share of Poland, Finland, the Baltic States, and Bessarabia in the event of a

German invasion of Poland, which began shortly thereafter, on September 1, 1939.

HIV epidemic The first cases of HIV-AIDS appeared in the late 1970s. As HIV-AIDS became a global crisis, international organizations recognized the need for an early, swift, and comprehensive response to future outbreaks of disease.

Thomas Hobbes (1588–1679) English political philosopher whose *Leviathan* (1651) argued that any form of government capable of protecting its subjects' lives and property might act as an all-powerful sovereign. This government should be allowed to trample over both liberty and property for the sake of its own survival and that of its subjects. For in his natural state, Hobbes argued, man was like "a wolf" toward other men.

Holy Roman Empire Loosely allied collection of lands in central and western Europe ruled by the kings of Germany (and later Austria) from the twelfth century until 1806. Its origins are usually identified with the empire of Charlemagne, the Frankish king who was crowned emperor of Rome by the pope in 800.

homage Ceremony in which an individual becomes the "man" (French: *homme*) of a lord.

Homer (fl. eighth century B.C.E.) Greek rhapsode ("weaver" of stories) credited with merging centuries of poetic tradition in the epics known as the *Iliad* and the *Odyssey*.

hoplite Greek foot-soldier armed with a spear or short sword and protected by a large round shield (*hoplon*). In battle, hoplites stood shoulder to shoulder in a close formation called a phalanx.

Huguenots French Protestants who endured severe persecution in the sixteenth and seventeenth centuries.

humanism Program of study associated with the movement known as the Renaissance; humanism aimed to replace the scholastic emphasis on logic and philosophy with the study of ancient languages, literature, history, and ethics.

human rights Principle that all people have the right to legal equality, freedom of religion and speech, and the right to participate in government. Human rights laws prohibit torture, cruel punishment, and slavery.

David Hume (1711–1776) Scottish writer who applied Newton's method of scientific inquiry and skepticism to the study of morality, the mind, and government.

Hundred Years' War (1337–1453) Series of wars between England and France, fought mostly on French soil and prompted by the territorial and political claims of English monarchs.

Jan Hus (c. 1373–1415) Czech reformer who adopted many of the teachings of the English theologian John Wycliffe, and who also demanded that the laity be allowed to receive both the consecrated bread and wine of the Eucharist. The Council of Constance burned him at the stake for heresy. In response, his supporters, the Hussites, revolted against the Church.

Saddam Hussein (1937–2006) Former dictator of Iraq who invaded Iran in 1980 and started the eight-year-long Iran-Iraq War; invaded Kuwait in 1990, which led to the Gulf War of 1991; and was overthrown when the United States invaded Iraq in 2003. Involved in Iraqi politics since the mid-1960s, Hussein became the official head of state in 1979.

Iconoclast Controversy (717–87) Serious and often violent theological debate that raged in Byzantium after Emperor Leo III ordered the destruction of religious art on the grounds that any image representing a divine or holy personage is prone to promote idol worship and blasphemy. Iconoclast means "breaker of icons." Those who supported the veneration of icons were called iconodules, "adherents of icons."

Il-khanate Mongol-founded dynasty in thirteenth-century Persia.

Indian National Congress Indian political party formed in 1885 to achieve Indian independence from British colonial control. The Congress was led by Mohandas Gandhi in the 1920s and 1930s.

Indian Rebellion of 1857 Uprising that began near Delhi when the military disciplined a regiment of Indian soldiers employed by the British for refusing to use rifle cartridges greased with pork fat—unacceptable to either Hindus or Muslims. Rebels attacked law courts and burned tax rolls, protesting debt and corruption. The mutiny spread through large areas of northwest India before being violently suppressed by British troops.

Indo-Europeans Group of people speaking variations of the same language who moved into the Near East and Mediterranean region shortly after 2000 B.C.E.

indulgences Grants exempting Catholic Christians from the performance of penance, either in life or after death. The abusive trade in indulgences was a major catalyst of the Protestant Reformation.

Incas People of the highly centralized South American empire that was toppled by the Spanish conquistador Francisco Pizarro in 1533.

Innocent III (1160/61–1216) Pope who wanted to unify all of Christendom under papal hegemony; he furthered this goal at the Fourth Lateran Council of 1215, which defined one of the Church's dogmas as the acknowledgment of papal supremacy. The council also took an unprecedented interest in the religious education and habits of every Christian.

Inquisition Tribunal of the Roman Catholic Church that aims to combat heresy by enforcing religious orthodoxy and conformity.

International Monetary Fund (IMF) Established in 1945 to ensure international cooperation regarding currency exchange and monetary policy, the IMF is a specialized agency of the United Nations.

Investiture Conflict Name given to a series of disputes over the limitations of spiritual and secular power in Europe during the eleventh and early twelfth century; it came to a head when Pope Gregory VII and Emperor Henry IV of Germany both claimed the right to appoint and invest bishops with the regalia of office. After years of diplomatic and military hostility, the conflict was partially settled by the Concordat of Worms in 1122.

Irish potato famine Period of agricultural blight from 1845 to 1849 whose devastating results produced widespread starvation and led to mass immigration to America.

Iron Curtain Term coined by Winston Churchill in 1946 to refer to the borders of Eastern European nations that lay within the zone of Soviet control.

Italian invasion of Ethiopia (1896) Italy invaded Ethiopia, which was the last major independent African kingdom. Menelik II, the Ethiopian emperor, soundly defeated them.

Ivan the Great (1440–1505) Russian ruler who annexed neighboring territories and consolidated his empire's position as a European power.

Jacobins Radical French political group during the French Revolution that took power after 1792, executed the French king, and sought to remake French culture.

Jacquerie Violent 1358 peasant uprising in northern France, incited by disease, war, and taxes.

James I (1566–1625) Monarch who ruled Scotland as James VI, and who succeeded Elizabeth I as king of England in 1603. He oversaw the English vernacular translation of the Bible known by his name.

James II of England King of England, Ireland, and Scotland (r. 1685–88) whose commitment to absolutism and the restoration of Roman Catholicism led to his exile to France in the Glorious Revolution of 1688.

Janissaries Corps of enslaved soldiers recruited as children from the Christian provinces of the Ottoman Empire and brought up to display intense personal loyalty to the Ottoman sultan, who used these forces to curb local autonomy and serve as his personal bodyguards.

Jerome (c. 340–420) One of the early "Fathers" of the Church; Jerome translated the Bible from Hebrew and Greek into a popular form of Latin—hence the name by which this translation is known: the Vulgate, or "vulgar" (popular) Bible.

Jesuits Religious order formally known as the Society of Jesus, founded in 1540 by Ignatius Loyola to combat the spread of Protestantism. The Jesuits would become active in politics, education, and missionary work.

Jesus (c. 4 B.C.E.–c. 30 C.E.) Jewish preacher and teacher in the rural areas of Galilee and Judea who was arrested for seditious political activity, tried, and crucified by the Romans. After his execution, his followers claimed that he had been resurrected from the dead and taken up into heaven. They began to teach that Jesus had been the divine representative of God, the Messiah (Christ) foretold by ancient Hebrew prophets, and that he had suffered for the sins of humanity and would return to judge all the world's inhabitants at the end of time.

Joan of Arc (c. 1412–1431) Peasant girl from the province of Lorraine who claimed to have been commanded by God to lead French forces against the English occupying army during the Hundred Years' War. Successful in her efforts, she was betrayed by the French king and handed over to the English, who condemned her to death for heresy. Her reputation underwent a process of rehabilitation, but she was not officially canonized as a saint until 1920.

Judaism Religion of the Hebrews as it developed in the centuries after the establishment of the Hebrew kingdoms under David and Solomon, especially during the period of Babylonian Captivity.

Justinian (527–565) Emperor of Rome who unsuccessfully attempted to reunite the eastern and western portions of the empire. Also known for his important codification of Roman law, in the *Corpus Juris Civilis*.

Justinian's Code of Roman Law Formally known as the *Corpus Juris Civilis* or "body of civil law," this compendium consisted of a systematic compilation of imperial statutes, the writings of Rome's great legal authorities, a textbook of legal principles, and the legislation of Justinian and his immediate successors. As the most authoritative collection of Roman law, it formed the basis of canon law (the legal system of the Roman Church) and became essential to the developing legal traditions of every European state as well as of many countries around the world.

Das Kapital (*Capital*) Book by Karl Marx that outlined the theory behind historical materialism and attacked the socioeconomic inequities of capitalism (1867).

Johannes Kepler (1571–1630) Mathematician and astronomer who elaborated on and corrected Copernicus's theory of a heliocentric solar system and is chiefly remembered for his discovery of the three laws of planetary motion that bear his name.

Keynesian Revolution Postdepression economic ideas developed by the British economist John Maynard Keynes (1883–1946), whereby the state took a greater role in managing the economy, stimulating it by increasing the money supply and creating jobs.

KGB Soviet political police and spy agency, first formed as the Cheka not long after the Bolshevik coup in October 1917. It grew to more than 750,000 operatives with military rank by the 1980s.

Genghis Khan (c. 1167–1227) "Oceanic Ruler," the title adopted by the Mongol chieftain Temujin, founder of a dynasty that conquered much of southern Asia.

Khanate Major political unit of the vast Mongol Empire. There were four Khanates, including the Yuan Empire in China, forged by Genghis Khan's grandson Kubilai in the thirteenth century.

Ruhollah Khomeini (1902–1989) Iranian Shi'ite religious leader who led the revolution in Iran after the abdication of the shah in 1979. His government allowed some limited economic and political populism combined with strict constructions of Islamic law, restrictions on women's public life, and the prohibition of ideas or activities linked to Western influence.

Nikita Khrushchev (1894–1971) Leader of the Soviet Union during the Cuban missile crisis, Khrushchev came to power after Stalin's death in 1953. His reforms and criticisms of the excesses of the Stalin regime led to his fall from power in 1964.

Kremlin Once synonymous with the Soviet government, the name *Kremlin* refers to Moscow's walled city center and the palace originally built by Ivan the Great.

Kristallnacht Known as the "Night of Broken Glass," an organized attack by Nazis and their supporters on the Jews of Germany following the assassination of a German embassy official by a Jewish man in Paris. Throughout Germany, thousands of stores, schools, cemeteries, and synagogues were attacked on November 9, 1938. Dozens of people were killed, and tens of thousands of Jews were arrested and held in camps, where many were tortured and killed in the ensuing months.

Labour party Party founded in Britain in 1900 to represent workers and promote socialist principles.

Latin West After the founding of Constantinople, the western Latin-speaking half of the Roman Empire became poorer and more peripheral, but it also fostered the emergence of new barbarian kingdoms. At the same time, the Roman pope claimed to have inherited both the authority of Jesus and the essential elements of Roman imperial authority.

League of Nations International organization founded after the First World War to solve international disputes through arbitration; it was dissolved in 1946 and its assets were transferred to the United Nations.

Leonardo da Vinci (1452–1519) Florentine inventor, sculptor, architect, and painter whose breadth of interests typifies the ideal of "the Renaissance man."

Vladimir Lenin (1870–1924) Leader of the Bolshevik Revolution in Russia (1917) and the first leader of the Soviet Union.

Leviathan Book by Thomas Hobbes (1588–1679) that recommended a ruler have unrestricted power (1651).

liberalism Political and social theory that judges the effectiveness of a government in terms of its ability to protect individual rights. Liberals support representative forms of government, free trade, and freedom of speech and religion. In the economic realm, liberals believe that individuals should be free to engage in commercial or business activities without interference from the state or their community.

lithograph Art form that involves incising writing or design on stone and producing printed impressions.

John Locke (1632–1704) English philosopher and political theorist known for his contributions to liberalism. Locke had great faith in human reason and believed that just societies were those that infringed the least on the natural rights and freedoms of individuals. This led him to assert that a government's legitimacy depended on the consent of the governed, a view that had a profound effect on the authors of the United States' Declaration of Independence.

Louis IX of France King of France from 1226 to his death on crusade in 1270, Louis was renowned for his piety and for his close attention to the administration of law and justice in his realm. He was officially canonized as Saint Louis in 1297.

Louis XIV (1638–1715) Called the "Sun King," he was known for his success at strengthening the institutions of the French absolutist state.

Louis XVI (1754–1793) Well-meaning but ineffectual king of France, finally deposed and executed during the French Revolution.

Ignatius Loyola (1491–1556) Spanish founder of the Society of Jesus (the Roman Catholic religious order commonly known as the Jesuits), whose members vow to serve God through poverty, chastity, and missionary work. He abandoned his first career as a mercenary after reading an account of Christ's life.

Lucretia According to Roman legend, Lucretia was a virtuous Roman wife who was raped by the son of Rome's last king and who virtuously committed suicide in order to avoid bringing shame on her family.

Luftwaffe Literally "air weapon," the name of the German air force, which was founded during the First World War, disbanded in 1945, and reestablished when West Germany joined NATO in 1950.

Lusitania British passenger liner that was sunk by a German U-boat (submarine) on May 7, 1915. Public outrage over the sinking contributed to the U.S. decision to enter the First World War.

Martin Luther (1483–1546) German monk and professor of theology whose critique of the papacy launched the Protestant Reformation.

ma'at Egyptian term for the serene order of the universe, with which the individual soul (*ka*) must remain in harmony. The power of the pharaoh was linked to *ma'at*, insofar as it ensured the prosperity of the kingdom. After the upheavals of the First Intermediate Period, the perception of the pharaoh's relationship with *ma'at* was revealed to be conditional, something that had to be earned.

Niccolò Machiavelli (1469–1527) As the author of *The Prince* and the *Discourses on Livy*, he looked to the Roman past for paradigms of greatness while at the same time hoping to win the patronage of contemporary rulers who would restore Italy's political independence.

Magna Carta Regarded now as a landmark in the development of constitutional government, the "Great Charter" of 1215 was enacted during the reign of King John of England in order to limit his powers. In its own time, its purpose was to restore the power of great lords.

Magyar nationalism National movement in the Hungarian region of the Habsburg Empire led by Lajos Kossuth, calling for national independence for Hungary in 1848. With the support of Russia, Habsburg troops crushed the movement and all other revolutionary activities in the empire. Kossuth fled into exile.

Moses Maimonides (c. 1137–1204) Jewish scholar, physician, and scriptural commentator whose *Mishneh Torah* is a fundamental exposition of Jewish law.

Thomas Malthus (1766–1834) British political economist who believed that populations inevitably grew faster than the available food supply. Societies that could not control their population growth would be checked only by famine, disease, poverty, and infant malnutrition. He argued that governments could not alleviate poverty. Instead, the poor had to exercise "moral restraint," postpone marriage, and have fewer children.

Nelson Mandela (1918–2013) South African opponent of apartheid who led the African National Congress and was imprisoned from 1962 until 1990. After his release from prison, he worked with Prime Minister Frederik Willem De Klerk to establish majority rule. Mandela became the first black president of South Africa in 1994.

Manhattan Project Secret U.S. government research project to develop the first nuclear bomb. The vast project involved dozens of sites across the United States, including New Mexico, Tennessee, Illinois, California, Utah, and Washington. The first test of a nuclear bomb was conducted near Alamogordo, New Mexico, on July 16, 1945.

manor Common farmland worked collectively by the inhabitants of an entire village, sometimes on their own initiative, sometimes at the behest of a lord.

Mao Zedong (1893–1976) Leader of the Chinese Revolution who defeated the Nationalists in 1949 and established the communist People's Republic of China.

Marne River in France and site of major battle of the First World War in September 1914, which halted the German invasion of France and led to protracted trench warfare on the war's Western Front.

Marshall Plan Economic aid package given to Europe by the United States after the Second World War to promote reconstruction and economic development and to secure Western European countries from a feared communist takeover.

Karl Marx (1818–1883) German philosopher and economist who believed that a revolution of the working classes would overthrow the capitalist order and create a classless society. Author of *Das Kapital* and co-author of *The Communist Manifesto*.

Marxists Followers of the socialist political economist Karl Marx who called for workers everywhere to unite and create an independent political force. Marxists believed that industrialization produced an inevitable struggle between laborers and the class of capitalist property owners, and that this struggle would culminate in a revolution that would abolish private property and establish a society committed to social equality.

Mary See **cult of the Virgin**.

Mary I (1516–1558) Catholic daughter of Henry VIII and his first wife, Catherine of Aragon, Mary Tudor was the first queen regnant of England. Her attempts to reinstitute Roman Catholicism in England met with limited success, and after her early death she was labeled "Bloody Mary" by the Protestant supporters of her half sister and successor, Elizabeth I.

mass culture The spread of literacy and public education in the nineteenth century created a new audience for print entertainment and a new class of entrepreneurs in the media to cater to this audience. The invention of radio, film, and television in the twentieth century carried this development to another level, as millions of consumers were now accessible to the producers of news, information, and entertainment. The rise of this "mass culture" has been celebrated as an expression of popular tastes but also criticized as a vehicle for the manipulation of populations through clever and seductive propaganda.

Mayans Native American peoples whose culturally and politically sophisticated empire encompassed lands in present-day Mexico and Guatemala.

Giuseppe Mazzini (1805–1872) Founder and ideological leader of the Italian nationalist movement Young Italy.

Mecca Center of an important commercial network of the Arabian Peninsula and birthplace of the prophet Muhammad. It is now considered the holiest site in the Islamic world.

Medici Powerful fourteenth- to eighteenth-century dynasty of Florentine bankers and politicians whose ancestors were originally apothecaries ("medics").

Meiji Empire Empire created under the leadership of Mutsuhito, emperor of Japan from 1868 until 1912. During the Meiji period Japan became a world industrial and naval power.

Mensheviks Within the Russian Social Democratic Party, the Mensheviks advocated slow changes and a gradual move toward socialism, in contrast with the Bolsheviks, who wanted to push for a proletarian revolution. Mensheviks believed that a proletarian revolution in Russia was premature and that the country needed to complete its capitalist development first.

mercantilism Theory and policy for directing the economy of monarchical states between 1600 and 1800 based on the assumption that wealth and power depended on a favorable balance of trade (more exports and fewer imports) and the accumulation of precious metals. Mercantilists advocated forms of economic protectionism to promote domestic production.

Maria Sybilla Merian (1647–1717) Scientific illustrator and an important early entomologist; Merian conducted research on two continents and published the well-received *Metamorphosis of the Insects of Surinam*.

Merovingian Frankish dynasty that claimed descent from a legendary ancestor called Merovic; the Merovingians were the only powerful family to establish a lasting kingdom in western Europe during the fifth and sixth centuries.

Mesopotamia Literally the "land between the Tigris and the Euphrates rivers" (Greek), where the civilization of Sumer, the first urban society, flourished.

Klemens von Metternich (1773–1859) Austrian foreign minister whose primary goals were to bolster the legitimacy of monarchies and, after the defeat of Napoleon, to promote a balance of power that would prevent another large-scale war in Europe. At the Congress of Vienna, he opposed social and political change and wanted to check Russian and French expansion.

Michelangelo Buonarroti (1475–1564) Virtuoso Florentine sculptor, painter, and poet who spent much of his career in the service of the papacy. He is best known for the decoration of the Sistine Chapel and for his monumental sculptures.

Middle Kingdom of Egypt (2055–1650 B.C.E.) Period following the First Intermediate Period of dynastic warfare, which ended with the reassertion of pharonic rule under Mentuhotep II.

Miletus Greek polis and Persian colony on the Ionian coast of Asia Minor. Influenced by the cultures of Mesopotamia, Egypt, and Lydia, it produced several of the ancient world's first scientists and sophist philosophers. Thereafter, a political conflict between the ruler of Miletus, Aristagoras, and the Persian Emperor, Darius, sparked the Persian Wars with Greece.

John Stuart Mill (1806–1873) English liberal philosopher whose faith in human reason led him to support a broad variety of civic and political freedoms for men and women, including the right to vote and the right to free speech.

Slobodan Milosevic (1941–2006) Serbian nationalist politician who became president of Serbia and whose policies during the Balkan wars of the early 1990s led to the deaths of thousands of Croatians, Bosnian Muslims, Albanians, and Kosovars. After leaving office in 2000, he was arrested and tried for war crimes at the International Court in The Hague. The trial ended before a verdict when he died in 2006.

Minoan Crete Maritime empire based at Knossos on the Greek island of Crete and named for the legendary King Minos. The Minoans dominated the Aegean for much of the second millennium B.C.E.

Modernism In the late-nineteenth and early twentieth centuries there were several different modernist movements in art and literature, but they shared three key characteristics. First, they had a sense that the world had radically changed and that this change should be embraced. Second, they believed that traditional aesthetic values and assumptions about creativity were ill-suited to the present. Third, they developed a new conception of what art could do that emphasized expression over representation and insisted on the value of novelty, experimentation, and creative freedom.

Mongols A nomadic people from the steppes of Central Asia who were united under the ruler Genghis Khan. His conquest of China was continued by his grandson Kubilai and his great-grandson son Ogedei, whose army also seized southern Russia and then moved through Hungary and Poland toward eastern Germany. The Mongol armies withdrew from eastern Europe after the death of Ogedei, but his descendants continued to rule his vast empire for much of the thirteenth century.

Michel de Montaigne (1533–1592) French philosopher and social commentator, best known for his *Essays*.

Montesquieu (1689–1755) French aristocrat and Enlightenment philosophe whose most influential work was *The Spirit of Laws*, in which he analyzed structures that shaped law and categorized governments into three types: republics, monarchies, and despotisms. His ideas about the separation of powers among the executive, the legislative, and the judicial branches of government influenced the authors of the U.S. Constitution.

Thomas More (1478–1535) Christian humanist, English statesman, and author of *Utopia*. In 1529, he was appointed lord chancellor of England but resigned because he opposed King Henry VIII's plans to establish a national church under royal control. He was eventually executed for refusing to take an oath acknowledging Henry to be the head of the Church of England and has since been canonized by the Roman Catholic Church.

mos maiorum Literally "the code of the elders" or "the custom of ancestors" (Latin). This unwritten code governed the lives of Romans under the Republic and stressed the importance of showing reverence to ancestral tradition. *Mos maiorum* was sacrosanct and essential to Roman identity, and an important influence on Roman culture, law, and religion.

Wolfgang Amadeus Mozart (1756–1791) Austrian composer, famous at a young age as a concert musician and later celebrated as a prolific composer of instrumental music and operas that are seen as the apogee of the Classical style in music.

Muhammad (570–632 c.e.) The founder of Islam, regarded by his followers as God's last and greatest prophet.

Munich Conference (1938) Hitler met with the leaders of Britain, France, and Italy and negotiated an agreement that gave Germany a major slice of Czechoslovakia. British prime minister Chamberlain believed that the agreement would bring peace to Europe. Instead, Germany invaded and seized the rest of Czechoslovakia.

Muscovy Duchy centered on Moscow whose dukes saw themselves as heirs to the Roman Empire. In the early fourteenth century, Moscow was under the control of the Mongol Khanate. After the collapse of the Khanate, the Muscovite grand duke, Ivan III, conquered all the Russian principalities between Moscow and the border of Poland-Lithuania, and then Lithuania itself. By the time of his death in 1505, Ivan had established Muscovy as a dominant power.

Muslim learning and culture The Crusades brought the Latin West into contact with the Islamic world, which affected European culture in myriad ways. Europeans adapted Arabic numerals and mathematical concepts as well as Arabic and Persian words. Through Arabic translations, Western scholars gained access to Greek learning, which had a profound influence on Christian theology. European scholars also learned from the Islamic world's accomplishments in medicine and science.

Benito Mussolini (1883–1945) Italian founder of the Fascist party who came to power in Italy in 1922 and allied himself with Hitler and the Nazis during the Second World War.

Mycenaean Greece (1600–1200 b.c.e.) Term used to describe the civilization of Greece in the late Bronze Age, when territorial kingdoms like Mycenae formed around a king, a warrior caste, and a palace bureaucracy.

Nagasaki Second Japanese city on which the United States dropped an atomic bomb. The attack took place on August 9, 1945; the Japanese surrendered shortly thereafter, ending the Second World War.

Napoleon III (1808–1873) Nephew of Napoleon Bonaparte, Napoleon III was elected president of the French Second Republic in 1848 and made himself emperor of France in 1852. During his reign (1852–70), he rebuilt the French capital of Paris. Defeated in the France-Prussian War of 1870, he went into exile.

Napoleonic Code Legal code drafted by Napoleon in 1804 and based on Justinian's *Corpus Iuris Civilis*; it distilled different legal traditions to create one uniform law. The code confirmed the abolition of feudal privileges of all kinds and set the conditions for exercising property rights.

Napoleon's military campaigns In 1805, the Russians, Prussians, Austrians, Swedes, and British attempted to contain Napoleon's French army, but he defeated them. Following his victories, Napoleon created a new empire of France and affiliated states. In 1808, he invaded Spain, but fierce resistance prevented Napoleon from achieving a complete victory. In 1812, Napoleon invaded Russia, and his army was decimated as it retreated from Moscow during the winter. After the Russian campaign, the united European powers defeated Napoleon and forced him into exile. He escaped and reassumed command of his army, but the European powers defeated him for the final time at the Battle of Waterloo in 1815.

Gamal Abdel Nasser (1918–1970) Former president of Egypt and the most prominent spokesman for secular pan-Arabism. He became a target for Islamist critics, such as Sayyid Qutb and the Muslim Brotherhood, who were angered by the Western-influenced policies of his regime.

National Assembly of France Governing body of France that succeeded the Estates General in 1789 during the French Revolution. It was composed of, and defined by, the delegates of the Third Estate.

National Association for the Advancement of Colored People (NAACP) U.S. civil rights organization founded in 1910 and dedicated to ending inequality and segregation for black Americans.

National Convention Governing body of France from September 1792 to October 1795. It declared France a republic and then tried and executed the French king. The Convention also confiscated the property of the enemies of the revolution, instituted a policy of de-Christianization, changed marriage and inheritance laws, abolished slavery in its colonies, placed a cap on the price of necessities, and ended the compensation of nobles for their lost privileges.

nationalism Movement to unify a country under one government based on perceptions of the population's common history, customs, and social traditions.

nationalism in Yugoslavia In the 1990s, Slobodan Milosevic and his allies reignited Serbian nationalism in the former Yugoslavia, which led non-Serb republics in Croatia and Slovenia to seek independence. The country erupted into war, with the worst violence taking place in Bosnia, a multi-ethnic region with Serb, Croatian, and Bosnian Muslim populations. European diplomats proved powerless to stop attempts by Croatian and Serbian military and paramilitary forces to claim territory through ethnic cleansing and violent intimidation. Atrocities were committed on all sides, but pro-Serb forces were responsible for the most deaths.

NATO The North Atlantic Treaty Organization, a 1949 military agreement among the United States, Canada, Great Britain, and eight Western European nations, which declared that an armed attack against any one of the members would be regarded as an attack against all. Created during the Cold War in the face of the Soviet Union's control of Eastern Europe, NATO continues to exist today and the current membership of twenty-eight states includes former members of the Warsaw Pact as well as Albania and Turkey.

Nazi party Founded in the early 1920s, the National Socialist German Workers' Party (NSDAP) gained control over Germany under the leadership of Adolf Hitler in 1933 and continued in power until Germany was defeated in 1945.

Nazism Political movement in Germany led by Adolf Hitler, which advocated a violent anti-Semitic, anti-Marxist, pan-German ideology.

Neo-Assyrian Empire (883–859 B.C.E.–612–605 B.C.E.) Assurnasirpal II laid the foundations of the Neo-Assyrian Empire through military campaigns against neighboring peoples. Eventually, the empire stretched from the Mediterranean Sea to western Iran. A military dictatorship governed the empire through its army, which it used to frighten and oppress both its subjects and its enemies. The empire's ideology was based on waging holy war in the name of its principal god, Assur, and the exaction of tribute through terror.

Neoliberalism Ideology emphasizing free markets, profit incentives, and restraints on both budget deficits and social welfare programs as the best guarantee of individual liberties. Beginning in the 1980s, neoliberal theory was used to structure the policy of financial institutions like the International Monetary Fund and the World Bank, which turned away from interventionist policies in favor of market-driven models of economic development.

Neolithic Revolution The "New" Stone Age, which began around 11,000 B.C.E., saw new technological and social developments, including managed food production, the beginnings of permanent settlements, and the rapid intensification of trade.

Neoplatonism School of thought based on the teachings of Plato and prevalent in the Roman Empire, which had a profound effect on the formation of Christian theology. Neoplatonists argued that nature is a book written by its creator to reveal the ways of God to humanity. Convinced that God's perfection

must be reflected in nature, neoplatonists searched for the ideal and perfect structures that they believed must lie behind the "shadows" of the everyday world.

New Deal President Franklin Delano Roosevelt's package of government reforms that were enacted during the depression of the 1930s to provide jobs for the unemployed, social welfare programs for the poor, and security for the financial markets.

New Economic Policy In 1921, the Bolsheviks abandoned war communism in favor of the New Economic Policy (NEP). Under NEP, the state still controlled all major industrial and financial concerns, while individuals could own private property, trade freely within limits, and farm their own land for their own benefit. Fixed taxes replaced grain requisition. The policy successfully helped Soviet agriculture recover from the civil war but was later abandoned in favor of collectivization.

Isaac Newton (1642–1727) One of the foremost scientists of all time, Newton was an English mathematician and physicist; he is noted for his development of calculus, work on the properties of light, and theory of gravitation.

Tsar Nicholas II (1868–1918) The last Russian tsar, who abdicated the throne in 1917; he and his family were executed by the Bolsheviks on July 17, 1918.

Friedrich Nietzsche (1844–1900) German philosopher who denied the possibility of knowing absolute "truth" or "reality," since all knowledge comes filtered through linguistic, scientific, or artistic systems of representation. He also criticized Judeo-Christian morality for instilling a repressive conformity that drained civilization of its vitality.

nongovernmental organizations (NGOs) Private organizations like the Red Cross that play a large role in international affairs.

Novum Organum Treatise by English statesman and scientist Francis Bacon (1561–1626) that advanced a philosophy of study through observation.

October Days (1789) The high price of bread and the rumor that the king was unwilling to cooperate with the assembly caused the women who worked in Paris's large central market to march to Versailles along with their supporters to address the king, Louis XVI. Not satisfied with their initial reception, they broke through the palace gates and called for the king to return to Paris from Versailles, which he did the following day.

Old Kingdom of Egypt (c. 2686–2160 B.C.E.) During this time, the pharaohs controlled a powerful and centralized bureaucratic state whose vast human and material resources are embodied by the pyramids of Giza. This period came to an end as the pharaoh's authority collapsed, leading to a period of dynastic warfare and localized rule.

OPEC (Organization of the Petroleum Exporting Countries) Organization created in 1960 by oil-producing countries in the Middle East, South America, and Africa to regulate the production and pricing of crude oil.

Operation Barbarossa Codename for Hitler's invasion of the Soviet Union in 1941.

Opium Wars (1839–42 and 1856–60) Wars fought between the British and Qing-era China to protect British trade in opium; the wars resulted in the ceding of Hong Kong to the British.

Oracle at Delphi The most important shrine in ancient Greece. The priestess of Apollo who attended the shrine was believed to have the power to predict the future.

Ottoman Empire (c.1300–1923) During the thirteenth century, the Ottoman dynasty established itself as leader of the Turks. From the fourteenth to sixteenth centuries, they conquered Anatolia, Armenia, Syria, and North Africa as well as parts of southeastern Europe, the Crimea, and areas along the Red Sea. Portions of the Ottoman Empire persisted up to the time of the First World War, but it was dismantled in the following years.

Reza Pahlavi (1919–1980) The Western-friendly shah of Iran who was installed during a 1953 coup supported by Britain and the United States. After a lengthy economic downturn, public unrest, and personal illness, he retired from public life under popular pressure in 1979.

Pan-African Conference Assembly in London in 1900 that sought to draw attention to the sovereignty of African people and their mistreatment by colonial powers.

Panhellenism The "all Greek" culture that allowed ancient Greek colonies to maintain a connection to their homeland and to each other through their shared language and heritage. These colonies also exported their culture into new areas and created new Greek-speaking enclaves, which permanently changed the cultural geography of the Mediterranean world.

pan-Slavism Cultural movement that sought to unite native Slavic peoples within the Russian and Habsburg Empires under Russian leadership.

Partition of India (1947) At independence, British India was partitioned into the nations of India and Pakistan. The majority of the population in India was Hindu and the majority of the population in Pakistan was Muslim. The process of partition brought brutal religious and ethnic warfare. More than 1 million Hindus and Muslims died and 12 million became refugees.

Blaise Pascal (1623–1662) Catholic philosopher who wanted to establish the truth of Christianity by appealing simultaneously to intellect and emotion. In his *Pensées*, he argued that faith alone can resolve the world's contradictions and that his own awe in the face of evil and uncertainty must be evidence of God's existence.

Paul of Tarsus Originally known as Saul, Paul was a Greek-speaking Jew and Roman citizen who underwent a miraculous conversion experience and became the most important exponent of Christianity in the 50s and 60s C.E.

Pax Romana (27 B.C.E.–180 C.E.) Literally translated as "the Roman Peace." During this time, the Roman world enjoyed an unprecedented period of peace and political stability.

Peace of Augsburg Settlement negotiated in 1555 among factions within the Holy Roman Empire; it formulated the principle *cuius regio, eius religio* ("he who rules, his religion"), meaning that the inhabitants of any given territory should follow the religion of its ruler, whether Catholic or Protestant.

Peace of Paris The 1919 Paris Peace Conference established the terms to end the First World War. Great Britain, France, Italy, and the United States signed five treaties with each of the defeated nations: Germany, Austria, Hungary, Turkey, and Bulgaria. The settlement is notable for the territory that Germany had to give up, including large parts of Prussia to the new state of Poland, and Alsace and Lorraine to France; the disarming of Germany; and the "war guilt" provision, which required Germany and its allies to pay massive reparations to the victors.

Peace of Westphalia (1648) Agreement reached at the end of the Thirty Years' War that altered the political map of Europe. France emerged as the predominant power on the Continent, while the Austrian Habsburgs had to surrender all the territories they had gained and could no longer use the office of the Holy Roman Emperor to dominate central Europe. Spain was marginalized and Germany became a volatile combination of Protestant and Catholic principalities.

Pearl Harbor American naval base in Hawaii that was bombed by the Japanese on December 7, 1941, bringing the United States into the Second World War.

peasantry Term used in continental Europe to refer to rural populations that lived from agriculture. Some peasants were free and could own land. Serfs were peasants who were legally bound to the land and subject to the authority of the local lord.

Peloponnesian War Name given to the series of wars fought between Sparta (on the Greek Peloponnesus) and Athens from 431 B.C.E. to 404 B.C.E., and which ended in the defeat of Athens and the loss of her imperial power.

perestroika Introduced by Soviet leader Mikhail Gorbachev in June 1987, *perestroika* (Russian for "restructuring") was the name given to economic and political reforms begun earlier in his tenure. It restructured the state bureaucracy, reduced the privileges of the political elite, and instituted a shift from the centrally planned economy to a mixed economy, combining planning with the operation of market forces.

Periclean Athens Following his election as *strategos* in 461 B.C.E., Pericles pushed through political reforms in Athens which gave poorer citizens greater influence in politics. He promoted Athenians' sense of superiority through ambitious public works projects and lavish festivals to honor the gods, thus ensuring his continual reelection. But eventually, Athens' growing arrogance and aggression alienated it from the rest of the Greek world.

Pericles (c. 495–429 B.C.E.) Athenian politician who occupied the office of *strategos* for thirty years and who presided over a series of civic reforms, building campaigns, and imperialist initiatives.

Persian Empire Consolidated by Cyrus the Great in 559, this empire eventually stretched from the Persian Gulf to the Mediterranean and also encompassed Egypt. Persian rulers were able to hold this empire together through a policy of tolerance and a mixture of local and centralized governance. This imperial model of government would be adopted by many future empires.

Persian Wars (490–479 B.C.E.) In 501 B.C.E., a political conflict between the Greek ruler of Miletus, Aristagoras, and the Persian Emperor, Darius, sparked the first of the Persian Wars when Darius sent an army to punish Athens for its intervention on the side of the Greeks. Despite being heavily outnumbered, Athenian hoplites defeated the Persian army at the plain of

Marathon. In 480 B.C.E., Darius's son Xerxes invaded Greece but was defeated at sea and on land by combined Greek forces under the leadership of Athens and Sparta.

Peter the Great (1672–1725) Energetic tsar who transformed Russia into a leading European country by centralizing government, modernizing the army, creating a navy, and reforming education and the economy.

Francesco Petrarca (Petrarch) (1304–1374) Italian scholar who revived interest in classical writing styles and was famed for his vernacular love sonnets.

pharaoh Term meaning "household" which became the title borne by the rulers of ancient Egypt. The pharaoh was regarded as the divine representative of the gods and the embodiment of Egypt itself. The powerful and centralized bureaucratic state ruled by the pharaohs was more stable and long-lived than any another civilization in world history, lasting (with few interruptions) for approximately 3,000 years.

Pharisees Group of Jewish teachers and preachers who emerged in the third century B.C.E. They insisted that all of Yahweh's (God's) commandments were binding on all Jews.

Philip II (382–336 B.C.E.) King of Macedonia and father of Alexander, he consolidated the southern Balkans and the Greek city-states under Macedonian domination.

Philip II of Spain King of Spain (r. 1556–98) and briefly king of England and Ireland during his marriage to Queen Mary I of England. As a staunch Catholic, Philip responded with military might to the desecration of Catholic churches in the Spanish Netherlands in the 1560s. When commercial conflict with England escalated, Philip sent the Spanish Armada (Navy) to conquer England in 1588, but it was largely destroyed by stormy weather.

Philip II Augustus (1165–1223) The first French ruler to use the title "king of France" rather than "king of the French." After he captured Normandy and its adjacent territories from the English, he built an effective system of local administration, which recognized regional diversity while promoting centralized royal control. This administrative pattern would characterize French government until the French Revolution.

Philip IV of France King of France from 1285 until his death, Philip's conflict with Pope Boniface VIII led to the transfer of the papal court to Avignon from 1309 to 1378.

Philistines Descendants of the Sea Peoples who fled to the region that now bears their name, Palestine, after their defeat at the hands of the pharaoh Ramses III. They dominated their neighbors, the Hebrews, who used writing as an effective means of discrediting them (the Philistines themselves did not leave a written record to contest the Hebrews' views).

philosophe During the Enlightenment, this French word referred to an intellectual whose reflections were unhampered by the constraints of religion or dogma.

Phoenicians A Semitic people known for their trade in exotic purple dyes and other luxury goods, they originally settled in present-day Lebanon around 1200 B.C.E. and from there established commercial colonies throughout the Mediterranean, notably Carthage.

Plato (429–349 B.C.E.) Student of Socrates who dedicated his life to transmitting his teacher's legacy through the writing of dialogues on philosophical subjects, in which Socrates himself plays the major role. The longest and most famous of these, known as the *Republic*, describes an idealized polis governed by a superior group of individuals chosen for their natural attributes of intelligence and character, who rule as "philosopher-kings."

Plotinus (204–270 C.E.) Neoplatonist philosopher who taught that everything in existence has its ultimate source in the divine, and that the highest goal of life should be the mystic reunion of the soul with this divine source, something that can be achieved through contemplation and asceticism. This outlook blended with that of early Christianity and was instrumental in the spread of that religion within the Roman Empire.

poleis One of the major political innovations of the ancient Greeks was the *polis*, or city-state (plural *poleis*). These independent social and political entities began to emerge in the ninth century B.C.E., each one organized around an urban center and fostering markets, meeting places, and religious worship; frequently, poleis also controlled some surrounding territory.

Marco Polo (1254–1324) Venetian merchant who traveled through Asia for twenty years and published his observations in a widely read memoir.

population growth In the nineteenth century, Europe experienced dramatic population growth. During this period, the spread of rural manufacturing allowed men and women to begin marrying younger and raising families earlier, which increased the size of the average family. As the population grew, the portion of young and fertile people also increased, which reinforced the population growth. By 1900, population growth was strongest in Britain and Germany, and slower in France.

portolan charts Also known as *portolani*, these special charts were invented by medieval mariners during the fourteenth century and were used to map locations of ports and sea routes, while also taking note of prevailing winds and other conditions at sea.

Potsdam (1945) At this conference, Truman, Churchill, and Stalin met to discuss issues that would be raised by the conclusion of the Second World War, including making territorial changes to Germany and its allies and the question of war reparations.

Prague spring Period of political liberalization in Czechoslovakia between January and August 1968 that was initiated by Alexander Dubček, the Czech leader. This period of expanding freedom and openness in this Eastern-bloc nation ended on August 20, when the USSR and Warsaw Pact countries invaded with 200,000 troops and 5,000 tanks.

pre-Socratics Group of philosophers in the Greek city of Miletus, who raised questions about humans' relationship with the natural world and the gods and who formulated rational theories to explain the physical universe they observed. Their name reflects the fact that they flourished prior to the lifetime of Socrates.

price revolution An unprecedented inflation in prices in the latter half of the sixteenth century, resulting in part from the enormous influx of silver bullion from Spanish America.

principate Modern term for the centuries of autocratic rule by the successors of Augustus, who seized power in 27 B.C.E.

and styled himself *princeps* or Rome's "first man." See **Roman Republic**.

printing press Introduced in Europe by Johannes Gutenberg of Mainz in 1453–55, this new technology quickly revolutionized communication and played a significant role in political, religious, and intellectual revolutions.

Protestantism Name given to the many dissenting varieties of Christianity that emerged during the Reformation in sixteenth-century western Europe. While Protestant beliefs and practices differed widely, all were united in their rejection of papal authority and the dogmas of the Roman Catholic Church.

provisional government After the collapse of the Russian monarchy in July 1917, leaders in the Duma organized this government and hoped to establish a democratic system under constitutional rule. They also refused to concede military defeat in the war against Germany, but it found impossible to institute domestic reforms and fight a war at the same time. As conditions worsened, the Bolsheviks gained support. In October 1917, they attacked the provisional government and seized control.

Claudius Ptolomeus, called Ptolemy (c. 85–165 C.E.) Greek-speaking geographer and astronomer active in Roman Alexandria, he rejected the findings of previous Hellenistic scientists in favor of the erroneous theories of Aristotle, publishing highly influential treatises that promulgated these errors and suppressed, for example, the accurate findings of Aristarchus (who had posited the Heliocentric universe) and Erathosthenes (who had calculated the circumference of the earth).

Ptolemaic system Ptolemy of Alexandria promoted Aristotle's understanding of cosmology. In this system, the heavens orbit the earth in an organized hierarchy of spheres, and the earth and the heavens are made of different matter and subject to different laws of motion. A prime mover (usually understood to be God) produces the motion of the celestial bodies.

Ptolemy (c. 367–c. 284 B.C.E.) One of Alexander the Great's trusted generals (and possibly his half brother), he became pharaoh of Egypt and founded a new dynasty that lasted until that kingdom's absorption into the Roman Empire in 30 B.C.E.

public sphere Between the official realm of state activities and the private realm of the household and individual, lies the "public sphere." The public sphere has a political dimension—it is the space of debate, discussion, and expressions of popular opinion. It also has an economic dimension—it is where business is conducted, where commercial transactions take place, where people enter into contracts, search for work, or hire employees.

Punic Wars (264–146 B.C.E.) Three periods of warfare between Rome and Carthage, two maritime empires who struggled for dominance of the Mediterranean. Rome emerged as the victor, destroyed the city of Carthage and took control of Sicily, North Africa, and Hispania (Spain).

pyramids Constructed in Egypt during the third millennium B.C.E., these structures were monuments to the power and divinity of the pharaohs entombed inside them.

Qur'an (often Koran) Islam's principal holy scriptures, comprised of the prophecies revealed to Muhammad and redacted during and after his death.

Raphael (Raffaelo Sanzio) (1483–1520) Italian painter active in Rome, his works include *The School of Athens*.

realism Artistic and literary style which emerged in the late nineteenth century and sought to portray common situations as they would appear in reality.

Realpolitik German term for a Political strategy based on advancing power for its own sake.

reason The human capacity to solve problems and discover truth in ways that can be verified intellectually. Philosophers distinguish the knowledge gained from reason from the teachings of instinct, imagination, and faith, which are verified according to different criteria.

Reformation Religious and political movement in sixteenth-century Europe that led to a break between dissenting forms of Christianity and the Roman Catholic Church; notable figures include Martin Luther and John Calvin.

Reich Term for the German state. The First Reich corresponded to the Holy Roman Empire (9th c.–1806), the Second Reich was from 1871 to 1919, and the Third Reich lasted from 1933 through May 1945.

Renaissance From the French word meaning "rebirth," this term came to be used in the nineteenth century to describe the artistic, intellectual, and cultural movement that emerged in Italy after 1300 and that sought to recover and emulate the heritage of the classical past.

Restoration period (1815–1848) European movement after the defeat of Napoleon to restore Europe to its pre–French Revolution status and to prevent the spread of revolutionary or liberal political movements.

Cardinal Richelieu (1585–1642) First minister to King Louis XIII, he is considered by many to have ruled France in all but name, centralizing political power and suppressing dissent.

Roman army Under the Republic, the Roman army was made up of citizen-soldiers who were required to serve in wartime. As Rome's empire grew, the need for more fighting men led to the extension of citizenship rights and, eventually, to the development of a vast, professional, standing army that numbered as many as 300,000 by the middle of the third century B.C.E. By that time, however, citizens were not themselves required to serve, and many legions were made up of paid conscripts and foreign mercenaries.

Roman citizenship The rights and responsibilities of Rome's citizens were gradually extended to the free (male) inhabitants of other Italian provinces and later to most provinces in the Roman world. In contrast to slaves and non-Romans, Romans had the right to be tried in an imperial court and could not be legally subjected to torture.

Roman Republic The Romans traced the founding of their republic to the overthrow of their last king and the establishment of a unique form of constitutional government, in which the power of the aristocracy (embodied by the Senate) was checked by the executive rule of two elected consuls and the collective will of the people. For hundreds of years, this balance of power provided the Republic with a measure of political stability and prevented any single individual or clique from gaining too much power.

Romanticism Beginning in Germany and England in the late eighteenth century and continuing up to the end of the nineteenth century, Romanticism was a movement in art, music, and literature that countered the rationalism of the Enlightenment by placing greater value on human emotions and the power of nature to stimulate creativity.

Jean-Jacques Rousseau (1712–1778) French philosopher and radical political theorist whose *Social Contract* attacked privilege and inequality. One of the primary principles of Rousseau's political philosophy is that politics and morality should not be separated.

Royal Society Scientific organization founded in Britain in 1660 with the goal of pursuing collective research. Members would conduct experiments, record the results, and share them with their peers, who would study the methods, reproduce the experiment, and assess the results. The arrangement gave English scientists a sense of common purpose as well as a system for reaching a consensus on facts.

Russian Revolution of 1905 After Russia's defeat in the Russo-Japanese War, Russians began clamoring for political reforms. Protests grew over the course of 1905, and the autocracy lost control of entire towns and regions as workers went on strike, soldiers mutinied, and peasants revolted. Forced to yield, Tsar Nicholas II issued the October Manifesto, which pledged individual liberties and provided for the election of a parliament (the Duma). The most radical of the revolutionary groups were put down with force, and the pace of political change remained very slow in the aftermath of the revolution.

Russo-Japanese War (1904–5) Japanese and Russian expansion collided in Mongolia and Manchuria. Russia was humiliated after the Japanese navy sank its fleet, which helped provoke a revolt in Russia and led to an American-brokered peace treaty.

sacrament Sacred rite. In the Roman Catholic tradition, the administration of the sacraments is considered necessary for salvation.

Saint Bartholomew's Day Massacre The mass murder of French Protestants (Huguenots) instigated by the French queen, Catherine de' Medici, and carried out by Catholics. It began in Paris on August 24, 1572, and spread to other parts of France, continuing into October of that year. More than 70,000 people were killed.

salons In the eighteenth century, informal gatherings of intellectuals and aristocrats devoted to discourse about Enlightenment ideas.

Sappho (c. 620–c. 550 B.C.E.) One of the most celebrated Greek poets, she was revered as "the Tenth Muse" and emulated by many male poets. Ironically, though, only two of her poems survive intact, and the rest must be pieced together from fragments quoted by later poets.

Sargon the Great (r. 2334–2279 B.C.E.) The Akkadian ruler who consolidated power in Mesopotamia.

SARS epidemic (2003) The successful containment of severe acute respiratory syndrome (SARS) is an example of how international health organizations can effectively work together to recognize and respond to a disease outbreak. The disease itself, however, is a reminder of the dangers that exist in a globalized economy with a high degree of mobility of both populations and goods.

Schlieffen Plan Devised by German general Alfred von Schlieffen in 1905 to avoid the dilemma of a two-front war against France and Russia. The Schlieffen Plan required that Germany attack France first through Belgium and secure a quick victory before wheeling to the east to meet the slower armies of the Russians on the Eastern Front. The Schlieffen Plan was put into operation on August 2, 1914, at the outset of the First World War.

scientific revolution of antiquity The Hellenistic period was the most brilliant age in the history of science before the seventeenth century C.E. Aristarchus of Samos posited the existence of a heliocentric universe. Eratosthenes of Alexandria accurately calculated the circumference of the earth. Archimedes turned physics into its own branch of experimental science. Hellenistic anatomists became the first to practice human dissection, greatly improving their understanding of human physiology. Ironically, most of these discoveries were suppressed by pseudo-scientists who flourished under the Roman Empire during the second century C.E., notably Claudius Ptolomaeus (Ptolemy) and Aelius Galenus (Galen).

second industrial revolution The technological developments in the last third of the nineteenth century, which included new techniques for refining and producing steel; increased availability of electricity for industrial, commercial, and domestic use; advances in chemical manufacturing; and the creation of the internal combustion engine.

Second World War Worldwide war that began in September 1939 in Europe, and even earlier in Asia (the Japanese invasion of Manchuria began in 1931), principally pitting Britain, the United States, and the Soviet Union (the Allies) against Nazi Germany, Italy, and Japan (the Axis). The war ended in 1945 with the defeat of Germany and Japan.

Seleucus (d. 280 B.C.E.) The Macedonian general who ruled the Persian heartland of the empire created by Alexander the Great.

Semitic The Semitic language family has the longest recorded history of any linguistic group and is the root for most languages of the Middle and Near East. Ancient Semitic languages include ancient Babylonian and Assyrian, Phoenician, the classical form of Hebrew, early dialects of Aramaic, and the classical Arabic of the Qur'an.

Sepoy Mutiny of 1857 See **Indian Rebellion of 1857**.

serfdom Peasant labor. Unlike slaves, serfs are "attached" to the land they work, and are not supposed to be sold apart from that land.

William Shakespeare (1564–1616) English playwright who flourished during the reigns of Elizabeth I and James I; Shakespeare received a basic education in his hometown of Stratford-upon-Avon and worked in London as an actor before achieving success as a dramatist and poet.

Shi'ites An often-persecuted minority within Islam, Shi'ites believe that only descendants of Muhammad's successor Ali and his wife Fatimah (Muhammad's daughter) can have any authority over the Muslim community. Today, Shi'ites constitute the ruling party in Iran and are numerous in Iraq but otherwise comprise only 10 percent of Muslims worldwide.

Abbé Sieyès (1748–1836) In 1789, he wrote the pamphlet "What is the Third Estate?" in which he posed fundamental questions about the rights of the Third Estate (the commons) and helped provoke its secession from the Estates-General. He was a leader at the Tennis Court Oath, but he later helped Napoleon seize power.

Sinn Féin Irish revolutionary organization that formed in 1900 to fight for Irish independence.

Sino-Japanese War (1894–95) Conflict over the control of Korea in which China was forced to cede the province of Taiwan to Japan.

slave revolt in Saint-Domingue (1791–1804) In September of 1791, the largest slave rebellion in history broke out in Saint-Domingue, the largest and most important French colony in the Caribbean. In 1794, the revolutionary government in France abolished slavery in the colonies, though this act was essentially only recognizing the liberty that the slaves had seized by their own actions. Napoleon reestablished slavery in the French Caribbean in 1802, but failed in his attempt to reconquer Saint-Domingue. Armies commanded by former slaves succeeded in winning independence for a new nation, Haiti, in 1804, making the revolt in Saint-Domingue the first successful slave revolt in history.

slavery The practice of subjugating people to a life of bondage, and of selling or trading these unfree people. For most of human history, slavery had no racial or ethnic basis, and was widely practiced by all cultures and civilizations. Anyone could become a slave, for example, by being captured in war or by being sold for the payment of a debt. It was only in the fifteenth century, with the growth of the African slave trade, that slavery came to be associated with particular races and peoples.

Adam Smith (1723–1790) Scottish economist and liberal philosopher who proposed that competition between self-interested individuals led naturally to a healthy economy. He became famous for his influential book, *The Wealth of Nations* (1776).

Social Darwinism Belief that Charles Darwin's theory of natural selection (evolution) was applicable to human societies and justified the right of the ruling classes or countries to dominate the weak.

social democracy Belief that democracy and social welfare go hand in hand and that diminishing the sharp inequalities of class society is crucial to fortifying democratic culture.

socialism Political ideology that calls for a classless society with collective ownership of all property.

Society of Jesus See **Jesuits**.

Socrates (469–399 B.C.E.) Athenian philosopher and teacher who promoted the careful examination of all inherited opinions and assumptions on the grounds that "the unexamined life is not worth living." A veteran of the Peloponnesian War, Socrates was tried and condemned by his fellow citizens for engaging in allegedly seditious activities and was executed in 399 B.C.E. His most influential pupils were the philosopher Plato and the historian and social commentator Xenophon.

Solon (d. 559 B.C.E.) Elected archon in 594 B.C.E., this Athenian aristocrat enacted a series of political and economic reforms that formed the basis of Athenian democracy.

Somme (1916) River in France and site of a battle of the First World War in which Allied forces attempted to take entrenched German positions from July to mid-November of 1916. Neither side was able to make any real gains despite massive casualties: 500,000 Germans, 400,000 British, and 200,000 French.

Soviet bloc International alliance that included the East European countries of the Warsaw Pact as well as the Soviet Union; it also came to include Cuba.

soviets Local councils elected by workers and soldiers in Russia. Socialists started organizing these councils in 1905, and the Petrograd soviet in the capital emerged as one of the centers of power after the Russian monarchy collapsed in 1917 in the midst of World War I. The soviets became increasingly powerful and pressed for social reform and the redistribution of land, and called for Russian withdrawal from the war against Germany.

Spanish-American War (1898) War between the United States and Spain in Cuba, Puerto Rico, and the Philippines. It ended with a treaty in which the United States took over the Philippines, Guam, and Puerto Rico; Cuba won partial independence.

Spanish Armada Supposedly invincible fleet of warships sent against England by Philip II of Spain in 1588 but vanquished by the English fleet and bad weather in the English Channel.

Sparta Region of Greece in the Peloponnesian peninsula; around 650 B.C.E., after the suppression of a slave revolt, Spartan rulers militarized their society in order to prevent future rebellions and to protect Sparta's superior position in Greece, orienting their society toward the maintenance of their army. Sparta briefly joined forces with Athens and other poleis in the second war with Persia in 480–479 B.C.E., but these two rivals ultimately fell out again in 431 B.C.E. when Sparta and her Peloponnesian allies went to war against Athens and her allies. This bloody conflict lasted until Athens was defeated in 404 B.C.E., after Sparta received military aid from the Persians.

Spartiate A full citizen of Sparta, hence a professional soldier of the hoplite phalanx.

spinning jenny Device invented by James Hargreaves (c. 1720–1774) that revolutionized the British textile industry by allowing a worker to spin much more thread than was possible on a hand spinner.

SS (Schutzstaffel) Formed in 1925 to serve as Hitler's personal security force and to guard Nazi party (NSDAP) meetings, the SS grew into a large militarized organization notorious for their participation in carrying out Nazi policies.

Joseph Stalin (1879–1953) Bolshevik leader who succeeded Lenin as the leader of the Soviet Union and ruled until his death in 1953.

Stalingrad (1942–43) The turning point on the Eastern Front during the Second World War came when the German army tried to take the city of Stalingrad in an effort to break the back of Soviet industry. The German and Soviet armies fought a bitter battle in which more than a half million German, Italian, and Romanian soldiers were killed and the Soviets suffered over a million casualties. The German army surrendered after more than five months of fighting. After Stalingrad, the Soviet army launched a series of attacks that pushed the Germans back.

Stoicism Ancient philosophy derived from the teachings of Zeno of Athens (fl. c. 300) and widely influential within the Roman Empire; it also affected the development of Christianity. Stoics believed in the essential orderliness of the cosmos, and that everything that occurs is for the best. Since everything is determined in accordance with rational purpose, no individual is master of his or her fate, and the only agency that human beings have consists in their responses to good fortune or adversity.

Sumerians The ancient inhabitants of southern Mesopotamia (modern Iraq and Kuwait) whose sophisticated civilization emerged around 4000 B.C.E.

Sunnis Proponents of Islam's customary religious practices (*sunna*) as they developed under the first two caliphs to succeed Muhammad, his father-in-law Abu-Bakr and his disciple Umar. Sunni orthodoxy is dominant within Islam but is opposed by the Shi'ites (from the Arabic word *shi'a*, "faction").

syndicalism Nineteenth-century political movement that embraced a strategy of strikes and sabotage by workers. Their hope was that a general strike of all workers would bring down the capitalist state and replace it with workers' syndicates or trade associations. Their refusal to participate in politics limited their ability to command a wide influence.

tabula rasa Term used by John Locke (1632–1704) to describe the human mind before it acquires ideas as a result of experience; Latin for "clean slate."

Tennis Court Oath (1789) Oath taken by representatives of the Third Estate in June 1789, in which they pledged to form a National Assembly and write a constitution limiting the powers of the king.

Reign of Terror (1793–94) Campaign at the height of the French Revolution in which violence, including systematic executions of opponents of the revolution, was used to purge France of its "enemies" and to extend the revolution beyond its borders; radicals executed as many as 40,000 persons who were judged to be enemies of the state.

Tetrarchy The result of Diocletian's political reforms of the late third century C.E., which divided the Roman Empire into four quadrants.

Theban Hegemony Term describing the period when the polis of Thebes dominated the Greek mainland, which reached its height after 371 B.C.E., under leadership of the Theban general Epaminondas. It was in Thebes that the future King Philip II of Macedon spent his youth, and it was the defeat of Thebes and Athens at the hands of Philip and Alexander—at the Battle of Chaeronea in 338—that Macedonian hegemony was forcefully asserted.

theory of evolution Darwin's theory that linked biology to history. Darwin believed that competition between different organisms and struggle with the environment were fundamental and unavoidable facts of life. In this struggle, those individuals who were better adapted to their environment survived, whereas the weak perished. This produced a "natural selection," or favoring of certain adaptive traits over time, leading to a gradual evolution of different species.

Third Estate The population of France under the Old Regime was divided into three "estates"—corporate bodies that determined an individual's rights or obligations under royal law. The clergy constituted the First Estate, the nobility the Second, and the commoners (the vast bulk of the population) made up the Third Estate.

Third Reich The German state from 1933 to 1945 under Adolf Hitler and the Nazi party.

Third World Nations—mostly in Asia, Latin America, and Africa—that are not highly industrialized.

Thirty Years' War (1618–48) Beginning as a conflict between Protestants and Catholics in Germany, this series of skirmishes escalated into a general European war fought on German soil by armies from Sweden, France, and the Holy Roman Empire.

Timur the Lame (1336–1405) Also known as Tamerlane, he was the last ruler of the Mongol Khans' Asian empire.

Marshal Tito (1892–1980) Yugoslavian communist and resistance leader who became the leader of Yugoslavia and fought to keep his government independent of the Soviet Union. In response, the Soviet Union expelled Yugoslavia from the communist countries' economic and military pacts.

towns Centers for markets and administration. Historically, towns have existed in a symbiotic relationship with the countryside, providing markets for surplus food from outlying farms as well as producing manufactured goods. In the Middle Ages, towns tended to grow up around a castle or monastery which afforded protection.

Treaty of Brest-Litovsk (1918) Separate peace between imperial Germany and the new Bolshevik regime in Russia. The treaty acknowledged the German victory on the Eastern Front and withdrew Russia from the war.

Treaty of Utrecht (1713) Resolution to the War of Spanish Succession that reestablished a balance of power in Europe, to the benefit of Britain and to the disadvantage of Spain, Holland, and France.

Treaty of Versailles Signed on June 28, 1919, this peace settlement ended the First World War and required Germany to surrender a large part of its most valuable territories and to pay huge reparations to the Allies.

trench warfare Weapons such as barbed wire and the machine gun gave a tremendous advantage to defensive positions in World War I, leading to prolonged battles between entrenched armies in fixed positions. The trenches eventually consisted of 25,000 miles of holes and ditches that stretched across the Western Front in northern France, from the Atlantic coast to the Swiss border. On the eastern front, the large expanse of territories made trench warfare less significant.

triangular trade The eighteenth-century commercial Atlantic shipping pattern that took rum from New England to Africa, traded it for slaves taken to the West Indies, and brought sugar back to New England to be processed into rum.

Triple Entente Alliance developed before the First World War that eventually included Britain, France, and Russia.

Truman Doctrine (1947) Declaration promising U.S. economic and military intervention to counter any attempt by the Soviet Union to expand its influence. Often cited as a key moment in the origins of the Cold War.

tsar Russian word for "emperor," derived from the Latin *caesar* and similar to the German *kaiser*, it was the title claimed by the rulers of medieval Muscovy and of the later Russian Empire.

Ubaid culture Early civilization that flourished in Mesopotamia between 5500 and 4000 B.C.E., it was characterized by large village settlements and temple complexes: a precursor to the more urban civilization of the Sumerians.

Umayyad Caliphate (661–930) The Umayyad family resisted the authority of the first two caliphs who succeeded Muhammad but eventually placed a member of their own family in that position of power. The Umayyad Caliphate ruled the Islamic world from 661 to 750, modeling their administration on that of the Roman Empire. After a rebellion led by the rival Abbasid family, the power of the Umayyad Caliphate was confined to their territories in al-Andalus (southern Spain).

Universal Declaration of Human Rights (1948) United Nations declaration that laid out the rights to which all human beings are entitled.

University of Paris The reputation of Peter Abelard and his students attracted many intellectuals to Paris in the twelfth century; some of them began offering instruction to aspiring scholars. By 1200, this loose association of teachers had formed themselves into a *universitas*, or corporation. They began collaborating in the higher academic study of the liberal arts, with a special emphasis on theology.

Pope Urban II (1042–1099) Instigator of the First Crusade (1096–99), who promised that anyone who fought or died in the service of the Church would receive absolution from sin.

urban populations During the nineteenth century, urban populations in Europe increased sixfold. For the most part, urban areas had medieval infrastructures that where overwhelmed by new populations and industries. As a result, many European cities became overcrowded and unhealthy.

Utopia Title of a semi-satirical social critique by the English statesman Sir Thomas More (1478–1535); the word derives from the Greek "best place" or "no place."

Lorenzo Valla (1407–1457) One of the first practitioners of scientific philology (the historical study of language), Valla's analysis of the so-called Donation of Constantine showed that the document could not possibly have been written in the fourth century C.E., but must have been forged centuries later.

vassal A person who pledges to be loyal and subservient to a lord in exchange for land, income, or protection.

velvet revolutions Peaceful political revolutions throughout Eastern Europe in 1989.

Verdun (1916) Site in France of a battle between German and French forces that lasted for ten months during the First World War. The Germans saw the battle as a chance to break French morale through a war of attrition, and the French believed the battle to be a symbol of France's strength. In the end, over 400,000 lives were lost and the German offensive failed.

Versailles Conference (1919) Peace conference following the First World War; it resulted in the Treaty of Versailles, which forced Germany to pay reparations and to give up territories to the victors.

Queen Victoria (1819–1901) Influential monarch who reigned from 1837 until her death; she presided over the expansion of the British Empire as well as the evolution of British politics and social and economic reforms.

Viet Cong Vietnamese communist group formed in 1954; committed to overthrowing the government of South Vietnam and reunifying North and South Vietnam.

Vikings (c. 800–c. 1000) The collapse of the Abbasid Caliphate disrupted Scandinavian commercial networks and turned traders into raiders (the word *viking* describes the activity of raiding). These raids often escalated into invasions that contributed to the collapse of the Carolingian Empire, resulted in the devastation of settled territories, and ended with the establishment of Viking colonies. By the tenth century, Vikings controlled large areas of eastern England, Scotland, Ireland, Iceland, Greenland, and parts of northern France. They had also established the beginnings of the kingdom that became Russia and made exploratory voyages to North America, founding a settlement at Newfoundland (Canada).

A Vindication of the Rights of Woman Book by Mary Wollstonecraft (1759–1797), English republican who applied Enlightenment political ideas to issues of gender.

Virgil (70–19 B.C.E.) Influential Roman poet who wrote under the patronage of the emperor Augustus. His *Aeneid* was modeled on the ancient Greek epics of Homer and told the mythical tale of Rome's founding by the Trojan refugee Aeneas.

Visigoths The tribes of "west" Goths who sacked Rome in 410 C.E. and later established a kingdom in the Roman province of Hispania (Spain).

Voltaire Pseudonym of French philosopher, deist, and satirist François Marie Arouet (1694–1778), who championed the cause of human dignity against state and church oppression in works such as the novel *Candide*.

Lech Wałęsa (b. 1943) Leader of the Polish labor movement Solidarity, which organized a series of strikes across Poland in 1980 to protest working conditions, shortages, and high prices. Above all, Solidarity demanded an independent labor union. Its leaders were imprisoned and the union banned, but a new series of strikes in 1988 led to the legalization of Solidarity and open elections.

war communism The Russian Civil War forced the Bolsheviks to take a more radical economic stance. They requisitioned grain from the peasantry and outlawed private trade in consumer goods as "speculation." They also militarized production facilities and abolished money.

Wars of the Roses Fifteenth-century civil conflict between the English dynastic houses of Lancaster and York, each of which was symbolized by the heraldic device of a rose (red and white, respectively). It was ultimately resolved by the accession of the Lancastrian king Henry VII, who married Elizabeth of York.

Warsaw Pact (1955–91) Military alliance between the USSR and other communist states that was established as a response to the creation of the NATO alliance.

The Wealth of Nations Treatise published in 1776 by Adam Smith, whose laissez-faire ideas predicted the economic boom of the Industrial Revolution.

Weimar Republic The government of Germany between 1919 and the rise of Hitler and the Nazi party.

Western Front Military front that stretched from the English Channel through Belgium and France to the Alps during the First World War.

Whites Term for the Russian "counterrevolutionaries" of the Bolshevik Revolution (1918–21) who fought the Bolsheviks (the "Reds"); they included former supporters of the tsar, Social Democrats, and large independent peasant armies.

William the Conqueror (1027–1087) Duke of Normandy who claimed the throne of England; in 1066, William invaded England and defeated the Anglo-Saxon king Harold at the Battle of Hastings. He and his Norman followers imposed imperial rule in England through a brutal campaign of military conquest, surveillance, and the suppression of the indigenous Anglo-Saxon (Old English) language.

William of Ockham (d. 1349) English philosopher and Franciscan friar who denied that human reason could prove fundamental theological truths, such as the existence of God; he argued that there is no necessary connection between the observable laws of nature and the unknowable essence of divinity. His theories, derived from the work of earlier scholastics, form the basis of the scientific method.

Woodrow Wilson (1856–1924) U.S. president who requested and received a declaration of war from Congress so that America could enter the First World War. After the war, his prominent role in the Paris Peace Conference signaled the rise of the United States as a world power. He also proposed the Fourteen Points, which influenced the peace negotiations.

Maria Winkelmann (1670–1720) German astronomer who worked with her husband in his observatory. Despite discovering a comet and preparing calendars for the Berlin Academy of Sciences, the academy would not let her take her husband's place within the Academy after he died.

witch craze Rash of persecutions against so-called witches that took place in both Catholic and Protestant countries of early modern Europe and their colonies, facilitated by both secular governments and religious authorities.

women's associations Because European women were excluded from the workings of parliamentary and mass politics, some women formed organizations to press for political and civil rights. Some groups focused on establishing educational opportunities for women while others, "suffragettes," campaigned energetically for the vote.

William Wordsworth (1770–1850) English Romantic poet whose central themes were nature, simplicity, and feeling. He considered nature to be man's most trustworthy teacher and source of sublime power that nourished the human soul.

World Bank International agency established in 1944 to provide economic assistance to war-torn nations in need of economic development.

John Wycliffe (c. 1330–1384) Professor of theology at the University of Oxford who urged the English king to confiscate ecclesiastical wealth and to replace corrupt priests and bishops with men who would live according to the apostolic standards of poverty and piety. Wycliffe advocated direct access to the scriptures and promoted an English translation of the Bible. His teachings played an important role in the Peasants' Revolt of 1381 and inspired the even more radical initiatives of a group known as Lollards.

Xerxes (c. 519–465 B.C.E.) Xerxes succeeded his father, Darius, as Great King of Persia. Seeking to avenge his father's shame and eradicate any future threats to Persian hegemony, he launched his own invasion of Greece in 480 B.C.E. An allied Greek army defeated his forces in 479 B.C.E.

Yalta Accords Meeting among U.S. president Franklin D. Roosevelt, British prime minister Winston Churchill, and Soviet premier Joseph Stalin that was held in the Crimea in 1945 shortly before the end of the Second World War to plan for the postwar order.

Young Turks Turkish reformist movement in 1908 that aimed to modernize the Ottoman Empire, restore parliamentary rule, and depose Sultan Abdul Hamid II.

ziggurats Temples constructed under the Dynasty of Ur in what is now Iraq, beginning around 2100 B.C.E.

Zionism Political movement dating to the end of the nineteenth century holding that the Jewish people constitute a nation and are entitled to a national homeland. Zionists rejected a policy of Jewish assimilation and advocated the reestablishment of a Jewish homeland in Palestine.

Zollverein Customs union, started by Prussia in 1834, which established free trade among the German states and a uniform tariff against the rest of the world. By the 1840s, the union included almost all of the German states except German Austria. It is considered an important forerunner of the political unification of Germany, which was completed in 1870 under Prussian leadership.

Zoroastrianism One of the three major universal faiths of the ancient world, alongside Judaism and Christianity; it was derived from the teachings of the Persian Zoroaster around 600 B.C.E. Zoroaster redefined religion as an ethical practice common to all, rather than as a set of rituals and superstitions unique to a particular group of people. Zoroastrianism teaches that there is one supreme god in the universe, Ahura-Mazda (Wise Lord), but that his goodness will be constantly assailed by the forces of evil until the arrival of a final "judgment day." Proponents of this faith should therefore help good to triumph over evil by leading a good life and by performing acts of compassion and charity. Zoroastrianism exercised a profound influence over many early Christians, including Augustine.

Ulrich Zwingli (1484–1531) Former priest from the Swiss city of Zurich who joined Luther and Calvin in attacking the authority of the Roman Catholic Church.

Text Credits

Aristophanes: 300 words from *Aristophanes: Lysistrata and Other Plays* translated with an introduction and notes by Alan H. Sommerstein (Penguin Books, 2002). Copyright © Alan H. Sommerstein, 2002. Reproduced by permission of Penguin Books Ltd.

Arrian: 365 words from *The Campaigns of Alexander* by Arrian, translated by Aubrey de Sélincourt, revised with an introduction and notes by J. R. Hamilton (Penguin Classics 1958, Revised edition 1971). Copyright © the Estate of Aubrey de Sélincourt, 1958. Introduction and Notes copyright © J.R. Hamilton, 1971. Reproduced by permission of Penguin Books Ltd.

Bernard of Angers: "A Miracle of St. Faith," by Bernard of Angers, from *Readings in Medieval History,* 2nd Edition, edited by Patrick J. Geary (Toronto, Ontario: University of Toronto Press, 2003). Copyright © 2003. Reprinted with permission of the publisher.

Henry Bettenson (ed.): "Obedience as a Jesuit Hallmark" from *Documents of the Christian Church,* 2nd Edition. Copyright © 1967, Oxford University Press. Reprinted by permission of Oxford University Press.

Gabriel Biel: "Execrabilis." Reprinted by permission of the publisher from *Defensorium Obedientiae Apostolicae Et Alia Documenta* by Gabriel Biel, edited and translated by Reiko A. Oberman, Daniel E. Zerfoss and William J. Courtenay, pp. 224–227, Cambridge, Mass.: The Belknap Press of Harvard University Press, Copyright © 1968 by the President and Fellows of Harvard College.

Boyer, Baker & Kirshner (eds.): "Declaration of the Rights of Man and of the Citizen" from *University of Chicago Readings in Western Civilization, Vol. 7.* Copyright © 1987 by The University of Chicago. Reprinted by permission of The University of Chicago Press.

Walter Bower: "A Declaration of Scottish Independence," from *Scotichronicon,* Volume 7, by Walter Bower. Edited by B. Scott and D. E. R. Watt. Reprinted by permission of Birlinn Limited.

Jean Baptiste Colbert: "Mercantilism and War" from *Colbert and a Century of French Mercantilism,* edited by Charles W. Cole. Copyright © 1939 Columbia University Press. Reprinted with permission of the publisher

Anna Comnena: pp. 308–311 from *The Alexiad of Anna Comnena,* translated by E.R.A. Sewter (Penguin Classics, 1969). Copyright © E.R.A. Sewter, 1969. Reproduced by permission of Penguin Books Ltd.

David Brion Davis: From *Encyclopédie,* Vol. 16, Neuchâtel, 1765, p. 532 as cited in David Brion Davis, *The Problem of Slavery in Western Culture.* (Ithaca, N.Y.: Cornell University Press, 1966), p. 416. Copyright © 1966 by David Brion Davis. Reprinted by permission.

Simone de Beauvoir: From *The Second Sex* by Simone de Beauvoir, translated by Constance Borde & Sheila Malovany-Chevalier, translation copyright © 2009 by Constance Borde and Sheila Malovany-Chevalier. Used by permission of Alfred A. Knopf, an imprint of the Knopf Doubleday Publishing Group, a division of Penguin Random House, LLC and The Random House Group Limited.

Marie de France: "Equitan" (pp. 56–57) from *The Lais of Marie de France,* by Marie de France, translated by Glyn S. Burgess and Keith Busby (Penguin Classics 1986, Second edition 1999). Copyright © Glyn S Burgess and Keith Busby, 1986, 1999. Reproduced by permission of Penguin Books Ltd.

Bartolome de las Casas: 500 words from *A Short Account of the Destruction of the Indies* by Bartolome de las Casas, edited and translated by Nigel Griffin, introduction by Anthony Pagden (Penguin Classics, 1992). Translation and Notes copyright © Nigel Griffin, 1992. Introduction copyright © Anthony Pagden 1992. Reproduced by permission of Penguin Books Ltd.

Michel de Montaigne: From *Montaigne: Selections from the Essays,* translated and edited by Donald M. Frame (Harlan Davidson, Inc., 1973), pp. 34–38.

Alexis de Tocqueville: From *Recollections: The French Revolution of 1848;* trans. George Lawrence, ed. J.P. Mayer, pp. 436–437. Copyright © 1987 by Transaction Publishers. Reprinted by permission of the publisher.

Rene Descartes: From *A Discourse on the Method of Correctly Conducting One's Reason,* trans. Ian Maclean. Copyright © Ian Maclean 2006. Reprinted by permission of Oxford University Press.

Armand J. du Plessis: "Cardinal Richelieu on the Common People of France," pp. 31–32 from Hill, Henry Bertram, *The Political Testament of Cardinal Richelieu.* © 1961 by the Board of Regents of the University of Wisconsin System. Reprinted by permission of The University of Wisconsin Press.

Ecumenical Councils: "Epitome of the Definition of the Iconoclastic Conciliabulum" from *A Select Library of Nicene and Post-Nicene Fathers of the Christian Church, Vol. XIV,* eds. Schaff & Wace (Grand Rapids, MI: Wm. B. Eerdmans Publishing Company, 1955), pp. 543–544.

Frantz Fanon: Excerpt from *The Wretched of the Earth* by Frantz Fanon, copyright © 1963 by *Présence Africaine.* Used by permission of Grove/Atlantic, Inc.

Robert Filmer: "Observations upon Aristotle's Politiques" (1652), in *Divine Right and Democracy: An Anthology of Political Writing in Stuart England,* edited by David Wootton. Pp 110–118. Copyright © 1986. Reproduced by permission of Hackett Publishing Company, Inc.

Betty Friedan: From *The Feminine Mystique* by Betty Friedan. Copyright © 1983, 1974, 1973, 1963 by Betty Friedan. Used by permission of Victor Gollancz, an imprint of The Orion Publishing Group, London and W.W. Norton & Company, Inc.

Galileo Galilei: From *Discoveries and Opinions of Galileo* by Galileo Galilei, translated by Stillman Drake, copyright © 1957 by Stillman Drake. Used by permission of Doubleday, an imprint of the Knopf Doubleday Publishing Group, a division of Penguin Random House LLC. All rights reserved.

Mohandas K. Gandhi: From *Hind Swaraj* or *Indian Home Rule* by M.K. Gandhi, p. 56, Ahmedabad: Navajivan Trust, 1946. Reprinted by permission of the publisher.

Pierre Gassendi: From *The Selected Works of Pierre Gassendi*, Edited by Craig B. Brush. (New York: Johnson Reprint Corporation, 1972) pp. 334–336.

Joseph Goebbels: "Why Are We Enemies of the Jews?" from Snyder, Louis, *Documents of German History*. Copyright © 1958 by Rutgers, the State University. Reprinted by permission of Rutgers University Press.

Homer: *Iliad*, translated by Stanley Lombardo, selections from pp. 115–118. Copyright © 1997 by Hackett Publishing Company, Inc. Reprinted by permission of Hackett Publishing Company, Inc. All rights reserved.

Rosemary Horrox (ed.): From *The Black Death*, by Horrox (Trans., Ed.), 1994, Manchester University Press, Manchester, UK. Reprinted with permission.

Juvenal: 224 words (pp. 138–139) from *The Sixteen Satires* by Juvenal, translated by Peter Green (Penguin Classics 1967, Revised edition 1974). Copyright © Peter Green 1967, 1974. Reproduced by permission of Penguin Books Ltd.

Nikita Khrushchev: "Report to the Communist Party Congress (1961)" from *Current Soviet Policies IV*, eds. Charlotte Saikowski and Leo Gruliow, from the translations of the Current Digest of the Soviet Press. Joint Committee on Slavic Studies, 1962, pp. 42–45. Copyright © East View Information Services, Inc. All rights reserved. Reprinted by permission.

Maureen Gallery Kovacs (trans.): Excerpts from *The Epic of Gilgamesh*, with an Introduction and Notes by Kovacs, Maureen Gallery, translator. Copyright © 1985, 1989 by the Board of Trustees of the Leland Stanford Junior University. All rights reserved. Used with the permission of Stanford University Press, www.sup.org.

Carolyne Larrington: "The Condemnation of Joan of Arc by the University of Paris" from *Women and Writing in Medieval Europe*, Carolyne Larrington, Copyright © 1995 Routledge. Reproduced by permission of Taylor & Francis Books UK.

L.R. Loomis (ed. and trans.): "Haec Sancta Synodus" and "Frequens" from *The Council of Constance*, edited by L.R. Loomis, pp. 229, 246–247. Copyright © 1962, Columbia University Press. Reprinted with permission of the publisher.

H.R. Loyn and John Percival: "Capitulary concerning the parts of Saxony" from *The Reign of Charlemagne: Documents on Carolingian Government and Administration* by H.R. Loyn and John Percival, copyright © 1976 by the author and reprinted by permission of Palgrave Macmillan. All Rights Reserved.

Niccolò Machiavelli: From *The Prince* by Niccolò Machiavelli, translated and edited by Thomas G. Bergin, pp. 75–78. Copyright © 1947 by Harlan Davidson, Inc.

Maganus Magnusson and Herman Pálsson: pp. 65–67 from *The Vinland Sagas* translated with an introduction by Magnus Magnusson and Hermann Pálsson (Penguin Classics, 1965). Copyright © Magnus Magnusson and Hermann Pálsson. Reproduced by permission of Penguin Books Ltd.

Karl Marx: "Neve Rheinische Zeitung" from *The Class Struggles in France*, pp. 57–58. And pp. 38–39 of Karl Mark, Frederick Engels: Collected Works, vol.38 (1982). Reprinted by permission of International Publishers Co., New York.

National Council of the Churches of Christ in the USA: Genesis 6:5–9:1, 1 Samuel 8:4–22, 9:1–10:1, 10:20–25, Acts of the Apostles 23:31–24:27 from the New Revised Standard Version of the Bible, copyright © 1989, Division of Christian Education of the National Council of the Churches of Christ in the United States of America. Used by permission. All rights reserved.

Nicholas Osterroth: "Clay Miner Autobiography" from *The German Worker: Working-Class Autobiographies from the Age of Industrialization*, translated and edited by Alfred Kelly, pp. 185–186. Copyright © 1987, The Regents of the University of California. Reprinted by permission of the University of California Press.

Ebenezer Pettigrew: "Notebook containing an account of the death of Ann. B Pettigrew, June 10, 1830," in the Pettigrew Family Papers #592, Southern Historical Collection, Wilson Library, The University of North Carolina at Chapel Hill. Reprinted by permission.

Phintys: From Lefkowitz, Mary R., and Maureen B. Fant, eds. *Women's Life in Greece and Rome: A Souce Book in Translation*, second edition, pp. 163–164. © 1982, 1992 M.B. Fant & M. R. Lefkowitz. Reprinted by permission of Bristol Classical Press, an imprint of Bloomsbury Publishing Plc. and Johns Hopkins University Press.

E.M. Plass: From *What Luther Says, Vol. II*, (pgs. 888–889) © 1959, 1987 Concordia Publishing House. Used with permission of CPH. All rights reserved.

Plato: 365 words (pp. 87–91) from *The Last Days of Socrates* by Plato, translated by Hugh Tredennick and Harold Tarrant, introduction and notes by Harold Tarrant (Penguin Classics 1954, Revised edition 1993).). Copyright © Hugh Tredennick, 1954, 1959, 1969. Copyright © Harold Tarrant, 1993. Reproduced by permission of Penguin Books Ltd.

Pliny the Younger, Letters from Book Ten of *Pliny the Younger: Complete Letters*, trans. P.G. Walsh. Copyright © P.G. Walsh 2006. Reprinted by permission of Oxford University Press.

Plutarch: From Lefkowitz, Mary R., and Maureen B. Fant, eds. *Women's Life in Greece and Rome: A Souce Book in Translation*, second edition. pp. 147–149. © 1982, 1992 M.B. Fant & M.R. Lefkowitz. Reprinted by permission of Bristol Classical Press, an imprint of Bloomsbury Publishing Plc. and Johns Hopkins University Press.

Polybius: 350 words from *The Rise of the Roman Empire* by Polybius, translated by Ian Scott-Kilvert, selected with an introduction by F.W. Walbank (Penguin Classics, 1979). Copyright © Ian Scott-Kilvert, 1979. Reproduced by permission of Penguin Books Ltd.

James B. Pritchard (ed.): "Cyrus (557–529)." From *Ancient Near Eastern Texts Relating to the Old Testament – Third Edition with Supplement*. © 1950, 1955, 1969, renewed 1978 by Princeton University Press. Reprinted by permission of Princeton University Press.

Tariq Ramadan: "Islam and Muslims in Europe: A Silent Revolution toward Rediscovery," *Muslims in the West, From Sojourners to Citizens*, ed. Yvonne Yazbeck Haddad, pp. 160–163. Copyright © 2002 by Oxford University Press. Inc. Reprinted by permission of Oxford University Press, Inc.

Martha T. Roth: Excerpts from "The Code of Hammurabi" from *Law Collections from Mesopotamia and Asia Minor*, edited by Martha T. Roth (Scholars Press, 1997), pp. 76–135. Reprinted by permission of Society of Biblical Literature.

Jean Rousseau: From *Rousseau's Political Writings: A Norton Critical Edition*, edited by Alan Ritter and Julia Conaway Bondanella, translated by Julia Conaway Bondanella. Copyright © 1988 by W.W. Norton & Company, Inc. Used by permission of W.W. Norton & Company, Inc.

Richard Sakwa: "Stalin on Industrialism" and "The Bolsheviks Must Seize Power" from *Rise and Fall of the Soviet Union 1917–1991*, by Richard Sakwa. Copyright © 1999 Routledge. Reproduced by permission of Taylor & Francis Books UK.

Sappho: "Fragment 16" from *The Poetry of Sappho*, translated and notes by Jim Powell, pp. 6–7. Copyright © 2007 by Jim Powell. Reprinted by permission of the author. "Sappho to Her Pupils," translated by Lachlan Mackinnon, *Times Literary Supplement*, July 15, 2005. © Lachlan Mackinnon / The Times Literary Supplement / nisyndication.com. Reprinted with permission.

Michael Sells (trans.): "81: The Overturning" from *Approaching the Qur'an: The Early Revelations*, translated by Michael Sells, pp. 48, 50. Copyright © 1999 by Michael A. Sells. Reprinted by permission of White Cloud Press.

Lewis Siegelbaum and Andrei Sokolov: "Letters from Anonymous Workers to the Newspaper Pravda" from *Stalinism as a Way of Life*, pp. 39–41. Copyright © 2004 by Yale University. Reprinted by permission of Yale University Press.

Denis Mack Smith: "Building the Italian Nation" from *The Making of Italy, 1796–1870* (New York: Harper & Row, 1968), pp. 47–49, 181–182, 224–225. Reprinted by permission of the author.

St. Ambrose: "The Memorial of Symmachus, Prefect of the City" from *A Select Library of Nicene and Post-Nicene Fathers of the Christian Church, Vol. X*, eds. Schaff & Wace (Grand Rapids, MI: Wm. B. Eerdmans Publishing Company, 1955), pp. 414–415.

St. Francis of Assisi: Excerpts from *St. Francis of Assisi: Omnibus of Sources, Volume One*, edited by Marion A. Habig. Reprinted by permission of Franciscan Media. All rights reserved.

Tacitus: 480 words from *The Annals of Imperial Rome* by Tacitus, translated with and introduction by Michael Grant (Penguin Classics 1956, Sixth revised edition 1989). Copyright © Michael Grant Publications Ltd, 1956, 1959, 1971, 1973, 1975, 1977, 1989. Reproduced by permission of Penguin Books Ltd.

Simon Taylor (ed.): "National Socialist Campaign Pamphlet" from *Germany, 1918–1933: Revolution, Counter-Revolution, and the Rise of Hitler* (London: Gerald Duckworth and Co., Ltd), p. 106.

Harry S. Truman: From *Memoirs*, Vol. 1 (Garden City, NY: Doubleday, 1955), pp. 419–421. Reprinted by permission.

Tyrtaeus: "Exhortation to the Young Hoplite" from *University of Chicago Readings in Western Civilization, Vol. 1*, eds. Adkins & White, pp. 23–24. Copyright © 1986 by The University of Chicago. Reprinted by permission of The University of Chicago Press.

United Nations: Excerpt from *Report of the Fourth World Conference on Women*, United Nations, 4–15 September 1995. Reprinted by permission of the United Nations.

Pope Urban II: "Pope Urban II's Call at Clermont, November 1195" from *The Crusades: A Reader*, edited by S.J. Allen and Emilie Amt. © University of Toronto Press 2010. Reprinted with permission of the publisher.

Ludvik Vaculik: Originally published as "Dva Tisice Slov," *Literarny Listy* (Prague) June 27, 1968. Translated by Mark Kramer, Joy Moss, and Ruth Tosek. From *The Prague Spring 1968,* edited by Jaromir Navrátil. Budapest–New York: Central European University Press, 1998, 177–181. Reprinted by permission.

Peter Waldo: "The Conversion of Peter Waldo" from *The Birth of Popular Heresy*, edited/translated by Robert I. Moore (Edward Arnold, 1975).

Sumner Willard and Charity Cannon Willard: Excerpts from pages 11–13 in *The Book of the Deeds of Arms and of Chivalry*, by Christine de Pizan, 1999. Copyright © 1999 Pennsylvania State University Press. Reprinted by permission of the Pennsylvania State University Press.

A59

Library; **p. 259:** Wikimedia Commons; **p. 261:** Bibliotheque Nationale, Paris, France/The Bridgeman Art Library; **p. 263 (top):** Danita Delimont/Getty; **p. 263 (bottom):** Wikimedia Commons; **p. 266:** Cameraphoto Arte, Venice/Art Resource, NY; **p. 267:** © Bob Battersby/Eye Ubiquitous/Corbis; **p. 268 (left):** The Granger Collection, NYC; **p. 268 (right):** Wikimedia Commons; **p. 269:** Wikimedia Commons; **p. 271:** Simone Martini/Wikimedia Commons; **p. 273:** Graham Bell/Getty Images; **p. 279 (left):** Wikimedia Commons; **p. 279 (right):** Associated Press.

Chapter 11: pp. 284–85: Réunion des Musées Nationaux/Art Resource, NY; **p. 286:** HIP/Art Resource, NY; **p. 288:** Réunion des Musées Nationaux/Art Resource, NY; **p. 289:** Réunion des Musées Nationaux/Art Resource, NY; **p. 290:** akg-images/British Library; **p. 292:** Wikimedia Commons; **p. 293 (left):** Bildarchiv Preussischer Kulturbesitz/Art Resource, NY; **p. 293 (right):** Scala/Art Resource, NY; **p. 299:** Werner Forman Archive/Topkapi Palace Library, Istanbul/Art Resource, NY; **p. 300:** Bibliothèque Royale Albert I, Brussels; **p. 301:** Réunion des Musées Nationaux/Art Resource, NY; **p. 304 (left):** Associated Press; **p. 304 (right):** The Bridgeman Art Library; **p. 309 (left):** Wikimedia Commons; **p. 309 (right):** The Art Archive/British Library.

Chapter 12: pp. 312–13: The Art Archive/Topkapi Museum Istanbul/Gianni Dagli Orti; **p. 319:** Erich Lessing/Art Resource, NY; **p. 320:** Erich Lessing/Art Resource, NY; **p. 322:** Scala/Art Resource, NY; **p. 323 (top):** Ted Spiegel/Corbis; **p. 323 (bottom):** Scala/Art Resource, NY; **p. 324 (left):** Nimatallah/Art Resource, NY; **p. 324 (right):** Scala/Art Resource, NY; **p. 324 (bottom):** Sandro Vannini/Corbis; **p. 325 (left):** DEA PICTURE LIBRARY/Getty Images; **p. 325 (right):** © University of Leicester/Corbis; **p. 326:** Louvre, Paris, France/Giraudon/The Bridgeman Art Library; **p. 328:** Bildarchiv Preussischer Kulturbesitz/Art Resource, NY; **p. 331:** Museo del Prado, Madrid/Art Archive; **p. 337:** Bibliotheque Nationale, Paris, France/Giraudon/The Bridgeman Art Library; **p. 338:** akg-images; **p. 340:** The Art Archive/Biblioteca Nacional de Madrid/Dagli Orti.

Chapter 13: pp. 342–43: The Art Archive/Nationalmuseet Copenhagen Denmark/Alfredo Dagli Orti; **p. 345:** Erich Lessing/Art Resource, NY; **p. 346:** Sandro Vannini/Corbis; **p. 347:** Bayerische Staatsgemäldesammlungen/Alte Pinakothek, Munich; **p. 348 (left):** Staatsbibliothek, Bern; **p. 348 (right):** Bibliothèque Royale; **p. 349 (left):** Staatliche Museen zu Berlin-Preußischer Kulturbesitz, Kupferstichkabinett; **p. 349 (right):** By permission of the British Library/Art Resource, NY; **p. 361 (left):** Scala/Art Resource, NY; **p. 361 (right):** Scala/Art Resource, NY; **p. 362 (left):** Erich Lessing/Art Resource, NY; **p. 362 (right):** MICHAL CIZEK/AFP/Getty Images/Newscom; **p. 364:** Kunsthistorisches Museum, Vienna; **p. 365:** Corbis.

Chapter 14: pp. 368–69: Wikimedia Commons; **p. 373:** Wikimedia Commons; **p. 375:** Peter Newark American Pictures/The Bridgeman Art Library; **p. 379:** British Museum/Wikimedia Commons; **p. 380:** Wikimedia Commons; **p. 387 (left):** The National Trust Photolibrary/Alamy; **p. 387 (right):** Wikimedia Commons; **p. 390:** Wikimedia Commons; **p. 391:** Interfoto/Alamy; **p. 395 (left):** © Franz-Marc Frei/Corbis; **p. 395 (right):** Icon Entertainment International/The Kobal Collection; **p. 396 (left):** Image copyright © The Metropolitan Museum of Art/Art Resource, NY; **p. 396 (right):** Wikimedia Commons; **p. 397 (top–left):** Erich Lessing/Art Resource, NY; **p. 397 (top–right):** Wikimedia Commons; **p. 397 (bottom–left):** © English Heritage Photo Library; **p. 397 (bottom–right):** Gift of Mr. and Mrs. Robert Woods Bliss, © 1997 Board of Trustees, National Gallery of Art, Washington, D.C.

Chapter 15: pp. 400–401: The Royal Collection © 2010 Her Majesty Queen Elizabeth II; **p. 402:** Wikimedia Commons; **p. 404 (left):** The Granger Collection, New York; **p. 404 (right):** Wikimedia

Commons; **p. 405 (top):** With kind permission of the University of Edinburgh/The Bridgeman Art Library International; **p. 405 (bottom):** Erich Lessing/Art Resource, NY; **p. 408 (left):** The Granger Collection, New York; **p. 408 (right):** Getty Images; **p. 411:** The Royal Collection © 2010 Her Majesty Queen Elizabeth II; **p. 412:** Snark/Art Resource, NY; **p. 417:** Bildarchiv Preussischer Kulturbesitz/Art Resource, NY; **p. 418:** Lebrecht Authors; **p. 420:** Courtesy Dr. Alexander Boguslawski, Professor of Russian Studies, Rollins College.

Chapter 16: pp. 424–25: Cellarius, Andreas/The Bridgeman Art Library; **p. 427:** Jeffrey Coolidge/Getty Images; **p. 428 (left):** Private Collection/The Bridgeman Art Library; **p. 428 (right):** © Peter Ginter/Science Faction/Corbis; **p. 429:** Erich Lessing/Art Resource, NY; **p. 431:** Private Collection/The Bridgeman Art Library; **p. 432 (left):** The Granger Collection, New York; **p. 432 (right):** Wikimedia Commons; **p. 433 (left):** Stapleton Collection/Corbis; **p. 433 (right):** Royal Astronomical Society/Photo Researchers, Inc.; **p. 435:** John P. McCaskey cropped by Smartse/wikimedia commons; **p. 436:** Rene Descartes, L'homme de René Descartes, et la formation du foetus . . . Paris: Compagnie des Libraires, 1729/Courtesy of Historical Collections & Services, Claude Moore Health Sciences Library, University of Virginia; **p. 437:** Bodleian Library; **p. 442:** *Thysania agrippina*, white witch—Caterpillar, cocoon and adults of a white witch moth (*Thysania agrippina*). Plate 20 from *Metamorphosis Insectorum* (1705) by Maria Sybilla Merian (1647–1717). ©The Natural History Museum, London/The Image Works; **p. 443 (left):** Newton, Sir Isaac (1642–1727)/© Courtesy of the Warden and Scholars of New College, Oxford/The Bridgeman Art Library; **p. 443 (right):** Bettmann/Corbis; **p. 444:** Bettmann/Corbis; **p. 445:** Giraudon/Art Resource, NY.

Chapter 17: pp. 448–49: Bridgeman Art Library; **p. 450:** Elizabeth Nesbitt Room Chapbook Collection/Information Sciences Library/University of Pittsburgh; **p. 452:** © Ali Meyer/CORBIS; **p. 453:** The New York Public Library/Art Resource, NY; **p. 456:** Historisches Museum der Stadt Wien; **p. 457:** Moritz Daniel Oppenheim, "Lavater and Lessing Visit Moses Mendelssohn." In the permanent collections, Judah L. Magnes Museum. Photo: Ben Ailes; **p. 460 (left):** Sir Joshua Reynolds/Omai of the Friendly Isles/nla.pic-an5600097/National Library of Australia; **p. 460 (right):** William Hodges/King of Otaheite//National Library of Australia; **p. 461:** Francesco Bartolozzi/A view of the inside of a house in the island of Ulietea, with the representation of a dance to the music of the country/nla.pic-an9184905/National Library of Australia; **p. 466:** Tate Gallery, London/Art Resource, NY; **p. 467:** Bridgeman Art Library; **p. 468:** Bettmann/Corbis; **p. 469 (left):** The Granger Collection, New York; **p. 469 (right):** Bluberries/iStock Photo; **p. 472:** Scala/ Art Resource, NY.

Chapter 18: pp. 476–77: Erich Lessing/Art Resource, NY; **p. 480:** akg-images; **p. 481:** Giraudon/The Bridgeman Art Library; **p. 482:** Chateau de Versailles, France /The Bridgeman Art Library; **p. 483:** Musee de la Ville de Paris, Musee Carnavalet, Paris, France/Giraudon/The Bridgeman Art Library; **p. 489:** Bibliotheque Nationale, Paris, France / The Bridgeman Art Library; **p. 492:** Erich Lessing/Art Resource, NY; **p. 493:** Scala/White Images/Art Resource, NY; **p. 494 (left):** Risma Archivo/Alamy; **p. 494 (right):** The Art Archive; **p. 495 (left):** Musee de la Ville de Paris, Musee Carnavalet, Paris, France/Lauros/Giraudon/The Bridgeman Art Library; **p. 495 (right):** Courtesy of the Warden and Scholars of New College, Oxford/The Bridgeman Art Library; **p. 496 (left):** The Gallery Collection/Corbis; **p. 496 (right):** Wikimedia Commons; **p. 500 (left):** The Granger Collection, New York; **p. 500 (right):** © Thorsten Strasas/Demotix/Corbis; **p. 501:** Gianni Dagli Orti/Corbis.

Chapter 19: pp. 504–5: National Gallery, London/Art Resource, NY; **p. 506:** Peak District National Park; **p. 508 (left):** The National

Archives of the UK; **p. 508 (right)**: The Granger Collection, New York; **p. 509**: Snark/Art Resource, NY; **p. 514**: HIP-Archive/Topham/The Image Works; **p. 515**: HIP-Archive/Topham/The Image Works; **p. 517**: Fotomas/Topham/The Image Works; **p. 518 (left)**: © Heritage Images/Corbis; **p. 518 (right)**: © ACE STOCK LIMITED/Alamy; **p. 519**: Geoffrey Clements/Corbis; **p. 525**: The Granger Collection, NY.

Chapter 20: pp. 530–31: Erich Lessing/Art Resource, NY; **p. 537**: Erich Lessing/Art Resource, NY; **p. 539**: Royal Collection Trust/© Her Majesty Queen Elizabeth II 2013; **p. 541**: The Trustees of the British Museum/Art Resource, NY; **p. 545**: The Stapleton Collection/The Bridgeman Art Library; **p. 546 (left)**: akg-images; **p. 546 (right)**: Time & Life Pictures/Getty Images; **p. 547**: Bettmann/Corbis; **p. 552**: Bettmann/Corbis; **p. 553 (left)**: Portrait of Mary Shelley (1797–1851) at the Age of Nineteen, c.1816 (litho) by English School (19th century), Russell-Cotes Art Gallery and Museum, Bournemouth, UK/Bridgeman Art Library; **p. 553 (right)**: Illustration from 'Frankenstein' by Mary Shelley (1797–1851) (engraving) (b/w photo) by English School (19th century), Private Collection/Bridgeman Art Library; **p. 555**: Archivo Iconografico S.A./Corbis; **p. 556**: Wikimedia Commons; **p. 557 (top)**: Wikimedia Commons; **p. 557 (bottom)**: Wikimedia Commons.

Chapter 21: pp. 560–61: Erich Lessing/Art Resource, NY; **p. 566 (left)**: Gianni Dagli Orti/The Art Archive at Art Resource, NY; **p. 566 (right)**: Erich Lessing/Art Resource, NY; **p. 567**: Bildarchiv Preussischer Kulturbesitz/Art Resource, NY; **p. 568 (left)**: Bildarchiv Preussischer Kulturbesitz/Art Resource, NY; **p. 568 (right)**: Image Source; **p. 570**: Bildarchiv Preussischer Kulturbesitz/Art Resource, NY; **p. 571 (left)**: Bildarchiv Preussischer Kulturbesitz/Art Resource, NY; **p. 571 (right)**: Corbis; **p. 572**: Imagno/Getty Images; **p. 577 (left)**: Rischgitz/Getty Images; **p. 577 (right)**: Scala/Art Resource, NY; **p. 578**: Charles E. Rotkin/Corbis; **p. 579**: Hulton-Deutsch Collection/Corbis; **p. 580**: Scala/Art Resource, NY; **p. 584**: Deutsches Historisches Museum; **p. 585 (left)**: Bildarchiv Preussischer Kulturbesitz/Art Resource, NY; **p. 585 (right)**: Bildarchiv Preussischer Kulturbesitz/Art Resource, NY; **p. 587**: Bettmann/Corbis; **p. 591**: Corbis.

Chapter 22: pp. 594–95: The Granger Collection, New York; **p. 596**: Bibliotheque des Arts Decoratifs, Paris, France/Archives Charmet/The Bridgeman Art Library; **p. 598 (left)**: Ken and Jenny Jacobson Orientalist Photography Collection/Research Library, The Getty Research Institute, Los Angeles (2008.R.3); **p. 598 (right)**: Hulton Archive/Getty Images; **p. 599 (left)**: The Granger Collection, New York/The Granger Collection; **p. 599 (right)**: © CHARLES PLATIAU/Reuters/Corbis; **p. 602 (left)**: Punchcartoons.com; **p. 602 (right)**: Bettmann/Corbis; **p. 604**: Oriental and India Office Collections, The British Library/Art Resource, NY; **p. 608**: Hulton-Deutsch/Corbis; **p. 612**: North Wind Picture Archives; **p. 615 (all)**: 1999 National Gallery of Art, Washington, D.C.

Chapter 23: pp. 618–19: akg-images; **p. 621**: akg-images; **p. 626**: Austrian Archives/Corbis; **p. 628 (top)**: Library of Congress; **p. 628 (bottom)**: Bettmann/Corbis; **p. 633 (left)**: The Granger Collection, New York; **p. 633 (middle)**: Charles Leandre (1862–1930) Private Collection/The Bridgeman Art Library Nationality; **p. 633 (right)**: Rue des Archives/The Granger Collection, New York; **p. 634 (left)**: Bettmann/Corbis; **p. 634 (right)**: Hulton-Deutsch Collection/CORBIS; **p. 634 (top)**: *Black Lines*, December 1913. Oil on canvas, 51 x 51 5/8 inches. Solomon R. Guggenheim Museum, Solomon R. Guggenheim Founding Collection, Gift, Solomon R. Guggenheim. 37.241. Vasily Kandinsky © 2007 Artists Rights Society (ARS), New York/ADAGP, Paris; **p. 643 (left)**: Scala/Art Resource, NY. © 2010 Estate of Pablo Picasso/

Artists Rights Society (ARS), New York; **p. 643 (right)**: Erich Lessing/Art Resource, NY.

Chapter 24: pp. 646–47: akg-images; **p. 648**: bpk,berlin/Art Resource; **p. 653**: Hulton-Deutsch Collection/Corbis; **p. 654 (both)**: Swim Ink 2, LLC/Corbis; **p. 655 (left)**: Hoover Institution, Stanford University; **p. 655 (right)**: Wikipedia; **p. 656**: Trustees of the Imperial War Museum, London; **p. 659**: Bettmann/Corbis; **p. 660**: Corbis; **p. 662**: Bildarchiv Preussischer Kulturbesitz; **p. 665**: Hulton-Deutsch Collection/Coribs; **p. 667**: Bettmann/Corbis; **p. 668**: National Archives; **p. 669 (left)**: © Bettmann/CORBIS; **p. 669 (right)**: © Wally McNamee/CORBIS.

Chapter 25: pp. 674–75: Erich Lessing/Art Resource, NY © VAGA; **p. 676**: The Art Artists Rights Society (ARS), New York; **p. 677**: Picture History; **p. 678**: Courtesy of Schickler-Lafaille Collection; **p. 679**: Hoover Institution, Stanford University; **p. 686 (left)**: © Daily Mail/Rex/Alamy; **p. 686 (right)**: Giorgio Cosulich/Getty Images; **p. 687**: Hulton-Deutsch Collection/Corbis; **p. 692**: Hulton-Deutsch Collection/Corbis; **p. 694 (left)**: Topham/The Image Works; **p. 694 (right)**: The Kobal Collection; **p. 695**: Photo by William Vanderson/Fox Photos/Getty Images; **p. 696 (top)**: The Museum of Modern Art, New York. Photograph courtesy the Museum of Modern Art, New York/Art Resource, NY. © 2013 Artists Rights Society (ARS), New York/VG Bild-Kunst, Bonn; **p. 696 (bottom)**: Musee National d'Art Moderne, Centre Georges Pompidou, Paris, France. Photo CNAC/MNAM/Dist. RMN/Art Resource, NY; **p. 697**: Granger Collection.

Chapter 26: pp. 700–701: Giraudon/Art Resource, NY. © 2010 Estate of Pablo Picasso/Artists Rights Society (ARS), New York; **p. 703**: The Southworth Collection, The Mandeville Special Collections Library of UC San Diego; **p. 704**: Giraudon/Art Resource, NY. © 2010 Estate of Pablo Picasso/Artists Rights Society (ARS), New York; **p. 708**: Hulton-Deutsch Collection/Corbis; **p. 710**: Bettmann/Corbis; **p. 712**: Hoover Institution, Stanford University; **p. 713**: akg-images/ullstein bild; **p. 714**: AP Photo; **p. 716**: Yad Vashem Archives; **p. 717**: Yad Vashem Archives; **p. 718 (left)**: Hulton-Deutsch Collection/Corbis; **p. 718 (right)**: © Egon Steiner/dpa/Corbis; **p. 720 (left)**: National Archives; **p. 720 (right)**: Library of Congress; **p. 721**: Library of Congress.

Chapter 27: pp. 726–27: Bettmann/Corbis; **p. 728**: Bettmann/Corbis; **p. 730 (both)**: Michael Nicholson/Corbis; **p. 731**: Michael Nicholson/Corbis; **p. 732**: The Granger Collection, NYC; **p. 733**: AP Photo; **p. 736**: © Giehr/dpa/Corbis; **p. 746**: ©ADAGP, Paris Corbis; **p. 748 (left)**: © STR/epa/Corbis; **p. 748 (right)**: © Bettmann/CORBIS; **p. 749**: The Granger Collection, NYC.

Chapter 28: pp. 752–53: Peter Turnley/Corbis; **p. 755**: Bettmann/Corbis; **p. 756 (top)**: © Keystone/Corbis; **p. 756 (bottom)**: Corbis; **p. 757**: Corbis; **p. 758**: Martha Holmes/Time & Life Pictures, Getty Images; **p. 760**: AP Photo; **p. 764**: Corbis; **p. 767**: © Peter Turnley/CORBIS; **p. 768**: Wally McNamee/Corbis; **p. 796 (left)**: © Boris Yurchenko/AP/AP/Corbis; **p. 769 (right)**: © Sysoyev Grigory/ITAR-TASS/Corbis; **p. 772**: Patrick Robert/Corbis Sygma; **p. 774**: Peter Turnley/Corbis; **p. 775 (both)**: dpa/Landov.

Chapter 29: pp. 778–79: Gerd Ludwig/Corbis; **p. 781**: Michale Brennan/Corbis; **p. 782**: Shaul Schwaz/Corbis; **p. 783**: Reuters/Corbis; **p. 785**: Reuters/Corbis; **p. 786**: Justin Guariglia/Corbis; **p. 787 (left)**: Gerd Ludwig/Corbis; **p. 787 (right)**: Reuters/Corbis; **p. 791**: Bettmann/Corbis; **p. 795**: Reuters/Corbis; **p. 801 (left)**: © Libor Hajsky/epa/Corbis; **p. 801 (right)**: Associated Press.

Index

Kassites, 33, 36, 42
Kay, John, 507
Kazakhstan, 606
Keats, John, 552
Kellogg-Briand Pact, 702
Kempe, Margery, 308
Kennedy, John Fitzgerald, 750, 761
Kennedy, Robert F., 764
Kennen, George, 733
Kenya, U.S. embassy bombing in, 794
Kepler, Johannes, 430–31, 447
Keynes, John Maynard, 445, 670, 693, 739
Khaldei, Evgeny, 714, 720
Khanate of the Golden Horde, 257–58, 258
Khasekhemwy, Queen of Egypt, 27
Khodorkovsky, Mikhail, 769, 769
Khomeini, Ayatollah Ruhollah, 791, 792
khora, 61
Khrushchev, Nikita, 733, 733–36, 750, 764
Khufu (Cheops), Pharaoh of Egypt, pyramid of, 24, 25, 59
Kiev, 195, 256
Kievan Rus', 256, 257
Kim Il Sung, 740
King, Martin Luther Jr., 760, 761, 764
kingship, concept of. See also absolutism
    absolutism, 402–3
    anointing and, 184
    Assyrian, 47–48
    Babylonian, 16
    Byzantine Empire and, 166
    Carolingian, 187
    Egyptian, 21, 24, 25, 35
    Magna Carta and, 226
    Persian, 51
    Stoicism and, 99
    Sumerian, 11, 21
King William's War, 414
Kinsey, Alfred, 759
Kinsey Reports, 759
Kipling, Rudyard, 598, 600–601
Kirch, Gottfried, 441
Kitchener, Horatio, 614
Klimt, Gustav, 586
Kline, Franz, 757
Kniazev, B.N., 681
knights, knighthood, 202–3, 213–14, 247, 247, 288
Knights Hospitaller, 233
Knights of the Temple (Knights Templar), 218
Knights Templar, 233, 273
Knossos, 38, 40, 40
Knox, John, 355
Kohl, Helmut, 769
Kollár, Jan, 572
Kollwitz, Käthe, 675–76, 676
Korb, Johann Georg, 419
Korean War, 740
Kosovo, 772, 773–74
Kosovo, battle of, 296
Kossuth, Lajos, 571, 571–73, 576
Kosygin, Aleksey, 791

Kovaly, Heda, 727
Kowloon Bay, 786
Krak des Chevaliers, 233, 233
Kremlin, 329
Krenz, Egon, 768
Kristallnacht, 692
Kublai Khan, 256–60
kulaks, 678, 679
Kulturkampf, 631
Kush, Kingdom of, 33
Kyoto Protocol, 784

labor politics, 625–27
labor unions, 625, 755
Labour Party (Great Britain), 626, 632, 692, 693, 739, 740, 743, 744
Labyrinth, 38
La Dolce Vita (film), 758
La Farina, Giuseppe, 574–75
Lais (Marie de France), 250
laissez-faire economics, 544
La Malinche, 338
Lamarck, Jean, 637
Lamartine, Alphonse de, 564
Landini, Francesco, 328
Lang, Fritz, 697
language. See literature and language
Laocoön (sculpture), 107, 107
las Casas, Bartolomé de, 339
Lascaux cave painting, 5
Last Judgment, The (Michelangelo), 322
Last Supper, The (Leonardo), 322, 322
latifundia, 121
Latin language, 294
Latin Right, 113, 114
Latins, 113
law, legal systems
    Alfred the Great and, 190
    in Athens, 68
    Bill of Rights (1689), 411
    in Byzantine Empire, 167
    canon law, 229–30, 232
    Hammurabi and, 16–19, 19
    Magna Carta, 226
    Napoleonic Code, 493, 496, 498
    Neo-Assyrian, 48
    Roman, 115, 121–23, 127, 134–36
    in Russia, 535
Lawrence, T.E., 658, 670
League of Nations, 668, 670, 702–4, 706
Le Corbusier (Charles Edouard Jeanneret), 696
legions, Roman, 114, 123–24, 127
Leibniz, Gottfried, 441
Leif Eiriksson, 262
Lenin, Vladimir Ilych (Vladimir Ilych Ulyanov), 613, 635, 664–66, 665, 677
Lennon, John, 757
Leo III, Byzantine Emperor, 168, 169
Leo III, Pope, 187
Leo IX, Pope, 209
Leonardo da Vinci, 320–22, 322, 427
Leopold I, King of Austria, 414–16

Leopold II, Emperor of Austria, 486
Leopold II, King of the Belgians, 608, 609
Leo X, Pope, 346, 347
Leo XIII, Pope, 642
Lepidus, Marcus Aemilius, 125, 129
Les Misérables (Hugo), 554
Lesseps, Ferdinand de, 596
Lessing, Gotthold, 457, 457
Letters on Sunspots (Galileo), 431
"Letters on the English Nation" (Voltaire), 454
Lever, Harold, 621
Levi, Primo, 715–16
Leviathan (Hobbes), 393
Levites, 54
Leyster, Judith, 397, 398
liberalism, 475, 482, 499, 514, 532, 542, 544
    and national politics, 629–37
    Prussia and, 561–79, 582, 587
    Whig Party and, 539
Liberal Party (Great Britain), 578, 632
Liber feudorum maior, 229, 231, 231
Liberty Leading the People (Delacroix), 537, 554
libraries
    at Alexandria, 93, 98, 100
    at Nineveh, 48
Libre Parole, La, 629, 633
Libya, Arab Spring and, 800, 802
Lichtenstein, Roy, 758
Licinius, 150
Liebknecht, Karl, 685
Liegnitz, battle of, 256
Lincoln, Abraham, 562
Lindisfarne Gospels, 181
Lingsberg Runestone, 195
List, Friedrich, 549, 567
literature and language
    Anglo-Saxon, 190
    Black Death's effect on, 289–90
    Carolingian, 187
    courtly literature, 248–49
    Egyptian, 29
    Etruscan, 112
    Greek, 65–67, 75–77, 88–90, 100
    Hellenistic, 108
    Indo-European, 32
    interwar, 695
    Linear A, 40
    Linear B, 40, 41, 60, 61
    literacy and books, 642–43
    nationalism and, 573
    Neo-Assyrian, 48
    Northern Renaissance, 327
    political satire, 76
    Roman, 112, 121, 131–32, 137
    Romanticism and, 551–53
    Semitic, 15, 32, 42
    Sumerian, 11–13
    vernacular in, 241, 247, 251–52
    women and, 241, 248–49, 467
Lithuania
    alliance with Poland, 299
    Ivan the Great's invasion of, 329

in literature after Black Death, 290
medieval literacy of, 241
in monasteries, 180–81, 239
Napoleonic Code and, 493
Nazi Germany and, 689
Plato on, 104–5
Reformation and, 357
in Renaissance, 295
romanticism and, 552–53
Rousseau on, 464–65
scientific revolution and, 441–42
second industrial revolution and, 627–28, 628
in Soviet Union, 681, 755
United Nations Report on the Fourth World Conference of Women, 796–97
Wollstonecraft on, 465, 466
working class, 526–27
in workplace, 681, 754–55, 755
World War I and, 654–55, 660, 660–61
Women of Algiers (Delacroix), 555
Women's Social and Political Union (WSPU), 627
women's suffrage, 579, 579, 612, 627–28, 632, 661, 760
Woolf, Virginia, 648, 695
Wordsworth, William, 487, 551
working class
 Industrial Revolution and, 525, 525–28
 labor politics and, 625–27
workplace, postwar changes in, 754–55
World Trade Center, September 11 attack on, 794–95, 795
World Trade Organization, 779
World War I, 647–73, 657
 airplanes in, 658
 assassination of Franz Ferdinand and, 648, 648–49
 Balkans in onset of, 648–49
 British entry into, 652
 causes of, 648–51
 compared to World War II, 701–2
 conscription in, 661
 consequences of, 672–73
 Eastern front of, 652
 financial costs of, 661–62
 food shortages in, 662, 662–63
 Gallipoli in, 653
 German invasion of Belgium in, 652
 German surrender in, 668
 home front in, 659–63, 660, 662
 in imperial colonies, 658–59
 inflation and, 662
 innovations of weaponry in, 648, 653, 656, 658, 667
 Ireland and, 659
 Italy in, 652, 653
 legacy of, 669
 Lusitania attack in, 653
 Marne in, 652

in Middle East, 658–59, 667, 671
 national boundaries redrawn after, 669, 670, 671, 684
 naval blockade of Germany in, 653
 naval warfare in, 653, 658
 Nivelle Offensive in, 658
 October offensive in, 667, 667
 Ottoman entry into, 653
 Paris Peace Settlement and. See Paris Peace Conference
 propaganda posters in, 654–55
 resource mobilization in, 661–62
 Russia in, 649, 652, 653, 654, 663–66
 Somme in, 647, 658
 submarines in, 653
 surrender of Austria-Hungary, 667
 tanks in, 658, 667
 as transformative, 663
 trench warfare in, 653, 654, 656, 658
 Triple Alliance and, 648
 Triple Entente and, 648
 U.S. entry into, 666, 667
 Verdun in, 656, 658
 Western Front, 656
 women and, 654–55, 660, 660–61
World War II, 701–25, 709
 aftermath of, 727–28, 749–50
 air power in, 708, 708
 annexation of Austria in, 706
 appeasement policy and, 703–4, 706
 Atlantic theater of, 708–9
 atomic bomb in, 719, 721, 722–24
 Battle of Britain in, 708, 708
 Blitzkrieg in, 701, 707
 causes of, 702–3
 civilian targets in, 702, 719
 compared to World War I, 701–2
 consequences of, 724, 725, 727–28
 D-Day in, 720, 721
 Dresden firebombing in, 719, 728, 728
 Dunkirk in, 707
 Eastern Front in, 711, 720–21
 French surrender in, 707
 home front in, 719
 invasion of Denmark and Norway in, 707
 Italy in, 708, 721
 moral dilemmas in, 712
 Munich conference and, 706–7
 Nazi invasion of Poland in, 707
 North African theater, 709
 occupation of France, 707
 outbreak of, 706
 Pacific theater in, 710, 711, 721–24
 Pearl Harbor attack in, 710, 710
 re-occupation of Rhineland, 706
 resistance groups, 712
 Soviet-Nazi nonaggression pact in, 707
 Stalingrad in, 720

submarines in, 708–9
 Sudetenland and, 706
 as total war, 718–19
 U.S. entry into, 710
 Vichy regime in, 707–8
 Warsaw Ghetto, 717–18
 Western front in, 721
Worms, Concordat of, 210
Wretched of the Earth, The (Fanon), 747, 748
Wright, Frank Lloyd, 696
writing. *See* alphabets and writing
WSPU (Women's Social and Political Union), 627
Wycliffe, John, 285, 309–10, 345

Xavier, Saint Francis, 364
Xenophanes, 72
xenophobia, 629
Xenophon, 62, 86–89, 92, 114
Xerxes, King of Persia, 50, 73–74
Ximenes de Cisneros, Cardinal Francisco, 361

Yahweh, 46, 47, 53–56, 141, 172
Yeltsin, Boris, 770
Yersinia pestis, 279
York, England, 290
York Castle, 203
Young Turks, 637
youth culture, 756, 756–57, 757
Ypres, first Battle of (1915), 653
Yugoslavia
 causes of violence in, 775–76
 creation of, 668
 Croatia war with, 772–73
 Dayton Peace talks, 773
 ethnic cleansing in Bosnia, 772–73
 international action, 773
 Kosovo war in, 772, 773–74
 national identity in, 772
 Slovenian secession from, 772

Zaire, 785
Zarathustra. *See* Zoroaster, Zoroastrianism
Zawahiri, Ayman al-, 794
Zealots, 141
Zeno, Eastern Roman Emperor, 157
Zeno of Citium, 101
Zetkin, Clara, 627
Zeus, 41, 62, 94
Ziggurat of Ur, 2, 15, 16, 16
zionism, 631, 659, 670
Zola, Émile, 629
Zollverein, 567
Zoroaster, Zoroastrianism, 51, 55, 57, 103, 142, 149
Zurbaran, Francisco, 402
Zwingli, Ulrich, 353

NORTH POLAR REGION

GLOBAL SATELLITE MOSAIC

The beauty and complexity of Earth's landscapes, oceans, and beneath the oceans are revealed with the Global Satellite Mosaic. The mosaic was created for the National Geographic Society by NASA's Jet Propulsion Laboratory and more than 500 satellite images from the National Oceanic and Atmospheric Administration. The cloud-free images show Earth in its natural colors as seen from space. One can easily identify the world's major glaciers, deserts, mountain ranges, and rain forests. For example, follow the green ribbon of lush vegetation along the Nile into the stark, dry Sahara. The mountain ranges seem to rise off the map thanks to digital elevation databases from the Department of Defense. The deepest areas of the ocean realm are colored dark blue in contrast to the light blue areas highlighting continental shelves, submarine ridges, and underwater mountains.

BIOSPHERE

Thousands of satellite images of the land and oceans were combined to show a picture of biosphere, or plant productivity, in the oceans, red, yellow, and green indicate waters rich in phytoplankton. On land, dark green areas show high potential plant productivity; tan areas suffer from productivity limitations due to aridity and temperature.

THE W

SATEL

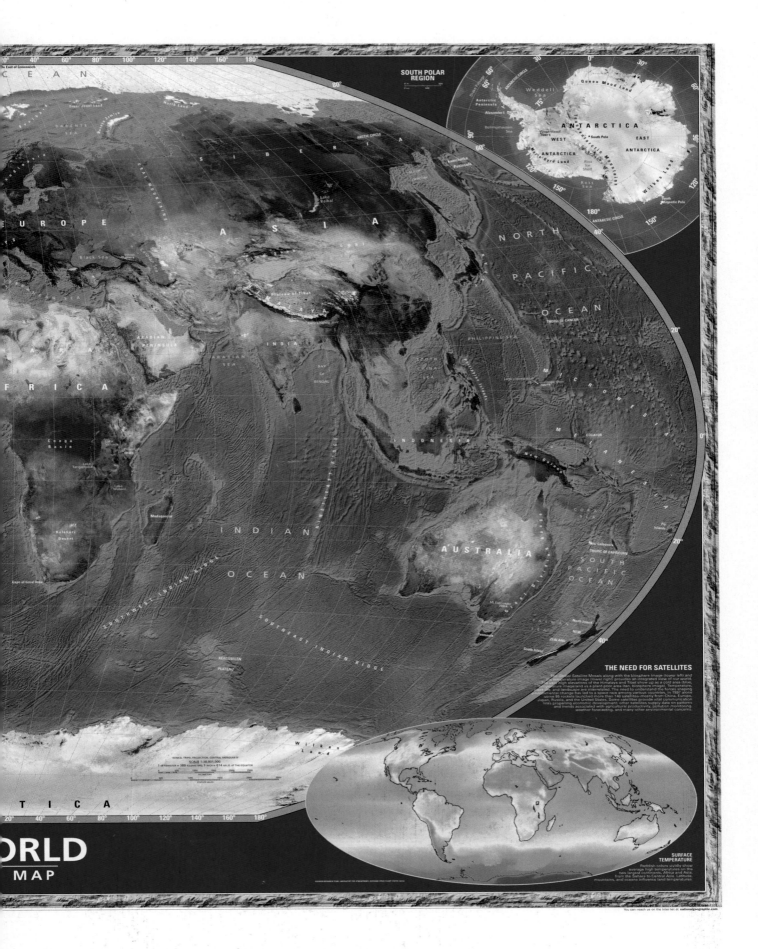

SOUTH POLAR REGION

ANTARCTICA

WEST ANTARCTICA

EAST ANTARCTICA

Queen Maud Land

Wilkes Land

Weddell Sea

Antarctic Peninsula

South Pole

South Magnetic Pole

Ross Ice Shelf

Ross Sea

Marie Byrd Land

ANTARCTIC CIRCLE

SIBERIA

ASIA

EUROPE

AFRICA

ARABIAN PENINSULA

INDIA

Lake Baikal

ARCTIC CIRCLE

Kamchatka Peninsula

NORTH PACIFIC OCEAN

TROPIC OF CANCER

PHILIPPINE SEA

SOUTH CHINA SEA

MICRONESIA

MELANESIA

EQUATOR

INDONESIA

Plateau of Tibet

ARABIAN SEA

BAY OF BENGAL

INDIAN OCEAN

Madagascar

Kalahari Desert

Cape of Good Hope

Congo Basin

Lake Tanganyika

Lake Malawi

SOUTHWEST INDIAN RIDGE

SOUTHEAST INDIAN RIDGE

KERGUELEN PLATEAU

AUSTRALIA

Great Barrier Reef

New Caledonia

TROPIC OF CAPRICORN

SOUTH PACIFIC OCEAN

Fiji Islands

TASMAN SEA

North Island

NEW ZEALAND

South Island

THE NEED FOR SATELLITES

This Biosphere Satellite Mosaic along with the biosphere image (lower left) and
the temperature image (lower right) provides an integrated view of our world.
The very high elevations of the Himalaya and Tibet show up as a cold area (blue,
in the temperature image) and as a giant pine area (tan, biosphere image). Temperature,
land use, and landscape are interrelated. The need to understand the forces shaping
environmental change has led to a space race among various countries. In 1997 alone
some 85 rockets launched more than 140 satellites—mostly from China, Europe,
Japan, Russia, and the United States. Some satellites provide vital communication
links propelling economic development; other satellites supply data on patterns
and trends associated with agricultural productivity, pollution monitoring,
weather forecasting, and many other environmental concerns.

Wilkes Land

WINKEL TRIPEL PROJECTION; CENTRAL MERIDIAN 0°
SCALE 1:38,931,000

SURFACE TEMPERATURE

Reddish colors vividly show
average high temperatures on the
two largest continents, Africa and Asia,
from the Sahara to Central Asia. Latitude,
mountains, and oceans influence land temperatures.

ORLD
MAP